The Little, Brown Reader

Ninth Edition

Marcia Stubbs
Wellesley College

Sylvan Barnet
Tufts University

William E. Cain
Wellesley College

Longman

New York • San Francisco • Boston
London • Toronto • Sydney • Tokyo • Singapore • Madrid
Mexico City • Munich • Paris • Cape Town • Hong Kong • Montreal

Senior Vice President/Publisher: Joseph Opiela
Acquisitions Editor: Lynn M. Huddon
Executive Marketing Manager: Ann Stypuloski
Supplements Editor: Donna Campion
Media Supplements Editor: Nancy Garcia
Senior Production Manager: Valerie Zaborski
Project Coordination, Text Design, and Electronic Page Makeup: Clarinda
    Publication Services
Cover Designer/Manager: Wendy Fredericks
Cover Photos: Front (left to right): *Katherine Graham:* Globe Photos; *Richard
    Rodriguez:* Roger Ressmeyer/CORBIS; *Maya Angelou:* AP/Wide World
    Photos; *John Updike:* AP/Wide World Photos. Back (left to right): *Virginia
    Woolf:* AP/Wide World Photos; *Amy Tan:* Reed Schumann/Reuters/CORBIS;
    Martin Luther King Jr.: Globe Photos; *Jimmy Carter:* Getty Images
    Newsmakers Liaison
Photo Researcher: Photosearch, Inc.
Print Buyer: Lucy Hebard
Printer and Binder: R. R. Donnelley & Sons/Crawfordsville
Cover Printer: The Lehigh Press, Inc.

For permission to use copyrighted material, grateful acknowledgment is made to
the copyright holders throughout the book and on page 911, which are hereby
made part of this copyright page.

Library of Congress Cataloging-in-Publication Data

The Little, Brown reader/[edited by] Marcia Stubbs, Sylvan Barnet, William E.
Cain.—9th ed.
    p. cm.
  Includes index.
  ISBN 0-321-09138-8
    1. College readers. 2. English language—Rhetoric—Problems, exercises, etc.
  3. Report writing—Problems, exercises, etc. I. Stubbs, Marcia. II. Barnet, Sylvan.
  III. Cain, William E.

PE1417 .L644 2003
808'.0427—dc21

                                                          2002018915

Please visit our website at
http://www.ablongman.com/stubbs

ISBN 0-321-09138-8

1 2 3 4 5 6 7 8 9 10–DOC–05 04 03 02

Detailed Contents

3   Academic Writing   43

4   Writing an Argument   63

5   Reading and Writing about Pictures   91

6   Memoirs: Discovering the Past   111

7 A Sense of Place   183

A Casebook on Barbie   308

9   Identities   321

A Casebook on Race   382

Picturing Identity   400

10   Teaching and Learning   413

A great teacher explains in a metaphor the progress of the mind from opinion to knowledge.

By age seven, Richard Rodriguez learns "the great lesson of school, that I had a public identity."

"The young must learn to learn as well as to play. Some even may enjoy learning once they try it."

"School is not a radio station or a television program."

The secret of success is nothing less than a national consensus on the importance of excellent education.

A psychiatrist discusses the ways in which adults shape children's behavior.

"Every woman, regardless of age, social class, ethnicity, and academic achievement needs to know that she is capable of intelligent thought. . . . "

According to Fan Shen, who migrated from China to Nebraska, "To try to be 'myself,' which I knew was a key to

A Casebook on the SAT   506

11   Work and Play   519

12   Messages   619

14   Law and Order   735

15   Body and Soul   789

16   Classic Essays   841

Rhetorical Contents

Analogy

Analysis

Argument

Cause and Effect

Comparison and Contrast

Definition

Description

Diction

Evaluation

Exposition

Irony

Narration

Style

Preface

Overview

Books have been put to all sorts of unexpected uses. Tolstoy used Tatishef's dictionaries as a test of physical endurance, holding them in his outstretched hand for five minutes, enduring "terrible pain." Books (especially pocket-sized Bibles) have served as armor by deflecting bullets. And they have served as weapons: two hundred years ago the poet and essayist Samuel Johnson knocked a man down with a large book.

In a course in writing, what is the proper use of the book in hand? This anthology contains some 150 essays, together with a few poems, stories, and fables, and numerous "Short Views," that is, paragraphs and aphorisms. But these readings are not the subject matter of the course; the subject matter of a writing course is writing, particularly the writing the students themselves produce. The responsibilities we felt as editors, then, were to include selections that encourage and enable students to write well, and to exclude selections that do not.

Our selections and writing exercises also reflect our own experience, over many years, as teachers of writing courses. We think it's important for the selections to lead not only to good written work by students, but also to lively discussion and debate. The more that students are engaged by the readings, and led to explore and examine their own responses in relation to those of their classmates, the more they feel there's something at stake in the writing they are doing. We have found, like all of our colleagues, that students improve the most when their work on papers is connected with lively classroom discussions about the readings, and we have tried to keep this point in mind in choosing selections and in preparing our Topics for Critical Thinking and Writing.

Purpose

To talk of "enabling" first: Students, like all other writers, write best when they write on fairly specific topics that can come within their experience and within their command in the time that they have available to write. A glance at our table of contents will reveal the general areas within which, we believe, students can find topics they have already given some thought to and are likely to be encountering in other courses as well: family relationships; love and courtship; schools; work, sports, and play.

Although other sections ("Messages" and "Art and Life") are also on familiar subjects—language, art, and popular culture—the selections themselves offer ways of thinking about these subjects that may be less familiar. Television commercials and films, for example, can be thought of as networks that articulate and transmit values implicit in a culture.

Other sections are about areas of experience that, while hardly remote from students' interest, are perhaps more difficult for all of us to grasp concretely: the tension between civil rights and liberties and the need for law and order; matters of gender and ethnic identity; relationships between mind and body or body and spirit. In these sections, therefore, we have taken particular care to exclude writing that is, for our purposes, too abstract, or too technical, or too elaborate. Finally, we conclude with "Classic Essays," ranging from Plato to Peter Singer.

As editors we have tried to think carefully about whether selections we were inclined to use—because they were beautifully written or on a stimulating topic—would encourage students to write. Such encouragement does not come, we feel, solely from the subject of an essay or from its excellence; it comes when the essay engenders in the reader a confidence in the writing process itself. No one quality in essays automatically teaches such confidence: not length or brevity, not difficulty or simplicity, not necessarily clarity, and almost certainly not brilliance. But essays that teach writing demonstrate, in some way, that the writers had some stake in what they were saying, took some pains to say what they meant, and took pleasure in having said it.

The selections we include vary in length, complexity, subtlety, tone, and purpose. Most were written by our contemporaries, but not all. The authors include historians, sociologists, scientists, saints, philosophers, and undergraduates, as well as journalists and other professional writers. And we have included some pictures in each section. The pictures, beautiful things in themselves, provide immediate or nearly immediate experiences for students to write about. We offer substantial help to students who want to write about pictures: in Chapter 5, "Reading and Writing about Pictures," we set forth our own ideas about the topic, and in Chapter 13 we reprint a helpful introductory essay, Lou Jacobs's "What Qualities Does a Good Photograph Have?" But we hope that everything in the book will allow students to establish connections between the activities that produced the words (and pictures) in these pages and their own work in putting critical responses to them on paper.

Flexible Arrangement

Although any arrangement of the selections—thematic, rhetorical, alphabetical, chronological, or random—would have suited our purposes, we prefer the thematic arrangement. For one thing, by narrowing our choices it helped us to make decisions. But more important, we know that in the real world what people write about is subjects, and we don't want to miss any opportunity to suggest that what goes on in writing courses is something like what goes on outside. The thematic categories are not intended to be rigid, however, and they do not pretend to be comprehensive; some of the questions following the selections suggest that leaping across boundaries is permitted, even encouraged. And, for instructors who prefer to organize their writing course rhetorically, we have added a selective table of contents organized rhetorically. Finally, we append a glossary of terms for students of writing.

What's New in the Ninth Edition?

William Hazlitt said that he always read an old book when a new one was published. We hope that this new edition allows instructors to read both at once. We have of course retained those essays and the special features (for example, Checklists for Writers, head notes, and the Topics for Critical Thinking and Writing at the end of each essay) that in our experience and the experience of many colleagues have consistently been of value to instructors and to students. But, guided by suggestions from users of the eighth edition, we have made many changes and additions. Among the most evident changes in the five introductory chapters devoted to reading and writing are

- in the chapter on "Writing an Agument," a new essay on violence in the media, followed by a paragraph-by-paragraph analysis
- in the chapter on "Reading and Writing about Pictures," new essays by a student (on Munch's *The Scream*) and by a professional writer (on a perfume advertisement), as well as a documented paper on Dorothea Lange, retained from the preceding edition

We have also added two new sections of readings:

- A Sense of Place
- Body and Soul

and there are new essays in every section. (Sixty-five readings are new to this edition.) Some of the new material is in casebooks that have been added to the ninth edition:

- A Casebook on Barbie
- A Casebook on the SAT

- A Casebook on E-Mail
- A Casebook on College Athletics

We have retained the popular casebook on race. In the chapter on "Identities," we have also added a four-color insert with eight pictures,

- Picturing Identity

which, in addition to providing visual pleasure, provides students with further material for writing. We assume that Chapter 5, "Reading and Writing about Pictures," will help students to think fruitfully about these images.

A new Companion Website, *The Little, Brown Reader Online* (at www. ablongman.com/stubbs), developed by Shaun Reno of Parkland Community College, offers chapter overviews, chapter review questions, and Web links for each chapter. Students will also find links to new reading selections for each chapter, additional information on selected writers in each chapter, and additional analysis, synthesis and response writing assignments. Sample syllabi, sample assignments, teaching suggestions, and other resources are also provided for instructors.

An updated Instructor's Manual, *Teaching The Little, Brown Reader*, is available to adopters of this Ninth Edition.

Acknowledgments

As usual, we are indebted to readers-in-residence. Morton Berman, William Burto, and Judith Stubbs have often read our material and then told us what we wanted to hear. At Longman, Lynn Huddon, Kristi Olson, and Teresa Ward have provided valuable assistance. We are grateful also to colleagues at other institutions who offered suggestions for the ninth edition: Jesse T. Airaudi, Baylor University; Jeanne Anderegg, University of North Dakota; Christine Gilmore, University of Toledo; Karen A. Kildahl, South Dakota State University; Nancy Kreml, Midlands Technical College; Joseph McDade, Houston Community College; Richard Nordquist, Armstrong Atlantic State University; Thomas Villano, Boston University.

Marcia Stubbs
Sylvan Barnet
William E. Cain

CHAPTER 1

A Writer Reads

One reads well only when one reads with some personal goal in mind. It may be to acquire some power. It may be out of hatred for the author.

Paul Valéry

Good writers are also good readers—of the works of other writers and of their own notes and drafts. The habits they develop as readers of others—for instance, evaluating assumptions, scrutinizing arguments, and perceiving irony—empower them when they write, read, and revise their own notes and drafts. Because they themselves are readers, when they write they have a built-in awareness of how their readers might respond. They can imagine an audience, and they write almost as if in dialogue with it.

Active reading (which is what we are describing) involves writing at the outset: annotating a text by highlighting or underlining key terms, putting question marks or brief responses in the margin, writing notes in a journal. Such reading, as you already may have experienced, helps you first of all to understand a text, to get clear what the writer seems to intend. Later, skimming your own notes will help you to recall what you have read.

But active reading also gives you confidence as a writer. It helps you to treat your own drafts with the same respect and disrespect with which you read the work of others. To annotate a text or a draft is to respect it enough to give it serious attention, but it is also to question it, to assume that the text or draft is not the last word on the topic.

But let's start at the beginning.

Previewing

By *previewing* we mean getting a tentative fix on a text before reading it closely.

If you know something about the **author,** you probably already know something about a work even before you read the first paragraph. An essay by Martin Luther King Jr. will almost surely be a deeply serious discussion centering on civil rights, and, since King was a Baptist clergyman, it is likely to draw on traditional religious values. An essay by Woody Allen will almost surely differ from King's in topic and tone. Allen usually writes about the arts, especially the art of film. Both writers are serious (though Allen also writes comic pieces), but they are serious about different things and serious in different ways. We can read both with interest, but when we begin with either of them, we know we will get something very different from the other.

King and Allen are exceptionally well known, but you can learn something about all of the authors represented in *The Little, Brown Reader* because they are introduced by means of biographical notes. Make it a practice to read these notes. They will give you some sense of what to expect. You may never have heard, for example, of J. H. Plumb—we include one of his essays later in this chapter—but when you learn from the note that he was a professor of history at the University of Cambridge and that he also taught in U. S. universities, you can tentatively assume that the essay will have a historical dimension. Of course, you may have to revise this assumption—the essay may be about the joys of trout fishing or the sorrows of being orphaned at an early age—but in all probability the biographical note will have given you some preparation for reading the essay.

The **original place of publication** may also give you some sense of what the piece will be about. The essays in *The Little, Brown Reader* originally were published in books, magazines, or newspapers, and these sources (specified, when relevant, in the biographical notes) may in themselves provide a reader with clues. For instance, since *The American Scholar* is published by Phi Beta Kappa and is read chiefly by college and university teachers or by persons with comparable education, articles in *The American Scholar* usually offer somewhat academic treatments of serious matters. They assume that the readers are serious and capable of sustained intellectual effort. Whereas a newspaper editorial runs about one thousand words, articles in *The American Scholar* may be fifteen or so pages long.

Some journals have an obvious political slant, and the articles they publish are to some degree predictable in content and attitude. For instance, William Buckley's *National Review* is politically conservative. Its subscribers want to hear certain things, and *National Review* tells them what they want to hear. Its readers know, too, that the essays will be lively and can be read fairly rapidly. Similarly, subscribers to *Ms.* expect highly readable essays with a strong feminist slant.

The **form,** or **genre** (a literary term for type or kind of literature), may provide another clue as to what will follow. For instance, you can expect a letter to the editor to amplify or contradict an editorial or to comment approvingly or disapprovingly on some published news item. It will almost surely be concerned with a current issue. Martin Luther King Jr.'s "Letter from Birmingham Jail," a response to a letter from eight clergymen, is a famous example of a letter arguing on behalf of what was then a current action.

The **title,** as we have already noted, may provide a clue. Again, King provides an example; even before studying "I Have a Dream," a reader can assume that the essay will be about King's vision of the future. Another example of a title that announces its topic is "We Have No 'Right to Happiness.'" This title is straightforward and informative, but suppose you pick up an essay called "Do-It-Yourself Brain Surgery." What do you already know about the essay?

Skimming

"Some books are to be tasted, others to be swallowed, and some few to be chewed and digested." You may already have encountered this wise remark by Francis Bacon, a very good reader (and a good writer, too—though he did not write Shakespeare's plays). The art of reading includes the art of skimming, that is, the art of gliding rapidly over a piece of writing and getting its gist.

Skimming has three important uses: to get through junk mail and other lightweight stuff; to locate what is relevant to your purpose in a mass of material, as, for instance, when you are working on a research paper; and (our topic now) to get an overview of an essay, especially to get the gist of its argument. Having discovered what you can from the name of the author, the title of the work, and the place of publication, you may want to skim the essay before reading it closely.

The **opening paragraph** will often give you a good idea of the **topic** or general area of the essay (for instance, the family). And if the essay is essentially an argument, it may announce the writer's **thesis,** the point that the writer will argue (for instance, that despite the high divorce rate, the family is still in good shape). Here is an example from J. H. Plumb's "The Dying Family." (The entire essay is printed later in this chapter.)

> I was rather astonished when a minibus drove up to my house and out poured ten children. They had with them two parents, but not one child had them both in common as mother and father, and two of them belonged to nei-ther parent, but to a former husband of the wife who had died. Both parents, well into middle age, had just embarked, one on his fourth, the other on her third marriage. The children, who came in all sizes, and ranged from blonde nordic to jet-haired Greek, bounded around the garden, young and old as happy as any children that I have seen. To them, as Californians, their situa-tion was not particularly odd; most of their friends had multiple parents. Indeed to them perhaps the odd family was the one which Western culture has held up as a model for two thousand years or more—the life-long union of man and wife. But it took me a very long time to believe that they could be either happy or adjusted. And yet, were they a sign of the future, a way the world was going?

Taking into account the author's profession (a historian), the title ("The Dying Family"), and the first paragraph, a reader assumes that the essay probably will examine the new family in relation to the traditional Western model. A reader probably also assumes, on the basis of the first paragraph, that Plumb will not go on to scold this California family; we can't of course be certain of his position, but thus far he seems willing to grant that the family may really be happy.

If the title and first paragraph do not seem especially informative (the first paragraph may be a sort of warmup, akin to the speech maker's "A funny thing happened to me on my way here"), look closely at the sec-ond. Then, as you scan subsequent paragraphs, look especially for **topic sentences** (often the first sentence in a paragraph), which summarize the paragraph, and look for passages that follow **key phrases** such as "the important point to remember," "these two arguments can be briefly put thus," "in short," "it is essential to recall," and so on. Plumb's third para-graph begins thus:

Basically the family has fulfilled three social functions—to provide a basic labor force, to transmit property and to educate and train children not only into an accepted social pattern, but also in the work skills upon which their future subsistence would depend.

Not surprisingly, Plumb goes on to amplify—to support with details—these assertions, and you won't be wrong if you guess that later in the essay he will indicate that a change in historical conditions has changed the role of the family.

In skimming an essay, pay special attention to the **final paragraph,** which usually reformulates the writer's thesis. Plumb's final paragraph is long, and we need not quote it in full here, but it ends thus:

Like any other human institution the family has always been molded by the changing needs of society, sometimes slowly, sometimes fast. And that bus load of children does no more than symbolize the failure, not of marriage, but of the role of the old-fashioned family unit in a modern, urbanized, scientific and affluent society.

Later, when you reread his essay carefully, you'll be on the lookout for the evidence that supports this view.

As you scan an essay, you'll find it useful to highlight phrases or sentences, or to draw vertical lines in the margin next to passages that seem to be especially concise bearers of meaning. In short, even while you are skimming you are using your pen.

If the essay is divided into sections, **headings** may give you an idea of the range of coverage. You probably won't need to highlight them—they already stand out—but there's no harm in doing so.

When you skim, you are seeking to get the gist of the author's **thesis,** or **point.** But you are also getting an idea of the author's **methods** and the author's **purpose.** For instance, skimming may reveal that the author is using statistics (or an appeal to common sense, or whatever) to set forth an unusual view. When Plumb begins by confessing he was "astonished" by the children in the minibus, he is using a bit of personal history to assure us that he is not a dry-as-dust historian whose understanding of life is based entirely on research in libraries. We immediately see that Plumb is writing for all of us, not just for professional historians, and we see that his purpose is to inform us in an engaging way. He will do a little preaching along the way, but even in skimming we can see that his chief purpose is to educate us, not to censure us for our high divorce rate. Another author might take the minibus as a symbol of what is wrong with the American family today, but such an author probably would, from the outset, let us sense what was coming, perhaps by depicting the children as quarreling or sulking.

During this preliminary trip through a piece of writing, you may get a pretty good idea of the writer's personality. More precisely, since you are not encountering the writer in the flesh but only the image that the writer presents in the essay, you may form an impression of the **voice,** or **persona,** that speaks in the essay. Something of Plumb's persona is evident in passages such as "I was rather astonished," "to them, as Californians, their situation was not particularly odd" (clearly the writer is *not* a Californian), and "it took me a very long time to believe that they could be either happy or adjusted." We will return to this important matter of persona later, on pages 16–17.

Let's now look at Plumb's essay. We suggest that in your first reading you skim it—perhaps highlighting, underlining, or drawing vertical lines next to passages that strike you as containing the chief ideas. To this extent, you are reading for information. But because you have ideas of your own and because you do not accept something as true simply because it appears in print, you may also want to put question marks or expressions of doubt ("Really?" "Check this") in the margin next to any passages that strike you as puzzling. Further, you may want to circle any words that you are not familiar with, but at this stage don't bother to look them up. In short, run through the essay, seeking to get the gist and briefly indicating your responses, but don't worry about getting every detail of the argument.

J. H. Plumb

The Dying Family

I was rather astonished when a minibus drove up to my house and out poured ten children. They had with them two parents, but not one child had them both in common as mother and father, and two of them belonged to neither parent, but to a former husband of the wife who had died. Both parents, well into middle age, had just embarked, one on his fourth, the other on her third marriage. The children, who came in all sizes, and ranged from blonde nordic to jet-haired Greek, bounded around the garden, young and old as happy as any children that I have seen. To them, as Californians, their situation was not particularly odd; most of their friends had multiple parents. Indeed to them perhaps the odd family was the one which Western culture has held up as a model for two thousand years or more—the lifelong union of man and wife. But it took me a very long time to believe that they could be either happy or

J. H. Plumb, "The Dying Family" from *In the Light of History* by J. H. Plumb. Published by Houghton Mifflin Company and Penguin Books Ltd. Reprinted by permission of Sir John Plumb.

adjusted. And yet, were they a sign of the future, a way the world was going?

Unlike anthropologists or sociologists, historians have not studied family life very closely. Until recently we knew very little of the age at which people married in Western Europe in the centuries earlier than the nineteenth or how many children they had, or what the rates of illegitimacy might be or whether, newly wed, they lived with their parents or set up a house of their own. Few of these questions can be answered with exactitude even now, but we can make better guesses. We know even less, however, of the detailed sexual practices that marriage covered: indeed this is a subject to which historians are only just turning their attention. But we do know much more of the function of family life—its social role—particularly if we turn from the centuries to the millennia and pay attention to the broad similarities rather than the fascinating differences between one region and another: and, if we do, we realize that the family has changed far more profoundly than ever the bus load of Californians might lead us to expect.

Basically the family has fulfilled three social functions—to provide a basic labor force, to transmit property and to educate and train children not only into an accepted social pattern, but also in the work skills upon which their future subsistence would depend. Until very recent times, the vast majority of children never went to any school: their school was the family, where they learned to dig and sow and reap and herd their animals, or they learned their father's craft of smith or carpenter or potter. The unitary family was particularly good at coping with the small peasant holdings which covered most of the world's fertile regions from China to Peru. In the primitive peasant world a child of four or five could begin to earn its keep in the fields, as they still can in India and Africa: and whether Moslem, Hindu, Inca or Christian, one wife at a time was all that the bulk of the world's population could support, even though their religion permitted them more. Indeed, it was the primitive nature of peasant economy which gave the family, as we know it, its wide diffusion and its remarkable continuity.

Whether or not it existed before the neolithic revolution we shall never know, but certainly it must have gained in strength as families became rooted to the soil. Many very primitive people who live in a pre-agrarian society of hunting and food-gathering often tend to have a looser structure of marriage and the women a far greater freedom of choice and easier divorce, as with the Esquimaux, than is permitted in peasant societies. There can be little doubt that the neolithic revolution created new opportunities for the family as we know it, partly because this revolution created new property relations. More importantly it created great masses of property, beyond anything earlier societies had known. True, there were a few hunting peoples, such as the Kwakiutl Indians, who had considerable possessions—complex lodges, great pieces of copper and piles of fibre blankets, which periodically they destroyed in great battles of raging pride—but the property, personal or communal, of most primitive hunting people is usually trivial.

After the revolution in agriculture, property and its transmission lay   5
at the very heart of social relations and possessed an actuality which we find hard to grasp. Although we are much richer, possessions are more anonymous, often little more than marks in a ledger, and what we own constantly changes. Whereas for the majority of mankind over this last seven thousand years property has been deeply personal and familial: a plot of land, if not absolute ownership over it, then valuable rights in it; sometimes a house, even though it be a hovel by our standards; perhaps no more than the tools and materials of a craft, yet these possessions were the route both to survival and to betterment. Hence they were endowed with manna, bound up with the deepest roots of personality. In all societies the question of property became embedded in every aspect of family life, particularly marriage and the succession and rights of children. Because of property's vital importance, subservience of women and children to the will of the father, limited only by social custom, became the pattern of most great peasant societies. Marriage was sanctified not only by the rites of religion, but by the transmission of property. Few societies could tolerate freedom of choice in marriage—too much vital to the success or failure of a family depended on it: an ugly girl with five cows was a far fairer prospect than a pretty girl with one. And because of the sexual drives of frail human nature, the customs of marriage and of family relationships needed to be rigorously enforced. Tradition sanctified them; religion blessed them. Some societies reversed the sexually restrictive nature of permanent marriage and permitted additional wives, but such permission was meaningless to the mass of the peasantry who fought a desperate battle to support a single family. And, as we shall see, the patterns of family life were always looser for the rich and the favored.

But a family was always more than property expressed clearly and visibly in real goods; it was for thousands of years both a school and a tribunal, the basic unit of social organization whose function in modern society has been very largely taken over by the state. In most peasant societies, life is regulated by the village community, by the patriarchs of the village, and the only officer of the central government these villagers see with any regularity is the tax-gatherer; but in societies that have grown more complex, and this is particularly true of the West during the last four hundred years, life has become regulated by the nation state or by the growth in power and importance of more generalized local communities—the town or county.

This has naturally weakened the authority of heads of families, a fact that can be symbolically illustrated by change in social custom. No child in Western Europe would sit unbidden in the presence of its parents until the eighteenth century: if it did it could be sure of rebuke and punishment. No head of a household would have thought twice about beating a recalcitrant young servant or apprentice before the end of the nineteenth century. For a younger brother to marry without the consent of his eldest brother would have been regarded as a social enormity; and sisters were disposable property. All of this power has vanished. Indeed the family ties of all of us have been so loosened that we find it hard to grasp the intensity of family relationships or their complexity, they have disintegrated so rapidly this last hundred years. Now nearly every child in the Western world, male or female, is educated outside the family from five years of age. The skills they learn are rarely, if ever, transmitted by parents: and what is more they learn about the nature of their own world, its social structure and its relationships in time outside the family. For millennia the family was the great transmitter and formulator of social custom; but it now only retains a shadow of this function, usually for very young children only.

Although the economic and education functions of the family have declined, most of us feel that it provides the most satisfactory emotional basis for human beings; that a secure family life breeds stability, a capacity not only for happiness, but also to adjust to society's demands. This, too, may be based on misjudgment, for family life in the past was not remarkable for its happiness. We get few glimpses into the private lives of men and women long dead, but when we do we often find strain, frustration, petty tyranny. For so many human beings family life was a prison from which they could not escape. And although it might create deep satisfactions here and there, the majority of the rich and affluent classes of the last four hundred years in Western Europe created for themselves a double standard, particularly as far as sex was concerned. In a few cities such as Calvin's Geneva, the purity of family life might be maintained, but the aristocracies of France, Italy and Britain tolerated, without undue concern, adultery, homosexuality and that sexual freedom which, for better or worse, we consider the hallmark of modern life. Indeed the family as the basic social group began firstly to fail, except in its property relations, amongst the aristocracy.

But what we think of as a social crisis of this generation—the rapid growth of divorce, the emancipation of women and adolescents, the sexual and educational revolutions, even the revolution in eating which is undermining the family as the basis of nourishment, for over a hundred years ago the majority of Europeans never ate in public in their lives—all of these things, which are steadily making the family weaker and weaker, are the inexorable result of the changes in society itself. The family as a unit of social organization was remarkably appropriate for a less complex world of agriculture and craftsmanship, a world which stretches back some seven thousand years, but ever since industry and highly urbanized societies began to take its place, the social functions of the family have steadily weakened—and this is a process that is unlikely to be halted. And there is no historical reason to believe that human beings could be less or more happy, less or more stable. Like any other human institution the family has always been molded by the changing needs of society, sometimes slowly, sometimes fast. And that bus load of children does no more than symbolize the failure, not of marriage, but of the role of the

old-fashioned family unit in a modern, urbanized, scientific and affluent
society.

Even a quick skimming reveals that Plumb offers, as you anticipated
he would, a historical view. He begins with a glance at one contemporary
family, but you probably noticed that by the second paragraph he speaks
as a historian, tracing the origins and development of the institution of
the family.

Highlighting, Underlining, Annotating

Now that you have the gist of Plumb's essay, go back and reread it; this
time, highlight or underline key passages as though you were marking
the text so that you might later easily review it for an examination. Your
purpose now is simply to make sure that you know what Plumb is getting at. You may strongly disagree with him on details or even on large
matters, and you would certainly make clear your differences with him if
you were to write about his essay; but for the moment your purpose is to
make sure that you know what his position is. See if in each paragraph
you can find a sentence that contains the topic idea of the paragraph. If
you find such sentences, mark them.

Caution: Do not allow yourself to highlight or underline whole paragraphs. Before you start to mark a paragraph, read it to the end, and then
go back and mark what you now see as the key word, phrase, or passage.
If you simply start marking a paragraph from the beginning, you may
end up marking the whole; and thus you will defeat your purpose, which
is to make highly visible the basic points of the essay.

You may also want to jot down, in the margins, questions or objections, and you may want to circle any words that puzzle you.

Time's up. Let's talk about the underlinings and highlightings.

No two readers of the essay will make exactly the same annotations.
To take a small example, a reader in Alaska would probably be more
likely to mark the passage about "the Esquimaux" in paragraph 4 than
would a reader in St Louis. But here is what one reader produced.

note
first
person

①was rather astonished when a minibus drove up
to my house and out poured <u>ten children</u>. They had
with them two parents, but <u>not one child</u> had them both   *new*
<u>in common as mother and father</u>, and two of them   *(California)*
belonged to neither parent, but to a former husband of   *style*
the wife who had died. Both parents, well into middle
age, had just embarked, one on his fourth, the other on
her third marriage. The children, who came in all sizes,
and ranged from blonde nordic to jet-haired Greek,
bounded around the garden, young and old as happy

as any children that Ⓘ have seen. To them, as
Californians, their situation was not particularly odd;
most of their friends had multiple parents. Indeed to
them perhaps the odd family was the one which
Western culture has held up as a model for two   *old style*
thousand years or more--the lifelong union of man and
wife. But it took me a very long time to believe that they
could be either happy or adjusted. And yet, were they   *who says*
a sign of the future, a way the world was going?   *they are*
                                                          happy?

first person   Unlike anthropologists or sociologists, ⟨historians⟩
again, but have not studied family life very closely. Until recently
less   ⟨we⟩ knew very little of the age at which people married
"personal" in Western Europe in the centuries earlier than the
nineteenth or how many children they had, or what the
rates of illegitimacy might be or whether, newly wed,
they lived with their parents or set up a house of their
own. Few of these questions can be answered with
exactitude even now, but ⟨we⟩ can make better guesses.
⟨We⟩ know even less, however, of the detailed sexual
practices that marriage covered: indeed this is a
subject to which historians are only just turning their
attention. But ⟨we⟩ do know much more of the function of
family life--its social role--particularly if we turn from
the centuries to the millennia and pay attention to the
broad similarities rather than the fascinating
differences between one region and another: and, if
we do, ⟨we⟩ realize that the family has changed far more   *change*
profoundly than even the bus load of Californians
might lead us to expect.

                 Basically the family has fulfilled three social   *1. provides*
3 functions functions--to provide a basic labor force, to transmit *labor*
property and to educate and train children not only   *2. transmits*
into an accepted social pattern, but also in the work   *property*
skills upon which their future subsistence would   *3. educates*
depend. Until very recent times, the vast majority of   *children*
children never went to any school: their school was the
family, where they learned to dig and sow and reap
and herd their animals, or they learned their father's
craft of smith or carpenter or potter. The ⟨unitary⟩ family *?*
was particularly good at coping with the small peasant
holdings, which covered most of the world's fertile
regions from China to Peru. In the primitive peasant
world a child of four or five could begin to earn its
keep in the fields, as they still can in India and Africa:
and whether Moslem, Hindu, Inca or Christian, one   *? couldn't*
wife at a time was all that the bulk of the world's   *wives earn*
population could support, even though their religion   *their keep?*
permitted them more. Indeed, it was the primitive
not also   nature of peasant economy, which gave the family, as
religious we know it, its wide diffusion and its remarkable
teachings? continuity.

Whether or not it existed before the (neolithic) (revolution) we shall never know, but certainly it must have gained in strength as families became rooted to the soil. Many very primitive people who live in a pre-agrarian society of hunting and food-gathering often tend to have a looser structure of marriage and the women a far greater freedom of choice and easier divorce, as with the Esquimaux, than is permitted in peasant societies. There can be little doubt that the neolithic revolution created new opportunities for the family as we know it, partly because this revolution created new property relations. More importantly it created great masses of property, beyond anything earlier societies had known. True, there were a few hunting peoples, such as the Kwakiutl Indians, who had considerable possessions--complex lodges, great pieces of copper and piles of fibre blankets, which periodically they destroyed in great battles of raging pride--but the property, personal or communal, of most primitive hunting people is usually trivial.

Of course different readers will find different passages of special interest and importance. Our personal histories, our beliefs, our preconceptions, our current preoccupations, to some extent determine how we read. For instance, when they come to the fifth paragraph some readers may mark Plumb's sexist language ("mankind"), and some may highlight the assertion that "Marriage was sanctified not only by the rites of religion, but by the transmission of property." Readers who are especially interested in class relations might also highlight and underline this sentence:

The patterns of family life were always looser for the rich and the favored.

Notice, by the way, that although Plumb makes this assertion he does not offer a value judgment. A reader might mark the sentence and add in the margin: *Still true, and outrageous!* Or, conversely, a reader may feel that the statement is false, and might write, *Really???*, or even *Not the rich, but the poor (free from bourgeois hangups) are sexually freer.*

As these last examples indicate, even when you simply set out to make a few notes that will help you to follow and to remember the essay-ist's argument, you may well find yourself making notes that record your **responses** (where you agree, what you question), notes that may start you thinking about the validity of the argument.

As we have already said, *what* you annotate will partly depend on what interests you, what your values are, and what your purpose is. True, you have read the essay because it was assigned, but Plumb's original readers read it for other reasons. It appeared first in a magazine and then in a collection of Plumb's essays. The original readers, then, were people who freely picked it up because they wanted to learn about the family or perhaps because they had read something else by Plumb, liked it, and wanted to hear more from this author.

Imagine yourself, for a moment, as a reader encountering this essay in a magazine that you have picked up. If you are reading because you want to know something about the family in an agrarian society, you'll annotate one sort of thing; if you are reading because as a child of divorced parents you were struck and possibly outraged by his first paragraph, you'll annotate another sort of thing; if you are reading because you admire Plumb as a historian, you'll annotate another sort of thing; and if you are reading because you dislike Plumb, you'll annotate something else. We remind you of a comment by Paul Valéry, quoted at the beginning of this chapter: "One reads well only when one reads with some personal goal in mind. It may be to acquire some power. It may be out of hatred for the author." An exaggeration, but there is something to it. (In the Book of Job, Job wishes that his "adversary had written a book.")

Summarizing

In your effort to formulate a brief version of what an essayist is saying, you may want to write a summary, especially if you found the essay difficult. A good way to begin is to summarize each paragraph in a sentence or two, or in some phrases. By summarizing each paragraph, you compile—without doing any additional work—an outline of the essay. Here is a student's outline of Plumb's essay.

1. Minibus in California: 10 children and 2 parents, but not one child was child of both adults. Different from traditional family. Sign of the way the world is going.
2. Many things not known about the past (age of marriage, sexual practices), but something known of the function of family life.
3. Three functions: providing a labor force, transmitting property, educating and training children. Peasant families today.
4, 5. After neolithic (agricultural?) revolution, family strengthened because people rooted to the soil (produced masses of property: land, house, or tools of a craft). Transmission of property sanctified marriage.
6, 7. Family was also school and basic social unit. Head of the household ruled (chose the mate for a child, etc.). In modern societies government has taken over many functions of patriarchs.
8. Despite loss of functions, most of us still feel that a family breeds stability, happiness. May be a misjudgment; family often was a prison. And for last 400 years the rich created a double standard, at least for sex.

9.   Decline of family (divorce, emancipation of women and adoles-
       cents, etc.) is result of historic <u>change in society itself</u>. Family ap-
       propriate for agricultural society but less in industrial and urban
       societies. Busload of kids symbolizes not the failure of marriage
       but the loss of role for old-fashioned family in a modern society.

Especially if an essay is complex, writing a summary of this sort can
help you to follow the argument. Glancing over your notes, you probably
can see, fairly easily, what the writer's *main* points are, as distinct from
the *subordinate* points and the examples that clarify the points.
Furthermore, since your summary is now a paragraph outline, you can
look it over to see not only what it adds up to, but also how the writer
shaped the material. Producing a summary, then, may be an activity that
is useful to you when you are *reading* an essay. It will almost surely help
you to grasp the essay and to remember its argument. And if you are
writing about the essay—perhaps to take issue with it or to amplify a
point that it makes—you may have to include in your essay a brief summary so that your readers will know what you are writing about.

How long should the summary be? Just long enough to give readers
what they need in order to follow your essay. If in a fairly long essay you
are going to take issue with several of Plumb's points, you may want to
give a fairly detailed summary—perhaps a page long.

For a short essay, however, something like the following passage
might be appropriate:

In "The Dying Family," J. H. Plumb argues that when society was
primarily agricultural, the family provided education and training, a labor
force, and a way of transmitting property. In today's industrialized society,
however, these functions are largely provided by the government, and
the traditional family is no longer functional.

(For further discussion of summaries, see the entry on pages 908–909 of
this book, in "A Writer's Glossary.")

Critical Thinking: Analyzing the Text

Writing a summary requires that you pay attention to the text, but it does
not require you to question the text, to think about such issues as whether
the author's assumptions are plausible and whether evidence supports
the generalizations. In reading an essay, in addition to being able to summarize it accurately you must engage in **critical thinking.** "Critical" here
does not mean finding fault ("Don't be so critical") but, rather, it means
paying close attention to the ways in which the parts form the whole. In
this sense, to read critically is to read analytically.

We have already said that you will probably find yourself putting
question marks in the margins next to words that you don't know and

that don't become clear in the context, and next to statements that you find puzzling or dubious. These marks will remind you to take action— perhaps to check a dictionary, to reread a paragraph, or to jot down your objection in the margin or at greater length in a journal.

But analytic readers also engage in another sort of questioning, though they may do so almost unconsciously. They are almost always asking themselves—or rather asking the text—several questions. You'll notice that these questions concern not only the writer's point but also the writer's craft. By asking such questions, you will learn about subject matter (for instance, about the history of the family in Plumb's essay) and also about some of the tricks of the writer's trade (for instance, effective ways of beginning). If you read actively, asking the following questions, you will find that reading is *not* a solitary activity; you are conversing with a writer.

- What is the writer's thesis?
- How does the writer support the thesis?
- What is the writer's purpose (to persuade, to rebut, to entertain, to share an experience, or whatever)?
- How do the writer's audience and purpose help shape the writing? (The place of publication is often a clue to the audience.) For instance, does the writer use humor or, on the other hand, speak earnestly? Are terms carefully defined, or does the writer assume that the audience is knowledgeable and does not need such information?
- What is the writer's tone?

These questions will help you to understand what you are reading and how writers go about their business. But you are also entitled to evaluate what you are reading, hence some other questions, of a rather different sort:

- How successful is the piece? What are its strengths and weaknesses? What do I especially like or dislike about it? Why?

We recommend that when you read an essay you ask each of these questions—not, of course, during an initial skimming, but during a second and third reading, after you have some sense of the essay.

These questions almost can be boiled down to one question:

What is the writer up to?

That is, a reader who is not content merely to take what the writer is handing out asks such questions as, Why *this* way of opening? Why *this* way of defining the term? The assumption that the writer has a purpose may be false. (We are reminded of a comment that Metternich, the keenly analytic Austrian statesman and diplomat, uttered when he learned that the Czar had died: "I wonder why he did that.") Yes, the writer may just be blundering along, but it's reasonable to begin with the assumption that the writer is competent. If under questioning the writer fails, you have at least learned that not everything in print is worthy.

Tone and Persona

Perhaps you know the line from Owen Wister's novel, *The Virginian:* "When you call me that, smile." Words spoken with a smile mean something different from the same words spoken through clenched teeth. But while speakers can communicate by facial gestures, body language, and changes in tone of voice, writers have only words in ink on paper. Somehow the writer has to help us to know whether, for instance, he or she is solemn, or joking, in earnest.

Consider the beginning of the first paragraph of J. H. Plumb's "The Dying Family."

> I was rather astonished when a minibus drove up to my house and out poured ten children. They had with them two parents, but not one child had them both in common as mother and father, and two of them belonged to neither parent, but to a former husband of the wife who had died. Both parents, well into middle age, had just embarked, one on his fourth, the other on her third marriage. The children, who came in all sizes, and ranged from blonde nordic to jet-haired Greek, bounded around the garden, young and old as happy as any children that I have seen.

Plumb's first sentence *could* have run thus:

> I noted with considerable surprise the fact that when a minibus drove up to my house, ten children got out of the vehicle.

This version contains nothing that is certifiably wrong—the grammar and spelling are satisfactory—but it lacks the energy of Plumb's version. In the original, Plumb is astonished rather than surprised, and the children don't just get out of the minibus, they "pour" out. Further, the original minibus is just a minibus; it doesn't become (as it unnecessarily does, in the revised version) a "vehicle." After all, who speaks of vehicles other than perhaps police officers when they say in an official report that they "apprehended the perpetrator in a speeding vehicle"?

Notice too, in the succeeding sentences, that the children "came in all sizes." If Plumb had said that the smallest child was about three feet tall, and the largest child must have been at least five feet tall, he might have been more exact, but he certainly would have been less engaging. As readers we probably enjoy the fairly colloquial tone that this distinguished professor is using.

What sort of person is Plumb? He seems to be a neighbor, chatting easily with us, not a remote professor delivering a lecture. And yet even in this paragraph, when he speaks of "two thousand years or more" of "Western culture" we realize that he is a historian who can speak with some authority. He may or may not be divorced, he may or may not be a loving parent, he may or may not be a good cook—there are countless things we don't know about him—so we can't really say what sort of person he is. We can, however, say what sort of *persona* (or personality) he conveys in his essay.

How do readers form an impression of a persona? By listening, so to speak, with a third ear, listening for the writer's attitude toward

- himself or herself,
- the subject, and
- the audience.

Still, different readers will, of course, respond differently. To take a simple example, readers who do not wish to hear arguments concerning new views of the family may dismiss Plumb as radical, or as lacking in basic moral values. But we think most readers will agree with us in saying that Plumb conveys the persona of someone who is (1) educated, (2) at least moderately engaging, (3) a good teacher, and (4) concerned with a significant issue. It's our guess, too, that Plumb hoped to be seen as this sort of person. If readers of his first paragraph conclude that he is conceited, stuffy, full of hot air, a threat to society, and so on, he has failed terribly, because he has turned his readers away.

There is a lesson for writers, too. When you reread your own drafts and essays, try to get out of yourself and into the mind of an imagined reader, say a classmate. Try to hear how your words will sound in this other person's ear; that is, try to imagine what impression this reader will form of your attitude toward yourself, your subject, and your reader.

A Reader Writes

All there is to writing is having ideas. To learn to write is to learn to have ideas.

Robert Frost

So far, the only writing that we have suggested you do is in the form of annotating, summarizing, and responding to some basic and some specific questions about the essayist's thesis and methods. All of these activities help you to think about what you are reading. "It is thinking," the philosopher John Locke wrote, "that makes what we read ours." But ultimately your thoughts will manifest themselves in your own essays, which probably will take off from one or more of the essays that you have read. Before we discuss writing about more than one essay, let's look at another essay, this one by C. S. Lewis (1898–1963).

Lewis taught English literature at Oxford and at Cambridge, but he is most widely known not for his books on literature but for his books on Christianity (*The Screwtape Letters* is one of the most famous), his children's novels (collected in a seven-volume set called *The Chronicles of Narnia*), and his science fiction (for instance, *Perelandra*). Lewis also wrote autobiographical volumes and many essays on literature and on morality. The essay printed here—the last thing that he wrote—was published in *The Saturday Evening Post* in December 1963, shortly after his death.

C. S. Lewis

We Have No "Right to Happiness"

After all," said Clare, "they had a right to happiness."

We were discussing something that once happened in our own neighborhood. Mr. A. had deserted Mrs. A. and got his divorce in order to marry Mrs. B., who had likewise got her divorce in order to marry Mr. A. And there was certainly no doubt that Mr. A. and Mrs. B. were very much in love with one another. If they continued to be in love, and if nothing went wrong with their health or their income, they might reasonably expect to be very happy.

It was equally clear that they were not happy with their old partners. Mrs. B. had adored her husband at the outset. But then he got smashed up in the war. It was thought he had lost his virility, and it was known that he had lost his job. Life with him was no longer what Mrs. B. had bargained for. Poor Mrs. A., too. She had lost her looks—and all her liveliness. It might be true, as some said, that she consumed herself by bearing his children and nursing him through the long illness that overshadowed their earlier married life.

You mustn't, by the way, imagine that A. was the sort of man who nonchalantly threw a wife away like the peel of an orange he'd sucked dry. Her suicide was a terrible shock to him. We all knew this, for he told us so himself. "But what could I do?" he said. "A man has a right to happiness. I had to take my one chance when it came."

I went away thinking about the concept of a "right to happiness."   5

At first this sounds to me as odd as a right to good luck. For I believe—whatever one school of moralists may say—that we depend for a very great deal of our happiness or misery on circumstances outside all human control. A right to happiness doesn't, for me, make much more sense than a right to be six feet tall, or to have a millionaire for your father, or to get good weather whenever you want to have a picnic.

I can understand a right as a freedom guaranteed me by the laws of the society I live in. Thus, I have a right to travel along the public roads because society gives me that freedom; that's what we mean by calling the roads "public." I can also understand a right as a claim guaranteed me by the laws, and correlative to an obligation on someone else's part. If I have a right to receive £100 from you, this is another way of saying that you have a duty to pay me £100. If the laws allow Mr. A. to desert his wife and seduce his neighbor's wife, then, by definition, Mr. A. has a legal right to do so, and we need bring in no talk about "happiness."

But of course that was not what Clare meant. She meant that he had not only a legal but a moral right to act as he did. In other words, Clare is—or would be if she thought it out—a classical moralist after the style of Thomas Aquinas, Grotius, Hooker and Locke. She believes that behind the laws of the state there is a Natural Law.[1]

I agree with her. I hold this conception to be basic to all civilization. Without it, the actual laws of the state become an absolute, as in Hegel. They cannot be criticized because there is no norm against which they should be judged.

The ancestry of Clare's maxim, "They have a right to happiness," is   10
august. In words that are cherished by all civilized men, but especially by Americans, it has been laid down that one of the rights of man is a right to "the pursuit of happiness." And now we get to the real point.

What did the writers of that august declaration mean?

It is quite certain what they did not mean. They did not mean that man was entitled to pursue happiness by any and every means—including, say, murder, rape, robbery, treason and fraud. No society could be built on such a basis.

---

[1]**Thomas Aquinas ... Natural Law** Lewis names some philosophers and theologians from the thirteenth century through the eighteenth who believed that certain basic moral principles are evident to rational people in all periods and in all cultures. (Editors' note)

They meant "to pursue happiness by all lawful means"; that is, by all means which the Law of Nature eternally sanctions and which the laws of the nation shall sanction.

Admittedly this seems at first to reduce their maxim to the tautology that men (in pursuit of happiness) have a right to do whatever they have a right to do. But tautologies, seen against their proper historical context, are not always barren tautologies. The declaration is primarily a denial of the political principles which long governed Europe: a challenge flung down to the Austrian and Russian empires, to England before the Reform Bills, to Bourbon France.[2] It demands that whatever means of pursuing happiness are lawful for any should be lawful for all; that "man," not men of some particular caste, class, status or religion, should be free to use them. In a century when this is being unsaid by nation after nation and party after party, let us not call it a barren tautology.

But the question as to what means are "lawful"—what methods of pursuing happiness are either morally permissible by the Law of Nature or should be declared legally permissible by the legislature of a particular nation—remains exactly where it did. And on that question I disagree with Clare. I don't think it is obvious that people have the unlimited "right to happiness" which she suggests.

For one thing, I believe that Clare, when she says "happiness," means simply and solely "sexual happiness." Partly because women like Clare never use the word "happiness" in any other sense. But also because I never heard Clare talk about the "right" to any other kind. She was rather leftist in her politics, and would have been scandalized if anyone had defended the actions of a ruthless man-eating tycoon on the ground that his happiness consisted in making money and he was pursuing his happiness. She was also a rabid teetotaler; I never heard her excuse an alcoholic because he was happy when he was drunk.

A good many of Clare's friends, and especially her female friends, often felt—I've heard them say so—that their own happiness would be perceptibly increased by boxing her ears. I very much doubt if this would have brought her theory of a right to happiness into play.

Clare, in fact, is doing what the whole western world seems to me to have been doing for the last forty-odd years. When I was a youngster, all the progressive people were saying, "Why all this prudery? Let us treat sex just as we treat all our other impulses." I was simple-minded enough to believe they meant what they said. I have since discovered that they meant exactly the opposite. They meant that sex was to be treated as no other impulse in our nature has ever been treated by civilized people. All the others, we admit, have to be bridled. Absolute obedience to your instinct for self-preservation is what we call cowardice; to your acquisitive impulse, avarice. Even sleep must be resisted if you're a sentry. But every

15

[2]**England . . . France** England before the bills that liberalized representation in Parliament in the nineteenth century, and France before the French Revolution of 1789–99. (Editors' note)

unkindness and breach of faith seems to be condoned provided that the object aimed at is "four bare legs in a bed."

It is like having a morality in which stealing fruit is considered wrong—unless you steal nectarines.

And if you protest against this view you are usually met with chatter about the legitimacy and beauty and sanctity of "sex" and accused of harboring some Puritan prejudice against it as something disreputable or shameful. I deny the charge. Foam-born Venus . . . golden Aphrodite . . . Our Lady of Cyprus[3] . . . I never breathed a word against you. If I object to boys who steal my nectarines, must I be supposed to disapprove of nectarines in general? Or even of boys in general? It might, you know, be stealing that I disapproved of.

The real situation is skillfully concealed by saying that the question of Mr. A.'s "right" to desert his wife is one of "sexual morality." Robbing an orchard is not an offense against some special morality called "fruit morality." It is an offense against honesty. Mr. A.'s action is an offense against good faith (to solemn promises), against gratitude (toward one to whom he was deeply indebted) and against common humanity.

Our sexual impulses are thus being put in a position of preposterous privilege. The sexual motive is taken to condone all sorts of behavior which, if it had any other end in view, would be condemned as merciless, treacherous and unjust.

Now though I see no good reason for giving sex this privilege, I think I see a strong cause. It is this.

It is part of the nature of a strong erotic passion—as distinct from a transient fit of appetite—that it makes more towering promises than any other emotion. No doubt all our desires make promises, but not so impressively. To be in love involves the almost irresistible conviction that one will go on being in love until one dies, and that possession of the beloved will confer, not merely frequent ecstasies, but settled, fruitful, deep-rooted, lifelong happiness. Hence *all* seems to be at stake. If we miss this chance we shall have lived in vain. At the very thought of such a doom we sink into fathomless depths of self-pity.

Unfortunately these promises are found often to be quite untrue. Every experienced adult knows this to be so as regards all erotic passions (except the one he himself is feeling at the moment). We discount the world-without-end pretensions of our friends' amours easily enough. We know that such things sometimes last—and sometimes don't. And when they do last, this is not because they promised at the outset to do so. When two people achieve lasting happiness, this is not solely because they are great lovers but because they are also—I must put it crudely—good people; controlled, loyal, fairminded, mutually adaptable people.

[3]**Foam-born Venus . . . Aphrodite . . . Cyprus** The Roman goddess Venus was identified with the Greek goddess of love, Aphrodite. Aphrodite sprang from the foam (*aphros*), and was especially worshipped in Cyprus. (Editors' note)

If we establish a "right to (sexual) happiness" which supersedes all the ordinary rules of behavior, we do so not because of what our passion shows itself to be in experience but because of what it professes to be while we are in the grip of it. Hence, while the bad behavior is real and works miseries and degradations, the happiness which was the object of the behavior turns out again and again to be illusory. Everyone (except Mr. A. and Mrs. B.) knows that Mr. A. in a year or so may have the same reason for deserting his new wife as for deserting his old. He will feel again that all is at stake. He will see himself again as the great lover, and his pity for himself will exclude all pity for the woman.

Two further points remain.

One is this. A society in which conjugal infidelity is tolerated must always be in the long run a society adverse to women. Women, whatever a few male songs and satires may say to the contrary, are more naturally monogamous than men; it is a biological necessity. Where promiscuity prevails, they will therefore always be more often the victims than the culprits. Also, domestic happiness is more necessary to them than to us. And the quality by which they most easily hold a man, their beauty, decreases every year after they have come to maturity, but this does not happen to those qualities of personality—women don't really care twopence about our *looks*—by which we hold women. Thus in the ruthless war of promiscuity women are at a double disadvantage. They play for higher stakes and are also more likely to lose. I have no sympathy with moralists who frown at the increasing crudity of female provocativeness. These signs of desperate competition fill me with pity.

Secondly, though the "right to happiness" is chiefly claimed for the sexual impulse, it seems to me impossible that the matter should stay there. The fatal principle, once allowed in that department, must sooner or later seep through our whole lives. We thus advance toward a state of society in which not only each man but every impulse in each man claims *carte blanche*.[4] And then, though our technological skill may help us survive a little longer, our civilization will have died at heart, and will—one dare not even add "unfortunately"—be swept away.

Responding to an Essay

After you have read Lewis's essay at least twice, you may want to jot down your responses to the basic questions that we introduced on page 15 after J. H. Plumb's essay. Here they are yet again, slightly abbreviated:

- What is the writer's thesis?
- How does the writer support the thesis?
- What is the writer's purpose?

---

[4]***Carte blanche*** full permission to act (French for "blank card") (Editors' note)

- How does the writer shape the purpose to the audience?
- What is the writer's tone?
- How successful is the piece? What are its strengths and weaknesses?

And here, to help you to think further about Lewis's essay, are some specific questions:

- Having read the entire essay, look back at Lewis's first five paragraphs and point out the ways in which he is not merely recounting an episode but is already conveying his attitude and seeking to persuade.
- Lewis argues that we do not have a "right to (sexual) happiness." What *duty* or *duties* do we have, according to Lewis?
- In paragraph 25 Lewis writes:

  When two people achieve lasting happiness, this is not solely because they are great lovers but because they are also—I must put it crudely—good people; controlled, loyal, fairminded, mutually adaptable people.

  If you know of a couple who in your opinion have achieved "lasting happiness," do you agree with Lewis's view that their achievement is largely because they are "good people"?
- Evaluate Lewis's comment in paragraph 28 on the differences between men and women.

If you find yourself roughing out responses to any of these questions, you may be on the way toward writing a first draft of an essay.

The Writing Process

An essay is a response to experience. J. H. Plumb saw (or says that he saw) a busload of people and was prompted to think about them and ultimately to write an essay on the family (page 6); C. S. Lewis heard (or says that he heard) someone utter a comment about a right to happiness, and he was set to thinking and then to writing about it (page 20). Their essays came out of their experience. By *experience* we do not mean only what they actually saw (since we can suspect that Plumb and Lewis may have invented the episodes they use at the start of their essays); their experience included things they had read about and had reflected on. After all, Plumb's bus and Lewis's report of Clare's remark were at most only triggers, so to speak. A good deal of previous experience and a good deal of later experience—chiefly in the form of reading and of *thinking* about what they had read—went into the production of their essays.

In short, writers think about their responses to experience. You have been actively reading their responses—engaging in a dialogue with these authors—and so you have been undergoing your own experiences. You have things to say, though on any given topic you probably are not yet certain of *all* that you have to say or of how you can best say it. You need to get further ideas, to do further thinking. How do you get ideas? The short answer is that you will get ideas if you engage in an imagined dialogue with the authors whom you are reading. When you read an essay, you will find yourself asking such questions as, What evidence supports this assertion? Is the writer starting from assumptions with which I don't agree? Why do I especially like (or dislike) this essay?

Many writers—professionals as well as students—have found it useful to get their responses down on paper, either as annotations in the margins or as entries in a journal, or both. Here, as a sample, are the annotations that one student jotted next to Lewis's third and fourth paragraphs.

It was equally clear that they were not happy with their old partners. Mrs. B. had adored her husband at the outset. But then he got smashed up in the war. It was thought he had lost his virility, and it was known that he had lost his job. Life with him was no longer what Mrs. B had <u>bargained</u> for. Poor Mrs. A., too. She had lost her looks--and all her liveliness. It might be true, as some said, that she consumed herself by bearing his children and nursing him through the long illness that overshadowed their earlier married life.

> *Loaded word. Makes her too calcu-lating*

> *These examples are caricatures. They really defeat L's purpose*

You musn't, by the way, imagine that A. was the sort of man who nonchalantly threw a wife away like the peel of an orange he'd sucked dry. Her suicide was a terrible shock to him. We all knew this, for <u>he told us so himself</u>. "But what could I do?" he said. "A man has a right to happiness. I had to take my one chance when it came."

> *Is CSL making him <u>too</u> awful?*

Annotations of this sort often are the starting point for entries in a journal.

Keeping a Journal

A journal is not a diary, a record of what the writer did during the day ("Today I read Lewis's 'We Have No "Right to Happiness"'"). Rather, a journal is a place to store some of the thoughts that you may have scribbled on a bit of paper or in the margin of the text—for instance, your initial response to the title of an essay or to something you particularly liked or disliked. It is also a place to jot down further reflections. You can record your impressions as they come to you in any order—almost as though you are talking to yourself. Since no one else is going to read your notes, you can be entirely free and at ease. The student whose annotations we reproduced a moment ago wrote the following entry in his journal:

> I find Lewis's writing is very clear and in its way persuasive, but I also think that his people--A. and B. and Clare--are not real people. They are almost caricatures. Anyway, he certainly has chosen people (or invented them?) who help him make his case. What if Mrs. B.'s husband had been a wife-beater, or maybe someone who molested their daughter? Would Lewis still think Mrs. B. was wrong to leave Mr. B.?

A second student wrote a rather different entry in her journal:

> Lewis at first seems to be arguing against a "right to happiness," but really he is arguing against adultery and divorce, against what we can call the Playboy morality--the idea that if a middle-aged man divorces his middle-aged wife because he now finds his young secretary attractive, he is acting maturely.

Here is a third entry:

> Terrific. That story about A. and B. really got to me. But is it true? Does it matter if it isn't true? Probably not; there are people like the A.'s and the B.'s. Lewis really is awfully good at holding my interest. And I was really grabbed by that business about a right to happiness being as strange as a right to be six feet tall. But my question is this: I agree that we don't have a right to be six feet tall, but why, then, do we have any rights? Lewis talks about Natural Law, but what is that?
>
> Is the idea of one husband and one wife "Natural Law"? If so, how come so many societies don't obey it? When Bertrand Russell talks about natural instincts and emotions "which we inherit from our animal ancestors," is this like Natural Law?
>
> Still, I think Lewis is terrific. And I think he is probably right about the difference between men and women. It seems obvious to me that men care more about a woman's looks than women care about a man's looks. How can this be checked?

You might even make a journal entry in the form of a letter to the author or in the form of a dialogue. Or you might have Mr. A. and Mrs. B. give *their* versions of the story that Clare reports.

Questioning the Text Again

We have already suggested that one way to increase your understanding of an essay and to get ideas that you may use in an essay of your own is to ask questions of the selection that you have read. Let's begin by thinking about the questions we asked following C. S. Lewis's "We Have No 'Right to Happiness'" (pages 24–25). All of these could provide topics for your own essays. Some were questions that might be asked of any essay, you'll recall—about the author's thesis, the way in which the author supports the thesis, the author's purpose, the author's persona or tone, and your evaluation of the essay. And there were questions specifically about Lewis's essay, concerning Lewis's comments on rights and his comments about the differences between men and women.

Probably the most obvious topic for an essay such as Lewis's is

What is the author's thesis, and how sound is it?

One student formulated the thesis as follows:

> We not only do not have a "right" to sexual happiness, but we probably cannot achieve lasting happiness if we allow sex to govern behavior that otherwise "would be condemned as merciless, treacherous and unjust."

An essay concerning Lewis's thesis might be narrowed, for example, to

Does Lewis give a one-sided view of divorce?

or

Does Lewis underestimate (or overestimate) the importance of sexual satisfaction?

But other topics easily come to mind, for instance:

- Lewis's methods as a writer
- The logic of Lewis's argument

Take the matter of Lewis's methods, a topic of special interest if you are trying to become a better writer. One student who planned to write about this topic made the following notes.

Summaries, Jottings, Outlines, and Lists

(Parenthetic numbers refer to Lewis's paragraphs.)

1. Purpose is obviously to persuade. How does he do it?
2. Very informal manner:
    a. Begins by telling of a conversation he had (1).
    b. Often uses "I"; for instance, "I went away thinking" (5); "this sounds to me" (6); "I can understand" (7); "I was simple-minded

enough to believe" (18). So the tone is personal, as if he and the reader were having a conversation.

3. Though informal, seems very educated:
    a. Cites authorities, apparently philosophers, in par. 8 (check these names); refers to Austrian, Russian, English, and French history (14).
    b. Educated vocabulary ("tautologies" in par. 14).

4. But also uses easy examples: Mr. and Mrs. A. and Mr. and Mrs. B. in first paragraph; stealing fruit (19-21).

5. Makes the abstract clear by being concrete. In par. 18, when he says that our impulses have to be controlled, he says, "Absolute obedience to your instinct for self-preservation is what we call cowardice. . . ."

6. Sentences are all clear. Some are very short ("I agree with her" 9), but even the long sentences--several lines of type--are clear. Give one (or maybe two) examples?

7. In next-to-last par., frankly speaks as a male: "domestic happiness is more necessary to them [that is, women] than to us." And "the quality by which they [that is, women] most easily hold a man," and "women don't really care twopence about our looks" (all in 28). Sense of a man talking heart-to-heart to men. But how might it strike a woman? Sexist? Ask Jane and Tina.

You may prefer to record your thoughts in the form of lists:

Methods:
    Examples
    Anecdote about A. and B. (par. 1)
    Stealing fruit (19-21)
Informal style:
    Uses "I" (many places)
    Also uses "we"
Clear sentences (give examples)
Vocabulary:
    Usually simple words
    A few hard words ("tautologies" in par. 14)
Beginning: an individual listening
End: rather authoritative: generalizes about men vs women

Further thinking and further readings of Lewis's essay produced more evidence, and of course the material then had to be reorganized into a clear and effective sequence, but these notes and lists were highly promising. The student who wrote them was well on the way to writing a strong first draft.

After converting his notes into a draft and then revising the draft, an interesting—yet rather common—thing happened. The student found himself dissatisfied with his point. He now felt that he wanted to say something different. The annotations and the drafts, it turned out, were a way of helping him to get to a deeper response to Lewis's essay, and so he rewrote his essay, changing his focus. But we are getting ahead of our story.

Getting Ready to Write a Draft

After jotting down notes (and further notes stimulated by rereading and further thinking), you probably will be able to formulate a tentative thesis, a point such as "Lewis argues with great skill," or "Lewis does not make clear the concept of Natural Law," or "Lewis generalizes too freely," or "Lewis has a narrow idea of why people divorce." At this point most writers find it useful to clear the air by glancing over their preliminary notes and by jotting down the thesis and a few especially promising notes—brief statements of what they think their key points may be. These notes may include some key quotations that the writer thinks will help support the thesis.

Draft of an Essay

On "We Have No 'Right to Happiness'"

When I first read the title of C. S. Lewis's essay, I was interested and also somewhat resistant. Without having given much thought to it, I believe that I do have a right to happiness. I don't want to give up this right or this belief. Still I was intrigued to know what Lewis had to say. After reading the essay, it seemed entirely reasonable to say that if there is a right to happiness there are also limits to it. So I decided to look at how Lewis managed to make me change my mind--at least part way.

C. S. Lewis is persuasive, especially because of three things. First, although Lewis (a professor) is obviously very learned, he uses an informal manner that sounds very natural and honest. Second, he gives clear examples. Three, his sentences are always clear. This is true even when they are not especially short. All of these things combine together to make his essay clear and interesting. Lewis is an Englishman, not an American.

Lewis's informal manner, especially seen in his use of the first-person pronoun, appears right away. In the second sentence, when he says "We were discussing something. . . ." He uses "I" in the fifth paragraph and in many later paragraphs.

Another sign of Lewis's informality is his use of such expressions as "It might be true, as some said," and "You mustn't, by the way, imagine," and "for one thing." It sounds like an ordinary person talking, even though Lewis also mentions the names of philosophers in paragraph 8, and in paragraph 14 mentions several historical matters.

Next I will deal with Lewis's examples. The examples help him to be clear to the reader. The essay begins with a story about four people. Two said they had a "right to happiness." In this story Lewis lets us see two people (Mr. A. and Mrs. B.) who behave very badly. They justify their behavior simply by saying they have a right to happiness. They behave so badly--Mr. A. deserts the wife who nursed him through a long illness, and Mrs. B. deserts her husband, who is a wounded veteran--that just to hear them talk about a "right to happiness" is almost enough to make you say they should not be happy and they certainly do not have a right to happiness. The example of Mr. and Mrs. A. and Mr. and Mrs. B. is the longest example that Lewis gives, but Lewis several times gives short examples. These short examples make his point clear. For instance, when he wants to show how silly it is to treat sex differently from all other impulses, he says that it is "like having a morality in which stealing fruit is considered wrong--unless you steal nectarines."

Another thing Lewis does to persuade the reader is to write very clear sentences. Some of his sentences are long--about three lines of print--but the reader has no trouble with them. Here is an example of this sort of sentence.

> A right to happiness doesn't, for me, make much more sense than a right to be six feet tall, or to have a millionaire for your father, or to get good weather whenever you want to have a picnic.

The only thing that causes any trouble is a few unfamiliar words such as "tautologies" (paragraph 14) and "tycoon" (paragraph 16), but you can understand the essay even without looking up such words.

Revising and Editing a Draft

To write a good essay you must be a good reader not only of the essay you are writing about but also of the essay you yourself are writing. We're not talking about proofreading or correcting spelling errors, though you must engage in those activities as well.

Revising. In revising their work, writers ask themselves such questions as,

> Do I mean what I say?
>
> Do I say what I mean? (Answering this question will cause you to ask yourself such questions as, Do I need to define my terms, add examples to clarify, reorganize the material so that a reader can grasp it?)

During this part of the process of writing, you do your best to read the draft in a skeptical frame of mind. In taking account of your doubts, you will probably unify, organize, clarify, and polish the draft.

- **Unity** is achieved partly by eliminating irrelevancies. In the second paragraph of the draft, for example, the writer says that "Lewis is an Englishman, not an American," but the fact that Lewis is English is not clearly relevant to the student's argument that Lewis writes persuasively. The statement should be deleted—or its relevance should be demonstrated.
- **Organization** is largely a matter of arranging material into a sequence that will assist the reader to grasp the point. If you reread your draft and jot down a paragraph outline of the sort shown on pages 13–14 and 28–29, you can then see if the draft has a reasonable organization—a structure that will let the reader move easily from the beginning to the end.
- **Clarity** is achieved largely by providing concrete details, examples, and quotations to support generalizations and by providing helpful transitions ("for instance," "furthermore," "on the other hand," "however").
- **Polish** is small-scale revision. For instance, one deletes unnecessary repetitions. In the first sentence of the second paragraph, "C. S. Lewis" can effectively be changed to "Lewis"—there really is no need to repeat his initials—and in the second sentence of the second paragraph "Lewis" can be changed to "he." Similarly, in polishing, a writer combines choppy sentences into longer sentences and breaks overly long sentences into shorter sentences.

Editing. After producing a draft that seems good enough to show to someone, writers engage in yet another activity. They edit; that is, they check the accuracy of quotations by comparing them with the original, check a dictionary for the spelling of doubtful words, check a handbook for doubtful punctuation—for instance, whether a comma or a semicolon is needed in a particular sentence.

A Revised Draft

Persuasive Strategies in C. S. Lewis's

~~On~~ "We Have No 'Right to Happiness'"

~~When I first read the title of C. S. Lewis's essay I was interested and also somewhat resistant. Without having given much thought to it, I believe that I do have a right to happiness. I don't want to give up this right or this belief. Still I was intrigued to know what Lewis has to say. After reading the essay it seemed entirely reasonable to say that if there is a right to happiness there are also limits to it. So I decided to look at how Lewis managed to make me change my mind, at least part way.~~

C. S. Lewis's "We Have No 'Right to Happiness'" is surprisingly persuasive-- "surprisingly" because I believe in the right to happiness which is mentioned in the Declaration of Independence. Lewis, an Englishman writing in an American magazine, probably knew he was facing an audience who did not hold his view, and he apparently decided to begin by stating his position as directly as possible in his title, "We Have No 'Right to Happiness'". How does he win his reader over?

C. S. Lewis is persuasive because in addition to thinking carefully, he writes effectively. Three features of his writing especially contribute to his effectiveness.

~~C. S. Lewis is persuasive especially because of three things.~~ First, although Lewis (a professor) is obviously very learned, he uses an informal manner that ~~sounds very natural and honest~~ helps to establish a bond between him and his reader. Second, he gives clear examples. ~~Three~~ Third, his sentences are always clear. This is true even when they are not especially short. All of these things combine together to make his essay clear and interesting. ~~Lewis is an Englishman, not an American.~~

Lewis's informal manner, especially seen in his use of the first-person pronoun, appears right away. ~~In~~ In the second sentence, when he says "We were discussing something. . . ." He uses "I" in the fifth paragraph and in many later paragraphs.

Another sign of Lewis's informality is his use of such expressions as "It might be true, as some said," and "You mustn't, by the way, imagine," and "for one thing." It sounds like an ordinary person talking, even though Lewis also mentions the names of philosophers in paragraph 8, and in paragraph 14 mentions several historical matters.

As for
~~Next I will deal with Lewis's~~ examples. *, which* ~~The examples~~ help him to be clear *, the story of Mr. & Mrs. A. and Mr. & Mrs. B. is a good illustration.* ~~to the reader. The essay begins with a story about four people.~~ *Mr. A. & Mrs. B. both of whom believed they* ~~Two said they~~ had a "right to happiness." ~~In this story Lewis lets us see two people (Mr. A. and Mrs. B.) who behave very badly. They justify their behavior simply by saying they have a right to happiness~~. They behave so badly--Mr. A. deserts the wife who nursed him through a long illness, and Mrs. B. deserts her husband, who is a wounded veteran--that just to hear them talk about a "right to happiness" is almost enough to make you *doubt that there can be such a right* ~~say they should not be happy and they certainly do not have a right to happiness~~. The example of Mr. and Mrs. A. and Mr. and Mrs. B. is the longest example that Lewis gives, but *he* ~~Lewis~~ several times gives short examples *, that* ~~These short examples~~ make his point clear. For instance, when he wants to show how silly it is to treat sex differently from all other impulses, he says that it is "like having a morality in which stealing fruit is considered wrong--unless you steal nectarines."

Lewis's third persuasive technique
~~Another thing Lewis does to persuade the reader~~ is to write very clear sentences. Some of his sentences are long--about three lines of print--but the reader has no trouble with them. Here is an example of this sort of sentence.

A right to happiness doesn't, for me, make much more

sense than a right to be six feet tall, or to have a

millionaire for your father, or to get good weather

whenever you want to have a picnic.
The sentence is fairly long, partly because the second half gives three examples, but because these examples are given in a parallel construction ("to be," "or to have," "or to get") the reader easily follows the thought.

True,
~~The only thing that causes any trouble is~~ a few unfamiliar words such as
                                    may cause a bit of trouble
tautologies (paragraph 14) and tycoon (paragraph 16), but ~~you~~ can
                                                        a reader
understand the essay even without looking up such words.

Of course Lewis has not absolutely proved that there is no "right to
happiness," but he has made a good, clear case. The clarity, in fact, is part
of the case. Everything that Lewis says here seems so obvious that a reader
is almost persuaded by Lewis's voice alone.

Rethinking the Thesis: Preliminary Notes

You'll probably agree that the student improved his draft, for instance by
deleting the original first paragraph and replacing it with a more focused
paragraph. But, as we mentioned earlier, when the student thought further about his revision, he was still dissatisfied with it because he no
longer fully believed his thesis.

He found that although he continued to admire Lewis's persuasive
techniques, he remained unpersuaded by Lewis's argument. He therefore
felt obliged to change the thesis of his essay from (approximately)
"Lewis's chief persuasive techniques are ..." to "Although Lewis is
highly skilled as a persuasive writer, even his rhetorical skill cannot overcome certain weaknesses in his thesis."

Here are some of the annotations that the student produced after he
recognized his dissatisfaction with his revised draft.

Mr. and Mrs. A. and B. may or may not be real people, but they cer-
     tainly seem UNREAL: too neatly suited (all good or bad) to L's
     purpose.

> The villains: Mr. A. (he tosses out his wife after she loses her
> looks, despite the fact that she wore herself out with his
> children and nursed him through long illness; even after
> wife commits suicide he doesn't see that he continues to talk
> selfishly); Mrs. B. (she leaves her husband when he gets
> wounded and he loses his "virility" and loses his job). Aren't
> these people a bit too awful? Are they really typical of
> people who divorce?

> The heroes--or saints? Mrs. A. (nursed husband through
> long illness, wore self out with the children); Mr. B. (injured
> in war; loses job).

Clare: She also seems too suited to CSL's thesis; she's pretty
     terrible, and stupid too.

Lewis on Divorce: He seems to think it is always motivated by a desire for
     sex, and that it is always wrong. But what if a husband abuses his

wife--maybe physically, or maybe verbally and emotionally? Maybe chronic alcoholic, refuses treatment, etc.? Or what if wife abuses husband--probably not physically, but verbally, and maybe she assaults kids? Or take another angle: what if woman married at too young an age, inexperienced, married to escape from an awful family, and now finds she made a mistake? Should she stay married to the man for life? In short, does Lewis see divorce from enough angles?

First five paragraphs are extremely interesting, but are unfair for three reasons:

1. Lewis <u>loads the dice</u>, showing us goodies and baddies, and then says (par. 5) that they set him to thinking about the ''right to happiness'';
2. He <u>overemphasizes the importance of sex</u>, neglects other possible reasons why people divorce;
3. His discussion of ''<u>Natural Law</u>,'' is not convincing to me. I simply am not convinced that there is a ''Law of Nature'' that ''eternally sanctions'' certain things.

Sexist??? Although CSL seems to be defending women (esp. par. 28, in which he says that promiscuity puts women at a double disadvantage), there is something sort of sexist in the essay, and I imagine that this will turn off women, and maybe even men. I know that <u>I'm</u> a little bothered by it.

The Final Version

We won't take you through the drafts that the student wrote, but in reading the final version, below, you will notice that although some of the points from the draft are retained, the thesis, as we said, has shifted. Notice, for instance, that the first paragraph of the revised draft is used in the final version but with two significant changes: in the first sentence the student now adds that he finds Lewis's essay "finally unconvincing," and in the last sentence of the paragraph he implies that he will discuss why the essay is "not finally convincing."

Jim Weinstein

Professor Valdez

English Composition 12

Style and Argument:

An Examination of C. S. Lewis's

''We Have No 'Right to Happiness'''

C. S. Lewis's ''We Have No 'Right to Happiness''' is, though finally unconvincing, surprisingly persuasive--''surprisingly'' because I believe in the right to happiness, which is mentioned in the Declaration of Independence. Lewis, an Englishman writing in an American magazine, probably knew he was facing an audience who did not hold his view, and he apparently decided to begin by stating his position as directly as possible in his title: "We Have No 'Right to Happiness.'" How does he nearly win his reader over? And why is he not finally convincing?

Lewis is highly (though not entirely) persuasive because he writes effectively. Three features of his writing especially contribute to his effectiveness. First, although Lewis (a professor) is obviously very learned, he uses an informal manner that helps to establish a bond between him and his reader. Second, he gives clear examples. Third, his sentences are always clear, even when they are not especially short. All of these things combine to make his essay clear and interesting--and almost convincing.

His informal manner, especially his use of the first-person pronouns, appears right away in the second sentence, when he says "We were discussing something. . . ." He uses "I" in the fifth paragraph and in many later paragraphs. Another sign of his informality is his use of such expressions as "It might be true, as some said," and "You mustn't, by the way, imagine." It sounds like an ordinary person talking.

Most of his examples, too, seem ordinary. They make his points seem almost obvious. For instance, when he wants to show how silly it is to treat sex differently from all other impulses, he says that it is "like having a morality in which stealing fruit is considered wrong--unless you steal nectarines" (p. 23). The touch of humor drives the point home.

Still, although Lewis seems thoughtful and he makes his argument very clear, the essay somehow does not finally persuade. The trouble may largely be Mr. and Mrs. A. and B., but there are other difficulties, too.

Mr. and Mrs. A. and B. are just too simple a case, too neat an illustration. Lewis of course wanted to make a clear-cut case, but a reader does not really believe in these people. They are caricatures: Mr. A. tosses out his wife after she loses her looks (and she lost them not only through the natural process of aging but through taking care of the family), and Mrs. B. leaves her husband, a wounded veteran. Of course it is conceivable that there really were a Mr. A. and a Mrs. B., but surely the pros and cons of divorce ought not to be based on cases like this, where it is so clear that Mr. A. and Mrs. B. are irresponsible. They are, one might say, as morally stupid as Clare is. But the fact that these people are selfish and stupid and that they each get a divorce does not prove that only selfish and stupid people seek divorce.

Nor do the experiences of the A.'s and the B.'s show that people who seek a divorce always are seeking sexual pleasure. We can imagine, for instance, a woman married to a wife-beater. Does she not have a right to be free of her abusive husband, a "right to happiness"? Nor need we limit our case to physical abuse. A husband (or a wife) can abuse a spouse verbally and emotionally and can be impossibly neglectful of the children. Or we can imagine a couple who married when very young-- perhaps partly for the sake of defying their parents, or maybe in order to escape from a bad family situation. In any case, we can imagine that one member of the couple now sees that a bad mistake was made. Need they stay tied to each other?

Lewis's essay is powerful, partly because it clearly advances a thesis that must seem strange to many Americans; and it is interesting, partly because Lewis makes his points clearly and he seems to be such a thoughtful and decent person. But in the end, the essay is not convincing. It is just a little too simple in its examples and in its suggestion that people who claim a right to happiness are really just saying that they want to get divorced so they can live legally with another sexual partner.

[New page]

Work Cited

Lewis, C.S. "We Have No 'Right to Happiness.'" The Little Brown Reader.

Ed. Marcia Stubbs, Sylvan Barnet, and William E. Cain. 9th ed. New

York: Longman, 2003. 20-24.

A Brief Overview of the Final Version

- First, a mechanical matter: A bibliographic note, on a separate page headed "Work Cited," tells the reader where the essay can be found.
- The title, though not especially engaging, is informative—more so than, say, "On an Essay by C. S. Lewis." Readers know that the writer will discuss Lewis's style and argument in a particular essay.
- The student's final essay is *not* simply a balanced debate, a statement of the pros and cons that remains inconclusive. Rather, the student argues a thesis: although Lewis's essay is in some ways admirable, it remains unconvincing.
- The student's thesis is stated early, in fact in the first paragraph. It's almost always a good idea to let your reader know early where you will be going.
- Quotations are used as evidence, not as padding. See, for example, paragraphs 3 and 4.
- The writer has kept his reader in mind. He has not summarized Lewis's essay in needless detail, but, on the other hand, he has not assumed that the reader knows the essay inside out. For instance, he does not simply assert that Mr. A. behaves very badly; rather, he reminds us that Mr. A. rejects his wife after she loses her looks. When he uses a quotation, he guides the reader to where in Lewis's essay the quotation can be found.
- He also keeps the reader in mind by using helpful transitions. In paragraph 2 notice "First," "Second," and "Third"; in paragraph 5, "Still" indicates a reversal of direction. Notice, too, that key words and phrases are repeated. Repetition of this sort, like transitions, makes it easy for the reader to follow the writer's train of thought. In the second paragraph, for example, he cites Lewis's "informal manner" as the first of three points of style. His next paragraph begins, "His informal manner. . . ." Similarly, the last sentence of paragraph 3 contains the words "ordinary person." The next paragraph begins, "Most of his examples, too, seem ordinary."
- So far we have talked about what is in the essay. But what is *not* in it is also worth comment. In the final essay, the student does *not* include all of the points he jotted down in his preliminary notes. He does not take up either Natural Law or the issue of sexism, probably because he felt unsure about both. Notes are points of departure; if when you get going you find you are going down a blind alley, don't hesitate to go back and drop the point.

A Checklist for Analyzing and Evaluating an Essay That You Are Writing About

When you read, try to read sympathetically, opening yourself to the writer's vision of things. But when you have finished a sympathetic reading—and an attentive reading—and you have made various sorts of notes, probably including an outline and a summary of the essay you are reading, you are ready to *analyze* the writer's methods and to *evaluate* the piece.

In **analyzing,** you will examine the relationships between the parts; that is, you will ask such questions as,

- What is the *topic* of the essay? Try to state it, preferably in writing, as specifically as possible. For example, broadly speaking, one might say that the subject of Lewis's essay is the right to happiness; but within this subject his topic, more specifically, is sexual freedom. Plumb's subject is the family, and his topic is the historical changes that the family has undergone.

- What is the essay's *thesis* (either stated or implied)? If you have located a *thesis sentence* in the essay, underline it and write *thesis* in the margin. If the thesis is implied, try to formulate it in a sentence of your own.

- What does the title do? What *purpose* does it suggest the writer holds?

- What is the function of the opening paragraph (or paragraphs)? What claim on our attention or beliefs does it make?

- What speaker or *persona* (see pages 16–17) does the writer create, and how does the writer create it?

- What is the tone? Does the tone (pages 16–17) shift as the essay progresses? If so, why?

- What *audience* is the writer addressing? The general, literate public, or a more specialized group?

- How is the argument set forth? By logic? By drawing on personal experience? What evidence is there that the writer is an authority on the topic? Are there other appeals to authority? What other kinds of evidence support the essay's claim? What are the author's underlying assumptions? Are they stated or implied, and are they acceptable to you, or can you challenge them?

- If there is a formal, explicit conclusion, underline or restate it. If the conclusion is not stated but is implied, what does the writer want us to conclude?

In **evaluating,** you will ask such questions as,

- Is the essay as clear as it can be, given the complexity of the material? For instance, do specific examples help to make the generalizations clear? Are crucial terms adequately defined? If the thesis is not explicitly stated, is the essay unclear or is it perhaps better because of the indirectness?

- If the conclusion is not stated but implied, why does the writer not state it?

- Is the argument (if the essay is chiefly an argument) convincing, or is it marred by faulty thinking? If statistics are used, are they sound and relevant? If authorities are quoted, are they indeed authorities (rather than just big names) on this topic?

- Is the essay interesting? If so, in what ways, and if not, why not—which gets us back to analysis. If there are passages of undisguised argument, for instance, are they clear without being repetitious and boring? Do specific examples clarify and enliven general assertions?

- If the essay includes narrative or descriptive passages, are they pertinent? Should they have been amplified, or should they have been reduced or even deleted?

- How is the essay organized? Is the organization effective? Does the essay build to a climax?

Another way of thinking about the criteria for evaluating an essay is to ask:

- Is the essay persuasive (whether because of its logic or because of the power of the speaker's personality)?
- Does the essay give pleasure?

Don't hesitate to demand that an essay give you pleasure. The author probably thought that he or she was writing well, and certainly hoped to hold your interest throughout the essay and to make you feel that you were learning something of interest. In short, the author hoped that you would like the essay. You have every right to evaluate the essay partly by considering the degree of pleasure that it affords. Of course, in your essay you cannot simply say that you enjoyed an essay or that you were bored by it. You will have to support your assertions with reasons based on evidence. To support your assertions you must have read the writer's words carefully, so we are back to an earlier point: the first thing to do if you are going to write about a piece of writing is to read it attentively, pen or pencil in hand.

As you read and reread the material that you are writing about, subjecting it to the kinds of questions we have mentioned, your understanding of it will almost surely deepen. You will probably come to feel that it is better—or worse—than you had thought at first, or in any case that it is somewhat different.

As you prepare to write your own essay and as you draft it, you are learning, feeling your way toward a considered analysis. But once having said something—whether in a mental question to yourself or in a note or a draft—you have to evaluate your thought and improve it if it doesn't stand up under further scrutiny.

CHAPTER 3

Academic Writing

Kinds of Prose

Traditionally, prose is said to be of four kinds: **Exposition** (its chief purpose is to explain), **Description** (it sets forth a detailed account of appearances or sensations), **Narration** (it recounts a sequence of events, telling a story), and **Persuasion** or **Argument** (it attempts to get readers to accept or act on your views). Thus, an essay or a book on how to improve our game of tennis chiefly will be an

- *exposition*—a putting forth of information.
- In fact, however, the essay or book on how to improve our game probably will also include a good deal of *description* (it will describe as accurately as possible the motion of the arm),
- and it may include some *narration* ("Tennis seems to have originated in the courts of fourteenth-century France, originally was played with balls stuffed with horse hair, and from France the game traveled to Germany and England . . . ," or "You may already be familiar with the story of how Venus Williams became the great player that she now is, but the story is worth repeating here").
- The discussion of how to improve our tennis probably will not, however, contain much *persuasive* writing, because the author assumes that the readers are already sold on the game. On the other hand, one can reasonably say that simply by writing about how to improve your game, the author is in effect persuading you to stay with the game, implicitly telling you that, gee, even *you* can become a pretty good player.

When you think about it, almost *all* writing is persuasive, since it says, in effect, "I find this interesting and I want you to find it interesting too." Even a note on a refrigerator door, "Egg salad sandwich and apple on lower shelf," is partly an attempt to persuade the reader to leave the cold roast beef and the ice cream alone. Consider for a moment Thomas Jefferson's *Declaration of Independence* (page 745). On the surface, it is chiefly *expository*. Jefferson explains why the time has come for certain people to declare their independence from England; that's the expository part, the setting forth of information, though it also includes a good deal of narration, since Jefferson tells us that the King of England did this ("He has dissolved Representative Houses repeatedly") and the king did that ("He has kept among us, in times of peace, Standing Armies"). Jefferson offers this information because he wishes to *persuade* the international community—especially the French—to support the revolution. Or consider a very different piece of writing, also by a political figure, Lincoln's *Gettysburg Address* (page 626). Surely Lincoln was not chiefly concerned with exposition or narration or description. True, he tells his hearers that "four score and seven years ago our fathers brought forth on this continent, a new nation" (narration), but they already knew *that* story; and he explains to them that they cannot dedicate the cemetery because the dead men have already hallowed it (exposition). But the speech essentially is meant to celebrate the heroism of the dead, and, by reminding the audience of the heroism of the fallen soldiers, the speech seeks to inspire—to persuade—the living to continue the battle. Of these two essays, *The Declaration of Independence* is closer to academic writing than is *The Gettysburg Address.*

More about Critical Thinking: Analysis and Evaluation

In Chapter 1 we talked briefly about critical thinking and about analysis, and we now want to amplify our discussion, but first we should devote a few more words to the term "academic writing."

Exactly what is "academic writing"? *Academic* comes from the Greek *Academos,* a garden near Athens where the philosopher Plato taught. Because of its connection with a great teacher, the name of the garden came to refer to any place where the arts or sciences or both are taught or fostered. Academic writing is the sort of writing done in the academy—in colleges and universities. Since each academic discipline requires its own sort of writing, however, several kinds of writing are done in an academic setting. In literature courses, students chiefly analyze and evaluate works of literature—but they may also be required to write a story, poem, or play. In sociology courses, students may be asked to analyze and evaluate the views of a particular sociologist—but they may also be asked to interview authorities or perhaps ordinary folk, and to present their findings in writing.

Still, at the heart of most academic writing—most of the writing that you will do in college—is an activity that can be called *critical thinking,* which consists chiefly of *analyzing* and *evaluating.* Exactly what is analysis? Literally, it is "separating into parts," and a good way to get going on an analysis is to ask what the parts are. Let's talk briefly about "hate speech," a topic addressed in Derek Bok's "Protecting Freedom of Expression on the Campus" (page 762), an essay that was prompted by the display of a Confederate flag hung from the window of a dormitory. Is the display of a Confederate flag "hate speech"? It's not literally speech, of course, but probably most people would agree that the act of displaying the flag might be closely comparable to verbally expressing some ideas. But exactly what is hate speech? Suppose X uses an ethnic term that Y finds offensive, but X says he used it playfully? Or suppose X admits that the word was used aggressively, and suppose we all agree that such aggressive language is bad; we still have to think about *how bad* it is. Bad enough so that it ought to be regulated by the college? Punishable by a reprimand? Suspension? Expulsion?

If in an effort to think analytically we ask ourselves such questions (and perhaps even take notes to help us advance our thoughts), we might find we are thinking along these lines:

- What is hate speech? How is it distinguished from mere unthinking expression, or high spirits? Must the speech concern race, religion, ethnicity, or sexual preference? If *X* calls *Y* a fat pig, does this show an offensive hatred of obesity? (In asking the question, "What is . . . ?" we are getting into matters of *definition*.)
- The First Amendment to the Constitution guarantees freedom of speech, but it does *not* protect *all* speech (for instance, libel, false advertising, incitements to violence). Does hate speech belong to protected speech, or does it belong to *un*protected speech? (Here we are concerned with *classification*, with trying to see to what larger class of things something belongs.)
- How bad, after all, is hate speech? Bad, yes, but probably no one would suggest that it is as bad as murder or rape, or that it should be punished by long-term jail sentences. By one day in jail? By a reprimand? (Here we are concerned with quality, with evaluation.)

As you ask yourself questions such as these, and as you seek to answer them, you will probably find that your views are changing, perhaps slightly (maybe you are refining them), perhaps radically. The writer E. M. Forster tells of a little girl who, when instructed to think before she spoke, shrewdly replied, "How do I know what I think until I hear what I say?" Only by the process of hearing what we say, and then testing and pressing further in a mental conversation with ourselves, can we hope to have ideas that our fellow students and our instructors will value. When you write an academic paper, your instructor will expect you to have done this sort of work, and if you have done it, you will recognize that you have indeed been thinking, been educating yourself. If your paper is connected to Derek Bok's essay, you may begin with a brief summary of his essay (we'll talk more about summaries later), in which your thinking doesn't go much beyond (1) understanding what Bok says, and (2) setting forth his thesis accurately and concisely; but soon you will get around to offering an *analysis* and probably an *evaluation*, to putting on paper the results of your serious, critical thinking.

The essays in *The Little, Brown Reader* contain a good deal of information, but chiefly you will read them not for the information they contain— as Robert Reich points out in his essay on the future of work, the world is changing and today's facts will not be tomorrow's facts; rather, you read these essays chiefly for the ideas they advance, and for the habits of thought that they display. And you will respond to them largely by setting forth arguments of your own. Writing based on serious *thinking* is what is expected of you. One of the reasons you are attending college is to acquire practice in thinking. As William Cory says (page 419), one goes to school not only for knowledge—facts, we might say—but for

the art of assuming at a moment's notice a new intellectual posture, for the art of entering quickly into another person's thought, for the habit of submit-

Sitting Bull and Buffalo Bill, 1886

ting to censure and refutation, for the art of indicating assent or dissent in graduated terms. . . .

For a moment let's put aside the writings in this book, and look at a photograph of Sitting Bull and Buffalo Bill, taken in 1886 by William Notman. William Cody got his nickname from his work as a supplier of meat for workers on the Kansas Pacific Railway, but he got his fame from his exploits as an army scout and a fighter against the Sioux Indians. Sitting Bull, a chief of the Sioux Indians, had defeated Custer at the battle of Little Big Horn some ten years before this picture was taken, but he soon fled to Canada. In 1879 he was granted amnesty and he returned to the United States, where for a while he appeared in Buffalo Bill's Wild West Show. In 1890 whites, fearful of an Indian uprising, attempted to arrest Sitting Bull, and he was killed during the encounter.

What you have just read cannot pass for an example of critical thinking. We hope the writing is clear, but about the only thinking that we were forced to do was to decide how much information to give. Should we have added that Sitting Bull encouraged the Sioux not to sell their lands, and thus he enraged the whites? Should we have added that Buffalo Bill rode for the Pony Express? Or that he invented some of his greatest exploits? Probably none of these points needs to be made here, in a brief introduction to the photograph. In short, we made some choices—we decided to give minimal information—and that was that. But now let's think—think critically—about the picture. We can begin (and this may sound like a contradiction) with our emotional response, our gut feelings. We are interested in this picture—but why?

We begin to ask ourselves questions, a method that, we have seen, almost always helps to develop one's thoughts. What is going on here? There are two figures, but they are so different. Buffalo Bill, head brightly illuminated, is looking off into the distance, rather like a modern-day political candidate, whose upward and outward glance implies that he or she is looking into the future. His right hand is on his heart, in a patriotic or noble gesture; his left leg is thrust forward. He wears a mammoth buckle, a fancy jacket, and shiny hip boots. His hand is above Sitting Bull's on the gun, and he is both behind Sitting Bull and (by virtue of his left leg) in front of Sitting Bull. Buffalo Bill, in short, is all show biz. If we look closely at the setting, we see that the meeting is not taking place in the great outdoors; rather, the setting is a sort of stage set, presumably in a photographer's studio.

What of Sitting Bull? Whereas Buffalo Bill clearly was striking a pose for the camera, Sitting Bull seems indifferent to the camera. Later in this chapter we will discuss comparing at length, but here we want only to mention that comparing is an excellent way to perceive what is unique about each of the things being compared. By comparing these two figures, we can more clearly see Buffalo Bill's flamboyance—and Sitting Bull's reserve. Sitting Bull seems withdrawn; his face, tilted downward, is mostly in shadow; his body seems inert; his right arm hangs lifelessly; his headdress is splendid, but his trousers are baggy and his belt dangles beneath his shirt. His hand on the rifle is subordinated to Buffalo Bill's.

May we say that now we are really *thinking* about the picture? An *un*thinking description would say, "The picture shows the two figures, dividing the space approximately equally, each in costume." This statement is true, and it might indeed find a place in the early stage of an analytic essay on the photograph, but your teachers—you are writing in an academy—expect more than an accurate, neatly typed description.

Here is the final paragraph from one of the best student essays we have received on this photograph. (The earlier paragraphs specified the differences in pose, costume, and so on, along the lines that we have just set forth.)

Buffalo Bill is obviously the dominant figure in this photograph, but he is not the outstanding one. His efforts to appear great only serve to make him appear small. His attempt to outshine Sitting Bull strikes us as faintly ridiculous. We do not need or want to know any more about Buffalo Bill's personality; it is spread before us in this picture. Sitting Bull's humility and dignity make him more interesting than Buffalo Bill, and make us wish to prove our intuition and to ascertain that this proud Sioux was a great chief.

Of course the photograph might lead a student to another, related topic. For instance, a student might want to know more about the photographer, William Notman. What did Notman think the photograph said to viewers? Was Notman setting forth a compassionate statement about the American Indian? Or was he just doing a job for Buffalo Bill? One might do some research on Notman, first, perhaps, by turning to a handsome book of his photographs, *Portrait of a Period*, edited by J. Russell Harper and Stanley Triggs. Research on Notman might lead you to conclude that his pictures often subtly undermine the pretensions of his heroic sitters, or you might find, on the contrary, that Notman celebrates heroism of all kinds, white and Indian. Or you might find that, for some strange reason, his pictures of Indians are far more interesting than his pictures of whites.

If a student writing about Notman's photographs does no more than tell us that the book has 75 pictures, that they are black and white, that all are portraits, that . . . , the student is not presenting the sort of writing expected in an academic community. Such information if presented briefly is acceptable as a start, acceptable as establishing a framework, but it is only a start; it is *not* critical thinking, it is *not* academic writing.

One last example of a related essay that would exemplify critical thinking. You might want to read the entries on Sitting Bull and Buffalo Bill in two versions of the *Encyclopaedia Britannica*, the 9th edition (1911) and the most recent edition. If you do, take note of the differences between the two versions, and then think about what these differences tell us about the early twentieth century and the last decade of the twentieth century.

Joining the Conversation: Writing about Differing Views

Your instructor will probably ask you to read more than one essay in some section of this book. The chief reason for such an assignment is to stimulate you to think about some complex issue. After all, no one essay on any topic of significance can claim to say all that needs to be said about the topic. Essays that advocate similar positions on, say, capital punishment may, because of slightly different emphases, usefully supplement one another; and even two radically opposed essays may both contain material that you find is essential to a thoughtful discussion of the topic.

Let's say that you read an essay supporting the death penalty. Perhaps, as an aid to grasping the author's argument, you prepared a summary of the essay, and you notice that the writer's chief points are these:

1. The death penalty serves as a deterrent.
2. Justice requires that murderers pay an appropriate price for their crimes.

These basic points probably are supported by some evidence, but you have been reading critically, and you have wondered whether this or that piece of evidence is compelling. You have also wondered if more can't be said on the other side—not only by specific refutation of certain arguments, but perhaps also by arguments that the first essayist has not raised. You turn to a second essayist, someone who opposes the death penalty, and who (you find when you summarize the essay) in effect offers these arguments:

1. The death penalty does not serve as a deterrent.
2. If the death penalty is inflicted mistakenly, the error cannot be corrected.
3. The death penalty is imposed unequally; statistics indicate that when blacks and whites are guilty of comparable offenses, blacks are more likely to be sentenced to death.

It is now evident that the two writers are and are not talking about the same thing. They are talking about the death penalty, but for the most part they are not confronting the same issues. On only one issue—deterrence—do they face each other. On this issue you will want to think hard about the evidence that each offers. Possibly you will decide that one author makes a compelling case at least on this issue, but it is also possible that you will decide that the issue cannot be resolved. Or you may find that you can make a better case than did either writer.

Think about the other arguments offered—on the one hand that justice requires the death penalty, and on the other hand that it can be mistakenly inflicted and is awarded unequally. You will not only want to think hard about each of these points, but you will also wonder why only one of the two essayists took them up. Is one or the other argument so clearly mistaken that it is not worth discussing? Or is a particular argument one that can't be proved either true of false? Or are the writers working from different **assumptions** (unexamined beliefs)? For instance, the writer who argues that the death penalty is capriciously enforced may assume that race prejudice cannot be overcome, whereas a writer who rejects the argument may assume that the courts can and will see to it that the death penalty is imposed impartially. As a critical reader, you will want to be alert to the assumptions that writers make. You'll have to ask yourself often, *What assumption lies beneath this assertion?* That is, what belief is so firmly held, and is assumed to be so self-evident, that the writer does not bother to assert it? Do I share this assumption? Why?

If you are asked to compare two essays that offer sharply differing views, you probably will want to point out where the two face each other and where they don't. You probably will want also to offer an evaluation of the two. Or, depending on the assignment, you may use the two merely as a point of departure for your own essay on the topic. That is, you may want to draw on one or both—giving credit of course—and then offer your own serious thoughts.

Writing about Essays That Are Not Directly Related: A Student's Notes and Journal Entries

Let's assume that your instructor has asked you to read Plumb's "The Dying Family" (page 6) and Lewis's "We Have No 'Right to Happiness'" (page 20), and has asked you to compare them. Both of these essays concern family relationships, but they do not take distinctly different positions on a single controversial topic. They are, we might say, thoughtful voices in a conversation that is consistently interesting but is wide-ranging rather than sharply focused.

Let's say that you settle on Plumb's and Lewis's attitudes toward their material. Perhaps your first thought is that Lewis very obviously offers value judgments, whereas Plumb, as a historian, simply reports what has happened in history.

On rereading the two essays, you may find yourself making notes somewhat like these notes that a student made:

1. Some of Plumb's assumptions:
   Family evolves: history a process (not static, not cyclical).
   Idea of parents wedded until death no longer needed in our urban, industrial society.
   Happiness not increasing or decreasing.
2. I'm surprised to find so many assumptions in the writings of a historian.
   I thought history was supposed to be an account, the "story" of what happened: in Social Studies we learned history is "value-free."
3. Some of Lewis's assumptions:
   Lewis very clearly makes assumptions, for instance, belief in the existence of "Natural Law" (par. 8) and belief that "domestic happiness is more necessary to them than to us" (to women, than to men), par. 28. Also assumes that women don't care much about men's looks (28)--but is this true? How might someone be able to prove it?
4. Big difference between Plumb and Lewis on assumptions. I think that Plumb makes assumptions but is hardly aware of them, whereas Lewis makes them and puts them right up front. With Lewis we know exactly where he stands. For instance, he obviously believes that we can use our free will to behave in ways that he considers proper. He even talks

about "good people; controlled, loyal, fairminded" (25). (It's hard to imagine Plumb talking about "good people"; he only talks about whether people are "happy" or "stable.") Lewis pretty clearly believes not only that it's our job to act decently but that we <u>can</u> act decently. Seems not to accept the idea that we can be overwhelmed by passion or by the unconscious. Probably very anti-Freud. Anyway, his position is clear (and I agree with it). With Plumb we can hardly argue--at least I can't--since I'm not a historian. I don't know if what he says about the past really is true, but his opening paragraph strikes me as completely made up.

5.   Attitudes toward change in family:
      For Lewis, a moralist, breakdown of family is a disaster; for Plumb, a fact of social evolution.

One student, whose thoughts were something like those that we have just presented, wrote two entries in his journal.

> Plumb: As I see it, he makes assumptions that pretty much go against what Lewis is arguing. Plumb looks at this family in California, and he says they are happy and he thinks everything is just fine. Well, maybe not fine, but at least he says that these children seem "as happy as any children that I have seen." I'm not so sure they are as happy as most. I <u>know</u> (from my own experience and from what I hear from friends) what divorced kids go through. Divorce may be normal (common, ordinary), but is it <u>right</u>? It seems to lead to so much unhappiness (for parents <u>and</u> children). Putting aside my own feelings, I can certainly see that my parents aren't especially happy with their new families. But there is Plumb, with his happy busload. Is he kidding? Or trying to fool us?

> Lewis: Lewis says we have no right to happiness--no right to divorce, remarry several times, and have families like that busload of people Plumb talks about. Lewis seems to be saying that divorce is morally wrong. Why? What are his reasons? I think he gives two: 1) it makes people unhappy (for instance, Mr. B., the wounded veteran, must have been miserable when Mrs. B. left him), and 2) it is against "Natural Law." But come to think of it, what <u>is</u> Natural Law? What makes divorce contrary to Natural Law? <u>Is</u> it really "<u>un</u>natural"? Why? Lots of religions--maybe most of them--accept <u>di</u>vorce. And certainly governments accept it. So what makes it unnatural? What is it that Bertrand Russell said about our animal instinct? Check this.

The next day, after rereading Lewis's essay and the two entries, he wrote two additional entries in his journal:

> I think that I agree with Lewis that we don't have a right to happiness, just as we don't have a right to be rich and handsome. But I wish Lewis had given some clear reasons instead of just saying

that we have to remain for life with one spouse--even if we see that we have made a bad choice--because "Natural Law" tells us that we can't change. Come to think of it, Lewis <u>does</u> give some reasons against giving sex a special privilege: we hurt others, and we kid ourselves if we think each passion will last.

Both Lewis and Plumb use short stories to make their points: Plumb's busload of Californians, Lewis's Mr. and Mrs. A. and Mr. and Mrs. B. Suppose these stories aren't true and Lewis and Plumb made these stories up. Does that matter?

The Student's Final Version

Drawing on this material, the student drafted and revised an essay and then submitted it to peer review. Then, in the light of the comments and further thinking, he wrote the final version, which we give here. Our marginal comments summarize some of the strengths that we find in the finished essay. (*Note:* The original essay was, of course, double-spaced.)

Title gives a clue to topic.

Opening paragraph names authors and essays, and indicates thesis— that the essays strongly differ.

Clear transition ("Despite these great differences").

Details support generalization.

Two Ways of Thinking about Today's Families

J. H. Plumb in "The Dying Family" and C. S. Lewis in "We Have No 'Right to Happiness'" both note that to-day's families often consist of adults who have been divorced. But that is about as much as they would agree on. Judging from an example Plumb gives of a minibus with ten happy children, none of whom had both parents in common, Plumb thinks there is no reason to regret, much less to condemn, the behavior that presumably has produced this sort of family. And judging from the examples Lewis gives of Mrs. B. who left her wounded husband and of Mr. A. who left his worn-out wife, Lewis thinks that the pursuit of happiness--sexual happiness at the expense of marriage--is immoral.

Despite these great differences, there are interesting similarities in the essays. The essays are both by Englishmen, are about the same length, were both written around the middle of the twentieth century, and both begin with an example. Plumb begins with his minibus of ten children and two adults, Lewis with his Mr. and Mrs. A. and Mr. and Mrs. B. Certainly both examples are striking. I'm not sure that, on rereading the essays, I believe either example is real, but they caught my attention. I must say, however, that I have more trouble believing in Plumb's happy busload than in Lewis's two couples. Putting aside my own experience as the child of divorced parents (each of whom has remarried), ten children--no <u>two</u> of whom have the same two parents--just seems like too many.

Again a clear transition ("In addition to").

In addition to these relatively superficial resemblances, there is also a deeper resemblance. Plumb and Lewis are both talking about the great change in sexual behavior that came about in the twentieth century, especially in the middle of the century when divorce became respectable and common. But there is a big difference in their response. Plumb, writing as a historian, tries to understand why the change came about. Having concluded that the family no longer serves the purposes that it served in earlier periods, Plumb is not disturbed by the change. He ends his essay by saying,

Quotation is used as evidence to support student's assertion that Plumb "is not disturbed."

"And that bus load of children does no more than symbolize the failure, not of marriage, but of the role of the old-fashioned family unit in a modern, urbanized, scientific and affluent society" (9). Lewis, on the other hand, writes as a moralist. He tries to understand why the A.'s and B.'s of this world do what they do, and he sees that they behave as they do because of "the sexual impulse" (23). But Lewis does more than see

Cites evidence.

what they do; he <u>judges</u> what they do, in particular he judges behavior against what he calls "Natural Law" (21) and "the Law of Nature" (22). And he makes it clear that he is not speaking only of sexual behavior. After saying that women are at a disadvantage in a society that tolerates conjugal infidelity, he makes a final point that goes far beyond matters of sex:

Quotation of more than four lines is indented five spaces at left.

> Secondly, though the "right to happiness" is chiefly claimed for the sexual impulse, it seems to me impossible that the matter should stay there. The fatal principle, once allowed in that department, must sooner or later seep through the whole of our lives. (24)

Transition ("For Plumb, then") by means of brief summary.

Parallel construction ("For Plumb. . . For Lewis") highlights similarities and differences.

For Plumb, then, the family is something produced by history, and it changes as history goes on. For Lewis, the family--two adults wedded for life--is something in accordance with Natural Law, and since this law does not change, the nature of the family does not change, or, rather, <u>should not</u> change. This difference between the essays, of course, is far more important than all of the similarities. Each essay is interesting to read, and maybe each is even convincing during the moments that someone is reading it. But finally the essays are strongly opposed to each other, and it is impossible to agree with both of them.

Student briefly
offers objections
to each essay.

Discloses
reasons.

How is a reader to decide between the two essays? Doubtless the earlier experience of a reader predisposes that reader to believe certain things and not to believe other things. Reading Plumb's essay, I find, drawing on my experience, that I cannot believe in his busload of happy children. Plumb does not seem to be aware that children are greatly pained by the divorce and remarriage of their parents. In short, Plumb seems to me to be too satisfied that everything is just fine and that we need not regret the loss of the old-style family. On the other hand, Lewis does not think that everything is just fine with the family. He sees the selfishness behind the "right to [sexual] happiness" that for the most part has destroyed the old-fashioned family. But Lewis rests his case entirely on Natural Law, something that perhaps not many people today believe in.

Student
imaginatively
extends the
discussion.

I can imagine Lewis and Plumb meeting and having a debate. Lewis points out to Plumb that divorce causes more unhappiness than Plumb has admitted, and Plumb points out to Lewis that if modern divorce causes much suffering, there must also have been much suffering when parents did <u>not</u> get divorced. Plumb and Lewis each grant the truth of these objections, and then, in my imagined debate, Plumb says to Lewis, "Furthermore, you build your case on 'Natural Law,' but I don't think there really is any such thing. I will grant that Mr. A. and Mrs. B. seem irresponsible, but I won't grant that married adults must for their entire lives remain with each other." Lewis replies: "If you don't think that some things are right--<u>always</u> right--and that some things are wrong--<u>always</u> wrong--what guides actions? You seem to care whether or not people are happy. But isn't it clear to you that some people seek their own happiness at the expense of others? What gives them such a right? If you don't believe in Natural Law, what do you believe in? Where do 'rights' come from?"

Transition and
conclusion about
the two essays.

And so the debate ends, not so much because they differ about whether people today are happier than people in the past, but because they differ in their assumptions. Plumb's assumption that history determines the rightness or wrongness of the family is unacceptable to Lewis, and Lewis's assumption that the family is based on Natural Law is unacceptable to Plumb.

Student
introduces a
personal note, but
relates it closely to
the two readings.

What is my own position? For the moment, I find <u>both</u> assumptions unacceptable. Intellectually I feel the force of Plumb's argument, but my experience tells me that he accepts the change in the family too easily. Intellectually I feel the force of Lewis's argument, but somehow I cannot convince myself that there is such a thing as Natural Law. Still, of the two writers, I feel that Lewis has a clearer picture of what people are like. I do know lots of people like Mr. and Mrs. A and Mr. and Mrs. B, but I don't know that busload of California kids.

Concludes with succinct references to both essays.

Documentation.

Works Cited

Lewis, C. S. "We Have No 'Right to Happiness.'" The Little, Brown Reader. Ed. Marcia Stubbs, Sylvan Barnet, William E. Cain. 9th ed. New York: Longman, 2003. 20-24.

Plumb, J. H. "The Dying Family." The Little, Brown Reader. Ed. Marcia Stubbs, Sylvan Barnet, and William E. Cain. 9th ed. New York: Longman, 2003. 6-10.

Interviewing

In preparing to write about some of the essays in *The Little, Brown Reader,* you may want to interview faculty members or students, or persons not on the campus. For instance, if you are writing about the essays by Plumb and Lewis, you may want to talk to instructors who teach sociology or ethics—or you may simply want to collect the views of people who have no special knowledge but who may offer thoughtful responses. Obviously topics such as divorce and the value of computers in the classroom and almost all of the other topics addressed in this book are matters that you might profitably discuss with someone whose experience is notably different from your own.

A college campus is an ideal place to practice interviewing. Faculties are composed of experts in a variety of fields, and distinguished visitors are a regular part of extracurricular life. In the next few pages, we'll offer some advice on conducting interviews and writing essays based on them. If you take our advice, you'll acquire a skill you may well put to further, more specialized use in social science courses; at the same time you'll be developing skill in asking questions and shaping materials relevant to all research and writing.

Guidelines for Conducting the Interview and Writing the Essay

You can conduct interviews over the telephone or online using electronic mail, but in the following pages we assume that you are conducting the interview face to face.

1. *Finding a subject for an interview.* If you are looking for an expert, in the college catalog scan the relevant department and begin to ask questions of students who have some familiarity with the department. Then, with a name or two in mind, you may want to see if these faculty members have written anything on the topic. Department secretaries are good sources of information not only about the special interests of the faculty but also about guest speakers scheduled by the department in the near future. Investigate the athletic department if you're interested in sports; or the departments of music, art, and drama, for the names of resident or visiting performing artists. Other sources of newsworthy personalities or events: the publicity office, the president's office, the college newspaper, bulletin boards. All are potential sources for information about recent awards, or achievements, or upcoming events that may lead you to a subject for an interview, and a good story.

2. Preliminary homework. Find out as much as you can about your potential interviewee's work, from the sources we mentioned above. If the subject of your interview is a faculty member, ask the department secretary if you may see a copy of that person's vita (Latin for "life," and pronounced vee-ta). Many departments have these brief biographical sketches on file for publicity purposes. The vita will list, among other things, publications and current research interests.

3. Requesting the interview. In making your request, don't hesitate to mention that you are fulfilling an assignment, but also make evident your own interest in the person's work or area of expertise. (Showing that you already know something about the work, that you've done some preliminary homework, is persuasive evidence of your interest.) Request the interview, preferably in writing, at least a week in advance, and ask for ample time (probably an hour to an hour and a half) for a thorough interview.

4. Preparing thoroughly. If your subject is a writer, read and take notes on the publications that most interest you. Read book reviews, if available; read reviews of performances if your subject is a performing artist. As you read, write out the questions that occur to you. As you work on them, try to phrase your questions so that they require more than a yes or no answer. A "why" or "how" question is likely to be productive, but don't be afraid of a general question such as "Tell me something about . . ."

Revise your questions and put them in a reasonable order. Work on an opening question that you think your subject will find both easy and interesting to answer. "How did you get interested in . . . " is often a good start. Type your questions or write them boldly so that you will find them easy to refer to.

Think about how you will record the interview. Although a tape recorder may seem like a good idea, there are good reasons not to rely on one. First of all, your subject may be made uneasy by its presence and freeze up. Second, the recorder (or the operator) may malfunction, leaving you with a partial record, or nothing at all. Third, even if all goes well, when you prepare to write you will face a mass of material, some of it inaudible, and all of it daunting to transcribe.

If, despite these warnings, you decide (with your subject's permission) to tape, expect to take notes anyway. It's the only way you can be sure you will have a record of what was important to you out of all that was said. Think beforehand, then, of how you will take notes, and if you can manage to, practice by interviewing a friend. You'll probably find that you'll want to devise some system of shorthand, perhaps no more than using initials for names that frequently recur, dropping the vowels in words that you transcribe—whatever assists you to write quickly but legibly. But don't think you must transcribe every word. Be prepared to do a lot more listening than writing.

   5. *Presenting yourself for the interview.* Dress appropriately, bring your prepared questions and a notebook or pad for your notes, and appear on time.

   6. *Conducting the interview.* At the start of the interview, try to engage briefly in conversation, without taking notes, to put your subject at ease. Even important people can be shy. Remembering that will help keep you at ease, too. If you want to use a tape recorder, ask your subject's permission, and if it is granted, ask where the microphone may be conveniently placed.

   As the interview proceeds, *keep your purpose in mind.* Are you trying to gain information about an issue or topic, or are you trying to get a portrait of a personality? Listen attentively to your subject's answers and be prepared to follow up with your own responses and spontaneous questions. Here is where your thorough preparation will pay off.

   A good interview develops like a conversation. Keep in mind that your prepared questions, however essential, are not sacred. At the same time don't hesitate to steer your subject, courteously, from apparent irrelevancies (what one reporter calls "sawdust") to something that interests you more. "I'd like to hear a little more about ..." you can say. Or "Would you mind telling me about how you ..." It's also perfectly acceptable to ask your subject to repeat a remark so that you can record it accurately, and if you don't understand something, don't be afraid to admit it. Experts are accustomed to knowing more than others do and are particularly happy to explain even the most elementary parts of their lore to an interested listener.

   7. *Concluding the interview.* Near the end of the time you have agreed upon, ask your subject if he or she wishes to add any material, or to clarify something said earlier. Express your thanks and, at the appointed time, leave promptly.

   8. *Preparing to write.* As soon as possible after the interview, review your notes, amplify them with details you wish to remember but might have failed to record, and type them up. You might have discovered during the interview, or you might see now, that there is something more that you want to read by or about your subject. Track it down and take further notes.

   9. *Writing the essay.* In writing your first draft, think about your audience. Unless a better idea occurs to you, consider your college newspaper or magazine, or a local newspaper, as the place you hope to publish your

story. Write with the readers of that publication in mind. Thinking of your readers will help you to be clear—for instance to identify names that have come up in the interview but which may be unfamiliar to your readers.

As with other writing, begin your draft with any idea that strikes you, and write at a fast clip until you have exhausted your material (or yourself).

When you revise, remember to keep your audience in mind; your material should, as it unfolds, tell a coherent and interesting story. Interviews, like conversations, tend to be delightfully circular or disorderly. But an essay, like a story, should reveal its contents in a sequence that captures and holds attention.

If you've done a thorough job of interviewing you may find that you have more notes than you can reasonably incorporate without disrupting the flow of your story. Don't be tempted to plug them in anyway. If they're really interesting, save them, perhaps by copying them into your journal; if not, chuck them out.

In introducing direct quotations from your source, choose those that are particularly characteristic, or vivid, or memorable. Paraphrase or summarize the rest of what is usable. Although the focus of your essay is almost surely the person you interviewed, it is your story, and most of it should be in your own words. Even though you must keep yourself in the background, your writing will gain in interest if your reader hears your voice as well as your subject's.

You might want to use a particularly good quotation for your conclusion. (Notice that both essays we've chosen as examples conclude this way.) Now make sure that you have an attractive opening paragraph. Identifying the subject of your interview and describing the setting is one way to begin. Give your essay an attractive title. Before you prepare your final draft, read your essay aloud. You're almost certain to catch phrases you can improve, and places where a transition will help your reader to follow you without effort. Check your quotations for accuracy; check with your subject any quotations or other details you're in doubt about. Type your final draft, then edit and proofread carefully.

10. Going public. Make two copies of your finished essay, one for the person you interviewed, one for yourself. The original is for your instructor; hand it in on time.

Topic for Writing

Write an essay based on an interview. You needn't be limited in your choice of subject by the examples we've given. A very old person, a recent immigrant, the owner or manager of an interesting store or business, a veteran of the war in Afghanistan, a gardener1 are only a few of the possibilities. If you can manage to do so, include a few photographs of your subject, with appropriate captions.

Using Quotations

Our marginal comments briefly call your attention to the student's use of quotations, but here we remind you of procedures for using quotations. These procedures are not noteworthy when handled properly, but they become noticeable and even ruinous to your essay when bungled. Read over the following reminders, check them against the student's essay that you have just read, and consult them again the first few times you write about an essay.

- *Quote.* Quotations from the work under discussion provide indispensable support for your analysis.
- *Don't overquote.* Most of your essay should consist of your own words.
- *Quote briefly.* Use quotations as evidence, not as padding.
- *Comment on what you quote*—immediately before or immediately after the quotation. Make sure your reader understands why you find the quotation relevant. Don't count on the quotation to make your point for you.
- *Take care with embedded quotations* (quotations within a sentence of your own). A quotation must make good sense and must fit grammatically into the sentence of which it is a part.

Incorrect:

> Plumb says he was "astonished when a minibus drove up to my house."

(In this example, the shift from Plumb to "my" is bothersome, especially since the student uses the first person in his essay.)

Improved:

> Plumb says that he was "astonished" when he saw a minibus arrive at his house.

Or:

> Plumb says, "I was astonished when a minibus drove up to my house."

Incorrect:

> Plumb implies he is well read because "Unlike anthropologists or sociologists, historians have not studied family life very closely."

Improved:

> Plumb implies he is well read in his assertion that "Unlike anthro-
> pologists or sociologists, historians have not studied family life
> very closely."

- Don't try to fit a long quotation into the middle of one of your own
  sentences. It is almost impossible for the reader to come out of the
  quotation and pick up the thread of your sentence. It is better to
  lead into a long quotation with "Plumb says," followed by a colon,
  and then, after quoting, to begin a new sentence of your own.
- *Quote exactly.* Any material that you add (to make the quotation
  coherent with your sentence) must be in square brackets. Thus:

> Plumb says that he "was rather astonished when a minibus drove
> up to [his] house and out poured ten children."

An ellipsis (any material that you omit from a quotation) must be indicated by three spaced periods:

> Plumb says he "was rather astonished when a minibus drove
> up . . . and out poured ten children."

If you end the quotation before the end of the author's sentence, add a period and then three spaced periods to indicate the omission:

> Plumb says he "was rather astonished when a minibus drove
> up. . . ."

- *Quote fairly.* It would not be fair, for instance, to say that Lewis says,
  "After all, . . . they had a right to happiness." The words do in fact
  appear in Lewis's essay, but he is quoting them in order, ultimately,
  to refute them.
- *Identify the quotation* clearly for your reader. Use such expressions as
  "Lewis says," "Plumb argues."
- *Identify the source of quotations* in a list called "Works Cited."
- *Check your punctuation.* Remember: Periods and commas go *inside*
  the closing quotation marks, semicolons and colons go outside.
  Question marks and exclamation points go inside if they are part of
  the quotation, outside if they are your own.

A Checklist for Editing: Thirteen Questions to Ask Yourself

- Is the title of my essay at least moderately informative?

- Do I identify the subject of my essay (author and title) early?
- What is my thesis? Do I state it soon enough (perhaps even in the title) and keep it in view?
- Is the organization reasonable? Does each point lead into the next, without irrelevancies and without anticlimaxes?
- Is each paragraph unified by a topic sentence or a topic idea? Are there adequate transitions from one paragraph to the next?
- Are generalizations supported by appropriate concrete details, especially by brief quotations from the text?
- Is the opening paragraph interesting and, by its end, focused on the topic? Is the final paragraph conclusive without being repetitive?
- Is the tone appropriate? No sarcasm, no apologies, no condescension?
- If there is a summary, is it as brief as possible, given its purpose?
- Are the quotations accurate? Do they serve a purpose other than to add words to the essay?
- Is documentation provided where necessary?
- Are the spelling and punctuation correct? Are other mechanical matters (such as margins, spacing, and citations) in correct form? Have I proofread carefully?
- Is the paper properly identified—author's name, instructor's name, course number, and date?

CHAPTER 4

Writing an Argument

Although in common usage an **argument** can be a noisy wrangle—baseball players argue about the umpire's decision, spouses argue about who should put out the garbage—in this chapter we mean a discourse that uses *reasons*—rather than, say, appeals to pity, or, for that matter, threats—in order to persuade readers to hold the writer's opinion, or at least to persuade readers that the writer's opinion is thoughtful and reasonable. In this sense, argument is a thoroughly respectable activity.

What distinguishes argument from **exposition** (for instance, the explanation of a process) is this: argument and exposition both consist of statements, but in argument some statements are offered as *reasons* for other statements. Essentially one builds an argument on the word *because*. Another characteristic of argument is that argument assumes there may be a substantial disagreement among informed readers. Exposition assumes that the reader is unfamiliar with the subject matter—let's say, the origins of jazz or the law concerning affirmative action—but it does *not* assume that the reader holds a different opinion. The writer of an argument, however, seeks to overcome disagreement (for instance about the value or the fairness of something) by offering reasons that are convincing or at least worth considering carefully. Here is Supreme Court Justice Louis Brandeis concluding a justly famous argument that government may not use evidence illegally obtained by wiretapping:

> Decency, security, and liberty alike demand that government officials shall be subjected to the same rules of conduct that are commands to the citizen. In a government of laws, existence of the government will be imperilled if it fails to observe the law scrupulously. Our Government is the potent, the omnipresent teacher. For good or for ill, it teaches the whole people by its example. Crime is contagious. If the Government becomes a lawbreaker, it breeds contempt for law; it invites every man to become a law unto himself; it invites anarchy. To declare that in the administration of the criminal law the end justifies the means—to declare that the Government may commit crimes in order to secure the conviction of a private criminal—would bring terrible retribution. Against that pernicious doctrine the Court should resolutely set its face.

Brandeis's reasoning is highlighted by his forceful style. Note the resonant use of parallel constructions ("Decency, security, and liberty," "For good or for ill," "it breeds. . . it invites," "To declare. . . to declare"), which convey a sense of dignity and authority. Notice, too, the effective variation between short and long sentences. The sentences range from three words ("Crime is contagious"—forceful because of its brevity and its alliteration) to thirty-seven words (the next-to-last sentence—impressive because of its length and especially because the meaning is suspended until the end, when we get the crucial verb and its object, "would bring terrible retribution"). Later in our discussion of argument we will talk about the importance of the writer's style.

The Aims of an Argumentative Essay

The aim might seem obvious—to persuade the reader to accept the writer's opinion. In fact, often there are other aims. First, writers draft argumentative essays partly in order to find out what they believe. In drafting a paper they come to see that certain of their unformed beliefs can't really be supported or that their beliefs need to be considerably modified. This point should not come as a surprise; in earlier chapters we have said that writers get ideas and refine their beliefs by the act of writing. Second, if you read argumentative essays in, say, *National Review* (a conservative magazine), in *The Nation* (a liberal magazine), or in just about any magazine, you will see that much of the writing is really a matter of preaching to the converted. Good arguments may be offered, but they are offered not to persuade readers but to reassure them that the views they already hold are sound. After all, few liberals read *National Review*, few conservatives read *The Nation*, and so on.

When you write an argumentative essay, although you may hope to convince all readers to adopt your view, you probably also realize that the subject is complex, and that other opinions are possible. What you want to do is to set forth your viewpoint as effectively as possible, not because you believe all readers will say, "Yes, of course, you have converted me," but because *you want your view to be given a hearing. You want to show that it is one that can be held by a reasonable person.* Because you are a person of good will, with an open mind, you realize that most issues are very complicated. You have formed some ideas, and now you are taking a stand and arguing on its behalf. However, you probably are not saying that no other view can possibly have the tiniest scrap of merit. As Virginia Woolf put it (with perhaps a bit of self-irony),

> When a subject is highly controversial. . . one cannot hope to tell the truth. One can only show how one came to hold whatever opinion one does hold. One can only give one's audience the chance of drawing their own conclusions as they observe the limitations, the prejudices, the idiosyncrasies of the speaker.

Again, we want to say that in drafting the paper your chief aim is to educate yourself; in offering it to readers your chief aim is to let others know that your views are worth considering because they are supported by reason. If you persuade your readers to accept your views, great; but you should at least persuade them that a reasonable person can hold these views.

Negotiating Agreements: The Approach of Carl R. Rogers

Carl H. Rogers (1902–87), best known for his book entitled *On Becoming a Person*, was a psychotherapist, not a writer, but he has exerted a great influence on teachers of writing. Rogers originally intended to become a

Protestant minister, but, as he tells in *On Becoming a Person*, during the course of a six-month visit to East Asia he came to recognize "that sincere and honest people could believe in very divergent religious doctrines." He turned to the study of psychology, and in the course of time developed the idea that a therapist must engage in "reflection," by which he meant that the therapist must reflect—must give back an image—of what the client said. (Rogers's use of the word "client" rather than "patient" is itself a clue to his approach; the therapist is not dealing with someone who is supposed passively to accept treatment from the all-powerful doctor.)

What has this to do with seeking to persuade a reader? Consider two lawyers arguing a case in court. Lawyer A may seem to be arguing with lawyer B, but neither lawyer really is trying to convince the other, and neither lawyer has the faintest interest in learning from the other. The lawyers are trying to persuade not each other, but the judge or jury. Similarly, the writer of a letter to a newspaper, taking issue with an editorial, probably has no thought of changing the newspaper's policy. Rather, the letter is really directed to another audience, readers of the newspaper. And we hear this sort of thing on radio and television shows with titles like *Crossfire*, *Firing Line*, and *Point Counterpoint*. For the most part the participants are not trying to learn from each other and are not trying to solve a complex problem, but rather are trying to convince the audience that one side is wholly right and the other side is wholly wrong. If they are talking about an issue that we don't know much about, the arguments on both sides may seem to be equally strong, and we are likely to side with the speaker whose *style* of talk (and maybe of dress) we prefer. This point is important, and we will return to it when we talk about the *persona* or character of the writer of an argument.

Suppose that unlike a participant on a radio or television show, and unlike a lawyer arguing a case, speaker X really does want to persuade speaker Y; that is, X really wants to bring Y around to X's point of view, or if X is mistaken in his or her views, X really is willing to learn from Y in the course of the give and take. Rogers points out that when we engage in an argument, if we feel that our integrity or our identity is threatened, we stiffen our resistance. Normally we may *want* to grow, to develop our thoughts, to act in accordance with sound reasons, but when we are threatened we erect defenses that in fact shut us off from communication. That is, we find ourselves within a circle that not only shuts others out but that also has the unintended effect of shutting us in. We—or our opponent—may have given very good reasons, but because each party has behaved in a threatening manner, and has felt threatened by the other side, we have scarcely listened to each other, and therefore little or nothing has been communicated. (If you think about your own experience, you probably can confirm Rogers's view.)

To avoid this deplorable lack of opportunity for growth, Rogers suggests that participants in arguments need to become partners, not adversaries. Here, with Rogers's insight in mind, we can digress for a moment, and call attention to the combative terms normally associated with argument. *Debate,* for instance, is from Latin *de-* (down) and *battere* (to beat), the same word that gives us *battery,* as in "assault and battery." We *marshal* our arguments (arrange them into a military formation), and we *attack our opponents,* seeking to *rebut* (from a Latin word meaning "to butt back") or *refute* (again from a Latin word, this time meaning "to drive back") their assertions. When we are engaged in these activities, (1) we are scarcely in a position to learn from those we are talking with—really, talking *at*—and (2) we are not likely to teach them anything, because, like us, they are busy *defending* (still another military word) their own position.

Rogers suggests, therefore, that a writer who wishes to communicate (as opposed to a lawyer or a debater who merely wishes to win) needs to reduce the threat. To repeat: The participants in an argument need to become partners rather than adversaries. "Mutual communication," he says, "tends to be pointed toward solving a problem rather than attacking a person or a group."

Take abortion, for instance. We hear about "pro-life" (or "anti-abortion") people, and about "pro-choice" (or "pro-abortion") people. It may seem that there is no common ground, nothing they can agree on. But polls reveal considerable ambiguity within some people. Consider, for instance, a finding of a New York Times/CBS News poll of representative Americans, in January 1998. Participants were asked which statement came nearer to their opinion: Is abortion the same thing as murdering a child, or Is abortion not murder because the fetus really isn't a child? Half the sample chose "the same thing as murdering a child," and 38 percent chose "the fetus really isn't a child." At the same time, however, 58 percent, including a third of those who chose "murdering a child," agreed that abortion was "sometimes the best course in a bad situation." These apparently inconsistent responses have been fairly consistent for the last fifteen years; some people who consider abortion equivalent to murdering a child will grant that there are situations in which abortion is "the best course," and, we should add, many pro-choice people, people who insist that a woman has a right to choose and that her choice is not the government's business, also agree that abortion should not be lightly entered into. Take a particular case: A pregnant woman who regards abortion as "the same thing as murdering a child" learns that her baby will probably have Down's Syndrome (such persons have an average IQ of about 50, are prone to hearing problems and vision problems, and have an increased risk of heart disease and leukemia). Despite her opposition to abortion, she may become one of the people who feel abortion is "sometimes the best course in a bad situation." Given the choice of bearing or aborting, she may very reluctantly decide to abort. Yet on the day we were drafting these pages we happened to come across a letter in a newspaper making a point that, however obvious, we had not thought of. The writer, Maureen K. Hogan, Executive Director of Adopt a Special Kid, reported in her letter that "There are thousands of families around the United States that would be happy to adopt such a child. . . . In 25 years, there hasn't been a single child for whom we have not been able to find a home." We can imagine that a woman who dreaded the idea of aborting a fetus but felt that she had no choice but abortion, might, on hearing this information, modify her intention, and engage in a course of behavior that she and all others concerned will find more satisfactory.

We should mention, too, that open-minded discussion between persons who hold differing views may reveal that some of their differences are verbal rather than substantial. One can wonder, for instance, if the poll would have produced the same results if the question had asked about "killing" rather than "murdering" a child. Patient, well-intentioned discussion may reveal that the parties are not as far apart as they at first seem to be; they share some ground, and once this common ground is acknowledged, differences can be discussed.

Consider, as another example, a proposal in 1997 by President Clinton to introduce voluntary national tests in reading and mathematics. Some people think this is a Bad Idea. Why?

- What is tested is what will get taught; teachers will soon start preparing students for the test, rather than teaching the things they think are important. Why would teachers do this? Because they want to look good, they want their school to stand high in the national ratings.
- A second objection is that testing introduces an unhealthy spirit of competition.
- A third objection concerns the issue of who will make the tests. Administrators? Professors of education? The teachers who are on the firing line?
- A fourth objection is that, no matter who makes the test, the testing board would have too much power, since it would in effect determine not only what things get taught but which students get to go on to college.
- A fifth objection is that a national test would have little meaning; some states have a relatively homogenous population, whereas others have a relatively heterogenous population. A sixth objection is that test scores don't have much value. After all, we know (or do we?) that the SAT is not really a good predictor of success in school, and that tests are especially likely to fail to recognize the offbeat creative students—just look at X, who had poor grades and dropped out of school and is now recognized as a genius.

Probably all of these objections have some weight, but replies (also of varying weight) can be made to them. To take only the first two: It may be a good thing if teachers are jolted out of their parochialism and are made to become aware of the values of others, and, second, what is wrong with some competition? Competition sometimes is healthy. But after all of the pros and the cons are laid out, a Rogerian thinker will want to see what the two sides can *agree* on. They can agree, probably, that American school children ought to do better in reading and in mathematics. They can also agree, probably, that testing has some validity. And they can also agree, probably, that national testing by itself will not solve the problem. For instance, other possibilities include a longer school year, better pay for teachers (to attract better teachers), national tests for teachers, and so on. If the disputants can first establish the positions they *share,* and realize that both sides are people of good will endowed with some good ideas, they may better be able to work out their differences.

Rogers was drawing on his experience as a psychotherapist, which means he was mostly writing about the relationship between two people who were literally talking to each other, whereas a writer can at best imagine a reader. But good writers do in fact bring their readers into their writings, by such devices as "It may be said that. . . "—here one summarizes or quotes a view other than one's own. Writers genuinely interested in contributing to the solution of a problem will not merely busy themselves in asserting their position but will also inform themselves of a variety of views, by listening and by reading. And when they listen and read, they must do so with an open mind, giving the speaker or author (at least at first) the benefit of the doubt. (Rogers's term for this sort of activity is "empathic listening," i.e., comprehension so complete that it grasps not only the thoughts but also the feelings and motives of another.) That is, they will listen and read sympathetically, and they will not be too quick to evaluate. They may even, in an effort to do justice to the material, listen and read with the mind of a believer. Or, if this is asking too much, they will act in the spirit advocated by the seventeenth-century essayist Francis Bacon: "Read not to contradict and confute; nor to believe and take for granted; nor to find talk and discourse; but to weigh and consider."

Writers genuinely interested in persuading others will educate themselves, by listening and reading. In their own writing, where they wish to contribute their views on a disputed matter, they simultaneously can reduce the psychological threat to those who hold views different from their own by doing several things: They can show sympathetic understanding of the opposing argument; they can recognize what is valid in it; and they can recognize and demonstrate that those who take a different view are nonetheless persons of goodwill.

A writer who takes Rogers seriously will, usually, in the first part of an argumentative essay

- state the problem, suggesting that it is an issue of concern, and that the reader has a stake in it;
- show respect for persons who hold differing views;
- set forth opposing positions, *stated in such a way that their proponents will agree that the statements of their positions are fair;* and
- find some shared values—that is, grant whatever validity the writer finds in those positions, for instance, by recognizing the circumstances in which they would indeed be acceptable.

Having accurately summarized other views and having granted some concessions, the writer presumably has won the reader's attention and goodwill; the writer can now

> • show how those who hold other positions will benefit if they accept the writer's position.

This last point is essentially an appeal to self-interest. In the example we gave a moment ago, concerning a pregnant woman who has contemplated aborting a fetus that, if born, probably will be a baby with Down Syndrome, the appeal to self-interest might run along the lines that if she bears the child she will be free from the remorse she might feel if she had aborted it.

Sometimes, of course, the differing positions will be so far apart that no reconciliation can be proposed, in which case the writer will probably seek to show how the issue can best be solved by adopting the writer's own position. But even in such an essay it is desirable to state the opposing view in such a way that proponents of that view will agree that that is indeed their position and not a caricature of it.

Rogers, again, was a psychologist, not a teacher of writing and not a logician. In fact, his writing shares with some recent feminist theory a distrust of logic, which can be seen as masculine and aggressive, concerned with winning, even with "annihilating the opposition." Rogers offers advice not so much on winning (in the sense of conquering) but in the sense of winning over, that is, gaining converts, or at least allies.

A Checklist for Rogerian Argument

- Have I treated other views with **respect**?
- Have I stated at least one other view **in a way that would satisfy its proponents, and thus demonstrated my familiarity with the issue?**
- Have I granted **validity to any aspects of other positions, and thus demonstrated my openmindedness?**
- Have I pointed out the **common ground,** the ground that we share, and thus prepared the reader to listen attentively to my proposals?
- Have I shown how the other position will be strengthened, at least in some contexts, by accepting some aspects of my position? (In short, have I **appealed to the reader's self-interest,** by showing that proponents of the other view(s) will benefit from accepting at least part of my view?

Three Kinds of Evidence: Examples, Testimony, Statistics

Writers of arguments seek to persuade by showing that they themselves are persons of goodwill, and—our topic here—by offering evidence to support their thesis. The chief forms of evidence used in argument are:

Examples

Testimony (the citation of authorities)

Statistics

We'll briefly consider each of these.

Examples

Example is from the Latin *exemplum*, which means "something taken out." An **example** is the sort of thing, taken from among many similar things, that one selects and holds up for view, perhaps after saying "for example" or "for instance."

Three sorts of examples are especially common in written arguments:

Real examples

Invented instances

Analogies

Real examples are just what they sound like—instances that have occurred. If we are arguing that gun control won't work, we point to those states that have adopted gun control laws and that nevertheless have had no reduction in crimes using guns. Or, if one wants to support the assertion that a woman can be a capable head of state, one may find oneself pointing to women who have actually served as heads of state, such as Cleopatra, Queen Elizabeth I of England, Golda Meir (prime minister of Israel), Indira Ghandi (prime minister of India), and Margaret Thatcher (prime minister of England).

The advantage of using real examples is, clearly, that they are real. Of course, an opponent might stubbornly respond that the persons whom you name could not, for some reason or other, function as the head of state in *our* country. One might argue, for instance, that the case of Golda Meir proves nothing, since the role of women in Israeli society is different from the role of women in the United States (a country in which a majority of the citizens are Christians). And one might argue that much of Mrs. Gandhi's power came from her being the daughter of Nehru, an immensely popular Indian statesman. Even the most compelling real example inevitably will be in some ways special or particular, and in the eyes of some readers may not seem to be a fair example.

Consider, for instance, a student who is arguing that peer review should be part of the writing course, pointing out that he or she found it of great help in high school. An opponent argues that things in college are different: college students should be able to help themselves, even highly gifted college students are not competent to offer college-level instruction, and so on. Still, as the feebleness of these objections (and the objections against Meir and Gandhi) indicates, real examples can be very compelling.

Invented instances are exempt from the charge that, because of some detail or other, they are not relevant as evidence. Suppose you are arguing against capital punishment, on the grounds that if an innocent person is executed, there is no way of even attempting to rectify the injustice. If you point to the case of X, you may be met with the reply that X was not in fact innocent. Rather than get tangled up in the guilt or innocence of a particular person, it may be better to argue that we can suppose—we can imagine—an innocent person convicted and executed, and we can imagine that evidence later proves the person's innocence.

Invented instances have the advantage of presenting an issue clearly, free from all of the distracting particularities (and irrelevancies) that are bound up with any real instance. But invented instances have the disadvantage of being invented, and they may seem remote from the real issues being argued.

Analogies are comparisons pointing out several resemblances between two rather different things. For instance, one might assert that a government is like a ship, and in times of stress—if the ship is to weather the storm—the authority of the captain must not be questioned.

But don't confuse an analogy with proof. An analogy is an extended comparison between two things: it can be useful in exposition, for it explains the unfamiliar by means of the familiar: "A government is like a ship, and just as a ship has a captain and a crew, so a government has. . . . "; "Writing an essay is like building a house; just as an architect must begin with a plan, so the writer must. . . ." Such comparisons can be useful, helping to clarify what otherwise might be obscure, but their usefulness goes only so far. Everything is what it is, and not something else. A government is not a ship, and what is true of a captain's power need not be true of a president's power; and a writer is not an architect. Some of what is true about ships may be roughly true of governments, and some of what is true about architects may be (again, roughly) true of writers, but there are differences too. Consider the following analogy between a lighthouse and the death penalty:

> The death penalty is a warning, just like a lighthouse throwing its beams out to sea. We hear about shipwrecks, but we do not hear about the ships the lighthouse guides safely on their way. We do not have proof of the number of ships it saves, but we do not tear the lighthouse down.

> J. Edgar Hoover

How convincing is Hoover's analogy as an argument, that is, as a reason for retaining the death penalty?

Testimony

Testimony, or the citation of authorities, is rooted in our awareness that some people are recognized as experts. In our daily life we constantly turn to experts for guidance: we look up the spelling of a word in the dictionary, we listen to the weather forecast on the radio, we take an ailing cat to the vet for a checkup. Similarly, when we wish to become informed about controversial matters, we often turn to experts, first to help educate ourselves and then to help convince our readers.

Don't forget that *you* are an authority on many things. For example, today's newspaper includes an article about the cutback in funding for teaching the arts in elementary and secondary schools. Educators are responding that arts education is not a frill, and that in fact the arts provide the analytical thinking, teamwork, motivation, and self-discipline that most people agree are needed to reinvigorate American schools. If you have studied the arts in school—for instance, if you painted pictures or learned to play a musical instrument—you are in a position to evaluate these claims. Similarly, if you have studied in a bilingual educational program, your own testimony will be invaluable.

There are at least two reasons for offering testimony in an argument. The obvious reason is that expert opinion does (and should) carry some weight with the audience; the less obvious one is that a change of voice (if the testimony is not your own) in an essay may afford the reader a bit of pleasure. No matter how engaging our own voice may be, a fresh voice— whether that of Thomas Jefferson, Albert Einstein, or Toni Morrison— may provide a refreshing change of tone.

But there are dangers. The chief dangers are that the words of authorities may be taken out of context or otherwise distorted, or that the authorities may not be authorities on the topic at hand. We are concerned quite rightly with what the framers of the U.S. Constitution said, but it is not entirely clear that their words can be fairly applied, on one side or the other, to such an issue as abortion. We are concerned quite rightly with what Einstein said, but it is not entirely clear that his eminence as a physicist qualifies him as an authority on, say, world peace. In a moment, when we discuss errors in reasoning, we'll have more to say about the proper and improper use of authorities.

Statistics

Statistics, another important form of evidence, are especially useful in arguments concerning social issues. If we want to argue for (or against) raising the driving age, we will probably do some research in the library, and will offer statistics about the number of accidents caused by people in certain age groups.

But a word of caution: the significance of statistics may be difficult to assess. For instance, opponents of gun control legislation have pointed out, in support of the argument that such laws are ineffectual, that homicides in Florida *increased* after Florida adopted gun control laws. Supporters of gun control laws cried "foul," arguing that in the years after adopting these laws Miami became (for reasons having nothing to do with the laws) the cocaine capital of the United States, and the rise in homicide was chiefly a reflection of murders involved in the drug trade. That is, a significant change in the population has made a comparison of the figures meaningless. This objection seems plausible, and probably the statistics therefore should carry little weight.

How Much Evidence Is Enough?

If you allow yourself ample time to write your essay, you probably will turn up plenty of evidence to illustrate your arguments, such as examples drawn from your own experience and imagination, from your reading, and from your talks with others. Examples not only will help to clarify and to support your assertions but also will provide a concreteness that will be welcome in a paper that might be, on the whole, fairly abstract. Your sense of your audience will have to guide you in making your selection of examples. Generally speaking, a single example may not fully illuminate a difficult point, and so a second example—a clincher—may be desirable. If you offer a third or fourth example you probably are succumbing to a temptation to include something that tickles your fancy. If it is as good as you think it is, the reader probably will accept the unnecessary example and may even be grateful. But before you pile on examples, try to imagine yourself in your reader's place, and ask if an example is needed. If not, ask yourself if the reader will be glad to receive the overload.

One other point: on most questions—say on the value of bilingual education or on the need for rehabilitation programs in prisons—it's not possible to make a strictly logical case, in the sense of an absolutely airtight proof. Don't assume that it is your job to make an absolute proof. What you are expected to do is to offer a reasonable argument. Remember Virginia Woolf's words: "When a subject is highly controversial. . . one cannot hope to tell the truth. One can only show how one came to hold whatever opinion one does hold."

Avoiding Fallacies

Let's further examine writing reasonable arguments by considering some obvious errors in reasoning. In logic these errors are called **fallacies** (from a Latin verb meaning "to deceive"). As Tweedledee says in *Through the*

Looking-Glass, "If it were so, it would be; but as it isn't, it ain't. That's logic."

To persuade readers to accept your opinions you must persuade them that you are reliable; if your argument includes fallacies, thoughtful readers will not take you seriously. More important, if your argument includes fallacies, you are misleading yourself. When you search your draft for fallacies, you are searching for ways to improve the quality of your thinking.

1. False Authority. Don't try to borrow the prestige of authorities who are not authorities on the topic in question—for example, a heart surgeon speaking on politics. Similarly, some former authorities are no longer authorities because the problems have changed or because later knowledge has superseded their views. Adam Smith, Thomas Jefferson, Eleanor Roosevelt, and Albert Einstein remain persons of genius, but an attempt to use their opinions when you are examining modern issues— even in their fields—may be questioned. Remember the last words of John B. Sedgwick, a Union Army general at the Battle of Spotsylvania in 1864: "They couldn't hit an elephant at this dist—."

In short, before you rely on an authority, ask yourself if the person in question *is* an authority on the topic. And don't let stereotypes influence your idea of who is an authority. There is an apt Yiddish proverb: "A goat has a beard, but that doesn't make him a rabbi."

2. False Quotation. If you do quote from an authority, don't misquote. For example, you may find someone who grants that "there are strong arguments in favor of abolishing the death penalty"; but if she goes on to argue that, on balance, the arguments in favor of retaining it seem stronger to her, it is dishonest to quote her words so as to imply that she favors abolishing it.

3. Suppression of Evidence. Don't neglect evidence that is contrary to your own argument. You owe it to yourself and your reader to present all the relevant evidence. Be especially careful not to assume that every question is simply a matter of *either/or.* There may be some truth on both sides. Take the following thesis: "Grades encourage unwholesome competition and should therefore be abolished." Even if the statement about the evil effect of grading is true, it may not be the whole truth, and therefore it may not follow that grades should be abolished. One might point out that grades do other things, too: they may stimulate learning, and they may assist students by telling them how far they have progressed. One might nevertheless conclude, on balance, that the fault outweighs the benefits. But the argument will be more persuasive now that the benefits of grades have been considered.

Concede to the opposition what it deserves and then outscore the opposition. Failure to confront the opposing evidence will be noticed; your readers will keep wondering why you do not consider some particular point, and may consequently dismiss your argument. However, if you confront the opposition, you will almost surely strengthen your own argument. As Edmund Burke said two hundred years ago, "He that wrestles with us strengthens our nerves, and sharpens our skill. Our antagonist is our helper."

4. Generalization from Insufficient Evidence. In rereading a draft of an argument that you have written, try to spot your own generalizations. Ask yourself if a reasonable reader is likely to agree that the generalization is based on an adequate sample.

A visitor to a college may sit in on three classes, each taught by a different instructor, and may find all three stimulating. That's a good sign, but can we generalize and say that the teaching at this college is excellent? Are three classes a sufficient sample? If all three are offered by the Biology Department, which includes only five instructors, perhaps we can tentatively say that the teaching of biology at this institution is good. If the Biology Department contains twenty instructors, perhaps we can still say—though more tentatively—that this sample indicates that the teaching of biology is good. But what does the sample say about the teaching of other subjects at the college? It probably does say something—the institution may be much concerned with teaching across the board—but then again it may not say a great deal, since the Biology Department may be exceptionally concerned with good teaching.

5. The Genetic Fallacy. Don't assume that something can necessarily be explained in terms of its birth or origin. "He wrote the novel to make money, so it can't be any good" is not a valid inference. The value of a novel does not depend on the author's motivations in writing it. Indeed, the value or worth of a novel needs to be established by reference to other criteria. Neither the highest nor the lowest motivations guarantee the quality of the product. Another example: "Capital punishment arose in days when men sought revenge, so now it ought to be abolished." Again, an unconvincing argument: capital punishment may have some current value; for example, it may serve as a deterrent to crime. But that's another argument, and it needs evidence if it is to be believed. Be on guard, too, against the thoughtless tendency to judge people by their origins: Mr. X has a foreign accent, so he is probably untrustworthy or stupid or industrious.

6. Begging the Question and Circular Reasoning. Don't assume the truth of the point that you should prove. The term "begging the question" is a trifle odd. It means, in effect, "You, like a beggar, are asking me to grant you something at the outset."

Examples: "The barbaric death penalty should be abolished"; "This senseless language requirement should be dropped." Both of these statements assume what they should prove—that the death penalty is barbaric, and that the language requirement is senseless. You can, of course, make such assertions, but you must go on to prove them.

Circular reasoning is usually an extended form of begging the question. What ought to be proved is covertly assumed. Example: "X is the best-qualified candidate for the office, because the most informed people say so." Who are the most informed people? Those who recognize X's superiority. Circular reasoning, then, normally includes intermediate steps absent from begging the question, but the two fallacies are so closely related that they can be considered one. Another example: "I feel sympathy for her because I identify with her." Despite the "because," no reason is really offered. What follows "because" is merely a restatement, in slightly different words, of what precedes; the shift of words, from *feel sympathy* to *identify with* has misled the writer into thinking she is giving a reason. Other examples: "Students are interested in courses when the subject matter and the method of presentation are interesting"; "There cannot be peace in the Middle East because the Jews and the Arabs will always fight." In each case, an assertion that ought to be proved is reasserted as a reason in support of the assertion.

7. *Post hoc ergo propter hoc.* Latin: "after this, therefore because of this." Don't assume that because X precedes Y, X must cause Y. For example: "He went to college and came back a boozer; college corrupted him." He might have taken up liquor even if he had not gone to college. Another example: "When a fifty-five-mile-per-hour speed limit was imposed in 1974, after the Arab embargo on oil, the number of auto fatalities decreased sharply, from 55,000 deaths in 1973 to 46,000 in 1974. Therefore, it is evident that a fifty-five-mile-per-hour speed limit—still adhered to in some states—saves lives." Not quite. Because gasoline was expensive after the embargo, the number of miles traveled decreased. The number of fatalities *per mile* remained constant. The price of gas, not the speed limit, seems responsible for the decreased number of fatalities. Moreover, the national death rate has continued to fall. Why? Several factors are at work: seat-belt and child-restraint laws, campaigns against drunk driving, improved auto design, and improved roads. Medicine, too, may have improved, so that today doctors can save accident victims who in 1974 would have died. In short, it probably is impossible to isolate the correlation between speed and safety.

8. *Argumentum ad hominem.* Here the argument is directed toward the person (*hominem* is Latin for *man*) rather than toward the issue. Don't shift from your topic to your opponent. A speaker argues against legalizing abortions, and her opponent, instead of facing the merits of the argument, attacks the character or the associations of the opponent: "You're a Catholic, aren't you?"

9. *False Assumption.* Consider the Scot who argued that Shakespeare must have been a Scot. Asked for his evidence, he replied, "The ability of the man warrants the assumption." Or take such a statement as "She goes to Yale, so she must be rich." Possibly the statement is based on faulty induction (the writer knows four Yale students, and all four are rich), but more likely he is just passing on a cliché. The Yale student in question may be on a scholarship, may be struggling to earn the money, or may be backed by parents of modest means who for eighteen years have saved money for her college education. Other examples: "I haven't heard him complain about French 10, so he must be satisfied";

"She's a writer, so she must be well read." A little thought will show how weak such assertions are; they *may* be true, but they may not.

The errors we have discussed are common. In revising your writing, try to spot them and eliminate or correct them. You have a point to make, and you should make it fairly. If you can only make it unfairly, you are doing an injustice to your reader and yourself; you should try to change your view of the topic. You don't want to be like the politician whose speech had a marginal note: "Argument weak; shout here."

Drafting an Argument

Imagining an Audience

A writer's job is made easier if the audience is known. Thus, if you are writing for the college newspaper, you can assume that your readers know certain things, and you can adopt a moderately familiar tone. Similarly, if you are writing a letter to the college trustees, you can assume that they know certain things—you will not have to tell them that the institution is a small, coeducational, undergraduate college located in northern Georgia—but you will probably adopt a somewhat more formal tone than you would use in writing for your fellow students.

Your instructor may tell you to imagine a particular audience—readers of the local newspaper, alumni, high school students, your representative in Congress, or any other group. But if your instructor does not specify an audience, you will probably do best if you imagine one of two possibilities: either write for the general reader (the person who reads *Time* or *Newsweek*) or for your classmates. Although these two audiences are similar in many respects, there is a significant difference. All of your classmates may be of the same gender or the same religion, they may be of approximately the same age, and they may come from the same area. In an essay written for your classmates, then, you may not have to explain certain things that you will indeed have to explain if you are writing for the general reader. To cite an obvious example: if the school is specialized (for instance, if it is a religious school or a military school), you can assume that your readers know certain things and share certain attitudes that you cannot assume in the general public.

Getting Started

If your essay is related to one or more of the readings in this book, of course you will read the essay(s) carefully—perhaps highlighting, underlining, annotating, summarizing, and outlining, as we suggest in our first chapter. You will question the text, and you probably will make entries in a journal, as we suggest in the second and third chapters. These entries may be ideas that come to you out of the blue, or they may emerge from conscious, critical thinking, perhaps in conversations with some of your classmates. (Critical thinking means, among other things, that you will question your own assumptions and evaluate your evidence as objectively as possible.)

Discussions—with yourself and with others—will help you to improve your ideas. At this stage, you will probably have some ideas that you did not have when you began thinking about the topic, and you will probably want to abandon some of your earlier ideas which now seem less strong than you had originally thought.

Writing a Draft

By now you probably have a fair idea of the strengths and (as you see it) the weaknesses of other positions. You also have a fair idea of what your thesis—your claim—is and what reasons you will offer to support it. And you also probably have at hand some of the supporting evidence—examples, statements by authorities, or personal experiences—that you intend to offer as support.

Some people, at this point—especially if they are writing on a word processor—like to sit down and write freely, pouring out their ideas. They then print out the material and, on rereading, highlight what seems useful, perhaps indicating in the margins how the material should be reorganized. They then (again, we are speaking of writing on a word processor) move blocks of material into some reasonable organization.

Our own preference (even though we also use a word processor when we write a first draft) is to prepare a rough outline on paper—really a list of topics. Then, after further thought, we add to it, circling items on the list and indicating (by means of arrows) better positions for these items.

Next, when we have a rough outline (perhaps a list of five or six chief items, under each of which we have written a word or phrase indicating how the point might be developed), we start writing on the word processor. It happens that our rough outline (later, much changed) for this section ran thus:

audience

    assigned? or general? or classmates

    starting

        annotating, journal? Refer to earlier chapters?

    writing

        brainstorming? outline first, then word processor

Revising

Revising a Draft

After you have written a first draft, you will read it and, almost surely, make extensive revisions. Some points will now strike you as not really worth making; others that do survive the cut you will now see as needing to be developed. You may see that you have not adequately set forth a commonly held view that you will in effect be largely rejecting. You now realize that you must summarize this view fairly, because many people hold it, and you now see the need to indicate that you are familiar with the view, that you see its merits, and that you think your own view is better and may at least in part be attractive even to those who hold this other view.

You may also see that the organization needs improvement. For instance, if you notice that a point you have made in the second paragraph is pretty much the same as one in the sixth paragraph, the two should be combined, rewritten, and perhaps put into an entirely new position.

Reorganizing, and providing the transitional words and phrases that make the organization clear to the reader ("moreover," "a second example," "on the other hand"), is usually not difficult, especially if you outline your draft. When you look at the outline of what you have written, you will probably see that portions of the draft have to be moved around or (in some cases) amplified or deleted, and new transitions written. Organizing an argument is so important that we will treat it separately, at some length, in a moment.

In revising, think carefully about how you use **quotations.** Keep in mind the following principles:

- Most quotations should be brief; present a long quotation only if it is extremely interesting and cannot be summarized effectively.
- Let the reader know who wrote the quotation. Identify an author who is not widely known, for example: "Judith Craft, a lawyer who specializes in constitutional matters, argues. . . "; "The warden of a maximum security prison, John Alphonso, testified that. . . "; "Anne Smith, a lesbian who has given birth to one child and adopted a second, suggests that families headed by lesbians. . . ." This sort of lead-in gives authority to the quotation.
- Let the reader know how the quotation was originally used. Examples: "The editor of the journal *Nature* argues. . . "; "The Pope rejects this view, saying. . . "; "Dr. Joycelyn Elders interprets the statistics as indicating that. . . ."
- Use the present tense: "X says," *not* "X said," though of course if you are treating the passage as something from the past, use the past tense: "X wrote, twenty years ago, that. . . , but today he argues that. . . ."

After revising your draft, you may want to show it to some classmates or friends; they will doubtless give you helpful advice if you make it clear that you really do want their assistance.

Organizing an Argument

The writer of a persuasive essay almost always has to handle, in some sequence or other, the following matters:

- The background (for instance, the need to consider the issue)
- The readers' preconceptions
- The thesis (claim)
- The evidence that supports the claim
- The counterevidence
- Responses to counterclaims and counterevidence (perhaps a refutation, but probably a concession that there *is* merit in the counterclaims although not as much as in the writer's thesis)
- Some sort of reaffirmation—for instance, that the topic needs attention, that the thesis advanced is the most plausible or the most workable or the most moral, and that even holders of other views may find their own values strengthened by adopting the writer's view

And here we repeat the organization that we suggested (page 69) for Rogerian argument:

- state the problem, suggesting that it is an issue of concern, and that the reader has a stake in it;
- show respect for persons who hold differing views;
- set forth opposing positions, *stated in such a way that their proponents will agree that the statements of their positions are fair;* and
- find some shared values—that is, grant whatever validity the writer finds in those positions, for instance, by recognizing the circumstances in which they would indeed be acceptable.

Having accurately summarized other views and having granted some concessions, the writer presumably has won the reader's attention and goodwill; the writer can now

- show how those who hold other positions will benefit if they accept the writer's position.

A Word about Beginnings and Endings

In the **introduction** (the first paragraph or first few paragraphs) you will usually indicate what the issue is, why it is of significance, and what your thesis is. You will also, through your tone, introduce yourself—which is to say that you will convey some sort of personality to the reader. Obviously, it is in your interest to come across as courteous, reasonable, and well informed. We will talk about this matter in a moment, when we discuss the writer's persona.

In the **ending** you probably will offer a paragraph of summary, but try to make it interesting by including something new. You might, for instance, include an interesting quotation, or reexamine a phrase from your opening paragraph in a new light. And you might appeal to your readers' self-interest, indicating how they will benefit by adopting your view.

Persona and Style

In Chapter 1 we talked about the writer's **persona**—the personality that the writer conveys through his or her words. More exactly, the persona is the image of the writer that *the readers* imagine. The writer tries to convey a certain image (courteous, fair-minded, authoritative, or all of the above, and more); but if readers find the writer discourteous, well, the writer *is* discourteous (or mean-spirited, or uninformed). It won't do for the writer, hearing of the readers' response, to insist that he or she did not mean to be discourteous (is not mean-spirited or is well-informed).

The persona is created by the impression that the words make—both the individual words and the kinds of sentences (long or short, complex or simple) in which they appear. A writer who says something like "It behooves us to exert all of our mental capacities on what I deem the primary issue of our era" will strike readers as a pompous ass. The writer may have a heart of gold and be well-informed, but he or she will still strike readers as a pompous ass—and the writer's argument will not get a very attentive hearing. A writer who uses many short sentences, much direct address to the reader, and lots of colloquial diction ("Let's get down to nuts and bolts. You've got to stop kidding yourselves. We all know what the problem is") probably will strike readers as aggressive—someone they are not keen on associating with. In short, the wrong persona can alienate readers. Even though the arguments are thoughtful, readers will be put off. We would live in a better world if we could listen objectively and separate the argument (very good) from the speaker (very unpleasant), but we can't usually do so. A hundred years ago Samuel Butler put it this way (he is overstating the case, but there is much to what he says): "We are not won by arguments that we can analyze but by tone and temper, by the manner."

Now, in fact one often *does* find aggressive writing in magazines, but this writing is, as we said earlier, a sermon addressed to the converted. The liberal readers of *The Nation* derive pleasure from seeing conservatives roughed up a bit, just as the conservative readers of *National Review* derive pleasure from seeing liberals similarly handled. But again, these writers—utterly ignoring the principles of Carl Rogers, which we set forth on pages 65–70—are not trying to gain a hearing for their ideas; rather, they are reassuring their readers that the readers' ideas are just fine.

What kind of persona should you, as the writer of an argument, try to project? You will want to be (you will *have to be*) yourself. But, just as you have different kinds of clothes, suitable for different purposes, you have several or even many selves—for instance, the self you are with a close friend, the self you are with your teachers, the self you are with customers (if you have a job), and so forth. The self that you will present in your essays—the self that you hope the readers will see from the words you put down on the page—will probably include certain specific qualities. You probably want your readers to see that you are informed and fair and are presenting a thoughtful case. You want them to be interested in hearing what you have to say. If you browse through the essays in this book, you will of course hear different voices. Although some may have an academic tone and some may sound folksy, almost all of them have one thing in common: they are the voices of people whom we would like to get to know.

An Overview: An Examination of an Argument

Now that we have covered the ground from a more or less theoretical point of view, let's look at a specific argument. The writer is Richard Rhodes, a journalist who has written for many newspapers and magazines, including *The New York Times, Newsweek, Harper's, Playboy,* and *Rolling Stone.* Rhodes is also known as a novelist and as a writer of books about science and technology. We reprint an essay that first appeared in *The New York Times* on September 17, 2000.

Richard Rhodes

Hollow Claims about Fantasy Violence

The moral entrepreneurs are at it again, pounding the entertainment 1 industry for advertising its Grand Guignolesque confections[1] to children. If exposure to this mock violence contributes to the development of violent behavior, then our political leadership is justified in its indignation at what the Federal Trade Commission has reported about the marketing of violent fare to children. Senators John McCain and Joseph Lieberman have been especially quick to fasten on the FTC report as they make an issue of violent offerings to children.

But is there really a link between entertainment and violent behavior? 2

Richard Rhodes, "Hollow Claims about Fantasy Violence." Originally published in *The New York Times,* 9/17/00. Reprinted by permission.

[1]**Grand Guignolesque confections** The Grand Guignol was a Parisian theater specializing in plays dealing with brutality.

The American Medical Association, the American Psychological   3
Association, the American Academy of Pediatrics, and the National
Institute of Mental Health all say yes. They base their claims on social science research that has been sharply criticized and disputed within the social science profession, especially outside the United States. In fact, no direct, causal link between exposure to mock violence in the media and
subsequent violent behavior has ever been demonstrated, and the few
claims of modest correlation have been contradicted by other findings,
sometimes in the same studies.

History alone should call such a link into question. Private violence   4
has been declining in the West since the media-barren late Middle Ages,
when homicide rates are estimated to have been 10 times what they are in
Western nations today. Historians attribute the decline to improving social controls over violence—police forces and common access to courts of
law—and to a shift away from brutal physical punishment in child-rearing (a practice that still appears as a common factor in the background of
violent criminals today).

The American Medical Association has based its endorsement of the   5
media violence theory in major part on the studies of Brandon
Centerwall, a psychiatrist in Seattle. Dr. Centerwall compared the murder
rates for whites in three countries from 1945 to 1974 with numbers for tel-
evision set ownership. Until 1975, television broadcasting was banned in
South Africa, and "white homicide rates remained stable" there, Dr.
Centerwall found, while corresponding rates in Canada and the United
States doubled after television was introduced.

A spectacular finding, but it is meaningless. As Franklin E. Zimring   6
and Gordon Hawkins of the University of California at Berkeley subsequently pointed out, homicide rates in France, Germany, Italy, and Japan
either failed to change with increasing television ownership in the same
period or actually declined, and American homicide rates have more recently been sharply declining despite a proliferation of popular media
outlets—not only movies and television but also video games and the
Internet.

Other social science that supposedly undergirds the theory, too, is   7
marginal and problematic. Laboratory studies that expose children to selected incidents of televised mock violence and then assess changes in the
children's behavior have sometimes found more "aggressive" behavior
after the exposure—usually verbal, occasionally physical.

But sometimes the control group, shown incidents judged not to be   8
violent, behaves more aggressively afterward than the test group; sometimes comedy produces the more aggressive behavior; and sometimes
there's no change. The only obvious conclusion is that sitting and watching television stimulates subsequent physical activity. Any kid could tell
you that.

As for those who claim that entertainment promotes violent behavior   9
by desensitizing people to violence, the British scholar Martin Barker offers this critique: "Their claim is that the materials they judge to be harm-

ful can only influence us by trying to make us be the same as them. So horrible things will make us horrible—not horrified. Terrifying things will make us terrifying—not terrified. To see something aggressive makes us feel aggressive—not aggressed against. This idea is so odd, it is hard to know where to begin in challenging it."

Even more influential on national policy has been a 22-year study by   10
two University of Michigan psychologists, Leonard I. Eron and L. Rowell Huesmann, of boys exposed to so-called violent media. The Telecommunications Act of 1996, which mandated the television V-chip, allowing parents to screen out unwanted programming, invoked these findings, asserting, "Studies have shown that children exposed to violent video programming at a young age have a higher tendency for violent and aggressive behavior later in life than children not so exposed."

Well, not exactly. Following 875 children in upstate New York from   11
third grade through high school, the psychologists found a correlation between a preference for violent television at age 8 and aggressiveness at age 18. The correlation—0.31—would mean television accounted for about 10 percent of the influences that led to this behavior. But the correlation only turned up in one of three measures of aggression: the assessment of students by their peers. It didn't show up in students' reports about themselves or in psychological testing. And for girls, there was no correlation at all.

Despite the lack of evidence, politicians can't resist blaming the me   12
dia for violence. They can stake out the moral high ground confident that the First Amendment will protect them from having to actually write legislation that would be likely to alienate the entertainment industry. Some use the issue as a smokescreen to avoid having to confront gun control.

But violence isn't learned from mock violence. There is good evi   13
dence—causal evidence, not correlational—that it's leaned in personal violent encounters, beginning with the brutalization of children by their parents or their peers.

The money spent on all the social science research I've described was   14
diverted from the National Institute of Mental Health budget by reducing support for the construction of community mental health centers. To this day there is no standardized reporting system for emergency-room findings of physical child abuse. Violence is on the decline in America, but if we want to reduce it even further, protecting children from real violence in their real lives—not the pale shadow of mock violence—is the place to begin.

The Analysis Analyzed

Let's go through Rhodes's argument step by step, looking not only at the points he makes, but also at the ways he makes them.

The title does not clearly announce the topic and the thesis, but it does give the reader a hint: Rhodes will be: concerned with "hollow claims" (i.e., with assertions he thinks are insubstantial) about something he calls "fantasy violence." At this stage the reader doesn't know what "fantasy violence" is—could it be fantasies of violence that some or all of us have, or could it be fantastic violence in films, or what? But "fantasy" and "violence" are words that interest most people, and the writer has therefore probably hooked the reader. (Give him a B + for the title.)

The first paragraph begins with a world-weary voice: "The moral entrepreneurs are at it again. . . ." The readers do not know exactly who "the moral entrepreneurs" are, and what they are doing again, but Rhodes's first words are catchy, and by the end of the sentence the readers know the main point: People who seem to be in the business of making moral judgments—"moral entrepreneurs"—are yet again criticizing the entertainment industry because it advertises its "Grand Guignolesque confections" to children. Notice how Rhodes *diminishes* or trivializes the violent productions, by calling them "Grand Guignolesque confections." For him, they are theatrical (showy but insubstantial) candies or pastries. He is already preparing us for his thesis.

The second sentence in this paragraph introduces the term "mock violence," and it makes clear Rhodes's topic: He will be concerned not with the real violence of life—assaults, robberies, rapes, murders—but with the fictional, unreal or "mock" violence of the media. If indeed "mock violence contributes to the development of violent behavior," then the moral entrepreneurs (he will name some names in a moment) are "justified" in their indignation. But readers by now can guess that Rhodes will argue that "mock violence" (the "fantasy violence" of his title) does *not* contribute to violent behavior. By the end of the paragraph we know what his topic is, and we have a pretty good idea of what his thesis will be. (Give him an A for his opening paragraph.)

The second paragraph consists of only one sentence: "But is there really a link between entertainment and violent behavior?" Your instructor has probably already told you, rightly, to beware of writing one-sentence paragraphs. A paragraph of one sentence is usually underdeveloped. But Rhodes knows what he is doing here. Since in an essay each paragraph is of roughly equal weight, a one-sentence paragraph must indeed contain a weighty sentence, a big point, and this one does. By letting a single sentence stand as a paragraph, Rhodes is telling us that it is very important. And clearly the answer to his question, "But is there really a link between entertainment and violent behavior?" will be, "No." (Give him an A for knowing how to make effective use of a short paragraph.)

The third paragraph shows us the opposing view. Rhodes cites the heavyweights, the medical associations who "all say yes," who all say there is a link between entertainment and violent behavior in real life. What is Rhodes doing, citing these people who hold a view different from his own? He is letting us know that of course he is familiar with the opposing view; his position is not (he thus assures us) based on ignorance of the other view. And then he firmly rejects this view: "In fact, no direct causal fink between exposure to mock violence in the media and subsequent violent behavior has ever been demonstrated." Gosh, readers think, we didn't know that; we thought that there are all sort of studies that prove. . . . But Rhodes's statement is so strong that it causes us to doubt what we thought we knew, and we realize that in fact we have not read the studies, we do *not* know of any study that really proves the connection. Gee, maybe he is right, after all. (Give him an A for writing a vigorous paragraph that begins to win us to his side.)

The fourth paragraph tells us to think about history, and it offers a statistic, admittedly an uncertain one ("homicide rates are estimated to have been 10 times what they are"). By now we can stop grading his paragraphs; he has probably won a writer's most important battle—not the battle to convince a reader, but the battle to keep a reader's attention. Almost surely the reader who has come this far will continue to read the essay to the end, and that's really as much as a writer can hope for. If the reader is also convinced, that's great, but it's an extra. When writers offer an argument, they want to tell people what their ideas are, and they want to explain why they hold these ideas. They offer reasons based on evidence, but they can offer them only to those readers who stay with them, so writers must write in ways that hold the attention of readers. The job of a writer is to make readers mentally say, "Very interesting, tell me more."

The fifth paragraph sets forth opposing evidence, statistics accepted by no less an authority than the American Medical Association. Why does he do this? Because, again, if writers are to be at all convincing they must show awareness of opposing viewpoints. We can be pretty sure, however, that Rhodes will go on to dispute this opposing view.

The sixth paragraph does exactly what the reader expects it to do: It rejects the AMA position. The statistical findings are "spectacular"—but they are "meaningless." Of course Rhodes cannot merely assert this, he must provide evidence. And he does. Whether this evidence is totally convincing is not our concern here; we are merely pointing out the techniques Rhodes uses in setting forth his argument.

The seventh paragraph returns to the strategy of setting forth the view Rhodes rejects, and we know what he will do in the eighth paragraph.

The eighth paragraph predictably offers evidence rejecting the view set forth in the preceding paragraph. It tells the reader that the experiments don't really prove what they are supposed to prove, and that they prove only that "sitting and watching television stimulates subsequent physical activity." And then, since Rhodes's aim is to discredit the experiments, he firmly dismisses the results with "Any kid could tell you that."

The ninth paragraph glances at a variation of the opposing view, and dismisses it by quoting an authority. Rhodes doubtless could have dismissed the view himself, but he wisely thought it was appropriate to let the reader know that someone else shares his view.

The tenth paragraph gives yet another glance at the opposing view— and we know what is coming next.

The eleventh paragraph dismisses the gist of the tenth, with "Well, not exactly." And Rhodes now offers statistics to support his position.

The twelfth paragraph begins by mentioning "politicians." Probably we are meant to recall Senators McCain and Lieberman, who were specifically named in the opening paragraph.

The thirteenth paragraph assumes that the reader has been following the argument, taking in the evidence, and perhaps is now convinced. It offers no evidence—doubtless Rhodes feels that he has made his case; the paragraph is content to state the thesis bluntly: "But violence isn't learned from mock violence."

The fourteenth (final) paragraph mentions the National Institute of Mental Health—an organization we met in paragraph 3—but the point now is that the money used for wrong-headed social science research could have been used more wisely by the NIMH "for the construction of community mental health centers". The paragraph ends by returning the "mock violence" of the first paragraph, a variation on the "fantasy violence" of the title.

In short,

- Rhodes's opening paragraph gets attention, though perhaps he took a risk by referring to the Grand Guignol, an allusion that not everyone will get;
- he shows he is familiar with arguments other than his own;
- his language, except for the reference to "Grand Guignolesque confections," is easily intelligible to the ordinary reader;
- his paragraphs are coherent and unified; readers are never confused about the point of a paragraph;
- his organization is clear; readers are never uncertain of how a paragraph is related to the previous paragraph;
- his concluding paragraph, with its reference to "mock violence," neatly ties things up by glancing back to the beginning of the essay.

You may strongly disagree with Rhodes's position, but if so, you ought to be able to offer some evidence. The evidence need not be the statements of authorities, or statistics that you have encountered; it may be your own experience. But whether or not you disagree with Rhodes's position, we hope you will agree with our view that he sets his position forth effectively.

Topics for Critical Thinking and Writing

1. Rhodes sets forth views other than his own, but he makes no effort to suggest that they have any merit, or that they can be held by reasonable people. His essay shows no awareness of the principles that Carl Rogers set forth (see pages 65–70). Do you think Rhodes comes across as overly aggressive, arrogant, stubborn, rude? Or on this issue can there be no middle

ground? In an essay of 250 words discuss Rhodes's tone as you perceive it, and its effectiveness here.

2. One reader of Rhodes's essay wrote a letter to *The New York Times,* asserting that even if violent movies and violent music cannot be directly tied to real violence, "they do set a tone and a mood. And they do send the message that in America, violence is an answer to almost any problem." If Rhodes were to write to this person, what do you think he would say? (Put your response in a letter of about 500 words.)

3. Another letter-writer said that, unfortunately, athletes are role models for young boys: "We continue to train boys to be violent men by offering them [as role models] highly paid athletes who fight, trash-talk, and assault officials." Write a 500-word essay supporting or taking issue with this position.

4. A third letter-writer said that "Society at large; endorses violence and killing," and went on to cite the death penalty as "society's ultimate violence." This "socially approved real violence," the letter-writer asserted, encourages violent behavior. In a 500-word essay, set forth your response to this position.

A Checklist for Revising Drafts of Arguments

- Does the introduction let the audience know what the topic is, why the topic is of some importance, and what your thesis is?
- Are the terms clearly defined?
- Are the assumptions likely to be shared by your readers? If not, are they reasonably argued rather than merely asserted?
- Does the essay summarize other views fairly, and grant that they have some merit, at least in some contexts?
- Are the facts verifiable? Is the evidence reliable?
- Is the reasoning sound?
- Are the authorities really authorities on this matter?
- Are quotations no longer than they need to be, are they introduced with useful lead-ins, and do they make good reading?
- Are all of the substantial counterarguments recognized and effectively responded to?
- Is the organization effective? Does the essay begin interestingly, keep the thesis in view, and end interestingly?
- Is the tone appropriate? (Avoid sarcasm, present yourself as fair-minded, and assume that people who hold views opposed to yours are also fair-minded.)

CHAPTER 5

Reading and Writing about Pictures

I am after the one unique picture whose composition possesses such vigor and richness, and whose content so radiates outwards from it, that this single picture is a whole story in itself.

Henri Cartier-Bresson

The Language of Pictures

It may sound odd to talk about "reading" pictures and about the "language" of pictures, but pictures, like words, convey messages. Advertisers know this, and that's why their advertisements for soft drinks include images of attractive young couples frolicking at the beach. The not-so-hidden message is that consumers of these products are healthy, prosperous, relaxed, and sexually attractive.

Like compositions made of words—stories, poems, even vigorous sentences—many pictures are carefully constructed things, built up in a certain way in order to make a statement. To cite an obvious example, in medieval religious pictures Jesus or Mary may be shown larger than the surrounding figures to indicate their greater spiritual status. But even in realistic paintings the more important figures are likely to be given a greater share of the light or a more central position than the lesser figures. Such devices of composition are fairly evident in paintings, but we occasionally forget that photographs too are almost always constructed things. The photographer—even the amateur just taking a candid snapshot—adjusts a pillow under the baby's head, or suggests that the subject may want to step out of the shadow, and then the photographer backs up a little and bends his or her knees before clicking the shutter. Even when photographing something inanimate, the photographer searches for the best view, waits for a cloud to pass, and perhaps pushes out of the range of the camera some trash that would spoil the effect of a lovely fern growing beside a rock. Minor White was speaking for almost all photographers when he said, "I don't take pictures, I make them."

And we often make our photographs for a particular purpose—perhaps to have a souvenir of a trip, or to show what we look like in uniform, or to show grandparents what the new baby looks like. Even professional photographers have a variety of purposes—for instance, to provide wedding portraits, to report the news, to sell automobiles, or to record some visual phenomena that they think must be recorded. Sometimes these purposes can be mingled. During the depression of the early 1930s, for instance, the Resettlement Administration employed photographers such as Dorothea Lange to help convince the nation that migrant workers and dispossessed farmers needed help. These photographers were, so to speak, selling something, but they were also reporting the news and serving a noble social purpose. Later in this chapter we will reproduce Lange's most famous picture, *Migrant Mother*, along with some comments on it that students wrote in journals. We will follow these entries from journals with a finished essay, submitted by a student at the end of the term.

But before we get to Lange's photograph, we will give some questions that may help you to think about pictures.

What are some of the basic things to look for in understanding the language of pictures? One can begin almost anywhere, but let's begin with the relationship among the parts:

> Do the figures share the space evenly, or does one figure overpower another, taking most of the space or the light?
>
> Are the figures harmoniously related, perhaps by a similar stance or shared action? Or are they opposed, perhaps by diagonals thrusting at each other? Generally speaking, diagonals may suggest instability, except when they form a triangle resting on its base. Horizontal lines suggest stability, as do vertical lines when connected by a horizontal line. Circular lines are often associated with motion, and sometimes—especially by men—with the female body and fertility. These simple formulas, however, must be applied cautiously, for they are not always appropriate.
>
> In a landscape, what is the relation between humans and nature? Are the figures at ease in nature, or are they dwarfed by it? Are they earthbound, beneath the horizon, or (because the viewpoint is low) do they stand out against the horizon and perhaps seem in touch with the heavens, or at least with open air? Do the natural objects in the landscape somehow reflect the emotions of the figures in it?
>
> If the picture is a portrait, how do the furnishings and the background and the angle of the head or the posture of the head and body (as well, of course, as the facial expression) contribute to our sense of the character of the person portrayed?
>
> What is the effect of light in the picture? Does it produce sharp contrasts, brightly illuminating some parts and throwing others into darkness? Or does it, by means of gentle gradations, unify most or all of the parts? Does the light seem theatrical or natural, disturbing or comforting? If the picture is in color, is the color realistic or is it expressive, or both?

You can stimulate responses to pictures by asking yourself two kinds of questions:

1. *What is this doing?* Why is this figure here and not there, why is this tree so brightly illuminated, why are shadows omitted, why is this seated figure leaning forward like that?

2. *Why do I have this response?* Why do I find this figure pathetic, this landscape oppressive, this child revoltingly sentimental but that child fascinating?

The first of these questions, "What is this doing?" requires you to identify yourself with the artist, wondering perhaps whether the fence or the side of the house is the better background for this figure, or whether both figures should sit or stand. The second question, "Why do I have this response?" requires you to trust your feelings. If you are amused, repelled, unnerved, or soothed, assume that these responses are appropriate and follow them up— at least until further study of the work provides other responses.

Sample Analyses of Pictures

If you take a course in art history you will probably be asked to write a formal analysis. In such a context, the word *formal* is not the opposite of *informal*, as in a formal dance or a formal dinner, but simply means "related to the form or structure." Here we print a short formal analysis written by a student in such a course, but, as you will see later in this chapter, formal analysis is not practiced only by students in art history courses. Anyone in the advertising business, and almost anyone who talks about advertising, in some degree engages in formal analysis. We follow the student's analysis of Edvard Munch's *The Scream* with a professional analysis of an advertisement.

Joan Daremo

Edvard Munch's *The Scream*

Is there a more unnerving work of art than Munch's lithograph of 1896? Even his painting of the same subject, two years earlier, seems by virtue of its color (rather than severely contrasting black and white spaces) to be less filled with anguish. This lithograph is almost unbearably agitated: Although the two little boats seem to rest easily on the water, our eyes cannot rest on them, for the thrusting diagonals pull the eyes to the left rear, but the compelling picture of the central anguished figure pulls them forward again. Maybe there is some calm in the heavens (although even in the sky the wavy horizontal lines are full of motion) as well as in the water, but the isolated figure in the center is surrounded by, and seems assaulted by, strongly conflicting lines—at the right, verticals that crash into horizontals, and at the left, the diagonals.

At the left, too, walking out of the picture and thus away from the chief figure, two figures stand near each other, forming, we might say, the

society from which the central figure is excluded. But even these two figures are separated from each other by a narrow space—this is not a world
in which someone can put an arm on another's shoulder. Even more important, these two figures are looking in different directions, again a suggestion of the lack of really close community in this world that Munch en-
visions. The two apparently muse on the water, but the screaming wobbly
figure, whose bones seem to have dissolved from terror, averts its eyes
from (and closes it ears to) the seething surrounding world; it (the figure
seems sexless, almost a skull, though some people perceive a female)
faces nothing but us, or, rather, it faces the empty space which we occupy,
because its eyes are not focused on us.

What the student has done is to look closely at the picture and to tell
us how it works—how it makes its effect on the viewer.

The Scream (or *The Shriek)*
Edvard Munch, 1896

Topics for Critical Thinking or Writing

1. Take any picture that you especially like in this book and write an essay in which you call attention to the ways in which the form of the work contributes to its effect on you.

2. If you have a favorite painting or picture not in the book, write an essay in which you tell the reader why you think it is something special.

3. The Metropolitan Museum of Art's WWW site (www.metmuseum.org) gives online access to 3,500 pieces in its collection. Visit this site, select a work of art that especially interests you, and then write a formal analysis.

Now let's look at a cultural historian's analysis of an advertisement. In the introduction to his book *Twenty Ads That Shook the World*, James B. Twitchell says he uses "a kind of art-historical approach in which the artifact of the ad is the basis of the interpretation. What makes it work?" (4). His chapter "She's Very Charlie" is an eleven-page analysis of a Revlon advertisement for a perfume called *Charlie*, popular in the 1970s and 1980s. The picture shows a rear view of a young woman and a young man; the woman holds an attaché case in her left hand, and her right hand pats the man's behind. In the lower right corner, an inset picture of a perfume bottle obscures part of the man's legs. We give only the portion of the chapter devoted to analyzing the picture; earlier in the chapter Twitchell talks about the sense of smell and about the recent history of perfume advertising. In the paragraph preceding our extract, he makes the point that the name of the scent is important.

James B. Twitchell

She's Very Charlie

But the best way to a perfect name was to have such a finely tuned antenna to the shifting sea changes of popular culture that you could find a distant tsunami and ride it all the way to shore. No one currently does this better than Calvin Klein. Who else knew to bring out Obsession in the 1980s, then Escape in the early 1990s, and the unisex CK One for today. This split-second marketing for scents that "last through the ages" started not with Calvin but with Charlie, Revlon's launch of a new jasmine-loaded scent in the late 1960s.

In a world where French names were *de rigueur,* the use of a male diminutive was startling. Many people thought "Charlie" was the last gasp of Charles Revson, the ailing CEO, who was in his last days, naming products after himself. Many insiders were concerned about the name. But not the customers. They liked it.

More startling to the customers was that the "Charlie" woman in the ads was younger than the usual perfume user. She was invariably pictured in the daytime, doing something *active,* and often doing it alone, like strutting around in front of the Eiffel Tower, hitching a ride on a luggage dolly in a hotel lobby, striding down a city street in a mannish tweed suit and boots with three-inch heels, or apparently nude in the water with nothing showing but an upswept hairdo and a pearl necklace. In fact, if men are in the picture, they are usually looking at her with awe, often with their faces blurred.

If she is with a recognizable man, as we see in this most famous example, the microecology of social relationships is profoundly rearranged. She's in charge. No doubt about it. For appreciators of irony, it might be noted that while the model for those ever-so-successful Charlie ads occasionally wore trousers, Mr. Revson wouldn't allow his women employees to wear trousers to work.

But in the magical world of advertising, Charlie is not just in charge, she is clearly enjoying dominance. She is taller than her partner, more confident. Presumably they are both going back to their respective offices (note that they carry the same sized work tools, the ubiquitous attaché case, and wear the same black-and-white business attire), but they are not of equal status. As they are saying their ta-ta's, she looks down, he looks askance. Not only does he have part of his anatomy removed from the picture so that the Charlie bottle can be foregrounded, and not only does she have the jaunty scarf and the cascading hair of a free spirit, but she is delivering that most masculine of signifiers, the booty pat.

The booty pat in this image is what the kiss is in the usual perfume ad. But the booty pat is most usually seen being delivered man to man, leader to follower, in a very controlled environment, usually an athletic event. In football especially, the pat signifies comradeship, dedication to business, and is applied dominant to submissive. After throwing his arm around the shoulder of a player, the coach delivers it to a hulking cub who is returning to the field of battle. After breaking the huddle, the quarterback delivers it to his massive linemen. When Charlie bestows it on her gentleman friend here in Downtown U.S.A., she is harvesting a rich crop of meaning. The tide has turned, and now men are getting their butts slapped by, of all people, women. Charlie has subverted sexism, turned it on its head, used it against itself, and she knows it.

The New York Times knew it as well and the editors initially refused to run the ad, saying it was in "poor taste." But eleven women's magazines knew better and did indeed recognize that often "poor taste" is just another word for "something really important going on." What was going on was, of course, the women's movement, and Charlie was out in front. She was giving the Old Spice man his sailing orders, and he was enjoying it.

Thinking About Dorothea Lange's
Migrant Mother, Nipomo, California

Let's look now at a photograph by Dorothea Lange, an American photographer who made her reputation with photographs of migrant laborers in California during the depression that began in 1929. Lange's *Migrant Mother, Nipomo, California* (1936) is probably the best-known image of the period. One of our students made the following entry in his journal. (The student was given no information about the photograph other than the name of the photographer and the title of the picture.)

> This woman seems to be thinking. In a way, the picture reminds me of a statue called The Thinker, of a seated man who is bent over, with his chin resting on his fist. But I wouldn't say that this photograph is really so much about thinking as it is about other things. I'd say that it is about several other things. First (but not really in any particular order), fear. The children must be afraid, since they have turned to their mother. Second, the picture is about love. The children press against their mother, sure of her love. The mother does not actually show her love--for instance, by kissing them, or even hugging them--but you feel she loves them. Third, the picture is about hopelessness. The mother doesn't seem to be able to offer any comfort. Probably they have very little food; maybe they are homeless. I'd say the picture is also about courage. Although the picture seems to me to show hopelessness, I also think the mother, even though she does not know how she will be able to help her children shows great strength in her face. She also has a lot of dignity. She hasn't broken down in front of the children: she is going to do her best to get through the day and the next day and the next.

Another student wrote:

> I remember from American Lit that good literature is not sentimental. (When we discussed the word, we concluded that "sentimental" meant "sickeningly sweet.") Some people might think that Lange's picture, showing a mother and two little children, is sentimental, but I don't think so. Although the children must be upset, and maybe they even are crying, the mother seems to be very strong. I feel that with a mother like this, the children are in very good hands. She is not "sickeningly sweet." She may be almost overcome with despair, but she doesn't seem to ask us to pity her.

Figure 1

Migrant Mother, Nipomo, California
Dorothea Lange, 1936

A third student wrote:

> It's like those pictures of the homeless in the newspapers and on
> TV. A photographer sees some man sleeping in a cardboard box,
> or a woman with shopping bags sitting in a doorway, and he takes
> their picture. I suppose the photographer could say that he is call-
> ing the public's attention to "the plight of the homeless," but I'm
> not convinced that he's doing anything more than making money
> by selling photographs. Homeless people have almost no pri-
> vacy, and then some photographer comes along and invades
> even their doorways and cardboard houses. Sometimes the peo-
> ple are sleeping, or even if they are awake they may be in so
> much despair that they don't bother to tell the photographer to
> get lost. Or they may be mentally ill and don't know what's hap-
> pening. In the case of this picture, the woman is not asleep, but
> she seems so preoccupied that she isn't aware of the photogra-
> pher. Maybe she has just been told there is no work for her, or
> maybe she has been told she can't stay if she keeps the children.

> Should the photographer have intruded on this woman's sorrow?
> This picture may be art, but it bothers me.

All of these entries seem to us to be thoughtful, interesting, and helpful, though even taken together they do not provide the last word.

Here are a few additional points. First, it happens that Lange has written about the picture. She said that she had spent the winter of 1935–36 taking photographs of migrants, and now, in March, she was preparing to drive five hundred miles to her home when she noticed a sign that said, "Pea-Pickers Camp." Having already taken hundreds of pictures, she drove on for twenty miles, but something preyed on her mind, and she made a U-turn and visited the camp. Here is part of what she wrote.

> I saw and approached the hungry and desperate mother, as if drawn by a magnet. I do not remember how I explained my presence or my camera to her, but I do remember she asked me no questions. I made five exposures, working closer and closer from the same direction. I did not ask her name or her history. She told me her age, that she was thirty-two. She said that they had been living on frozen vegetables from the surrounding fields, and birds that the children killed. She had just sold the tires from her car to buy food. There she sat in that lean-to tent with her children huddled around her, and seemed to know that my pictures might help her, and so she helped me. There was a sort of equality about it. . . . What I am trying to tell other photographers is that had I not been deeply involved in my undertaking on that field trip, I would not have had to turn back. What I am trying to say is that I believe this inner compulsion to be the vital ingredient in our work.

Lange does not say anything about posing the woman and her child, and we can assume that she had too much decency to ask a woman and children in these circumstances to arrange themselves into an interesting pictorial composition. Furthermore, it seems obvious that unlike, say, a figure in a wedding portrait, the woman is not striking a pose. She has not deliberately prepared herself for a picture that will represent her to the public. Nevertheless, the composition—the way things are put together—certainly contributes to the significance of the picture. Of course the subject matter, a mother with children, may suggest the traditional Madonna and Child of the Middle Ages and the Renaissance, but the resemblance is not just in the subject matter. Lange's photograph may remind us of paintings in which the Madonna and the infant Jesus form a unified composition, their heads and limbs harmonizing and echoing each other.

The photograph, with its near-balance—a child on each side, the mother's bare left arm balanced by the child's bare arm, the mother's hand at one side of her neck echoed by the child's hand at the other side—achieves a stability, or harmony, that helps make the painfulness of the subject acceptable. That is, although the subject may be painful, it is possible to take some pleasure in the way in which it is presented. That the faces of the children are turned away probably helps make the subject acceptable. If we saw not only the woman's face but also the faces of two hungry children, we might feel that Lange was tugging too vigorously at our heartstrings. Finally, speaking of faces, it is worth mentioning that the woman does not look at us. We don't know why, but we can guess that she takes no notice of us because she is preoccupied with issues far beyond us.

A Sample Essay by a Student

We have already given extracts from the journals of three students. A week after the journals were due, students were asked to write essays on the picture. Notice in the following essay that the student draws not only on his own experience as an amateur photographer but also on material that he found in the college library.

Did Dorothea Lange Pose Her Subject for Migrant Mother?

In doing research for this essay, I was surprised to find that Dorothea Lange's Migrant Mother (figure 1) is one of six pictures of this woman and her children. Migrant Mother is so much an image of the period, an icon of the Depression, that it is hard to believe it exists in any other form than the one we all know.[1]

In addition to the famous picture, four other pictures of this subject (figures 2–5) are illustrated in a recent book, Vincent Virga's Eyes of the Nation, and still another picture (figure 6) is illustrated in Karen Tsujimoto's Dorothea Lange. When you think about it, it is not surprising

---

[1]Curiously, Lange in her short essay on the picture, "The Assignment I'll Never Forget: Migrant Mother," in Popular Photography 46 (February 1960): 43, says that she made five exposures. A slightly abridged version of the essay is reprinted in Milton Meltzer, Dorothea Lange: A Photographer's Life (New York: Farrar Straus Giroux 1978): 132-33. Because Meltzer's book is more available than the magazine, when I quote from the article I quote from his book.

that Lange would take several pictures of this woman and her children. Anyone who takes snapshots knows that if photographers have the opportunity they will take several pictures of a subject. What is surprising is that the picture we all know, the one that has become an icon for the period, is so much more moving than the others.

Two of the pictures include an older child, apparently a teenager, sitting in a chair, so in a sense they are "truer" to the fact, because they give us more information about the family. The trunk, for instance, tells us that these people are on the move, and the setting--a messy field, with a shabby tent or lean-to--tells us that they are homeless. But sometimes less is more; the pictures showing the tent, trunk, and all of the children seem to sprawl. Perhaps we find ourselves wondering why people who seem to have only a trunk and some canvas would carry with them so bulky an object as a rocker. In saying that the two more inclusive pictures are less

Figure 2

Figure 3

effective--less impressive, less moving--than the others, then, I don't think that I am simply expressing a personal preference. I think that most or maybe even all viewers would agree.

Putting aside the two pictures that show the setting, and also putting aside for the moment the most famous picture, we probably can agree that the three remaining pictures of the woman are approximately equally effective, one viewer might prefer one picture, another viewer another, but compared with the two that show the larger setting, all three of these pictures have the advantage of emphasizing the mother-and-child motif. But the remaining picture, the famous one, surely is far more memorable than even the other three close-up pictures. Why? Partly, perhaps, because it is a closer view, eliminating the tent pole and most of the hanging cloth. Partly it is more effective because the children have turned their faces from the camera, thereby conveying their isolation from everything in the world except their mother. And partly it is more effective

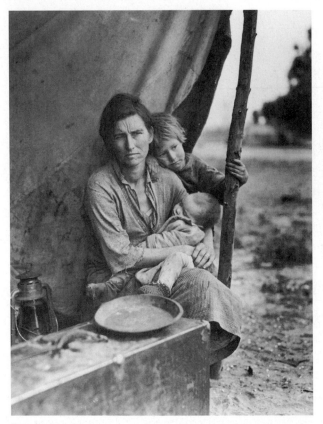

Figure 4

because the woman, touching the side of her face, has a faraway look of anxiety.

Thinking about this picture in the context of the other five, if one has a cynical mind one might wonder if Lange staged it. And this is exactly what Charles J. Shindo says she did, in his recent book:

> In the course of this encounter Lange took six exposures, starting with a long shot of the lean-to with the mother and four children inside. . . . For the final shot Lange called back another of the children and had the children lean upon their mother with their backs to the camera. The woman raised her hand to her chin and struck the now famous pose of the <u>Migrant Mother</u>. . . . (50)

Figure 5

Figure 6

What evidence does Shindo give for his claim that "Lange called back another of the children" and that she "had the children lean upon their mother"? Absolutely none. He does not cite Lange, or an eyewitness, or anyone who suggests that Lange customarily posed her subjects. He ignores the basic evidence, Lange's own words about how she took the picture:

> I saw and approached the hungry and desperate mother, as if drawn by a magnet. I do not remember how I explained my presence or my camera to her, but I do remember she asked me no questions. I made five exposures, working closer and closer from the same direction. I did not ask her name or her history. She told me her age, that she was thirty-two. She said that they had been living on frozen vegetables from the surrounding fields, and birds that the children killed. She had just sold the tires from her car to buy food. There she sat in that lean-to tent with her children huddled around her, and seemed to know that my pictures might help her, and so she helped me. There was a sort of equality about it.
>
> The pea crop at Nipomo had frozen and there was no work for anybody. But I did not approach the tents and shelters of other stranded pea-pickers. It was not necessary; I knew I had recorded the essence of my assignment. . . . (qtd. in Meltzer 133)

This is the _only_ eye-witness account of how Lange photographed the woman and her children. Of course she may not have been telling the truth, but none of her contemporaries ever challenged the truth of her statement. Furthermore, everything that we know about Lange suggests that she did not pose her subjects. For instance, Rondal Partridge, a longtime friend and sometimes a co-worker, gave this description of

Lange's method: "She did not ask people to hold a pose or repeat an action, instead she might ask a question: 'How much does that bag of cotton weigh?' And the man, wanting to give her a precise answer, would lift it onto the scales and Lange would make her photograph" (qtd. in Ohrn 61).

Rondal Partridge's comment harmonizes with comments that Lange herself made about her method. Asked about her approach to photography, she said, "First--hands off! Whatever I photograph, I do not molest or tamper with or arrange" (qtd. in Dixon 68). Elsewhere she explained that since she worked with a large camera, "You have to wait until certain decisions are made by the subject--what he's going to give to the camera, which is a very important decision; and the photographer-- what he's going to choose to take" (qtd. in Ohrn 233). If I may add a personal comment, I want to say that as an amateur portrait photographer I know from my experience and from talking to other photographers, that posed photographs just don't come out successfully. You can't say to children, "Turn your faces toward your mother," and then say to the mother, "Please put your hand on your cheek," and get a good picture. Every photographer quickly learns that when the photographer specifies the poses, the pictures will be lifeless. The way to get a picture that is convincing is, as Lange's friend said, for the photographer to engage in some talk with the subject, which allows the subject to respond in some significant way. I imagine that while Lange talked, the children may have become uneasy at the sight of the woman with the big camera, and they may have turned and sought the security of their mother. (This is only a guess, but it is very different from Shindo's assertion, made without evidence, that "Lange called back another of the children and had the children lean upon their mother with their backs to the camera"). And perhaps Lange asked the woman something like, "What do you think you will do now?" or "Do you think you can get a friend to give your family a hitch to another work-site?" or some such thing, and the woman responded naturally. Again my view is different from Shindo's, who says that the woman "struck the pose of the <u>Migrant Mother,</u>" where "struck the pose," in the context of his preceding sentences about Lange coldly setting up the image, suggests that the whole thing is a performance, with Lange as stage-manager and the woman as the chief actor.

Anyone who has read a book about Dorothea Lange, and has studied Lange's numerous comments about her ways of working in <u>Dorothea Lange</u>, ed. Howard M. Levin and Katherine Northrup, knows that posing figures was utterly foreign to her. In 1923 she posted on her darkroom door these words from Francis Bacon, and they guided her for the remaining thirty-odd years of her career:

> The contemplation of things as they are
>
> without substitution or imposture
>
> without error or confusion
>
> is in itself a nobler thing
>
> than a whole harvest of invention. (qtd. in Stein 59)

In her photography Lange sought to show the viewer "things as they are." She believed it was nobler to show life as it is than it is to invent compositions.

There are, of course, questions about this picture, such as "Exactly what is the mother thinking about?" Is she thinking that the situation is hopeless? Or that somehow she and the children will get through? Does her face show despair, or does it show determination? These are questions that we cannot answer definitively. But if we ask the question, "Did Lange tell the children and the woman how to position themselves?" we must answer that all of the evidence suggests that she did not set the scene. She spoke to the woman, and she moved about, looking for the best shot, but a picture as great as this one can only have come from (to repeat Lange's own belief) what the subject is "going to give to the camera" and what the photographer is "going to choose to take."

Works Cited

Dixon, Daniel. "Dorothea Lange." Modern Photography 16 (Dec 1952).
    68-77, 138-41.

Levin, Howard M., and Katherine Northrup. Dorothea Lange. 2 vols.
    Glencoe: Text-Fiche Press, 1980.

Meltzer, Milton. Dorothea Lange: A Photographer's Life. New York: Farrar,
    1978.

Ohrn, Karin Becker. Dorothea Lange and the Documentary Tradition.
    Baton Rouge: Louisiana State UP, 1980.

Shindo, Charles J. Dust Bowl Migrants in the American Imagination.
    Lawrence: UP of Kansas, 1997.

Stein, Sally. "Peculiar Grace: Dorothea Lange and the Testimony of the
    Body." Dorothea Lange: A Visual Life. Ed. Elizabeth Partridge.
    Washington, D. C.: Smithsonian Institution, 1994. 57-89.

Last Words

If your instructor asks you to write about a picture—perhaps one in this book—and if even after thinking about the questions on pages 93–94 you don't quite know where to begin, you may want to think about it partly in terms of one of the following remarks by distinguished photographers. (But remember: a remark need not be true just because it was made by someone who is highly regarded as a photographer.)

> A great photograph is a full expression of what one feels about what is being photographed in the deepest sense, and is, thereby, a true expression of what one feels about life in its entirety.
>
> Ansel Adams

> It's the subject-matter that counts. I'm interested in revealing the subject in a new way to intensify it.
>
> Harry Callahan

> Documentary photography records the social scene of our time. It mirrors the present and documents for the future. Its focus is man in his relations to mankind.
>
> Dorothea Lange

Photography is the simultaneous recognition, in a fraction of a second, of the significance of an event as well as of the precise organization of forms which give that event its proper expression.

Henri Cartier-Bresson

I am a passionate lover of the snapshot because of all photographic images it comes closest to truth. The snapshot is a specific spiritual moment. . . . What the eye sees is different from what the camera records. Whereas the eye sees in three dimensions, images are projected on a surface of two dimensions, which for every image-maker is a great problem. The snap-shooter disregards this problem, and the result is that his pictures have an apparent disorder and imperfection, which is exactly their appeal and their style. . . . Out of this imbalance, and out of this not knowing, and out of this real innocence toward the medium comes an enormous vitality and expression of life.

Lisette Model

Or you might begin by thinking about a statement by Janet Malcolm, who in *Diana and Nikon* (a book about photography) said:

If "the camera can't lie," neither is it inclined to tell the truth, since it can reflect only the usually ambiguous, and sometimes outright deceitful surface of reality.

Exercise: Find a picture that interests you, and write two or three paragraphs about it. Say whatever you want to say, but, like Benson, you may want to take a picture that allows you to draw on your technical knowledge, so that you can educate your reader. If you read any specialized magazines, for instance about sports or computers or automobiles or fashion or beekeeping, you probably know more about this area than the average person. From a magazine on this topic, take a picture that interests you—a picture that (a) stimulates you to reflect, as Benson does in his first paragraph, and that (b) allows you to educate your reader by elucidating technical details, as Benson does in his second paragraph.

CHAPTER 6

Memoirs: Discovering the Past

Wedding in the Poitou (1957–58)
Robert Doisneau

Oneida Family Portrait
Mark R. Harrington, 1907

Vietnam Veterans Memorial
(AP/Wide World Photos)

Short Views

Know myself? If I knew my self, I'd run away.
Johann Wolfgang von Goethe

The true art of memory is the art of attention.
Samuel Johnson

The charm, one might say the genius of memory, is that it is
choosy, chancy, and temperamental: It rejects the edifying cathedral and indelibly photographs the small boy outside, chewing a
hunk of melon in the dust.
Elizabeth Bowen

Our memory is like a shop in the window of which is exposed now
one, now another photograph of the same person. And as a rule the
most recent exhibit remains for some time the only one to be seen.
Marcel Proust

It's a pleasure to share one's memories. Everything remembered is
dear, endearing, touching, precious. At least the past is safe—
though we didn't know it at the time. We know it now. Because it's
in the past; because we have survived.
Susan Sontag

Not the power to remember, but its very opposite, the power to
forget, is a necessary condition for our existence.
Sholem Asch

Memory is the thing you forget with.
Alexander Chase

A retentive memory may be a good thing, but the ability to forget
is the true token of greatness.
Elbert Hubbard

Better by far you should forget and smile
Than that you should remember and be sad.
Christina Rossetti

We are now at the 24th of March 1856, and from this point of time, my journal, let us renew our daily intercourse without looking back. Looking back was not intended by nature, evidently, from the fact that our eyes are in our faces and not in our hind heads. Look straight before you, then, Jane Carlyle, and, if possible, not over the heads of things either, away into the distant vague. Look, above all, at the duty nearest hand, and what's more, do it. Ah, the spirit is willing, but the flesh is weak, and four weeks of illness have made mine weak as water.
    Jane Welsh Carlyle

I did, I think, nothing.
    Evelyn Waugh

Went to bed, and slept dreamlessly, but not refreshingly. Awoke, and up an hour before being called; but dawdled three hours in dressing. When one subtracts from life infancy (which is vegetation)—sleep, eating, and swilling—buttoning and unbuttoning— how much remains of downright existence? The summer of a dormouse.
    Lord Byron

To be able to enjoy one's past life is to live twice.
    Martial

Memory . . . is the diary that we all carry about with us.
    Oscar Wilde

Mary Karr

Mary Karr (b. 1965) is a poet and essayist who has won numerous prizes, awards, and grants for her work. In The Liars' Club, *published by Penguin in 1995, she describes a troubled and at times traumatic childhood with her parents and sister in East Texas. Critics have called her memoir "dazzling" and "wickedly funny."*

Ms. Karr teaches literature and creative writing at Syracuse University, and lives with her son in upstate New York.

Texas, 1961

Maybe it's wrong to blame the arrival of Grandma Moore for much of the worst hurt in my family, but she was such a ring-tailed bitch that I do. She sat like some dissipated empress in Mother's huge art deco chair (mint-green vinyl with square black arms), which she turned to face right out of our front picture window like she was about to start issuing proclamations any minute.

All day, she doled out criticisms that set my mother to scurrying around with her face set so tight her mouth was a hyphen. The drapes were awful; let's make some new. When was the last time we'd cleaned our windows? (Never.) Had Mother put on weight? She seemed pudged up. I looked plumb like a wetback I was so dark. (Lecia had managed to come out blond like her people, but Grandma never got over my looking vaguely Indian like Daddy.) And I was *pore-looking*, a term she reserved for underfed farm animals and the hookworm-ridden Cajun kids we saw trying to catch crawfish on summer afternoons on the edge of Taylor's Bayou. (Marvalene Seesacque once described her incentive for craw-dadding all day: "You don't catch, you don't eat.")

In a house where I often opened a can of tamales for breakfast and ate them cold (I remember sucking the cuminy tomato sauce off the paper each one was wrapped in) Grandma cut out a *Reader's Digest* story on the four major food groups and taped it to the refrigerator. Suddenly our family dinners involved dishes you saw on TV, like meatloaf—stuff you had to light the oven to make, which Mother normally didn't even bother doing for Thanksgiving.

Our family's habit of eating meals in the middle of my parents' bed also broke overnight. Mother had made the bed extra big by stitching two mattresses together and using coat hangers to hook up their frames. She'd said that she needed some spread-out space because of the humidity, a word Lecia and I misheard for a long time as *stupidity*. (Hence, our tendency to say, *It ain't the heat, it's the stupidity*.) It was the biggest bed I ever saw, and filled their whole bedroom wall-to-wall. She had to stitch up special sheets for it, and even the chest of drawers had to be put out in the hall. The only pieces of furniture that still fit next to the bed were a standing brass ashtray shaped like a Viking ship on Daddy's side and a tall black reading lamp next to a wobbly tower of hardback books on Mother's.

Anyway, the four of us tended to eat our family meals sitting cross-legged on the edges of that bed. We faced opposite walls, our backs together, looking like some four-headed totem, our plates balanced on the spot of quilt between our legs. Mother called it picnic-style, but since I've been grown, I recall it as just plain odd. I've often longed to take out an ad in a major metropolitan paper and ask whether anybody else's family ate back-to-back in the parents' bed, and what such a habit might signify.

With Grandma there, we used not just the table but table linens. Mother hired a black woman named Mae Brown to wash and iron the tablecloth and napkins when they got greased up. And we couldn't just come in out of the heat at midday and pull off our clothes anymore with Grandma there. We'd had this habit of stripping down to underwear or putting on pajamas in the house, no matter what the time. In the serious heat, we'd lie for hours half-naked on the wooden floor in front of the black blade-fan sucking chipped ice out of wadded-up dish towels. Now Grandma even tried to get us to keep shoes and socks on. Plus we had to take baths every night. One of these first baths ended with the old woman holding me in a rough towel on her lap while she scrubbed at my neck with fingernail-polish remover. (It had supposedly accumulated quite a crust.)

She undertook to supervise our religious training, which had until then consisted of sporadic visits to Christian Science Sunday school alternating with the exercises from a book Mother had on yoga postures. (I could sustain a full-lotus position at five.) Grandma bought Lecia and me each white leather Bibles that zipped shut. "If you read three chapters a day and five on Sunday, you can read the Holy Bible in one year," she said. I don't remember ever unzipping mine once after unwrapping it, for Grandma was prone to abandoning any project that came to seem too daunting, as making us into Christians must have seemed.

Much later, when Mother could be brought to talk about her own childhood, she told stories about how peculiar her mother's habits had been. Grandma Moore didn't sound like such a religious fanatic back then. She just seemed like a fanatic in general. For instance, she had once sent away for a detective-training kit from a magazine. The plan was for her and Mother to spy on their neighbors—this, back when the Lubbock population still fit into three digits. According to Mother, this surveillance went on for weeks. Grandma would stirrup Mother up to the parson's curtained windows—and not because of any suspected adultery or flagrant sinning, but to find out whether his wife did her cakes from scratch or not. She kept the answers to these kinds of questions in an alphabetized log of prominent families. She would also zero in on some particular person who troubled her and keep track of all his comings and goings for weeks on end. She knew the procedure for taking fingerprints and kept

Mother's on a recipe card, in case she was ever kidnapped. Grandma even began to collect little forensic envelopes of hair and dust that she found on people's furniture when she visited them. Mother said that for the better part of a year, they'd be taking tea at some lady's house, when her mother would suddenly sneak an envelope with something like a dust-ball in it into the pocket of her pinafore. Whatever became of this *evidence* Mother couldn't say. The whole detective-training deal got dropped as abruptly as it had been undertaken.

When Grandma came to our house, she brought with her that same kind of slightly deranged scrutiny. Before, our lives had been closed to outsiders. The noise of my parents' fights might leak out through the screens at night, and I might guess at the neighbors' scorn, but nobody really asked after our family, about Mother's being Nervous. We didn't go to church. No one came to visit. We probably seemed as blurry to the rest of the neighborhood as bad TV. Suddenly Grandma was staring at us with laser-blue eyes from behind her horn rims, saying *Can I make a suggestion?* or beginning every sentence with *Why don't you . . . ?*

Also, she was herself secretive. She bustled around as if she had some   10 earnest agenda, but God knows what it was. She carried, for instance, an enormous black alligator doctor's bag, which held, along with the regular lady stuff in there—cosmetics and little peony-embroidered hankies—an honest-to-God hacksaw. It was the kind you see only in B movies, when criminals need it to saw through jail bars. Lest you think I fabricate, Lecia saw it, too. We even had a standing joke that we were keeping Grandma prisoner, and she was planning to bust out.

I had always thought that what I lacked in my family was some attentive, brownie-baking female to keep my hair curled and generally Donna-Reed over me. But my behavior got worse with Grandma's new order. I became a nail-biter. My tantrums escalated to the point where even Daddy didn't think they were funny anymore. I tore down the new drapes they'd hung across the dining room windows and clawed scratch marks down both of Lecia's cheeks. Beating me didn't seem to discourage me one whit. Though I was a world-famous crybaby, I refused to cry during spankings. I still can recall Daddy holding a small horse quirt, my calves striped with its imprint and stinging and my saying, "Go on and hit me then, if it makes you feel like a man to beat on a little girl like me." End of spanking.

Lecia was both better-tempered and better at kissing ass than I was, so she fared better. But the pressure must have gotten to her too. It was during Grandma's residency that my sister stuffed me struggling into the clothes hamper that pulled out from the bathroom wall, and left me screaming among the mildewed towels till Mae Brown came back from getting groceries. Also, she took to plastering down her bangs with so much hair spray that neither wind nor rain could move them. (I called her Helmet-head.) And she lengthened all her skirts so her knees didn't show anymore. In pictures from then, she looks like a child trying to impersonate an adult and coming out some strange gargoyle neither adult nor child. Once she even had me climb up on her shoulders, then draped a brown corduroy painter's smock to hang from my shoulders to her knees. We staggered from house to house pretending we were some lady collecting for the American Cancer Society. I remember holding a coffee can out to various strangers as I listed side to side on her shoulders. We didn't clear a dime.

In fairness to Grandma, she was dying of cancer at fifty, which can't do much for your disposition. Still, I remember not one tender feeling for or from her. Her cheek was withered like a bad apple and smelled of hyacinth. I had to be physically forced to kiss this cheek, even though I was prone to throwing my arms around the neck of any vaguely friendly grown-up—vacuum-cleaner salesman, mechanic, checkout lady.

The worst part wasn't all the change she brought, but the silence that came with it. Nobody said anything about how we'd lived before. It felt as if the changes themselves had just swept over us like some great wave, flattening whatever we'd once been. I somehow knew that suggesting a dinner in the middle of the bed, or stripping down when I came in from playing, would have thrown such a pall of shame over the household that I couldn't even consider it. Clearly, we had, all this time, been doing everything all wrong.

Topics for Critical Thinking and Writing

1. In the opening sentence of this section of her memoir, Karr calls Grandma Moore "a ring-tailed bitch." Do you remember how you felt, reading that description? Were you surprised? How do you explain your reaction, whatever it was?

2. How did Mary feel about her parents? About her sister? What passages best reveal how she felt about them?

3. Karr doesn't reveal until her next-to-last paragraph that her grandmother was dying of cancer. Should she have revealed this earlier? What does the narrative gain (or lose) by her postponing this revelation?

4. Imagine that you were a social worker in East Texas and the Karrs were on your case list. In three or four sentences, describe the family.

5. How does Karr feel about her childhood? Is she angry? Regretful? Stoic? Note some instances of humor in her account. How do they help you to understand her feelings?

6. A writing assignment: Think of a relative or close family friend whom you disliked or who made you uncomfortable. Write an account of that person within your family, including two or three incidents that reveal the person as you then perceived him or her.

Frank McCourt

Frank McCourt was born in Brooklyn to Irish immigrant parents. The family returned to Ireland, settling in a Limerick slum, enduring bitter poverty. The father, when he worked, drank away his wages; the mother, Angela, repeatedly pregnant, nursed her sick infants and was forced to beg for money to feed them. McCourt returned to America at 19, where he was later joined by his mother and 3 surviving brothers. Frank managed to get a college education and then taught writing in high schools in New York City. He published Angela's Ashes, *his first book, at the age of 66. It has sold several million copies and has won numerous awards, including a Pulitzer Prize.*

Brooklyn and Limerick

Brooklyn

When Dad gets a job Mam is cheerful and she sings,

> Anyone can see why I wanted your kiss,
> It had to be and the reason is this
> Could it be true, someone like you
> Could love me, love me?

When Dad brings home the first week's wages Mam is delighted she can pay the lovely Italian man in the grocery shop and she can hold her head up again because there's nothing worse in the world than to owe and be beholden to anyone. She cleans the kitchen, washes the mugs and plates, brushes crumbs and bits of food from the table, cleans out the icebox and orders a fresh block of ice from another Italian. She buys toilet paper that we can take down the hall to the lavatory and that, she says, is better than having the headlines from the *Daily News* blackening your arse. She boils water on the stove and spends a day at a great tin tub washing our shirts and socks, diapers for the twins, our two sheets, our three towels. She hangs everything out on the clotheslines behind the apartment house and we can watch the clothes dance in wind and sun. She says you wouldn't want the neighbors to know what you have in the way of a wash but there's nothing like the sweetness of clothes dried by the sun.

When Dad brings home the first week's wages on a Friday night we know the weekend will be wonderful. On Saturday night Mam will boil water on the stove and wash us in the great tin tub and Dad will dry us. Malachy will turn around and show his behind. Dad will pretend to be shocked and we'll all laugh. Mam will make hot cocoa and we'll be able to stay up while Dad tells us a story out of his head. All we have to do is say a name, Mr. MacAdorey or Mr. Leibowitz down the hall, and Dad will

---

have the two of them rowing up a river in Brazil chased by Indians with green noses and puce shoulders. On nights like that we can drift off to sleep knowing there will be a breakfast of eggs, fried tomatoes and fried bread, tea with lashings of sugar and milk and, later in the day, a big dinner of mashed potatoes, peas and ham, and a trifle Mam makes, layers of fruit and warm delicious custard on a cake soaked in sherry.

When Dad brings home the first week's wages and the weather is fine Mam takes us to the playground. She sits on a bench and talks to Minnie MacAdorey. She tells Minnie stories about characters in Limerick and Minnie tells her about characters in Belfast and they laugh because there are funny people in Ireland, North and South. Then they teach each other sad songs and Malachy and I leave the swings and seesaws to sit with them on the bench and sing,

> A group of young soldiers one night in a camp
> Were talking of sweethearts they had.
> All seemed so merry except one young lad,
> And he was downhearted and sad.
> Come and join us, said one of the boys,
> Surely there's someone for you.
> But Ned shook his head and proudly he said
> I am in love with two, Each like a mother to me,
> From neither of them shall I part.
> For one is my mother, God bless her and love her,
> The other is my sweetheart.

Malachy and I sing that song and Mam and Minnie laugh till they cry at the way Malachy takes a deep bow and holds his arms out to Mam at the end. Dan MacAdorey comes along on his way home from work and says Rudy Vallee better start worrying about the competition. 5

When we go home Mam makes tea and bread and jam or mashed potatoes with butter and salt. Dad drinks the tea and eats nothing. Mam says, God above, How can you work all day and not eat? He says, The tea is enough. She says, You'll ruin your health, and he tells her again that food is a shock to the system. He drinks his tea and tells us stories and shows us letters and words in the *Daily News* or he smokes a cigarette, stares at the wall, runs his tongue over his lips.

When Dad's job goes into the third week he does not bring home the wages. On Friday night we wait for him and Mam gives us bread and tea. The darkness comes down and the lights come on along Classon Avenue. Other men with jobs are home already and having eggs for dinner because you can't have meat on a Friday. You can hear the families talking upstairs and downstairs and down the hall and Bing Crosby is singing on the radio, Brother, can you spare a dime?

Malachy and I play with the twins. We know Mam won't sing Anyone can see why I wanted your kiss. She sits at the kitchen table talking to herself, What am I going to do? till it's late and Dad rolls up the stairs singing Roddy McCorley. He pushes in the door and calls for us, Where are my troops? Where are my four warriors?

Mam says, Leave those boys alone. They're gone to bed half hungry because you have to fill your belly with whiskey.

He comes to the bedroom door. Up, boys, up. A nickel for everyone   10
who promises to die for Ireland.

> Deep in Canadian woods we met
> From one bright island flown.
> Great is the land we tread, but yet
> Our hearts are with our own.

Up, boys, up. Francis, Malachy, Oliver, Eugene. The Red Branch Knights, the Fenian Men, the IRA. Up, up.

Mam is at the kitchen table, shaking, her hair hanging damp, her face wet. Can't you leave them alone? she says. Jesus, Mary and Joseph, isn't it enough that you come home without a penny in your pocket without making fools of the children on top of it?

She comes to us. Go back to bed, she says.

I want them up, he says. I want them ready for the day Ireland will be free from the center to the sea.

Don't cross me, she says, for if you do it'll be a sorry day in your   15
mother's house.

He pulls his cap down over his face and cries, My poor mother. Poor Ireland. Och, what are we going to do?

Mam says, You're pure stone mad, and she tells us again to go to bed.

On the morning of the fourth Friday of Dad's job Mam asks him if he'll be home tonight with his wages or will he drink everything again? He looks at us and shakes his head at Mam as if to say, Och, you shouldn't talk like that in front of the children.

Mam keeps at him. I'm asking you, Are you coming home so that we can have a bit of supper or will it be midnight with no money in your pocket and you singing Kevin Barry and the rest of the sad songs?

He puts on his cap, shoves his hands into his trouser pockets, sighs   20
and looks up at the ceiling. I told you before I'll be home, he says.

Later in the day Mam dresses us. She puts the twins into the pram and off we go through the long streets of Brooklyn. Sometimes she lets Malachy sit in the pram when he's tired of trotting along beside her. She tells me I'm too big for the pram. I could tell her I have pains in my legs from trying to keep up with her but she's not singing and I know this is not the day to be talking about my pains.

We come to a big gate where there's a man standing in a box with windows all around. Mam talks to the man. She wants to know if she can go inside to where the men are paid and maybe they'd give her some of Dad's wages so he wouldn't spend it in the bars. The man shakes his head. I'm sorry, lady, but if we did that we'd have half the wives in

Brooklyn storming the place. Lotta men have the drinking problem but there's nothing we can do long as they show up sober and do their work.

We wait across the street. Mam lets me sit on the sidewalk with my back against the wall. She gives the twins their bottles of water and sugar but Malachy and I have to wait till she gets money from Dad and we can go to the Italian for tea and bread and eggs.

When the whistle blows at half five men in caps and overalls swarm through the gate, their faces and hands black from the work. Mam tells us watch carefully for Dad because she can hardly see across the street her-self, her eyes are that bad. There are dozens of men, then a few, then none. Mam is crying, Why couldn't ye see him? Are ye blind or what?

She goes back to the man in the box. Are you sure there wouldn't be   25
one man left inside?

No, lady, he says. They're out. I don't know how he got past you.

We go back through the long streets of Brooklyn. The twins hold up their bottles and cry for more water and sugar. Malachy says he's hungry and Mam tells him wait a little, we'll get money from Dad and we'll all have a nice supper. We'll go to the Italian and get eggs and make toast with the flames on the stove and we'll have jam on it. Oh, we will, and we'll all be nice and warm.

It's dark on Atlantic Avenue and all the bars around the Long Island Railroad Station are bright and noisy. We go from bar to bar looking for Dad. Mam leaves us outside with the pram while she goes in or she sends me. There are crowds of noisy men and stale smells that remind me of Dad when he comes home with the smell of the whiskey on him.

The man behind the bar says, Yeah, sonny, whaddya want? You're not supposeta be in here, y'know.

I'm looking for my father. Is my father here?   30

Naw, sonny, how'd I know dat? Who's your fawdah?

His name is Malachy and he sings Kevin Barry.

Malarkey?

No, Malachy.

Malachy? And he sings Kevin Barry?   35

He calls out to the men in the bar, Youse guys, youse know guy Malachy what sings Kevin Barry?

Men shake their heads. One says he knew a guy Michael sang Kevin Barry but he died of the drink which he had because of his war wounds.

The barman says, Jeez, Pete, I didn't ax ya to tell me history o' da woild, did I? Naw, kid. We don't let people sing in here. Causes trouble. Specially the Irish. Let 'em sing, next the fists are flying. Besides, I never hoid a name like dat Malachy. Naw, kid, no Malachy here.

The man called Pete holds his glass toward me. Here, kid, have a sip, but the barman says, Whaddya doin', Pete? Tryina get the kid drunk? Do that again, Pete, an' I'll come out an' break y'ass.

Mam tries all the bars around the station before she gives up. She   40
leans against a wall and cries. Jesus, we still have to walk all the way to

Classon Avenue and I have four starving children. She sends me back into the bar where Pete offered me the sip to see if the barman would fill the twins' bottles with water and maybe a little sugar in each. The men in the bar think it's very funny that the barman should be filling baby bottles but he's big and he tells them shut their lip. He tells me babies should be drinking milk not water and when I tell him Mam doesn't have the money he empties the baby bottles and fills them with milk. He says, Tell ya mom they need that for the teeth an' bones. Ya drink water an' sugar an' all ya get is rickets. Tell ya Mom.

Mam is happy with the milk. She says she knows all about teeth and bones and rickets but beggars can't be choosers.

When we reach Classon Avenue she goes straight to the Italian grocery shop. She tells the man her husband is late tonight, that he's probably working overtime, and would it be at all possible to get a few things and she'll be sure to see him tomorrow?

The Italian says, Missus, you always pay your bill sooner or later and you can have anything you like in this store.

Oh, she says, I don't want much.

Anything you like, missus, because I know you're an honest woman   45
and you got a bunch o'nice kids there.

We have eggs and toast and jam though we're so weary walking the long streets of Brooklyn we can barely move our jaws to chew. The twins fall asleep after eating and Mam lays them on the bed to change their diapers. She sends me down the hall to rinse the dirty diapers in the lavatory so that they can be hung up to dry and used the next day. Malachy helps her wash the twins' bottoms though he's ready to fall asleep himself.

I crawl into bed with Malachy and the twins. I look out at Mam at the kitchen table, smoking a cigarette, drinking tea, and crying. I want to get up and tell her I'll be a man soon and I'll get a job in the place with the big gate and I'll come home every Friday night with money for eggs and toast and jam and she can sing again Anyone can see why I wanted your kiss.

The next week Dad loses the job. He comes home that Friday night, throws his wages on the table and says to Mam, Are you happy now? You hang around the gate complaining and accusing and they sack me. They were looking for an excuse and you gave it to them.

He takes a few dollars from his wages and goes out. He comes home late roaring and singing. The twins cry and Mam shushes them and cries a long time herself.

Limerick

On a Saturday morning Mam finishes her tea and says, You're going to   50
dance.

Dance? Why?

You're seven years old, you made your First Communion, and now 'tis time for the dancing. I'm taking you down to Catherine Street to Mrs. O'Connor's Irish dancing classes. You'll go there every Saturday morning and that'll keep you off the streets. That'll keep you from wandering around Limerick with hooligans.

She tells me wash my face not forgetting ears and neck, comb my hair, blow my nose, take the look off my face, what look? never mind, just take it off, put on my stockings and my First Communion shoes which, she says, are destroyed because I can't pass a canister or a rock without kicking it. She's worn out standing in the queue at the St. Vincent de Paul Society begging for boots for me and Malachy so that we can wear out the toes with the kicking. Your father says it's never too early to learn the songs and dances of your ancestors.

What's ancestors?

Never mind, she says, you're going to dance.

I wonder how I can die for Ireland if I have to sing and dance for Ireland, too. I wonder why they never say, You can eat sweets and stay home from school and go swimming for Ireland.

Mam says, Don't get smart or I'll warm your ear.

Cyril Benson dances. He has medals hanging from his shoulders to his kneecaps. He wins contests all over Ireland and he looks lovely in his saffron kilt. He's a credit to his mother and he gets his name in the paper all the time and you can be sure he brings home the odd few pounds. You don't see him roaming the streets kicking everything in sight till the toes hang out of his boots, oh, no, he's a good boy, dancing for his poor mother.

Mam wets an old towel and scrubs my face till it stings, she wraps the towel around her finger and sticks it in my ears and claims there's enough wax there to grow potatoes, she wets my hair to make it lie down, she tells me shut up and stop the whinging, that these dancing lessons will cost her sixpence every Saturday, which I could have earned bringing Bill Galvin his dinner and God knows she can barely afford it. I try to tell her, Ah, Mam, sure you don't have to send me to dancing school when you could be smoking a nice Woodbine and having a cup of tea, but she says, Oh, aren't you clever. You're going to dance if I have to give up the fags forever.

If my pals see my mother dragging me through the streets to an Irish dancing class I'll be disgraced entirely. They think it's all right to dance and pretend you're Fred Astaire because you can jump all over the screen with Ginger Rogers. There is no Ginger Rogers in Irish dancing and you can't jump all over. You stand straight up and down and keep your arms against yourself and kick your legs up and around and never smile. My uncle Pa Keating said Irish dancers look like they have steel rods up their arses, but I can't say that to Mam, she'd kill me.

There's a gramophone in Mrs. O'Connor's playing an Irish jig or a reel and boys and girls are dancing around kicking their legs out and keeping

55

60

their hands to their sides. Mrs. O'Connor is a great fat woman and when she stops the record to show the steps all the fat from her chin to her ankles jiggles and I wonder how she can teach the dancing. She comes over to my mother and says, So, this is little Frankie? I think we have the makings of a dancer here. Boys and girls, do we have the makings of a dancer here?

We do, Mrs. O'Connor.

Mam says, I have the sixpence, Mrs. O'Connor.

Ah, yes, Mrs. McCourt, hold on a minute.

She waddles to a table and brings back the head of a black boy with kinky hair, big eyes, huge red lips and an open mouth. She tells me put the sixpence in the mouth and take my hand out before the black boy bites me. All the boys and girls watch and they have little smiles. I drop in the sixpence and pull my hand back before the mouth snaps shut. Everyone laughs and I know they wanted to see my hand caught in the mouth. Mrs. O'Connor gasps and laughs and says to my mother, Isn't that a howl, now? Mam says it's a howl. She tells me behave myself and come home dancing. 65

I don't want to stay in this place where Mrs. O'Connor can't take the sixpence herself instead of letting me nearly lose my hand in the black boy's mouth. I don't want to stay in this place where you have to stand in line with boys and girls, straighten your back, hands by your sides, look ahead, don't look down, move your feet, move your feet, look at Cyril, look at Cyril, and there goes Cyril, all dressed up in his saffron kilt and the medals jingling, medals for this and medals for that and the girls love Cyril and Mrs. O'Connor loves Cyril for didn't he bring her fame and didn't she teach him every step he knows, oh, dance, Cyril, dance, oh, Jesus, he floats around the room, he's an angel out of heaven and stop the frowning, Frankie McCourt, or you'll have a puss on you like a pound of tripe, dance, Frankie, dance, pick up your feet for the love o'Jesus, onetwothreefourfive-sixseven onetwothree and a onetwothree, Maura, will you help that Frankie McCourt before he ties his two feet around his poll entirely, help him, Maura.

Maura is a big girl about ten. She dances up to me with her white teeth and her dancer's dress with all the gold and yellow and green figures that are supposed to come from olden times and she says, Give me your hand, little boy, and she wheels me around the room till I'm dizzy and making a pure eejit of myself and blushing and foolish till I want to cry but I'm saved when the record stops and the gramophone goes hoosh hoosh.

Mrs. O'Connor says, Oh, thank you, Maura, and next week, Cyril, you can show Frankie a few of the steps that made you famous. Next week, boys and girls, and don't forget the sixpence for the little black boy.

Boys and girls leave together. I make my own way down the stairs and out the door hoping my pals won't see me with boys who wear kilts and girls with white teeth and fancy dresses from olden times.

Mam is having tea with Bridey Hannon, her friend from next door.   70
Mam says, What did you learn? and makes me dance around the kitchen,
onetwothreefourfivesixseven onetwothree and a onetwothree. She has a
good laugh with Bridey. That's not too bad for your first time. In a month
you'll be like a regular Cyril Benson.

I don't want to be Cyril Benson. I want to be Fred Astaire.

They turn hysterical, laughing and squirting tea out of their mouths,
Jesus love him, says Bridey. Doesn't he have a great notion of himself.
Fred Astaire how are you.

Mam says Fred Astaire went to his lessons every Saturday and didn't
go around kicking the toes out of his boots and if I wanted to be like him
I'd have to go to Mrs. O'Connor's every week.

The fourth Saturday morning Billy Campbell knocks at our door.
Mrs. McCourt, can Frankie come out and play? Mam tells him, No, Billy.
Frankie is going to his dancing lesson.

He waits for me at the bottom of Barrack Hill. He wants to know why   75
I'm dancing, that everyone knows dancing is a sissy thing and I'll wind
up like Cyril Benson wearing a kilt and medals and dancing all over with
girls. He says next thing I'll be sitting in the kitchen knitting socks. He
says dancing will destroy me and I won't be fit to play any kind of football, soccer, rugby or Gaelic football itself because the dancing teaches
you to run like a sissy and everyone will laugh.

I tell him I'm finished with the dancing, that I have sixpence in my
pocket for Mrs. O'Connor that's supposed to go into the black boy's
mouth, that I'm going to the Lyric Cinema instead. Sixpence will get the
two of us in with tuppence left over for two squares of Cleeves' toffee,
and we have a great time looking at *Riders of the Purple Sage*.

Dad is sitting by the fire with Mam and they want to know what
steps I learned today and what they're called. I already did "The Siege
of Ennis" and "The Walls of Limerick," which are real dances. Now I
have to make up names and dances. Mam says she never heard of a
dance called "The Siege of Dingle" but if that's what I learned go ahead,
dance it, and I dance around the kitchen with my hands down by my
sides making my own music, diddley eye di eye di eye diddley eye do
you do you, Dad and Mam clapping in time with my feet. Dad says,
Och, that's a fine dance and you'll be a powerful Irish dancer and a
credit to the men who died for their country. Mam says, That wasn't
much for a sixpence.

Next week it's a George Raft film and the week after that a cowboy film
with George O'Brien. Then it's James Cagney and I can't take Billy because
I want to get a bar of chocolate to go with my Cleeves' toffee and I'm having
a great time till there's a terrible pain in my jaw and it's a tooth out of my
gum stuck in my toffee and the pain is killing me. Still, I can't waste the toffee so I pull out the tooth and put it in my pocket and chew the toffee on the
other side of my mouth blood and all. There's pain on one side and delicious toffee on the other and I remember what my uncle Pa Keating would
say. There are times when you wouldn't know whether to shit or go blind.

I have to go home now and worry because you can't go through the world short a tooth without your mother knowing. Mothers know every-thing and she's always looking into our mouths to see if there's any class of disease. She's there by the fire and Dad is there and they're asking me the same old questions, the dance and the name of the dance. I tell them I learned "The Walls of Cork" and I dance around the kitchen trying to hum a made-up tune and dying with the pain of my tooth. Mam says, "Walls o'Cork," my eye, there's no such dance, and Dad says, Come over here. Stand there before me. Tell us the truth, Did you go to your dancing classes today?

I can't tell a lie anymore because my gum is killing me and there's   80
blood in my mouth. Besides, I know they know everything and that's what they're telling me now. Some snake of a boy from the dancing school saw me going to the Lyric Cinema and told and Mrs. O'Connor sent a note to say she hadn't seen me in ages and was I all right because I had great promise and could follow in the footsteps of the great Cyril Benson.

Dad doesn't care about my tooth or anything. He says I'm going to confession and drags me over to the Redemptorist church because it's Saturday and confessions go on all day. He tells me I'm a bad boy, he's ashamed of me that I went to the pictures instead of learning Ireland's na-tional dances, the jig, the reel, the dances that men and women fought and died for down those sad centuries. He says there's many a young man that was hanged and now moldering in a lime pit that would be glad to rise up and dance the Irish dance.

The priest is old and I have to yell my sins at him and he tells me I'm a hooligan for going to the pictures instead of my dancing lessons al-though he thinks himself that dancing is a dangerous thing almost as bad as the films, that it stirs up thoughts sinful in themselves, but even if dancing is an abomination I sinned by taking my mother's sixpence and lying and there's a hot place in hell for the likes of me, say a decade of the rosary and ask God's forgiveness for you're dancing at the gates of hell it-self, child.

 Topics for Critical Thinking and Writing

1. *Angela's Ashes*, the book from which these selections come, is flooded with memories of poverty, hunger, alcoholism, depression, and infant death. Nevertheless, the book has been an international best-seller ever since it was published in 1996. What qualities do you detect in these early episodes that account for the enormous popularity of this dark memoir?

2. Notice that McCourt persistently uses the present tense. Reread a passage or two and then try to describe the effect of the present tense. One way to think about it is to recast some sentences using the past tense. Then try to describe the difference.

3. When you were a child did you ever use money given to you for one purpose on another? An easier question, did you ever lie about where you had
spent an afternoon or an evening? Write a brief essay, 3 to 4 pages, describing your experience. Try to capture your voice at your age at the time
of the incident.

Bobbie Ann Mason

*Bobbie Ann Mason was born in 1940 in rural western Kentucky and graduated from the
University of Kentucky with a major in journalism. She took a master's degree at the State
University of New York at Binghamton, and a Ph.D. at the University of Connecticut, where she
wrote a dissertation on a novel by Vladimir Nabokov. Between graduate degrees she worked in
New York for various magazines, including* TV Star Parade. *In 1974 she published her first
book—a revised version of the dissertation on Nabokov—and in 1975 she published her second,*
The Girl Sleuths: A Guide to the Bobbsey Twins, Nancy Drew and Their Sisters. *In her late
thirties she started to write short fiction, publishing her first story in 1980, in* The New Yorker.
She has written three volumes of short stories and a novel, Love Life *(1985), as well as a memoir
about her childhood and family life,* Clear Springs *(1999), which is the book from which we
draw the following pages.*

In an interview about Clear Springs *Mason said, "I realized that your memories over time
are really lost, or they're transformed. They become memories of memories, and you lose sight of
the original. And finally, there are a lot of things you remember that you can't prove really happened, and there are a lot of things you don't remember that did happen."*

First Memories

My very first memory is a scene fading into . . . oblivion. It was a pleasant summer Sunday afternoon. I was still an only child. I was three. We had
company, and Granny made vanilla ice cream, churned in a freezer filled
with salted ice. I was wearing a blue-print dress and white socks and sandals. Mama had made my dress from a muslin feedsack. It felt luxurious
and finely textured, like Granny's damask tablecloth. The kinfolks gathered
on the front porch, where they could see anybody passing along the road,
and I was sitting alone for a few minutes at the top of the steps to the back
porch. The concrete stairway had a tubular metal rail, smooth and round to
hold. When I got a little older, I would swing out under this rail to the
ground, and the metal would make a slight squeak against my moist hands.
But that day I sat on the top step in a quiet moment that has stayed with me
always. I was concentrating deeply on a Coca-Cola bottle cap that Daddy
had fastened onto my dress. He had separated the cork lining from the
metal cap and then fitted the cap and cork together again, capturing the

dress material snugly between. The texture of thin cork was like skin, pleasant to touch. The metal cap was cool, hard, and fluted, like the ones in Granny's bottle-capper for the grape juice she bottled from the grapes on her arbor. I tested out the fitting of this marvelous wonder—the cap separated and then reunited on my dress—and I remember feeling that I was making a discovery about how the world works in clever ways—disparate objects making delightful, unexpected connections for no real reason other than for our pleasure in discovering them.

I remember the ice cream that day, vanilla and heavenly, with the occasional tang of salt from a crumb of salted ice flicked into the cream tub. (Granny and Granddaddy called ice cream "cream.") Ice cream and Coca-Cola were imprinted on the appetite center of my brain that day. They became part of my mind's unfolding, like the patterns on my dress.

That same year a much more significant scene occurred, but I have no memory of it. I climbed onto the kitchen table, and—no doubt pleased with myself—I stood there surveying the room from my new vantage point. Granny and Granddaddy had forbidden me to climb on the kitchen table.

"I was outside when I heard you squalling," Mama says. "And I ran from the wash-house, up the back steps, to the kitchen. Bob was standing there with the razor strop in his hand. You were screaming like you'd been kilt, and he was fixing to thrash again. I jerked that thing out of his hand so hard it burnt the skin off of my fingers. Then I grabbed you up and run into the bedroom. I was bawling as hard as you were."

When my mother tells her memory, it is as if she is going through it again. I can see the hurt on her face. "Your little legs were purely black," she says. "I don't know how many times he hit you, but you stayed bruised a long time. Wilburn didn't say anything to his daddy that I know of. But Bob never hurt you again."

"I don't remember it at all," I say. I think about how mothers report they never remember the pain of giving birth. I wonder if forgetting applies to all kinds of pain, and if pain is the reason so much of our history has been forgotten. I cannot remember the savagery of the razor strop, its sting, my squalling, the black welts on my legs, the shudder of my mother's sobs. I loved my grandfather.

 ## Topic for Critical Thinking and Writing

In this brief extract from her memoir, *Clear Springs*, Mason recounts her first memory and then a second more important scene, which she had forgotten. What is your earliest memory? Is there another scene which you have been told about but which you have forgotten? Write some journal entries in which you recall early memories, and scenes you know about only because someone else described them to you.

Jimmy Carter

Jimmy Carter, born in Plains, Georgia, in 1924, served as thirty-ninth president of the United States. After leaving the White House, he and his wife, Rosalynn, founded the Carter Center, which works to prevent and resolve conflicts, promote freedom and democracy, and improve health around the world. President Carter has written thirteen books, including Talking Peace: A Vision for the Next Generation *(1993),* Always a Reckoning and Other Poems *(1995), and* An Hour before Daylight *(2001), from which the following pages are reprinted. Another excerpt appears on page 384.*

My Boyhood Home

Although I was born in Plains and actually lived next door to my future wife, Rosalynn, when she was a baby, the first thing I remember clearly was when I was four years old and my father took us out to show us our new home on the farm. There were four of us, including my sister, Gloria, who was two years younger than I. The front door was locked when we got there, and Daddy realized that he had forgotten the key. He tried to raise one of the windows that opened onto the front porch, but a wooden bar on the inside let it come up only about six inches. So he slid me through the crack and I came around to unlock the door from the inside. The approval of my father for my first useful act has always been one of my most vivid memories.

Our house was typical of those occupied by middle-income landowners of the time. Set back about fifty feet from the dirt road, it was square, painted tan to match the dust, and had a broad front porch and split-shingle roof. The rooms were laid out in "shotgun" style, with a hall that went down the middle of the house dividing the living room, dining room, and kitchen on the left side from three bedrooms on the right. We also had a screened porch that extended across the back of the house, where we worked and stored things such as well water, corn for the chickens, and extra wood to keep it dry. The front porch was where our family congregated in warm weather, which was about nine months of the year. We had a swing suspended from the ceiling and some rocking chairs out there, and Daddy often used the slightly sloping floor for a quick nap after dinner and before going back to work in the afternoon. I relished lying beside him as a little boy, long before I could do useful work in the fields.

There is little doubt that I now recall those days with more fondness than they deserve. We drew water from a well in the yard, and every day of the year we had the chore of keeping extra bucketfuls in the kitchen and on the back porch, combined with the constant wood-sawing and chopping to supply the cooking stove and fireplaces. In every bedroom was a slop jar (chamber pot) that was emptied each morning into the outdoor privy, about twenty yards from our back door. This small shack had a large hole for adults and a lower and smaller one for children; we wiped with old newspapers or pages torn from Sears, Roebuck catalogues. These were much better facilities than those I knew when I was with the other families on the place, who squatted behind bushes and wiped with corn-cobs or leaves.

It was a great day for our family in 1935 when Daddy purchased from a mail-order catalogue and erected a windmill with a high wooden tank and pipes that provided running water for the kitchen and a bathroom with toilet. We even had a rudimentary shower made from a large tin can with its bottom perforated by nail holes. One extra benefit was that the top platform of the windmill, up near the fan blades, gave a good view of the nearby fields.

Our house was surrounded by a white-sanded yard, which we had to   5
sweep frequently to remove fowl and animal droppings and leaves from our pecan, magnolia, mulberry, and chinaberry trees. Most of our brush brooms were made of small saplings or limbs of dogwood, which were resilient and long lasting. Several times a year we took a two-mule wagon about three miles to a pit and loaded it with fresh sand, which was scattered on the yard to give it a new white surface. Behind our house and surrounded by fenced fields were a small garage (never used for a car), a smokehouse, a chicken house, and a large woodpile.

Our artificial light came from kerosene lamps, and it was considered almost sinful to leave one burning in an unoccupied room. The only exception was in the front living room, where we had an Aladdin lamp about five feet high whose asbestos wick miraculously provided illumination bright enough for reading in a wide area. We turned this flame way down when we went to eat a meal, both to conserve fuel and to avoid the lamp's tendency to flame up and blacken the fragile wick with thick soot. When this happened—a mishap for which someone always had to be identified as the culprit—we had to endure an extended period of careful flame control while we waited in near darkness for the soot to burn off enough for us to read again.

One significant difference between my parents was their reading habits. Daddy mostly limited his reading to the daily and weekly newspapers and farm journals, but he also owned a small library, which I still have, that included Halliburton's *Royal Road to Romance*, a collection of A. Conan Doyle's Sherlock Holmes stories, and a complete set of Edgar Rice Burroughs's Tarzan books, each carefully signed and numbered by my father to indicate their proper sequence. By contrast, my mother read constantly and encouraged us children to do the same. Since we stayed busy most of the time, Mama and I always had a magazine or book to read while eating our meals, and this became a lifetime habit for my own family and me. The only exception was Sunday dinner, which, for some reason, had too formal an atmosphere for literature at the table. At night, at suppertime, there was no such restraint.

I didn't know of any rural families that had electric lights until the rural-electrification program came along in the late 1930s. We had a large battery-powered radio in the front room that we used sparingly, and only at night, as we all sat around looking at it during "Amos and Andy," "Fibber McGee and Molly," "Jack Benny," or "Little Orphan Annie." When its power failed, we would sometimes bring in the battery from the pickup truck to keep it playing for a special event. I recall some rare baseball games re-created by the announcer from telegraph reports, a few boxing matches, and the late night in 1936 when Alfred Landon was chosen as the Republican nominee for president. The voting went on so long that the battery in our house gave out, and we took the radio outside and set it on the hood of the pickup until the convention made its choice, hours after midnight.

The most memorable radio broadcast was in 1938, the night of the return match between heavyweight boxers Joe Louis and Max Schmeling. The German champion had defeated the black American two years earlier, and the world's attention was focused on the return bout. For our community, this fight had heavy racial overtones, with almost unanimous support at our all-white school for the European over the American. A delegation of our black neighbors came to ask Daddy if they could listen to the broadcast, and we put the radio in the window so the assembled crowd in the yard could hear it. The fight ended abruptly, in the first round, with Louis almost killing Schmeling. There was no sound from outside—or inside—the house. We heard a quiet "Thank you, Mr. Earl," and then our visitors walked silently out of the yard, crossed the road and the railroad tracks, entered the tenant house, and closed the door. Then all hell broke loose, and their celebration lasted all night. Daddy was tight-lipped, but all the mores of our segregated society had been honored.

I don't remember much about the summer heat, but I have vivid memories of how cold it was in winter. The worst job was getting up in the morning to start a fire going somewhere in the frigid house. We kept a good supply of pine kindling, which we called "lighterd," to start the blaze that would eventually ignite the long-burning hickory and oak, but I always hoped that some live coals were still smoldering under the ashes so the fire would start quickly. There was an open fireplace in the living room that we lit only late in the afternoon, when the family would gather there, but the fire (later a wood-burning heater) in the bedroom where Mama and Daddy slept was made at dawn, so we shivering children would rush there in the mornings to put on our clothes. I had the northeast corner room, which had no source of heat. We never thought about pajamas, which would have been warmer than the BVDs that Daddy and I wore on cold days under our shirts and trousers, and then slept in at night.

Almost all our food was produced in our pasture, fields, garden, and yard. My mother did not enjoy cooking, but was good at preparing

a few basic dishes, and Daddy liked to cook special meals such as bat-
ter cakes, all-too-rare waffles, and fried fish. At hog-killing time, he
fixed souse meat, a conglomeration of meat from heads, feet, and other
animal parts that were boiled to a thick, soft mush, heavily spiced, and
then congealed into a loaf that could be sliced for later consumption.
He also assumed the responsibility of preparing homemade mayonnaise
throughout the year and eggnog at Christmas. Whichever farm woman
who came in to cook for us when Mama was working as a nurse just
embellished the basic meals of her own family with a few of our fancier
foods, like rice, cheese, peanut butter, macaroni, and canned goods.
Nothing went to waste around our house, and we were expected to eat
whatever was prepared and to clean our plates before leaving the table.

Corn was our staple grain, and rarely would we have a meal without grits, lye hominy, roasting ears, or one of the half-dozen recipes for
corn bread. We always had chickens available, either hens or fryers, and
it was usually my job to catch and kill them so they could be dressed
and then baked, fried, or made into a pie for dinner or supper. (We
never heard the word "lunch" applied to sitting down at a table.)
Chicken was standard for Sunday dinner after church, when we also
had fresh vegetables: peas, potatoes, string beans, butter beans, okra,
rutabagas, and all kinds of greens, with collards our favorite, but never
any spinach. We also had mashed Irish potatoes or rice and gravy, biscuits, and a pie made from seasonal fruit or sweet potatoes. Cured pork
products were available most of the year, and it was surprising how often we ate seafood that Daddy bought from two local men who made
regular truck trips from Plains to the Gulf and brought back mullet,
mackerel, shrimp, and oysters. Canned salmon, which sold for either a
nickel or a dime depending on the quality or size of the can, was usually
transformed into fried croquettes and eaten with gobs of catsup.
Another staple was kit fish, which was dried mackerel packed with salt
in small wooden kegs. We soaked the pieces in clear water overnight to
reduce the saltiness, and fried them for breakfast to go with our grits
and biscuits.

I still have vivid memories of the home place where I spent my boyhood. There was a dirt tennis court next to our house, unknown on any
other farm in our area, which Daddy laid out as soon as we moved there
and kept clean and relatively smooth with a piece of angle iron nailed to a
pine log that a mule could drag over it every week or so. Next was my father's commissary store, with the windmill in back, and then a large
fenced-in garden. A two-rut wagon road ran from our back yard to the
barn, which would become the center of my life as I matured and eagerly
assumed increasing responsibilities for the work of a man.

Beyond the garden and alongside this small road was a combination
blacksmith and carpenter shop surrounded by piles of all kinds of scrap
metal, where everyone on the farm knew that rattlesnakes loved to breed.

This is where we shod mules and horses, sharpened plow points, repaired machinery, made simple iron implements, and did woodwork, with Daddy providing the overall supervision. He was skilled with the forge and anvil, and did fairly advanced blacksmith work. This is one of the first places I was able to work alongside him. I could turn the hand crank on the forge blower fast enough to keep the charcoal fire ablaze, and to hold some of the red-hot pieces on the anvil with tongs while Daddy shaped them with a hammer and then plunged them, hissing, into water or oil for tempering. It required some skill to keep a plow point completely flat on the steel surface; otherwise a hammer blow would bring a violent and painful twisting, with the tongs and red-hot metal sometimes flying out of my hands. There was almost always something broken around the farm, and only rarely would anything be taken to town for welding. I learned a lot from Daddy, and also from Jack Clark, a middle-aged black man who was something of a supervisor on our farm and did most of the mule- and horse-shoeing.

In front of the shop was a large Sears, Roebuck grinding stone, and we would sit on a wooden seat and pedal to keep the thick disc spinning, with the bottom of the stone running in half an automobile tire filled with water. This was a busy place where we sharpened hoes, axes, scythes, knives, and scissors. Daddy didn't believe in paying for something we could do ourselves, so he also had an iron shoemaker's last in the shop that he used for replacing worn-out heels and soles for the family's shoes. As I got older, I helped with all the jobs in the shop, but was always most interested in working with wood, especially in shaping pieces with froe, plane, drawknife, and spokeshave.

The centerpiece of our farm life, and a place of constant exploration for me, was our large, perfectly symmetrical barn. It had been built by an itinerant Scottish carpenter named Mr. Valentine, whose basic design was well known in our farming region. Daddy was very proud of its appearance and its practical arrangement, which minimized labor in handling the large quantities of feed needed for our livestock. There were special cribs, bins, and tanks for storing oats, ear corn, velvet beans, hay, fodder, and store-bought supplements, including molasses, a bran called "shorts," and cottonseed meal. The sheep, goats, and cattle were usually kept in stalls separate from each other and from the mules and horses, and animals requiring veterinary care could also be isolated while being treated. Hogs had their own pens, and were not permitted inside the barn.

Before I was big enough for real fieldwork, Daddy encouraged me to spend time with Jack Clark, knowing that it was the best way for me to be educated about farm life, as Jack kept up a constant stream of comments about the world as he knew or envisioned it.

Jack was very black, of medium height, and strongly built. He had surprisingly long arms, and invariably wore clean overalls, knee-high rubber boots, and a straw hat. Knowing (or at least claiming) that he spoke for my father, he issued orders or directions to the other hands in a somewhat gruff voice, always acting as the final arbiter over which field each hand would plow and which mule he would harness. He ignored the grumbled complaints. When all the other workers were off to their assigned duties, Jack was the sole occupant of the barn and the adjacent lots—except when I was following behind him like a puppy dog and bombarding him with questions. We became close friends, but there was always some restraint as to intimacy between us. For instance, although my daddy would pick me up on occasion to give me a hug or let me ride on his shoulders, this would have been inconceivable with Jack, except when he might lift me over a barbed-wire fence or onto the back of a mule or horse.

Radiating from the barn was a maze of fences and gates that let us move livestock from one place to another with minimal risk of their escape. This was one of my earliest tasks, requiring only a modicum of skill and the ability to open and close the swinging gates. Within the first array of enclosures was a milking shed that would hold four cows at a time, adequate to accommodate our usual herd of eight to a dozen Jerseys and Guernseys that we milked in two shifts, twice a day. Later, we had a dozen A-frame hog-farrowing structures, which I helped my daddy build after bringing the innovative design home from my Future Farmer class in school. One shelter was assigned to each sow when birthing time approached, and the design kept the animals dry, provided a convenient place for feed and water, and minimized the inadvertent crushing of the baby pigs by their heavy mamas. Except during extended dry seasons, the constantly used lots for hogs and milk cows were always ankle deep in mud and manure, which made bare feet much superior to brogans.

A little open shed near the barn enclosed a pump that lifted about two cups of water from our shallow well with each stroke. It was driven by a small two-cycle gasoline engine that we cranked up and let run once or twice a day, just long enough to fill several watering troughs around the barn and sheds. This was the only motor-driven device on the farm, and was always viewed with a mixture of suspicion and trepidation. We were justifiably doubtful that it would crank when we needed it most, dreading the hour or two of hand pumping as the only alternative source of water for all the animals. Between the pump house and barn was a harness shed, an open-ended building where we stored a buggy, two wagons, and all the saddles, bridles, and other harness needed for an operating farm. Also near the barn was a concrete dipping-vat about four feet deep, filled with a pungent mixture containing creosote, through which we would drive our cattle, goats, and newly sheared sheep to protect them, at least temporarily, from flies and screwworms. 20

The farm operation always seemed to me a fascinating system, like a huge clock, with each of its many parts depending on all the rest. Daddy was the one who designed, owned, and operated the complicated mechanism, and Jack Clark wound it daily and kept it on time. I had dreams that one day I would be master of this machine, with its wonderful intricacies.

The workers on our place, all black, lived in five small clapboard houses, three right on the highway, one set farther back from the road, and another across the railroad tracks directly in front of our house. This was the community in which I grew up, all within a stone's throw of the barn.

 ## Topics for Critical Thinking and Writing

1. At the end of his first paragraph President Carter says, "The approval of my father for my first useful act has always been one of my most vivid memories." Try to recall the first time you felt *useful* in your family. How old were you, and what did you do? Did the grownups around you demonstrate their approval? Did the act and its consequences remain important to you as Jimmy Carter's did to him? Why, or why not? (If this topic interests you, write an essay of about 500 words on it.)

2. In paragraph 3, President Carter says, "There is little doubt that I now recall those days with more fondness than they deserve." Explain this sentence. Why do the recollections deserve little fondness? And what evidence of fondness do you find in President Carter's recollections?

3. At the end of paragraph 9, after recalling listening to the Joe Louis/Max Schmeling match on the radio, President Carter writes, "Daddy was tight-lipped, but all the mores of our segregated society had been honored." What does he mean?

4. President Carter describes a Southern setting during the depression that was full of hardships. Do you agree with us, however, that his tone is cheerful? If you agree, locate two or three passages that express his pleasure in his memories. And what were the hardships? To put this topic another way, would you like to have grown up in Earl Carter's household?

Black Elk

Black Elk, a wichasha wakon (holy man) of the Oglala Sioux, as a small boy witnessed the battle of the Little Bighorn (1876). He lived to see his people all but annihilated and his hopes for them extinguished. In 1931, toward the end of his life, he told his life story to the poet and scholar John G. Neihardt to preserve a sacred vision given him. Another excerpt from Black Elk Speaks *appears on page 289.*

"War Games" (editors' title) is from Black Elk Speaks.

War Games

When it was summer again we were camping on the Rosebud, and I did not feel so much afraid, because the Wasichus seemed farther away and there was peace there in the valley and there was plenty of meat. But all the boys from five or six years up were playing war. The little boys would gather together from the different bands of the tribe and fight each other with mud balls that they threw with willow sticks. And the big boys played the game called Throwing-Them-Off-Their-Horses, which is a battle all but the killing; and sometimes they got hurt. The horsebacks from the different bands would line up and charge upon each other, yelling; and when the ponies came together on the run, they would rear and flounder and scream in a big dust, and the riders would seize each other, wrestling until one side had lost all its men, for those who fell upon the ground were counted dead.

When I was older, I, too, often played this game. We were always naked when we played it, just as warriors are when they go into battle if it is not too cold, because they are swifter without clothes. Once I fell off on my back right in the middle of a bed of prickly pears, and it took my mother a long while to pick all the stickers out of me. I was still too little to play war that summer, but I can remember watching the other boys, and I thought that when we all grew up and were big together, maybe we could kill all the Wasichus or drive them far away from our country. . . .

There was a war game that we little boys played after a big hunt. We went out a little way from the village and built some grass tepees, playing we were enemies and this was our village. We had an adviser, and when it got dark he would order us to go and steal some dried meat from the big people. He would hold a stick up to us and we had to bite off a piece of it. If we bit a big piece we had to get a big piece of meat, and if we bit a little piece, we did not have to get so much. Then we started for the big people's village, crawling on our bellies, and when we got back without getting caught, we would have a big feast and a dance and make kill talks, telling of our brave deeds like warriors. Once, I remember, I had no brave deed to tell. I crawled up to a leaning tree beside a tepee and there was meat hanging on the limbs. I wanted a tongue I saw up there in the moonlight, so I climbed up. But just as I was about to reach it, the man in the tepee yelled "Ye-a-a!" He was saying this to his dog, who was stealing some meat too, but I thought the man had seen me, and I was so scared I fell out of the tree and ran away crying.

Then we used to have what we called a chapped breast dance. Our adviser would look us over to see whose breast was burned most from not having it covered with the robe we wore; and the boy chosen would lead the dance while we all sang like this:

I have a chapped breast.
My breast is red.
My breast is yellow.

And we practiced endurance too. Our adviser would put dry sun-flower seeds on our wrists. These were lit at the top, and we had to let them burn clear down to the skin. They hurt and made sores, but if we knocked them off or cried Owh!, we would be called women.

 Topics for Critical Thinking and Writing

1. Notice the subjective passages in Black Elk's descriptions of the games he played as a child. What do they reveal about Black Elk as a child and as an adult? How appropriate are these revelations to his topic?

2. The Duke of Wellington is reported to have said that the battle of Waterloo was won on the playing fields of Eton. Try to describe a game that is a small version of an adult activity and that teaches adult habits—good or bad. As an experiment, write the description as objectively as you can. Then rewrite it, allowing your description to reveal your attitudes—as a child and now—to the game, to other children, and to the adult world.

Katharine Graham

Katharine Graham (1917–2001) in Personal History *(1997) candidly records her life as the daughter of a multimillionaire and the wife and then the widow of a talented, charming man, whose mental illness culminated in his suicide. Mrs. Graham then piloted* The Washington Post, *the newspaper published by her father and then by her husband, into publishing stories on the Pentagon Papers and Watergate, and through a pressman's strike. Mrs. Graham received many honors and awards, and* Personal History, *from which we have selected the following pages, won the Pulitzer Prize for biography. The title of the selection is the editors'.*

On Money, Religion, and Sex

Sᴇɴsɪᴛɪᴠᴇ sᴜʙᴊᴇᴄᴛs were rarely mentioned at our house, but three were particularly taboo—money, my father's being Jewish, and sex. None of the three was ever articulated by any of us in the family; in fact, *nothing* difficult or personal was discussed among us. There was such an aversion to talking about money or our wealth that, ironically, there was, in some odd ways, a fairly Spartan quality to our lives. We were not showered with conspicuous possessions, elaborate toys, or clothes. At one point, when Florence was eleven, my mother wrote in her diary that she had gotten Flo very modest presents for her birthday—"books, pralines and other simple things." Though Mother felt that she had been a bit mean, she also felt that "it is the best way to continue their chance for happiness to restrain the desire for possessions."

I had less than most of the girls in my class—certainly fewer clothes. My spare wardrobe in grammar school consisted of one or two jumpers and blouses for school, and one best dress. We were also treated strictly in the matter of allowance. I still remember a telegram Bis sent my father from Vassar: "Allowance early or bust." He wired back, "Bust." The only discussion I do remember relating to wealth had to do with being told that you couldn't just be a rich kid, that you had to do something, to be engaged in useful, productive work; you couldn't and shouldn't do *nothing*. Working was always a part of my life. I remember one Christmas vacation, when I was probably about fifteen, spent at the Federal Reserve Board learning to draw graphs.

My mother's ambivalence about money and what it brought to her no doubt contributed to her own unwillingness to talk about it. Once, in 1922, after a visit to a Utah copper mine that had yielded my father great financial gains, she wrote in her diary: "[The mine] was an interesting sight but the village that led up to it appalled me. . . . This is where [the money] comes from and I spend it on Chinese art but it was a shock to think that we live on money that is produced under such conditions."

Remarkably, the fact that we were half Jewish was never mentioned any more than money was discussed. I was totally—incredibly—unaware of anti-Semitism, let alone of my father's being Jewish. I don't think this was deliberate; I am sure my parents were not denying or hiding my father's Jewishness from us, nor were they ashamed of it. But there was enough sensitivity so that it was never explained or taken pride in. Indeed, we had a pew in St. John's Episcopal Church— the president's church, on Lafayette Square—but mainly because the rector was a friend of the family. When I was about ten, all of us Meyer children were baptized at home to satisfy my devout Lutheran maternal grandmother, who thought that without such a precaution we were all headed for hell. But for the most part, religion was not part of our lives.

One of the few memories I have of any reference to my being Jewish   5 is of an incident that took place when I was ten or eleven. At school we were casting for reading aloud *The Merchant of Venice*, and one classmate suggested I should be Shylock because I was Jewish. In the same way I had once innocently asked my mother whether we were millionaires—after someone at school accused my father of being one—I asked if I was Jewish and what that meant. She must have avoided the subject, because I don't remember the answer. This confusion about religion was not limited to me: my sister Bis recalls that at lunch in our apartment in New York once, with guests present, she blurted out, "Say, who is this guy Jesus everyone is talking about?'

My identity as Jewish did not become an issue until I reached college and a discussion arose with a girl from Chicago who was leaving Vassar. She had been asked if she would see another acquaintance, a Jewish girl, also from Chicago. "Oh, no," she replied, "you can't have a Jew in your house in Chicago." My best friend, Connie Dimock, later told me how horrified she was to have this said in front of me. Only then did I "get it"—and this was 1935, with Hitler already a factor in the world.

About the third thing that was never discussed in our family, sex, I knew nothing for a surprisingly long time. I had no idea what sex was or how babies were conceived. In fact, it was as if our rigorous schedules and exercise and athletic program were constructed to keep us from thinking too much about it. I once asked my mother what really happened during sex, telling her I'd read about the sperm and the ova but wondered how it all worked. She responded, "Haven't you seen dogs in the street?" Although unfortunately I hadn't, I naturally said, "Of course," and that was the end of the conversation. Mother finally brought herself to speak to me about having periods, or "becoming a woman." "Don't worry about it, Mother," I replied, "it happened months ago."

Because these matters were never discussed, I was almost totally unaware of all of them—money, religion, and sex. It's peculiar: I realized, of course, that the houses were big and that we had a lot of servants, but I didn't know we were rich any more than I knew we were Jewish. In some ways it was quite bizarre; in others, quite healthy. Equally odd was how little we were taught about the practical aspects of life. I didn't know how to manage the simplest tasks. I didn't know how to dress, sew, cook, shop, and, rather more important, relate to people of any kind, let alone young men. My governess and I did some minor shopping, but as I grew up I mostly inherited party dresses from my sisters, until, when I was eighteen, Mother took me to Bergdorf Goodman for French clothes of staggering beauty and sophistication, which were well beyond my years and whose quality was wasted on young people who dressed appropriately. There was nothing in between for everyday.

I was always well fed and cared for, of course. In fact, my mother was constantly reminding us of how lucky we were, how much we owed our parents, how far-seeing and wonderful my father was to have taken care of us all. And we were indeed lucky. We had vast privileges. We had parents with solid values. Our interests were aroused in art and politics and books. But to all of this I brought my own feelings of inability and inferiority—not only to my mother, but to my older sisters and brother. I was, I thought, realistic about my own assets and abilities as I grew older. I was not very pretty. I grew tall early, and therefore seemed ungainly to myself. I didn't think I could excel, and was sure I'd never attract a man whom I would like and who would not be viewed with condescension by my parents and siblings.

In all the turmoil of the family and our strange isolation both from   10
our parents and from the outside world, we children were left to bring
ourselves up emotionally and intellectually. We were leading lives
fraught with ambivalence. It was hard to have an identity. An early example of this came one day when the telephone rang in the playroom and
there was no grown-up present. Bis very fearfully picked up the phone
and said hello. A male voice impatiently asked, "Who is this? Who is
this?," to which Bis replied, "This is the little girl that Mademoiselle takes
care of." That was the only way she could think of to describe herself to a
strange grown-up.

So the question of who we really were and what our aspirations were,
intellectual or social, was always disquieting. The more subtle inheritance
of my strange childhood was the feeling, which we all shared to some extent, of believing we were never quite going about things correctly. Had I
said the right thing? Had I worn the right clothes? Was I attractive? These
questions were unsettling and self-absorbing, even overwhelming at
times, and remained so throughout much of my adult life, until, at last, I
grew impatient with dwelling on the past.

Topics for Critical Thinking and Writing

1. Graham says of her family, "*nothing* difficult or personal was discussed
    among us." Compare the Graham family with your own, and then judge
    whether the Grahams' failure to discuss "difficult or personal" topics was a
    good or a bad thing.

2. In the sixth paragraph Graham recounts an anti-Semitic remark she heard
    in college and, after a friend's horrified response to it, says "Only then did I
    'get it'—this was 1935, with Hitler already a factor in the world." What did
    Graham then "get," and why does she here write of Hitler?

3. In paragraph 8 Graham says, "I didn't know we were rich any more than I
    knew we were Jewish. In some ways it was quite bizarre; in others, quite
    healthy." Do you agree that Graham's ignorance of the family's wealth and
    religion was both "bizarre" and "healthy"? Again compare the Grahams with
    your own family. In an essay of 500 words, indicate how aware you were
    of your family's financial status, and how conscious you were of your fam-
    ily's religion, and indicate why you think your degree of awareness was
    healthy or unhealthy.

4. "Had I said the right thing? Had I worn the right clothes? Was I attractive?"
    Graham writes that these questions were "unsettling and self-absorbing,
    even overwhelming at times." In your view were these questions the result
    of her "strange childhood," or do they strike you as typical for a person her
    age? Explain.

5. Having read this excerpt from *Personal History*, do you find Katharine
    Graham a person you would have liked to know? What personal qualities
    does her writing reveal? Again, having read this excerpt, do you think you

may someday read the autobiography? In a paragraph try to characterize Graham's writing and offer your opinion of it.

Maya Angelou

Maya Angelou, born in St. Louis, Missouri, in 1938, grew up in Arkansas and California. She studied music, dance, and drama (she had a role in the televised version of Alex Haley's Roots*), and she is now a professor of American studies at Wake Forest University. She has also worked as a cook, streetcar conductor, and waitress. In addition to writing books of poetry, she has written six autobiographical volumes.*

"Graduation" (editors' title) comes from her first autobiography, I Know Why the Caged Bird Sings *(1969).*

Graduation

The children in Stamps trembled visibly with anticipation. Some adults were excited too, but to be certain the whole young population had come down with graduation epidemic. Large classes were graduating from both the grammar school and the high school. Even those who were years removed from their own day of glorious release were anxious to help with preparations as a kind of dry run. The junior students who were moving into the vacating classes' chairs were tradition-bound to show their talents for leadership and management. They strutted through the school and around the campus exerting pressure on the lower grades. Their authority was so new that occasionally if they pressed a little too hard it had to be overlooked. After all, next term was coming, and it never hurt a sixth grader to have a play sister in the eighth grade, or a tenth-year student to be able to call a twelfth grader Bubba. So all was endured in a spirit of shared understanding. But the graduating classes themselves were the nobility. Like travelers with exotic destinations on their minds, the graduates were remarkably forgetful. They came to school without their books, or tablets or even pencils. Volunteers fell over themselves to secure replacements for the missing equipment. When accepted, the willing workers might or might not be thanked, and it was of no importance to the pregraduation rites. Even teachers were respectful of the now quiet and aging seniors, and tended to speak to them, if not as equals, as beings only slightly lower than themselves. After tests were returned and grades given, the student body, which acted like an extended family, knew who did well, who excelled, and what piteous ones had failed.

Unlike the white high school, Lafayette County Training School distinguished itself by having neither lawn, nor hedges, nor tennis court, nor climbing ivy. Its two buildings (main classrooms, the grade school and home economics) were set on a dirt hill with no fence to limit either its boundaries or those of bordering farms. There was a large expanse to the left of the school which was used alternately as a baseball diamond or a basketball court. Rusty hoops on the swaying poles represented the permanent recreational equipment, although bats and balls could be borrowed from the P.E. teacher if the borrower was qualified and if the diamond wasn't occupied.

Over this rocky area relieved by a few shady tall persimmon trees the graduating class walked. The girls often held hands and no longer bothered to speak to the lower students. There was a sadness about them, as if this old world was not their home and they were bound for higher ground. The boys, on the other hand, had become more friendly, more outgoing. A decided change from the closed attitude they projected while studying for finals. Now they seemed not ready to give up the old school, the familiar paths and classrooms. Only a small percentage would be continuing on to college—one of the South's A & M (agricultural and mechanical) schools, which trained Negro youths to be carpenters, farmers, handymen, masons, maids, cooks and baby nurses. Their future rode heavily on their shoulders, and blinded them to the collective joy that had pervaded the lives of the boys and girls in the grammar school graduating class.

Parents who could afford it had ordered new shoes and ready-made clothes for themselves from Sears and Roebuck or Montgomery Ward. They also engaged the best seamstresses to make the floating graduating dresses and to cut down secondhand pants which would be pressed to a military slickness for the important event.

Oh, it was important, all right. Whitefolks would attend the ceremony, and two or three would speak of God and home, and the Southern way of life, and Mrs. Parsons, the principal's wife, would play the graduation march while the lower-grade graduates paraded down the aisles and took their seats below the platform. The high school seniors would wait in empty classrooms to make their dramatic entrance. 5

In the Store I was the person of the moment. The birthday girl. The center. Bailey had graduated the year before, although to do so he had had to forfeit all pleasures to make up for his time lost in Baton Rouge.

My class was wearing butter-yellow piqué dresses, and Momma launched out on mine. She smocked the yoke into tiny crisscrossing puckers, then shirred the rest of the bodice. Her dark fingers ducked in and out of the lemony cloth as she embroidered raised daisies around the hem. Before she considered herself finished she had added a crocheted cuff on the puff sleeves, and a pointy crocheted collar.

I was going to be lovely. A walking model of all the various styles of fine hand sewing and it didn't worry me that I was only twelve years old and merely graduating from the eighth grade. Besides, many teachers in Arkansas Negro schools had only that diploma and were licensed to impart wisdom.

The days had become longer and more noticeable. The faded beige of former times had been replaced with strong and sure colors. I began to see my classmates' clothes, their skin tones, and the dust that waved off pussy willows. Clouds that lazed across the sky were objects of great concern to me. Their shiftier shapes might have held a message that in my new happiness and with a little bit of time I'd soon decipher. During that period I looked at the arch of heaven so religiously my neck kept a steady ache. I had taken to smiling more often, and my jaws hurt from the unaccustomed activity. Between the two physical sore spots, I suppose I could have been uncomfortable, but that was not the case. As a member of the winning team (the graduating class of 1940) I had outdistanced unpleasant sensations by miles. I was headed for the freedom of open fields.

Youth and social approval allied themselves with me and we trammeled memories of slights and insults. The wind of our swift passage remodeled my features. Lost tears were pounded to mud and then to dust. Years of withdrawal were brushed aside and left behind, as hanging ropes of parasitic moss. ¹⁰

My work alone had awarded me a top place and I was going to be one of the first called in the graduating ceremonies. On the classroom blackboard, as well as on the bulletin board in the auditorium, there were blue stars and white stars and red stars. No absences, no tardinesses, and my academic work was among the best of the year. I could say the preamble to the Constitution even faster than Bailey. We timed ourselves often: "WethepeopleoftheUnitedStatesinordertoformamore perfectunion . . . " I had memorized the Presidents of the United States from Washington to Roosevelt in chronological as well as alphabetical order.

My hair pleased me too. Gradually the black mass had lengthened and thickened, so that it kept at last to its braided pattern, and I didn't have to yank my scalp off when I tried to comb it.

Louise and I had rehearsed the exercises until we tired out ourselves. Henry Reed was class valedictorian. He was a small, very black boy with hooded eyes, a long, broad nose and an oddly shaped head. I had admired him for years because each term he and I vied for the best grades in our class. Most often he bested me, but instead of being disappointed I was pleased that we shared top places between us. Like many Southern Black children, he lived with his grandmother, who was as strict as Momma and as kind as she knew how to be. He was courteous, respectful and soft-spoken to elders, but on the playground he chose to play the roughest games. I admired him. Anyone, I reckoned, sufficiently afraid or sufficiently dull could be polite. But to be able to operate at a top level with both adults and children was admirable.

His valedictory speech was entitled "To Be or Not To Be." The rigid tenth-grade teacher helped him to write it. He'd been working on the dramatic stresses for months.

The weeks until graduation were filled with heady activities. A group of small children were to be presented in a play about buttercups and daisies and bunny rabbits. They could be heard throughout the building practicing their hops and their little songs that sounded like silver bells. The older girls (non-graduates, of course) were assigned the task of making refreshments for the night's festivities. A tangy scent of ginger, cinnamon, nutmeg and chocolate wafted around the home economics building as the budding cooks made samples for themselves and their teachers.

In every corner of the workshop, axes and saws split fresh timber as the woodshop boys made sets and stage scenery. Only the graduates were left out of the general bustle. We were free to sit in the library at the back of the building or look in quite detachedly, naturally, on the measures being taken for our event.

Even the minister preached on graduation the Sunday before. His subject was, "Let your light so shine that men will see your good works and praise your Father, Who is in Heaven." Although the sermon was purported to be addressed to us, he used the occasion to speak to backsliders, gamblers, and general ne'er-do-wells. But since he had called our names at the beginning of the service we were mollified.

Among Negroes the tradition was to give presents to children going only from one grade to another. How much more important this was when the person was graduating at the top of the class. Uncle Willie and Momma had sent away for a Mickey Mouse watch like Bailey's. Louise gave me four embroidered handkerchiefs. (I gave her three crocheted doilies.) Mrs. Sneed, the minister's wife, made me an underskirt to wear for graduation, and nearly every customer gave me a nickel or maybe even a dime with the instruction "Keep on moving to higher ground," or some such encouragement.

Amazingly the great day finally dawned and I was out of bed before I knew it. I threw open the back door to see it more clearly, but Momma said, "Sister, come away from that door and put your robe on."

I hoped the memory of that morning would never leave me. Sunlight was itself still young, and the day had none of the insistence maturity would bring it in a few hours. In my robe and barefoot in the backyard, under cover of going to see about my new beans, I gave myself up to the gentle warmth and thanked God that no matter what evil I had done in my life He had allowed me to live to see this day. Somewhere in my fatalism I had expected to die, accidentally, and never have the chance to walk up the stairs in the auditorium and gracefully receive my hard-earned diploma. Out of God's merciful bosom I had won reprieve.

Bailey came out in his robe and gave me a box wrapped in Christmas paper. He said he had saved his money for months to pay for it. It felt like

15

20

a box of chocolates, but I knew Bailey wouldn't save money to buy candy when we had all we could want under our noses.

He was as proud of the gift as I. It was a soft-leather-bound copy of a collection of poems by Edgar Allan Poe, or, as Bailey and I called him, "Eap." I turned to "Annabel Lee" and we walked up and down the garden rows, the cool dirt between our toes, reciting the beautifully sad lines.

Momma made a Sunday breakfast although it was only Friday. After we finished the blessing, I opened my eyes to find the watch on my plate. It was a dream of a day. Everything went smoothly and to my credit I didn't have to be reminded or scolded for anything. Near evening I was too jittery to attend to chores, so Bailey volunteered to do all before his bath.

Days before, we had made a sign for the Store and as we turned out the lights Momma hung the cardboard over the doorknob. It read clearly: CLOSED. GRADUATION.

My dress fitted perfectly and everyone said that I looked like a sunbeam in it. On the hill, going toward the school, Bailey walked behind with Uncle Willie, who muttered, "Go on, Ju." He wanted him to walk ahead with us because it embarrassed him to have to walk so slowly. Bailey said he'd let the ladies walk together, and the men would bring up the rear. We all laughed, nicely. 25

Little children dashed by out of the dark like fireflies. Their crepe-paper dresses and butterfly wings were not made for running and we heard more than one rip, dryly, and the regretful "uh uh" that followed.

The school blazed without gaiety. The windows seemed cold and unfriendly from the lower hill. A sense of ill-fated timing crept over me, and if Momma hadn't reached for my hand I would have drifted back to Bailey and Uncle Willie, and possibly beyond. She made a few slow jokes about my feet getting cold, and tugged me along to the now-strange building.

Around the front steps, assurance came back. There were my fellow "greats," the graduating class. Hair brushed back, legs oiled, new dresses and pressed pleats, fresh pocket handkerchiefs and little hand-bags, all homesewn. Oh, we were up to snuff, all right. I joined my comrades and didn't even see my family go in to find seats in the crowded auditorium.

The school band struck up a march and all classes filed in as had been rehearsed. We stood in front of our seats, as assigned, and on a signal from the choir director, we sat. No sooner had this been accomplished than the band started to play the national anthem. We rose again and sang the song, after which we recited the pledge of allegiance. We remained standing for a brief minute before the choir director and the principal signaled to us, rather desperately I thought, to take our seats. The command was so unusual that our carefully rehearsed and smooth-running machine was thrown off. For a full minute we fumbled for our chairs and bumped into each other awkwardly. Habits change or solidify under pressure, so in our state of nervous tension we had been ready to follow our usual assembly pattern: the American National Anthem, then the pledge of allegiance, then the song every Black person I knew called the Negro National Anthem. All done in the same key, with the same passion and most often standing on the same foot.

Finding my seat at last, I was overcome with a presentiment of worse   30 things to come. Something unrehearsed, unplanned, was going to happen, and we were going to be made to look bad. I distinctly remember being explicit in the choice of pronoun. It was "we," the graduating class, the unit, that concerned me then.

The principal welcomed "parents and friends" and asked the Baptist minister to lead us in prayer. His invocation was brief and punchy, and for a second I thought we were getting back on the high road to right action. When the principal came back to the dais, however, his voice had changed. Sounds always affected me profoundly and the principal's voice was one of my favorites. During assembly it melted and lowed weakly into the audience. It had not been in my plan to listen to him, but my curiosity was piqued and I straightened up to give him my attention.

He was talking about Booker T. Washington, our "late great leader," who said we can be as close as the fingers on the hand, etc. . . . Then he said a few vague things about friendship and the friendship of kindly people to those less fortunate than themselves. With that his voice nearly faded, thin, away. Like a river diminishing to a stream and then to a trickle. But he cleared his throat and said, "Our speaker tonight, who is also our friend, came from Texarkana to deliver the commencement address, but due to the irregularity of the train schedule, he's going to, as they say, 'speak and run.'" He said that we understood and wanted the man to know that we were most grateful for the time he was able to give us and then something about how we were willing always to adjust to another's program, and without more ado—"I give you Mr. Edward Donleavy."

Not one but two white men came through the door offstage. The shorter one walked to the speaker's platform, and the tall one moved over to the center seat and sat down. But that was our principal's seat, and already occupied. The dislodged gentleman bounced around for a long breath or two before the Baptist minister gave him his chair, then with more dignity than the situation deserved, the minister walked off the stage.

Donleavy looked at the audience once (on reflection, I'm sure that he wanted only to reassure himself that we were really there), adjusted his glasses and began to read from a sheaf of papers.

He was glad "to be here and to see the work going on just as it was in   35 the other schools."

At the first "Amen" from the audience I willed the offender to immediate death by choking on the word. But Amen's and Yes, sir's began to fall around the room like rain through a ragged umbrella.

He told us of the wonderful changes we children in Stamps had in store. The Central School (naturally, the white school was Central) had already been granted improvements that would be in use in the fall. A well-known artist was coming from Little Rock to teach art to them. They were going to have the newest microscopes and chemistry equipment for their laboratory. Mr. Donleavy didn't leave us long in the dark over who made these improvements available to Central High. Nor were we to be ignored in the general betterment scheme he had in mind.

He said that he had pointed out to people at a very high level that one of the first-line football tacklers at Arkansas Agricultural and Mechanical College had graduated from good old Lafayette County Training School. Here fewer Amen's were heard. Those few that did break through lay dully in the air with the heaviness of habit.

He went on to praise us. He went on to say how he had bragged that "one of the best basketball players at Fisk sank his first ball right here at Lafayette County Training School."

40

The white kids were going to have a chance to become Galileos and Madame Curies and Edisons and Gauguins, and our boys (the girls weren't even in on it) would try to be Jesse Owenses and Joe Louises.

Owens and the Brown Bomber were great heroes in our world, but what school official in the white-goddom of Little Rock had the right to decide that those two men must be our only heroes? Who decided that for Henry Reed to become a scientist he had to work like George Washington Carver, as a bootblack, to buy a lousy microscope? Bailey was obviously always going to be too small to be an athlete, so which concrete angel glued to what county seat had decided that if my brother wanted to become a lawyer he had to first pay penance for his skin by picking cotton and hoeing corn and studying correspondence books at night for twenty years?

The man's dead words fell like bricks around the auditorium and too many settled in my belly. Constrained by hard-learned manners I couldn't look behind me, but to my left and right the proud graduating class of 1940 had dropped their heads. Every girl in my row had found something new to do with her handkerchief. Some folded the tiny squares into love knots, some into triangles, but most were wadding them, then pressing them flat on their yellow laps.

On the dais, the ancient tragedy was being replayed. Professor Parsons sat, a sculptor's reject, rigid. His large, heavy body seemed devoid of will or willingness, and his eyes said he was no longer with us. The other teachers examined the flag (which was draped stage right) or their notes, or the windows which opened on our now-famous playing diamond.

Graduation, the hush-hush magic time of frills and gifts and congratulations and diplomas, was finished for me before my name was called. The accomplishment was nothing. The meticulous maps, drawn in three colors of ink, learning and spelling decasyllabic words, memorizing the whole of *The Rape of Lucrece*—it was nothing. Donleavy had exposed us.

We were maids and farmers, handymen and washerwomen, and any-   45
thing higher that we aspired to was farcical and presumptuous. Then I
wished that Gabriel Prosser and Nat Turner had killed all white-folks in
their beds and that Abraham Lincoln had been assassinated before the
signing of the Emancipation Proclamation, and that Harriet Tubman had
been killed by that blow on her head and Christopher Columbus had
drowned in the *Santa Maria*.

It was awful to be Negro and have no control over my life. It was brutal to be young and already trained to sit quietly and listen to charges
brought against my color and no chance of defense. We should all be dead.
I thought I should like to see us all dead, one on top of the other. A pyramid
of flesh with the whitefolks on the bottom, as the broad base, then the
Indians with their silly tomahawks and teepees and wigwams and treaties,
the Negroes with their mops and recipes and cotton sacks and spirituals
sticking out of their mouths. The Dutch children should all stumble in
their wooden shoes and break their necks. The French should choke to
death on the Louisiana Purchase (1803) while silkworms ate all the
Chinese with their stupid pigtails. As a species, we were an abomination.
All of us.

Donleavy was running for election, and assured our parents that if he
won we could count on having the only colored paved playing field in
that part of Arkansas. Also—he never looked up to acknowledge the
grunts of acceptance—also, we were bound to get some new equipment
for the home economics building and the workshop.

He finished, and since there was no need to give any more than the
most perfunctory thank-you's, he nodded to the men on the stage, and
the tall white man who was never introduced joined him at the door.
They left with the attitude that now they were off to something really important. (The graduation ceremonies at Lafayette County Training School
had been a mere preliminary.)

The ugliness they left was palpable. An uninvited guest who wouldn't
leave. The choir was summoned and sang a modern arrangement of
"Onward, Christian Soldiers," with new words pertaining to graduates
seeking their place in the world. But it didn't work. Elouise, the daughter
of the Baptist minister, recited "Invictus," and I could have cried at the im-
pertinence of "I am the master of my fate, I am the captain of my soul."

My name had lost its ring of familiarity and I had to be nudged to go   50
and receive my diploma. All my preparations had fled. I neither marched
up to the stage like a conquering Amazon, nor did I look in the audience
for Bailey's nod of approval. Marguerite Johnson, I heard the name again,
my honors were read, there were noises in the audience of appreciation,
and I took my place on the stage as rehearsed.

I thought about colors I hated: ecru, puce, lavender, beige and black.

There was shuffling and rustling around me, then Henry Reed was
giving his valedictory address, "To Be or Not to Be." Hadn't he heard the
whitefolks? We couldn't *be*, so the question was a waste of time. Henry's

voice came out clear and strong. I feared to look at him. Hadn't he got the message? There was no "nobler in the mind" for Negroes because the world didn't think we had minds, and they let us know it. "Outrageous fortune"? Now, that was a joke. When the ceremony was over I had to tell Henry Reed some things. That is, if I still cared. Not "rub," Henry, "erase." "Ah, there's the erase." Us.

Henry had been a good student in elocution. His voice rose on tides of promise and fell on waves of warnings. The English teacher had helped him to create a sermon winging through Hamlet's soliloquy. To be a man, a doer, a builder, a leader, or to be a tool, an unfunny joke, a crusher of funky toadstools. I marveled that Henry could go through with the speech as if we had a choice.

I had been listening and silently rebutting each sentence with my eyes closed; then there was a hush, which in an audience warns that something unplanned is happening. I looked up and saw Henry Reed, the conservative, the proper, the A student, turn his back to the audience and turn to us (the proud graduating class of 1940) and sing, nearly speaking,

> *Lift ev'ry voice and sing*
> *Till earth and heaven ring*
> *Ring with the harmonies of Liberty . . .*

It was the poem written by James Weldon Johnson. It was the music composed by J. Rosamond Johnson. It was the Negro National Anthem. Out of habit we were singing it. 55

Our mothers and fathers stood in the dark hall and joined the hymn of encouragement. A kindergarten teacher led the small children onto the stage and the buttercups and daisies and bunny rabbits marked time and tried to follow:

> *Stony the road we trod*
> *Bitter the chastening rod*
> *Felt in the days when hope, unborn, had died.*
> *Yet with a steady beat*
> *Have not our weary feet*
> *Come to the place for which our fathers sighed?*

Every child I knew had learned that song with his ABC's and along with "Jesus Loves Me This I Know." But I personally had never heard it before. Never heard the words, despite the thousands of times I had sung them. Never thought they had anything to do with me.

On the other hand, the words of Patrick Henry had made such an impression on me that I had been able to stretch myself tall and trembling and say, "I know not what course others may take, but as for me, give me liberty or give me death."

And now I heard, really for the first time:

We have come over a way that with tears has been watered,
We have come, treading our path through the blood of the slaughtered.

While echoes of the song shivered in the air, Henry Reed bowed his   60
head, said "Thank you," and returned to his place in the line. The tears
that slipped down many faces were not wiped away in shame.

We were on top again. As always, again. We survived. The depths
had been icy and dark, but now a bright sun spoke to our souls. I was no
longer simply a member of the proud graduating class of 1940; I was a
proud member of the wonderful, beautiful Negro race.

Oh, Black known and unknown poets, how often have your auc-
tioned pains sustained us? Who will compute the lonely nights made less
lonely by your songs, or the empty pots made less tragic by your tales?

If we were a people much given to revealing secrets, we might raise
monuments and sacrifice to the memories of our poets, but slavery cured
us of that weakness. It may be enough, however, to have it said that we
survive in exact relationship to the dedication of our poets (include
preachers, musicians and blues singers).

Topics for Critical Thinking and Writing

1. In paragraph 1 notice such overstatements as "glorious release," "the gradu-
    ating classes themselves were the nobility," and "exotic destinations." Find
    further examples in the next few pages. What do you think is the function
    of this diction?

2. Characterize the writer as you perceive her through paragraph 28. Support
    your characterization with references to specific passages. Next, characterize
    her in paragraph 46, which begins. "It was awful to be Negro." Next, charac-
    terize her on the basis of the entire essay. Finally, in a sentence, try to de-
    scribe the change, telling the main attitudes or moods that she goes through.

3. How would you define *poets* as Angelou uses the word in the last sentence?

Richard Wright

Richard Wright (1908–60), the grandson of a slave and the son of an impoverished share-
cropper family, was born on a cotton plantation near Natchez, Mississippi. He dropped out of
school after completing the ninth grade, took a variety of odd jobs, and in 1927 moved to
Chicago, where he worked as a porter, dishwasher, and postal clerk. In 1937 he moved to

New York, where he became the Harlem editor of The Daily Worker, *a Communist newspaper. In 1947 he and his family moved to Paris, where they lived until he suffered a fatal heart attack in 1960.*

With Native Son *(1940), a militant novel attacking racism, Wright became the first African-American writer to reach a large white audience. His next best-selling work was an autobiography,* Black Boy *(1945), part of which we reprint below. (The title is the editors'.)*

Writing and Reading

The eighth grade days flowed in their hungry path and I grew more conscious of myself; I sat in classes, bored, wondering, dreaming. One long dry afternoon I took out my composition book and told myself that I would write a story; it was sheer idleness that led me to it. What would the story be about? It resolved itself into a plot about a villain who wanted a widow's home and I called it *The Voodoo of Hell's Half-Acre*. It was crudely atmospheric, emotional, intuitively psychological, and stemmed from pure feeling. I finished it in three days and then wondered what to do with it.

The local Negro newspaper! That's it . . . I sailed into the office and shoved my ragged composition book under the nose of the man who called himself the editor.

"What is that?" he asked.

"A story," I said.

"A news story?"   5

"No, fiction."

"All right. I'll read it," he said.

He pushed my composition book back on his desk and looked at me curiously, sucking at his pipe.

"But I want you to read it *now*," I said.

He blinked. I had no idea how newspapers were run. I thought that   10
one took a story to an editor and he sat down then and there and read it and said yes or no.

"I'll read this and let you know about it tomorrow," he said.

I was disappointed; I had taken time to write it and he seemed distant and uninterested.

"Give me the story," I said, reaching for it.

He turned from me, took up the book and read ten pages or more.

"Won't you come in tomorrow?" he asked. "I'll have it finished then."   15

I honestly relented.

"All right," I said. "I'll stop in tomorrow."

I left with the conviction that he would not read it. Now, where else could I take it after he had turned it down? The next afternoon, en route to my job, I stepped into the newspaper office.

"Where's my story?" I asked.

"It's in galleys," he said.   20

"What's that?" I asked; I did not know what galleys were.

"It's set up in type," he said. "We're publishing it."

"How much money will I get?" I asked, excited.

"We can't pay for manuscript," he said.

"But you sell your papers for money," I said with logic.   25

"Yes, but we're young in business," he explained.

"But you're asking me to *give* you my story, but you don't *give* your papers away," I said.

He laughed.

"Look, you're just starting. This story will put your name before our readers. Now, that's something," he said.

"But if the story is good enough to sell to your readers, then you   30
ought to give me some of the money you get from it," I insisted.

He laughed again and I sensed that I was amusing him.

"I'm going to offer you something more valuable than money," he said. "I'll give you a chance to learn to write."

I was pleased, but I still thought he was taking advantage of me.

"When will you publish my story?"

"I'm dividing it into three installments," he said.   35

"The first installment appears this week. But the main thing is this: Will you get news for me on a space rate basis?"

"I work mornings and evenings for three dollars a week," I said.

"Oh," he said. "Then you better keep that. But what are you doing this summer?"

"Nothing."

"Then come to see me before you take another job," he said. "And   40
write some more stories."

A few days later my classmates came to me with baffled eyes, holding copies of the *Southern Register* in their hands.

"Did you really write that story?" they asked me.

"Yes."

"Why?"

"Because I wanted to."   45

"Where did you get it from?"

"I made it up."

"You didn't. You copied it out of a book."

"If I had, no one would publish it."

"But what are they publishing it for?"   50

"So people can read it."

"Who told you to do that?"

"Nobody."

"Then why did you do it?"

"Because I wanted to," I said again.   55

They were convinced that I had not told them the truth. We had never had any instruction in literary matters at school; the literature of the nation or the Negro had never been mentioned. My schoolmates could not understand why anyone would want to write a story; and, above all, they could not understand why I had called it *The Voodoo of Hell's Half-Acre*. The mood out of which a story was written was the most alien thing conceivable to them. They looked at me with new eyes, and a distance, a suspiciousness came between us. If I had thought anything in writing the story, I had thought that perhaps it would make me more acceptable to them, and now it was cutting me off from them more completely than ever.

At home the effects were no less disturbing. Granny came into my room early one morning and sat on the edge of my bed.

"Richard, what is this you're putting in the papers?" she asked.

"A story," I said.

"About what?" 60

"It's just a story, granny."

"But they tell me it's been in three times."

"It's the same story. It's in three parts."

"But what is it about?" she insisted.

I hedged, fearful of getting into a religious argument. 65

"It's just a story I made up," I said.

"Then it's a lie," she said.

"Oh, Christ," I said.

"You must get out of this house if you take the name of the Lord in vain," she said.

"Granny, please . . . I'm sorry," I pleaded. "But it's hard to tell you 70 about the story. You see, granny, everybody knows that the story isn't true, but . . . "

"Then why write it?" she asked.

"Because people might want to read it."

"That's the Devil's work," she said and left.

My mother also was worried.

"Son, you ought to be more serious," she said. "You're growing up 75 now and you won't be able to get jobs if you let people think that you're weak-minded. Suppose the superintendent of schools would ask you to teach here in Jackson, and he found out that you had been writing stories?"

I could not answer her.

"I'll be all right, mama," I said.

Uncle Tom, though surprised, was highly critical and contemptuous. The story had no point, he said. And whoever heard of a story by the title of *The Voodoo of Hell's Half-Acre*? Aunt Addie said that it was a sin for anyone to use the word "hell" and that what was wrong with me was that I had nobody to guide me. She blamed the whole thing upon my upbringing.

In the end I was so angry that I refused to talk about the story. From no quarter, with the exception of the Negro newspaper editor, had there come a single encouraging word. It was rumored that the principal wanted to know why I had used the word "hell." I felt that I had committed a crime. Had I been conscious of the full extent to which I was pushing against the current of my environment, I would have been frightened altogether out of my attempts at writing. But my reactions were limited to the attitude of the people about me, and I did not speculate or generalize.

I dreamed of going north and writing books, novels. The North sym-   80 bolized to me all that I had not felt and seen; it had no relation whatever to what actually existed. Yet, by imagining a place where everything was possible, I kept hope alive in me. But where had I got this notion of doing something in the future, of going away from home and accomplishing something that would be recognized by others? I had, of course, read my Horatio Alger stories, my pulp stories, and I knew my Get-Rich-Quick Wallingford series from cover to cover, though I had sense enough not to hope to get rich; even to my naïve imagination that possibility was too remote. I knew that I lived in a country in which the aspirations of black people were limited, marked-off. Yet I felt that I had to go somewhere and do something to redeem my being alive.

I was building up in me a dream which the entire educational system of the South had been rigged to stifle. I was feeling the very thing that the state of Mississippi had spent millions of dollars to make sure that I would never feel; I was becoming aware of the thing that the Jim Crow laws had been drafted and passed to keep out of my consciousness; I was acting on impulses that southern senators in the nation's capital had striven to keep out of Negro life; I was beginning to dream the dreams that the state had said were wrong, that the schools had said were taboo.

Had I been articulate about my ultimate aspirations, no doubt someone would have told me what I was bargaining for; but nobody seemed to know, and least of all did I. My classmates felt that I was doing something that was vaguely wrong, but they did not know how to express it. As the outside world grew more meaningful, I became more concerned, tense; and my classmates and my teachers would say: "Why do you ask so many questions?" Or: "Keep quiet."

I was in my fifteenth year; in terms of schooling I was far behind the average youth of the nation, but I did not know that. In me was shaping a yearning for a kind of consciousness, a mode of being that the way of life about me had said could not be, must not be, and upon which the penalty of death had been placed. Somewhere in the dead of the southern night my life had switched onto the wrong track and, without my knowing it, the locomotive of my heart was rushing down a dangerously steep slope, heading for a collision, heedless of the warning red lights that blinked all about me, the sirens and the bells and the screams that filled the air. . . .

One morning I arrived early at work and went into the bank lobby where the Negro porter was mopping. I stood at a counter and picked up the Memphis *Commercial Appeal* and began my free reading of the press. I came finally to the editorial page and saw an article dealing with one H. L. Mencken. I knew by hearsay that he was the editor of the *American Mercury*, but aside from that I knew nothing about him. The article was a furious denunciation of Mencken, concluding with one, hot, short sentence: Mencken is a fool.

I wondered what on earth this Mencken had done to call down upon   85
him the scorn of the South. The only people I had ever heard denounced in the South were Negroes, and this man was not a Negro. Then what ideas did Mencken hold that made a newspaper like the *Commercial Appeal* castigate him publicly? Undoubtedly he must be advocating ideas that the South did not like. Were there, then, people other than Negroes who criticized the South? I knew that during the Civil War the South had hated northern whites, but I had not encountered such hate during my life. Knowing no more of Mencken than I did at that moment, I felt a vague sympathy for him. Had not the South, which had assigned me the role of a non-man, cast at him its hardest words?

Now, how could I find out about this Mencken? There was a huge library near the riverfront, but I knew that Negroes were not allowed to patronize its shelves any more than they were the parks and playgrounds of the city. I had gone into the library several times to get books for the white men on the job. Which of them would now help me to get books? And how could I read them without causing concern to the white men with whom I worked? I had so far been successful in hiding my thoughts and feelings from them, but I knew that I would create hostility if I went about this business of reading in a clumsy way.

I weighed the personalities of the men on the job. There was Don, a Jew; but I distrusted him. His position was not much better than mine and I knew that he was uneasy and insecure; he had always treated me in an offhand, bantering way that barely concealed his contempt. I was afraid to ask him to help me to get books; his frantic desire to demonstrate a racial solidarity with the whites against Negroes might make him betray me.

Then how about the boss? No, he was a Baptist and I had the suspicion that he would not be quite able to comprehend why a black boy would want to read Mencken. There were other white men on the job whose attitudes showed clearly that they were Kluxers or sympathizers, and they were out of the question.

There remained only one man whose attitude did not fit into an anti-Negro category, for I had heard the white men refer to him as a "Pope lover." He was an Irish Catholic and was hated by the white Southerners. I knew that he read books, because I had got him volumes from the library several times. Since he, too, was an object of hatred, I felt that he might refuse me but would hardly betray me. I hesitated, weighing and balancing the imponderable realities.

One morning I paused before the Catholic fellow's desk.   90

"I want to ask you a favor," I whispered to him.

"What is it?"

"I want to read. I can't get books from the library. I wonder if you'd let me use your card?"

He looked at me suspiciously.

"My card is full most of the time," he said.   95

"I see," I said and waited, posing my question silently.

"You're not trying to get me into trouble, are you, boy?" he asked, staring at me.

"Oh, no, sir."

"What book do you want?"

"A book by H. L. Mencken."   100

"Which one?"

"I don't know. Has he written more than one?"

"He has written several."

"I didn't know that."

"What makes you want to read Mencken?"   105

"Oh, I just saw his name in the newspaper," I said.

"It's good of you to want to read," he said. "But you ought to read the right things."

I said nothing. Would he want to supervise my reading?

"Let me think," he said. "I'll figure out something."

I turned from him and he called me back. He stared at me quizzically.   110

"Richard, don't mention this to the other white men," he said.

"I understand," I said. "I won't say a word."

A few days later he called me to him.

"I've got a card in my wife's name," he said. "Here's mine."

"Thank you, sir."   115

"Do you think you can manage it?"

"I'll manage fine," I said.

"If they suspect you, you'll get in trouble," he said.

"I'll write the same kind of notes to the library that you wrote when you sent me for books," I told him. "I'll sign your name."

He laughed.   120

"Go ahead. Let me see what you get," he said.

That afternoon I addressed myself to forging a note. Now, what were the names of books written by H. L. Mencken? I did not know any of them. I finally wrote what I thought would be a foolproof note: *Dear Madam: Will you please let this nigger boy*—I used the word "nigger" to make the librarian feel that I could not possibly be the author of the note—*have some books by H. L. Mencken?* I forged the white man's name.

I entered the library as I had always done when on errands for whites, but I felt that I would somehow slip up and betray myself. I doffed my hat, stood a respectful distance from the desk, looked as un-bookish as possible, and waited for the white patrons to be taken care of. When the desk was clear of people, I still waited. The white librarian looked at me.

"What do you want, boy?"

As though I did not possess the power of speech, I stepped forward   125
and simply handed her the forged note, not parting my lips.

"What books by Mencken does he want?" she asked.

"I don't know, ma'am," I said, avoiding her eyes.

"Who gave you this card?"

"Mr. Falk," I said.

"Where is he?"   130

"He's at work, at the M——Optical Company," I said. "I've been in here for him before."

"I remember," the woman said. "But he never wrote notes like this."

Oh, God, she's suspicious. Perhaps she would not let me have the books? If she had turned her back at that moment, I would have ducked out the door and never gone back. Then I thought of a bold idea.

"You can call him up, ma'am," I said, my heart pounding.

"You're not using these books, are you?" she asked pointedly.   135

"Oh, no, ma'am. I can't read."

"I don't know what he wants by Mencken," she said under her breath.

I knew now that I had won; she was thinking of other things and the race question had gone out of her mind. She went to the shelves. Once or twice she looked over her shoulder at me, as though she was still doubtful. Finally she came forward with two books in her hand.

"I'm sending him two books," she said. "But tell Mr. Falk to come in next time, or send me the names of the books he wants. I don't know what he wants to read."

I said nothing. She stamped the card and handed me the books. Not   140
daring to glance at them, I went out of the library, fearing that the woman would call me back for further questioning. A block away from the library I opened one of the books and read a title: *A Book of Prefaces*. I was nearing my nineteenth birthday and I did not know how to pronounce the word "preface." I thumbed the pages and saw strange words and strange names. I shook my head, disappointed. I looked at the other book; it was called *Prejudices*. I knew what that word meant; I had heard it all my life. And right off I was on guard against Mencken's books. Why would a man want to call a book *Prejudices?* The word was so stained with all my memories of racial hate that I could not conceive of anybody using it for a title. Perhaps I had made a mistake about Mencken? A man who had prejudices must be wrong.

When I showed the books to Mr. Falk, he looked at me and frowned.

"That librarian might telephone you," I warned him.

"That's all right," he said. "But when you're through reading those books, I want you to tell me what you get out of them."

That night in my rented room, while letting the hot water run over my can of pork and beans in the sink, I opened *A Book of Prefaces* and began to read. I was jarred and shocked by the style, the clear, clean, sweeping sentences. Why did he write like that? And how did one write like that? I pictured the man as a raging demon, slashing with his pen, consumed with hate, denouncing everything American, extolling everything European or

German, laughing at the weaknesses of people, mocking God, authority. What was this? I stood up, trying to realize what reality lay behind the meaning of the words. . . . Yes, this man was fighting, fighting with words. He was using words as a weapon, using them as one would use a club. Could words be weapons? Well, yes, for here they were. Then, maybe, perhaps, I could use them as a weapon? No. It frightened me. I read on and what amazed me was not what he said, but how on earth anybody had the courage to say it.

Occasionally I glanced up to reassure myself that I was alone in the room. Who were these men about whom Mencken was talking so passionately? Who was Anatole France? Joseph Conrad? Sinclair Lewis, Sherwood Anderson, Dostoevski, George Moore, Gustave Flaubert, Maupassant, Tolstoy, Frank Harris, Mark Twain, Thomas Hardy, Arnold Bennett, Stephen Crane, Zola, Norris, Gorky, Bergson, Ibsen, Balzac, Bernard Shaw, Dumas, Poe, Thomas Mann, O. Henry, Dreiser, H. G. Wells, Gogol, T. S. Eliot, Gide, Baudelaire, Edgar Lee Masters, Stendhal, Turgenev, Huneker, Nietzsche, and scores of others? Were these men real? Did they exist or had they existed? And how did one pronounce their names?

I ran across many words whose meanings I did not know, and I either looked them up in a dictionary or, before I had a chance to do that, encountered the word in a context that made its meaning clear. But what strange world was this? I concluded the book with the conviction that I had somehow overlooked something terribly important in life. I had once tried to write, had once reveled in feeling, had let my crude imagination roam, but the impulse to dream had been slowly beaten out of me by experience. Now it surged up again and I hungered for books, new ways of looking and seeing. It was not a matter of believing or disbelieving what I read, but of feeling something new, of being affected by something that made the look of the world different.

As dawn broke I ate my pork and beans, feeling dopey, sleepy. I went to work, but the mood of the book would not die; it lingered, coloring everything I saw, heard, did. I now felt that I knew what the white men were feeling. Merely because I had read a book that had spoken of how they lived and thought, I identified myself with that book. I felt vaguely guilty. Would I, filled with bookish notions, act in a manner that would make the whites dislike me?

I forged more notes and my trips to the library became frequent. Reading grew into a passion. My first serious novel was Sinclair Lewis's *Main Street*. It made me see my boss, Mr. Gerald, and identify him as an American type. I would smile when I saw him lugging his golf bags into the office. I had always felt a vast distance separating me from the boss, and now I felt closer to him, though still distant. I felt now that I knew him, that I could feel the very limits of his narrow life. And this had happened because I had read a novel about a mythical man called George F. Babbitt.

145

The plots and stories in the novels did not interest me so much as the point of view revealed. I gave myself over to each novel without reserve, without trying to criticize it; it was enough for me to see and feel something different. And for me, everything was something different. Reading was like a drug, a dope. The novels created moods in which I lived for days. But I could not conquer my sense of guilt, my feeling that the white men around me knew that I was changing, that I had begun to regard them differently.

Whenever I brought a book to the job, I wrapped it in newspaper—a habit that was to persist for years in other cities and under other circumstances. But some of the white men pried into my packages when I was absent and they questioned me.   150

"Boy, what are you reading those books for?"

"Oh, I don't know, sir."

"That's deep stuff you're reading, boy."

"I'm just killing time, sir."

"You'll addle your brains if you don't watch out."   155

I read Dreiser's *Jennie Gerhardt* and *Sister Carrie* and they revived in me a vivid sense of my mother's suffering; I was overwhelmed. I grew silent, wondering about the life around me. It would have been impossible for me to have told anyone what I derived from these novels, for it was nothing less than a sense of life itself. All my life had shaped me for the realism, the naturalism of the modern novel, and I could not read enough of them.

Steeped in new moods and ideas, I bought a ream of paper and tried to write; but nothing would come, or what did come was flat beyond telling. I discovered that more than desire and feeling were necessary to write and I dropped the idea. Yet I still wondered how it was possible to know people sufficiently to write about them? Could I ever learn about life and people? To me, with my vast ignorance, my Jim Crow station in life, it seemed a task impossible of achievement. I now knew what being a Negro meant. I could endure the hunger. I had learned to live with hate. But to feel that there were feelings denied me, that the very breath of life itself was beyond my reach, that more than anything else hurt, wounded me. I had a new hunger.

In buoying me up, reading also cast me down, made me see what was possible, what I had missed. My tension returned, new, terrible, bitter, surging, almost too great to be contained. I no longer *felt* that the world about me was hostile, killing; I *knew* it. A million times I asked myself what I could do to save myself, and there were no answers. I seemed forever condemned, ringed by walls.

I did not discuss my reading with Mr. Falk, who had lent me his library card; it would have meant talking about myself and that would have been too painful. I smiled each day, fighting desperately to maintain my old behavior, to keep my disposition seemingly sunny. But some of the white men discerned that I had begun to brood.

"Wake up there, boy!" Mr. Olin said one day.

"Sir!" I answered for the lack of a better word.

"You act like you've stolen something," he said.

I laughed in the way I knew he expected me to laugh, but I resolved to be more conscious of myself, to watch my every act, to guard and hide the new knowledge that was dawning within me.

If I went north, would it be possible for me to build a new life then? But how could a man build a life upon vague, unformed yearnings? I wanted to write and I did not even know the English language. I bought English grammars and found them dull. I felt that I was getting a better sense of the language from novels than from grammars. I read hard, discarding a writer as soon as I felt that I had grasped his point of view. At night the printed page stood before my eyes in sleep.

Mrs. Moss, my landlady, asked me one Sunday morning: 165

"Son, what is this you keep on reading?"

"Oh, nothing. Just novels."

"What you get out of 'em?"

"I'm just killing time," I said.

"I hope you know your own mind," she said in a tone which implied   170
that she doubted if I had a mind.

I knew of no Negroes who read the books I liked and I wondered if any Negroes ever thought of them. I knew that there were Negro doctors, lawyers, newspapermen, but I never saw any of them. When I read a Negro newspaper I never caught the faintest echo of my preoccupation in its pages. I felt trapped and occasionally, for a few days, I would stop reading. But a vague hunger would come over me for books, books that opened up new avenues of feeling and seeing, and again I would forge another note to the white librarian. Again I would read and wonder as only the naïve and unlettered can read and wonder, feeling that I carried a secret, criminal burden about with me each day.

That winter my mother and brother came and we set up housekeeping, buying furniture on the installment plan, being cheated and yet knowing no way to avoid it. I began to eat warm food and to my surprise found that regular meals enabled me to read faster. I may have lived through many illnesses and survived them, never suspecting that I was ill. My brother obtained a job and we began to save toward the trip north, plotting our time, setting tentative dates for departure. I told none of the white men on the job that I was planning to go north; I knew that the moment they felt I was thinking of the North they would change toward me. It would have made them feel that I did not like the life I was living, and because my life was completely conditioned by what they said or did, it would have been tantamount to challenging them.

I could calculate my chances for life in the South as a Negro fairly clearly now.

I could fight the southern whites by organizing with other Negroes, as my grandfather had done. But I knew that I could never win that way; there were many whites and there were but few blacks. They were strong and we were weak. Outright black rebellion could never win. If I fought openly I would die and I did not want to die. News of lynchings were frequent.

I could submit and live the life of a genial slave, but that was impossi- 175 ble. All of my life had shaped me to live by my own feelings and thoughts. I could make up to Bess and marry her and inherit the house. But that, too, would be the life of a slave; if I did that, I would crush to death something within me, and I would hate myself as much as I knew the whites already hated those who had submitted. Neither could I ever willingly present myself to be kicked, as Shorty had done. I would rather have died than do that.

I could drain off my restlessness by fighting with Shorty and Harrison. I had seen many Negroes solve the problem of being black by transferring their hatred of themselves to others with a black skin and fighting them. I would have to be cold to do that, and I was not cold and I could never be.

I could, of course, forget what I had read, thrust the whites out of my mind, forget them; and find release from anxiety and longing in sex and alcohol. But the memory of how my father had conducted himself made that course repugnant. If I did not want others to violate my life, how could I voluntarily violate it myself?

I had no hope whatever of being a professional man. Not only had I been so conditioned that I did not desire it, but the fulfillment of such an ambition was beyond my capabilities. Well-to-do Negroes lived in a world that was almost as alien to me as the world inhabited by whites.

What, then, was there? I held my life in my mind, in my consciousness each day, feeling at times that I would stumble and drop it, spill it forever. My reading had created a vast sense of distance between me and the world in which I lived and tried to make a living, and that sense of distance was increasing each day. My days and nights were one long, quiet, continuously contained dream of terror, tension, and anxiety. I wondered how long I could bear it.

Topics for Critical Thinking and Writing

1. In this section of his autobiography, Wright recounts his illegal use of the public library. Why was his use of the library illegal? And why was the library so important to him? Compare Wright's experience with your own introduction to a public library.

2. At the end of the first part of the narrative (paragraph 83), Wright tells of his "yearning for a kind of consciousness, a mode of being . . . upon which the

penalty of death had been placed." To what extent can we change the consciousness that we have? Is Wright exaggerating when he says that "the penalty of death had been placed" on the changes he desires?

3. Wright frequently uses dialogue to tell his story. Select a passage of dialogue, of about a page, and then summarize it without using dialogue. Then, in a brief paragraph, explain what has been gained or lost. We suggest Wright's conversations with the editor of the newspaper or with "the Catholic fellow."

Doris Kearns Goodwin

Doris Kearns Goodwin was born in Rockville Centre, New York, in 1943, and educated at Colby College (BA) and Harvard University (Ph.D.). As an undergraduate she served in Washington as a State Department intern, and between college and graduate school she served as a House of Representatives intern. In 1968, the year she received her Ph.D., she served as special assistant to President Lyndon Johnson—a rather remarkable appointment, since Johnson offered it to her knowing that in 1967 she had published an article urging the Democrats not to renominate him for the 1968 election.

One product of her work with Johnson was a highly acclaimed biography (which she published under the name of Doris Helen Kearns), Lyndon Johnson and the American Dream *(1976). She has also written two more books which are widely regarded as major works:* The Fitzeralds and the Kennedys: An American Saga *(1987) and* No Ordinary Time: Franklin and Eleanor Roosevelt *(1994), which won the Pulitzer Prize in 1995.* Wait till Next Year, *her book about the Dodgers and her memories of baseball, the source of the following passage, was published in 1997. Goodwin is a regular panelist on television programs and was the first woman journalist to enter the locker room of the Boston Red Sox.*

Fan

My continuing love of baseball is inseparably linked to memories of my father. On summer nights, when he came home from work, the two of us would sit together on our porch, reliving that day's Brooklyn Dodger game, which I had permanently preserved in the large red scorebook he'd given me for my seventh birthday.

I can still remember how proud I was when I first mastered all the miniature symbols that allowed me to record every movement, play by play, of our favorite players, Jackie Robinson and Duke Snider. Pee Wee Reese and Gil Hodges. With the scorebook spread between us, my dad would ask me questions about different plays, whether a strikeout was called or swinging, and if I'd been careful in my scoring, I would know the answers.

At such moments, when he smiled at me, I could not help but smile, too, for he had one of those contagious smiles that started in his eyes and traveled across his face, leaving laugh lines on either side of his mouth.

Sometimes a particular play would trigger in my dad a memory of a similar situation framed forever in his mind, and suddenly we were back in time recalling the Dodgers of his childhood—Casey Stengel, Zack Wheat, and Jimmy Johnston. Mingling together the present and the past, our conversations nurtured within me an irresistible fascination with history, which has remained to this day.

It fell to me to be the family scorekeeper not only because I was the third daughter and youngest child, but because my idea of a perfect afternoon was lying in front of our ten-inch-screen television, watching baseball. What is more, there was real power in being the one to keep score. For all through my early childhood, my father kept from me the knowledge that the daily papers printed daily box scores, permitting me to imagine that without my symbolic renderings of all the games he had missed while he was at work, he would never have been able to follow the Dodgers in the only proper way a team should be followed, day by day, inning by inning. In other words, without me, his love for baseball would be forever unrequited.

In our neighborhood in Rockville Centre, New York, allegiance was   5
equally divided among Dodger, Yankee, and Giant fans. As families emigrated from different parts of the city to the suburbs of Long Island, the old loyalties remained intact, creating rival enclaves on every street. Born and bred in Brooklyn, my father would always love the Dodgers, fear the Giants, and hate the abominable Yankees.

The butcher shop in our neighborhood was owned by a father and son, Old Joe and Young Joe Schmidt. They were both rabid Giant fans, as was Max, the man in charge of the vegetables. Knowing how much I loved baseball, they all took great delight in teasing me. They called me Ragmop, in honor of my unruly hair, and they constantly made fun of my Dodgers. I'd pretend to be angry, but the truth was that I loved going into their shop; I loved the sawdust on the floor, the sides of beef hanging from the ceiling, the enormous walk-in freezer behind the counter. And most of all, I loved the attention I received.

During the glorious summer of 1951, when I was eight years old and the Dodgers seemed invincible, I visited my friends in the butcher shop every day. Jackie Robinson was awesome that year, hitting .338; Roy Campanella was the MVP; Gil Hodges hit 40 homers. It seemed that no one could beat us. But then, in the third week of August, the Giants began an astonishing stretch that whittled the Dodger lead away until the season ended in a tie.

When the deciding play-off began, I was so nervous I couldn't sit by the television. Each time the Giants came to bat in the early innings, I left the room, returning only when I knew they were out and the Dodgers were up. I began to relax slightly as the Dodgers pulled ahead 4–1, but when the Giants came to bat in the last of the ninth, I could hear the beating of my heart. Then, as Bobby Thomson stepped to the plate, with one run in and two men on base, my sister Charlotte predicted that he would hit a home run and win the game for the Giants. When Thomson did precisely that, crushing Ralph Branca's pitch into the left field stand, I thought for a moment my sister had made it happen and I hated her with all my heart.

In the days that followed, I refused to go into the butcher shop, unable to face the mocking laughter that I imagined would accompany my first steps into the store. I was wrong. After a week's absence, a bouquet of flowers arrived at my door. "Ragmop, come back," the card read. "We miss you. Your friends at Bryn Mawr Meat Market."

"Wait till next year," my father consoled, repeating a refrain that   10
would become all too familiar in the years ahead. But at eight years of age, it was easy to gamble in expectation, to believe that as soon as winter gave way to spring, a splendid new season would begin.

This indomitable belief in the future was vitally important to me when I was a child, for my mother's life was slowly ebbing away. The rheumatic fever she had when she was young had left her heart permanently damaged; every year, it seemed, she suffered another heart attack, which sent her to the hospital for days or weeks at a time. I was never made privy to the full extent of her illness; on the contrary, I took great comfort from the ritual of knowing that each time she went away, she came back. It's only a matter of time. I kept telling myself, as the ambulance carried her away, until she'll walk through the door again and everything will be all right.

In my prayers, the Dodgers figured prominently. Every night I said two sets of Hail Marys and Our Fathers. Believing that each prayer was worth a certain number of days off my inevitable sentence to purgatory, I dedicated the first set of prayers to my account in heaven. At the end of the week I would add up my nightly prayers and fold the total into a note. "Dear God. I have said 935 days worth of prayers this week. Please put this to my account. I live at 125 Southard Avenue." My second set of prayers was directed toward more earthly desires, chief among them the wish for the Dodgers to win the World Series at least once before I died.

It took tens of thousands of Hail Marys and Our Fathers, but finally on October 4, 1955, the Dodgers won their first-ever world championship. It was one of the happiest moments of my life, made all the more special because this time, I predicted the outcome. In the sixth inning, Sandy Amoros made a spectacular catch in left field of a wicked fly ball that would have tied the score with two Yankee runs. I knew then that the Dodgers would win, just as, on other occasions, a failed sacrifice or a double play signaled an inevitable loss.

Everything happened quickly after that until, stunningly, it was the bottom of the ninth with the Dodgers up 2–0. And this time there was no Bobby Thomson to destroy the cherished dreams of delirious Brooklyn fans. When my father came home that night, we celebrated by recreating the entire game, play by play, and there was more. When the newspaper arrived on our lawn the next morning with the fabulous headline THIS *IS* NEXT YEAR, we relished every word as if we were hearing about the game for the first time.

Things fell apart all too quickly after that magical summer. When I first heard the rumor that Brooklyn owner Walter O'Malley was contemplating taking the Dodgers to Los Angeles, I refused to believe it, assuming he was simply jockeying for a new stadium. I hated all the talk about the need for a new stadium. When they said Ebbets Field was too small, too dilapidated, I took it as a personal insult. I couldn't imagine a more beautiful place.

I dreamed one night I was being ushered into O'Malley's office to make the case for Brooklyn. He was standing behind his desk, a diabolic look on his face that chilled my heart. But as I started to talk, his face softened and when I finished, he threw his arms around me and promised to stay at Ebbets Field. I had saved the Dodgers for Brooklyn!

In reality, of course, neither I nor anyone else could prevent the unforgivable O'Malley from completing his invidious act of betrayal. When the move was officially announced in the fall of 1957, I felt as if I, too, were being uprooted. Never again to sit in the stands at Ebbets Field, never again to watch the papers for the first news out of spring training, it was impossible to imagine.

My sense of being uprooted was real. As the 1958 season got under way, a weird, empty season with neither the Dodgers nor the Giants in New York, my mother suffered another heart attack. As before, she was taken away, but this time she didn't return. Six months later, we sold our house and moved to an apartment. My father couldn't bear sleeping in his bedroom without my mother.

Suddenly, my feelings for baseball seemed an aspect of my departing youth, to be discarded along with my childhood freckles and my collection of *Archie* comics. I didn't entirely forget about baseball during those last years in high school, but without a team to root for, my emotions became detached; my heart wasn't in it anymore.

Then, one September day, having settled in Massachusetts while getting my Ph.D. at Harvard, I agreed, half reluctantly, to go to Fenway Park. There it was again: the cozy ball field scaled to human dimensions so that every word of encouragement and every scornful yell could be heard on the field; the fervent crowd that could, with equal passion, curse a player for today's failures after cheering his heroics the day before; the team that always seemed to break your heart in the last weeks of the season. It was love at first sight as I found myself directing all my old intensities toward my new team—the Boston Red Sox.

By this time, my dad had become a Mets fan so there was no need to feel guilty about my new love. Indeed, my return to baseball reinforced the old link between my father and me: providing endlessly absorbing topics for conversation. Once again our talks produced a sequence of

15

20

mental images, vivid recollections of similar plays from the past; once again, we were united by an easy affection.

In the summer of 1972, while I was still single and teaching at Harvard, my father died. He had just settled down in his favorite chair to watch the Mets when he suffered a fatal heart attack. I remember the inconsolable feeling that the children I hoped to have someday would never know this extraordinary man, who had given me such steadfast love for so many years.

When I got married and had children my passion for the Sox assumed a strange urgency: at times I felt almost as if I were circling back to my childhood, as I found myself following the same rituals with my sons that I had practiced with my father. At Fenway Park, there are a number of ramps one can take to get from the crowded concession stands selling hot dogs, Cokes, tacos, and beer to the interior of the park itself. Ramp 33 is "my" ramp—with a curious attachment to a ritual my father followed by entering Ebbets Field at the same angle each time, I find myself walking up exactly the same ramp every game so that my first sight of the field comes at the same angle.

Indeed, sometimes when I close my eyes against the sun as I sit with my boys at Fenway, I am suddenly back at Ebbets Field, a young girl once more in the presence of my father, watching the players of my youth on the grassy field below. There is magic in these moments, for when I open my eyes and see my sons in the place where my father once sat, I feel an invisible bond among our three generations, an anchor of loyalty linking my sons to the grandfather whose face they have never seen, but whose person they have come to know through this most timeless of all sports.

When the Sox won the pennant in 1986, my boys were absolutely certain they would win the World Series. I, of course, was less sure, having been at the edge of victory so many times before only to see my hopes dashed at the final moment. Yet by the sixth game, with the Sox leading 3 games to 2 over the Mets and ahead 5–3 in the bottom of the tenth, I told my husband to break out the champagne. Then, of course, in an agonizing replay of the Bobby Thomson fiasco, Boston first baseman Bill Buckner let a routine grounder slip through his legs and the Mets came back to win both the game and the World Series.

25

I tried to control my emotions but I couldn't. "Mom, it's all right," my boys consoled me. "They'll win next year. Don't worry."

Oh, my God, I thought. These kids don't know yet that the Sox haven't won since 1918, that this may be as close as they will ever come in any of our lifetimes. Suddenly I felt possessed of a terrible wisdom that I did not ever want to impart to my children.

"Right," I said. "Wait till next year."

Topics for Critical Thinking and Writing

1. In paragraph 17 Goodwin says "neither I nor anyone else could prevent the unforgivable O'Malley from completing his invidious act of betrayal." What was O'Malley's "act of betrayal"? And how would you characterize Goodwin's style here?

2. In paragraph 20 how does Goodwin characterize baseball? What does she *leave out* of her characterization? In a paragraph try to create an impression of a game, focusing on a particular angle to highlight.

3. In her next-to-last paragraph Goodwin writes of a "terrible wisdom" but does not define it. What was the wisdom?

4. If you ever have been a fan of baseball or some other sport, write a narrative essay explaining how you came to be a fan and whether or not your enthusiasm continues.

Ted Solotaroff

Ted Solotaroff, a distinguished editor and writer, was an editor of Commentary *and the editor of* Bookweek. *He founded the literary journal* American Review *and is the author of* The Red-Hot Vacuum *(1970) and* A Few Good Voices in My Head *(1987), two acclaimed books of criticism and cultural commentary.* Truth Comes in Blows *(1998), for which he won the PEN award for memoirs, is about Solotaroff's coming-of-age: at home, in school, and on the playing fields of Elizabeth, New Jersey. It is, in particular, a memorable story of his resistance to the assaults of an irascible and domineering father.*

You're Not Catholic, Are You?

My crush on the St. Genevieve guys was specific and long-standing. One Saturday evening that July, seven or eight of them, including the three vaunted Ward brothers, turned up at the school playground and got a softball game going. It was sort of like the summer league again, and again I was put in the outfield as one of the younger and weaker players. But I made a couple of nice catches and threw out a runner at third, and the positive image of myself took over, which I was then calling "rangy."

Until that evening I had been just another one of the playground kids hanging around on the fringe of the St. Genevieve crowd, a secret fan of their athletic skills, parochial prep school culture, Irish Catholic ways. George Tiernan, whom I knew best, since he lived across from the school, was on the track team at Seton Hall in South Orange. Howie Newhart pitched for the junior varsity at St. Benedict's in Newark. Miles Gilson, the "brain" in the group, went to Xavier in New York. Jim and Jack Ward, the twins, had gone to my junior high, where they were star ends on the football team and forwards on the basketball team. Next year their brother Shrimp would go there and become the dominant athlete, because he was even tougher than the twins. (He would later be an All-American lineman at Maryland.) The others traveled to prep schools an hour or more from

Elizabeth and had to handle hours of homework in Latin and Ethics and something called Rhetoric as well as much tougher versions of the math, science, and history that were taught in the public schools. It all seemed very strict and yet bracing, a Marine boot camp for the mind.

Over the last summer or two I had become friendly with George Tiernan, a quiet, solid teenager, two years older than I. We had listened at his house to the All-Star game, which Ted Williams had won with a home run in the ninth, a great climax to a game that was particularly memorable because it had taken me into my first Catholic home. George lived with his aunt, because his mother had died. She was an elderly woman whose face was covered in faded freckles, and her presence seemed as stiff and dry as a carton of old curtains. For refreshments she gave us a box of Vermont maple sugar to share. I had never tasted it before, and its too-sweet, crumbly texture in my mouth also seemed part of this austere atmosphere where a mother had died. This, too, was somehow Catholic, death being easily associated in my fervent curiosity with the severe clothes and faces of real-life priests who gave people last rites all the time, and the even more perturbing black-and-white habits and the bare, pallid faces of nuns that made them seem like God's witches.

Normally after an evening game like this one the St. Genevieve guys went off together and I went home by myself. But tonight George asked me if I wanted to come along. They were going to Felber's for a soda, then they all had to go to confession, but after that they would hang out somewhere. There was a welcome in the others' faces as well, at least some of them, including Jim Ward's, the nicest of the Ward brothers. He had always called me Ted instead of Solly or Sol as the others did, one or two of them with a mock-Yiddish "Sz." But tonight they were all calling me Ted or Sol without a smirk in it, dealing me into the conversation, as I elatedly straggled along with them up Shelley Avenue, as though a new person, a confident, rangy athlete and full American, was being born inside of me.

A half hour later I was sitting by myself on the front steps of Miles Gilson's nice house across the street from St. Genevieve's, where they had left me while they went inside for confession. Tommy Hopkins and Jim Curry, who were my age, were serving as altar boys at mass the next day, but they all had to confess their sins, as George Tiernan had explained to me, so that they could do penance for them and receive Holy Communion at mass. On the way over, there had been a lot of casual talk about the priests and even jokes and teasing about serving and confession and so forth, but these practices of their religion invested it with a moral and spiritual aura in my mind and made its rules loom with a compelling power. Here were the best athletes and the toughest fighters in my end of Elmora, who for all of their horsing around about it took their religion seriously and respected its obligations.

5

As I sat there in the quiet darkness, gazing through the spiked iron fence at the handsome gray stone church, the words "serve" and "confession," "penance" and "Holy Communion" and "high mass," entered and rose in my mind like solemn, thrilling music. It was like the moment in a movie when some unlikely person steps forward and sings "Ave Maria" beautifully, and a great hush of reverence descends on all of the characters, even if they are in prison. I had no idea what a mass was or why people believed that a little wafer and a sip of wine could contain the body and blood of Jesus Christ, but the idea of getting your sins off your chest by saying a few prayers that cleaned up your conscience seemed like a wonderful gift from your religion, particularly for someone like myself who kept doing things he was ashamed of.

As I sat there pondering the trade-off between going to confession and having to go to a school for eight years where the priests cuffed your ear and the nuns rapped your knuckles hard with a ruler, a figure came out of the church, and as he passed through the gate of the spiked fence, I saw that he was a priest. Nervously, I watched him cross the street and turn and walk toward the Gilson house as though my presence in this Catholic neighborhood had been reported to him. I looked away as he drew near, but he stopped and began peering at me.

"Good evening, my son," he said. "Are you staying with the Gilsons?"

I was seized by confusion. I didn't know how to address him. Half of me wanted to call him Father and half of me didn't. I managed to shake my head.

"Cat got your tongue?" he asked, his eyes crinkling. He was a small,   10
slender, elderly man, with a brisk, businesslike manner rather than a stern one.

"I'm just waiting here," I said. "I'm a friend of George Tiernan's. He and Miles and the others are at confession and Miles said I could wait here for them."

"I don't think I've seen you before. Do you live in the neighborhood?"

"No . . . " I said, my mind again tripping and falling flat over the Father word. But I wanted to say something that would show him respect, that would use my good manners, so that he wouldn't think that I was some dumb Italian or Greek kid from the Port, or one of the Jewish louts who shot pool at the YMHA, which were the ways I saw myself in his eyes. So I said, "No, sir. I'm from the Shelley Avenue neighborhood, near where George lives. We were all playing softball together."

"I see," he said. "Just cooling off." He continued looking at me. "You're not Catholic, are you?"

I shook my head.   15

"I thought for a moment you might be. You look Italian. What's your name?"

I told him. I had to say it twice and then spell it for him to get it. Then I said, "It's Jewish."

"It sounds Russian," he said in his brisk way. "Is your nationality Russian?"

"No, it's American. My parents were both born here."

"I was wondering about your extraction. Of course we're all Americans now," he said. "And we all worship the same God, don't we?"   20

I nodded, not wanting him to know that I didn't worship God in the way he meant. I was afraid he would ask me why I wasn't home or at temple on my Sabbath, though by now it was already over.

After he went on, I thought about what it would be like to be Catholic, to have someone like him in my life who was in charge of the part of me that wanted to behave better and whom I could call Father. I said the word aloud several times, trying it out. "Yes, Father." "No, Father." Then I said, "Father, I have sinned." It seemed the best thing of all about being Catholic.

But also, as I realized, the thing that made being Catholic most remote from me. My taking bar mitzvah lessons had nothing to do with worshiping God in the way that George and Miles and the others were doing right now. I liked and respected Rabbi Halberstadter, but he was not someone I could go to and say, "Rabbi, I have sinned. I have jerked off every night this week and twice today at The Shop," or "I have teased my sister until she cried," or "I have broken three windows in the Shelley Avenue school and can't stop." Learning my *haftorah* from him had nothing to do with my conscience or with the feelings that made me pray on the beach in Belmar.

Once I started thinking about Rabbi Halberstadter I came in touch again with what prevented me from calling the priest Father, what made the word as I breathed it now both a self-mockery and a betrayal. I looked across the street again at St. Genevieve's, but what I saw now was not the graceful portals and arches but the black iron fence in front of it with its grim spikes on which it was said a boy climbing over them was once so badly injured that he'd almost lost his leg from blood poisoning. While the building receded again into the remoteness of its doctrines and practices, the fence came forbiddingly forward as a barrier not only to it but to the different person I had felt like with the St. Genevieve boys. Now there was just me again; a few good catches didn't change anything, didn't make me belong with the St. Genevieve guys. I got to my feet and hurried away before they came out of confession.

Topics for Critical Thinking and Writing

1. Observe the passages of description in this excerpt, of George's aunt, for example, and of St. Genevieve's church. As you reread them, ask yourself: What is the effect of these passages? What do they disclose about the narrator?

2. Solotaroff recalls his difficulty in addressing the priest, who approaches him while he is waiting for his friends, and in the concluding paragraph he calls

his breathing the word "father" a "self-mockery and a betrayal." What does he mean here? A betrayal of what or of whom?

3. Have you ever imagined what it would be like to be someone very different from yourself? If so, what made you realize that you could not become that person?

Eudora Welty

Eudora Welty (1909–2001) was born in Jackson, Mississippi. Although she earned a bachelor's degree at the University of Wisconsin, and she spent a year studying advertising in New York City at the Columbia University Graduate School of Business, she lived almost all of her life in Jackson.

In the preface to her Collected Stories *she says:*

I have been told, both in approval and in accusation, that I seem to love all my characters. What I do in writing of any character is to try to enter into the mind, heart and skin of a human being who is not myself. Whether this happens to be a man or a woman, old or young, with skin black or white, the primary challenge lies in making the jump itself. It is the act of a writer's imagination that I set most high.

In addition to writing stories and novels, Welty wrote a book about fiction, The Eye of the Story *(1977), and a memoir,* One Writer's Beginnings *(1984), from which we reprint the following excerpt.*

The Secret

It was when my mother came out onto the sleeping porch to tell me goodnight that her trial came. The sudden silence in the double bed meant my younger brothers had both keeled over in sleep, and I in the single bed at my end of the porch would be lying electrified, waiting for this to be the night when she'd tell me what she'd promised for so long. Just as she bent to kiss me I grabbed her and asked: "Where do babies come from?"

My poor mother! But something saved her every time. Almost any night I put the baby question to her, suddenly, as if the whole outdoors exploded, Professor Holt would start to sing. The Holts lived next door; he taught penmanship (the Palmer Method), typing, bookkeeping and shorthand at the high school. His excitable voice traveled out of their diningroom windows across the two driveways between our houses, and up to our upstairs sleeping porch. His wife, usually so quiet and gentle, was his uncannily spirited accompanist at the piano.

"High-ho! Come to the Fair!" he'd sing, unless he sang "Oho ye oho ye, who's bound for the ferry, the briar's in bud and the sun's going down!"

"Dear, this isn't a very good time for you to hear Mother, is it?"

She couldn't get started. As soon as she'd whisper something, Professor Holt galloped into the chorus, "And 'tis but a penny to Twickenham town!" "Isn't that enough?" she'd ask me. She'd told me that the mother and the father had to both *want* the baby. This couldn't be enough. I knew she was not trying to fib to me, for she never did fib, but also I could not help but know she was not really *telling* me. And more than that, I was afraid of what I was going to hear next. This was partly because she wanted to tell me in the dark. I thought *she* might be afraid. In something like childish hopelessness I thought she probably *couldn't* tell, just as she *couldn't* lie.

On the night we came the closest to having it over with, she started to tell me without being asked, and I ruined it by yelling, "Mother, look at the lightning bugs!"

In those days, the dark was dark. And all the dark out there was filled with the soft, near lights of lightning bugs. They were everywhere, flashing on the slow, horizontal move, on the upswings, rising and subsiding in the soundless dark. Lightning bugs signaled and answered back without a stop, from down below all the way to the top of our sycamore tree. My mother just gave me a businesslike kiss and went on back to Daddy in their room at the front of the house. Distracted by lightning bugs, I had missed my chance. The fact is she never did tell me.

I doubt that any child I knew ever was told by her mother any more than I was about babies. In fact, I doubt that her own mother ever told her any more than she told me, though there were five brothers who were born after Mother, one after the other, and she was taking care of babies all her childhood.

Not being able to bring herself to open that door to reveal its secret, one of those days, she opened another door.

In my mother's bottom bureau drawer in her bedroom she kept treasures of hers in boxes, and had given me permission to play with one of them—a switch of her own chestnut-colored hair, kept in a heavy bright braid that coiled around like a snake inside a cardboard box. I hung it from her doorknob and unplaited it; it fell in ripples nearly to the floor, and it satisfied the Rapunzel in me to comb it out. But one day I noticed in the same drawer a small white cardboard box such as her engraved calling cards came in from the printing house. It was tightly closed, but I opened it, to find to my puzzlement and covetousness two polished buffalo nickels, embedded in white cotton. I rushed with this opened box to my mother and asked if I could run out and spend the nickels.

"No!" she exclaimed in a most passionate way. She seized the box into her own hands. I begged her; somehow I had started to cry. Then she sat down, drew me to her, and told me that I had had a little brother who had come before I did, and who had died as a baby before I was born. And these two nickels that I'd wanted to claim as my find were his. They had lain on his eyelids, for a purpose untold and unimaginable. "He was a fine little baby, my first baby, and he shouldn't have died. But he did. It was because your mother almost died at the same time," she told me. "In looking after me, they too nearly forgot about the little baby."

She'd told me the wrong secret—not how babies could come but how they could die, how they could be forgotten about.

I wondered in after years: how could my mother have kept those two coins? Yet how could someone like herself have disposed of them in any way at all? She suffered from a morbid streak which in all the life of the family reached out on occasions—the worst occasions—and touched us, clung around us, making it worse for her; her unbearable moments could find nowhere to go.

The future story writer in the child I was must have taken unconscious note and stored it away then: one secret is liable to be revealed in the place of another that is harder to tell, and the substitute secret when nakedly exposed is often the more appalling.

Perhaps telling me what she did was made easier for my mother by the two secrets, told and still not told, being connected in her deepest feeling, more intimately than anyone ever knew, perhaps even herself. So far as I remember now, this is the only time this baby was ever mentioned in my presence. So far as I can remember, and I've tried, he was never mentioned in the presence of my father, for whom he had been named. I am only certain that my father, who could never bear pain very well, would not have been able to bear it.

It was my father (my mother told me at some later date) who saved her own life, after that baby was born. She had in fact been given up by the doctor, as she had long been unable to take any nourishment. (That was the illness when they'd cut her hair, which formed the switch in the same bureau drawer.) What had struck her was septicemia, in those days nearly always fatal. What my father did was to try champagne.

I once wondered where he, who'd come not very long before from an Ohio farm, had ever heard of such a remedy, such a measure. Or perhaps as far as he was concerned he invented it, out of the strength of desperation. It would have been desperation augmented because champagne couldn't be bought in Jackson. But somehow he knew what to do about that too. He telephoned to Canton, forty miles north, to an Italian orchard grower, Mr. Trolio, told him the necessity, and asked, begged, that he put a bottle of his wine on Number 3, which was due in a few minutes to stop in Canton to "take on water" (my father knew everything about train schedules). My father would be waiting to meet the train in Jackson. Mr. Trolio did—he sent the bottle in a bucket of ice and my father snatched it off the baggage car. He offered my mother a glass of chilled champagne and she drank it and kept it down. She was to live, after all.

15

Now, her hair was long again, it would reach in a braid down her back, and now I was her child. She hadn't died. And when I came, I hadn't died either. Would she ever? Would I ever? I couldn't face *ever*. I must have rushed into her lap, demanding her like a baby. And she had to put her first-born aside again, for me.

 ## Topics for Critical Thinking and Writing

1. Welty writes, "I doubt that any child I knew ever was told by her mother any more than I was about babies." This was probably true for her generation. How true is it of yours?

2. In the biographical note we quote Welty as saying: "What I do in writing of any character is to try to enter into the mind, heart and skin of a human being who is not myself." Here she is doubtless writing about her fiction, but how well does her note apply to her portrait of her mother? In your own words, describe Welty's mother and then explain where in the manuscript you located the evidence.

3. What secret or secrets were there in your family or among your friends? Write an essay, 750 to 1000 words, describing your attempt to have the secret disclosed and your success or failure.

Tobias Wolff

*Tobias Wolff was born in Alabama in 1945, but he grew up in the state of Washington. He left high school before graduating, served as an apprentice seaman and as a weight-guesser in a carnival, and then joined the army, where he served four years as a paratrooper. After his discharge from the army, he hired private tutors to enable him to pass the entrance degree to Oxford University. At Oxford be did spectacularly well, graduating with First Class Honors in English. Wolff has written stories, novels, and an autobiography (*This Boy's Life*); he now teaches writing at Syracuse University.*

Powder

Just before Christmas my father took me skiing at Mount Baker. He'd had to fight for the privilege of my company, because my mother was still angry with him for sneaking me into a nightclub during his last visit, to see Thelonius Monk.

He wouldn't give up. He promised, hand on heart, to take good care of me and have me home for dinner on Christmas Eve, and she relented.

Tobias Wolff, from *This Boy's Life*. Copyright © 1989 by Tobias Wolff. Used by permission of Grove/Atlantic, Inc.

But as we were checking out of the lodge that morning it began to snow, and in this snow he observed some quality that made it necessary for us to get in one last run. We got in several last runs. He was indifferent to my fretting. Snow whirled around us in bitter, blinding squalls, hissing like sand, and still we skied. As the lift bore us to the peak yet again, my father looked at his watch and said: "Criminey. This'll have to be a fast one."

By now I couldn't see the trail. There was no point in trying. I stuck to him like white on rice and did what he did and somehow made it to the bottom without sailing off a cliff. We returned our skis and my father put chains on the Austin-Healy while I swayed from foot to foot, clapping my mittens and wishing I were home. I could see everything. The green table-cloth, the plates with the holly pattern, the red candles waiting to be lit.

We passed a diner on our way out. "You want some soup?" my father asked. I shook my head. "Buck up," he said. "I'll get you there. Right, doctor?"

I was supposed to say, "Right, doctor," but I didn't say anything.   5

A state trooper waved us down outside the resort. A pair of saw-horses were blocking the road. The trooper came up to our car and bent down to my father's window. His face was bleached by the cold. Snowflakes clung to his eyebrows and to the fur trim of his jacket and cap.

"Don't tell me," my father said.

The trooper told him. The road was closed. It might get cleared, it might not. Storm took everyone by surprise. So much, so fast. Hard to get people moving. Christmas Eve. What can you do?

My father said: "Look. We're talking about four, five inches. I've taken this car through worse than that."

The trooper straightened up, boots creaking. His face was out of sight   10
but I could hear him. "The road is closed."

My father sat with both hands on the wheel, rubbing the wood with his thumbs. He looked at the barricade for a long time. He seemed to be trying to master the idea of it. Then he thanked the trooper, and with a weird, old-maidy show of caution turned the car around. "Your mother will never forgive me for this," he said.

"We should have left before," I said. "Doctor."

He didn't speak to me again until we were in a booth at the diner, waiting for our burgers. "She won't forgive me," he said. "Do you understand? Never."

"I guess," I said, but no guesswork was required; she wouldn't forgive him.

"I can't let that happen." He bent toward me. "I'll tell you what I   15
want. I want us to be all together again. Is that what you want?"

"Yes, sir."

He bumped my chin with his knuckles. "That's all I needed to hear."

When we finished eating he went to the pay phone in the back of the diner, then joined me in the booth again. I figured he'd called my mother, but he didn't give a report. He sipped at his coffee and stared out the window at the empty road. "Come on, come on," he said. A little while later he said, "Come on!" When the trooper's car went past, lights flashing, he got up and dropped some money on the check. "O.K. Vámonos."

The wind had died. The snow was falling straight down, less of it now; lighter. We drove away from the resort, right up to the barricade. "Move it," my father told me. When I looked at him he said, "What are you waiting for?" I got out and dragged one of the sawhorses aside, then put it back after he drove through. He pushed the door open for me. "Now you're an accomplice," he said. "We go down together." He put the car into gear and gave me a look. "Joke, doctor."

"Funny, doctor."   20

Down the first long stretch I watched the road behind us, to see if the trooper was on our tail. The barricade vanished. Then there was nothing but snow: snow on the road, snow kicking up from the chains, snow on the trees, snow in the sky; and our trail in the snow. I faced around and had a shock. The lie of the road behind us had been marked by our own tracks, but there were no tracks ahead of us. My father was breaking virgin snow between a line of tall trees. He was humming "Stars Fell on Alabama." I felt snow brush along the floorboards under my feet. To keep my hands from shaking, I clamped them between my knees.

My father grunted in a thoughtful way and said, "Don't ever try this yourself."

"I won't."

"That's what you say now, but someday you'll get your license and then you'll think you can do anything. Only you won't be able to do this. You need, I don't know—a certain instinct."

"Maybe I have it."   25

"You don't. You have your strong points, but not . . . this. I only mention it, because I don't want you to get the idea this is something just anybody can do. I'm a great driver. That's not a virtue, O.K.? It's just a fact, and one you should be aware of. Of course you have to give the old heap some credit, too—there aren't many cars I'd try this with. Listen!"

I listened. I heard the slap of the chains, the stiff, jerky rasps of the wipers, the purr of the engine. It really did purr. The car was almost new. My father couldn't afford it, and kept promising to sell it, but here it was.

I said, "Where do you think that policeman went to?"

"Are you warm enough?" He reached over and cranked up the blower. Then he turned off the wipers. We didn't need them. The clouds had brightened. A few sparse, feathery flakes drifted into our slipstream and were swept away. We left the trees and entered a broad field of snow that ran level for a while and then tilted sharply downward. Orange stakes had been planted at intervals in two parallel lines and my father steered a course between them, though they were far enough apart to leave considerable doubt in my mind as to where exactly the road lay. He was humming again, doing little scat riffs around the melody.

"O.K. then. What are my strong points?"   30
"Don't get me started," he said. "It'd take all day."
"Oh, right. Name one."
"Easy. You always think ahead."

True. I always thought ahead. I was a boy who kept his clothes on numbered hangers to insure proper rotation. I bothered my teachers for homework assignments far ahead of their due dates so I could make up schedules. I thought ahead, and that was why I knew that there would be other troopers waiting for us at the end of our ride, if we got there. What I did not know was that my father would wheedle and plead his way past them—he didn't sing "O Tannenbaum" but just about—and get me home for dinner, buying a little more time before my mother decided to make the split final. I knew we'd get caught; I was resigned to it. And maybe for this reason I stopped moping and began to enjoy myself.

Why not? This was one for the books. Like being in a speedboat, but   35
better. You can't go downhill in a boat. And it was all ours. And it kept coming, the laden trees, the unbroken surface of snow, the sudden white vistas. Here and there I saw hints of the road, ditches, fences, stakes, but not so many that I could have found my way. But then I didn't have to. My father was driving. My father in his 48th year, rumpled, kind, bankrupt of honor, flushed with certainty. He was a great driver. All persuasion, no coercion. Such subtlety at the wheel, such tactful pedalwork. I actually trusted him. And the best was yet to come—the switchbacks and hairpins. Impossible to describe. Except maybe to say this: If you haven't driven fresh powder, you haven't driven.

Topics for Critical Thinking and Writing

1. How would you characterize the father?

2. How does the boy feel about his father?

Countee Cullen

Countee Cullen (1903–46) was born Countee Porter in New York City, raised by his grandmother, and then adopted by the Reverend Frederick A. Cullen, a Methodist minister in Harlem. Cullen received a bachelor's degree from New York University (Phi Beta Kappa) and a master's degree from Harvard. He earned his living as a high school teacher of French, but his literary gifts were recognized in his own day.

Incident
(For Eric Walrond)

Once riding in old Baltimore,
   Heart-filled, head-filled with glee.
I saw a Baltimorean
   Keep looking straight at me.

Now I was eight and very small.   5
   And he was no whit bigger.
And so I smiled, but he poked out
   His tongue, and called me, "Nigger."

I saw the whole of Baltimore
   From May until December;   10
Of all the things that happened there
   That's all that I remember.

 Topics for Critical Thinking and Writing

1. How would you define an "incident"? A serious occurrence? A minor occurrence, or what? Think about the word, and then think about Cullen's use of
   it as a title for the event recorded in this poem. Test out one or two other
   possible titles as a way of helping yourself to see the strengths or weaknesses of Cullen's title.

2. The dedicatee, Eric Walrond (1898–1966), was an African-American essayist and writer of fiction, who in an essay, "On Being Black," had described
   his experiences of racial prejudice. How does the presence of the dedication
   bear on our response to Cullen's account of the "incident"?

3. What is the tone of the poem? Indifferent? Angry? Or what? What do you
   think is the speaker's attitude toward the "incident"? What is your attitude?

4. Ezra Pound, poet and critic, once defined literature as "news that *stays*
   news." What do you think he meant by this? Do you think that the definition fits Cullen's poem?

CHAPTER 7

A Sense of Place

Navajo Dancers Entertaining a Tourist Train, June 1963, Durango, Colorado
George Hight

Pearblossom Hwy.
David Hockney, April 11–18, 1986

Buzz Aldrin on the Moon
Neil Armstrong, 1969

Short Views

All places are distant from heaven alike.
> *Robert Burton*

One always begins to forgive a place as soon as it's left behind.
> *Charles Dickens*

A place belongs forever to whoever claims it hardest, remembers it most obsessively, wrenches it from itself, shapes it, renders it, loves it so radically that he remakes it in his own image.
> *Joan Didion*

Why do you wonder that globe-trotting does not help you, seeing that you always take yourself with you? The reason which set you wandering is ever at your heels.
> *Seneca the Younger*

I have traveled a good deal in Concord.
> *Henry David Thoreau*

Walden Pond
9900 12th Avenue West
Everett, Washington 98204
BRAND NEW AND BEAUTIFUL! Presenting Walden Pond, the residential community catering to those who have come to expect a quality residence to welcome them home. Conveniently located near schools, Walter Hall Golf Course, Everett Mall, Boeing, ferry, restaurants, shopping, Puget Sound, Mukilteo and other recreation / entertainment.
> *Greater Puget Sound Apartment Guide*

I had to leave home so I could find myself, find my own intrinsic nature buried under the personality that had been imposed on me.
> *Gloria Anzaldúa*

Mid pleasures and palaces though we may roam,
Be it ever so humble, there's no place like home.
> *John Howard Payne*

Home is the place where, when you have to go there,
They have to take you in.
> *Robert Frost*

Home is the place you can go when you're whipped.
> *Muhammad Ali*

It is typical, in America, that a person's hometown is not the place
where he is living now but is the place he left behind.
> *Margaret Mead and Rhoda Metraux*

Washington is a city of Southern efficiency and Northern charm.
> *John F. Kennedy*

A book of verses underneath the bough,
A jug of wine, a loaf of bread—and Thou
  Beside me singing in the wilderness—
Oh, Wilderness were Paradise enow!
> *Omar Khayyam, trans. Edward FitzGerald*

To me heaven would be a big bull ring with me holding two bar-
rera seats and a trout stream outside that no one else was allowed
to fish in and two lovely houses in the town; one where I would
have my wife and children and be monogamous and love them
truly and well and the other where I would have my nine beautiful mistresses on nine different floors.
> *Ernest Hemingway*

Louis Owens

Louis Owens, born in 1948, describes himself as "a mixed-blood American of Choctaw, Cherokee, and Irish-American heritage." He is a professor of English at the University of California at Davis, where he specializes in Native American writing, but before he became a teacher and a writer he worked as a firefighter and wilderness ranger.

Owens's essay should be read in the context of the Wilderness Act of 1964, which defines a wilderness thus: "A wilderness, in contrast with those areas where man and his own works dominate the landscape, is hereby recognized as an area where the earth itself and its community of life are untrammeled by man, where man himself is a visitor who does not remain."

The American Indian Wilderness

In the center of the Glacier Peak Wilderness in northern Washington, a magnificent, fully glaciated white volcano rises over a stunningly beautiful region of the North Cascades. On maps, the mountain is called Glacier Peak. To the Salishan people who have always lived in this part of the Cascades, however, the mountain is *Dakobed*, or the Great Mother, the place of emergence. For more than eighty years, a small, three-sided log shelter stood in a place called White Pass just below one shoulder of the great mountain, tucked securely into a meadow between thick stands of mountain hemlock and alpine fir.

In the early fall of seventy-six, while working as a seasonal ranger for the U.S. Forest Service, I drew the task of burning the White Pass shelter. After all those years, the shelter roof had collapsed like a broken bird wing under the weight of winter snow, and the time was right for fire and replanting. It was part of a Forest Service plan to remove all human-made objects from wilderness areas, a plan of which I heartily approved. So I backpacked eleven miles to the pass and set up camp, and for five days, while a bitter early storm sent snow driving horizontally out of the north, I dismantled the shelter and burned the old logs, piling and burning and piling and burning until nothing remained. The antique, hand-forged spikes that had held the shelter together I put into gunny sacks and cached to be packed out later by mule. I spaded up the earth beaten hard for nearly a century by boot and hoof, and transplanted plugs of vegetation from hidden spots on the nearby ridge.

At the end of those five days, not a trace of the shelter remained, and I felt good, very smug in fact, about returning the White Pass meadow to its "original" state. As I packed up my camp, the snowstorm had subsided to a few flurries and a chill that felt bone-deep with the promise of winter. My season was almost over, and as I started the steep hike down to the trailhead my mind was on the winter I was going to spend in sunny Arizona.

Louis Owens, "The American Indian Wilderness" from the *American Nature Writing Newsletter*, Fall 1994. Reprinted by permission of the author.

A half-mile from the pass I saw the two old women. At first they were dark, hunched forms far down on the last long switchback up the snowy ridge. But as we drew closer to one another, I began to feel a growing amazement that, by the time we were face-to-face, had become awe. Almost swallowed up in their baggy wool pants, heavy sweaters and parkas, silver braids hanging below thick wool caps, they seemed ancient, each weighted with at least seventy years as well as a small backpack. They paused every few steps to lean on their staffs and look out over the North Fork drainage below, a deep, heavily forested river valley that rose on the far side to the glaciers and sawtoothed black granite of the Monte Cristo Range. And they smiled hugely upon seeing me, clearly surprised and delighted to find another person in the mountains at such a time.

We stood and chatted for a moment, and as I did with all backpack-   5
ers, I reluctantly asked them where they were going. The snow quickened a little, obscuring the view, as they told me that they were going to White Pass.

"Our father built a little house up here," one of them said, "when he worked for the Forest Service like you. Way back before we was born, before this century."

"We been coming up here each year since we was little," the other added. "Except last year when Sarah was not well enough."

"A long time ago, this was all our land," the one called Sarah said. "All Indi'n land everywhere you can see. Our people had houses up in the mountains, for gathering berries every year."

As they took turns speaking, the smiles never leaving their faces, I wanted to excuse myself, to edge around these elders and flee to the trail-head and my car, drive back to the district station and keep going south. I wanted to say, "I'm Indian too. Choctaw from Mississippi; Cherokee from Oklahoma"—as if mixed blood could pardon me for what I had done. Instead, I said, "The shelter is gone." Cravenly I added, "It was crushed by snow, so I was sent up to burn it. It's gone now."

I expected outrage, anger, sadness, but instead the sisters continued   10
to smile at me, their smiles changing only slightly. They had a plastic tarp and would stay dry, they said, because a person always had to be prepared in the mountains. They would put up their tarp inside the hemlock grove above the meadow, and the scaly hemlock branches would turn back the snow. They forgave me without saying it—my ignorance and my part in the long pattern of loss which they knew so well.

Hiking out those eleven miles, as the snow of the high country became a drumming rain in the forests below, I had long hours to ponder my encounter with the sisters. Gradually, almost painfully, I began to understand that what I called "wilderness" was an absurdity, nothing more than a figment of the European imagination. Before the European invasion, there was no wilderness in North America; there was only the fertile continent where people lived in a hardlearned balance with the natural world. In embracing a philosophy that saw the White Pass shelter—and all traces of humanity—as a shameful stain upon the "pure" wilderness, I had succumbed to a five-hundred-year-old pattern of deadly thinking that separates us from the natural world. This is not to say that what we call wilderness today does not need careful safeguarding. I believe that White Pass really is better off now that the shelter doesn't serve as a magnet to backpackers and horsepackers who compact the soil, disturb and kill the wildlife, cut down centuries-old trees for firewood, and leave their litter strewn about. And I believe the man who built the shelter would agree. But despite this unfortunate reality, the global environmental crisis that sends species into extinction daily and threatens to destroy all life surely has its roots in the Western pattern of thought that sees humanity and "wilderness" as mutually exclusive.

In old-growth forests in the North Cascades, deep inside the official Wilderness Area, I have come upon faint traces of log shelters built by Suiattle and Upper Skagit people for berry harvesting a century or more ago—just as the sisters said. Those human-made structures were as natural a part of the Cascade ecosystem as the burrows of marmots in the steep scree slopes. Our Native ancestors all over this continent lived within a complex web of relations with the natural world, and in doing so they assumed a responsibility for their world that contemporary Americans cannot even imagine. Unless Americans, and all human beings, can learn to imagine themselves as intimately and inextricably related to every aspect of the world they inhabit, with the extraordinary responsibilities such relationship entails—unless they can learn what the indigenous peoples of the Americas knew and often still know—the earth simply will not survive. A few square miles of something called wilderness will become the sign of failure everywhere.

Topics for Critical Thinking and Writing

1. The Forest Service commissioned Owens to "dismantle" the shelter and then to burn the logs. Does it make sense to use human beings to create a "natural" space? Explain.

2. Suppose someone said to you that human beings are a part of nature, and that their creations—let's say the three-sided shelter at White Pass—are just as "natural" as a bird's nest. What response might you make?

3. In his second paragraph Owen tells us that the Forest Service had a plan "to remove all human-made objects from wilderness areas." What can be said in behalf of such a plan? What can be said against it? By the way, given the realities of life today, can we reasonably say that parts of the country can be unshaped by human activity? If, for instance, we restore wolves to a certain area that they have long been absent from, is this area of nature really natural?

4. In his final paragraph Owens says that unless people come to understand that they are "inextricably related to every aspect of the world, . . . a few square miles of something called wilderness will become the sign of failure everywhere." What does he mean?

Sallie Bingham

Sallie Bingham, born in 1937, is known as an author (plays, fiction, a memoir) and as a strong supporter of feminist causes. She has, for instance, established the Kentucky Foundation for Women, which makes grants to women artists and which publishes a quarterly, The American Voice, *and she supports theater groups in Santa Fe and New York. By birth she is in a position to offer financial support; her grandfather, a man of immense wealth (derived largely from money he inherited from his second wife) founded the* Louisville Courier-Journal, *a major newspaper, and her father was the publisher of the paper. Sallie Bingham was active on the board of directors of the family's communications empire, but in the 1980s she was forced off the board, and she decided to sell her shares. Her memoir,* Passion and Prejudice *(1989), provides a view of life among the Binghams.*

Since 1991 Bingham has lived in Santa Fe, but "A Woman's Land" was published when she was living outside of Louisville.

A Woman's Land

Four years ago I bought a piece of wild land. Parts of it had been farmed in a haphazard sort of way, but most of it was woods, or fields on their way back to being woods. Since moving to this piece of land, which is often called a farm, I have begun to wonder about its appropriate uses and about my relation to it, as one of the very few women who own land.

So few women own land that the phrase, woman landowner, seems curious. At once we wonder how she came to own it, how she afforded it—and that recognition of the financial inequities women face obscures another question—can a woman *own* land?

We are in new territory here because we have no myths or legends, no sayings or parables to guide us. We few who own the half-acre our house stands on, or the several acres left from an old farm, or the piece of property that descended through the family, must weave our own theories; we have nothing to go on except the words of the land-patriarchs, and they have little to offer that does not offend.

Women do not usually exploit, even in situations where exploitation is possible or expected; we do not often sell our children, for example. Where poor women have been brought to barter their unborn babies for money, a concept vital to the community breaks down. The mother's heartbreak reflects the disease of her times.

Generally we are not farmers, but gardeners. We may raise a few   5
flowers or some vegetables for the table. We take from the earth what we can use, or what we can enjoy without depleting the supply. Women are not usually hunters or real-estate developers. We do not always seek to convert gifts into power or cash.

The deer in the woods seems to me to have been placed there not for my purposes or for the purposes of the hunter, but to fulfill the law of her existence: to graze, sleep, procreate, or run away from danger, without reference even to my appreciation of her beauty.

The old fields in front of and behind my house seem to exist without reference to their potential productivity. Once they were treed; now, the trees and brush would return if the farmer who rents them for corn kept his machinery in the barn for one season. The land would be revitalized, no longer scoured and soured by chemical sprays and fertilizers. Perhaps in my lifetime those elements the soil has lost would be restored—if the machinery continued to stay in the barn. But soon the "field" would no longer be a field, but a wild place, accessible only to birds and small animals that can move through briars on their hidden paths.

Yet, this would not seem to me to be the land's intention either, but that cycle of change might, once again, bring beeches into maturity on this stretch. The land is given only to itself—it exists for me as the ground under my feet, but not as a possibility, a future, a hope of gain.

Does my attitude make the land into a luxury, affordable only by the very rich, who do not need to consider productivity? If so, women must find another way, for women are not rich, almost by definition, in a sexist society where we are always in charge of the spiritual and social work that holds the community together and pays poorly.

Perhaps I can form a theory based on the communal use of my land, 10
which recognizes several purposes for this piece of common acreage: relief for my eyes and for my soul, a place for my husband's sheep to graze, a horizon for my sons to escape from and through, a place for the barn cat and her kitten to fatten off grain-fed mice, and for my friends to house and tend their special animals—the llama, the three-legged deer. These two curious animals bear, symbolically, the weight of the whole place: they exist outside of the money exchange. Does that make them the curiosities of the rich? Not quite. Their caretakers are not wealthy, and yet their wealth or lack of it does not enter into the exchange. These animals live outside of the area of commerce, or are excluded from it. They are gifts.

The sheep are not gifts. They were bought with a certain end in view: to be converted into cash. However, the sheep's symbolic meaning has changed as they have begun to share the barn with the llama and the three-legged deer. They have names, or at least some of them do. Their purpose is no longer clear.

Is this sheer sentimentality? Again, a luxury of the rich, who do not toil, nor do they spin? Or is it a recognition of the ultimate independence of the sheep (an odd expression for such dumb and dumbly obedient beasts) from our aims or plans?

What defines the land is what escapes definition: the Canada geese who light on the pond and take off with a wild flurry of wings in the morning, always towards the south; the heron outside my studio window who stood for a short while on a stone in the river. These birds did not arrive here, and pause briefly, for our edification. They exist in their own worlds, which we can barely appreciate, which we cannot penetrate or convert into cash.

But what was the motive that brought a hunter to shoot one of our rare bald eagles, so well-marked with spray paint and electronic devices? Surely the hunter was a boy or a man. Surely he sought in the killing something he could take away with him, a talisman or a boast. The need to "make something out of" the experience perhaps defines the male. A woman might have wanted to make the sighting into a story or a painting. But she would not have figured, necessarily, in that story or painting, as the hunter must figure in the shooting of the eagle. The eagle would have lived to see another day, free of the woman—the artist—and her transitory usage; the eagle did not outlive the man's aim.

I am uncomfortable suggesting that a woman's use of the land might   15
be better than a man's. Notions of women's superiority always have a sting in the tail. We carry enough weight in the world without taking on the weight of being morally superior. Yet, the fact remains that women do not destroy land, either as owners who sell off pastures for shopping centers or as employees who operate bulldozers that push down trees. Is it enough to say that we are powerless to commit this evil? I think not. A woman who is able to buy land probably learned something about its care from the way a woman without financial power tended her African violets.

But perhaps the difference in attitudes towards the land is not gender-related. Perhaps the artist, male or female, is able to see trees and open stretches as gifts, not as possibilities for conversion. Perhaps our addictive needs are satisfied by the manufacturing of words out of the landscape, rather than by the manufacturing of tract houses.

Artists who are men are often perceived as living on the fringes of their gender, stripling lads even in old age, Apollos without followers. Often they lack power and money. To the extent that their androgyny is corrupted by power and money, they become more male-like, more interested in conversion, in "making something out of." The rare successful artist who purchases land is perhaps more likely to sell off parts of it for subdivisions than the equally rare woman who can afford to buy and will preserve it.

If the gift survives the addiction, however, as it seems capable of doing, there will still be a need for a woman or an artist to appreciate it—although to all intents and purposes, that appreciation is inessential. Appreciation, if it is converted into action, can save land.

There will always be a few rich women who will endow a piece of land and will it to perpetuity, although for the land to survive, her heirs must accept that it does not belong to them. In how many cases has a woman been able to surmount her heirs' ideas of their rights and leave the land to continue "undeveloped"?

In the case of my land, the woman landowner's heirs despoiled it   20
with their motorcycles and logged out all the old trees and would have

sold it to the highest bidder for any purpose whatsoever if the lack of city water and sewage hadn't hampered their aims. It came to me almost by default.

Now, as I work on my will, I am trying to insure that the land remains open forever. This means that it will not be inherited by my sons, but will remain, as it is now, a gift. This is difficult, if not impossible, to do, first on a personal level. All children long to inherit what is of value to the parent; it is a way of receiving commitment and memories. In the case of my sons, their inevitable immersion in the patriarchy means that they will want to "make something out of" the land, should it pass to them. Leaving it to lie fallow, to grow up again with weeds, would seem an eccentric choice for a male landowner.

On another level, the patriarchy itself is dead set against my decision. The right of sons to inherit is fundamental to capitalism, and to the more secretive continuation of a ruling class. How then can heirs be taught to see the land as a gift? Only by stroking the three-legged deer and looking at the silent llama.

Topics for Critical Thinking and Writing

1. What sort of persona does Bingham reveal? Point to specific passages that in your view especially clearly establish her persona.

2. Bingham says (paragraph 2) that "few" women own land. Think of the landowners whom you know. Do the men greatly outnumber the women? Do the women who own land seem different from those who don't? Explain.

3. In paragraph 10 Bingham very briefly introduces two "special animals—the llama, the three-legged deer." She goes on to say, in the same paragraph, "These two curious animals bear, symbolically, the weight of the whole place: they exist outside of the money exchange." What does she mean? (Notice that these animals return in the final—crucial—paragraph.)

4. In several passages Bingham wonders whether her views are possible only for the rich. Consider, for example, the first sentence in paragraph 9: "Does my attitude make the land into a luxury, affordable only by the very rich, who do not need to consider productivity?" Does she, in your view, have anything to say to persons who are not in a position to own land without putting it to use?

5. In the last sentence of paragraph 15 Bingham says, "A woman who is able to buy land probably learned something about its care from the way a woman without financial power tended her African violets." What does she mean? Do you think she is right? Explain.

6. In paragraph 4 Bingham says that "women do not usually exploit, even in situations where exploitation is possible or expected; we do not often sell

our children, for example." Assuming the truth of Bingham's earlier assertion that women landowners are few, consider other areas in which exploitation may occur. As you think about this issue, consider whether you know women who exploit other women, or their spouses, or their children, or their parents, or their co-workers. And then consider the men whom you know, and the degree to which they exploit land or people. Based on your firsthand knowledge, write an essay of about 250–500 words, evaluating Bingham's assertion that "women do not usually exploit."

Bill McKibben

Bill McKibben, born in California in 1960 and educated at Harvard, became a staff writer for The New Yorker, *and then became a freelance writer, publishing in numerous magazines including the* New York Review of Books, Rolling Stone, *and* The New Republic. *Among his many books are* The End of Nature *(1989),* The Age of Missing Information *(1992), and* A Year of Living Strenuously *(2000).*

Now or Never

When global warming first emerged as a potential crisis in the late '80s, one academic analyst called it "the public policy problem from hell." The years since have only proven him more astute—15 years into our understanding of climate change, we have yet to figure out how we're going to tackle it. And environmentalists are just as clueless as anyone else: Do we need to work on lifestyles or on lobbying, on politics or on photovoltaics? And is there a difference? How well we handle global warming will determine what kind of century we inhabit—and indeed what kind of planet we leave behind to everyone and everything that follows us down into geologic time. It is *the* environmental question, the one that cuts closest to home and also floats off most easily into the abstract. So far it has been the ultimate "can't get there from here" problem, but the time has come to draw a roadmap—one that may help us deal with the handful of other issues on the list of real, world-shattering problems.

The first thing to know about global warming is this: The science is sound. In 1988, when scientists first testified before Congress about the potential for rapid and destabilizing climate change, they were still describing a hypothesis. It went like this: Every time human beings burn coal, gas, oil, wood or any other carbon-based fuel, they emit large quantities of carbon dioxide. (A car emits its own weight in carbon annually if

Bill McKibben, "Now or Never," *In These Times*, April 10, 2001. Reprinted by permission of the publisher.

you drive it the average American distance.) This carbon dioxide accumulates in the atmosphere. It's not a normal pollutant—it doesn't poison you, or change the color of the sunset. But it does have one interesting property: Its molecular structure traps heat near the surface of the planet that would otherwise radiate back out to space. It acts like the panes of glass on a greenhouse.

The hypothesis was that we were putting enough carbon dioxide into the atmosphere to make a difference. The doubters said no—that the earth would compensate for any extra carbon by forming extra clouds and cooling the planet, or through some other feedback mechanism. And so, as scientists will, they went at it. For five years—lavishly funded by governments that wanted to fund research instead of making politically unpopular changes—scientists produced paper after paper. They studied glacial cores and tree rings and old pollen sediments in lake beds to understand past climates; they took temperature measurements on the surface and from space; they refined their computer models and ran them backward in time to see if they worked. By 1995 they had reached a conclusion. That year the Intergovernmental Panel on Climate Change (IPCC), a group of all the world's climatologists assembled under the auspices of the United Nations, announced that human beings were indeed heating up the planet.

The scientists kept up the pace of their research for the next five years, and in the past five months have published a series of massive updates to their findings. These results are uniformly grimmer than even five years before. They include:

- The prediction that humans will likely heat the planet 4 to 6 degrees Fahrenheit in this century, twice as much as earlier forecast, taking global temperatures to a level not seen in millions of years, and never before in human history.
- The worst-case possibility that we will raise the temperature by as much as 11 degrees Fahrenheit, a true science-fiction scenario that no one had seriously envisaged before.
- The near certainty that these temperature increases will lead to rises in sea level of at least a couple of feet.
- The well-documented fear that disease will spread quickly as vectors like mosquitoes expand their range to places that used to be too cool for their survival.

But it isn't just the scientists who are hard at work on this issue. For the past five years, it's almost as if the planet itself has been peer-reviewing their work. We've had the warmest years on record—including 1998, which was warmer than any year for which records exist. And those hot years have shown what even small changes in temperature—barely a degree Fahrenheit averaged globally—can do to the earth's systems.

Consider hydrology, for instance. Warm air holds more water vapor than cold air, so there is an increase in evaporation in dry areas, and hence

5

more drought—something that has been documented on every continent. Once that water is in the atmosphere, it's going to come down some-where—and indeed we have seen the most dramatic flooding ever recorded in recent years. In 1998, 300 million humans, one in 20 of us, had to leave their homes for a week, a month, a year, forever because of rising waters.

Or look at the planet's cryosphere, its frozen places. Every alpine gla-cier is in retreat; the snows of Kilimanjaro will have vanished by 2015; and the Arctic ice cap is thinning fast—data collected by U.S. and Soviet nuclear submarines show that it is almost half gone compared with just four decades ago.

In other words, human beings are changing the planet more funda-mentally in the course of a couple of decades than in all the time since we climbed down from the trees and began making clever use of our oppos-able thumbs. There's never been anything like this.

Yet to judge from the political response, this issue ranks well below, say, the estate tax as a cause for alarm and worry. In 1988, there was enough public outcry that George Bush the Elder promised to combat "the greenhouse effect with the White House effect." In 1992, Bill Clinton promised that Americans would emit no more carbon dioxide by 2000 than they had in 1990—and that his administration would do the work of starting to turn around our ocean liner of an economy, laying the founda-tion for the transition to a world of renewable energy.

That didn't happen, of course. Fixated on the economy, Clinton and Gore presided over a decade when Americans, who already emitted a quarter of the world's carbon dioxide, actually managed to increase their total output by 12 percent. Now we have a president who seems unsure whether global warming is real, and far more concerned with increasing power production than with worrying about trifles like the collapse of the globe's terrestrial systems. In November, the hope of global controls on carbon dioxide production essentially collapsed at an international con-ference in the Hague, when the United States refused to make even mod-est concessions on its use of fossil fuels, and the rest of the world finally walked away from the table in disgust.

In the face of all this, what is an environmentalist to do? The normal answer, when you're mounting a campaign, is to look for self-interest, to scare people by saying what will happen to us if we don't do something: all the birds will die, the canyon will disappear beneath a reservoir, we will choke to death on smog.

But in the case of global warming, those kind of answers don't exactly do the trick, at least in the timeframe we're discussing. At this latitude, cli-mate change will creep up on us. Severe storms have already grown more frequent and more damaging. The seasons are less steady in their pro-gression. Some agriculture is less reliable. But face it: Our economy is so enormous that it handles those kinds of changes in stride. Economists who work on this stuff talk about how it will shave a percentage or two off GNP over the next few decades—not enough to notice in the kind of generalized economic boom they describe. And most of us live lives so divorced from the natural world that we hardly notice the changes anyway. Hotter? Turn up the air conditioning. Stormier? Well, an enormous percentage of Americans commute from remote-controlled garage to office parking garage—they may have gone the last year without getting good and wet in a rainstorm. By the time the magnitude of the change is truly in our faces, it will be too late to do much about it: There's such a lag time with carbon dioxide in the atmosphere that we need to be making the switch to solar and wind and hydrogen right about now. Yesterday, in fact.

So maybe we should think of global warming in a different way—as the great moral crisis of our moment, the equivalent in our time of the civil rights movement of the '60s.

Why a moral question? In the first place, because we've never figured out a more effective way to screw the marginalized and poor of this planet. Having taken their dignity, their resources and their freedom under a variety of other schemes, we now are taking the very physical stability on which they depend for the most bottom-line of existences.

Our economy can absorb these changes for a while, but for a moment consider Bangladesh. A river delta that houses 130 million souls in an area the size of Wisconsin, Bangladesh actually manages food self-sufficiency most years. But in 1998, the sea level in the Bay of Bengal was higher than normal, just the sort of thing we can expect to become more frequent and severe. The waters sweeping down the Ganges and the Brahmaputra from the Himalayas could not drain easily into the ocean—they backed up across the country, forcing most of its inhabitants to spend three months in thigh-deep water. The fall rice crop didn't get planted. We've seen this same kind of disaster in the last few years in Mozambique or Honduras or Venezuela or any of a dozen other wretched spots.

And a moral crisis, too, if you place any value on the rest of creation. Coral reef researchers indicate that these spectacularly intricate ecosystems are also spectacularly vulnerable—rising water temperatures will likely bleach them to extinction by mid-century. In the Arctic, polar bears are 20 percent scrawnier than they were a decade ago: As pack ice melts, so does the opportunity for hunting seals. All in all, this century seems poised to see extinctions at a rate not observed since the last big asteroid slammed into the planet. But this time the asteroid is us.

A moral question, finally, if you think we owe any debt to the future. No one ever has figured out a more thorough-going way to stripmine the present and degrade what comes after. Forget the seventh generation—we're talking 70th generation, and 700th. All the people that will ever be related to you. Ever. No generation yet to come will ever forget us—we are the ones present at the moment when the temperature starts to spike,

15

and so far we have not reacted. If it had been done to us, we would loathe the generation that did it, precisely as we will one day be loathed.

But trying to make a moral campaign is no easy task. In most moral crises, there is a villain—some person or class or institution that must be overcome. Once they're identified, the battle can commence. But you can't really get angry at carbon dioxide, and the people responsible for its production are, well, us. So perhaps we need some symbols to get us started, some places to sharpen the debate and rally ourselves to action. There are plenty to choose from: our taste for ever bigger houses and the heating and cooling bills that come with them; our penchant for jumping on airplanes at the drop of a hat; and so on. But if you wanted one glaring example of our lack of balance, you could do worse than point the finger at sport utility vehicles.

SUVs are more than mere symbol. They are a major part of the problem—one reason we emit so much more carbon dioxide now than we did a decade ago is because our fleet of cars and trucks actually has gotten steadily less fuel efficient for the past 10 years. If you switched today from the average American car to a big SUV, and drove it for just one year, the difference in carbon dioxide that you produced would be the equivalent of opening your refrigerator door and then forgetting to close it for six years. SUVs essentially are machines for burning fossil fuel that just happen to also move you and your stuff around.

But what makes them such a perfect symbol is the brute fact that they are simply unnecessary. Go to the parking lot of the nearest suburban supermarket and look around: the only conclusion you can draw is that to reach the grocery, people must drive through three or four raging rivers and up the side of a trackless canyon. These are semi-military machines (some, like the Hummer, are not semi at all), Brinks trucks on a slight diet. They don't keep their occupants safer, they do wreck whatever they plow into—they are the perfect metaphor for a heedless, supersized society. And a gullible one, which has been sold on these vast vehicles partly by the promise that they somehow allow us to commune with nature.

That's why we need a much broader politics than the White House–lobbying that's occupied the big enviros for the past decade, or the mass-market mailing that has been their stock in trade for the past quarter century. We need to take all the brilliant and energetic strategies of local grassroots groups fighting dumps and cleaning up rivers, and we need to make those tactics national and international. So that's why some pastors are starting to talk with their congregations about what car they're going to buy, and why some college seniors are passing around petitions pledging to stay away from the Ford Explorers and Excursions and Extraneouses, and why some few auto dealers have begun to notice informational picketers outside on Saturday mornings urging their customers to think about gas mileage when they go inside.

20

The point is not that by themselves such actions—any individual actions—will make any real dent in the production of carbon dioxide pouring into our atmosphere. Even if you got 10 percent of Americans really committed to changing energy use, their solar homes wouldn't make much of a dent in our national totals. But 10 percent would be enough to change the politics of the issue, to insure the passage of the laws that would cause us all to shift our habits. And so we need to begin to take an issue that is now the province of technicians and turn it into a political issue—just as bus boycotts began to take the issue of race and make it public, forcing the system to respond. That response is likely to be ugly—there are huge companies with a lot to lose, and many people so tied in to their current ways of life that advocating change smacks of subversion. But this has to become a political issue—and fast. The only way that may happen, short of a hideous drought or monster flood, is if it becomes a personal issue first.

Topics for Critical Thinking and Writing

1. McKibben argues that global warming constitutes "a moral crisis" (paragraph 13). What reasons does he offer?

2. In paragraphs 19–20 McKibben talks about SUVs. In 20 he says "they are simply unnecessary." Do you agree? If you don't, explain why. And if you do agree, explain why SUVs are popular.

3. What *persona* does McKibben convey in this essay? (On *persona*, see pages 16–17.) Thoughtful? Belligerent? Hysterical? Concerned but eccentric? Support your answer with evidence.

4. McKibben often varies the length of his sentences, sometimes perhaps surprisingly. For instance, in the first paragraph the first sentence contains 24 words, the second 29 words, the third 24, but the fourth—a question—contains only 5 words. What effect does he gain? Take another passage in his essay where there is a sharp contrast, and explain the effect.

5. Now that you have read McKibben's essay, and thought further about it, do you plan to change your behavior in any way? Explain.

Jane Jacobs

Jane Jacobs was born in Scranton, Pennsylvania, in 1916. After graduating from high school she took an unpaid job on the local newspaper, but soon left for New York City, where she worked at various jobs and sometimes—this was during the Depression—didn't work. The jobs included free-lance work for the New York Herald *and for* Vogue. *During World War II she worked for the Office of War Information, and from 1952 until 1962 she served as an associate editor of* Architectural Forum. *Among her many books are* The Death and Life of Great American Cities *(1961),* Systems of Survival *(1992), and* The Nature of Economics *(2000). "A Good Neighborhood" (editors' title) comes from the first of these books.*

A Good Neighborhood

Anthropologist Elena Padilla, author of *Up from Puerto Rico*, describing Puerto Rican life in a poor and squalid district of New York, tells how much people know about each other—who is to be trusted and who not, who is defiant of the law and who upholds it, who is competent and well informed and who is inept and ignorant—and how these things are known from the public life of the sidewalk and its associated enterprises. These are matters of public character. But she also tells how select are those permitted to drop into the kitchen for a cup of coffee, how strong are the ties, and how limited the number of a person's genuine confidants, those who share in a person's private life and private affairs. She tells how it is not considered dignified for everyone to know one's affairs. Nor is it considered dignified to snoop on others beyond the face presented in public. It does violence to a person's privacy and rights. In this, the people she describes are essentially the same as the people of the mixed, Americanized city street on which I live, and essentially the same as the people who live in high-income apartments or fine town houses, too.

A good city street neighborhood achieves a marvel of balance between its people's determination to have essential privacy and their simultaneous wishes for differing degrees of contact, enjoyment or help from the people around. This balance is largely made up of small, sensitively managed details, practiced and accepted so casually that they are normally taken for granted.

Perhaps I can best explain this subtle but all-important balance in terms of the stores where people leave keys for their friends, a common custom in New York. In our family, for example, when a friend wants to use our place while we are away for a weekend or everyone happens to be out during the day, or a visitor for whom we do not wish to wait up is spending the night, we tell such a friend that he can pick up the key at the delicatessen across the street. Joe Cornacchia, who keeps the delicatessen, usually has a dozen or so keys at a time for handing out like this. He has a special drawer for them.

Now why do I, and many others, select Joe as a logical custodian for keys? Because we trust him, first, to be a responsible custodian, but equally important because we know that he combines a feeling of good will with a feeling of no personal responsibility about our private affairs. Joe considers it no concern of his whom we choose to permit in our places and why.

Around on the other side of our block, people leave their keys at a   5
Spanish grocery. On the other side of Joe's block, people leave them at the candy store. Down a block they leave them at the coffee shop, and a few hundred feet around the corner from that, in a barber shop. Around one corner from two fashionable blocks of town houses and apartments in the Upper East Side, people leave their keys in a butcher shop and a bookshop; around another corner they leave them in a cleaner's and a drug store. In unfashionable East Harlem keys are left with at least one florist, in bakeries, in luncheonettes, in Spanish and Italian groceries.

The point, wherever they are left, is not the kind of ostensible service that the enterprise offers, but the kind of proprietor it has.

A service like this cannot be formalized. Identifications... questions... insurance against mishaps. The all-essential line between public service and privacy would be transgressed by institutionalization. Nobody in his right mind would leave his key in such a place. The service must be given as a favor by someone with an unshakable understanding of the difference between a person's key and a person's private life, or it cannot be given at all.

Or consider the line drawn by Mr. Jaffe at the candy store around our corner—a line so well understood by his customers and by other storekeepers too that they can spend their whole lives in its presence and never think about it consciously. One ordinary morning last winter, Mr. Jaffe, whose formal business name is Bernie, and his wife, whose formal business name is Ann, supervised the small children crossing at the corner on the way to P.S. 41, as Bernie always does because he sees the need; lent an umbrella to one customer and a dollar to another; took custody of two keys; took in some packages for people in the next building who were away; lectured two youngsters who asked for cigarettes; gave street directions; took custody of a watch to give the repair man across the street when he opened later; gave out information on the range of rents in the neighborhood to an apartment seeker; listened to a tale of domestic difficulty and offered reassurance; told some rowdies they could not come in unless they behaved and then defined (and got) good behavior; provided an incidental forum for half a dozen conversations among customers who dropped in for oddments; set aside certain newly arrived papers and magazines for regular customers who would depend on getting them; advised a mother who came for a birthday present not to get the ship-model kit because another child going to the same birthday party was giving that; and got a back copy (this was for me) of the previous day's newspaper out of the deliverer's surplus returns when he came by.

After considering this multiplicity of extra-merchandising services I asked Bernie, "Do you ever introduce your customers to each other?"

He looked startled at the idea, even dismayed. "No," he said thoughtfully. "That would just not be advisable. Sometimes, if I know two customers who are in at the same time have an interest in common, I bring up the subject in conversation and let them carry it on from there if they want to. But oh no, I wouldn't introduce them."

When I told this to an acquaintance in a suburb, she promptly assumed that Mr. Jaffe felt that to make an introduction would be to step above his social class. Not at all. In our neighborhood, storekeepers like the Jaffes enjoy an excellent social status, that of businessmen. In income they are apt to be the peers of the general run of customers and in independence they are the superiors. Their advice, as men or women of common sense and experience, is sought and respected. They are well known as individuals, rather than unknown as class symbols. No; this is that almost unconsciously enforced, well-balanced line showing the line between the city public world and the world of privacy.

This line can be maintained, without awkwardness to anyone, because of the great plenty of opportunities for public contact in the enterprises along the sidewalks, or on the sidewalks themselves as people move to and fro or deliberately loiter when they feel like it, and also because of the presence of many public hosts, so to speak, proprietors of meeting places like Bernie's where one is free either to hang around or dash in and out, no strings attached.

Under this system, it is possible in a city street neighborhood to know all kinds of people without unwelcome entanglements, without boredom, necessity for excuses, explanations, fears of giving offense, embarrassments respecting impositions or commitments, and all such paraphernalia of obligations which can accompany less limited relationships. It is possible to be on excellent sidewalk terms with people who are very different from oneself, and even, as time passes, on familiar public terms with them. Such relationships can, and do, endure for many years, for decades; they could never have formed without that line, much less endured. They form precisely because they are by-the-way to people's normal public sorties.

⟨ℛ⟩ Topics for Critical Thinking and Writing

1. In the first two paragraphs Jacobs defines "a good city street neighborhood." Are her standards applicable to suburban or rural neighborhoods? If not, how might they be adapted?

2. What other qualities define a good neighborhood for you? What makes for a bad neighborhood?

3. Jacobs doesn't speak here of how good neighborhoods, or bad, come into existence. What forces, in your opinion, create good or bad neighborhoods? Can the evolution of neighborhoods be predicted, or controlled?

4. If you reread the first paragraph, you will notice that the first sentence is un-usually long and that the second is unusually short; the third is fairly long and the fourth fairly short. What is the effect of these two shorter sentences, beyond mere variety? Elsewhere in the essay, too, Jacobs's prose includes some very long sentences, but they probably did not confuse you. Why?

A Tale of Two Cities

The New York Times every Sunday publishes a feature devoted to a particular city, "What's Doing in . . . . " It is designed to assist persons who may visit the city, or perhaps better, it is designed to suggest that readers should consider making a visit to the city that is discussed. Each article follows this formula:

- An introduction of a few short paragraphs, designed to engage the reader's interest by giving bits of history and a hint of the atmosphere
- "Events," a few short paragraphs listing local celebrations such as parades, musical events, and sporting events
- "Sightseeing," a few short paragraphs describing some of the chief sights, with comments such as "You will need a car," "A short walk from here," "More to most children's tastes . . . "
- "Where to Stay," a selected list of hotels and motels, with brief eval-uations, prices, addresses, and phone numbers
- "Where to Eat," a guide to a range of selected eating-places, from luxury restaurants to local pizza parlors

We reprint portions of two of these articles, one by Jim Yardley, the chief of the Houston Bureau of *The New York Times*, the other by Micheline Maynard, a resident of Michigan who often writes for the *Times* about the automobile industry. Please note that we *omit* the sections headed "Events" and "Where to Stay."

Jim Yardley

What's Doing in San Antonio

There wasn't much that Mark Twain liked, but he did like San Antonio. When he famously rated it as one of only four unique cities in the United States—the others being Boston, New Orleans and San Francisco—he touched on a complaint about many American cities that apparently was valid even a century ago: one place was not much different from another.

Today, San Antonio remains unique, if not undiscovered. For decades, in fact, much civic energy has been dedicated to making certain that San Antonio gets discovered, and as a result the city is now a favorite tourist and convention destination. So much so that Twain might have had some different opinions on the city's handful of theme parks and other tourism lures.

But he would still find much to love. In this melting-pot era, San Antonio is a true cultural crossroads, a place where Spanish and English or a mix of both are heard on the street; where the relics of the past have not been razed and covered in concrete, as they have been in other Texas cities. San Antonio is also simply a lot of fun.

Like New Orleans, the city is parochial in the best sense of the word, isolated enough to nurture its own music, its own food and a civic appreciation of both. There is a sense upon arriving, checking into a hotel and stepping down to the banks of the Riverwalk that you have gotten away, that you can exhale. And why not do it sitting beside the river and sipping a margarita?

Fiesta is a rollicking San Antonio celebration in which schools close   5
and city employees get the day off for the Battle of Flowers parade. Local officials say that more than 3.5 million people participate, from the volunteers who stage events to the tourists who attend the parades. That is far different from the first Battle of Flowers Parade in 1891, when a women's charitable organization rode past the Alamo in horse-drawn carriages. There is no shortage of fake royalty as various private organizations crown various monarchs, including King Antonio, who presides over the River Parade, and El Rey Feo, the Ugly King, at the Fiesta Flambeau.

Spring is a wonderful time to visit. Fall is a rumor here, a close cousin to summer. Information: Convention and Visitors Bureau, (800) 843–2526; www.sanantoniovisit.com.

Sightseeing

The centerpiece of San Antonio remains the Alamo, the old stone mission at 300 Alamo Plaza that is the lodestone of Texas history. In 1836 Davy Crockett and Jim Bowie and 187 other defenders died at the hands of Santa Anna and the Mexican Army. But their deaths inspired the famous battle cry that Texas shouted in defeating Santa Anna's army later at the Battle of San Jacinto. Today, with 2.5 million visitors a year, the Alamo is the state's top tourist attraction. Inside are exhibits on the Bowie knife; artifacts from a recent archaeological dig relating to the retreat of Santa Anna's army back to Mexico; and pieces commemorating William Barret Travis, the garrison's doomed commander. Open Monday through Saturday 9 A.M. to 5:30 P.M., Sunday 10 A.M. to 5:30. Admission is free. Information: (210) 225–1391, www.thealamo.org.

It is a very short walk from there to the Riverwalk, or the Paseo del Rio, the twisting tourist district built along the bank of the San Antonio River. In the 1920's, city officials considered paving over Riverwalk. Now it is the centerpiece of the city's leisure life. Lined with shops, sidewalk cafes, restaurants and hotels, the Riverwalk stretches about three miles, punctuated by W.P.A.-era arched bridges and entrance steps. Boat ride: $5.25.

You will need a car to visit San Antonio's Spanish missions, but they are worth the effort. Four missions make up the San Antonio Missions National Historical Park, all of them established in the early 1700's by Franciscan friars and all of them along the river. (The Alamo is also a mission, originally called the Mission San Antonio de Valero, but it is separate from the historical park.)

Mission San Jose, 6701 San Jose Drive, (210) 932–1001, established in   10
1720, is famous for its rose window, carved from limestone with sculptured pomegranates. Mission Concepion, (210) 534–1540, is best known for its frescoes. Mission San Juan Capistrano, (210) 534–0749, features the remnants of an extensive irrigation system built by Indians, and Mission Espada, (210) 627–2021, features a Moorish arch leading to the chapel doorway. www.nps.gov/saan.

More to most children's tastes is SeaWorld, 10500 SeaWorld Drive, (210) 523–3611, www.seaworld.com, the largest marine-life theme park in the country. The park offers the Steel Eel roller coaster and all sorts of water rides. The main attraction is Shamu, the killer whale, but there are also beluga whales, seals, otters and penguins. SeaWorld opens daily at 10 A.M. Memorial Day through Aug. 12, weekends till Nov. 25. General admission: $33.95.

Where to Eat

The contemporary French restaurant, Le Reve, 152 East Pecan, (210) 212–2221, was rated the top restaurant in Texas last year by Gourmet magazine. The chef, Andrew Weissman, emphasizes seafood entrees— monkfish on braised baby leeks is one of his signature dishes. For appetizers, the caramelized onion tart on flaky pastry dough or the crispy veal sweetbread scented with white truffles are excellent. Jackets required. Dinner for two with wine: $150.

At Biga on the Banks, 203 South St. Mary's Street, (210) 225–0722, the chef, Bruce Auden, changes the menu daily and offers a tour of world cuisine without ever betraying its Texas roots. Appetizers include chicken fried oysters or tasso-spiked shrimp dumplings; entrees range from sesame tempura crusted swordfish to a Big A bone-on beef tenderloin garnished with onion rings and potato slices. Dinner for two with drinks: $110.

Anyone looking for grand decor will not find it at Liberty Bar, 328 East Josephine Street, (210) 227–1187, a short ride from downtown. But the quality of the food and the airy, unpretentious interior lend a casual elegance to a corner restaurant where the old walls connect at odd angles and the hardwood floors slope noticeably. From the mesquite charcoal grill comes everything from lamb sausage to center-cut pork chops to peppered tenderloin. Among the appetizers, the chile relleno en nogada is wonderful. Lunch for two is about $45, dinner about $55.

Mi Tierra, 218 Produce Row, (210) 225–1262, is in Market Square. Great for families, this sprawling coliseum of Mexican food is open 24 hours a day, with strolling mariachi groups, year-round Christmas lights, a fabulous bakery and good margaritas. It's a tourist favorite, but the locals come, too. A couple was having a small wedding reception the day I visited. From a menu that has everything, the chicken gorditas were delicious. Dinner for two, about $40.

15

Another favorite Mexican restaurant is El Mirador, 722 South St. Mary's Street, (210) 225–9444. Every Saturday the owner's mother makes spinach and chicken soups ($4.95) considered so miraculous that they help nurse natives through the flu season. Dinner for two with margaritas, about $50.

Anyone with a taste for Texas barbecue should try Bob's Smokehouse, 3306 Roland Avenue, (210) 333–9338. Dinner for two is about $20. The family special ($24.24) is made up of a pound each of brisket, sausage and pork ribs with a pint of beans and a pint of potato salad.

Micheline Maynard

What's Doing in Detroit

The United States auto industry, always on a roller coaster, seems to be swooping downward again. Each week seems to bring news of cutbacks at factories, rising gasoline prices, or safety concerns that threaten to slow car sales. But the sluggish economy isn't getting in the way of a wave of festivities planned to mark Detroit's 300th birthday this summer.

The French explorer Antoine de la Mothe Cadillac, leading a party of 200 countrymen and American Indians (paddling canoes, not driving), set foot at what is now Hart Plaza in 1701. Cadillac founded a fort and fur-trading post at the narrow place in the river where he went ashore, which came to be called Ville d'etroit—city of the strait. For its first 95 years, Detroit was under French control. The United States took over in 1796, surrendered it to the British during the War of 1812, then regained it the following year under Gen. William Henry Harrison.

By the time the automobile industry arrived in the early 1900's, Detroit was already a bustling port and business center. This year, the city has been preoccupied by both the auto industry problems and the decision of its popular mayor, Dennis Archer, not to seek a third term. Detroit's sports teams haven't helped lift spirits—the Red Wings exited the Stanley Cup playoffs this year in the first round, and the Tigers, in their second year in a grand new ball park, have been struggling once again. But the mood should improve with the raft of activities associated with the tricentennial, for which billboards have been popping up all around town.

Sightseeing

While Detroit's downtown is fairly compact, it is often advisable for visitors to rent a car to reach outlying attractions.

One site within walking distance of downtown is Comerica Park, home of the Detroit Tigers. More than just a ball field, the year-old park, at 2100 Woodward Avenue, boasts a Ferris wheel and a merry-go-round. Friday is fireworks night, and children are allowed to run the bases on Monday nights. Detroit 300 Day will be celebrated when the Tigers play the Yankees on July 18. Tickets range from $8 to $75. Information, (313) 962–4000, or www.detroittigers.com.

The Motown Historical Museum, 2648 West Grand Boulevard, (313) 875–2264, aka "Hitsville USA," is made up of two modest homes that gave birth to the Motown sound. The lively tour includes Studio A, where many Motown hits were recorded; a replica of the apartment of Motown's founder, Berry Gordy Jr., as well as the chance to dance like a Temptation or sing like a Supreme while listening to the music. General admission, $6.

None of the area's auto plants hold regularly scheduled tours, but it is possible to visit the homes of the auto barons. Two such places have ties to the Ford family. Fairlane, the Henry Ford Estate, at 4901 Evergreen Road in Dearborn on the University of Michigan-Dearborn campus, (313) 593–5590, or at www.umd.umich.edu/fairlane, is about 15 minutes west of downtown Detroit. It was the home of the auto company founder and his wife, Clara. Begun in 1914, the 56-room mansion is built from massive cuts of Marblehead limestone and has a powerhouse designed by Thomas Edison that still supplies heat. Summer tours are at 10 and 11 A.M. and at 1, 2 and 3 P.M. Monday through Saturday, and on the half-hour from 1 through 4:30 P.M. on Sunday. General admission, $8.

The Edsel and Eleanor Ford House, 1100 Lake Shore Drive in Grosse Pointe Shores, (313) 884–4222, www.fordhouse.org, was built by Henry's only child, Edsel, the father of Henry Ford II and the Ford board member William Clay Ford Sr., whose son, William Jr., is the company's current chairman. The house and grounds are on the Lake St. Clair shore in one of Detroit's wealthiest areas. Decorated largely in antique English and French styles, the house features an Art Deco study used by Edsel's children to entertain their friends. General admission, $6.

Meadow Brook Hall, on the grounds of Oakland University near Adams Road in Rochester, 25 miles north of downtown, (248) 370–3140, www.meadowbrookhall.org, dwarfs the Fords' homes in size and lavishness. Completed in 1929 for $4 million, the 110-room manor, one of the largest private residences in the nation, was the home of Matilda Dodge Wilson, widow of the automotive pioneer John Dodge. It has a hidden pipe organ, 24 fireplaces, and sprawling, hilly grounds. Tours Monday through Saturday at 1:30 P.M. until July 1, when they leave hourly on the half-hour from 10:30 A.M. through 3:30 P.M. General admission, $8.

Where to Eat

Tribute, 31425 West 12 Mile Road, Farmington Hills, just northwest of Detroit, (248) 848–9393, offers contemporary French cuisine with an Asian flair, prepared by Takashi Yagihashi. The menu changes seasonally. Choices may include sashimi of yellowfin tuna, Japanese barbecue beef short ribs, or roasted rack of lamb with couscous. The imaginative pastry chef Michael Laiskonis prepares treats such as a three-souffle plate that includes chocolate, Turkish coffee and banana-pistachio. Dinner for two with wine, about $160. Weekend reservations required at least a week in advance.

At 111 years old, the Roma Cafe, 3401 Riopelle Street, (313) 831–5940, is Detroit's oldest Italian restaurant. It continues to pack in customers who ignore its slight shabbiness and concentrate on the classic Italian-American food. Waiters, some of whom have been at the Roma 30 years, are never afraid to advise diners on what to order. Homemade pastas include paglia and fieno (green and white noodles with peas and prosciutto) and ravioli Genovese. Dinner for two with wine, $60. The Roma is set in a far corner of the Eastern Market, which bustles by day but can seem deserted at night. It's safe if visited by car or taxi.

The Traffic Jam and Snug, 511 West Canfield Street, (313) 831–9470, has long been a favorite with students and faculty at Wayne State University. The restaurant's funky brick walls and stained-glass windows provide a backdrop to an equally eclectic menu. With its own brewery and bakery, Traffic Jam features a number of vegetarian choices such as black-eyed pea and hominy soup and a black bean burrito, and there is

10

the big, meaty Jam burger, one of the city's best. Desserts, including homemade ice cream, are worth saving room for. Dinner for two with beer, $40.

Dearborn is home to one of the largest Arab populations in the country, and Warren Avenue abounds with Middle Eastern bakeries, food shops and restaurants, with extremely reasonable prices. Expect a warm welcome at Al-Ameer, 12710 West Warren, (313) 582–8185, where pita bread is baked in a vestibule oven alongside a juice-squeezing booth. A daily $6.95 special, like baked lamb, comes with soup and salad. Lunch for two with juice or iced tea, $20.

 ## Topics for Critical Thinking and Writing

1. If some sentences in either essay struck you as particularly engaging, point them out and explain why you think they are interesting.

2. You are a journalist, and have been asked by *The New York Times* to write a piece for its "What's Doing" series. You may want to write about a place where you have lived for years, or the place where you attend college, or a place you have visited with interest—perhaps more than once. In any event, taking the two preceding articles as models, write your piece for *The New York Times*.

3. If you have ever been prompted to visit a place because of something you had read about it, write an essay of 500 words in which you explain what prompted you, and your responses during and after the visit. Did the place turn out to be the same as, or different from, the place that you had read about?

4. Invent a place and write a "What's Doing" piece about it, taking the two preceding essays as models.

Kevin Sack

Kevin Sack is the Atlanta bureau chief of The New York Times. *The following essay appeared in* The New York Times Magazine, *March 4, 2001.*

Atlanta: In Its Heart, It's a Southern Town

John Shelton Reed, a sociologist of the South, once wrote that Atlanta is what a quarter of a million Confederate soldiers died to prevent. I think about that sometimes while idling in traffic on the downtown connector, staring emptily at the Soviet-style dormitories that were built for the Olympics and now block the view of the gently scaled Georgia Tech campus. Maybe he's right, I think. After all, Mr. Reed, who writes from the smug perch of Chapel Hill, N.C., certainly hit the mark when he wrote of Atlanta's civic slogan—"The City Too Busy to Hate"—that it was "a pretty sorry reason not to hate." But then, just as I am prepared to surrender to Mr. Reed's insight, I am always stopped by his implicit suggestion: that Atlanta is not really Southern. What's worse, he seems to be saying, Atlanta is the North come South.

Clearly, there are elements of truth to the suggestion that Atlanta has little to define its character as regional. The South has not been spared the homogenization of American commerce and culture, certainly not in the age of Webvan. And as the region's capital, Atlanta sets the trend with its ubiquitous strips of Starbucks coffee shops, Blockbuster video stores and CVS pharmacies.

Just as clearly, each Northerner who moves to Atlanta dilutes the city's Southernness. A fourth of the 2.8 million people who lived in the 20-county metropolitan area in 1990 were born outside the South. With the population growing to nearly four million, spurred by an influx of Hispanics and Asians, that proportion can only have grown.

And yet Atlanta, in my experience, does remain distinctly Southern, Southern in its manners and language, Southern in its culture and history, Southern in its pace and values.

It is not a museum piece. It is not the same static South you see in   5
Charleston, S.C., and Savannah, Ga., or Natchez, Miss., and New Orleans, and for travelers looking to step back in time those may be better destinations.

Atlanta is the classic example of the dynamic South, a South that is changing in infinite ways. Indeed, it is both the best and the worst of the new South, and has been for decades. And just because it is the new South does not make it any less Southern than the old one.

"The bottom line is this," explains Jim Auchmutey, an Atlanta native who writes about city history and Southern culture for *The Atlanta Journal-Constitution*, "people who say Atlanta isn't Southern have a very old-fashioned notion of what the South is. But if you allow for the possibility that whole stretches of the region have never been scenes out of a Faulkner novel, and that most Southerners for decades have lived in metropolitan areas, then, of course, Atlanta is Southern."

The question is not an insignificant one in a city that drew 17 million tourists and conventioneers last year. With few physical assets—no water other than the Chattahoochee River, no highlands other than Stone Mountain—its regional flavor is largely what it has to sell, along with a vast convention center and a surfeit of hotels with glass elevators.

Above all, Atlanta is home to the quintessential Southern story, the civil rights movement, which can be relived at Dr. Martin Luther King Jr.'s birthplace and at his crypt, just blocks away from each other on Auburn Avenue. In recent years, the National Park Service has taken over Dr. King's former pulpit, the Ebenezer Baptist Church, and now plays recordings of his sermons there, while the congregation has moved across Auburn to a gleaming new sanctuary in the shape of a horn of plenty. At the original church, members felt crowded by Sunday-morning tourists but the new building offers ample room to enjoy the choir's exuberant renditions of gospel standards and the Rev. Joseph Roberts's stem-winding sermons.

More than any other American city, Atlanta remains the civil rights   10
movement's living legacy, a city that elected its first black mayor in 1973 and will almost certainly elect its fourth this year.

Want to see the real South? Walk the crowded corridors of Lenox Square, the mega-mall in Buckhead where well-dressed shoppers of both races are united by their mutual taste for Coach bags and Bernini suits. Stroll the aisles of the DeKalb Farmers Market in Decatur along with immigrants from Cambodia and Jamaica, searching for bok choy and Scotch bonnet peppers. While in Decatur, just east of town, drop in on Gabe Feldman, originally of Brooklyn, who opened Atlanta's first kosher barbecue joint last December (without pulled pork, of course). He named it Twelve Oaks, after Ashley Wilkes's plantation in "Gone With the Wind."

Just because the city's Southernness has been trampled a bit in the second Yankee invasion does not mean that it has been eradicated altogether. You hear it whenever a waitress at one of Atlanta's more than 200 Waffle Houses asks, "What y'all having?" (even if it's only you in the booth). You see it when a businessman holds open the door of a downtown office building for a stream of women leaving for lunch.

It is, of course, an increasing challenge to maintain gentle manners when stalled in traffic on smoggy highways. But Atlantans work at sustaining the hospitality that once seemed congenital. "Y'all drive nice now," begged the bumper sticker that a friend recently spied on a sport utility vehicle racing down Georgia 400—"This is still the South."

Over the years, Atlanta has bulldozed much of its past to make room for its current clash of eclectic, frequently uninspired architecture. But there are corners that still reveal a Southern grace and appreciation for classicism. In the Colony Square area, the Greek Revival First Church of Christ, Scientist, built of beige brick in 1914, somehow finds a balance with its modernist neighbor across Peachtree Street, Richard Meier's High Museum of Art, which is wrapped in steel panels covered with white porcelain.

While there never was a Tara, the South's antebellum elegance is cap-   15
tured in the columned mansions of Buckhead, the old-money neighborhood where in spring dogwoods and azaleas turn vast lawns into a Pointillist blur of pinks and whites. It also remains in Marietta's quaint

town square and in the grand old homes of Ansley Park and Druid Hills, where Miss Daisy was driven.

Southernness is preserved in the collection of Howard Finster's folk art at the High Museum of Art, in the nightly blues sessions at Blind Willie's in Virginia-Highlands and in the campy reconstruction of the Battle of Atlanta at the Cyclorama in Grant Park (while there, be sure to visit Zoo Atlanta and the city's most celebrated Asian immigrants, the pandas Lun Lun and Yang Yang). It is redolent inside the majestic, 72-year-old Fox Theater in midtown, with its fanciful turrets and twinkling, starlit ceiling, and in the languorous pace of an afternoon Braves game at Turner Field. It can be found in the excellent Civil War exhibits at the Atlanta History Center and on the face of Stone Mountain, the Confederate Mount Rushmore, with its giant carvings of Robert E. Lee, Jefferson Davis and Stonewall Jackson astride their steeds. Considered the world's largest relief carving, the project began in 1915 but was not dedicated until 1970. In classic Atlanta fashion, the quiet cul-de-sacs surrounding the mountain are now populated by upper-middle-class black families who hike up the granite face on Sunday outings.

For every chain restaurant (O.K., maybe not for every one), there is a Harold's Barbecue, hard by the federal penitentiary in southeast Atlanta, where you can dunk crispy cracklin' corn bread into a thick bowl of smoky Brunswick stew, made these days with chicken instead of rabbit or squirrel. Or a Mary Mac's Tea Room, where you can order pot likker with your fried chicken livers, or a Colonnade Restaurant, where blue-haired Buckhead matrons and gay men knock back stiff cocktails at adjacent tables.

At a host of vibrant new restaurants like South City Kitchen, Southern cooking has been updated so that you can try your fried green tomatoes with goat cheese and a red pepper coulis. The city is now a solid restaurant town, with places like Seeger's and Bluepointe winning raves.

There is one other thing that makes Atlanta Southern. It is a city of strivers, a town molded by its lingering insecurity over the loss of a war and generations of slights. That insecurity, that compulsive need for approval, is basic to Atlanta's boosterism, its civic ethos. It is what led city leaders to dream the audacious dream that they could stage the Olympics in Atlanta and force the world to take notice.

But after using its Southern charm and civil rights legacy to win the Games, Atlanta debated just how much of the South—and which aspects of it—it wanted to show the world. Its solution was telling. During the opening ceremonies, Dr. King's taped voice boomed from amplifiers, reminding the world anew of his dream for his native region. And then, a parade of 30 chrome Chevy pickups took the field, roaring around a cluster of giddy cheerleaders.

20

Topics for Critical Thinking and Writing

1. Evaluate the title and the first sentence. The first paragraph forms a sort of introduction. How would you describe and evaluate Sack's opening strategy?

2. Paragraph 16 says that "Southernness is preserved in"—among other things—"the campy reconstruction of the Battle of Atlanta." What makes something "campy," and does a campy reconstruction of the Battle of Atlanta preserve Southernness because it is campy, or because it is the Battle of Atlanta, or both?

3. The essay is rich in concrete details concerning, for instance, buildings, monuments, people, and food. Does the author have an underlying thesis that holds all of these details together, or, to put it differently, do all these details help to communicate an underlying thesis? If so, what is the thesis?

4. Did you enjoy reading the essay? Why, or why not? If tomorrow you had a chance to go to Atlanta, perhaps on a tour with your glee club or football team, would you look forward to the visit? Why, or why not?

Joan Didion

Joan Didion, born in Sacramento in 1934 and educated at the University of California, Berkeley, worked for a while as a features editor at Vogue, *but then turned to freelance writing. Among her novels are* Play It as It Lays *(1970),* A Book of Common Prayer *(1977), and* The Last Thing He Wanted *(1996). Collections of her magazine essays include* Slouching Towards Bethlehem *(1968), which is the source of the piece we reprint, and* The White Album *(1979).*

On Going Home

I am home for my daughter's first birthday. By "home" I do not mean the house in Los Angeles where my husband and I and the baby live, but the place where my family is, in the Central Valley of California. It is a vital although troublesome distinction. My husband likes my family but is uneasy in their house, because once there I fall into their ways, which are difficult, oblique, deliberately inarticulate, not my husband's ways. We live in dusty houses ("D-U-S-T," he once wrote with his finger on surfaces all over the house, but no one noticed it) filled with mementos quite without value to him (what could the Canton dessert plates mean to him? how could he have known about the assay scales, why should he care if he did know?), and we appear to talk exclusively about people we know who have been committed to mental hospitals, about people we know who have been booked on drunk-driving charges, and about property, particularly about property, land, price per acre and C-2 zoning and assessments and freeway access. My brother does not understand my husband's inability to perceive the advantage in the rather common real-estate transaction known as "sale-leaseback," and my husband in turn does not understand why so many of the people he hears about in my father's house have recently been committed to mental hospitals or booked on drunk-driving charges. Nor does he understand that when we talk about sale-leasebacks and right-of-way condemnations we are talking in code about the things we like best, the yellow fields and the cottonwoods and the rivers rising and falling and the mountain roads closing when the heavy snow comes in. We miss each other's points, have another drink and regard the fire. My brother refers to my husband, in his presence, as "Joan's husband." Marriage is the classic betrayal.

Or perhaps it is not any more. Sometimes I think that those of us who are now in our thirties were born into the last generation to carry the burden of "home," to find in family life the source of all tension and drama. I had by all objective accounts a "normal" and a "happy" family situation, and yet I was almost thirty years old before I could talk to my family on the telephone without crying after I had hung up. We did not fight. Nothing was wrong. And yet some nameless anxiety colored the emotional charges between me and the place that I came from. The question of whether or not you could go home again was a very real part of the sentimental and largely literary baggage with which we left home in the fifties; I suspect that it is irrelevant to the children born of the fragmentation after World War II. A few weeks ago in a San Francisco bar I saw a pretty young girl on crystal take off her clothes and dance for the cash prize in an "amateur-topless" contest. There was no particular sense of moment about this, none of the effect of romantic degradation, of "dark journey," for which my generation strived so assiduously. What sense could that girl possibly make of, say, *Long Day's Journey into Night*? Who is beside the point?

That I am trapped in this particular irrelevancy is never more apparent to me than when I am home. Paralyzed by the neurotic lassitude engendered by meeting one's past at every turn, around every corner, inside every cupboard, I go aimlessly from room to room. I decide to meet it head-on and clean out a drawer, and I spread the contents on the bed. A bathing suit I wore the summer I was seventeen. A letter of rejection from *The Nation*, an aerial photograph of the site for a shopping center my father did not build in 1954. Three teacups hand-painted with cabbage roses and signed "E.M.," my grandmother's initials. There is no final solution for letters of rejection from *The Nation* and teacups hand-painted in 1900. Nor is there any answer to snapshots of one's grandfather as a young man on skis, surveying around Donner Pass in the year 1910. I smooth out the snapshot and look into his face, and do and do not see my own. I close the drawer, and have another cup of coffee with my mother. We get along very well, veterans of a guerrilla war we never understood.

Days pass. I see no one. I come to dread my husband's evening call, not only because he is full of news of what by now seems to me our remote life in Los Angeles, people he has seen, letters which require attention, but because he asks what I have been doing, suggests uneasily that I get out, drive to San Francisco or Berkeley. Instead I drive across the river to a family graveyard. It has been vandalized since my last visit and the monuments are broken, overturned in the dry grass. Because I once saw a rattlesnake in the grass I stay in the car and listen to a country-and-Western station. Later I drive with my father to a ranch he has in the foothills. The man who runs his cattle on it asks us to the roundup, a week from Sunday, and although I know that I will be in Los Angeles I say, in the oblique way my family talks, that I will come. Once home I mention the broken monuments in the graveyard. My mother shrugs.

I go to visit my great-aunts. A few of them think now that I am my cousin, or their daughter who died young. We recall an anecdote about a relative last seen in 1948, and they ask if I still like living in New York City. I have lived in Los Angeles for three years, but I say that I do. The baby is offered a horehound drop, and I am slipped a dollar bill "to buy a treat." Questions trail off, answers are abandoned, the baby plays with the dust motes in a shaft of afternoon sun.

It is time for the baby's birthday party: a white cake, strawberry-marshmallow ice cream, a bottle of champagne saved from another party. In the evening, after she has gone to sleep, I kneel beside the crib and touch her face, where it is pressed against the slats, with mine. She is an open and trusting child, unprepared for and unaccustomed to the ambushes of family life, and perhaps it is just as well that I can offer her little of that life. I would like to give her more. I would like to promise her that she will grow up with a sense of her cousins and of rivers and of her great-grandmother's teacups, would like to pledge her a picnic on a river with fried chicken and her hair uncombed, would like to give her *home* for her birthday, but we live differently now and I can promise her nothing like that. I give her a xylophone and a sundress from Madeira, and promise to tell her a funny story.

◎ Topics for Critical Thinking and Writing

1. Didion reveals that members of her family are difficult, inarticulate, poor housekeepers, and so forth. Do you find these revelations about her family distasteful? Would you mind seeing in print similarly unflattering things you had written about your own family? How might such revelations be justified? Are they justified in this essay?

2. Summarize the point of the second paragraph. Do you find Didion's speculations about the difference between her generation and succeeding generations meaningful? Are they accurate for your generation?

3. Do you think that growing up necessarily involves estrangement from one's family? Explain.

Nicholas Negroponte

Nicholas Negroponte, born in 1943, was trained in architecture at the Massachusetts Institute of Technology, where he now teaches and serves as director of the Media Lab. He is author of influential books including The Architecture Machine *(1970) and* Being Digital *(1995), and a monthly columnist for* Wired *magazine. In the Introduction to* Being Digital *Negroponte says that "computing is not about computers anymore. It is about living." What he means is evident in the selection that we give from* Being Digital. *In our casebook on e-mail we include another essay from* Being Digital.

Place without Space

In the same ways that hypertext removes the limitations of the printed page, the post-information age will remove the limitations of geography. Digital living will include less and less dependence upon being in a specific place at a specific time, and the transmission of place itself will start to become possible.

If I really could look out the electronic window of my living room in Boston and see the Alps, hear the cowbells, and smell the (digital) manure in summer, in a way I am very much in Switzerland. If instead of going to work by driving my atoms into town, I log into my office and do my work electronically, exactly where is my workplace?

In the future, we will have the telecommunications and virtual reality technologies for a doctor in Houston to perform a delicate operation on a patient in Alaska. In the nearer term, however, a brain surgeon will need to be in the same operating theater at the same time as the brain; many activities, like those of so-called knowledge workers, are not as dependent on time and place and will be decoupled from geography much sooner.

Today, writers and money managers find it practicable and far more appealing to be in the Caribbean or South Pacific while preparing their manuscripts or managing their funds. However, in some countries, like Japan, it will take longer to move away from space and time dependence, because the native culture fights the trend. (For example: one of the main reasons that Japan does not move to daylight savings time in the summer is because going home "after dark" is considered necessary, and workers try not to arrive after or go home before their bosses.)

In the post-information age, since you may live and work at one or   5
many locations, the concept of an "address" now takes on new meaning.

When you have an account with America Online, CompuServe, or Prodigy, you know your own e-mail address, but you do not know where it physically exists. In the case of America Online, your Internet address is your ID followed by @aol.com—usable anywhere in the world. Not only do you not know where @aol.com is, whosoever sends a message to that address has no idea of where either it or you might be. The address becomes much more like a Social Security number than a street coordinate. It is a virtual address.

In my case, I happen to know where my address, @hq.media.mit.edu, is physically located. It is a ten-year-old HP Unix machine in a closet near my office. But when people send me messages they are sending them to me, not to that closet. They might infer I am in Boston (which is usually not the case). In fact, I am usually in a different time zone, so not only space but time is shifted as well.

 ## Topics for Critical Thinking and Writing

1. In his first paragraph Negroponte says that "digital living will include less and less dependence upon being in a specific place at a specific time, and the transmission of place itself will start to become possible." If you can now, at midnight, read on your computer screen the text of an article that is in a library that closes at 9:00 P.M., no doubt we can say that this act of reading no longer depends on "being in a specific place at a specific time." But is it reasonable to speak of this condition as "the transmission of place itself"?

2. What is your answer to the question Negroponte asks at the end of his second paragraph?

3. Which if any of Negroponte's predictions seem highly likely to you? Which seem highly unlikely? Explain.

4. Negroponte is a professor at Massachusetts Institute of Technology, in Cambridge, Massachusetts. Do you think you would like to sit in his classroom in Cambridge, on, say, Monday, Wednesday, and Friday at 10:00 A.M.? Or would you be just as happy staying where you are, and watching him on a screen?

John Updike

John Updike (b. 1932) grew up in Shillington, Pennsylvania, where his father was a teacher and his mother was a writer. After receiving a B.A. degree from Harvard he studied drawing at Oxford for a year, but an offer from The New Yorker *magazine brought him back to the United States. He at first served as a reporter for the magazine, but soon began contributing poetry, essays, and fiction. Today he is one of America's most prolific and well-known writers.*

The following essay on the destruction of the World Trade Center (September 11, 2001) was published in The New Yorker *less than a week after the attack.*

September 11, 2001

Suddenly summoned to witness something great and horrendous, we keep fighting not to reduce it to our own smallness. From the viewpoint of a tenth-floor apartment in Brooklyn Heights, where I happened to be visiting some kin, the destruction of the World Trade Center twin towers had the false intimacy of television, on a day of perfect reception. A four-year-old girl and her babysitter called from the library, and pointed out through the window the smoking top of the north tower, not a mile away. It seemed, at that first glance, more curious than horrendous: smoke speckled with bits of paper curled into the cloudless sky, and strange inky rivulets ran down the giant structure's vertically corrugated surface. The W.T.C. had formed a pale background to our Brooklyn view of lower Manhattan, not beloved, like the stony, spired midtown thirties skyscrapers it had displaced as the city's tallest, but, with its pre-postmodern combination of unignorable immensity and architectural reticence, in some lights beautiful. As we watched the second tower burst into ballooning flame (an intervening building had hidden the approach of the second airplane), there persisted the notion that, as on television, this was not quite real; it could be fixed; the technocracy the towers symbolized would find a way to put out the fire and reverse the damage.

And then, within an hour, as my wife and I watched from the Brooklyn building's roof, the south tower dropped from the screen of our viewing; it fell straight down like an elevator, with a tinkling shiver and a groan of concussion distinct across the mile of air. We knew we had just witnessed thousands of deaths; we clung to each other as if we ourselves were falling. Amid the glittering impassivity of the many buildings across the East River, an empty spot had appeared, as if by electronic command, beneath the sky that, but for the sulfurous cloud streaming south toward the ocean, was pure blue, rendered uncannily pristine by the absence of jet trails. A swiftly expanding burst of smoke and dust hid the rest of lower Manhattan; we saw the collapse of the second tower only on television, where the

New York City, September 11, 2001

Krista Niles/*The New York Times*

footage of hellbent airplane, exploding jet fuel, and imploding tower was played and replayed, much-rehearsed moments from a nightmare ballet.

The nightmare is still on. The bodies are beneath the rubble, the last-minute cell-phone calls—remarkably calm and loving, many of them—are still being reported, the sound of an airplane overhead still bears an unfamiliar menace, the thought of boarding an airplane with our old blasé blitheness keeps receding into the past. Determined men who have transposed their own lives to a martyr's afterlife can still inflict an amount of destruction that defies belief. War is conducted with a fury that requires abstraction—that turns a planeful of peaceful passengers, children included, into a missile the faceless enemy deserves. The other side has the abstractions; we have only the mundane duties of survivors—to pick up the pieces, to bury the dead, to take more precautions, to go on living.

American freedom of motion, one of our prides, has taken a hit. Can we afford the openness that lets future kamikaze pilots, say, enroll in Florida flying schools? A Florida neighbor of one of the suspects remembers him saying he didn't like the United States: "He said it was too lax. He said, 'I can go anywhere I want to, and they can't stop me.'" It is a weird complaint, a begging perhaps to be stopped. Weird, too, the silence of the heavens these days, as flying has ceased across America. But fly again we must; risk is a price of freedom, and walking around Brooklyn Heights that afternoon, as ash drifted in the air and cars were few and open-air lunches continued as usual on Montague Street, renewed the impression that, with all its failings, this is a country worth

A Week after September 11, 2001

fighting for. Freedom, reflected in the street's diversity and daily ease, felt palpable. It is mankind's elixir, even if a few turn it to poison. The next morning, I went back to the open vantage from which we had watched the tower so dreadfully slip from sight. The fresh sun shone on the eastward façades, a few boats tentatively moved in the river, the ruins were still sending out smoke, but New York looked glorious.

Topics for Critical Thinking and Writing

1. Do you think that Updike's first sentence works well? Would the essay be more effective if it began with the second sentence?

2. How would you characterize the style of this essay? In your view, does Updike describe the event, or, instead, his own experience of the event? Is it possible to make a distinction between the two—a description of an event, on

the one hand, and the description of one's personal experience of it, on the other?

3. Does Updike make a specific point in this piece of writing, or does he have some other intention in mind?

4. This essay was written and published very soon after the events of September 11th. What is its impact when you read it today? How do you imagine that its first readers responded to it?

5. If you were the editor of *The New Yorker* and this essay was submitted to you, a few days after September 11th, would you accept it for publication or not? What kind of letter would you write to the author, accepting or rejecting his essay, and/or asking for revisions?

Edward Bellamy

Edward Bellamy (1850–98) was born in Chicopee Falls, in western Massachusetts. His ancestors included many ministers, and for a while Bellamy thought he would follow their footsteps, but when he was unable to experience the requisite rebirth in Christ he abandoned the family profession, studied law and was admitted to the bar, and then turned to journalism and the writing of fiction. Three novels brought him modest success, but Looking Backward, 2000–1887 *(1888) made his name a household word.*

The book belongs to a genre called utopian fiction, named for Sir Thomas More's Utopia (1516). Greek for "no place," Utopia is (on the whole) More's view of an ideal society. (For a selection from More's book, see page 564.) More's story, narrated by a man who supposedly traveled to remote places with Amerigo Vespucci, reports the doings of people in a geographically remote society. Bellamy's Looking Backward, 2000–1887, *though published in 1888, supposedly reports the doings of people remote in time, the year 2000. That is, Bellamy, writing in the late nineteenth century, purports to tell his readers what life will be like in the year 2000. The fictional device is this: A young Bostonian, Julian West, is hypnotized in 1887 (i.e., the time when Bellamy was writing the book), falls asleep, and wakes up 113 years later, in the year 2000. When West, a rather naive fellow, tells the people of this new society about what life was a century ago—the present for Bellamy's readers—Bellamy is of course able to present an unflattering view of the age; and when the people of the year 2000 tell West what life is now like, Bellamy is in effect able to suggest to his readers that it is this sort of life that we should strive for.*

We give about one-tenth of the book.

Looking Backward

Chapter V

When in the course of the evening the ladies retired, leaving Dr. Leete and myself alone, he sounded me as to my disposition for sleep, saying that if I felt like it my bed was ready for me; but if I was inclined to wakefulness nothing would please him better than to bear me company. "I am a late bird, myself," he said, "and, without suspicion of flattery, I may say that a companion more interesting than yourself could scarcely be imagined. It is decidedly not often that one has a chance to converse with a man of the nineteenth century."

Now I had been looking forward all the evening with some dread to the time when I should be alone, on retiring for the night. Surrounded by these most friendly strangers, stimulated and supported by their sympathetic interest, I had been able to keep my mental balance. Even then, however, in pauses of the conversation I had had glimpses, vivid as lightning flashes, of the horror of strangeness that was waiting to be faced when I could no longer command diversion. I knew I could not sleep that night, and as for lying awake and thinking, it argues no cowardice, I am sure, to confess that I was afraid of it. When, in reply to my host's question, I frankly told him this, he replied that it would be strange if I did not feel just so, but that I need have no anxiety about sleeping; whenever I wanted to go to bed, he would give me a dose which would insure me a sound night's sleep without fail. Next morning, no doubt, I would awake with the feeling of an old citizen.

"Before I acquire that," I replied, "I must know a little more about the sort of Boston I have come back to. You told me when we were upon the house-top that though a century only had elapsed since I fell asleep, it had been marked by greater changes in the conditions of humanity than many a previous millennium. With the city before me I could well believe that, but I am very curious to know what some of the changes have been. To make a beginning somewhere, for the subject is doubtless a large one, what solution, if any, have you found for the labor question? It was the Sphinx's riddle[1] of the nineteenth century, and when I dropped out the Sphinx was threatening to devour society, because the answer was not forthcoming. It is well worth sleeping a hundred years to learn what the right answer was, if, indeed, you have found it yet."

"As no such thing as the labor question is known nowadays," replied Dr. Leete, "and there is no way in which it could arise, I suppose we may claim to have solved it. Society would indeed have fully deserved being devoured if it had failed to answer a riddle so entirely simple. In fact, to speak by the book, it was not necessary for society to solve the riddle at all. It may be said to have solved itself. The solution came as the result of a process of industrial evolution which could not have terminated otherwise. All that society had to do was to recognize and coöperate with that evolution, when its tendency had become unmistakable."

"I can only say," I answered, "that at the time I fell asleep no such evolution had been recognized."   5

"It was in 1887 that you fell into this sleep, I think you said."

"Yes, May 30th, 1887."

My companion regarded me musingly for some moments. Then he observed, "And you tell me that even then there was no general recognition of the nature of the crisis which society was nearing? Of course, I fully credit your statement. The singular blindness of your contemporaries to

---

[1]In Greek mythology, the sphinx, a winged monster with the head of a woman and the body of a lion, asked this riddle: "What goes on four legs in the morning, two at noon, and three in the evening?" Those who did not know the answer—man—were killed. (Editors' note)

the signs of the times is a phenomenon commented on by many of our historians, but few facts of history are more difficult for us to realize, so obvious and unmistakable as we look back seem the indications, which must also have come under your eyes, of the transformation about to come to pass. I should be interested, Mr. West, if you would give me a little more definite idea of the view which you and men of your grade of intellect took of the state and prospects of society in 1887. You must, at least, have realized that the widespread industrial and social troubles, and the underlying dissatisfaction of all classes with the inequalities of society, and the general misery of mankind, were portents of great changes of some sort."

"We did, indeed, fully realize that," I replied. "We felt that society was dragging anchor and in danger of going adrift. Whither it would drift nobody could say, but all feared the rocks."

"Nevertheless," said Dr. Leete, "the set of the current was perfectly perceptible if you had but taken pains to observe it, and it was not toward the rocks, but toward a deeper channel." 10

"We had a popular proverb," I replied, "that 'hindsight is better than foresight,' the force of which I shall now, no doubt, appreciate more fully than ever. All I can say is, that the prospect was such when I went into that long sleep that I should not have been surprised had I looked down from your house-top to-day on a heap of charred and moss-grown ruins instead of this glorious city."

Dr. Leete had listened to me with close attention and nodded thoughtfully as I finished speaking. "What you have said," he observed, "will be regarded as a most valuable vindication of Storiot, whose account of your era has been generally thought exaggerated in its picture of the gloom and confusion of men's minds. That a period of transition like that should be full of excitement and agitation was indeed to be looked for; but seeing how plain was the tendency of the forces in operation, it was natural to believe that hope rather than fear would have been the prevailing temper of the popular mind."

"You have not yet told me what was the answer to the riddle which you found," I said. "I am impatient to know by what contradiction of natural sequence the peace and prosperity which you now seem to enjoy could have been the outcome of an era like my own."

"Excuse me," replied my host, "but do you smoke?" It was not till our cigars were lighted and drawing well that he resumed. "Since you are in the humor to talk rather than to sleep, as I certainly am, perhaps I cannot do better than to try to give you enough idea of our modern industrial system to dissipate at least the impression that there is any mystery about the process of its evolution. The Bostonians of your day had the reputation of being great askers of questions, and I am going to show my descent by asking you one to begin with. What should you name as the most prominent feature of the labor troubles of your day?"

"Why, the strikes, of course," I replied. 15

"Exactly; but what made the strikes so formidable?"

"The great labor organizations."

"And what was the motive of these great organizations?"

"The workmen claimed they had to organize to get their rights from the big corporations," I replied.

"That is just it," said Dr. Leete; "the organization of labor and the strikes were an effect, merely, of the concentration of capital in greater masses than had ever been known before. Before this concentration began, while as yet commerce and industry were conducted by innumerable petty concerns with small capital, instead of a small number of great concerns with vast capital, the individual workman was relatively important and independent in his relations to the employer. Moreover, when a little capital or a new idea was enough to start a man in business for himself, workingmen were constantly becoming employers and there was no hard and fast line between the two classes. Labor unions were needless then, and general strikes out of the question. But when the era of small concerns with small capital was succeeded by that of the great aggregations of capital, all this was changed. The individual laborer, who had been relatively important to the small employer, was reduced to insignificance and powerlessness over against the great corporation, while at the same time the way upward to the grade of employer was closed to him. Self-defense drove him to union with his fellows.

"The records of the period show that the outcry against the concentration of capital was furious. Men believed that it threatened society with a form of tyranny more abhorrent than it had ever endured. They believed that the great corporations were preparing for them the yoke of a baser servitude than had ever been imposed on the race, servitude not to men but to soulless machines incapable of any motive but insatiable greed. Looking back, we cannot wonder at their desperation, for certainly humanity was never confronted with a fate more sordid and hideous than would have been the era of corporate tyranny which they anticipated.

"Meanwhile, without being in the smallest degree checked by the clamor against it, the absorption of business by ever larger monopolies continued. In the United States there was not, after the beginning of the last quarter of the century, any opportunity whatever for individual enterprise in any important field of industry, unless backed by a great capital. During the last decade of the century, such small businesses as still remained were fast-failing survivals of a past epoch, or mere parasites on the great corporations, or else existed in fields too small to attract the great capitalists. Small businesses, as far as they still remained, were reduced to the condition of rats and mice, living in holes and corners, and counting on evading notice for the enjoyment of existence. The railroads had gone on combining till a few great syndicates controlled every rail in the land. In manufactories, every important staple was controlled by a syndicate. These syndicates, pools, trusts, or whatever their name, fixed prices and crushed all competition except when combinations as

20

vast as themselves arose. Then a struggle, resulting in a still greater consolidation, ensued. The great city bazaar crushed its country rivals with branch stores, and in the city itself absorbed its smaller rivals till the business of a whole quarter was concentrated under one roof, with a hundred former proprietors of shops serving as clerks. Having no business of his own to put his money in, the small capitalist, at the same time that he took service under the corporation, found no other investment for his money but its stocks and bonds, thus becoming doubly dependent upon it.

"The fact that the desperate popular opposition to the consolidation of business in a few powerful hands had no effect to check it proves that there must have been a strong economical reason for it. The small capitalists, with their innumerable petty concerns, had in fact yielded the field to the great aggregations of capital, because they belonged to a day of small things and were totally incompetent to the demands of an age of steam and telegraphs and the gigantic scale of its enterprises. To restore the former order of things, even if possible, would have involved returning to the day of stage-coaches. Oppressive and intolerable as was the régime of the great consolidations of capital, even its victims, while they cursed it, were forced to admit the prodigious increase of efficiency which had been imparted to the national industries, the vast economies effected by concentration of management and unity of organization, and to confess that since the new system had taken the place of the old the wealth of the world had increased at a rate before undreamed of. To be sure this vast increase had gone chiefly to make the rich richer, increasing the gap between them and the poor; but the fact remained that, as a means merely of producing wealth, capital had been proved efficient in proportion to its consolidation. The restoration of the old system with the subdivision of capital, if it were possible, might indeed bring back a greater equality of conditions, with more individual dignity and freedom, but it would be at the price of general poverty and the arrest of material progress.

"Was there, then, no way of commanding the services of the mighty wealth-producing principle of consolidated capital without bowing down to a plutocracy like that of Carthage? As soon as men began to ask themselves these questions, they found the answer ready for them. The movement toward the conduct of business by larger and larger aggregations of capital, the tendency toward monopolies, which had been so desperately and vainly resisted, was recognized at last, in its true significance, as a process which only needed to complete its logical evolution to open a golden future to humanity.

"Early in the last century the evolution was completed by the final consolidation of the entire capital of the nation. The industry and commerce of the country, ceasing to be conducted by a set of irresponsible corporations and syndicates of private persons at their caprice and for their profit, were intrusted to a single syndicate representing the people, to be conducted in the common interest for the common profit. The nation, that is to say, organized as the one great business corporation in which all other corporations were absorbed; it became the one capitalist in the place of all other capitalists, the sole employer, the final monopoly in which all previous and lesser monopolies were swallowed up, a monopoly in the profits and economies of which all citizens shared. The epoch of trusts had ended in The Great Trust. In a word, the people of the United States concluded to assume the conduct of their own business, just as one hundred odd years before they had assumed the conduct of their own government, organizing now for industrial purposes on precisely the same grounds that they had then organized for political purposes. At last, strangely late in the world's history, the obvious fact was perceived that no business is so essentially the public business as the industry and commerce on which the people's livelihood depends, and that to entrust it to private persons to be managed for private profit is a folly similar in kind, though vastly greater in magnitude, to that of surrendering the functions of political government to kings and nobles to be conducted for their personal glorification."

"Such a stupendous change as you describe," said I, "did not, of course, take place without great bloodshed and terrible convulsions."

"On the contrary," replied Dr. Leete, "there was absolutely no violence. The change had been long foreseen. Public opinion had become fully ripe for it, and the whole mass of the people was behind it. There was no more possibility of opposing it by force than by argument. On the other hand the popular sentiment toward the great corporations and those identified with them had ceased to be one of bitterness, as they came to realize their necessity as a link, a transition phase, in the evolution of the true industrial system. The most violent foes of the great private monopolies were now forced to recognize how invaluable and indispensable had been their office in educating the people up to the point of assuming control of their own business. Fifty years before, the consolidation of the industries of the country under national control would have seemed a very daring experiment to the most sanguine. But by a series of object lessons, seen and studied by all men, the great corporations had taught the people an entirely new set of ideas on this subject. They had seen for many years syndicates handling revenues greater than those of states, and directing the labors of hundreds of thousands of men with an efficiency and economy unattainable in smaller operations. It had come to be recognized as an axiom that the larger the business the simpler the principles that can be applied to it; that, as the machine is truer than the hand, so the system, which in a great concern does the work of the master's eye in a small business, turns out more accurate results. Thus it came about that, thanks to the corporations themselves, when it was proposed that the nation should assume their functions, the suggestion implied nothing which seemed impracticable even to the timid. To be sure it was a step beyond any yet taken, a broader generalization, but the very fact that the nation would be the sole corporation in the field would, it was seen, relieve the undertaking of many difficulties with which the partial monopolies had contended."

Chapter IX

Dr. and Mrs. Leete were evidently not a little startled to learn, when they presently appeared, that I had been all over the city alone that morning, and it was apparent that they were agreeably surprised to see that I seemed so little agitated after the experience.

"Your stroll could scarcely have failed to be a very interesting one," said Mrs. Leete, as we sat down to table soon after. "You must have seen a good many new things."

"I saw very little that was not new," I replied. "But I think what surprised me as much as anything was not to find any stores on Washington Street, or any banks on State. What have you done with the merchants and bankers? Hung them all, perhaps, as the anarchists wanted to do in my day?"

"Not so bad as that," replied Dr. Leete. "We have simply dispensed with them. Their functions are obsolete in the modern world."

"Who sells you things when you want to buy them?" I inquired.   5

"There is neither selling nor buying nowadays; the distribution of goods is effected in another way. As to the bankers, having no money we have no use for those gentry."

"Miss Leete," said I, turning to Edith, "I am afraid that your father is making sport of me. I don't blame him, for the temptation my innocence offers must be extraordinary. But, really, there are limits to my credulity as to possible alterations in the social system."

"Father has no idea of jesting, I am sure," she replied, with a reassuring smile.

The conversation took another turn then, the point of ladies' fashions in the nineteenth century being raised, if I remember rightly, by Mrs. Leete, and it was not till after breakfast, when the doctor had invited me up to the house-top, which appeared to be a favorite resort of his, that he recurred to the subject.

"You were surprised," he said, "at my saying that we got along with-   10
out money or trade, but a moment's reflection will show that trade existed and money was needed in your day simply because the business of production was left in private hands, and that, consequently, they are superfluous now."

"I do not at once see how that follows," I replied.

"It is very simple," said Dr. Leete. "When innumerable different and independent persons produced the various things needful to life and comfort, endless exchanges between individuals were requisite in order that they might supply themselves with what they desired. These exchanges constituted trade, and money was essential as their medium. But as soon as the nation became the sole producer of all sorts of commodities, there was no need of exchanges between individuals that they might get what they required. Everything was procurable from one source, and nothing could be procured anywhere else. A system of direct distribution from the national storehouses took the place of trade, and for this money was unnecessary."

"How is this distribution managed?" I asked.

"On the simplest possible plan," replied Dr. Leete. "A credit corresponding to his share of the annual product of the nation is given to every citizen on the public books at the beginning of each year, and a credit card issued him with which he procures at the public storehouses, found in every community, whatever he desires whenever he desires it. This arrangement, you will see, totally obviates the necessity for business transactions of any sort between individuals and consumers. Perhaps you would like to see what our credit cards are like.

"You observe," he pursued as I was curiously examining the piece of pasteboard he gave me, "that this card is issued for a certain number of dollars. We have kept the old word, but not the substance. The term, as we use it, answers to no real thing, but merely serves as an algebraical symbol for comparing the values of products with one another. For this purpose they are all priced in dollars and cents, just as in your day. The value of what I procure on this card is checked off by the clerk, who pricks out of these tiers of squares the price of what I order."

"If you wanted to buy something of your neighbor, could you transfer part of your credit to him as consideration?" I inquired.

"In the first place," replied Dr. Leete," our neighbors have nothing to sell us, but in any event our credit would not be transferable, being strictly personal. Before the nation could even think of honoring any such transfer as you speak of, it would be bound to inquire into all the circumstances of the transaction, so as to be able to guarantee its absolute equity. It would have been reason enough, had there been no other, for abolishing money, that its possession was no indication of rightful title to it. In the hands of the man who had stolen it or murdered for it, it was as good as in those which had earned it by industry. People nowadays interchange gifts and favors out of friendship, but buying and selling is considered absolutely inconsistent with the mutual benevolence and disinterestedness which should prevail between citizens and the sense of community of interest which supports our social system. According to our ideas, buying and selling is essentially anti-social in all its tendencies. It is an education in self-seeking at the expense of others, and no society whose citizens are trained in such a school can possibly rise above a very low grade of civilization."

"What if you have to spend more than your card in any one year?" I asked.

"The provision is so ample that we are more likely not to spend it all," replied Dr. Leete. "But if extraordinary expenses should exhaust it, we can obtain a limited advance on the next year's credit, though this practice is not encouraged, and a heavy discount is charged to check it. Of course if a man showed himself a reckless spendthrift he would receive his allowance monthly or weekly instead of yearly, or if necessary not be permitted to handle it all."

"If you don't spend your allowance, I suppose it accumulates?"   20

"That is also permitted to a certain extent when a special outlay is anticipated. But unless notice to the contrary is given, it is presumed that the citizen who does not fully expend his credit did not have occasion to do so, and the balance is turned into the general surplus."

"Such a system does not encourage saving habits on the part of citizens," I said.

"It is not intended to," was the reply. "The nation is rich, and does not wish the people to deprive themselves of any good thing. In your day, men were bound to lay up goods and money against coming failure of the means of support and for their children. This necessity made parsimony a virtue. But now it would have no such laudable object, and, having lost its utility, it has ceased to be regarded as a virtue. No man any more has any care for the morrow, either for himself or his children, for the nation guarantees the nurture, education, and comfortable maintenance of every citizen from the cradle to the grave."

"That is a sweeping guarantee!" I said. "What certainty can there be that the value of a man's labor will recompense the nation for its outlay on him? On the whole, society may be able to support all its members, but some must earn less than enough for their support, and others more; and that brings us back once more to the wages question, on which you have hitherto said nothing. It was at just this point, if you remember, that our talk ended last evening; and I say again, as I did then, that here I should suppose a national industrial system like yours would find its main difficulty. How, I ask once more, can you adjust satisfactorily the comparative wages or remuneration of the multitude of avocations, so unlike and so incommensurable, which are necessary for the service of society? In our day the market rate determined the price of labor of all sorts, as well as of goods. The employer paid as little as he could, and the worker got as much. It was not a pretty system ethically, I admit; but it did, at least, furnish us a rough and ready formula for settling a question which must be settled ten thousand times a day if the world was ever going to get forward. There seemed to us no other practicable way of doing it."

"Yes," replied Dr. Leete, "it was the only practicable way under a sys-   25
tem which made the interests of every individual antagonistic to those of every other; but it would have been a pity if humanity could never have devised a better plan, for yours was simply the application to the mutual relations of men of the devil's maxim, "Your necessity is my opportunity." The reward of any service depended not upon its difficulty, danger, or hardship, for throughout the world it seems that the most perilous, severe, and repulsive labor was done by the worst paid classes; but solely upon the strait of those who needed the service."

"All that is conceded," I said. "But, with all its defects, the plan of settling prices by the market rate was a practical plan; and I cannot conceive what satisfactory substitute you can have devised for it. The government being the only possible employer, there is of course no labor market or market rate. Wages of all sorts must be arbitrarily fixed by the government. I cannot imagine a more complex and delicate function than that must be, or one, however performed, more certain to breed universal dissatisfaction."

"I beg your pardon," replied Dr. Leete, "but I think you exaggerate the difficulty. Suppose a board of fairly sensible men were charged with settling the wages for all sorts of trades under a system which, like ours, guaranteed employment to all, while permitting the choice of avocations. Don't you see that, however unsatisfactory the first adjustment might be, the mistakes would soon correct themselves? The favored trades would have too many volunteers, and those discriminated against would lack them till the errors were set right. But this is aside from the purpose, for, though this plan would, I fancy, be practicable enough, it is no part of our system."

"How, then, do you regulate wages?" I once more asked.

Dr. Leete did not reply till after several moments of meditative silence. "I know, of course," he finally said, "enough of the old order of things to understand just what you mean by that question; and yet the present order is so utterly different at this point that I am a little at loss how to answer you best. You ask me how we regulate wages; I can only reply that there is no idea in the modern social economy which at all corresponds with what was meant by wages in your day."

"I suppose you mean that you have no money to pay wages in," said I. "But the credit given the worker at the government storehouse answers to his wages with us. How is the amount of the credit given respectively to the workers in different lines determined? By what title does the individual claim his particular share? What is the basis of allotment?"   30

"His title," replied Dr. Leete, "is his humanity. The basis of his claim is the fact that he is a man."

"The fact that he is a man!" I repeated, incredulously. "Do you possibly mean that all have the same share?"

"Most assuredly."

The readers of this book never having practically known any other arrangement, or perhaps very carefully considered the historical accounts of former epochs in which a very different system prevailed, cannot be expected to appreciate the stupor of amazement into which Dr. Leete's simple statement plunged me.

"You see," he said, smiling, "that it is not merely that we have no   35 money to pay wages in, but, as I said, we have nothing at all answering to your idea of wages."

By this time I had pulled myself together sufficiently to voice some of the criticisms which, man of the nineteenth century as I was, came uppermost in my mind, upon this to me astounding arrangement. "Some men do twice the work of others!" I exclaimed. "Are the clever workmen content with a plan that ranks them with the indifferent?"

"We leave no possible ground for any complaint of injustice," replied Dr. Leete, "by requiring precisely the same measure of service from all."

"How can you do that, I should like to know, when no two men's powers are the same?"

"Nothing could be simpler," was Dr. Leete's reply. "We require of each that he shall make the same effort; that is, we demand of him the best service it is in his power to give."

"And supposing all do the best they can," I answered, "the amount of the product resulting is twice greater from one man than from another."   40

"Very true," replied Dr. Leete; "but the amount of the resulting product has nothing whatever to do with the question, which is one of desert. Desert is a moral question, and the amount of the product a material quantity. It would be an extraordinary sort of logic which should try to determine a moral question by a material standard. The amount of the effort alone is pertinent to the question of desert. All men who do their best, do the same. A man's endowments, however godlike, merely fix the measure of his duty. The man of great endowments who does not do all he might, though he may do more than a man of small endowments who does his best, is deemed a less deserving worker than the latter, and dies a debtor to his fellows. The Creator sets men's tasks for them by the faculties he gives them; we simply exact their fulfillment."

"No doubt that is very fine philosophy," I said; "nevertheless it seems hard that the man who produces twice as much as another, even if both do their best, should have only the same share."

"Does it, indeed, seem so to you?" responded Dr. Leete. "Now, do you know, that seems very curious to me? The way it strikes people nowadays is, that a man who can produce twice as much as another with the same effort, instead of being rewarded for doing so, ought to be punished if he does not do so. In the nineteenth century, when a horse pulled a heavier load than a goat, I suppose you rewarded him. Now, we should have whipped him soundly if he had not, on the ground that, being much stronger, he ought to. It is singular how ethical standards change." The doctor said this with such a twinkle in his eye that I was obliged to laugh.

"I suppose," I said, "that the real reason that we rewarded men for their endowments, while we considered those of horses and goats merely as fixing the service to be severally required of them, was that the animals, not being reasoning beings, naturally did the best they could, whereas men could only be induced to do so by rewarding them according to the amount of their product. That brings me to ask why, unless human nature has mightily changed in a hundred years, you are not under the same necessity."

"We are," replied Dr. Leete. "I don't think there has been any change in   45
human nature in that respect since your day. It is still so constituted that

special incentives in the form of prizes, and advantages to be gained, are requisite to call out the best endeavors of the average man in any direction."

"But what inducement," I asked, "can a man have to put forth his best endeavors when, however much or little he accomplishes, his income remains the same? High characters may be moved by devotion to the common welfare under such a system, but does not the average man tend to rest back on his oar, reasoning that it is of no use to make a special effort, since the effort will not increase his income, nor its withholding diminish it?"

"Does it then really seem to you," answered my companion, "that human nature is insensible to any motives save fear of want and love of luxury, that you should expect security and equality of livelihood to leave them without possible incentives to effort? Your contemporaries did not really think so, though they might fancy they did. When it was a question of the grandest class of efforts, the most absolute self-devotion, they depended on quite other incentives. Not higher wages, but honor and the hope of men's gratitude, patriotism and the inspiration of duty, were the motives which they set before their soldiers when it was a question of dying for the nation, and never was there an age of the world when those motives did not call out what is best and noblest in men. And not only this, but when you come to analyze the love of money which was the general impulse to effort in your day, you find that the dread of want and desire of luxury was but one of several motives which the pursuit of money represented; the others, and with many the more influential, being desire of power, of social position, and reputation for ability and success. So you see that though we have abolished poverty and the fear of it, and inordinate luxury with the hope of it, we have not touched the greater part of the motives which underlay the love of money in former times, or any of those which prompted the supremer sorts of effort. The coarser motives, which no longer move us, have been replaced by higher motives wholly unknown to the mere wage earners of your age. Now that industry of whatever sort is no longer self-service, but service of the nation, patriotism, passion for humanity, impel the worker as in your day they did the soldier. The army of industry is an army, not alone by virtue of its perfect organization, but by reason also of the ardor of self-devotion which animates its members.

"But as you used to supplement the motives of patriotism with the love of glory, in order to stimulate the valor of your soldiers, so do we. Based as our industrial system is on the principle of requiring the same unit of effort from every man, that is, the best he can do, you will see that the means by which we spur the workers to do their best must be a very essential part of our scheme. With us, diligence in the national service is the sole and certain way to public repute, social distinction, and official power. The value of a man's services to society fixes his rank in it. Compared with the effect of our social arrangements in impelling men to be zealous in business, we deem the object-lessons of biting poverty and wanton luxury on which you depended a device as weak and uncertain as it was barbaric. The lust of honor even in your sordid day notoriously impelled men to more desperate effort than the love of money could."

Topics for Critical Thinking and Writing

1. Let's assume that, like Bellamy in 1887, you are writing a book in which the narrator chats with people who are living a hundred years from now. Write the opening paragraphs, using Bellamy's device of setting forth a view of life that you hope in the future will be regarded as barbaric. (The present, as Bellamy saw it, was ruthlessly capitalistic, and the future he envisioned was ideally socialistic, but of course your own view may be very different.) *Alternative topic*: You may want to envision a *dystopia*, a horrific society (George Orwell's *1984* is a famous example), in which case your narrator, speaking around 2100, will probably ironically see our time as wicked (though the reader should understand that what is being condemned is good), and the society of 2100 as good (though the reader should understand that what is being praised is evil).

2. The questions that are always asked about books such as *Looking Backward* are: (1) is the writer's vision practical; that is, might this imagined world really come into existence, or has the writer misunderstood human nature?, and (2) is the writer's vision desirable; that is, would we want to live in the world described in the book? In an essay of 500 to 750 words, give your response to both of these questions, as applied to *Looking Backward*.

James Joyce

James Joyce (1882–1941) was born into a middle-class family in Dublin, Ireland. His father drank, becoming increasingly irresponsible and unemployable, and the family sank in the social order. Still, Joyce received a strong classical education at excellent Jesuit schools and at University College, Dublin, where he studied modern languages. In 1902, at the age of twenty, he left Ireland so that he might spend the rest of his life writing about life in Ireland. ("The shortest way to Tara," he said, "is via Holyhead," i.e., the shortest way to the heart of Ireland is to take ship away.) In Trieste, Zurich, and Paris he supported his family in a variety of ways, sometimes teaching English in a Berlitz language school. His fifteen stories, collected under the title of Dubliners, *were written between 1904 and 1907, but he could not get them published until 1914. Next came a highly autobiographical novel,* A Portrait of the Artist as a Young Man *(1916).* Ulysses *(1922), a large novel covering eighteen hours in Dublin, was for some years banned by the United States Post Office, though few if any readers today find it offensive. Joyce spent most of the rest of his life working on* Finnegans Wake *(1939).*

Nine years before he succeeded in getting Dubliners *published he described the manuscript in these terms:*

My intention was to write a chapter of the moral history of my country and I chose Dublin for the scene because that city seemed to me the centre of paralysis. . . . I have written it for the most part in a style of scrupulous meanness and with the conviction that he is a very bold man who dares to alter in the presentment, still more to deform, whatever he has seen and heard.

Araby

North Richmond Street, being blind,[1] was a quiet street except at the hour when the Christian Brothers' School set the boys free. An uninhabited house of two stories stood at the blind end, detached from its neighbors in a square ground.

The other houses of the street, conscious of decent lives within them, gazed at one another with brown imperturbable faces.

The former tenant of our house, a priest, had died in the back drawingroom. Air, musty from having long been enclosed, hung in all the rooms, and the waste room behind the kitchen was littered with old useless papers. Among these I found a few papercovered books, the pages of which were curled and damp: *The Abbot*, by Walter Scott, *The Devout Communicant* and *The Memoirs of Vidocq*.[2] I liked the last best because its leaves were yellow. The wild garden behind the house contained a central apple-tree and a few straggling bushes under one of which I found the late tenant's rusty bicycle-pump. He had been a very charitable priest; in his will he had left all his money to institutions and the furniture of his house to his sister.

When the short days of winter came dusk fell before we had well eaten our dinners. When we met in the street the houses had grown sombre. The space of sky above us was the colour of everchanging violet and towards it the lamps of the street lifted their feeble lanterns. The cold air stung us and we played till our bodies glowed. Our shouts echoed in the silent street. The career of our play brought us through the dark muddy lanes behind the houses where we ran the gauntlet of the rough tribes from the cottages, to the back doors of the dark dripping gardens where odours arose from the ashpits, to the dark odorous stables where a coachman smoothed and combed the horse or shook music from the buckled harness. When we returned to the street light from the kitchen windows had filled the areas. If my uncle was seen turning the corner we hid in the shadow until we had seen him safely housed. Or if Mangan's sister came out on the doorstep to call her brother in to his tea we watched her from our shadow peer up and down the street. We waited to see whether she would remain or go in and, if she remained, we left our shadow and walked up to Mangan's steps resignedly. She was waiting for us, her figure defined by the light from the half-opened door. Her brother always

---

[1]**blind** a dead-end street (All notes are by the editors.)

[2]*The Abbot* was one of Scott's popular historical romances. *The Devout Communicant* was a Catholic religious manual; *The Memoirs of Vidocq* were the memoirs of the chief of the French detective force.

teased her before he obeyed and I stood by the railings looking at her. Her dress swung as she moved her body and the soft rope of her hair tossed from side to side.

Every morning I lay on the floor in the front parlour watching her door. The blind was pulled down to within an inch of the sash so that I could not be seen. When she came out on the doorstep my heart leaped. I ran to the hall, seized my books and followed her. I kept her brown figure always in my eye and, when we came near the point at which our ways diverged, I quickened my pace and passed her. This happened morning after morning. I had never spoken to her, except for a few casual words, and yet her name was like a summons to all my foolish blood.

Her image accompanied me even in places the most hostile to romance. On Saturday evenings when my aunt went marketing I had to go to carry some of the parcels. We walked through the flaring streets, jostled by drunken men and bargaining women, amid the curses of labourers, the shrill litanies of shop-boys who stood on guard by the barrels of pigs' cheeks, the nasal chanting of street-singers, who sang a *come-all-you* about O'Donovan Rossa,[3] or a ballad about the troubles in our native land. These noises converged in a single sensation of life for me: I imagined that I bore my chalice safely through a throng of foes. Her name sprang to my lips at moments in strange prayers and praises which I myself did not understand. My eyes were often full of tears (I could not tell why) and at times a flood from my heart seemed to pour itself out into my bosom. I thought little of the future. I did not know whether I would ever speak to her or not or, if I spoke to her, how I could tell her of my confused adoration. But my body was like a harp and her words and gestures were like fingers running upon the wires.

One evening I went into the back drawing-room in which the priest had died. It was a dark rainy evening and there was no sound in the house. Through one of the broken panes I heard the rain impinge upon the earth, the fine incessant needles of water playing in the sodden beds. Some distant lamp or lighted window gleamed below me. I was thankful that I could see so little. All my senses seemed to desire to veil themselves and, feeling that I was about to slip from them, I pressed the palms of my hands together until they trembled, murmuring: *O love! O love!* many times.

At last she spoke to me. When she addressed the first words to me I was so confused that I did not know what to answer. She asked me was I going to Araby.

I forget whether I answered yes or no. It would be a splendid bazaar, she said; she would love to go.

—And why can't you? I asked.

---

[3]Jeremiah O'Donovan (1831–1915), a popular Irish leader who was jailed by the British for advocating violent rebellion. A "come-all-you" was a topical song that began "Come all you gallant Irishmen."

While she spoke she turned a silver bracelet round and round her   10
wrist. She could not go, she said, because there would be a retreat that
week in her convent. Her brother and two other boys were fighting for
their caps and I was alone at the railings. She held one of the spikes, bowing her head towards me. The light from the lamp opposite our door
caught the white curve of her neck, lit up her hair that rested there and,
falling, lit up the hand upon the railing. It fell over one side of her dress
and caught the white border of a petticoat, just visible as she stood at ease.

—It's well for you, she said.

—If I go, I said, I will bring you something.

What innumerable follies laid waste my waking and sleeping
thoughts after that evening! I wished to annihilate the tedious intervening days. I chafed against the work of school. At night in my bedroom
and by day in the classroom her image came between me and the page I
strove to read. The syllables of the word *Araby* were called to me through
the silence in which my soul luxuriated and cast an Eastern enchantment
over me. I asked for leave to go to the bazaar on Saturday night. My aunt
was surprised and hoped it was not some Freemason[4] affair. I answered
few questions in class, I watched my master's face pass from amiability to
sternness; he hoped I was not beginning to idle. I could not call my wandering thoughts together. I had hardly any patience with the serious work
of life which, now that it stood between me and my desire, seemed to me
child's play, ugly monotonous child's play.

On Saturday morning I reminded my uncle that I wished to go to the
bazaar in the evening. He was fussing at the hallstand, looking for the
hat-brush, and answered me curtly:

—Yes, boy, I know.   15

As he was in the hall I could not go into the front parlour and lie at
the window. I left the house in bad humour and walked slowly towards
the school. The air was pitilessly raw and already my heart misgave me.

When I came home to dinner my uncle had not yet been home. Still it
was early. I sat staring at the clock for some time and, when its ticking began to irritate me, I left the room. I mounted the staircase and gained the
upper part of the house. The high cold empty gloomy rooms liberated me
and I went from room to room singing. From the front window I saw my
companions playing below in the street. Their cries reached me weakened
and indistinct and, leaning my forehead against the cool glass, I looked
over at the dark house where she lived. I may have stood there for an
hour, seeing nothing but the brown-clad figure cast by my imagination,
touched discreetly by the lamplight at the curved neck, at the hand upon
the railings and at the border below the dress.

When I came downstairs again I found Mrs Mercer sitting at the fire.
She was an old garrulous woman, a pawnbroker's widow, who collected
used stamps for some pious purpose. I had to endure the gossip of the

---

[4]Irish Catholics viewed the Masons as their Protestant enemies.

tea-table. The meal was prolonged beyond an hour and still my uncle did not come. Mrs Mercer stood up to go: she was sorry she couldn't wait any longer, but it was after eight o'clock and she did not like to be out late, as the night air was bad for her. When she had gone I began to walk up and down the room, clenching my fists. My aunt said:

—I'm afraid you may put off your bazaar for this night of Our Lord.

At nine o'clock I heard my uncle's latchkey in the halldoor. I heard 20
him talking to himself and heard the hallstand rocking when it had received the weight of his overcoat. I could interpret these signs. When he was midway through his dinner I asked him to give me the money to go to the bazaar. He had forgotten.

—The people are in bed and after their first sleep now, he said.

I did not smile. My aunt said to him energetically:

—Can't you give him the money and let him go? You've kept him late enough as it is.

My uncle said he was very sorry he had forgotten. He said he believed in the old saying: *All work and no play makes Jack a dull boy*. He asked me where I was going and, when I had told him a second time he asked me did I know *The Arab's Farewell to His Steed*.[5] When I left the kitchen he was about to recite the opening lines of the piece to my aunt.

I held a florin tightly in my hand as I strode down Buckingham Street 25
towards the station. The sight of the streets thronged with buyers and glaring with gas recalled to me the purpose of my journey. I took my seat in a third-class carriage of a deserted train. After an intolerable delay the train moved out of the station slowly. It crept onward among ruinous houses and over the twinkling river. At Westland Row Station a crowd of people pressed to the carriage doors; but the porters moved them back, saying that it was a special train for the bazaar. I remained alone in the bare carriage. In a few minutes the train drew up beside an improvised wooden platform. I passed out on to the road and saw by the lighted dial of a clock that it was ten minutes to ten. In front of me was a large building which displayed the magical name.

I could not find any sixpenny entrance and, fearing that the bazaar would be closed, I passed in quickly through a turnstile, handing a shilling to a weary-looking man. I found myself in a big hall girdled at half its height by a gallery. Nearly all the stalls were closed and the greater part of the hall was in darkness. I recognised a silence like that which pervades a church after a service. I walked into the center of the bazaar timidly. A few people were gathered about the stalls which were still open. Before a curtain, over which the words *Café Chantant* were written in coloured lamps, two men were counting money on a salver. I listened to the fall of the coins.

Remembering with difficulty why I had come I went over to one of the stalls and examined porcelain vases and flowered tea-sets. At the door of the

[5]"The Arab to His Favorite Steed" was a popular sentimental poem by Caroline Norton (1808–1877).

stall a young lady was talking and laughing with two young gentlemen. I remarked their English accents and listened vaguely to their conversation.

—O, I never said such a thing!

—O, but you did!

—O, but I didn't! 30

—Didn't she say that?

—Yes! I heard her.

—O, there's a . . . fib!

Observing me the young lady came over and asked me did I wish to buy anything. The tone of her voice was not encouraging; she seemed to have spoken to me out of a sense of duty. I looked humbly at the great jars that stood like eastern guards at either side of the dark entrance to the stall and murmured:
—No, thank you. 35
The young lady changed the position of one of the vases and went back to the two young men. They began to talk of the same subject. Once or twice the young lady glanced at me over her shoulder.

I lingered before her stall, though I knew my stay was useless, to make my interest in her wares seem the more real. Then I turned away slowly and walked down the middle of the bazaar. I allowed the two pennies to fall against the sixpence in my pocket. I heard a voice call from one end of the gallery that the light was out. The upper part of the hall was now completely dark.

Gazing up into the darkness I saw myself as a creature driven and derided by vanity; and my eyes burned with anguish and anger.

Topics for Critical Thinking and Writing

1. How old, approximately, is the narrator of "Araby" at the time of the experience he describes? How old is he at the time he tells his story? On what evidence do you base your estimates?

2. The boy, apparently an only child, lives with an uncle and aunt, rather than with parents. Why do you suppose Joyce put him in this family setting rather than some other?

3. The story is rich in images of religion. This in itself is not surprising, for the story is set in Roman Catholic Ireland, but the religious images are not simply references to religious persons or objects. In an essay of 500 to 750 words, discuss how these images reveal the narrator's state of mind.

4. In an essay of about 500 words, consider the role of images of darkness and blindness and what they reveal to us about "Araby" as a story of the fall from innocence into painful awareness.

James Wright

James Wright (1927–80) was born in Martins Ferry, Ohio, which provided him with the locale for many of his poems. He is often thought of as a poet of the Midwest, but (as in the example that we give) his poems move beyond the scenery. Wright was educated at Kenyon College in Ohio and at the University of Washington. He wrote several books of poetry and published many translations of European and Latin American poetry.

Lying in a Hammock at William Duffy's Farm in Pine Island, Minnesota

Over my head, I see the bronze butterfly,
Asleep on the black trunk,
Blowing like a leaf in green shadow.
Down the ravine behind the empty house,
The cowbells follow one another   5
Into the distances of the afternoon.
To my right,
In a field of sunlight between two pines,
The droppings of last year's horses
Blaze up into golden stones.   10
I lean back, as the evening darkens and comes on.
A chicken hawk floats over, looking for home.
I have wasted my life.

 Topics for Critical Thinking and Writing

1. How important is it that the poet is "lying in a hammock"? That he is at some place other than his own home?

2. Do you take the last line as a severe self-criticism, or as a joking remark, or as something in between, or what?

3. Write an imitation of Wright's poem, placing yourself somewhere specific, your eye taking in the surroundings. End with a judgment or concluding comment, as Wright does. Try to imitate the sentence structure as well as

the form of Wright's poem. Here is an imitation written by a student at Wellesley College:

Near my side, I feel his strong body,
Asleep on the blue sheet,
Smiling like a babe in soft blankets,
Behind the house, past the blooming garden,
The children chase one another
Through the haziness of the morning.
In the yard,
In a pool of shadow behind high hedges,
The hummings of late summer's honeybees
Sound among the yellow flowers.
I stand up, as the morning brightens and comes on.
A wild goose cries somewhere, looking for the path.
I have enjoyed my life.

CHAPTER 8

All in the Family

Sonia
Joanne Leonard, 1966

Why One's Parents Got Married
R. Chast

Mrs. Brown and Catherine
Faith Ringgold, 1973

The Acrobat's Family with a Monkey
Pablo Picasso, 1905

Short Views

Higamus hogamus,
Woman's monogamous;
Hogamus higamus,
Man is polygamous.
> *Anonymous (often attributed to William James)*

After a certain age, the more one becomes oneself, the more obvious one's family traits become.
> *Marcel Proust*

All happy families resemble one another; every unhappy family is unhappy in its own fashion.
> *Leo Tolstoy*

On Tuesday, March 31, he and I dined at General Paoli's. A question was started, whether the state of marriage was natural to man. Johnson. "Sir, it is so far from being natural for a man and woman to live in a state of marriage, that we find all the motives which they have for remaining in that connection, and the restraints which civilized society imposes to prevent separation, are hardly sufficient to keep them together." The General said, that in a state of nature a man and woman uniting together would form a strong and constant affection, by the mutual pleasure each would receive; and that the same causes of dissension would not arise between them, as occur between husband and wife in a civilized state. Johnson. "Sir, they would have dissensions enough, though of another kind. One would choose to go a hunting in this wood, the other in that; one would choose to go a fishing in this lake, the other in that; or, perhaps, one would choose to go a hunting, when the other would choose to go a fishing; and so they would part. Besides, Sir, a savage man and a savage woman meet by chance; and when the man sees another woman that pleases him better, he will leave the first."
> *James Boswell*

Marriage is the best of human statuses and the worst, and it will continue to be. And that is why, though its future in some form or other is as assured as anything can be, this future is as equivocal as its past. The demands that men and women make on marriage will never be fully met; they cannot be.
> *Jessie Bernard*

A slavish bondage to parents cramps every faculty of the mind; and Mr. Locke very judiciously observes, that "if the mind be curbed and humbled too much in children, if their spirits be abased and broken much by too strict an hand over them, they lose all their vigour and industry." This strict hand may in some degree account for the weakness of women; for girls, from various causes, are more kept down by their parents, in every sense of the word, than boys. The duty expected from them is, like all the duties arbitrarily imposed on women, more from a sense of propriety, more out of respect for decorum, than reason; and thus taught slavishly to submit to their parents, they are prepared for the slavery of marriage. I may be told that a number of women are not slaves in the marriage state. True, but they then become tyrants; for it is not rational freedom, but a lawless kind of power resembling the authority exercised by the favourites of absolute monarchs, which they obtain by debasing means.

    Mary Wollstonecraft

Nobody who has not been in the interior of a family can say what the difficulties of any individual of that family may be.

    Jane Austen

When I was young enough to still spend a long time buttoning my shoes in the morning, I'd listen toward the hall: Daddy upstairs was shaving in the bathroom and Mother downstairs was frying the bacon. They would begin whistling back and forth to each other up and down the stairwell. My father would whistle his phrase, my mother would try to whistle, then hum hers back. It was their duet. I drew my buttonhook in and out and listened to it—I knew it was "The Merry Widow." The difference was, their song almost floated with laughter: how different from the record, which growled from the beginning, as if the Victrola were only slowly being wound up. They kept it running between them, up and down the stairs where I was now just about ready to run clattering down and show them my shoes.

    Eudora Welty

Lewis Coser

Lewis Coser, born in Berlin in 1913, was educated at the Sorbonne in Paris and at Columbia University, where he received a Ph.D. in sociology in 1954. For many years he taught at the State University of New York, Stony Brook, where he held the title Distinguished Professor. The passage given below is from a textbook designed for college students.

The Family

Following the French anthropologist Claude Lévi-Strauss, we can define the family as a group manifesting these characteristics: it finds its origin in marriage; it consists of husband, wife and children born in their wedlock—though other relatives may find their place close to that nuclear group; and the members of the group are united by moral, legal, economic, religious, and social rights and obligations. These include a network of sexual rights and prohibitions and a variety of socially patterned feelings such as love, attraction, piety, awe, and so on.

The family is among the few universal institutions of mankind. No known society lacks small kinship groups of parents and children related through the process of reproduction. But recognition of the universality of this institution must immediately be followed by the acknowledgment that its forms are exceedingly varied. The fact that many family organizations are not monogamic, as in the West, led many nineteenth-century observers to the erroneous conclusion that in "early" stages of evolution there existed no families, and that "group marriage," institutionalized promiscuity, prevailed. This is emphatically not the case; even though patterned wife-lending shocked the sensibilities of Victorian anthropologists, such an institution is evidently predicated on the fact that men have wives in the first place. No matter what their specific forms, families in all known societies have performed major social functions—reproduction, maintenance, socialization, and social placement of the young.

Families may be monogamous or polygamous—there are systems where one man is entitled to several wives and others where several husbands share one wife. A society may recognize primarily the small nuclear, conjugal unit of husband and wife with their immediate descendants or it may institutionalize the large extended family linking several generations and emphasizing consanguinity more than the conjugal bond. Residence after marriage may be matrilocal, patrilocal or neolocal; exchanges of goods and services between families at the time of marriage may be based on bride price, groom price or an equal exchange;

endogamous or exogamous regulations may indicate who is and who is not eligible for marriage; the choice of a mate may be controlled by parents or it may be left in large measure to the young persons concerned. These are but a few of the many differences which characterize family structures in variant societies.

 Topics for Critical Thinking and Writing

1. At the end of paragraph 2, Coser writes: "No matter what their specific forms, families in all known societies have performed major social functions—reproduction, maintenance, socialization, and social placement of the young." What does "socialization" mean? How does it differ from "social placement of the young"? What specific forms does each take in our society?

2. What examples can you give of "moral, legal, economic, religious, and social rights and obligations" (paragraph 1) that unite members of a family?

3. Compare Coser and Plumb (page 6) on the social functions of the family. According to Plumb, what responsibility does the family in our society have in performing the social functions Coser lists? How do other institutions compete with the family in performing some of these functions?

4. As you read other selections in this chapter, what variations in form of the family do you encounter? Are there any variations in form that Coser did not mention or anticipate?

William J. Doherty

William J. Doherty is a family therapist and director of the Marriage and Family Programs at the University of Minnesota. We reprint a passage from his book, The Intentional Family *(1997).*

Doherty explains intentional thus: "An intentional family is one whose members create a working plan for maintaining and building family ties, and then implement the plan as best they can."

Rituals of Passage: Weddings

Most family rituals occur at home, away from the gaze and judgment of the community. No one is around to evaluate the quality of your family dinner or bedtime rituals. But weddings and funerals are planned by the family to share with their community, which is why they are so packed with meaning and stress.

Weddings and funerals have always been public events because they are too important to be left to individuals. We all have a stake in the start of a new family and in the death of a member of the community. But being intentional about these two central family rituals, in the face of community traditions and pressures, is a major challenge for families.

Weddings

Wedding rituals occur in every human society because marriage in its various forms has enormous social significance. In the Western world, the weddings of royalty and the upper class were always highly ritualized because of their political importance. By the eighteenth century, families of the middle class were also celebrating weddings in a big way. But it wasn't until the nineteenth century in Europe and America that almost all families, rich and poor, began putting substantial time and resources into weddings. It was during this period that what we think of as the "traditional wedding" came into being.

The traditional wedding is American society's classic example of a rite of passage. Anthropologists studying premodern cultures realized that rituals served as transitions from one state of being to another, for example, from childhood to adolescence. (Confirmations and bar mitzvahs serve the same purpose today for Christians and Jews, respectively.) Traditional rites of passage involved a separation from the community, a transitional event, and then reemergence with a new social identity. In other words, you go away, you are transformed, and you return with a new role in the community.[1] Traditional wedding ceremonies involved all three stages.

Although there are regional, ethnic, and religious variations, the general outline of a traditional American wedding ceremony is as follows: At the outset, the groom stands at the front of the church with his best man, awaiting his bride. Before that, he has been mingling about, whereas the bride is in seclusion getting prepared. Immediate family members are escorted to their assigned places on either side of the aisle. There is a pause. The rite of transition begins in earnest when the music shifts and the bride's party starts walking down the aisle. The first high point of the ritual occurs when the bride appears, resplendent in a white gown, accompanied by her father or other significant man. The couple are reunited at the front when the parents hand her over to her groom. The rite of transition culminates with the couple's exchange of vows in solemn tones in front of a member of the clergy. Sometimes at the end of the service, particularly if the woman has taken the man's family name, the clergyperson introduces the couple to the congregation as Mr. and Mrs. They are now legally and religiously married, with all the accompanying rights and responsibilities, before God and the state. The transformation of identity now complete, the couple walk back down the aisle in more informal

5

---

[1]Arnold van Gennep was the anthropologist who pioneered the study of rites of passage. See *The Rites of Passage* (Chicago: University of Chicago Press, 1960), originally published in 1909.

fashion to joyous music. The receiving line then initiates the postcere-
mony rituals of congratulations and celebration.

However, this traditional wedding ritual is packed with a number of
fascinating contradictions:[2]

- *Traditional weddings are public ceremonies that are nevertheless organized
  by individual families.* Virtually every other public ceremony in our
  society is organized by clergy, officials, or other professionals. No
  wonder families feel so much pressure, and why they rely on
  wedding guides and other "expert" opinions.
- *Weddings follow strict guidelines of propriety, with a personal touch.*
  Dear Abby and Ann Landers have made a living responding to
  irate family members and guests who all have complaints about violations of wedding protocol, everything from the invitations to
  what the bride wore and the lack of thank-you notes. Although
  there are clear rights and wrongs in traditional weddings, the couple is also expected to put its own stamp on the ritual in details
  such as the invitations, flowers, cake, music, wedding attire, vows,
  and order of service. These personal choices must also be "correct,"
  that is, not out of line with community expectations. The double-
  bind is thus manifest: To be unoriginal is to not measure up, but to
  be too original is to invite social disapproval.
- *Even couples with little religious affiliation often want religious weddings.* Couples who do not make time for the "sacred" in their daily
  lives nevertheless frequently want this religious aspect to their
  weddings. In American society, only religious surroundings make
  possible the traditional wedding pomp and circumstance of the
  majestic bridal procession up a long aisle, high-vaulted ceilings, the
  engulfing organ music, and the sense that something profound and
  holy is occurring. An office wedding by a justice of the peace carries far less ritual power. The traditional wedding ritual is even
  more potent if held at the place of one's baptism, bar mitzvah or bat
  mitzvah, and the weddings and funerals of loved ones. The walls
  reverberate with family memories.
- *Traditional religious weddings combine the sense of the sacred and the sexual, elements that are rarely connected in society.* In all cultures and all   10
  religions, the sexual bond is what makes marriage unique. Sexual
  themes, therefore, pervade the wedding ritual, from the presumed
  virginity of the bride in her white gown and the readings from the
  erotic Song of Songs in the Bible to the expectation that the bride and
  groom will exchange a lover's kiss. The couple is expected to consummate their union on the wedding night. Traditional religious
  rituals also refer to the outcome of their sexual activity—children,

[2]See Diana Leonard Barker, "A Proper Wedding," in Marie Corbin (ed.), *The Couple* (New
York Penguin Books, 1978), pp. 56–77; and Diana Leonard Barker, *Sex and Generation: A
Study of Courtship and Wedding* (New York: Tavistock Publications, 1980).

the continuity of the family, and the community. Failure to consummate the marriage is in fact grounds for annulment in most religions. This combination of the sacred and the sexual gives weddings special power in our consciousness.

- *The couple are elevated and celebrated by the community, but also teased and embarrassed.* After honoring the bride and groom with gifts and special attention, guests at the traditional wedding reception expect the couple to submit to embarrassing, silly rituals such as feeding each other cake, dancing on command, having people pay to dance with them, removing and tossing a garter belt, having to kiss whenever the guests tinkle their glasses, and enduring practical jokes as they prepare to leave for their honeymoon. The same kinds of rituals occur in many other cultures; in Hindu weddings, for example, the couple is required to play various games for the benefit of the guests. It is as if the community wants to remind the couple not to feel above those who know and love them the best.

- *Weddings in contemporary society are expected to bring a man and woman together as equal partners in marriage, but the traditional ceremony suggests an imbalance.* The bride's white dress is the key symbol. The white color symbolizes youth and virginity, two elements not regarded as important for the groom. She purchases her dress, often at considerable expense, and is expected to keep it. The groom generally rents his tuxedo unless he happens to own one. The bride is the object of much more attention than the groom before, during, and after the ceremony. In the traditional ceremony, she is given away by her family; no one gives him away. In the past, she received a ring; he did not. In many cases, she still changes her family name to his. All of these elements make it clear that the change in identity is more significant for the woman than for the man, implying that her status in the world will be dependent on his. Although most contemporary couples aspire to equality in marriage, they enthusiastically go through a ritual that emphasizes the woman's inequality.[3]

- *Traditionally only first marriages are allowed the full ritual.* Actually, the key is the bride's prior marriages, not the groom's. A woman supposedly only has the right to wear white once. After that, she is expected to be more discreet about what she wears—she is clearly no longer a virgin—and what she expects in the way of attention and gifts. If the man has been married three times before but the woman has never been married, they are still eligible to have a traditional wedding—another clear illustration of how a wedding is thought to change a woman's identity more than a man's. But Intentional Couples today sometimes ignore these strictures for second marriages and have all the bells and

[3]*Ibid.*, p. 71.

whistles at their wedding. I know one woman who had eloped for her first wedding and decided to make the second one a grand production. It was her groom's first marriage and he was all for it.

 Topics for Critical Thinking and Writing

1. In these pages, Doherty lists what he calls the "fascinating contradictions" of the traditional wedding ritual. What are the contradictions? Were you aware that these contradictions existed? Which of them strikes you as most interesting?

2. If you have been married, how many of the contradictions that Doherty lists did your wedding ritual include? If you expect (sometime) to be married, how traditional do you want your wedding to be?

3. In an essay of about 750 words, report a wedding that you have attended. Comment on the contradictions—or lack of contradictions—that you observed and remember.

Gabrielle Glaser

Gabrielle Glaser is the author of a recent book, Strangers to the Tribe: Portraits of Interfaith Marriage *(1997). We reprint an essay that was originally published in* The New York Times Magazine *in 1997.*

Scenes from an Intermarriage

As Alfred and Eileen Ono sit down late one evening to discuss their family's religious life, even the seating arrangement seems to reveal their spiritual divide. On one side of their sumptuous living room in Portland, Ore., Eileen settles into a comfortable wing chair. Al is across from her, on the couch, next to their 22-year-old daughter, Sarah. From time to time during the conversation, father and daughter link hands.

Sarah and her 18-year-old brother, Alistair, a college freshman, have been raised in the Buddhist faith of their Japanese-American father. Eileen, a Middle Westerner with Dutch, Lithuanian and German roots, has remained a Catholic. The Onos decided how to raise the children long ago, even before they were married, and Eileen insists that her solitary spirituality is of little import. But the religious differences in this family, in which both children shave their heads in the style of Buddhist monks and nuns, exert a gravitational pull on each relationship—between the

Gabrielle Glaser, "Faith is a Gamble: Scenes from an Intermarriage" published in *The New York Times Magazine*, December 7, 1997. By permission of Gabrielle Glaser.

parents and the children, between the siblings and between husband and wife.

Perhaps surprisingly, it is Eileen who is most relaxed about the family's complicated spiritual life. Over the years, her husband has become more doctrinaire. When Sarah was in her early teens and interested in Catholicism, for example, Al insisted that she continue to attend temple every Sunday. Then, in college, when she dated a devout Irish Catholic and began going to Mass with him, Al expressed his disappointment outright.

The Onos say that they try to live up to the ideal of tolerance in all matters. But it isn't any easier for them than it is for the other 33 million Americans who live in interfaith households. The United States, founded by religious dissidents and shaped by a Christian revival in the 19th century, has evolved into a rich religious pluralism. As racial and ethnic barriers have become hazier, intermarriage has become more common: according to recent surveys, 52 percent of Jews, 32 percent of Catholics and 57 percent of Buddhists marry outside the faith.

Many couples split their religious differences in the interest of family harmony, but the Onos' choice not to is evident the moment you enter their splendid turn-of-the-century home. A gold Japanese panel rests on the living room mantel, and in the library sits a black lacquer *obutsudan*, or Buddhist shrine, where Alistair, Sarah and Al recite chants over prayer beads. The three practice Jodoshinshu, a form of Japanese Buddhism, although in recent years Sarah has also included elements of Tibetan Buddhism. (Alistair refers teasingly to Sarah's interest in Tibetan Buddhism as an "upper-middle-class white thing.")

Al, a gentle man with thick gray hair and a kind but intense face, speaks in the drawn-out vowels of his native Minnesota. His parents, George and Masaye, were born in California; their marriage was arranged by a match-maker. They later settled in St. Louis Park, and helped to found the state's first Buddhist temple. Growing up, Al flourished there and relished the simple truths of his faith: There is suffering. There is a cause for suffering. Suffering can be overcome by thinking and living in the right way. His Buddhism, which he describes as "logical and linear," built on wisdom, knowledge, truth and compassion, filters into all aspects of his life: as a doctor—he has a thriving OB-GYN practice in Portland—a father and a husband. "When patients come to me and say, 'Oh, my God, it's cancer, I should have come to you sooner,'" Al says, "I say: 'This is not because you've done anything wrong or because you missed your last appointment. Don't blame yourself. Bodies are always changing. Now it's time to put it back on track.'"

Eileen, on the other hand, has always had questions about her faith. A plain-spoken woman with pale, luminous skin and large, hazel eyes, she was raised in a Minnesota farming town where about half the population was Catholic. As a child, she liked the music and pageantry the church offered, but some things didn't make sense to her. "I'd go to confession and have to make up sins," she says. "I just hadn't done anything horrible."

5

By the time she married, Eileen had also begun to find much of church doctrine—on birth control and the role of women, for example—outdated. Still, she considers herself Catholic. "It's how I was brought up, and it's in my soul," she says.

From time to time, she has second thoughts about the choice she made 27 years ago to raise children in a religion not her own. "I sometimes wish we could be all the same thing," she says softly. "Sure, I do." Sometimes an "Our Father" or "Hail, Mary" will cross her lips before she falls asleep, or when she learns that someone has died. But she rarely goes to church, and like the crossword puzzles she does on Sunday mornings when the rest of her family is at temple, or the meticulous squares of fabric she sews together in her award-winning quilts, Eileen's faith lies apart, boxed and separate, from the rest of her family. "I'm happy with how my spiritual life is," she says. She pauses, then adds, "It's others who have a problem with it."

Those others included her relatives, at least at first. When Al and Eileen began dating in the late 1960's as students at the University of Minnesota, their parents couldn't believe the relationship was serious. When Al told his parents of the couple's plans to marry, his parents accepted the announcement with grim resignation. Eileen's parents reacted with similar reticence.

The wedding was to take place in Minneapolis, and the closest 10 English-speaking Buddhist clergyman lived hundreds of miles away, in Chicago, so the couple settled on a Catholic priest. They were married in a campus chapel, amid burlap banners reading "Peace" and "Love." Led by the priest, they recited Buddhist wedding vows, emphasizing not love or miracles but truth, honor and respect.

Yet the occasion did not flow as smoothly as they had hoped. Eileen's father, an Army veteran, had been stationed in the Philippines during World War II, and after the surrender had hunted the country for Japanese deserters. After several glasses of champagne at the reception, he approached George Ono's best friend with a powerful slap on the back. "Whoever would have guessed that my daughter would be marrying a Jap 25 years after I was over there shooting at them?" he declared. Eileen and Al stared at each other in disbelief. "We'd been so worried about the religious aspects of the wedding that we had overlooked the racial ones," Eileen says. "Our families had always been very cordial to each other." There were other not-so-subtle messages. As a gift, an aunt gave them a plaster statue of Christ, engraved with their names and wedding date.

The couple moved to Portland, and a few years after Sarah's birth the family started going to the Oregon Buddhist Temple there. But at first it was Eileen who took the children to and from services—while Al, caught up in building his medical practice, rarely went. Over time, she began to feel a resistance to being so involved and told Al that he would have to take the lead. "I don't care if you're in the middle of a delivery, you're going to have to be the point man on this," she finally said to him. When Al started going, she stopped.

Sometimes during the ride to temple an image would flash through his head. Of all things, he envisioned a Norman Rockwell painting he once saw, of a family driving off to church, all together. He would dismiss the picture by reminding himself: "But she's not Japanese! She doesn't even relate to this stuff. This was the agreement."

These days, Eileen attends temple occasionally and has incorporated Buddhist thought into her life as a *hakujin*, or white person, as she jokingly calls herself. Indeed, the flies she once swatted are now gently shooed outdoors, in keeping with the Buddhist belief that all forms of life deserve dignity and respect. "They get several chances," she says with a smile. But she has retained a few of her rituals, and Christmas is one of them. The family chooses a tree together, and on Dec. 24 Al and Sarah attend midnight Mass—because they like the music. Eileen doesn't go. "I'm not practicing Catholicism, so I don't feel good just going to church for the highlights," she says, "but I do encourage them to go." The next morning, the whole family opens presents together.

Al says that Christ embodied the wisdom and compassion to which Buddhists aspire, so honoring his birthday has never been an issue. Even so, the holiday Eileen loved as a child, and dreamed of sharing someday with her children, is a bit of a compromise. But religious differences can't take all of the blame: Dec. 25 is also Alistair's birthday, and at noon the day turns from celebrating Christ's arrival to celebrating Alistair's.

Other holidays follow Japanese tradition. For New Year's, Al spends days preparing a feast of special rice cakes and sashimi, and the family toasts one another with sake. "It's never been, 'Well, if you get sushi, tomorrow we have to have schnitzel,'" Eileen says. "I never denied my heritage. It just wasn't a big deal."

Her children's upbringing was a world away from memorizing catechism lessons. Sarah and Alistair spent Sundays at dharma school, learning to chant and meditate. At home, they drank green tea and, as toddlers, learned to use chopsticks. (So accustomed was the family to eating rice at every meal that Alistair thought mashed potatoes were a delicacy. "I thought there was a religious meaning to having them at Thanksgiving," he says with a grin. "That's the only time we ever had them.")

Yet growing up Buddhist in Portland wasn't easy. Children taunted Sarah and Alistair on the playground. In his advanced-placement English class, Alistair once suggested that perhaps not everyone was able to recognize Biblical allusions in literature. The teacher replied, "If you don't know the story of Moses, you don't belong here."

Sarah, a recent graduate of Connecticut College, is back at home doing part-time work while she looks for a job. As a child, she could see only what her religion didn't offer her. "Buddhism didn't have any perks," she says. "Until high school, it was weird. There's no Buddhist rite of passage. My Jewish friends got bas mitzvahs, my Catholic friends got big parties at their first Communion. When you're 9 or 10, you don't want to be anything but what your friends are." So she "tried out" Catholicism and at night would drop to her knees, hands clasped together, and pray at her bedside. She thought it might be easier to "talk to God" than to sit in silent meditation and clear her head of all thoughts. She even attended Catholic summer camp. Her friends taught her prayers, walked her through the steps of Mass, including Communion. She wanted, she says, "to pass," and told people that her mother was Catholic. When a counselor found out that Sarah had taken Communion without being Catholic, she scolded her. Sarah was mortified.

In time, Sarah, a small woman with delicate Asian features, made   20
peace with Buddhism. She studied in Asia for several months and welcomed living in a Buddhist society. Her faith, she says, has taught her one true thing: "to focus on the present."

In some ways, Eileen and Al's decision to raise their children as Buddhists was reinforced by society at large. Because of their Japanese surname and their tea-with-cream-colored skin, both Alistair and Sarah say that they found themselves identifying more readily with their Asian roots than their European ones. Alistair in particular has immersed himself in Japanese culture and credits the dynamic young minister at the Portland temple with inspiring his deeper involvement in Buddhism. At a special ceremony last spring, he received his Buddhist name, a great honor. Days later, he had the name, Gu-Sen—"widespread proclamation"—tattooed in Japanese on his lower back.

Yet guilt also lurks behind Alistair's enthusiasm for his father's faith and heritage. He half-facetiously calls himself a "mama's boy," and frequently E-mails Eileen from college; he worries that he has neglected her in some way. When a high-school history teacher gave out an assignment to research family trees, Alistair filled out the Ono branches practically by heart. When he asked his mother for help with her side, she pulled out photo albums and scrapbooks and recounted details of little-known relatives. "I had never asked about them before," he says. "I felt kind of bad."

Al, too, wonders quietly if he has inadvertently dampened his wife's religious life or her ties to her culture. They don't talk about it much; Al shies from confrontation. But he does remember that on a trip to Ireland some years ago they stumbled one afternoon into a stone church in the middle of Mass. Al turned to Eileen and asked, "Do you want to take Communion?" She brushed him off, he says, by saying she couldn't, since she hadn't been to confession in years. "Was it that she didn't want to be bothered?" he wonders. "Or was it just too complicated with me there, and she didn't want to mess with it?"

What may become of the religious divide between Al and Eileen now, with both children grown, is hard to say. Their marriage is a solid one. They take trips together, go to movies, make elaborate meals, enjoy their children. As middle age gives way to senior discounts, however, the Onos are likely to have disquieting moments. For them, death poses yet another separation. "I don't necessarily believe that God will forgive all at the last minute," Eileen says. "But I do think our spirits go somewhere." Al shakes his head gently. "I'm not so sure there's any connection between this life and another one. The Buddhist perspective doesn't believe we'll all be together again somewhere. I kid Eileen sometimes, telling her: 'Gee, Eileen, if you get last rites, you'll go to heaven. We'll all go to hell, so we'll still be in different places.' "

 Topics for Critical Thinking and Writing

1. Glaser writes of the Ono family's "complicated spiritual life" (paragraph 3). What are the complications, and what produces them?

2. Glaser casts her first paragraph in the present tense. What advantage does this focus give her?

3. Think of an intermarriage with which you are acquainted, in your family or among your friends. Then jot down a list of "scenes" that represent it; for example, religious services, holidays, weddings, funerals. Would you label the intermarriage "complicated"?

4. In an essay of 750 to 1000 words, write your own "Scenes from an Intermarriage" through which you reveal its ease, or strains, or both.

Anonymous

The anonymous author of this essay has revealed only that he was forty when he wrote it, is married, and is the father of three children. The essay originally appeared in The New Republic, *a magazine that was, at the time, regarded as liberal.*

Confessions of an Erstwhile Child

Some years ago I attempted to introduce a class of Upward Bound students to political theory via More's *Utopia*. It was a mistake: I taught precious little theory and earned More a class full of undying enemies on account of two of his ideas. The first, that all members of a Utopian family were subject to the lifelong authority of its eldest male. The second, the Utopian provision that should a child wish to follow a profession different from that of his family, he could be transferred by adoption to a family that practiced the desired trade. My students were not impressed with my claim that the one provision softened the other and made for a fair compromise—for what causes most of our quarrels with our parents but our choice of life-patterns, of occupation? In objecting to the first provision my students were picturing themselves as children, subject to an unyielding authority. But on the second provision they surprised me by taking the parents' role and arguing that this form of ad lib adoption denied them a fundamental right of ownership over their children. It occurred to me that these reactions were two parts of the same pathology: having suffered the discipline of unreasonable parents, one has earned the right to be unreasonable in turn to one's children. The phenomenon has well-known parallels, such as frantic martinets who have risen from the ranks. Having served time as property, my Upward Bound students wanted theirs back as proprietors. I shuddered. It hardly takes an advanced course in Freudian psychology to realize that the perpetuation, generation after generation, of psychic lesions must go right to this source, the philosophically dubious notion that children are the property of their biological parents, compounded with the unphilosophic certitude so many parents harbor, that their children must serve an apprenticeship as like their own as they can manage.

The idea of the child as property has always bothered me, for personal reasons I shall outline. I lack the feeling that I own my children and I have always scoffed at the idea that what they are and do is a continuation or a rejection of my being. I like them, I sympathize with them, I acknowledge the obligation to support them for a term of years—but I am not so fond or foolish as to regard a biological tie as a lien on their loyalty or respect, nor to imagine that I am equipped with preternatural powers of guidance as to their success and happiness. Beyond inculcating some of the obvious social protocols required in civilized life, who am I to pronounce on what makes for a happy or successful life? How many of us can say that we have successfully managed our own lives? Can we do better with our children? I am unimpressed, to say no more, with parents who have no great track record, presuming to oracular powers in regard to their children's lives.

The current debate over the Equal Rights Amendment frequently turns to custody questions. Opponents of ERA have made the horrifying discovery that ERA will spell the end of the mother's presumed rights of custody in divorce or separation cases, and that fathers may begin custody rights. Indeed a few odd cases have been so settled recently in anticipation of the ratification of ERA. If ratified, ERA would be an extremely blunt instrument for calling the whole idea of custody into question, but I for one will applaud anything that serves to begin debate. As important as equal rights between adults may be, I think that the rights of children are a far more serious and unattended need. To me, custody by natural parents, far from being a presumed right only re-examined in case of collapsing marriages, should be viewed as a privilege.

At this point I have to explain why I can so calmly contemplate the denial of so-called parental rights.

I am the only child of two harsh and combative personalities who married, seemingly, in order to have a sparring partner always at hand. My parents have had no other consistent or lasting aim in life but to win out over each other in a contest of wills. They still live, vigorous and angry septuagenarians, their ferocity little blunted by age or human respect. My earliest memories—almost my sole memories—are of unending combat, in which I was sometimes an appalled spectator, more often a hopeless negotiator in a war of no quarter, and most often a bystander accused of covert belligerency on behalf of one side or the other, and frequently of both! I grew up with two supposed adults who were absorbed in their hatreds and recriminations to the exclusion of almost all other reality. Not only did I pass by almost unnoticed in their struggle, the Depression and World War II passed them by equally unnoticed. I figured mainly as a practice target for sarcasm and invective, and occasionally as the ultimate culprit responsible for their unhappiness. ("If it weren't for you," my mother would sometimes say, "I could leave that SOB," a remark belied by her refusal to leave the SOB during these 20 long years since I left their "shelter.")

The reader may ask, "How did you survive if your parents' house was all that bad?" I have three answers. First, I survived by the moral equivalent of running away to sea or the circus, i.e., by burying myself in books and study, especially in the history of faraway and (I thought) more idealistic times than our own, and by consciously shaping my life and tastes to be as different as possible from those of my parents (this was a reproach to them, they knew, and it formed the basis of a whole secondary area of conflict and misunderstanding). Second, I survived because statistically most people "survive" horrible families, but survival can be a qualified term, as it is in my case by a permanently impaired digestive system and an unnatural sensitivity to raised voices. And third, though I found solace in schooling and the rationality, cooperation and basic fairness in teachers that I missed in my parents, I must now question whether it is healthy for a child to count so heavily on schooling for the love and approval that he deserves from his home and family. Even if schooling can do this well, in later life it means that one is loyal and affectionate toward schooling, not toward parents, who may in some sense need affection even if they don't "deserve" it. I am not unaware that however fair and rational I may be in reaction to my parents' counter-examples, I am a very cold-hearted man. I might have done better transferred to a new family, not just by receiving love, but through learning to give it—a lack I mourn as much or more than my failure to receive.

It is little wonder then that I have an acquired immunity to the notion that parental custody is by and large a preferable thing. In my case, almost anything else would have been preferable, including even a rather callously run orphanage—anything for a little peace and quiet. Some people are simply unfit, under any conditions, to be parents, even if, indeed especially if, they maintain the charade of a viable marriage. My parents had no moral right to custody of children, and I cannot believe that my experience is unique or particularly isolated. There are all too many such marriages, in which some form of horror, congenial enough to adults too sick or crazed to recognize it, works its daily ruination on children. Surely thousands of children conclude at age 10 or 11, as I did, that marriage is simply an institution in which people are free to be as beastly as they have a mind to, which may lead either to a rejection of marriage or to a decision to reduplicate a sick marriage a second time, with another generation of victims. It is time to consider the rights of the victims.

How to implement a nascent theory of justice for children is difficult to say. One cannot imagine taking the word of a five-year-old against his parents, but what about a ten- or twelve-year-old? At *some* point, children should have the right to escape the dominance of impossible parents. The matter used to be easier than it has been since World War I. The time-honored solution—for boys—of running away from home has been made infeasible by economic conditions, fingerprints, social security and minimum wage laws. No apprenticeship system exists any more, much less its upper-class medieval version—with required exchange of boys at puberty among noble families to serve as pages and so forth. The adoption system contemplated in More's *Utopia* is a half-remembered echo of a medieval life, in which society, wiser than its theory, decreed a general exchange of children at or just before puberty, whether through apprenticeship or page-service, or more informal arrangements, like going to a university at 14 or running away with troubadors or gypsies.

Exchanging children is a wisely conceived safety valve against a too traumatic involvement between the biological parent and the child. Children need an alternative to living all their formative life in the same biological unit. They should have the right to petition for release from some sorts of families, to join other families, or to engage in other sorts of relationships that may provide equivalent service but may not be organized as a family. The nuclear family, after all, is not such an old or proven vehicle. Phillippe Aries' book, *Centuries of Childhood*, made the important point that the idea of helpless childhood is itself a notion of recent origin, that grew up simultaneously in the 16th and 17th centuries with the small and tight-knit nuclear family, sealed off from the world by another recent invention, "privacy." The older *extended* family (which is the kind More knew about) was probably more authoritarian on paper but much less productive of dependency in actual operation. There ought to be more than one way a youngster can enter adult society with more than half of his sanity left. At least no one should be forced to remain in a no-win game against a couple of crazy parents for 15–18 years. At 10 or 12, children in really messy situations should have the legal right to petition for removal from impossible families, and those rights should be reasonably easy to exercise. (This goes on de facto among the poor, of course, but it is not legal, and usually carries both stigma and danger.) The minimum wage laws should be modified to exempt such persons, especially if they wish to continue their education, working perhaps for public agencies, if they have no other means of support. If their parents can support them, then the equivalent of child support should be charged them to maintain their children, not in luxury, but adequately. Adoption of older children should be facilitated by easing of legal procedures (designed mainly to govern the adoption of *infants*) plus tax advantages for those willing to adopt older children on grounds of goodwill. Indeed children wishing to escape impossible family situations should be allowed a fair degree of initiative in finding and negotiating with possible future families.

Obviously the risk of rackets would be very high unless the exact 10 terms of such provisions were framed very carefully, but the possibility of rackets is less frightening to anyone who thinks about it for long than the dangers of the present situation, which are evident and unrelieved by any signs of improvement. In barely a century this country has changed from a relatively loose society in which Huckleberry Finns were not uncommon, to a society of tense, airless nuclear families in which unhealthy and neurotic tendencies, once spawned in a family, tend to repeat themselves at a magnifying and accelerating rate. We may soon gain the distinction of being the only nation on earth to need not just medicare but "psychi-care." We have invested far too heavily in the unproved "equity" called the nuclear family; that stock is about to crash and we ought to begin finding escape options. In colonial days many New England colonies passed laws imposing fines or extra taxes on parents who kept their children under their own roofs after age 15 or 16, on the sensible notion that a person of that age ought to be out and doing on his own, whether going to Yale or apprenticing in a foundry. Even without the benefit of Freud, the colonial fathers had a good sense of what was wrong with a closely bound and centripetal family structure—it concentrates craziness like compound interest, and so they hit it with monetary penalties, a proper Protestant response, intolerant at once of both mystery and excuses. But this was the last gasp of a medieval and fundamentally Catholic idea that children, God help them, while they may be the children of *these* particular parents biologically, spiritually are the children of God, and more appositely are the children of the entire community, for which the entire community takes responsibility. The unguessed secret of the middle ages was not that monasteries relieved parents of unwanted children; more frequently, they relieved children of unwanted parents!

Topics for Critical Thinking and Writing

1. What is the author's thesis? (Quote the thesis sentence.) Apart from his own experience, what evidence or other means does he offer to persuade you to accept his thesis?

2. What part does the *tone* of his article play in persuading you to agree with him or in alienating you? Does his tone strike you, perhaps, as vigorous or belligerent, as ironic or bitter, as reasonable or hysterical?

3. The author admits (paragraph 6) that he is "a very cold-hearted man." Do you remember your initial reaction to that sentence? What was it? Overall, does the author strengthen or jeopardize his argument by this admission? Explain.

4. If you did not find the article persuasive, did you find it interesting? Can you explain why?

Julie Matthaei

Julie Matthaei teaches economics at Wellesley College and is active with the Economic Literacy Project of Women for Economic Justice of Boston. She is the author of several books, including An Economic History of Women in America *(1982) and* Race, Gender, and Work, *rev.ed. (1996).*

Political Economy and Family Policy

Our current, "natural" family system, based on biological similarities and differences, is in crisis. Not only are its institutions breaking down, they are also under attack as unjust, unequal, and unfree. The "natural" family system needs to be replaced by a consciously social family system; this means socializing parenting costs and pursuing policies which attack the sexual division of labor and better integrate economic and family life.

The family plays a central role in the distribution of income and wealth in our society, reproducing class, race, and gender inequalities. This paper will 1) present a radical and feminist analysis of the "traditional" family system, 2) discuss the recent breakdown of this system, 3) present a radical and feminist critique of the traditional family system, and 4) indicate social policies which would build a family system more consistent with the principles of equality, freedom, and social justice.

The "Natural" Family

The development of capitalism and wage labor in the nineteenth-century U.S. brought with it new familial institutions. The family con-

Julie Matthaei, "Political Economy and Family Policy." Reprinted from Union for Radical Political Economics, *The Imperiled Economy, Book II: Through the Safety Net.* Copyright 1988. By permission of the author.

tinued to be patriarchal—ruled by the husband/father—but was less defined by and involved in commodity production, either as a family firm, or as a family enslaved to producing for others. The family emerged as an increasingly personal and feminine sphere, physically separate and distinct from the competitive and masculine economy (Matthaei 1982). Since, in the nineteenth century, "scientific" explanations of social life were replacing the former religious ones, the new familial institutions were viewed as "natural," and stress was placed on their determination by biological similarities and differences. This "natural,"[1] family system has three, interconnected parts:

1. *"Natural" Marriage.* Marriage is seen as a union of naturally different and complementary beings: men/males and women/females (biological sex and social gender are equated). Men and women are believed to be instinctually heterosexual; those who form homosexual liaisons are viewed as unnatural and perverted.[2] Men are seen as natural bread-winners, competing in the economy, and women as natural homemakers, caring for their husbands and children in the home, and segregated into dead-end, low paid "women's jobs." Forced into this sexual division of labor, men and women need one another to be socially complete, and in order to undertake the essential function of marriage, which is seen as . . .

2. *"Natural" Parenting.* Parenting is seen as the biological production of offspring, a process in which adults pass on their identities and wealth to their children, to "their own flesh and blood." Children are seen as the responsibility and property of their parents. Women/females are seen as naturally endowed with special maternal instincts which make them more qualified than men/males for parenting.

3. *"Natural" Community.* Connected to the view of family life as natural is a white racist view of society which divides people into races and views whites as the biologically superior race. Whites rationalize their political and economic domination of people of color not only as natural but also as part of "white man's burden to civilize the savages."[3] Races and white supremacy are perpetuated as social entities by the prohibition of racial intermarriage; by the passing down of wealth or poverty, language and culture to one's children; and by racially segregated institutions such as housing and job markets.

The Breakdown of the "Natural" Family System

In the last fifteen years, the "natural" family system has been breaking down and coming under increasing attack by feminists and others.

---

[1]*Natural* is in quotes because the "natural" family system is actually a social product.
[2]In contrast, previous times viewed homosexual attractions as natural (and shared by all) but immoral and not to be acted on (Weeks 1979).
[3]Similarly, whites in the Eugenics movement argued that poor whites had inferior genes, and worked to limit their reproduction (Gould 1981).

1. *Married women have entered the labor force and "men's jobs" in growing numbers, challenging the "natural" sexual division of labor.* Now over half of married women are in paid jobs at any one time. Women are demanding entry into the better-paid "men's jobs," and pressing their husbands to do "women's work" in the home. The "natural" marriage union between a bread-winning husband and a homemaking wife has become the exception rather than the rule, characterizing only 29% of husband/wife couples in 1985 (Current Population Reports March 1985).

2. *Married women's labor force participation has created a crisis in day care: there is a severe shortage of day care facilities, especially affordable ones.* In New York, for example, between 830,000 and 1.2 million preschool and school-age children vie for the fewer than 135,000 available licensed child care placements (Select Committee on Children 1987). The shortage of day care, combined with the absence of flexible jobs, forces parents to use makeshift arrangements: 2.1 million or 7% of 5–13-year-olds whose mothers work outside the home are admittedly left unsupervised; actual numbers are much higher (Children's Defense Fund 1987).

3. *Growing numbers are not living in husband/wife families*; only 57% of all households include married couples. Adults are marrying later, spending more time living alone (23.4% of all households) or with friends or lovers. Homosexuality appears to be on the rise, and gays are coming out of the closet and demanding their rights. Marriages have become very unstable; divorce rates more than tripled between 1960 and 1982, more than doubling the number of female-headed households (1986 and 1987 Statistical Abstracts). 10

4. *"Natural" parenting is on the wane.* Divorces create "unnatural" female-headed households, most with dependent children. Unwed mothering has increased to comprise 1 in 5 births and over half of all births among blacks (1987 Statistical Abstract). Remarriages create "unnatural" families, with step-parents and -siblings. More "unnatural" is the trend for sterile couples, gays, and singles to obtain children through artificial insemination, surrogate mothers, and inter-country inter-racial adoptions.

What do these trends mean? Members of the so-called Moral Majority interpret them as the breakdown of *the* family; their solution, embodied in the Family Protection Act of the late 1970s and early 1980s, is to put the "natural" family back together: encourage marriage; discourage divorce, unwed mothering, homosexuality; and get married women out of men's jobs and back into the home. The radical perspective is the opposite; the "natural" family is only one of many possible family systems, a very oppressive and ineffective one at that, as the next section will show. Growing numbers are rejecting the "natural" family system, and trying to create alternative family structures. What society needs is a radical family policy to focus and facilitate this process of dismantling of the old family system and constructing a new and more liberated one.

The Radical Critique of the "Natural" Family

The radical critique of the "natural" family has many prongs. All of these are underlain by a common claim—the "natural" family is not natural, necessary, or optimal, and a more adequate family system needs to be developed.

1. *The "natural" family system is not natural.* Biological differences in skin color or sex organs, and biological similarities between parent and child, do not necessitate a particular family form, or hierarchy and difference between the sexes and races. Past family systems have been very different from the "natural" family.[4] It is not nature but our society which is producing and reproducing the "natural" family, and its associated institutions of gender and race difference and inequality, through parenting practices, laws, labor market structures, and culture.

2. *The "natural" family system is classist and racist.* The conception of the "natural" family is generated by the dominant culture of upper-class, native-born whites, who then claim it applies to all. Since being a man means bread-winning and supporting a homebound homemaker and children, men without "family wage" jobs due to unemployment, class, or race discrimination are seen (and often see themselves) as less than manly. Black women, forced into the labor force to compensate for their husbands' lack of economic opportunity, are viewed as unfeminine, castrating "matriarchs," and the extended and chosen family system which blacks have developed to combat poverty and economic insecurity is condemned as deviant (Stack 1974). The inability of the poor to properly parent their children because of their meager resources is seen as a fault in their characters, and they are criticized for having children at all, as if the poor do not have a right to parent.

3. *The "natural" family system impoverishes female-headed households.* Women and children face high risks of poverty. Married women are to specialize in unpaid homemaking and mothering, complementing their husbands' bread-winning. Divorce or widowhood leaves women with little access to income, but with major if not full emotional and financial responsibility for the children.[5] "Women's jobs" do not pay enough to cover

15

---

[4]Among the Rangiroa, adopted children were given equal status and rights as biological offspring, and considered "one belly" (from the same mother) with one another and with their other siblings (Sahlins 1976). In the New England and Southern colonies, mothering among the wealthy was essentially biological, producing one's husband's children, who were then nursed and cared for by poor white or slave women. Mead (1935) found societies where men and women shared the early care of children. Many societies see polygamy as the norm for marriage; others have allowed females to live as men and take wives after having cross-sex dreams (Blackwood 1984). Among the ancient Greeks, the highest form of love for an adult man was homosexual love for a younger man.

[5]In 1983, only 35% of mothers caring for their children with absent fathers received any child support, and the average yearly payment was only $2,341; only 6% of separated or divorced women received any alimony (1987 Statistical Abstract).

child care and keep female households with young children out of poverty. The present welfare system (Aid to Families with Dependent Children), structured to support the "natural" family system, does not even provide female-headed families with poverty-level income. The result: the majority of black and Hispanic female-headed families (50 and 53%, respectively), and 27% of white female-headed families, are poor. Children are penalized the most: 54% of children in such families are poor (Current Population Reports 1985).

4. *"Natural" marriage creates inequality between the sexes.* Since wives are relegated to unpaid housework and low paid jobs, they are economically dependent upon their husbands. Fear of losing this financial support can force women into subservience to their husbands, and into staying in unsatisfying marriages. Indeed, some feminists see "natural" marriage as a struggle in which men have gained the upper hand by monopolizing the higher-paid jobs (Hartmann 1981). Whatever its origins, "natural" marriage is clearly unequal, making mutual love and respect difficult.

5. *"Natural" parenting is oppressive and unjust.* Along with financial responsibility, parents are given almost total power over children. Children have no rights, and no system through which they can complain about mistreatment or find alternative parents (Rodham 1976). In a society where most men are under the power of bosses, and women under that of their husbands, parenting provides an arena where adults have total power and authority. It is easy to forget one's children's needs and use or abuse them to fill one's own needs. What results is not only an epidemic of child physical and sexual abuse,[6] but also the training of each child to accept and participate in hierarchical and authoritarian systems, from schools to workplaces to politics (Miller 1981).

6. *The "natural" family perpetuates inequality between families* through the generations, because parents pass down their economic position to their children. Inheritance keeps ownership of the means of production in the hands of a few, mostly white, families.[7] Children born into higher-income families receive better nutrition, housing, health care, and schooling than their poor counterparts, have the "insurance" of wealthy relatives to back them up and encourage risk-taking, and can expect to inherit wealth. On the other hand, 11 million children (one in five) must live without even the most basic goods and services (Current Population Reports 1985). This is not only unjust but also irrational: it is in society's interest to guarantee quality health care and education to its future workers and citizens.

---

[6]The media have focussed on child abuse by strangers—on day care scandals and missing children—whereas the vast majority of children are abused by their parents or relatives (Eliasoph 1986).
[7]The wealthiest 2.4% of households owns 65% of the income-producing wealth (Edwards, Reich, Weisskopf 1986).

7. *The "natural" family system discourages the formation of alternative families, while forcing many into unwanted "natural" families.* Its broad and virulent anti-gay discrimination from education, employment, housing, and marriage laws to media images—makes it very difficult for people to love and share their lives with people of the same sex. It discriminates against couples who are unable to have children biologically by treating adoption and artificial insemination as "unnatural" and undesirable options. On the other hand, the "natural" family's equation of sex, reproduction, and marriage creates unwanted children by creating opposition to sex education, birth control for unmarried teens, and abortion. Forty percent of all births are mistimed or unwanted—for those under 24, a disastrous 53%—forcing millions of women into premature or unwanted motherhood and/or marriages (1987 Statistical Abstract).

Conceptualizing a Social Family System

The "natural" family system is inadequate, oppressive, and is coming apart at the seams. At the same time, all need the love and warmth and sharing and parenting which family relationships provide.[8] Hence criticism is not enough; an *alternative* and better vision of family life needs to be delineated, along with a set of concrete policies to bring such a new family system into being.

The oppressiveness of the "natural" family system was accepted because its institutions were seen as natural and inevitable. Our new family system would be a *consciously* social one, its institutions developed through study, discussion, struggle and compromise, and continually criticized and improved so as to maximize freedom, equality, self-fulfillment, democracy, and justice. Here are some of the central principles of such a system; while it may appear utopian, many are living out parts of this vision now.

Social Marriage. Marriage would become a symmetrical relationship between whole, equal, and socially independent human beings, each participating in a similar range of familial, economic and political activities.[9] Its basis would be mutual love of the other, i.e., liking of, respect for, and sexual attraction to the person the other is, as providing the reason for intimate sharing of lives and living spaces and, if desired, parenting. Couples would not be expected to stay together "for better or for worse . . . as long as ye both shall live"; nor would they need to, since each would have earnings.

---

[8]Some feminists and gays have taken an "anti-family" position, as if the "natural" family is the only family form (Barrett and McIntosh 1982); however they usually advocate some alternative, family-like institutions.

[9]If this seems far-fetched, an October 1977 CBS–*New York Times* National Survey found that 50% of 30–44 year olds, and 67% of 18–29-year-olds, preferred a symmetrical marriage (of a man and woman who both had jobs, did housework, and cared for the children) over the traditional, complementary one.

Social Parenting. Parenting would be recognized as a quintessentially social activity which, by shaping our unconsciousnesses, bodies, and minds, shapes the future of our society. Society would ensure that each child is well cared for and educated, since the upbringing of children as physically and psychologically healthy, creative, educated, and socially-conscious citizens is essential both to society's well-being, and to our belief in equal opportunity. This would include providing children and their parents with economic and institutional support, as well as seeking out optimal parenting practices and educating prospective parents in them.

Social Community. Cultural and economic differences between groups of people would be acknowledged to be social rather than natural products. All human beings would be recognized as equally human citizens of the world, and a concept of basic human rights, both political and economic, developed. Intercultural marriages would be encouraged to further social understanding. [25]

Bringing the Social Family into Being: A Policy Checklist

Although the "natural" family system is in decline, the social family system cannot replace it unless there are many changes in our economic and social institutions. Here are some of the policies which will help bring about these changes; many are now in place in other countries.

1. *Policies which socialize parenting.*
    a. *Policies which establish the right of all adults to choose when and if they wish to parent.* Universal sex education and parenting training for adolescents, as well as access of all to free, safe, 100% effective birth control, abortions, and adoption placement, are needed to make every child a wanted child. At the same time, society must recognize the right of those who are infertile, gay, or single to parent, and support the development of alternative modes of obtaining children from adoption to artificial insemination and in-vitro fertilization.[10] The right to parent must also be protected by programs to help low-income parents with the costs of child-rearing (see 1b). Finally, the right to parent must be seen as socially established, rather than inhering in the genetic connection between a parent and a child; parenting rights must be revocable if a parent neglects or abuses a child, and society should seek to prevent child abuse through an effective system of child advocates and parenting support and training.

---

[10]Most doctors refuse to artificially inseminate single or lesbian women. The developing practice of surrogate mothering is very controversial among feminists and radicals. Since eggs can be fertilized outside of a womb, and embryos can be raised in incubators from the age of a few months, there are many other possibilities, including impregnating men, or even producing infants entirely outside of human bodies, as Marge Piercy (1976) and Shulamith Firestone (1970) have envisioned.

b. *Policies which ensure a basic, social inheritance for every child.* The best way to ensure healthy and provided-for children is to ensure this health and income to all families through a system of national health insurance and a combination of anti-poverty measures, from full employment, to comparable worth, to a guaranteed annual income. In addition, since having children does increase a family's poverty risk, family allowances should be provided to parents according to need.[11] Furthermore, all children need to have access to high quality, free or sliding-scale education, from preschool day care when their parents are at work, to elementary and secondary school and college. This "social inheritance" program would be paid for by high inheritance taxes and very progressive income and/or luxury taxes. Such taxes would, in themselves, help reduce the present gross inequalities of opportunity among children.[12]

c. *Policies which socialize child-care costs: government- and business-subsidized day care.* Making quality child care available and affordable to all should be the joint financial responsibility of business and government, since it benefits both employers and society at large. A few trend-setting employers now provide child-care benefits to their workers, having found that these more than pay for themselves by decreasing worker absenteeism, increasing productivity, and attracting top workers (Blau and Ferber 1986). Current federal funding through Title 20 is woefully inadequate; many states are serving less than 30% of their eligible populations (Select Committee on Children 1987). One survey found that ¼ of all full-time homemakers, and ½ of all single parents, were kept from employment and training programs by the unavailability of child care (Cal. Governor's Task Force on Child Care 1986). Again, Sweden provides the example to follow: the government pays 100% of the child-care costs of public day care centers, which are used by over half of children with employed mothers (Blau and Ferber 1986).

On the other hand, to permit parents with job commitments to spend more time with their children, especially their infants, a system of paid leaves from work without loss of one's job or seniority must be established. The U.S. does not even have laws guaranteeing prospective

---

[11]Sweden and France give housing allowances to parents (Kamerman and Kahn 1979); many European countries have national health insurance and family allowances. Swedish policy is to guarantee all citizens a minimum standard of living (Ibid.); in the U. S., the needy only receive support through "entitlement" programs, which require certain qualifications (such as being a female household head with children) other than being poor, and which do not, in any event, raise incomes up to the poverty level.

[12]See Chester (1982) for a review of Western thought on inheritance.

parents an *unpaid* leave when they have or adopt a child.[13] In a few states, women can use their temporary disability insurance to pay for 4 to 10 weeks of pregnancy/infant care leave (Kamerman et al. 1983). Again, Sweden is the model in this area, with: 1) paid, year-long parental leaves, 2) up to 60 days a year paid leave to care for sick children, and 3) the right for all full-time employed parents with children under 8 to reduce their work weeks (with reduced pay) to 30 hours a week (Ginsberg 1983). Radicals have advocated a shorter work week without reduction in pay as a solution to unemployment and low productivity, for it would create more jobs, reduce unemployment, and increase output (Bowles, Gordon, and Weisskopf 1983); a consideration of the needs of parents makes such policies even more desirable. Other innovations which allow adults to combine work with parenting are flex-time and flex-place (working at home); the extension of health, pension, and other benefits to part-time workers; and the cafeteria benefit plan, which allows dual-career couples to eliminate doubly-covered benefits in favor of more of other benefits, such as leaves or child-care support (Farley 1983; Kamerman and Hayes 1982).

    2.   *Policies to support egalitarian, symmetrical marriages* in which partners participate equally in parenting, housework, the labor force, and political life.[14]

> a. *Comparable worth, affirmative action, increased unionization.* Comparable worth would increase the pay of women's jobs to that of men's jobs requiring comparable skill, effort, and responsibility. Affirmative action encourages women to enter into traditionally masculine jobs. Women need to organize in unions to fight for the above, and for general wage increases; one platform is "solidarity wages," again practiced in Sweden, in which workers agree to take part of their wage increase to reduce inequalities among them. Together these policies would stop the segregation of women into low-paid, dead-end, less-satisfying jobs, reduce women's economic dependence upon men, and encourage more similar work and family participation by the sexes.
>
> b. *Socialization of parenting* (see #1 above) would support symmetrical marriage, for it would allow adults to combine parenting with labor force commitments, reducing the pressure to specialize as in "natural" marriage.
>
> c. *Repeal of the laws that discourage formation of "unnatural" marriages and non-traditional households.* This includes repealing

35

---

[13]Kamerman and Kingston (in Kamerman and Hayes 1982) found that paid maternity leave was available to fewer than one-third of all employed women in 1978, and averaged only about six weeks of benefits.

[14]Cuba encourages such marriages through its "Family Code," adopted in 1975 (Randall 1981); however, it still discriminates against gay couples.

sodomy laws and advocating legislation prohibiting discrimination against gays in employment, housing, insurance, foster parenting, adoption, and other areas.[15] Gay relationships must be legitimized in marriage laws, to give spouses health insurance, pension, inheritance, and other benefits and rights enjoyed by heterosexual spouses.[16] The repeal of co-residence laws, which in many states prohibit the cohabitation of more than two unrelated adults, is needed to allow the formation of non-biologically-based extended families.

d. *Individual rather than joint taxation of married couples.* Our present income tax system is progressive and married couples are discouraged from entering the labor force since, when a woman's earnings raise the household's tax bracket, much of her earnings are paid to the government in taxes.[17] Taxing adults individually (as is currently done in Sweden), rather than jointly, would instead encourage both members of a couple to participate in the labor force.

e. *Policies to aid the casualties of the "natural" marriage system.* Until the above changes are achieved, women and children will continue to face high poverty risks when they live in female-headed households. Many feminists advocate the strengthening of alimony and child-support laws; however, this both reinforces the "natural" marriage notion that husbands should be the main providers, and reproduces class and race inequality, because wives' and children's incomes depend on that of their husbands/fathers. Extensive welfare reform, combined with the policies above, is a better solution.

3. *Policies to create social community.* Labor market reforms (2a) must always aim at eliminating both race and sex segregation and discrimination. These, along with social inheritance policies, will go far in stopping the economic reproduction of racial inequality in the U.S. The decline of "natural" parenting views of children as "one's own flesh and blood" will foster, and in turn be fostered by, the decline of conceptions of

---

[15]Sodomy laws, which outlaw forms of "unnatural sex" (e.g., anal intercourse and oral/genital sex, either heterosexual or homosexual), still exist in many states, and were recently upheld by the Supreme Court, although they are seldom enforced. Many cities and a few states have passed gay rights legislation, and more and more employers have extended their non-discrimination policy to include sexual preference or orientation.

[16]In June 1987, the Swedish Parliament approved a bill which gave gay couples the same rights as heterosexuals married by common law; it will allow couples to sign housing leases as couples, regulate the division of property after a break-up, and grant lovers the right to inherit property in the absence of a will (*Gay Community News*, June 14–20, 1987).

[17]Even though the recent tax reform reduced the progressivity of the tax system, and a 1983 reform exempted 10% of the income of the lower-earning partner from taxation, the "marriage penalty" persists (Blau and Ferber 1986).

race, as both are replaced by a view of a human community reproduced through social parenting.

Bibliography

Barrett, Michele, and Mary McIntosh. 1982. *The Anti-Social Family*. London: New Left Books.

Blackwood, Evelyn. 1984. Sexuality and Gender in Certain Native Tribes: The Case of Cross-Gender Females. *Signs* 10(1):27–42.

Blau, Francine, and Marianne Ferber. 1986. *The Economics of Women, Men, and Work*. Upper Saddle River, N.J.: Prentice-Hall.

Bowles, Samuel, David M. Gordon, and Thomas E. Weisskopf. 1983. *Beyond the Wasteland: A Democratic Alternative to Economic Decline*. New York: Anchor Doubleday.

Chester, Ronald. 1982. *Inheritance, Wealth, and Society*. Bloomington: Indiana University Press.

Children's Defense Fund. 1987. Unpublished paper.

Edwards, Richard, Michael Reich, and Thomas Weisskopf. 1986. *The Capitalist System*. Upper Saddle River, N.J.: Prentice-Hall. Third Edition.

Eliasoph, Nina. 1986. Drive-In Mortality, Child Abuse, and the Media. *Socialist Review* #90, 16(6):7–31.

Farley, Jennie, ed. 1983. *The Woman in Management*. New York: ILR Press.

Firestone, Shulamith. 1970. *The Dialectic of Sex*. New York: Morrow.

Ginsberg, Helen. 1983. *Full Employment and Public Policy: The United States and Sweden*. Lexington, Mass.: D.C. Heath and Co.

Gould, Stephen J. 1981. *The Mismeasure of Man*. New York: Norton.

Hartmann, Heidi. 1981. The Unhappy Marriage of Marxism and Feminism. In *Women and Revolution: A Discussion of the Unhappy Marriage of Marxism and Feminism*, Lydia Sargent (ed.), pp. 1–41. Boston: South End Press.

Kamerman, Sheila, and Alfred Kahn. 1979. *Family Policy: Government and Families in Fourteen Countries*. New York: Columbia University Press.

Kamerman, Sheila, and Cheryl Hayes, eds. 1982. *Families That Work: Children in a Changing World*. Washington: National Academy Press.

Kamerman, Sheila, et al., eds. 1983. *Maternity Policies and Working Women*. New York: Columbia University Press.

Matthaei, Julie. 1982. *An Economic History of Women in America: Women's Work, the Sexual Division of Labor, and the Development of Capitalism*. New York: Schocken Books.

Mead, Margaret. 1935. *Sex and Temperament in Three Primitive Societies*. New York: William Morrow and Co.

Miller, Alice. 1981. *The Drama of the Gifted Child*, trans. by Ruth Ward. New York: Basic Books.

Piercy, Marge. 1976. *Woman on the Edge of Time*. New York: Fawcett.

Randall, Margaret. 1981. *Women in Cuba: Twenty Years Later*. New York: Smyrna Press.

Rodham, Hillary. 1976. Children under the Law. In *Rethinking Childhood*, Arlene Skolnick (ed.). Boston: Little, Brown and Co.

Sahlins, Marshall. 1976. *The Use and Abuse of Biology: An Anthropological Critique of Sociobiology*. Ann Arbor: University of Michigan Press.

Select Committee on Children, Youth and Families, U.S. House of Representatives. 1987. Fact Sheet: Hearing on Child Care, Key to Employment in a Changing Economy. March 10.

Stack, Carol. 1974. *All Our Kin*. New York: Harper & Row.

U.S. Bureau of the Census, Current Population Reports. 1985. Household and Family Characteristics: March 1985.

—. 1985. Money Income and Poverty Status of Families and Persons in the United States.

—. 1986, 1987. Statistical Abstract of the United States.

Weeks, Jeffrey. 1979. *Coming Out: Homosexual Politics in Britain, from the Nineteenth Century to the Present*. London: Quartet Books.

Topics for Critical Thinking and Writing

1. What, if anything, strikes you as "radical" in Matthaei's "radical analysis" of the "'natural' family" (paragraph 3)? Do any parts of this analysis strike you as misleading, dated, or wrong? If so, which parts, and what do you find wrong with them?

2. In paragraph 7 Matthaei says that "adults are marrying later." Assuming this statement to be true, what do you think are the causes? What do you think may be the consequences, good and bad?

3. In paragraph 10 Matthaei denies that the "natural" family is natural. Do you think she proves her case? If not, in what way(s) does she fail?

4. Matthaei argues (paragraph 18) that the idea of the "natural" family can lead easily to child abuse. Can one argue in response that the "natural" family is better suited to assist children in growing into healthy, responsible, happy adults than is any conceivable alternative arrangement? If you think so, what arguments might you offer? (For an interesting argument that children should be granted legal rights to escape impossible families, see "Confessions of an Erstwhile Child," page 261.)

5. In paragraph 20 Matthaei argues that the idea of the "natural" family "discriminates against couples who are unable to have children biologically." Is she saying that all adults—including the sterile, the infertile, and those who do not wish to engage in heterosexual sex—have a right to have children? If she is saying this, on what might she base this right? In her next paragraph she says that "all need the love and warmth and sharing and parenting which family relationships provide." Is this need perhaps the basis for a right—possessed by all adults—to have children? (See also the discussion in paragraph 24.)

6. Much of the essay is devoted to arguing on behalf of various kinds of equality. For example, in paragraph 23, in discussing "social marriage,"

Matthaei says that "marriage would become a symmetrical relationship between whole, equal, and socially independent human beings." The two persons involved would participate "in a similar range of familial, economic,
and political activities." But what if both persons do not share an interest in,
for example, political activities? Should they therefore not marry? Or suppose that one person enjoyed the world of paid work and the other preferred to engage, at least for a while, chiefly in the role of parenting and
housekeeping. Do you think such a marriage would be inherently unstable?

7. In paragraph 29, Matthaei argues for programs and policies that would re-
distribute wealth—for example, a guaranteed annual income. Suppose
someone argued (or at least asserted) that he or she saw no reason to support the families of the poor. What reply might you make?

8. Matthaei apparently sees marriage as involving only two adults. Do you assume that she rejects polygamy (a practice not unknown in the United
States and elsewhere)? And what about polyandry (one woman with two or
more husbands)? If you accept Matthaei's arguments, or most of them, how
do *you* feel about polygamy and polyandry? What argument(s) can you
imagine for these?

Andrew Sullivan

*Andrew Sullivan grew up in England, but he earned a doctorate in government at Harvard
University. Sullivan for several years served as the editor of* The New Republic, *where the following essay was originally published in 1989.*

Here Comes the Groom

A (Conservative) Case for Gay Marriage

Last month in New York, a court ruled that a gay lover had the right
to stay in his deceased partner's rent-control apartment because the lover
qualified as a member of the deceased's family. The ruling deftly annoyed
almost everybody. Conservatives saw judicial activism in favor of gay
rent control: three reasons to be appalled. Chastened liberals (such as the
New York Times editorial page), while endorsing the recognition of gay relationships, also worried about the abuse of already stretched entitlements that the ruling threatened. What neither side quite contemplated is
that they both might be right, and that the way to tackle the issue of un-
conventional relationships in conventional society is to try something
both more radical and more conservative than putting courts in the busi-

Andrew Sullivan, "Here Comes the Groom: A (Conservative) Case for Gay Marriage," *The
New Republic*, August 28, 1989. Reprinted by permission of *The New Republic*. © 1989, The
New Republic, Inc.

ness of deciding what is and is not a family. That alternative is the legalization of civil gay marriage.

The New York rent-control case did not go anywhere near that far, which is the problem. The rent-control regulations merely stipulated that a "family" member had the right to remain in the apartment. The judge ruled that to all intents and purposes a gay lover is part of his lover's family, inasmuch as a "family" merely means an interwoven social life, emotional commitment, and some level of financial interdependence.

It's a principle now well established around the country. Several cities have "domestic partnership" laws, which allow relationships that do not fit into the category of heterosexual marriage to be registered with the city and qualify for benefits that up till now have been reserved for straight married couples. San Francisco, Berkeley, Madison, and Los Angeles all have legislation, as does the politically correct Washington, D.C. suburb, Takoma Park. In these cities, a variety of interpersonal arrangements qualify for health insurance, bereavement leave, insurance, annuity and pension rights, housing rights (such as rent-control apartments), adoption and inheritance rights. Eventually, according to gay lobby groups, the aim is to include federal income tax and veterans' benefits as well. A recent case even involved the right to use a family member's accumulated frequent-flier points. Gays are not the only beneficiaries; heterosexual "live-togethers" also qualify.

There's an argument, of course, that the current legal advantages extended to married people unfairly discriminate against people who've shaped their lives in less conventional arrangements. But it doesn't take a genius to see that enshrining in the law a vague principle like "domestic partnership" is an invitation to qualify at little personal cost for a vast array of entitlements otherwise kept crudely under control.

To be sure, potential DPs have to prove financial interdependence, shared living arrangements, and a commitment to mutual caring. But they don't need to have a sexual relationship or even closely mirror old-style marriage. In principle, an elderly woman and her live-in nurse could qualify. A couple of uneuphemistically confirmed bachelors could be DPs. So could two close college students, a pair of seminarians, or a couple of frat buddies. Left as it is, the concept of domestic partnership could open a Pandora's box of litigation and subjective judicial decision-making about who qualifies. You either are or are not married; it's not a complex question. Whether you are in a "domestic partnership" is not so clear.

More important, the concept of domestic partnership chips away at the prestige of traditional relationships and undermines the priority we give them. This priority is not necessarily a product of heterosexism. Consider heterosexual couples. Society has good reason to extend legal advantages to heterosexuals who choose the formal sanction of marriage over simply living together. They make a deeper commitment to one another and to society; in exchange, society extends certain benefits to them. Marriage provides an anchor, if an arbitrary and weak one, in the chaos of

5

sex and relationships to which we are all prone. It provides a mechanism for emotional stability, economic security, and the healthy rearing of the next generation. We rig the law in its favor not because we disparage all forms of relationships other than the nuclear family, but because we recognize that not to promote marriage would be to ask too much of human virtue. In the context of the weakened family's effect upon the poor, it might also invite social disintegration. One of the worst products of the New Right's "family values" campaign is that its extremism and hatred of diversity has disguised this more measured and more convincing case for the importance of the marital bond.

The concept of domestic partnership ignores these concerns, indeed directly attacks them. This is a pity, since one of its most important objectives—providing some civil recognition for gay relationships—is a noble cause and one completely compatible with the defense of the family. But the way to go about it is not to undermine straight marriage; it is to legalize old-style marriage for gays.

The gay movement has ducked this issue primarily out of fear of division. Much of the gay leadership clings to notions of gay life as essentially outsider, antibourgeois, radical. Marriage, for them, is co-optation into straight society. For the Stonewall[1] generation, it is hard to see how this vision of conflict will ever fundamentally change. But for many other gays—my guess, a majority—while they don't deny the importance of rebellion twenty years ago and are grateful for what was done, there's now the sense of a new opportunity. A need to rebel has quietly ceded to a desire to belong. To be gay and to be bourgeois no longer seems such an absurd proposition. Certainly since AIDS, to be gay and to be responsible has become a necessity.

Gay marriage squares several circles at the heart of the domestic partnership debate. Unlike domestic partnership, it allows for recognition of gay relationships, while casting no aspersions on traditional marriage. It merely asks that gays be allowed to join in. Unlike domestic partnership, it doesn't open up avenues for heterosexuals to get benefits without the responsibilities of marriage, or a nightmare of definitional litigation. And unlike domestic partnership, it harnesses to an already established social convention the yearnings for stability and acceptance among a fast-maturing gay community.

Gay marriage also places more responsibilities upon gays: It says for the first time that gay relationships are not better or worse than straight relationships, and that the same is expected of them. And it's clear and dignified. There's a legal benefit to a clear, common symbol of commitment. There's also a personal benefit. One of the ironies of domestic part-

10

[1]The Stonewall Inn was a gay bar in New York City. When the police closed it in June 1966, the gays did not submit (as they had done in the past) but attacked the police. The event is regarded as a turning point in gay history.

nership is that it's not only more complicated than marriage, it's more demanding, requiring an elaborate statement of intent to qualify. It amounts to a substantial invasion of privacy. Why, after all, should gays be required to prove commitment before they get married in a way we would never dream of asking of straights?

Legalizing gay marriage would offer homosexuals the same deal society now offers heterosexuals: general social approval and specific legal advantages in exchange for a deeper and harder-to-extract-yourself-from commitment to another human being. Like straight marriage, it would foster social cohesion, emotional security, and economic prudence. Since there's no reason gays should not be allowed to adopt or be foster parents, it could also help nurture children. And its introduction would not be some sort of radical break with social custom. As it has become more acceptable for gay people to acknowledge their loves publicly, more and more have committed themselves to one another for life in full view of their families and their friends. A law institutionalizing gay marriage would merely reinforce a healthy social trend. It would also, in the wake of AIDS, qualify as a genuine public health measure. Those conservatives who deplore promiscuity among some homosexuals should be among the first to support it. Burke[2] could have written a powerful case for it.

The argument that gay marriage would subtly undermine the unique legitimacy of straight marriage is based upon a fallacy. For heterosexuals, straight marriage would remain the most significant—and only legal—social bond. Gay marriage could only delegitimize straight marriage if it were a real alternative to it, and this is clearly not true. To put it bluntly, there's precious little evidence that straights could be persuaded by any law to have sex with—let alone marry—someone of their own sex. The only possible effect of this sort would be to persuade gay men and women who force themselves into heterosexual marriage (often at appalling cost to themselves and their families) to find a focus for their family instincts in a more personally positive environment. But this is clearly a plus, not a minus: Gay marriage could both avoid a lot of tortured families and create the possibility for many happier ones. It is not, in short, a denial of family values. It's an extension of them.

Of course, some would claim that any legal recognition of homosexuality is a de facto attack upon heterosexuality. But even the most hardened conservatives recognize that gays are a permanent minority and aren't likely to go away. Since persecution is not an option in a civilized society, why not coax gays into traditional values rather than rail incoherently against them?

There's a less elaborate argument for gay marriage: It's good for gays. It provides role models for young gay people who, after the exhilaration

---

[2]Edmund Burke (1729–97), conservative British politician.

of coming out, can easily lapse into short-term relationships and insecurity with no tangible goal in sight. My own guess is that most gays would embrace such a goal with as much (if not more) commitment as straights. Even in our society as it is, many lesbian relationships are virtual textbook cases of monogamous commitment. Legal gay marriage could also help bridge the gulf often found between gays and their parents. It could bring the essence of gay life—a gay couple—into the heart of the traditional straight family in a way the family can most understand and the gay off-spring can most easily acknowledge. It could do as much to heal the gay-straight rift as any amount of gay rights legislation.

If these arguments sound socially conservative, that's no accident. It's   15
one of the richest ironies of our society's blind spot toward gays that essentially conservative social goals should have the appearance of being so radical. But gay marriage is not a radical step. It avoids the mess of domestic partnership: it is humane; it is conservative in the best sense of the word. It's also practical. Given the fact that we already allow legal gay relationships, what possible social goal is advanced by framing the law to encourage those relationships to be unfaithful, undeveloped, and insecure?

Topics for Critical Thinking and Writing

1. In his second paragraph Sullivan summarizes a judge's definition of a family. How satisfactory do you find the definition? Explain.

2. What is "conservative"—Sullivan's word, in his title—about this case for gay and lesbian marriages?

3. A common argument in support of the financial privileges that the state awards to the traditional family is that it is in the state's interest for children to be brought up by adults committed to each other. However, divorce is now common, and, of course, many married couples do not have children, for one reason or another. Can any justification, then, be offered for allowing a spouse—but not an unmarried heterosexual or homosexual lover—to inherit without payment of taxes the partner's share of property jointly held?

4. In Sullivan's view why is marriage better than mere cohabitation? What is your view of this matter?

5. In paragraph 11 Sullivan says that "there's no reason gays should not be allowed to adopt or be foster parents." This issue is highly controversial. Construct the strongest argument you can, on one side or the other. (Remember, a strong argument faces the opposing arguments.)

6. In his next-to-last paragraph Sullivan says that "legal gay marriage could also help bridge the gulf often found between gays and their parents." If you are aware of gays who are separated from their parents by a "gulf," do you think that legal marriage might reduce that gulf? Explain.

Arlie Hochschild

Arlie Hochschild, born in Boston in 1940, holds a bachelor's degree from Swarthmore and a Ph.D. from the University of California, Berkeley, where he is now a professor in the Department of Sociology. He is the author of several important books, including The Second Shift: Working Parents and the Revolution at Home *(1989, written with Anne Machung). The material that we give below comes from this book.*

The Second Shift: Employed Women Are Putting in Another Day of Work at Home

Every American household bears the footprints of economic and cultural trends that originate far outside its walls. A rise in inflation eroding the earning power of the male wage, an expanding service sector opening up jobs for women, and the inroads made by women into many professions—all these changes do not simply go on around the American family. They occur *within* a marriage or living-together arrangement and transform it. Problems between couples, problems that seem "unique" or "marital," are often the individual ripples of powerful economic and cultural shock waves. Quarrels between husbands and wives in households across the nation result mainly from a friction between faster-changing women and slower-changing men.

The exodus of women from the home to the workplace has not been accompanied by a new view of marriage and work that would make this transition smooth. Most workplaces have remained inflexible in the face of the changing needs of workers with families, and most men have yet to really adapt to the changes in women. I call the strain caused by the disparity between the change in women and the absence of change elsewhere the "stalled revolution."

If women begin to do less at home because they have less time, if men do little more, and if the work of raising children and tending a home requires roughly the same effort, then the questions of who does what at home and of what "needs doing" become a source of deep tension in a marriage.

Over the past 30 years in the United States, more and more women have begun to work outside the home, and more have divorced. While some commentators conclude that women's work *causes* divorce, my research into changes in the American family suggests something else. Since all the wives in the families I studied (over an eight-year period) worked outside the home, the fact that they worked did not account for why some marriages were happy and others were not. What *did* contribute to happiness was the husband's willingness to do the work at home. Whether they were traditional or more egalitarian in their relationship, couples were happier when the men did a sizable share of housework and child care.

In one study of 600 couples filing for divorce, researcher George 5 Levinger found that the second most common reason women cited for wanting to divorce—after "mental cruelty"—was their husbands' "neglect of home or children." Women mentioned this reason more often than financial problems, physical abuse, drinking, or infidelity.

A happy marriage is supported by a couple's being economically secure, by their enjoying a supportive community, and by their having compatible needs and values. But these days it may also depend on a shared appreciation of the work it takes to nurture others. As the role of the homemaker is being abandoned by many women, the homemaker's work has been continually devalued and passed on to low-paid housekeepers, baby-sitters, or day-care workers. Long devalued by men, the contribution of cooking, cleaning, and care-giving is now being devalued as mere drudgery by many women, too.

In the era of the stalled revolution, one way to make housework and child care more valued is for men to share in that work. Many working mothers are already doing all they can at home. Now it's time for men to make the move.

If more mothers of young children are working at full-time jobs outside the home, and if most couples can't afford household help, who's doing the work at home? Adding together the time it takes to do a paid job and to do housework and child care and using estimates from major studies on time use done in the 1960s and 1970s, I found that women worked roughly 15 more hours each week than men. Over a year, they worked an extra month of 24-hour days. Over a dozen years, it was an extra year of 24-hour days. Most women without children spend much more time than men on housework. Women with children devote more time to both housework and child care. Just as there is a wage gap between men and women in the workplace, there is a "leisure gap" between them at home. Most women work one shift at the office or factory and a "second shift" at home.

In my research, I interviewed and observed 52 couples over an eight-year period as they cooked dinner, shopped, bathed their children, and in general struggled to find enough time to make their complex lives work. The women I interviewed seemed to be far more deeply torn between the demands of work and family than were their husbands. They talked more about the abiding conflict between work and family. They felt the second shift was *their* issue, and most of their husbands agreed. When I telephoned one husband to arrange an interview with him, explaining that I wanted to ask him how he managed work and family life, he replied genially, "Oh, this will *really* interest my *wife*."

Men who shared the load at home seemed just as pressed for time as their wives, and as torn between the demands of career and small children. But of the men I surveyed, the majority did not share the load at home. Some refused outright. Others refused more passively, often offering a loving shoulder to lean on, or an understanding ear, as their working wife faced the conflict they both saw as hers. At first it seemed to me that the problem of the second shift *was* hers. But I came to realize that those husbands who helped very little at home were often just as deeply affected as their wives—through the resentment their wives felt toward them and through their own need to steel themselves against that resentment.

A clear example of this phenomenon is Evan Holt, a warehouse furniture salesman who did very little housework and played with his four-year-old son, Joey, only at his convenience. His wife, Nancy, did the second shift, but she resented it keenly and half-consciously expressed her frustration and rage by losing interest in sex and becoming overly absorbed in Joey.

Even when husbands happily shared the work, their wives *felt* more responsible for home and children. More women than men kept track of doctor's appointments and arranged for kids' playmates to come over. More mothers than fathers worried about a child's Halloween costume or a birthday present for a school friend. They were more likely to think about their children while at work and to check in by phone with the baby-sitter.

Partly because of this, more women felt torn between two kinds of urgency, between the need to soothe a child's fear of being left at day-care and the need to show the boss she's "serious" at work. Twenty percent of the men in my study shared housework equally. Seventy percent did a substantial amount (less than half of it, but more than a third), and 10 percent did less than a third. But even when couples more equitably share the work at home, women do two thirds of the daily jobs at home, such as cooking and cleaning up—jobs that fix them into a rigid routine. Most women cook dinner, for instance, while men change the oil in the family car. But, as one mother pointed out, dinner needs to be prepared every evening around six o'clock, whereas the car oil needs to be changed every six months, with no particular deadline. Women do more child care than men, and men repair more household appliances. A child needs to be tended to daily, whereas the repair of household appliances can often wait, said the men, "until I have time." Men thus have more control over when they make their contributions than women do. They may be very busy with family chores, but, like the executive who tells his secretary to "hold my calls," the man has more control over his time.

Another reason why women may feel under more strain than men is that women more often do two things at once—for example, write checks and return phone calls, vacuum and keep an eye on a three-year-old, fold laundry and think out the shopping list. Men more often will either cook dinner *or* watch the kids. Women more often do both at the same time.

Beyond doing more at home, women also devote proportionately more of their time at home to housework than men and proportionately less of it to child care. Of all the time men spend working at home, a growing amount of it goes to child care. Since most parents prefer to tend to their children than to clean house, men do more of what they'd rather do. More men than women take their children on "fun" outings to the park, the zoo, the movies. Women spend more time on maintenance, such as feeding and bathing children—enjoyable activities, to be sure, but often less leisurely or "special" than going to the zoo. Men also do fewer of the most undesirable household chores, such as scrubbing the toilet.

As a result, women tend to talk more intensely about being overtired, sick, and emotionally drained. Many women interviewed were fixated on the topic of sleep. They talked about how much they could "get by on": six and a half, seven, seven and a half, less, more. They talked about who they knew who needed more or less. Some apologized for how much sleep they needed—"I'm afraid I need eight hours of sleep"—as if eight was "too much." They talked about how to avoid fully waking up when a child called them at night, and how to get back to sleep. These women talked about sleep the way a hungry person talks about food.

If, all in all, the two-job family is suffering from a speedup of work and family life, working mothers are its primary victims. It is ironic, then, that often it falls to women to be the time-and-motion experts of family life. As I observed families inside their homes, I noticed it was often the mother who rushed children, saying, "Hurry up! It's time to go." "Finish your cereal now," "You can do that later," or "Let's go!" When a bath needed to be crammed into a slot between 7:45 and 8:00, it was often the mother who called out. "Let's see who can take their bath the quickest!" Often a younger child would rush out, scurrying to be first in bed, while the older and wiser one stalled, resistant, sometimes resentful: "Mother is always rushing us." Sadly, women are more often the lightning rods for family tensions aroused by this speedup of work and family life. They are the villains in a process in which they are also the primary victims. More than the longer hours and the lack of sleep, this is the saddest cost to women of their extra month of work each year.

Raising children in a nuclear family is still the overwhelming preference of most people. Yet in the face of new problems for this family model we have not created an adequate support system so that the nuclear family can do its job well in the era of the two-career couple. Corporations have done little to accommodate the needs of working parents, and the government has done little to prod them.

We really need, as sociologist Frank Furstenberg has suggested, a Marshall Plan for the family. After World War II we saw that it was in our best interests to aid the war-torn nations of Europe. Now—it seems obvi-

15

ous in an era of growing concern over drugs, crime, and family instability—it is in our best interests to aid the overworked two-job families right
here at home. We should look to other nations for a model of what could be
done. In Sweden, for example, upon the birth of a child every working couple is entitled to 12 months of paid parental leave—nine months at 90 percent of the worker's salary, plus an additional three months at about three
hundred dollars a month. The mother and father are free to divide this year
off between them as they wish. Working parents of a child under eight
have the opportunity to work no more than six hours a day, at six hours'
pay. Parental insurance offers parents money for work time lost while visiting a child's school or caring for a sick child. That's a true pro-family policy.

A pro-family policy in the United States could give tax breaks to com-   20
panies that encourage job sharing, part-time work, flex time, and family
leave for new parents. By implementing comparable worth policies we
could increase pay scales for "women's" jobs. Another key element of a
pro-family policy would be instituting fewer-hour, more flexible options—called "family phases"—for all regular jobs filled by parents of
young children.

Day-care centers could be made more warm and creative through
generous public and private funding. If the best form of day-care comes
from the attention of elderly neighbors, students, or grandparents, these
people could be paid to care for children through social programs.

In these ways, the American government would create a safer environment for the two-job family. If the government encouraged corporations to consider the long-range interests of workers and their families,
they would save on long-range costs caused by absenteeism, turnover,
juvenile delinquency, mental illness, and welfare support for single
mothers.

These are real pro-family reforms. If they seem utopian today, we
should remember that in the past the eight-hour day, the abolition of child
labor, and the vote for women seemed utopian, too. Among top-rated employers listed in *The 100 Best Companies to Work for in America* are many offering country-club memberships, first-class air travel, and million-dollar
fitness centers. But only a handful offer job sharing, flex time, or part-
time work. Not one provides on-site day-care, and only three offer child-
care deductions: Control Data, Polaroid, and Honeywell. In his book
Megatrends, John Naisbitt reports that 83 percent of corporate executives
believed that more men feel the need to share the responsibilities of parenting; yet only 9 percent of corporations offer paternity leave.

Public strategies are linked to private ones. Economic and cultural
trends bear on family relations in ways it would be useful for all of us to
understand. The happiest two-job marriages I saw during my research
were ones in which men and women shared the housework and parenting. What couples called good communication often meant that they
were good at saying thanks to one another for small aspects of taking
care of the family. Making it to the school play, helping a child read,

cooking dinner in good spirit, remembering the grocery list, taking responsibility for cleaning up the bedrooms—these were the silver and gold of the marital exchange. Until now, couples committed to an equal sharing of housework and child care have been rare. But, if we as a culture come to see the urgent need of meeting the new problems posed by the second shift, and if society and government begin to shape new policies that allow working parents more flexibility, then we will be making some progress toward happier times at home and work. And as the young learn by example, many more women and men will be able to enjoy the pleasure that arises when family life is family life, and not a second shift.

 ## Topics for Critical Thinking and Writing

1. Here is Hochschild's opening sentence: "Every American household bears the footprints of economic and cultural trends that originate far outside its walls." Explain what Hochschild means and then, using the household you know best, test the truth of Hochschild's sentence.

2. What does Hochschild mean by the phrase "stalled revolution"?

3. Hochschild writes that "Most workplaces have remained inflexible in the face of the changing needs of workers with families" (second paragraph). Assuming that he is correct, why do you think this is so?

4. The rest of the sentence we just quoted is "and most men have yet to really adapt to the changes in women." To what changes does he refer? And do you think he is right? If so, how do you account for the failure of men to adapt?

5. According to Hochschild, women "are the villains in a process in which they are also the primary victims." What does he mean? In your own experience, have you been aware that women have been cast as the villains?

6. Hochschild lists conditions in Sweden for working families and refers to them as a "pro-family policy." What are some of the conditions? Why, in your opinion, does a similar pro-family policy not exist in the United States?

7. In your own family, what was the division of labor for raising children and doing household chores? Who did what (and how often)? Write a brief essay (500–750 words) in which you reveal both the division of labor and your attitude toward it.

Black Elk

Black Elk, a wichasha wakon(holy man) of the Oglala Sioux, as a small boy witnessed the battle of the Little Bighorn (1876). He lived to see his people all but annihilated and his hopes for them extinguished. In 1931, toward the end of his life, he told his life story to the poet and scholar John G. Neihardt to preserve a sacred vision given him.

"High Horse's Courting" is a comic interlude in Black Elk Speaks, *a predominantly tragic memoir.*

High Horse's Courting

You know, in the old days, it was not very easy to get a girl when you wanted to be married. Sometimes it was hard work for a young man and he had to stand a great deal. Say I am a young man and I have seen a young girl who looks so beautiful to me that I feel all sick when I think about her. I cannot just go and tell her about it and then get married if she is willing. I have to be a very sneaky fellow to talk to her at all, and after I have managed to talk to her, that is only the beginning.

Probably for a long time I have been feeling sick about a certain girl because I love her so much, but she will not even look at me, and her parents keep a good watch over her. But I keep feeling worse and worse all the time; so maybe I sneak up to her tepee in the dark and wait until she comes out. Maybe I just wait there all night and don't get any sleep at all and she does not come out. Then I feel sicker than ever about her.

Maybe I hide in the brush by a spring where she sometimes goes to get water, and when she comes by, if nobody is looking, then I jump out and hold her and just make her listen to me. If she likes me too, I can tell that from the way she acts, for she is very bashful and maybe will not say a word or even look at me the first time. So I let her go, and then maybe I sneak around until I can see her father alone, and I tell him how many horses I can give him for his beautiful girl, and by now I am feeling so sick that maybe I would give him all the horses in the world if I had them.

Well, this young man I am telling about was called High Horse, and there was a girl in the village who looked so beautiful to him that he was just sick all over from thinking about her so much and he was getting sicker all the time. The girl was very shy, and her parents thought a great deal of her because they were not young any more and this was the only child they had. So they watched her all day long, and they fixed it so that she would be safe at night too when they were asleep. They thought so much of her that they had made a rawhide bed for her to sleep in, and after they knew that High Horse was sneaking around after her, they took rawhide thongs and tied the girl in bed at night so that nobody could steal her when they were asleep, for they were not sure but that their girl might really want to be stolen.

Well, after High Horse had been sneaking around a good while and hiding and waiting for the girl and getting sicker all the time, he finally caught her alone and made her talk to him. Then he found out that she liked him maybe a little. Of course this did not make him feel well. It made him sicker than ever, but now he felt as brave as a bison bull, and so he went right to her father and said he loved the girl so much that he would give two good horses for her—one of them young and the other one not so very old.

But the old man just waved his hand, meaning for High Horse to go away and quit talking foolishness like that.

High Horse was feeling sicker than ever about it; but there was another young fellow who said he would loan High Horse two ponies and when he got some more horses, why, he could just give them back for the ones he had borrowed.

Then High Horse went back to the old man and said he would give four horses for the girl—two of them young and the other two not hardly old at all. But the old man just waved his hand and would not say anything.

So High Horse sneaked around until he could talk to the girl again, and he asked her to run away with him. He told her he thought he would just fall over and die if she did not. But she said she would not do that; she wanted to be bought like a fine woman. You see she thought a great deal of herself too.

That made High Horse feel so very sick that he could not eat a bite, and he went around with his head hanging down as though he might just fall down and die any time.

Red Deer was another young fellow, and he and High Horse were great comrades, always doing things together. Red Deer saw how High Horse was acting, and he said: "Cousin, what is the matter? Are you sick in the belly? You look as though you were going to die."

Then High Horse told Red Deer how it was, and said he thought he could not stay alive much longer if he could not marry the girl pretty quick.

Red Deer thought awhile about it, and then he said: "Cousin, I have a plan, and if you are man enough to do as I tell you, then everything will be all right. She will not run away with you; her old man will not take four horses; and four horses are all you can get. You must steal her and run away with her. Then afterwhile you can come back and the old man cannot do anything because she will be your woman. Probably she wants you to steal her anyway."

So they planned what High Horse had to do, and he said he loved the girl so much that he was man enough to do anything Red Deer or anybody else could think up. So this is what they did.

That night late they sneaked up to the girl's tepee and waited until it sounded inside as though the old man and the old woman and the girl were sound asleep. Then High Horse crawled under the tepee with a knife. He had to cut the rawhide thongs first, and then Red Deer, who was pulling up the stakes around that side of the tepee, was going to help drag the girl outside and gag her. After that, High Horse could put her across his pony in front of him and hurry out of there and be happy all the rest of his life.

When High Horse had crawled inside, he felt so nervous that he could hear his heart drumming, and it seemed so loud he felt sure it would 'waken the old folks. But it did not, and afterwhile he began cutting the thongs. Every time he cut one it made a pop and nearly scared him to death. But he was getting along all right and all the thongs were cut down as far as the girl's thighs, when he became so nervous that his knife slipped and stuck the girl. She gave a big, loud yell. Then the old folks jumped up and yelled too. By this time High Horse was outside, and he and Red Deer were running away like antelope. The old man and some other people chased the young men but they got away in the dark and nobody knew who it was.

Well, if you ever wanted a beautiful girl you will know how sick High Horse was now. It was very bad the way he felt, and it looked as though he would starve even if he did not drop over dead sometime.

Red Deer kept thinking about this, and after a few days he went to High Horse and said: "Cousin, take courage! I have another plan, and I am sure, if you are man enough, we can steal her this time." And High Horse said: "I am man enough to do anything anybody can think up, if I can only get that girl."

So this is what they did.

They went away from the village alone, and Red Deer made High Horse strip naked. Then he painted High Horse solid white all over, and after that he painted black stripes all over the white and put black rings around High Horse's eyes. High Horse looked terrible. He looked so terrible that when Red Deer was through painting and took a good look at what he had done, he said it scared even him a little.

"Now," Red Deer said, "if you get caught again, everybody will be so scared they will think you are a bad spirit and will be afraid to chase you."

So when the night was getting old and everybody was sound asleep, they sneaked back to the girl's tepee. High Horse crawled in with his knife, as before, and Red Deer waited outside, ready to drag the girl out and gag her when High Horse had all the thongs cut.

High Horse crept up by the girl's bed and began cutting at the thongs. But he kept thinking, "If they see me they will shoot me because I look so terrible." The girl was restless and kept squirming around in bed, and when a thong was cut, it popped. So High Horse worked very slowly and carefully.

But he must have made some noise, for suddenly the old woman awoke and said to her old man: "Old Man, wake up! There is somebody in this tepee!" But the old man was sleepy and didn't want to be bothered. He said: "Of course there is somebody in this tepee. Go to sleep and don't bother me." Then he snored some more.

But High Horse was so scared by now that he lay very still and as flat to the ground as he could. Now, you see, he had not been sleeping very well for a long time because he was so sick about the girl. And while he was lying there waiting for the old woman to snore, he just forgot everything, even how beautiful the girl was. Red Deer who was lying outside ready to do his part, wondered and wondered what had happened in there, but he did not dare call out to High Horse.   25

Afterwhile the day began to break and Red Deer had to leave with the two ponies he had staked there for his comrade and girl, or somebody would see him.

So he left.

Now when it was getting light in the tepee, the girl awoke and the first thing she saw was a terrible animal, all white with black stripes on it, lying asleep beside her bed. So she screamed, and then the old woman screamed and the old man yelled. High Horse jumped up, scared almost to death, and he nearly knocked the tepee down getting out of there.

People were coming running from all over the village with guns and bows and axes, and everybody was yelling.

By now High Horse was running so fast that he hardly touched the ground at all, and he looked so terrible that the people fled from him and let him run. Some braves wanted to shoot at him, but the others said he might be some sacred being and it would bring bad trouble to kill him.   30

High Horse made for the river that was near, and in among the brush he found a hollow tree and dived into it. Afterwhile some braves came there and he could hear them saying that it was some bad spirit that had come out of the water and gone back in again.

That morning the people were ordered to break camp and move away from there. So they did, while High Horse was hiding in his hollow tree.

Now Red Deer had been watching all this from his own tepee and trying to look as though he were as much surprised and scared as all the others. So when the camp moved, he sneaked back to where he had seen his comrade disappear. When he was down there in the brush, he called, and High Horse answered, because he knew his friend's voice. They washed off the paint from High Horse and sat down on the river bank to talk about their troubles.

High Horse said he never would go back to the village as long as he lived and he did not care what happened to him now. He said he was going to go on the war-path all by himself. Red Deer said: "No, cousin, you are not going on the war-path alone, because I am going with you."

So Red Deer got everything ready, and at night they started out on the war-path all alone. After several days they came to a Crow camp just   35 about sundown, and when it was dark they sneaked up to where the Crow horses were grazing, killed the horse guard, who was not thinking about enemies because he thought all the Lakotas were far away, and drove off about a hundred horses.

They got a big start because all the Crow horses stampeded and it was probably morning before the Crow warriors could catch any horses to ride. Red Deer and High Horse fled with their herd three days and nights before they reached the village of their people. Then they drove the whole herd right into the village and up in front of the girl's tepee. The old man was there, and High Horse called out to him and asked if he thought maybe that would be enough horses for his girl. The old man did not wave him away that time. It was not the horses that he wanted. What he wanted was a son who was a real man and good for something.

So High Horse got his girl after all, and I think he deserved her.

 ## Topics for Critical Thinking and Writing

Although High Horse's behavior is amusing and at times ridiculous, how does Black Elk make it clear that he is not ridiculing the young man, but is instead in sympathy with him? Consider the following questions:

1. What is the effect of the first three paragraphs? Think about the first two sentences, and then the passage beginning "Say I am a young man . . ." and ending ". . . I would give him all the horses in the world if I had them."

2. Describe the behavior of the young girl and of her father and mother. How do they contribute to the comedy? How does their behavior affect your understanding of Black Elk's attitude toward High Horse?

3. What is the function of Red Deer?

4. The narrative consists of several episodes. List them in the order in which they occur and then describe the narrative's structure. How does this structure affect the tone?

Josh Quittner

Josh Quittner, co-author of Masters of Deception: The Gang That Ruled Cyberspace *(1995) and author of* Speeding the Net: The Inside Story of Netscape *(1998), is the managing editor of* On *magazine, where the following essay first appeared. In writing this essay he drew on reporting by Roy B. White.*

Keeping Up with Your Kids

I have never been too worried about what my kids do online. I have been using the Web for about as long as there was a Web to use, and I am not an alarmist. But all that changed recently, when a good friend confessed that his 14-year-old daughter had become involved with a 30-year-old man—an adult she met in a chat room.

My friend—I'll call him Frank—is just like me. He's been using computers for decades and is as comfortable online as he is off. Though he too has two PC-using kids, he ignored the Internet's red-light zones. Frank had always assumed that as far as the bad stuff was concerned, most of it was either hype or manageable.

The first hint of trouble came when he found a picture of a strange man—a much older guy—secreted in his daughter's room. "Just a friend," she said, clearly stonewalling. Given how much time his daughter spends online, Frank decided to do a quick search of the family's PC. There he found records of sexually charged chat that his daughter had logged. The chats were apparently with this man.

This story has a happy ending; that is, Frank was able to intervene in time. What technology enabled, technology solved. Frank used the Internet to hunt down the predator and find his home—which, as it turned out, was only a few towns away. Then he got a judge to sign an order barring this creep from having any contact with his daughter.

The whole affair left Frank shaken; he felt guilty and frustrated. "She   5
needs her computer for school. I can't take it away from her. What would you do?"

That's the question I'm wrestling with now—as are, I know, a growing number of parents. My computer-savvy daughters are 12 and 10 years old, and so much of their social lives are online; instant messaging is as much a part of their culture as the telephone. But giving children immediate and unbridled access to the Internet without preparing them is a little like giving them the keys to the car without subjecting them to any driver's education. And unbridled access is what they want from the moment they hear the crash-bang of two modems colliding. The population of teenagers online is soaring: more than 30 million kids under the age of 18 are online, according to the Pew Internet and American Life Project; that's 45% of the age group. And though the windows the Web opens up for a child are powerful portals to the world, there is also some pretty kid-unfriendly stuff out there: according to *Kids Marketing Report*, a British newsletter, there are now 7 million pornography sites on the Web. Plug an innocuous term into a search engine, and porn sites may turn up along with the bull's-eye hits. X-rated junk e-mail does not discriminate by age—it arrives unbidden in all our inboxes. And, as my friend Frank learned, the Net makes it possible for the worst kind of people to slither into your home.

A whole cottage industry aimed at concerned parents has arisen as a result. The "solutions" range from software that allows you to spy on your kids to filters that prevent access to certain websites and chat rooms to secret software agents that will surreptitiously e-mail you when Junior is going someplace online that he shouldn't. You can even get a software timer that ends your child's online session after a set period every day.

Here's a look at some of the more popular approaches.

Doug Fowler is president of SpectorSoft (*www.spectorsoft.com*), the Vero Beach, Fla., maker of Spector ($69.95), one of the most popular programs for spying on your kids (or, for that matter, your spouse or employees). There are a dozen other programs like it, with names like Investigator and 007 Stealth Activity Recorder & Reporter. "The biggest draw is its simplicity," Fowler says of his product. It's easy to install and use. Like its competitors, it secretly records everything that happens on your PC—every e-mail, every chat session, every website visited, every keystroke. It does this by taking a "snapshot" of the screen every 30 seconds and saving the lot in a hidden, password-protected folder that supposedly can hold over a day's worth of activity. The session can then be replayed later, as if you were watching it on a VCR. You can hit Play or fast-forward through the whole thing. You can pause at the interesting bits. EBlaster, also from SpectorSoft, does the same thing, but it e-mails reports to any address you want, so you can spy from a remote location.

Fowler describes Spector as an "essential way to see what your children are doing online." You can't watch over their shoulders all the time, he says. Still, to me spying feels like a violation. Naturally, Fowler disagrees: "I don't have any moral qualms whatsoever." 10

Bob Watkins, a machinery salesman from Memphis, Tenn., was suspicious of how much time his 13-year-old stepdaughter was spending with her music teacher. The girl denied any involvement with the 37-year-old man, so Watkins did some preliminary snooping on his family's PC and found sexually explicit e-mail in her account. Because it was unclear who, exactly, sent the message, Watkins decided to plant Spector and find out. Why didn't he just report his suspicions to the school principal? Watkins says he was worried that he lacked evidence.

So he installed the program. Within 36 hours, he had collected enough incriminating e-mail to turn the matter over to the police, who arrested the teacher. In February, Mark E. Johnson, who had in fact had sex with the girl, pleaded guilty to statutory rape; he received a $500 fine, a suspended sentence and a year of probation.

Watkins says that spying was his only recourse: "I don't believe a child under the roof and protection of a parent should have any expectation of total privacy."

Clearly, this was a last-resort kind of a thing. I can imagine being reduced to spying on my children if I believed that it was the only way to protect them from impending harm, but I am entirely opposed to doing such a thing routinely, proactively. There has to be a better way.

I was relieved to find out that Dr. T. Berry Brazelton, the noted clinical professor of pediatrics emeritus at Harvard Medical School and author of *Touchpoints*, a well-regarded book on child-related issues, agrees that spyware is not the answer—and says it may even create additional problems for children. The child will "just end up acting out against authority," he says. "By devaluing the children, you're only setting them up to do everything you don't want them to do."   15

One way to stay ahead of the game, he says, is to talk frequently with your children about what they're doing online. Sit with them at the computer and discuss what they see. Says Dr. Brazelton, "Share with them the values of your home and use the media to bring them out." Talking is essential. Using surveillance software, he cautions, "is not a communication system."

So what about other technologies that might help parents keep an eye on their kids when they're online? With the advent of the federal Children's Internet Protection Act, which forces publicly funded institutions to implement safety procedures on PCs, libraries across the U.S. have started to install filters. A filter, in this case, is nothing more than a piece of software that prevents the Web surfer from visiting "banned" sites; the banned-site list usually comes from the filter-maker. Dr. Brazelton is surprisingly open to filters. At the very least, he says, parents ought to be aware of them.

I confess that when my daughters were younger, one of the features that I liked most about AOL (the parent company of this magazine) was how easy it was to control my kids' access to the online world. Initially, I prevented them from accessing the Web, and blocked their use of Instant Messenger and chat. They were allowed to receive mail from people on a list that I set up, but not from anyone else. As they got older, I gradually increased their freedom until today, they enjoy full e-mail, IM, chat and even Web access. But I would never use a filter—it just feels too heavy-handed.

Still, approximately 6% of parents with young children use filters, according to Jupiter Research, an Internet market-research firm. A dozen programs for blocking access to objectionable websites, including Cyber Patrol (*www.cyberpatrol.com*), Cyber-sitter (*www.cybersitter.com*) and Net Nanny (*www.netnanny.com*), are being marketed to parents and educators. These filters have been around nearly as long as the Web itself.

At first, the filter approach may sound simple, but in reality it is
rather Sisyphean: to do its job, a filter has to figure out which of the more
than 50 million websites out there are inappropriate, note the addresses
and make them unavailable to your browser. How can any program possibly keep up with all the new porn sites that come online every day, especially if they rely on humans to spot them? If a filter uses an automatic
approach—searching for and blocking sites that use certain forbidden
words, for example—good content is too often blocked along with the
bad. (The classic example is the word *breasts*—porn sites, breast-cancer
pages and grocery stores that sell chicken breasts would all be blocked.)
Finally, many filters reflect their manufacturers' hidden political agendas
and fail to disclose which sites they block. Gay sex-education sites, for example, are blocked by most filters.

If you want to understand why filters don't work, visit Peacefire
(*www.peacefire.org*), a Seattle-based website run by Bennett Haselton.
Last summer, Peacefire checked 1,000 commercial sites (those ending in
.com, rather than .org or .edu) listed with Network Solutions, the primary domain-name administrator. Two popular filters, Cyber Patrol and
Surf-Watch (owned by SurfControl), showed an 80% error rate, even
blocking sites that were not sexually explicit while allowing pornographic sites to get through. (To look at results, go to *www.peacefire.org/
error-rates*.) The filters' makers, by the way, dispute the accuracy of the
test. Haselton is such a pebble in the shoe of the censorware business
that a number of filters actually block access to Peacefire's website. "The
only people who have a problem with the Internet are those who don't
want their kids to have access to alternative points of view," Haselton
claims.

SurfControl spokesperson Sydney Rubin firmly disagrees with that
notion. Filtering, she says, "prevents children from accessing material
they never intended to look for, which could shock and harm them. It's
not about passing judgment on material." For the record, Cyber Patrol
blocks access to Peacefire because, Rubin says, information on the website
might help children circumvent filters. "It's not for the political views,"
she says.

A number of companies, acting as middlemen, have begun to offer
screening services. Instead of actually running a filter on your PC, locally,
you connect to a third party that does the filtering for you. One example
is FamilyClick, which works with many ISPs (but not AOL) and is run by
Tim Robertson, son of evangelist Pat Robertson. The service is not affiliated with the senior Robertson.

Tim Robertson maintains that his service is family-friendly and has
nothing to do with a particular religious perspective. Users can even
customize their comfort zone by selecting one of six access levels. He
says he came up with the idea a few years ago when his daughter accidentally stumbled on a sexually explicit website. He was incensed: "It's

interesting to me that people somehow differentiate between physical danger and intellectual or moral danger. But moral dangers are just as severe—and in some cases, can have more lasting damage than physical injury."

For $4.95 a month, the service filters out objectionable websites, screens any search results and even provides special chat rooms where adults monitor kids' conversations. To begin, users download software that helps them customize their FamilyClick connection; from then on, connections to the Internet are mediated by this service, which presumably keeps everything clean.   25

While that approach clearly works for many people, it won't work for me. I don't like relinquishing control over what my kids can or can't see to a third party.

So I turned to Jean Armour Polly, whom I've come to think of over the years as the voice of sanity where the Net and kids are concerned. Polly, a former librarian, is the author of *The Internet Kids & Family Yellow Pages*, a frequently updated book that describes more than 3,000 great sites for children. "Having a good relationship with your kids," says Polly, "is better than installing special software."

Like Dr. Brazelton, she favors heart-felt and frequent communication with kids. She even suggests that parents and children enter into a written contract that enumerates the kids' rights and responsibilities. While a child might earn the right, say, to instant-message his peers, he also has the responsibility never to give out personal information to anyone online—even if the person appears to know him.

Likewise, parents need to do their homework. Do you know your child's screen name for instant messaging or if she has a website? Visit her page or search for it (and her screen name) on Google. You need to know what your kid is telling the world about herself. Why? Put yourself in the shoes of someone who would do her harm: Is she disclosing personal details or information that a creep could leverage to get into her confidence?

Because we've always kept our computer in a public space, our kids think nothing of us hovering. I often check the History file on my browser to see who's been going where. On Microsoft Internet Explorer, that's easy—you just click on the History button on the navigation bar at the top of your browser window.   30

Some of this stuff might have helped my friend Frank. Most of it probably wouldn't. But one piece of software that he might consider now is PC-Timer (*www.pctimer.com*), which allows you to limit the time your child spends online. You set the time and specify which programs, such as Internet Explorer or Netscape, you want to limit; the timer pulls the plug.

Or Frank could act on a tip I heard from Marc Pellier, CEO of Sympatico-Lycos, Canada's biggest Web portal: buy your kids a whopping 21-inch monitor. They'll love you for it—and you'll be able to keep an eye on things from another room. That's not spying. It's just parenting.

Topics for Critical Thinking and Writing

1. Do you think that the behavior of children online is the responsibility of their parents, or, instead, the government? If you have children, do you worry about what they are doing on-line, in their e-mailing and exploring of the Net?

2. Do you think Quittner's opening is effective? Is it too personal? Why, in your view, did he choose to start this way?

3. In paragraphs 9 and 10 Quittner says that SpectorSoft and comparable devices allow parents to "spy." Fowler, the president of SpectorSoft, says, "I don't have any moral qualms whatsoever." Is "spying" the right word? And, if so, is Fowler deficient in a moral sense? Or obtuse? Explain. Note, by the way, that Quittner returns to the issue of spying in his final paragraph.

4. Paragraphs 11–13 tell of a father, Bob Watkins, who discovered that his thirteen-year-old stepdaughter was having sex with a teacher. Watkins said, "I don't believe a child under the roof and protection of a parent should have any expectation of total privacy." Your view? (You might put your ideas into the form of a letter of 250 words addressed to Mr. Watkins, or perhaps addressed to the readers of *On* magazine, where Quittner's essay first appeared.)

5. Paragraphs 15–16 suggest that parents should talk with their children "about what they're doing online." How effective do you imagine such a strategy is? Do you think surveillance is necessary?

6. If you had an adolescent child, would you use a filter to prevent the child from visiting certain sites? Why, or why not?

7. What is your response overall to this article? Did you enjoy reading it? Did you learn anything new from it? Does an article need to tell us something new to make it worth our time? What else might it do?

8. In your view, is there really a problem, or is Quittner making a fuss about nothing? In an essay of 250 words, explain.

9. If the college you are attending informed you that from now on, it would be keeping a record during the academic year of all the WWW sites you visited while using the college's computer system, would that bother you? If so, would it bother you on general principle? Or for some other reason? What reply might be made to the assertion that the college has a right to keep a record of what students do online when they are using the college's computer system?

Celia E. Rothenberg

Celia E. Rothenberg graduated from Wellesley College in 1991. A history major with a special interest in the lives of Middle Eastern women, she was awarded a Marshall fellowship and studied modern Middle Eastern history at Oxford. She has served as an intern in an Israeli-Palestinian women's peace group in Jerusalem, and she plans to continue working for understanding between these two groups.

Rothenberg wrote the following essay while she was an undergraduate.

Child of Divorce

Over this past winter vacation my parents, brother, and I spent a few days together—a rare event now that the four of us live in four different states. As I watched my parents and brother engage in our usual laughter and reminiscing, accompanied by an occasional tear at a past both bitter and sweet, I listened more closely than ever before to what is a frequent topic of discussion, our relationship as a family.

Perhaps because my parents divorced when I was a small child, it seems to surprise my friends that my family's recollections of those years are filled with many pleasant memories. After all, those who don't know my family have reason to assume that the memories of growing up with divorced parents in some tough economic times might be rather dreary. In fact, however, my memories center on the results of the thoughtfulness and conscious effort exerted by both my parents to create a sense of love and protection for my brother and me. I have always felt that my family was a team, a team that sometimes fumbled, and sometimes seemed to have two, three, or even four captains, and a team that underwent a change in plan mid-game, but a team nevertheless. It is only recently, however, that I have realized how much patience and understanding went into achieving that sense of belonging and love, and how achieving it was part of the long and often painful process for us of divorce and healing.

My parents divorced, after fifteen years of marriage, when I was six. I have nearly no memories of living in a two-parent household. From the time of my earliest memories, my mother has always studied or worked full time. Immediately after the divorce, she, like many women who find themselves single after many years as a "housewife," went back to school. My brother at the time was twelve. Although I remember my Cinderella-shaped cake for my seventh birthday, a few of my favorite pets, and a well-loved school teacher, I remember very little of my mom's return to school, or my own or brother's adjustment to our new surroundings. Perhaps the gaps in my memory serve as some kind of mental defense mechanism to protect me from the reality of the harder times; no

---

matter the reason for my memory voids, however, my brother's recollections are so vivid, and my mom and dad so open about those years, that my scattered memories have been augmented by their story-telling—to the point that I often confuse my memories with theirs.

It is only recently, in fact, that I have realized how difficult the initial years following the divorce were for my mother, brother and father. Over this past winter vacation, my mom told me for the first time how taxing even the simplest tasks seemed to be. For example, locking the doors to our new, small house conjured up all the difficulties and sadnesses of this new beginning. Because my dad had customarily locked up, she had rarely been the one to lock each lock and turn off each light. Doing these tasks in a new house in a new city was a constant reminder of her changed circumstances. Late in the evening she would carefully plot the order in which to turn off the lights, so as not to be alone in the dark. She would lock a door, and then a window, pausing in between the locks to distract her mind from the task at hand—and the frightening and lonely feelings these new responsibilities brought with them.

My family now openly recalls that those years were a difficult time of   5
adjustment to new schools, a new city, and a new life. We had moved from a small suburb of St. Louis to Champaign-Urbana, a community largely centered on the life of the University of Illinois. Our first house in Champaign and my mom's tuition for the Master's degree in Library and Information Science were largely financed by the sale of the lovely Steinway baby grand piano that had graced my parents' living room since before I was born. Before the divorce, my father was an attorney until he found himself in legal difficulties, which ultimately led him to give up the practice of law. His reduced income and my mom's tuition bills placed us under a great financial strain.

My brother, who was twelve at the time of the divorce, particularly recalls how difficult communication was between the three of us and my father, and at times even among the three of us. To help ease the tension of my dad's monthly visits and maintain a relationship which included some fun, my brother and dad played checkers through the mail. They carefully conceived of a plan of multiple paper copies of the checker board and colored pencils for their game. One of my few early memories of those years focusses on the checker board we set up on the dining room table to represent the game my brother and dad played on paper. One evening, the cat we brought with us from (as my mother often said) our "other life," jumped on the board, knocking the pieces all over the table. Steve was inconsolable, and only a prolonged long-distance phone call to figure out where each piece belonged resolved the situation.

That first year my brother escaped into a world of books, often reading fiction and plays when he should have been doing homework, a coping behavior he practiced until he was nearly through high school.

But even the deepest hurts can heal over time. With encouragement and support from both my parents, Steve channeled his considerable energy and anger into planning for an early graduation from high school and a year in Israel between high school and college. The only conditions set were that he had to earn enough money to buy his own plane ticket and he had to have a college acceptance letter in hand before he left. These goals gave him something to work for at a time when he felt that he had lost friends and status in coming to a new, very different, and less comfortable environment than had been part of his early days.

As for me, perhaps because I was six years younger, I appeared to go blithely along, oblivious to most of the tensions and strains that Steve seemed to feel. With my mother studying for her classes and Steve spending almost all his time reading, I became an avid reader myself, almost in self defense. I found new friends and reveled in my new elementary school, a magnet school where we studied French every day. I wrote long, detailed stories of a young girl who lived on a farm with both parents and a dozen brothers and sisters and a beautiful horse. Perhaps I, too, was seeking some consolation in an imaginary life far removed from our little house.

It can take years for wounds to heal, and I am happy to say that my family healed more quickly than most. Perhaps we got past that initial phase early on because my parents did not make too many mistakes. They avoided some common pitfalls of divorcing families. The divorce was quick—the process was completed a few months after my parents sold their house and moved to their new homes—there were no court battles, no screaming fights, no wrenching decisions that we children were required to make. Steve and I were never asked—or allowed—to choose sides or express a preference for one parent over the other. Although my own memories are blurry, the few recollections I have of those first five years focus on my dad's regular monthly visits (he lived a few hours away by car). By the time I was ten, he was spending nearly every weekend with us at the house, a pattern which continued for the next decade, until I was out of high school and off to Wellesley.

Nothing worthwhile, my mother has always told me, is ever easy. It could not have always been easy for either of my parents to spend so much of their free time together when they had chosen to create separate lives, but at the time Steve and I rarely saw anything but civility and fondness. As parents they were determined not to let their children suffer for mistakes they may have made in their marriage. It is one of their greatest gifts to Steve and me, for it was the ultimate lesson in learning about the commitment and cost of love and the lifelong responsibilities of family.

The stories we have accumulated over the years have become more hilarious as I have grown older. My dad, determined not to be a "Disneyland daddy," showing up on the weekends for shopping and dinners out, was not uncomfortable in our new home. In fact, he helped us figure out how

10

to do various home improvement projects. Under his direction, we rewired our house (and nearly electrocuted Steve in the process), insulated our attic (the family story lingers that we nearly blew off the roof), and painted the house (and, of course, ourselves). Our projects probably didn't save us very much money, since we seemed to spend as much money on fixing the mistakes we made as on the project itself, yet we were not merely building the house, or growing gardens, or mowing the lawn. We were rebuilding our lives, making memories, and creating a sense of togetherness.

My own clear and more complete memories begin at the age of eleven, when my mother, brother, and I began a new life-style, which reflected a newly achieved flexibility and confidence in our ability to manage our lives. When my brother entered the University of Illinois, we moved into a big old house and I began high school. The house was what a real estate broker fondly calls a "fixer-upper," and was perfect for my mom's income (she worked for the University after she finished her Master's degree) and our need for space for friends of mine and Steve's. Steve, in particular, brought home countless Jewish college students whom he knew from his involvement in the campus Jewish student organization. They often needed a good meal, a shoulder to lean on, an opinion on a paper, or a good night's sleep.

I remember our dining room on Shabbos, furnished with a dining room set probably beautiful in my grandmother's day but battered after three generations of use, packed with college students eating dinner. I remember vividly the talk and the laughter, the jesting and the endless debates. My mom was not only an intellectual support for those students but also an inspiration, someone who had experienced a marriage gone bad, the trials and tribulations of parenting alone (at least during the week), and the tough economics of a single-parent household. Conversations stretched from the abstract to the concrete, from the politics of the Eastern bloc to the intricacies of love and sex.

Over the years it has become clear that the divorce, although traumatic, opened our minds, enriched our relationships with each other, and loosened restraints we did not know we were subject to. I vividly remember my high school years as a busy time full of my friends and my brothers' who simply enjoyed being around the house. The slightly chaotic, easy-going atmosphere of the house was fostered in large part by our mom; she had disliked the isolated feeling of life in suburbia when she was married. She wanted to create a different atmosphere for Steve and me, a place where young people were comfortable to come and go.

My friends in high school were fascinated by my home, and I enjoyed it as much as they did. My dad was able to watch us grow and change from weekend to weekend, his place secure and comfortable at the head of the Shabbos table surrounded by students. He helped us with science projects, participated in countless car-pools, and, most of all, was there when we needed him. Although from the point of view of the Census Bureau we were a "single parent household," in actuality we were a *family* that happened to have divorced parents. Perhaps our experience was not typical of some families in which there has been a divorce, but the labels obscure our understanding of the needs and hopes of all families, which I think are probably the same, divorced or not. My parent's expectations for Steve and me were not altered by their marital status, nor do I think that Steve and I let them get away with very much on the excuse that they were divorced!

I have always loved my family, but I find that I admire each of them increasingly as time goes on. Now, when we gather from different corners of the country and world during vacations a few times a year, we admit that the best and the worst, but always the most precious times, were when we were together on the weekends in that big old house, sometimes with the students and sometimes with only each other. On special occasions, we have a (very patient) long-distance operator connect the four of us on the same phone line, and we talk as if there is no tomorrow. We are fiercely proud of one another; I often have to restrain myself from blurting out the merits of my exceptional family to my unsuspecting friends.

At times I wonder how different we would be if we had not gone through the divorce, but for that question I can conjure up no really meaningful speculation. I know that we immensely value our time together, freely share our money (or, I should say, our student loans, as my brother is now in law school, my mom is a full-time doctoral student and my father shoulders the Wellesley burden), and exorbitantly rejoice in each other's company. What more could any of us want from family? So often, it seems to me, I see families that do not realize they possess a great wealth—time. They are together all the time. They don't miss the moments of their mother/father/brother/sister's lives that are irreplaceable.

There is no question that it is often difficult to be a family. My own family's life took a path with an unexpected curve. We weathered times of tough adjustments, economic difficulties, and typical adolescent rebellion. Through it all, though, there was a guiding (if unspoken until many years later) principle of life: family is family forever, and there is no escaping either the trials or the rewards. My parents expect my brother and me to extend ourselves and do work that in some way will bring more light into the world. I have parents who, on modest incomes and budgets, have endowed me with dreams and a sense that the impossible is possible. I have parents for whom I am extremely grateful.

When I told my family that Wellesley asked me to write an article on [20] growing up in a single parent household, they responded in their typical chaotic fashion. My brother forced each of us to sit and write a page about the "Single-Parent Thing" before he let us eat dinner. My mother began plotting a book made up of chapters written from the different perspectives of mother, father, son, and daughter in the single-parent household. My dad insisted we discuss it over dinner (and promised to write his page immediately after dessert). In the end, I took their contributions with me back to Wellesley and wrote down my own feelings, late at night in Munger Hall.

 ## Topics for Critical Thinking and Writing

1. What are your earliest memories of your family? How would you account for the fact that Rothenberg has "nearly no memories of living in a two-parent household"?

2. Rothernberg calls her family "exceptional." What do you find to be her strongest evidence for this claim?

3. In paragraph 2 Rothenberg refers to assumptions that her friends make about a child who grew up with divorced parents. What are or were your assumptions? On what are (or were) they based?

4. A highly personal essay runs the risk of being of little interest to persons other than the author. If you found this essay interesting, try to account for its appeal.

Jamaica Kincaid

Jamaica Kincaid was born in 1949 in St. Johns, Antigua, in the West Indies. She was educated at the Princess Margaret School in Antigua and, briefly, at Westchester Community College and Franconia College. Since 1974 she has been a contributor to The New Yorker, *where "Girl" first was published. "Girl" was later included in the first of Kincaid's six books,* At the Bottom of the River.*

Ms. Kincaid informs us that "benna," mentioned early in "Girl," refers to "songs of the sort your parents didn't want you to sing, at first calypso and later rock and roll."*

Girl

Wash the white clothes on Monday and put them on the stone heap; wash the color clothes on Tuesday and put them on the clothesline to dry; don't walk barehead in the hot sun; cook pumpkin fritters in very hot sweet oil; soak your little clothes right after you take them off; when buying cotton to make yourself a nice blouse, be sure that it doesn't have gum on it, because that way it won't hold up well after a wash; soak salt fish overnight before you cook it; is it true that you sing benna in Sunday school?; always eat your food in such a way that it won't turn someone else's stomach; on Sundays try to walk like a lady and not like the slut you are so bent on becoming; don't sing benna in Sunday school; you mustn't speak to wharf-rat boys, not even to give directions; don't eat fruits on the street—flies will follow you; *but I don't sing benna on Sundays at all and never in Sunday school*; this is how to sew on a button; this is how to make a buttonhole for the button you have just sewed on; this is how to hem a dress when you see the hem coming down and so to prevent yourself from looking like the slut I know you are so bent on becoming; this is how you iron your father's khaki shirt so that it doesn't have a crease; this is how you iron your father's khaki pants so that they don't have a crease; this is how you grow okra—far from the house, because okra tree harbors red ants; when you are growing dasheen, make sure it gets plenty of water or else it makes your throat itch when you are eating it; this is how you sweep a corner; this is how you sweep a whole house; this is how you sweep a yard; this is how you smile to someone you don't like too much; this is how you smile to someone you don't like at all; this is how you smile to someone you like completely; this is how you set a table for tea; this is how you set a table for dinner; this is how you set a table for dinner with an important guest; this is how you set a table for lunch; this is how you set a table for breakfast; this is how to behave in the presence of men who don't know you very well, and this way they won't recognize immediately the slut I have warned you against becoming; be sure to wash every day, even if it is with your own spit; don't squat down to play marbles—you are not a boy, you know; don't pick people's flowers—you might catch something; don't throw stones at blackbirds, because it might not be a blackbird at all; this is how to make a bread pudding; this is how to make doukona; this is how to make pepper pot; this is how to make a good medicine for a cold; this is how to make a good medicine to throw away a child before it even becomes a child; this is how to catch a fish; this is how to throw back a fish you don't like, and that way something bad won't fall on you; this is how to bully a man; this is how a man bullies you; this is how to love a man, and if this doesn't work there are other ways, and if they don't work don't feel too bad about giving up; this is how to spit up in the air if you feel like it, and this is how to move quick so that it doesn't fall on you; this is how to make ends meet; always squeeze bread to make sure it's fresh; *but what if the baker won't let me feel the bread?*; you mean to say that after all you are really going to be the kind of woman who the baker won't let near the bread?

 Topic for Critical Thinking and Writing

In a paragraph, identify the two characters whose voices we hear in this story. Explain what we know about them (their circumstances and their relationship). Cite specific evidence from the text. For example, what is the effect of the frequent repetition of "this is how"? Are there other words or phrases frequently repeated?

   Try reading a section of "Girl" out loud in a rhythmical pattern, giving the principal and the second voices. Then reread the story, trying to incorporate this rhythm mentally into your reading. How does this rhythm contribute to the overall effect of the story? How does it compare to or contrast with speech rhythms that are familiar to you?

Robert Hayden

Robert Hayden (1913–80) was born in Detroit, Michigan. His parents divorced when he was a child, and he was brought up by a neighboring family, whose name he adopted. In 1942, at the age of 29, he graduated from Detroit City College (now Wayne State University), and he received a master's degree from the University of Michigan. He taught at Fisk University from 1946 to 1969 and after that, for the remainder of his life, at the University of Michigan. In 1979 he was appointed Consultant in Poetry to the Library of Congress, the first African American to hold the post.

Those Winter Sundays

Sundays too my father got up early
and put his clothes on in the blueblack cold,
then with cracked hands that ached
from labor in the weekday weather made
banked fires blaze. No one ever thanked him.   5

I'd wake and hear the cold splintering, breaking.
When the rooms were warm, he'd call,
and slowly I would rise and dress,
fearing the chronic angers of that house.

Speaking indifferently to him,   10
who had driven out the cold
and polished my good shoes as well.
What did I know, what did I know
of love's austere and lonely offices?

 Topics for Critical Thinking and Writing

1. In line 1, what does the word "too" tell us about the father? What does it suggest about the speaker and the implied hearer of the poem?

2. How old do you believe the speaker was at the time he recalls in the second and third stanzas? What details suggest this age?

3. What is the meaning of "offices" in the last line? What does this word suggest that other words Hayden might have chosen do not?

4. What do you take to be the speaker's present attitude toward his father? What circumstances, do you imagine, prompted his memory of "Those Winter Sundays"?

5. In a page or two, try to get down the exact circumstances when you spoke "indifferently," or not at all, to someone who had deserved your gratitude.

A Casebook on Barbie

Barbie is said to be the most popular toy ever made. Here is an abbreviated chronology, listing the chief events in her life.

1959   Barbie is introduced by Mattel. Historians say that she was a knock-off of a German doll that was designed for men, a sort of three-dimensional pin-up, to be put on dashboards. Barbie's measurements, if she were a human, supposedly would be a most unrealistic 38-18-34. (Another estimate is 38-19-34.)

1961   Ken is created; in due time he will be (among many other roles) an airline captain, a doctor, a soldier, a sailor, a cowboy, a college student, a life guard, and a rock star. Rather slender at first, he later became hunkier.

1965   Ken and Barbie get bendable legs.

1967   The revised Barbie gains eyelashes and a rotating waist ("Twist 'N Turn Barbie").

1970   Barbie swivels at the waist, wrists, knees, ankles; arms swing around (the advertisement says that Barbie is "As posable as you are").

1980   Black Barbie appears, and also several International Barbies (e.g. French, Spanish, Hawaiian).

1998   Barbie's bust is decreased, her waist is increased, and she is able to stand on her own two feet.

2000   "Barbie for President" is introduced, in three models: black, Hispanic, white. The absence of an Asian-American model is noticed, and some groups protest the absence.

Although we now have Doctor Barbie, Businesswoman Barbie, and so on, and we have Barbies of various colors, some people have protested that the essential message conveyed by the doll is still that successful women are blonde, pretty, slender, and big-busted. In this casebook we offer essays and poems that take various points of view.

"Barbie" is big business, and the buyers are not always the parents of little girls. This browser at a Barbie convention may well be looking to add a doll to his own collection.

Astronaut Barbie dolls at the Smithsonian's National Air and Space Museum. Left to right: from the 60s, the 80s, and the 90s. There were Barbie astronauts before the U.S. space program took the idea of women astronauts seriously.

Stephanie Claire Oliver, age eight, and the owner of 62 Barbie dolls, looks at the world's most expensive Barbie doll. Valued at $80,000, this Barbie's gown is decorated with 160 diamonds.

Anonymous

The following editorial appeared in the San Francisco Chronicle *on November 19, 1997. The same issue of the newspaper included an article by Kevin Leary, which we reprint after the editorial.*

Beauty and the Barbie Doll

Ask most any grade-school girl to cite an example of glamour, and chances are good the name "Barbie" will figure in the response. Then take a look at the stacks of Barbies in any toy store, and you have an overpowering message about how society defines beauty—blonde hair and exaggeratedly large breasts, tiny waists and curved buttocks.

Oh, Mattel has made a few concessions since the days when success could only mean a date at the prom with the androgynous Ken. Today's Barbie also can be gainfully employed, such as the popular "Sea World" worker in a sleek black wetsuit. And then there's "Doctor Barbie," an African American with smock and stethoscope—and, of course, high heels and clingy mini-dress.

Barbie is hardly the only purveyor of an unsettling message about the importance of a certain "look," but she is a powerful one. The consequences of this tortured ideal of beauty are very real. They are apparent in the dieting school-age girls of average build who view themselves as woefully overweight. They are apparent in the number of women who assume the risk of breast implants, or other cosmetic surgery, to attain a beauty denied by nature.

Mattel has just announced that some of its 1999 Barbies will have more realistic proportions. The healthy change is just what Doctor Barbie would have ordered.

Kevin Leary

Kevin Leary writes editorials for the San Francisco Chronicle. *We give here his response to the* Chronicle *editorial that is printed above.*

Barbie Curtsies to Political Correctness

Chalk up a victory for political correctness in Toyland. Barbie Doll, the shapely, 11 1/2-inch tall, plastic queen of the toy world, has become a victim of her own elaborate beauty and is about to be overhauled to look more like her critics.

Mattel Inc., the El Segundo–based toy company, has decided to downgrade the doll with a thicker waist, slimmer hips and a bust reduction.

It will give the doll a "more contemporary" and "natural" look, they say.

Why not give her a mustache, cellulite and varicose veins, too? And while they're at it, how about giving Skipper acne and Ken a beer gut and a receding hairline?

Have they gone mad at Mattel? They have marketed the most successful toy in the history of the world, a glamorous fantasy vehicle for little girls that has become an international icon. And they want to change it.   5

More than a billion Barbies have been sold since it was introduced in 1959. Placed head to toe that many dolls would circle the Earth more than seven times. Worldwide sales this year will be about $2 billion. One is sold every two seconds.

The average American girl, ages 3 to 11, owns 10 Barbies. Little girls—and many boys—appreciate Barbie the way she is, exquisitely slim, with long, well-formed legs, a tiny waist and extraordinary mamelonation for her size.

It didn't take long for salacious adults to calculate that if she were a life-size 5-foot-6, her measurements would be 38-19-34. That set off more feminist cawing about sexuality and impossible physical standards of beauty.

Shrieking Barbie-bashers—with a lot of time on their hands—insist the doll is a brainless clotheshorse and a symbol of materialism and sexist stereotyping. They blame Barbie for an epidemic of anorexia and low self-esteem among young girls.

That, of course, is thoroughgoing nonsense. Barbie dolls are toys.   10
They are not meant to be role models or major influences in a kid's life.

But even as mere toys, the dolls have been models of women's liberation and success, as well as physical attractiveness. During her 38 years, Barbie has been a doctor, a nurse, a stewardess, a broadcaster, an Olympic gold medalist in several sports. She was an astronaut in 1965, nearly 20 years before Sally Ride.

She has broken barriers of race and disability. There are black Barbies, Latina Barbies, Asian Barbies and a Barbie in a wheelchair. All of them shapely.

The relentless criticism frequently focuses on the doll's physique. But anyone who has observed young girls playing with Barbies—including Skipper, Ken, Courtney, Tommy and the rest of the doll gang—knows that the dolls are not about sex and materialism.

They are simply attractive dolls with lots of clothes and accessories that encourage children to be anything or do anything they can imagine.

Barbie and her plastic companions provide the characters that chil-   15
dren use to create a magical world of unlimited imagination where everyone is beautiful, rich and accomplished. It's a gilded world of pure fun—beach houses, fancy cars, boats, mobile homes, exciting jobs and a vast wardrobe. It's a world without the warped political correctness that is trying to take the fun out of childhood.

It's too bad that Mattel is bowing to decades of relentless silliness, but the company's marketeers are not stupid. Mattel will introduce 24 new Barbie models in January, and only one of them will bear the new dumpy look.

The others will retain the familiar tush conformation that has contributed to Barbie's huge popularity in 150 countries around the world. We'll see how the new, homelier model sells.

Meg Wolitzer

Meg Wolitzer, a resident of New York, is the author of short stories, novels, and essays. This essay originally appeared in a collection of essays edited by Yona Zeldis McDonough, Barbie Chronicles *(1999).*

Barbie as Boy Toy

My boys are playing with Barbie again. They have spent much of the day building a hideout, talking on the walkie-talkie headphones sent to them by their aunt, and watching Scooby-Doo cartoons on TV, and now it is nighttime and Barbie has been extracted from the toy chest and brought into the fray. It wouldn't have occurred to me to buy a Barbie doll for my sons, but through a series of events too boring to recount here, one happened to find its way into our home. I never thought the doll would be of more than a passing interest to my sons, since, throughout their lives, neither has ever showed the slightest interest in dolls. They have always, however, responded to all things vehicular; the soundtrack in our household is often a low-level *Vrrrrmmm* . . . as a car is pushed along the arm of a sofa. But the day Barbie arrived in the household, my sons quickly liberated her from her plastic box, and she has remained a surprisingly popular plaything ever since.

"Barbieeeeee!" screams Charlie, who's three, as he flings the doll across the living room toward his seven-year-old brother, Gabriel. Gabriel reaches out and neatly catches the doll in one hand. As I head across the living room, the doll whizzes back toward my younger son like a well-dressed missile. If I was the mother of girls, I might fear that the presence of a Barbie doll in their lives was sending them subliminal antifeminist messages about women. I would have to work hard to teach them that looks aren't everything, and try to get them to give the doll interests beyond dressing up in front of a vanity mirror in order to entice the male doll in her life.

My own mother worried about such matters back in the late sixties and early seventies, and when my sister and I requested a Barbie doll, the request was denied. My mother never came right out and said that she disapproved of Barbie on political grounds; actually, I don't think she'd ever really given it that much thought. But I feel that she had an innate sense of Barbie as being somehow illicit, an object that should be kept out of our home if at all possible. A compromise eventually was reached; my sister and I were never given an actual Barbie doll, but were instead given Barbie's younger sister, Skipper: a less-threatening, presexual version of Barbie. Whether my mother's precautions had any tangible effect can't be known, although I do remain a strong feminist with little interest in "accessories," and my sister is a lesbian.

But as far as my two boys go, I don't need to worry unduly about the political "message" aspect of Barbie, because, for the most part, neither of my sons dwells on her anatomy or wardrobe or vacuous, made-up face. (Although I have to say that just the other day, Charlie did peer under Barbie's blouse and, noticing her two nipple-free swells, commented admiringly, "She's got big muscles!") No, for them Barbie is merely another *thing* to be played with, manipulated, occasionally talked to, but mostly flung. Barbie is highly throwable, and highly catchable, too, what with that ample head of hair. I needn't worry that my boys are learning to be disrespectful of women through their behavior toward this doll. In truth, she has never actually been humanized by them.

I have a friend whose little boy was given a baby doll when he was   5 eighteen months old. At first he ignored her, but finally, when he saw that her eyes opened and closed, he became interested. From then on, he would move the doll repeatedly up and down so he could see this mechanical phenomenon in action. When someone asked him what his doll's name was, he proudly said, "Eye."

Dolls as machines; dolls as projectiles. Why is it that most boys don't simply sit down and dress and feed and pamper and talk to dolls? Why is it that most boys don't even *like* dolls? Back in the 1970s, *Free to Be You and Me* was a popular TV special devoted to promoting nonsexist attitudes in children. One of the song-stories was about a little boy who, to his parents' chagrin, craves a doll. His mother and father buy him a baseball and bat to try and distract him, but these gifts don't do the trick. One day, his grandmother arrives bearing a coveted, verboten doll. While William's parents begin to freak out, his grandmother explains that a doll is a wonderful present for a boy because it will teach him how to be a loving father someday.

Before I had children of my own, this story used to move me; if I had a boy someday, I swore, I would definitely let him have a doll. I would be the kind of nonsexist parent who allowed my son to express himself freely. He could have a doll—oh, what the hell, he could have an entire, well-equipped Dream House! But I never imagined that I would one day have two boys who enjoyed dolls only insofar as they could serve as rough-and-tumble objects.

Which isn't to say that my sons aren't loving and tender; they certainly are. They are kind to other children, and surprisingly sensitive to people's feelings. But these qualities don't always overtly appear in the actual *ways* in which they play. I've watched a mother in my son's preschool sit discreetly to the side of the room and beam as her daughter took care of a "sick" doll. "Oh, poor thing, you're burning hot!" the girl said, and she stuck a pretend digital thermometer in the doll's ear and announced that her fever was quite high. Liquid Tylenol was dispensed, as were a series of kisses and hugs, and the doll was tucked into bed and sung an entire medley of lullabies. It was gratifying for that mother to see the way in which her daughter used that doll as a vessel for empathy, for burgeoning maternal feelings. The little girl had clearly been treated similarly, and the results of good mothering were evident.

But what about boys, my own and others? What can be said about who they are from the way in which they go *Vrmmmm, vrmmm*, or scrutinize the moving parts of a toy, or toss a Barbie doll around a room? The truth is that I beam, too, when I watch my sons deeply involved in their play. I see how free they are in the world, how comfortable they are taking an object and creating an entire imagined universe for it. And if Barbie's tiny rosebud mouth could ever speak, I'm certain she would say she has a lot more fun with Gabriel and Charlie than she ever did with Ken.

Yona Zeldis McDonough

Yona Zeldis McDonough is the author of Anne Frank, *a biography for children. The essay that we reprint originally appeared in* The New York Times Magazine, *on January 25, 1998.*

Sex and the Single Doll

Now that my son is six and inextricably linked to the grade school social circuit, he gets invited to birthday parties. Lots of them. Whenever I telephone to say he's coming, I always ask for hints on what might be a particularly coveted gift for the birthday child. And whenever that child is a girl, I secretly hope that the answer will be the dirty little word I am longing to hear. *Barbie.*

No such luck. In the liberal Brooklyn neighborhood where we live, there is a definite bias against the poor doll, a veritable Barbie backlash. "My daughter loves her, but I can't stand her," laments one mother. "I won't let her in the house," asserts another. "Oh, please!" sniffs a third.

But I love Barbie. I loved her in 1963, when she first made her entrance into my life. She was blond, with a Jackie Kennedy bouffant hairdo. Her thickly painted lids (carved out of plastic) and pouty, unsmiling mouth gave her a look both knowing and sullen. She belonged to a grown-up world of cocktail dresses, cigarette smoke, and perfume. I loved her in the years that followed, too, when she developed bendable joints; a twist-and-turn waist; long, silky ash-blond hair; and feathery, lifelike eyelashes. I never stopped loving her. I never will.

I've heard all the arguments against her: She's a bimbo and an airhead; she's an insatiable consumer—for tarty clothes, a dream house filled with garish pink furniture, a pink Barbie-mobile—who teaches little girls that there is nothing in life quite so exciting as shopping. Her body, with its buoyant breasts, wasplike waist, and endless legs, defies all human proportion. But at six, I inchoately understood Barbie's appeal: pure sex. My other dolls were either babies or little girls, with flat chests and chubby legs. Even the other so-called fashion dolls—Tammy, in her aqua-and-white playsuit, and Tressy, with that useless hank of hair, couldn't compete. Barbie was clearly a woman doll, and a woman was what I longed to be.

When I was eight, and had just learned about menstruation, I fash-   5
ioned a small sanitary napkin for her out of neatly folded tissues. Rubber bands held it in place. "Oh, look," said my bemused mother, "Barbie's got her little period. Now she can have a baby." I was disappointed, but my girlfriends all snickered in a much more satisfying way. You see, I wanted Barbie to be, well, dirty. We all did.

Our Barbies had sex, at least our childish version of it. They hugged and kissed the few available boy dolls we had—cleancut and oh-so-square Ken, the more relaxed and sexy Allan. They also danced, pranced, and strutted, but mostly they stripped, showing off their amazing, no-way-in-the-world human bodies. An adult friend tells me how she used to put her Barbie's low-backed bathing suit on backwards so the doll's breasts were exposed. I liked dressing mine in her pink-and-white candy-striped baby-sitter's apron—and nothing else.

I've also heard that Barbie is a poor role model for little girls. Is there such widespread contempt for the intelligence of children that we really imagine they are stupid enough to be shaped by a doll? Girls learn how to be women not from their dolls but from the women around them. Most often this means Mom. My own was a march-to-a-different-drummer bohemian in the early sixties. She eschewed the beauty parlor, cards, and mah-jongg that the other moms in the neighborhood favored. Instead, she wore her long black hair loose, her earrings big and dangling, and her lipstick dark. She made me a Paris bistro birthday party with candles stuck in old wine bottles, red-and-white-checked tablecloths for decorations; she read the poetry of T. S. Eliot to the assembled group of enchanted ten-year-olds. She was, in those years, an aspiring painter, and her work graced not only the walls of our apartment, but also the shower curtain, bathroom mirror, and a chest of drawers in my room. She—not an eleven-and-half-a-inch doll—was the most powerful female role model in my life. What she thought of Barbie I really don't know, but she had the good sense to back off and let me use the doll in my own way.

Barbie has become more politically correct over the years. She no longer looks so vixenish, and has traded the sultry expression I remember for one that is more wholesome and less covert. She now exists in a variety of "serious" incarnations: teacher, Olympic athlete, dentist. And Mattel recently introduced the Really Rad Barbie, a doll whose breasts and hips are smaller and whose waist is thicker, thus reflecting a more real (as if children wanted their toys to be real) female body. None of this matters one iota. Girls will still know the real reason they love her—and it has nothing to do with new professions or a subtly amended figure.

Fortunately, my Barbie love will no longer have to content itself with buying gifts for my son's friends and the daughters of my own. I have a daughter now, and although she is just two, she already has half a dozen Barbies.

They are, along with various articles of clothing, furniture, and other essential accoutrements, packed away like so many sleeping princesses in translucent pink plastic boxes that line my basement shelves. But the magic for which they wait is no longer the prince's gentle kiss. Instead, it is the heart and mind of my little girl as she picks them up and begins to play. I can hardly wait.

Marge Piercy

Marge Piercy, born in Detroit in 1936, was the first member of her family to attend college. After earning a bachelor's degree from the University of Michigan in 1957 and a master's degree from Northwestern University in 1958, she moved to Chicago. There she worked at odd jobs while writing novels (unpublished) and engaging in action on behalf of women and African Americans and against the war in Vietnam. In 1970—the year she moved to Wellfleet, Massachusetts, where she still lives—she published her first book, a novel. Since then she has published other novels, short stories, poems, and essays.

Barbie Doll

This girlchild was born as usual
and presented dolls that did pee-pee
and miniature GE stoves and irons
and wee lipsticks the color of cherry candy.
Then in the magic of puberty, a classmate said: 5
You have a great big nose and fat legs.

She was healthy, tested intelligent,
possessed strong arms and back,
abundant sexual drive and manual dexterity.
She went to and fro apologizing.   10
Everyone saw a fat nose on thick legs.

She was advised to play coy,
exhorted to come on hearty,
exercise, diet, smile and wheedle.
Her good nature wore out   15

like a fan belt.
So she cut off her nose and her legs
and offered them up.

In the casket displayed on satin she lay
with the undertaker's cosmetics painted on,   20
a turned-up putty nose,
dressed in a pink and white nightie.
Doesn't she look pretty? everyone said.
Consummation at last.
To every woman a happy ending.   25

Denise Duhamel

Denise Duhamel was born in 1961 in Woonsocket, Rhode Island, and educated at Emerson College and Sarah Lawrence College. She has published several books of poems, and she has received a New York Foundation for the Arts Fellowship and the Poets and Writers' Exchange Award. Her most recent book is Queen for a Day: Selected and New Poems *(2001).*

In the following poem, Gautama (line 3) refers to Siddhartha Gautama, who became the Buddha ("The Enlightened"). ("Gautama" is the family or clan name.) He was born c. 560 BC in what is now Nepal, near the Indian border, and he is thought to have died c. 480 BC. Although Gautama is the Buddha, or The Historical Buddha, anyone who achieves enlightenment can become a Buddha. Enlightenment begins with comprehending the Four Noble Truths: (1) human life is characterized by suffering (physical and mental); (2) suffering is caused by craving (desire, for instance lust, or even the desire for approval); (3) it is possible to end suffering; (4) the way to end suffering is to follow the Eightfold Path, which includes such things as "Right Speech" (e.g., avoid telling lies, avoid angry words) and "Right Action" (e.g., avoid killing any living creature, avoid drinking intoxicants). (Any book on Buddhism will explain the Eightfold Path in detail, or begin with an account in an encyclopedia and then, if you are taken with what you find, consult some of the references it cites.) The idea is to recognize that nothing has a fixed, independent nature, hence "all is emptiness" (line 3 of Duhamel's poem) and "There is no self" (line 4). (The Sanskrit word translated as "emptiness" is sunyata or shunyata, pronounced shoon-YA-ta; the word translated as "no self" is anatman, pronounced un-AT-mun.) If we understand that all is emptiness, that there is no enduring self, we can empty our transient selves of desire, of attachment to things—even of desire for or attachment to things we can consider noble, such as love of humanity, or of our parents or our country.

Images of the Buddha vary—sometimes he is shown as an ascetic, the bones evident beneath the skin, sometimes as fleshy, but the pot-bellied laughing or smiling figures (see lines 7–8 of Duhamel's poem) in shops that sell Asian knickknacks do not represent the Buddha. Rather, they are representations of a Chinese folk deity, Putai (Japanese: Hotei), widely regarded as a god of Good Luck, though indeed Putai came to be regarded as a Buddha-to-be.

Buddhist Barbie

In the 5th century B.C.
an Indian philosopher

Gautama teaches "All is emptiness"
and "There is no self."
In the 20th century A.D.
Barbie agrees, but wonders how a man
with such a belly could pose,
smiling, and without a shirt.

 ## Topics for Critical Thinking and Writing

1. The essay by Leary is pretty much a reply to the anonymous editorial that precedes it. Write your own reply, either to the anonymous essay or to Leary's. Or write a dialogue setting forth what these two writers might say to each other after each had read the other's essay.

2. What evidence can you offer to support or refute the idea that Barbie has had a bad effect on young women? Speaking more generally, do you think that toys help to shape behavior? Does anything in your own experience confirm or refute this view?

3. Write a dialogue in which Pollitt and McDonough discuss Barbie.

4. Write a poem—or an essay of 50 words—about Ken, Barbie's companion doll. If you wish, closely imitate Marge Piercey's poem.

5. Write—in verse or prose—Gautama's response to Duhamel's Buddhist Barbie.

CHAPTER 9

Identities

Grandfather and Grandchildren Awaiting Evacuation Bus,
Hayward, California, May 9, 1942
Dorothea Lange

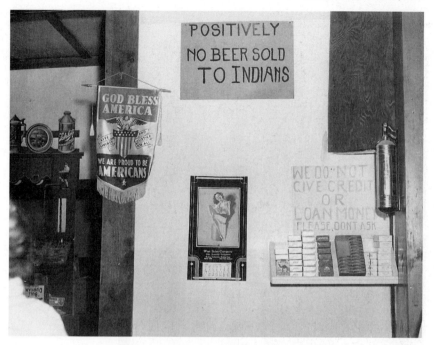

American Gothic
Grant Wood, 1930

American Gothic
Gordon Parks

Short Views

In every known society, the male's need for achievement can be recognized. Men may cook, or weave, or dress dolls or hunt hummingbirds, but if such activities are appropriate occupations of men, then the whole society, men and women alike, votes them as important. When the same occupations are performed by women, they are regarded as less important.

Margaret Mead

There is no female mind. The brain is not an organ of sex. As well speak of a female liver.

Charlotte Perkins Gilman

This has always been a man's world, and none of the reasons hitherto brought forward in explanation of this fact has seemed adequate.

Simone de Beauvoir

We all have been put into categories which fix us in a position which lasts the whole of our lives. Girls are called "feminine" beings and are taught the appropriate feminine behavior; boys are labelled "masculine" and have their behavior defined for them too. No one escapes. Failure to conform to our assigned behavior means that we feel wrong and bad about ourselves. We are not encouraged to break the laws of sex and gender; and certainly no one questions whether the demands of society are contrary to the demands of being human. There ought to be questions asked, though. For what society does is not in our best interest as persons. Society's interest is concerned with how effective we will be as economic and political and cultural supports, not how human we will be.

Heather Formaini

America is God's crucible, the great melting pot where all the races of Europe are melting and re-forming.

Israel Zangwill

No metaphor can capture completely the complexity of ethnic dynamics in the U. S. "Melting pot" ignores the persistence and reconfiguration of ethnicity over the generations. "Mosaic," much more apt for pluralistic societies such as Kenya or India, is too static a metaphor; it fails to take into account the easy penetration of many ethnic boundaries. Nor is "salad bowl" appropriate; the ingredients of a salad bowl are mixed but do not change. "Rainbow" is a tantalizing metaphor, but rainbows disappear. "Symphony," like "rainbow," implies near perfect harmony; both fail to take into account the variety and range of ethnic conflict in the United States.

The most accurately descriptive metaphor, the one that best explains the dynamics of ethnicity, is "kaleidoscope." American ethnicity is kaleidoscopic, i.e. "complex and varied, changing form, pattern, color . . . continually shifting from one set of relations to another; rapidly changing." When a kaleidoscope is in motion, the parts give the appearance of rapid change and extensive variety in color and shape and in their interrelationships. The viewer sees an endless variety of variegated patterns, just as takes place on the American ethnic landscape.

Lawrence Fuchs

We have room for but one language here and that is the English language, for we intend to see that the crucible turns out our people as Americans, of American nationality and not as dwellers in a polyglot boarding house, and we have room for but one loyalty and that is a loyalty to the American people.

Theodore Roosevelt

I cannot say too often—any man who carries a hyphen about him carries a dagger which he is ready to plunge into the vitals of the Republic.

Woodrow Wilson

Capitalism is a machine for the suppression of one class by another.

Vladimir I. Lenin

Through our own efforts and concerted good faith in learning to know, thus to respect, the wonderfully rich and diverse subcommunities of America, we can establish a new vision of America: a place where "community" may mean many things, yet retains its deeper spiritual significance. We may even learn to coincide with

the 500th anniversary of the "discovery" of America by Columbus, that America, in its magnificent variety, has yet to be discovered.
Joyce Carol Oates

I have a dream that my four little children will one day live in a nation where they will not be judged by the color of their skin but by the content of their character.
Martin Luther King Jr.

Light came to me when I realized that I did not have to consider any racial group as a whole. God made them duck by duck and that was the only way I could see them.
Zora Neale Hurston

Racism is so universal in this country, so wide-spread and deep-seated, that it is invisible because it is so normal.
Shirley Chisholm

Stephen Jay Gould

Stephen Jay Gould (1941–2002) taught paleontology, biology, and the history of science at Harvard University. The essays he wrote for the magazine Natural History *have been collected in several highly readable books.*

Women's Brains

In the Prelude to *Middlemarch*, George Eliot lamented the unfulfilled lives of talented women:

> Some have felt that these blundering lives are due to the inconvenient indefiniteness with which the Supreme Power has fashioned the natures of women: if there were one level of feminine incompetence as strict as the ability to count three and no more, the social lot of women might be treated with scientific certitude.

Eliot goes on to discount the idea of innate limitation, but while she wrote in 1872, the leaders of European anthropometry were trying to measure "with scientific certitude" the inferiority of women. Anthropometry, or measurement of the human body, is not so fashionable a field these days, but it dominated the human sciences for much of the nineteenth century and remained popular until intelligence testing replaced skull measurement as a favored device for making invidious comparisons among races, classes, and sexes. Craniometry, or measurement of the skull, commanded the most attention and respect. Its unquestioned leader, Paul Broca (1824–80), professor of clinical surgery at the Faculty of Medicine in Paris, gathered a school of disciples and imitators around himself. Their work, so meticulous and apparently irrefutable, exerted great influence and won high esteem as a jewel of nineteenth-century science.

Broca's work seemed particularly invulnerable to refutation. Had he not measured with the most scrupulous care and accuracy? (Indeed, he had. I have the greatest respect for Broca's meticulous procedure. His numbers are sound. But science is an inferential exercise, not a catalog of facts. Numbers, by themselves, specify nothing. All depends upon what you do with them.) Broca depicted himself as an apostle of objectivity, a man who bowed before facts and cast aside superstition and sentimentality. He declared that "there is no faith, however respectable, no interest, however legitimate, which must not accommodate itself to the progress of human knowledge and bend before truth." Women, like it or not, had smaller brains than men and, therefore, could not equal them in intelligence. This fact, Broca argued, may reinforce a common prejudice in male society, but it is also a scientific truth. L. Manouvrier, a black sheep in Broca's fold, rejected the inferiority of women and wrote with feeling about the burden imposed upon them by Broca's numbers:

> Women displayed their talents and their diplomas. They also invoked philosophical authorities. But they were opposed by *numbers* unknown to Condorcet or to John Stuart Mill. These numbers fell upon poor women like a sledge hammer, and they were accompanied by commentaries and sarcasms more ferocious than the most misogynist imprecations of certain church fathers. The theologians had asked if women had a soul. Several centuries later, some scientists were ready to refuse them a human intelligence.

Broca's argument rested upon two sets of data: the larger brains of men in modern societies, and a supposed increase in male superiority through time. His most extensive data came from autopsies performed personally in four Parisian hospitals. For 292 male brains, he calculated an average weight of 1,325 grams; 140 female brains averaged 1,144 grams for a difference of 181 grams, or 14 percent of the male weight. Broca understood, of course, that part of this difference could be attributed to the greater height of males. Yet he made no attempt to measure the effect of size alone and actually stated that it cannot account for the entire difference because we know, a priori, that women are not as intelligent as men (a premise that the data were supposed to test, not rest upon):

> We might ask if the small size of the female brain depends exclusively upon the small size of her body. Tiedemann has proposed this explanation. But we must not forget that women are, on the average, a little less intelligent than men, a difference which we should not exaggerate but which is, nonetheless, real. We are therefore permitted to suppose that the relatively small size of the female brain depends in part upon her physical inferiority and in part upon her intellectual inferiority.

In 1873, the year after Eliot published *Middlemarch*, Broca measured the cranial capacities of prehistoric skulls from L'Homme Mort cave. Here he found a difference of only 99.5 cubic centimeters between males and females, while modern populations range from 129.5 to 220.7. Topinard, Broca's chief disciple, explained the increasing discrepancy through time as a result of differing evolutionary pressures upon dominant men and passive women:

> The man who fights for two or more in the struggle for existence, who has all the responsibility and the cares of tomorrow, who is constantly active in combating the environment and human rivals, needs more brain than the woman whom he must protect and nourish, the sedentary woman, lacking any interior occupations, whose role is to raise children, love, and be passive.

In 1879, Gustave Le Bon, chief misogynist of Broca's school, used these data to publish what must be the most vicious attack upon women in modern scientific literature (no one can top Aristotle). I do not claim his views were representative of Broca's school, but they were published in France's most respected anthropological journal. Le Bon concluded:

> In the most intelligent races, as among the Parisians, there are a large number of women whose brains are closer in size to those of gorillas than to the most developed male brains. This inferiority is so obvious that no one can contest it for a moment; only its degree is worth discussion. All psychologists who have studied the intelligence of women, as well as poets and novelists, recognize today that they represent the most inferior forms of human evolution and that they are closer to children and savages than to an adult, civilized man. They excel in fickleness, inconstancy, absence of thought and logic, and incapacity to reason. Without doubt there exist some distinguished women, very superior to the average man, but they are as exceptional as the birth of any monstrosity, as, for example, of a gorilla with two heads; consequently, we may neglect them entirely.

Nor did Le Bon shrink from the social implications of his views. He was horrified by the proposal of some American reformers to grant women higher education on the same basis as men:

> A desire to give them the same education, and, as a consequence, to propose the same goals for them, is a dangerous chimera . . . . The day when, misunderstanding the inferior occupations which nature has given her, women leave the home and take part in our battles; on this day a social revolution will begin, and everything that maintains the sacred ties of the family will disappear.

Sound familiar?[1]

I have reexamined Broca's data, the basis for all this derivative pronouncement, and I find his numbers sound but his interpretation ill-founded, to say the least. The data supporting his claim for increased difference through time can be easily dismissed. Broca based his contention on the samples from L'Homme Mort alone—only seven male and six female skulls in all. Never have so little data yielded such far ranging conclusions.

In 1888, Topinard published Broca's more extensive data on the Parisian hospitals. Since Broca recorded height and age as well as brain size, we may use modern statistics to remove their effect. Brain weight decreases with age, and Broca's women were, on average, considerably older than his men. Brain weight increases with height, and his average

---

[1]When I wrote this essay, I assumed that Le Bon was a marginal, if colorful, figure. I have since learned that he was a leading scientist, one of the founders of social psychology, and best known for a seminal study on crowd behavior, still cited today (*La psychologie des foules*, 1895), and for his work on unconscious motivation.

man was almost half a foot taller than his average woman. I used multiple regression, a technique that allowed me to assess simultaneously the influence of height and age upon brain size. In an analysis of the data for women, I found that, at average male height and age, a woman's brain would weigh 1,212 grams. Correction for height and age reduces Broca's measured difference of 181 grams by more than a third, to 113 grams.

I don't know what to make of this remaining difference because I cannot assess other factors known to influence brain size in a major way. Cause of death has an important effect: degenerative disease often entails a substantial diminution of brain size. (This effect is separate from the decrease attributed to age alone.) Eugene Schreider, also working with Broca's data, found that men killed in accidents had brains weighing, on average, 60 grams more than men dying of infectious diseases. The best modern data I can find (from American hospitals) records a full 100-gram difference between death by degenerative arteriosclerosis and by violence or accident. Since so many of Broca's subjects were very elderly women, we may assume that lengthy degenerative disease was more common among them than among the men.

More importantly, modern students of brain size still have not agreed on a proper measure for eliminating the powerful effect of body size. Height is partly adequate, but men and women of the same height do not share the same body build. Weight is even worse than height, because most of its variation reflects nutrition rather than intrinsic size—fat versus skinny exerts little influence upon the brain. Manouvrier took up this subject in the 1880s and argued that muscular mass and force should be used. He tried to measure this elusive property in various ways and found a marked difference in favor of men, even in men and women of the same height. When he corrected for what he called "sexual mass," women actually came out slightly ahead in brain size.

Thus, the corrected 113-gram difference is surely too large; the true figure is probably close to zero and may as well favor women as men. And 113 grams, by the way, is exactly the average difference between a 5 foot 4 inch and a 6 foot 4 inch male in Broca's data. We would not (especially us short folks) want to ascribe greater intelligence to tall men. In short, who knows what to do with Broca's data? They certainly don't permit any confident claim that men have bigger brains than women.

To appreciate the social role of Broca and his school, we must recognize that his statements about the brains of women do not reflect an isolated prejudice toward a single disadvantaged group. They must be weighed in the context of a general theory that supported contemporary social distinctions as biologically ordained. Women, blacks, and poor people suffered the same disparagement, but women bore the brunt of Broca's argument because he had easier access to data on women's brains. Women were singularly denigrated but they also stood as surrogates for other disenfranchised groups. As one of Broca's disciples wrote in 1881: "Men of the black races have a brain scarcely heavier than that of white women." This juxtaposition extended into many other realms of anthropological argument, particularly to claims that, anatomically and emotionally, both women and blacks were like white children—and that white children, by the theory of recapitulation, represented an ancestral (primitive) adult stage of human evolution. I do not regard as empty rhetoric the claim that women's battles are for all of us.

Maria Montessori did not confine her activities to educational reform for young children. She lectured on anthropology for several years at the University of Rome, and wrote an influential book entitled *Pedagogical Anthropology* (English edition, 1913). Montessori was no egalitarian. She supported most of Broca's work and the theory of innate criminality proposed by her compatriot Cesare Lombroso. She measured the circumference of children's heads in her schools and inferred that the best prospects had bigger brains. But she had no use for Broca's conclusions about women. She discussed Manouvrier's work at length and made much of his tentative claim that women, after proper correction of the data, had slightly larger brains than men. Women, she concluded, were intellectually superior, but men had prevailed heretofore by dint of physical force. Since technology has abolished force as an instrument of power, the era of women may soon be upon us: "In such an epoch there will really be superior human beings, there will really be men strong in morality and in sentiment. Perhaps in this way the reign of women is approaching, when the enigma of her anthropological superiority will be deciphered. Woman was always the custodian of human sentiment, morality and honor."

This represents one possible antidote to "scientific" claims for the constitutional inferiority of certain groups. One may affirm the validity of biological distinctions but argue that the data have been misinterpreted by prejudiced men with a stake in the outcome, and that disadvantaged groups are truly superior. In recent years, Elaine Morgan has followed this strategy in her *Descent of Woman*, a speculative reconstruction of human prehistory from the woman's point of view—and as farcical as more famous tall tales by and for men.

I prefer another strategy. Montessori and Morgan followed Broca's philosophy to reach a more congenial conclusion. I would rather label the whole enterprise of setting a biological value upon groups for what it is: irrelevant and highly injurious. George Eliot well appreciated the special tragedy that biological labeling imposed upon members of disadvantaged groups. She expressed it for people like herself—women of extraordinary talent. I would apply it more widely—not only to those whose dreams are flouted but also to those who never realize that they may dream—but I cannot match her prose. In conclusion, then, the rest of Eliot's prelude to *Middlemarch*:

The limits of variation are really much wider than anyone would imagine from the sameness of women's coiffure and the favorite love stories in prose and verse. Here and there a cygnet is reared uneasily among the ducklings in the brown pond, and never finds the living stream in fellowship with its own oary-footed kind. Here and there is born a Saint Theresa, foundress of nothing, whose loving heartbeats and sobs after an unattained goodness tremble off and are dispersed among hindrances instead of centering in some long-recognizable deed.

Topics for Critical Thinking and Writing

1. What is your understanding of anthropometry from paragraph 2? According to Gould, what does intelligence testing have in common with anthropometry? Characterize his attitude toward both. How does he reveal his attitude in this paragraph?

2. In paragraph 3, what does Gould mean when he says, "But science is an inferential exercise, not a catalog of facts"?

3. In paragraph 13 Gould says, "I do not regard as empty rhetoric the claim that women's battles are for all of us." What does he mean? What foundation for this opinion have this paragraph and paragraph 2 provided?

4. Who was Maria Montessori, and what does her work have to do with Gould's argument? If her relevance is not entirely clear to you, or was not on first reading, what might Gould have done to make it clearer?

5. What, according to Gould, are the social consequences of what he calls in paragraph 16 *biological labeling*? If on the whole you agree with him, what is the basis of your agreement?

6. In paragraph 13 Gould refers to the "social role of Broca and his school." What does he mean by that? On the basis of this essay (and others of Gould's that you may have read) formulate in a sentence or two the social role of Gould.

Katha Pollitt

Katha Pollitt (b. 1949) writes chiefly on literary, political, and social topics. In addition to writing essays, she writes poetry; her first collection of poems, Antarctic Traveller *(1982), won the National Book Critics Circle Award. She publishes widely, especially in* The Nation, The New Yorker, *and* The New York Times. *We reprint an article that originally appeared in* The New York Times Magazine.

Why Boys Don't Play with Dolls

It's twenty-eight years since the founding of NOW,[1] and boys still like trucks and girls still like dolls. Increasingly, we are told that the source of these robust preferences must lie outside society—in prenatal hormonal influences, brain chemistry, genes—and that feminism has reached its natural limits. What else could possibly explain the love of preschool girls for party dresses or the desire of toddler boys to own more guns than Mark from Michigan?

True, recent studies claim to show small cognitive differences between the sexes: He gets around by orienting himself in space; she does it by remembering landmarks. Time will tell if any deserve the hoopla with which each is invariably greeted, over the protests of the researchers themselves. But even if the results hold up (and the history of such research is not encouraging), we don't need studies of sex-differentiated brain activity in reading, say, to understand why boys and girls still seem so unalike.

The feminist movement has done much for some women, and something for every woman, but it has hardly turned America into a playground free of sex roles. It hasn't even got women to stop dieting or men to stop interrupting them.

Instead of looking at kids to "prove" that differences in behavior by sex are innate, we can look at the ways we raise kids as an index to how unfinished the feminist revolution really is, and how tentatively it is embraced even by adults who fully expect their daughters to enter previously male-dominated professions and their sons to change diapers.

I'm at a children's birthday party. "I'm sorry," one mom silently mouths to the mother of the birthday girl, who has just torn open her present—Tropical Splash Barbie. Now, you can love Barbie or you can hate Barbie, and there are feminists in both camps. But *apologize* for Barbie? Inflict Barbie, against your own convictions, on the child of a friend you know will be none too pleased?

Every mother in that room had spent years becoming a person who had to be taken seriously, not least by herself. Even the most attractive,

5

[1]**NOW** National Organization for Women (Editors' note)

I'm willing to bet, had suffered over her body's failure to fit the impossible American ideal. Given all that, it seems crazy to transmit Barbie to the next generation. Yet to reject her is to say that what Barbie represents—being sexy, thin, stylish—is unimportant, which is obviously not true, and children know it's not true.

Women's looks matter terribly in this society, and so Barbie, however ambivalently, must be passed along. After all, there are worse toys. The Cut and Style Barbie styling head, for example, a grotesque object intended to encourage "hair play." The grown-ups who give that probably apologize, too.

How happy would most parents be to have a child who flouted sex conventions? I know a lot of women, feminists, who complain in a comical, eye-ball-rolling way about their sons' passion for sports: the ruined weekends, obnoxious coaches, macho values. But they would not think of discouraging their sons from participating in this activity they find so foolish. Or do they? Their husbands are sports fans, too, and they like their husbands a lot.

Could it be that even sports-resistant moms see athletics as part of manliness? That if their sons wanted to spend the weekend writing up their diaries, or reading, or baking, they'd find it disturbing? Too antisocial? Too lonely? Too gay?

Theories of innate differences in behavior are appealing. They let parents off the hook—no small recommendation in a culture that holds moms, and sometimes even dads, responsible for their children's every misstep on the road to bliss and success.   10

They allow grown-ups to take the path of least resistance to the dominant culture, which always requires less psychic effort, even if it means more actual work: Just ask the working mother who comes home exhausted and nonetheless finds it easier to pick up her son's socks than make him do it himself. They let families buy for their children, without *too* much guilt, the unbelievably sexist junk that the kids, who have been watching commercials since birth, understandably crave.

But the thing the theories do most of all is tell adults that the *adult* world—in which moms and dads still play by many of the old rules even as they question and fidget and chafe against them—is the way it's supposed to be. A girl with a doll and a boy with a truck "explain" why men are from Mars and women are from Venus, why wives do housework and husbands just don't understand.

The paradox is that the world of rigid and hierarchical sex roles evoked by determinist theories is already passing away. Three-year-olds may indeed insist that doctors are male and nurses female, even if their own mother is a physician. Six-year-olds know better. These days, something like half of all medical students are female, and male applications to nursing school are inching upward. When tomorrow's three-year-olds play doctor, who's to say how they'll assign the roles?

With sex roles, as in every area of life, people aspire to what is possible, and conform to what is necessary. But these are not fixed, especially today. Biological determinism may reassure some adults about their present, but it is feminism, the ideology of flexible and converging sex roles, that fits our children's future. And the kids, somehow, know this.

That's why, if you look carefully, you'll find that for every kid who fits   15
a stereotype, there's another who's breaking one down. Sometimes it's the same kid—the boy who skateboards *and* takes cooking in his after school program; the girl who collects stuffed animals *and* A-pluses in science.

Feminists are often accused of imposing their "agenda" on children. Isn't that what adults always do, consciously and unconsciously? Kids aren't born religious, or polite, or kind, or able to remember where they put their sneakers. Inculcating these behaviors, and the values behind them, is a tremendous amount of work, involving many adults. We don't have a choice, really, about *whether* we should give our children messages about what it means to be male and female—they're bombarded with them from morning till night.

Topics for Critical Thinking and Writing

1. In a paragraph set forth Pollitt's answer to the question she poses in her title.

2. In paragraph 7 Pollitt says, "Women's looks matter terribly in this society." Do you agree with this generalization? If they do matter "terribly," do they matter more than men's? What evidence can you give, one way or the other? Set forth your answer in an essay of 250 words.

3. Look at the last sentence in paragraph 12: "A girl with a doll and a boy with a truck 'explain' why men are from Mars and women are from Venus, why wives do housework and husbands just don't understand." Why does Pollitt put "explain" within quotation marks? What is she getting at by speaking of Mars and Venus? "Do housework" and "don't understand" are not the parallel construction that a reader probably expects. Do you think Pollitt's writing is deficient here, or is the variation purposeful? Explain.

4. In paragraph 14 Pollitt says that "the ideology of flexible and converging sex roles" is the one that "fits our children's future." What would be examples of "flexible and converging sex roles"? And do you agree that this ideology is the one that suits the immediate future? Why?

5. Do you believe that you have been influenced by Barbie or by any other toy? Explain.

6. In her final paragraph Pollitt says that adults always impose an "agenda" on their children, consciously or unconsciously. What agenda did your parents (or other adults charged with your upbringing) impose or try to impose? What was your response? As you think back on it, were the agenda and the responses appropriate? Set forth your answers in an essay of 500 to 750 words.

7. If you have heard that "brain chemistry" or "genes" (paragraph 1) account for "innate differences in behavior" (paragraph 10) in boys and girls, in a paragraph set forth the view, and in another paragraph evaluate it, drawing perhaps on your reading of Pollitt's essay.

Malcolm Gladwell

Malcolm Gladwell is a staff writer for The New Yorker.

The Sports Taboo

The education of any athlete begins, in part, with an education in the racial taxonomy of his chosen sport—in the subtle, unwritten rules about what whites are supposed to be good at and what blacks are supposed to be good at. In football, whites play quarterback and blacks play running back; in baseball whites pitch and blacks play the outfield. I grew up in Canada, where my brother Geoffrey and I ran high-school track, and in Canada the rule of running was that anything under the quarter-mile belonged to the West Indians. This didn't mean that white people didn't run the sprints. But the expectation was that they would never win, and, sure enough, they rarely did. There was just a handful of West Indian immigrants in Ontario at that point—clustered in and around Toronto—but they *owned* Canadian sprinting, setting up under the stands at every major championship, cranking up the reggae on their boom boxes, and then humiliating everyone else on the track. My brother and I weren't from Toronto, so we weren't part of that scene. But our West Indian heritage meant that we got to share in the swagger. Geoffrey was a magnificent runner, with powerful legs and a barrel chest, and when he was warming up he used to do that exaggerated, slow-motion jog that the white guys would try to do and never quite pull off. I was a miler, which was a little outside the West Indian range. But, the way I figured it, the rules meant that no one should ever out-kick me over the final two hundred metres of any race. And in the golden summer of my fourteenth year, when my running career prematurely peaked, no one ever did.

When I started running, there was a quarter-miler just a few years older than I was by the name of Arnold Stotz. He was a bulldog of a runner, hugely talented, and each year that he moved through the sprinting ranks he invariably broke the existing four-hundred-metre record in his age class. Stotz was white, though, and every time I saw the results of a big track meet I'd keep an eye out for his name, because I was convinced

Malcolm Gladwell, "The Sports Taboo" from *The New Yorker*, May 19, 1997. Reprinted with permission from *The New Yorker*.

that he could not keep winning. It was as if I saw his whiteness as a degenerative disease, which would eventually claim and cripple him. I never asked him whether he felt the same anxiety, but I can't imagine that he didn't. There was only so long that anyone could defy the rules. One day, at the provincial championships, I looked up at the results board and Stotz was gone.

Talking openly about the racial dimension of sports in this way, of course, is considered unseemly. It's all right to say that blacks dominate sports because they lack opportunities elsewhere. That's the "Hoop Dreams" line, which says whites are allowed to acknowledge black athletic success as long as they feel guilty about it. What you're not supposed to say is what we were saying in my track days—that we were better *because* we were black, because of something intrinsic to being black. Nobody said anything like that publicly last month when Tiger Woods won the Masters or when, a week later, African men claimed thirteen out of the top twenty places in the Boston Marathon. Nor is it likely to come up this month, when African-Americans will make up eighty per cent of the players on the floor for the N.B.A. playoffs. When the popular television sports commentator Jimmy (the Greek) Snyder did break this taboo, in 1988—infamously ruminating on the size and significance of black thighs—one prominent N.A.A.C.P. official said that his remarks "could set race relations back a hundred years." The assumption is that the whole project of trying to get us to treat each other the same will be undermined if we don't all agree that under the skin we actually are the same.

The point of this, presumably, is to put our discussion of sports on a par with legal notions of racial equality, which would be a fine idea except that civil-rights law governs matters like housing and employment and the sports taboo covers matters like what can be said about someone's jump shot. In his much heralded new book "Darwin's Athletes," the University of Texas scholar John Hoberman tries to argue that these two things are the same, that it's impossible to speak of black physical superiority without implying intellectual inferiority. But it isn't long before the argument starts to get ridiculous. "The spectacle of black athleticism," he writes, inevitably turns into "a highly public image of black retardation." Oh, really? What, exactly, about Tiger Woods's victory in the Masters resembled "a highly public image of black retardation"? Today's black athletes are multimillion-dollar corporate pitchmen, with talk shows and sneaker deals and publicity machines and almost daily media opportunities to share their thoughts with the world, and it's very hard to see how all this contrives to make them look stupid. Hoberman spends a lot of time trying to inflate the significance of sports, arguing that how we talk about events on the baseball diamond or the track has grave consequences for how we talk about race in general. Here he is, for example, on Jackie Robinson:

> The sheer volume of sentimental and intellectual energy that has been invested in the mythic saga of Jackie Robinson has discouraged further thinking about what his career did and did not accomplish. . . . Black America has

paid a high and largely unacknowledged price for the extraordinary prominence given the black athlete rather than other black men of action (such as
military pilots and astronauts), who represent modern aptitudes in ways that
athletes cannot.

Please. Black America has paid a high and largely unacknowledged   5
price for a long list of things, and having great athletes is far from the top
of the list. Sometimes a baseball player is just a baseball player, and sometimes an observation about racial difference is just an observation about
racial difference. Few object when medical scientists talk about the significant epidemiological differences between blacks and whites—the fact
that blacks have a higher incidence of hypertension than whites and twice
as many black males die of diabetes and prostate cancer as white males,
that breast tumors appear to grow faster in black women than in white
women, that black girls show signs of puberty sooner than white girls. So
why aren't we allowed to say that there might be athletically significant
differences between blacks and whites?

According to the medical evidence, African-Americans seem to have,
on the average, greater bone mass than do white Americans—a difference
that suggests greater muscle mass. Black men have slightly higher circu-
lating levels of testosterone and human-growth hormone than their white
counterparts, and blacks over all tend to have proportionally slimmer
hips, wider shoulders, and longer legs. In one study, the Swedish physiologist Bengt Saltin compared a group of Kenyan distance runners with a
group of Swedish distance runners and found interesting differences in
muscle composition: Saltin reported that the Africans appeared to have
more blood-carrying capillaries and more mitochondria (the body's cellular power plant) in the fibres of their quadriceps. Another study found
that, while black South African distance runners ran at the same speed as
white South African runners, they were able to use more oxygen—eighty-
nine per cent versus eighty-one per cent—over extended periods: somehow, they were able to exert themselves more. Such evidence suggested
that there were physical differences in black athletes which have a bearing on activities like running and jumping, which should hardly come as
a surprise to anyone who follows competitive sports.

To use track as an example—since track is probably the purest measure of athletic ability—Africans recorded fifteen out of the twenty fastest
times last year in the men's ten-thousand-metre event. In the five thousand metres, eighteen out of the twenty fastest times were recorded by
Africans. In the fifteen hundred metres, thirteen out of the twenty fastest
times were African, and in the sprints, in the men's hundred metres, you
have to go all the way down to the twenty-third place in the world rankings—to Geir Moen, of Norway—before you find a white face. There is a
point at which it becomes foolish to deny the fact of black athletic
prowess, and even more foolish to banish speculation on the topic.
Clearly, something is going on. The question is what.

If we are to decide what to make of the differences between blacks and whites, we first have to decide what to make of the word "difference," which can mean any number of things. A useful case study is to compare the ability of men and women in math. If you give a large, representative sample of male and female students a standardized math test, their mean scores will come out pretty much the same. But if you look at the margins, at the very best and the very worst students, sharp differences emerge. In the math portion of an achievement test conducted by Project Talent—a nationwide survey of fifteen-year-olds—there were 1.3 boys for every girl in the top ten per cent, 1.5 boys for every girl in the top five per cent, and seven boys for every girl in the top one per cent. In the fifty-six-year history of the Putnam Mathematical Competition, which has been described as the Olympics of college math, all but one of the winners have been male. Conversely, if you look at people with the very lowest math ability, you'll find more boys than girls there, too. In other words, although the average math ability of boys and girls is the same, the distribution isn't: there are more males than females at the bottom of the pile, more males than females at the top of the pile, and fewer males than females in the middle. Statisticians refer to this as a difference in variability.

This pattern, as it turns out, is repeated in almost every conceivable area of gender difference. Boys are more variable than girls on the College Board entrance exam and in routine elementary-school spelling tests. Male mortality patterns are more variable than female patterns; that is, many more men die in early and middle age than women, who tend to die in more of a concentrated clump toward the end of life. The problem is that variability differences are regularly confused with average differences. If men had higher average math scores than women, you could say they were better at the subject. But because they are only more variable the word "better" seems inappropriate.

The same holds true for differences between the races. A racist stereotype is the assertion of average difference—it's the claim that the typical white is superior to the typical black. It allows a white man to assume that the black man he passes on the street is stupider than he is. By contrast, if what racists believed was that black intelligence was simply more variable than white intelligence, then it would be impossible for them to construct a stereotype about black intelligence at all. They wouldn't be able to generalize. If they wanted to believe that there were a lot of blacks dumber than whites, they would also have to believe that there were a lot of blacks smarter than they were. This distinction is critical to understanding the relation between race and athletic performance. What are we seeing when we remark black domination of élite sporting events—an average difference between the races or merely a difference in variability?

This question has been explored by geneticists and physical anthropologists, and some of the most notable work has been conducted over the past few years by Kenneth Kidd, at Yale. Kidd and his colleagues have

10

been taking DNA samples from two African Pygmy tribes in Zaire and the Central African Republic and comparing them with DNA samples taken from populations all over the world. What they have been looking for is variants—subtle differences between the DNA of one person and another—and what they have found is fascinating. "I would say, without a doubt, that in almost any single African population—a tribe or however you want to define it—there is more genetic variation than in all the rest of the world put together," Kidd told me. In a sample of fifty Pygmies, for example, you might find nine variants in one stretch of DNA. In a sample of hundreds of people from around the rest of the world, you might find only a total of six variants in that same stretch of DNA—and probably every one of those six variants would also be found in the Pygmies. If everyone in the world was wiped out except Africans, in other words, almost all the human genetic diversity would be preserved.

The likelihood is that these results reflect Africa's status as the homeland of *Homo sapiens:* since every human population outside Africa is essentially a subset of the original African population, it makes sense that everyone in such a population would be a genetic subset of Africans, too. So you can expect groups of Africans to be more variable in respect to almost anything that has a genetic component. If, for example, your genes control how you react to aspirin, you'd expect to see more Africans than whites for whom one aspirin stops a bad headache, more for whom no amount of aspirin works, more who are allergic to aspirin, and more who need to take, say, four aspirin at a time to get any benefit—but far fewer Africans for whom the standard two-aspirin dose would work well. And to the extent that running is influenced by genetic factors you would expect to see more really fast blacks—and more really slow blacks—than whites but far fewer Africans of merely average speed. Blacks are like boys. Whites are like girls.

There is nothing particularly scary about this fact, and certainly nothing to warrant the kind of gag order on talk of racial differences which is now in place. What it means is that comparing élite athletes of different races tells you very little about the races themselves. A few years ago, for example, a prominent scientist argued for black athletic supremacy by pointing out that there had never been a white Michael Jordan. True. But, as the Yale anthropologist Jonathan Marks has noted, until recently there was no black Michael Jordan, either. Michael Jordan, like Tiger Woods or Wayne Gretzky or Cal Ripken, is one of the best players in his sport not because he's like the other members of his own ethnic group but precisely because he's not like them—or like anyone else, for that matter. Élite athletes are élite athletes because, in some sense, they are on the fringes of genetic variability. As it happens, African populations seem to create more of these genetic outliers than white populations do, and this is what underpins the claim that blacks are better athletes than whites. But that's all the claim amounts to. It doesn't say anything at all about the rest of us, of all races, muddling around in the genetic middle.

There is a second consideration to keep in mind when we compare blacks and whites. Take the men's hundred-metre final at the Atlanta Olympics. Every runner in that race was of either Western African or Southern African descent, as you would expect if Africans had some genetic affinity for sprinting. But suppose we forget about skin color and look just at country of origin. The eight-man final was made up of two African-Americans, two Africans (one from Namibia and one from Nigeria), a Trinidadian, a Canadian of Jamaican descent, an Englishman of Jamaican descent, and a Jamaican. The race was won by the Jamaican-Canadian, in world-record time, with the Namibian coming in second and the Trinidadian third. The sprint relay—the 4 × 100—was won by a team from Canada, consisting of the Jamaican-Canadian from the final, a Haitian-Canadian, a Trinidadian-Canadian, and another Jamaican-Canadian. Now it appears that African heritage is important as an initial determinant of sprinting ability, but also that the most important advantage of all is some kind of cultural or environmental factor associated with the Caribbean.

Or consider, in a completely different realm, the problem of hypertension. Black Americans have a higher incidence of hypertension than white Americans, even after you control for every conceivable variable, including income, diet, and weight, so it's tempting to conclude that there is something about being of African descent that makes blacks prone to hypertension. But it turns out that although some Caribbean countries have a problem with hypertension, others—Jamaica, St. Kitts, and the Bahamas—don't. It also turns out that people in Liberia and Nigeria—two countries where many New World slaves came from—have similar and perhaps even lower blood-pressure rates than white North Americans, while studies of Zulus, Indians, and whites in Durban, South Africa, showed that urban white males had the highest hypertension rates and urban white females had the lowest. So it's likely that the disease has nothing at all to do with Africanness.

15

The same is true for the distinctive muscle characteristic observed when Kenyans were compared with Swedes. Saltin, the Swedish physiologist, subsequently found many of the same characteristics in Nordic skiers who train at high altitudes and Nordic runners who train in very hilly regions—conditions, in other words, that resemble the mountainous regions of Kenya's Rift Valley, where so many of the country's distance runners come from. The key factor seems to be Kenya, not genes.

Lots of things that seem to be genetic in origin, then, actually aren't. Similarly, lots of things that we wouldn't normally think might affect athletic ability actually do. Once again, the social-science literature on male and female math achievement is instructive. Psychologists argue that when it comes to subjects like math, boys tend to engage in what's known as ability attribution. A boy who is doing well will attribute his success to the fact that he's good at math, and if he's doing badly he'll blame his teacher or his own lack of motivation—anything but his ability. That makes it easy for him to bounce back from failure or disappointment, and gives him a lot of confidence in the face of a tough new challenge. After all, if you think you do well in math because you're good at math, what's stopping you from being good at, say, algebra, or advanced calculus? On the other hand, if you ask a girl why she is doing well in math she will say, more often than not, that she succeeds because she works hard. If she's doing poorly, she'll say she isn't smart enough. This, as should be obvious, is a self-defeating attitude. Psychologists call it "learned help-lessness"—the state in which failure is perceived as insurmountable. Girls who engage in effort attribution learn helplessness because in the face of a more difficult task like algebra or advanced calculus they can conceive of no solution. They're convinced that they can't work harder, because they think they're working as hard as they can, and that they can't rely on their intelligence, because they never thought they were that smart to begin with. In fact, one of the fascinating findings of attribution research is that the smarter girls are, the more likely they are to fall into this trap. High achievers are sometimes the most helpless. Here, surely, is part of the explanation for greater math variability among males. The fe-male math whizzes, the ones who should be competing in the top one and two per cent with their male counterparts, are the ones most often paralyzed by a lack of confidence in their own aptitude. They think they belong only in the intellectual middle.

The striking thing about these descriptions of male and female stereo-typing in math, though, is how similar they are to black and white stereo-typing in athletics—to the unwritten rules holding that blacks achieve through natural ability and whites through effort. Here's how *Sports Illustrated* described, in a recent article, the white basketball player Steve Kerr, who plays alongside Michael Jordan for the Chicago Bulls. According to the magazine, Kerr is a "hard-working overachiever," dis-tinguished by his "work ethic and heady play" and by a shooting style "born of a million practice shots." Bear in mind that Kerr is one of the best shooters in basketball today, and a key player on what is arguably one of the finest basketball teams in history. Bear in mind, too, that there is no evidence that Kerr works any harder than his teammates, least of all Jordan himself, whose work habits are legendary. But you'd never guess that from the article. It concludes, "All over America, whenever quicker, stronger gym rats see Kerr in action, they must wonder, How can that guy be out there instead of me?"

There are real consequences to this stereotyping. As the psychologists Carol Dweck and Barbara Licht write of high-achieving schoolgirls, "[They] may view themselves as so motivated and well disciplined that they cannot entertain the possibility that they did poorly on an academic task because of insufficient effort. Since blaming the teacher would also be out of character, blaming their abilities when they confront difficulty may seem like the most reasonable option." If you substitute the words "white athletes" for "girls" and "coach" for "teacher," I think you have part of the reason that so many white athletes are underrepresented at the highest levels of professional sports. Whites have been saddled with the athletic equivalent of learned helplessness—the idea that it is all but fruitless to try and compete at the highest levels, because they have only effort on their side. The causes of athletic and gender discrimination may be diverse, but its effects are not. Once again, blacks are like boys, and whites are like girls.

When I was in college, I once met an old acquaintance from my high-school running days. Both of us had long since quit track, and we talked about a recurrent fantasy we found we'd both had for getting back into shape. It was that we would go away somewhere remote for a year and do nothing but train, so that when the year was up we might finally know how good we were. Neither of us had any intention of doing this, though, which is why it was a fantasy. In adolescence, athletic excess has a certain appeal—during high school, I happily spent Sunday afternoons running up and down snow-covered sandhills—but with most of us that obsessiveness soon begins to fade. Athletic success depends on having the right genes and on a self-reinforcing belief in one's own ability. But it also depends on a rare form of tunnel vision. To be a great athlete, you have to *care*, and what was obvious to us both was that neither of us cared anymore. This is the last piece of the puzzle about what we mean when we say one group is better at something than another: sometimes different groups care about different things. Of the seven hundred men who play major-league baseball, for example, eighty-six come from either the Dominican Republic or Puerto Rico, even though those two islands have a combined population of only eleven million. But then baseball is something that Dominicans and Puerto Ricans care about—and you can say the same thing about African-Americans and basketball, West Indians and sprinting, Canadians and hockey, and Russians and chess. Desire is the great intangible in performance, and unlike genes or psychological affect we can't measure it and trace its implications. This is the problem, in the end, with the question of whether blacks are better at sports than whites. It's not that it's offensive, or that it leads to discrimination. It's that, in some sense, it's not a terribly interesting question; "better" promises a tidier explanation than can ever be provided.

I quit competitive running when I was sixteen—just after the summer I had qualified for the Ontario track team in my age class. Late that August, we had travelled to St. John's, Newfoundland, for the Canadian championships. In those days, I was whippet-thin, as milers often are, five feet six and not much more than a hundred pounds, and I could skim along the ground so lightly that I barely needed to catch my breath. I had two white friends on that team, both distance runners, too, and both, improbably, even smaller and lighter than I was. Every morning, the three of us would run through the streets of St. John's, charging up the hills and flying down the other side. One of these friends went on to have a distinguished college running career, the other became a world-class miler; that summer, I myself was the Canadian record holder in the fifteen hundred

20

metres for my age class. We were almost terrifyingly competitive, without a shred of doubt in our ability, and as we raced along we never stopped talking and joking, just to prove how absurdly easy we found running to be. I thought of us all as equals. Then, on the last day of our stay in St. John's, we ran to the bottom of Signal Hill, which is the town's principal geographical landmark—an abrupt outcrop as steep as anything in San Francisco. We stopped at the base, and the two of them turned to me and announced that we were all going to run straight up Signal Hill *backward*. I don't know whether I had more running ability than those two or whether my Africanness gave me any genetic advantage over their whiteness. What I do know is that such questions were irrelevant, because, as I realized, they were willing to go to far greater lengths to develop their talent. They ran up the hill backward. I ran home.

 ## Topics for Critical Thinking and Writing

1. In paragraph 6 Gladwell, referring to scientific studies, says that one difference between blacks and whites "suggests" something, and another study found that blacks "appeared" to have a certain quality. We notice the cautious words. Should Gladwell have refrained from citing these studies, which apparently are not conclusive? Why, or why not?

2. Why in an article about athletes does Gladwell discuss (paragraph 17) the attitudes of boys and girls with respect to achievement in mathematics?

3. In a paragraph explain why, in your view, "the claim that blacks are better athletes than whites" (paragraph 13) is taboo.

4. In paragraphs 3 and 4 Gladwell implies that Tiger Woods is black—and indeed he is widely perceived as black. In fact his father is half African American, one quarter Native American, and one quarter Chinese; his mother is half Thai, one quarter Chinese, and one quarter white. In an essay of 250 words explain why, in your view, Tiger Woods is often regarded as black.

5. Gladwell devotes his long final paragraph to an anecdote about running backward. What is the point of the anecdote? In an essay of 250 words set forth the point, and indicate why this paragraph does or does not make an effective ending to the essay.

6. This essay was first published in 1997. Do you think it is dated? If so, what is your evidence?

Carol Tavris

Carol Tavris, born in Los Angeles in 1944, holds a bachelor's degree from Brandeis University and a Ph.D. from the University of Michigan. Among her many publications are The Female Experience *(1973),* Anger: the Misunderstood Emotion *(1983), and* The Mismeasure of Woman: Why Women Are Not the Better Sex, the Inferior Sex, or the Opposite Sex, and How Using Men as the Yardstick for Normalcy Has Given Women the Short End of the Stick *(1992). We reprint an essay that first appeared in* The New York Times *in 1997.*

How Friendship Was "Feminized"

Once upon a time and not so very long ago, everyone thought that men had the great and true-blue friendships. The cultural references stretched through time and art: Damon and Pythias, Hamlet and Horatio, Butch Cassidy and the Sundance Kid. The Lone Ranger never rode off with anyone but Tonto, and Laurel never once abandoned Hardy in whatever fine mess he got them into.

Male friendships were said to grow from the deep roots of shared experience and faithful camaraderie, whereas women's friendships were portrayed as shallow, trivial and competitive, like Scarlett O'Hara's with her sisters. Women, it was commonly claimed, would sell each other out for the right guy, and even for a good time with the wrong one.

Some social scientists told us that this difference was hard-wired, a result of our evolutionary history. In the early 1970's, for example, the anthropologist Lionel Tiger argued in "Men in Groups" that "male bonding" originated in prehistoric male hunting groups and was carried on today in equivalent pack-like activities: sports, politics, business and war.

Apparently, women's evolutionary task of rummaging around in the garden to gather the odd yam or kumquat was a solo effort, so females do not bond in the same way. Women prattle on about their feelings, went the stereotype, but men act.

My, how times have changed. Today, we are deluged in the wave of best-selling books that celebrate female friendships—"Girlfriends," "Sisters," "Mothers and Daughters" and its clever clone, "Daughters and Mothers." The success of this genre is partly because the book market is so oriented to female readers these days.

But it is also a likely result of two trends that began in the 1970's and 1980's: Female scholars began to dispel the men-are-better stereotype in all domains and women became the majority of psychotherapists. The result was a positive reassessment of the qualities associated with women, including a "feminizing" of definitions of intimacy and friendship.

5

Accordingly, female friendships are now celebrated as the deep and abiding ones, based as they are on shared feelings and confidences. Male friendships are scorned as superficial, based as they are on shared interests in, say, the Mets and Michelle Pfeiffer.

In our psychologized culture, "intimacy" is defined as what many women like to do with their friends: talk, express feelings and disclose worries. Psychologists, most of whom are good talkers, validate this definition as the true measure of intimacy. For example, in a study of "intimacy maturity" in marriage, published in the *Journal of Personality and Social Psychology*, researchers equated "most mature" with "most verbally expressive." As a woman, I naturally think this is a perfectly sensible equation, but I also know it is an incomplete one. To label people mature or immature, you also have to know how they actually behave toward others.

What about all the men and women who support their families, put the wishes of other family members ahead of their own or act in moral and considerate ways when conflicts arise? They are surely mature, even if they are inarticulate or do not express their feelings easily. Indeed, what about all the men and women who define intimacy in terms of deeds rather than words: sharing activities, helping one another or enjoying companionable silence? Too bad for them. That's a "male" definition, and out of favor in these talky times.

Years ago, my husband had to have some worrisome medical tests,   10
and the night before he was to go to the hospital we went to dinner with one of his best friends who was visiting from England. I watched, fascinated, as male stoicism combined with English reserve produced a decidedly unfemale-like encounter. They laughed, they told stories, they argued about movies, they reminisced. Neither mentioned the hospital, their worries or their affection for each other. They didn't need to.

It is true that women's style of intimacy has many benefits. A large body of research in health psychology and social psychology finds that women's greater willingness to talk about feelings improves their mental and physical health and makes it easier to ask for help.

But as psychologists like Susan Nolen-Hoeksema of Stanford University have shown, women's fondness for ruminating about feelings can also prolong depression, anxiety and anger. And it can keep women stuck in bad jobs or relationships, instead of getting out of them or doing what is necessary to make them better.

Books and movies that validate women's friendships are overdue, and welcome as long as they don't simply invert the stereotype. Playing the women-are-better game is fun, but it blinds us to the universal need for intimacy and the many forms that friendship takes. Maybe men could learn a thing or two about friendship from women. But who is to say that women couldn't learn a thing or two from them in exchange?

Topics for Critical Thinking and Writing

1. Evaluate Tavris's first paragraph as an opening paragraph. (In your evaluation you may want to consider such topics as: Did it attract your interest? Is it clear? Is it appropriate to what follows?)

2. In a sentence or two, formulate Tavris's thesis.

3. How would you characterize Tavris's style? Formal? Chatty? Vulgar? Or what? In a paragraph set forth your view, supporting it with specific examples drawn from her essay.

4. In her first paragraph Tavris cites some famous examples of male friendships. What additional examples can you cite? What comparable examples of female friendship can you cite? If female examples come less easily to mind, why do you suppose this is so?

5. Drawing on your own experience, write an essay (250–500 words) on male versus female friendships. Since your experience now includes familiarity with Tavris's essay, you can, if you wish, make use of it in your own writing. You may even want to put your essay into the form of a reply to hers.

6. Take one of the following passages and write an essay of 500 words, using the quotation as an epigraph.

> Friendships, in general, are suddenly contracted, and therefore it is no wonder they are easily dissolved.
>
> Joseph Addison (1974)

> No man can be friends with a woman he finds attractive. He always wants to have sex with her. Sex is always out there. Friendship is ultimately doomed and that is the end of the story.
>
> Nora Ephron (1989)

> If a man does not make new acquaintance as he advances through life, he will soon find himself left alone. A man, Sir, should keep his friendship in constant repair.
>
> Samuel Johnson (1755) (*Note:* Johnson probably is using "man" generically, to stand for any human being. Take the remark as *not* referring only to men.)

Scott Russell Sanders

Scott Russell Sanders first published this essay in Milkweed Chronicle, *Spring/Summer 1984, and then reprinted it in his book,* Paradise of Bombs.

The Men We Carry in Our Minds . . . and How They Differ from the Real Lives of Most Men

"This must be a hard time for women," I say to my friend Anneke. "They have so many paths to choose from, and so many voices calling them."

"I think it's a lot harder for men," she replies.

"How do you figure that?"

"The women I know feel excited, innocent, like crusaders in a just cause. The men I know are eaten up with guilt."

"Women feel such pressure to be everything, do everything," I say. "Career, kids, art, politics. Have their babies and get back to the office a week later. It's as if they're trying to overcome a million years' worth of evolution in one lifetime."

"But we help one another. And we have this deep-down sense that we're in the *right*—we've been held back, passed over, used—while men feel they're in the wrong. Men are the ones who've been discredited, who have to search their souls."

I search my soul. I discover guilty feelings aplenty—toward the poor, the Vietnamese, Native Americans, the whales, an endless list of debts. But toward women I feel something more confused, a snarl of shame, envy, wary tenderness, and amazement. This muddle troubles me. To hide my unease I say, "You're right, it's tough being a man these days."

"Don't laugh," Anneke frowns at me. "I wouldn't be a man for anything. It's much easier being the victim. All the victim has to do is break free. The persecutor has to live with his past."

How deep is that past? I find myself wondering. How much of an inheritance do I have to throw off?

When I was a boy growing up on the back roads of Tennessee and Ohio, the men I knew labored with their bodies. They were marginal farmers, just scraping by, or welders, steelworkers, carpenters; they swept floors, dug ditches, mined coal, or drove trucks, their forearms ropy with muscle; they trained horses, stoked furnaces, made tires, stood on assembly lines wrestling parts onto cars and refrigerators. They got up before light, worked all day long whatever the weather, and when they came home at night they looked as though somebody had been whipping them. In the evenings and on weekends they worked on their own places, tilling gardens that were lumpy with clay, fixing broken-down cars, hammering on houses that were always too drafty, too leaky, too small.

The bodies of the men I knew were twisted and maimed in ways visible and invisible. The nails of their hands were black and split, the hands tattooed with scars. Some had lost fingers. Heavy lifting had given many of them finicky backs and guts weak from hernias. Racing against conveyor belts had given them ulcers. Their ankles and knees ached from years of standing on concrete. Anyone who had worked for long around machines was hard of hearing. They squinted, and the skin of their faces was creased like the leather of old work gloves. There were times, studying them, when I dreaded growing up. Most of them coughed, from dust or cigarettes, and most of them drank cheap wine or whiskey, so their eyes looked bloodshot and bruised. The fathers of my friends always seemed older than the mothers. Men wore out sooner. Only women lived into old age.

As a boy I also knew another sort of men, who did not sweat and break down like mules. They were soldiers, and so far as I could tell they scarcely worked at all. But when the shooting started, many of them would die. This was what soldiers were *for*, just as a hammer was for driving nails.

Warriors and toilers: these seemed, in my boyhood vision, to be the chief destinies for men. They weren't the only destinies, as I learned from having a few male teachers, from reading books, and from watching television. But the men on television—the politicians, the astronauts, the generals, the savvy lawyers, the philosophical doctors, the bosses who gave orders to both soldiers and laborers—seemed as remote and unreal to me as the figures in Renaissance tapestries. I could no more imagine growing up to become one of these cool, potent creatures than I could imagine becoming a prince.

A nearer and more hopeful example was that of my father, who had escaped from a red-dirt farm to a tire factory, and from the assembly line to the front office. Eventually he dressed in a white shirt and tie. He carried himself as if he had been born to work with his mind. But his body, remembering the earlier years of slogging work, began to give out on him in his fifties, and it quit on him entirely before he turned 65.

A scholarship enabled me not only to attend college, a rare enough feat in my circle, but even to study in a university meant for the children of the rich. Here I met for the first time young men who had assumed from birth that they would lead lives of comfort and power. And for the first time I met women who told me that men were guilty of having kept all the joys and privileges of the earth for themselves. I was baffled. What privileges? What joys? I thought about the maimed, dismal lives of most of the men back home. What had they stolen from their wives and daughters? The right to go five days a week, 12 months a year, for 30 or 40 years

15

to a steel mill or a coal mine? The right to drop bombs and die in war? The right to feel every leak in the roof, every gap in the fence, every cough in the engine as a wound they must mend? The right to feel, when the layoff comes or the plant shuts down, not only afraid but ashamed?

I was slow to understand the deep grievances of women. This was because, as a boy, I had envied them. Before college, the only people I had ever known who were interested in art or music or literature, the only ones who read books, the only ones who ever seemed to enjoy a sense of ease and grace were the mothers and daughters. Like the men-folk, they fretted about money, they scrimped and made do. But, when the pay stopped coming in, they were not the ones who had failed. Nor did they have to go to war, and that seemed to me a blessed fact. By comparison with the narrow, ironclad days of fathers, there was an expansiveness, I thought, in the days of mothers. They went to see neighbors, to shop in town, to run errands at school, at the library, at church. No doubt, had I looked harder at their lives, I would have envied them less. It was not my fate to become a woman, so it was easier for me to see the graces. I didn't see, then, what a prison a house could be, since houses seemed to me brighter, handsomer places than any factory. I did not realize—because such things were never spoken of—how often women suffered from men's bullying. Even then I could see how exhausting it was for a mother to cater all day to the needs of young children. But if I had been asked, as a boy, to choose between tending a baby and tending a machine, I think I would have chosen the baby. (Having now tended both, I know I would choose the baby.)

So I was baffled when the women at college accused me and my sex of having cornered the world's pleasures. I think something like my bafflement has been felt by other boys (and by girls as well) who grew up in dirt-poor farm country, in mining country, in black ghettos, in Hispanic barrios, in the shadows of factories, in Third World nations— any place where the fate of men is just as grim and bleak as the fate of women.

When the women I met at college thought about the joys and privileges of men, they did not carry in their minds the sort of men I had known in my childhood. They thought of their fathers, who were bankers, physicians, architects, stockbrokers, the big wheels of the big cities. They were never laid off, never short of cash at month's end, never lined up for welfare. These fathers made decisions that mattered. They ran the world.

The daughters of such men wanted to share in this power, this glory. So did I. They yearned for a say over their future, for jobs worthy of their abilities, for the right to live at peace, unmolested, whole. Yes, I thought, yes yes. The difference between me and these daughters was that they saw me, because of my sex, as destined from birth to become like their fathers, and therefore as an enemy to their desires. But I knew better. I wasn't an enemy, in fact or in feeling. I was an ally. If I had known, then, how to tell them so, would they have believed me? Would they now?

🕮 Topics for Critical Thinking and Writing

1. Look at Sanders's introductory paragraphs (1–9). What do you think he hoped to accomplish by these paragraphs? To put it another way, suppose the essay began with paragraph 10, "When I was a boy growing up. . . ." What would be changed or lost?

2. Look at the second sentence of paragraph 10. It's a rather long sentence, with three independent clauses and lists of parallel phrases. How would you describe the verbs he uses? What effect does the structure of the sentence produce?

3. What is the topic sentence of paragraph 11? How does Sanders develop the paragraph, and what does the paragraph contribute to his argument?

4. What advantages did women enjoy that Sanders says he envied when he was a boy? What disadvantages does he mention (in paragraph 15)? What disadvantages does he *not* mention?

5. In paragraphs 16, 17, and 18, Sanders shifts from focusing on issues of gender to issues of class. How has he prepared us for this shift?

6. Evaluate Sanders's argument. How would you answer the questions he poses in his final paragraph?

7. When you were growing up, which lives seemed to have the most advantages or disadvantages, those of men or of women? Why did you think so? Did your opinion change as you grew older? Explain.

Paul Theroux

Paul Theroux was born in 1941 in Medford, Massachusetts, and was educated at the University of Maine, the University of Massachusetts, and Syracuse University. He served as a Peace Corps volunteer in Africa and has spent much of his adult life abroad, in Africa, Asia, Europe, and Central America. Though best known as a novelist and writer of travel books, he is also a poet and essayist. This essay originally appeared in The New York Times Magazine.

The Male Myth

There is a pathetic sentence in the chapter "Fetishism" in Dr. Norman Cameron's book *Personality Development and Psychopathology*. It goes: "Fetishists are nearly always men; and their commonest fetish is a woman's shoe." I cannot read that sentence without thinking that it is just one more awful thing about being a man—and perhaps it is the most important thing to know about us.

I have always disliked being a man. The whole idea of manhood in America is pitiful, a little like having to wear an ill-fitting coat for one's entire life. (By contrast, I imagine femininity to be an oppressive sense of nakedness.) Even the expression "Be a man!" strikes me as insulting and abusive. It means: Be stupid, be unfeeling, obedient and soldierly, and stop thinking. Man means "manly"—how can one think "about men" without considering the terrible ambition of manliness? And yet it is part of every man's life. It is a hideous and crippling lie; it not only insists on difference and connives at superiority, it is also by its very nature destructive—emotionally damaging and socially harmful.

The youth who is subverted, as most are, into believing in the masculine ideal is effectively separated from women—it is the most savage tribal logic—and he spends the rest of his life finding women a riddle and a nuisance. Of course, there is a female version of this male affliction. It begins with mothers encouraging little girls to say (to other adults), "Do you like my new dress?" In a sense, girls are traditionally urged to please adults with a kind of coquettishness, while boys are enjoined to behave like monkeys toward each other. The 9-year-old coquette proceeds to become womanish in a subtle power game in which she learns to be sexually indispensable, socially decorative and always alert to a man's sense of inadequacy.

Femininity—being ladylike—implies needing a man as witness and seducer; but masculinity celebrates the exclusive company of men. That is why it is so grotesque; and that is also why there is no manliness without inadequacy—because it denies men the natural friendship of women.

It is very hard to imagine any concept of manliness that does not belittle women, and it begins very early. At an age when I wanted to meet girls—let's say the treacherous years of 13 to 16—I was told to take up a sport, get more fresh air, join the Boy Scouts, and I was urged not to read so much. It was the 1950's and, if you asked too many questions about sex, you were sent to camp—boy's camp, of course; the nightmare. Nothing is more unnatural or prisonlike than a boys' camp, but if it were not for them, we would have no Elks' Lodges, no pool-rooms, no boxing matches, no marines.

5

And perhaps no sports as we know them. Everyone is aware of how few in number are the athletes who behave like gentlemen. Just as high-school basketball teaches you how to be a poor loser, the manly attitude toward sports seems to be little more than a recipe for creating bad marriages, social misfits, moral degenerates, sadists, latent rapists and just plain louts. I regard high-school sports as a drug far worse than marijuana, and it is the reason that the average tennis champion, say, is a pathetic oaf.

Any objective study would find the quest for manliness essentially right wing, puritanical, cowardly, neurotic and fueled largely by a fear of women. It is also certainly philistine. There is no book hater like a Little League coach. But, indeed, all the creative arts are obnoxious to the manly ideal, because at their best the arts are pursued by uncompetitive and essentially solitary people. It makes it very hard for a creative youngster, for any boy who expresses the desire to be alone seems to be saying that there is something wrong with him.

It ought to be clear by now that I have an objection to the way we turn boys into men. It does not surprise me that when the President of the United States has his customary weekend off, he dresses like a cowboy—it is both a measure of his insecurity and his willingness to please. In many ways, American culture does little more for a man than prepare him for modeling clothes in the L. L. Bean catalogue. I take this as a personal insult because for many years I found it impossible to admit to myself that I wanted to be a writer. It was my guilty secret, because being a writer was incompatible with being a man.

There are people who might deny this, but that is because the American writer, typically, has been so at pains to prove his manliness. But first there was a fear that writing was not a manly profession—indeed, not a profession at all. (The paradox in American letters is that it has always been easier for a woman to write and for a man to be published.) Growing up, I had thought of sports as wasteful and humiliating, and the idea of manliness as a bore. My wanting to become a writer was not a flight from that oppressive role playing, but I quickly saw that it was at odds with it. Everything in stereotyped manliness goes against the life of the mind. The Hemingway personality is too tedious to go into here, but certainly it was not until this aberrant behavior was examined by feminists in the 1960's that any male writer dared question the pugnacity in Hemingway's fiction. All that bullfighting and arm-wrestling and elephant shooting diminished Hemingway as a writer: One cannot be a male writer without first proving that one is a man.

It is normal in America for a man to be dismissive or even somewhat apologetic about being a writer. Various factors make it easier. There is a heartiness about journalism that makes it acceptable—journalism is the manliest form of American writing and, therefore, the profession the most independent-minded women seek (yes, it is an illusion, but that is my point). Fiction writing is equated with a kind of dispirited failure and is only manly when it produces wealth. Money is masculinity. So is drinking. Being a drunkard is another assertion, if misplaced, of manliness. The American male writer is traditionally proud of his heavy drinking. But we are also very literal-minded people. A man proves his manhood in America in old-fashioned ways. He kills lions, like Hemingway; or he hunts ducks, like Nathanael West; or he makes pronouncements, like "A man should carry enough knife to defend himself with," as James Jones is said to have once told an interviewer. And we are familiar with the

10

lengths to which Norman Mailer is prepared, in his endearing way, to prove that he is just as much a monster as the next man.

When the novelist John Irving was revealed as a wrestler, people took him to be a very serious writer. But what interests me is that it is inconceivable that any woman writer would be shown in such a posture. How surprised we would be if Joyce Carol Oates were revealed as a sumo wrestler or Joan Didion enjoyed pumping iron. "Lives in New York City with her three children" is the typical woman-writer's biographical note, for just as the male writer must prove he has achieved a sort of muscular manhood, the woman writer—or rather her publicists—must prove her motherhood.

There would be no point in saying any of this if it were not generally accepted that to be a man is somehow—even now in feminist-influenced America—a privilege. It is on the contrary an unmerciful and punishing burden. Being a man is bad enough; being manly is appalling. It is the sinister silliness of men's fashions that inspires the so-called dress code of the Ritz-Carlton Hotel in Boston. It is the institutionalized cheating in college sports. It is a pathetic and primitive insecurity.

And this is also why men often object to feminism, but are afraid to explain why: Of course women have a justified grievance, but most men believe—and with reason—that their lives are much worse.

Topics for Critical Thinking and Writing

1. In paragraph 6 Theroux says that "high-school basketball teaches you how to be a poor loser." Think about this, and then write a paragraph that in effect offers a definition of a "poor loser" but that also shows how a high school sport teaches one to be a poor loser.

2. Theroux speaks of "the Hemingway personality" and of "the pugnacity in Hemingway's fiction." If you have read a work by Hemingway, write a paragraph in which you explain (to someone unfamiliar with Hemingway) what Theroux is talking about.

3. Let's assume that a reader says he or she doesn't quite understand Theroux's final paragraph. Write a paragraph explaining it.

4. Theroux makes some deliberately provocative statements, for example:

> Nothing is more unnatural or prisonlike than a boys' camp.
> Everyone is aware of how few in number are the athletes who behave like gentlemen.
> The quest for manliness . . . [is] fueled largely by a fear of women.

Choose one such statement from the essay and consider what you would need to do to argue effectively against it. You needn't produce the argument, but simply consider how such an argument might be constructed.

Andrew Lam

Andrew Lam is an associate editor of the Pacific News Service. This essay originally appeared as an op-ed piece in The New York Times *in 1993.*

Goodbye, Saigon, Finally

Flipping through my United States passport as if it were a comic book, the customs man at the Noi Bai Airport, near Hanoi, appeared curious. "Brother, when did you leave Vietnam?"

"One day before National Defeat Day," I said without thinking. It was an exile's expression, not his.

"God! When did that happen?"

"The 30th of April, 1975."

"But, brother, don't you mean National Liberation Day?"   5

If this conversation had occurred a decade earlier, the difference would have created a dangerous gap between the Vietnamese and the returning Vietnamese-American. But this happened in 1992, when the walls were down, and as I studied the smiling young official, it occurred to me that there was something about this moment, an epiphany. "Yes, brother, I suppose I do mean liberation day."

Not everyone remembers the date with humor. It marked the Vietnamese diaspora, boat people, refugees.

On April 29, 1975, my family and I escaped from Saigon in a crowded C-130. We arrived in Guam the next day, to hear the BBC's tragic account of Saigon's demise: U.S. helicopters flying over the chaotic city, Vietcong tanks rolling in, Vietnamese climbing over the gate into the U.S. Embassy, boats fleeing down the Saigon River toward the South China Sea.

In time, April 30 became the birth date of an exile's culture built on defeatism and a sense of tragic ending. For a while, many Vietnamese in America talked of revenge, of blood debts, of the exile's anguish. Their songs had nostalgic titles: "The Day When I Return" and "Oh, Mother Vietnam, We Are Still Here."

April 30, 1976: A child of 12 with nationalistic fervor, I stood in front   10
of San Francisco City Hall with other refugees. I waved the gold flag with three horizontal red stripes. I shouted (to no one in particular): "Give us back South Vietnam!"

April 30, 1979: An uncle told me there was an American plan to retake our homeland by force: "The way Douglas MacArthur did for the South Koreans in the 50's." My 17-year-old brother declared that he would join the anti-Communist guerrilla movement in Vietnam. My father sighed.

Andrew Lam, "Goodbye Saigon, Finally." Originally published in *The New York Times*, 4/30/93. Reprinted by permission.

April 30, 1983: I stayed awake all night with Vietnamese classmates from Berkeley to listen to monotonous speeches by angry old men. "National defeat must be avenged by sweat and blood!" one vowed.

But through the years, April 30 has come to symbolize something entirely different to me. Although I sometimes mourn the loss of home and land, it's the American landscape and what it offers that solidify my hyphenated identity. This date of tragic ending, from an optimist's point of view, is also an American rebirth, something close to the Fourth of July.

I remember whispering to a young countryman during one of those monotonous April 30 rallies in the mid-1980's: "Even as the old man speaks of patriotic repatriation, we've already become Americans."

Assimilation, education, the English language, the American "I"— these have carried me and many others further from that beloved tropical country than the C-130 ever could. Each optimistic step the young Vietnamese takes toward America is tempered with a little betrayal of Little Saigon's parochialism, its sentimentalities and the old man's outdated passion.   15

When did this happen? Who knows? One night, America quietly seeps in and takes hold of one's mind and body, and the Vietnamese soul of sorrows slowly fades away. In the morning, the Vietnamese American speaks a new language of materialism: his vocabulary includes terms like career choices, down payment, escrow, overtime.

My brother never made it to the Indochinese jungle. The would-be guerrilla fighter became instead a civil engineer. My talk of endless possibilities is punctuated with favorite verbs—transcend, redefine, become. "I want to become a writer," I declared to my parents one morning. My mother gasped.

April 30, 1975: defeat or liberation?

"It was a day of joyous victory," said a retired Communist official in Hanoi. "We fought and realized Uncle Ho's dream of national independence." Then he asked for Marlboro cigarettes and a few precious dollars.

Nhon Nguyen, a real estate salesman in San Jose, a former South Vietnamese naval officer, said: "I could never forget the date. So many people died. So much blood. I could never tolerate Communism, you know."   20

Mai Huong, a young Vietnamese woman in Saigon, said that, of course, it was National Liberation Day. "But it's the South," she said with a wink, "that liberated the North." Indeed, conservative Uncle Ho has slowly admitted defeat to entrepreneurial and cosmopolitan Miss Saigon. She has taken her meaning from a different uncle, you know, Uncle Sam.

"April 30, 1975?" said Bobby To, my 22-year-old cousin in San Francisco. "I don't know that date. I don't remember Vietnam at all." April 29, 1992, is more meaningful to him, Bobby said. "It's when the race riots broke out all over our country. To me it's more realistic to worry about what's going on over here than there."

Sighing, the customs man, who offered me a ride into Hanoi, said: "In truth, there are no liberators. We are all defeated here." There is no job, no future, no direction, only a sense of collective malaise, something akin to the death of the national soul. He added: "You're lucky, brother. You left Vietnam and became an American."

April 30, 1993: My friends and I plan to watch *Gone with the Wind* for the umpteenth time and look for a scene of our unrequited romantic longings: Scarlett, teary-eyed with wind-blown hair, returning to forlorn Tara. We no longer can. Children of defeat, self-liberating adults, we promise to hug instead and recount to each other our own stories of flight.

Topics for Critical Thinking and Writing

1. Lam sets up at once the distinction between National Defeat Day and National Liberation Day and calls the moment for him an *epiphany*. How does he do it? And what is an epiphany?

2. In paragraph 8 Lam remembers the escape from Vietnam in 1975, and then April 30 in 1976, 1979, 1983. Assuming that you were not around to notice those dates—or even if you were—what techniques does Lam use to make them vivid?

3. In paragraph 15 Lam says, "Each optimistic step the young Vietnamese takes toward America is tempered with a little betrayal of Little Saigon's parochialism, its sentimentalities and the old man's outdated passion." What does he mean?

4. At the essay's conclusion, Lam says that he and his friends will watch *Gone with the Wind* and "recount to each other our own stories of flight." Why do they watch *Gone with the Wind* (instead of a Vietnamese film)? What does Lam's choice of the film tell us?

5. If you have a story similar to Lam's, or one that in many ways is opposed to Lam's, try to tell it in an essay that begins with a narrative and may end with one too.

Bharati Mukherjee

Bharati Mukherjee, born in Calcutta, India, in 1940, spent much of her childhood in London with her parents and sisters, but returned to India in 1951. She earned a bachelor's and a master's degree in India, then moved to London, and to the United States, where she studied for a doctorate at the University of Iowa Writers Workshop. At Iowa she met and married a novelist, and the couple later moved to Canada. While living in Canada she published two novels, and in 1980 she came to the United States to teach at the University of Iowa. She has also taught at Skidmore College, Queens College, and Columbia University. We reprint an essay that originally appeared in The New York Times.

Bharati Mukherjee, "Two Ways to Belong in America." Originally published in *The New York Times*, 9/22/96. Reprinted by permission.

Two Ways to Belong in America

This is a tale of two sisters from Calcutta, Mira and Bharati, who have lived in the United States for some 35 years, but who find themselves on different sides in the current debate over the status of immigrants. I am an American citizen and she is not. I am moved that thousands of long-term residents are finally taking the oath of citizenship. She is not.

Mira arrived in Detroit in 1960 to study child psychology and pre-school education. I followed her a year later to study creative writing at the University of Iowa. When we left India, we were almost identical in appearance and attitude. We dressed alike, in saris; we expressed identical views on politics, social issues, love and marriage in the same Calcutta convent-school accent. We would endure our two years in America, secure our degrees, then return to India to marry the grooms of our father's choosing.

Instead, Mira married an Indian student in 1962 who was getting his business administration degree at Wayne State University. They soon acquired the labor certifications necessary for the green card of hassle-free residence and employment.

Mira still lives in Detroit, works in the Southfield, Mich., school system, and has become nationally recognized for her contributions in the fields of pre-school education and parent-teacher relationships. After 36 years as a legal immigrant in this country, she clings passionately to her Indian citizenship and hopes to go home to India when she retires.

In Iowa City in 1963, I married a fellow student, an American of 5 Canadian parentage. Because of the accident of his North Dakota birth, I bypassed labor-certification requirements and the race-related "quota" system that favored the applicant's country of origin over his or her merit. I was prepared for (and even welcomed) the emotional strain that came with marrying outside my ethnic community. In 33 years of marriage, we have lived in every part of North America. By choosing a husband who was not my father's selection, I was opting for fluidity, self-invention, blue jeans and T-shirts, and renouncing 3,000 years (at least) of caste-observant, "pure culture" marriage in the Mukherjee family. My books have often been read as unapologetic (and in some quarters over-enthusiastic) texts for cultural and psychological "mongrelization." It's a word I celebrate.

Mira and I have stayed sisterly close by phone. In our regular Sunday morning conversations, we are unguardedly affectionate. I am her only blood relative on this continent. We expect to see each other through the looming crises of aging and ill health without being asked. Long before Vice President Gore's "Citizenship U.S.A." drive, we'd had our polite arguments over the ethics of retaining an overseas citizenship while expecting the permanent protection and economic benefits that come with living and working in America.

Like well-raised sisters, we never said what was really on our minds, but we probably pitied one another. She, for the lack of structure in my life, the erasure of Indianness, the absence of an unvarying daily core. I, for the narrowness of her perspective, her uninvolvement with the mythic depths or the superficial pop culture of this society. But, now, with the scapegoating of "aliens" (documented or illegal) on the increase, and the targeting of long-term legal immigrants like Mira for new scrutiny and new self-consciousness, she and I find ourselves unable to maintain the same polite discretion. We were always unacknowledged adversaries, and we are now, more than ever, sisters.

"I feel used," Mira raged on the phone the other night. "I feel manipulated and discarded. This is such an unfair way to treat a person who was invited to stay and work here because of her talent. My employer went to the I.N.S. and petitioned for the labor certification. For over 30 years, I've invested my creativity and professional skills into the improvement of *this* country's pre-school system. I've obeyed all the rules, I've paid my taxes, I love my work, I love my students, I love the friends I've made. How dare America now change its rules in midstream? If America wants to make new rules curtailing benefits of legal immigrants, they should apply only to immigrants who arrive after those rules are already in place."

To my ears, it sounded like the description of a long-enduring, comfortable yet loveless marriage, without risk or recklessness. Have we the right to demand, and to expect, that we be loved? (That, to me, is the subtext of the arguments by immigration advocates.) My sister is an expatriate, professionally generous and creative, socially courteous and gracious, and that's as far as her Americanization can go. She is here to maintain an identity, not to transform it.

I asked her if she would follow the example of others who have decided to become citizens because of the anti-immigration bills in Congress. And here, she surprised me. "If America wants to play the manipulative game, I'll play it too," she snapped. "I'll become a U.S. citizen for now, then change back to Indian when I'm ready to go home. I feel some kind of irrational attachment to India that I don't to America. Until all this hysteria against legal immigrants, I was totally happy. Having my green card meant I could visit any place in the world I wanted to and then come back to a job that's satisfying and that I do very well."   10

In one family, from two sisters alike as peas in a pod, there could not be a wider divergence of immigrant experience. America spoke to me—I married it—I embraced the demotion from expatriate aristocrat to immigrant nobody, surrendering those thousands of years of "pure culture," the saris, the delightfully accented English. She retained them all. Which of us is the freak?

Mira's voice, I realize, is the voice not just of the immigrant South Asian community but of an immigrant community of the millions who have stayed rooted in one job, one city, one house, one ancestral culture, one cuisine, for the entirety of their productive years. She speaks for greater numbers than I possibly can. Only the fluency of her English and the anger, rather than fear, born of confidence from her education, differentiate her from the seamstresses, the domestics, the technicians, the shop owners, the millions of hard-working but effectively silenced documented immigrants as well as their less fortunate "illegal" brothers and sisters.

Nearly 20 years ago, when I was living in my husband's ancestral homeland of Canada, I was always well-employed but never allowed to feel part of the local Quebec or larger Canadian society. Then, through a Green Paper that invited a national referendum on the unwanted side effects of "nontraditional" immigration, the Government officially turned against its immigrant communities, particularly those from South Asia.

I felt then the same sense of betrayal that Mira feels now. I will never forget the pain of that sudden turning, and the casual racist outbursts the Green Paper elicited. That sense of betrayal had its desired effect and drove me, and thousands like me, from the country.

Mira and I differ, however, in the ways in which we hope to interact   15
with the country that we have chosen to live in. She is happier to live in America as expatriate Indian than as an immigrant American. I need to feel like a part of the community I have adopted (as I tried to feel in Canada as well). I need to put roots down, to vote and make the difference that I can. The price that the immigrant willingly pays, and that the exile avoids, is the trauma of self-transformation.

 ## Topics for Critical Thinking and Writing

1. Analyze the first paragraph as an opening paragraph. Why do you think it is or is not effective? (Some suggestions: Does the phrase "a tale of two sisters" ring a bell? Do the variations in the lengths of the sentences contribute to the meaning?)

2. Given what you now know about Mira, do you think she has a case? List her arguments and evaluate each. If you believe they don't add up to much, do you think she should be required to leave? Set forth your evaluation of her arguments, and your view about granting permanent status to aliens who do not wish to become citizens, in an essay of 500 words.

3. If you are an American citizen, can you imagine living most of your adult life in another country—perhaps because you believe you are contributing a needed skill, or perhaps because your spouse is a citizen of that country—and *not* becoming a citizen, even though you enjoy your life there? Or put the reverse question: Can you imagine *becoming* a citizen of that country? Perhaps much would depend on the country. Choose a country that you are likely to find highly attractive, and in an essay of 500 words set forth your position.

4. Mukherjee in her final paragraph speaks of the "price" that the immigrant willingly pays when he or she becomes a citizen. Interview two immigrants who have become citizens, and report their views on what (if anything) it cost them spiritually to become a citizen. (On interviewing, see pages 56–59.)

Emily Tsao

Emily Tsao wrote this essay when she was a sophomore at Yale University. It was originally published in Newsday.

Thoughts of an Oriental Girl

I am an Oriental girl. Excuse me, I forgot to use my politically correct dictionary. Let me rephrase that, I am an Asian-American woman. Yes, that sounds about right. Excuse me again; I mean politically correct.

When I first stepped onto the campus scene last year, I, like many other anxious freshmen, wanted to fit in. I wanted to wear the right clothes, carry the right bookbag and, most important, say the right things. Speaking to upperclassmen, however, I realized that I had no command of the proper "PC" language.

Girls, it became clear, were to be called women. Freshmen who were girls were to be called freshwomen. Mixed groups of both sexes were to be labeled freshpeople, and upperclassmen were to be referred to as upperclasspeople. Orientals were to be called Asian Americans, blacks were to be called African Americans and Hispanics Latinos.

To me, most of this seemed pointless. Being called a girl doesn't bother me. I'm 18 years old. My mom is a woman. I'm her kid. I don't expect her to refer to me as a woman.

I have always referred to my female friends as girls, and still do. I   5
want my boyfriend to call me his girlfriend, not his woman friend.

My friends and I refer to the male students at college as boys or guys. Never men. Kevin Costner and Robert Redford are men. Men don't drink themselves sick at keg parties every weekend, ask Dad for money, or take laundry home to Mom.

For 12 years of high school and grade school, the female students were always girls and the males were boys. Why does going to college with these same peers suddenly make me a woman and the boys men? I certainly don't feel much older or wiser than I did last year. When people refer to me as a woman, I turn around to see who might be standing behind me.

Another fad now is for people to spell women with a "y" in place of the "e"—"womyn." These people want to take the "men" out of "women." Next perhaps they'll invent "femyle."

I've always been gender conscious with my language when it seemed logical. In third grade I referred to the mailman as a mailperson because our mail was sometimes delivered by a woman. I don't think I ever said mailwoman, though, because it just didn't sound right.

From elementary through high school, I told people I was Chinese,   10
and if I wanted to refer to all Asians, I used the word "Orientals." I guess
I was young and foolish and didn't know any better.

At college I was told that the proper label for me was Asian
American, that "Oriental" was a word to describe furniture, not people.
But what is the difference? All Asians are still being clumped together,
even though each group—Chinese, Korean, Japanese, Indians,
Vietnamese and Filipinos, to name just a few—comes from a different
country with a different language and culture.

The new "PC" term to describe Asian Americans and all other minorities is "people of color." The reason, I am told, is that the "minority"
population has grown to be the majority. But even if that's true, the phrase
seems contradictory. Since many African Americans no longer want to be
referred to as blacks, why should the term for minorities once again refer
to skin color? The same is true for Asians, most of whom find the label
"yellow" more offensive than Oriental. And isn't white also a color?

As long as we're throwing out all the old labels, why not replace
"white" with "European American." Wasps could be EAASPS (European-
American Anglo Saxon Protestants). Well, maybe not. Minority groups
want new labels to give themselves a more positive image, but unless the
stereotypes disappear as well, is it really going to help very much?

Look at the word "sophomore," which comes from Greek roots
meaning "wise fool." PC-conscious sophomores ought to revolt against
this offensive phrase. I, however, will not be among them. Changing the
word won't make me any smarter, humbler or wiser.

◎ Topics for Critical Thinking and Writing

1. Tsao doesn't comment on stereotypical views of persons of Asian background, but one commonly hears that the chief stereotypes are these: The
   men are asexual, effeminate, and sly; the women are malevolent (Dragon
   Lady) or passive (Madam Butterfly). If you are familiar with any of the images that perhaps have helped to perpetuate these or other stereotypes,
   set forth your response, for instance to a Charlie Chan film (the clever
   Asian).

2. In paragraph 11 Tsao rightly insists that "each group—Chinese, Korean,
   Japanese, Indians, Vietnamese and Filipinos, to name just a few—comes
   from a different country with a different language and culture." If we can
   speak of "culture"—whether Chinese or Anglo or Italian or Italian American—
   how does culture differ from stereotypical behavior?

3. In her first three paragraphs Tsao says that the word "Oriental" is now in
   disfavor, but she doesn't say why. The reasons apparently are two: (1) The
   word (from Latin *oriri*, "to arise") means, in effect, the east, where the sun
   arises. The word is now regarded as Eurocentric; China, Korea, and Japan
   are eastern relative to Europe, but they are not eastern in an absolute
   sense. (2) "Oriental," used of Chinese, Koreans, Japanese, Indonesians and

others, suggests racial identity, and overlooks important cultural differences. The preferred terms today are East Asia and East Asian. Given this background, do you think it is foolish to abandon the terms "Orient" and "Oriental"? In an essay of 250 words set forth your response.

4. In paragraph 3 Tsao talks about the word "freshman." If you were a college dean or president, in other words someone in a position to set the tone for the institution, would you abandon "freshman" and "freshwoman" for "freshperson," or perhaps for "first-year student"? In a paragraph explain why you would or would not drop "freshman" for all first-year students.

5. In paragraph 12 Tsao comments on the use of the term "people of color." Does the term seem to you to have some value, or is it something we should avoid using? Set forth your views in one or two paragraphs.

Gloria Naylor

Gloria Naylor–university teacher, essayist, and novelist–holds an M.A. in Afro-American Studies from Yale University. Her first novel, The Women of Brewster Place *(1983), won an American Book Award. "A Question of Language" originally appeared in* The New York Times.

A Question of Language

Language is the subject. It is the written form with which I've managed to keep the wolf away from the door and, in diaries, to keep my sanity. In spite of this, I consider the written word inferior to the spoken, and much of the frustration experienced by novelists is the awareness that whatever we manage to capture in even the most transcendent passages falls far short of the richness of life. Dialogue achieves its power in the dynamics of a fleeting moment of sight, sound, smell, and touch.

I'm not going to enter the debate here about whether it is language that shapes reality or vice versa. That battle is doomed to be waged whenever we seek intermittent reprieve from the chicken and egg dispute. I will simply take the position that the spoken word, like the written word, amounts to a nonsensical arrangement of sounds or letters without a consensus that assigns "meaning." And building from the meanings of what we hear, we order reality. Words themselves are innocuous; it is the consensus that gives them true power.

I remember the first time I heard the word *nigger*. In my third-grade class, our math tests were being passed down the rows, and as I handed the papers to a little boy in back of me, I remarked that once again he had received a much lower mark than I did. He snatched his test from me and spit out that word. Had he called me a nymphomaniac or a necrophiliac, I couldn't have been more puzzled. I didn't know what a nigger was, but I knew that whatever it meant, it was something he shouldn't have called me. This was verified when I raised my hand, and in a loud voice repeated what he had said and watched the teacher scold him for using a "bad" word. I was later to go home and ask the inevitable question that every black parent must face—"Mommy, what does 'nigger' mean?"

And what exactly did it mean? Thinking back, I realize that this could not have been the first time the word was used in my presence. I was part of a large extended family that had migrated from the rural South after World War II and formed a close-knit network that gravitated around my maternal grandparents. Their ground-floor apartment in one of the buildings they owned in Harlem was a weekend mecca for my immediate family, along with countless aunts, uncles, and cousins who brought along assorted friends. It was a bustling and open house with assorted neighbors and tenants popping in and out to exchange bits of gossip, pick up an old quarrel or referee the ongoing checkers game in which my grandmother cheated shamelessly. They were all there to let down their hair and put up their feet after a week of labor in the factories, laundries, and shipyards of New York.

Amid the clamor, which could reach deafening proportions—two or three conversations going on simultaneously, punctuated by the sound of a baby's crying somewhere in the back rooms or out on the street—there was still a rigid set of rules about what was said and how. Older children were sent out of the living room when it was time to get into the juicy details about "you-know-who" up on the third floor who had gone and gotten herself "p.r.e.g.n.a.n.t!" But my parents, knowing that I could spell well beyond my years, always demanded that I follow the others out to play. Beyond sexual misconduct and death, everything else was considered harmless for our young ears. And so among the anecdotes of the triumphs and disappointments in the various workings of their lives, the word *nigger* was used in my presence, but it was set within contexts and inflections that caused it to register in my mind as something else.

In the singular, the word was always applied to a man who had distinguished himself in some situation that brought their approval for his strength, intelligence, or drive:

"Did Johnny really do that?"

"I'm telling you, that nigger pulled in $6,000 of overtime last year. Said he got enough for a down payment on a house."

When used with a possessive adjective by a woman—"my nigger"—it became a term of endearment for husband or boyfriend. But it could be more than just a term applied to a man. In their mouths it became the pure essence of manhood—a disembodied force that channeled their past history of struggle and present survival against the odds into a victorious statement of being: "Yeah, that old foreman found out quick enough—you don't mess with a nigger."

5

In the plural, it became a description of some group within the community that had overstepped the bounds of decency as my family defined it: Parents who neglected their children, a drunken couple who fought in public, people who simply refused to look for work, those with excessively dirty mouths or unkempt households were all "trifling niggers." This particular circle could forgive hard times, unemployment, the occasional bout of depression—they had gone through all of that themselves—but the unforgivable sin was lack of self-respect.

A woman could never be a *nigger* in the singular, with its connotation of confirming worth. The noun *girl* was its closest equivalent in that sense, but only when used in direct address and regardless of the gender doing the addressing. *Girl* was a token of respect for a woman. The one-syllable word was drawn out to sound like three in recognition of the extra ounce of wit, nerve or daring that the woman had shown in the situation under discussion.

"G.i.r.l, stop. You mean you said that to his face?"

But if the word was used in a third-person reference or shortened so that it almost snapped out of the mouth, it always involved some element of communal disapproval. And age became an important factor in these exchanges. It was only between individuals of the same generation, or from an older person to a younger (but never the other way around), that "girl" would be considered a compliment.

I don't agree with the argument that use of the word *nigger* at this social stratum of the black community was an internalization of racism. The dynamics were the exact opposite: the people in my grandmother's living room took a word that whites used to signify worthlessness or degradation and rendered it impotent. Gathering there together, they transformed *nigger* to signify the varied and complex human beings they knew themselves to be. If the word was to disappear totally from the mouths of even the most liberal of white society, no one in that room was naive enough to believe it would disappear from white minds. Meeting the word head-on, they proved it had absolutely nothing to do with the way they were determined to live their lives.

So there must have been dozens of times that the word *nigger* was spoken in front of me before I reached the third grade. But I didn't "hear" it until it was said by a small pair of lips that had already learned it could be a way to humiliate me. That was the word I went home and asked my mother about. And since she knew that I had to grow up in America, she took me in her lap and explained.

✑ Topics for Critical Thinking and Writing

1. Why, according to Naylor (in paragraph 1) is written language inferior to spoken language? Can you think of any way or any circumstance in which written language is superior? How does Naylor's essay support her position here? Or does it?

2. In paragraph 2 Naylor says "Words themselves are innocuous; it is the consensus that gives them true power." What does this mean? In the rest of the essay Naylor discusses meanings of the word *nigger*. To what extent does her discussion demonstrate that consensus "assigns meaning" and gives words power?

3. If as a child you were the victim of an ethnic slur, explain how you reacted to it and how others (perhaps a parent or teacher) reacted to it. Or, if you ever delivered an ethnic slur, explain how you felt then and how you feel now about the incident or incidents.

Jeanne Wakatsuki Houston

Jeanne Wakatsuki, the daughter of immigrants from Japan, was born in Inglewood, California. When she was seven, the Japanese attack on Pearl Harbor aroused such fear and resentment that Japanese and Japanese Americans on the Pacific coast of the United States were relocated, and her family was forced to spend three and a half years at Manzanar, a camp in Owens Valley, California. Later she graduated from San Jose State University, married James D. Houston, and took up writing as a career.

Her first book, written with her husband, was Farewell to Manzanar *(1973), a memoir of her experience of the years during World War II. We reprint an essay from a later collection,* Beyond Manzanar *(1985).*

Double Identity

The memories surrounding my awareness of being female fall into two categories: those of the period before World War II, when the family made up my life, and those after the war when I entered puberty, and my world expanded to include the ways and values of my Caucasian peers. I did not think about my Asian-ness and how it influenced my self-image as a female until I married.

In remembering myself as a small child, I find it hard to separate myself from the entity of the family. I was too young to be given "duties" according to my sex, and I was unaware that this was the organizational basis for operating the family. I took it for granted that everyone just did what had to be done to keep things running smoothly. My five older sisters helped my mother with domestic duties. My four older brothers helped my father in the fishing business. What I vaguely recall about the sensibility surrounding our sex differences was that my sisters and I all liked to please our brothers. Moreover, we tried to attract positive attention from Papa. A smile or affectionate pat from him was like a gift from heaven. Somehow, we never felt this way about Mama. We took her love for granted. But there was something special about Papa.

I never identified this as one of the blessings of maleness. After all, I played with my brother Kiyo, two years older than myself, and I never felt there was anything special about him. I could even make him cry. My older brothers were fun-loving, boisterous and very kind to me, especially when I made them laugh with my imitations of Carmen Miranda dancing, or Bonnie Baker singing "Oh, Johnny." But Papa was different. His specialness came not from being male, but from being the authority.

After the war, and the closing of the camps, my world drastically changed. The family had disintegrated, my father was no longer "God-like" despite my mother's attempt to sustain that pre-war image of him. I was spending most of my time with my new Caucasian friends and learning new values that clashed with the values of my parents. It was also time that I assumed the duties girls were supposed to do—cooking, cleaning the house, washing and ironing clothes. I remember washing and ironing my brothers' shirts, careful to press the collars correctly, trying not to displease them. I cannot ever remember my brothers performing domestic chores while I lived at home. Yet, even though they may not have been working "out there," as the men were supposed to do, I did not resent it. It would have embarrassed me to see my brothers doing the dishes. Their reciprocation came in a different way. They were very protective of me and made me feel good and important for being a female. If my brother Ray had extra money, he would sometimes buy me a sexy sweater like my Caucasian friends wore, which Mama wouldn't buy for me. My brothers taught me to ride a bicycle, to drive a car, took me to my first dance, and proudly introduced me to their friends.

Although the family had changed, my identity as a female within it did not differ much from my older sisters' who grew up before the war. The males and females supported each other but for different reasons. No longer was the survival of the family as a group our primary objective; we cooperated to help each other survive "out there" in the complicated world that had weakened Papa.

We were living in Long Beach then. My brothers encouraged me to run for school office, to try out for majorette and song leader, and to run for Queen of various festivities. They were proud that I was breaking social barriers still closed to them. It was acceptable for an Oriental male to excel academically and in sports. But to gain recognition socially in a society that had been fed the stereotyped model of the Asian male as cook, houseboy or crazed *Kamikaze* pilot, was almost impossible. The more alluring myth of mystery and exotica that surrounds the Oriental female made it easier, though no less inwardly painful.

Whenever I succeeded in the *hakujin*[1] world, my brothers were supportive, whereas Papa would be disdainful, undermined by my obvious

5

---
[1]*hakujin*, Caucasian.

capitulation to the ways of the West. I wanted to be like my Caucasian friends. Not only did I want to look like them, I wanted to act like them. I tried hard to be outgoing and socially aggressive, and to act confidently, like my girl friends. At home I was careful not to show these traits to my father. For him it was bad enough that I did not even look very Japanese; I was too big, and I walked too assertively. My breasts were large, and besides that I showed them off with those sweaters the *hakujin* girls wore! My behavior at home was never calm and serene, but around my father I still tried to be as Japanese as I could.

As I passed puberty and grew more interested in boys, I soon became aware that an Oriental female evoked a certain kind of interest from males. I was still too young to understand how or why an Oriental female fascinated Caucasian men, and of course, far too young to see then that it was a form of "not being seen." My brothers would warn me, "Don't trust the *hakujin* boys. They only want one thing. They'll treat you like a servant and expect you to wait on them hand and foot. They don't know how to be nice to you." My brothers never dated Caucasian girls. In fact, I never really dated Caucasian boys until I went to college. In high school, I used to sneak out to dances and parties where I would meet them. I wouldn't even dare to think what Papa would do if he knew.

What my brothers were saying was that I should not act towards Caucasian males as I did towards them. I must not "wait on them" or allow them to think I would, because they wouldn't understand. In other words, be a Japanese female around Japanese men and act *hakujin* around Caucasian men. This double identity within a "double standard" resulted not only in confusion of my role or roles as female, but also in who or what I was racially. With the admonitions of my brothers lurking deep in my consciousness, I would try to be aggressive, assertive and "come on strong" towards Caucasian men. I mustn't let them think I was submissive, passive and all-giving, like Madame Butterfly.[2] With Asian males I would tone down my natural enthusiasm and settle into patterns instilled in me through the models of my mother and my sisters. I was not comfortable in either role.

I found I was more physically attracted to Caucasian men. Although T.V. and film were not nearly as pervasive as they are now, we still had an abundance of movie magazines and films from which to garner our idols for crushes and fantasy. For years I was madly in love with Lon McAllister and Alan Ladd. Bruce Lee and O.J. Simpson were absent from the idol-making media. Asian men became like "family" to me: they were my brothers. Of course, no one was like my father. He was so powerful. The only men who might possess some of that power were those whose

10

---

[2]*Madame Butterfly*: In Puccini's opera with this title, a young Japanese woman falls in love with an American naval officer in Japan, becomes pregnant, and is abandoned by him.

control and dominance over his life diminished his. Those would be the men who interested me.

Although I was attracted to males who looked like someone in a Coca-Cola ad, I yearned for the expressions of their potency to be like that of Japanese men, like that of my father: unpredictable, dominant, and brilliant—yet sensitive and poetic. I wanted a blond Samurai.[3]

When I met him during those college years in San Jose, I was surprised to see how readily my mother accepted the idea of our getting married. My father had passed away, but I was still concerned about her reaction. All of my married brothers and sisters had Japanese American mates. I would be the first to marry a Caucasian. "He's a strong man and will protect you. I'm all for it," she said. Her main concern for me was survival. Knowing that my world was the world of the *hakujin*, she wanted me to be protected, even if it meant marriage to one. It was 1957, and inter-racial couples were a rare sight to see. She felt that my husband-to-be was strong because he was acting against the norms of his culture, perhaps even against his parent's wishes. From her vantage point, where family and group opinion outweighed the individual's, this willingness to oppose them was truly a show of strength.

When we first married I wondered if I should lay out his socks and underwear every morning like my mother used to do. But my brothers' warning would float up from the past: don't be subservient to Caucasian men or they will take advantage. So I compromised and laid them out whenever I thought to do it . . . which grew less and less often as the years passed. His first reaction to this wifely gesture was to be uncomfortably pleased. Then he was puzzled by its sporadic occurrence, which did not seem to be an act of apology, or a sign that I wanted something. On the days when I felt I should be a good Japanese wife, I did it. On other days, when I felt American and assertive, I did not.

When my mother visited us, as she often did, I had to be on good behavior, much to my husband's pleasure and surprise. I would jump up from the table to fill his empty water glass (if she hadn't beat me to it) or butter his roll. If I didn't notice that his plate needed refilling, she would kick me under the table and reprimand me with a disapproving look. Needless to say, we never had mother-in-law problems. He would often ask with hope in his voice "when is your mother coming to visit?"

Despite the fact that early in our marriage we had become aware of   15
the "images" we had married and were trying to relate to each other as the real people we were, he still hoped deep in his heart that I was his exotic, mysterious but ever available *Cho-Cho san*.[4] And I still saw him as my Anglo Samurai, wielding his sword of integrity, slaying the dragons

[3]*Samurai*: A member of the Japanese warrior class.
[4]*Cho-Cho san*, Madam Butterfly.

that prevented my acceptance as an equal human being in his world, now mine.

My mother dutifully served my father throughout their marriage. I never felt she resented it. I served my brothers and father and did not resent it. I was made to feel not only important for performing duties of my role, but absolutely integral for the functioning of the family. I realized a very basic difference in attitude between Japanese and American culture towards serving another. In my family, to serve another could be uplifting, a gracious gesture that elevated oneself. For many white Americans it seems that serving another is degrading, an indication of dependency or weakness in character, or a low place in the social ladder. To be ardently considerate is to be "self-effacing" or apologetic.

My father used to say, "Serving humanity is the greatest virtue. Giving service of yourself is more worthy than selling the service or goods of another." He would prefer that we be maids in someone's home, serving someone well, than be salesgirls where our function would be to exchange someone else's goods, handling money. Perhaps it was his way to rationalize and give pride to the occupations open to us as Orientals. Nevertheless, his words have stayed with me, giving me spiritual sustenance at times when I perceived that my willingness to give was misconstrued as a need to be liked or an act of manipulation to get something.

I was talking about this subject with an Asian American woman friend, recently widowed, whose husband had also been Asian American. He had been a prominent surgeon, highly thought of in the community where we live. She is forty-two, third generation Chinese, born in San Francisco, articulate, intelligent and a professional therapist for educationally handicapped children. She "confessed" her reticence to let her Caucasian friends know she served her husband. "There is such a stereotyped view that is laid on us. They just don't understand *why* we do what we do!"

She told me of an incident when she remarked to a Caucasian friend that she polished her husband's shoes. Her friend turned on her in mock fury and said, "Don't you dare let my husband know you do that!" My friend said she felt ashamed, humiliated, that she had somehow betrayed this woman by seeming subordinate to her husband.

"I served him in many ways," she said. "Even though he was a graduate of Stanford and professionally successful, he drove himself to work harder and longer to compete because he felt he was handicapped by being Chinese. You know our Asian men, the ones raised with values from the old country are not equipped to compete like white American men. They are not conditioned to be outwardly aggressive and competitive. It was agony for my husband, and I knew he was out there doing it for us, so I tried to make it easier for him at home." As I looked at her I could see her compassion, and for a flickering moment I saw my mother. A generation had passed, but some things had not changed that much.

20

My husband and I often joke that the reason we have stayed married for so long is that we continually mystify each other with responses and attitudes that are plainly due to our different backgrounds. For years I frustrated him with unpredictable silences and accusative looks. I felt a great reluctance to tell him what I wanted or what needed to be done in the home. I was inwardly furious that I was being put into the position of having to *tell* him what to do. I felt my femaleness, in the Japanese sense, was being degraded. I did not want to be the authority. That would be humiliating for him and for me. He, on the other hand, considering the home to be under my dominion, in the American sense, did not dare to impose on me what he thought I wanted. He wanted me to tell him or make a list, like his parents.

Entertaining socially was also confusing. Up to recent times, I still hesitated to sit at one head of our rectangular dining table when my husband sat at the other end. It seemed right to be seated next to him, helping him serve the food. Sometimes I did it anyway, but only with our close friends who didn't misread my physical placement as psychological subservience.

At dinner parties I always served the men first, until I noticed the women glaring at me. I became self-conscious about it and would try to remember to serve the women first. Sometimes I would forget and automatically turn to a man. I would catch myself abruptly, dropping a bowl of soup all over him. Then I would have to serve him first anyway, as a gesture of apology. My unconscious Japanese instinct still managed to get what it wanted.

Now I just entertain according to how I feel that day. If my Japanese sensibility is stronger I act accordingly and feel comfortable. If I want to go all-American I can do that too. I have come to accept the cultural hybridness of my personality, to recognize it as a strength and not weakness. Because I am culturally neither pure Japanese nor pure American does not mean I am less of a person. It means I have been enriched with the heritage of both.

As I look back on my marriage and try to compare it to the marriage of my parents, it seems ludicrous to do so—like comparing a sailboat to a jet airliner. Both get you there, but one depends on the natural element of wind and the other on modern technology. What does emerge as a basic difference is directly related to the Japanese concept of cooperation for group survival and the American value of competition for the survival of the individual. My Japanese family cooperated to survive economically and spiritually. Although sibling rivalry was subtly present, it was never allowed the ferocity of expression we allow our children. I see our children compete with each other. I have felt my husband and I compete with each other—not always in obvious ways, such as professional recognition or in the comparison of role responsibilities, but in attitudes toward self-fulfillment. "I love you more than you love me," or "My doing nothing is more boring than your doing nothing."

Competition does provide some challenge and excitement in life. Yet carried to extremes in personal relationships it can become destructive.

How can you fully trust someone you are in competition with? And when trust breaks down, isolation and alienation set in.

I find another basic difference between my mother and myself in how we relate to sons. I try very consciously not to indulge my son, as my mother indulged my brothers. My natural inclination is to do as she did. So I try to restrain it. In fact, I find myself being harder on him, afraid that my constrained Japanese training to please the male might surface, crippling instead of equipping him for future relationships with females who may not be of my background, hampering his emotional survival in the competitive and independent world he will face when he leaves the nest.

How my present attitudes will affect my children in later years remains to be seen. My world is radically different from mother's world, and all indications point to an even wider difference in our world from our children's. Whereas my family's struggle and part of my own was racially based, I do not foresee a similar struggle for our children. Their biracialness is, indeed, a factor in their identity and self-image, but I feel their struggle will be more to sustain human dignity in a world rapidly dehumanizing itself with mechanization and technology. My hope is they have inherited that essential trait ethnic minorities in this country have so sharply honed: a strong will to survive.

Topics for Critical Thinking and Writing

1. In her fifth paragraph Jeanne Wakatsuki Houston recalls how her brothers and sisters cooperated to "help each other survive 'out there' in the complicated world that had weakened Papa." What do we suppose had happened to reduce Papa's "Godlike" image? And in the next paragraph, Houston speaks of how her brothers encouraged her "to run for school office, to try out for majorette and song leader, and to run for Queen of various festivities." How had her brothers encouraged her here?

2. Houston tells us in paragraph 7 that, although now past puberty, she was "still too young to understand how or why an Oriental female fascinated Caucasian men." Nowadays, Houston would probably not use the word *Oriental*. Can you explain why? (Hint: See the entry on *Orient* in "A Writer's Glossary.")

3. We are told that there are differences in the Houston household that stem from the writer and her husband coming from different cultures. Which of these differences most resemble those that are *not* a result of being a Japanese/American couple? Can you explain why?

4. In her last paragraph Houston projects some differences for her children from those of her world with her husband. What are these differences? Do you find them similar to the challenges you face or not? Explain.

5. Houston contrasts her Japanese environment, which emphasized service in her family, with the Caucasian environment, which emphasizes competi-

tion. She calls it her *cultural hybridness* and is proud of it. Compare this essay with Fan Shen's, page 000. Is he also proud of his "hybridness"? Explain.

Brent Staples

Brent Staples, born in 1951, holds a Ph.D. in psychology from the University of Chicago. He taught briefly and then turned to journalism. He is now assistant metropolitan editor at The New York Times. *We reprint an essay that appeared in this paper in 1994.*

The "Scientific" War on the Poor

Everyone knows the stereotype of the fair-haired executive who owes the office with the view and the six-figure salary to an accident of birth—like relatives in the halls of power. What about merit, for heaven's sake? Why not give I.Q. tests, grant the best jobs to those who score well and send the laggards to the mailroom?

That would never happen, nor should it. I.Q. scores in themselves tell you almost nothing. This was clearly explained by the Frenchman Alfred Binet, who invented the first usable I.Q. test in 1905. The test had one purpose: to help identify learning-disabled children who needed special schools. Binet warned that a "brutal pessimism" would follow if his test was ever mistaken as a measure of a fixed, unchangeable intelligence.

You wouldn't know it from the I.Q. worship in progress today, but using the tests to draw finer distinctions than Binet intended amounts to overreaching, if not scientific fraud. Most scientists concede that they don't really know what "intelligence" is. Whatever it might be, paper and pencil tests aren't the tenth of it.

The fair-haired executive gets a pass for other reasons entirely. First, because the world works more on insiderism and inherited privilege than on "pure merit," whatever that might be. Second, because the charge of innate stupidity has historically been reserved for the poor.

That charge surfaced during the immigrant influx of the teens and   5
20's, and again during the affirmative-action 60's and 70's—both times when America found "scientific" justifications of poverty very appealing. Misgivings about the "underclass" have made them appealing again. By way of example, consider Senator Daniel Patrick Moynihan's ludicrous claim that out-of-wedlock births in modern America amounted to the creation of a new species.

Alfred Binet's American imitators embraced "brutal pessimism" right away. In 1912, after Eastern and Southern Europeans began to out-number Northern Europeans at Ellis Island, immigration authorities asked the psychologist Henry Goddard to do "quality control," through intelligence testing. Goddard and his colleagues believed that Nordic peoples were civilization's best and that the rest were genetically second-rate or worse. The test was merely a means of proving it.

Not surprisingly, Goddard's testing of what he called a representative sample of immigrants showed that 80 percent of all Jews, Italians and Hungarians and nearly 90 percent of Russians were "feeble-minded." As a result, hundreds each year were deported.

At the start of World War I, two million draftees were also tested. The results showed a gap between blacks and whites, but at the time, few were interested. The passion then was proving a connection between "mental deficiency" and national origin among white immigrants. The testers didn't bother with translation; non-English-speakers were instructed in pantomime.

Once again, British immigrants were classified as first-rate, with Poles, Italians and Russians labeled stupid and undesirable. The data were published by the National Academy of Sciences in 1921, and contributed to the introduction of temporary limits on immigration. I.Q. hysteria also resulted in sterilization laws that were enforced only against the poor.

The I.Q. believers worked with messianic zeal. Like many before him, 10 the British psychologist Sir Cyril Burt went way beyond science in defense of his beliefs. Burt alleged that intelligence was so wired into the genes, so indifferent to environment, that identical twins reared apart had virtually identical I.Q. scores. Statisticians now agree that Burt made much of it up.

The I.Q. worshipers of today remain essentially unchanged from Goddard's time. Despite the impression that there is something new in *The Bell Curve*, its authors, Charles Murray and Richard Herrnstein, have merely reasserted the long-unproven claim that I.Q. is mainly inherited. The language is calmer, the statistical gimmicks slicker, but the truth remains the same: There exist no plausible data to make the case. Belief to the contrary rests mainly on brutal preconceptions about poverty, but also on a basic confusion between pseudoscience and the real thing.

◐ Topics for Critical Thinking and Writing

1. In his first paragraph Staples outlines the "stereotype of the fair-haired executive who owes the office with the view and the six-figure salary to an accident of birth." Why, he asks, don't we give I.Q. tests for such jobs? In the next paragraph, however, he says "That would never happen, nor should it." Why does he believe that it should *not* happen? Do *you* believe it should or should not happen? Why?

2. In paragraph 5 Staples mentions two earlier times when "'scientific' justifica-tions of poverty" were appealing. Why were these "justifications" appeal-ing? Why are they appealing now? And why does Staples use quotation marks around "scientific"?

3. What happened in 1912 on Ellis Island that prompted authorities to ask Henry Goddard for "quality control"? What did he do? Staples offers no ex-amples for the "affirmative-action 60's and 70's." Should he have?

4. In his last paragraph Staples states that "brutal preconceptions about poverty" underlie arguments for I.Q. scores. If Staples had removed the word *brutal*, would the sentence remain the same?

Amy Tan

Amy Tan was born in Oakland, California, in 1952, of Chinese immigrant parents. When she was eight, she won first prize among elementary students with an essay entitled "What the Library Means to Me." In due time she attended Linfield College in Oregon, then transferred to San Jose State University where, while working two part-time jobs, she became an honors student and a President's Scholar. In 1973 she earned an M.A. in linguistics, also at San Jose, and she later en-rolled as a doctoral student at the University of California, Berkeley, though she left this program after the murder of a close friend. For the next five years she worked as a language development consultant and a project director, and then she became a freelance business writer. In 1986 she published her first short story, and it was reprinted in Seventeen, *where it was noticed by an agent, who encouraged her to continue writing fiction. In 1989* The Joy Luck Club *was pub-lished. Other books include* The Kitchen God's Wife *(1991),* The Hundred Secret Senses *(1995), and* The Bonesetter's Daughter *(2001). She has also written two books for children,* The Moon Lady *(1992) and* SAGWA the Chinese Siamese Cat *(1994).*

The essay that we reprint appeared in Life *magazine in April 1991.*

Snapshot: Lost Lives of Women

When I first saw this photo as a child, I thought it was exotic and re-mote, of a faraway time and place, with people who had no connection to my American life. Look at their bound feet! Look at that funny lady with the plucked forehead!

The solemn little girl is, in fact, my mother. And leaning against the rock is my grandmother, Jingmei. "She called me Baobei," my mother told me. "It means Treasure."

The picture was taken in Hangzhou, and my mother believes the year was 1922, possibly spring or fall, judging by the clothes. At first glance, it appears the women are on a pleasure outing.

But see the white bands on their skirts? The white shoes? They are in mourning. My mother's grandmother, known to the others as Divong,

Courtesy Amy Tan

"The Replacement Wife," has recently died. The women have come to this place, a Buddhist retreat, to perform yet another ceremony for Divong. Monks hired for the occasion have chanted the proper words. And the women and little girl have walked in circles clutching smoky sticks of incense. They knelt and prayed, then burned a huge pile of spirit money so that Divong might ascend to a higher position in her new world.

This is also a picture of secrets and tragedies, the reasons that warnings have been passed along in our family like heirlooms. Each of these women suffered a terrible fate, my mother said. And they were not peasant women but big city people, very modern. They went to dance halls and wore stylish clothes. They were supposed to be the lucky ones.

Look at the pretty woman with her finger on her cheek. She is my mother's second cousin, Nunu Aiji, "Precious Auntie." You cannot see this, but Nunu Aiyi's entire face was scarred from smallpox. Lucky for her, a year or so after this picture was taken, she received marriage proposals from two families. She turned down a lawyer and married another man. Later she divorced her husband, a daring thing for a woman to do. But then, finding no means to support herself or her young daughter, Nunu eventually accepted the lawyer's second proposal—to become his number two concubine. "Where else could she go?" my mother asked. "Some people said she was lucky the lawyer still wanted her."

Now look at the small woman with a sour face (*third from left*). There's a reason that Jyou Ma, "Uncle's Wife," looks this way. Her husband, my great-uncle often complained that his family had chosen an ugly woman for his wife. To show his displeasure, he often insulted Jyou Ma's cooking. One time Great-Uncle tipped over a pot of boiling soup, which fell all over his niece's four-year-old neck and nearly killed her. My mother was the little niece, and she still has that soup scar on her neck. Great-Uncle's family eventually chose a pretty woman for his second wife. But the complaints about Jyou Ma's cooking did not stop.

Doomma, "Big Mother," is the regal-looking woman seated on a rock. (The woman with the plucked forehead, far left, is a servant, remembered only as someone who cleaned but did not cook.) Doomma was the daughter of my great-grandfather and Nu-pei, "The Original Wife." She was shunned by Divong, "The Replacement Wife," for being "too strong," and loved by Divong's daughter, my grandmother. Doomma's first daughter was born with a hunchback—a sign, some said, of Doomma's own crooked nature. Why else did she remarry, disobeying her family's orders to remain a widow forever? And why did Doomma later kill herself, using some mysterious means that caused her to die slowly over three days? "Doomma died the same way she lived," my mother said, "strong, suffering lots."

Jingmei, my own grandmother, lived only a few more years after this picture was taken. She was the widow of a poor scholar, a man who had the misfortune of dying from influenza when he was about to be appointed a vice-magistrate. In 1924 or so, a rich man, who liked to collect pretty women, raped my grandmother and thereby forced her into becoming one of his concubines. My grandmother, now an outcast, took her young daughter to live with her on an island outside of Shanghai. She left her son behind, to save his face. After she gave birth to another son she killed herself by swallowing raw opium buried in the New Year's rice cakes. The young daughter who wept at her deathbed was my mother.

At my grandmother's funeral, monks tied chains to my mother's ankles so she would not fly away with her mother's ghost. "I tried to take them off," my mother said. "I was her treasure. I was her life."   10

My mother could never talk about any of this, even with her closest friends. "Don't tell anyone," she once said to me. "People don't understand. A concubine was like some kind of prostitute. My mother was a good woman, high-class. She had no choice."

I told her I understood.

"How can you understand?" she said, suddenly angry. "You did not live in China then. You do not know what it's like to have no position in life. I was her daughter. We had no face! We belonged to nobody! This is a shame I can never push off my back." By the end of the outburst, she was crying.

On a recent trip with my mother to Beijing, I learned that my uncle found a way to push the shame off his back. He was the son my grandmother left behind. In 1936 he joined the Communist party—in large part, he told me, to overthrow the society that forced his mother into concubinage. He published a story about his mother. I told him I had written about my grandmother in a book of fiction. We agreed that my grandmother is the source of strength running through our family. My mother cried to hear this.

My mother believes my grandmother is also my muse, that she helps   15
me write. "Does she still visit you often?" she asked while I was writing

my second book. And then she added shyly, "Does she say anything about me?"

"Yes," I told her. "She has lots to say. I am writing it down."

This is the picture I see when I write. These are the secrets I was supposed to keep. These are the women who never let me forget why stories need to be told.

 ## Topics for Critical Thinking and Writing

1. Consider the title of this essay. Why are the women's lives described as "lost lives"? Can you imagine a companion piece, "Lost Lives of Men"? If not, why not?

2. In paragraph 5, what does Tan communicate by "And they were not peasant women but big city people, very modern"? What does she imply about the lives of those who *were* peasants?

3. In the fifth paragraph and in the last, Tan refers to "secrets" that she "was supposed to keep." What were the secrets? Why does she reveal them?

4. In the first paragraph Tan reports, "When I first saw this photo as a child, I thought it was exotic and remote, of a faraway time and place, with people who had no connection to my American life." What does she imply in this paragraph about their "connection to [her] American life" now? Where in the essay is that connection revealed or explained?

5. If you are lucky enough to have photographs of your ancestors, explore the images of the people in them and what you have been told about their lives. Do you feel "connected" or not? Explain.

Pat Mora

Pat Mora did her undergraduate work at Texas Western College and then earned a master's degree at the University of Texas at El Paso, where she later served as Assistant to the Vice President for Academic Affairs, Director of the University Museum, and then (1981–89) as Assistant to the President. She has published essays on Hispanic culture as well as a children's book, Tomás and the Library Lady, *but she is best known for her books of poems. Mora has received several awards, including one from the Southwest Council of Latin American Studies.*

Immigrants

wrap their babies in the American flag,
feed them mashed hot dogs and apple pie,
name them Bill and Daisy,
buy them blonde dolls that blink blue
eyes or a football and tiny cleats   5
before the baby can even walk,
speak to them in thick English,
   hallo, babee, hallo.
whisper in Spanish or Polish
when the babies sleep, whisper   10
in a dark parent bed, that dark
parent fear, "Will they like
our boy, our girl, our fine american
boy, our fine american girl?"

 Topics for Critical Thinking and Writing

1. To say that someone—for example, a politician—"wraps himself in the American flag" is to suggest disapproval or even anger or contempt. What behavior does the phrase usually describe? What does Mora mean when she says that immigrants "wrap their babies in the American flag"?

2. What do you suppose is Mora's attitude toward the immigrants? Do you think the poet fully approves of their hopes? On what do you base your answer?

3. Does Mora's description of the behavior of immigrants ring true of the immigrant group you are part of or know best? What is your attitude toward their efforts to assimilate? Explain in an essay of 750 to 1000 words.

A Casebook on Race

Because *The Columbia Encyclopedia* is amazingly comprehensive and, for its size, relatively inexpensive, many people rightly believe that (like a good dictionary) it should be part of one's home reference library. We reprint the unsigned essay on "Race."

Race

Race, one of the group of populations constituting humanity. The differences among races are essentially biological and are marked by the hereditary transmission of physical characteristics. Genetically a race may be defined as a group with gene frequencies differing from those of the other groups in the human species (see HEREDITY; GENETICS; GENE). However, the genes responsible for the hereditary differences between humans are few when compared with the vast number of genes common to all human beings regardless of the race to which they belong. All human groups belong to the same species (*Homo sapiens*) and are mutually fertile. The term *race* is inappropriate when applied to national, religious, geographic, linguistic, or cultural groups, nor can the biological criteria of race be equated with any mental characteristics such as intelligence, personality, or character. Races arose as a result of MUTATION, selection, and adaptational changes in human populations. Most scholars hold that there has been a common evolution for all races and that differentiation occurred relatively late in history. Even to classify humans on the basis of physiological traits is difficult, for the coexistence of races since earliest times through conquests, invasions, migrations, and mass deportations has produced a heterogeneous world population. Nevertheless, by limiting the criteria to such traits as skin pigmentation, color and form of hair, shape of head, stature, and form of nose, most anthropologists agree on the existence of three relatively distinct groups: the Caucasoid, the Mongoloid, and the Negroid. The Caucasoid, found in Europe, N Africa, and the Middle East to N India, is characterized as pale reddish white to olive brown in color, of medium to tall stature, with a long or broad head form. The hair is light blond to dark brown in color, of a fine texture, and straight or wavy. The color of the eyes is light blue to dark brown and the nose bridge is usually high. The Mongoloid race, including most peoples of E Asia and the Indians of the Americas, has been described as saffron to yellow or reddish brown in color, of medium stature, with a broad head form. The hair is dark, straight, and coarse; body hair is sparse. The eyes are black to dark brown. The epicanthic fold, imparting an almond shape to the eye, is common, and the nose bridge is usually low or medium. The Negroid race is characterized by brown to brown-black skin, usually a long head form, varying stature, and thick, everted lips. The hair is dark and coarse, usually kinky. The eyes are dark, the nose bridge low, and the nostrils broad. To the Negroid race belong the peoples of Africa south of the Sahara, the Pygmy groups of Indonesia, and the inhabitants of New Guinea and Melanesia. Each of these broad groups can be divided into subgroups. General agreement is lacking as to the classification of such people as the aborigines of Australia, the Dravidian people of S India, the Polynesians, and the Ainu of N Japan. Attempts have been made to classify humans since the 17th cent., when scholars first began to separate types of flora and fauna. Johann Friedrich BLUMENBACH was the first to divide mankind according to skin color. In the 19th and early 20th cent., men such as Joseph Arthur GOBINEAU and Houston Stewart CHAMB-ERLAIN, mainly interested in pressing forward the supposed superiority of their own kind of culture or nationality, began to attribute cultural and psychological values to race. This approach, called racism, culminated in the vicious racial doctrines of Nazi Germany, and especially in ANTI-SEMITISM. This same approach complicated the INTEGRATION movement in the United States and underlies segregation policies in the Republic of South Africa (see APARTHEID). See Ruth Benedict, *Race: Science and Politics* (rev. ed. 1943, repr. 1968); C. S. Coon, *The Origin of Races* (1962) and *Living Races of Man* (1965); Margaret Mead et al., ed., *Science and the Concept of Race* (1968); S. M. Garn, ed., *Readings on Race* (2d ed. 1968) and *Human Races* (3d ed. 1971); J. C. King, *The Biology of Race* (1971); L. L. Cavalli-Sforza, *The Origin and Differentiation of Human Races* (1972).

Jimmy Carter

Jimmy Carter, born in Plains, Georgia, in 1924, served as thirty-ninth president of the United States. After leaving the White House, he and his wife, Rosalynn, founded the Carter Center, which works to prevent and resolve conflicts, promote freedom and democracy, and improve health around the world. President Carter has written thirteen books, including Talking Peace: A Vision for the Next Generation *(1993),* Always a Reckoning and Other Poems *(1995), and* An Hour Before Daylight *(2001), from which the following pages are reprinted. Another excerpt appears on page 000.*

A Note on a Segregated Society

Until my last two years of high school, the black boys at Archery were my closest friends; I had a more intimate relationship with them than with any of my white classmates in town. This makes it more difficult for me to justify or explain my own attitudes and actions during the segregation era. A turning point in my relationship with A.D. and my other friends occurred when we were about fourteen years old. Until then, there had never been any distinction among us, despite the great difference between our economic circumstances. I lived in the "big house" and they lived in tenant shacks; I had a bicycle, my parents owned an automobile, and we went to separate churches and schools. I was destined to go to college, and few of them would finish their high school work. But there were no acknowledged differences of rank or status when we were together in the fields, on the creek banks, or playing in our yard or theirs, and we never thought about being of different color.

Around age fourteen, I began to develop closer ties with the white community. I was striving for a place on the varsity basketball team and developed a stronger relationship with my classmates, including a growing interest in dating girls. One day about this time, A.D., Edmund, and I approached the gate leading from our barn to the pasture. To my surprise, they opened it and stepped back to let me go through first. I was immediately suspicious that they were playing some trick on me, but I passed through without stumbling over a tripwire or having them slam the gate in my face.

It was a small act, but a deeply symbolic one. After that, they often treated me with some deference. I guess that their parents had done or said something that caused this change in my black friends' attitude. The constant struggle for leadership among our small group was resolved, but a precious sense of equality had gone out of our personal relationship, and things were never again the same between them and me.

It seems strange now that I never discussed this transition in our lives with either my black friends or my own parents. We still competed equally while on the baseball field, fishing, or working in the field, but I was not reluctant to take advantage of my new stature by assuming, on occasion, the authority of my father. Also, we were more inclined to go our separate ways if we had an argument, since I was increasingly involved with my white friends in Plains. I guess all of us just assumed that this was one more step toward maturity and that we were settling into our adult roles in an unquestioned segregated society.

Sharon Begley

Sharon Begley, a senior writer for Newsweek, *published this essay in an issue (February 13, 1995) whose cover story was "What Color is Black?"*

Three Is Not Enough

To most Americans race is as plain as the color of the nose on your face. Sure, some light-skinned blacks, in some neighborhoods, are taken for Italians, and some Turks are confused with Argentines. But even in the children of biracial couples, racial ancestry is writ large—in the hue of the skin and the shape of the lips, the size of the brow and the bridge of the nose. It is no harder to trace than it is to judge which basic colors in a box of Crayolas were combined to make tangerine or burnt umber. Even with racial mixing, the existence of primary races is as obvious as the existence of primary colors.

Or is it? C. Loring Brace has his own ideas about where race resides, and it isn't in skin color. If our eyes could perceive more than the superficial, we might find race in chromosome 11: there lies the gene for hemoglobin. If you divide humankind by which of two forms of the gene each person has, then equatorial Africans, Italians and Greeks fall into the "sickle-cell race"; Swedes and South Africa's Xhosas (Nelson Mandela's ethnic group) are in the healthy-hemoglobin race. Or do you prefer to group people by whether they have epicanthic eye folds, which produce the "Asian" eye? Then the !Kung San (Bushmen) belong with the Japanese and Chinese. Depending on which trait you choose to demarcate races, "you won't get anything that remotely tracks conventional [race] categories," says anthropologist Alan Goodman, dean of natural science at Hampshire College.

The notion of race is under withering attack for political and cultural reasons—not to mention practical ones like what to label the child of a Ghanaian and a Norwegian. But scientists got there first. Their doubts about the conventional racial categories—black, white, Asian—have nothing to do with a sappy "we are all the same" ideology. Just the reverse. "Human variation is very, very real," says Goodman. "But race, as a way of organizing [what we know about that variation], is incredibly simplified and bastardized." Worse, it does not come close to explaining the astounding diversity of humankind—not its origins, not its extent, not its meaning. "There is no organizing principle by which you could put 5 billion people into so few categories in a way that would tell you anything important about humankind's diversity," says Michigan's Brace, who will lay out the case against race at the annual meeting of the American Association for the Advancement of Science.

About 70 percent of cultural anthropologists, and half of physical anthropologists, reject race as a biological category, according to a 1989 survey by Central Michigan University anthropologist Leonard Liebermnan and colleagues. The truths of science are not decided by majority vote, of course. Empirical evidence, woven into a theoretical whole, is what matters. The threads of the argument against the standard racial categories:

• **Genes:** In 1972, population biologist Richard Lewontin of Harvard   5
University laid out the genetic case against race. Analyzing 17 genetic markers in 168 populations such as Austrians, Thais and Apaches, he found that there is more genetic difference within one race than there is between that race and another. Only 6.3 percent of the genetic differences could be explained by the individuals' belonging to different races. That is, if you pick at random any two "blacks" walking along the street, and analyze their 23 pairs of chromosomes, you will probably find that their genes have less in common than do the genes of one of them with that of a random "white" person. Last year the Human Genome Diversity Project used 1990s genetics to extend Lewontin's analysis. Its conclusion: genetic variation from one individual to another of the same "race" swamps the average differences between racial groupings. The more we learn about humankind's genetic differences, says geneticist Luca Cavalli-Sforza of Stanford University, who chairs the committee that directs the biodiversity project, the more we see that they have almost nothing to do with what we call race.

• **Traits:** As sickle-cell "races" and epicanthic-fold "races" show, there are as many ways to group people as there are traits. That is because "racial" traits are what statisticians call non-concordant. Lack of concordance means that sorting people according to *these* traits produces different groupings than you get in sorting them by *those* (equally valid) traits. When biologist Jared Diamond of UCLA surveyed half a dozen traits for a recent issue of *Discover* magazine, he found that, depending on which traits you pick, you can form very surprising "races." Take the scooped-out shape of the back of the front teeth, a standard "Asian" trait. Native Americans and Swedes have these shovel-shaped incisors, too, and so would fall in the same race. Is biochemistry better? Norwegians, Arabians, north Indians and the Fulani of northern Nigeria, notes Diamond, fall into the "lactase race" (the lactase enzyme digests milk sugar). Everyone else—other Africans, Japanese, Native Americans—forms the "lactase-deprived race" (their ancestors did not drink milk from cows or goats and hence never evolved the lactase gene). How about blood types, the familiar A, B and O groups? Then Germans and New Guineans, populations that have the same percentages of each type, are in one race; Estonians and Japanese comprise a separate one for the same reason, notes anthropologist Jonathan Marks of Yale University. Depending on which traits are chosen, "we could place Swedes in the same race as either Xhosas, Fulani, the Ainu of Japan or Italians," writes Diamond.

• **Subjectivity:** If race is a valid biological concept, anyone in any culture should be able to look at any individual and say, Aha, you are a . . . It should not be the case, as French tennis star Yannick Noah said a few years ago, that "in Africa I am white, and in France I am black" (his mother is French and his father is from Cameroon). "While biological traits give the impression that race is a biological unit of nature," says anthropologist George Armelagos of Emory University, "it remains a cultural construct. The boundaries between races depends on the classifier's own cultural norms."

• **Evolution:** Scholars who believe in the biological validity of race argue that the groupings reflect human pre-history. That is, populations that evolved together, and separately from others, constitute a race. This school of thought holds that blacks should all be in one race because they are descended from people who stayed on the continent where humanity began. Asians, epitomized by the Chinese, should be another race because they are the children of groups who walked north and east until they reached the Pacific. Whites of the pale, blond variety should be another because their ancestors filled Europe. Because of their appearance, these populations represent the extremes, the archetypes, of human diversity—the reds, blues and yellows from which you can make every other hue. "But if you use these archetypes as your groups you have classified only a very tiny proportion of the world's people, which is not very useful," says Marks, whose incisive new book "Human Biodiversity" deconstructs race. "Also, as people walked out of Africa, they were differentiating along the way. Equating 'extreme' with 'primordial' is not supported by history."

Often, shared traits are a sign of shared heritage—racial heritage. "Shared traits are not random," says Alice Brues, an anthropologist at the University of Colorado. "Within a continent, you of course have a number of variants [on basic traits], but some are characteristic of the larger area, too. So it's natural to look for these major divisions. It simplifies your thinking." A wide distribution of traits, however, makes them suspect as evidence of a shared heritage. The dark skin of Somalis and Ghanaians, for instance, indicates that they evolved under the same elective force (a sunny climate). But that's all it shows. It does *not* show that they are any more closely related, in the sense of sharing more genes, than either is to Greeks. Calling Somalis and Ghanaians "black" therefore sheds no further light on their evolutionary history and implies—wrongly—that they are more closely related to each other than either is to someone of a different "race." Similarly, the long noses of North Africans and northern Europeans reveal that they evolved in dry or cold climates (the nose moistens air before the air reaches the lungs, and longer noses moisten more air). The tall, thin bodies of Kenya's Masai evolved to dissipate heat; Eskimos evolved short, squat bodies to retain it. Calling these peoples "different races" adds nothing to that understanding.

Where did the three standard racial divisions come from? They entered the social, and scientific, consciousness during the Age of Exploration. Loring Brace doesn't think it's a coincidence that the standard races represent peoples who, as he puts it, "lived at the end of the Europeans' trade routes"—in Africa and China—in the days after Prince Henry the Navigator set sail. Before Europeans took to the seas, there was little perception of races. If villagers began to look different to an Englishman riding a horse from France to Italy and on to Greece, the change was too subtle to inspire notions of races. But if the English sailor left Lisbon Harbor and dropped anchor off the Kingdom of Niger, people looked so different he felt compelled to invent a scheme to explain the world—and, perhaps, distance himself from the Africans.

This habit of sorting the world's peoples into a small number of groups got its first scientific gloss from Swedish taxonomist Carolus Linnaeus. (Linnaeus is best known for his system of classifying living things by genus and species—*Escherichia coli, Homo sapiens* and the rest.) In 1758 he declared that humanity falls into four races: white (Europeans), red (Native Americans), dark (Asians), and black (Africans). Linnaeus said that Native Americans (who in the 1940s got grouped with Asians) were ruled by custom. Africans were indolent and negligent, and Europeans were inventive and gentle, said Linnaeus. Leave aside the racist undertones (not to mention the oddity of ascribing gentleness to the group that perpetrated the Crusades and Inquisition): that alone should not undermine its validity. More worrisome is that the notion and the specifics of race predate genetics, evolutionary biology and the science of human origins. With the revolutions in those fields, how is it that the 18th-century scheme of race retains its powerful hold? Consider these arguments:

• **If I parachute into Nairobi, I know I'm not in Oslo:** Colorado's Alice Brues uses this image to argue that denying the reality of race flies in the face of common sense. But the parachutists, if they were familiar with the great range of human diversity, could also tell that they were in Nairobi rather than Abidjan—east Africans don't look much like west Africans. They could also tell they were in Istanbul rather than Oslo, even though Turks and Norwegians are both called Caucasian.

• **DOA, male, 58119 . . . black:** When U.S. police call in a forensic anthropologist to identify the race of a skeleton, the scientist comes through 80 to 85 percent of the time. If race has no biological validity, how can the sleuths get it right so often? The forensic anthropologist could, with enough information about bone structure and genetic markers, identify the region from which the corpse came—south and west Africa, Southeast Asia and China, Northern and Western Europe. It just so happens that the police would call corpses from the first two countries black, from the middle two Asian, and the last pair white. But lumping these six distinct populations into three groups of two serves no biological purpose, only a social convention. The larger grouping may reflect how society views humankind's diversity, but does not explain it.

• **African-Americans have more hypertension:** If race is not real, how can researchers say that blacks have higher rates of infant mortality, lower rates of osteoporosis and a higher incidence of hypertension? Because a social construct can have biological effects, says epidemiologist Robert Hahn of the U.S. Centers for Disease Control and Prevention. Consider hypertension among African-Americans. Roughly 34 percent have high blood pressure, compared with about 16 percent of whites. But William Dressler finds the greatest incidence of hypertension among blacks who are upwardly mobile achievers. "That's probably because in mundane interactions, from the bank to the grocery store, they are treated in ways that do not coincide with their self-image as respectable achievers," says Dressler, an anthropologist at the University of Alabama. "And the upwardly mobile are more likely to encounter discriminatory white culture." Lab studies show that stressful situations—like being followed in grocery stores as if you were a shoplifter—elevate blood pressure and lead to vascular changes that cause hypertension. "In this case, race captures social factors such as the experience of discrimination," says sociologist David Williams of the University of Michigan. Further evidence that hypertension has more to do with society than with biology: black Africans have among the lowest rates of hypertension in the world.

If race is not a biological explanation of hypertension, can it offer a biological explanation of something as complex as intelligence? Psychologists are among the strongest proponents of retaining the three conventional racial categories. It organizes and explains their data in the most parsimonious way, as Charles Murray and Richard Herrnstein argue in "The Bell Curve." But anthropologists say that such conclusions are built on a foundation of sand. If nothing else, argues Brace, every ethnic group evolved under conditions where intelligence was a requirement for survival. If there are intelligence "genes," they must be in all ethnic groups equally: differences in intelligence must be a cultural and social artifact.

Scientists who doubt the biological meaningfulness of race are not nihilists. They just prefer another way of capturing, and explaining, the great diversity of humankind. Even today most of the world's peoples marry within their own group. Intramarriage preserves features—fleshy lips, small ears, wide-set eyes—that arose by a chance genetic mutation long ago. Grouping people by geographic origins—better known as ethnicity—"is more correct both in a statistical sense and in under-standing the history of human variation," says Hampshire's Goodman. Ethnicity also serves as a proxy for differences—from diet to a history of discrimination—that can have real biological and behavioral effects.

In a 1942 book, anthropologist Ashley Montagu called race "Man's Most Dangerous Myth." If it is, then our most ingenuous myth must be that we sort humankind into groups in order to understand the meaning and origin of humankind's diversity. That isn't the reason at all; a greater number of smaller groupings, like ethnicities, does a better job. The obsession with broad categories is so powerful as to seem a neurological imperative. Changing our thinking about race will require a revolution in thought as profound, and profoundly unsettling, as anything science has ever demanded. What these researchers are talking about is changing the way in which we see the world—and each other. But before that can happen, we must do more than understand the biologist's suspicions about race. We must ask science, also, why it is that we are so intent on sorting humanity into so few groups—us and Other—in the first place.

Shelby Steele

Shelby Steele, a research fellow at the Hoover Institution, was educated at Coe College, Southern Illinois University, and the University of Utah. In 1990 one of his books, The Content of Our Character: A New Vision of Race in America, *was awarded the National Book Critics Circle Award for nonfiction. His most recent book is* A Dream Deferred: The Second Betrayal of Black Freedom in America. *Steele publishes widely in major journals, including* The New York Times *and (the source of the following article)* Time *magazine.*

Hailing While Black

IN MANHATTAN RECENTLY I ATTEMPTED SOMETHING THAT is thought to be all but impossible for a black man: I tried to hail a cab going uptown toward Harlem after dark. And I'll admit to feeling a new nervousness. This simple action—black man hailing cab—is now a tableau in America's ongoing culture war. If no cab swerves in to pick me up, America is still a racist country, and the entire superstructure of contemporary liberalism is bolstered. If I catch a ride, conservatives can breath easier. So, as I raise my hand and step from the curb, much is at stake.

It's all the talk these days of racial profiling that has set off my nerves in this way. Having grown up in the era of segregation, I know I can survive the racial profiling of a cabby. What makes me most nervous is the anxiety that I have wrongly estimated the degree of racism in American life. I am a conservative. But conservatism is a misunderstood identity in blacks that would be much easier to carry in a world where New York City cab drivers stopped for black fares, even after dark.

It is easy to believe that racial profiling is a serious problem in America. It fits the American profile, and now politicians have stepped forward to give it credence as a problem. But is it a real problem? Is dark skin a shorthand for criminality in the mind of America's law-enforcement officers? Studies show that we blacks are stopped in numbers higher than our percentage in the population but lower than our documented involvement in crime. If you're trying to measure racism, isn't it better to compare police stops to actual black involvement in crime than to the mere representation of blacks in the population? The elephant in the living room—and the tragedy in black America—is that we commit crimes vastly out of proportion to our numbers in society.

But I can already hear "so what?" from those who believe profiling is a serious problem. And I know that the more energetic among them will move numbers and points of reference around like shells in a shill game to show racism. In other words, racial profiling is now an "identity" issue like affirmative action, black reparations or even O.J.'s innocence. It is less a real issue than a coded argument over how much racism exists in society today. We argue these issues fiercely—make a culture war around them—because the moral authority of both the left and right political identities hangs in the balance.

Racial profiling is a boon to the left because this political identity justifies its demand for power by estimating racism to be high. The more racism, the more power the left demands for social interventions that go beyond simple fairness under the law. Profiling hurts the right because it makes its fairness-under-the-law position on race seem inadequate, less than moral considering the prevalence of racism. The real debate over racial profiling is not about stops and searches on the New Jersey Turnpike. It is about the degree of racism in America and the distribution of power it justifies.

Even as individuals, we Americans cannot define our political and moral identities without making them accountable to an estimate of racism's potency in American life. Our liberalism or conservatism, our faith in government intervention or restraint and our concept of social responsibility on issues from diversity to school reform—all these will be, in part, a response to how bad we think racism is. The politically liberal identity I was born into began to fade as my estimate of American racism declined. I could identify with a wider range of American ideas and possibilities when I thought they were no longer tainted by racism. Many whites I know today, who are trying to separate themselves from the shame of America's racist past, will overestimate racism to justify a liberal identity that they hope proves that separateness. First the estimation, then the identity.

Recently, after a talk on a college campus, a black girl stood up and told me that she was "frequently" stopped by police while driving in this bucolic and liberal college town. A professor on the same campus told me that blacks there faced an "unwelcome atmosphere"—unwelcomeness being a newly fashionable estimation of racism's potency on college campuses today. Neither of these people offered supporting facts. But I don't think they were lying so much as "spinning" an estimation of racism that shored up their political identities.

We are terrible at discussing our racial problems in America today because we just end up defending our identities and the political power we hope those identities will align us with. On that day in Manhattan, I caught the first cab that came along. And I should have been happy just for the convenience of good service. That I also saw this minor event as evidence of something, that I was practicing a kind of political sociology as well as catching a cab—that is the problem.

Stanley Crouch

Stanley Crouch, born in Los Angeles in 1945, is a playwright, actor, drummer and band leader, and author of several books of social criticism in which he explores such topics as feminism, black power, and the films of Spike Lee. In his early years he was a black nationalist, but he is now regarded as conservative—though his essays almost always contain surprises even for readers who think they are familiar with his work.

Race Is Over

Even though error, chance and ambition are at the nub of the human future, I am fairly sure that race, as we currently obsess over it, will cease to mean as much 100 years from today. The reasons are basic— some technological, others cultural. We all know that electronic media have broken down many barriers, that they were even central to the fall of the Soviet Union because satellite dishes made it impossible for the Government to control images and ideas about life outside the country. People there began to realize how far behind they were from the rest of the modern world. The international flow of images and information will continue to make for a greater and greater swirl of influences. It will increasingly change life on the globe and also change our American sense of race.

In our present love of the mutually exclusive, and our pretense that we are something less than a culturally miscegenated people, we forget our tendency to seek out the exotic until it becomes a basic cultural taste, the way pizza or sushi or tacos have become ordinary fare. This approach guarantees that those who live on this soil a century from now will see and accept many, many manifestations of cultural mixings and additions.

In that future, definition by racial, ethnic and sexual groups will most probably have ceased to be the foundation of special-interest power. Ten decades up the road, few people will take seriously, accept or submit to any forms of segregation that are marching under the intellectually ragged flag of "diversity." The idea that your background will determine your occupation, taste, romantic preference or any other thing will dissolve in favor of your perceived identity as defined by your class, livelihood and cultural preferences. Americans of the future will find themselves surrounded in every direction by people who are part Asian, part Latin, part African, part European, part American Indian. What such people will look like is beyond my imagination, but the sweep of body types, combinations of facial features, hair textures, eye colors and what are now unexpected skin tones will be far more common, primarily because the current paranoia over mixed marriages should by then be largely a superstition of the past.

In his essay "The Little Man at Chehaw Station," Ralph Ellison described a young "light-skinned, blue-eyed, Afro-American-featured individual who could have been taken for anything from a sun-tinged white Anglo-Saxon, an Egyptian, or a mixed-breed American Indian. . . . " He used the young man as an example of our central problem—"the challenge of arriving at an adequate definition of American cultural identity. . . . " While the youth's feet and legs were covered by riding boots and breeches, he wore a multicolored dashiki and "a black homburg hat tilted at a jaunty angle." For Ellison, "his clashing of styles nevertheless sounded an integrative, vernacular tone, an American compulsion to improvise upon the given."

The vernacular tone Ellison wrote of is what makes us improvise   5
upon whatever we actually like about one another, no matter how we might pretend we feel about people who are superficially different. Furthermore, the social movements of minorities and women have greatly aided our getting beyond the always culturally inaccurate idea that the United States is "a white man's country."

We sometimes forget how much the Pilgrims learned from the American Indians, or look at those lessons in only the dullest terms of exploitation, not as a fundamental aspect of our American identity. We forget that by the time James Fenimore Cooper was inventing his back-woodsmen, there were white men who had lived so closely to the land and to the American Indian that the white man was, often quite proudly, a cultural mulatto. We forget that we could not have had the cowboy without the

Mexican vaquero. We don't know that our most original art-music, jazz, is a combination of African, European and Latin elements. Few people are aware that when the Swiss psychoanalyst Carl Jung came to this country he observed that white people walked, talked and laughed like Negroes. He also reported that the two dominant figures in the dreams of his white American patients were the Negro and the American Indian.

Are we destined to become one bland nation of interchangeables? I do not think so. What will fall away over the coming decades, I believe, is our present tendency to mistake something borrowed for something ethnically "authentic." Regions will remain regions and within them we will find what we always find: variations on the overall style and pulsation. As the density of cross-influences progresses, we will get far beyond the troubles the Census Bureau now has with racial categories, which are growing because we are so hung up on the barbed wire of tribalism and because we fear absorption, or "assimilation." We look at so-called "assimilation" as some form of oppression, some loss of identity, even a way of "selling out." In certain cases and at certain times, that may have been more than somewhat true. If you didn't speak with a particular command of the language—or at a subdued volume—you might have been dismissed as crude. If you hadn't been educated in what were considered the "right places," you were seen as some sort of a peasant.

But anyone who has observed the dressing, speaking and dancing styles of Americans since 1960 can easily recognize the sometimes startling influences that run from the top to the bottom, the bottom to the top. Educated people of whatever ethnic group use slang and terms scooped out from the disciplines of psychology, economics and art criticism. In fact, one of the few interesting things about the rap idiom is that some rappers pull together a much richer vocabulary than has ever existed in black pop music, while peppering it to extremes with repulsive vulgarity.

One hundred years from today, Americans are likely to look back on the ethnic difficulties of our time as quizzically as we look at earlier periods of human history, when misapprehension defined the reality. There will still be squabbling, and those who supposedly speak in the interest of one group or another will hector the gullible into some kind of self-obsession that will influence the local and national dialogues. But those squabbles are basic to upward mobility and competition. It is the very nature of upward mobility and competition to ease away superficial distinctions in the interest of getting the job done. We already see this in the integration of the workplace, in the rise of women and in the increase of corporations that grant spousal-equivalent benefits to homosexuals because they want to keep their best workers, no matter what they do privately as consenting adults. In the march of the world economy, the imbalances that result from hysterical xenophobia will largely melt away because Americans will be far too busy standing up to the challenges of getting as many international customers for their wares as they can. That is, if they're lucky.

Edward Rothstein

Edward Rothstein writes regularly for The New York Times, *where this article appeared, on December 14, 1997.*

Ethnicity and Disney: It's a Whole New Myth

In Julie Taymor's triumphant Broadway reinterpretation of the Walt Disney Company's "Lion King," the movie's shamanesque baboon, Rafiki, is transmuted into a Zulu-chanting priestess, an African griot-storyteller, hooting and hollering, grunting knowingly and guiding the young lion Simba to his destiny. In the show, Rafiki is thrust to the story's center, just as the generic African background of the animated feature film is thrust into the foreground by Ms. Taymor, with muscular dance and music, ritualistic images and carnivalesque ensemble pieces.

With this new ethnic emphasis, Rafiki's closest Disney ancestor may be James Baskett, who starred as the black plantation-style story-teller Uncle Remus in "Song of the South" 51 years ago. That film has never been released on video and probably never will be (it is available only on laser disk from Japan). In it, Mr. Baskett, whose voice was known from the "Amos 'n' Andy" radio show, charmed the movie's post-Reconstruction Southern children with Joel Chandler Harris's vernacular tales of Brer Rabbit and Brer Fox. His performance won him a special Oscar, but the charm had its limits. *The New Yorker* said that the film consisted of "the purest sheep-dip about happy days on the old plantation." Adam Clayton Powell Jr. said it was an "insult to American minorities" and to "everything that America as a whole stands for."

The ethnic romance of the Broadway "Lion King," with its mixture of Zulu chant and songs by Elton John and Tim Rice, might also have turned into caricature. But it was saved by Ms. Taymor's genius, along with something else: the show's attitude toward ethnicity is not patronizing because ethnicity is no longer being treated as the mark of an outsider. Instead, ethnicity defines a society itself.

This represents a major change in the Disney vision of ethnicity, which is no small matter. Disney films may be the only cultural experience shared by American children, while ethnicity and race are probably the most charged words in American politics.

Ethnically defined characters have been a crucial part of Disney films   5
for many years, both before Walt Disney died in 1966 and after. These
characters include the broadly sketched black-American crows of
"Dumbo" (1941) singing "I be done seen 'bout everything"; the alley cats
of "Aristocats" (1970), who break out into an infectious jazz rendition of
"Ev'rybody Wants to Be a Cat," led by the voice of Scatman Crothers; and
Sebastian the crab in "The Little Mermaid" (1989), sung by Samuel E.
Wright, who gives advice to a calypso beat ("Go on and kiss the girl").
Isn't there also a hint of caricature of black Americans when the Ape King
in "The Jungle Book" (1967) yearns to learn the secret of civilization and
sings (in the voice of Louis Prima), "I wan'na be like you"?

And not just black culture has preoccupied the Disney empire.
Throughout the films—pre-Walt and post, animated and live action—ethnic types abound, sometimes associated with national caricatures and
even social class. "The Three Caballeros" (1945) is a veritable tour of Latin
American stereotypes. "Peter Pan" (1953) has an "Injun" powwow,
"Pocahontas" (1995) an American Indian potlatch. In "Mary Poppins"
(1964), the middle-class Banks family comes up against the Cockney
chimney sweep Bert. "Aladdin" (1992) offended some viewers with its
references to Arab culture. "The Hunchback of Notre-Dame" (1996) has
the magically beguiling Gypsy Esmeralda.

Why is ethnicity so central to the Disney oeuvre? The word ethnic,
which comes from the Greek word ethnos, meaning heathen or pagan, is
a title given to an outsider and implies condescension: the ethnic heathen
has rejected the civilized mainstream and has also been rejected by it.
And the Disney ethnic character has tended to be interpreted as evidence
of racism and insularity shared by Walt Disney and generations of Disney
animators, writers and directors.

But while American racial attitudes have changed dramatically over
the course of Disney history, the nature of the Disney view of ethnicity
has been remarkably consistent until recently. And despite whiffs of condescension (and rare mean-spiritedness, as in the portrait of the Siamese
cats in "Lady and the Tramp" in 1955), the ethnic character is treated with
unusual affection. The Disney ethnic characters are loaded down by
cliché—in accent, character and mannerism—but are also admired, even
envied (they also get the best songs).

The crows in "Dumbo," for example, are more knowledgeable and
witty than any of the flying elephant's circus colleagues. The alley cats in
"Aristocrats" turn out to be the heroes, possessing far more important
skills than the upper-crust "white" kittens. Esmeralda, the Gypsy of
"Hunchback," comprehends the trials of Quasimodo because of her own
beleaguered ethnic status.

This is no accident. Ethnicity involves complicated relationships be-   10
tween an outsider and a supposed center, between an immigrant and the
mainstream, an aspiring lower class and a complacent middle. And these
relationships are often the very subjects of the films themselves. Disney
movies do not just incorporate ethnicity; they are, in a broad sense, about it.

This is true even if the key characters are not explicitly ethnic. Dumbo is a misfit, Pinocchio a boy without a purpose. Ariel the mermaid is out of place in her underwater world, yearning to be human. In "Beauty and the Beast," Belle is "so different from the rest of us." The outsider—the hunchback, the child, the disenfranchised princess, the beast—struggles to join the center or change it.

Meanwhile, the identifiably ethnic characters aid in those struggles: Geppetto tries to help Pinocchio become a boy; Sebastian helps the little mermaid become human; the dwarfs help Snow White; the inner-city cats help the Aristocats. The typical Disney film presents a joint triumph: the ethnic character ends up becoming mainstream, and the mainstream ends up learning from and accepting the ethnic character.

In this light, the Disney oeuvre seems an embodiment of old-fashioned liberalism, something that seems bizarre given Walt Disney's reputation as a man of the right (any chance of his obtaining true liberal credentials ended with his anti-Communist testimony before the House Un-American Activities Committee in 1947). Still, until the recent past, when their view of ethnicity began to shift, Disney films—reaching back to "Dumbo," and even encompassing the paternalistic "Song of the South"—proclaimed a melting-pot liberalism. The dominant idea was not conformity but mutual accommodation.

Walt Disney's latest biographer, Steven Watts, points out in his forthcoming book, *Magic Kingdom*,[1] that in the 1950s the Disney studios also engaged in an almost radical celebration of American self-reliance. But this tendency, too, became a celebration of the melting pot, in which ethnic characters, like the Mexican-born Zorro, were heroic iconoclasts. In Disneyland, Disney envisioned an idealized America that incorporated exotic lands and foreign climes. Even the star of "The Mickey Mouse Club" on television was the young Italian-American Annette Funicello.

In fact, in contrast with many other popular forms of entertainment, few ethnic characters, even in the early Disney films, are villains. In "Bambi" (1942), which in its eco pieties anticipates "The Lion King," the enemy is man himself, the hunter and fire maker. In "Dumbo" the most unlikable characters are the other elephants, who dislike anyone different from themselves. In "Hunchback," the villain hates Gypsies, the poor and the crippled. Evil is far more often associated with pretense and social climbing than with being ethnically different.

This then was the central myth of the Disney entertainment empire, a variation on the American dream that tapped into children's fantasies and adult political hopes. In a way, it was almost opposite of the grandly popular myths of opera that dominated 19th-century European culture.

15

---

[1] Watts's *Magic Kingdom: Walt Disney and the American Way of Life* was published in 1998.

Opera, like Disney genre films, came into its own with the efforts to create unified nations out of disparate peoples. But in opera, the outsider often threatens the social order and the conflict between the ethnic character (think Carmen) and the mainstream (think Don José) often ended in tragedy. No triumph came without pain and complication. Disney's optimism allowed none of this; the view of society was ethnically rich, but it was a civilization without discontents.

Such optimism couldn't be sustained. In the 90's, the Disney myth started to dissolve leading to a string of meandering, strained films. Ethnicity remained prominent in "Aladdin," as if out of habit, but was unrelated to anything else in the film. "Pocahontas" signaled the first real signs of change, overturning Disney liberalism and exchanging it for assertions of ethnic independence. The film "The Lion King" rejected the Disney myth more completely by focusing on a new notion of ethnicity: its hero was not an outsider yearning to join the center or thriving outside it but a disinherited heir who had to recapture his ethnic kingdom. "The Lion King" is not about accommodation and influence but about ethnic identity.

This means that the outsider is not someone to be admired or learned from, like the Tramp or Uncle Remus or Sebastian. He is a villain who threatens the ethnic future. Scar is literally a heathen, a pagan who rejects the Circle of Life and African animal society; he is portrayed as an ethnic caricature who is really an anti-ethnic. Simba tells Scar he is strange; the villain replies in a precious drawl, "You have no idea."

Partly because the film never makes much of Simba's native culture, the ethnic stakes never seem very high. But Ms. Taymor has fully uncovered the new Disney myth with her production's African-style celebrations and chants. The film's subtext comes to the surface. The ethnic world is being threatened by Scar; it is that world that Simba must preserve by accepting his identity and celebrating its centrality.   20

This transformation of the Disney myth reflects changes in the larger society as well. The melting pot is out; ethnic identity is in. Accommodation is no longer the issue; self-assertion is. But nuance is hardly more plentiful. It will be revealing to see what happens if Disney comes through with its proposed version of Verdi's opera "Aida." That opera focuses on the demands made by ethnic and national identity and their conflicts with personal desire. Private and public clash; tragedy emerges from the fray.

Will Disney allow itself to reveal the dangers behind its new myth? Is there room in the Disney universe for a sense of complication, or even for old-style reconciliation? The issues are not Disney's alone.

⌾ Topics for Critical Thinking and Writing

1. The *Columbia Encyclopedia* article on "Race" (page 382) refers to inappropriate applications of the word "race." What applications does it list as inappropriate? The author also states that "biological criteria of race" cannot "be equated with any mental characteristics such as intelligence, personality, or

character." If, in a conversation, you were to hear an inappropriate use of the word "race," or an equation of race with mental characteristics, what would you do?

2. In "A Note on a Segregated Society" (page 384) President Carter recalls a painful childhood experience. Most of us have had the experience of drifting away from close childhood friends. If you can recall this happening to you, write a brief essay (500 words) describing and explaining your experience, comparing it, if it's helpful, with President Carter's.

3. In "Three Is Not Enough" (page 385) Sharon Begley quotes George Armelagos as saying that race is "a cultural construct" (paragraph 7). What does Armelagos mean? Begley also quotes Robert Hahn (paragraph 14) as saying that "a social construct can have biological effects." What does Hahn mean? What examples of this phenomenon does Begley offer?

4. Shelby Steele in his essay "Hailing While Black" (page 390) refers to "racial profiling." What is "racial profiling"? How does the idea of racial profiling, according to Steele, affect what he calls "the left" and "the right"? Explain Steele's last sentence to someone who has read the article but didn't "get it."

5. In "Race Is Over" (page 392) Stanley Crouch foresees changes in our thinking in 100 years. What changes does he foresee? What, in Crouch's opinion, will cause these changes?

6. Edward Rothstein in "Ethnicity and Disney: It's a Whole New Myth" (page 395) claims that "Disney movies do not just incorporate ethnicity; they are, in a broad sense, about it." What does he mean? Has his article changed your view of Disney movies? To what extent do you agree with him, for example, in his analysis of *The Lion King*?

7. Since the attacks on the World Trade Center and the Pentagon on September 11, 2001, we have heard increasingly of ethnic profiling. How is it similar to and different from racial profiling? Are there occasions when, in your opinion, ethnic profiling is acceptable? Or is it always unacceptable? Explain.

8. The articles in the Casebook on Race define or refer to inappropriate applications of the word race, racial prejudice, and racial profiling. Explain what is meant by each term, and then how they differ.

9. Have you ever been the victim, the perpetrator, or a witness to racial or ethnic profiling or prejudice? If so, in an essay of 750–1000 words, recount the circumstances of the event, and your reaction to it, then and now. Use President Carter's essay or Shelby Steele's as models, if either or both are helpful.

Picturing Identity

John Updike

John Updike, born in 1932, grew up in Shillington, Pennsylvania, where his father was a teacher and his mother was a writer. After receiving a B.A. degree from Harvard he studied drawing at Oxford for a year, but an offer from The New Yorker *magazine brought him back to the United States. He at first served as a reporter for the magazine, but soon began contributing poetry, essays, and fiction. Today he is one of America's most prolific and well-known writers.*

Before the Mirror

How many of us still remember
when Picasso's *Girl Before a Mirror* hung
at the turning of the stairs in the pre-expansion
Museum of Modern Art?
Millions of us, maybe, but we form   5
a dwindling population. Garish
and brush-slashed and yet as balanced
as a cardboard queen in a deck of giant cards,
the painting proclaimed, *Enter here*
and abandon preconception. She bounced   10
the erotic balls of herself back and forth
between reflection and reality.

Now I discover, in the recent retrospective
at the same establishment,
that the dazzling painting dates   15
from March of 1932,
the very month in which I first saw light,
squinting in quick nostalgia for the womb.
Inspecting, I bend closer. The blacks,
the stripy cyanide greens are still uncracked.   20
I note with satisfaction; the cherry reds
and lemon yellows full of childish juice.
No sag, no wrinkle. Fresh as paint. *Back then.*
I reflect, *they knew just how to lay it on.*

Girl Before a Mirror
Pablo Picasso, 1932

Marxism Will Give Health to the Sick
Frida Kahlo, 1954

The Gulf Stream
Winslow Homer, 1899

Self-Portrait
Vincent van Gogh

Nude Descending a Staircase, No. 2
Marcel Duchamp, 1912*

*Marcel Duchamp's *Nude Descending a Staircase, No. 2* (1912) was exhibited in 1913 in the Armory Show, an international exhibition held at an armory in New York, and later in Chicago and Boston. The Armory Show gave America its first good look at contemporary European art, for instance, cubism, which had influenced Duchamp's painting.

Just what is it that makes today's homes so different, so appealing?
Richard Hamilton, 1956

Gold Marilyn Monroe
Andy Warhol, 1962

Two Women Dressing Their Hair
Kitagawa Utamaro*

*Kitagawa Utamaro (1754–1806) lived in Edo (now called Tokyo). He special-
ized in designing pictures of courtesans and actors that were then used to
make woodblock prints. Brothels and the theatre were important parts of
what was called the Floating World, that is, the world of transient pleasure.

Cathy Song

Cathy Song was born in Honolulu in 1952 of a Chinese mother and a Korean father. She holds a bachelor's degree from Wellesley College and a master's degree in creative writing from Boston University. A manuscript that she submitted to the Yale Series of Younger Poets was chosen as the winner and in 1983 was published under the title of Picture Bride.

Beauty and Sadness

for Kitagawa Utamaro

He drew hundreds of women
in studies unfolding
like flowers from a fan.
Teahouse waitresses, actresses,
geishas, courtesans and maids.   5
They arranged themselves
before this quick, nimble man
whose invisible presence
one feels in these prints
is as delicate   10
as the skinlike paper
he used to transfer
and retain their fleeting loveliness.

Crouching like cats,
they purred amid the layers of kimono   15
swirling around them
as though they were bathing
in a mountain pool with irises
growing in the silken sunlit water.
Or poised like porcelain vases,   20
slender, erect and tall; their heavy
brocaded hair was piled high
with sandalwood combs and blossom sprigs
poking out like antennae.
They resembled beautiful iridescent insects,   25
creatures from a floating world.

Utamaro absorbed these women of Edo
in their moments of melancholy
He captured the wisp of shadows,   30

the half-draped body
emerging from a bath; whatever
skin was exposed
was powdered white as snow.
A private space disclosed.   35
Portraying another girl
catching a glimpse of her own vulnerable
face in the mirror, he transposed
the trembling plum lips
like a drop of blood   40
soaking up the white expanse of paper.

At times, indifferent to his inconsolable
eye, the women drifted
through the soft gray feathered light,
maintaining stillness, the moments in between.   45
Like the dusty ash-winged moths
that cling to the screens in summer
and that the Japanese venerate
as ancestors reincarnated;
Utamaro graced these women with immortality   50
in the thousand sheaves of prints
fluttering into the reverent hands of keepers:
the dwarfed and bespectacled painter
holding up to a square of sunlight
what he had carried home beneath his coat   55
one afternoon in winter.

Topics for Critical Thinking and Writing

1. Do pictures have "meanings," or should we simply enjoy looking, and not try to interpret? For instance, do you think Winslow Homer in *The Gulf Stream* (page 403) is making some sort of statement about the relationship between human beings and nature, or about persons of color? Similarly, is Picasso, in his picture of a woman looking into a mirror (pag 401), saying something about vanity, or mortality, or . . . ? If you think many famous paintings do not have meanings, do you think viewers should simply enjoy the patterns and colors, and not fret about interpreting the picture? Explain.

2. The paintings by Kahlo (page 402) and van Gogh (page 404) are both self-portraits. What sort of "self" does each artist depict? If you could paint a self-portrait, what "self" would you want to convey? Do you in fact have a self, or rather, do you have several or even many selves?

3. Most of these pictures are not realisitc; they could not possibly be confused with photographs. Take, for instance, the pictures by Hamilton (page 406)—

even though this image does include photographs—and Utamaro (page 408). What is the point of artistic distortion? Why shouldn't artists aim to depict things as we see them?

4. The first twelve lines of Updike's poem (page 400) describe the speaker's thoughts "then," when he first saw Picasso's picture, and the last twelve lines describe his ideas "now." In two paragrahs, or in one extended paragraph, write a "Then and Now," describing a picture, a song, or a scene (a lake, a house, a kitchen, a person) then and now.

5. Invent a dialogue (about two double-spaced typed pages) between any two of these artists, in which they discuss the nature of painting. Among the issues you may have them discuss are (a) their intentions when they paint and (b) the functions of pictures.

6. If one of these pictures especially appeals to you, explain why (in an essay of 500 words). You may want to structure your essay as a comparison, contrasting your favorite image with your least favorite image.

CHAPTER 10

Teaching and Learning

Blackboard
Winslow Homer, 1877

The Lesson—Planning a Career
Ron James, 1963

Knowledge is power.
> *Francis Bacon*

Hard students are commonly troubled with gouts, catarrahs, rheums, cachexia, bradypepsia, bad eyes, stone, and collick, crudities, oppilations, vertigo, winds, consumptions, and all such diseases as come by over-much sitting: they are most part lean, dry, ill-colored . . . and all through immoderate pains and extraordinary studies.
> *Robert Burton*

In my opinion, the only justification for high schools is as therapeutic halfway houses for the deranged. Normal adolescents can find themselves and grow further only by coping with the jobs, sex, and chances of the real world—it is useless to feed them curricular imitations. I would simply abolish the high schools, substituting apprenticeships and other alternatives and protecting the young from gross exploitation by putting the school money directly in their pockets. The very few who have authentic scholarly interests will gravitate to their own libraries, teachers, and academies, as they always did in the past, when they could afford it. In organic communities, adolescents cluster together in their own youth houses, for their fun and games and loud music, without bothering sober folk. I see no reason whatsoever for adults to set up or direct such nests or to be there at all unless invited.
> *Paul Goodman*

I can judge one of the main effects of personal grading by the attitudes of students who land in my remedial course in college. They hate and fear writing more than anything else they have had to do in school. If they see a blank sheet of paper on which they are expected to write something, they look as though they want to scream. Apparently they have never written anything that anyone thought was good. At least, no one ever told them that anything in their writing was good. All their teachers looked for were mistakes, and there are so many kinds of mistakes in writing that their students despair of ever learning to avoid them.

The attitude toward writing that these students have developed is well illustrated by a story told by the Russian writer Chekhov about a kitten that was given to his uncle. The uncle wanted to make the kitten a champion killer of mice, so while it was still very young, he showed it a live mouse in a cage. Since the kitten's hunt-

ing instinct had not yet developed, it examined the mouse curiously but without any hostility. The uncle wanted to teach it that such fraternizing with the enemy was wrong, so he slapped the kitten, scolded it, and sent it away in disgrace. The next day the same mouse was shown to the kitten again. This time the kitten regarded it rather fearfully but without any aggressive intent. Again the uncle slapped it, scolded it, and sent it away. This treatment went on day after day. After some time, as soon as the kitten saw or smelled that mouse, it screamed and tried to climb up the walls. At that point the uncle lost patience and gave the kitten away, saying that it was stupid and would never learn. Of course the kitten had learned perfectly, and had learned exactly what it had been taught, but unfortunately not what the uncle intended to teach. "I can sympathize with that kitten," says Chekhov, "because that same uncle tried to teach me Latin."
> *Paul B. Diederich*

A woman came to Rabbi Israel, the great maggid or teacher in Koznitz, and told him, with many tears, that she had been married a dozen years and still had not borne a son. "What are you willing to do about it?" he asked her. She did not know what to say. "My mother," so the maggid told her, "was aging and still had no child. Then she heard that the holy Baal Shem was stopping over in Apt in the course of a journey. She hurried to his inn and begged him to pray she might bear a son. 'What are you willing to do about it?' he asked. 'My husband is a poor book-binder,' she replied, 'but I do have one fine thing that I shall give to the rabbi.' She went home as fast as she could and fetched her good cape, her 'Katinka,' which was carefully stowed away in a chest. But when she returned to the inn with it, she heard that the Baal Shem had already left for Mezbizh. She immediately set out after him and since she had no money to ride, she walked from town to town with her 'Katinka' until she came to Mezbizh. The Baal Shem took the cape and hung it on the wall. 'It is well,' he said. My mother walked all the way back, from town to town, until she reached Apt. A year later, I was born."

"I, too," cried the woman, "will bring you a cape of mine so that I may get a son."

"That won't work," said the maggid. "You heard the story. My mother had no story to go by."
> *Hasidic Tale*

You go to a great school not for knowledge so much as for arts and habits; for the habit of attention, for the art of expression, for the art of assuming at a moment's notice a new intellectual posture, for the art of entering quickly into another person's thought, for the habit of submitting to censure and refutation, for the art of indicating assent or dissent in graduated terms, for the habit of regarding minute points of accuracy, for the habit of working out what is possible in a given time, for taste, for discrimination, for mental courage and mental soberness. Above all, you go to a great school for self-knowledge.

William Cory

How people keep correcting us when we are young! There's always some bad habit or other they tell us we ought to get over. Yet most bad habits are tools to help us through life.

Johann Wolfgang von Goethe

Supposing anyone were to suggest that the best results for the individual and society could be derived through compulsory feeding, would not the most ignorant rebel against such a stupid procedure? And yet the stomach has far greater adaptability to almost any situation than the brain. With all that, we find it quite natural to have compulsory mental feeding.

Indeed, we actually consider ourselves superior to other nations, because we have evolved a compulsory brain tube through which, for a certain number of hours every day, and for so many years, we can force into the child's mind a large quantity of mental nutrition.

. . . The great harm done by our system of education is not so much that it teaches nothing worth knowing, that it helps to perpetuate privileged classes, that it assists them in the criminal procedure of robbing and exploiting the masses; the harm of the system lies in its boastful proclamation that it stands for true education, thereby enslaving the masses a great deal more than could an absolute ruler.

Emma Goldman

The education of women should always be relative to that of men. To please, to be useful to us, to make us love and esteem them, to educate us when young, to take care of us when grown up; to advise, to console us, to render our lives easy and agreeable. These are the duties of women at all times, and what they should be taught in their infancy.

Jean-Jacques Rousseau

If Johnny can't learn because he is hungry, that's the fault of poverty. But if Johnny can't pay attention because he is sleepy, that's the fault of parents.

What does it matter if we have a new book or an old book, if
we open neither?
        Jesse Jackson

Universities are, of course, hostile to geniuses.
        Ralph Waldo Emerson

The man who can make hard things easy is the educator.
        Ralph Waldo Emerson

It is perhaps idle to wonder what, from my present point of view,
would have been an ideal education. If I could provide such a curriculum for my own children they, in their turn, might find it all a
bore. But the fantasy of what I would have liked to learn as a child
may be revealing, since I feel unequipped by education for problems that lie outside the cloistered, literary domain in which I am
competent and at home. Looking back, then, I would have
arranged for myself to be taught survival techniques for both natural and urban wildernesses. I would want to have been instructed
in self-hypnosis, in aikido (the esoteric and purely self-defensive
style of judo), in elementary medicine, in sexual hygiene, in vegetable gardening, in astronomy, navigation, and sailing; in cookery
and clothesmaking, in metalwork and carpentry, in drawing and
painting, in printing and typography, in botany and biology, in op-
tics and acoustics, in semantics and psychology, in mysticism and
yoga, in electronics and mathematical fantasy, in drama and dancing, in singing and in playing an instrument by ear; in wandering,
in advanced daydreaming, in prestidigitation, in techniques of escape from bondage, in disguise, in conversation with birds and
beasts, in ventriloquism, in French and German conversation, in
planetary history, in morphology, and in classical Chinese. Actually, the main thing left out of my education was a proper love for
my own body, because one feared to cherish anything so obviously
mortal and prone to sickness.
        Alan Watts

Education! Which of the various me's do you propose to educate,
and which do you propose to suppress?
        D. H. Lawrence

Think about the kind of world you want to live and work in.
What do you need to know to build the world? Demand that your
teachers teach you that.
        Prince Kropotkin

The entire object of true education is to make people not merely do the right things, but enjoy the right things.
John Ruskin

Learning without thought is labor lost; thought without learning is dangerous.
Confucius

Nan-in, a Japanese master during the Meiji era (1868–1912), received a university professor who came to inquire about Zen.

Nan-in served tea. He poured his visitor's cup full, and then kept on pouring.

The professor watched the overflow until he no longer could restrain himself. "It is overfull. No more will go in!"

"Like this cup," Nan-in said, "you are full of your own opinions and speculations. How can I show you Zen unless you first empty your cup?"
Anonymous Zen Anecdote

I think [Raymond Weaver] first attracted my attention as someone worth watching when, while we were both new instructors, I heard from a bewildered freshman about the quiz he had just given. The first question written on the blackboard was, "Which of the required readings in this course did you find least interesting?" Then, after members of the class had had ten minutes in which to expatiate on what was certainly to many a congenial topic, he wrote the second question: "To what defect in yourself do you attribute this lack of interest?"
Joseph Wood Krutch

It is not sufficiently understood that a child's education should include at least a rudimentary grasp of religion, sex, and money. Without a basic knowledge of these three primary facts in a normal human being's life—subjects which stir the emotions, create events and opportunities, and if they do not wholly decide must greatly influence an individual's personality—no human being's education can have a safe foundation.
Phyllis Bottome

Plato

Plato (427–347 BC), born in Athens, the son of an aristocratic family, wrote thirty dialogues in which Socrates is the chief speaker. Socrates, about twenty-five years older than Plato, was a philosopher who called himself a gadfly to Athenians. For his efforts at stinging them into thought the Athenians executed him in 399 BC. "The Myth of the Cave" is the beginning of Book VII of Plato's dialogue entitled The Republic. *Socrates is talking with Glaucon.*

For Plato, true knowledge is philosophic insight or awareness of the Good, not mere opinion or the knack of getting along in this world by remembering how things have usually worked in the past. To illustrate his idea that awareness of the Good is different from the ability to recognize the things of this shabby world, Plato (through his spokesman Socrates) resorts to an allegory: men imprisoned in a cave see on a wall in front of them the shadows or images of objects that are really behind them, and they hear echoes, not real voices. (The shadows are caused by the light from a fire behind the objects, and the echoes by the cave's acoustical properties.) The prisoners, unable to perceive the real objects and the real voices, mistakenly think that the shadows and the echoes are real, and some of them grow highly adept at dealing with this illusory world. Were Plato writing today, he might have made the cave a movie theater: we see on the screen in front of us images caused by an object (film, passing in front of light) that is behind us. Moreover, the film itself is an illusory image, for it bears only the traces of a yet more real world—the world that was photographed—outside of the movie theater. And when we leave the theater to go into the real world, our eyes have become so accustomed to the illusory world that we at first blink with discomfort—just as Plato's freed prisoners do when they move out of the cave—at the real world of bright day, and we long for the familiar darkness. So too, Plato suggests, dwellers in ignorance may prefer the familiar shadows of their unenlightened world ("the world of becoming") to the bright world of the eternal Good ("the world of being") that education reveals.

We have just used the word education. You will notice that the first sentence in the translation (by Benjamin Jowett) says that the myth will show "how far our nature is enlightened or unenlightened." In the original Greek the words here translated enlightened *and* unenlightened *are* paideia *and* apaideusia. *No translation can fully catch the exact meanings of these elusive words. Depending on the context,* paideia *may be translated as* enlightenment, education, civilization, culture, knowledge of the good.

The Myth of the Cave

And now, I said, let me show in a figure how far our nature is enlightened or unenlightened—Behold! human beings living in an underground den, which has a mouth open toward the light and reaching all along the den; here they have been from their childhood, and have their legs and necks chained so that they cannot move, and can only see before them, being prevented by the chains from turning round their heads. Above and behind them a fire is blazing at a distance, and between the fire and the prisoners there is a raised way; and you will see, if you look, a low wall built along the way, like the screen which marionette players have in front of them, over which they show the puppets.

I see.

And do you see, I said, men passing along the wall carrying all sorts of vessels, and statues and figures of animals made of wood and stone and various materials, which appear over the wall? Some of them are talking, others silent.

You have shown me a strange image, and they are strange prisoners.

Like ourselves, I replied; and they see only their own shadows, or the 5
shadows of one another, which the fire throws on the opposite wall of the
cave?

True, he said; how could they see anything but the shadows if they
were never allowed to move their heads?

And of the objects which are being carried in like manner they would
only see the shadows?

Yes, he said.

And if they were able to converse with one another, would they not
suppose that they were naming what was actually before them?

Very true. 10

And suppose further that the prison had an echo which came from
the other side, would they not be sure when one of the passerby spoke
that the voice which they heard came from the passing shadow?

No question, he replied.

To them, I said, the truth would be literally nothing but the shadows
of the images.

That is certain.

And now look again, and see what will naturally follow if the prison- 15
ers are released and disabused of their error. At first, when any of them is
liberated and compelled suddenly to stand up and turn his neck round
and walk and look toward the light, he will suffer sharp pains; the glare
will distress him, and he will be unable to see the realities of which in his
former state he had seen the shadows; and then conceive some one saying
to him, that what he saw before was an illusion, but that now, when he is
approaching nearer to being and his eye is turned toward more real existence, he has a clearer vision—what will be his reply? And you may further imagine that his instructor is pointing to the objects as they pass and
requiring him to name them—will he not be perplexed? Will he not fancy
that the shadows which he formerly saw are truer than the objects which
are now shown to him?

Far truer.

And if he is compelled to look straight at the light, will he not have a
pain in his eyes which will make him turn away to take refuge in the objects of vision which he can see, and which he will conceive to be in reality clearer than the things which are now being shown to him?

True, he said.

And suppose once more, that he is reluctantly dragged up a steep
and rugged ascent, and held fast until he is forced into the presence of the
sun himself, is he not likely to be pained and irritated? When he approaches the light his eyes will be dazzled, and he will not be able to see
anything at all of what are now called realities.

Not all in a moment, he said. 20

He will require to grow accustomed to the sight of the upper world.
And first he will see the shadows best, next the reflections of men and

other objects in the water, and then the objects themselves; then he will gaze upon the light of the moon and the stars and the spangled heaven; and he will see the sky and the stars by night better than the sun or the light of the sun by day?

Certainly.

Last of all he will be able to see the sun, and not mere reflections of him in the water, but he will see him in his own proper place, and not in another; and he will contemplate him as he is.

Certainly.

He will then proceed to argue that this is he who gives the season and the years, and is the guardian of all that is in the visible world, and in a certain way the cause of all things which he and his fellows have been accustomed to behold?

25

Clearly, he said, he would first see the sun and then reason about him.

And when he remembered his old habitation, and the wisdom of the den and his fellow-prisoners, do you not suppose that he would felicitate himself on the change, and pity them?

Certainly, he would.

And if they were in the habit of conferring honors among themselves on those who were quickest to observe the passing shadows and to remark which of them went before, and which followed after, and which were together; and who were therefore best able to draw conclusions as to the future, do you think that he would care for such honors and glories, or envy the possessors of them? Would he not say with Homer,

Better to be the poor servant of a poor master,

and to endure anything, rather than think as they do and live after their manner?

Yes, he said, I think that he would rather suffer anything than entertain these false notions and live in this miserable manner.

30

Imagine once more, I said, such an one coming suddenly out of the sun to be replaced in his old situation; would he not be certain to have his eyes full of darkness?

To be sure, he said.

And if there were a contest, and he had to compete in measuring the shadows with the prisoners who had never moved out of the den, while his sight was still weak, and before his eyes had become steady (and the time which would be needed to acquire this new habit of sight might be very considerable), would he not be ridiculous? Men would say of him that up he went and down he came without his eyes; and that it was better not even to think of ascending; and if any one tried to loose another and lead him up to the light, let them only catch the offender, and they would put him to death.

No question, he said.

This entire allegory, I said, you may now append, dear Glaucon, to
the previous argument; the prison-house is the world of sight, the light of
the fire is the sun, and you will not misapprehend me if you interpret the
journey upwards to be the ascent of the soul into the intellectual world
according to my poor belief, which, at your desire, I have expressed—
whether rightly or wrongly God knows. But, whether true or false, my
opinion is that in the world of knowledge the idea of good appears last of
all, and is seen only with an effort; and, when seen, is also inferred to be
the universal author of all things beautiful and right, parent of light and
of the lord of light in this visible world, and the immediate source of reason and truth in the intellectual; and that this is the power upon which he
who would act rationally either in public or private life must have his eye
fixed.

I agree, he said, as far as I am able to understand you.

Moreover, I said, you must not wonder that those who attain to this
beatific vision are unwilling to descend to human affairs; for their souls
are ever hastening into the upper world where they desire to dwell;
which desire of theirs is very natural, if our allegory may be trusted.

Yes, very natural.

And is there anything surprising in one who passes from divine con-
templations to the evil state of man, misbehaving himself in a ridiculous
manner; if, while his eyes are blinking and before he has become accustomed to the surrounding darkness, he is compelled to fight in courts of
law, or in other places, about the images or the shadows of images of justice, and is endeavoring to meet the conceptions of those who have never
yet seen absolute justice?

Anything but surprising, he replied.

Any one who has common sense will remember that the bewilder-
ments of the eyes are of two kinds, and arise from two causes, either from
coming out of the light or from going into the light, which is true of the
mind's eye, quite as much as of the bodily eye; and he who remembers this
when he sees any one whose vision is perplexed and weak, will not be too
ready to laugh; he will first ask whether that soul of man has come out of
the brighter life, and is unable to see because unaccustomed to the dark, or
having turned from darkness to the day is dazzled by excess of light. And
he will count the one happy in his condition and state of being, and he will
pity the other; or, if he have a mind to laugh at the soul which comes from
below into the light, there will be more reason in this than in the laugh
which greets him who returns from above out of the light into the den.

That, he said, is a very just distinction.

But then, if I am right, certain professors of education must be wrong
when they say that they can put a knowledge into the soul which was not
there before, like sight into blind eyes.

They undoubtedly say this, he replied.

Whereas, our argument shows that the power and capacity of learning exists in the soul already; and that just as the eye was unable to turn

from darkness to light without the whole body, so too the instrument of knowledge can only by the movement of the whole soul be turned from the world of becoming into that of being, and learn by degrees to endure the sight of being, and of the brightest and best of being, or in other words, of the good.

Very true.

And must there not be some art which will effect conversion in the easiest and quickest manner; not implanting the faculty of sight, for that exists already, but has been turned in the wrong direction, and is looking away from the truth?

Yes, he said, such an art may be presumed.

And whereas the other so-called virtues of the soul seem to be akin to bodily qualities, for even when they are not originally innate they can be implanted later by habit and exercise, the virtue of wisdom more than anything else contains a divine element which always remains, and by this conversion is rendered useful and profitable; or, on the other hand, hurtful and useless. Did you never observe the narrow intelligence flashing from the keen eye of a clever rogue—how eager he is, how clearly his paltry soul sees the way to his end; he is the reverse of blind, but his keen eyesight is forced into the service of evil, and he is mischievous in proportion to his cleverness?

Very true, he said.

But what if there had been a circumcision of such natures in the days of their youth; and they had been severed from those sensual pleasures, such as eating and drinking, which, like leaden weights, were attached to them at their birth, and which drag them down and turn the vision of their souls upon the things that are below—if, I say, they had been released from these impediments and turned in the opposite direction, the very same faculty in them would have seen the truth as keenly as they see what their eyes are turned to now.

Very likely.

Yes, I said; and there is another thing which is likely, or rather a necessary inference from what has preceded, that neither the uneducated and uninformed of the truth, nor yet those who never make an end of their education, will be able ministers of State; not the former, because they have no single aim of duty which is the rule of all their actions, private as well as public; nor the latter, because they will not act at all except upon compulsion, fancying that they are already dwelling apart in the islands of the blest.

Very true, he replied.

Then, I said, the business of us who are the founders of the State will be to compel the best minds to attain that knowledge which we have already shown to be the greatest of all—they must continue to ascend until they arrive at the good; but when they have ascended and seen enough we must not allow them to do as they do now.

What do you mean?

I mean that they remain in the upper world: but this must not be allowed; they must be made to descend again among the prisoners in the den, and partake of their labors and honors, whether they are worth having or not.

But is not this unjust? he said; ought we to give them a worse life, when they might have a better?

You have again forgotten, my friend, I said, the intention of the legislator, who did not aim at making any one class in the State happy above the rest; the happiness was to be in the whole State, and he held the citizens together by persuasion and necessity, making them benefactors of the State, and therefore benefactors of one another; to this end he created them, not to please themselves, but to be his instruments in binding up the State.

True, he said, I had forgotten.   60

Observe, Glaucon, that there will be no justice in compelling our philosophers to have a care and providence of others; we shall explain to them that in other States, men of their class are not obliged to share in the toils of politics: and this is reasonable, for they grow up at their own sweet will, and the government would rather not have them. Being self-taught, they cannot be expected to show any gratitude for a culture which they have never received. But we have brought you into the world to be rulers of the hive, kings of yourselves and of the other citizens, and have educated you far better and more perfectly than they have been educated, and you are better able to share in the double duty. Wherefore each of you, when his turn comes, must go down to the general underground abode, and get the habit of seeing in the dark. When you have acquired the habit, you will see ten thousand times better than the inhabitants of the den, and you will know what the several images are, and what they represent, because you have seen the beautiful and just and good in their truth. And thus our State which is also yours will be a reality, and not a dream only, and will be administered in a spirit unlike that of other States, in which men fight with one another about shadows only and are distracted in the struggle for power, which in their eyes is a great good. Whereas the truth is that the State in which the rulers are most reluctant to govern is always the best and most quietly governed, and the State in which they are most eager, the worst.

Quite true, he replied.

And will our pupils, when they hear this, refuse to take their turn at the toils of State, when they are allowed to spend the greater part of their time with one another in the heavenly light?

Impossible, he answered; for they are just men, and the commands which we impose upon them are just; there can be no doubt that every one of them will take office as a stern necessity, and not after the fashion of our present rulers of State.

Yes, my friend, I said; and there lies the point. You must contrive for   65
your future rulers another and a better life than that of a ruler, and then you may have a well-ordered State; for only in the State which offers this,

will they rule who are truly rich, not in silver and gold, but in virtue and wisdom, which are the true blessing of life. Whereas if they go to the administration of public affairs, poor and hungering after their own private advantage, thinking that hence they are to snatch the chief good, order there can never be; for they will be fighting about office, and the civil and domestic broils which thus arise will be the ruin of the rulers themselves and of the whole State.

Most true, he replied.

And the only life which looks down upon the life of political ambition is that of true philosophy. Do you know of any other?

Indeed, I do not, he said.

And those who govern ought not to be lovers of the task? For, if they are, there will be rival lovers, and they will fight.

No question.   70

Who then are those whom we shall compel to be guardians? Surely they will be the men who are wisest about affairs of State, and by whom the State is best administered, and who at the same time have other honors and another and a better life than that of politics?

They are the men, and I will choose them, he replied.

And now shall we consider in what way such guardians will be produced, and how they are to be brought from darkness to light—as some are said to have ascended from the world below to the gods?

By all means, he replied.

The process, I said, is not the turning over of an oyster-shell,[1] but the   75
turning round of a soul passing from a day which is little better than night to the true day of being, that is, the ascent from below which we affirm to be true philosophy?

Quite so.

Topics for Critical Thinking and Writing

1. Plato is not merely reporting one of Socrates's conversations; he is teaching. What advantages does a dialogue have over a narrative or an essay as a way of teaching philosophy? How is the form of a dialogue especially suited to solving a problem?

2. If you don't know the etymology of the word *conversion,* look it up in a dictionary. How is the etymology appropriate to Plato's idea about education?

3. In paragraph 19, describing the prisoner as "reluctantly dragged" upward and "forced" to look at the sun, Socrates asks: "Is he not likely to be pained and irritated?" Can you recall experiencing pain and irritation while learning something you later were glad to have learned? Can you recall learning something new *without* experiencing pain and irritation?

---

[1]An allusion to a game in which two parties fled or pursued according as an oyster shell that was thrown into the air fell with the dark or light side uppermost. (Translator's note)

4. "The State in which rulers are most reluctant to govern is always the best and most quietly governed, and the State in which they are most eager, the worst" (paragraph 61). What does Socrates mean? Using examples from contemporary politics, defend this proposition or argue against it.

5. Can you account for the power of this myth or fable? In our introductory comment (page 423), we tried to clarify the message by saying that a movie theater might serve as well as cave. But, in fact, if the story were recast using a movie theater, would the emotional power be the same? Why or why not?

6. The metaphors of education as conversion and ascent are linked by the metaphor of light. Consider such expressions as "I see" (meaning "I understand") and "Let me give an illustration" (from the Latin *in* = in, and *lustrare* = to make bright). What other expressions about light are used metaphorically to describe intellectual comprehension?

Richard Rodriguez

Richard Rodriguez, the son of immigrants from Mexico, was born in San Francisco in 1944. He was educated at Stanford University, Columbia University, and the University of California, Berkeley, where he specialized in English literature of the Renaissance. In his book, The Hunger of Memory *(1982), he reports how his progress in the Anglo world was accompanied by estrangement from the Spanish-speaking world. We print an excerpt from the book; the title of the excerpt is our own.*

Public and Private Language

Supporters of bilingual education today imply that students like me miss a great deal by not being taught in their family's language. What they seem not to recognize is that, as a socially disadvantaged child, I considered Spanish to be a private language. What I needed to learn in school was that I had the right—and the obligation—to speak the public language of *los gringos*. The odd truth is that my first-grade classmates could have become bilingual, in the conventional sense of that word, more easily than I. Had they been taught (as upper-middle-class children are often taught early) a second language like Spanish or French, they could have regarded it simply as that: another public language. In my case such bilingualism could not have been so quickly achieved. What I did not believe was that I could speak a single public language.

Without question, it would have pleased me to hear my teachers address me in Spanish when I entered the classroom. I would have felt much less afraid. I would have trusted them and responded with ease.

But I would have delayed—for how long postponed?—having to learn the language of public society. I would have evaded—and for how long could I have afforded to delay?—learning the great lesson of school, that I had a public identity.

Fortunately, my teachers were unsentimental about their responsibility. What they understood was that I needed to speak a public language. So their voices would search me out, asking me questions. Each time I'd hear them, I'd look up in surprise to see a nun's face frowning at me. I'd mumble, not really meaning to answer. The nun would persist, "Richard, stand up. Don't look at the floor. Speak up. Speak to the entire class, not just to me!" But I couldn't believe that the English language was mine to use. (In part, I did not want to believe it.) I continued to mumble. I resisted the teacher's demands. (Did I somehow suspect that once I learned public language my pleasing family life would be changed?) Silent, waiting for the bell to sound, I remained dazed, diffident, afraid.

Because I wrongly imagined that English was intrinsically a public language and Spanish an intrinsically private one, I easily noted the difference between classroom language and the language of home. At school, words were directed to a general audience of listeners. ("Boys and girls.") Words were meaningfully ordered. And the point was not self-expression alone but to make oneself understood by many others. The teacher quizzed: "Boys and girls, why do we use that word in this sentence? Could we think of a better word to use there? Would the sentence change its meaning if the words were differently arranged? And wasn't there a better way of saying much the same thing?" (I couldn't say. I wouldn't try to say.)

Three months. Five. Half a year passed. Unsmiling, ever watchful, my teachers noted my silence. They began to connect my behavior with the difficult progress my older sister and brother were making. Until one Saturday morning three nuns arrived at the house to talk to our parents. Stiffly, they sat on the blue living room sofa. From the doorway of another room, spying the visitors, I noted the incongruity—the clash of two worlds, the faces and voices of school intruding upon the familiar setting of home. I overheard one voice gently wondering, "Do your children speak only Spanish at home, Mrs. Rodriguez?" While another voice added, "That Richard especially seems so timid and shy."

That Rich-heard!

With great tact the visitors continued, "Is it possible for you and your husband to encourage your children to practice their English when they are home?" Of course, my parents complied. What would they not do for their children's well-being? And how could they have questioned the Church's authority which those women represented? In an instant, they agreed to give up the language (the sounds) that had revealed and accentuated our family's closeness. The moment after the visitors left, the change was observed. "*Ahora,* speak to us *en inglés,*" my father and mother united to tell us.

At first, it seemed a kind of game. After dinner each night, the family gathered to practice "our" English. (It was still then *inglés,* a language

5

foreign to us, so we felt drawn as strangers to it.) Laughing, we would try to define words we could not pronounce. We played with strange English sounds, often over-anglicizing our pronunciations. And we filled the smiling gaps of our sentences with familiar Spanish sounds. But that was cheating, somebody shouted. Everyone laughed. In school, meanwhile, like my brother and sister, I was required to attend a daily tutoring session. I needed a full year of special attention. I also needed my teachers to keep my attention from straying in class by calling out, *Rich-heard*—their English voices slowly prying loose my ties to my other name, its three notes. *Ri-car-do*. Most of all I needed to hear my mother and father speak to me in a moment of seriousness in broken—suddenly heartbreaking—English. The scene was inevitable: One Saturday morning I entered the kitchen where my parents were talking in Spanish. I did not realize that they were talking in Spanish however until, at the moment they saw me, I heard their voices change to speak English. Those *gringo* sounds they uttered startled me. Pushed me away. In that moment of trivial misunderstanding and profound insight, I felt my throat twisted by unsounded grief. I turned quickly and left the room. But I had no place to escape to with Spanish. (The spell was broken.) My brother and sisters were speaking English in another part of the house.

Again and again in the days following, increasingly angry, I was obliged to hear my mother and father: "Speak to us *en inglés*." (*Speak*). Only then did I determine to learn classroom English. Weeks after, it happened: One day in school I raised my hand to volunteer an answer. I spoke out in a loud voice. And I did not think it remarkable when the entire class understood. That day, I moved very far from the disadvantaged child I had been only days earlier. The belief, the calming assurance that I belonged in public, had at last taken hold.

Shortly after, I stopped hearing the high and loud sounds of *los gringos*. A more and more confident speaker of English, I didn't trouble to listen to *how* strangers sounded, speaking to me. And there simply were too many English-speaking people in my day for me to hear American accents anymore. Conversations quickened. Listening to persons who sounded eccentrically pitched voices, I usually noted their sounds for an initial few seconds before I concentrated on *what* they were saying. Conversations became content-full. Transparent. Hearing someone's *tone* of voice—angry or questioning or sarcastic or happy or sad—I didn't distinguish it from the words it expressed. Sound and word were thus tightly wedded. At the end of a day, I was often bemused, always relieved, to realize how "silent," though crowded with words, my day in public had been. (This public silence measured and quickened the change in my life.)

At last, seven years old, I came to believe what had been technically true since my birth: I was an American citizen.

But the special feeling of closeness at home was diminished by then. Gone was the desperate, urgent, intense feeling of being at home: rare was the experience of feeling myself individualized by family intimates. We remained a loving family, but one greatly changed. No longer so close; no longer bound tight by the pleasing and troubling knowledge of our public separateness. Neither my older brother nor sister rushed home after school anymore. Nor did I. When I arrived home there would often be neighborhood kids in the house. Or the house would be empty of sounds.

Following the dramatic Americanization of their children, even my parents grew more publicly confident. Especially my mother. She learned the names of all the people on our block. And she decided we needed to have a telephone installed in the house. My father continued to use the word *gringo*. But it was no longer charged with the old bitterness or distrust. (Stripped of any emotional content, the word simply became a name for those Americans not of Hispanic descent.) Hearing him, sometimes, I wasn't sure if he was pronouncing the Spanish word *gringo* or saying gringo in English.

Matching the silence I started hearing in public was a new quiet at home. The family's quiet was partly due to the fact that, as we children learned more and more English, we shared fewer and fewer words with our parents. Sentences needed to be spoken slowly when a child addressed his mother or father. (Often the parent wouldn't understand.) The child would need to repeat himself. (Still the parent misunderstood.) The young voice, frustrated, would end up saying, "Never mind"—the subject was closed. Dinners would be noisy with the clinking of knives and forks against dishes. My mother would smile softly between her remarks; my father at the other end of the table would chew and chew at his food, while he stared over the heads of his children.

My *mother!* My *father!* After English became my primary language, I   15
no longer knew what words to use in addressing my parents. The old Spanish words (those tender accents of sound) I had used earlier—*mamá* and *papá*—I couldn't use anymore. They would have been too painful reminders of how much had changed in my life. On the other hand, the words I heard neighborhood kids call *their* parents seemed equally unsatisfactory. *Mother* and *Father; Ma, Papa, Pa, Dad, Pop* (how I hated the all-American sound of that last word especially)—all these terms I felt were unsuitable, not really terms of address for *my* parents. As a result, I never used them at home. Whenever I'd speak to my parents, I would try to get their attention with eye contact alone. In public conversations, I'd refer to "my parents" or "my mother and father."

My mother and father, for their part, responded differently, as their children spoke to them less. She grew restless, seemed troubled and anxious at the scarcity of words exchanged in the house. It was she who would question me about my day when I came home from school. She smiled at small talk. She pried at the edges of my sentences to get me to say something more. (What?) She'd stopped her children's talking. By contrast, my father seemed reconciled to the new quiet. Though his English improved somewhat, he retired into silence. At dinner he spoke very little. One night his children and even his wife helplessly giggled at his garbled English pronunciation of the Catholic Grace before Meals. Thereafter he made his wife recite the prayer at the start of each meal, even on formal occasions, when there were guests in the house. Hers became the public voice of the family. On official business, it was she, not my father, one would usually hear on the phone or in stores, talking to strangers. His children grew so accustomed to his silence that, years later, they would speak routinely of his shyness. (My mother would often try to explain: Both his parents died when he was eight. He was raised by an uncle who treated him like little more than a menial servant. He was never encouraged to speak. He grew up alone. A man of few words.) But my father was not shy, I realized, when I'd watch him speaking Spanish with relatives. Using Spanish, he was quickly effusive. Especially when talking with other men, his voice would spark, flicker, flare alive with sounds. In Spanish, he expressed ideas and feelings he rarely revealed in English. With firm Spanish sounds, he conveyed confidence and authority English would never allow him.

The silence at home, however, was finally more than a literal silence. Fewer words passed between parent and child, but more profound was the silence that resulted from my inattention to sounds. At about the time I no longer bothered to listen with care to the sounds of English in public, I grew careless about listening to the sounds family members made when they spoke. Most of the time I heard someone speaking at home and didn't distinguish his sounds from the words people uttered in public. I didn't even pay much attention to my parents' accented and ungrammatical speech. At least not at home. Only when I was with them in public would I grow alert to their accents. Though, even then, their sounds caused me less and less concern. For I was increasingly confident of my own public identity.

I would have been happier about my public success had I not sometimes recalled what it had been like earlier, when my family had conveyed its intimacy through a set of conveniently private sounds. Sometimes in public, hearing a stranger, I'd hark back to my past. A Mexican farmworker approached me downtown to ask directions to somewhere. "Hijito . . . ?" he said. And his voice summoned deep longing. Another time, standing beside my mother in the visiting room of a Carmelite convent, before the dense screen which rendered the nuns shadowy figures, I heard several Spanish-speaking nuns—their busy, singsong overlapping voices—assure us that yes, yes, we were remembered, all our family was remembered in their prayers. (Their voices echoed faraway family sounds.) Another day, a dark-faced old woman—her hand light on my shoulder—steadied herself against me as she boarded a bus. She murmured something I couldn't quite comprehend. Her Spanish voice came near, like the face of a never-before-seen relative in the instant before I was kissed. Her voice, like so many of the Spanish voices I'd hear in public, recalled the golden age of my youth. Hearing Spanish then, I continued to be a careful, if sad, listener to sounds. Hearing a Spanish-speaking family walking behind me, I turned to look. I smiled for an instant, before my glance found the Hispanic-looking faces of strangers in the crowd going by.

Topics for Critical Thinking and Writing

1. We have called this selection from Richard Rodriguez's *The Hunger of Memory* "Public and Private Language," and, indeed, the words occur often in the text. But, from reading these pages, how would you identify what is "public language" and what is "private"? What words and images would you associate with each?

2. In his first paragraph Rodriguez identifies himself as a "socially disadvantaged child." What does he mean?

3. At the end of his second paragraph Rodriguez identifies "the great lesson of school," that he "had a public identity." What does Rodriguez mean by his "public identity," and would you say that your elementary school also aided you in achieving one? Explain.

4. In his eleventh and twelfth paragraphs Rodriguez comes "to believe what had been technically true since [his] birth"—he was now an "American citizen." He seems to associate this truth with a change in his family relationships. Was there a period in your life when you felt such a change in your family—with or without a change in language? If so, how would you characterize it?

Ernest van den Haag

Ernest van den Haag (1914–2002), born in The Hague, Netherlands, came to the United States in 1940 and became a U.S. citizen in 1947. During a long and highly productive career, he practiced psychoanalysis and taught psychology, sociology, and law at several universities.

In the following essay, reprinted from the National Review, *van den Haag offers several steps to help youngsters learn more—the first of which is for adults to decide that children ought to learn.*

Why Do American Kids Learn So Little?

biased

American children learn far less in school than European and Japanese children do, although America spends far more per pupil. Why is so little education achieved for so much money? The answer may lie in a major oddity in the American creed.

Europeans have always regarded children as barbarians to be painfully civilized by schooling. Childhood is thought to be merely, or mainly, a means to adult achievement. Children are apprentice adults. Schools are to teach them what they will need, even if they cannot see the use of it: language (including grammar), arithmetic, science, history, classics. In Europe there are hardly any of those undemanding classes so frequent in the U.S., such as current events, or home economics.

Of course, the young have never liked the stern demands the schools made. They have preferred to enjoy being young—*gaudeamus igitur juvenes dum sumus,*[1] the students sang—instead of using their young years to prepare for adult careers. But the young could sing all they wanted (in the Latin they learned in school), they had little choice. Without parental support—inheritance and connections—they could never hope to make their way in the world, for which the schools served as gatekeepers. Thus, in Europe—and in Japan, which has swallowed the European idea hook, line, and sinker—the power of the older generation is used to make children spend most of their time doing schoolwork. Occasionally they have rebelled, but, on the whole, they have submitted, become literate, and gone on their way.

In America, however, youth is seen as an end in itself, never merely a means to adult achievement. Children rarely are expected to work at anything they don't enjoy. Teachers are expected to "motivate" their students and to make learning a pleasure, even if this means going easy on unavoidably tedious stretches. The young themselves tend to see adulthood as a hard-to-avoid postscript, almost a decline. Many adults nostalgically agree.

Parents seldom can make unwilling children do homework, and   5
teachers wisely don't ask for what they can't get. To demand vexatious schoolwork of children seems almost immoral in the American context.

Unlike Europeans, Americans do not expect their children to continue in their own social position: they regard their children as the hope of the future. Far from imposing the civilization of the past, education is to help the young to "find themselves," to unfold their innate creativity. The young will do better if less encumbered by the past. Margaret Mead even told parents that they must learn from the young, who "have the knowledge."

To most Americans the future always has been more real than the past. This notion makes teaching hard, for teaching requires, at least temporarily, submission to the authority of ancient ideas, and of teachers who transmit them. All learning initially must rest on the authority of the past; after all, the past is all that can be learned.

Pupils must first accept the teachers' authority. Teachers cannot explain to an eight-year-old why words are spelled as they are, or why two

[1]*gaudeamus igitur juvenes dum sumus,* let us be joyful while we are young (Latin, from a medieval university song).

and two make four, not five. It is only after much material has been absorbed by rote—children fortunately like learning by rote, although progressive teachers don't like to let them—that students can begin to examine critically and usefully what they are learning. If the authority of the older generation is weak, little knowledge will be absorbed.

We largely let students elect the classes they prefer, assuming that they know enough to fashion their own curriculum, although they cannot yet have learned how to evaluate the importance of various kinds of knowledge. Of course, they elect the easy classes, sometimes of dubious value. They get the same credit toward a diploma for easy classes as they get for harder ones, the same for Contemporary Drama as for Advanced Algebra.

Via Media[2]

There must be a reasonable middle way between a joyous childhood   10
and an exclusively instrumental use of it, a way of combining the civilizing influence of science, history, and literature with the enjoyment of youth. The young must learn to learn as well as to play. Some even may enjoy learning once they try it. Is there anything that can be done to bring about the necessary changes? Consider some beginning steps.

Public schools currently have a monopoly on tax money, which they jealously guard, and because public schools do not compete with one another—pupils are assigned—each public school is in a near monopoly position. The usual effects of monopoly occur: shoddy products at high cost to the involuntary purchasers (taxpayers). A voucher system, entitling parents to choose any public school in the state for their children—and, later on, any approved private school as well—would introduce some competition and might eliminate the worst effects of the monopoly. Schools never should be subsidized; *schooling* should be, by granting vouchers to parents.

Other monopoly features should be dismantled as well. Currently nobody, however capable, is allowed to teach without first attending courses in education. This functions as a barrier to entry, strengthening the entrenched monopoly defended by unions. Private schools hire teachers able to teach their subjects well, in spite (or because) of not having attended a school of education. Usually these teachers are much less well paid than public-school teachers; yet their students, on the average, learn more according to all available tests.

In other countries children spend more time in school. It has been suggested therefore that the school day should be lengthened and summer vacations shortened. I doubt that this will help much. It is not that children spend too little time in school; rather they learn too little in the time they spend. More homework might indeed help, if only marginally.

---

[2]*Via Media*, the middle way (Latin).

What ails American schools is not lack of money. We spend much more per pupil (adjusted for inflation) than we did in the past, and far more than other countries do. But the returns in learning are remarkably low. Where does the money go? Far too much goes into non-teaching activities. There is far too much administration, as can be shown irrefutably by comparing the ratio of teaching to non-teaching personnel in private and public schools. I do not claim that these administrators, counselors, et al. do not work hard. Rather, the work doesn't contribute much to the education of children. They keep each other busy.

Then there is the quality of the teachers themselves. Children cannot   15
learn much from teachers who do not command basic skills. Scandalously few do.

Teachers have some reasonable complaints. They get many children from homes to which learning is as alien as discipline. Still, most children can learn to spell and to read, can learn elementary grammar and arithmetic—if teachers are allowed to impose the necessary discipline, as they are not now. There are some things that can be learned by doing—in fact, only by doing: carefulness, punctuality, manners, discipline are among them. Anybody can acquire these; but schools make little effort to help. They do not feel they are charged with helping to forge the character of students, many of whom graduate functionally illiterate, with slovenly work habits and manners.

Minimum requirements for a high-school diploma (to which each school should be able to add its own) should be imposed by every state, fulfilled only by passing examinations, including essay tests, graded by teachers from schools other than the one attended by the student.

Public schools also should be allowed to expel students unwilling to learn (or to submit to discipline), as private schools are now. Contrary to much opinion, not only would the schools be better off, the expelled students themselves are likely to do better by not being kept when schooling is unproductive for them.

We should stop assuming complacently that our children are being educated just because we have many schools with lots of teachers and myriad administrators. Currently they learn very little, not because they are stupid, but because they are taught very little. It is easier that way for everybody, the kids, the teachers, the parents. But we can't afford it any longer. If we want to avoid a rapid decline of America we must make sure that our children are educated rather than just entertained and kept in school. This will require more changes than I proposed. But we have to begin somewhere.

Topics for Critical Thinking and Writing

1. Do you agree with van den Haag (paragraph 2) that courses in current events and home economics are necessarily "undemanding"? Explain.

2. In paragraph 4 van den Haag speaks of "unavoidably tedious stretches," and in paragraph 5 of "vexatious schoolwork." Do you agree that there must be such things? If so, how would you as a teacher proceed? Or do you assume that material is "tedious" and "vexatious" only because it is not properly taught? If so, give an example of how a skilled teacher presented material that might otherwise have been tedious or vexatious and made it exciting or enjoyable.

3. In paragraph 6 van den Haag quotes what he implies is a wrong-headed statement by Margaret Mead, to the effect that parents must learn from their young, who "have the knowledge." He does not cite his source, but do you think that he has said enough to indicate that the idea is preposterous? Or on the other hand do you think that the young do indeed have certain kinds of "knowledge" and that their parents can learn some things from them? Explain.

4. Do you agree with the remarks in paragraph 8 about authority and rote learning? If not, explain your position.

5. In paragraph 9 van den Haag dismisses the idea of youngsters electing courses. Drawing on your own experience in secondary school, evaluate his reason.

6. As you look back on your elementary or high school education, what do you think were the greatest strengths? The greatest weaknesses? (You may want to compare one kind of schooling with the other.)

7. Van den Haag implies that many teachers "do not command basic skills." Drawing on your experience, do you agree? (If you write about particular teachers, do not use their real names.)

8. In paragraph 16 van den Haag suggests that schools should teach "carefulness, punctuality, manners, discipline"—in short, aspects of character. Do you agree? Did some or all of your teachers teach any or all of these things? Explain.

9. Consider the strategies that van den Haag uses in his final paragraph. Do you think it provides a good ending for this argumentative essay? Explain.

Neil Postman

Neil Postman, born in New York City in 1931, has taught in elementary and secondary schools and is now a professor of communication arts and sciences at New York University.

Order in the Classroom

William O'Connor, who is unknown to me in a personal way, was once a member of the Boston School Committee, in which capacity he made the following remark: "We have no inferior education in our schools. What we have been getting is an inferior type of student."

The remark is easy to ridicule, and I have had some fun with it in the past. But there are a couple of senses in which it is perfectly sound.

In the first place, a classroom is a technique for the achievement of certain kinds of learning. It is a workable technique provided that both the teacher and the student have the skill and, particularly, the attitudes that are fundamental to it. Among these, from the student's point of view, are tolerance for delayed gratification, a certain measure of respect for and fear of authority, and a willingness to accommodate one's individual desires to the interests of group cohesion and purpose. These attitudes cannot be taught easily in school because they are a necessary component of the teaching situation itself. The problem is not unlike trying to find out how to spell a word by looking it up in the dictionary. If you do not know how a word is spelled, it is hard to look it up. In the same way, little can be taught in school unless these attitudes are present. And if they are not, to teach them is difficult.

Obviously, such attitudes must be learned during the years before a child starts school; that is, in the home. This is the real meaning of the phrase "preschool education." If a child is not made ready at home for the classroom experience, he or she usually cannot benefit from any normal school program. Just as important, the school is defenseless against such a child, who, typically, is a source of disorder in a situation that requires order. I raise this issue because education reform is impossible without order in the classroom. Without the attitudes that lead to order, the classroom is an entirely impotent technique. Therefore, one possible translation of Mr. O'Connor's remark is, "We have a useful technique for educating youth but too many of them have not been provided at home with the attitudes necessary for the technique to work."

In still another way Mr. O'Connor's remark makes plain sense. The electronic media, with their emphasis on visual imagery, immediacy, non-linearity, and fragmentation, do not give support to the attitudes that are

5

fundamental to the classroom; that is, Mr. O'Connor's remark can be translated as, "We would not have an inferior education if it were the nineteenth century. Our problem is that we have been getting students who are products of the twentieth century." But there is nothing nonsensical about this, either. The nineteenth century had much to recommend it, and we certainly may be permitted to allow it to exert an influence on the twentieth. The classroom is a nineteenth-century invention, and we ought to prize what it has to offer. It is one of the few social organizations left to us in which sequence, social order, hierarchy, continuity, and deferred pleasure are important.

The problem of disorder in the classroom is created largely by two factors: a dissolving family structure, out of which come youngsters who are "unfit" for the presuppositions of a classroom; and a radically altered information environment, which undermines the foundation of school. The question, then, is, What should be done about the increasing tendency toward disorder in the classroom?

Liberal reformers, such as Kenneth Keniston, have answers, of a sort. Keniston argues that economic reforms should be made so that the integrity and authority of the family can be restored. He believes that poverty is the main cause of family dissolution, and that by improving the economic situation of families, we may kindle a sense of order and aspiration in the lives of children. Some of the reforms he suggests in his book *All Our Children* seem practical, although they are long-range and offer no immediate response to the problem of present disorder. Some Utopians, such as Ivan Illich, have offered other solutions; for example, dissolving the schools altogether, or so completely restructuring the school environment that its traditional assumptions are rendered irrelevant. To paraphrase Karl Kraus's epigram about psychoanalysis, these proposals are the Utopian disease of which they consider themselves the cure.

One of the best answers comes from Dr. Howard Hurwitz, who is neither a liberal reformer nor a Utopian. It is a good solution, I believe, because it tries to respond to the needs not only of children who are unprepared for school because of parental failure but of children of all backgrounds who are being made strangers to the assumptions of school by the biases of the electronic media.

During the eleven years Dr. Hurwitz was principal at Long Island City High School, the average number of suspensions each year was three, while in many New York City high schools the average runs close to one hundred. Also, during his tenure, not one instance of an assault on a teacher was reported, and daily student attendance averaged better than 90 percent, which in the context of the New York City school scene represents a riot of devotion.

Although I consider some of Dr. Hurwitz's curriculum ideas uninspired and even wrong-headed, he understands a few things of overriding importance that many educators of more expansive imagination do

10

not. The first is that educators must devote at least as much attention to the immediate consequences of disorder as to its abstract causes. Whatever the causes of disorder and alienation, the consequences are severe and, if not curbed, result in making the school impotent. At the risk of becoming a symbol of reaction, Hurwitz ran "a tight ship." He holds to the belief, for example, that a child's right to an education is terminated at the point where the child interferes with the right of other children to have one.

Dr. Hurwitz also understands that disorder expands proportionately to the tolerance for it, and that children of all kinds of home backgrounds can learn, in varying degrees, to function in situations where disorder is not tolerated at all. He does not believe that it is inevitably or only the children of the poor who are disorderly. In spite of what the "revisionist" education historians may say, poor people still regard school as an avenue of social and economic advancement for their children, and do not object in the least to its being an orderly and structured experience.

All this adds up to the common sense view that the school ought not to accommodate itself to disorder, or to the biases of other communication systems. The children of the poor are likely to continue to be with us. Some parents will fail to assume competent responsibility for the preschool education of their children. The media will increase the intensity of their fragmenting influence. Educators must live with these facts. But Dr. Hurwitz believes that as a technique for learning, the classroom can work if students are oriented toward its assumptions, not the other way around. William O'Connor, wherever he is, would probably agree. And so do I. The school is not an extension of the street, the movie theater, a rock concert, or a playground. And it is certainly not an extension of the psychiatric clinic. It is a special environment that requires the enforcement of certain traditional rules of controlled group interaction. The school may be the only remaining public situation in which such rules have any meaning, and it would be a grave mistake to change those rules because some children find them hard or cannot function within them. Children who cannot ought to be removed from the environment in the interests of those who can.

Wholesale suspensions, however, are a symptom of disorder, not a cure for it. And what makes Hurwitz's school noteworthy is the small number of suspensions that have been necessary. This is not the result of his having "good" students or "bad" students. It is the result of his having created an unambiguous, rigorous, and serious attitude—a nineteenth-century attitude, if you will—toward what constitutes acceptable school behavior. In other words, Dr. Hurwitz's school turns out to be a place where children of all backgrounds—fit and unfit—can function, or can learn to function, and where the biases of our information environment are emphatically opposed.

At this point I should like to leave the particulars of Dr. Hurwitz's solution and, retaining their spirit, indicate some particulars of my own.

Let us start, for instance, with the idea of a dress code. A dress code   15
signifies that school is a special place in which special kinds of behavior
are required. The way one dresses is an indication of an attitude toward a
situation. And the way one is *expected* to dress indicates what that attitude
ought to be. You would not wear dungarees and a T-shirt that says "Feel
Me" when attending a church wedding. That would be considered an
outrage against the tone and meaning of the situation. The school has
every right and reason, I believe, to expect the same sort of consideration.

Those who are inclined to think this is a superficial point are probably forgetting that symbols not only reflect our feelings but to some extent create them. One's kneeling in church, for example, reflects a sense
of reverence but also engenders reverence. If we want school to *feel* like
a special place, we can find no better way to begin than by requiring
students to dress in a manner befitting the seriousness of the enterprise
and the institution. I should include teachers in this requirement. I
know of one high school in which the principal has put forward a dress
code of sorts for teachers. (He has not, apparently, had the courage to
propose one for the students.) For males the requirement is merely a
jacket and tie. One of his teachers bitterly complained to me that such a
regulation infringed upon his civil rights. And yet, this teacher will accept without complaint the same regulation when it is enforced by an
elegant restaurant. His complaint and his acquiescence tell a great deal
about how he values schools and how he values restaurants.

I do not have in mind, for students, uniforms of the type sometimes
worn in parochial schools. I am referring here to some reasonable standard of dress which would mark school as a place of dignity and seriousness. And I might add that I do not believe for one moment the argument
that poor people would be unable to clothe their children properly if such
a code were in force. Furthermore, I do not believe that poor people have
advanced that argument. It is an argument that middle-class education
critics have made on behalf of the poor.

Another argument advanced in behalf of the poor and oppressed is
the students' right to their own language. I have never heard this argument come from parents whose children are not competent to use
Standard English. It is an argument, once again, put forward by "liberal"
education critics whose children *are* competent in Standard English but
who in some curious way wish to express their solidarity with and charity for those who are less capable. It is a case of pure condescension, and I
do not think teachers should be taken in by it. Like the mode of dress, the
mode of language in school ought to be relatively formal and exemplary,
and therefore markedly different from the custom in less rigorous places.
It is particularly important that teachers should avoid trying to win their
students' affection by adopting the language of youth. Such teachers frequently win only the contempt of their students, who sense that the language of teachers and the language of students ought to be different; that
is to say, the world of adults is different from the world of children.

In this connection, it is worth saying that the modern conception of childhood is a product of the sixteenth century, as Philippe Aries has documented in his *Centuries of Childhood*. Prior to that century, children as young as six and seven were treated in all important respects as if they were adults. Their language, their dress, their legal status, their responsibilities, their labor, were much the same as those of adults. The concept of childhood as an identifiable stage in human growth began to develop in the sixteenth century and has continued into our own times. However, with the emergence of electronic media of communication, a reversal of this trend seems to be taking place. In a culture in which the distribution of information is almost wholly undifferentiated, age categories begin to disappear. Television, in itself, may bring an end to childhood. In truth, there is no such thing as "children's programming," at least not for children over the age of eight or nine. Everyone sees and hears the same things. We have already reached a point where crimes of youth are indistinguishable from those of adults; and we may soon reach a point where the punishments will be the same.

I raise this point because the school is one of our few remaining institutions based on firm distinctions between childhood and adulthood, and on the assumption that adults have something of value to teach the young. That is why teachers must avoid emulating in dress and speech the style of the young. It is also why the school ought to be a place for what we might call "manners education": the adults in school ought to be concerned with teaching youth a standard of civilized interaction.   20

Again those who are inclined to regard this as superficial may be underestimating the power of media such as television and radio to teach how one is to conduct oneself in public. In a general sense, the media "unprepare" the young for behavior in groups. A young man who goes through the day with a radio affixed to his ear is learning to be indifferent to any shared sound. A young woman who can turn off a television program that does not suit her needs at the moment is learning impatience with any stimulus that is not responsive to her interests.

But school is not a radio station or a television program. It is a social situation requiring the subordination of one's own impulses and interests to those of the group. In a word, manners. As a rule, elementary school teachers will exert considerable effort in teaching manners. I believe they refer to this effort as "socializing the child." But it is astonishing how precipitously this effort is diminished at higher levels. It is certainly neglected in the high schools, and where it is not, there is usually an excessive concern for "bad habits," such as smoking, drinking, and in some nineteenth-century schools, swearing. But, as William James noted, our virtues are as habitual as our vices. Where is the attention given to the "Good morning" habit, to the "I beg your pardon" habit, to the "Please forgive the interruption" habit?

The most civilized high school class I have ever seen was one in which students and teacher said "Good morning" to each other and in which the students stood up when they had something to say. The teacher, moreover, thanked each student for any contribution made to the class, did not sit with his feet on the desk, and did not interrupt a student unless he had asked permission to do so. The students, in turn, did not interrupt each other, or chew gum, or read comic books when they were bored. To avoid being a burden to others when one is bored is the essence of civilized behavior.

Of this teacher, I might also say that he made no attempt to entertain his students or model his classroom along the lines of a TV program. He was concerned not only to teach his students manners but to teach them how to attend in a classroom, which is partly a matter of manners but also necessary to their intellectual development. One of the more serious difficulties teachers now face in the classroom results from the fact that their students suffer media-shortened attention spans and have become accustomed, also through intense media exposure, to novelty, variety, and entertainment. Some teachers have made desperate attempts to keep their students "tuned in" by fashioning their classes along the lines of *Sesame Street* or the *Tonight* show. They tell jokes. They change the pace. They show films, play records, and avoid *anything* that would take more than eight minutes. Although their motivation is understandable, this is what their students least need. However difficult it may be, the teacher must try to achieve student attention and even enthusiasm through the attraction of ideas, not razzmatazz. Those who think I am speaking here in favor of "dull" classes may themselves, through media exposure, have lost an understanding of the potential for excitement contained in an idea. The media (one prays) are not so powerful that they can obliterate in the young, particularly in the adolescent, what William James referred to as a "theoretic instinct," a need to know reasons, causes, abstract conceptions. Such an "instinct" can be seen in its earliest stages in what he calls the "sporadic metaphysical inquiries of children as to who made God, and why they have five fingers. . . ."

I trust that the reader is not misled by what I have been saying. As I 25 see it, nothing in any of the above leads to the conclusion that I favor a classroom that is authoritarian or coldhearted, or dominated by a teacher insensitive to students and how they learn. I merely want to affirm the importance of the classroom as a special place, aloof from the biases of the media; a place in which the uses of the intellect are given prominence in a setting of elevated language, civilized manners, and respect for social symbols.

Topics for Critical Thinking and Writing

1. In paragraph 3 what does Postman mean by "tolerance for delayed gratification"? By the way, two paragraphs later Postman uses an expression that is approximately synonymous with "delayed gratification." What is this expression?

2. Postman in part blames "the electronic media," because (he says in paragraph 5) they emphasize "fragmentation." Does he give any examples in his

essay? Do you think you know what he means? And do you think he is right?

3. Who is Postman's audience? High school students? Parents and teachers? Professors of education? And who is Postman—that is, putting aside the biographical note on page 440, what sort of person does the author of the essay reveal himself to be? A frustrated high school teacher? A professor of education? An intelligent layperson? Does he seem to know what he is talking about?

4. In paragraph 10 we are told, with approval, that a principal named Dr. Howard Hurwitz "ran 'a tight ship.'" First, make sure that you know what the phrase means, and then write an essay of five hundred words evaluating the degree of success of some instructor or administrator who ran a tight ship in your school. Your essay will, of course, have to give us a sense of what the instructor or administrator did, as well as your evaluation of the results of his or her teaching or administrating.

5. If you disagree with Postman on the value of a dress code, set forth your disagreement in a persuasive essay of five hundred words.

6. Write an editorial—as an alumnus or alumna—for your high school newspaper, summarizing Postman's essay in a paragraph, and then comparing your school with Postman's idea of a good school, and, finally, evaluating your school and Postman's essay. You may, for example, conclude that, thank heavens, your school was nothing like Postman's ideal school.

Merry White

Merry White is the author of The Japanese Educational Challenge *(1987) and* Japan: The Material Child *(1993). She is also the author of a book on noodles. White, who has served as an administrator of Harvard's East Asian Studies Program, now teaches anthropology at Boston University. This essay was originally published in 1984, hence the salaries specified in paragraph 19 and comments on world trends must be adjusted in view of later developments.*

Japanese Education

How Do They Do It?

Japan has become the new reference point for the developing nations and the West, and comparisons with Japan cause increasing wonder and sometimes envy. Travel agents continue to profit from the curiosity of

Merry White, "Japanese Education: How Do They Do It," *The Public Interest*, No. 76, Summer 1984. Copyright © 1984 by National Affairs, Inc. By permission of the author and the publisher.

Americans, particularly businessmen, who take regular tours of Japan seeking the secrets of Japanese industry. They come back with photographs and full notebooks, convinced they have learned secrets that can be transplanted to their own companies.

Even the Japanese have entered the pop-sociological search for the secrets of their own success; their journalists suggest that they emphasize problem *prevention* while Americans make up for their lack of prescience and care through *remediation* (in the case of cars, recalls for flawed models). The explanation given by a European Economic Community report—that the Japanese are workaholics willing, masochistically, to live in "rabbit hutches" without complaint—was met with amused derision in Japan. But it seems that those who do not look for transportable "secrets" are nonetheless willing to believe that the source of Japanese success is genetic, and thus completely untransferable. There are alternatives to these positions, and an examination of Japanese education provides us with a backdrop for considering them.

The Social Consensus

The attention given to the decline of both American industry and American education has not yet led to an awareness here of the close relationship between the development of people and the development of society, an awareness we see everywhere in Japanese thought and institutions, and whose effects we can see in the individual achievements of Japanese children. If Americans realized how powerful the relationship is between Japanese school achievement and social and economic successes we might see the same kind of protectionist language aimed at the Japanese educational system that we see directed at their automobile industry. ("The Japanese must stop producing such able and committed students because *it isn't fair*.")

The Japanese understand how important it is to have not just a high level of literacy (which they have had since well before modernization), but also a high level of education in the whole population. It has been said that the Japanese high school graduate is as well educated as an American college graduate, and indeed it is impressive that any worker on the factory floor can be expected to understand statistical material, work from complex graphs and charts, and perform sophisticated mathematical operations. This consensus that education is important, however simple it may sound, is the single most important contributor to the success of Japanese schools. Across the population, among parents, at all institutional and bureaucratic levels, and highest on the list of national priorities, is the stress on excellence in education. This is not just rhetoric. If the consensus, societal mobilization, and personal commitment—all focused on education—are not available to Americans, the reason is not genetic, nor are we locked in an immutable cultural pattern. We simply have not mobilized around our children.

There are dear advantages to being a Japanese child: a homogeneous   5
population focused on perpetuating its cultural identity; an occupational
system where selection and promotion are based on educational credentials; a relatively equal distribution of educational opportunities; a universal core curriculum; highly trained and rewarded teachers; and families, especially mothers, devoted to enhancing the life chances of children
and working cooperatively with the educational system. Finally, there are
high standards for performance in every sector, and a carefully graded series of performance expectations in the school curriculum.

It is clear from these assertions that the measurable cognitive achievements of Japanese education represent only part of the picture. The
American press stresses these achievements and accounts for them in
terms of government expenditures, longer school years, and early use of
homework. While the International Association for the Evaluation of
Educational Achievement (IEA) test scores certainly indicate that
Japanese children are testing higher than any children in the world (especially in math and science), and while some researchers have even
claimed that Japanese children on average score 11 points more than
American children on IQ tests, the social and psychological dimensions of
Japanese education are similarly impressive and are primary contributors
to cognitive achievement. The support given by family and teachers to
the emotional and behavioral development of the child provides a base
for the child's acquisition of knowledge and problem-solving skills. But
beyond this, the Japanese think a major function of education is the development of a happy, engaged, and secure child, able to work hard and cooperate with others.

Inside the Japanese School

In order to understand the context of the Japanese educational system, some basic information is necessary:

1. Education is compulsory for ages six to 15, or through lower
secondary school. (Age is almost always correlated with grade level, by
the way, because only rarely is a child "kept back" and almost never "put
ahead.") Non-compulsory high school attendance (both public and
private) is nearly universal, at 98 percent.

2. There is extensive "non-official" private education. Increasing
numbers of children attend pre-schools. Currently, about 95 percent of the
five-year olds are in kindergarten or nursery school, 70 percent of the
four-year olds and 10 percent of three-year olds. Many older children attend *juku* (after school classes) as well. These are private classes in a great
variety of subjects, but most enhance and reinforce the material to be
learned for high school or college entrance examinations. There are also
yobiko (cram schools) for those taking an extra year between high school
and college to prepare for the exams.

3.   While competition for entrance to the most prestigious universi-   10
ties is very stiff, nearly 40 percent of the college-age group attend college
or university. (The rates are slightly higher for women, since many attend
two-year junior colleges.)

4.   Japanese children attend school 240 days a year, compared to 180
in the U.S. Many children spend Sundays in study or tutoring, and vacation classes are also available. Children do not necessarily see this as oppressive, and younger children often ask their parents to send them to
juku as a way of being with their friends after school. Homework starts in
first grade, and children in Japan spend more time in home study than
children in any other country except Taiwan. In Japan, 8 percent of the
high school seniors spend less than five hours per week on homework,
compared to 65 percent of American seniors.[1]

5.   Primary and lower secondary schools provide what we would
call a core curriculum: a required and comprehensive course of study pro-
gressing along a logical path, with attention given to children's develop-
mental levels. In elementary and lower secondary school, language learning dominates the school curriculum, and takes up the greatest number of
classroom hours, particularly from second to fourth grade. The large
number of characters to be learned requires an emphasis on memorization and drill that is not exhibited in the rest of the curriculum. Arithmetic
and math are next in number of class hours, followed by social studies.
The curriculum includes regular physical education and morning exercise as part of a "whole-child" program. In high school all students take
Japanese, English, math, science, and social studies each year, and all students have had courses in chemistry, biology, physics, and earth sciences.
All high school students take calculus.

6.   Computers and other technology do not play a large role in
schools. The calculator is used, but has not replaced mental calculations
or, for that matter, the abacus. There is no national program to develop
high technology skills in children. Americans spend much more money
on science and technology in the schools; the Japanese spend more on
teacher training and salaries.

These features should be seen in the context of a history of emphasis
on education in Japan. To begin with, an interest in mass (or at least widespread) education greatly antedated the introduction of Western schools
to Japan. Literacy, numeracy, and a moral education were considered important for people of all classes. When Western style universal compulsory schooling was introduced in 1872, it was after a deliberate and wide-
ranging search throughout the world that resulted in a selection of
features from German, French, and American educational systems that
would advance Japan's modernization and complement her culture.
While uniform, centralized schooling was an import, it eventually

[1]Thomas Rohlen, *Japan's High Schools* (Berkeley: University of California Press, 1983), p. 277.

brought out Japan's already refined powers of adaptation—not the ability to adapt to a new mode as much as *the ability to adapt the foreign mode to Japanese needs and conditions.*

Also striking was the rapidity with which Japan developed a modern   15
educational system and made it truly universal. In 1873, one year after the Education Act, there was 28 percent enrollment in primary schools, but by 1904 enrollment had already reached 98 percent—one percent less than the current rate. The rush to educate children was buttressed both by the wish to catch up with the West and by a cultural interest in schooling.

A Truly National System

Tradition, ideology, and international competition are not, however, the only motive forces in Japanese education: other factors are as significant. First, Japan has a relatively homogeneous population. Racially and economically there is little variety. Minority groups, such as Koreans and the former out-castes, exist and do suffer some discrimination, but all children have equal access to good schooling. Income is more evenly distributed in Japan than in America and most people (96 percent in a recent Prime Minister's Office poll) consider themselves middle class. There are few remaining regional differences that affect the educational system, except perhaps local accents.

Second, educational financing and planning are centralized. While American educational policy sees the responsibility for schooling as a local matter, Japanese planners can rely on a centralized source of funding, curriculum guidance, and textbook selection. In terms of educational spending as a percentage of total GNP, the U.S. and Japan are not so far apart: The U.S. devotes 6.8 percent of its GNP to education, and Japan devotes 8.6 percent. But in Japan about 50 percent of this is national funding, while in the U.S. the federal government provides only 8 percent of the total expenditure on education, most of which is applied to special education, not to core schooling. Moreover, in the U.S. there exist no national institutions to build a consensus on what and how our children are taught. The most significant outcome of centralization in Japan is the even distribution of resources and quality instruction across the country. National planners and policymakers can mobilize a highly qualified teaching force and offer incentives that make even the most remote areas attractive to good teachers.

Third (but perhaps most important in the comparison with the United States), teachers enjoy respect and high status, job security, and good pay. More than in any other country, teachers in Japan are highly qualified: Their mastery of their fields is the major job qualification, and all have at least a bachelor's degree in their specialty. Moreover, they have a high degree of professional involvement as teachers: 74 percent are said to belong to some professional teachers' association in which teaching methods and curriculum are actively discussed.[2]

---

[2]William Cummings, *Education and Equality in Japan* (Princeton: Princeton University Press, 1980), p. 159.

Teachers are hired for life, at starting salaries equivalent to starting salaries for college graduates in the corporate world. Elementary and junior high school teachers earn $18,200 per year on the average, high school teachers $19,000. Compared to other Japanese public sector workers, who earn an average of $16,800, this is a high salary, but it is less than that of managers in large companies or bureaucrats in prestigious ministries. In comparison with American teachers, whose salaries average $17,600, it is an absolutely higher wage. The difference is especially striking when one considers that over all professions, salaries are lower in Japan than in the U.S. In fact, American teachers' salaries are near the bottom of the scale of jobs requiring a college degree. Relative status and prestige correlate with salary in both countries. Japanese teachers' pay increases, as elsewhere in Japan, are tied to a seniority ladder, and older "master teachers" are given extra pay as teacher supervisors in each subject.[3]

Japanese teachers see their work as permanent: Teaching is not a waystation on a path to other careers. Teachers work hard at improving their skills and knowledge of their subject, and attend refresher courses and upgrading programs provided by the Ministry of Education. While there are tendencies, encouraged by the Teachers' Union, to downplay the traditional image of the "devoted, selfless teacher" (since this is seen as exploitative), and to redefine the teacher as a wage laborer with regular hours, rather than as a member of a "sacred" profession, teachers still regularly work overtime and see their job's sphere extending beyond classroom instruction. Classes are large: The average is about 40 students to one teacher. Teachers feel responsible for their students' discipline, behavior, morality, and for their general social adjustment as well as for their cognitive development. They are "on duty" after school hours and during vacations, and supervise vacation play and study. They visit their students' families at home, and are available to parents with questions and anxieties about their children. The Teachers' Union protests strongly against this extensive role, but both teachers and parents reinforce this role, tied as it is to the high status of the teacher.

Fourth, there is strong ideological and institutional support for education because the occupational system relies on schools to select the right person for the right organization. Note that this is not the same as the "right job" or "slot": A new company recruit, almost always a recent graduate, is not expected to have a skill or special identity, but to be appropriate in general educational background and character for a company. The company then trains recruits in the skills they will need, as well as in the company style. Of course, the basic skill level of the population of high school and college graduates is extremely high. But the important fact is that the social consensus supports an educational system that creates a committed, productive labor force. And although the emphasis

[3]There is a debate in Japan today concerning rewarding good teachers with higher pay: Professor Sumiko Iwao, of Keio University, reports that when quality is measured in yen, the commitment of teachers to good teaching declines.

seems to be on educational credentials, the quality of graduates possessing these credentials is indisputably high.

Mom

The background I have presented—of national consensus, institutional centralization, and fiscal support—alone does not explain the successes of Japanese education. There are other, less tangible factors that derive from cultural conceptions of development and learning, the valued
role of maternal support, and psychological factors in Japanese pedagogy,
and which distinguish it from American schooling.

The role of mothers is especially important. The average Japanese
mother feels her child has the potential for success: Children are believed
to be born with no distinguishing abilities (or disabilities) and can be mobilized to achieve and perform at high levels. Effort and commitment are
required, and, at least at the beginning, it is the mother's job to engage the
child. One way of looking at Japanese child development is to look at the
words and concepts related to parental goals for their children. A "good
child" has the following, frequently invoked characteristics: He is
otonashii (mild or gentle), *sunao* (compliant, obedient, and cooperative),
akarui (bright, alert), and *genki* (energetic and spirited). *Sunao* has frequently been translated as "obedient," but it would be more appropriate
to use "open minded," "nonresistant," or "authentic in intent and cooperative in spirit." The English word "obedience" implies subordination and
lack of self-determination, but *sunao* assumes that what we call compliance (with a negative connotation) is really cooperation, an act of affirma-
tion of the self. A child who is *sunao* has not yielded his personal autonomy for the sake of cooperation; cooperation does not imply giving up
the self, but in fact implies that working with others is the appropriate
setting for expressing and enhancing the self.

One encourages a *sunao* child through the technique, especially used
by mothers and elementary school teachers, of *wakaraseru*, or "getting the
child to understand." The basic principle of child rearing seems to be:
Never go against the child. *Wakaraseru* is often a long-term process that
ultimately engages the child in the mother's goals, and makes her goals
the child's own, thus producing an authentic cooperation, as in *sunao*. The
distinction between external, social expectations and the child's own personal goals becomes blurred from this point on. An American might see
this manipulation of the child through what we would call "indulgence"
as preventing him from having a strong will of his own, but the Japanese
mother sees long term benefits of self-motivated cooperation and real
commitment.

Japanese mothers are active teachers as well, and have a real curricu-   25
lum for their pre-school children: Games, teaching aids, ordinary activities
are all focused on the child's development. There are counting games for
very small babies, songs to help children learn new words, devices to fo-

cus the child's concentration. Parents buy an average of two or three new books every month for their preschoolers, and there are about 40 monthly activity magazines for preschoolers, very highly subscribed. The result is that most, at least most urban children, can read and write the phonetic syllabary before they enter school, and can do simple computations.

Maternal involvement becomes much more extensive and "serious" once she and the child enter the elementary school community. In addition to formal involvement in frequent ceremonies and school events, PTA meetings and visiting days, the mother spends much time each day helping the child with homework (sometimes to the point at which the teachers joke that they are really grading the mothers by proxy). There are classes for mothers, called *mamajuku*, that prepare mothers in subjects their children are studying. Homework is considered above all a means for developing a sense of responsibility in the child, and like much in early childhood education, it is seen as a device to train character.

The Japanese phenomenon of maternal involvement recently surfaced in Riverdale, New York, where many Japanese families have settled. School teachers and principals there noted that each Japanese family was purchasing two sets of textbooks. On inquiring, they found that the second set was for the mother, who could better coach her child if she worked during the day to keep up with his lessons. These teachers said that children entering in September with no English ability finished in June at the top of their classes in every subject.

The effort mothers put into their children's examinations has been given a high profile by the press. This is called the *kyoiku mama* syndrome—the mother invested in her children's progress. In contrast to Western theories of achievement, which emphasize individual effort and ability, the Japanese consider academic achievement to be an outgrowth of an interdependent network of cooperative effort and planning. The caricature of the mother's over-investment, however, portrays a woman who has totally identified with her child's success or failure, and who has no separate identity of her own. The press emphasizes the negative aspects of this involvement with accounts of maternal nervous breakdowns, reporting a murder by a mother of the child next-door, who made too much noise while her child was studying. But the press also feeds the mother's investment by exhorting her to prepare a good work environment for the studying child, to subscribe to special exam-preparation magazines, to hire tutors, and to prepare a nutritious and exam-appropriate diet.

High-schoolers from outlying areas taking entrance exams in Tokyo come with their mothers to stay in special rooms put aside by hotels. They are provided with special food, study rooms, counselors, and tension release rooms, all meant to supply home-care away from home. The home study-desk bought by most parents for their smaller children symbolizes the hovering care and intensity of the mother's involvement: All models have a high front and half-sides, cutting out distractions and enclosing the workspace in womb-like protection. There is a built-in study light, shelves, a clock, electric pencil sharpener, and built-in calculator. The most popular model includes a push-button connecting to a buzzer in the kitchen to summon mother for help or for a snack.

How Do You Feel about Cubing?

Not much work has been done yet to analyze the relationship between the strongly supportive learning atmosphere and high achievement in Japan. In the home, mothers train small children in a disciplined, committed use of energy through what Takeo Doi has called the encouragement of "positive dependency"; in the schools as well there is a recognition that attention to the child's emotional relationship to his work, peers, and teachers is necessary for learning.

A look at a Japanese classroom yields some concrete examples of this. Many Westerners believe that Japanese educational successes are due to an emphasis on rote learning and memorization, that the classroom is rigidly disciplined. This is far from reality. An American teacher walking into a fourth grade science class in Japan would be horrified: children all talking at once, leaping and calling for the teacher's attention. The typical American's response is to wonder, "Who's in control of this room?" But if one understands the content of the lively chatter, it is clear that all the noise and movement is focused on the work itself—children are shouting out answers, suggesting other methods, exclaiming in excitement over results, and not gossiping, teasing, or planning games for recess. As long as it is the result of this engagement, the teacher is not concerned over the noise, which may measure a teacher's success. (It has been estimated that American teachers spend about 60 percent of class time on organizing, controlling, and disciplining the class, while Japanese teachers spend only 10 percent.)

A fifth grade math class I observed reveals some elements of this pedagogy. The day I visited, the class was presented with a general statement about cubing. Before any concrete facts, formulae, or even drawings were displayed, the teacher asked the class to take out their math diaries and spend a few minutes writing down their feelings and anticipations over this new concept. It is hard for me to imagine an American math teacher beginning a lesson with an exhortation to examine one's emotional predispositions about cubing (but that may be only because my own math training was antediluvian).

After that, the teacher asked for conjectures from the children about the surface and volume of a cube and asked for some ideas about formulae for calculation. The teacher asked the class to cluster into its component *han* (working groups) of four or five children each, and gave out materials for measurement and construction. One group left the room with large pieces of cardboard, to construct a model of a cubic meter. The groups worked internally on solutions to problems set by the teacher and competed with each other to finish first. After a while, the cubic meter group returned, groaning under the bulk of its model, and everyone gasped over its size. (There were many comments and guesses as to how many children could fit inside.) The teacher then set the whole class a very challenging problem, well over their heads, and gave them the rest of the class time to work on it. The class ended without a solution, but the teacher made no particular effort to get or give an answer, although she exhorted them to be energetic. (It was several days before the class got the answer—there was no deadline but the excitement did not flag.)

Several characteristics of this class deserve highlighting. First, there was attention to feelings and predispositions, provision of facts, and opportunities for discovery. The teacher preferred to focus on process, engagement, commitment, and performance rather than on discipline (in our sense) and production. Second, the *han:* Assignments are made to groups, not to individuals (this is also true at the workplace) although individual progress and achievement are closely monitored. Children are supported, praised, and allowed to make mistakes through trial and error within the group. The group is also pitted against other groups, and the group's success is each person's triumph, and vice versa. Groups are made up by the teacher and are designed to include a mixture of skill levels—there is a *hancho* (leader) whose job it is to choreograph the group's work, to encourage the slower members, and to act as a reporter to the class at large.

Japanese teachers seem to recognize the emotional as well as the intellectual aspects of engagement. Japanese pedagogy (and maternal socialization) are based on the belief that effort is the most important factor in achievement, and that the teacher's job is to get the child to commit himself positively and energetically to hard work. This emphasis is most explicit in elementary school, but persists later as a prerequisite for the self-discipline and effort children exhibit in high school. 35

American educational rhetoric does invoke "the whole child," does seek "self-expression," and does promote emotional engagement in "discovery learning." But Japanese teaching style, at least in primary schools, effectively employs an engaging, challenging teaching style that surpasses most American attempts. In the cubing class, I was struck by the spontaneity, excitement, and (to American eyes) "unruly" dedication of the children to the new idea, and impressed with the teacher's ability to create this positive mood. It could be a cultural difference: We usually separate cognition and emotional affect, and then devise artificial means of reintroducing "feeling" into learning. It is rather like the way canned fruit juices are produced—first denatured by the preserving process and then topped up with chemical vitamins to replace what was lost.

The Role of Competition

The frequent accusation that Japanese education involves children in hellish competition must also be examined. In the elementary school classroom, competition is negotiated by means of the *han*. The educational system tries to accommodate both the ideology of harmony and the interest in hierarchy and ranking. The introduction of graded, competitive Western modes of education into societies where minimizing differences between people is valued has often produced severe social and psychological dislocation (as in Africa and other parts of the Third World). In Japan, the importance of the modern educational system as a talent selector and the need to preserve harmony and homogeneity have produced complementary rather than conflicting forces. The regular classroom is a place where the individual does not stick out, but where individual needs are met and goals are set. Children are not held back nor advanced by ability: The cohesion of the age group is said to be more important. Teachers focus on pulling up the slower learners, rather than tracking the class to suit different abilities. For the most part, teachers and the school system refuse to engage in examination preparation hysteria. Part of the reason for this is pressure from the Teachers' Union, a very large and powerful labor union which consistently resists any moves away from the egalitarian and undifferentiating mode of learning. Turning teachers into drill instructors is said to be dehumanizing, and the process of cramming a poor substitute for education.

So where is the competitive selection principle served? In the *juku*. *Juku* are tough competitive classes, often with up to 500 in one lecture hall. The most prestigious are themselves very selective and there are examinations (and preparation courses for these) to enter the *juku*. Some *juku* specialize in particular universities' entrance exams, and they will boast of their rate of admission into their universities. It is estimated that one third of all primary school students and one half of all secondary school students attend *juku*, but in Tokyo the rate rises to 86 percent of junior high school students. The "king of *juku*," Furukawa Noboru, the creator of a vast chain of such classes, says that *juku* are necessary to bridge the gap of present realities in Japan. He says that public schools do not face the fact of competition, and that ignoring the reality does not help children. The Ministry of Education usually ignores this non-accredited alternative and complementary system, and permits this functional division to take the pressure off the public schools. While there is considerable grumbling by parents, and while it is clear that the *juku* introduce an inegalitarian element into the process of schooling (since they do cost money), they do, by their separation from the regular school, permit the persistence of more traditional modes of learning, while allowing for a fast track in the examinations.

It is important to note that in Japan there really is only one moment of critical importance to one's career chances—the entrance examination to college. There are few opportunities to change paths or retool. Americans' belief that one can be recreated at any time in life, that the self-made person can get ahead, simply is not possible in Japan—thus the intense focus on examinations.

The Problems—In Context

This rapid tour through the Japanese educational system cannot neglect the problems. However, two things must be kept in mind when considering these well-publicized difficulties: One is that although problems
do exist, the statistical reality is that, compared to the West, Japan still
looks very good indeed. The other is that the Japanese themselves tend to
be quite critical, and educational problems are given attention. But this attention should be seen in context: Not that people are not truly concerned
about real problems, but that the anxiety seems related to a sense of national insecurity. The Japanese focus on educational issues may emanate
from a sense of the importance of intellectual development in a society
where there are few other resources. Any educational problem seems to
put the nation truly at risk.

Japanese parents are critical and watchful of the schools and are not
complacent about their children's successes. There was a telling example of this in a recent comparative study of American and Japanese education. Mothers in Minneapolis and in Sendai, roughly comparable
cities, were asked to evaluate their children's school experiences. The
Minneapolis mothers consistently answered that the schools were fine
and that their children were doing well, while the Sendai mothers were
very critical of their schools and worried that their children were not
performing up to potential. Whose children were, in objective tests, doing better? The Sendai group—in fact so much better that the poorest
performer in the Japanese group was well ahead of the best in the
American group. Mothers in Japan and the U.S. have very different perspectives on performance: Japanese mothers attribute failure to lack of
effort while American mothers explain it as lack of ability. Japanese children have an external standard of excellence to which they can aspire,
while an American child normally can only say he will "do his best."

Problems have surfaced, of course. Psychotherapists report a syndrome among children related to school and examination pressure.
School phobia, psychosomatic symptoms, and juvenile suicide are most
frequently reported. Japan does lead the world in school-related suicides
for the 15- to 19-year old age group, at about 300 per year. Recently, the
"battered teacher" and "battered parent" syndromes have received much
attention. There are cases where teenagers have attacked or killed parents
and teachers, and these have been related to examination pressure. The
numbers involved in these case are very small—at least in comparison
with American delinquency patterns and other juvenile pathologies.
Dropouts, drug use, and violent juvenile crimes are almost non-existent
in Japan. The crimes reported in one year among school-age children in
Osaka, for example, are equal to those reported in one day in New York.

Criticism leveled at Japanese education by Western observers focuses
on what they regard as a suppression of genius and individuality, and a
lack of attention to the development of creativity in children. The first may

indeed be a problem—for the geniuses—because there is little provision for tracking them to their best advantage. There has been discussion of introducing tracking so that individual ability can be better served, but this has not been implemented. The superbright may indeed be disadvantaged.

On the other hand, creativity and innovation *are* encouraged, but their manifestations may be different from those an American observer would expect. We must look at our own assumptions, to see if they are too limited. Americans see creativity in children as a fragile blossom that is stifled by rigid educational systems or adult standards. Creativity involves a necessary break with traditional content and methods, and implies the creation of a new idea or artifact. Whether creativity is in the child or in the teaching, and how it is to be measured, are questions no one has answered satisfactorily. Why we emphasize it is another question, probably related to our theories of progress and the importance we attach to unique accomplishments that push society forward. The fact is that, if anything, our schools do less to encourage creativity than do the Japanese, especially in the arts. All children in Japan learn two instruments and how to read music in elementary school, have regular drawing and painting classes, and work in small groups to create projects they themselves devise. It is true, though, that if everyone must be a soloist or composer to be considered creative, then most Japanese are not encouraged to be creative.

It is not enough to claim that the Japanese have been successful in   45
training children to take exams at the expense of a broader education. And it is not at all appropriate to say that they are unable to develop children's individuality and create the geniuses who make scientific breakthroughs. The first is untrue and the second remains to be shown as false by the Japanese themselves, who are now mobilizing to produce more scientists and technologists. In fact, the scales are tipped in favor of Japan, and to represent it otherwise would be a distortion.

The success of the Japanese model has led to its use in other rapidly developing countries, including south Korea, Taiwan, and Singapore. There, education is seen as the linchpin for development, and attention to children has meant the allocation of considerable resources to schools. The results are similar to those seen in Japanese schools: Highly motivated, hard-working students who like school and who have achieved very high scores on international achievement tests.

Seeing Ourselves through Japanese Eyes

What *America* can learn from Japan is rather an open question. We can, to begin with, learn more *about* Japan, and in doing so, learn more about ourselves. Japanese advancements of the past 20 years were based on American principles of productivity (such as "quality control"), not on samurai management skills and zen austerities. Looking for Japanese secrets, or worse, protesting that they are inhuman or unfair, will not get us very far. They have shown they can adjust programs and policies to the needs and resources of the times; we must do the same. We need to regain the scientific literacy we lost and reacquire the concrete skills and participatory techniques we need. We should see Japan as establishing a new standard, not as a model to be emulated. To match that standard we have to aim at general excellence, develop a long-term view, and act consistently over time with regard to our children's education.

 Topics for Critical Thinking and Writing

1. In paragraph 4 White contrasts Japanese commitment to education with our own. Where in our society might one look for evidence of commitment or lack of commitment to education?

2. In paragraph 5 White lists many "clear advantages to being a Japanese child." Considering your education, or any other grounds you choose, which of these "advantages" would you like to have? Are there any you would gladly do without? Can you explain why? How many of the Japanese advantages appear to be dependent on the first that White lists, "a homogeneous population"? Are you aware of advantages to growing up in a heterogeneous population? (For an explanation of Japanese homogeneity, see paragraph 16.)

3. At the end of paragraph 6 White says that "the Japanese think a major function of education is the development of a happy, engaged, and secure child, able to work hard and cooperate with others." Complete the following sentence: "Americans think a major function of education is . . ."

4. In paragraph 11 White discusses the amount of time Japanese students spend on homework. What were your own experiences with homework? Did homework contribute significantly to your education? Were there assignments you now regard as counterproductive?

5. In paragraph 13 White says that computers do not play a large role in Japanese schools. If computers played a fairly large role in your education, what do you think you learned from them, aside from how to operate them?

6. In paragraph 18 White reports that Japanese teachers are highly qualified. Do you think that, on the whole, your high school teachers were highly qualified? If you were able to do so, what measures would you take to insure well-qualified teachers in *all* American high schools? (White's paragraph 19 may provide some ideas.)

7. In paragraph 32 White briefly describes a math class about to study cubing. Does the procedure followed in the class strike you as being of any value? Why or why not? And what about the procedure described in the next paragraph? (In thinking about this, consider also White's comments in paragraphs 34–35). Looking back at a class in which you learned a good deal, what "elements of this pedagogy" (White's words, paragraph 32) made the class successful?

8. In paragraph 37 White says that children in Japanese schools are almost never held back or advanced because of ability, and there is no tracking system. What do you think of this system? (Consider also paragraphs 43 and 44.)

9. In paragraph 39 White writes of the belief of Americans that "one can be recreated at any time in life, that the self-made person can get ahead." To what extent do you share these beliefs? To what extent did the schools you attended promote them?

10. Japan has produced relatively few winners of the Nobel Prize. Did White's essay help you to understand why this might be so? Do you take the lack of Nobel Prize winners to be a significant criticism of the Japanese educational system?

11. Given the great differences between our societies, what, if anything, do you think our educational system can learn from the Japanese system? (For example, we are far less homogeneous. And the mothers in our society often hold paying jobs, whereas few Japanese mothers do. Further, two thirds of our teenagers hold part-time jobs, whereas almost no Japanese teenagers hold jobs.)

Robert Coles

Robert Coles is a psychiatrist and a professor at Harvard. He is the author of many books, including Children of Crisis *(5 volumes, 1967–77), which won the Pulitzer Prize, and* The Spiritual Lives of Children *(1990). "On Raising Moral Children" is an excerpt from* The Moral Intelligence of Children, *published by Random House in 1997.*

On Raising Moral Children

The Child as Witness

I first heard the term "moral intelligence" many years ago, from Rustin McIntosh, a distinguished pediatrician who was teaching a group of us how to work with young patients who were quite ill. When we asked him to explain what he had in mind by that phrase, "moral intelligence," he did not respond with an elegantly precise definition. Rather, he told us about boys and girls he'd known and treated who had it—who were "good," who were kind, who thought about others, who extended themselves toward those others, who were "smart" that way. He told us stories of clinical moments he found unforgettable: a girl dying of leukemia who worried about the "burden" she'd put upon her terribly saddened mother; a boy who lost the effective use of his right arm due to an automobile injury, and who felt sorry less for himself than he did for his dad, who loved baseball, loved coaching his son and others in a neighborhood Little League team.

Moral intelligence isn't only acquired by memorization of rules and regulations, by dint of abstract classroom discussion or kitchen compliance. We grow morally as a consequence of learning how to be with others, how to behave in this world, a learning prompted by taking to heart what we have seen and heard. The child is an ever attentive witness of grownup morality.

Of course, some children don't explicitly tell us what they have witnessed, the sense they've made of us, our moral ways of being. It can be hard for our sons and daughters to stand up to us, their parents, and teachers, point things out that trouble them. I once realized this all too memorably when I was driving my nine-year-old son to the hospital. He had injured himself in an accident—he had disobeyed his mother and me by "playing" with some carpentry tools we had set aside in our garage. I was upset because he'd sustained a deep cut that obviously would require surgical attention and that he'd ignored our "rule." I raced with him to the hospital on a rainy morning, careless that my car was splashing pedestrians, and at one point, I ignored a yellow light, then a red light. Amidst this headlong rush to an emergency ward, my son said, "Dad, if we're not careful, we'll make more trouble on our way to getting out of trouble."

A boy was pointing out, tactfully, respectfully, and yes, a bit fearfully, a major irony—that this effort to get us out of "trouble" could lead to more trouble; and he was also giving me a reproving as well as an anxious look: Be careful, lest you hurt people on your all too hurried journey. I realized the ethical implications of my son's admonitory if not admonishing remark: There's something important at stake here, the lives of others. A boy had reached outside himself, thought of those others, no matter his own ordeal, with its justification of a heightened self-regard. That is what our children can offer us and what we can offer them—a chance to learn from them, even as we try to teach them.

Day One

"I think we start sending signals to our kids from Day One," said a mother in one of my discussion groups. "My sister, Maisie, has a son who had a great appetite right from the beginning. They're going along fine— six months, seven months, and you know what? He'd be sitting in the bassinet or the high chair, and he'd gulp down that milk, and as he got bigger, and had a little more control, he started throwing the bottle away, throwing it on the floor. He knew what he was doing, he heard the 'bang', the 'thump', and he was obviously pleased with himself. A neighbor told my sister, 'He's just flexing his muscles, so let him do it—be glad he's like that.' But Maisie said no, no; she said she wasn't going to let her kid get the idea that he could behave like that: toss something away, when he was through with it, and see other people come running to clean up the mess he'd made! You know what she did? She didn't shout or get real tough with him; she just made sure she was there, right there, her hand ready, as the baby took his last bit of milk, and she took the bottle from him, while talking to him, or cleaning his face. In a while, the baby lost interest—she tested him a few times by not being so quick to ease the bottle away. Now, to my mind, my sister had started teaching her son right versus wrong—how he should behave, and what he shouldn't do, as early as it was, as young as the boy was."

Maisie had been smart enough to move in her mind from a boy who teased his mother, so she saw it, to an older child who had a similarly cavalier attitude toward his parents and others in authority. The parent has an opportunity to teach even a baby under one, and certainly a baby who is two or three, how to come to terms with wishes and yearnings, with times of disappointment and frustration that are part of love, of life. Some lucky babies have parents who show them love, and who love, in return—but do not become slaves to their child's demands, nor to their own nervous wish, natural for all of us, to give as much as we have, and as often as we can, to our sons and daughters. Other parents are less sure of themselves, or are lacking in self-restraint, and so let concern and affection deteriorate into an indulgence that can turn a child's head.

The Age of Conscience

In elementary school, maybe as never before or ever afterwards, the child becomes an intensely moral creature, quite interested in figuring out the reasons of this world—how and why things work, but also, how and why he or she should behave in various situations. "This is the age of conscience," Anna Freud once observed to me, and she went further: "This is the age that a child's conscience is built—or isn't; it is the time when a child's character is built and consolidated, or isn't." These are the years when a new world of knowledge and possibility arrives in the form of books, music, art, athletics, and, of course, the teachers and coaches who offer all that, the fellow students who share in the experiences. These are years of magic, of eager, lively searching on the part of children, whose parents and teachers are often hard put to keep up with them, as they try to understand things.

I once asked a six-year-old boy about his keen interest in telescopes. "When I look in it," he said, "it's like going on a long trip, and I'm far away, but I'm still here too." That child then took me on another kind of voyage, further into his mind and the thinking of other children than I had thought possible. "Those stars," he told me, "are moving fast, even if it looks like they're not moving one inch. A friend of mine said that God is keeping them from bumping into each other, but I told him, no, God isn't like that. He lets things happen—he doesn't keep interfering! He made everything, and then everything is on its own, and people too. In Sunday school, they say it's up to you, whether you'll be good or bad, and it's like that with the stars: they keep moving, and if they go off track, that's because something has gone wrong—it's an accident, it's not God falling asleep, or getting mad, something like that." He decided to complete his presentation: "Here it's different—there are people here. We're the star with people! That's why we could mess things up. The stars could hit each other—one star gets in the way of the other. That would be bad luck for both of them. But we could do something bad to this place, this star—and it would be as bad as if another star hit it, worse even!" A boy seemingly detoured by intellectual inclination from this planet's problems in favor of abiding interests in other planets was quite interested in addressing the biggest questions confronting all of us human beings—how our behavior might influence the very nature of existence.

Adolescence

Young people coming of age quite naturally command a good deal of our notice. They are understandably self-conscious, hence apt to call attention to themselves (while often claiming to want no such thing), and they bring us back to our own momentous time of adolescence—a second birth of sorts, only now accompanied by a blaze of self-awareness. Perhaps no other aspect of our life has prompted more writing on the part of our novelists, social scientists, journalists—it is as if these youths, in their habits, their interests, their language and dress, their music and politics, and not least, their developing sexuality, have a hold on us that is tied to our own memories.

Even if they have a good number of friends, many young people   10
have a loneliness that has to do with a self-imposed judgment of sorts: I am pushed and pulled by an array of urges, yearnings, worries, fears, that I can't share with anyone, really. This sense of utter difference makes for a certain moodiness well known among adolescents, who are, after all, constantly trying to figure out exactly how they ought to and might live.

I remember a young man of 15 who engaged in light banter, only to shut down, keep shaking his head, refuse to talk at all when his own life became the subject at hand. (He had stopped going to school, begun using large amounts of pot; he sat in his room for hours, listening to rock music.) After calling him, to myself, a host of psychiatric names—withdrawn, depressed, possibly psychotic—I asked him about his head-shaking behavior. I wondered whom he was thereby addressing. He did reply: "No one." I hesitated, gulped a bit as I took a chance: "Not yourself?" He looked right at me now in a sustained stare, for the first time. "Why do you say that?"

I decided not to answer the question in the manner that I was trained to reply—an account of what I had surmised about him, what I thought was happening inside him. Instead, with some unease, I heard myself saying this: "I've been there; I remember being there, when I felt I couldn't say a word to anyone." I can still remember those words, still remember feeling that I ought not have spoken them—a breach in "technique." The young man kept staring at me, didn't speak, at least through his mouth. When he took out his handkerchief and wiped his eyes, I realized they had begun to fill.

From there, we began a very gradual climb upward, step by step. As Anna Freud told me, "We are not miracle workers, who can say something, and—presto!—the trouble in a life has vanished. But I have noticed that in most of the adolescents that I see, in most of them a real effort at understanding . . . can go a long way."

To Parents and Teachers

Ralph Waldo Emerson once said, "Character is higher than intellect." Marian, a student of mine several years ago, much admired Emerson. She had arrived at Harvard from the Midwest and was trying hard to work her way through college by cleaning the rooms of her fellow students. Again and again she met classmates who had forgotten the meaning of please, of thank you, no matter their high SAT scores. They did not hesitate to be rude, even crude toward her. One day she was not so subtly propositioned by a young man she knew to be very bright. She quit her job, and was preparing to quit going to school. She came to see me full of anxiety and anger. "I've been taking all these philosophy courses," she said to me at one point, "and we talk about what's true, what's important, what's good. Well, how do you teach people to be good?"

Rather obviously, community service offers us all a chance to put our money where our mouths are. Books and classroom discussion, the skepticism of Marian notwithstanding, can be of help in this matter. But ultimately we must heed the advice of Henry James. When asked by his nephew what he ought to do in life, James replied, "Three things in human life are important. The first is to be kind. The second is to be kind. And the third is to be kind." The key to those words is the hortatory verb—the insistence that one find an existence that enables one to be kind. How to do so? By wading in, over and over, with that purpose in mind, with a willingness to sail on, tacking and tacking again, helped by those we aim to help, guided by our moral yearnings on behalf of others, on behalf of ourselves with others: a commitment to others that won't avoid squalls and periods of drift, a commitment that will become the heart of the journey itself.

15

Topics for Critical Thinking and Writing

1. Rustin McIntosh, from whom Coles first heard the term "moral intelligence," does not define it. Based on Cole's article, how would you define it? And how do children acquire it?

2. In his third and fourth paragraphs, Coles relates a personal anecdote. What is it, and what point is he making through it? What other anecdotes does he use, and why does he use them?

3. In his final paragraph, Coles uses a metaphor. What is it? Evaluate its effectiveness.

4. In a paragraph or two reveal through an anecdote a moral lesson.

Mary Field Belenky, Blythe McVicker Clinchy, Nancy Rule Goldberger, and Jill Mattuck Tarule

Mary Belenky is an assistant research professor at the University of Vermont. Blythe Clinchy taught psychology at Wellesley College, Nancy Goldberger is a visiting scholar in psychology at New York University, and Jill Tarule is Dean of Education at the University of Vermont. The essay printed here is part of Chapter 9 of their book, Women's Ways of Knowing, *a study of how women's intellectual abilities develop. (The title of the extract is the editors'.)*

How Women Learn

We begin with the reminiscences of two ordinary women, each recalling an hour during her first year at college. One of them, now middle-aged, remembered the first meeting of an introductory science course. The professor marched into the lecture hall, placed upon his desk a large jar filled with dried beans, and invited the students to guess how many beans the jar contained. After listening to an enthusiastic chorus of wildly inaccurate estimates the professor smiled a thin, dry smile, revealed the correct answer, and announced, "You have just learned an important lesson about science. Never trust the evidence of your own senses."

Thirty years later, the woman could guess what the professor had in mind. He saw himself, perhaps, as inviting his students to embark upon an exciting voyage into a mysterious underworld invisible to the naked eye, accessible only through scientific method and scientific instruments. But the seventeen-year-old girl could not accept or even hear the invitation. Her sense of herself as a knower was shaky, and it was based on the belief that she could use her own firsthand experience as a source of truth. This man was saying that this belief was fallacious. He was taking away her only tool for knowing and providing her with no substitute. "I remember feeling small and scared," the woman says, "and I did the only thing I could do. I dropped the course that afternoon, and I haven't gone near science since."

The second woman, in her first year at college, told a superficially similar but profoundly different story about a philosophy class she had attended just a month or two before the interview. The teacher came into class carrying a large cardboard cube. She placed it on the desk in front of her and asked the class what it was. They said it was a cube. She asked what a cube was, and they said a cube contained six equal square sides. She asked how they knew that this object contained six equal square sides. By looking at it, they said. "But how do you know?" the teacher asked again. She pointed to the side facing her and, therefore, invisible to the students; then she lifted the cube and pointed to the side that had been face down on the desk, and, therefore, also invisible. "We can't look at all six sides of a cube at once, can we? So we can't exactly *see* a cube. And yet, you're right. You know it's a cube. But you know it not just because you have eyes but because you have intelligence. You invent the sides you cannot see. You use your intelligence to create the 'truth' about cubes."

The student said to the interviewer,

> It blew my mind. You'll think I'm nuts, but I ran back to the dorm and I called my boyfriend and I said, "Listen, this is just incredible," and I told him all about it. I'm not sure he could see why I was so excited. I'm not sure I understand it myself. But I really felt, for the first time, like I was really in college, like I was—I don't know—sort of *grown up*.

Both stories are about the limitations of firsthand experience as a source of knowledge—we cannot simply see the truth about either the jar of beans or the cube—but there is a difference. We can know the truth about cubes. Indeed, the students did know it. As the science professor pointed out, the students were wrong about the beans; their senses had deceived them. But, as the philosophy teacher pointed out, the students were right about the cube; their minds had served them well.

The science professor was the only person in the room who knew how many beans were in that jar. Theoretically, the knowledge was available to the students; they could have counted the beans. But faced with that tedious prospect, most would doubtless take the professor's word for it. He is authority. They had to rely upon his knowledge rather than their own. On the other hand, every member of the philosophy class knew that the cube had six sides. They were all colleagues.

The science professor exercised his authority in a benign fashion, promising the students that he would provide them with the tools they needed to excavate invisible truths. Similarly, the philosophy teacher planned to teach her students the skills of philosophical analysis, but she was at pains to assure them that they already possessed the tools to construct some powerful truths. They had built cubes on their own, using only their own powers of inference, without the aid of elaborate procedures or fancy apparatus or even a teacher. Although a teacher might have told them once that a cube contained six equal square sides, they did

5

not have to take the teacher's word for it; they could have easily verified it for themselves.

The lesson the science professor wanted to teach is that experience is a source of error. Taught in isolation, this lesson diminished the student, rendering her dumb and dependent. The philosophy teacher's lesson was that although raw experience is insufficient, by reflecting upon it the student could arrive at truth. It was a lesson that made the student feel more powerful ("sort of grown up").

No doubt it is true that, as the professor in May Sarton's novel *The Small Room* says, the "art" of being a student requires humility. But the woman we interviewed did not find the science lesson humbling; she found it humiliating. Arrogance was not then and is not now her natural habitat. Like most of the women in our sample she lacked confidence in herself as a thinker; and the kind of learning the science teacher demanded was not only painful but crippling.

In thinking about the education of women, Adrienne Rich writes,   10
"Suppose we were to ask ourselves, simply: What does a woman need to know?" A woman, like any other human being, does need to know that the mind makes mistakes; but our interviews have convinced us that every woman, regardless of age, social class, ethnicity, and academic achievement, needs to know that she is capable of intelligent thought, and she needs to know it right away. Perhaps men learn this lesson before going to college, or perhaps they can wait until they have proved themselves to hear it; we do not know. We do know that many of the women we interviewed had not yet learned it.

⟡ Topics for Critical Thinking and Writing

1. How is the professor in the first anecdote characterized? Look particularly at the words used in paragraphs 1 and 2 to describe him. How is the student characterized? Look back at the first sentence: Why do the writers use the word *ordinary* to describe both students? Why did they not simply say, "We begin with the reminiscences of two women"?

2. In paragraph 5 the writers say, "Both stories are about the limitations of firsthand experience as a source of knowledge." What else do the stories have in common? What are the important differences? What particular difference is most relevant to the main point of the essay?

3. Look again at paragraph 6. The science teacher is described as being "authority." The students "had to rely upon his knowledge rather than their own." Is this relationship between teacher and students more likely in science courses than in philosophy or literature courses? Is it inevitable in sciences courses? If so, why?

4. What is the main point of the concluding paragraph? Do the two anecdotes support this point? To what extent does your own experience confirm it or not confirm it?

Fan Shen

Fan Shen came to the United States from the People's Republic of China. A translator and writer, he also teaches at Rockland Community College in Suffern, New York.

The Classroom and the Wider Culture

Identity as a Key to Learning English Composition

One day in June 1975, when I walked into the aircraft factory where I was working as an electrician, I saw many large-letter posters on the walls and many people parading around the workshops shouting slogans like "Down with the word 'I'!" and "Trust in masses and the Party!" I then remembered that a new political campaign called "Against Individualism" was scheduled to begin that day. Ten years later, I got back my first English composition paper at the University of Nebraska—Lincoln. The professor's first comments were: "Why did you always use 'we' instead of 'I'?" and "Your paper would be stronger if you eliminated some sentences in the passive voice." The clashes between my Chinese background and the requirements of English composition had begun. At the center of this mental struggle, which has lasted several years and is still not completely over, is the prolonged, uphill battle to recapture "myself."

In this paper I will try to describe and explore this experience of reconciling my Chinese identity with an English identity dictated by the rules of English composition. I want to show how my cultural background shaped—and shapes—my approaches to my writing in English and how writing in English redefined—and redefines—my *ideological* and *logical* identities. By "ideological identity" I mean the system of values that I acquired (consciously and unconsciously) from my social and cultural background. And by "logical identity" I mean the natural (or Oriental) way I organize and express my thoughts in writing. Both had to be modified or redefined in learning English composition. Becoming aware of the process of redefinition of these different identities is a mode of learning that has helped me in my efforts to write in English, and, I hope, will be of help to teachers of English composition in this country. In presenting my case for this view, I will use examples from both my composition courses and literature courses, for I believe that writing papers for both kinds of courses contributed to the development of my "English

Fan Shen, "The Classroom and the Wider Culture: Identity as a Key to Learning English Composition," *College Composition and Communication*, 40, December 1989. Copyright 1989 by the National Council of Teachers of English. Reprinted with permission.

identity." Although what I will describe is based on personal experience, many Chinese students whom I talked to said that they had had the same or similar experiences in their initial stages of learning to write in English.

Identity of the Self: Ideological and Cultural

Starting with the first English paper I wrote, I found that learning to compose in English is not an isolated classroom activity, but a social and cultural experience. The rules of English composition encapsulate values that are absent in, or sometimes contradictory to, the values of other societies (in my case, China). Therefore, learning the rules of English composition is, to a certain extent, learning the values of Anglo-American society. In writing classes in the United States I found that I had to reprogram my mind, to redefine some of the basic concepts and values that I had about myself, about society, and about the universe, values that had been imprinted and reinforced in my mind by my cultural background, and that had been part of me all my life.

Rule number one in English composition is: Be yourself. (More than one composition instructor has told me, "Just write what *you* think.") The values behind this rule, it seems to me, are based on the principle of protecting and promoting individuality (and private property) in this country. The instruction was probably crystal clear to students raised on these values, but, as a guideline of composition, it was not very clear or useful to me when I first heard it. First of all, the image or meaning that I attached to the word "I" or "myself" was, as I found out, different from that of my English teacher. In China, "I" is always subordinated to "We"—be it the working class, the Party, the country, or some other collective body. Both political pressure and literary tradition require that "I" be somewhat hidden or buried in writings and speeches; presenting the "self" too obviously would give people the impression of being disrespectful of the Communist Party in political writings and boastful in scholarly writings. The word "I" has often been identified with another "bad" word, "individualism," which has become a synonym for selfishness in China. For a long time the words "self" and "individualism" have had negative connotations in my mind, and the negative force of the words naturally extended to the field of literary studies. As a result, even if I had brilliant ideas, the "I" in my papers always had to show some modesty by not competing with or trying to stand above the names of ancient and modern authoritative figures. Appealing to Mao or other Marxist authorities became the required way (as well as the most "forceful" or "persuasive" way) to prove one's point in written discourse. I remember that in China I had even committed what I can call "reversed plagiarism"—here, I suppose it would be called "forgery"—when I was in middle school: willfully attributing some of my thoughts to "experts" when I needed some arguments but could not find a suitable quotation from a literary or political "giant."

Now, in America, I had to learn to accept the words "I" and "self" as   5
something glorious (as Whitman did), or at least something not to be
ashamed of or embarrassed about. It was the first and probably biggest
step I took into English composition and critical writing. Acting upon my
professor's suggestion, I intentionally tried to show my "individuality"
and to "glorify" "I" in my papers by using as many "I's" as possible—"I
think," "I believe," "I see"—and deliberately cut out quotations from authorities. It was rather painful to hand in such "pompous" (I mean immodest) papers to my instructors. But to an extent it worked. After a
while I became more comfortable with only "the shadow of myself." I felt
more at ease to put down *my* thoughts without looking over my shoulder
to worry about the attitudes of my teachers or the reactions of the Party
secretaries, and to speak out as "bluntly" and "immodestly" as my
American instructors demanded.

But writing many "I's" was only the beginning of the process of redefining myself. Speaking of redefining myself is, in an important sense,
speaking of redefining the word "I." By such a redefinition I mean not
only the change in how I envisioned myself, but also the change in how *I*
perceived the world. The old "I" used to embody only one set of values,
but now it had to embody multiple sets of values. To be truly "myself,"
which I knew was a key to my success in learning English composition,
meant *not to be my Chinese self* at all. That is to say, when I write in English
I have to wrestle with and abandon (at least temporarily) the whole system of ideology which previously defined me in myself. I had to forget
Marxist doctrines (even though I do not see myself as a Marxist by choice)
and the Party lines imprinted in my mind and familiarize myself with a
system of capitalist/bourgeois values. I had to put aside an ideology of
collectivism and adopt the values of individualism. In composition as
well as in literature classes, I had to make a fundamental adjustment: If I
used to examine society and literary materials through the microscopes of
Marxist dialectical materialism and historical materialism, I now had to
learn to look through the microscopes the other way around, i.e., to learn
to look at and understand the world from the point of view of "idealism."
(I must add here that there are American professors who use a Marxist
approach in their teaching.)

The word "idealism," which affects my view of both myself and the
universe, is loaded with social connotations, and can serve as a good example of how redefining a key word can be a pivotal part of redefining
my ideological identity as a whole.

To me, idealism is the philosophical foundation of the dictum of
English composition: "Be yourself." In order to write good English, I
knew that I had to be myself, which actually meant not to be my Chinese
self. It meant that I had to create an English self and be *that* self. And to be
that English self, I felt, I had to understand and accept idealism the way a
Westerner does. That is to say, I had to accept the way a Westerner sees
himself in relation to the universe and society. On the one hand, I knew a

lot about idealism. But on the other hand, I knew nothing about it. I mean I knew a lot about idealism through the propaganda and objections of its opponent, Marxism, but I knew little about it from its own point of view. When I thought of the word "materialism"—which is a major part of Marxism and in China has repeatedly been "shown" to be the absolute truth—there were always positive connotations, and words like "right," "true," etc., flashed in my mind. On the other hand, the word "idealism" always came to me with the dark connotations that surround words like "absurd," "illogical," "wrong," etc. In China "idealism" is depicted as a ferocious and ridiculous enemy of Marxist philosophy. Idealism, as the simplified definition imprinted in my mind had it, is the view that the material world does not exist; that all that exists is the mind and its ideas. It is just the opposite of Marxist dialectical materialism which sees the mind as a product of the material world. It is not too difficult to see that idealism, with its idea that mind is of primary importance, provides a philosophical foundation for the Western emphasis on the value of individual human minds, and hence individual human beings. Therefore, my final acceptance of myself as of primary importance—an importance that overshadowed that of authority figures in English composition—was, I decided, dependent on an acceptance of idealism.

My struggle with idealism came mainly from my efforts to understand and to write about works such as Coleridge's *Biographia Literaria* and Emerson's "Over-Soul." For a long time I was frustrated and puzzled by the idealism expressed by Coleridge and Emerson—given their ideas, such as "I think, therefore I am" (Coleridge obviously borrowed from Descartes) and "the transparent eyeball" (Emerson's view of himself)—because in my mind, drenched as it was in dialectical materialism, there was always a little voice whispering in my ear "You are, therefore you think." I could not see how human consciousness, which is not material, could create apples and trees. My intellectual conscience refused to let me believe that the human mind is the primary world and the material world secondary. Finally, I had to imagine that I was looking at a world with my head upside down. When I imagined that I was in a new body (born with the head upside down) it was easier to forget biases imprinted in my subconsciousness about idealism, the mind, and my former self. Starting from scratch, the new inverted self—which I called my "English Self" and into which I have transformed myself—could understand and *accept*, with ease, idealism as "the truth" and "himself" (i.e., my English Self) as the "creator" of the world.

Here is how I created my new "English Self." I played a "game" similar to ones played by mental therapists. First I made a list of (simplified) features about writing associated with my old identity (the Chinese Self), both ideological and logical, and then beside the first list I added a column of features about writing associated with my new identity (the English Self). After that I pictured myself getting out of my old identity, the timid, humble, modest Chinese "I," and creeping into my new identity (often in the form of a new skin or a mask), the confident, assertive,

10

and aggressive English "I." The new "Self" helped me to remember and accept the different rules of Chinese and English composition and the values that underpin these rules. In a sense, creating an English Self is a way of reconciling my old cultural values with the new values required by English writing, without losing the former.

An interesting structural but not material parallel to my experiences in this regard has been well described by Min-zhan Lu in her important article, "From Silence to Words: Writing as Struggle" (*College English* 49 [April 1987]: 437–48). Min-zhan Lu talks about struggles between two selves, an open self and a secret self, and between two discourses, a mainstream Marxist discourse and a bourgeois discourse her parents wanted her to learn. But her struggle was different from mine. Her Chinese self was severely constrained and suppressed by mainstream cultural discourse, but never interfused with it. Her experiences, then, were not representative of those of the majority of the younger generation who, like me, were brought up on only one discourse. I came to English composition as a Chinese person, in the fullest sense of the term, with a Chinese identity already fully formed.

Identity of the Mind: Illogical and Alogical

In learning to write in English, besides wrestling with a different ideological system, I found that I had to wrestle with a logical system very different from the blueprint of logic at the back of my mind. By "logical system" I mean two things: the Chinese way of thinking I used to approach my theme or topic in written discourse, and the Chinese critical/logical way to develop a theme or topic. By English rules, the first is illogical, for it is the opposite of the English way of approaching a topic; the second is alogical (nonlogical), for it mainly uses mental pictures instead of words as a critical vehicle.

The Illogical Pattern. In English composition, an essential rule for the logical organization of a piece of writing is the use of a "topic sentence." In Chinese composition, "from surface to core" is an essential rule, a rule which means that one ought to reach a topic gradually and "systematically" instead of "abruptly."

The concept of a topic sentence, it seems to me, is symbolic of the values of a busy people in an industrialized society, rushing to get things done, hoping to attract and satisfy the busy reader very quickly. Thinking back, I realized that I did not fully understand the virtue of the concept until my life began to rush at the speed of everyone else's in this country. Chinese composition, on the other hand, seems to embody the values of a leisurely paced rural society whose inhabitants have the time to chew and taste a topic slowly. In Chinese composition, an introduction explaining how and why one chooses this topic is not only acceptable, but often regarded as necessary. It arouses the reader's interest in the topic little by little (and this is seen as a virtue of composition) and gives him/her a sense of refinement. The famous Robert B. Kaplan "noodles" contrasting a spiral Oriental thought process with a straight-line Western approach ("Cultural Thought Patterns in Inter-Cultural Education," *Readings on English as a Second Language,* ed. Kenneth Croft, 2nd ed., Winthrop, 1980, 403–10) may be too simplistic to capture the preferred pattern of writing in English, but I think they still express some truth about Oriental writing. A Chinese writer often clears the surrounding bushes before attacking the real target. This bush-clearing pattern in Chinese writing goes back two thousand years to Kong Fuzi (Confucius). Before doing anything, Kong says in his *Luen Yu (Analects),* one first needs to call things by their proper names (expressed by his phrase "Zheng Ming"). In other words, before touching one's main thesis, one should first state the "conditions" of composition: how, why, and when the piece is being composed. All of this will serve as a proper foundation on which to build the "house" of the piece. In the two thousand years after Kong, this principle of composition was gradually formalized (especially through the formal essays required by imperial examinations) and became known as "Ba Gu," or the eightlegged essay. The logic of Chinese composition, exemplified by the eightlegged essay, is like the peeling of an onion: Layer after layer is removed until the reader finally arrives at the central point, the core.

Ba Gu still influences modern Chinese writing. Carolyn Matalene has 15 an excellent discussion of this logical (or illogical) structure and its influence on her Chinese students' efforts to write in English ("Contrastive Rhetoric: An American Writing Teacher in China," *College English* 47 [November 1985]: 789–808). A recent Chinese textbook for composition lists six essential steps (factors) for writing a narrative essay, steps to be taken in this order: time, place; character, event, cause, and consequence (*Yuwen Jichu Zhishi Liushi Jiang [Sixty Lessons on the Basics of the Chinese Language],* ed. Beijing Research Institute of Education, Beijing Publishing House, 1981, 525–609). Most Chinese students (including me) are taught to follow this sequence in composition.

The straightforward approach to composition in English seemed to me, at first, illogical. One could not jump to the topic. One had to walk step by step to reach the topic. In several of my early papers I found that the Chinese approach—the bush-clearing approach—persisted, and I had considerable difficulty writing (and in fact understanding) topic sentences. In what I deemed to be topic sentences, I grudgingly gave out themes. Today, those papers look to me like Chinese papers with forced or false English openings. For example, in a narrative paper on a trip to New York, I wrote the forced/false topic sentence, "A trip to New York in winter is boring." In the next few paragraphs, I talked about the weather, the people who went with me, and so on, before I talked about what I learned from the trip. My real thesis was that one could always learn something even on a boring trip.

The Alogical Pattern. In learning English composition, I found that there was yet another cultural blueprint affecting my logical thinking. I found from my early papers that very often I was unconsciously under the influence of a Chinese critical approach called the creation of "yijing," which is totally non-Western. The direct translation of the word "yijing" is: yi, "mind or consciousness," and jing, "environment." An ancient approach which has existed in China for many centuries and is still the subject of much discussion, yijing is a complicated concept that defies a universal definition. But most critics in China nowadays seem to agree on one point, that yijing is the critical approach that separates Chinese literature and criticism from Western literature and criticism. Roughly speaking, yijing is the process of creating a pictorial environment while reading a piece of literature. Many critics in China believe that yijing is a creative process of inducing oneself, while reading a piece of literature or looking at a piece of art, to create mental pictures, in order to reach a unity of nature, the author, and the reader. Therefore, it is by its very nature both creative and critical. According to the theory, this nonverbal, pictorial process leads directly to a higher ground of beauty and morality. Almost all critics in China agree that yijing is not a process of logical thinking—it is not a process of moving from the premises of an argument to its conclusion, which is the foundation of Western criticism. According to yijing, the process of criticizing a piece of art or literary work has to involve the process of creation on the reader's part. In yijing, verbal thoughts and pictorial thoughts are one. Thinking is conducted largely in pictures and then "transcribed" into words. (Ezra Pound once tried to capture the creative aspect of yijing in poems such as "In a Station of the Metro." He also tried to capture the critical aspect of it in his theory of imagism and vorticism, even though he did not know the term "yijing.") One characteristic of the yijing approach to criticism, therefore, is that it often includes a description of the created mental pictures on the part of the reader/critic and his/her mental attempt to bridge (unite) the literary work, the pictures, with ultimate beauty and peace.

In looking back at my critical papers for various classes, I discovered that I unconsciously used the approach of yijing, especially in some of my earlier papers when I seemed not yet to have been in the grip of Western logical critical approaches. I wrote, for instance, an essay entitled "Wordsworth's Sound and Imagination: The Snowdon Episode." In the major part of the essay I described the pictures that flashed in my mind while I was reading passages in Wordsworth's long poem, *The Prelude*.

> I saw three climbers (myself among them) winding up the mountain in silence "at the dead of night," absorbed in their "private thoughts." The sky was full of blocks of clouds of different colors, freely changing their shapes, like oily pigments disturbed in a bucket of water. All of a sudden, the moonlight broke the darkness "like a flash," lighting up the mountain tops. Under the "naked moon," the band saw a vast sea of mist and vapor, a silent ocean. Then the silence was abruptly broken, and we heard the "roaring of waters, torrents, streams/Innumerable, roaring with one voice" from a "blue chasm," a fracture in the vapor of the sea. It was a joyful revelation of divine truth to the human mind: the bright, "naked" moon sheds the light of

"higher reasons" and "spiritual love" upon us; the vast ocean of mist looked like a thin curtain through which we vaguely saw the infinity of nature beyond; and the sounds of roaring waters coming out of the chasm of vapor cast us into the boundless spring of imagination from the depth of the human heart. Evoked by the divine light from above, the human spring of imagination is joined by the natural spring and becomes a sustaining source of energy, feeding "upon infinity" while transcending infinity at the same time.

Here I was describing my own experience more than Wordsworth's. The picture described by the poet is taken over and developed by the reader. The imagination of the author and the imagination of the reader are thus joined together. There was no "because" or "therefore" in the paper. There was little *logic*. And I thought it was (and it is) criticism. This seems to me a typical (but simplified) example of the yijing approach. (Incidentally, the instructor, a kind professor, found the paper interesting, though a bit "strange.")

In another paper of mine, "The Note of Life: Williams's 'The Orchestra'," I found myself describing my experiences of pictures of nature while reading William Carlos Williams's poem, "The Orchestra." I "painted" these fleeting pictures and described the feelings that seemed to lead me to an understanding of a harmony, a "common tone," between man and nature. A paragraph from that paper reads:

20

The poem first struck me as a musical fairy tale. With rich musical sounds in my ear, I seemed to be walking in a solitary, dense forest on a spring morning. No sound from human society could be heard. I was now sitting under a giant pine tree, ready to hear the grand concert of Nature. With the sun slowly rising from the east, the cello (the creeping creek) and the clarinet (the rustling pine trees) started with a slow overture. Enthusiastically the violinists (the twittering birds) and the French horn (the mumbling cow) "interpose[d] their voices," and the bass (bears) got in at the wrong time. The orchestra did not stop, they continued to play. The musicians of Nature do not always play in harmony. "Together, unattuned," they have to seek "a common tone" as they play along. The symphony of Nature is like the symphony of human life: both consist of random notes seeking a "common tone." For the symphony of life

> Love is that common tone
> shall raise his fiery head
> and sound his note.

Again, the logical pattern of this paper, the "pictorial criticism," is illogical to Western minds but "logical" to those acquainted with yijing. (Perhaps I should not even use the words "logical" and "think" because they are so conceptually tied up with "words" and with culturally-based conceptions, and therefore very misleading if not useless in a discussion of yijing. Maybe I should simply say that yijing is neither illogical nor logical, but alogical.)

I am not saying that such a pattern of "alogical" thinking is wrong—in fact some English instructors find it interesting and acceptable—but it is very non-Western. Since I was in this country to learn the English language and English literature, I had to abandon Chinese "pictorial logic," and to learn Western "verbal logic."

If I Had to Start Again

The change is profound: Through my understanding of new meanings of words like "individualism," "idealism," and "I," I began to accept the underlying concepts and values of American writing, and by learning to use "topic sentences" I began to accept a new logic. Thus, when I write papers in English, I am able to obey all the general rules of English composition. In doing this I feel that I am writing through, with, and because of a new identity. I welcome the change, for it has added a new dimension to me and to my view of the world. I am not saying that I have entirely lost my Chinese identity. In fact I feel that I will never lose it. Any time I write in Chinese, I resume my old identity, and obey the rules of Chinese composition such as "Make the 'I' modest," and "Beat around the bush before attacking the central topic." It is necessary for me to have such a Chinese identity in order to write authentic Chinese. (I have seen people who, after learning to write in English, use English logic and sentence patterning to write Chinese. They produce very awkward Chinese texts.) But when I write in English, I imagine myself slipping into a new "skin," and I let the "I" behave much more aggressively and knock the topic right on the head. Being conscious of these different identities has helped me to reconcile different systems of values and logic, and has played a pivotal role in my learning to compose in English.

Looking back, I realize that the process of learning to write in English is in fact a process of creating and defining a new identity and balancing it with the old identity. The process of learning English composition would have been easier if I had realized this earlier and consciously sought to compare the two different identities required by the two writing systems from two different cultures. It is fine and perhaps even necessary for American composition teachers to teach about topic sentences, paragraphs, the use of punctuation, documentation, and so on, but can anyone design exercises sensitive to the ideological and logical differences that students like me experience—and design them so they can be introduced at an early stage of an English composition class? As I pointed out earlier, the traditional advice "Just be yourself" is not clear and helpful to students from Korea, China, Vietnam, or India. From "Be yourself" we are likely to hear either "Forget your cultural habit of writing" or "Write as you would write in your own language." But neither of the two is what the instructor meant or what we want to do. It would be helpful if he or she pointed out the different cultural/ideological connotations of the word "I," the connotations that exist in a group-centered culture and an individual-centered culture. To sharpen the contrast, it might be useful to design papers on topics like "The Individual vs. The Group: China vs. America" or "Different 'I's' in Different Cultures."

Carolyn Matalene mentioned in her article (789) an incident concerning American businessmen who presented their Chinese hosts with gifts of cheddar cheese, not knowing that the Chinese generally do not like cheese. Liking cheddar cheese may not be essential to writing English prose, but being truly accustomed to the social norms that stand behind ideas such as the English "I" and the logical pattern of English composition—call it "compositional cheddar cheese"—is essential to writing in English. Matalene does not provide an "elixir" to help her Chinese students like English "compositional cheese," but rather recommends, as do I, that composition teachers not be afraid to give foreign students English "cheese," but to make sure to hand it out slowly, sympathetically, and fully realizing that it tastes very peculiar in the mouths of those used to a very different cuisine.

25

 Topics for Critical Thinking and Writing

1. In his second paragraph Fan Shen says, "I will try to describe and explore this experience of reconciling my Chinese identity with an English identity." What does the article tell us is part of a "Chinese identity," and what is part of an "English identity"? How does your experience in answering this question account for the value of beginning his article with two narratives?

2. His article is based, primarily, on "personal experience." Is this part of his "English identity" or "Chinese identity"? Explain.

3. In paragraph 4 Fan Shen says that "Rule number one in English composition is: Be yourself." Whether you are from the United States or from another culture, try to explain why "being yourself" is (or is not) difficult when you enter college writing. Why did Fan Shen find it difficult?

4. Does Fan Shen's explanation (paragraphs 13–15) of the value of the topic sentence in English help to explain it to you, or do you have some other account of it? Explain.

5. In his next-to-last paragraph Fan Shen suggests topics for instructors to assign to international students. One of the two, "Different 'I's'" in Different Cultures," strikes us as a good project to assign to native students as well as those from other cultures. We suggest here that you write a journal entry taking notes on the "different 'I's'" you have experienced before attending college and now. If it suits you to do this, divide your journal entry in two down the middle, taking notes on the "I" before and the "I" after.

Paul Goodman

Paul Goodman (1911–72) received his bachelor's degree from City College in New York and his Ph.D. from the University of Chicago. He taught in several colleges and universities, and he was a prolific writer on literature, politics, and education. Goodman's view that students were victims of a corrupt society made him especially popular on campuses–even in the 1960s when students tended to distrust anyone over thirty. "A Proposal to Abolish Grading" (editors' title) is an extract from Compulsory Mis-Education and the Community of Scholars *(1966).*

A Proposal to Abolish Grading

Let half a dozen of the prestigious Universities—Chicago, Stanford, the Ivy League—abolish grading, and use testing only and entirely for pedagogic purposes as teachers see fit.

Anyone who knows the frantic temper of the present schools will understand the transvaluation of values that would be effected by this modest innovation. For most of the students, the competitive grade has come to be the essence. The naïve teacher points to the beauty of the subject and the ingenuity of the research; the shrewd student asks if he is responsible for that on the final exam.

Let me at once dispose of an objection whose unanimity is quite fascinating. I think that the great majority of professors agree that grading hinders teaching and creates a bad spirit, going as far as cheating and plagiarizing. I have before me the collection of essays, *Examining in Harvard College*, and this is the consensus. It is uniformly asserted, however, that the grading is inevitable; for how else will the graduate schools, the foundations, the corporations *know* whom to accept, reward, hire? How will the talent scouts know whom to tap?

By testing the applicants, of course, according to the specific task-requirements of the inducting institution, just as applicants for the Civil Service or for licenses in medicine, law, and architecture are tested. Why should Harvard professors do the testing *for* corporations and graduate-schools?

The objection is ludicrous. Dean Whitla, of the Harvard Office of Tests, points out that the scholastic-aptitude and achievement tests used for *admission* to Harvard are a super-excellent index for all-around Harvard performance, better than high-school grades or particular Harvard course-grades. Presumably, these college-entrance tests are tailored for what Harvard and similar institutions want. By the same logic, would not an employer do far better to apply his own job-aptitude test rather than to rely on the vagaries of Harvard sectionmen. Indeed, I doubt that many employers bother to look at such grades; they are more

5

likely to be interested merely in the fact of a Harvard diploma, whatever that connotes to them. The grades have most of their weight with the graduate schools—here, as elsewhere, the system runs mainly for its own sake.

It is really necessary to remind our academics of the ancient history of Examination. In the medieval university, the whole point of the gruelling trial of the candidate was whether or not to accept him as a peer. His disputation and lecture for the Master's was just that, a masterpiece to enter the guild. It was not to make comparative evaluations. It was not to weed out and select for an extra-mural licensor or employer. It was certainly not to pit one young fellow against another in an ugly competition. My philosophic impression is that the medievals thought they knew what a good job of work was and that we are competitive because we do not know. But the more status is achieved by largely irrelevant competitive evaluation, the less will we ever know.

(Of course, our American examinations never did have this purely guild orientation, just as our faculties have rarely had absolute autonomy; the examining was to satisfy Overseers, Elders, distant Regents—and they as paternal superiors have always doted on giving grades, rather than accepting peers. But I submit that this set-up itself makes it impossible for the student to *become* a master, to *have* grown up, and to commence on his own. He will always be making A or B for some overseer. And in the present atmosphere, he will always be climbing on his friend's neck.)

Perhaps the chief objectors to abolishing grading would be the students and their parents. The parents should be simply disregarded; their anxiety has done enough damage already. For the students, it seems to me that a primary duty of the university is to deprive them of their props, their dependence on extrinsic valuation and motivation, and to force them to confront the difficult enterprise itself and finally lose themselves in it.

A miserable effect of grading is to nullify the various uses of testing. Testing, for both student and teacher, is a means of structuring, and also of finding out what is blank or wrong and what has been assimilated and can be taken for granted. Review—including high-pressure review—is a means of bringing together the fragments, so that there are flashes of synoptic insight.

There are several good reasons for testing, and kinds of test. But if the aim is to discover weakness, what is the point of down-grading and punishing it, and thereby inviting the student to conceal his weakness, by faking and bulling, if not cheating? The natural conclusion of synthesis is the insight itself, not a grade for having had it. For the important purpose of placement, if one can establish in the student the belief that one is testing *not* to grade and make invidious comparisons but for his own advantage, the student should normally seek his own level, where he is challenged and yet capable, rather than trying to get by. If the student dares to accept himself as he is, a teacher's grade is a crude instrument compared with a

10

student's self-awareness. But it is rare in our universities that students are encouraged to notice objectively their vast confusion. Unlike Socrates, our teachers rely on power-drives rather than shame and ingenuous idealism.

Many students are lazy, so teachers try to goad or threaten them by grading. In the long run this must do more harm than good. Laziness is a character-defense. It may be a way of avoiding learning, in order to protect the conceit that one is already perfect (deeper, the despair that one *never* can). It may be a way of avoiding just the risk of failing and being down-graded. Sometimes it is a way of politely saying, "I won't." But since it is the authoritarian grown-up demands that have created such attitudes in the first place, why repeat the trauma? There comes a time when we must treat people as adult, laziness and all. It is one thing courageously to fire a do-nothing out of your class; it is quite another thing to evaluate him with a lordly F.

Most important of all, it is often obvious that balking in doing the work, especially among bright young people who get to great universities, means exactly what it says: The work does not suit me, not this subject, or not at this time, or not in this school, or not in school altogether. The student might not be bookish; he might be school-tired; perhaps his development ought now to take another direction. Yet unfortunately, if such a student is intelligent and is not sure of himself, he *can* be bullied into passing, and this obscures everything. My hunch is that I am describing a common situation. What a grim waste of young life and teacherly effort! Such a student will retain nothing of what he has "passed" in. Sometimes he must get mononucleosis to tell his story and be believed.

And ironically, the converse is also probably commonly true. A student flunks and is mechanically weeded out, who is really ready and eager to learn in a scholastic setting, but he has not quite caught on. A good teacher can recognize the situation, but the computer wreaks its will.

Topics for Critical Thinking and Writing

1. In his opening paragraph Goodman limits his suggestion about grading and testing to "half a dozen of the prestigious Universities." Does he offer any reason for this limitation? Can you?

2. In paragraph 3 Goodman says that "the great majority of professors agree that grading hinders teaching." What evidence does he offer to support this claim? What arguments might be made that grading assists teaching? Should Goodman have made them?

3. As a student, have grades helped you to learn, or have grades hindered you? Explain.

4. If you have been a student in an ungraded course, describe the course and evaluate the experience.

Diane Ravitch

Diane Ravitch has taught history and education at Teachers College, Columbia University, and has served as Assistant Secretary of Education. Her latest book is Left Back: A Century of Failed School Reforms *(2000). The following essay was originally published in* Time *(September 11, 2000).*

In Defense of Testing

No one wants to be tested. We would all like to get a driver's license without answering questions about right of way or showing that we can parallel park a car. Many future lawyers and doctors probably wish they could join their profession without taking an exam.

But tests and standards are a necessary fact of life. They protect us—most of the time—from inept drivers, hazardous products, and shoddy professionals. In schools too, exams play a constructive role. They tell public officials whether new school programs are making a difference and where new investments are likely to pay off. They tell teachers what their students have learned—and have not. They tell parents how their children are doing compared with others their age. They encourage students to exert more effort.

It is important to recall that for most of this century, educators used intelligence tests to decide which children should get a high-quality education. The point of IQ testing was to find out how much children were capable of learning rather than to test what they had actually learned. Based on IQ scores, millions of children were assigned to dumbed-down programs instead of solid courses in science, math, history, literature, and foreign languages.

This history reminds us that tests should be used to improve education, not ration it. Every child should have access to a high-quality education. Students should have full opportunity to learn what will be tested; otherwise their test scores will merely reflect whether they come from an educated family.

In the past few years, we have seen the enormous benefits that flow   5 to disadvantaged students because of the information provided by state tests. Those who fall behind are now getting extra instruction in after-school classes and summer programs. In their efforts to improve student performance, states are increasing teachers' salaries, testing new teachers, and insisting on better teacher education.

Good tests should include a mix of essay, problem-solving, short-answer, and even some multiple-choice questions. On math quizzes, students should be able to show how they arrived at their answer. The tests widely used today often rely too much on multiple-choice questions, which encourage guessing rather than thinking. Also, they frequently ignore the importance of knowledge. Today's history tests, for example, seldom expect the student to know any history—sometimes derided as "mere facts"—but only to be able to read charts, graphs, and cartoons.

Performance in education means the mastery of both knowledge and skills. This is why it is reasonable to test teachers to make sure they know their subject matter, as well as how to teach it to young children. And this is why it is reasonable to assess whether students are ready to advance to the next grade or graduate from high school. To promote students who cannot read or do math is no favor to them. It is like pushing them into a deep pool before they have learned to swim. If students need extra time and help, they should get it, but they won't unless we first carefully assess what they have learned.

 ## Topics for Critical Thinking and Writing

1. In her second paragraph, Ravitch says of tests that "they tell teachers what their students have learned—and have not." Thinking back on tests you took in school, to what extent do you agree with Ravitch's assertion? Do you agree with her claim that tests "encourage students to exert more effort"? Is that true of you?

2. In her fourth paragraph Ravitch seems to link testing to her assertion that "every child should have access to a high-quality education." Do you believe that testing and improving education are linked? Explain.

3. In her sixth paragraph Ravitch says that history tests "seldom expect the student to know any history." What history courses did you take in high school? To what extent did the tests you took support Ravitch's claim?

4. In paragraph 7 Ravitch asserts that "it is reasonable to test teachers to make sure they know their subject matter, as well as how to teach it to young children." In your schools were teachers ever tested? If not, do you think that testing your teachers would have led to improvement in your education? What measures other than testing are there to assess the competence of teachers?

E. B. White

E[lwyn] B[rooks] White (1899–1985) wrote poetry and fiction, but he is most widely known as an essayist and as the coauthor (with William Strunk Jr.) of Elements of Style. *After a long career at* The New Yorker *he retired to Maine, but he continued to write until the year before his death at the age of 86.*

Education

I have an increasing admiration for the teacher in the country school where we have a third-grade scholar in attendance. She not only undertakes to instruct her charges in all the subjects of the first three grades, but she manages to function quietly and effectively as a guardian of their health, their clothes, their habits, their mothers, and their snowball engagements. She has been doing this sort of Augean task for twenty years, and is both kind and wise. She cooks for the children on the stove that heats the room, and she can cool their passions or warm their soup with equal competence. She conceives their costumes, cleans up their messes, and shares their confidences. My boy already regards his teacher as his great friend, and I think tells her a great deal more than he tells us.

The shift from city school to country school was something we worried about quietly all last summer. I have always rather favored public school over private school, if only because in public school you meet a greater variety of children. This bias of mine, I suspect, is partly an attempt to justify my own past (I never knew anything but public schools) and partly an involuntary defense against getting kicked in the shins by a young ceramist on his way to the kiln. My wife was unacquainted with public schools, never having been exposed (in her early life) to anything more public than the washroom of Miss Winsor's. Regardless of our backgrounds, we both knew that the change in schools was something that concerned not us but the scholar himself. We hoped it would work out all right. In New York our son went to a medium-priced private institution with semi-progressive ideas of education, and modern plumbing. He learned fast, kept well, and we were satisfied. It was an electric, colorful, regimented existence with moments of pleasurable pause and giddy incident. The day the Christmas angel fainted and had to be carried out by one of the Wise Men was educational in the highest sense of the term. Our scholar gave imitations of it around the house for weeks afterward, and I doubt if it ever goes completely out of his mind.

His days were rich in formal experience. Wearing overalls and an old sweater (the accepted uniform of the private seminary), he sallied forth at morn accompanied by a nurse or a parent and walked (or was pulled) two blocks to a corner where the school bus made a flag stop. This flashy vehicle was as punctual as death: seeing us waiting at the cold curb, it would sweep to a halt, open its mouth, suck the boy in, and spring away with an angry growl. It was a good deal like a train picking up a bag of mail. At school the scholar was worked on for six or seven hours by half a dozen teachers and a nurse, and was revived on orange juice in mid-morning. In a cinder court he played games supervised by an athletic instructor, and in a cafeteria he ate lunch worked out by a dietitian. He soon learned to read with gratifying facility and discernment and to make Indian weapons of a semi-deadly nature. Whenever one of his classmates fell low of a fever the news was put on the wires and there were breathless phone calls to physicians, discussing periods of incubation and allied magic.

In the country all one can say is that the situation is different, and somehow more casual. Dressed in corduroys, sweatshirt, and short rubber boots, and carrying a tin dinner-pail, our scholar departs at the crack of dawn for the village school, two and a half miles down the road, next to the cemetery. When the road is open and the car will start, he makes the journey by motor, courtesy of his old man. When the snow is deep or the motor is dead or both, he makes it on the hoof. In the afternoons he walks or hitches all or part of the way home in fair weather, gets transported in foul. The schoolhouse is a two-room frame building, bungalow type, shingles stained a burnt brown with weather-resistant stain. It has a chemical toilet in the basement and two teachers above the stairs. One takes the first three grades, the other the fourth, fifth, and sixth. They have little or no time for individual instruction, and no time at all for the esoteric. They teach what they know themselves, just as fast and as hard as they can manage. The pupils sit still at their desks in class, and do their milling around outdoors during recess.

There is no supervised play. They play cops and robbers (only they call it "Jail") and throw things at one another—snowballs in winter, rose hips in fall. It seems to satisfy them. They also construct darts, pinwheels, and "pick-up sticks" (jackstraws), and the school itself does a brisk trade in penny candy, which is for sale right in the classroom and which contains "surprises." The most highly prized surprise is a fake cigarette, made of cardboard, fiendishly lifelike.

The memory of how apprehensive we were at the beginning is still strong. The boy was nervous about the change too. The tension, on that first fair morning in September when we drove him to school, almost blew the windows out of the sedan. And when later we picked him up on the road, wandering along with his little blue lunch-pail, and got his laconic report "All right" in answer to our inquiry about how the day had gone, our relief was vast. Now, after almost a year of it, the only difference we can discover in the two school experiences is that in the country he sleeps better at night—and *that* probably is more the air than the edu-

5

cation. When grilled on the subject of school-in-country vs. school-in-city, he replied that the chief difference is that the day seems to go so much quicker in the country. "Just like lightning," he reported.

 Topics for Critical Thinking and Writing

1. Which school, public or private, does White prefer? Since White doesn't state his preference outright, from what evidence were you able to infer it?

2. In the first half of paragraph 2 White admits to a bias in favor of public schools, and he speculates, half-seriously, about the origins of his bias. If his intention here is not simply to amuse us, what is it?

3. What is White's strongest argument in favor of the school he prefers? Where in the essay do you find it?

Katie Zernike

Katie Zernike is an education reporter for The New York Times, *where this essay appeared, in the issue of August 5, 2001.*

Zernike uses the term feng shui *in a relatively untechnical sense. One might even argue that she misunderstands it. (Our first question, printed after the essay, raises issues concerning her title.) Feng shui, a Chinese term pronounced "fung shwee," literally means "wind and water." It refers to the Chinese art of siting graves, buildings, and cities in auspicious places, specifically where there is a concentration of the vital energy of the earth and sky. In this view, the earth is alive, and cosmic forces (qi, pronounced chee) flow in conduits just below its surface. In locating any architectural construction, specialists take into account the configuration of hills and the presence of streams and vegetation. A deficient site can be improved by the addition of vegetation, artificial mounds, ponds, walls, etc. The goal is (speaking metaphorically) to enable the residents to sail with the current and the wind, or to design a place which (again speaking metaphorically) serves as a garment that lets the wearer take in the vital energy. Some versions of feng shui emphasize not only the physical aspects of the site but also the individual's character, moral awareness, and sense of wholeness.*

The Feng Shui of Schools

Can the shape of a hallway discourage bullying in schools? Can more windows even out the gap between rich and poor students? Can a simple change of paint increase test scores, or carpeting make a math whiz out of the class clown?

Researchers pooh-poohed such ideas for years, referring in particular to a 1997 study by the Educational Testing Service that found no connection between test scores and how much a school spent on construction and maintenance. But a growing number of architects, educators and environmental psychologists now point to other research showing clear links between elements of design and student achievement. Part of this is a matter of message: If jails are cleaner and better designed than schools, what does that say to children about the relative importance of education? But there is also a kind of feng shui—a way of thinking about how to structure and decorate a classroom to enhance learning.

The opportunity is great. By some estimates the nation is expected to spend $500 billion on new schools over the next decade. Ray Bordwell, an architect with Perkins & Will in Chicago, one of the nation's oldest school design firms, says that the country will need 6,000 new schools between now and 2006. And that is just to meet enrollment increases. The average school is more than 40 years old, so existing buildings, too, will need upgrades.

The Incredible Lightness

Experts agree most on the importance of daylight and windows in the classroom. Consider the results of a 1999 study done for the California Board for Energy Efficiency, which tracked 21,000 students in three school districts in three states.

5

In Capistrano, Calif., students in classrooms with the most daylight improved 20 percent faster on math tests and 26 percent faster on reading tests over one year than students in classrooms with the least. Moving a child from the classroom with the least daylight to one with the most produced the same improvement as moving that child from the lowest to the highest performing school in the district.

In Seattle, the second of the three districts, the amount of daylight was "a more potent predictor" of student performance than sex, class size or whether the student came from a single-parent household, the study found. There and in Fort Collins, Colo., students in classrooms with more daylight had scores 7 to 18 percent higher than those in classrooms without daylight.

The three districts had students with similar backgrounds but different teaching styles, building designs and climates. The consistent results, researchers say, indicate the importance of lighting, no matter what else happens in the classroom.

C. Kenneth Tanner, a professor at the School Design and Planning Laboratory at the University of Georgia, argues that students in windowless classrooms—built especially in the 1970's as architects tried to make buildings more efficient in heating and cooling—are experiencing a kind of jet lag because their circadian rhythms are depressed by lack of natural light.

Windows also improve airflow, another critical element in school design. In the California study, students in classrooms with windows that could open progressed about 8 percent faster over one year than those in classrooms with fixed windows, regardless of whether there was air-conditioning. The key, said Jeffery A. Lackney, an assistant professor of engineering at the University of Wisconsin at Madison, is that the air completely recirculate one and a half times an hour. Reading comprehension declines as room temperature rises above 74 degrees, he said, and addition and subtraction skills decline when a room becomes warmer than 77 degrees.

Quiet Is Golden

National and state commissions have recommended lengthening the amount of time students spend on academics—"time on task," in the jargon. That time is often lost because of noise, whether from traffic, airplanes or other students. Not only are students less likely to hear what a teacher is saying, they are also more likely to give up on an academic challenge.

Lorraine E. Maxwell, an environmental psychologist at Cornell University who specializes in the effect of noise on learning, gives the example of a preschool in Corning, N.Y. It had been designed for beauty, with soaring, rounded 16-foot ceilings and walls that reached only partway to the ceiling. But that design was not one for learning. "The ceiling was the perfect place for sound to go up and whirl around and around," Professor Maxwell said. "That's why you do round ceilings in a concert hall. But you shouldn't do it for classrooms."

The decibel level was higher than schools she had studied near New York City airports. "It was a tiring environment," she said. "It was an effort to make yourself heard." After the preschool installed baffles of gym-mat-like material on the walls, the children improved in language skills, using more words and more complete sentences.

Professor Maxwell reserves particular disdain for traditional lunchrooms with their long narrow tables, which require shouting to be heard. Round tables are more expensive, but they allow students to talk, not shout, reducing overall noise in a school. She and others advocate carpet in the hallways, which can muffle footsteps, chatter and the slamming of lockers.

Even in small doses, bad design can impede learning, says Gay Elliott, head of interior design at Fanning/Howey Associates, the nation's biggest school design firm. "If you're in a theater and somebody's cell phone goes off, doesn't that ruin the mood and the moment? It's the same in the classroom."

Color Them Teal

A change of color is the least expensive and fastest way to improve a school's environment. In general, bright colors stimulate brain activity and respiration. Cool colors promote muscle relaxation and reduction in blood pressure—especially good for calming budding teenagers in the middle grades. But don't use too much of any one color. Designers recommend mild colors for walls and floors to minimize glare and restful colors for, say, a reading area. Stronger colors are reserved for areas that demand attention, in particular the "teaching wall" behind the chalkboard or marker board. They also encourage a broader range than has been traditional. "Young children are bored with primary colors," Ms. Elliott said. "It's overdone, and just as adults get sick of looking at white walls, they get sick of looking at red, blue and yellow."

Schools also have to consider endurance. Teal, for example, is now a trendy color in school walls. But Ms. Elliott recommends painting one wall that color and the others a more classic butter yellow. That way, when the trend runs its course, only one wall needs repainting.

She also cautions schools to consider their context. In Minnesota, with its relentlessly gray winters, otherwise sophisticated taupe walls become depressing. In Florida, with its beating sunshine, orange will overstimulate children.

Size Matters

The long debate over the importance of class size has pretty much given way to the consensus that smaller is better; California state law even limits the number of students in elementary-grade classes to 20. But how small should the learning environment be?

Attention spans wane as students get farther than 12 feet from the teacher, says Professor Lackney, and students in the front and center have been shown to have higher test scores. Of course, children who are less serious about achievement do tend to seek the anonymity of the rear rows.

Architects and planners have their own prescriptions. They recommend students sit at a large table (u-shaped or trapezoidal) instead of desks or, if new furniture is too expensive, arranging desks into tables.

It is almost impossible, Ms. Elliott says, to have all students within the appropriate range of a teacher at all times, so her firm now gives teachers desks with casters so they can move around the room, engaging more students.

The standard classroom minimum used to be 30 square feet for each student, but that, Mr. Bordwell says, is getting to seem crowded as technology eats up space.

Research at the school design lab in Georgia shows that elementary schools with less than 100 square feet per student overall have significantly lower scores on the Iowa Test of Basic Skills, a commonly used measure of achievement. So architects now design schools with pods or wings dividing the larger student body into smaller groups to create intimacy in a large setting.

School as Home

The arrangement of space is crucial. The open classrooms popular in the 1960's and 70's are now considered a disaster—too loud, too little light. But the more traditional classrooms, like boxes off a hallway, are seen as too limited for today's technology and teaching needs. The key is flexibility. As the model, many architects look to the Celebration School, part of the Disney Company's planned community in Florida. The school is arranged in 10 neighborhoods, about 6,000 square feet and holding 100 students with four teachers each. Within that space are rooms for large- and small-group meetings, places for teachers and students to talk quietly, and a hearth area for reading and other quiet activities. Each neighborhood has its own restroom.

The goal is to make the space less institutional and more like home. George Luaces, an architect with the Hillier Group in Newark, talks of the school of the future as a cluster of apartments. (Presumably, the ideal is more a penthouse with a terrace than a fourth-floor walkup.)

The message of the entryway is important, Mr. Luaces says. The school he designed for Niagara Falls, N.Y., is arranged around a glass-enclosed atrium with a library and media center inside. It is the first thing students see as they walk in, setting a tone of research, activity and learning. From the entryway, Mr. Luaces says, schools should proceed to smaller rooms as the relationships become more intimate and more important—from student-to-school to student-to-teacher. At Public School 69 in the Dyker Heights section of Brooklyn, designed by Hardy Holzman Pfeiffer Associates and set to open next January, each classroom will have its own small entry niche with a sitting area, display case and bulletin board wall covering.

Architects also encourage space of one's own for teachers and for students. "If you can't regulate your privacy, it has a psychological impact," Professor Lackney said. "It affects your motivation and your stamina if you can't break away for a moment."

The traditional spaces for students—the lockers—give architects fits. They are noisy and, as Mr. Bordwell says, "a good place for kids to get together and start shoving each other." In the ideal school, students have their own library carrels or benches where they can plug in a laptop. At Celebration, small groups of students share a walk-in closet.

School design may also enhance safety. The new model school is arranged around a hexagonal common space, with short hallways. The long corridors in traditional schools, architects say, send a message to "run"—not exactly the way to reduce truancy and rebellion. And 90 percent of behavior problems, Mr. Bordwell says, happen in the hallways between classes.

While some educators doubt assertions that design can affect behavior—and academic achievement—planners warn not to underestimate its impact. "If you were going to ask me the most important thing in a classroom," Ms. Elliott said, "other than a good teacher, I'd say carpet."

 Topics for Critical Thinking and Writing

1. The words "feng shui" appear in the title of the article and at the end of the second paragraph. What do you understand feng shui to mean? Would you have advised Zernike to define the term, or to omit it? Why, or why not? We

offer a brief description of *feng shui* in our headnote, but readers of the original article did not have this information. Is our headnote helpful, or intrusive?

2. Describe and evaluate the opening paragraph.

3. What evidence does Zernike offer to link school design with student behavior and achievement? How persuasive do you find her argument?

4. According to this article, what would be the ideal school design? In an essay of about 750 words, describe a school you attended and compare it with this ideal. In your essay, estimate the effect of the design of your school on your behavior and academic achievement.

5. Perhaps you have children; if not, imagine that you have children. How likely are you to examine the design of a school building before enrolling your children in the school? Explain in one well-developed paragraph.

6. A box accompanying the article said, "Designers recommend bright colors for areas that demand attention, like behind the teacher, and cool shades for reading areas." (See also paragraph 15.) What are "cool shades"? Are you convinced that a cool shade behind the teacher would be undesirable? How might one prove or disprove this business about the effectiveness of colors?

David Gelernter

David Gelernter, a professor of computer science at Yale University, originally published this essay in The New Republic *in 1994.*

Unplugged

Over the last decade an estimated $2 billion has been spent on more than 2 million computers for America's classrooms. That's not surprising. We constantly hear from Washington that the schools are in trouble and that computers are a godsend. Within the education establishment, in poor as well as rich schools, the machines are awaited with nearly religious awe. An inner-city principal bragged to a teacher friend of mine recently that his school "has a computer in every classroom . . . despite being in a bad neighborhood!"

Computers should be in the schools. They have the potential to accomplish great things. With the right software, they could help make science tangible or teach neglected topics like art and music. They could help students form a concrete idea of society by displaying on screen a version of the city in which they live—a picture that tracks real life moment by moment.

David Gelernter, "Unplugged," *The New Republic*, September 19, 1994. Reprinted by permission of *The New Republic*. © 1994, The New Republic, Inc.

In practice, however, computers make our worst educational nightmares come true. While we bemoan the decline of literacy, computers discount words in favor of pictures and pictures in favor of video. While we fret about the decreasing cogency of public debate, computers dismiss linear argument and promote fast, shallow romps across the information landscape. While we worry about basic skills, we allow into the classroom software that will do a student's arithmetic or correct his spelling.

Take multimedia. The idea of multimedia is to combine text, sound and pictures in a single package that you browse on screen. You don't just *read* Shakespeare; you watch actors performing, listen to songs, view Elizabethan buildings. What's wrong with that? By offering children candy-coated books, multimedia is guaranteed to sour them on unsweetened reading. It makes the printed page look even more boring than it used to look. Sure, books will be available in the classroom, too—but they'll have all the appeal of a dusty piano to a teen who has a Walkman handy.

So what if the little nippers don't read? If they're watching Olivier instead, what do they lose? The text, the written word along with all of its attendant pleasures. Besides, a book is more portable than a computer, has a higher-resolution display, can be written on and dog-eared and is comparatively dirt cheap.

Hypermedia, multimedia's comrade in the struggle for a brave new classroom, is just as troubling. It's a way of presenting documents on screen without imposing a linear start-to-finish order. Disembodied paragraphs are linked by theme; after reading one about the First World War, for example, you might be able to choose another about the technology of battleships, or the life of Woodrow Wilson, or hemlines in the '20s. This is another cute idea that is good in minor ways and terrible in major ones. Teaching children to understand the orderly unfolding of a plot or a logical argument is a crucial part of education. Authors don't merely agglomerate paragraphs; they work hard to make the narrative read a certain way, prove a particular point. To turn a book or a document into hypertext is to invite readers to ignore exactly what counts—the story.

The real problem, again, is the accentuation of already bad habits. Dynamiting documents into disjointed paragraphs is one more expression of the sorry fact that sustained argument is not our style. If you're a newspaper or magazine editor and your readership is dwindling, what's the solution? Shorter pieces. If you're a politician and you want to get elected, what do you need? Tasty sound bites. Logical presentation be damned.

Another software species, "allow me" programs, is not much better. These programs correct spelling and, by applying canned grammatical and stylistic rules, fix prose. In terms of promoting basic skills, though, they have all the virtues of a pocket calculator.

In Kentucky, as *The Wall Street Journal* recently reported, students in grades K–3 are mixed together regardless of age in a relaxed environ-

5

ment. It works great, the *Journal* says. Yes, scores on computation tests have dropped 10 percent at one school, but not to worry: "Drilling addition and subtraction in an age of calculators is a waste of time," the principal reassures us. Meanwhile, a Japanese educator informs University of Wisconsin mathematician Richard Akey that in his country, "calculators are not used in elementary or junior high school because the primary emphasis is on helping students develop their mental abilities." No wonder Japanese kids blow the pants off American kids in math. Do we really think "drilling addition and subtraction in an age of calculators in a waste of time"? If we do, then "drilling reading in an age of multimedia is a waste of time" can't be far behind.

Prose-correcting programs are also a little ghoulish, like asking a   10
computer for tips on improving your personality. On the other hand, I ran this article through a spell-checker, so how can I ban the use of such programs in schools? Because to misspell is human; to have no idea of correct spelling is to be semiliterate.

There's no denying that computers have the potential to perform inspiring feats in the classroom. If we are ever to see that potential realized, however, we ought to agree on three conditions. First, there should be a completely new crop of children's software. Most of today's offerings show no imagination. There are hundreds of similar reading and geography and arithmetic programs, but almost nothing on electricity or physics or architecture. Also, they abuse the technical capacities of new media to glitz up old forms instead of creating new ones. Why not build a time-travel program that gives kids a feel for how history is structured by zooming you backward? A spectrum program that lets users twirl a frequency knob to see what happens?

Second, computers should be used only during recess or relaxation periods. Treat them as fillips, not as surrogate teachers. When I was in school in the '60s, we all loved educational films. When we saw a movie in class, everybody won: teachers didn't have to teach, and pupils didn't have to learn. I suspect that classroom computers are popular today for the same reasons.

Most important, educators should learn what parents and most teachers already know: you cannot teach a child anything unless you look him in the face. We should not forget what computers are. Like books—better in some ways, worse in others—they are devices that help children mobilize their own resources and learn for themselves. The computer's potential to do good is modestly greater than a book's in some areas. Its potential to do harm is vastly greater, across the board.

❧ Topics for Critical Thinking and Writing

1. If you used computers in your elementary or secondary school, evaluate their contribution to your education. (This need not be an all-or-nothing is-

sue; it may be that computers were useless in some courses, moderately useful in others, and highly useful in still others.)

2. One of Gelernter's complaints (paragraph 3) is that "computers discount words in favor of pictures and pictures in favor of video." Is this true—and if it is true, is it necessarily a bad thing? Explain.

3. Paragraph 9 touches on whether "drilling addition and subtraction in an age of calculators is a waste of time." Your views?

Hubert B. Herring

Hubert B. Herring, an editor of the Business Section of The New York Times, *published this essay in the newspaper on June 13, 2001.*

On the Eve of Extinction: Four Years of High School

Rumor has it that high school lasts four years. Don't believe it.

From what I can see, the second half of senior year has become an unscheduled holiday, interrupted only by decisions on college, a comically expensive prom and relatively meaningless final exams.

Senioritis, or senior slump, has become so severe that soon we might have to drop the pretense and say high school lasts three and a half years, followed by a six-month break. A training-wheels sabbatical.

Students hit an invisible "off" switch, with all but a handful dropping all pretense of studying—and, if questioned by pesky parents, saying: "Hey, come *on!* No one's studying anymore." Now, when your son says, "All the other kids have BMW's," you can chalk that up to hyperbole, but on this point, alas, he's not far off. Senioritis does seem nearly universal.

One senior of my acquaintance (he shall remain anonymous; otherwise I'll never get him to clean up his room) recently managed to extend lunch to three full school periods. But enough said on that front.   5

A friend recalls that when he was in high school, one teacher said: "When I was a kid, if you cut classes, showed up late and didn't do any work, they called you a bum. Now they call you a senior." And that was *then*.

The startling extremity of this phenomenon brings to mind a marvelous notion called "landfall syndrome." That's when sailors, perfectly content while far at sea, grow desperately impatient the instant they sight land. But for today's seniors, the syndrome strikes in January, roughly 10 seconds after the last midyear exam. They haven't spied land; they just heard that another ship knew about another ship that had spied land.

Why does this happen? Well, either students have already been accepted into college or they have all their applications in and are simply awaiting word. In either case, the colleges' decisions are based on grades already awarded, so what's the point of studying hard now, students ask. They've worked hard for years, they say—and, in many cases, they have indeed. So chill out, Dad.

And it's surely gotten worse as colleges admit more students early. If the check's in the mail in December, and if you're already picking out those extra-long dorm sheets and pestering your parents for the very best laptop ("and of course I'll need a cell phone"), it's hard to keep up the grind come March.

Peer pressure—or its equally potent cousin, peer example—surely   10
comes into it. When they were juniors, they were fully aware of the partying of the exalted seniors. No way are they going to be nerds and study any more than their predecessors.

But dangers abound in all this. Students could get out of the routine of studying and find it hard to rev up again come fall. And they might miss out on crucial lessons, which could mean doing poorly on college placement exams or even being forced to take remedial classes.

Don't think educators aren't taking notice. In September, a national commission was set up to ponder this increasingly dysfunctional year.

"By the time many high school students reach their senior year, they are ready to check out," Richard W. Riley, then the education secretary, told the group. This period "should really be a more well-structured transition into adulthood."

And Michael W. Kirst, a Stanford University professor and author of a recent report called "Overcoming the High School Senior Slump," called this lost half-year a luxury "we can no longer afford."

What to do? Basically, I see two solutions. First, high schools and col-   15
leges could get tough—high schools by withholding diplomas from those who slack off, colleges by being strict about withdrawing acceptances if grades slide (they say they will, but rarely mean it).

The second would be, basically, to follow the kind of strategy adopted by one college we visited, which laid out a lawn, watched where students walked and only then installed walkways. In other words, admit that this semester is an educational sinkhole and make that sabbatical official. End school in January, and let students get jobs or do community service for six months.

The virtues of this idea are abundant: it's an ideal compromise for those who espouse taking a year off to taste the world, and students can earn some money to make a dent in that often-crippling tuition, giving them a stake in their own future.

Most important, perhaps, it's honest: it would end the sham of students' nominally being in school but in reality having a months-long graduation party. It can make the first lesson of adulthood that you can't pretend to be doing one thing while you're really doing something else entirely.

 Topics for Critical Thinking and Writing

1. How would you describe the tone of Herring's opening paragraph? Where else in his essay do you find a similar tone?

2. In paragraph 3, Herring calls the second semester of senior year "a training-wheels sabbatical." What does he mean? What is a sabbatical?

3. What is "senioritis"? How does Herring account for it?

4. Did you suffer from what Herring calls "a dysfunctional senior year"? If so, describe it. Does Herring accurately account for its causes? If not, how did you avoid it?

5. What solutions for "senioritis" does Herring propose? What is your view of these solutions?

Nadya Labi

A reporter and staff writer for Time, *Nadya Labi published this essay in* Time, *April 19, 1999. The research was based on reporting by Richard Woodbury (Denver), Melissa August (Washington), and Maggie Sieger (Chicago).*

Classrooms for Sale

Solve this problem: the staff and students of School District 11 in Colorado Springs, Colo., drank 30,000 cases of Coke beverages last year. District 11 has a 10-year, $8 million contract with the soft-drink company that calls for the yearly consumption of 1.68 million bottles of Coke products. If a case contains 24 bottles, which answer is correct? A) District 11 met its goal, and its students will sing back-up to Aretha Franklin in a new ad campaign. B) District 11 is 960,000 bottles in the red. C) Students should drink lots more Coke.

The best answer is B, but a District 11 administrator chose C. "If 35,439 staff and students buy one Coke product every other day for a school year," wrote John Bushey in a September missive to area principals, "we will double the required quota." His advice: allow Coke products in class and place vending machines in easily accessible areas. "Location, location, location is the key," he wrote, signing his memo "the Coke Dude."

Schools need money. Students have plenty of it to spend: $72 billion for all kids through high school, according to the most recent figures from Consumers Union. Those twin economic pressures have led to a disturbing trend on school grounds. In the past nine months, public school exclusivity deals with cola companies have soared 300%, to a record 150. And that's just the most obvious signal that schools are open for business. Calvin Klein models pout on the covers of textbooks; homecoming may be sponsored by Dr. Pepper; Taco Bell dishes up burritos at a school cafeteria near you; and that new overhead projector may be just one company's way of saying thanks—for eating Campbell's soup.

Commercialism in classrooms has become so rampant that last week a California education committee voted to restrict the use of brand names in taxpayer-funded textbooks. Parents were upset about a McGraw-Hill math textbook that is filled with references to products like Volkswagen automobiles, Jif peanut butter and Beanie Babies. McGraw-Hill representatives point out that the company receives no compensation for mentioning the products, which are used simply to get kids' attention. "The practice of using real-life examples is a technique that's been around for 12 to 15 years," says Roger Rogalin, president of the publishing company's school division. "We live in a branded society, and these are the things kids are talking about."

The product placements in textbooks do seem innocent of any overt   5
commercial intent. Still, if you think Toys "R" Us and MTV are the only

places where kids are being trained as consumers, take a walk through any elementary school or high school. Those splashy book covers? Chances are they're distributed by Cover Concepts, a company that sells advertising space on book covers to companies like Nestlé and Calvin Klein. That new weight-lifting machine? The school may participate in any of the incentive programs run by General Mills, Campbell's soup or AT&T. Schools earn points for every box top, soup label or long-distance phone call—which can then be redeemed for athletic and educational equipment. Or the school may be flush with prize money won in a contest sponsored by Chips Ahoy!, which asked students to confirm that there really are 1,000 chips in each bag, or Kellogg's, which had kids make sculptures out of Rice Krispies and melted marshmallows. "Is it proper for public institutions to become salespeople and build brand loyalty?" asks Andrew Hagelshaw, senior program director at the Center for Commercial-Free Public Education in Oakland, Calif. "Advertisers realize that schools are the perfect place to develop new markets. Kids can't switch the channel."

That's literally true in the case of ZapMe! Corp., which gives schools a free ride on the information superhighway, providing high-speed PCs, Internet access, laser printers and technical support. The catch? Students must use the computers for a minimum of four hours daily, while staring at a 2-in. x 4-in. billboard of rotating ads. Students earn "ZapPoints" that can be redeemed at an e-commerce mall. "There's a huge gap between what schools need and what they can afford," says Frank Vigil, president of the San Ramon–based company. "We want to provide the solution." He has signed up 5,000 schools in his first four months of marketing.

School resistance to these kinds of ventures has been steadily worn down, ever since Channel One began offering schools free video equipment in return for showing kids a daily TV newscast filled with commercials. Now some companies are allowed into schools to do their market research. Noggin, an interactive TV network created by Nickelodeon and the Children's Television Network, meets with more than 300 students at a New Jersey school during lunch and recess for the express purpose of finding out "what sparks kids." To thank Watchung School for its cooperation, the network has "contributed" $7,000 worth of keyboards. Education Market Resources conducts focus groups in schools on behalf of Kentucky Fried Chicken, McDonald's, Mattel and advertising giant Leo Burnett. "We are strictly a kids' market-research firm," says Bob Reynolds, president of the Kansas-based company. "We never promote or market goods." But the information it collects is provided to other companies that then promote and market their own goods.

Secretary of Education Richard Riley is fond of saying, "Better education is everybody's business." In Plymouth, Mich., they take that slogan to heart. District administrators are considering auctioning off school names to the highest-bidding corporation. No takers yet, but it could be the ultimate product placement: imagine your kid one day graduating from McDonald's Middle School and heading off to Coke High.

Topics for Critical Thinking and Writing

1. When you first saw the title of the essay, what was your response? Something like "This is a good thing"? Or "What? That's outrageous"? Or "Well, let me think about this; it may be good, it may be bad"? *Why* did the title generate this response?

2. The third paragraph begins, "Schools need money." Do you think the writer takes this need to be an adequate justification for the activities that she reports? What evidence in the text supports your answer?

3. The fourth paragraph begins, "Commercialism in classrooms has become so rampant that last week a California education committee voted to restrict the use of brand names in taxpayer-funded textbooks." Exactly what does "rampant" mean? What does the use of this word tell us about the writer's point of view?

4. Reread the entire fourth paragraph. Does the business about McGraw-Hill support the assertion, made in the first sentence of the paragraph, that commercialism in classrooms is "rampant"?

5. Reread the final paragraph. Do you suppose that the writer believes that this "ultimate product placement" might in fact occur? And what do you think her attitude toward it is? What makes you think you can guess her attitude?

6. Look closely at the last part of the last sentence of the essay: "imagine your kid one day graduating from McDonald's Middle School and heading off to Coke High." Would the effect be at all different if this part of the sentence ran, "imagine your kid one day graduating from Coke Middle School and heading off to McDonald's High"? If you think there is a difference, explain it.

Toni Cade Bambara

Toni Cade Bambara (1939–95), an African-American writer, was born in New York City in 1939, received her B.A. from Queens College in 1959 and her M.A. from City College in 1964. Both schools are part of the City University of New York. She taught at Livingston College of Rutgers University, and served as writer in residence at Spelman College in Atlanta.

The Lesson

Back in the days when everyone was old and stupid or young and foolish and me and Sugar were the only ones just right, this lady moved on our block with nappy hair and proper speech and no makeup. And

---

quite naturally we laughed at her, laughed the way we did at the junk man who went about his business like he was some bigtime president and his sorry-ass horse his secretary. And we kinda hated her too, hated the way we did the winos who cluttered up our parks and pissed on our handball walls and stank up our hallways and stairs so you couldn't halfway play hide-and-seek without a goddamn gas mask. Miss Moore was her name. The only woman on the block with no first name. And she was black as hell, cept for her feet, which were fish-white and spooky. And she was always planning these boring-ass things for us to do, us being my cousin, mostly, who lived on the block cause we all moved North the same time and to the same apartment then spread out gradual to breathe. And our parents would yank our heads into some kinda shape and crisp up our clothes so we'd be presentable for travel with Miss Moore, who always looked like she was going to church, though she never did. Which is just one of the things the grownups talked about when they talked behind her back like a dog. But when she came calling with some sachet she'd sewed up or some gingerbread she'd made or some book, why then they'd all be too embarrassed to turn her down and we'd get handed over all spruced up. She'd been to college and said it was only right that she should take responsibility for the young ones' education, and she not even related by marriage or blood. So they'd go for it. Specially Aunt Gretchen. She was the main gofer in the family. You got some ole dumb shit foolishness you want somebody to go for, you send for Aunt Gretchen. She been screwed into the go-along for so long, it's a blood-deep natural thing with her. Which is how she got saddled with me and Sugar and Junior in the first place while our mothers were in a la-de-da apartment up the block having a good ole time.

So this one day Miss Moore rounds us all up at the mailbox and it's puredee hot and she's knockin herself out about arithmetic. And school suppose to let up in summer I heard, but she don't never let up. And the starch in my pinafore scratching the shit outta me and I'm really hating this nappy-head bitch and her goddamn college degree. I'd much rather go to the pool or to the show where it's cool. So me and Sugar leaning on the mailbox being surly, which is a Miss Moore word. And Flyboy checking out what everybody brought for lunch. And Fat Butt already wasting his peanut-butter-and-jelly sandwich like the pig he is. And Junebug punchin on Q.T.'s arm for potato chips. And Rosie Giraffe shifting from one hip to the other waiting for somebody to step on her foot or ask her if she from Georgia so she can kick ass, preferably Mercedes'. And Miss Moore asking us do we know what money is, like we a bunch of retards. I mean real money, she say, like it's only poker chips or monopoly papers we lay on the grocer. So right away I'm tired of this and say so. And would much rather snatch Sugar and go to the Sunset and terrorize the West Indian kids and take their hair ribbons and their money too. And Miss Moore files that remark away for next week's lesson on brotherhood, I can tell. And finally I say we oughta get to the subway cause it's cooler and besides we might meet some cute boys. Sugar done swiped her mama's lipstick, so we ready.

So we heading down the street and she's boring us silly about what things cost and what our parents make and how much goes for rent and how money ain't divided up right in this country. And then she gets to the part about we all poor and live in the slums, which I don't feature. And I'm ready to speak on that, but she steps out in the street and hails two cabs just like that. Then she hustles half the crew in with her and hands me a five-dollar bill and tells me to calculate 10 percent tip for the driver. And we're off. Me and Sugar and Junebug and Flyboy hangin out the window and hollering to everybody, putting lipstick on each other cause Flyboy a faggot anyway, and making farts with our sweaty armpits. But I'm mostly trying to figure how to spend this money. But they all fascinated with the meter ticking and Junebug starts laying bets to how much it'll read when Flyboy can't hold his breath no more. Then Sugar lays bets as to how much it'll be when we get there. So I'm stuck. Don't nobody want to go for my plan, which is to jump out at the next light and run off to the first bar-b-que we can find. Then the driver tells us to get the hell out cause we there already. And the meter reads eighty-five cents. And I'm stalling to figure out the tip and Sugar say give him a dime. And I decide he don't need it as bad as I do, so later for him. But then he tries to take off with Junebug's foot still in the door so we talk about his mama something ferocious. Then we check out that we on Fifth Avenue and everybody dressed up in stockings. One lady in a fur coat, hot as it is. White folks crazy.

"This is the place," Miss Moore say, presenting it to us in the voice she uses at the museum. "Let's look in the windows before we go in."

"Can we steal?" Sugar asks very serious like she's getting the ground   5
rules squared away before she plays. "I beg your pardon," say Miss Moore, and we fall out. So she leads us around the windows of the toy store and me and Sugar screamin, "This is mine, that's mine, I gotta have that, that was made for me, I was born for that," till Big Butt drowns us out.

"Hey, I'm goin to buy that there."

"That there? You don't even know what it is, stupid."

"I do so," he say punchin on Rosie Giraffe. "It's a microscope."

"Whatcha gonna do with a microscope, fool?"

"Look at things."   10

"Like what, Ronald?" ask Miss Moore. And Big Butt ain't got the first notion. So here go Miss Moore gabbing about the thousands of bacteria in a drop of water and the somethinorother in a speck of blood and the million and one living things in the air around us is invisible to the naked eye. And what she say that for? Junebug go to town on that "naked" and we rolling. Then Miss Moore ask what it cost. So we all jam into the window smudgin it up and the price tag say $300. So then she ask how long'd take for Big Butt and Junebug to save up their allowances. "Too long," I say. "Yeh," adds Sugar, "outgrown it by that time." And Miss Moore say no, you never outgrow learning instruments. "Why, even medical students and interns and," blah, blah, blah. And we ready to choke Big Butt for bringing it up in the first damn place.

"This here costs four hundred eighty dollars," say Rosie Giraffe. So we pile up all over her to see what she pointin out. My eyes tell me it's a chunk of glass cracked with something heavy, and different-color inks dripped into the splits, then the whole thing put into a oven or something. But for $480 it don't make sense.

"That's a paperweight made of semi-precious stones fused together under tremendous pressure," she explains slowly, and her hands doing the mining and all the factory work.

"So what's a paperweight?" asks Rosie Giraffe.

"To weigh paper with, dumbbell," say Flyboy, the wise man from the   15
East.

"Not exactly," say Miss Moore, which is what she say when you warm or way off too. "It's to weigh paper down so it won't scatter and make your desk untidy." So right away me and Sugar curtsy to each other and then to Mercedes who is more the tidy type.

"We don't keep paper on top of the desk in my class," say Junebug, figuring Miss Moore crazy or lyin one.

"At home, then," she say. "Don't you have a calendar and a pencil case and a blotter and a letter-opener on your desk at home where you do your homework?" And she know damn well what our homes look like cause she nosys around in them every chance she gets.

"I don't even have a desk," say Junebug. "Do we?"

"No. And I don't get no homework neither," says Big Butt.   20

"And I don't even have a home," say Flyboy like he do at school to keep the white folks off his back and sorry for him. Send this poor kid to camp posters, is his specialty.

"I do," says Mercedes. "I have a box of stationery on my desk and a picture of my cat. My godmother bought the stationery and the desk. There's a big rose on each sheet and the envelopes smell like roses."

"Who wants to know about your smelly-ass stationery," say Rosie Giraffe fore I can get my two cents in.

"It's important to have a work area all your own so that . . ."

"Will you look at this sailboat, please," say Flyboy, cuttin her off and   25
pointin to the thing like it was his. So once again we tumble all over each other to gaze at this magnificent thing in the toy store which is just big enough to maybe sail two kittens across the pond if you strap them to the posts tight. We all start reciting the price tag like we in assembly. "Handcrafted sailboat of fiberglass at one thousand one hundred ninety-five dollars."

"Unbelievable," I hear myself say and am really stunned. I read it again for myself just in case the group recitation put me in a trance. Same thing. For some reason this pisses me off. We look at Miss Moore and she lookin at us, waiting for I dunno what.

"Who'd pay all that when you can buy a sailboat set for a quarter at Pop's, a tube of glue for a dime, and a ball of string for eight cents? It must have a motor and a whole lot else besides," I say. "My sailboat cost me about fifty cents."

"But will it take water?" say Mercedes with her smart ass.

"Took mine to Alley Pond Park once," say Flyboy. "String broke. Lost it. Pity."

"Sailed mine in Central Park and it keeled over and sank. Had to ask   30
my father for another dollar."

"And you got the strap," laugh Big Butt. "The jerk didn't even have a string on it. My old man wailed on his behind."

Little Q.T. was staring hard at the sailboat and you could see he wanted it bad. But he too little and somebody'd just take it from him. So what the hell. "This boat for kids, Miss Moore?"

"Parents silly to buy something like that just to get all broke up," say Rosie Giraffe.

"That much money it should last forever," I figure.

"My father'd buy it for me if I wanted it."   35

"Your father, my ass," say Rosie Giraffe getting a chance to finally push Mercedes.

"Must be rich people shop here," say Q.T.

"You are a very bright boy," say Flyboy. "What was your first clue?" And he rap him on the head with the back of his knuckles, since Q.T. the only one he could get away with. Though Q.T. liable to come up behind you years later and get his licks in when you half expect it.

"What I want to know is," I says to Miss Moore though I never talk to her, I wouldn't give the bitch that satisfaction, "is how much a real boat costs? I figure a thousand'd get you a yacht any day."

"Why don't you check that out," she says, "and report back to the   40
group?" Which really pains my ass. If you gonna mess up a perfectly good swim day least you could do is have some answers. "Let's go in," she say like she got something up her sleeve. Only she don't lead the way. So me and Sugar turn the corner to where the entrance is, but when we get there I kinda hang back. Not that I'm scared, what's there to be afraid of, just a toy store. But I feel funny, shame. But what I got to be shamed about? Got as much right to go in as anybody. But somehow I can't seem to get hold of the door, so I step away for Sugar to lead. But she hangs back too. And I look at her and she looks at me and this is ridiculous. I mean, damn, I have never ever been shy about doing nothing or going nowhere. But then Mercedes steps up and then Rosie Giraffe and Big Butt crowd in behind and shove, and next thing we all stuffed into the doorway with only Mercedes squeezing past us, smoothing out her jumper and walking right down the aisle. Then the rest of us tumble in like a glued-together jigsaw done all wrong. And people lookin at us. And it's like the time me and Sugar crashed into the Catholic church on a dare. But once we got in there and everything so hushed and holy and the can-

dles and the bowin and the handkerchiefs on all the drooping heads, I just couldn't go through with the plan. Which was for me to run up to the altar and do a tap dance while Sugar played the nose flute and messed around in the holy water. And Sugar kept givin me the elbow. Then later teased me so bad I tied her up in the shower and turned it on and locked her in. And she'd be there till this day if Aunt Gretchen hadn't finally figured I was lyin about the boarder takin a shower.

Same thing in the store. We all walkin on tiptoe and hardly touchin the games and puzzles and things. And I watched Miss Moore who is steady watchin us like she waitin for a sign. Like Mama Drewery watches the sky and sniffs the air and takes note of just how much slant is in the bird formation. Then me and Sugar bump smack into each other, so busy gazing at the toys, 'specially the sailboat. But we don't laugh and go into our fatlady bump-stomach routine. We just stare at that price tag. Then Sugar run a finger over the whole boat. And I'm jealous and want to hit her. Maybe not her, but I sure want to punch somebody in the mouth.

"Whatcha bring us here for, Miss Moore?"

"You sound angry, Sylvia. Are you mad about something?" Givin me one of them grins like she tellin a grown-up joke that never turns out to be funny. And she's lookin very closely at me like maybe she plannin to do my portrait from memory. I'm mad, but I won't give her that satisfaction. So I slouch around the store bein very bored and say, "Let's go."

Me and Sugar at the back of the train watchin the tracks whizzin by large then small then gettin gobbled up in the dark. I'm thinkin about this tricky toy I saw in the store. A clown that somersaults on a bar then does chin-ups just cause you yank lightly at his leg. Cost $35. I could see me askin my mother for a $35 birthday clown. "You wanna who that costs what?" she'd say, cocking her head to the side to get a better view of the hole in my head. Thirty-five dollars and the whole household could go visit Granddaddy Nelson in the country. Thirty-five dollars would pay for the rent and the piano bill too. Who are these people that spend that much for performing clowns and $1000 for toy sailboats? What kinda work they do and how they live and how come we ain't in on it? Where we are is who we are, Miss Moore always pointin out. But it don't necessarily have to be that way, she always adds then waits for somebody to say that poor people have to wake up and demand their share of the pie and don't none of us know what kind of pie she talkin about in the first damn place. But she ain't so smart cause I still got her four dollars from the taxi and she sure ain't gettin it. Messin up my day with this shit. Sugar nudges me in my pocket and winks.

Miss Moore lines us up in front of the mailbox where we started from, seem like years ago, and I got a headache for thinkin so hard. And we lean all over each other so we can hold up under the draggy-ass lecture

45

she always finishes us off with at the end before we thank her for borin us to tears. But she just looks at us like she readin tea leaves. Finally she say, "Well, what do you think of F.A.O. Schwartz?"

Rosie Giraffe mumbles, "White folks crazy."

"I'd like to go there again when I get my birthday money," says Mercedes, and we shove her out the pack so she has to lean on the mailbox by herself.

"I'd like a shower. Tiring day," say Flyboy.

Then Sugar surprises me by sayin, "You know, Miss Moore, I don't think all of us here put together eat in a year what that sailboat costs." And Miss Moore lights up like somebody goosed her. "And?" she say, urging Sugar on. Only I'm standin on her foot so she don't continue.

"Imagine for a minute what kind of society it is in which some people   50
can spend on a toy what it would cost to feed a family of six or seven. What do you think?"

"I think," say Sugar pushing me off her feet like she never done before, cause I whip her ass in a minute, "that this is not much of a democracy if you ask me. Equal chance to pursue happiness means an equal crack at the dough, don't it?" Miss Moore is besides herself and I am disgusted with Sugar's treachery. So I stand on her foot one more time to see if she'll shove me. She shuts up, and Miss Moore looks at me, sorrowfully I'm thinkin. And somethin weird is goin on, I can feel it in my chest.

"Anybody else learn anything today?" lookin dead at me. I walk away and Sugar has to run to catch up and don't even seem to notice when I shrug her arm off my shoulder.

"Well, we got four dollars anyway," she says.

"Un hunh."

"We could go to Hascombs and get half a chocolate layer and then go   55
to the Sunset and still have plenty money for potato chips and ice cream sodas."

"Uh hunh."

"Race you to Hascombs," she say.

We start down the block and she gets ahead which is O.K. by me cause I'm going to the West End and then over to the Drive to think this day through. She can run if she want to and even run faster. But ain't nobody gonna beat me at nuthin.

Topics for Critical Thinking and Writing

1. What is the point of Miss Moore's lesson? Why does Sylvia resist it?

2. Describe the relationship between Sugar and Sylvia. What is Sugar's function in the story?

3. What does the last line of the story suggest?

Wu-tsu Fa-yen

Wu-tsu Fa-yen (1025–1104) was a Chinese Zen Buddhist priest. More exactly, he was a Ch'an priest: Zen is Japanese for the Chinese Ch'an.

The practitioner of Zen (to use the more common name) seeks satori, "enlightenment" or "awakening." The awakening is from a world of blind strivings (including those of reason and of morality). The awakened being, free from a sense of the self in opposition to all other things, perceives the unity of all things. Wu-tsu belonged to the branch of Zen that uses "shock therapy, the purpose of which is to jolt the student out of his analytical and conceptual way of thinking and lead him back to his natural and spontaneous faculty" (Kenneth Ch'en, Buddhism in China *[1964, rptd. 1972], p. 359).*

The title of this story, from The Sayings of Goso Hōyen, *is the editors'.*

Zen and the Art of Burglary

If people ask me what Zen is like, I will say that it is like learning the art of burglary. The son of a burglar saw his father growing older and thought, "If he is unable to carry on his profession, who will be the bread-winner of the family, except myself? I must learn the trade." He intimated the idea to his father, who approved of it.

One night the father took the son to a big house, broke through the fence, entered the house, and, opening one of the large chests, told the son to go in and pick out the clothing. As soon as the son got into it, the father dropped the lid and securely applied the lock. The father now came out to the courtyard and loudly knocked at the door, waking up the whole family; then he quietly slipped away by the hole in the fence. The residents got excited and lighted candles, but they found that the burglar had already gone.

The son, who remained all the time securely confined in the chest, thought of his cruel father. He was greatly mortified, then a fine idea flashed upon him. He made a noise like the gnawing of a rat. The family told the maid to take a candle and examine the chest. When the lid was unlocked, out came the prisoner, who blew out the light, pushed away the maid, and fled. The people ran after him. Noticing a well by the road, he picked up a large stone and threw it into the water. The pursuers all gathered around the well trying to find the burglar drowning himself in the dark hole.

In the meantime he went safely back to his father's house. He blamed his father deeply for his narrow escape. Said the father, "Be not offended, my son. Just tell me how you got out of it." When the son told him all about his adventures, the father remarked, "There you are, you have learned the art."

Topics for Critical Thinking and Writing

1. What assumptions about knowledge did the father make? Can you think of any of your own experiences that substantiate these assumptions?

2. Is there anything you have studied or are studying to which Zen pedagogical methods would be applicable? If so, explain by setting forth a sample lesson.

A Casebook on the SAT

Because most colleges and universities require the SAT, about two million people will take the tests this year. But the SAT recently has come in for a good deal of criticism, and one can hardly pick up a newspaper or a popular magazine without reading something about the pros and cons of this test, and, for that matter, the pros and cons of all kinds of testing. In February 2001, when Richard C. Atkinson, the president of the University of California, announced that he was recommending that the University of California no longer require applicants to submit SAT I scores, the issue became inescapable.

Richard C. Atkinson

Richard C. Atkinson has been president of the University of California since 1995. Before assuming the presidency he served for fifteen years as chancellor of the University of California's San Diego campus. His research has centered on problems of memory and cognition.

On February 18, 2001, at the American Council on Education Conference, Atkinson called for the elimination of SAT I as a requirement for students applying to the University of California. Atkinson assumed that the change, if adopted, would strengthen high school curricula and teaching and would help students to focus on mastering of subject matter rather than on preparing for tests. The speech drew nationwide attention; we give a brief extract from the speech, and then some of the responses.

Standardized Tests and Access to American Universities

Recently, I asked the Academic Senate of the University of California to consider two major changes in our admissions policies.

Richard C. Atkinson, from "Standardized Tests and Access to American Universities," presented at the American Council on Education Conference, February 18, 2001. Reprinted by permission.

First, I recommended that the university require only standardized tests that assess mastery of specific subject areas rather than undefined notions of "aptitude" or "intelligence." To facilitate this change, I recommended that we no longer require the SAT I for students applying to U.C.

Second, I recommended that all campuses move away from admission processes that use quantitative formulas and instead adopt evaluative procedures that look at applicants in a comprehensive, holistic way. While this recommendation is intended to provide a fairer basis on which to make admission decisions, it would also help ensure that standardized tests do not have an undue influence but rather are used to illuminate the student's total record.

In the short term, these proposals will not result in earth-shaking changes in determining which students are admitted and which are rejected. In the long term, however, they will help strengthen high school curricula and pedagogy, create a stronger connection between what students accomplish in high school and their likelihood of being admitted to U.C., and focus student attention on mastery of subject matter rather than test preparation.

For many years, I have worried about the use of the SAT, but last year my concerns coalesced. I visited an upscale private school and observed a class of 12-year-old students studying verbal analogies in anticipation of the SAT. I learned that they spend hours each month—directly and indirectly—preparing for the SAT, studying long lists of verbal analogies such as "untruthful is to mendaciousness" as "circumspect is to caution." The time involved was not aimed at developing the students' reading and writing abilities but rather their test-taking skills.

What I saw was disturbing and prompted me to spend time taking sample SAT tests and reviewing the literature. I concluded what many others have concluded: that America's overemphasis on the SAT is compromising our educational system.

Alfie Kohn

*Alfie Kohn was educated at Brown University and the University of Chicago. Among his eight
book on education and human behavior are* What To Look for in a Classroom *(1998),* The
Schools Our Children Deserve: Moving beyond Traditional Classrooms and "Tougher
Standards" *(1999), and* The Case against Standardized Testing *(2000).*

Two Cheers for an End to the SAT

One imagines the folks at the College Board blushing deeply when,
a few years back, they announced that the "A" in SAT no longer stood for
"Aptitude." Scarlet, after all, would be an appropriate color to turn
while, in effect, conceding that the test wasn't—and, let's face it, never
had been—a measure of intellectual aptitude. For a brief period, the examination was rechristened the Scholastic Assessment Test, a name presumably generated by the Department of Redundancy Department.
Today, literally—and perhaps figuratively—SAT doesn't stand for anything at all.

It wasn't the significance of the shift in the SAT's name that recently
produced an epiphany for Richard C. Atkinson, president of the
University of California. Rather, the tipping point in deciding to urge the
elimination of the SAT as a requirement for admission came last year during a visit to the upscale private school his grandchildren attend. There,
he watched as 12-year-olds were drilled on verbal analogies, part of an
extended training that, he said in announcing his proposal, "was not
aimed at developing the students' reading and writing abilities but rather
their test-taking skills." More broadly, he argued, "America's overemphasis on the SAT is compromising our educational system."

Of course, it must be pointed out that U.C., assuming its policy-mak-
ing bodies accept their president's advice, would not be the first institution to drop the SAT. Hundreds of colleges and universities, including
Bates, Bowdoin, Connecticut, and Mount Holyoke Colleges, no longer require the SAT or ACT. A survey by FairTest, a Cambridge, Mass.-based
advocacy group, reported that such colleges are generally well-satisfied
that "applicant pools and enrolled classes have become more diverse
without any loss in academic quality."

On balance, this latest and most significant challenge to the reign of
the SAT is very welcome news indeed. There is a possible downside as
well, but we should begin by recognizing that even before colleges began
hopping off the SAT bandwagon, the assumption that they needed something like the test to help them decide whom to admit was difficult to de-

fend, if only because of a powerful counterexample to our north: No such test is used in Canada. But the more one learns about the SAT in particular, the more one wonders what took Atkinson so long, and what is taking many of his counterparts even longer. Consider:

- The SAT is a measure of resources more than of reasoning. Year after year, the College Board's own statistics depict a virtually linear correlation between SAT scores and family income. Each rise in earnings (measured in $10,000 increments) brings a commensurate rise in scores. Other research, meanwhile, has found that more than half the difference among students' scores can be explained purely on the basis of parents' level of education.
- Aggregate scores don't reflect educational achievement. SAT results are still sometimes used to compare one state with another or one year with another. Unfortunately, not only is the test voluntary, but participation rates vary enormously by state and district. The researchers Brian Powell and Lala Carr Steelman, writing in a 1996 issue of the *Harvard Educational Review*, reported that those rates account for a whopping 85 percent of the variance in scores; when fewer students take the test, a state's results end up looking much better. Similarly, even if it is true that average national scores have declined over the decades (once we factor in the statistical readjustment that took place in 1996), that is mostly because more students, relatively speaking, are now taking the test.
- Individual scores don't reflect a student's intellectual depth. The verbal section of the SAT is basically just a vocabulary test. It is not a measure of aptitude or of subject-area competency. So what does it measure, other than the size of students' houses?

An interesting 1995 study with students at East Carolina University classified them as taking a "surface" approach to their assignments (meaning they memorized facts and did as little as possible); a "deep" approach (informed by a genuine desire to understand and a penchant for connecting current lessons with previous knowledge); or an "achieving" approach (where performance, particularly as compared with that of others, mattered more than learning). SAT scores turned out to be significantly correlated with both the surface and achieving approaches, but not at all with the deep approach. (That finding has been replicated with the results of other standardized tests taken by younger students, lending support to the criticism that such examinations tend to measure what matters least.)

- SAT's don't predict the future. A considerable amount of research, including but not limited to a summary of more than 600 studies published by the College Board in 1984, has found that only about 12 to 16 percent of the variance in freshman grades could be explained by SAT scores, suggesting that they are not particularly useful even with respect to that limited variable—and virtually worthless at predicting how students will fare after their freshman year (and whether they will graduate).

• SAT's don't contribute to diversity. Far from offering talented minority students a way to prove their worth, the overall effect of the SAT has been to ratify entrenched patterns of discrimination. Maria Blanco, a regional counsel with the Mexican American Legal Defense and Educational Fund, remarked recently that the SAT "has turned into a barrier to students of color," because it "keeps out very qualified kids who have overcome obstacles but don't test very well." Colleges looking to put together a racially and ethnically diverse student body are, therefore, already likely to minimize the significance of standardized-test scores.

Unhappily, though, some people committed to affirmative action— and even more who are opposed to it—have treated the SAT as a marker for merit and then argued about whether it is legitimate to set scores aside. Should a desire for equity sometimes override the desire for excellence? But that question is utterly misconceived. SAT's, like other standardized tests, do not further the cause of equity *or* excellence. Such tests privilege the privileged and reflect a skill at taking tests. Few people— other than those who profit handsomely from its administration—will mourn the SAT when it finally breathes its last.

And now the bad news: Unless we are very careful, a long-overdue move to jettison SAT scores may simply ratchet up the significance accorded to other admissions criteria that are little better and possibly even worse. Atkinson suggested that, at least in the short run, colleges might switch to the SAT 2, better known as achievement tests. While that may be a step forward in some respects, it may have the effect of creating a standardized, exam-based high-school curriculum that could squeeze out other kinds of teaching. That is already beginning to happen as states impose their own exit tests: Teachers feel compelled to cover vast amounts of content, often superficially, rather than letting students discover ideas.

The more ominous threat, though, is that, as the SAT fades, it will be replaced by high-school grades. There is a widespread assumption that less emphasis on scores as an admission criterion has to mean more emphasis on grades, as though nature has decreed an inverse relationship between the two. But for grades to be given more emphasis would be terribly unfortunate. On the most obvious level, grades are unreliable indicators of student achievement. A "B" from one teacher or school doesn't equate to a "B" from somewhere else; in fact, some studies have shown that a given assignment may even receive two different grades from a single teacher who reads it at two different times. Most people know that is true; tests like the SAT are more dangerous because they are falsely assumed to be objective.

What is far more disturbing about even the current emphasis on grades, let alone the prospect of enhancing their significance, is the

5

damage they do when students are led to compulsively groom their transcripts.

Researchers have found three consistent effects of focusing attention on traditional grades. First, interest in the learning itself tends to decline. Many studies have shown that the more people are rewarded for doing something, the more they tend to lose interest in whatever they had to do to get the reward. While it's not impossible for a student to be concerned about getting high marks and also to enjoy playing with ideas, the practical reality is that there is a negative correlation between a grade orientation and a learning orientation.

Second, focusing on grades tends to reduce the quality of students' thinking. One series of studies by the researcher Ruth Butler found that graded students were significantly less creative than those who received only qualitative feedback. The more the task required creative thinking, in fact, the worse the performance of students who knew they were going to receive a grade. In another experiment by two University of Rochester researchers, reported in 1987, students who were told they would be graded on how well they learned a social-studies lesson had more trouble understanding the main point of the assigned text than did students who were told that no grades would be involved. Even on a measure of rote recall, the graded group remembered fewer facts a week later.

Finally, concern about grades often reduces a student's preference for challenging tasks. Those who cut corners—who choose short books, undemanding projects, and "gut" courses—are not being lazy so much as rational; they are responding to the imperative to bring up their grade-point averages.

If it's worrisome that SAT coaching sessions take time away from meaningful intellectual pursuits, then it's worse that an admissions policy that causes students to become obsessed with grades could undermine the intellectual value of virtually everything they do in high school. Indeed, it can create intellectual dispositions that persist in and beyond college. From that perspective, complaints about "grade inflation" are a spectacular exercise in missing the point. The problem isn't that too many students are getting A's; the problem is that too many students are getting the idea that the whole point of school is to get A's.

The only thing worse than placing added emphasis on the G.P.A. is placing added emphasis on *relative* G.P.A. Some state systems now want to guarantee acceptance to all students in a top percentage of their class. Here, the emphasis is not merely on performance (as opposed to learning), but on victory. A considerable body of data demonstrates that creating competition among students is decidedly detrimental with respect to achievement and motivation to learn. The urgent question should not be whether high-school class rank is correlated with college grades, but whether secondary schools can maintain (or create) a focus on intellectual exploration when their students are forced to view their classmates as obstacles to their own success.

Where does all this leave us? Those willing to ask the truly radical questions about college admissions might consider an observation offered 30 years ago during a public lecture at the Educational Testing Service by the psychologist David McClelland. Rather than asking what criteria best predict success in higher education, he asked whether colleges should even be looking for the most-qualified students. "One would think that the purpose of education is precisely to improve the performance of those who are not doing very well," he mused. "If the colleges were interested in proving that they could educate people, high-scoring students might be poor bets because they would be less likely to show improvement in performance."

Many of us will find that challenge too unsettling, preferring that we continue to admit those students who will probably be easiest to educate. But even if we are looking for the "best" students, we ought to see G.P.A. numbers and SAT scores as a matched set of flawed criteria. Grades-and-tests, at best, will predict future grades-and-tests. Although some would dispute that, there is good evidence that grades don't predict later-life success, in occupational or intellectual terms. In the 1980's, a review of 35 studies, published in the *American Educational Research Journal*, concluded that academic indicators (grades and tests) from college—never mind high school—accounted for less than 3 percent of the variance in eventual occupational performance as judged by income, job-effectiveness ratings, and job satisfaction. Moreover, those indicators had no predictive power whatsoever for M.D.'s and Ph.D.'s. 15

When Mount Holyoke College, after a lengthy study by faculty members, announced last year that it would stop requiring students to submit SAT scores, the president, Joanne Creighton, did not limit her criticism to that test. "There has been a kind of reductionism in higher education, reducing students and institutions to numbers," she said. Similarly, Atkinson said that he had recommended "that all campuses move away from admission processes that use narrowly defined quantitative formulas and instead adopt procedures that look at applicants in a comprehensive, holistic way."

Doing so will not be an easy sell, if only because it is faster and therefore cheaper for universities that hear from tens of thousands of applicants to continue reducing each one to a numerical formula, rather than to weigh each as an individual. A move from SAT to G.P.A.—or SAT 1 to SAT 2—will merely fine-tune the formula. That would be a pity, because the attention given Atkinson's proposal has provided us with an opportunity to confront larger and more lasting issues.

Gary M. Lavergne

Gary M. Lavergne, director of admissions research at the University of Texas, Austin, is a former employee of the College Board. The essay that we reprint appeared originally in The New York Times, *March 4, 2001.*

Is This the End for the SAT?

Richard Atkinson, president of the University of California system, recently observed a classroom of 12-year-olds using analogies to extend their mastery of English. Dr. Atkinson realized that these children were preparing for the SAT. They should not have to take the test for another five years. But some students will take it at 12 and then over and over again until it's "for real."

Dr. Atkinson told his story at the start of a controversial speech last month recommending that the University of California system no longer require scores for the SAT I—the "aptitude SAT"—in deciding admissions. His concerns are less about whether SAT's work for colleges than about unintended consequences, like the impact of the test on curriculums and massive investments in test preparation. He said misuse of the SAT is so widespread that the overemphasis on it "is compromising our educational system"—probably the most serious challenge the SAT has ever faced.

The maker of the SAT, the College Board, has contributed to the crisis. It is a nonprofit organization, but its survival depends on a certain level of sales. The board seeks to provide expert services, develop tests and expand its markets. Added to the mixture is a zeal to spread its influence over education. The relationship between the College Board's wish to test children properly and its wish to raise revenue and expand its influence has gone from being a mild conflict to being a troubling contradiction.

The board needs to admit unambiguously that the SAT and its relative, the PSAT/NMSQT, have become unhealthy obsessions. The board should actively discourage the use of tests for anything for which they were not developed. For example, political decision makers in several states, including California and Texas, look to the SAT to perform inappropriate tasks. In its College Bound Senior Reports, the board asserts that using SAT scores "to compare or evaluate teachers, schools, districts, states or other educational units is not valid" and says it "strongly discourages such uses." Other than these buried phrases, however, there is no serious attempt to discourage them. On the contrary, the board provides massive amounts of data to states for "school report cards" to make such comparisons.

Gary M. Lavergne, "Is This the End for the SAT?" Originally published in *The New York Times*, 3/4/01. Reprinted by permission.

A similar muddle characterizes the questions of curriculums and   5
"teaching to the test." In a 1989 monograph, "The Common Yardstick: A
Case for the SAT," the board argued that the SAT was necessary in a nation with a vast diversity of educational curriculums. The report described the SAT as "curriculum-neutral" and said it "presumes no particular pattern of course work or course content." But upper management,
through the board's regional offices, has often advocated "curricular
alignment" between state standards and the SAT and PSAT (which is
made up of retired SAT questions). For a fee, schools and districts can secure a PSAT Summary of Answers Report to fine-tune their curriculums
and so improve performance on this supposedly curriculum-neutral test.

Just a few years ago, the PSAT was considered a test for college-
bound 11th graders. Today, the board markets it as an all-student test.
The number of eighth graders taking the PSAT increased by 125 percent
from 1995 through 1999. Dr. Atkinson's outrage at seeing 12-year-olds
practicing for the SAT is exceeded by the anger of test-center supervisors forced to counsel frightened middle schoolers facing a test designed
for college-bound seniors. As the tested population grows younger and
younger, the test's original college-admissions focus nearly disappears.

The greatest challenge before the College Board, however, is to seriously re-evaluate its messages on SAT test preparation and coaching. Is
the SAT coachable or not? In 1989, in response to claims that prep courses
could result in 120- to 140-point increases, and thus that the test favored
wealthy students who could afford coaching, the board teamed with an
Educational Testing Service scientist, Donald Powers, to study the effects
of prep courses. Mr. Powers presented compelling arguments and data
showing that coaching had very little effect on score increases. Yet the
board sells an extensive suite of test preparation materials, often advertised as "Test Prep from the Test Makers."

All is not lost for the SAT. For most universities, the SAT actually
works, in that the exam does do well at predicting future achievement.
And the "holistic" approach embraced by testing opponents has dangers
of its own. How can a college admissions officer explain to an applicant
that "other applicants had richer life experiences than you" or "we were
hoping to admit someone from another high school"?

The ACT and the SAT are important to universities. The problem is
that this incredible expanding test is being asked to do far more than it
should. The SAT program needs to shrink, a change College Board administrators are not likely to make unless the board's member organizations—representatives of high schools, colleges, universities and larger
school districts—force it to.

The SAT, as an aptitude test, did once help level the playing field so   10
that bright students from poor schools would have a greater chance to secure college admissions. This was the intended mission of the SAT—and
this is the mission from which the SAT has, in Dr. Atkinson's view,
strayed so far that the test should be abandoned.

But the problem is really with misuse of the test rather than the test itself. The College Board would do well to restrain the uses made of its tests and listen carefully to friendly advice, its own research and some not so friendly criticism. Otherwise we will probably see the end of the SAT.

Jack E. White

After serving on the staff of The Washington Post, *Jack E. White joined* Time *magazine as Nation editor and a senior correspondent in the New York Bureau. He then left* Time *to serve as senior producer for domestic news for ABC World News Tonight with Peter Jennings—the first African American to hold such a position. In 1993 he returned to* Time *as a national correspondent based in Washington, D.C. A regular columnist for* Time, *White also has written freelance articles for the* Columbia Journalism Review, Ebony, *and* Black Enterprise.

Why Dropping the SAT Is Bad for Blacks

If I had my way, the University of California would keep using the SAT until black students catch up with whites, Asians and immigrants from the Caribbean. It's a matter of ethnic pride. I'm as fed up with the tortuous theories experts have concocted to explain why our kids' scores are the lowest of any racial group as I am with the bigots who claim that proves they can't ever measure up. There's simply no excuse for black youngsters with college-educated parents to perform worse than white youths whose folks only finished high school. The only way to silence the critics is to close the black achievement gap, not to throw out the test because we're embarrassed by the results.

I can already hear my black and white liberal friends howling that I've bought into Ward Connerly's crusade against affirmative action. So be it. I'm less interested in what right-wingers like him think than I am in what we think, and frankly, I don't understand why so many of us continue to pour so much more energy into attacking the alleged biases of standardized tests than we invest in improving our children's scores. I suspect it's because we're afraid that the racists are right when they claim that our kids can't cut it intellectually, so why bother trying. That's nonsense, of course—an echo of the sense of inferiority that afflicted blacks during the bad old days of Jim Crow. But despite our growing affluence and our gains from the civil rights movement, a lot of African Americans seem to have been unable to put those nagging racial self-doubts behind them. In my opinion, such inner fears constitute the most difficult obstacle to our continued progress.

This doesn't mean that African Americans on the whole are suffering from a "cult of anti-intellectualism," as John McWhorter, a black professor at the University of California, Berkeley, claims in his recent book, *Losing the Race: Self-Sabotage in Black America.* Despite all the fuss about some black teenagers' disparaging their more studious peers for "acting white," most of us, regardless of age or where we stand on the economic ladder, value high achievement as much as anyone. Our problem is not cultural. It's political and psychological. Too many of us have forgotten that we are still engaged in a struggle for racial redemption that involves, among other things, beating whites at their own game in the classroom as well as on the playing field. We've got to start hitting the books with the same passion and moral courage that we used to overcome slavery and segregation. Our honor demands it. And so does our history.

The sad truth is that as long as we're lagging behind academically, we can't call ourselves equal. Now that our civil rights are legally secure and many of us have become prosperous, we need to erase every last, lingering scintilla of doubt about black intellectual ability. It doesn't matter that such beliefs are totally specious and rooted in racism. They influence decision makers in colleges, the government and corporations. If the powers that be believe in their hearts that blacks aren't as smart as everyone else (as many of them do—even if they would never admit it), we will be patronized, not treated with respect.

That's one of the reasons why thoughtful blacks in higher education like H. Patrick Swygert, president of Howard University, aren't willing to jettison the SAT. He's adamantly opposed to "any abandonment of standardized tests that would carry with it the implication that we just can't meet the mark." He doesn't think the SAT by itself is an adequate measure of students' potential (nor do I). But it is an important indicator of how well prepared they are for demanding college work. As a consequence, Howard (where my dad taught for 40 years) has been raising its admissions standards. The average SAT score of incoming freshmen has gone up from about 900 to 1062 in the five years that Swygert has been president. Yet Howard is attracting more applicants than ever, welcoming 1,432 freshmen this year, the largest incoming class in decades. Swygert insists there's only one way to ensure that the opportunities created by the civil rights movement won't be slammed shut again: by meeting the same standards as everyone else. "We can't let those openings be constricted because we somehow either failed to make the cut or were viewed as being unable to make it," says he.

What I hear in those words is an appeal to black pride and determination as we fight to attain the elusive commodity that economist Glenn Loury once described as "equal respect in the eyes of one's fellow citizens." It's going to require, among other things, installing tougher classes, especially in math, sciences and literature, and making sure our kids take them; better teachers; changes in study habits; and above all else, a new burst of self-confidence. We've got to believe that even at their most bigoted, whites never came up with a test blacks couldn't ace, including the SAT. We've got to make second-class scholarship—and low test scores—as intolerable to us as second class citizenship used to be.

 ## Topics for Critical Thinking and Writing

1. On March 12, 2001, *Time* Magazine ran an article, "Should SATs Matter?" Predictably the article evoked letters from readers. One reader, whose letter was published in the issue of April 2, 2001, picked up a comment made on page 64 of the article: "Assuming we can measure innate intelligence, do we want a society that rewards genes? Are we afraid of what kind of society that might be? Or should we instead reward only the achievements of a life— what we do with our gifts, not what we start with?" The letter asserted that the United States is already a society that rewards genes: "We reward the genes of physical beauty, musical and artistic talent, and athletic ability with fame, fortune and special treatment." The letter-writer continued: "The only genetic gift that we do not reward on its own merits is intelligence. In fact, we try our best to be politically correct by saying intelligence is not genetic."

   What *assumptions* about the nature of a good society did the writer of the original essay make when he or she asked if we "want a society that rewards genes?" What *assumptions* does the letter-writer make about a good society? Respond to one of these in an essay of 200–250 words.

2. Now for a second letter responding to the article in *Time*. In a sidebar (March 12, 2001, page 76), the author reported that experimenters were developing alternatives to the SAT. In one of these tests, nicknamed the Lego Test, "Small groups of students [are asked] to reproduce a relatively complicated Lego robot. One at a time, students are allowed to go and look at the structure, which is placed in another room, but they can't take notes." In other tests, aimed at evaluating the students' creativity, "Students write the caption for a cartoon or design the logo for a company." The suggestion that the SAT might be replaced by tests along these lines evoked a letter that granted that although the SAT has been given too much weight, "knowing mathematical formulas is still more reasonable for a standardized test than constructing Lego robots or writing cartoon captions."

   Do you think, contrary to the writer of the second letter, that the Lego Test and the Cartoon Test may well have considerable merit? If you were on an admissions committee, would you recommend that such tests be given a try? Why, or why not? Set forth your answer either in the form of a letter (200–250 words) to the letter writer or to your colleagues on the committee.

3. If you were an admissions officer at a college, how would you weight the SAT in comparison with (a) high school grades, (b) letters of recommendation, and (c) a sample of the candidate's writing? (Let's assume that interviews are not feasible because of the expense involved, both for the candidate and for the institution.)

4. If you have taken the SATs, do you think that your scores give valuable information to the college's admissions office? Explain.

5. A common objection against the SATs is that "teachers teach for the test," that is, they gear their instruction toward helping students score well, rather than toward helping students to become thoughtful persons. Given your experience in high school, is there some truth to the charge? And even if it is true, is it a bad thing?

6. Should a distinction be made between testing for basics (reading, writing, and mathematics), where students indeed should be prepared to meet certain tests, and testing in other fields, such as literature, the social sciences, and the physical sciences, where perhaps there is little general agreement about the goals? For instance: In chemistry, should instruction focus on chemical formulas, or on basic concepts in chemistry? In history, should it focus on names and dates, or on issues such as racism, ideas of freedom, and changing conceptions of women?

Work and Play

Short Views

Work and play are words used to describe the same thing under differing conditions.
  Mark Twain

The Battle of Waterloo was won on the playing fields of Eton.
  Attributed to the Duke of Wellington

The competitive spirit goes by many names. Most simply and directly, it is called "the work ethic." As the name implies, the work ethic holds that labor is good in itself; that a man or woman at work not only makes a contribution to his fellow man, but becomes a better person by virtue of the act of working. That work ethic is ingrained in the American character. That is why most of us consider it immoral to be lazy or slothful—even if a person is well off enough not to have to work or deliberately avoids work by going on welfare.
  Richard Milhous Nixon

In the laws of political economy, the alienation of the worker from his product is expressed as follows: the more the worker produces, the less he has to consume; the more value he creates, the more valueless, the more unworthy he becomes; the better formed is his product, the more deformed becomes the worker; the more civilized his product, the more brutalized becomes the worker; the mightier the work, the more powerless the worker; the more ingenious the work, the duller becomes the worker and the more he becomes nature's bondsman.

  Political economy conceals the alienation inherent in labor by avoiding any mention of the evil effects of work on those who work. Thus, whereas labor produces miracles for the rich, for the worker it produces destitution. Labor produces palaces, but for the worker, hovels. It produces beauty, but it cripples the worker. It replaces labor by machines, but how does it treat the worker? By throwing some workers back into a barbarous kind of work, and by turning the rest into machines. It produces intelligence, but for the worker, stupidity and cretinism.
  Karl Marx

My young men shall never work. Men who work cannot dream, and wisdom comes in dreams.
    Smohalla, of the Nez Perce

Everyone who is prosperous or successful must have dreamed of something. It is not because he is a good worker that he is prosperous, but because he dreamed.
    Lost Star, of the Maricopa

The possible quantity of play depends on the possible quantity of pay.
    John Ruskin

It can't be just a job. It's not worth playing just for money. It's a way of life. When we were kids there was the release in playing, the sweetness in being able to move and control your body. This is what play is. Beating somebody is secondary. When I was a kid, to really move was my delight. I felt released because I could move around anybody. I was free.
    Eric Nesterenko, Professional Hockey Player

Winning is not the most important thing; it's everything.
    Vince Lombardi

The games don't matter to me. I have no interest in the games. The only things that interested me in sports were the issues. I was interested in Muhammad Ali, in Jackie Roosevelt Robinson, in Curtis Flood. That's the kind of thing that mattered to me. Curtis Flood's assault on baseball, the reserve clause. I remember going to see Flood, who was tending bar in a place called The Rustic Inn. . . . He told me, "There's something in my heart and in my mind that says, 'No, you can't trade me. You can't sell me. This is the United States of America, and I will not be traded as a slave.'" I was fulfilled by his attitude and his behavior. That mattered to me. I was never interested in these silly games. I can't think of anything less important in life than who wins or loses a game. There are certain causes in sports that transcend sport, that have to do with constitutional law, that have to do with the nature of society.
    Howard Cosell

Serious sport has nothing to do with fair play. It is bound up with hatred, jealousy, boastfulness, disregard of all rules and sadistic pleasure in witnessing violence: in other words, it is war minus the shooting.

> *George Orwell*

The maturity of man—that means to have reacquired the seriousness that one has as a child at play.

> *Friedrich Nietzsche*

I see great things in baseball. It's our game—the American game. It will take our people out-of-doors, fill them with oxygen, give them a larger physical stoicism. Tend to relieve us from being a nervous, dyspeptic set. Repair these losses, and be a blessing to us.

> *Walt Whitman*

It's great because it has no clock. You can play forever. You can't kill that clock or run a few plays up the middle as you can do in the other sports.

It's great because it is a sport of rigid, complex rules, but every field is unique. No park is the same, and no other sport can make that claim.

It's great because you can do things in foul territory; you can win a game, you can lose a game, outside the field.

It's great because it not only follows the rhythms of the seasons but it is as much about loss as it is about winning. The greatest baseball players fail seven times out of ten.

It's great because you can't go to your best player every time as you can in other sports. Even Babe Ruth came up only once every nine times.

> *Ken Burns*

The boys throw stones at the frogs in sport, but the frogs die not in sport but in earnest.

> *Bion*

Bertrand Russell

Bertrand Russell (1872–1970) was educated at Trinity College, Cambridge. He published his first book, The Study of German Social Democracy, *in 1896; subsequent books on mathematics and on philosophy quickly established his international reputation. His pacifist opposition to World War I cost him his appointment at Trinity College and won him a prison sentence of six months. While serving this sentence he wrote his* Introduction to Mathematical Philosophy. *In 1940 an appointment to teach at the College of the City of New York was withdrawn because of Russell's unorthodox moral views. But he was not always treated shabbily; he won numerous awards, including (in 1950) a Nobel Prize. After World War II he devoted most of his energy to warning the world about the dangers of nuclear war.*

In reading the first sentence of the essay that we reprint, you should know that the essay comes from a book called The Conquest of Happiness, *published in 1930.*

Work

Whether work should be placed among the causes of happiness or among the causes of unhappiness may perhaps be regarded as a doubtful question. There is certainly much work which is exceedingly irksome, and an excess of work is always very painful. I think, however, that, provided work is not excessive in amount, even the dullest work is to most people less painful than idleness. There are in work all grades, from mere relief of tedium up to the profoundest delights, according to the nature of the work and the abilities of the worker. Most of the work that most people have to do is not in itself interesting, but even such work has certain great advantages. To begin with, it fills a good many hours of the day without the need of deciding what one shall do. Most people, when they are left free to fill their own time according to their own choice, are at a loss to think of anything sufficiently pleasant to be worth doing. And whatever they decide on, they are troubled by the feeling that something else would have been pleasanter. To be able to fill leisure intelligently is the last product of civilization, and at present very few people have reached this level. Moreover the exercise of choice is in itself tiresome. Except to people with unusual initiative it is positively agreeable to be told what to do at each hour of the day, provided the orders are not too unpleasant. Most of the idle rich suffer unspeakable boredom as the price of their freedom from drudgery. At times, they may find relief by hunting big game in Africa, or by flying round the world, but the number of such sensations is limited, especially after youth is past. Accordingly the more intelligent rich men work nearly as hard as if they were poor, while rich women for the most part keep themselves busy with innumerable trifles of whose earth-shaking importance they are firmly persuaded.

Work therefore is desirable, first and foremost, as a preventive of boredom, for the boredom that a man feels when he is doing necessary though uninteresting work is as nothing in comparison with the boredom that he feels when he has nothing to do with his days. With this advantage of work another is associated, namely that it makes holidays much more delicious when they come. Provided a man does not have to work so hard as to impair his vigor, he is likely to find far more zest in his free time than an idle man could possibly find.

The second advantage of most paid work and of some unpaid work is that it gives chances of success and opportunities for ambition. In most work success is measured by income, and while our capitalistic society continues, this is inevitable. It is only where the best work is concerned that this measure ceases to be the natural one to apply. The desire that men feel to increase their income is quite as much a desire for success as for the extra comforts that a higher income can procure. However dull work may be, it becomes bearable if it is a means of building up a reputation, whether in the world at large or only in one's own circle. Continuity of purpose is one of the most essential ingredients of happiness in the long run, and for most men this comes chiefly through their work. In this respect those women whose lives are occupied with housework are much less fortunate than men, or than women who work outside the home. The domesticated wife does not receive wages, has no means of bettering herself, is taken for granted by her husband (who sees practically nothing of what she does), and is valued by him not for her housework but for quite other qualities. Of course this does not apply to those women who are sufficiently well-to-do to make beautiful houses and beautiful gardens and become the envy of their neighbors; but such women are comparatively few, and for the great majority housework cannot bring as much satisfaction as work of other kinds brings to men and to professional women.

The satisfaction of killing time and of affording some outlet, however modest, for ambition, belongs to most work, and is sufficient to make even a man whose work is dull happier on the average than a man who has no work at all. But when work is interesting, it is capable of giving satisfaction of a far higher order than mere relief from tedium. The kinds of work in which there is some interest may be arranged in a hierarchy. I shall begin with those which are only mildly interesting and end with those that are worthy to absorb the whole energies of a great man.

Two chief elements make work interesting; first, the exercise of skill, and second, construction. 5

Every man who has acquired some unusual skill enjoys exercising it until it has become a matter of course, or until he can no longer improve himself. This motive to activity begins in early childhood: a boy who can stand on his head becomes reluctant to stand on his feet. A great deal of work gives the same pleasure that is to be derived from games of skill. The work of a lawyer or a politician must contain in a more delectable form a great deal of the same pleasure that is to be derived from playing bridge. Here of course there is not only the exercise of skill but the outwitting of a skilled opponent. Even where this competitive element is absent, however, the performance of difficult feats is agreeable. A man who can do stunts in an aeroplane finds the pleasure so great that for the sake of it he is willing to risk his life. I imagine that an able surgeon, in spite of the painful circumstances in which his work is done, derives satisfaction from the exquisite precision of his operations. The same kind of pleasure, though in a less intense form, is to be derived from a great deal of work of a humbler kind. All skilled work can be pleasurable, provided the skill required is either variable or capable of indefinite improvement. If these conditions are absent, it will cease to be interesting when a man has acquired his maximum skill. A man who runs three-mile races will cease to find pleasure in this occupation when he passes the age at which he can beat his own previous record. Fortunately there is a very considerable amount of work in which new circumstances call for new skill and a man can go on improving, at any rate until he has reached middle age. In some kinds of skilled work, such as politics, for example, it seems that men are at their best between sixty and seventy, the reason being that in such occupations a wide experience of other men is essential. For this reason successful politicians are apt to be happier at the age of seventy than any other men of equal age. Their only competitors in this respect are the men who are the heads of big businesses.

There is, however, another element possessed by the best work, which is even more important as a source of happiness than is the exercise of skill. This is the element of constructiveness. In some work, though by no means in most, something is built up which remains as a monument when the work is completed. We may distinguish construction from destruction by the following criterion. In construction the initial state of affairs is comparatively haphazard, while the final state of affairs embodies a purpose: in destruction the reverse is the case; the initial state of affairs embodies a purpose, while the final state of affairs is haphazard, that is to say, all that is intended by the destroyer is to produce a state of affairs which does not embody a certain purpose. This criterion applies in the most literal and obvious case, namely the construction and destruction of buildings. In constructing a building a previously made plan is carried out, whereas in destroying it no one decides exactly how the materials are to lie when the demolition is complete. Destruction is of course necessary very often as a preliminary to subsequent construction; in that case it is part of a whole which is constructive. But not infrequently a man will engage in activities of which the purpose is destructive without regard to any construction that may come after. Frequently he will conceal this from himself by the belief that he is only sweeping away in order to build afresh, but it is generally possible to unmask this pretense, when it is a pretense, by asking him what the subsequent construction is to be. On this subject it will be found that he will speak vaguely and without enthusiasm, whereas on the preliminary destruction he has spoken precisely and with zest. This applies to not a few revolutionaries and militarists and other apostles of violence. They are actuated, usually without their own knowledge, by hatred: the destruction of what they hate is their real purpose, and they are comparatively indifferent to the question what is to come after it. Now I cannot deny that in the work of destruction as in the work of construction there may be joy. It is a fiercer joy, perhaps at moments more intense, but it is less profoundly satisfying, since the result is one in which little satisfaction is to be found. You kill your enemy, and when he is dead your occupation is gone, and the satisfaction that you derive from victory quickly fades. The work of construction, on the other hand, when completed is delightful to contemplate, and moreover is never so fully completed that there is nothing further to do about it. The most satisfactory purposes are those that lead on indefinitely from one success to another without ever coming to a dead end; and in this respect it will be found that construction is a greater source of happiness than destruction. Perhaps it would be more correct to say that those who find satisfaction in construction find in it greater satisfaction than the lovers of destruction can find in destruction, for if once you have become filled with hate you will not easily derive from construction the pleasure which another man would derive from it.

At the same time few things are so likely to cure the habit of hatred as the opportunity to do constructive work of an important kind.

The satisfaction to be derived from success in a great constructive enterprise is one of the most massive that life has to offer, although unfortunately in its highest forms it is open only to men of exceptional ability. Nothing can rob a man of the happiness of successful achievement in an important piece of work, unless it be the proof that after all his work was bad. There are many forms of such satisfaction. The man who by a scheme of irrigation has caused the wilderness to blossom like the rose enjoys it in one of its most tangible forms. The creation of an organization may be a work of supreme importance. So is the work of those few statesmen who have devoted their lives to producing order out of chaos, of whom Lenin is the supreme type in our day. The most obvious examples are artists and men of science. Shakespeare says of his verse: "So long as men can breathe, or eyes can see, so long lives this." And it cannot be doubted that the thought consoled him for misfortune. In his sonnets he maintains that the thought of his friend reconciled him to life, but I cannot help suspecting that the sonnets he wrote to his friend were even more effective for this purpose than the friend himself. Great artists and great men of science do work which is in itself delightful; while they are doing it, it secures them the respect of those whose respect is worth having, which gives them the most fundamental kind of power, namely power over men's thoughts and feelings. They have also the most solid reasons for thinking well of themselves. This combination of fortunate circumstances ought, one would think, to be enough to make any man happy. Nevertheless it is not so. Michelangelo, for example, was a profoundly unhappy man, and maintained (not, I am sure, with truth) that he would not have troubled to produce works of art if he had not had to pay the debts of his impecunious relations. The power to produce great art is very often, though by no means always, associated with a temperamental unhappiness, so great that but for the joy which the artist derives from his work, he would be driven to suicide. We cannot, therefore, maintain that even the greatest work must make a man happy; we can only maintain that it must make him less unhappy. Men of science, however, are far less often temperamentally unhappy than artists are, and in the main the men who do great work in science are happy men, whose happiness is derived primarily from their work.

One of the causes of unhappiness among intellectuals in the present day is that so many of them, especially those whose skill is literary, find no opportunity for the independent exercise of their talents, but have to hire themselves out to rich corporations directed by Philistines, who insist upon their producing what they themselves regard as pernicious nonsense. If you were to inquire among journalists in either England or America whether they believed in the policy of the newspaper for which they worked, you would find, I believe, that only a small minority do so; the rest, for the sake of a livelihood, prostitute their skill to purposes which they believe to be harmful. Such work cannot bring any real satisfaction, and in the course of reconciling himself to the doing of it, a man has to make himself so cynical that he can no longer derive wholehearted satisfaction from anything whatever. I cannot condemn men who undertake work of this sort, since starvation is too serious an alternative, but I think that where it is possible to do work that is satisfactory to a man's constructive impulses without entirely starving, he will be well advised from the point of view of his own happiness if he chooses it in preference to work much more highly paid but not seeming to him worth doing on its own account. Without self-respect genuine happiness is scarcely possible. And the man who is ashamed of his work can hardly achieve self-respect.

The satisfaction of constructive work, though it may, as things are, be the privilege of a minority, can nevertheless be the privilege of a quite large minority. Any man who is his own master in his work can feel it; so can any man whose work appears to him useful and requires considerable skill. The production of satisfactory children is a difficult constructive work capable of affording profound satisfaction. Any woman who has achieved this can feel that as a result of her labor the world contains something of value which it would not otherwise contain.

Human beings differ profoundly in regard to the tendency to regard their lives as a whole. To some men it is natural to do so, and essential to happiness to be able to do so with some satisfaction. To others life is a series of detached incidents without directed movement and without unity. I think the former sort are more likely to achieve happiness than the latter, since they will gradually build up those circumstances from which they can derive contentment and self-respect, whereas the others will be blown about by the winds of circumstances now this way, now that, without ever arriving at any haven. The habit of viewing life as a whole is an essential part both of wisdom and of true morality, and is one of the things which ought to be encouraged in education. Consistent purpose is not enough to make life happy, but it is an almost indispensable condition of a happy life. And consistent purpose embodies itself mainly in work.

 ## Topics for Critical Thinking and Writing

1. Russell says (paragraph 3): "The desire that men feel to increase their income is quite as much a desire for success as for the extra comforts that a higher income can procure." In its context, what does *success* mean? In your experience, do Russell's words ring true? Why or why not?

2. In paragraphs 7–11 Russell develops a contrast between what he calls "destructive" and "constructive" work. Is the contrast clarified by the examples he offers? What examples from your own experience or knowledge can you add?

3. In paragraph 10 Russell speaks of workers who "prostitute their skills to purposes which they believe to be harmful." What work does he use as an example here? What other examples can you offer? Imagine yourself doing work that you do not respect or that you even find "harmful." Then imagine being offered work that you do respect but at a much lower salary. How helpful would you find Russell's advice? What would you do? (Specific examples of work that you respect and work that you don't respect will help you to form a clear idea of the choice and a clear argument to support it.)

4. What new point does Russell introduce in his last paragraph? How well does this last paragraph work as a conclusion?

5. Russell is generally admired for his exceptionally clear prose. List some of the devices that make for clarity in this essay.

6. Through most of his essay, Russell writes as if only men were engaged in work. What references to women working do you find? From these references and from the predominant references to men, would you describe Russell as sexist? Why or why not?

7. Compare Russell with Steinem (page 539) on the value of work.

W. H. Auden

W[ystan] H[ugh] Auden (1907–73) was born and educated in England. In 1939 he came to the United States and became an American citizen, but in 1972 he returned to England to live. Although Auden established his reputation chiefly with his poetry, he also wrote excellent plays, libretti, and essays.

   One of Auden's most unusual works, A Certain World: A Commonplace Book, is an anthology of some of his favorite passages from other people's books, along with brief reflections on his reading. The passage we print here begins with a reference to Hannah Arendt's The Human Condition.

Work, Labor, and Play

So far as I know, Miss Hannah Arendt was the first person to define the essential difference between work and labor. To be happy, a man must feel, firstly, free and, secondly, important. He cannot be really happy if he is compelled by society to do what he does not enjoy doing, or if what he enjoys doing is ignored by society as of no value or importance. In a society where slavery in the strict sense has been abolished, the sign that what a man does is of social value is that he is paid money to do it, but a laborer today can rightly be called a wage slave. A man is a laborer if the job society offers him is of no interest to himself but he is compelled to take it by the necessity of earning a living and supporting his family.

The antithesis to labor is play. When we play a game, we enjoy what we are doing, otherwise we should not play it, but it is a purely private activity; society could not care less whether we play it or not.

Between labor and play stands work. A man is a worker if he is personally interested in the job which society pays him to do; what from the point of view of society is necessary labor is from his own point of view voluntary play. Whether a job is to be classified as labor or work depends, not on the job itself, but on the tastes of the individual who undertakes it. The difference does not, for example, coincide with the difference between a manual and a mental job; a gardener or a cobbler may be a worker, a bank clerk a laborer. Which a man is can be seen from his attitude toward leisure. To a worker, leisure means simply the hours he needs to relax and rest in order to work efficiently. He is therefore more likely to take too little leisure than too much; workers die of coronaries and forget their wives' birthdays. To the laborer, on the other hand, leisure means freedom from compulsion, so that it is natural for him to imagine that the fewer hours he has to spend laboring, and the more hours he is free to play, the better.

What percentage of the population in a modern technological society are, like myself, in the fortunate position of being workers? At a guess I would say sixteen per cent, and I do not think that figure is likely to get bigger in the future.

Technology and the division of labor have done two things: by eliminating in many fields the need for special strength or skill, they have made a very large number of paid occupations which formerly were enjoyable work into boring labor, and by increasing productivity they have reduced the number of necessary laboring hours. It is already possible to imagine a society in which the majority of the population, that is to say, its laborers, will have almost as much leisure as in earlier times was enjoyed by the aristocracy. When one recalls how aristocracies in the past actually behaved, the prospect is not cheerful. Indeed, the problem of dealing with boredom may be even more difficult for such a future mass society than it was for aristocracies. The latter, for example, ritualized their time; there was a season to shoot grouse, a season to spend in town, etc. The masses are more likely to replace an unchanging ritual by fashion which it will be in the economic interest of certain people to change as often as possible. Again, the masses cannot go in for hunting, for very soon there would be no animals left to hunt. For other aristocratic amusements like gambling, dueling, and warfare, it may be only too easy to find equivalents in dangerous driving, drug-taking, and senseless acts of violence. Workers seldom commit acts of violence, because they can put their aggression into their work, be it physical like the work of a smith, or mental like the work of a scientist or an artist. The role of aggression in mental work is aptly expressed by the phrase "getting one's teeth into a problem."

 Topics for Critical Thinking and Writing

1. Some readers have had trouble following Auden in his first three paragraphs, although by the end of the third paragraph the difficulties have disappeared. Can you summarize the first paragraph in a sentence? If you think that the development of the idea in these first three paragraphs could be clearer, insert the necessary phrases or sentences, or indicate with arrows the places to which sentences should be moved.

2. Compare Auden with Russell (page 526) on the relationship between work and happiness.

Malcolm X

Malcolm X, born Malcolm Little in Nebraska in 1925, was the son of a Baptist minister. He completed the eighth grade, but then he got into trouble and was sent to a reformatory. After his release he became a thief, dope peddler, and pimp. In 1944 he was sent to jail, where he spent six and a half years. During his years in jail he became a convert to the Black Muslim faith. Paroled in 1950, he served as a minister and founded Muslim temples throughout the United States. In 1964, however, he broke with Elijah Muhammad, leader of the Black Muslims and a powerful advocate of separation of whites and blacks. Malcolm X formed a new group, the Organization of Afro-American Unity, but a year later he was assassinated in New York. His Autobiography, *written with Alex Haley, was published in 1964. Haley (1921–92) is also the author of* Roots, *a study tracing a black family back through seven generations.*

"The Shoeshine Boy" (editors' title) is from The Autobiography of Malcolm X, *chapter 3.*

The Shoeshine Boy

When I got home, Ella said there had been a telephone call from somebody named Shorty. He had left a message that over at the Roseland State Ballroom, the shoeshine boy was quitting that night, and Shorty had told him to hold the job for me.

"Malcolm, you haven't had any experience shining shoes," Ella said. Her expression and tone of voice told me she wasn't happy about my taking that job. I didn't particularly care, because I was already speechless thinking about being somewhere close to the greatest bands in the world. I didn't even wait to eat any dinner.

The ballroom was all lighted when I got there. A man at the front door was letting in members of Benny Goodman's band. I told him I wanted to see the shoeshine boy, Freddie.

"You're going to be the new one?" he asked. I said I thought I was, and he laughed, "Well, maybe you'll hit the numbers and get a Cadillac, too." He told me that I'd find Freddie upstairs in the men's room on the second floor.

But downstairs before I went up, I stepped over and snatched a   5
glimpse inside the ballroom. I just couldn't believe the size of that waxed floor! At the far end, under the soft, rose-colored lights, was the bandstand with the Benny Goodman musicians moving around, laughing and talking, arranging their horns and stands.

A wiry, brown-skinned, conked fellow upstairs in the men's room greeted me. "You Shorty's homeboy?" I said I was, and he said he was Freddie. "Good old boy," he said. "He called me, he just heard I hit the big number, and he figured right I'd be quitting." I told Freddie what the man at the front door had said about a Cadillac. He laughed and said, "Burns them white cats up when you get yourself something. Yeah, I told them I was going to get me one—just to bug them."

Freddie then said for me to pay close attention, that he was going to be busy and for me to watch but not get in the way, and he'd try to get me ready to take over at the next dance, a couple of nights later.

As Freddie busied himself setting up the shoeshine stand, he told me, "Get here early . . . your shoeshine rags and brushes by this footstand . . . your polish bottles, paste wax, suede brushes over here . . . everything in place, you get rushed, you never need to waste motion . . ."

While you shined shoes, I learned, you also kept watch on customers inside, leaving the urinals. You darted over and offered a small white hand towel. "A lot of cats who ain't planning to wash their hands, sometimes you can run up with a towel and shame them. Your towels are really your best hustle in here. Cost you a penny apiece to launder—you always get at least a nickel tip."

The shoeshine customers, and any from the inside rest room who took a towel, you whiskbroomed a couple of licks. "A nickel or a dime tip, just give 'em that," Freddie said. "But for two bits, Uncle Tom a little— white cats especially like that. I've had them to come back two, three times a dance." 10

From down below, the sound of the music had begun floating up. I guess I stood transfixed. "You never seen a big dance?" asked Freddie. "Run on awhile, and watch."

There were a few couples already dancing under the rose-covered lights. But even more exciting to me was the crowd thronging in. The most glamorous-looking white women I'd ever seen—young ones, old ones, white cats buying tickets at the window, sticking big wads of green bills back into their pockets, checking the women's coats, and taking their arms and squiring them inside.

Freddie had some early customers when I got back upstairs. Between the shoeshine stand and thrusting towels to me just as they approached the wash basin, Freddie seemed to be doing four things at once. "Here, you can take over the whiskbroom," he said, "just two or three licks—but let 'em feel it."

When things slowed a little, he said, "You ain't seen nothing tonight. You wait until you see a spooks' dance! Man, our own people carry *on!*" Whenever he had a moment, he kept schooling me. "Shoelaces, this drawer here. You just starting out, I'm going to make these to you as a present. Buy them for a nickel a pair, tell cats they need laces if they do, and charge two bits."

Every Benny Goodman record I'd ever heard in my life, it seemed, was filtering faintly into where we were. During another customer lull, Freddie let me slip back outside again to listen. Peggy Lee was at the mike singing. Beautiful! She had just joined the band and she was from North Dakota and had been singing with a group in Chicago when Mrs. Benny Goodman discovered her, we had heard some customers say. She finished the song and the crowd burst into applause. She was a big hit. 15

"It knocked me out, too, when I first broke in here," Freddie said, grinning, when I went back in there. "But, look, you ever shined any shoes?" He laughed when I said I hadn't, excepting my own. "Well, let's get to work. I never had neither." Freddie got on the stand and went to work on his own shoes. Brush, liquid polish, brush, paste wax, shine rag, lacquer sole dressing . . . step by step, Freddie showed me what to do.

"But you got to get a whole lot faster. You can't waste time!" Freddie showed me how fast on my own shoes. Then, because business was ta-pering off, he had time to give me a demonstration of how to make the shine rag pop like a firecracker. "Dig the action?" he asked. He did it in slow motion. I got down and tried it on his shoes. I had the principle of it. "Just got to do it faster," Freddie said. "It's a jive noise, that's all. Cats tip better, they figure you're knocking yourself out!"

 ## Topics for Critical Thinking and Writing

1. In this selection Malcolm X is more concerned with Benny Goodman than with learning about shining shoes. Freddie is concerned with teaching Malcolm the trade. What are we concerned with in this selection?

2. How would you characterize Freddie's attitude toward his job?

3. In paragraph 17 Freddie demonstrates a "jive noise." Using evidence from this selection, the library, mother wit, or what you will, define *jive*.

4. On what date did Malcolm begin his apprenticeship as a shoeshine boy? How did you arrive at that date?

John Updike

John Updike (b. 1932) grew up in Shillington, Pennsylvania, where his father was a teacher and his mother was a writer. After receiving a B.A. degree from Harvard he studied drawing at Oxford for a year, but an offer from The New Yorker *magazine brought him back to the United States. He at first served as a reporter for the magazine, but soon began contributing poetry, essays, and fiction. Today he is one of America's most prolific and well-known writers.*

Early Inklings

"**Y**ou're hired": sweet words, in this life of getting and spending. I have heard them rather rarely; my last regular paycheck was issued when I was twenty-five and poised to anoint myself a self-employed writer. My first paying job that I can recall was swatting flies ten for a penny on my family's side porch. The pay rate, considering the number and sluggishness of Pennsylvania flies, seems high; perhaps I broke my employers' bank. Though I was keen and eager, at the age of six or so, the job did not open out into a career.

Next, at the age of twelve, I worked for a weekly pass to the local movie theatre. I and some six or eight other boys would gather at the Shillington, with its triangular marquee and slanting lobby, on Saturday mornings, and be entrusted with bundles of little tinted leaflets, folded once like a minimal book, advertising the week's coming attractions. Shows, some of them double features, changed every other day and took Sundays off—gangster films, musicals, Disney cartoons, romantic comedies, Abbott and Costello, Biblical epics, all offering a war-beset, Depression-haunted America ninety minutes of distraction from its troubles. We boys were dispatched in pairs, some of us to territories as remote as Mohnton and Sinking Spring, and scampered up and down the concrete steps of hilly Pennsylvania to leave our slithering beguilements on expectant porches where tin boxes held empty milk bottles and rubber mats said in raised letters "Welcome." When the leaflets were gone—some very bad boys, it was rumored, would dump theirs down a storm drain—we returned to the theatre for our magic pass. More than once, to save the seven cents the movie-house proprietor had given us for the trolley car, my partner and I would saunter the several miles back to Shillington, between the shining tracks.

Next, a dark chapter. I must have been sixteen when I was deemed eligible to work in a lens factory in the gritty city of Reading. They were sunglass lenses, at least in our end of the plant—they came mounted on hemispheres fitted, in turn, onto upright hubs that held them under rotating caps in a long trough full of a red liquid abrasive called "mud." They had to be changed every twenty minutes, as I remember; I was always falling behind, and a foreman kept coming around to chalk rejection marks—white X's—on my overcooked hemispheres, with their blank and slippery eyes. The red sludge got all over you, inexpungeably, into hair, ears, and fingernails. A wan, Dickensian boy about my age tried to teach me the ropes, but my only prowess emerged at the brief lunch break, when a country skill at quoits enabled me to outscore my malnourished city-dwelling co-workers.

On the vast factory floor, various machines mercilessly thrummed around me, and my stomach churned. In my nervous moments of repose, I smoked cigarettes, flipping the butts right onto the scarred old floor. I could smoke all I wanted; the adults around me didn't care. But the consolation fell short: if this thrumming, churning misery marked the entrance to adulthood, childhood wasn't so bad. I quit after three days, promising my parents to work profitably instead at my strawberry patch on the farm to which we had moved. Agricultural labor is as mirthless as industrial, but the strawberry season lasted only three weeks of straddling the wide rows, as the sun baked your bare back and daddy longlegs waltzed up your arms. For the rest of the summer, I tried to write a mystery novel.

When I was eighteen, between high school and college, the editor of   5
the Reading *Eagle* told me I was hired, as a summer copyboy. This was
even better than swatting flies. It paid a bit better, too—thirty-four dollars
and change in a small brown envelope every Friday. My duties were to
hang around the editorial room, doing a breakfast run for the doughnut-
prone, coffee-addicted staff and carrying copy into the Linotype room,
where men in green eyeshades tickled the keyboards of the towering
Mergenthaler Linotype machines. Their activity was noisily industrial,
and smelled of hot lead and human confinement, but its product made
sense to me. A copyboy's last duty of the day was to bring up a stack of
fresh, warm newspapers (the *Eagle* was an afternoon paper) from the
roaring pressroom and distribute them, with a touch of ceremony, to the
editors, the reporters, and even the paper's owner, a local magnate who
sat patiently in his grand front office. He always thanked me. I felt part of
a meaningful process, a daily distillation, an installment of life's ceaseless
poetry. This was my element, ink on paper.

Topics for Critical Thinking and Writing

1. The title, "Early Inklings," contains a pun. What is it? Do you find it appealing?

2. The first sentence refers to a sonnet by William Wordsworth that begins,

   > The world is too much with us; late and soon,
   > Getting and spending, we lay waste our powers.

   The editors of *The Little, Brown Reader*—teachers of writing and literature—
   enjoy this echo, for its relevance and wit. Choose two or three phrases or
   passages from the essay that you enjoy, and explain why you enjoy them.

3. Updike's first job was swatting flies on his family's side porch. What was
   your first job, and how much were you paid for it? Respond in a paragraph.

4. The fourth paragraph begins "Next, a dark chapter." If you had a job for
   which you were ill prepared or ill suited, explain, in an essay of 500 words,
   what it was and how long you kept at it.

Gloria Steinem

Gloria Steinem was born in Toledo in 1934 and educated at Smith College. An active figure in politics, civil rights affairs, and feminist issues, she was a co-founder of the Women's Action Alliance and a co-founder and editor of Ms. *magazine. We reprint an essay from one of her books,* Outrageous Acts and Everyday Rebellions *(1983).*

The Importance of Work

Toward the end of the 1970s, *The Wall Street Journal* devoted an eight-part, front-page series to "the working woman"—that is, the influx of women into the paid-labor force—as the greatest change in American life since the Industrial Revolution.

Many women readers greeted both the news and the definition with cynicism. After all, women have always worked. If all the productive work of human maintenance that women do in the home were valued at its replacement cost, the gross national product of the United States would go up by 26 percent. It's just that we are now more likely than ever before to leave our poorly rewarded, low-security, high-risk job of home-making (though we're still trying to explain that it's a perfectly good one and that the problem is male society's refusal both to do it and to give it an economic value) for more secure, independent, and better-paid jobs outside the home.

Obviously, the real work revolution won't come until all productive work is rewarded—including child rearing and other jobs done in the home—and men are integrated into so-called women's work as well as vice versa. But the radical change being touted by the *Journal* and other media is one part of that long integration process: the unprecedented flood of women into salaried jobs, that is, into the labor force as it has been male-defined and previously occupied by men. We are already more than 41 percent of it—the highest proportion in history. Given the fact that women also make up a whopping 69 percent of the "discouraged labor force" (that is, people who need jobs but don't get counted in the unemployment statistics because they've given up looking), plus an official female unemployment rate that is substantially higher than men's, it's clear that we could expand to become fully half of the national work force by 1990.

Faced with this determination of women to find a little independence and to be paid and honored for our work, experts have rushed to ask: "Why?" It's a question rarely directed at male workers. Their basic motivations of survival and personal satisfaction are taken for granted. Indeed, men are regarded as "odd" and therefore subjects for sociological study and journalistic reports only when they *don't* have work, even if they are rich and don't need jobs or are poor and can't find them. Nonetheless, pollsters and sociologists have gone to great expense to prove that women work outside the home because of dire financial need, or if we persist despite the presence of a wage-earning male, out of some desire to buy "little extras" for our families, or even out of good old-fashioned penis envy.

Job interviewers and even our own families may still ask salaried   5
women the big "Why?" If we have small children at home or are in some job regarded as "men's work," the incidence of such questions increases. Condescending or accusatory versions of "What's a nice girl like you doing in a place like this?" have not disappeared from the workplace.

How do we answer these assumptions that we are "working" out of some pressing or peculiar need? Do we feel okay about arguing that it's as natural for us to have salaried jobs as for our husbands—whether or not we have young children at home? Can we enjoy strong career ambitions without worrying about being thought "unfeminine"? When we confront men's growing resentment of women competing in the work force (often in the form of such guilt-producing accusations as "You're taking men's jobs away" or "You're damaging your children"), do we simply state that a decent job is a basic human right for everybody?

I'm afraid the answer is often no. As individuals and as a movement, we tend to retreat into some version of a tactically questionable defense: "Womenworkbecausewehaveto." The phrase has become one word, one key on the typewriter—an economic form of the socially "feminine" stance of passivity and self-sacrifice. Under attack, we still tend to present ourselves as creatures of economic necessity and familial devotion. "Womenworkbecausewehaveto" has become the easiest thing to say.

Like most truisms, this one is easy to prove with statistics. Economic need *is* the most consistent work motive—for women as well as men. In 1976, for instance, 43 percent of all women in the paid-labor force were single, widowed, separated, or divorced, and working to support themselves and their dependents. An additional 21 percent were married to men who had earned less than ten thousand dollars in the previous year, the minimum then required to support a family of four. In fact, if you take men's pensions, stocks, real estate, and various forms of accumulated wealth into account, a good statistical case can be made that there are more women who "have" to work (that is, who have neither the accumulated wealth, nor husbands whose work or wealth can support them for the rest of their lives) than there are men with the same need. If we were going to ask one group "Do you really need this job?" we should ask men.

But the first weakness of the whole "have to work" defense is its deceptiveness. Anyone who has ever experienced dehumanized life on welfare or any other confidence-shaking dependency knows that a paid job may be preferable to the dole, even when the hand-out is coming from a family member. Yet the will and self-confidence to work on one's own can diminish as dependency and fear increase. That may explain why—contrary to the "have to" rationale—wives of men who earn less than three thousand dollars a year are actually *less* likely to be employed than wives whose husbands make ten thousand dollars a year or more.

Furthermore, the greatest proportion of employed wives is found   10
among families with a total household income of twenty-five to fifty thousand dollars a year. This is the statistical underpinning used by some sociologists to prove that women's work is mainly important for boosting families into the middle or upper middle class. Thus, women's incomes are largely used for buying "luxuries" and "little extras": a neat double-whammy that renders us secondary within our families, and makes our jobs expendable in hard times. We may even go along with this interpretation (at least, up to the point of getting fired so a male can have our job). It preserves a husbandly ego-need to be seen as the primary breadwinner, and still allows us a safe "feminine" excuse for working.

But there are often rewards that we're not confessing. As noted in *The Two-Career Couple*, by Francine and Douglas Hall: "Women who hold jobs by choice, even blue-collar routine jobs, are more satisfied with their lives than are the full-time housewives."

In addition to personal satisfaction, there is also society's need for all its members' talents. Suppose that jobs were given out on only a "have to work" basis to both women and men—one job per household. It would be unthinkable to lose the unique abilities of, for instance, Eleanor Holmes Norton, the distinguished chair of the Equal Employment Opportunity Commission. But would we then be forced to question the important work of her husband, Edward Norton, who is also a distinguished lawyer? Since men earn more than twice as much as women on the average, the wife in most households would be more likely to give up her job. Does that mean the nation could do as well without millions of its nurses, teachers, and secretaries? Or that the rare man who earns less than his wife should give up his job?

It was this kind of waste of human talents on a society-wide scale that traumatized millions of unemployed or underemployed Americans during the Depression. Then, a one-job-per-household rule seemed somewhat justified, yet the concept was used to displace women workers only, create intolerable dependencies, and waste female talent that the country needed. That Depression experience, plus the energy and example of women who were finally allowed to work during the manpower shortage created by World War II, led Congress to reinterpret the meaning of the country's full-employment goal in its Economic Act of 1946. Full employment was officially defined as "the employment of those who want to work, without regard to whether their employment is, by some definition, necessary. This goal applies equally to men and to women." Since bad economic times are again creating a resentment of employed women—as well as creating more need for women to be employed—we need such a goal more than ever. Women are again being caught in a tragic double bind: We are required to be strong and then punished for our strength.

Clearly, anything less than government and popular commitment to this 1946 definition of full employment will leave the less powerful groups, whoever they may be, in danger. Almost as important as the financial penalty paid by the powerless is the suffering that comes from being shut out of paid and recognized work. Without it, we lose much of our self-respect and our ability to prove that we are alive by making some difference in the world. That's just as true for the suburban woman as it is for the unemployed steel worker.

But it won't be easy to give up the passive defense of "weworkbe-   15
causewehaveto."

When a woman who is struggling to support her children and grand-children on welfare sees her neighbor working as a waitress, even though that neighbor's husband has a job, she may feel resentful; and the waitress (of course, not the waitress's husband) may feel guilty. Yet unless we establish the obligation to provide a job for everyone who is willing and able to work, that welfare woman may herself be penalized by policies that give out only one public-service job per household. She and her daughter will have to make a painful and divisive decision about which of them gets that precious job, and the whole household will have to survive on only one salary.

A job as a human right is a principle that applies to men as well as women. But women have more cause to fight for it. The phenomenon of the "working woman" has been held responsible for everything from an increase in male impotence (which turned out, incidentally, to be attributable to medication for high blood pressure) to the rising cost of steak (which was due to high energy costs and beef import restrictions, not women's refusal to prepare the cheaper, slower-cooking cuts). Unless we see a job as part of every citizen's right to autonomy and personal fulfillment, we will continue to be vulnerable to someone else's idea of what "need" is, and whose "need" counts the most.

In many ways, women who do not have to work for simple survival, but who choose to do so nonetheless, are on the frontier of asserting this right for all women. Those with well-to-do husbands are dangerously easy for us to resent and put down. It's easier still to resent women from families of inherited wealth, even though men generally control and benefit from that wealth. (There is no Rockefeller Sisters Fund, no J. P. Morgan & Daughters, and sons-in-law may be the ones who really sleep their way to power.) But to prevent a woman whose husband or father is wealthy from earning her own living, and from gaining the self-confidence that comes with that ability, is to keep her needful of that unearned power and less willing to disperse it. Moreover, it is to lose forever her unique talents.

Perhaps modern feminists have been guilty of a kind of reverse snobbism that keeps us from reaching out to the wives and daughters of wealthy men; yet it was exactly such women who refused the restrictions of class and financed the first wave of feminist revolution.

For most of us, however, "womenworkbecausewehaveto" is just true   20
enough to be seductive as a personal defense.

If we use it without also staking out the larger human right to a job, however, we will never achieve that right. And we will always be subject to the false argument that independence for women is a luxury affordable only in good economic times. Alternatives to layoffs will not be explored, acceptable unemployment will always be used to frighten those with jobs into accepting low wages, and we will never remedy the real cost, both to families and to the country, of dependent women and a massive loss of talent.

Worst of all, we may never learn to find productive, honored work as a natural part of ourselves and as one of life's basic pleasures.

Topics for Critical Thinking and Writing

1. In paragraph 2 Steinem characterizes homemaking as a "poorly rewarded, low-security, high-risk job." How might she justify each of these descriptions of homemaking? Do you agree that homemaking is rightly classified as a job? If so, do you agree with her description of it?

2. Restate in your own words Steinem's explanation (paragraph 9) of why "wives of men who earn *less* than three thousand dollars a year are actually *less* likely to be employed than wives whose husbands make ten thousand dollars a year or more." The salary figures are, of course, out of date. Is the point nevertheless still valid? Explain.

3. To whom does Steinem appear to address her remarks? Cite evidence for your answer. In your opinion, is this audience likely to find her argument persuasive? Would a different audience find it more or less persuasive? Explain.

4. In addition to arguments, what persuasive devices does Steinem use? How, for example, does she persuade you that she speaks with authority? What other authorities does she cite? How would you characterize her diction and tone, for instance in paragraph 18? (On diction, see page 903; on tone, see pages 16–17 and 909.)

5. Steinem suggests two reasons for working: "personal satisfaction" and "society's need for all its members' talents." Suppose that you had no financial need to work. Do you imagine that you would choose to work in order to gain "personal satisfaction"? Or, again if you had no need to work, would you assume that you are morally obligated to contribute to society by engaging in paid work?

6. Summarize, in a paragraph of about 100 to 150 words, Steinem's argument that it is entirely proper for wealthy women to work for pay. In the course of your paragraph, you may quote briefly from the essay.

7. Compare Steinem with Russell (page 526) on the value of work.

Felice N. Schwartz

Felice N. Schwartz is founder and president of Catalyst, a not-for-profit organization that works with corporations to foster the career development of women.

In 1989 Schwartz published in the Harvard Business Review *an article that was widely interpreted as advising women to limit their expectations of advancement if they entered the business world. The controversy was reported in the newspapers, and Schwartz took the opportunity to reach a mass audience by writing an essay–printed below–for* The New York Times.

The "Mommy Track" Isn't Anti-Woman

"The cost of employing women in business is greater than the cost of employing men."

This sentence, the first of my recent article in the *Harvard Business Review*, has provoked an extraordinary debate, now labeled by others "the Mommy track." The purpose of the article was to urge employers to create policies that help mothers balance career and family responsibilities, and to eliminate barriers to female productivity and advancement.

But two fears have emerged in the debate. One is that, by raising the issue that it costs more to employ women, we will not be hired and promoted. The other is the fear that if working mothers are offered a variety of career paths, including a part-time option, all women will be left with the primary responsibility for child care.

Acknowledging that there are costs associated with employing women will not lead companies to put women in dead-end jobs. Time taken from work for childbearing, recovery and child care, as well the counterproductive attitudes and practices women face in a male-dominated workplace, do take their toll on women's productivity. But in our competitive marketplace, the costs of employing women pale beside the payoffs.

Current "baby-bust" demographics compel companies to employ women at every level, no matter what the cost. Why? Women comprise half the talent and competence in the country. The idea that companies are looking for excuses to send women home again is untrue. Companies are looking for solutions, not excuses.   5

Over and over, corporate leaders tell me that their most pressing concern is not why but *how* to respond cost-effectively to the needs of women. Some take bold steps to provide women with the flexibility and family supports they need; others implement ground-breaking programs to remove barriers to women's leadership. The farsighted do both.

Felice Schwartz, "The 'Mommy Track' Isn't Anti-Woman." Originally published in *The New York Times*, 3/22/89. Reprinted by permission.

Their programs address the needs of women as individuals. There can be no one career "track" to which women, or men, can be expected to adhere throughout their lives. Few can know from the start to what degree they will be committed to career or to family. Raising the issue of the costs of employing women motivates companies to find solutions that work for individuals with diverse and sometimes changing goals and needs.

The second fear voiced in this debate is that making alternative career paths available to women may freeze them in the role of primary caretakers of children.

Today, men are more involved in their children's upbringing, from fixing breakfast to picking up kids at school—enriching our children's lives. But despite increased sharing of parental responsibilities, women remain at the center of family life. According to a recent study, 54 percent of married women who work full-time said child care was their responsibility—contrasted with two percent of surveyed men.

The danger of charting our direction on the basis of wishful thinking is clear. Whether or not men play a greater role in child rearing, companies must reduce the family-related stresses on working women. The flexibility companies provide for women now will be a model in the very near future for men—thus women will not be forced to continue to take primary responsibility for child care. Giving men flexibility will benefit companies in many ways, including greater women's productivity.   10

What I advocate is that companies create options that allow employees to set their own pace, strive for the top, find satisfaction at the midlevel or cut back for a period of time—not to be penalized for wanting to make a substantial commitment to family. Achievement should not be a function of whether an employee has children. Success is the reward of talent, hard work and commitment.

What benefits women benefits companies. In reducing the cost of employing women—by clearing obstacles to their advancement and providing family benefits—companies create an environment in which all can succeed. But employers will not be motivated to reduce the costs if it remains taboo to discuss them. Only by putting the facts on the table will employers and women—and men—be able to form a partnership in addressing the issues.

 Topic for Critical Thinking and Writing

Read the following letters, and then consult the topics on page 550.

Pat Schroeder, Lois Brenner, Hope Dellon, Anita M. Harris, Peg McAuley Byrd

The following letters were published in The New York Times *shortly after Schwartz's article appeared.*

Letters Responding to Felice N. Schwartz

To the Editor:

Felice N. Schwartz might have had the best of intentions when she wrote "Management Women and the New Facts of Life" for the *Harvard Business Review* and reiterated her thesis in "The 'Mommy Track' Isn't Anti-Woman" (Op-Ed, March 22). Her arguments, however, are hardly supported by her scholarship, which relies on unidentified studies at unnamed corporations about undefined "turnover" rates, assertions that begin with phrases like "we know" and "what we know to be true," and an undocumented assumption that women in business cost more.

The linchpin of Ms. Schwartz's thesis is an unidentified study at a single multinational corporation where the turnover rate for female managers was allegedly two and a half times that for male managers. Ms. Schwartz does not say whether the actual rates were an insignificant 1 percent for men and 2.5 percent for women, a significant 40 percent for men and 100 percent for women or something between. Moreover, she fails to explore the reasons for the difference. These might include poor personnel policies, like rigid relocation demands or a lack of parental leave, better job opportunities at other corporations or downturns in the company's fortunes that prompted more recently hired female managers to seek greener pastures.

Ms. Schwartz cites a second unidentified study (apparently of all female employees, not just managers) at another unnamed company, where "half of the women who take maternity leave return to their jobs late or not at all." That is, half returned as scheduled, and an unspecified number did not return, but for unexplained reasons.

Singling out turnover rates among female employees, whether clerks or managers, is a dubious approach. The days of an employee's spending 50 years with a single employer and retiring with a gold watch and a handshake are over. (Indeed, thanks to the buyout, merger and acquisition mania of the 1980s, the days of a company's lasting even a few years under the same ownership, management or even the same name, are diminishing.)

A January 1983 Bureau of Labor Statistics job-tenure survey that rep-   5
resented 54 million male and 42 million female workers reported that
fewer that 10 percent of workers of either sex had been with their current
employers 25 years or more. Of the 14 million male and 9.5 million female
managers and executives covered by the survey, the median tenure was
6.6 years for males and 4.7 years for females.

The survey also showed that 60 percent of the male managers and executives and 74 percent of their female counterparts had the same employer for 9 years or less. Only 11 percent of the males and 3 percent of
the females had the same employer for 25 years or more.

In short, few men or women remain with one employer for their entire careers, and women's somewhat lower managerial tenures might be
explained partly by women's having only recently entered the executive
ranks in significant numbers.

If Ms. Schwartz's scholarship is suspect, her two-track career model
(future mommies in this corner, future nonmommies in that corner) is
quaint—indeed Victorian—in view of what businesses are doing for men
and women.

Impelled by the changing American work force and striving to remain competitive, corporations like U S West, I.B.M., A.T. & T., Time Inc.,
Corning Glass, Quaker Oats and Merck have concluded that productivity
and family obligations are not mutually exclusive, that the almighty dollar and the family are not enemies. To accommodate these new realities
companies have instituted such employment practices as parental leave,
flexible and part-time schedules, sabbaticals, child care, telecommuting
and job sharing.

But workers are not the only beneficiaries of these new practices.   10
Employers are finding that meeting the needs of employees makes companies more productive and more competitive.

Pat Schroeder
Member of Congress, 1st Dist., Colo.
Washington, March 27, 1989

The writer of the following letter heads the family law department of a law firm and is co-
author of *Getting Your Share: A Woman's Guide to Successful Divorce Strategies* (1989).

To the Editor:

Corporations may welcome Felice Schwartz's discovery of the "career and family" woman and "her willingness to accept lower pay and little advancement in return for a flexible schedule" (news story, March 8),
but such women should consider the recent history of divorce laws before
agreeing to this definition.

Although the law says marriage is an economic partnership that values child rearing and other domestic contributions as well as earning

power, the reality is that when a marriage ends, women are not adequately compensated for having devoted themselves to their families at the expense of pursuing their career development.

If young women are going to be doubly penalized this way for choosing "the mommy track," they would do well to look closely at the experience of a generation of middle-aged women who have been left divorced and financially derailed by that choice.

Lois Brenner
New York, March 19, 1989

To the Editor:

Felice N. Schwartz, in her attempt to persuade us that "The 'Mommy Track' Isn't Anti-Woman" (Op-Ed, March 22), cites an intriguing statistic. According to a recent study, she says, 54 percent of married women working full-time regard child care as their responsibility, whereas only 2 percent of men say the same.

Does this mean that 46 percent of women in these circumstances see child care as a shared responsibility—presumably because men are sharing in the work? While not a majority, such a figure would be a significant enough minority to lend force to the argument for the importance of making businesses more responsive to the needs of both mothers and fathers—and, perhaps more compellingly, to the needs of the nation's children.

While Ms. Schwartz's assurance that "current 'baby-bust' demographics compel companies to employ women at every level" may be true, it is also true that few mothers have reached the top.

The idea of tracks has always had its limitations—whether in junior high school or in the corporate world. But if we must have such tracks in business, the chances of discrimination are surely much less for a "parent track" than for a "mommy track." Corporations may or may not believe that they can get along without mothers in high places, but they must realize that they cannot function without parents.

Hope Dellon
New York, March 24, 1989

The writer of the following letter, on assistant professor of communications at Simmons College in Boston, is the author of *Broken Patterns: Professional Women and the Quest for a New Feminine Identity* (1995).

To the Editor:

Another problem with Felice Schwartz's proposal to track working women according to the likelihood they will want to raise children is that it is impossible to tell ahead of time which women are which.

In interviewing highly successful career women in predominantly male fields, I found that some women who as late as age 34 said adamantly that they did not want children had, by 40, had them. One executive who had had her tubes tied at 29, with the idea that she wanted a career and no children was, at 35, about to be married; she wanted desperately to have the ligation reversed and was seriously contemplating a completely different line of work.

Women who in their 20's had expected to quit work to have families found themselves in their 30's still single or divorced and enjoying their careers. Most women, married or single, with or without children, expressed ambivalence both about children and about their careers.

The problem is not that women don't know what they want, but that women, like men, grow and change along the life cycle. Stereotyping women early on into mothers and nonmothers would hamper their ability to develop fully both as individuals and as productive employees.

Even worse, it would perpetuate a cycle in which generations of women have been depreciated, divided and weakened through a paradoxical message that says women are inferior if they—and unless they—compete in terms that are set by and for men.

Anita M. Harris
Cambridge, Mass., March 13, 1989

To the Editor:

While I mostly agree with your response to "Management Women and the New Facts of Life" (editorial, March 13), your perspective does not include or explore the profoundly different attitudes men and women have toward money, which is, after all, why people work. There has been a spate of surveys highlighting these different attitudes.

Men see money as a means to power, heightening their visibility for selection for leadership within society. Looked at this way, the insatiable appetite for money, frequently bordering on greed, makes sense, albeit an insane sense. Capital accumulation is seen as primarily a male activity.

Women, on the other hand, see money as a means of power to purchase. Money purchases food, clothing, shelter or the means of nurturing. This idea too has its insane side, giving rise to gross materialism. Excessive spending is seen as a female trait.

Both these traits cross gender, but a greater number fall within a male-female perspective.

Women cannot satisfy their primary need, nurturing family and society, with the same single-minded directness that men can bring to their primary need of territory (capital accumulation). The marketplace, a male invention, reflects this bias, presenting women with unnatural choices, creating for them a practical as well as psychological disadvantage.

We must force the news media to include differing economic attitudes in covering the brave woman who daily deals with the multifaceted pressures of family life and living up to her potential as described by others.

Peg McAulay Byrd
Madison, N.J., March 20, 1989

Topics for Critical Thinking and Writing

1. In paragraph 5 Schwartz says that "'baby-bust' demographics compel companies to employ women at every level, no matter what the cost." Exactly what does she mean?

2. In paragraph 9 Schwartz says that "Today, men are more involved in their children's upbringing. . . " One often hears comparable statements, but are they true? How would one verify such a statement? In any case, if *you* have any reason to agree or disagree with the statement, express the grounds. To what extent do you think men *ought* to be involved in child-rearing?

3. Schwartz begins her final paragraph by asserting, "What benefits women benefits companies." What evidence or arguments does she offer to support this claim? Or do you think the point is self-evident and needs no support?

4. List the three most cogent arguments the letter-writers make against Schwartz's position.

5. Imagine that you are Schwartz. Write a letter to *The New York Times* in which you reply to one of the letters.

Barbara Ehrenreich and Annette Fuentes

Barbara Ehrenreich writes regularly for The New York Times *and for* Ms. *magazine. Annette Fuentes, the editor of* Sisterhood is Global, *has also written for* Ms., *where this article originally appeared. Because the article was originally published in 1981, the figures for wages are out of date.*

Life on the Global Assembly Line

In Ciudad Juárez, Mexico, Anna M. rises at 5 A.M. to feed her son before starting on the two-hour bus trip to the maquiladora (factory). He will spend the day along with four other children in a neighbor's one-room home. Anna's husband, frustrated by being unable to find work for himself, left for the United States six months ago. She wonders, as she carefully applies her new lip gloss, whether she ought to consider herself still married. It might be good to take a night course, become a secretary. But she seldom gets home before eight at night, and the factory, where she stitches brassieres that will be sold in the United States through J. C. Penney, pays only $48 a week.

In Penang, Malaysia, Julie K. is up before the three other young women with whom she shares a room, and starts heating the leftover rice from last night's supper. She looks good in the company's green-trimmed uniform, and she's proud to work in a modern, American-owned factory. Only not

Barbara Ehrenreich and Annette Fuentes, "Life on the Global Assembly Line" from *Ms.*, June 1981. Reprinted by permission of the authors.

quite so proud as when she started working three years ago—she thinks as she squints out the door at a passing group of women. Her job involves peering all day through a microscope, bonding hair-thin gold wires to a silicon chip destined to end up inside a pocket calculator, and at 21, she is afraid she can no longer see very clearly.

Every morning, between four and seven, thousands of women like Anna and Julie head out for the day shift. In Ciudad Juárez, they crowd into *ruteras* (rundown vans) for the trip from the slum neighborhoods to the industrial parks on the outskirts of the city. In Penang they squeeze, 60 or more at a time, into buses for the trip from the village to the low, modern factory buildings of the Bayan Lepas free trade zone. In Taiwan, they walk from the dormitories—where the night shift is already asleep in the still-warm beds—through the checkpoints in the high fence surrounding the factory zone.

This is the world's new industrial proletariat: young, female, Third World. Viewed from the "first world," they are still faceless, genderless "cheap labor," signaling their existence only through a label or tiny imprint—"made in Hong Kong," or Taiwan, Korea, the Dominican Republic, Mexico, the Philippines. But they may be one of the most strategic blocs of womanpower in the world of the 1980s. Conservatively, there are 2 million Third World female industrial workers employed now, millions more looking for work, and their numbers are rising every year. Anyone whose image of Third World women features picturesque peasants with babies slung on their backs should be prepared to update it. Just in the last decade, Third World women have become a critical element in the global economy and a key "resource" for expanding multinational corporations.

It doesn't take more than second-grade arithmetic to understand what's happening. In the United States, an assembly-line worker is likely to earn, depending on her length of employment, between $3.10 and $5 an hour. In many Third World countries, a woman doing the same work will earn $3 to $5 a *day*. According to the magazine *Business Asia*, in 1976 the average hourly wage for unskilled work (male or female) was 55 cents in Hong Kong, 52 cents in South Korea, 32 cents in the Philippines, and 17 cents in Indonesia. The logic of the situation is compelling: Why pay someone in Massachusetts $5 an hour to do what someone in Manila will do for $2.50 a day? Or, as a corollary, why pay a male worker anywhere to do what a female worker will do for 40 to 60 percent less?

And so, almost everything that can be packed up is being moved out to the Third World; not heavy industry, but just about anything light enough to travel—garment manufacture, textiles, toys, footwear, pharmaceuticals, wigs, appliance parts, tape decks, computer components, plastic goods. In some industries, like garment and textile, American jobs are lost in the process, and the biggest losers are women, often black and Hispanic. But what's going on is much more than a matter of runaway shops. Economists are talking about a "new international division of labor," in which the process of production is broken down and the fragments are dispersed to different parts of the world. In general, the low-skilled jobs are farmed out to the Third World, where labor costs are minuscule, while control over the overall process and technology remains safely at company headquarters in "first world" countries like the United States and Japan.

The American electronics industry provides a classic example: circuits are printed on silicon wafers and tested in California; then the wafers are shipped to Asia for the labor-intensive process by which they are cut into tiny chips and bonded to circuit boards; final assembly into products such as calculators or military equipment usually takes place in the United States. Garment manufacture too is often broken into geographically separated steps, with the most repetitive, labor-intensive jobs going to the poor countries of the southern hemisphere. Most Third World countries welcome whatever jobs come their way in the new division of labor, and the major international development agencies—like the World Bank and the United States Agency for International Development (AID)—encourage them to take what they can get.

So much any economist could tell you. What is less often noted is the *gender* breakdown of the emerging international division of labor. Eighty to 90 percent of the low-skilled assembly jobs that go to the Third World are performed by women—in a remarkable switch from earlier patterns of foreign-dominated industrialization. Until now, "development" under the aegis of foreign corporations has usually meant more jobs for men and—compared to traditional agricultural society—a diminished economic status for women. But multinational corporations and Third World governments alike consider assembly-line work—whether the product is Barbie dolls or missile parts—to be "women's work."

One reason is that women can, in many countries, still be legally paid less than men. But the sheer tedium of the jobs adds to the multinationals' preference for women workers—a preference made clear, for example, by this ad from a Mexican newspaper: *We need female workers; older than 17, younger than 30; single and without children; minimum education primary school, maximum education one year of preparatory school [high school]; available for all shifts.*

It's an article of faith with management that only women can do, or will do, the monotonous, painstaking work that American business is exporting to the Third World. Bill Mitchell, whose job is to attract United States businesses to the Bermudez Industrial Park in Ciudad Juárez, told us with a certain macho pride: "A man just won't stay in this tedious kind of work. He'd walk out in a couple of hours." The personnel manager of a light assembly plant in Taiwan told anthropologist Linda Gail Arrigo: "Young male workers are too restless and impatient to do monotonous work with no career value. If displeased, they sabotage the machines and even threaten the foreman. But girls? At most, they cry a little."

10

In fact, the American businessmen we talked to claimed that Third World women genuinely enjoy doing the very things that would drive a man to assault and sabotage. "You should watch these kids going into work," Bill Mitchell told us. "You don't have any sullenness here. They smile." A top-level management consultant who specializes in advising American companies on where to relocate their factories gave us this global generalization: "The [factory] girls genuinely enjoy themselves. They're away from their families. They have spending money. They can buy motorbikes, whatever. Of course it's a regulated experience too— with dormitories to live in—so it's a healthful experience."

What is the real experience of the women in the emerging Third World industrial work force? The conventional Western stereotypes leap to mind: You can't really compare, the standards are so different. . . . Everything's easier in warm countries. . . . They really don't have any alternatives. . . . Commenting on the low wages his company pays its women workers in Singapore, a Hewlett-Packard vice-president said, "They live much differently here than we do . . . ." But the differences are ultimately very simple. To start with, they have less money.

The great majority of the women in the new Third World work force live at or near the subsistence level for one person, whether they work for a multinational corporation or a locally owned factory. In the Philippines, for example, starting wages in U.S.-owned electronics plants are between $34 to $46 a month, compared to a cost of living of $37 a month; in Indonesia the starting wages are actually about $7 a month less than the cost of living. "Living," in these cases, should be interpreted minimally: a diet of rice, dried fish, and water—a Coke might cost a half-day's wages—lodging in a room occupied by four or more other people. Rachael Grossman, a researcher with the Southeast Asia Resource Center, found women employees of U.S. multinational firms in Malaysia and the Philippines living four to eight in a room in boardinghouses, or squeezing into tiny extensions built onto squatter huts near the factory. Where companies do provide dormitories for their employees, they are not of the "healthful," collegiate variety implied by our corporate informant. Staff from the American Friends Service Committee report that dormitory space is "likely to be crowded, with bed rotation paralleling shift rotation—while one shift works, another sleeps, as many as twenty to a room." In one case in Thailand, they found the dormitory "filthy," with workers forced to find their own place to sleep among "splintered floorboards, rusting sheets of metal, and scraps of dirty cloth."

Wages do increase with seniority, but the money does not go to pay for studio apartments or, very likely, motorbikes. A 1970 study of young women factory workers in Hong Kong found that 88 percent of them were turning more than half their earnings over to their parents. In areas that are still largely agricultural (such as parts of the Philippines and

Malaysia), or places where male unemployment runs high (such as northern Mexico), a woman factory worker may be the sole source of cash income for an entire extended family.

But wages on a par with what an 11-year-old American could earn on   15
a paper route, and living conditions resembling what Engels found in nineteenth-century Manchester are only part of the story. The rest begins at the factory gate. The work that multinational corporations export to the Third World is not only the most tedious, but often the most hazardous part of the production process. The countries they go to are, for the most part, those that will guarantee no interference from health and safety inspectors, trade unions, or even freelance reformers. As a result, most Third World factory women work under conditions that already have broken or will break their health—or their nerves—within a few years, and often before they've worked long enough to earn any more than a subsistence wage.

Consider first the electronics industry, which is generally thought to be the safest and cleanest of the exported industries. The factory buildings are low and modern, like those one might find in a suburban American industrial park. Inside, rows of young women, neatly dressed in the company uniform or T-shirt, work quietly at their stations. There is air conditioning (not for the women's comfort, but to protect the delicate semiconductor parts they work with), and high-volume piped-in Bee Gees hits (not so much for entertainment, as to prevent talking).

For many Third World women, electronics is a prestige occupation, at least compared to other kinds of factory work. They are unlikely to know that in the United States the National Institute on Occupational Safety and Health (NIOSH) has placed electronics on its select list of "high health-risk industries using the greatest number of toxic substances." If electronics assembly work is risky here, it is doubly so in countries where there is no equivalent of NIOSH to even issue warnings. In many plants toxic chemicals and solvents sit in open containers, filling the work area with fumes that can literally knock you out. "We have been told of cases where ten to twelve women passed out at once," an AFSC field worker in northern Mexico told us, "and the newspapers report this as 'mass hysteria.'"

In one stage of the electronics assembly process, the workers have to dip the circuits into open vats of acid. According to Irene Johnson and Carol Bragg, who toured the National Semiconductor plant in Penang, Malaysia, the women who do the dipping "wear rubber gloves and boots, but these sometimes leak, and burns are common." Occasionally, whole fingers are lost. More commonly, what electronics workers lose is the 20/20 vision they are required to have when they are hired. Most electronics workers spend seven to nine hours a day peering through microscopes, straining to meet their quotas. One study in South Korea found that most electronics assembly workers developed severe eye problems after only one year of employment: 88 percent had chronic conjunctivitis; 44 percent became nearsighted; and 19 percent developed astigmatism. A manager for Hewlett-Packard's Malaysia plant, in an interview with Rachael Grossman, denied that there were any eye problems: "These girls are used to working with 'scopes.' We've found no eye problems. But it sure makes me dizzy to look through those things."

Electronics, recall, is the "cleanest" of the exported industries. Conditions in the garment and textile industry rival those of any nineteenth-century sweatshop. The firms, generally local subcontractors to large American chains such as J. C. Penney and Sears, as well as smaller manufacturers, are usually even more indifferent to the health of their employees than the multinationals. Some of the worst conditions have been documented in South Korea, where the garment and textile industries have helped spark that country's "economic miracle." Workers are packed into poorly lit rooms, where summer temperatures rise above 100 degrees. Textile dust, which can cause permanent lung damage, fills the air. When there are rush orders, management may require forced overtime of as much as 48 hours at a stretch, and if that seems to go beyond the limits of human endurance, pep pills and amphetamine injections are thoughtfully provided. In her diary (originally published in a magazine now banned by the South Korean government) Min Chong Suk, 30, a sewing-machine operator, wrote of working from 7 A.M. to 11:30 P.M. in a garment factory: "When [the apprentices] shake the waste threads from the clothes, the whole room fills with dust, and it is hard to breathe. Since we've been working in such dusty air, there have been increasing numbers of people getting tuberculosis, bronchitis, and eye diseases. Since we are women, it makes us so sad when we have pale, unhealthy, wrinkled faces like dried-up spinach. . . . It seems to me that no one knows our blood dissolves into the threads and seams, with sighs and sorrow."

In all the exported industries, the most invidious, inescapable health   20
hazard is stress. On their home ground United States corporations are not likely to sacrifice productivity for human comfort. On someone else's home ground, however, anything goes. Lunch breaks may be barely long enough for a woman to stand in line at the canteen or hawkers' stalls. Visits to the bathroom are treated as privilege; in some cases, workers must raise their hands for permission to use the toilet, and waits up to a half hour are common. Rotating shifts—the day shift one week, the night shift the next—wreak havoc with sleep patterns. Because inaccuracies or failure to meet production quotas can mean substantial pay losses, the pressures are quickly internalized; stomach ailments and nervous problems are not unusual in the multinationals' Third World female work force. In some situations, good work is as likely to be punished as slow or shoddy work. Correspondent Michael Flannery, writing for the AFL-CIO's *American Federationist*, tells the story of 23-year-old Basilia Altagracia, a seamstress who stitched collars onto ladies' blouses in the La Romana (Dominican Republic) free trade zone (a heavily guarded industrial zone owned by Gulf & Western Industries, Inc.):

"A nimble veteran seamstress, Miss Altagracia eventually began to earn as much as $5.75 a day. . . . 'I was exceeding my piecework quota by a lot.' . . . But then, Altagracia said, her plant supervisor, a Cuban emigré, called her into his office. 'He said I was doing a fine job, but that I and some other of the women were making too much money, and he was being forced to lower what we earned for each piece we sewed.' On the best days, she now can clear barely $3, she said. 'I was earning less, so I started working six and seven days a week. But I was tired and I could not work as fast as before.'" Within a few months, she was too ill to work at all.

As if poor health and the stress of factory life weren't enough to drive women into early retirement, management actually encourages a high turnover in many industries. "As you know, when seniority rises, wages rise," the management consultant to U.S. multinationals told us. He explained that it's cheaper to train a fresh supply of teenagers than to pay experienced women higher wages. "Older" women, aged 23 or 24, are likely to be laid off and not rehired.

We estimate, based on fragmentary data from several sources, that the multinational corporations may already have used up (cast off) as many as 6 million Third World workers—women who are too ill, too old (30 is over the hill in most industries), or too exhausted to be useful any more. Few "retire" with any transferable skills or savings. The lucky ones find husbands.

The unlucky ones find themselves at the margins of society—as bar girls, "hostesses," or prostitutes.

At 21, Julie's greatest fear is that she will never be able to find a husband.   25
She knows that just being a "factory girl" is enough to give anyone a bad reputa-
tion. When she first started working at the electronics company, her father re-
fused to speak to her for three months. Now every time she leaves Penang to go
back to visit her home village she has to put up with a lecture on morality from
her older brother—not to mention a barrage of lewd remarks from men outside
her family. If they knew that she had actually gone out on a few dates, that she
had been to a discotheque, that she had once kissed a young man who said he was
a student. . . . Julie's stomach tightens as she imagines her family's reaction. She
tries to concentrate on the kind of man she would like to marry: an engineer or
technician of some sort, someone who had been to California, where the company
headquarters are located and where even the grandmothers wear tight pants and
lipstick—someone who had a good attitude about women. But if she ends up hav-
ing to wear glasses, like her cousin who worked three years at the "scopes," she
might as well forget about finding anyone to marry her.

One of the most serious occupational hazards that Julie and millions of women like her may face is the lifelong stigma of having been a "factory girl." Most of the cultures favored by multinational corporations in their search for cheap labor are patriarchal in the grand old style: any young woman who is not under the wing of a father, husband, or older brother must be "loose." High levels of unemployment among men, as in Mexico, contribute to male resentment of working women. (Ironically, in some places the multinationals have increased male unemployment—for example, by paving over fishing and farming villages to make way for industrial parks.) Add to all this the fact that certain companies—American electronics firms are in the lead—actively promote Western-style sexual objectification as a means of insuring employee loyalty: there are company-sponsored cosmetics classes, "guess whose legs these are" contests, and swim-suit-style beauty contests where the prize might be a free night *for two* in a fancy hotel. Corporate-promoted Westernization only heightens the hostility many men feel toward any independent working women—having a job is bad enough, wearing jeans and mascara to work is going too far.

Anthropologist Patricia Fernandez, who has worked in a *maquiladora* herself, believes that the stigmatization of working women serves, indirectly, to keep them in line. "You have to think of the kind of socialization that girls experience in a very Catholic—or, for that matter, Muslim—society. The fear of having a 'reputation' is enough to make a lot of women bend over backward to be 'respectable' and ladylike, which is just what management wants." She points out that in northern Mexico, the tabloids delight in playing up stories of alleged vice in the *maquiladoras*—indiscriminate sex on the job, epidemics of venereal disease, fetuses found in factory rest rooms. "I worry about this because there are those who treat you differently as soon as they know you have a job at a *maquiladora*," one woman told Fernandez. "Maybe they think that if you have to work, there is a chance you're a whore."

And there is always a chance you'll wind up as one. Probably only a small minority of Third World factory workers turn to prostitution when their working days come to an end. But it is, as for women everywhere, the employment of last resort, the only thing to do when the factories don't need you and traditional society won't—or, for economic reasons, can't—take you back. In the Philippines, the brothel business is expanding as fast as the factory system. If they can't use you one way, they can use you another.

 Topics for Critical Thinking and Writing

1. Consider the title of the essay. When you first saw it, what connotations did "global assembly line" immediately suggest? Now that you have finished reading the essay, evaluate the title.

2. Before you read this essay, what was your image of the multinational corporation? Was it mostly positive, or negative, or neutral? To what extent has the article affected the way you think about multinational corporations? If, for example, you were offered a managerial job in a multinational, would you be inclined to ask questions about their employment practices abroad that you might not have asked before reading this article?

3. Paragraph 1, which gives us a quick portrait of Anna, tells us that "Anna's husband, frustrated by being unable to find work for himself, left for the United States six months ago." Why do the authors bother to include this detail? Is it in any way relevant to their thesis, or is it simply for human interest?

4. According to paragraph 10, management believes "that only women can do, or will do, the monotonous, painstaking work that American business is exporting to the Third World." Do the authors of the essay believe this? Do you believe that women by nature—or by training—are more suited than men "to do monotonous work with no career value"?

5. Paragraph 11 reports some statements businessmen offer as reasons why Third World women supposedly enjoy their jobs. Do you think these reasons (or some of them) have any merit? Do paragraphs 12–14 and 17–21 adequately refute these reasons?

6. In paragraph 14 we learn that 88 percent of the young female workers in Hong Kong turned more than half of their wages over to their parents. What conclusions can one reasonably draw from this assertion?

7. Why do you suppose that Julie (paragraphs 2 and 25) works in a factory?

8. In paragraph 26 the author tells us that "high levels of unemployment among men, as in Mexico, contribute to male resentment of working women." Does this analysis strike you as probably true? If so, what do you think American business can do about the Mexican economy?

9. What is the effect of using the second person pronoun (*you*) in the final paragraph?

10. Given what you have read about the working conditions of women in Third World countries, when you buy your next sweater (or tennis racquet or calculator or whatever) will you reject products made in Third World countries?

Henry Louis Gates Jr.

Henry Louis Gates Jr., born in West Virginia in 1950, holds degrees from Yale University and Clare College in Cambridge, England. Returning to the United States, Gates quickly established a reputation as a leading scholar of African-American literature. He is now chair of Harvard's program in African-American Studies, and he is also the director of the W. E. B. Du Bois Institute.
We reprint an essay that originally appeared in Sports Illustrated.

Delusions of Grandeur

Standing at the bar of an all-black VFW post in my home-town of Piedmont, W.Va., I offered five dollars to anyone who could tell me how many African-American professional athletes were at work today. There are 35 million African-Americans, I said.

"Ten million!" yelled one intrepid soul, too far into his cups.

"No way . . . more like 500,000," said another.

"You mean *all* professional sports," someone interjected, "including golf and tennis, but not counting the brothers from Puerto Rico?" Everyone laughed.

"Fifty thousand, minimum," was another guess.   5

Here are the facts:

There are 1,200 black professional athletes in the U.S.

There are 12 times more black lawyers than black athletes.

There are 2½ times more black dentists than black athletes.

There are 15 times more black doctors than black athletes.   10

Nobody in my local VFW believed these statistics; in fact, few people would believe them if they weren't reading them in the pages of *Sports Illustrated*. In spite of these statistics, too many African-American youngsters still believe that they have a much better chance of becoming another Magic Johnson or Michael Jordan than they do of matching the achievements of Baltimore Mayor Kurt Schmoke or neurosurgeon Dr. Benjamin Carson, both of whom, like Johnson and Jordan, are black.

In reality, an African-American youngster has about as much chance of becoming a professional athlete as he or she does of winning the lottery. The tragedy for our people, however, is that few of us accept that truth.

Let me confess that I love sports. Like most black people of my generation—I'm 40—I was raised to revere the great black athletic heroes, and I never tired of listening to the stories of triumph and defeat that, for blacks, amount to a collective epic much like those of the ancient Greeks: Joe Louis's demolition of Max Schmeling; Satchel Paige's dazzling repertoire of pitches; Jesse Owens's in-your-face performance in Hitler's 1936 Olympics; Willie Mays's over-the-shoulder basket catch; Jackie Robinson's quiet strength when assaulted by racist taunts; and a thousand other grand tales.

Nevertheless, the blind pursuit of attainment in sports is having a devastating effect on our people. Imbued with a belief that our principal avenue to fame and profit is through sport, and seduced by a win-at-any-cost system that corrupts even elementary school students, far too many black kids treat basketball courts and football fields as if they were classrooms in an alternative school system. "O.K., I flunked English," a young athlete will say. "But I got an A plus in slam-dunking."

The failure of our public schools to educate athletes is part and parcel   15
of the schools' failure to educate almost everyone. A recent survey of the Philadelphia school system, for example, stated that "more than half of all students in the third, fifth and eighth grades cannot perform minimum math and language tasks." One in four middle school students in that city fails to pass to the next grade each year. It is a sad truth that such statistics are repeated in cities throughout the nation. Young athletes—particularly young black athletes—are especially ill-served. Many of them are functionally illiterate, yet they are passed along from year to year for the greater glory of good old Hometown High. We should not be surprised to

learn, then, that only 26.6% of black athletes at the collegiate level earn their degrees. For every successful educated black professional athlete, there are thousands of dead and wounded. Yet young blacks continue to aspire to careers as athletes, and it's no wonder why; when the University of North Carolina recently commissioned a sculptor to create archetypes of its student body, guess which ethnic group was selected to represent athletes?

Those relatively few black athletes who do make it in the professional ranks must be prevailed upon to play a significant role in the education of all of our young people, athlete and nonathlete alike. While some have done so, many others have shirked their social obligations: to earmark small percentages of their incomes for the United Negro College Fund; to appear on television for educational purposes rather than merely to sell sneakers; to let children know the message that becoming a lawyer, a teacher or a doctor does more good for our people than winning the Super Bowl; and to form productive liaisons with educators to help forge solutions to the many ills that beset the black community. These are merely a few modest proposals.

A similar burden falls upon successful blacks in all walks of life. Each of us must strive to make our young people understand the realities. Tell them to cheer Bo Jackson but to emulate novelist Toni Morrison or businessman Reginald Lewis or historian John Hope Franklin or Spelman College president Johnetta Cole—the list is long.

Of course, society as a whole bears responsibility as well. Until colleges stop using young blacks as cannon fodder in the big-business wars of so-called nonprofessional sports, until training a young black's mind becomes as important as training his or her body, we will continue to perpetuate a system akin to that of the Roman gladiators, sacrificing a class of people for the entertainment of the mob.

Topics for Critical Thinking and Writing

1. Strictly speaking, the first five paragraphs are not necessary to Gates's argument. Why do you suppose he included them? Evaluate his strategy for opening the essay.

2. In his next-to-last paragraph Gates says that "successful blacks in all walks of life" have a special obligation. In his last paragraph he widens his vision, saying that "society as a whole bears responsibility as well." Two questions: (a) In what ways is society responsible? (b) How effective do you think the final paragraph is, and why? (Consider especially the comparison to gladiatorial games.)

3. In paragraph 13 Gates mentions Joe Louis, Satchel Paige, Jesse Owens, Willie Mays, and Jackie Robinson. Do a little research on one of these men and write a short paragraph explaining Gates's reference to him. For instance, *when* did Joe Louis defeat Max Schmeling (and who *was* Schmeling)—in what year, in what round, and with what sort of punches?

4. In paragraph 13 Gates says the he "never tired of listening to the stories of triumph and defeat that, for blacks, amount to a collective epic much like those of the ancient Greeks. . . ." The appeal of stories of triumph is evident, but what is the appeal of stories of defeat? If you are familiar with stories of defeat that concern your heritage, analyze the sources of their appeal.

Margaret A. Whitney

Margaret A. Whitney wrote this essay while she was a doctoral candidate at Rensselaer Polytechnic Institute, in Troy, New York. It was originally published in The New York Times Magazine.

Playing to Win

My daughter is an athlete. Nowadays, this statement won't strike many parents as unusual, but it does me. Until her freshman year in high school, Ann was only marginally interested in sport of any kind. When she played, she didn't swing hard, often dropped the ball, and had an annoying habit of tittering on field or court.

Indifference combined with another factor that did not bode well for a sports career. Ann was growing up to be beautiful. By the eighth grade, nature and orthodontics had produced a 5-foot-8-inch, 125-pound, brown-eyed beauty with a wonderful smile. People told her, too. And, as many young women know, it is considered a satisfactory accomplishment to be pretty and stay pretty. Then you can simply sit still and enjoy the unconditional positive regard. Ann loved the attention too, and didn't consider it demeaning when she was awarded "Best Hair," female category, in the eighth-grade yearbook.

So it came as a surprise when she became a jock. The first indication that athletic indifference had ended came when she joined the high-school cross-country team. She signed up in early September and ran third for the team within three days. Not only that. After one of those 3.1-mile races up hill and down dale on a rainy November afternoon, Ann came home muddy and bedraggled. Her hair was plastered to her head, and the mascara she had applied so carefully that morning ran in dark circles under her eyes. This is it, I thought. Wait until Lady Astor sees herself. But the kid with the best eighth-grade hair went on to finish the season and subsequently letter in cross-country, soccer, basketball and softball.

I love sports, she tells anyone who will listen. So do I, though my midlife quest for a doctorate leaves me little time for either playing or watching. My love of sports is bound up with the goals in my life and my hopes for my three daughters. I have begun to hear the message of sports. It is very different from many messages that women receive about living, and I think it is good.

My husband, for example, talked to Ann differently when he realized   5
that she was a serious competitor and not just someone who wanted to get in shape so she'd look good in a prom dress. Be aggressive, he'd advise. Go for the ball. Be intense.

Be intense. She came in for some of the most scathing criticism from her dad, when, during basketball season, her intensity waned. You're pretending to play hard, he said. You like it on the bench? Do you like to watch while your teammates play?

I would think, how is this kid reacting to such advice? For years, she'd been told at home, at school, by countless advertisements, "Be quiet, Be good, Be still." When teachers reported that Ann was too talkative, not obedient enough, too flighty. When I dressed her up in frilly dresses and admonished her not to get dirty. When ideals of femininity are still, quiet, cool females in ads whose vacantness passes for sophistication. How can any adolescent girl know what she's up against? Have you ever really noticed intensity? It is neither quiet nor good. And it's definitely not pretty.

In the end, her intensity revived. At half time, she'd look for her father, and he would come out of the bleachers to discuss tough defense, finding the open player, squaring up on her jump shot. I'd watch them at the edge of the court, a tall man and a tall girl, talking about how to play.

Of course I'm particularly sensitive at this point in my life to messages about trying hard, being active, getting better through individual and team effort. Ann, you could barely handle a basketball two years ago. Now you're bringing the ball up against the press. Two defenders are after you. You must dribble, stop, pass. We're depending on you. We need you to help us. I wonder if my own paroxysms of uncertainty would be eased had more people urged me—be active, go for it!

Not that dangers don't lurk for the females of her generation. I occa-   10
sionally run this horror show in my own mental movie theater: an unctuous but handsome lawyer-like drone of a young man spies my Ann. Hmmm, he says unconsciously to himself, good gene pool, and wouldn't she go well with my BMW and the condo? Then I see Ann with a great new hairdo kissing the drone goodbyehoney and setting off to the nearest mall with splendid-looking children to spend money.

But the other night she came home from softball tryouts at 6 in the evening. The dark circles under her eyes were from exhaustion, not make-up. I tried too hard today, she says. I feel like I'm going to puke.

After she has revived, she explains. She wants to play a particular position. There is competition for it. I can't let anybody else get my spot, she says,

I've got to prove that I can do it. Later we find out that she has not gotten the much-wanted third-base position, but she will start with the varsity team. My husband talks about the machinations of coaches and tells her to keep trying. You're doing fine, he says. She gets that I-am-going-to-keep-trying look on her face. The horror-show vision of Ann-as-Stepford-Wife fades.

Of course, Ann doesn't realize the changes she has wrought, the power of her self-definition. I'm an athlete, Ma, she tells me when I suggest participation in the school play or the yearbook. But she has really caused us all to rethink our views of existence: her younger sisters who consider sports a natural activity for females, her father whose advocacy of women has increased, and me. Because when I doubt my own abilities, I say to myself, Get intense, Margaret. Do you like to sit on the bench?

And my intensity revives.

I am not suggesting that participation in sports is the answer for all young women. It is not easy—the losing, jealousy, raw competition and intense personal criticism of performance.

And I don't wish to imply that the sports scene is a morality play either. Girls' sports can be funny. You can't forget that out on that field are a bunch of people who know the meaning of the word cute. During one game, I noticed that Ann had a blue ribbon tied on her ponytail, and it dawned on me that every girl on the team had an identical bow. Somehow I can't picture the Celtics gathered in the locker room of the Boston Garden agreeing to wear the same color sweatbands.

No, what has struck me, amazed me and made me hold my breath in wonder and in hope is both the ideal of sport and the reality of a young girl not afraid to do her best.

I watch her bringing the ball up the court. We yell encouragement from the stands, though I know she doesn't hear us. Her face is red with exertion, and her body is concentrated on the task. She dribbles, draws the defense to her, passes, runs. A teammate passes the ball back to her. They've beaten the press. She heads toward the hoop. Her father watches her, her sisters watch her, I watch her. And I think, drive, Ann, drive.

⟨ Topics for Critical Thinking and Writing

1. In her second paragraph Whitney claims that "nature and orthodontics had produced a . . . brown-eyed beauty with a wonderful smile." We find (and hope that you find) this passage amusing. What other instances of humor do you find in "Playing to Win"? Humor is always agreeable. Does it have any other function in this essay?

2. In her fourth paragraph Whitney says "I have begun to hear the message of sports." Does she say what that message is? If not, can you put it in your own words?

3. In her tenth paragraph Whitney implies that "dangers" "lurk" for females of her daughter's generation. What are the dangers?

4. In paragraph 16 Whitney mentions the blue ribbon Ann wore on her pony-tail. Why does she mention it? What is her point?

5. In her final paragraph, Whitney uses the present tense. Why? What is the effect?

6. In paragraph 7 Whitney refers to "countless advertisements" in which women are portrayed as "still, quiet, cool" and vacant. Whitney's essay was published in 1998. Are women still so portrayed? Look at a half dozen ads and then choose one to write about. In the first paragraph, describe the ad clearly enough so that someone who hasn't seen it can make a reasonably good sketch of it. In the second paragraph, analyze the ad, revealing what the composition and text say and imply about women. Indicate in your first paragraph the source of the ad, and include a copy of the ad with your essay.

Sir Thomas More

Sir Thomas More (1478–1535) was an extremely able English administrator and diplomat who rose to high rank in the government of King Henry VIII, but when he opposed the King's break with Roman Catholicism (Henry demanded that his subjects recognize him as Supreme Head of the Church), More was beheaded. Four hundred years later, in 1935, he was canonized.

More wrote Utopia *in Latin (the international language of the Renaissance) in 1516. The word is Greek for* no place, *with a pun on the Greek prefix,* eu, *meaning "good," so More's* Utopia *is both "no where" and a "good place." The Greek-sounding names for officials in this imaginary land—a syphogrant is elected by a group of thirty households, and a tranibor governs a group of ten syphogrants—have no meaning. Though the book is fictional, setting forth a playful vision of an ideal society, there is no story: it is not a novel but a sort of essay.*

"Work and Play" (editors' title) represents about one-tenth of the book.

Work and Play in Utopia

Their Occupations

Agriculture is the one occupation at which everyone works, men and women alike, with no exceptions. They are trained in it from childhood, partly in the schools where they learn theory, and partly through field trips to nearby farms, which make something like a game of practical instruction. On these trips they not only watch the work being done, but frequently pitch in and get a workout by doing the jobs themselves.

Besides farm work (which, as I said, everybody performs), each person is taught a particular trade of his own, such as wool-working, linen-making, masonry, metal-work, or carpentry. There is no other craft that is practiced by any considerable number of them. Throughout the island

Sir Thomas More, from *Utopia: A Norton Critical Edition*, Second Edition by Sir Thomas More, translated by Robert M. Adams. Translation copyright © 1992, 1975 by W. W. Norton & Company, Inc. Used by permission of W. W. Norton & Company, Inc.

people wear, and down through the centuries they have always worn, the same style of clothing, except for the distinction between the sexes, and between married and unmarried persons. Their clothing is attractive, does not hamper bodily movement, and serves for warm as well as cold weather; what is more, each household can make its own.

Every person (and this includes women as well as men) learns a second trade, besides agriculture. As the weaker sex, women practice the lighter crafts, such as working in wool or linen; the heavier crafts are assigned to the men. As a rule, the son is trained to his father's craft; for which most feel a natural inclination. But if anyone is attracted to another occupation, he is transferred by adoption into a family practicing the trade he prefers. When anyone makes such a change, both his father and the authorities make sure that he is assigned to a grave and responsible householder. After a man has learned one trade, if he wants to learn another, he gets the same permission. When he has learned both, he pursues whichever he likes better, unless the city needs one more than the other.

The chief and almost the only business of the syphogrants is to manage matters so that no one sits around in idleness, and assure that everyone works hard at his trade. But no one has to exhaust himself with endless toil from early morning to late at night, as if he were a beast of burden. Such wretchedness, really worse than slavery, is the common lot of workmen in all countries, except Utopia. Of the day's twenty-four hours, the Utopians devote only six to work. They work three hours before noon, when they go to dinner. After dinner they rest for a couple of hours, then go to work for another three hours. Then they have supper, and at eight o'clock (counting the first hour after noon as one), they go to bed and sleep eight hours.

The other hours of the day, when they are not working, eating, or sleeping, are left to each man's individual discretion, provided he does not waste them in roistering or sloth, but uses them busily in some occupation that pleases him. Generally these periods are devoted to intellectual activity. For they have an established custom of giving public lectures before daybreak; attendance at these lectures is required only of those who have been specially chosen to devote themselves to learning, but a great many other people, both men and women, choose voluntarily to attend. Depending on their interests, some go to one lecture, some to another. But if anyone would rather devote his spare time to his trade, as many do who don't care for the intellectual life, this is not discouraged; in fact, such persons are commended as especially useful to the commonwealth.

After supper, they devote an hour to recreation, in their gardens when the weather is fine, or during winter weather in the common halls where they have their meals. There they either play music or amuse themselves with conversation. They know nothing about gambling with dice, or other such foolish and ruinous games. They do play two games not unlike our own chess. One is a battle of numbers, in which one number captures another. The other is a game in which the vices fight a battle against the virtues. The game is set up to show how the vices oppose one

5

another, yet readily combine against the virtues; then, what vices oppose what virtues, how they try to assault them openly or undermine them in secret; how the virtues can break the strength of the vices or turn their purposes to good; and finally, by what means one side or the other gains the victory.

But in all this, you may get a wrong impression, if we don't go back and consider one point more carefully. Because they allot only six hours to work, you might think the necessities of life would be in scant supply. This is far from the case. Their working hours are ample to provide not only enough but more than enough of the necessities and even the conveniences of life. You will easily appreciate this if you consider how large a part of the population in other countries exists without doing any work at all. In the first place, hardly any of the women, who are a full half of the population, work; or, if they do, then as a rule their husbands lie snoring in the bed. Then there is a great lazy gang of priests and so-called religious men. Add to them all the rich, especially the landlords, who are commonly called gentlemen and nobility. Include with them their retainers, that mob of swaggering bullies. Finally, reckon in with these the sturdy and lusty beggars, who go about feigning some disease as an excuse for their idleness. You will certainly find that the things which satisfy our needs are produced by far fewer hands than you had supposed.

And now consider how few of those who do work are doing really essential things. For where money is the standard of everything, many superfluous trades are bound to be carried on simply to satisfy luxury and licentiousness. Suppose the multitude of those who now work were limited to a few trades, and set to producing more and more of those conveniences and commodities that nature really requires. They would be bound to produce so much that the prices would drop, and the workmen would be unable to gain a living. But suppose again that all the workers in useless trades were put to useful ones, and that all the idlers (who now guzzle twice as much as the workingmen who make what they consume) were assigned to productive tasks—well, you can easily see how little time each man would have to spend working, in order to produce all the goods that human needs and conveniences require—yes, and human pleasure too, as long as it's true and natural pleasure.

The experience of Utopia makes this perfectly apparent. In each city and its surrounding countryside barely five hundred of those men and women whose age and strength make them fit for work are exempted from it. Among these are the syphogrants, who by law are free not to work; yet they don't take advantage of the privilege, preferring to set a good example to their fellow-citizens. Some others are permanently exempted from work so that they may devote themselves to study, but only on the recommendation of the priests and through a secret vote of the syphogrants. If any of these scholars disappoints their hopes, he becomes a workman again. On the other hand, it happens from time to time that a craftsman devotes his leisure so earnestly to study, and makes such progress as a result, that he is relieved of manual labor, and promoted to the class of learned men. From this class of scholars are chosen ambassadors, priests, tranibors, and the prince himself, who used to be called Barzanes, but in their modern tongue is known as Ademus. Since all the rest of the population is neither idle nor occupied in useless trades, it is easy to see why they produce so much in so short a working day.

Apart from all this, in several of the necessary crafts their way of life   10
requires less total labor than does that of people elsewhere. In other coun-
tries, building and repairing houses requires the constant work of many men, because what a father has built, his thriftless heirs lets fall into ruin; and then his successor has to repair, at great expense, what could easily have been maintained at a very small charge. Further, even when a man has built a splendid house at large cost, someone else may think he has finer taste, let the first house fall to ruin, and then build another one somewhere else for just as much money. But among the Utopians, where everything has been established, and the commonwealth is carefully regulated, building a brand-new home on a new site is a rare event. They are not only quick to repair damage, but foresighted in preventing it. The re-
sult is that their buildings last for a very long time with minimum repairs; and the carpenters and masons sometimes have so little to do, that they are set to hewing timber and cutting stone in case some future need for it should arise.

Consider, too, how little labor their clothing requires. Their work clothes are loose garments made of leather which last as long as seven years. When they go out in public, they cover these rough working-clothes with a cloak. Throughout the entire island, everyone wears the same col-
ored cloak, which is the color of natural wool. As a result, they not only need less wool than people in other countries, but what they do need is less expensive. They use linen cloth most, because it requires least labor. They like linen cloth to be white and wool cloth to be clean; but they put no price on fineness of texture. Elsewhere a man is not satisfied with four or five woolen cloaks of different colors and as many silk shirts, or if he's a show-off, even ten of each are not enough. But a Utopian is content with a single cloak, and generally wears it for two seasons. There is no reason at all why he should want any others, for if he had them, he would not be better protected against the cold, nor would he appear in any way better dressed.

When there is an abundance of everything, as a result of everyone working at useful trades, and nobody consuming to excess, then great numbers of the people often go out to work on the roads, if any of them need repairing. And when there is no need even for this sort of public work, then the officials very often proclaim a short work day, since they never force their citizens to perform useless labor. The chief aim of their constitution and government is that, whenever public needs permit, all citizens should be free, so far as possible, to withdraw their time and energy from the service of the body, and devote themselves to the freedom and culture of the mind. For that, they think, is the real happiness of life. . . .

Their Moral Philosophy

They conclude, after carefully considering and weighing the matter, that all our actions and the virtues exercised within them look toward pleasure and happiness at their ultimate end.

By pleasure they understand every state or movement of body or mind in which man naturally finds delight. They are right in considering man's appetites natural. By simply following his senses and his right reason a man may discover what is pleasant by nature—it is a delight which does not injure others, which does not preclude a greater pleasure, and which is not followed by pain. But a pleasure which is against nature, and which men call "delightful" only by the emptiest of fictions (as if one could change the real nature of things just by changing their names), does not really make for happiness; in fact they say, it destroys happiness. And the reason is that men whose minds are filled with false ideas of pleasure have no room left for true and genuine delight. As a matter of fact, there are a great many things which have no sweetness in them, but are mainly or entirely bitter—yet which through the perverse enticements of evil lusts are considered very great pleasures, and even the supreme goals of life.

Among those who pursue this false pleasure the Utopians include 15 those whom I mentioned before, the men who think themselves finer fellows because they wear finer clothes. These people are twice mistaken: first in thinking their clothes better than anyone else's, and then in thinking themselves better because of their clothes. As far as a coat's usefulness goes, what does it matter if it was woven of thin thread or thick? Yet they act as if they were set apart by nature herself, rather than their own fantasies; they strut about, and put on airs. Because they have a fancy suit, they think themselves entitled to honors they would never have expected if they were poorly dressed, and they get very angry if someone passes them by without showing special respect.

It is the same kind of absurdity to be pleased by empty, ceremonial honors. What true and natural pleasure can you get from someone's bent knee or bared head? Will the creaks in your own knees be eased thereby, or the madness in your head? The phantom of false pleasure is illustrated by other men who run mad with delight over their own blue blood, plume themselves on their nobility, and applaud themselves for all their rich ancestors (the only ancestors worth having nowadays), and all their ancient family estates. Even if they don't have the shred of an estate themselves, or if they've squandered every penny of their inheritance, they don't consider themselves a bit less noble.

In the same class the Utopians put those people I described before, who are mad for jewelry and gems, and think themselves divinely happy if they find a good specimen, especially of the sort which happens to be fashionable in their country at the time—for stones vary in value from one market to another. The collector will not make an offer for the stone till it's taken out of its setting, and even then he will not buy unless the dealer guarantees and gives security that it is a true and genuine stone. What he fears is that his eyes will be deceived by a counterfeit. But if you consider the matter, why should a counterfeit give any less pleasure when your eyes cannot distinguish it from a real gem? Both should be of equal value to you, as they would be, in fact, to a blind man.

Speaking of false pleasure, what about those who pile up money, not because they want to do anything with the heap, but so they can sit and look at it? Is that true pleasure they experience, or aren't they simply cheated by a show of pleasure? Or what of those with the opposite vice, the men who hide away money they will never use and perhaps never even see again? In their anxiety to hold onto their money, they actually lose it. For what else happens when you deprive yourself, and perhaps other people too, of a chance to use money, by burying it in the ground? And yet when the miser has hidden his treasure, he exults over it as if his mind were now free to rejoice. Suppose someone stole it, and the miser died ten years later, knowing nothing of the theft. During all those ten years, what did it matter whether the money was stolen or not? In either case, it was equally useless to the owner.

To these false and foolish pleasures they add gambling, which they have heard about, though they've never tried it, as well as hunting and hawking. What pleasure can there be, they wonder, in throwing dice on a table? If there were any pleasure in the action, wouldn't doing it over and over again quickly make one tired of it? What pleasure can there be in listening to the barking and yelping of dogs—isn't that rather a disgusting noise? Is there any more real pleasure when a dog chases a rabbit than there is when a dog chases a dog? If what you like is fast running, there's plenty of that in both cases; they're just about the same. But if what you really want is slaughter, if you want to see a living creature torn apart under your eyes, then the whole thing is wrong. You ought to feel nothing but pity when you see the hare fleeing from the hound, the weak creature tormented by the stronger, the fearful and timid beast brutalized by the savage one, the harmless hare killed by the cruel dog. The Utopians, who regard this whole activity of hunting as unworthy of free men, have assigned it, accordingly, to their butchers, who as I said before, are all slaves. In their eyes, hunting is the lowest thing even butchers can do. In the slaughterhouse, their work is more useful and honest—besides which, they kill animals only from necessity; but in hunting they seek merely their own pleasure from the killing and mutilating of some poor little creature. Taking such relish in the sight of death, even if it's only beasts, reveals, in the opinion of the Utopians, a cruel disposition. Or if he isn't cruel to start with, the hunter quickly becomes so through the constant practice of such brutal pleasures.

Most men consider these activities, and countless others like them, to   20
be pleasures; but the Utopians say flatly they have nothing at all to do with real pleasure since there's nothing naturally pleasant about them. They often please the senses, and in this they are like pleasure, but that does not alter their basic nature. The enjoyment doesn't arise from the experience itself, but only from the perverse mind of the individual, as a result of which he mistakes the bitter for the sweet, just as pregnant women, whose taste has been turned awry, sometimes think pitch and tallow taste sweeter than honey. A man's taste may be similarly depraved, by disease or by custom, but that does not change the nature of pleasure, or of anything else.

Topics for Critical Thinking and Writing

1. What does More assume are the only functions of clothing? Do you agree with More, or do you find other important reasons why people wear the clothes that they wear?

2. The "work ethic" assumes that labor is good in itself—that there is some sort of virtue in work. (See Nixon's remark on page 523). Further, many people assume that work, at least certain kinds of work done under certain conditions, affords happiness to the worker. What does More's attitude seem to be on these two related points?

3. What is More's opinion of hunting? What arguments in support of hunting are commonly offered? In your opinion, does More successfully counter those arguments?

4. In approximately five hundred words set forth More's assumptions about the sources of happiness.

5. More says that each Utopian is free to do what he wishes with leisure hours, "provided he does not waste them in roistering or sloth." (By the way, since the Utopians work six hours a day, if they sleep eight hours they have ten hours of free time.) In five hundred words develop an argument for or against this proviso concerning the pursuit of happiness. (You may want to recall that our own government to some degree regulates our pleasure, for instance by outlawing bullfights.)

6. Note the passage (paragraph 6) in which More describes two games enjoyed by Utopians. Imitating More's style in describing the second game, write a paragraph describing a video game as a Utopian or anti-Utopian recreation.

Marie Winn

Marie Winn, born in Czechoslovakia in 1936, came to New York when she was still a child. She later attended Radcliffe College and received her degree from Columbia University. Our selection comes from Children without Childhood *(1983), a book based in part on interviews with hundreds of children and parents.*

The End of Play

Of all the changes that have altered the topography of childhood, the most dramatic has been the disappearance of childhood play. Whereas a decade or two ago children were easily distinguished from the adult world by the very nature of their play, today children's occupations do not differ greatly from adult diversions.

Infants and toddlers, to be sure, continue to follow certain timeless patterns of manipulation and exploration; adolescents, too, have not changed their free-time habits so very much, turning as they ever have towards adult pastimes and amusements in their drive for autonomy, self-mastery, and sexual discovery. It is among the ranks of school-age children, those six-to-twelve-year-olds who once avidly filled their free moments with childhood play, that the greatest change is evident. In the place of traditional, sometimes ancient childhood games that were still popular a generation ago, in the place of fantasy and make-believe play—"You be the mommy and I'll be the daddy"—doll play or toy-soldier play, jump-rope play, ball-bouncing play, today's children have substituted television viewing and, most recently, video games.

Many parents have misgivings about the influence of television. They sense that a steady and time-consuming exposure to passive entertainment might damage the ability to play imaginatively and resourcefully, or prevent this ability from developing in the first place. A mother of two school-age children recalls: "When I was growing up, we used to go out into the vacant lots and make up week-long dramas and sagas. This was during third, fourth, fifth grades. But my own kids have never done that sort of thing, and somehow it bothers me. I wish we had cut down on the TV years ago, and maybe the kids would have learned how to play."

The testimony of parents who eliminate television for periods of time strengthens the connection between children's television watching and changed play patterns. Many parents discover that when their children don't have television to fill their free time, they resort to the old kinds of imaginative, traditional "children's play." Moreover, these parents often observe that under such circumstances "they begin to seem more like children" or "they act more childlike." Clearly, a part of the definition of childhood, in adults' minds, resides in the nature of children's play.

Children themselves sometimes recognize the link between play and their own special definition as children. In an interview about children's books with four ten-year-old girls, one of them said: "I read this story about a girl my age growing up twenty years ago—you know, in 1960 or so,—and she seemed so much younger than me in her behavior. Like she might be playing with dolls, or playing all sorts of children's games, or jump-roping or something." The other girls all agreed that they had noticed a similar discrepancy between themselves and fictional children in books of the past: those children seemed more like children. "So what do *you* do in your spare time, if you don't play with dolls or play make-believe games or jump rope or do things kids did twenty years ago?" they were asked. They laughed and answered, "We watch TV." 5

But perhaps other societal factors have caused children to give up play. Children's greater exposure to adult realities, their knowledge of adult sexuality, for instance, might make them more sophisticated, less likely to play like children. Evidence from the counterculture communes of the sixties and seventies adds weight to the argument that it is television above all that has eliminated children's play. Studies of children raised in a variety of such communes, all television-free, showed the little communards continuing to fill their time with those forms of play that have all but vanished from the lives of conventionally reared American children. And yet these counterculture kids were casually exposed to all sorts of adult matters—drug taking, sexual intercourse. Indeed, they sometimes incorporated these matters into their play: "We're mating," a pair of six-year-olds told a reporter to explain their curious bumps and grinds. Nevertheless, to all observers the commune children preserved a distinctly childlike and even innocent demeanor, an impression that was produced mainly by the fact that they spent most of their time playing. Their play defined them as belonging to a special world of childhood.

Not all children have lost the desire to engage in the old-style childhood play. But so long as the most popular, most dominant members of the peer group, who are often the most socially precocious, are "beyond" playing, then a common desire to conform makes it harder for those children who still have the drive to play to go ahead and do so. Parents often report that their children seem ashamed of previously common forms of play and hide their involvement with such play from their peers. "My fifth-grader still plays with dolls," a mother tells, "but she keeps them hidden in the basement where nobody will see them." This social check on the play instinct serves to hasten the end of childhood for even the least advanced children.

What seems to have replaced play in the lives of great numbers of preadolescents these days, starting as early as fourth grade, is a burgeoning interest in boy-girl interactions—"going out" or "going together." These activities do not necessarily involve going anywhere or doing anything sexual, but nevertheless are the first stage of a sexual process that used to commence at puberty or even later. Those more sophisticated children who are already involved in such manifestly unchildlike interest make plain their low opinion of their peers who still *play*. "Some of the kids in the class are real weird," a fifth-grade boy states. "They're not interested in going out, just in trucks and stuff, or games pretending they're monsters. Some of them don't even *try* to be cool."

Video Games versus Marbles

Is there really any great difference, one might ask, between that gang of kids playing video games by the hour at their local candy store these days and those small fry who used to hang around together spending equal amounts of time playing marbles? It is easy to see a similarity between the two activities: each requires a certain amount of manual dexterity, each is almost as much fun to watch as to play, each is simple and yet challenging enough for that middle-childhood age group for whom time can be so oppressive if unfilled.

One significant difference between the modern pre-teen fad of video games and the once popular but now almost extinct pastime of marbles is economic: playing video games costs twenty-five cents for approximately three minutes of play; playing marbles, after a small initial investment, is free. The children who frequent video-game machines require a considerable outlay of quarters to subsidize their fun; two, three, or four dollars is not an unusual expenditure for an eight-or nine-year-old spending an hour or two with his friends playing Asteroids or Pac-Man or Space Invaders. For most of the children the money comes from their weekly allowance. Some augment this amount by enterprising commercial ventures—trading and selling comic books, or doing chores around the house for extra money.

But what difference does it make *where* the money comes from? Why should that make video games any less satisfactory as an amusement for children? In fact, having to pay for the entertainment, whatever the source of the money, and having its duration limited by one's financial resources changes the nature of the game, in a subtle way diminishing the satisfactions it offers. Money and time become intertwined, as they so often are in the adult world and as, in the past, they almost never were in the child's world. For the child playing marbles, meanwhile, time has a far more carefree quality, bounded only by the requirements to be home by suppertime or by dark.

But the video-game-playing child has an additional burden—a burden of choice, of knowing that the money used for playing Pac-Man could have been saved for Christmas, could have been used to buy something tangible, perhaps something "worthwhile," as his parents might say, rather than being "wasted" on video games. There is a certain sense of adultness that spending money imparts, a feeling of being a consumer,

10

which distinguishes a game with a price from its counterparts among the traditional childhood games children once played at no cost.

There are other differences as well. Unlike child-initiated and child-organized games such as marbles, video games are adult-created mechanisms not entirely within the child's control, and thus less likely to impart a sense of mastery and fulfillment: the coin may get jammed, the machine may go haywire, the little blobs may stop eating the funny little dots. Then the child must go to the storekeeper to complain, to get his money back. He may be "ripped off" and simply lose his quarter, much as his parents are when they buy a faulty appliance. This possibility of disaster gives the child's play a certain weight that marbles never imposed on its lighthearted players.

Even if a child has a video game at home requiring no coin outlay, the play it provides is less than optimal. The noise level of the machine is high—too high, usually, for the child to conduct a conversation easily with another child. And yet, according to its enthusiasts, this very noisiness is a part of the game's attraction. The loud whizzes, crashes, and whirrs of the video-game machine "blow the mind" and create an excitement that is quite apart from the excitement generated simply by trying to win a game. A traditional childhood game such as marbles, on the other hand, has little built-in stimulation; the excitement of playing is generated entirely by the players' own actions. And while the pace of a game of marbles is close to the child's natural physiological rhythms, the frenzied activities of video games serve to "rev up" the child in an artificial way, almost in the way a stimulant or an amphetamine might. Meanwhile the perceptual impact of a video game is similar to that of watching television—the action, after all, takes place on a television screen—causing the eye to defocus slightly and creating a certain alteration in the child's natural state of consciousness.

Parents' instinctive reaction to their children's involvement with video games provides another clue to the difference between this contemporary form of play and the more traditional pastimes such as marbles. While parents, indeed most adults, derive open pleasure from watching children at play, most parents today are not delighted to watch their kids flicking away at the Pac-Man machine. This does not seem to them to be real play. As a mother of two school-age children anxiously explains, "We used to do real childhood sorts of things when I was a kid. We'd build forts and put on crazy plays and make up new languages, and just generally we *played*. But today my kids don't play that way at all. They like video games and of course they still go in for sports outdoors. They go roller skating and ice skating and skiing and all. But they don't seem to really *play*." 15

Some of this feeling may represent a certain nostalgia for the past and the old generation's resistance to the different ways of the new. But it is more likely that most adults have an instinctive understanding of the importance of play in their own childhood. This feeling stokes their fears that their children are being deprived of something irreplaceable when they flip the levers on the video machines to manipulate the electronic images rather than flick their fingers to send a marble shooting towards another marble.

Play Deprivation

In addition to television's influence, some parents and teachers ascribe children's diminished drive to play to recent changes in the school curriculum, especially in the early grades.

"Kindergarten, traditionally a playful port of entry into formal school, is becoming more academic, with children being taught specific skills, taking tests, and occasionally even having homework," begins a report on new directions in early childhood education. Since 1970, according to the United States census, the proportion of three- and four-year-olds enrolled in school has risen dramatically, from 20.5 percent to 36.7 percent in 1980, and these nursery schools have largely joined the push towards academic acceleration in the early grades. Moreover, middle-class nursery schools in recent years have introduced substantial doses of academic material into their daily programs, often using those particular devices originally intended to help culturally deprived preschoolers in compensatory programs such as Headstart to catch up with their middle-class peers. Indeed, some of the increased focus on academic skills in nursery schools and kindergartens is related to the widespread popularity among young children and their parents of *Sesame Street*, a program originally intended to help deprived children attain academic skills, but universally watched by middle-class toddlers as well.

Parents of the *Sesame Street* generation often demand a "serious," skill-centered program for their preschoolers in school, afraid that the old-fashioned, play-centered curriculum will bore their alphabet-spouting, number-chanting four- and five-year-olds. A few parents, especially those whose children have not attended television classes or nursery school, complain of the high-powered pace of kindergarten these days. A father whose five-year-old daughter attends a public kindergarten declares: "There's a lot more pressure put on little kids these days than when we were kids, that's for sure. My daughter never went to nursery school and never watched *Sesame*, and she had a lot of trouble when she entered kindergarten this fall. By October, just a month and a half into the program, she was already flunking. The teacher told us our daughter couldn't keep up with the other kids. And believe me, she's a bright kid! All the other kids were getting gold stars and smiley faces for their work, and every day Emily would come home in tears because she didn't get a gold star. Remember when we were in kindergarten? We were *children* then. We were allowed just to play!"

A kindergarten teacher confirms the trend towards early academic pressure. "We're expected by the dictates of the school system to push a lot of curriculum," she explains. "Kids in our kindergarten can't sit

20

around playing with blocks any more. We've just managed to squeeze in one hour of free play a week, on Fridays."

The diminished emphasis on fantasy and play and imaginative activities in early childhood education and the increased focus on early academic-skill acquisition have helped to change childhood from a play-centered time of life to one more closely resembling the style of adulthood: purposeful, success-centered, competitive. The likelihood is that these preschool "workers" will not metamorphose back into players when they move on to grade school. This decline in play is surely one of the reasons why so many teachers today comment that their third- or fourth-graders act like tired businessmen instead of like children.

What might be the consequences of this change in children's play? Children's propensity to engage in that extraordinary series of behaviors characterized as "play" is perhaps the single great dividing line between childhood and adulthood, and has probably been so throughout history. The make-believe games anthropologists have recorded of children in primitive societies around the world attest to the universality of play and to the uniqueness of this activity to the immature members of each society. But in those societies, and probably in Western society before the middle or late eighteenth century, there was always a certain similarity between children's play and adult work. The child's imaginative play took the form of imitation of various aspects of adult life, culminating in the gradual transformation of the child's play from make-believe work to *real* work. At this point, in primitive societies or in our own society of the past, the child took her or his place in the adult work world and the distinctions between adulthood and childhood virtually vanished. But in today's technologically advanced society there is no place for the child in the adult work world. There are not enough jobs, even of the most menial kind, to go around for adults, much less for children. The child must continue to be dependent on adults for many years while gaining the knowledge and skills necessary to become a working member of society.

This is not a new situation for children. For centuries children have endured a prolonged period of dependence long after the helplessness of early childhood is over. But until recent years children remained childlike and playful far longer than they do today. Kept isolated from the adult world as a result of deliberate secrecy and protectiveness, they continued to find pleasure in socially sanctioned childish activities until the imperatives of adolescence led them to strike out for independence and self-sufficiency.

Today, however, with children's inclusion in the adult world both through the instrument of television and as a result of a deliberately preparatory, integrative style of child rearing, the old forms of play no longer seem to provide children with enough excitement and stimulation. What then are these so-called children to do for fulfillment if their desire to play has been vitiated and yet their entry into the working world of adulthood must be delayed for many years? The answer is precisely to get involved in those areas that cause contemporary parents so much distress: addictive television viewing during the school years followed, in adolescence or even before, by a search for similar oblivion via alcohol and drugs; exploration of the world of sensuality and sexuality before achieving the emotional maturity necessary for altruistic relationships.

Psychiatrists have observed among children in recent years a marked   25
increase in the occurrence of depression, a state long considered antithetical to the nature of childhood. Perhaps this phenomenon is at least somewhat connected with the current sense of uselessness and alienation that children feel, a sense that play may once upon a time have kept in abeyance.

Topics for Critical Thinking and Writing

1. In a sentence or two sum up Winn's thesis.

2. When you were a child, what did you do in your "spare time"? Judging from your own experience, is Winn's first paragraph true, or at least roughly true?

3. Assuming that children today do indeed spend many hours watching television and playing video games, is it true that these activities "do not differ greatly from adult diversions"? To test Winn's assertion, list the diversions of adults and of children that you know of from your own experience. Are the two lists indeed strikingly similar? Or do the lists reveal important differences? Explain.

4. Winn's argument is largely composed of a series of comparisons between the play of children before access to TV and after; between traditional and contemporary kindergarten; between childhood in "primitive" (and our own preindustrial) society and in technologically advanced societies. List the points she makes to develop each of these comparisons. How well does each comparison support her thesis?

5. Winn obviously prefers that children play by making up stories rather than watching television. What reasons can be given to prefer making up stories, or reading stories in a book, to watching stories on television? In this section of her book, Winn does not mention being read to by an adult as an activity of childhood. Draw your own comparison between traditional bedtime story-reading and night-time TV-watching. Would such a comparison have strengthened or weakened Winn's argument?

6. Speaking of video games (paragraph 11), Winn argues that "having to pay for the entertainment . . . changes the nature of the game, in a subtle way diminishing the satisfactions it offers." Can one reply that having to pay helps a child to appreciate the value of money? In short, can it be argued that paying for one's pleasure is a way of becoming mature?

John Podhoretz

John Podhoretz is a columnist for the New York Post *and a contributing editor at the* Weekly Standard. *The following article originally appeared in* Commentary *magazine in November 2000.*

Survivor and the End of Television

The finest piece of political rhetoric to be heard in this election year did not come from the mouth of a candidate for office, or from the pen of his highly paid speechwriter. Rather, it was delivered on a blisteringly hot night in a clearing on a South Seas island by a thirty-eight-year-old female truck driver from Wisconsin, speaking extemporaneously and directing her words at a woman she believed had betrayed her in their common quest for a prize of $1 million.

"I was your friend at the beginning of this," said Susan Hawk to Kelly Wigglesworth:

> At the time you were sweeter than me. I'm not a very openly nice person. I'm just frank, forward, and tell you the way it is. But . . . you're very two-faced and manipulative to get where you're at anywhere in life. That's why you fail all the time. . . .
>
> What goes around comes around. It's here. You will not get my vote. My vote will go to Richard. And I hope that it is the one vote that makes you lose the money. If not, so be it. I'll shake your hand, and I'll go on from here. But if I ever pass you along in life again and you were lying there dying of thirst, I would not give you a drink of water. I would let the vultures take you and do whatever they want with you. With no regrets. . . .
>
> This island is pretty much full of only two things: snakes and rats. And in the end we have Richard the snake, who knowingly went after prey, and Kelly, who turned into the rat that ran around like rats do on the island, trying to run from the snake.
>
> I feel we owe it to this island's spirit that we have come to know to let it be in the end the way Mother Nature intended it to be. For the snake to eat the rat.

Susan Hawk's invective blasted forth on national television before an audience of 40 million people. It erupted in the 13th and final episode of *Survivor*—the much-discussed game show featuring sixteen hitherto anonymous Americans who were flown to a deserted island, divided into teams, forced to compete in occasionally stomach-churning challenges of strength and nerve (like eating live earthworms), and then winnowed one at a time over the course of more than five weeks by a vote of the island-mates themselves until only one remained to collect the $1-million prize—not to mention a spanking new Plymouth Aztec.

What was so striking about Susan Hawk's speech, and what induced gasps across the country, was its unvarnished biliousness. (The object of her scorn, Kelly Wigglesworth, had voted against her the previous day when there were only three contestants remaining.) In some ways, her vituperative eloquence turned out to be the real climax of the show, even more so than the surprise victory of Richard Hatch, an openly gay Machiavellian fellow from Rhode Island who had spent a great deal of time cavorting in the nude and to whom much of America had taken a distinct dislike. But the two taken together—Hatch's bad-guy victory, Hawk's raw fury—hold the keys to understanding the extraordinary success of *Survivor*.

Whatever its faults, and they were manifold, *Survivor* became a sensation in part because it offered viewers a heady and original mix of fantasy fulfillment and honest emotion. The fantasy element was the free 39-day vacation to the South Seas, at the end of which lay the prospect of a pot of gold and a car. The honest emotions on display were all the churning feelings engendered by a summer at sleepaway camp—resentment, quick intimacy, disappointment, momentary kindness, the thrill of joining a secret clique. But it was the possibility of the unexpected—the surprise ending, the uncontrolled outburst, and, throughout, similar if less spectacular violations of the central tenets of popular culture—that set *Survivor* apart and made it such a success.

Not that it was without precedent. The "reality-television" genre, of which *Survivor* is by far the most popular example, had its origins nine years ago when the cable channel MTV premiered *The Real World*, a show that is still running. This program brings together seven college-age youngsters in a glamorous living space and follows them for four months "to see what happens when people stop being polite and start getting real." What happens, for the most part, is some pretty lousy behavior— racial and sexual strife as well as heavy-duty flirting and a tendency toward spring-break-like exhibitionism—that usually leads to one member's being expelled by the others. The only prize offered by *The Real World* is the chance to be on a television show that is edited like a music video and structured like a multicharacter situation comedy, with impossibly good-looking and colorful people who play to the camera like pros.

Survivor, based on a Dutch program, was in the same mold but more original. For one thing, the people on the show (with the exception of a very impressive seventy-two-year-old retired Navy SEAL named Rudy Boesch) were far more mundane in appearance and spirit. For another, they seemed to respond in authentic ways to the situation in which they had been placed. For television, that really was revolutionary. The question is, what does it signify?

Ever since it staged its blitzkrieg through American popular culture 50 years ago, television has been a medium notable for sheer unadulterated meretriciousness. It is a 24-hours-a-day, seven-days-a-week, in-home reductio ad absurdum—only without a trace of irony. Television takes people—actors, newscasters, pundits, everybody else who flickers there—and shrinks them down to fit literally in a box usually no larger than two feet across. Indeed, everything on TV is shrunk to fit. Politics is reduced to the 30-second commercial and the four-second soundbite; drama and comedy are reduced to purposeless incident. Every 30-minute sitcom and 60-minute police drama is drenched in plot, but at the end of each week's episode the central characters are left so unchanged by their experiences that they can go through the same gyrations a week later as if nothing had happened.

Americans have been around the television track for five decades now, and are thoroughly expert in its cliches and devices. No wonder, then, that over the past ten years there has occurred what a psychiatrist might call a withdrawal of affect. Americans still watch television, if not as much as they once did; but they are simply not as involved. The last prime-time hit to draw an audience of the size networks once expected of their most-watched shows was *ER*, and it premiered six years ago. Although some shows still have passionate followers, those followers number, for television, relatively few. Two decades ago, *The X Files*, a program about the supernatural, would have survived for only a matter of weeks before cancellation for lack of audience; but these days, driven by the enthusiasm of about 10 million viewers, it has lasted seven years on the Fox network.

Some of this decline is due to the cable-TV explosion, which has   10
eroded the networks' market share from 90 percent before 1980 to just about 50 percent today, and has altogether atomized the viewing audience. In 1970 it was a fair bet that almost everybody was watching the same shows. If there was a common culture in this large and heterogeneous country, it was the television culture: an Oregonian and a Vermonter who had never been more than 10 miles from home but suddenly found themselves standing next to each other on a line at Disneyland could at least conduct a passable conversation about the previous week's episode of *The Mary Tyler Moore Show*.

Now there is no common television culture. A medium that once cast a large net and built an audience the way a presidential campaign builds a voter coalition—providing a daddy character for men, a mommy character for women, a maid character for the urban working class, and three children of various ages for the kids—is now driven by demographics. Networks are no longer broadcasters; instead, they are increasingly what marketers call "narrowcasters." Programs like *Sabrina the Teenage Witch* appeal exclusively to girls between the ages of six and eighteen; others appeal exclusively to blacks (the most-watched network program among blacks, *The Parkers*, ranks 120th among television programs overall); and so forth.

This is where *Survivor* appeared to break the mold. It was the first new TV show in years to generate something like a common cultural experience across the United States, and only one of two old-style broadcast hits to debut on network television since *ER*. The other is *Who Wants to Be a Millionaire?*, a more conventional trivia/game show that unexpectedly revived the sagging fortunes of ABC just as *Survivor* brought new life to the moribund CBS.

Like *Survivor*, *Millionaire* offers the promise of a pot of gold. Again like *Survivor*, it also offers a glance at something real. Contestants have to answer multiple-choice questions; in the highly unlikely event that they get all sixteen right, they win. But, in contrast to other game shows, there is no clock—contestants have taken up to 40 minutes to answer a single question. And so they sit in what the host, Regis Philbin, calls the "hot seat," worried and excited, trying to puzzle out an answer, while the sympathetic Philbin encourages them to take their time. The whole business can prove truly nerve-wracking, especially if the viewer at home happens to know the correct answer.

What, then, does it all mean? The rise of "reality television" has given pundits new cause to maunder over the nation's moral health. Their exegeses, Gibbon-like in tone if not in style, suggest that we have developed a late-empire hunger for spectacles involving the humiliation and degradation of ordinary people. This alarming thesis, which applies as much to participants as to the audiences that watch them, was first advanced in the early 1980's when the talk-show host Phil Donahue added a new spice to the pablum served up on daytime television by encouraging citizens to share their most intimate secrets in exchange for a free trip to Chicago and a night in a hotel.

Have Americans become so immodest that large numbers of them are willing to violate their own privacy for the temporary pleasure of appearing on television? Or, to put it another way, has the "thymotic urge"—the hunger for recognition—that Francis Fukuyama diagnosed as the existential condition at the "end of history" so infiltrated the American soul that we have become willing to submit ourselves to the voyeuristic fetishes of others?   15

Before we collapse into an anxious heap awaiting the second Flood, however, we would do well to remember that 270 million people live in the United States. If you add up those who have applied to appear on *Survivor* and other such shows and those willing to appear on daytime talk shows, the actual or potential participants in "reality television" number around 50,000. That is one-fiftieth of 1 percent of the population.

As for viewers, here too the picture is at least somewhat more complicated than the pundits allow. Reality television offers a series of temptations simultaneously repellent and irresistible. Like highway rubbernecking—wherein everybody slows down in hopes of glimpsing a mangled car or body—reality TV offers us the chance to see human wreckage and to feel superior to the people involved in it or victimized by it. But it also gives us a chance to admire people when they do well or soar above their circumstances, as the contestants on *Survivor* did every day by toughing it out under difficult conditions. It is not so easy to separate the illicit pleasures of voyeurism—the secretly hoped-for injury—from the higher pleasures of admiration. In its own way, what is on offer in reality television resembles the combination of elements that has provided sports fans with compelling entertainment for millennia, minus the rules.

America is not coming to an end as a result of *Survivor*. But neither does the show signify something truly new, a breakthrough departure; the hour is too late for that. Rather, it represents the extreme, logical conclusion of the first era of the television age.

Topics for Critical Thinking and Writing

1. Did you watch *Survivor* in its first or second season? How do you rate it as entertainment? How do you account for its success? How does Podhoretz account for it?

2. In paragraph 4 Podhoretz says, "Everything on TV is shrunk to fit." What does he mean? In an essay of 250–500 words evaluate his view.

3. If there is a program you regularly watch, explain its attraction. Do friends of yours watch it also, and are you likely to talk about it? Set forth your responses in an essay of 500–750 words.

4. Define "reality television." What is its appeal? In your opinion, what is its future? Respond in an essay of 500 words.

Ted C. Fishman

Ted C. Fishman, a contributing editor to Harper's *magazine, wrote the following article for* The New York Times Magazine, *where it appeared on June 10, 2001.*

The Play's the Thing

The roar inside the Los Angeles Convention Center during last month's Electronic Entertainment Expo (E3) would have made even a gladiator shudder. Trigger-happy commandos. Screeching zombies. Robots with howitzers. Starfighters. Formula One race cars. Sprites, pixies, Spiderman and Mickey Mouse. And overpowering all the rest, on the floor's biggest display, Madden N.F.L., the No. 1 selling title for the new Sony PlayStation 2, with tackles, groans and bodies hitting the turf at volumes loud enough, it seemed, to shake the very concrete of the convention center. I felt like a Lilliputian trapped in the TV section at Crazy Eddie's with every set turned all the way up. And that was the point. The greatest good in the latest generation of video entertainment is to be "immersive." What the best games scream is, "Let me swallow you!"

Of course, the games, and the companies that make them, are also screaming at people like me, the bursars of families with kids who crave games, to hand them money. Lots of it. Repeatedly, like month after month. Consider: A Sony PlayStation 2 game console costs about $300. Microsoft's coming Xbox will cost about the same. Nintendo's next machine will run $200. Games cost $50 each; the industry's target consumer will buy 6 to 12 games a year. Online games, which can pull in thousands of players worldwide, cost as much as $20 per month.

All that can add up to a quick $1,000 a year, or roughly more than half the typical entertainment budget for American families with households that have annual incomes of $40,000 to $50,000. The game drain leaves the other half of the entertainment budget to cover cable television, Internet connections, nights out, vacations and the books, lessons, instruments and art supplies that link families to pre-Atari civilization. And the squeeze is likely to increase—time-wise as well as budget-wise. Over the next five years, the game industry expects to grow 71 percent, to $86 billion a year (almost six times as large as the current U.S. music-recording industry). Ed Fries, the head of games at Microsoft, wields a pie chart divided into three pieces —sleep, work and play—that presents play as a zero-sum wedge of life: more games means less play of other kinds. More electronic diversions mean fewer soccer games in the local youth league, no games of Robin Hood in the park, no games of tag in the alley.

Resistance is futile. How could it be otherwise when nearly every conceivable childhood, teenager and adult fantasy comes to life in 3-D, true-to-life animation and is interactive to boot? No wonder critics say these games are too powerful. The families of children shot at Columbine High School name Sega, Nintendo and Sony (among others) in a $5 billion lawsuit, arguing that the murders never would have happened had the killers not been primed by shoot-'em-up video games; the worrywart child psychologists trotted out by the media advise parents to monitor the games kids play (as if it were possible to know in the 45th hour of a game that the golems will spill minotaur blood). I suppose it is natural that where children's worlds are deeply mysterious, nervous parents see all sorts of correlations with bad behavior. But I can't believe that a game of stick swords or of army on a sand hill is any less violent than its video equivalent. Stabbing and shooting are essential to both; in the older version, you just pretend on real friends.

Instead, another correlation comforts me. As the video-game industry has exploded over the last decade, every category of juvenile crime has plummeted. It could just be that video games offer an improved form of fantasy.   5

At E3, Activision set up a 20-foot-high halfpipe with real skateboarders. It attracted the expo's biggest crowds. And yet almost as crowded were the Activision booths where the newest Tony Hawk's Pro Skater could be played. The "physics" and pace of this game have been programmed to recreate the sensation of skateboarding; there's a moment in the halfpipe, for example, when you're weightless in midair over the halfpipe, and your gut actually feels like it. Looking up at the real skateboarders rising perilously close to the ceiling lights, acting out various fantasies of flight and immortality and watching the video players do essentially the same, I realized why I'll be happily spending more on games for my kids.

Games are not a weak substitute for derring-do on a halfpipe or for mock swordplay in the woods. Nor are they secondhand thrills. They are real adventure. In a top video game, a player needs 50 hours or more to work through the puzzles or vanquish the bad guys. In a good sports game, the action never repeats. When my 9-year-old son and 13-year-old daughter play—often there's a friend beside them, holding a second controller—they slip into another realm and escape the overscheduled, nag-packed world of the urban child. Inside the box is where kids are allowed to be most outside the box. In there, their own problem-solving skills are brought to bear on situations I know nothing about; in there, my children find freedom from me. They may be on the couch, but with controller in hand, they are as far away as kids in the woods.

Except, thankfully, they are out of the woods. We live on the South Side of Chicago. Sending a kid to play swords out where street gangs enact wholly different fantasies would be madness. Tag in the alley is no smarter. And if they're inside on an animated skateboard, I won't complain. When they pick up a real skateboard, I'll know they've been tutored. Gaming isn't just pretend; it is a practicum for autonomy. I will gladly pay for that.

Topics for Critical Thinking and Writing

1. What is your experience with video games, and your attitude toward them? What is Fishman's experience and attitude?

2. In paragraph 7 Fishman writes, "Inside the box is where kids are allowed to be most outside the box." What does he mean, and do you agree? Explain.

3. Fishman summarizes arguments against video games by critics. What are those arguments, and how does Fishman respond to them? Is Fishman being fair to the critics? Explain.

4. Fishman compares video games with games played by children outdoors. Which does he favor, and why? In an essay of 250 words set forth your own view of this topic of indoor versus outdoor play.

James C. McKinley Jr.

James C. McKinley writes regularly for The New York Times, where this article originally appeared on August 11, 2000.

It Isn't Just a Game: Clues to Avid Rooting

It has long been assumed that ardent sports fans derive excitement and a sense of community from rooting for a big-time team. But a growing body of scientific evidence suggests that for some fans, the ties go much deeper.

Some researchers have found that fervent fans become so tied to their teams that they experience hormonal surges and other physiological changes while watching games, much as the athletes do.

The self-esteem of some male and female fans also rises and falls with a game's outcome, with losses affecting their optimism about everything from getting a date to winning at darts, one study showed.

Science is still grappling with many questions about why people form such deep ties to sports teams, and it has not yet rigorously confronted what may be the core question: is avidly rooting for a team good or bad for someone's health? But there are early clues, some of them surprising.

Psychologists have long suspected that many die-hard fans are lonely, alienated people searching for self-esteem by identifying with a sports team. But a study at the University of Kansas suggests just the opposite—that sports fans suffer fewer bouts of depression and alienation than do people who are uninterested in sports.

One theory traces the roots of fan psychology to a primitive time when human beings lived in small tribes, and warriors fighting to protect tribes were true genetic representatives of their people, psychologists say.

In modern society, professional and college athletes play a similar role for a city in the stylized war on a playing field, the theory goes. Even though professional athletes are mercenaries in every sense, their exploits may re-create the intense emotions in some fans that tribal warfare might have in their ancestors. It may also be these emotions that have in large part fueled the explosion in the popularity of sports over the last two decades.

"Our sports heroes are our warriors," Robert Cialdini, a professor of psychology at Arizona State, said about sports fans. "This is not some light diversion to be enjoyed for its inherent grace and harmony. The self is centrally involved in the outcome of the event. Whoever you root for represents you."

Dr. Cialdini pioneered research on fans in the 1970's. He began by documenting that college sports fans were far more likely to wear clothing with their team's logo on the day after victories than after defeats, a phenomenon he called "basking in reflected glory."

"It becomes possible to attain some sort of respect and regard not by one's own achievements but by one's connection to individuals of attainment," he said. 10

His later research showed that sports fans tend to claim credit for a team's success, saying "we won" to describe a victory, but tend to distance themselves from a team's failure, saying "they lost" when describing a defeat.

But Dr. Cialdini's initial theories did not cover all spectators, because some deeply committed fans, like the long suffering souls who love the Chicago Cubs, remain loyal and fiercely attached to their idols despite years of failure.

Studies over the last decade showed that while the run-of-the-mill spectator may abandon a team once it starts losing, more committed fans ride the same emotional roller coaster as the athletes.

Highs and Lows of Rooting

In 1993 psychologists at the University of Kansas came up with a survey for measuring a fan's attachment to his team. The scale divides fans into high, low and moderate identification, based on their responses to seven written questions.

A raft of studies since then has found that "highly identified" fans— both men and women—are not only less likely to abandon a team when it is doing poorly, but tend to blame their team's failures on officiating or bad luck rather than the other team's skill. 15

They also exhibit higher levels of physiological arousal at games, spend more money on tickets and merchandise and enjoy generally higher self-esteem than people uninterested in sports.

"It's the highly identified fans who demonstrate this fierce connection and feel elation and dejection along with the team," Dr. Cialdini said.

Gene Hamm, a 37-year-old elevator mechanic from Staten Island, says his passion for the Mets, ignited as a boy during the 1969 season, has never been extinguished. He watches every game he can on television, his emotions rising and falling with every pitch, every hit, every managerial decision.

"I actually feel myself sitting on the couch managing the team," he said.

Mr. Hamm spent months at home last year, recuperating from a job-related injury, and he said watching the Mets kept him from slipping into depression. Then Kenny Rogers walked in the winning run to seal the Atlanta Braves' victory over the Mets in the playoffs. 20

"You don't walk in the winning run," he said, looking as if he had swallowed a glass of lemon juice. "I really wish they could have won last year.

"That would have made me feel so much better."

Some recent studies suggest that some fans experience physiological changes during a game or when shown photos of their team.

A study in Georgia has shown, for instance, that testosterone levels in male fans rise markedly after a victory and drop just as sharply after a defeat. The same pattern has been documented in male animals who fight over a mate: biologists theorize that mammals may have evolved this way to ensure quick resolutions to conflicts.

James Dabbs, a psychologist at Georgia State University, tested saliva samples from different groups of sports fans before and after important games.   25

In one test, Dr. Dabbs took saliva samples from 21 Italian and Brazilian men in Atlanta before and after Brazil's victory over Italy in soccer's 1994 World Cup. The Brazilians' testosterone rose an average of 28 percent, while the Italians' levels dropped 27 percent.

In another study, at the University of Utah, Dr. Dabbs and a colleague, Paul Bernhardt, found that male college basketball fans whose responses to a questionnaire indicated they had a low opinion of themselves registered the highest surges in testosterone after a victory.

Dr. Dabbs said in an interview that the results suggest fans empathize with the competitors to such a degree that they mentally project themselves into the game and experience the same hormonal surges athletes do. The contest, however, must be an important one, like a playoff game, he said.

"We really are tribal creatures," he said.

Physiological Arousal

Charles Hillman, a psychologist now at the University of Illinois, found that ardent football fans at the University of Florida experienced extreme physiological arousal when they viewed pictures of Gator football stars making game-winning plays, but responded indifferently to pictures of other athletes and teams.   30

"Individuals that are highly identified with the team show extreme arousal compared to the average fan," he said.

Among zealous male and female fans, Dr. Hillman's study found, the level of arousal—measured by heart rate, brain waves and perspiration —was comparable to what the fans registered when shown erotic photos or pictures of animal attacks, he said.

For some fans, the emotional roller coaster of watching a game can be addictive. John Herde, a 65-year-old accountant in Manhattan, has been attending Rangers games since he was a teenager and owns season tickets. He remembers sitting in the upper rows of the old Madison Square Garden as a boy and banging on the ceiling when the team scored.

What has brought him back to hockey games again and again, he says, is the catharsis he feels when he gives free rein to his anger or gloats openly in triumph.

"It's a release," he said. "You can yell and scream and do whatever.   35
It's like therapy."

Edward Hirt of Indiana University has demonstrated that an ardent fan's self-esteem tends to track a team's performance.

Working with fans of Indiana University's basketball teams, Dr. Hirt showed zealous fans pictures of very attractive members of the opposite sex after a game and asked them to rate their ability to get a date with them.

The results demonstrated that men and women who were die-hard fans were much more optimistic about their sex appeal after a victory. They were also more sanguine about their ability to perform well at mental and physical tests, like darts and word games, Dr. Hirt found. When the team lost, that optimism evaporated.

"People identify themselves with a team through thick and thin," he said. "Your self-esteem will go up and down as your team does well or poorly."

Dr. Hirt said the desire to belong to a group or a society—a need once   40
fulfilled mostly by religious and political organizations—may explain why some fans remain loyal despite the repeated failure of their teams. Fans of the Cubs, he pointed out, have not enjoyed a World Series championship since 1908. Yet Wrigley Field sells out almost every game.

Fans of the Jets present another example. The team has not won a championship since 1969, when Joe Namath led the Jets to a Super Bowl. In 1985 the Jets moved from Shea Stadium in Queens to Giants Stadium in New Jersey, where they are a tenant in another team's home.

Edward Anzalone, a New York City firefighter, said he became fascinated with the Jets when he was a boy in the 1960's, and despite 30 years without a championship, has never lost faith in the team.

"It's an obsession," he says. "The fans went over to New Jersey and are still hanging tough, even with no stadium and not winning a Super Bowl since 1969."

These days, Mr. Anzalone, who is 40, is better known as Fireman Eddie to Jets fans. Every game, he rides on his brother Frank's shoulders, wearing a green-and-white fire helmet and leading the fans in a J-E-T-S chant. His devotion to the team has gained him some notoriety.

Mr. Anzalone's house in College Point, Queens, is painted green, the   45
Jets' color. He will drive only a green car. The room of his 3-year-old son, Tyler, is a shrine to the team, with footballs signed by several Jets most valuable players, a hat signed by Bill Parcells and a team jacket from 1966.

He says he still suffers with every loss. When Vinny Testaverde, the team's quarterback, ruptured his Achilles' tendon early in the opening game last season, Mr. Anzalone went to bed. "I was sick to my stomach," he said. "I was sick that day. I knew the year was shot."

In most cases, this deep attachment to a team can be healthy, studies have found. Daniel Wann, a psychologist at Murray State University in

Kentucky, has done several studies showing that an intense interest in a team can buffer people from depression and foster feelings of self-worth and belonging.

In 1991 Dr. Wann studied students at the University of Kansas, demonstrating that ardent fans of basketball and baseball teams had higher levels of self-esteem and suffered fewer bouts of depression than did people who were not followers of sports.

"So many of the traditional institutions are beginning to break down, religion and family," Dr. Wann said. "The human psyche is the same and something has to take the place of that. Sports fills an important void."

Coping with Loneliness

Michelle Musler, one of the most visible Knick fans in New York, acknowledges that her 27-year love affair with the team may have had its genesis in loneliness.   50

It began in the early 1970's. She was working, had been through a divorce, and had five children to raise. Once in a while, she said, she got tickets from her company to Knicks games.

"My ex-husband ran away with the lady next door and I didn't seem to fit into suburbia anymore," she said. "The Knicks gave me a purpose, something to do, a place to go. As a fan, I guess, there is a sense of belonging. That you are a part of something."

Ms. Musler, 63, became a season ticket-holder in 1974 and has missed only a handful of games since. A business consultant, she plans her travel each year around the Knicks' schedule, tapes road games to watch later and hoards newspaper accounts of her team. She once flew through the night after an 18-hour day of work to make it back from Hong Kong in time for a game.

She has lost some friends over the Knicks, when she turned down invitations to weddings and graduations because they conflicted with the playoffs. These sacrifices, however, have repaid her, she says, with new friends who share her obsession: sports writers, team officials, season ticket-holders and other fans.

"What has happened through the years is that the Knicks have become my social life," she said.   55

 Topics for Critical Thinking and Writing

1. Why, according to this article, do people become sports fans?

2. According to the research summarized in this article, is rooting for a team good or bad for the fan's health? To what extent does your own experience confirm this research?

3. Identify a sports fan whom you know (it could be yourself). Would you rate that person's identification with a team high, low, or moderate? (Use the

text, if it's helpful, to rate the identification.) Do you think that his or her identification affects the fan's self-esteem? Write a paragraph describing the fan's behavior before, during, and after a game, and a second paragraph describing the effect of the team's fortunes on the fan's well-being.

4. Several studies have linked the ardor of sports fans and their aggressive behavior. One claim often heard is that on Super Bowl Sunday there is an increase in wife-battering. If there is a connection between sports fans and aggression, does that, in your opinion, conflict with the other findings reported by McKinley? Explain.

5. Here is a brief questionnaire. Ask three fellow-students to answer the questions, and then write an essay of 500 words in which you tell your reader whether the responses in any way gave you additional insight into the respondees.

How important is it to you that [name of local team] wins?

    Not important   1   2   3   4   5   Very important

During the season, do you follow the activities of the team on radio, television, or newspaper?

    Not at all   1   2   3   4   5   As much as possible

How much do you dislike [name of most obvious rival]?

    Not at all   1   2   3   4   5   Very strongly

To what extent does the success or failure of the team you root for affect your mood or your health?

    Not at all   1   2   3   4   5   Very strongly

A Casebook on College Athletics

Sean Colclough

Sean Colclough wrote this article for the Daily Aztec, *the newspaper of San Diego State University.*

The Money Game: Is It Exploiting College Athletes?

Forget student-athlete. Ignore school pride. It's all about money in the powerful and secret world of college athletics. Money the athletes legally don't see. Money that is sometimes kept quiet.

As the only athletic program that turns a profit at San Diego State, the football program is big business. It supports not only its own players, but those on other programs as well. Without Aztec football, it's possible SDSU would not have an athletic program. It's possible every sport would be shut down. It's also likely that SDSU Athletic Director Rick Bay would be out of a job and an occupation Bay says he would run differently if it was only for profit purposes. "If I was running this as a pro team and as a business enterprise, I would run it entirely different," Bay said. "I would not have sports that didn't make money. I would not have swimming, track, volleyball or soccer. The only sport I'd have is football. That is the only sport that makes money. Football goes a long way in dictating other sports we have here. It generates the revenue to have those other sports."

For their role as the SDSU athletic life support, the football players and the coaches reprise the role of the three monkeys: hear nothing, see nothing, say nothing. "The money is out of our control, they keep us blind to it and they shade it from us," said Aztec cornerback and All-American candidate Ricky Parker. "That's under the table, what we don't see." What anyone can see is that the football players, most likely, are being exploited by the university. What anyone can see is the #43 San Diego State football jersey that hangs innocently on the wall at the SDSU bookstore. It's a jersey that belongs to George Jones, the Aztecs' star running back who was suspended for allegedly accepting extra benefits, benefits some say he probably deserved. Regardless if Jones plays this season, SDSU benefits. The cash register at Aztec Shops still collects money for his jersey. It's ironic that the earnings the bookstore makes on Jones' $150 jersey go directly to the president's office. Some of it could go to the athletic department, but none of it goes to Jones. For some reason, the

Sean Colclough, "The Money Game: Is It Exploiting College Athletes?," *The Daily Aztec,* October 9, 1996. Reprinted by permission.

earnings on the shirt are distributed to various campus programs, some-times including athletics.

"Aztec Shops gives a portion of its earnings to the president's office," Aztec Shops marketing manager Laura Gropen said. "Any money that is made on a football shirt does not go to the football program or directly to the athletic department. The university profits from the sale of all football apparel sold at Aztec Shops."

The obvious question is simple: By selling and marketing a student-athlete's uniform, are universities exploiting its athletes? "I don't think they're being exploited," Bay said. "If it wasn't for SDSU, that athlete wouldn't be in that uniform to begin with. He wouldn't even have that opportunity if it wasn't for the school. If there are athletes who feel they are being exploited and deserve more because they're scoring more touchdowns or their jersey number is being sold, I think it's time for them to turn professional."

One expert who thinks they are being exploited is Walter Byers, the NCAA executive director from 1951 to 1986. Byers has been openly criti-cal of the business of college athletics. In 1995, he wrote *Unsportsmanlike Conduct: Exploiting College Athletes*, a book that ripped the NCAA about monetary gifts, endorsements, legal battles, and advertising. Byers says participation in college sports is no longer a student activity, but a profes-sion. More importantly, he says, athletes should have access to the same free market that coaches and colleges have. In an interview with *Sports Illustrated*, Byers said, "We're in a situation where we, the colleges, say it's improper for athletes to get, for example, a new car. . . . Well, is that morally wrong? Or is that wrong because we say it's wrong?"

Today's version of college football is a game that is controlled by the NCAA and athletic directors. It's the NCAA who sets the rules, while the coaches and athletic directors act like cops in making sure the rules and the system are obeyed. "You can't break the system," SDSU head coach Ted Tollner said. "If you say, 'OK, they deserve this,' but the system can't finance it, then you break the system. If money is a factor, then they're not getting enough. They need to have a little bit more so they have more of a monthly living allowance." Tollner has been around this money game for 28 years. He has seen the business of college sports explode during the last few decades and he says there isn't much that can be done to change the rules. "Whether it is fair or not, it's the rules," Tollner said. "Right now the players can't share in the revenues because it's against the NCAA rules. Until it changes, there's nothing that can be done."

Until anything is done, Aztec players on scholarship continue to live at the poverty level while they help run the multi-million dollar business of college football. They are somehow expected to live on only $484 a month for rent and other living expenses. "You have to go through family to get more money," senior linebacker Craigus Thompson said. "The NCAA pro-vides you with what they think is enough money, but actually it's not. The

NCAA needs to provide college athletes with more than they have right now." The players are grateful they get a free education. They're also grateful they don't have to worry about books or food. But they're not stupid. They're not naive to the fact that SDSU is benefiting more than they are. They realize they're marketed and profited by SDSU for free. "I think in some ways we're being exploited," Parker said. "But that's the way it is, you know? That's the way it's run, and there isn't much we can do about it."

Dayna's Struggle

Temptation. Players might be exploited while they're in college, but what they're offered before they ever see a football field may be worse. When you have nothing your entire life, it's hard to resist. It's hard to say "no thanks" to the prospects of a better life. Universities, alumni and outside interests can manipulate a student-athlete and the choices he makes when picking a college, especially an athlete who has nothing. Someone who could use that new car or free cash.

Ask Aztec Running Back Dayna Overton

Growing up in Jeffersonville, Ind., Overton didn't have much. He wasn't the kid on the corner with the fancy new sneakers or the sweet new bike. For Overton, life wasn't exactly Forrest Gump and a box of chocolates. His stepfather supported an eight-member family on $13,000 a year. "Since I was 14, I never received anything," he said. "I never asked my parents for anything. I just went to school and played ball. As far as money and Christmas, I always sacrificed that for my little brothers and sisters." Overton knew his only way out was through football. His way to college and a good life was through his hands and his feet, because he was a star running back and a Super-Prep Magazine high school All-American. He had his pick of elite schools: Tennessee, Michigan, Washington, Purdue and Georgia were all drooling for him to sign. During his recruiting, Overton saw it all. He saw how some athletes lived and how some schools made sure they lived well. "When I visited Tennessee, they had a football dormitory and it was like a resort," Overton said. "It had Jacuzzis, video games, air conditioning and big screen televisions. I mean it was nice." During the entire process, Overton also saw how corrupt college football is. He saw how universities lie to get recruits. "The whole recruiting process at first was fun and then it turned into a nightmare," Overton said. "Everybody was trying to stab each other in the back. Purdue was telling me stuff that Washington was doing illegally. Indiana was telling me things that Michigan was doing wrong. It got to the point where I would try to skip phone calls."

Despite the many perks he openly saw from other schools, Overton finally decided on Michigan. But even after he committed to the Wolverines, the illegal offers didn't stop. Schools offered him things he had never had before, things that would have made his life very different.

10

"My counselor at Tennessee was an alumnus, and he said if I went there they would give me anything I want," Overton said. "My parents said they got offered, like, $5,000 and my dad got offered a job. They got offered these things by other universities after I had already committed to Michigan." During it all, Overton says the University of Washington may have been the worst. "Washington was probably the most corrupt," Overton said. "The guy that recruited me said, 'Dayna, we're going to take care of you. We have jobs lined up for $20 an hour and you don't have to do anything.'"

Michigan was not all it was cracked up to be for Overton, and after one season on the bench, he transferred to SDSU. He has seen a lot of differences in how college football is operated. Overton is now a veteran of how the business of college football is run. He has seen it in the Big Ten and he has seen it now in the Western Athletic Conference. "The Big Ten is luxury," Overton said. "The food was better and the living was better. Everything all around was better. We had a training table where they had tons of food; you could have fed Ethiopia with everything we had in Michigan."

As one of the Aztecs' backup running backs, Overton doesn't live in the sweet dorm with Jacuzzis, he doesn't drive a brand-new car; instead, he lives in an off-campus apartment for $180 a month. Overton says it's not the place he thought he would be in three years ago. "There is a lot of college people there, and it's rowdy," Overton said. "It's probably lower income people that live there, and there's a lot of kids running around. The main problem is it's loud and I can't really study. I wanted to move into these condos, but they were $350 a month and I couldn't afford that, no way."

The Answers

What should athletes get? How much do they actually deserve? When your day consists of 12 units and four hours of practice and films, how can you be compensated? The easiest answer would be for the NCAA to raise what an athlete can receive for a scholarship, says SDSU Associate Athletic Director Reggie Blaylock. The former Aztec offensive lineman, who is in charge of all student-athletes on campus, says the football team should not be singled out in receiving more benefits; all student-athletes deserve more. "You don't want to take out one sport and isolate football versus tennis and golf," Blaylock said. "In our program we have 17 sports. Everyone could always use more, but we try to treat every athlete the same. The cost for an apartment, food and living expenses is the same for every student-athlete."

SDSU's men's and women's soccer coach Chuck Clegg says the best answer would be to allow student-athletes to work. "I think the NCAA is finally opening up," Clegg said. "What they have to do is open it up so they allow athletes to work during the season. A person from a needy background should be able to maximize their financial aid resources. If

15

the NCAA allows student-athletes to work in the off-season it could equal it out."

While working in the off-season may be the answer for Clegg, Tollner says he would like to see his football players receive more on their scholarships because it's impossible for them to work during or after the season. "I would like to see a greater percentage allowed to them that is legal," Tollner said. "So they can go to school, have their tuition paid for and have a reasonable amount of spending money. How much is that? I don't know. Is that another couple hundred a month?"

The answer from the NCAA may come as soon as January when legislation might be passed that would allow student-athletes to work in the off-season. More importantly, this past June, the heads of 32 NCAA Division I athletic conferences met and discussed proposals to provide more financial aid to student-athletes. "We want to provide for the full needs of students," Jim Delany, president of the Collegiate Commissioners Association, told the Associated Press. But the truth is, unless something is done by the NCAA, the money game will continue to run across the nation. Somewhere, another Dayna Overton will be promised illegal benefits, and somewhere else another George Jones will be accused of accepting them. Unless something is done by the NCAA, the money game will always overpower the real game. And unless something is done, college athletics will always be looking over its shoulder.

Murray Sperber

Murray Sperber, the author of four books on college sports and college life, is a professor of English and American Studies at Indiana University, Bloomington. A paperback edition of his most recent book, Beer & Circus: How Big-Time College Sports Is Crippling Undergraduate Education *(Henry Holt & Co., New York), appeared in fall 2001. The essay "Myth versus Reality in Big-Time College Sports" is an updated revision of the "Introduction" of his book* College Sports Inc.: The Athletic Department Versus the University *(Henry Holt & Co., New York, 1990).*

Myth versus Reality in Big-Time College Sports

In interviews with UK [University of Kentucky] students, faculty members and administrators, a picture of two UK's emerges. One is a top-of-the-line . . . athletic program [a $40 million operation], run largely by and for off-campus supporters; the other is a chronically under-financed,

Murray Sperber, from *College Sports, Inc.: The Athletic Department Versus the University.* New York: Henry Holt & Co., 1990. Updated 2002 by Murray Sperber. Reprinted by permission of John W. Wright, literary agent for the author.

"fair-to-middlin" academic institution that seems to languish in the shadow of the "Big Blue" [athletic] monolith.[1]

A great number of myths shield college sports from casual scrutiny and burden any discussion of the subject. The following refutations of the most common myths try to introduce the reader to the reality of contemporary intercollegiate athletics.

Myth: College sports are part of the educational mission of American colleges and universities.

Reality: The main purpose of college sports is commercial entertain- 10
ment. Within most universities with big-time programs, the athletic department operates as a separate business and has almost no connection to the educational departments and functions of the school—even the research into and teaching of sports is done by the physical education department.

The reason elite athletes are in universities has nothing to do with the educational missions of their schools. Athletes are the only group of students recruited for commercial entertainment—not academic—purposes, and they are the only students who go through school on grants based not on educational aptitude, but on their talent and potential as commercial entertainers.

If colleges searched for and gave scholarships to upcoming rock stars 5
so that they could entertain the university community and earn money for their schools through concerts and tours, educational authorities and the public would call this "a perversion of academic values" and not allow it. Yet every year, American institutions of higher education hand out over a hundred thousand full or partial athletic scholarships, worth at least $1 billion, for reasons similar to the proposed grants to rock performers.

Myth: The alumni support—in fact, demand—that their alma maters have large and successful college sports programs.

Reality: Studies indicate that most alumni—people who attended a particular school—contribute mainly to the academic units of their colleges and universities and that less than 5% of them donate to its athletic programs. Moreover, alumni contributions correlate mainly to satisfaction about the quality of education that alums received as undergraduates: if they feel positive about their academic experiences, they tend to give; if not, they keep their checkbooks closed. The superiority of their alma maters' athletic teams has little to do with annual alumni giving. In fact, alumni sometimes withhold contributions from their schools when the athletic teams are too successful or are involved in sports scandals: they are embarrassed by their schools becoming "jock factories" and/or angered by the bad publicity from scandals, and they believe that their college degrees are being devalued.

An on-going indication of the nature of alumni giving are the rankings on that item in *U.S. News & World Report*'s annual college issue. With

---

[1]Item in the *Louisville (Kentucky) Courier-Journal*.

few exceptions, the universities and colleges that continually rank highest
in alumni giving are schools that do not participate in big-time college
sports, and that provide a quality undergraduate education. Most of the
big-time college sports schools rank far down the list.

Myth: College sports is incredibly profitable, earning huge sums of
money for American colleges and universities.

Reality: One of the best-kept secrets about intercollegiate athletics—   10
well guarded because athletic departments are extremely reluctant to open
their financial books—is that the vast majority of college sports programs
lose money. If profit-and-loss is defined according to ordinary business
practices, of the close to 600 members in the National Collegiate Athletic
Association (NCAA) Divisions I and II (those schools granting athletic
scholarships) only a small percentage of their athletic departments make a
consistent albeit small profit and, in any given year, another small cohort
breaks even or does better. All of the rest, approximately 500 athletic departments, consistently drop anywhere from a few dollars to millions annually
on their college sports programs. Moreover, the hundreds of schools in
NCAA Division III and the NAIA (National Association of Intercollegiate
Athletics) do not even try to break even with their college sports programs.

The financial numbers must be placed within context: traditionally,
athletic departments engage in "creative" accounting practices, moving
such legitimate costs as utilities and facilities maintenance bills (million-
dollar expenses for many programs) off their ledger sheets and onto their
universities' financial books; in addition, the multimillion-dollar debt
servicing on their facilities is frequently paid by regular students in the
form of mandatory and often hidden fees on students' university bills.
Actual athletic department losses are much higher than reported. These
deficits grew in the 1990s, a period of increasing television and ticket sale
revenue for college sports, and they show no signs of stabilizing. What
will occur during the first decade of the 21st century when, according to
many sports industry experts, TV payouts for college sports events and
ticket sales will level off?

Myth: The profits from college sports programs help all parts of the
university.

Reality: Because athletic department expenses usually exceed revenue, profits do not exist, and on those occasions when an intercollegiate
athletic program actually makes a few dollars, invariably it keeps every
penny. Moreover, athletic departments admit that they have no intention
of sharing their revenue; an NCAA survey reported that less than 1% of
all athletic programs defined their "fiscal objective" as earning money "to
support non-athletics activities of the institution." Every so often, the media carries a story about an athletic department donating money to the
university library or an academic fund, but these are almost always public relations ploys: the athletic department wants to overcome a history of
scandal and negative publicity, and usually makes this donation one
time, not annually or regularly.

Rather than financially aid the university, most athletic departments siphon money from it, not only by moving a multitude of expenditures onto the university's books, but also by having the school cover their annual deficits. Universities must "zero out" athletic department books at the end of the financial year, and, to do so, schools divert money from their general operating funds and other financial resources to cover the college sports deficits. Thus, money that could go to academic programs, student scholarships and loans, and many other educational purposes, disappears annually down the athletic department financial hole.

Myth: Schools receive millions of dollars when their teams play in   15
football bowl games.

Reality: Often the numbers in the media are for the "projected payout," whereas the actual payout can be much lower. Moreover, most participating schools must split their bowl revenue with other members of their conferences. As a result, when the headline announces that a Pac-10 team received $1 million for a bowl appearance, that school kept only $100,000 because of the conference's ten-way split.

In addition, athletic departments like to turn bowl and tournament trips into all-expenses-paid junkets for hundreds of people, including their employees and friends. Their travel, hotel, and entertainment costs often eat up the actual bowl or tourney payouts and transform post-season play into a deficit item!

Myth: Thanks to the NCAA's billion-dollar TV contract for its Division I men's basketball tournament, and the great crowds at the games, schools make millions of dollars when their teams participate in "March Madness."

Reality: Of the total annual revenue from the tournament—$228 million in the NCAA's most recent budget—the association distributes less than 3% directly to participating schools, and about 21% to their conferences (for a total distribution of $55 million). Many schools with a team eliminated in the first round (32 of 64 teams) receive a low-six-figure check, sometimes failing to cover their traveling party expenses. On the other hand, if several teams from the same conference reach the final rounds, they and their fellow conference members gain low-seven-figure payouts. Considering the 310 members in NCAA Division I men's basketball eligible for the tournament, the small minority that receive the million-dollar payouts resemble lottery winners. But, like addicted gamblers, all 310 schools spend big bucks to enter the Division I basketball season lottery, and a majority end their year with losing or small payout tickets.

Myth: Colleges and universities gain wonderful publicity from col-   20
lege sports, and almost all of it is free.

Reality: Publicity from college sports is a two-edged sword. When a school's teams, particularly in high-profile sports like basketball and football, are winning and achieving victory without cheating, the sword cuts through lots of media noise and focuses a large amount of attention on an athletic program. However, when a scandal or negative incident occurs, reporters do not disappear—in fact, many more than usual descend upon a school to cover the bad news, and the publicity sword can draw buckets of adverse publicity and public disapproval.

Indiana University experienced a great deal of positive recognition in the 1980s when the teams of men's basketball coach Bob Knight won two NCAA titles. However, in the year 2000, when Knight's inappropriate conduct attracted national media attention and derision, the sword swung back and, for many months, the school received an amazing volume of negative publicity. Indiana bled "crimson," one of its school colors.

University administrators sometimes justify the financial losses in their college sports programs by claiming that they "generate great free publicity." These officials never mention what occurs when the publicity sword swings back at a school.

Myth: College sports builds school spirit and campus community.

Reality: In interviews for *Beer & Circus* with hundreds of students, faculty members, and administrators across the country—whether the interviewee loved, hated, or was indifferent to big-time college sports—they all told stories about special deals, often illegal, that athletes at their school received, e.g. "Joey Jock was in my Chem class but he rarely came and a team manager took the exams for him." The tales were universal, and rather than reflect school spirit, they indicate cynicism.

As to building campus community: on occasion, particularly when a school's team wins a national championship, this appears true; however, in a deeper sense, because of the idiosyncratic and artificial nature of the event—the necessity of sweeping through an entire season and/or tournament—big-time sports schools mainly develop random, occasional communities, not permanent ones.

Historically, colleges and universities have built communities on shared ideals, discourse, study, and goals among their members. Often these communities were fragile and dissolved, but sometimes they coalesced, providing their participants with extremely valuable experiences. Some schools today, particularly those with adequate funding and a faculty commitment to undergraduate education, still foster college communities; but big-time intercollegiate athletics mainly produces the superficial coming together of fans in a stadium, arena, or bar for a few hours' duration. At these schools, administrators often promote sports teams as a way of creating the illusion of community; usually these officials know the impossibility of constructing a real community at their universities.

Myth: College coaches deserve their high annual incomes because they generate huge profits for their athletic programs.

Reality: John Wooden, the most successful men's basketball coach in NCAA history, was never paid more than $25,000 a year by his university, UCLA. Today, only a minority of coaches generate as much or more revenue for their schools as Wooden did for his, and the vast majority direct programs that lose money for their institutions. Nevertheless, an increasing number of coaches have joined the Millionaires Club, with annual incomes exceeding that figure, and a few have topped $2 million a year. As significant, the annual income of at least 100 NCAA Division I men's basketball coaches, and 75 Division I-A football coaches, approaches or surpasses $300,000, and many program heads in the "non-revenue sports" (so termed because they always lose money), like soccer, baseball, track, and swimming earn over $150,000 a year. At most colleges and universities in big-time college sports, a football and/or basketball coach has the highest annual income at the institution. But schools claim that they are in the education, not the entertainment, business.

Myth: College coaches deserve their high annual incomes because   30
they are the key to producing winning teams and are irreplaceable.

Reality: Sonny Smith, a longtime Division I men's basketball coach, commented, "It's a make-it-while-you-can thing. . . . If I quit tomorrow, there'd be 300 names in the ring." Except for a handful of truly outstanding and innovative coaches, most of the others are interchangeable and can be replaced by any number of the "300 names in the ring." When Bill Frieder, making over $400,000 a year, quit the University of Michigan on the eve of the 1989 NCAA men's basketball tournament, an unknown assistant, earning a fraction of Frieder's income, was given the top job. Under Steve Fisher, Michigan swept through the tourney and won the national championship.

The most amazing element of the high annual income of coaches is that it defies the laws of economic gravity. For every game won by a coach, another coach must lose, and many coaches have lost as many or more games in their careers than they have won. Because the supply of coaches far exceeds the demand, why do schools pay such exorbitantly high amounts to so many mediocre coaches? The only explanation is that coaches' annual income is one more absurd operating practice in big-time college sports, the most dysfunctional business in America.

Myth: Hired to be fired—that's the fate of most college coaches.

Reality: Firings are not the reason most college coaches change jobs. Coaches leave schools for a variety of reasons, most often, to take better paying positions; also to quit jobs that are not working out or to keep one step ahead of the NCAA sheriff; and, in a minority of cases, when asked to leave.

An analysis of the major coaching appointments listed weekly in *The*   35
Chronicle of Higher Education for over a decade reveals the following typical sequence: the head man at Big-Time Sports U. quits in mid-contract to go to the pros or to become an A.D.; the coach at Southern Jock State leaves his school to take the more lucrative package at Big-Time U.; the coach at Western Boondock sees a chance to move up and he grabs the job at Southern; finally, if Western cannot hire another head coach, it offers its smaller package to an assistant at a major program or, in desperation, it promotes one of its own assistants. When this Coach in Motion Play ends, at least three head coaches, as well as innumerable assistants, have changed jobs—not one of them fired by a college or university.

Myth: College athletic programs provide a wonderful opportunity for African-American coaches.

Reality: White athletic directors and program heads keep college coaching lily white by hiring their duplicates. Many studies, including some by the NCAA, of the racial backgrounds of head coaches in football, baseball, and men's track at Division I schools indicate the single-digit percentage of African-American head coaches in these sports. In men's basketball the total number of black coaches broke into double digits in the 1990s; however, only one hand was needed to count black head football coaches in Division IA. In contrast, over 50% of the football players and 70% of the men's basketball players, as well as a high percentage of track athletes in big-time programs, are African-American. Yet, the NCAA, athletic directors, and coaches deny that a white "old boy's club," hiring its own, exists.

Myth: College athletic programs provide a wonderful opportunity for women coaches.

Reality: Women head coaches, unlike African-American coaches, once had a strong position in college sports. However, in the 1970's and early 1980's, male athletic directors and program heads took over women's college sports as well as the jobs of female A.D.'s and many coaches. The most comprehensive study of this phenomenon shows that in the early 1970's, 90% of the athletic directors of women's college sports programs were female, whereas by 1988, the percentage had dropped to 16. In the same time span, the percent of female coaches of women's sports teams went from the mid-90's to 48. Those numbers improved slightly in the 1990s, but female coaches and A.D.'s never regained the control of women's sports that they held before the NCAA take-over of the AIAW (the Association of Intercollegiate Athletics for Women).

Myth: Talented athletes, like other high school graduates, should attend university.

Reality: Only about 33% of American high school students go on to four-year colleges and universities; one sub-section of these students, often with little interest in and preparation for higher education, is nevertheless required to attend university—aspiring professional athletes in football and men's basketball (only a handful of high school basketball players go directly to the NBA, and no high school football player has managed to move immediately to the NFL).

An anomaly of American history—that intercollegiate football and basketball began before the professional versions of those games and excluded viable minor leagues in those sports—has created a situation that is unknown and unthinkable in other countries: to become a major league player in a number of sports, an athlete must pass through an institution of higher learning. To compound the problem, American schools now take on the training of young athletes in sports, particularly baseball

40

and hockey, for which there are excellent minor professional leagues, as well as Olympic sport athletes for which there is a strong club system.

For young athletes who wish to concentrate on their athletic careers and to make the pros, a university education at this point in their lives does not make a lot of sense. They want to work full time on their sport and not be burdened by taking full college course loads. Possibly at another point in their lives, when their pro careers are over or never began, they will want to enroll in a college or university but not when they are fresh out of high school. For this cohort of athletes, higher education frustrates rather than helps them.

Myth: College athletes are amateurs, and their athletic scholarships do not constitute professional payment for playing sports.

Reality: A school gives an athlete a "full ride" grant worth   45
$10,000–$30,000 a year in exchange for the athlete's services in a commercial entertainment venture, i.e., playing on one of the school's sports teams. If the athlete fails to keep his or her part of the agreement and quits the team, the institution withdraws the financial package—even if the athlete continues in school as a regular student.

At one time in NCAA history, athletic scholarships were for four years and, once awarded, could not be revoked. In 1973, under pressure from coaches who wanted greater control over their players and the ability to "fire" them for poor athletic performances, the NCAA instituted one-year scholarships, renewed annually at the athletic department's behest. This turned athletic scholarships into one-year contracts, and many coaches treat them as such, terminating players' scholarships for performing athletically, not academically, below the coach's expectations.

Athletic scholarships, under their current terms, appear indistinguishable from what the IRS calls "barter payment for services rendered," thus making college athletes professional wage-earners. Possibly within the next decade, the courts will find that one-year grants constitute an employer-employee relationship between a school and an athlete. In addition, if an athlete sues to break the NCAA's rules on college players as amateurs and the courts order schools to pay their athletes, the fiction of amateurism will shatter and disappear forever.

Myth: College sports provides an excellent opportunity for African-American youngsters to get out of the ghetto and to contribute to American society.

Reality: Research by Harry Edwards, professor of sociology at the University of California, Berkeley, indicates that many athletic programs treat black athletes as "gladiators," bringing them to campus only to play sports, not for an education. The low graduation rates of black college athletes support Edwards' thesis.

Most schools with major athletic programs, as well as many with   50
smaller ones, recruit black athletes much more intensively and systematically than they do regular black students. Moreover, some schools fund their "black gladiators" by diverting money from scholarship sources,

such as Opportunity Grants, earmarked for academically motivated minority students. Thus, not only do the "black gladiators" fail to receive college educations, but, thanks to College Sports Inc., many black high school graduates—whose academic potential is far greater than the athletes—are deprived of the chance of entering university.

Myth: Athletes like Bill Bradley, who were outstanding in sports and in the classroom, prove that college sports works.

Reality: In any large sample of people in any endeavor, there are always a few at the top end of the bell curve. In fact, the widespread notice taken of Bradley's success in both sports and academics suggests that intercollegiate athletics is a system that works for only a few. No one bothers to name all of the outstanding Americans who were once top college students but not athletes, because they are not unusual and colleges and universities are supposed to produce them.

Myth: Schools like Duke and Stanford, giving their athletes good educations and graduating a high percentage of them, also win at the highest collegiate level. Duke and Stanford prove that college sports works.

Reality: Demography works. Every year, a small number of graduating high school football and basketball players with NFL and NBA potential (the "blue-chippers") score 1,200 or higher on their SAT exams or the equivalent on their ACTs. Recruiting experts estimate that annually there are about 300 football and 50 basketball players in this select pool. Through shrewdness and some luck, Duke coach Mike Krzyzewski positioned his basketball program to get players from this pool; as a result Duke "blue-chippers" like Grant Hill and Shane Battier have led the team to championships and have received excellent educations. But what about Duke football? Its coaches cannot obtain the "blue-chippers" with high SAT scores, and, because the school will not lower its admissions standards, Duke finishes at the bottom of its conference football standings.

Stanford sits in California, a state with a huge population and a good number of "blue-chippers" with high SAT scores. Stanford can sign enough players from this select pool to compete at the championship level. However, Stanford's main academic and athletic rival, the University of California at Berkeley, has failed to obtain many athletes from the select pool. As a result, Cal finishes in the lower regions of the Pac-10. The athletes at Cal receive as good an education as those at Stanford, they just cannot play sports at the same level.

Every coach in America would like to sign athletes with high SAT scores and "blue-chip" talent. But the pool is small, and only Duke men's basketball and Stanford seem able to gain more than a few players from the pool every year. Therefore, the triumphs of Duke men's basketball and Stanford sports are exceptional and prove that demography works, not college sports.

Myth: Most college athletes are dumb jocks.

Reality: Some dumb jocks—athletes who cannot do academic work at a college level—exist on college campuses, but much more common are

55

physically and mentally exhausted athletes who academically under-achieve. Coaches expect their players to spend at least 30 hours a week in their sport, and often this escalates to 40 or 50 or even more hours per week when travel and other time-consuming, sports-related activities are added in. This turns most Division I athletic scholarship holders into vo-cational students, young men and women working full time at very de-manding jobs and also trying to carry regular course loads. As a result of having to work their way through college in this manner, many athletes experience academic problems, particularly if they are taking challenging and meaningful courses.

To their credit, some athletes fight the intercollegiate athletic system as soon as they enter college, and they manage, through amazing effort, to ob-tain a good education while playing sports—often they have to defy athletic department attempts to steer them to "gut" courses and "mickey" majors. Other athletes, when they realize that they will never play at the pro level, begin to work hard on their education; nevertheless, because of time and physical constraints, they often academically underachieve. And some ath-letes, after they end their college athletic careers—because of either injury or the completion of their playing eligibility—become excellent students. Finally able to concentrate full time on their studies, they bring the disci-pline that they learned in sports to their academic endeavors.

The reality of the life of a college athlete is far more complex than the media and public realize, and labeling athletes as dumb jocks is far easier than engaging the reality of their lives.

Myth: The graduation rates of athletes announced each year by the NCAA and member institutions are accurate, particularly their compar-isons to the graduation rates of regular students at the same schools.

Reality: Comparing the graduation rates of athletic scholarship hold-ers to those of regular students is like comparing apples to alligators. The main reason that regular students at most Division I and II schools, par-ticularly those with residential campuses, fail to graduate is financial, not academic. In an era of ever-increasing tuition, room-and-board, and other college costs, many students run out of money and/or do not want to assume more debt; they then transfer to a less expensive institution, often in their hometown, to complete their degrees. Very few regular stu-dents actually flunk out of a school and depart in bad academic standing.

On the other hand, no athlete on a full athletic scholarship fails to pay his or her tuition, room-and-board, and every other school bill, including book and tutoring expenses. The athletic department pays the bills for the athlete. Therefore, when an athletic scholarship holder drops out of school, it is often for academic reasons. Yes, some athletes leave early to go into the NBA and NFL drafts, but they constitute such a tiny percentage of total athlete non-graduates as to be almost statistically meaningless.

Beyond the apples-to-alligators grad rate comparison, many athletic departments play sleight-of-numbers by making such pronouncements as, "90 percent of our seniors in football will graduate this June." In fact,

60

they mean that nine of the ten football players who made it to the senior class—out of the twenty-five-plus players who entered their program as freshmen or transfers—will receive diplomas. In other words, at least fifteen of the players in this class dropped out, and the actual grad rate is no higher than 36 percent.

Despite all of the attempts by the NCAA and member schools to massage the numbers, the graduation rates for many intercollegiate athletes, particularly in high-profile sports like basketball and football, remain low, and show no signs of improving. But the NCAA and athletic departments will persist in comparing apples to alligators as long as they can fool the public and the grad statistics do not rise up and bite them.

Myth: The NCAA represents the will of its member colleges and universities, and it tries to keep intercollegiate athletics in line with their educational objectives.

Reality: The NCAA functions mainly as a trade association for athletic directors and college coaches, implementing their wishes regardless of whether these are in the best interests of the member schools. Real power in the association resides in its various councils and committees; for many years, a large majority of council members have been athletic directors, most of them former coaches. Even the Division I presidents' committee (now called "cabinet") defers to the wishes of athletic directors and "power coaches." In addition, since the late 1980s, the executive directors of the association, first Dick Schultz and now Cedric Dempsey, came to this job from positions as athletic directors at big-time college sports schools, and they were coaches before becoming A.D.'s.

Not surprisingly, the NCAA never passes measures to reform big-time college sports in a systemic manner. Such reforms would help a majority of member schools as well as the athletes, but would go against the wishes and interests of a majority of coaches and athletic directors. For example, many reformers have called for a return to guaranteed four-year athletic scholarships as a way of moving athletes out from under their coaches' thumbs, i.e., removing the threat that a coach will not renew an athlete's one-year athletic scholarship. However, most coaches and athletic directors totally oppose this proposal, and they will never allow the NCAA to pass it.

Myth: NCAA athletic programs sponsor teams in many sports, including Olympic events, because they want to give those sports a chance to grow.

Reality: Most athletic directors and program heads are empire-builders. Through their control of the NCAA, they have instituted key legislation that ensures expanding budgets—even though increasing athletic department costs is not in the financial or academic interests of most of their schools.

The NCAA sets minimum requirements for big-time Division IA participation, currently 15 teams (men's and women's) in at least eight sports, almost all of them non-revenue (money-losing) operations. If an institution fails to meet the requirement, the NCAA drops it to "unclassified membership," bars all of its teams from NCAA play, and penalizes it in various other ways.

The NCAA's rationale for the sports and team minimum numbers—and similar rules apply to all divisions—is that schools should have "well-balanced athletic programs." In practice, these regulations serve the college sports establishment's self-interest: A.D.'s and coaches want their programs to be as big as possible, and to employ as many administrators, assistant coaches, and athletes as possible. The NCAA, by locking athletic departments into a high number of sports and teams, deprives member institutions of a large degree of autonomy over their athletic budgets.

Within the context of American higher education, these NCAA rules are an anomaly—no other outside agency forces universities to lose money in this way. Currently, this situation occurs during a period of tremendous financial constraints within higher education, when other parts of the university are experiencing severe cutbacks.

Myth: The NCAA can correct the problems in college sports.

Reality: The athletic directors and coaches who control the NCAA   75
deny the existence of any systemic problems in college sports. For them, the present system works well—after all, it provides them with extremely comfortable livings—and they see no need to repair it, except for some minor tinkerings.

Bo Schembechler, former head football coach and A.D. at Michigan, speaking for his fellow coaches and athletic directors, once shouted at an audience of reform-minded college presidents, "We are not the enemy." Bo was wrong. But he was true to the NCAA's self-serving denials of responsibility for the current problems.

The bottom line on meaningful NCAA reform is clear: the NCAA cannot solve the systemic problems in college sports because the coaches and A.D.'s who control it are a central source of those problems. Moreover, the association will fight any attempts at real reform, even if—as is probable in the future—College Sports Inc. begins to destroy the academic and fiscal integrity of some member institutions.

James L. Shulman and William G. Bowen

James L. Shulman is a financial and administrative officer of the Andrew W. Mellon Foundation. William G. Bowen, former president of Princeton University, is now president of the Mellon Foundation. Together they wrote The Game of Life: College Sports and Educational Values *(2001), an analysis of intercollegiate sports.*

Playing Their Way In

It's almost March, a month of games and meets that decide college winter sports championships. Soon afterward comes another kind of final—the weeks in April when many 17-year-olds who applied to selective colleges will open thin envelopes containing the disappointing news that they are not being offered places at schools like Bowdoin, the University of Michigan or Columbia. These two emotionally charged events of spring are far more closely connected than most of us probably suspect— even at the most selective colleges.

After looking at records of 90,000 students who entered 30 selective schools in 1951, 1976 and 1989, we found that sports today have a significant impact on the schools' admissions and the academic performance of their students. That impact is even more significant at small liberal arts colleges and Ivy League universities than at the large universities, simply because athletics directly affect a higher proportion of their students. Athletes in intercollegiate sports make up less than 5 percent of the male student body at a large school like Michigan, but 32 percent at the liberal arts colleges in our study.

Athletes who were actively recruited for teams at the 30 schools in our group—those on "the coach's list"—had a great advantage in admissions over others with similar S.A.T. scores, whether high-scoring, low-scoring or in between. The advantage was greater for athletes than for minority students or children of alumni.

All athletes at the 30 schools—whether recruited or not—entered college with appreciably lower test scores and high school grades than their classmates, and they ended up disproportionately low in their classes: among those we studied who entered in the fall of 1989, the proportions falling in the bottom third at graduation were 58 percent of all male athletes; 72 percent of the male athletes in the high-profile sports of football, basketball and ice hockey; and 39 percent of female athletes.

The academic performance was not only worse than that of classmates, but worse than what would have been expected on the basis of the athletes' test scores. Time pressure does not seem to be the only reason: classmates

5

James L. Shulman and William G. Bowen, "Playing Their Way In." Originally published in *The New York Times*, 2/22/01. Reprinted by permission.

who participated in other time-intensive extracurricular activities, like editing the student newspaper, tended to overperform academically.

What does distinguish campus life for these athletes is their membership in what might be called an athletic culture. They are highly concentrated in certain fields of study and in certain campus residences. In this atmosphere, athletics are naturally emphasized, and the upcoming game might easily get more attention than the term paper. The evidence of disappointing academic performance is found not only in football and basketball, but in lower-profile sports like tennis and swimming, and among both women and men.

In the 1950's, male athletes at the schools we looked at did well academically and were likely to be leaders of their classes as well as of their teams. In the 1970's, female athletes showed a similar pattern, excelling at athletics and academics, but the recruited male athletes were underperforming academically. By the 1990's, significant gaps in academic performance had appeared for women as well as men athletes. The directional signs are unmistakable.

The great emphasis placed on intercollegiate athletics is often attributed to a desire to please alumni, but when we surveyed alumni, we found that in general they favored decreasing their schools' emphasis on intercollegiate competition, not increasing it. Those who made the biggest donations assigned lower priority to intercollegiate athletics than to nearly every other aspect of college or university life that they were asked to rank.

Of course, sports are and should be fun and healthy and a positive way to build community spirit on a campus. But trustees, parents, faculty and society should consider what role specialized sports talent—as opposed to participation in sports as one part of a well-rounded application—should play in admission. Does it make sense for a liberal arts college or university to assign a large share of its scarce admissions places to students who, on average, fail to take full advantage of academic opportunities?

The root question is broader: With intellectual capital ever more important, how great a role should hand-eye coordination play in deciding who is given educational opportunity?   10

Louis Menand

Louis Menand, educated at Pomona College and Columbia University, and a specialist in Victorian and modern literature, teaches at the Graduate Center, City University of New York. We reprint an essay that originally appeared in The New Yorker *in 2001.*

Sporting Chances: The Cost of College Athletics

At many of the best colleges and universities in the United States today, there is a group of students who can be identified by an attribute that has nothing to do with academic ability. These students have, on average, lower S.A.T. scores than their classmates; they underperform in college (their grades are even lower than their S.A.T. scores predict) and are more likely than other students to rank in the bottom third of the class; their lives after graduation are relatively unaffected by their college experience; and they tend to feel isolated from other students—on some campuses, they live in separate dormitories. These students are aggressively recruited; admissions offices give them preferential treatment; and at some schools they are awarded scholarships regardless of financial need or academic merit. Any attempt to compromise the privileges or reduce the opportunities enjoyed by this special class of students, or to suggest that they somehow do not belong on campus, is met by threats and protests from outside groups. These students are varsity athletes.

"The Game of Life" (Princeton; $27.95), by James L. Shulman and William G. Bowen, is a study of intercollegiate sports. Shulman and Bowen are foundation officers by occupation—Bowen is the president and Shulman the financial and administrative officer of the Andrew W. Mellon Foundation—and statisticians by inclination. They are the sort of people who think that no observation is so intuitive that it can't be improved by a regression analysis. "The Game of Life" contains almost two hundred charts and tables, and its prose is cautious, methodical, and somewhat repetitive. But it may be one of the most important books on higher education published in the last twenty years. It is certainly one of the most interesting.

Bowen is a former president of Princeton. He came to the Mellon Foundation in 1988, and under his leadership the foundation created a database for the study of higher education. It gathered comprehensive information about the entering classes of 1951, 1976, and 1989 at thirty-two institutions: four large public universities, including Michigan and North Carolina; four Ivy League schools; nine other private universities, including Tulane and Stanford; seven coed liberal-arts colleges, including Swarthmore and Williams; four all-women's colleges; and four historically black colleges.

The schools in the Mellon database are not representative of American higher education, a system comprising almost four thousand institutions and enrolling more than fourteen million students. But they are representative of the small segment of that system in which admission is genuinely competitive. Most of the public debate over higher education—over racial diversity, the price of tuition, and the future of the liberal arts—concerns this segment. Achieving racial diversity may be a problem at Swarthmore; it is not a problem at Sonoma State, and most American colleges are more like Sonoma State, committed to providing access to higher education for everyone who qualifies, than they are like Swarthmore, committed to producing a cadre of élites. The Mellon Foundation's database was designed to facilitate the study of the education of future élites.

The database has been used in a number of studies that the founda-   5
tion has supported. In 1998, Bowen and Derek Bok, the former president of Harvard, used it to produce "The Shape of the River," a study of affirmative action in college admissions, which provided empirical support for the claim that the benefits of affirmative action (such as the professional advancement of non-whites) outweigh the costs (such as the disadvantaging of white applicants). "The Game of Life" is drawn from the same database, and although affirmative action is barely mentioned in its pages, it is a kind of companion to the earlier book.

Most people are likely to associate the term "varsity athlete" with a large state university somewhere in the Midwest. You might imagine that if you were to walk around the campus of a place like the University of Michigan you would be continually running into guys with twenty-inch necks on their way to football practice, while if you were to walk around the campus of a small liberal-arts college like Williams you would be running into tweedy ectomorphs on their way to French class.

In fact, in 1997–98 (the most recent year for which complete enrollment data are available) there were six hundred and sixty-six varsity athletes enrolled at the University of Michigan and seven hundred and fifteen enrolled at Williams—and Michigan is more than ten times as big. Thirty-six per cent of Williams students play intercollegiate sports and only three per cent of Michigan's do. Princeton has nine hundred and forty-two athletes, half again as many as Michigan.

This may seem a surprising contrast, but it is not a new one. Students at small private colleges have played sports for a long time. Intercollegiate athletic competition originated at Ivy League colleges in the nineteenth century. (The Ivy League is, in fact, a sports league. The only formal connection the so-called Ivy League colleges have is that they compete athletically against one another.) For many years, the Harvard-Yale game was what the Super Bowl is now—a national event for football fans. There was college football long before there was professional football. Today, most of America little notes nor long remembers who won the Harvard-Yale game, but Harvard and Yale still have football teams. They also have fencing teams, golf teams, field-hockey teams, cross-country teams, lacrosse teams, squash teams, and many more. The reason Princeton has half again as many varsity athletes as Michigan is that Princeton competes in half again as many sports: Princeton fields teams in thirty-one sports, Michigan in twenty-one. Michigan has to play schools like Ohio State, where the necks are truly large, and Princeton gets to play Columbia, but the number of athletes at a school obviously has nothing to do with the level of competition. Even in the Peewee League, you have to put eleven players on the field.

Shulman and Bowen's point is not that there are more athletes at small liberal-arts colleges than there are at large state universities. Twenty-seven per cent of Ivy League students are athletes today; twenty per cent were athletes in 1951. What has changed is the relation of the athletes to the rest of the student body. In 1951, the academic profile of a varsity wrestler or swimmer at a place like Princeton or Williams was indistinguishable from the academic profile of his non-athletic classmates. By 1989, the varsity athlete at every type of school except all-women's colleges was highly distinguishable from the rest of the class—not only in terms of academic aptitude and achievement but in terms of values and interests as well. College athletes today are more likely than their classmates to identify themselves as conservative, to name being "very well off financially" as an "essential" or "very important" goal in life, and to enter a business-related field (in the case of male athletes) or psychology (in the case of female athletes).

And they know they're different. Shulman and Bowen tell the story of a female graduate of one of the schools in the database who, when asked by a job interviewer why she had chosen the college she attended, replied, "Well, I'm a catcher, and I was recruited to come here to play on the softball team." This tendency of athletes to define themselves in non-academic terms seems to be reinforced by peer effects ("jock culture"), and it helps explain why athletes under-perform in class. (It's not, apparently, because they spend so much time at practice. Shulman and Bowen found that students engaged in other time-consuming extracurricular activities, like editing the student paper, tend to overperform.) Again, conventional assumptions are misleading. It's true, as you would expect, that the S.A.T. scores of the typical football or basketball player at a big-time sports school like Michigan or North Carolina are much lower than his classmates', but the S.A.T. scores of the typical varsity tennis player at a coed liberal-arts college are also much lower—a hundred and forty-three points lower—than his classmates'.

Today, all college sports—not just sports like football, basketball, and hockey, which are watched by thousands, but sports like squash and   10 wrestling, which are watched mainly by the boyfriends and girlfriends of the contestants (assuming that they don't have a match themselves some-where)—are played by students who have been recruited specifically to play them. In 1951, the Princeton squash player was an academically qual-ified man who happened to enjoy competitive squash. He was a sports "walk-on": he simply showed up for tryouts one day and made the team. Now there are almost no varsity-sports walk-ons at the colleges in the Mellon database. Athletes are recruited out of high school. Even squash players are identified during the admissions process as people qualified to play intercollegiate squash. There are many striking tables in "The Game of Life," but the most revealing are two that show the admissions advan-tage enjoyed in 1999 by different groups of applicants at an unnamed col-lege in the database which does not offer athletic scholarships (meaning that it cannot require potential athletes to play a sport after they enter) and where coaches do not have the final word in admissions. Among men, if you were black you had an eighteen-per-cent better chance of getting into this college than a white student with the same S.A.T. scores had. If you were what is known in admissions talk as a "legacy"—that is, the child of an alumnus—you had a twenty-five-per-cent better chance. But if you were an athlete you had a forty-eight-per-cent better chance. If you were a female athlete, your advantage was fifty-three per cent.

Large state universities are practically obliged to field teams in popular sports like football and basketball because those institutions are dependent on the largesse and good will of state legislators and other public officials. A nationally ranked football team brings a lot of attention to the campus and the state. It puts taxpayers and other possible irritants in a boosterish frame of mind. It also generates gate revenues, television revenues, and licensing revenues (from the sale of T-shirts and so on)—although in fact, as Shulman and Bowen show, it is so expensive to maintain a big-time college football program that virtually no college in the country makes money from football, no matter how successful its team. In 1998–99, the University of Michigan's football team had an average home attendance of 110,965 (a national record) and won the Citrus Bowl; the men's hockey team made it to the second round of the N.C.A.A. tournament, which it had won the year before; the men's gymnastics team won the national championship; and at the end of the year the athletic department had a $3.8-million shortfall. Still, for a school like Michigan or North Carolina, state pride is at stake. What is at stake for Stanford or Swarthmore? Why should colleges like those set aside slots for golfers, oarsmen, and badminton players in their entering classes? Michigan can make room for a hundred and fifty athletes in each class and still have more than five thousand places left. At Williams, which admits about five hundred students a year, more than a third of the places are taken by athletes.

Shulman and Bowen crunch their way through all the standard ratio-nales for college sports, and they cannot come up with empirical corrobo-ration for any of them. It is not the case that having winning teams in-

creases alumni giving; or that recruiting athletes enhances the racial or so-
cioeconomic diversity of the student body (people who play sports like
squash, tennis, crew, and golf are unlikely to be either non-white or un-
derprivileged); or that athletes are more likely than other graduates to assume leadership roles at work or in civic activities (apart from coaching
youth sports, such as Little League). Like other people who were involved in extracurricular activities in college, athletes give more as
alumni (except for graduates of big-time football and basketball programs, who actually give much less: "I gave my knee to Stanford" is the
kind of thing these alumni say when they are approached for a donation).
But, unlike other people active in alumni affairs, former athletes are primarily interested in the welfare of the college's sports teams. Their gifts
tend to be given specifically for athletics, and they are the first to protest
when a school tries to reduce the budget for one of its teams.

Some of the current institutional investment in sports is due to a belief in one or more of these myths about the civic virtues of good athletes
and the financial benefits of winning teams, but some, as Shulman and
Bowen explain, is the natural consequence of competition. Success in
sports is purely relative. You don't want your field-hockey team to be the
perennial doormat in its division, so you construct a new arena, with artificial turf, in the hope of attracting a better class of field-hockey player. If
you are successful, the rest of the schools in your division will discover
that they have to have artificial turf for their field-hockey teams, too, and
the level of commitment gets ratcheted up for everyone. Once you undertake to have a first-class badminton team, you are in the position of having to respond to every effort made by your intercollegiate rivals to improve their badminton squads. The greater the pressure to win, or at least
to make a respectable showing in intercollegiate competition, the more
willing colleges are to put money into coaching and facilities, and to trade
academic promise for athletic talent in admissions.

The other thing keeping colleges shackled to their athletics programs
is the notorious legal hammer of Title IX. Title IX of the Education
Amendment of 1972 forbids sex discrimination in any program at an educational institution that gets money from the federal government, even if
the program in question is not funded by the government. Since virtually
every nonprofit college and university in the country is dependent on
some form of federal aid, there is no escape from Title IX. And the provision has been interpreted to mean that a college is not only obliged to
fund men's and women's athletics equally (a major hurdle to clear if you
have a football team); it is also obliged to provide an equal number of ros-
ter spots for both sexes, on the theory that having fewer openings sends
the message that women are not expected to play sports.

The classic test of Title IX, touched on briefly in "The Game of Life," is   15
the case against Brown. In May, 1991, the university decided to cut its athletic budget by reducing four teams—men's golf and water polo and
women's volleyball and gymnastics—to club status. This meant that

those teams had to get donations from outside sources if they wanted to continue to participate in intercollegiate competition. (Total projected savings to the university: $77,823.) The gymnasts sued. Brown offered sixteen sports for men and sixteen for women, but sixty-two per cent of its varsity athletes were men and thirty-eight per cent were women, in a student body that is roughly fifty-fifty. The university argued that it was committed to providing athletic opportunities for any female students who wanted to play, but that the simple fact was that more men than women at Brown elected to play sports every year. The gymnasts replied that this was just the kind of sexist thinking that Title IX was designed to remedy—it reflected the attitude that girls don't like sports—and the First Circuit Court agreed. Brown was ordered to keep its women's gymnastics and volleyball programs. The university wasn't simply being required to support those teams on pain of losing its federal funding; it was effectively being compelled to recruit female gymnasts and volleyball players.

"The Game of Life" intends to make the case against intercollegiate athletics on their present scale, and readers not personally invested in college sports are likely to feel that it succeeds. Whether there are enough of these readers to lead to a change in policy is another matter. Shulman and Bowen are not optimistic, and with reason. In December, just before their book came out, Swarthmore announced that it was eliminating its football program. The college had fifty-five football players in a coed student body of fourteen hundred. It also voted to eliminate its wrestling team and to reduce women's badminton to club status. Swarthmore had concluded that to continue to participate in intercollegiate competition it would have to reserve thirty-two per cent of its places in each incoming class for athletes; it preferred, it said, to reserve only ten to fifteen per cent. Swarthmore is not exactly fabled for its prowess on the gridiron: its football team recently broke a twenty-eight-game losing streak. But the reaction of some alumni and trustees to the decision was swift, and a month later, on January 3rd, the college announced that it was reconsidering.

What's fascinating about "The Game of Life," though, isn't the shadow it casts on college sports. It's the light it sheds, almost inadvertently, on college in general. Nearly everything Shulman and Bowen say about students who are athletes has implications for the way we think about students who are not. Many people believe, for example, that athletic virtues translate into social virtues. Shulman and Bowen are fairly certain that the main thing athletes carry off the playing field and into life after college is the belief that competition is good, which, as they point out, is not the belief a liberal-arts education was designed to inculcate. Still, it is difficult to disabuse educators of the notion that certain skills are transferrable, because much of the rationale for liberal-arts education relies on exactly that notion. Almost everything students do in liberal-arts colleges is exogenous to "real life." Life isn't like a football game, but it isn't like a Joyce seminar, either. If athletic skills are not transferrable, why should we believe that the ability to interpret "Finnegans Wake" is?

One of the ways that Shulman and Bowen try to determine whether playing college sports makes people "better" is to distinguish between what they call "selection effects" and "treatment effects." They conclude that college athletes have the personal traits they do because they have consistently been selected—by admissions offices, by high-school coaches, and by the grownups who first encouraged them to play a sport—precisely for those traits. College athletes do not have team spirit because they play team sports, in other words; they play team sports because they have team spirit. There seems to be no evidence that actually playing the sport enhances the qualities athletes already have when they arrive on campus. Shulman and Bowen also find that the preference of male athletes for careers in business-related fields is present even before they start college, and that four years of liberal-arts education typically does little to change their goals or values. What Shulman and Bowen don't say, since it is not within the purview of their study, is just what "treatment effects" college has on anybody. Does a liberal-arts education make people more imaginative, open-minded, and humane, or is it that imaginative, open-minded, and humane people are the kind of people selected to receive a liberal-arts education? If the liberal arts genuinely liberalize, maybe there would be a greater social benefit if colleges recruited a class of bigots and highly intelligent dogmatists.

Shulman and Bowen think that one of the reasons college sports has become a problem is an increase in the level of athletic ability. Today's athletes consistently outperform yesterday's in both professional and amateur sports. This, Shulman and Bowen believe, is the result of specialization. Athletes train more intensively, from an earlier age, to perform a particular task. People decide to become a goalie or a breaststroker when they are still in grade school, and they spend years developing a high level of expertise in that one small area of human endeavor. Admissions offices are therefore obliged to find not just football players but quarterbacks, punters, inside line-backers, and so on. You can't simply take the twenty-two football players in your applicant pool with the highest S.A.T. scores. You could end up with twenty-two placekickers. Similarly, if you support a wrestling team you have to come up with at least one person in each weight class every four years. The reason Swarthmore eliminated its wrestling team is that it was able to send only three wrestlers to its first match.

But what is true of college athletes today is also true of college students generally. The admissions-office ideal used to be the all-around achiever— the Princeton squash player of 1951. Now the ideal is the gifted specialist. Colleges look for world-class squash players, cello virtuosi, filmmakers, math geniuses, and so on—students who are highly accomplished in a single field. Instead of the well-rounded student, Shulman and Bowen explain, admissions offices now seek the well-rounded class. They attribute this trend to larger social forces, but they neglect a more systemic one. Though liberal-arts colleges may tell you otherwise, most of them below the very top tier cannot fill a class with academically highly qualified tuition-paying applicants alone. In the nineteen-sixties and early nineteen-seventies, there was an explosion of new state-college campuses across the country, offering a much cheaper B.A. than Williams or Oberlin. When, soon afterward, the baby-boom college-student cohort tailed off, many élite liberal-arts colleges were left with a lot of empty dormitory beds to fill. This is why there are virtually no all-male colleges in the United States anymore: schools could not restrict their applicant pool to men and continue to maintain selectivity. The trend toward "diversity"—a term that refers not only to a variety of racial and ethnic backgrounds but to a variety of special talents and skills—is a way of broadening admissions criteria. Defining the ability to complete a forward pass as a kind of "excellence" extends the concept of selectivity beyond grades and test scores.

This raises, finally, the real, though almost entirely implicit, point of "The Game of Life." In "The Shape of the River," Bowen and Bok estimated that in 1976, at the twenty-eight predominately white schools in the Mellon database, a total of seven hundred black students were admitted who would probably have been rejected in a race-neutral admissions process. According to "The Game of Life," in the same year twenty-four of those schools (leaving out the all-women's colleges) admitted approximately twenty-six hundred athletes. The male athletes' S.A.T. scores were, on average, ninety-four points lower than their classmates'. In 1989, those colleges admitted approximately thirty-three hundred athletes; the S.A.T. scores of the men averaged a hundred and eighteen points lower.

Many articles and books have been written to explain why admissions policies that take race into account are pernicious and ought to be abandoned. The University of California is now required by law not to use race as a criterion in admissions. That black Americans have historically been denied access to higher education is indisputable. That affirmative-action policies at élite colleges and universities have increased the number of black Americans in the higher-status professions is established by Bowen and Bok's book. By 1992, of the seven hundred black students who had entered selective colleges under affirmative-action criteria sixteen years earlier, seventy were doctors, roughly sixty were lawyers, a hundred and twenty-five were business executives, and more than three hundred had become civic leaders. How many crusaders against affirmative action in college admissions will now speak out against the preferential treatment of athletes?

Topics for Critical Thinking and Writing

1. Does your college emphasize its sports programs? Do some sports receive more attention than others? Are women's teams given the same amount of attention as the men's teams? Should they be?

2. Sean Colclough says that sports in colleges and universities are "all about money." What is his evidence? Do you find his argument convincing, or is he exaggerating?

3. How is Murray Sperber's article both the same as and different from Colclough's? if you could select only one for an anthology, which would you choose and why?

4. Sperber contends that college sports programs are a drain on university resources and produce other bad effects. But doesn't a successful, exciting football or basketball team do a lot that's positive for campus life? Aren't the critics being narrow-minded?

5. Do you know any athletes at your college? Are any of them good students, or do they all seem unserious about education and committed only to their teams?

6. Whose application do you think should be given greater priority—a star high-school quarterback or a very gifted violinist? If you had only one space available, would you give it to the quarterback, the violinist, or a straight-A student?

7. Why are the authors of these articles so concerned about college athletics? Is this issue really as important as they claim? Aren't there other issues affecting higher education that are more important?

8. Louis Menand states that admissions offices now look for the "gifted specialist" rather than someone who—though not especially gifted in any one thing—is "well-rounded." What kind of person are you? Do you envy the other kind?

W. H. Auden

W[ystan] H[ugh] Auden (1907–73) was born and educated in England. In 1939 he came to the United States and later became an American citizen; but in 1972 he returned to England to live. Auden established his reputation chiefly with his poetry, but he also wrote plays, libretti, and essays (we include two of his essays in this book), all bearing the stamp of his highly original mind.

The Unknown Citizen

(To JS/O7/M/378 This Marble Monument Is Erected by the State)

He was found by the Bureau of Statistics to be
One against whom there was no official complaint,
And all the reports on his conduct agree
That, in the modern sense of an old-fashioned word, he was a saint,
For in everything he did he served the Greater Community.   5

Except for the War till the day he retired
He worked in a factory and never got fired,
But satisfied his employers, Fudge Motors Inc.
Yet he wasn't a scab or odd in his views,
For his Union reports that he paid his dues,   10
(Our report on his Union shows it was sound)
And our Social Psychology workers found
That he was popular with his mates and liked a drink.
The press are convinced that he bought a paper every day
And that his reactions to advertisements were normal in
    every way.   15
Policies taken out in his name prove that he was fully insured,
And his Health-card shows he was once in hospital but left it cured.
Both Producers Research and High-Grade Living declare
He was fully sensible to the advantages of the Installment Plan
And had everything necessary to the Modern Man,   20
A phonograph, radio, a car and a frigidaire.
Our researchers into Public Opinion are content
That he held the proper opinions for the time of year;
When there was peace, he was for peace; when there was war, he
    went.
He was married and added five children to the population,   25
Which our Eugenist says was the right number for a parent of his
    generation,
And our teachers report that he never interfered with their
    education.
Was he free? Was he happy? The question is absurd:
Had anything been wrong, we should certainly have heard.

 ## Topics for Critical Thinking and Writing

1. Who is the speaker, and on what occasion is he supposed to be speaking?

2. What do the words "The Unknown Citizen" suggest to you?

3. How does Auden suggest that he doesn't share the attitudes of the speaker and is, in fact, satirizing them? What else does he satirize?

4. If Auden were writing the poem today, what might he substitute for "Installment Plan" in line 19 and the items listed in line 21?

5. Explicate the last two lines.

6. Write a tribute to The Unknown Student or The Unknown Professor or Politician or Professional Athlete or some other object of your well-deserved scorn.

CHAPTER 12

Messages

Short Views

Men . . . employ speech only to conceal their thoughts.
Voltaire

We must be as clear as our natural reticence allows us to be.
Marianne Moore

To change your language you must change your life.
Derek Walcott

I personally think we developed language because of our deep inner need to complain.
Jane Wagner

If you saw a bullet hit a bird, and he told you he wasn't shot, you might weep at his courtesy, but you would certainly doubt his word.
Emily Dickinson

While I am thinking about metaphor, a flock of purple finches arrives on the lawn. Since I haven't seen these birds for some years, I am only fairly sure of their being in fact purple finches, so I get down Peterson's Field Guide and read his description: "Male: About size of House Sparrow, rosy-red, brightest on head and rump." That checks quite well, but his next remark—"a sparrow dipped in raspberry juice," is decisive: it fits. I look out the window again, and now I know that I am seeing purple finches.
Howard Nemerov

We will understand the world, and preserve ourselves and our values in it, only insofar as we have a language that is alert and responsive to it, and careful of it. I mean that literally. When we give our plows such brand names as "Sod Blaster," we are imposing on their use conceptual limits which raise the likelihood that they will be used destructively. When we speak of man's "war against nature," or of a "peace offensive," we are accepting the limitations of a metaphor that suggests, and even proposes, violent solutions. When students ask for the right of "participatory input" at the meetings of a faculty organization, they are thinking of democratic process, but they are speaking of a convocation of robots, and are thus devaluing the very traditions that they invoke.

Wendell Berry

Sticks and stones may break my bones, but words will never hurt me.

Anonymous

Language both reflects and shapes society. The textbook on American government that consistently uses male pronouns for the president, even when not referring to a specific individual (e.g., "a president may cast his veto"), reflects the fact that all our presidents have so far been men. But it also shapes a society in which the idea of a female president somehow "doesn't sound right."

Rosalie Maggio

The search is for the just word, the happy phrase, that will give expression to the thought, but somehow the thought itself is transfigured by the phrase when found.

Benjamin Cardozo

"Wild and Free." An American dream-phrase loosing images; a long-maned stallion racing across the grasslands, a V of Canada Geese high and honking, a squirrel chattering and leaping limb to limb overhead in an oak. It also sounds like an ad for a Harley-Davidson. Both words, profoundly political and sensitive as they are, have become consumer baubles.

Gary Snyder

There can be too much communication between people.

Ann Beattie

Abraham Lincoln

Abraham Lincoln (1809–65), sixteenth president of the United States, is not usually thought of as a writer, but his published speeches and writings comprise about 1,078,000 words, the equivalent of about four thousand pages of double-spaced typing. They were all composed without the assistance of a speech writer.

The Gettysburg campaign—a series of battles fought near Gettysburg in southeastern Pennsylvania—took place in June and July of 1863. Each side lost something like twenty-three thousand men. The battle is regarded as a turning point in the war, but the Confederate army escaped and the war continued until April 1865.

On November 19, 1863, Lincoln delivered a short speech (printed below) at the dedication of a national cemetery on the battlefield at Gettysburg.

Address at the Dedication of the Gettysburg National Cemetery

Four score and seven years ago our fathers brought forth on this continent, a new nation, conceived in Liberty, and dedicated to the proposition that all men are created equal.

Now we are engaged in a great civil war; testing whether that nation, or any nation so conceived and so dedicated, can long endure. We are met on a great battlefield of that war. We have come to dedicate a portion of that field as a final resting-place for those who here gave their lives that that nation might live. It is altogether fitting and proper that we should do this.

But, in a larger sense, we cannot dedicate—we cannot consecrate—we cannot hallow—this ground. The brave men, living and dead, who struggled here have consecrated it, far above our poor power to add or detract. The world will little note, nor long remember, what we say here, but it can never forget what they did here. It is for us the living, rather, to be dedicated here to the unfinished work which they who fought here have thus far so nobly advanced. It is rather for us to be here dedicated to the great task remaining before us—that from these honored dead we take increased devotion to that cause for which they gave the last full measure of devotion; that we here highly resolve that these dead shall not have died in vain; that this nation, under God, shall have a new birth of freedom; and that government of the people, by the people, for the people, shall not perish from the earth.

Gilbert Highet

Gilbert Highet (1906–78) was born in Glasgow, Scotland, and was educated at Glasgow University and at Oxford University. In 1937 he came to the United States, and in 1951 he was naturalized. Until his retirement in 1972 he taught Latin, Greek, and comparative literature at Columbia University. In addition to writing scholarly studies of classical authors, he wrote several general and more popular books.

The Gettysburg Address

Fourscore and seven years ago. . . .

These five words stand at the entrance to the best-known monument of American prose, one of the finest utterances in the entire language, and surely one of the greatest speeches in all history. Greatness is like granite: it is molded in fire, and it lasts for many centuries.

Fourscore and seven years ago. . . . It is strange to think that President Lincoln was looking back to the 4th of July 1776, and that he and his speech are now further removed from us than he himself was from George Washington and the Declaration of Independence. Fourscore and seven years before the Gettysburg Address, a small group of patriots signed the Declaration. Fourscore and seven years after the Gettysburg Address, it was the year 1950, and that date is already receding rapidly into our troubled, adventurous, and valiant past.

Inadequately prepared and at first scarcely realized in its full importance, the dedication of the graveyard at Gettysburg was one of the supreme moments of American history. The battle itself had been a turning point of the war. On the 4th of July 1863, General Meade repelled Lee's invasion of Pennsylvania. Although he did not follow up his victory, he had broken one of the most formidable aggressive enterprises of the Confederate armies. Losses were heavy on both sides. Thousands of dead were left on the field, and thousands of wounded died in the hot days following the battle. At first, their burial was more or less haphazard; but thoughtful men gradually came to feel that an adequate burying place and memorial were required. These were established by an interstate commission that autumn, and the finest speaker in the North was invited to dedicate them. This was the scholar and statesman Edward Everett of Harvard. He made a good speech—which is still extant: not at all academic, it is full of close strategic analysis and deep historical understanding.

Lincoln was not invited to speak, at first. Although people knew him as an effective debater, they were not sure whether he was capable of making a serious speech on such a solemn occasion. But one of the impressive things about Lincoln's career is that he constantly strove to *grow*. He was anxious to appear on that occasion and to say something worthy of it. (Also, it has been suggested, he was anxious to remove the impression that he did not know how to behave properly—an impression which had been strengthened by a shocking story about his clowning on the battlefield of Antietam the previous year.) Therefore when he was invited he took considerable care with his speech. He drafted rather more than half of it in the White House before leaving, finished it in the hotel at Gettysburg the night before the ceremony (not in the train, as sometimes reported), and wrote a fair copy next morning.

There are many accounts of the day itself, 19 November 1863. There are many descriptions of Lincoln, all showing the same curious blend of grandeur and awkwardness, or lack of dignity, or—it would be best to call it humility. In the procession he rode horseback: a tall lean man in a high plug hat, straddling a short horse, with his feet too near the ground. He arrived before the chief speaker, and had to wait patiently for half an hour or more. His own speech came right at the end of a long and exhausting ceremony, lasted less than three minutes, and made little impression on the audience. In part this was because they were tired, in part because (as eyewitnesses said) he ended almost before they knew he had begun, and in part because he did not speak the Address, but read it, very slowly, in a thin high voice, with a marked Kentucky accent, pronouncing "to" as "toe" and dropping his final R's.

Some people of course were alert enough to be impressed. Everett congratulated him at once. But most of the newspapers paid little attention to the speech, and some sneered at it. The *Patriot and Union* of Harrisburg wrote, "We pass over the silly remarks of the President; for the credit of the nation we are willing . . . that they shall no more be repeated or thought of"; and the London *Times* said, "The ceremony was rendered ludicrous by some of the sallies of that poor President Lincoln," calling his remarks "dull and commonplace." The first commendation of the Address came in a single sentence of the Chicago *Tribune*, and the first discriminating and detailed praise of it appeared in the Springfield *Republican*, the Providence *Journal*, and the Philadelphia *Bulletin*. However, three weeks after the ceremony and then again the following spring, the editor of *Harper's Weekly* published a sincere and thorough eulogy of the Address, and soon it was attaining recognition as a masterpiece.

At the time, Lincoln could not care much about the reception of his words. He was exhausted and ill. In the train back to Washington, he lay down with a wet towel on his head. He had caught smallpox. At that moment he was incubating it, and he was stricken down soon after he reentered the White House. Fortunately it was a mild attack, and it evoked one of his best jokes: he told his visitors, "At last I have something I can give to everybody."

He had more than that to give to everybody. He was a unique person, far greater than most people realize until they read his life with care. The wisdom of his policy, the sources of his statesmanship—these were things too complex to be discussed in a brief essay. But we can say something about the Gettysburg Address as a work of art.[1]

A work of art. Yes: for Lincoln was a literary artist, trained both by others and by himself. The textbooks he used as a boy were full of difficult exercises and skillful devices in formal rhetoric, stressing the qualities he practiced in his own speaking: antithesis, parallelism, and verbal harmony. Then he read and reread many admirable models of thought and expression: the King James Bible, the essays of Bacon, the best plays of Shakespeare. His favorites were *Hamlet, Lear, Macbeth, Richard III,* and *Henry VIII,* which he had read dozens of times. He loved reading aloud, too, and spent hours reading poetry to his friends. (He told his partner Herndon that he preferred getting the sense of any document by reading it aloud.) Therefore his serious speeches are important parts of the long and noble classical tradition of oratory which begins in Greece, runs through Rome to the modern world, and is still capable (if we do not neglect it) of producing masterpieces.

The first proof of this is that the Gettysburg Address is full of quotations—or rather of adaptations—which give it strength. It is partly religious, partly (in the highest sense) political: therefore it is interwoven with memories of the Bible and memories of American history. The first and the last words are Biblical cadences. Normally Lincoln did not say "fourscore" when he meant eighty; but on this solemn occasion he recalled the important dates in the Bible—such as the age of Abraham when his first son was born to him, and he was "fourscore and six years old." Similarly, he did not say there was a chance that democracy might die out: he recalled the somber phrasing in the Book of Job—where Bildad speaks of the destruction of one who shall vanish without a trace, and says that "his branch shall be cut off; his remembrance shall perish from the earth." Then again, the famous description of our State as "government of the people, by the people, for the people" was adumbrated by Daniel Webster in 1830 (he spoke of "the people's government, made for the people, made by the people, and answerable to the people") and then elaborated in 1854 by the abolitionist Theodore Parker (as "government of all the people, by all the people, for all the people"). There is good reason to think that Lincoln took the important phrase "under God" (which he interpolated at the last moment) from Weems, the biographer of Washington; and we know that it had been used at least once by Washington himself.

Analyzing the Address further, we find that it is based on a highly imaginative theme, or group of themes. The subject is—how can we put it

10

---

[1]For further reference, see W. E. Barton, *Lincoln at Gettysburg* (Indianapolis: Bobbs-Merrill, 1930); R. P. Basler, "Abraham Lincoln's Rhetoric." *American Literature* 11 (1939–40), 167–82; and L. E. Robinson, *Abraham Lincoln as a Man of Letters* (Chicago, 1918).

so as not to disfigure it?—the subject is the kinship of life and death, that mysterious linkage which we see sometimes as the physical succession of birth and death in our world, sometimes as the contrast, which is perhaps a unity, between death and immortality. The first sentence is concerned with birth:

> Our *fathers brought forth a new* nation, *conceived* in liberty.

The final phrase but one expresses the hope that

> this nation, under God, shall have a *new birth* of freedom.

And that last phrase of all speaks of continuing life as the triumph over death. Again and again throughout the speech, this mystical contrast and kinship reappear: "those who *gave their lives* that that nation might *live*," "the brave men *living and dead*," and so in the central assertion that the dead have already consecrated their own burial place, while "it is for us, the *living*, rather to be dedicated . . . to the great task remaining." The Gettysburg Address is a prose poem; it belongs to the same world as the great elegies, and the adagios of Beethoven.

Its structure, however, is that of a skillfully contrived speech. The oratorical pattern is perfectly clear. Lincoln describes the occasion, dedicates the ground, and then draws a larger conclusion by calling on his hearers to dedicate themselves to the preservation of the Union. But within that, we can trace his constant use of at least two important rhetorical devices.

The first of these is *antithesis*: opposition, contrast. The speech is full of it. Listen:

The world will little	*note*		
nor long	*remember*	what	*we say* here
but it can never	*forget*	what	*they did* here

And so in nearly every sentence: "brave men, *living* and *dead*"; "to *add* or *detract*." There is the antithesis of the Founding Fathers and men of Lincoln's own time:

> Our *fathers brought forth* a new nation . . .
>
> now *we* are testing whether that nation . . . can *long endure*.

And there is the more terrible antithesis of those who have already died and those who still live to do their duty. Now, antithesis is the figure of contrast and conflict. Lincoln was speaking in the midst of a great civil war.

The other important pattern is different. It is technically called   15
tricolon—the division of an idea into three harmonious parts, usually of
increasing power. The most famous phrase of the Address is a tricolon:

> government of the people
> > by the people
> > for the people.

The most solemn sentence is a tricolon:

> we cannot dedicate
> we cannot consecrate
> we cannot hallow   this ground.

And above all, the last sentence (which has sometimes been criticized
as too complex) is essentially two parallel phrases, with a tricolon growing out of the second and then producing another tricolon: a trunk, three
branches, and a cluster of flowers. Lincoln says that it is for his hearers to
be dedicated to the great task remaining before them. Then he goes on.

> that from these honored dead

—apparently he means "in such a way that from these honored
dead"—

> we take increased devotion to that cause.

Next, he restates this more briefly:

> that we here highly resolve. . .

And now the actual resolution follows, in three parts of growing
intensity:

> that these dead shall not have died in vain

> that this nation, under God, shall have a new birth of freedom

and that (one more tricolon)

> government of the people
> > by the people
> > for the people
> shall not perish from the earth.

Now, the tricolon is the figure which, through division, emphasizes basic harmony and unity. Lincoln used antithesis because he was speaking to a people at war. He used the tricolon because he was hoping, planning, praying for peace.

No one thinks that when he was drafting the Gettysburg Address, Lincoln deliberately looked up these quotations and consciously chose these particular patterns of thought. No, he chose the theme. From its development and from the emotional tone of the entire occasion, all the rest followed, or grew—by that marvelous process of choice and rejection which is essential to artistic creation. It does not spoil such a work of art to analyze it as closely as we have done; it is altogether fitting and proper that we should do this: for it helps us to penetrate more deeply into the rich meaning of the Gettysburg Address, and it allows us the very rare privilege of watching the workings of a great man's mind.

Topics for Critical Thinking and Writing

1. At the start of his essay, after quoting the opening words of Lincoln's speech, Highet uses a metaphor and a simile: he says that the words "stand at the entrance to the best-known monument," and that "greatness is like granite: it is molded in fire, and it lasts for many centuries." Are these figures of speech effective? Why or why not? How are the two figures related to each other?

2. Analyze the structure of Highet's essay.

3. This essay was a talk given on the radio, presumably to a large general public. Find passages in the essay that suggest oral delivery to an unspecialized audience. How would you describe Highet's tone?

4. It has been suggested that "government of the people, by the people" is redundant; a government *of* the people, it is argued, must be the same as a government *by* the people. Did Lincoln repeat himself merely to get a triad: "of the people, by the people, for the people"? If so, is this a fault? Or can it be argued that "government of the people" really means "government over the people"? If so, what does the entire expression mean?

5. Highet claims that Lincoln was not only a great statesman but also a literary artist. According to Highet, what was Lincoln's training as a literary artist? Highet implies that such training is still available. To what extent has it been available to you? Traditionally, studying "admirable models of thought and expression," including poetry, was an important part of writing instruction, but it is less common now. Should such study be included in writing courses? Why, or why not?

6. In paragraph 11 Highet points out that "the Gettysburg Address is full of quotations—or rather of adaptations," and he analyzes several examples of Lincoln's adaptations of sources. How is such adaptation different from plagiarism? Or is it?

Robin Lakoff

Robin Lakoff was born in 1943 and educated at Radcliffe College and Harvard University. A professor of linguistics at the University of California at Berkeley, she has been especially interested in the language that women use. The essay that we give here was first published in Ms. *magazine in 1974.*

You Are What You Say

Women's language is that pleasant (dainty?), euphemistic never-aggressive way of talking we learned as little girls. Cultural bias was built into the language we were allowed to speak, the subjects we were allowed to speak about, and the ways we were spoken of. Having learned our linguistic lesson well, we go out in the world, only to discover that we are communicative cripples—damned if we do, and damned if we don't.

If we refuse to talk "like a lady," we are ridiculed and criticized for being unfeminine. ("She thinks like a man" is, at best, a left-handed compliment.) If we do learn all the fuzzy-headed, unassertive language of our sex, we are ridiculed for being unable to think clearly, unable to take part in a serious discussion, and therefore unfit to hold a position of power.

It doesn't take much of this for a woman to begin feeling she deserves such treatment because of inadequacies in her own intelligence and education.

"Women's language" shows up in all levels of English. For example, women are encouraged and allowed to make far more precise discriminations in naming colors than men do. Words like *mauve, beige, ecru, aquamarine, lavender,* and so on, are unremarkable in a woman's active vocabulary, but largely absent from that of most men. I know of no evidence suggesting that women actually *see* a wider range of colors than men do. It is simply that fine discriminations of this sort are relevant to women's vocabularies, but not to men's; to men, who control most of the interesting affairs of the world, such distinctions are trivial—irrelevant.

In the area of syntax, we find similar gender-related peculiarities of 5
speech. There is one construction, in particular, that women use conversationally far more than men: the tag question. A tag is midway between an outright statement and a yes-no question; it is less assertive than the former, but more confident than the latter.

A *flat statement* indicates confidence in the speaker's knowledge and is fairly certain to be believed; a *question* indicates a lack of knowledge on some point and implies that the gap in the speaker's knowledge can and will be remedied by an answer. For example, if, at a Little League game, I have had my glasses off, I can legitimately ask someone else: "Was the player out at third?" A *tag question*, being intermediate between statement and question, is used when the speaker is stating a claim, but lacks full confidence in the truth of that claim. So if I say, "Is Joan here?" I will probably not be surprised if my respondent answers "no"; but if I say, "Joan is here, isn't she?" instead, chances are I am already biased in favor of a positive answer, wanting only confirmation. I still want a response, but I have enough knowledge (or think I have) to predict that response. A tag question, then, might be thought of as a statement that doesn't demand to be believed by anyone but the speaker, a way of giving leeway, of not forcing the addressee to go along with the views of the speaker.

Another common use of the tag question is in small talk when the speaker is trying to elicit conversation: "Sure is hot here, isn't it?"

But in discussing personal feelings or opinions, only the speaker normally has any way of knowing the correct answer. Sentences such as "I have a headache, don't I?" are clearly ridiculous. But there are other examples where it is the speaker's opinions, rather than perceptions, for which corroboration is sought, as in "The situation in Southeast Asia is terrible, isn't it?"

While there are, of course, other possible interpretations of a sentence like this, one possibility is that the speaker has a particular answer in mind—"yes" or "no"—but is reluctant to state it baldly. This sort of tag question is much more apt to be used by women than by men in conversation. Why is this the case?

The tag question allows a speaker to avoid commitment, and thereby 10 avoid conflict with the addressee. The problem is that, by so doing, speakers may also give the impression of not really being sure of themselves, or looking to the addressee for confirmation of their views. This uncertainty is reinforced in more subliminal ways, too. There is a peculiar sentence-intonation pattern, used almost exclusively by women, as far as I know, which changes a declarative answer into a question. The effect of using the rising inflection typical of a yes-no question is to imply that the speaker is seeking confirmation, even though the speaker is clearly the only one who has the requisite information, which is why the question was put to her in the first place:

(Q) When will dinner be ready?
(A) Oh . . . around six o'clock. . . ?

It is as though the second speaker was saying, "Six o'clock—if that's okay with you, if you agree." The person being addressed is put in the position of having to provide confirmation. One likely consequence of this sort of speech pattern in a woman is that, often unbeknownst to herself, the speaker builds a reputation of tentativeness, and others will refrain from taking her seriously or trusting her with any real responsibilities, since she "can't make up her mind," and "isn't sure of herself."

Such idiosyncrasies may explain why women's language sounds much more "polite" than men's. It is polite to leave a decision open, not impose your mind, or views, or claims, on anyone else. So a tag question is a kind of polite statement, in that it does not force agreement or belief on the addressee. In the same way a request is a polite command, in that it does not force obedience on the addressee, but rather suggests something be done as a favor to the speaker. A clearly stated order implies a threat of certain consequences if it is not followed, and—even more impolite—implies that the speaker is in a superior position and able to enforce the order. By couching wishes in the form of a request, on the other hand, a speaker implies that if the request is not carried out, only the speaker will suffer; noncompliance cannot harm the addressee. So the decision is really left up to the addressee. The distinction becomes clear in these examples:

Close the door.

Please close the door.

Will you close the door?

Will you please close the door?

Won't you close the door?

In the same ways as words and speech patterns used *by* women undermine their image, those used to *describe* women make matters even worse. Often a word may be used of both men and women (and perhaps of things as well); but when it is applied to women, it assumes a special meaning that, by implication rather than outright assertion, is derogatory to women as a group.

The use of euphemisms has this effect. A euphemism is a substitute for a word that has acquired a bad connotation by association with something unpleasant or embarrassing. But almost as soon as the new word comes into common usage, it takes on the same old bad connotations, since feelings about the things or people referred to are not altered by a change of name; thus new euphemisms must be constantly found.

There is one euphemism for *woman* still very much alive. The word, of course, is *lady*. *Lady* has a masculine counterpart, namely *gentleman*, occasionally shortened to *gent*. But for some reason *lady* is very much commoner than *gent(leman)*.

The decision to use *lady* rather than *woman*, or vice versa, may considerably alter the sense of a sentence, as the following examples show: 15

a. A woman (lady) I know is a dean at Berkeley.
b. A woman (lady) I know makes amazing things out of shoelaces and old boxes.

The use of *lady* in (a) imparts a frivolous, or nonserious, tone to the sentence: the matter under discussion is not one of great moment.

Similarly, in (b), using *lady* here would suggest that the speaker considered the "amazing things" not to be serious art, but merely a hobby or an aberration. If *woman* is used, she might be a serious sculptor. To say *lady doctor* is very condescending, since no one ever says *gentleman doctor* or even *man doctor*. For example, mention in the San Francisco *Chronicle* of January 31, 1972, of Madalyn Murray O'Hair as the *lady atheist* reduces her position to that of scatterbrained eccentric. Even *woman atheist* is scarcely defensible: sex is irrelevant to her philosophical position.

Many women argue that, on the other hand, *lady* carries with it overtones recalling the age of chivalry: conferring exalted stature on the person so referred to. This makes the term seem polite at first, but we must also remember that these implications are perilous: they suggest that a "lady" is helpless, and cannot do things by herself.

Lady can also be used to infer frivolousness, as in titles of organizations. Those that have a serious purpose (not merely that of enabling "the ladies" to spend time with one another) cannot use the word *lady* in their titles, but less serious ones may. Compare the *Ladies' Auxiliary* of a men's group, or the *Thursday Evening Ladies' Browning and Garden Society* with *Ladies' Liberation* or *Ladies' Strike for Peace*.

What is curious about this split is that *lady* is in origin a euphemism—a substitute that puts a better face on something people find uncomfortable—for *woman*. What kind of euphemism is it that subtly denigrates the people to whom it refers? Perhaps *lady* functions as a euphemism for *woman* because it does not contain the sexual implications present in *woman*: it is not "embarrassing" in that way. If this is so, we may expect that, in the future, *lady* will replace woman as the primary word for the human female, since *woman* will have become too blatantly sexual. That this distinction is already made in some contexts at least is shown in the following examples, where you can try replacing *woman* with *lady*:

a. She's only twelve, but she's already a woman.
b. After ten years in jail, Harry wanted to find a woman.
c. She's my woman, see, so don't mess around with her.

Another common substitute for *woman* is *girl*. One seldom hears a man past the age of adolescence referred to as a boy, save in expressions like "going out with the boys," which are meant to suggest an air of adolescent frivolity and irresponsibility. But women of all ages are "girls": one can have a man—not a boy—Friday, but only a girl—never a woman or even a lady—Friday; women have girlfriends, but men do not—in a nonsexual sense—have boyfriends. It may be that this use of *girl* is euphemistic in the same way the use of *lady* is: in stressing the idea of immaturity, it removes the sexual connotations lurking in *woman*. *Girl* brings to mind irresponsibility: you don't send a girl to do a woman's errand (or even, for that matter, a boy's errand). She is a person who is both too immature and too far from real life to be entrusted with responsibilities or with decisions of any serious or important nature.

20

Now let's take a pair of words which, in terms of the possible relationships in an earlier society, were simple male-female equivalents, analogous to *bull: cow*. Suppose we find that, for independent reasons, society has changed in such a way that the original meanings now are irrelevant. Yet the words have not been discarded, but have acquired new meanings, metaphorically related to their original senses. But suppose these new metaphorical uses are no longer parallel to each other. By seeing where the parallelism breaks down, we discover something about the different roles played by men and women in this culture. One good example of such a divergence through time is found in the pair, *master: mistress*. Once used with reference to one's power over servants, these words have become unusable today in their original master-servant sense as the relationship has become less prevalent in our society. But the words are still common.

Unless used with reference to animals, *master* now generally refers to a man who has acquired consummate ability in some field, normally nonsexual. But its feminine counterpart cannot be used this way. It is practically restricted to its sexual sense of "paramour." We start out with two terms, both roughly paraphrasable as "one who has power over another." But the masculine form, once one person is no longer able to have absolute power over another, becomes usable metaphorically in the sense of "having power over *something*." *Master* requires as its object only the name of some activity, something inanimate and abstract. But *mistress* requires a masculine noun in the possessive to precede it. One cannot say: "Rhonda is a mistress." One must be *someone's* mistress. A man is defined by what he does, a woman by her sexuality, that is, in terms of one particular aspect of her relationship to men. It is one thing to be an *old master* like Hans Holbein,[1] and another to be an *old mistress*.

The same is true of the words *spinster* and *bachelor*—gender words for "one who is not married." The resemblance ends with the definition. While *bachelor* is a neuter term, often used as a compliment, *spinster* normally is used pejoratively, with connotations of prissiness, fussiness, and so on. To be a bachelor implies that one has a choice of marrying or not, and this is what makes the idea of a bachelor existence attractive, in the popular literature. He has been pursued and has successfully eluded his pursuers. But a spinster is one who has not been pursued, or at least not seriously. She is old, unwanted goods. The metaphorical connotations of *bachelor* generally suggest sexual freedom; of *spinster*, puritanism or celibacy.

These examples could be multiplied. It is generally considered a *faux pas*, in society, to congratulate a woman on her engagement, while it is correct to congratulate her fiancé. Why is this? The reason seems to be that it is impolite to remind people of things that may be uncomfortable to them. To congratulate a woman on her engagement is really to say, "Thank goodness! You had a close call!" For the man, on the other hand,

---

[1]German painter of the sixteenth century.

there was no such danger. His choosing to marry is viewed as a good thing, but not something essential.

The linguistic double standards holds throughout the life of the relationship. After marriage, bachelor and spinster become man and wife, not man and woman. The woman whose husband dies remains "John's widow"; John, however, is never "Mary's widower."   25

Finally, why is it that salesclerks and others are so quick to call women customers "dear," "honey," and other terms of endearment they really have no business using? A male customer would never put up with it. But women, like children, are supposed to enjoy these endearments, rather than being offended by them.

In more ways than one, it's time to speak up.

Topics for Critical Thinking and Writing

1. Lakoff's first example of "women's language" (paragraph 4) has to do with colors. She says that women are more likely than men to use such words as *mauve, beige,* and *lavender* not because women see a wider range of colors but because men, "who control most of the interesting affairs of the world," regard distinctions of color as trivial and presumably leave them to the women. How adequate does this explanation seem to you?

2. For a day or so, try to notice if Lakoff's suggestion is correct that women are more inclined than men to use "tag questions" and to use a "rising inflection" with a declarative sentence. Jot down examples you hear, and write an essay of about five hundred words, either supporting or refuting Lakoff.

3. While you are eavesdropping, you might notice, too, whether or not in mixed company women talk more than men. Many men assume that "women talk a lot," but is it true? If, for instance, you spend an evening with an adult couple, try to form an impression about which of the two does more of the talking. Of course this is too small a sample to allow for a generalization; still, it is worth thinking about. If you are at a meeting—perhaps a meeting of a committee with men and women—again try to see whether the males or the females do most of the talking. Try also to see whether one sex interrupts the other more often than the other way around. And try to make some sense out of your findings.

4. In paragraph 11 Lakoff says, "Women's language sounds much more 'polite' than men's," and she implies that this politeness is a way of seeming weak. Do you associate politeness with weakness?

5. The essay originally appeared in *Ms.*, a feminist magazine, rather than in an academic journal devoted to language or to sociology. Why do you suppose Lakoff chose *Ms.*? What would you say her purpose was in writing and publishing the essay?

6. This essay was first published in 1974. Do you think it is dated? You might begin by asking yourself if women today use "women's language."

Barbara Lawrence

Barbara Lawrence was born in Hanover, New Hampshire, and educated at Connecticut College and New York University. She teaches at the State University of New York, at Old Westbury. This essay first appeared in The New York Times.

Four-Letter Words Can Hurt You

Why should any words be called obscene? Don't they all describe natural human functions? Am I trying to tell them, my students demand, that the "strong, earthy, gut-honest"—or, if they are fans of Norman Mailer, the "rich, liberating, existential"—language they use to describe sexual activity isn't preferable to "phony-sounding, middle-class words like 'intercourse' and 'copulate'?" "Cop You Late!" they say with fancy inflections and gagging grimaces. "Now, what is *that* supposed to mean?"

Well, what is it supposed to mean? And why indeed should one group of words describing human functions and human organs be acceptable in ordinary conversation and another, describing presumably the same organs and functions, be tabooed—so much so, in fact, that some of these words still cannot appear in print in many parts of the English-speaking world?

The argument that these taboos exist only because of "sexual hangups" (middle-class, middle-age, feminist), or even that they are a result of class oppression (the contempt of the Norman conquerors for the language of their Anglo-Saxon serfs), ignores a much more likely explanation, it seems to me, and that is the sources and functions of the words themselves.

The best known of the tabooed sexual verbs, for example, comes from the German *ficken*, meaning "to strike"; combined, according to Partridge's etymological dictionary *Origins*, with the Latin sexual verb *futuere*; associated in turn with the Latin *fustis*, "a staff or cudgel"; the Celtic *buc*, "a point, hence to pierce"; the Irish *bot*, "the male member"; the Latin *battuere*, "to beat"; the Gaelic *batair*, "a cudgeller"; the Early Irish *bualaim*, "I strike"; and so forth. It is one of what etymologists sometimes call "the sadistic group of words for the man's part in copulation."

The brutality of this word, then, and its equivalents ("screw," "bang," etc.), is not an illusion of the middle class or a crotchet of Women's Liberation. In their origins and imagery these words carry undeniably painful, if not sadistic, implications, the object of which is almost always female. Consider, for example, what a "screw" actually does to the wood it penetrates; what a painful, even mutilating, activity this kind of analogy suggests. "Screw" is particularly interesting in this context, since the

5

noun, according to Partridge, comes from words meaning "groove," "nut," "ditch," "breeding sow," "scrofula" and "swelling," while the verb, besides its explicit imagery, has antecedent associations to "write on," "scratch," "scarify," and so forth—a revealing fusion of a mechanical or painful action with an obviously denigrated object.

Not all obscene words, of course, are as implicitly sadistic or denigrating to women as these, but all that I know seem to serve a similar purpose: to reduce the human organism (especially the female organism) and human functions (especially sexual and procreative) to their least organic, most mechanical dimension; to substitute a trivializing or deforming resemblance for the complex human reality of what is being described.

Tabooed male descriptives, when they are not openly denigrating to women, often serve to divorce a male organ or function from any significant interaction with the female. Take the word "testes," for example, suggesting "witnesses" (from the Latin *testis*) to the sexual and procreative strengths of the male organ; and the obscene counterpart of this word, which suggests little more than a mechanical shape. Or compare almost any of the "rich," "liberating" sexual verbs, so fashionable today among male writers, with that much-derided Latin word "copulate" ("to bind or join together") or even that Anglo-Saxon phrase (which seems to have had no trouble surviving the Norman Conquest) "make love."

How arrogantly self-involved the tabooed words seem in comparison to either of the other terms, and how contemptuous of the female partner. Understandably so, of course, if she is only a "skirt," a "broad," a "chick," a "pussycat" or a "piece." If she is, in other words, no more than her skirt, or what her skirt conceals; no more than a breeder, or the broadest part of her; no more than a piece of a human being or a "piece of tail."

The most severely tabooed of all the female descriptives, incidentally, are those like a "piece of tail," which suggest (either explicitly or through antecedents) that there is no significant difference between the female channel through which we are all conceived and born and the anal outlet common to both sexes—a distinction that pornographers have always enjoyed obscuring.

This effort to deny women their biological identity, their individuality, their humanness, is such an important aspect of obscene language that one can only marvel at how seldom, in an era preoccupied with definitions of obscenity, this fact is brought to our attention. One problem, of course, is that many of the people in the best position to do this (critics, teachers, writers) are so reluctant today to admit that they are angered or shocked by obscenity. Bored, maybe, unimpressed, aesthetically displeased, but—no matter how brutal or denigrating the material—never angered, never shocked.

And yet how eloquently angered, how piously shocked many of these same people become if denigrating language is used about any minority group other than women; if the obscenities are racial or ethnic, that

10

is, rather than sexual. Words like "coon," "kike," "spic," "wop," after all, deform identity, deny individuality and humanness in almost exactly the same way that sexual vulgarisms and obscenities do.

No one that I know, least of all my students, would fail to question the values of a society whose literature and entertainment rested heavily on racial or ethnic pejoratives. Are the values of a society whose literature and entertainment rest as heavily as ours on sexual pejoratives any less questionable?

 Topics for Critical Thinking and Writing

1. In addition to giving evidence to support her view, what persuasive devices (such as irony, analogy) does Lawrence use? (On Irony, see pages 905–906; on analogy, see page 902.)

2. Not all authorities agree with all of Lawrence's etymologies. Is her argument, therefore, weakened?

3. Examine your own use or nonuse of four-letter words. How and when did you learn to use them or to avoid using them? If you have reasons to avoid them other than the ones Lawrence provides, what are they? If you do use such words, under what circumstances are you likely to use them? Will Lawrence's analysis persuade you to avoid them altogether? Why or why not?

Edward T. Hall

Edward T. Hall, born in Missouri in 1914, was for many years a professor of anthropology at Northwestern University.

Hall is especially concerned with "proxemics," a word derived from the Latin proximus, "nearest." Proxemics is the study of people's responses to spatial relationships—for example, their ways of marking out their territory in public places and their responses to what they consider to be crowding. In these pages from his book The Hidden Dimension *(1966), Hall suggests that Arabs and Westerners must understand the proxemic customs of each other's culture; without such understanding, other communications between them are likely to be misunderstood.*

Proxemics in the Arab World

In spite of over two thousand years of contact, Westerners and Arabs still do not understand each other. Proxemic research reveals some insights into this difficulty. Americans in the Middle East are immediately struck by two conflicting sensations. In public they are compressed and overwhelmed by smells, crowding, and high noise levels; in Arab homes Americans are apt to rattle around, feeling exposed and often somewhat inadequate because of too much space! (The Arab houses and apartments of the middle and upper classes which Americans stationed abroad commonly occupy are much larger than the dwellings such Americans usually inhabit.) Both the high sensory stimulation which is experienced in public places and the basic insecurity which comes from being in a dwelling that is too large provide Americans with an introduction to the sensory world of the Arab.

Behavior in Public

Pushing and shoving in public places is characteristic of Middle Eastern culture. Yet it is not entirely what Americans think it is (being pushy and rude) but stems from a different set of assumptions concerning not only the relations between people but how one experiences the body as well. Paradoxically, Arabs consider northern Europeans and Americans pushy, too. This was very puzzling to me when I started investigating these two views. How could Americans who stand aside and avoid touching be considered pushy? I used to ask Arabs to explain this paradox. None of my subjects was able to tell me specifically what particulars of American behavior were responsible, yet they all agreed that the impression was widespread among Arabs. After repeated unsuccessful attempts to gain insight into the cognitive world of the Arab on this particular point, I filed it away as a question that only time would answer. When the answer came, it was because of a seemingly inconsequential annoyance.

While waiting for a friend in a Washington, D.C., hotel lobby and wanting to be both visible and alone, I had seated myself in a solitary chair outside the normal stream of traffic. In such a setting most Americans follow a rule, which is all the more binding because we seldom think about it, that can be stated as follows: as soon as a person stops or is seated in a public place, there balloons around him a small sphere of privacy which is considered inviolate. The size of the sphere varies with the degree of crowding, the age, sex, and the importance of the person, as well as the general surroundings. Anyone who enters this zone and stays there is intruding. In fact, a stranger who intrudes, even for a specific purpose, acknowledges the fact that he has intruded by beginning his request with "Pardon me, but can you tell me. . . ?"

To continue, as I waited in the deserted lobby, a stranger walked up to where I was sitting and stood close enough so that not only could I easily touch him but I could even hear him breathing. In addition, the dark mass of his body filled the peripheral field of vision on my left side. If the lobby had been crowded with people, I would have understood his behavior, but in an empty lobby his presence made me exceedingly uncomfortable. Feeling annoyed by this intrusion, I moved my body in such a way as to communicate annoyance. Strangely enough, instead of moving away, my actions seemed only to encourage him, because he moved even closer. In spite of the temptation to escape the annoyance, I put aside thoughts of abandoning my post, thinking, "To hell with it. Why should I move? I was here first and I'm not going to let this fellow drive me out even if he is a boor." Fortunately, a group of people soon arrived whom my tormentor immediately joined. Their mannerisms explained his behavior, for I knew from both speech and gestures that they were Arabs. I had not been able to make this crucial identification by looking at my subject when he was alone because he wasn't talking and he was wearing American clothes.

In describing the scene later to an Arab colleague, two contrasting   5
patterns emerged. My concept and my feelings about my own circle of privacy in a "public" place immediately struck my Arab friend as strange and puzzling. He said, "After all, it's a public place, isn't it?" Pursuing this line of inquiry, I found that an Arab thought I had no rights whatsoever by virtue of occupying a given spot; neither my place nor my body was inviolate! For the Arab, there is no such thing as an intrusion in public. Public means public. With this insight, a great range of Arab behavior that had been puzzling, annoying, and sometimes even frightening began to make sense. I learned, for example, that if *A* is standing on a street corner and *B* wants his spot, *B* is within his rights if he does what he can to make *A* uncomfortable enough to move. In Beirut only the hardy sit in the last row in a movie theater, because there are usually standees who want seats and who push and shove and make such a nuisance that most people give up and leave. Seen in this light, the Arab who "intruded" on my space in the hotel lobby had apparently selected it for the very reason I had: it was a good place to watch two doors and the elevator. My show of annoyance, instead of driving him away, had only encouraged him. He thought he was about to get me to move.

Another silent source of friction between Americans and Arabs is in an area that Americans treat very informally—the manners and rights of the road. In general, in the United States we tend to defer to the vehicle that is bigger, more powerful, faster, and heavily laden. While a pedestrian walking along a road may feel annoyed he will not think it unusual to step aside for a fast-moving automobile. He knows that because he is moving he does not have the right to the space around him that he has when he is standing still (as I was in the hotel lobby). It appears that the reverse is true with the Arabs who apparently *take on rights to space as they move.* For someone else to move into a space an Arab is also moving into is a violation of his rights. It is infuriating to an Arab to have someone else cut in front of him on the highway. It is the American's cavalier treatment of moving space that makes the Arab call him aggressive and pushy.

Concepts of Privacy

The experience described above and many others suggested to me that Arabs might actually have a wholly contrasting set of assumptions concerning the body and the rights associated with it. Certainly the Arab tendency to shove and push each other in public and to feel and pinch women in public conveyances would not be tolerated by Westerners. It appeared to me that they must not have any concept of a private zone outside the body. This proved to be precisely the case.

In the Western world, the person is synonymous with an individual inside a skin. And in northern Europe generally, the skin and even the clothes may be inviolate. You need permission to touch either if you are a stranger. This rule applies in some parts of France, where the mere touching of another person during an argument used to be legally defined as assault. For the Arab the location of the person in relation to the body is quite different. The person exists somewhere down inside the body. The ego is not completely hidden, however, because it can be reached very easily with an insult. It is protected from touch but not from words. The dissociation of the body and the ego may explain why the public amputation of a thief's hand is tolerated as standard punishment in Saudi Arabia. It also sheds light on why an Arab employer living in a modern apartment can provide his servant with a room that is a box-like cubicle approximately 5 by 10 by 4 feet in size that is not only hung from the ceiling to conserve floor space but has an opening so that the servant can be spied on.

As one might suspect, deep orientations toward the self such as the one just described are also reflected in the language. This was brought to my attention one afternoon when an Arab colleague who is the author of an Arab-English dictionary arrived in my office and threw himself into a chair in a state of obvious exhaustion. When I asked him what had been going on, he said: "I have spent the entire afternoon trying to find the Arab equivalent of the English word 'rape.' There is no such word in Arabic. All my sources, both written and spoken, can come up with no more than an approximation, such as 'He took her against her will.' There is nothing in Arabic approaching your meaning as it is expressed in that one word."

Differing concepts of the placement of the ego in relation to the body are not easily grasped. Once an idea like this is accepted, however, it is possible to understand many other facets of Arab life that would otherwise be difficult to explain. One of these is the high population density of Arab cities like Cairo, Beirut, and Damascus. According to the animal studies described [elsewhere], the Arabs should be living in a perpetual behavioral sink. While it is probable that Arabs are suffering from population pressures, it is also just as possible that continued pressure from the desert has resulted in a cultural adaptation to high density which takes the form described above. Tucking the ego down inside the body shell not only would permit higher population densities but would explain why it is that Arab communications are stepped up as much as they are when compared to northern European communication patterns. Not only is the sheer noise level much higher, but the piercing look of the eyes, the touch

10

of the hands, and the mutual bathing in the warm moist breath during conversation represent stepped-up sensory inputs to a level which many Europeans find unbearably intense.

The Arab dream is for lots of space in the home, which unfortunately many Arabs cannot afford. Yet when he has space, it is very different from what one finds in most American homes. Arab spaces inside their upper middle-class homes are tremendous by our standards. They avoid partitions because Arabs *do not like to be alone*. The form of the home is such as to hold the family together inside a single protective shell, because Arabs are deeply involved with each other. Their personalities are intermingled and take nourishment from each other like the roots and soil. If one is not with people and actively involved in some way, one is deprived of life. An old Arab saying reflects this value: "Paradise without people should not be entered because it is Hell." Therefore, Arabs in the United States often feel socially and sensorially deprived and long to be back where there is human warmth and contact.

Since there is no physical privacy as we know it in the Arab family, not even a word for privacy, one could expect that the Arabs might use some other means to be alone. Their way to be alone is to stop talking. Like the English, an Arab who shuts himself off in this way is not indicating that anything is wrong or that he is withdrawing, only that he wants to be alone with his own thoughts or does not want to be intruded upon. One subject said that her father would come and go for days at a time without saying a word, and no one in the family thought anything of it. Yet for this very reason, an Arab exchange student visiting a Kansas farm failed to pick up the cue that his American hosts were mad at him when they gave him the "silent treatment." He only discovered something was wrong when they took him to town and tried forcibly to put him on a bus to Washington, D.C., the headquarters of the exchange program responsible for his presence in the U.S.

Arab Personal Distances

Like everyone else in the world, Arabs are unable to formulate specific rules for their informal behavior patterns. In fact, they often deny that there are any rules, and they are made anxious by suggestions that such is the case. Therefore, in order to determine how the Arab sets distances, I investigated the use of each sense separately. Gradually, definite and distinctive behavioral patterns began to emerge.

Olfaction occupies a prominent place in the Arab life. Not only is it one of the distance-setting mechanisms, but it is a vital part of a complex system of behavior. Arabs consistently breathe on people when they talk. However, this habit is more than a matter of different manners. To the Arab good smells are pleasing and a way of being involved with each other. To smell one's friend is not only nice but desirable, for to deny him your breath is to act ashamed. Americans, on the other hand, trained as they are not to breathe in people's faces, automatically communicate shame in trying to be polite. Who would expect that when our highest diplomats are putting on their best manners they are also communicating shame? Yet this is what occurs constantly, because diplomacy is not only "eyeball to eyeball" but breath to breath.

By stressing olfaction, Arabs do not try to eliminate all the body's   15
odors, only to enhance them and use them in building human relationships. Nor are they self-conscious about telling others when they don't like the way they smell. A man leaving his house in the morning may be told by his uncle, "Habib, your stomach is sour and your breath doesn't smell too good. Better not talk too close to people today." Smell is even considered in the choice of a mate. When couples are being matched for marriage, the man's go-between will sometimes ask to smell the girl, who may be turned down if she doesn't "smell nice." Arabs recognize that smell and disposition may be linked.

In a word, the olfactory boundary performs two roles in Arab life. It enfolds those who want to relate and separates those who don't. The Arab finds it essential to stay inside the olfactory zone as a means of keeping tab on changes in emotion. What is more, he may feel crowded as soon as he smells something unpleasant. While not much is known about "olfactory crowding," this may prove to be as significant as any other variable in the crowding complex because it is tied directly to the body chemistry and hence to the state of health and emotions. It is not surprising, therefore, that the olfactory boundary constitutes for the Arabs an informal distance-setting mechanism in contrast to the visual mechanisms of the Westerner.

Facing and Not Facing

One of my earliest discoveries in the field of intercultural communication was that the position of the bodies of people in conversation varies with the culture. Even so, it used to puzzle me that a special Arab friend seemed unable to walk and talk at the same time. After years in the United States, he could not bring himself to stroll along, facing forward while talking. Our progress would be arrested while he edged ahead, cutting slightly in front of me and turning sideways so we could see each other. Once in this position, he would stop. His behavior was explained when I learned that for the Arabs to view the other person peripherally is regarded as impolite, and to sit or stand back-to-back is considered very rude. You must be involved when interacting with Arabs who are friends.

One mistaken American notion is that Arabs conduct all conversations at close distance. This is not the case at all. On social occasions, they may sit on opposite sides of the room and talk across the room to each other. They are, however, apt to take offense when Americans use what are to them ambiguous distances, such as the four- to seven-foot social-consultative distance. They frequently complain that Americans are cold or aloof or "don't care." This was what an elderly Arab diplomat in an

American hospital thought when the American nurses used "professional" distance. He had the feeling that he was being ignored, that they might not take good care of him. Another Arab subject remarked, referring to American behavior, "What's the matter? Do I smell bad? Or are they afraid of me?"

Arabs who interact with Americans report experiencing a certain flatness traceable in part to a very different use of the eyes in private and in public as well as between friends and strangers. Even though it is rude for a guest to walk around the Arab home eying things, Arabs look at each other in ways which seem hostile or challenging to the American. One Arab informant said that he was in constant hot water with Americans because of the way he looked at them without the slightest intention of offending. In fact, he had on several occasions barely avoided fights with American men who apparently thought their masculinity was being challenged because of the way he was looking at them. As noted earlier, Arabs look each other in the eye when talking with an intensity that makes most Americans highly uncomfortable.

Involvement

As the reader must gather by now, Arabs are involved with each other on many different levels simultaneously. Privacy in a public place is foreign to them. Business transactions in the bazaar, for example, are not just between buyer and seller, but are participated in by everyone. Anyone who is standing around may join in. If a grownup sees a boy breaking a window, he must stop him even if he doesn't know him. Involvement and participation are expressed in other ways as well. If two men are fighting, the crowd must intervene. On the political level, *to fail to intervene* when trouble is brewing is to take sides, which is what our State Department always seems to be doing. Given the fact that few people in the world today are even remotely aware of the cultural mold that forms their thoughts, it is normal for Arabs to view *our* behavior as though it stemmed from *their* own hidden set of assumptions.

20

Feelings about Enclosed Spaces

In the course of my interviews with Arabs the term "tomb" kept cropping up in conjunction with enclosed space. In a word, Arabs don't mind being crowded by people but hate to be hemmed in by walls. They show a much greater overt sensitivity to architectural crowding than we do. Enclosed space must meet at least three requirements that I know of if it is to satisfy the Arabs: there must be plenty of unobstructed space in which to move around (possibly as much as a thousand square feet); very high ceilings—so high in fact that they do not normally impinge on the visual field; and, in addition, there must be an unobstructed view. It was spaces such as these in which the Americans referred to earlier felt so uncomfortable. One sees the Arab's need for a view expressed in many ways, even negatively, for to cut off a neighbor's view is one of the most effective ways of spiting him. In Beirut one can see what is known locally as the "spite house." It is nothing more than a thick, fourstory wall, built at the end of a long fight between neighbors, on a narrow strip of land, for the express purpose of denying a view of the Mediterranean to any house built on the land behind. According to one of my informants, there is also a house on a small plot of land between Beirut and Damascus which is completely surrounded by a neighbor's wall built high enough to cut off the view from all windows!

Boundaries

Proxemic patterns tell us other things about Arab culture. For example, the whole concept of the boundary as an abstraction is almost impossible to pin down. In one sense, there are no boundaries. "Edges" of towns, yes, but permanent boundaries out in the country (hidden lines), no. In the course of my work with Arab subjects I had a difficult time translating our concept of a boundary into terms which could be equated with theirs. In order to clarify the distinctions between the two very different definitions, I thought it might be helpful to pinpoint acts which constituted trespass. To date, I have been unable to discover anything even remotely resembling our own legal concept of trespass.

Arab behavior in regard to their own real estate is apparently an extension of, and therefore consistent with, their approach to the body. My subjects simply failed to respond whenever trespass was mentioned. They didn't seem to understand what I meant by this term. This may be explained by the fact that they organize relationships with each other according to closed social systems rather than spatially. For thousands of years Moslems, Marinites, Druses, and Jews have lived in their own villages, each with strong kin affiliations. Their hierarchy of loyalties is: first to one's self, then to kinsman, townsman, or tribesman, coreligionist and/or countryman. Anyone not in these categories is a stranger. Strangers and enemies are very closely linked, if not synonymous, in Arab thought. Trespass in this context is a matter of who you are, rather than a piece of land or a space with a boundary that can be denied to anyone and everyone, friend and foe alike.

In summary, proxemic patterns differ. By examining them it is possible to reveal hidden cultural frames that determine the structure of a given people's perceptual world. Perceiving the world differently leads to differential definitions of what constitutes crowded living, different interpersonal relations, and a different approach to both local and international politics.

 Topics for Critical Thinking and Writing

1. According to Hall, why do Arabs think Americans are pushy? And, again according to Hall, why do Arabs not consider themselves pushy?

2. Explain what Hall means by "cognitive world" (paragraph 2); by "ego" (paragraph 10); by "behavioral sink" (in the same paragraph). Then explain, for the benefit of someone who does not understand the terms, how you know what Hall means by each.

3. In paragraph 9 Hall points out that there is no Arabic equivalent of the English word *rape*. Can you provide an example of a similar gap in English or in another language? Does a cultural difference account for the linguistic difference?

4. In paragraph 3 Hall says of a rule that it "is all the more binding because we seldom think about it." Is this generally true of rules? What examples or counterexamples support your view?

Deborah Tannen

Deborah Tannen holds a Ph.D. in linguistics from the University of California, Berkeley, and is an associate professor of linguistics at Georgetown University. She is the author of scholarly articles and books as well as of popular articles in such magazines as New York *and* Vogue. *We reprint a chapter from one of her books,* That's Not What I Meant!

The Workings of Conversational Style

The Meaning is the Metamessage

You're sitting at a bar—or in a coffee shop or at a party—and suddenly you feel lonely. You wonder, "What do all these people find to talk about that's so important?" Usually the answer is, Nothing. Nothing that's so important. But people don't wait until they have something important to say in order to talk.

Very little of what is said is important for the information expressed in the words. But that doesn't mean that the talk isn't important. It's crucially important, as a way of showing that we are involved with each other, and how we feel about being involved. Our talk is saying something about our relationship.

Information conveyed by the meanings of words is the message. What is communicated about relationships—attitudes toward each other, the occasion, and what we are saying—is the metamessage. And it's metamessages that we react to most strongly. If someone says, "I'm not angry," and his jaw is set hard and his words seem to be squeezed out in a hiss, you won't believe the message that he's not angry; you'll believe the

---

metamessage conveyed by the way he said it—that he is. Comments like
"It's not what you said but the way you said it" or "Why did you say it
like that?" or "Obviously it's not nothing; something's wrong" are responses to metamessages of talk.

Many of us dismiss talk that does not convey important information
as worthless—meaningless small talk if it's a social setting or "empty
rhetoric" if it's public. Such admonitions as "Skip the small talk," "Get to
the point," or "Why don't you say what you mean?" may seem to be reasonable. But they are reasonable only if information is all that counts. This
attitude toward talk ignores the fact that people are emotionally involved
with each other and that talking is the major way we establish, maintain,
monitor, and adjust our relationships.

Whereas words convey information, how we speak those words—   5
how loud, how fast, with what intonation and emphasis—communicates
what we think we're doing when we speak: teasing, flirting, explaining,
or chastising; whether we're feeling friendly, angry, or quizzical; whether
we want to get closer or back off. In other words, how we say what we
say communicates social meanings.

Although we continually respond to social meaning in conversation,
we have a hard time talking about it because it does not reside in the dictionary definitions of words, and most of us have unwavering faith in the
gospel according to the dictionary. It is always difficult to talk about—
even to see or think about—forces and processes for which we have no
names, even if we feel their impact. Linguistics provides terms that describe the processes of communication and therefore make it possible to
see, talk, and think about them.

This chapter introduces some of the linguistic terms that give names
to concepts that are crucial for understanding communication—and
therefore relationships. In addition to the concept of metamessages—underlying it, in a sense—there are universal human needs that motivate
communication: the needs to be connected to others and to be left alone.
Trying to honor these conflicting needs puts us in a double bind. The linguistic concept of politeness accounts for the way we serve these needs
and react to the double bind—through metamessages in our talk.

Involvement and Independence

The philosopher Schopenhauer gave an often-quoted example of porcupines trying to get through a cold winter. They huddle together for
warmth, but their sharp quills prick each other, so they pull away. But
then they get cold. They have to keep adjusting their closeness and distance to keep from freezing and from getting pricked by their fellow porcupines—the source of both comfort and pain.

We need to get close to each other to have a sense of community, to
feel we're not alone in the world. But we need to keep our distance from
each other to preserve our independence, so others don't impose on or

engulf us. This duality reflects the human condition. We are individual and social creatures. We need other people to survive, but we want to survive as individuals.

Another way to look at this duality is that we are all the same—and all different. There is comfort in being understood and pain in the impossibility of being understood completely. But there is also comfort in being different—special and unique—and pain in being the same as everyone else, just another cog on the wheel.

Valuing Involvement and Independence

We all keep balancing the needs for involvement and independence, but individuals as well as cultures place different relative values on these needs and have different ways of expressing those values. America as a nation has glorified individuality, especially for men. This is in stark contrast to people in many parts of the world outside Western Europe, who more often glorify involvement in family and clan, for women and men.

The independent pioneers—and later our image of them—have served us well. The glorification of independence served the general progress of the nation as (traditionally male) individuals have been willing to leave their hometowns—the comfort of the familiar and familial—to find opportunity, get the best education, travel, work wherever they could find the best jobs or wherever their jobs sent them. The yearning for involvement enticed (traditionally female) individuals to join them.

The values of the group are reflected in personal values. Many Americans, especially (but not only) American men, place more emphasis on their need for independence and less on their need for social involvement. This often entails paying less attention to the metamessage level of talk—the level that comments on relationships—focusing instead on the information level. The attitude may go as far as the conviction that only the information level really counts—or is really there. It is then a logical conclusion that talk not rich in information should be dispensed with. Thus, many daughters and sons of all ages, calling their parents, find that their fathers want to exchange whatever information is needed and then hang up, but their mothers want to chat, to "keep in touch."

American men's information-focused approach to talk has shaped the American way of doing business. Most Americans think it's best to "get down to brass tacks" as soon as possible, and not "waste time" in small talk (social talk) or "beating around the bush." But this doesn't work very well in business dealings with Greek, Japanese, or Arab counterparts for whom "small talk" is necessary to establish the social relationship that must provide the foundation for conducting business.

Another expression of this difference—one that costs American tourists huge amounts of money—is our inability to understand the logic behind bargaining. If the African, Indian, Arab, South American, or

Mediterranean seller wants to sell a product, and the tourist wants to buy it, why not set a fair price and let the sale proceed? Because the sale is only one part of the interaction. Just as important, if not more so, is the interaction that goes on during the bargaining: an artful way for buyer and seller to reaffirm their recognition that they're dealing with—and that they are—humans, not machines.

Believing that only the information level of communication is important and real also lets men down when it comes to maintaining personal relationships. From day to day, there often isn't any significant news to talk about. Women are negatively stereotyped as frivolously talking at length without conveying significant information. Yet their ability to keep talking to each other makes it possible for them to maintain close friendships. *Washington Post* columnist Richard Cohen observed that he and the other men he knows don't really have friends in the sense that women have them. This may be at least partly because they don't talk to each other if they can't think of some substantive topic to talk about. As a result, many men find themselves without personal contacts when they retire.

The Double Bind

No matter what relative value we place on involvement and independence, and how we express these values, people, like porcupines, are always balancing the conflicting needs for both. But the porcupine metaphor is a little misleading because it suggests a sequence: alternately drawing close and pulling back. Our needs for involvement and independence—to be connected and to be separate—are not sequential but simultaneous. We must serve both needs at once in all we say.

And that is why we find ourselves in a double bind. Anything we say to show we're involved with others is in itself a threat to our (and their) individuality. And anything we say to show we're keeping our distance from others is in itself a threat to our (and their) need for involvement. It's not just a conflict—feeling torn between two alternatives—or ambivalence—feeling two ways about one thing. It's a double bind because whatever we do to serve one need necessarily violates the other. And we can't step out of the circle. If we try to withdraw by not communicating, we hit the force field of our need for involvement and are hurled back in.

Because of this double bind, communication will never be perfect; we cannot reach stasis. We have no choice but to keep trying to balance independence and involvement, freedom and safety, the familiar and the strange—continually making adjustments as we list to one side or the other. The way we make these adjustments in our talk can be understood as politeness phenomena.

Information and Politeness in Talk

A language philosopher, H. P. Grice, codified the rules by which conversation would be constructed if information were its only point: 20

Say as much as necessary and no more.

Tell the truth.

Be relevant.

Be clear.

[handwritten: philosopher (non-important)]

These make perfect sense—until we start to listen to and think about real conversations. For one thing, all the seeming absolutes underlying these injunctions are really relative. How much is necessary? Which truth? What is relevant? What is clear?

But even if we could agree on these values, we wouldn't want simply to blurt out what we mean, because we're juggling the needs for involvement and independence. If what we mean shows involvement, we want to temper it to show we're not imposing. If what we mean shows distance, we want to temper it with involvement to show we're not rejecting. If we state what we want to believe, others may not agree or may not want the same thing, so our statement could introduce disharmony; therefore we prefer to get an idea of what others want or think, or how they feel about what we want or think, before we commit ourselves to— maybe even before we make up our minds about—what we mean.

This broad concept of the social goals we serve when we talk is called "politeness" by linguists and anthropologists—not the pinky-in-the-air idea of politeness, but a deeper sense of trying to take into account the effect of what we say on other people.

Linguist Robin Lakoff devised another set of rules that describe the motivations behind politeness—that is, how we adjust what we say to take into account its effects on others. Here they are as Lakoff presents them:

1. Don't impose; keep your distance.
2. Give options; let the other person have a say.
3. Be friendly; maintain camaraderie.

[handwritten: Lakoff (not Tannen)]

Following Rule 3, Be friendly, makes others comfortable by serving their need for involvement. Following Rule 1, Don't impose, makes others comfortable by serving their need for independence. Rule 2, Give options, falls between Rules 1 and 3. People differ with respect to which rules they tend to apply, and when, and how.

To see how these rules work, let's consider a fairly trivial but common conversation. If you offer me something to drink, I may say, "No, thanks," even though I am thirsty. In some societies this is expected; you insist, and I give in after about the third offer. This is polite in the sense of Rule 1, Don't impose. If you expect this form of politeness and I accept on the first offer, you will think I'm too forward—or dying of thirst. If you don't expect this form of politeness, and I use it, you will take my refusal at face value—and I might indeed die of thirst while waiting for you to ask again.

I may also say, in response to your offer, "I'll have whatever you're having." This is polite in the sense of Rule 2, Give options: I'm letting you decide what to give me. If I do this, but you expect me to refuse the first offer, you may still think I'm pushy. But if you expect Rule 3, Be friendly, you may think me wishy-washy. Don't I know what I want?

Exercising Rule 3-style politeness, Be friendly, I might respond to your offer of something to drink by saying, "Yes, thanks, some apple juice, please." In fact, if this is my style of politeness, I might not wait for you to offer at all, but ask right off, "Have you got anything to drink?," or even head straight for your kitchen, throw open the refrigerator door, and call out, "Got any juice?"

If you and I both feel this is appropriate, my doing it will reinforce our rapport because we both subscribe to the rule of breaking rules; not having to follow the more formal rule sends a metamessage: "We are such good friends, we don't have to stand on ceremony." But if you don't subscribe to this brand of politeness, or don't want to get that chummy with me, you will be offended by my way of being friendly. If we have only recently met, that could be the beginning of the end of our friendship.

Of course, these aren't actually rules, but senses we have of the "natural" way to speak. We don't think of ourselves as following rules, or even (except in formal situations) of being polite. We simply talk in ways that seem obviously appropriate at the time they pop out of our mouths—seemingly self-evident ways of being a good person.

Yet our use of these "rules" is not unconscious. If asked about why we said one thing or another in this way or that, we are likely to explain that we spoke the way we did "to be nice" or "friendly" or "considerate." These are commonsense terms for what linguists refer to, collectively, as politeness—ways of taking into account the effect on others of what we say.

The rules, or senses, of politeness are not mutually exclusive. We don't choose one and ignore the others. Rather we balance them all to be appropriately friendly without imposing, to keep appropriate distance without appearing aloof.

Negotiating the offer of a drink is a fairly trivial matter, though the importance of such fleeting conversations should not be underestimated. The way we talk in countless such daily encounters is part of what constitutes our image of ourselves, and it is on the basis of such encounters that we form our impressions of each other. They have a powerful cumulative effect on our personal and interactive lives.

Furthermore, the process of balancing these conflicting senses of politeness—serving involvement and independence—is the basis for the most consequential of interactions as well as the most trivial. Let's consider the linguistic means we have of serving these needs—and their inherent indeterminacy, which means they can easily let us down.

The Two-Edged Sword of Politeness

Sue was planning to visit Amy in a distant city, but shortly before she was supposed to arrive, Sue called and canceled. Although Amy felt disappointed, she tried to be understanding. Being polite by not imposing, and respecting Sue's need for independence, Amy said it was really okay if Sue didn't come. Sue was very depressed at that time, and she got more depressed. She took Amy's considerateness—a sign of caring, respecting Sue's independence—as indifference—not caring at all, a lack of involvement. Amy later felt partly responsible for Sue's depression because she hadn't insisted that Sue visit. This confusion was easy to fall into and hard to climb out of because ways of showing caring and indifference are inherently ambiguous.

You can be nice to some one either by showing your involvement or by not imposing. And you can be mean by refusing to show involvement—cutting her off—or by imposing—being "inconsiderate." You can show someone you're angry by shouting at her—imposing—or refusing to talk to her at all: the silent activity called snubbing.

You can be kind by saying something or by saying nothing. For example, if someone has suffered a misfortune—failed an exam, lost a job, or contracted a disease—you may show sympathy by expressing your concern in words or by deliberately not mentioning it to avoid causing pain by bringing it up. If everyone takes the latter approach, silence becomes a chamber in which the ill, the bereaved, and the unemployed are isolated.

If you choose to avoid mentioning a misfortune, you run the risk of seeming to have forgotten, or of not caring. You may try to circumvent that interpretation by casting a knowing glance, making an indirect reference, or softening the impact with euphemisms ("your situation"), hedges and hesitations ("your ... um ... well ... er ... you know"), or apologies ("I hope you don't mind my mentioning this"). But meaningful glances and verbal hedging can themselves offend by sending the metamessage "This is too terrible to mention" or "Your condition is shameful." A person thus shielded may feel like shouting, "Why don't you just say it!?"

An American couple visited the husband's brother in Germany, where he was living with a German girlfriend. One evening during dinner, the girlfriend asked the brother where he had taken his American guests that day. Upon hearing that he had taken them to the concentration camp at Dachau, she exclaimed in revulsion that that was an awful place to take them; why would he do such a stupid thing? The brother cut off her exclamations by whispering to her while glancing at the American woman. His girlfriend immediately stopped complaining and

35

nodded in understanding, also casting glances at the American, who was not appreciative of their discretion. Instead, she was offended by the assumption that being Jewish is cause for whispering and furtive glances.

Any attempt to soften the impact of what is said can have the opposite effect. For example, a writer recalled the impression that a colleague had written something extremely critical about the manuscript of her book. Preparing to revise the manuscript, she returned to his comments and was surprised to see that the criticism was very mild indeed. The guilty word was the one that preceded the comment, not the comment itself. By beginning the sentence with "Frankly," her colleague sent a metamessage: "Steel yourself. This is going to hurt a lot."

Such layers of meaning are always at work in conversation; anything you say or don't say sends metamessages that become part of the meaning of the conversation.

Mixed Metamessages at Home

Parental love puts relative emphasis on involvement, but as children grow up, most parents give more and more signs of love by respecting their independence. Usually this comes too late for the children's tastes. The teenager who resents being told to put on a sweater or eat breakfast interprets the parent's sign of involvement as an imposition. Although this isn't in the message, the teenager hears a metamessage to the effect "You're still a child who needs to be told how to take care of yourself." 40

Partners in intimate relationships often differ about how they balance involvement and independence. There are those who show love by making sure the other eats right, dresses warmly, or doesn't drive alone at night. There are others who feel this is imposing and treating them like children. And there are those who feel that their partners don't care about them because they aren't concerned with what they eat, wear, or do. What may be meant as a show of respect for their independence is taken as lack of involvement—which it also might be.

Maxwell wants to be left alone, and Samantha wants attention. So she gives him attention, and he leaves her alone. The adage "Do unto others as you would have others do unto you" may be the source of a lot of anguish and misunderstanding if the doer and the done unto have different styles.

Samantha and Maxwell might feel differently if the other acted differently. He may want to be left alone precisely because she gives him so much attention, and she may want attention precisely because he leaves her alone. With a doting spouse she might find herself craving to be left alone, and with an independent spouse, he might find himself craving attention. It's important to remember that others' ways of talking to you are partly a reaction to your style, just as your style with them is partly a reaction to their style—with you.

The ways we show our involvement and considerateness in talk seem self-evidently appropriate. And in interpreting what others say, we assume they mean what we would mean if we said the same thing in the same way. If we don't think about differences in conversational style, we see no reason to question this. Nor do we question whether what we perceive as considerate or inconsiderate, loving or not, was *intended* to be so.

In trying to come to an understanding with someone who has misinterpreted our intentions, we often end up in a deadlock, reduced to childlike insistence:

"You said so."

"I said no such thing!"

"You did! I heard you!"

"Don't tell me what I said."

In fact, both parties may be sincere—and both may be right. He recalls what he meant, and she recalls what she heard. But what he intended was not what she understood—which was what she would have meant if she had said what he said in the way he said it.

These paradoxical metamessages are recursive and potentially confusing in all conversations. In a series of conversations between the same people, each encounter bears the burdens as well as the fruits of earlier ones. The fruits of ongoing relationships are an ever-increasing sense of understanding based on less and less talk. This is one of the great joys of intimate conversations. But the burdens include the incremental confusion and disappointment of past misunderstandings, and hardening conviction of the other's irrationality or ill will.

The benefits of repeated communication need no explanation; all our conventional wisdom about "getting to know each other," "working it out," and "speaking the same language" gives us ways to talk about and understand that happy situation. But we need some help—and some terms and concepts—to understand why communicating over time doesn't always result in understanding each other better, and why some times it begins to seem that one or the other is speaking in tongues.

Mixed Metamessages across Cultures

The danger of misinterpretation is greatest, of course, among speakers who actually speak different native tongues, or come from different cultural backgrounds, because cultural difference necessarily implies different assumptions about natural and obvious ways to be polite.

Anthropologist Thomas Kochman gives the example of a white office worker who appeared with a bandaged arm and felt rejected because her black fellow worker didn't mention it. The (doubly) wounded worker assumed that her silent colleague didn't notice or didn't care. But the co-worker was purposely not calling attention to something her colleague might not want to talk about. She let her decide whether or not to mention it: being considerate by not imposing. Kochman says, based on his research, that these differences reflect recognizable black and white styles.

An American woman visiting England was repeatedly offended—even, on bad days, enraged—when Britishers ignored her in settings in which she thought they should pay attention. For example, she was sitting at a booth in a railroad-station cafeteria. A couple began to settle into the opposite seat in the same booth. They unloaded their luggage; they laid their coats on the seat; he asked what she would like to eat and went off to get it; she slid into the booth facing the American. And throughout all this, they showed no sign of having noticed that someone was already sitting in the booth.

When the British woman lit up a cigarette, the American had a concrete object for her anger. She began ostentatiously looking around for another table to move to. Of course there was none; that's why the British couple had sat in her booth in the first place. The smoker immediately crushed out her cigarette and apologized. This showed that she had noticed that someone else was sitting in the booth, and that she was not inclined to disturb her. But then she went back to pretending the American wasn't there, a ruse in which her husband collaborated when he returned with their food and they ate it.

To the American, politeness requires talk between strangers forced to share a booth in a cafeteria, if only a fleeting "Do you mind if I sit down?" or a conventional "Is anyone sitting here?" even if it's obvious no one is. The omission of such talk seemed to her like dreadful rudeness. The American couldn't see that another system of politeness was at work. (She could see nothing but red.) By not acknowledging her presence, the British couple freed her from the obligation to acknowledge theirs. The American expected a show of involvement; they were being polite by not imposing.

An American man who had lived for years in Japan explained a similar politeness ethic. He lived, as many Japanese do, in frightfully close quarters—a tiny room separated from neighboring rooms by paper-thin walls. In this case the walls were literally made of paper. In order to preserve privacy in this most unprivate situation, his Japanese neighbors simply acted as if no one else lived there. They never showed signs of having overheard conversations, and if, while walking down the hall, they caught a neighbor with the door open, they steadfastly glued their gaze ahead as if they were alone in a desert. The American confessed to feeling what I believe most Americans would feel if a next-door neighbor passed within a few feet without acknowledging their presence—snubbed. But he realized that the intention was not rudeness by omitting to show involvement, but politeness by not imposing.

The fate of the earth depends on cross-cultural communication. Nations must reach agreements, and agreements are made by individual representatives of nations sitting down and talking to each other—public analogues of private conversations. The processes are the same, and so are the pitfalls. Only the possible consequences are more extreme.

We Need the Eggs

Despite the fact that talking to each other frequently fails to yield the understanding we seek, we keep at it, just as nations keep trying to negotiate and reach agreement. Woody Allen knows why, and tells, in his film *Annie Hall*, which ends with a joke that is heard in a voice-over: 55

> This guy goes to a psychiatrist and says, "Doc my brother's crazy. He thinks he's a chicken." And the doctor says, "Well, why don't you turn him in?" And the guy says, "I would, but I need the eggs." Well, I guess that's pretty much how I feel about relationships.

Even though intimate as well as fleeting conversations don't yield the perfect communication we crave—and we can see from past experience and from the analysis presented here that they can't—we still keep hoping and trying because we need the eggs of involvement and independence. The communication chicken can't give us these golden eggs because of the double bind: Closeness threatens our lives as individuals, and our real differences as individuals threaten our needs to be connected to other people.

But because we can't step out of the situation—the human situation—we keep trying to balance these needs. We do it by not saying exactly what we mean in our messages, while at the same time negotiating what we mean in metamessages. Metamessages depend for their meaning on subtle linguistic signals and devices.

Notes

[The page references have been changed to accord with pages in *The Little, Brown Reader*, 9th ed., and the bibliographic citations have been amplified where necessary.]

pp. 649, 650. The terms *metamessage* and *double bind* are found in Gregory Bateson, *Steps to an Ecology of Mind* (1972). For Bateson, a double bind entailed contradictory orders at different levels: the message and metamessage conflict. I use the term, as do other linguists (for example, Scollon, "The Rhythmic Integration of Ordinary Talk," in *Analyzing Discourse: Text and Talk*, Deborah Tannen, ed. [1981]), simply to describe the state of receiving contradictory orders without being able to step out of the situation.

p. 650. I am grateful to Pamela Gerloff for bringing to my attention Bettelheim's reference (in *Surviving* [1979]) to Schopenhauer's porcupine metaphor.

p. 651. Mary Catherine Bateson, *With a Daughter's Eye: A Memoir of Margaret Mead and Gregory Bateson* (1984), discusses G. Bateson's idea that living systems (biological processes as well as human interaction) never achieve a static state of balance, but achieve balance only as a series of adjustments within a range.

p. 652. For his conversational maxims see H. P. Grice, "Logic and Conservation," rptd. in *Syntax and Semantics*, vol. 3, *Speech Acts*, eds. Peter Cole and Jerry Morgan (1975).

p. 653. Lakoff's original statement of the rules of politeness is in Lakoff, "The Logic of Politeness, or Minding Your P's and Q's," *Papers from the Ninth Regional Meeting of the Chicago Linguistics Society* (1973). She also presents this system in the context of discussing male/female differences (Lakoff, *Language and Woman's Place* [1975]). Penelope Brown and Stephen Levinson, "Universals in Language Usage: Politeness Phenomena," in *Questions and Politeness*, ed. Esther Goody (1978), provide an extended and formalized discussion of politeness phenomena.

p. 657. Thomas Kochman presents an extended analysis of *Black and White Styles in Conflict* (1981).

p. 659. The quotation from *Annie Hall* is taken from the screenplay by Woody Allen and Marshall Brickman in *Four Films of Woody Allen* (NY: Random House, 1982).

 ## Topics for Critical Thinking and Writing

1. Tannen begins this chapter using the second person ("You're sitting at a bar—or in a coffee shop or at a party—and suddenly you feel lonely. You wonder . . ."), a usage often prohibited in high school English classes and textbooks. How well do you think it works here? Try to make the same point without using the second person. *Have* you made the same point? What has been left out?

2. How does Tannen define *metamessages*? The word will not appear in most dictionaries, but we can probably guess what it means, even without Tannen's explanation. What does *meta* usually mean as a prefix to a word? (Most dictionaries do define *meta* as a prefix.)

3. Why, according to Tannen, has the word *metamessages* been invented? What other linguistic terms does she introduce, and what do they mean?

4. What is the example of porcupines introduced to explain? Why do you suppose it is easier to remember the example than to remember what it explains?

5. In paragraph 11 Tannen says "individuals as well as cultures place different relative values" on the "needs for involvement and independence." In the same paragraph and in the next several paragraphs, she says that Americans

glorify independence and she offers an historical explanation of the glorification of independence and other values that flow from it. What does she assume here about "Americans," American culture, and American history?

6. In paragraph 16 Tannen contrasts women talking to women and men talking to men. What does she *assume* here, in addition to what she says, about the differences? On the whole, do you agree with her about women's talk and men's talk?

7. In paragraphs 47–53 Tannen talks about misinterpretations between persons of different cultural backgrounds. If possible, provide an example from your own experience.

8. Write an essay or a journal entry analyzing an encounter that illustrates the "double bind," a "politeness phenomenon," or "mixed metamessages," as Tannen defines these terms and situations. Or summarize this chapter in 750 words.

Steven Pinker

Steven Pinker, professor of brain and cognitive sciences at the Massachusetts Institute of Technology, is the author of The Language Instinct *(1994). We reprint an essay that originally appeared in* The New York Times, *5 April 1994.*

The Game of the Name

The *Los Angeles Times*'s new "Guidelines on Racial and Ethnic Identification," for its writers and editors, bans or restricts some 150 words and phrases such as "birth defect," "Chinese fire drill," "crazy," "dark continent," "stepchild," "WASP" and "to welsh."

Defying such politically correct sensibilities, *The Economist* allows the use of variants of "he" for both sexes (as in "everyone should watch his language"), and "crippled" for disabled people.

One side says that language insidiously shapes attitudes and that vigilance against subtle offense is necessary to eliminate prejudice. The other bristles at legislating language, seeing a corrosion of clarity and expressiveness at best, and thought control at worst, changing the way reporters render events and opinions.

Both arguments make assumptions about language and how it relates to thoughts and attitudes—a connection first made in 1946 by George Orwell in his essay "Politics and the English Language," which suggested that euphemisms, clichés and vague writing could be used to reinforce orthodoxy and defend the indefensible. We understand language and

Steven Pinker, "The Game of the Name." Originally published in *The New York Times,* 4/5/94. Reprinted by permission.

thought better than we did in Orwell's time, and our discoveries offer insights about the P.C. controversy.

First, words are not thoughts. Despite the appeal of the theory that   5
language determines thought, no cognitive scientist believes it. People coin new words, grapple for *le mot juste*[1], translate from other languages and ridicule or defend P.C. terms. None of this would be possible if the ideas expressed by words were identical to the words themselves. This should alleviate anxiety on both sides, reminding us that we are talking about style manuals, not brain programming.

Second, words are arbitrary. The word "duck" does not look, walk or quack like a duck, but we all know it means duck because we have memorized an arbitrary association between a sound and a meaning.

Some words can be built out of smaller pieces and their meanings can be discerned by examining how the pieces are arranged (a dishwasher washes dishes), but even complex words turn opaque, and people become oblivious to the logic of their derivation, memorizing them as arbitrary symbols. (Who last thought of "breakfast" as "breaking a fast"?)

The Los Angeles Times style manual seems to assume that readers are reflexive etymologists; for it bans "invalid" (literally "not valid" and thus an offensive reference to a disabled person), "New World" (ignores the indigenous cultures that preceded Columbus's voyage) and "Dutch treat" (offensive, presumably, to Netherlanders). But I doubt if Americans associate the dozen-odd idioms in which Dutch means "ersatz" ("Dutch uncle," "Dutch oven") with the Dutch; presumably, the sting has worn off in the three centuries since the English coined such terms to tweak their naval rivals.

The bewildering feature of political correctness is the mandated replacement of formerly unexceptionable terms by new ones: "Negro" by "black" by "African-American"; "Spanish-American" by "Hispanic" by "Latino"; "slum" by "ghetto" by "inner city" by, according to *The Los Angeles Times*, "slum" again.

How should a thoughtful person react to this carousel? Respect   10
means treating people as they wish to be treated, beginning with names. That is why there is a clear need for guidelines. One wonders, though, why *The Los Angeles Times*'s style panel apparently did not consult those it defends. Many deaf people insist on being called "deaf," not "individuals who cannot hear," and as one who was taught to revere the Wailing Wall, I was surprised to learn that the term is "highly offensive" rather than merely obsolete.

But if users of new ethnic terms have responsibilities, so do those who promulgate the terms. What are their motives? What are the effects?

Occasionally, neologisms are defended with some semantic rationale: "black" emphasized parity with the corresponding "white." "Native American" reminds us of who was here first and eschews the

---

[1]*Le mot juste,* the most suitable word.

inaccurate European label "Indian." But when new terms replace ones that had been justified in their own day with equal moral force and when offensive and sanctioned terms are near-synonyms—"colored people," "people of color"; "Afro-American," "African-American"; Negro (Spanish for "black"), "black"—something else must be driving the process.

To a linguist, the phenomenon is familiar: the euphemism treadmill. People invent new "polite" words to refer to emotionally laden or distasteful things, but the euphemism becomes tainted by association and the new one that must be found acquires its own negative connotations.

"Water closet" becomes "toilet" (originally a term for any body care, as in "toilet kit"), which becomes "bathroom," which becomes "rest room," which becomes "lavatory." "Garbage collection" turns into "sanitation," which turns into "environmental services."

The euphemism treadmill shows that concepts, not words, are in charge; give a concept a new name, and the name becomes colored by the concept; the concept does not become freshened by the name. (We will know we have achieved equality and mutual respect when names for minorities stay put.)   15

People learn a word by witnessing other people using it, so when they use a word, they provide a history of their reading and listening. Using the latest term for a minority often shows not sensitivity but subscribing to the right magazines or going to the right cocktail parties.

Shifts in terms have an unfortunate side effect. Many people who don't have a drop of malice or prejudice but happen to be older or distant from university, media and government spheres find themselves tainted as bigots for innocently using passé terms like "Oriental" or "crippled." Arbiters of the changing linguistic fashions must ask themselves whether this stigmatization is really what they set out to accomplish.

Topic for Critical Thinking and Discussion

In paragraph 8 Pinker expresses the opinion that because three centuries have passed since the English used the term *Dutch* to refer to something that is not quite the real thing, the term is no longer offensive. Do you suppose that an American of Dutch ancestry is bothered by such a term as *Dutch oven* (a heavy pot with a cover)? In any case, does the length of time since a phrase was originated have anything to do with whether the phrase is offensive today? Explain.

James B. Twitchell

James B. Twitchell teaches English and advertising at the University of Florida. He is the author of several books, including Carnival Culture: The Trashing of Taste in America (1992) and Twenty Ads That Shook the World: The Century's Most Groundbreaking Advertising and How It Changed Us All (2000). The following essay comes from Twenty Ads. We printed another selection from Twenty Ads earlier in The Little, Brown Reader on page 96, in our chapter on "Reading and Writing about Pictures."

The Marlboro Man:
The Perfect Campaign

Although advertising agencies love giving themselves prizes, there has been no award for the perfect campaign. If there were, Marlboro would win. Suffice it to say that this brand went from selling less than one quarter of one percent of the American market in the early 1950s to being the most popular in the entire world in just twenty years. Every fourth cigarette smoked is a Marlboro. Leo Burnett's brilliant campaign made Marlboro the most valuable brand in the world.

First, let's dispense with the politics of the product. We all know that cigarettes are the most dangerous legal product in the world. They kill more people each year than do guns. And yes, it is dreadful that the myth of independence is used to sell addiction. But never forget as well that it is exactly this danger that animates the Marlboro Man. He came into being just as smoking became problematic and, ironically, as long as anxiety exists, so will he.

And, second, cigarettes, like domestic beer and bottled water, build deep affiliations that have absolutely nothing to do with taste. As David Ogilvy said, "Give people a taste of Old Crow and *tell* them it's Old Crow. Then give them another taste of Old Crow, *but tell them it's Jack Daniels*. Ask them which they prefer. They'll think the two drinks are quite different. *They are tasting images*" (Ogilvy 1985, 87).

In fact, it was the cigarette companies that found this out first. In the 1920s they blindfolded brand-dedicated smokers and put them into dark rooms. Then they gave them Luckies, Pall Malls, Chesterfields, and Camels, as well as European smokes, and asked the smokers to identify "their own brand"—the one they were sure they knew. By now we all know the results. Taste has basically little or nothing to do with why people choose specific brands of cigarettes.

Just as we drink the label, we smoke the advertising. So what's so   5
smokable, so tasty, about this ad?

First, everything fits around the dominant image. The heading and the logotype fall naturally in place. Product name mediates between visual and verbal. Let's start with the name, *Marlboro*. Like so many cigarette brand names, it is English and elegant and, like its counterpart Winston, deceptively vague. Like the joke about how there's gotta be a pony in there somewhere, there's gotta be prestige in here somewhere. (Oddly enough, Marlboro was first created in Victorian England, then transported to the States as a cigarette for women.) The ersatz PM crest at the apex of the "red roof" chevron on the package hints of a bloodline, and the Latin motto "Veni, Vidi, Vici"[1] (!) conveys ancient warrior strength. Clearly, the power is now both in the pack and in the buckaroo.

The buckaroo is, of course, the eponymous Marlboro Man. He is what we have for royalty, distilled manhood. (Alas, the Winston man barely exists. What little of him there is is opinionated, urbane, self-assured—and needs to tell you so.) The Marlboro Man needs to tell you nothing. He carries no scepter, no gun. He never even speaks. Doesn't need to. The difference between Marlboro and Winston is the difference between myth and reality. Winston needed to break the rules publicly to be independent ("Winston tastes good *like* a cigarette should"); the Marlboro Man has already been there, done that. Little wonder the Viceroy man ("a thinking man's filter, a smoking man's taste") couldn't even make the cut.

Generating prestige *and* independence is a crucial aspect of cigarette selling. If you are targeting those who are just entering the consumption community, and if the act of consumption is dangerous, then you do not need to stress rebellion—that's a given. What you need to announce is initiation into the pack.

When R.J. Reynolds tested Marlboro on focus groups, they found that it was not rugged machismo that was alluring to young Marlboro smokers, but separation from restraints (the tattoo) *and* a sense of belonging (Marlboro Country). This "secret" RJR report, now available on the World Wide Web, is one reason why the "I'd walk a mile for a Camel" man was subsumed into the more personable, intelligent, and independent "Cool Joe" Camel.

Let's face it, the Camel man was downright stupid. In the most   10
repeated of his ill-fated "walk a mile" ads he is shown carrying a tire (instead of rolling it) across the desert (with no canteen), wearing no shade-providing hat. That he seemingly forgot the spare tire is as stupid as his choosing to smoke. Little wonder Cool Joe pushed him aside. A camel seems intelligent in comparison.

The Marlboro Man's transformation was less traumatic, but no less meaningful. In fact, it is a reversal of the most popular tabloid story of the 1950s. It was to be, as David Ogilvy would say, one of the "riskiest decisions ever made" and one "which few advertisers would take." Here's the cultural context on a thumbnail and what Philip Morris did about it:

[1]**Veni, Vidi, Vici** Latin: I came, I saw, I conquered (Julius Caesar's announcement of a victory)

On February 13, 1953, George Jorgenson went to Denmark and returned as Christine. The idea that one could change one's sex was profoundly unsettling to American culture. Once back at home, she uttered the perhaps apocryphal testament to his journey: "Men are wary of me and I'm wary of the ones who aren't."

At almost the same time, another repositioning was occurring. Now, as any modern ten-year-old can tell you, objects have sexual characteristics, too. Philip Morris had a female cigarette, Marlboro, that wouldn't sell. So they sent her up to Chicago to be regendered by Leo Burnett. Miss Marlboro was a "sissy smoke ... a tea room smoke," Burnett said. Although she had been in and out of production for most of the century, in her most recent incarnation she had a red filter tip (called the "beauty tip," to hide lipstick stains) and a long-running theme: "Mild as May." Men wouldn't touch her, nor would many women.

In December 1954, Burnett took Miss Marlboro out to his gentleman's farm south of Chicago and invited some of his agency cohorts over to brainstorm. Something had to be done to put some hair on her chest, to change her out of pinafores and into cowboy chaps, anything to get her out of the suffocating tea room.

"What is the most masculine figure in America?" Burnett asked. "Cab driver, sailor, marine, pilot, race car driver" came the replies. Then someone simply said, "Cowboy." Bingo! Copywriter Draper Daniels filled in the blank: this smoke "Delivers the Goods on Flavor." 15

But these admen were not thinking of a real cowboy, not some dirty, spitting, toothless, smelly wrangler. They were city boys who knew cowboys in bronzes and oils by Frederic Remington, or in oils and watercolors by Charles Russell, or in the purple prose of Owen Wister's *The Virginian* or in the pulp of Zane Grey's countless novels. Philip Morris and Leo Burnett now love to tell you that the Marlboro Man was always a "real cowboy." Just don't remind them that almost half of the real cowpunchers were black or Mexican.

No matter, Leo Burnett had just the image in mind. He remembered seeing one C. H. Long, a thirty-nine-year-old foreman at the JA Ranch in the Texas panhandle, a place described as "320,000 acres of nothing much," who had been heroically photographed by Leonard McCombe for a cover of *Life* magazine in 1949. In other words, this Marlboro cowboy was a real/reel cowboy, something like what Matt Dillon, played by James Arness, was on television. A slightly roughed-up, *High Noon* Gary Cooper, a lite-spaghetti Clint Eastwood.

To get to this image, the Leo Burnett Company tried out all manner of windblown wranglers, some professional models, some not. Then, in 1963, just as the health concerns about lung cancer really took hold, they discovered Carl "Big-un" Bradley at the 6666 Ranch in Guthrie, Texas. Carl was the first real cowboy they used, and from then on the Marlboro Men were honest-to-God cowboys, rodeo riders, and stuntmen.

One look at him and you know: no Ralph Lauren jeans, no 401(k) plans, no wine spritzers, nothing with little ducks all over it, just independence, pure and simple. He doesn't concern himself with the Surgeon General. He's his own sheriff. To make sure he stayed that way, all background was airbrushed out. Later he got a grubstake in Marlboro Country.

Even today the Philip Morris Company receives letters from all over the world, mostly at the beginning of the summer, from travelers wishing to know how to get to Marlboro Country.   20

But there's more to the ad than the free-ranging cowboy. That package with the insignia, built truck-tough as a flip-top *box*, was a badge. With its hearty red, white, and black lettering, the smoker pinned it to his chest on the average of twenty-three times a day. This *vade mecum*[2] of a package was designed by Frank Gianninoto and carefully tested through consumer surveys by Elmo Roper & Associates and the Color Research Institute. Now the *Veni, Vidi, Vici* starts making sense. With this package you are the decorated conqueror. You burn bridges, bust broncos, confront stuff like lung cancer.

Sure, the girlie filter was there for the women (incidentally, the famous Marlboro red came from the lipstick red of the original "beauty filter"), but it was battled by the box, the medallion—the manliness of it all.

Should you still not be convinced, there was always the brand, the literal brand—the tattoo. Remember, this was the 1950s, when tattoos were not a fashion accessory, but an unambiguous sign of antisocial "otherness." But this brand was not on the biceps to signify Charles Atlas manliness; rather it was on the back of the smoking hand, or on the wrist. A strange place for a tattoo, to be sure, but appropriate.

Although research departments may cringe to hear this, the tattoo was not the result of motivational research showing that the image would be super macho. Leo Burnett supposedly thought the tattoo would "say to many men that here is a successful man who used to work with his hands," while "to many women, we believe it will suggest a romantic past."

But there is another story that also may be true. Alas, it doesn't emphasize virility and romance but the bugaboo of interpretation, namely, happenstance. It seems someone at the agency had scribbled on the hand of the *Life* magazine cowboy that there was no copyright clearance for this particular image. The agency sent this image in a paste-up to Philip Morris and then made another version from another cowboy photo to avoid copyright problems. It, too, went to the client. Back came the reaction: "Where's the tattoo on the second cowboy?" Perplexed agency people dug up the original photo and saw the warning scribbled across the wrist (McGuire 1989, 23).   25

No matter what the story, the tattoo stuck, not because of any massive testing but because everyone knew the branding itself was compelling. You are what you smoke.

---

[2]**vade mecum** Latin: "come with me"

When a campaign "works," every part seems compelling. In fact, in great ads, as in great works of art, the sum of the parts is always more than the whole. The visual and verbal rhetoric is so strong that they seem to have always been in place. They seem indestructible. In truth, however, often the greatest act of creativity is knowing when to leave well enough alone. "I have learned that any fool can write a bad ad," Burnett says in one of his pithy *100 Leo's*, "but that it takes a real genius to keep his hands off a good one" (Burnett 1995, 53).

Most of the tinkering with this campaign has been by the government. For instance, many people thought that by removing the Marlboro Man from television in the early 1970s the feds would send him into the sunset. No such luck. You can take down all the billboards and remove him from magazines. "Just a little dab" of this rhetoric "will do ya."

When Philip Morris attempted to introduce brand extension—Marlboro Light—after all the advertising bans were in place, all they did was unsaddle the cowboy and foreground the horse. Now that even mentioning the cigarette by name is becoming taboo, they are mining the original campaign by making Marlboro Country into Marlboro Unlimited and selling lots of logo'd stuff to smokers, calling it Gear Without Limits. By selling annually some 20 million T-shirts, caps, jackets, and other items bearing Marlboro logos, Philip Morris was, for a time, the nation's third-largest mail-order house.

This attempt to get around the fear of legal restrictions on advertising   30
is called "sell-through," and you see it happening with almost all the major cigarette and beer brands. So Smokin' Joe, the super-cool Camel musician, appears on a host of nontobacco products like clothing, beach towels, baseball caps, while at the same time he also appears on the hit list of the FTC as a public nuisance.

And so what is Gear Without Limits for people who want to go to the Land That Knows No Limits? Well, what about products from the Marlboro Country Store like Snake River Fishing Gear ("An outfit made to go where the cold rivers run"), the Marlboro Folding Mountain Bike, a Mountain Lantern in Marlboro red, and the Marlboro Country Cookbook (complete with their green salsa recipe for couch cowpokes). Marlboro has so captured the iconography of cowboydom that they now have ads in mass-circulation magazines consisting *only* of recipes for such grub as Huevos Rancheros, Barkeeper's Burger, and Whiskey Beef Sandwiches.

My favorite Marlboro ad, however, is an English one in which a Harleyesque motorcycle is set out in the bleak Western plains. The only color in the bleached scene is on the bike's gas tank—Marlboro red. In art lingo, this trope is called *metonymy*.

Metonymy transfers meaning because the host image, the Marlboro cowboy, is imbedded so deep not just in American culture but in world culture that we close the circuit. Ironically, slow learners are helped by the appearance of the warning box telling you that smoking is dangerous! The Marlboro Man may indeed be Dracula to his foes, but he is still the perfect icon of adolescent independence.

Ironically, the greatest danger faced by the Marlboro Man is not from lawmen armed with scientific studies, but from some wiseguy MBA in Manhattan who will try to earn his spurs by tinkering with the campaign. This almost happened on April 22, 1993, as Michael Miles, CEO of Philip Morris, thought he could play chicken with the generics who were rustling his customers. Overnight, Miles cut the price of Marlboro by sixty cents a pack.

But the only critter he scared was the stock market, which lopped 23 percent off the price of PM stock in a single day. This day, still called "Marlboro Friday," will live in infamy as it seemed for a moment that other advertisers might follow. The whole point of branding is to make sure the consumer *pays* for the advertising by thinking that the interchangeable product is unique. He knows this when he pays a premium for it. When *Forbes* magazine (February 2, 1987) offered Marlboro smokers their chosen brand in a generic brown box at half the price, only 21 percent were interested. Just as the price of Marlboro is what economists call "inelastic," so is the advertising. Michael Miles lost his job and the company lost $13 billion in shareholder equity, but marketers learned a lesson: you don't fool with Mother Nature or a great campaign.

35

The Marlboro Man of the 1950s

The Marlboro Woman of the 1940s

Works Cited

Burnett, Leo. *100 Leo's: The Wit and Wisdom of Leo Burnett.* Lincolnwood, Ill.: NTC Business Books, 1995.

McGuide, John M. "How the Marlboro Cowboy Acquired His Tattoo." *St. Louis Post-Dispatch*, November 12, 1989.

Ogilvy, David. *On Advertising.* New York: Vintage, 1985.

 Topics for Critical Thinking and Writing

1. Reread the first two sentences of this essay. Does Twitchell prove the claim that he makes?

2. Did anything in this essay surprise you? Before you read it, were you familiar with the Marlboro man? If so, in what contexts? If not, why do you think this is the case?

3. Early on, Twitchell contends that smokers and drinkers in fact cannot tell the difference between their favorite brand and other brands. Did you believe this before you read Twitchell's essay? Do you believe it now? Couldn't you tell the difference between your favorite brand of soft drink and other brands?

4. If you are a smoker, what brand do you smoke? How much influence, do you suppose, has advertising had on your choice? If you are not a smoker, think of a product you use (e.g., jeans, underwear, sneakers) and, again, evaluate the effect of advertising on your choice.

5. What is Twitchell's conclusion about the importance of the Marlboro Man's tattoo? Do you have a tattoo? What made you decide to get one, or perhaps more than one? If you do not have a tattoo, do you think that you might get one at some point? And what would that tattoo be?

6. Reread the essay, noting the devices Twitchell uses to persuade. Then write a paragraph listing and analyzing these devices, providing examples for your reader.

7. The following sentences may puzzle some readers. Choose one, and explain it.

   a. [The Marlboro Man] came into being just as smoking became problematic and, ironically, as long as anxiety exists, so will he. (paragraph 2)
   b. The ersatz PM crest at the apex of the "red roof" chevron on the package hints of a bloodline, and the Latin motto "Vini, Vidi, Vici" (!) conveys ancient warrior strength. (paragraph 6)
   c. The Marlboro Man may indeed be Dracula to his foes, but he is still the perfect icon of adolescent independence. (paragraph 33)

A Casebook on E-Mail

Nicholas Negroponte

Nicholas Negroponte, born in 1943, holds degrees in architecture from the Massachusetts Institute of Technology, where he now teaches. Among his influential books are The Architecture Machine *and (the source of the following brief essay)* Being Digital *(1995).*

Being Asynchronous

A face-to-face or telephone conversation is real time and synchronous. Telephone tag is a game played to find the opportunity to be synchronous. Ironically, this is often done for exchanges, which themselves require no synchrony whatsoever, and could just as well be handled by non-real-time message passing. Historically, asynchronous communication, like letter writing, has tended to be more formal and less off-the-cuff exchanges. This is changing with voice mail and answering machines.

I have met people who claim they cannot understand how they (and we all) lived without answering machines at home and voice mail at the office. The advantage is less about voice and more about off-line processing and time shifting. It is about leaving messages versus engaging somebody needlessly in online discussion. In fact, answering machines are designed slightly backward. They should not only activate when you are not there or don't want to be there, but they should *always* answer the telephone and give the caller the opportunity to simply leave a message.

One of the enormous attractions of e-mail is that it is not interruptive like a telephone. You can process it at your leisure, and for this reason you may reply to messages that would not stand a chance in hell of getting through the secretarial defenses of corporate, telephonic life.

E-mail is exploding in popularity because it is *both* an asynchronous and a computer-readable medium. The latter is particularly important, because interface agents will use those bits to prioritize and deliver messages differently. Who sent the message and what it is about could determine the order in which you see it—no different from the current secretarial screening that allows a call from your six-year-old daughter to go right through, while the CEO of the XYZ Corporation is put on hold. Even on a busy workday, personal e-mail messages might drift to the top of the heap.

Not nearly as much of our communications need to be contemporaneous or in real time. We are constantly interrupted or forced into being

5

punctual for things that truly do not merit such immediacy or prompt-ness. We are forced into regular rhythms, not because we finished eating at 8:59 p.m., but because the TV program is about to start in one minute. Our great-grandchildren will understand our going to the theater at a given hour to benefit from the collective presence of human actors, but they will not understand the synchronous experiencing of television sig-nals in the privacy of our home—until they look at the bizarre economic model behind it.

Judith Kleinfeld

Judith Kleinfeld is a professor of psychology at the University of Alaska Fairbanks. This article originally appeared in the Minneapolis Star Tribune *in 1999.*

Check Your E-Mail; You May Be Fired

"**Y**our project has been canceled . . . you didn't get the promotion . . . you have to rewrite the report." Nobody likes to hear bad news, and few of us like to deliver it.

Consider using e-mail.

Delivering bad news by e-mail can be more accurate and less painful, business school professors Stephanie Sussman and Lee Sproull contend. They report their research in a study, "Straight Talk: Delivering Bad News Through Electronic Communication." Their results fly in the face of the generally accepted notion that bad news should be delivered in person. But e-mail is threatening to change what we consider right and proper. Is it good manners to send a thank-you note through e-mail? I wouldn't have thought so. But I get thank-you notes by e-mail all the time. Does it count as an affair when you carry on an intimate e-mail cor-respondence with someone you're not married to? The new consensus seems to be "Yes, that's an affair!" even if nobody mentions sex. Is it wrong to break up with someone through e-mail? A lot of people would say "yes." You need to give the other person a chance to sling it to you to your face.

But certain kinds of bad news may best be delivered over e-mail. Take the experience of my friend Paul, who was fired through e-mail. He was working from his home as an outside consultant, due to start full time at the first of the month. Two weeks into the job, Paul opened an e-mail from his boss. Buried in a routine message were these words: "The company no longer needs your services." In shock, Paul thought about heading for the company office and confronting his boss face-to-face. Instead, he decided to send an e-mail asking what he had done wrong. He did not push the "send" button until his message was cool and professional. His boss replied immediately. A long-term employee in another division was about to lose his job in a reorganization, he said, and had been given the job Paul was promised. But he would give Paul a sterling reference.

E-mail prevented Paul from ruining his recommendation.

Psychologists call people's reluctance to deliver bad news the "mum effect." Dreading the task of delivering bad news, people delay and sugar-coat the message. "However, in organizations, receiving bad news can be a first step toward improvement," Sussman and Sproull point out. Keeping bad news from the boss can jeopardize the company. To find out if electronic communication would increase honesty, they asked 117 students at the Boston University School of Management to deliver bad news.

The students were told that the career services center was short-staffed and they were needed to give feedback to other students on their draft resumes. Some of the draft resumes had congratulatory comments all over them while others were marked up with negative comments. Some students were told to schedule face-to-face appointments to deliver the news. Others were told to use the telephone. Some were told to use e-mail. The students delivered far more honest and useful information when they used e-mail to deliver the bad news. Good news was delivered accurately, no matter what the method of communication.

I asked Paul what he thought about getting bad news by e-mail. Did he think getting fired by e-mail was heartless? Or did he see it as more humane?

Paul came down in favor of e-mail. He could digest the bad news in private and get his emotions under control before he had to respond. "I do think e-mail is great for breaking bad news, at least in some administrative matters," was Paul's verdict. "But it's got its limits. Breaking up with someone over e-mail is kind of chicken."

Rob Nixon

Rob Nixon, a professor of English at the University of Wisconsin at Madison, published this essay in the Chronicle of Higher Education *in 2000.*

Please Don't E-Mail Me about This Article

It's Saturday morning, and I've sought refuge in my favorite place to write: a café a few blocks from home. Ten years ago, I would have found the infant mewling, the bleats of laughter, the cup clatter, and the chatter way too distracting. But these days, I find them easy to screen out. I relish the mental solitude I can achieve here against a backdrop of buzzing human sociability. But what I value most is the sanctuary the café offers from the supreme distraction of our age: the silent and unceasing cacophony of e-mail.

To judge from the testimony of friends and colleagues, the volume of e-mail we process daily has reached some kind of crisis point. More and more, the medium has become both utterly integral and a major source of exhaustion and disquiet. I don't know any academics who feel they would become better teachers or intellectuals if they received and sent more e-mail. I hasten to add that I can't claim to speak from the thick of the phenomenon. I am just a regular 25-to-30-e-mails-a-day guy. They arrive from colleagues, electronic mailing lists, administrators, students, ex-students, publishers, friends, family, and solicitous strangers (some wonderful, others out-and-out crackpots).

But even that moderate amount makes me rail against the merciless immediacy of e-mail, and feel as if I am constantly treading water. How, I wonder, do deans and chairs survive the e-mail tsunamis (80, 90 messages a day?) that crash down on them unceasingly?

Sometimes, one gets an inkling of the frustration at the top. A dean at my university sent a mass mailing accompanied by this appeal: "Do not reply to this e-mail. Please do not say yes, do not say no. Just come if you can"—thus sparing some administrative assistant carpal-tunnel syndrome from punching the delete button all the way to the hospital.

The distribution of my online affections has undergone a radical reversal. A decade ago, I found the Internet laborious, insubstantial, unenticing.   5

E-mail, on the other hand, charmed me totally. I adored the frisson, the serendipity, the quick-flaring intimacy. I remember reading W. H. Auden's line—"Now he is scattered among a hundred cities"—and thinking he had

---

no idea just how scattered identity would become. Or how exhilarating that could feel.

However, my romance with e-mail is now on the rocks. E-mail must rank as one of the most time-devouring timesavers of all time. Too often it makes nothing happen—fast. I don't say this out of some Luddite sensibility: I'd make a very feeble Luddite. I've come to delight in the Internet at large, which appeals to both the hunter-gatherer and the pastoralist browser in me. My research and teaching alike are unthinkable without it. Unlike e-mail, the Internet doesn't insistently demand responses. It seems less controlling, less of an imposition, and more of a resource. Once upon a time e-mail looked as if it would become an invigorating part of university life. By now, however, it has come to feel like a Sisyphean labor akin to hauling out the garbage or shoveling snow.

E-mail has become efficient to the point of counterefficiency, threatening to overwhelm the primary activities—teaching, reading, writing, and thinking—that we once hoped it might help sustain. The best teaching and writing require some professional space within which to give the illusion of inefficiency. It is in this space that we are most likely to be surprised by new ideas or to discover compelling ways to give fresh life to old ones. E-mail's demands for metronomic efficiency threatens such expanses of "idle" creativity.

At the heart of the problem is e-mail's paradoxical status. It is and isn't writing. You bend over the same computer, tapping the same keys, straining the same muscles you use to write your lectures, your articles, your books. But what you're composing is mostly ephemeral: It's not writing but meta-writing. A reply to a reply to a reply. The challenge is how to keep a technology with a rodentlike reproductive rate supplementary, not something that overruns our days.

Going to the café is one of my coping strategies. There my computer is reduced to a one-dimensional technology temporarily severed from interactive temptations and distractions. But such trips are a rare luxury. More often, I impose on myself a kind of inverted curfew: I try never to check e-mail before 4 P.M. Like many people, I experience my best energy in the mornings. I try to reserve that dream-inflected, caffeine-charged creativity for the activities that matter most: writing, teaching, reading, and one-on-one meetings with students. It's all too easy to go online first thing (and then again, and again) and scatter a day's worth of concentration within an hour or two of breakfast.

Certainly, e-mail can have a lingering seductiveness. Not least because it appears to resolve a central, often painful tension in the life of anyone who writes. As the editor Betsy Lerner puts it in her new book, *The Forest for the Trees*, "the great paradox of the writer's life is how much time he spends alone trying to connect with other people." We feel that paradox most acutely when we're writing books. But even composing lectures demands deferred connection. E-mail seems to resolve the para-

10

dox by transforming writing into a quick feedback loop. This is writing on the no-solitude, no-sweat, no-deferral plan.

To move from that mode of expectation back to real writing takes energy and discipline. Writing is hardest when you set out. It usually takes me an hour or two, after my first faltering starts, to enter "the zone." Historically, writers have used all kinds of ingenious and desperate acts to try to kick start the process—like John McPhee's strapping himself into his chair with a seat belt. I've made the mistake often enough of using e-mail to kick start me. In my experience, it warms you up for nothing but dispersion; the real writing is less likely to get done.

These days the buzz—and the money that follows the buzz—is all about connection. However, if we don't force ourselves into regular periods of disconnectedness, our students will be shortchanged. Academics have less time than ever to read and write. That's why intervals of withdrawal remain essential to our jobs as educators. Our task is to redeem information and yeast it, through research, reflection, and passion, into communicable knowledge. "Only connect," E.M. Forster exhorted his readers 90 years ago, in what became a celebrated liberal mantra. But connecting has become the easy part. Disconnection (in order to connect more deeply later) now requires the greater discipline and resourcefulness.

I wish e-mail were routed through some other apparatus than a computer—like, say, the DustBuster. That would have two primary advantages. First, we wouldn't be as prone to equate writing proper with e-mail, writing's easy surrogate. Second, we wouldn't have two physically unhealthy activities compressed into one posture. It's bad enough that writing locks us into a computer stoop. Now we must assume the same stance to absorb the ephemeral communications that used to pass through the telephone. No wonder our deltoid, trapezius, and infraspinatus muscles go into revolt.

I have friends (retirees, artists, writers) who lead more isolated lives than I do, without a matrix of institutional responsibilities. I'm talking about the 5-or-6-e-mails-a-day folk, for whom the medium can still feel like something of a pastime. Often they'll send me letter-length dispatches: long, witty, eloquent, and intimate. I feel the need, the desire, to respond in kind. But mostly I'm e-mailed out and can't endure more time filling up boxes on my computer screen. I watch with horror as my friends' long missives sink into the sedimentary layers of unanswered e-mail, turning into the digital equivalent of anthracite. These days, I'm more likely to respond by picking up the telephone.

This summer, I spent a month at an artists' colony in New Hampshire. The setup there was my idea of e-mail heaven. Thirty artists shared a single phone link. You had to pack up your computer and hike half a mile to the main residence to plug into it. What I adored was the sheer inconvenience of it all. Going online became a conscious choice, not a facile reflex that could derail your train of thought. I checked my e-mail every three days or so. In between, I could build up a head of steam, without the temptation of logging on for an incidental glance and finding, an hour later, that I was still inside e-mail's thrall and that the writing zone had fled.

The colony experience reminded me that I don't want e-mail to disappear. I just need periods in my life when it is less relentless and less convenient.

In moderation, e-mail is a boon. And yes, it can save time. But we'd do well to recall the Buddha's response on being told that a sprinter had shaved 0.1 seconds off the 100-meter record. "What," the Buddha inquired, "did she do with the time she saved?" To which I'd add: Write more e-mail?

Ed Boland

Ed Boland is a frequent contributor to The New York Times *and* The New York Times Sunday Magazine.

In Modern E-Mail Romances "Trash" Is Just a Click Away

One night this summer, Jason Kellogg, a 24-year-old publishing assistant, left a bar in Brooklyn after spending a good deal of time talking with a woman he had met that evening. When he left the bar, his friends demanded the requisite information: How old is she? Is she from the area? Does she have any good-looking friends? And most important, did you get a phone number?

Mr. Kellogg hesitated on the last question. "Well, not exactly," he said. "She gave me her e-mail."

That was a first for Mr. Kellogg. He sent her an e-mail message a few days later, although nothing came of their correspondence. "I suppose it was better than a flat-out rejection," he said. "She was probably turned off by my bad spelling."

E-mail, which has long been an indispensable tool in business, is beginning to influence more romantic relationships as well. With more and more Americans in front of a computer at work and spending time on them at home, e-mail is changing the ways people meet, court and even break up.

"It's changed every aspect of dating," said Sherry Amatenstein, a dating expert for the iVillage online network and author of "The Q & A Dating Book" (Adams Media, 2000). "Our new technology is both boon and curse for the modern dater."

5

One reason for the change in etiquette from requesting a phone number to requesting an e-mail address is comfort, particularly for women. "It's safer than a phone number," said Brenda Ross, dating adviser for About.com and creator of the Dating Advice for Geeks Web site. "With a few e-mails you can get some details, find out what a guy is like and then decide if you want to go out with him. It takes a lot of pressure off."

Some women are now using e-mail as a way to avoid people they have no intention of ever going out with. In many instances, Ms. Ross said, a woman doesn't want to give out her phone number, but she also doesn't want to be pestered all night for it by some libidinous Neanderthal. Solution: give him your e-mail address and never respond, or give an e-mail address that you never use, an updating of the time-honored dating tradition of giving a wrong phone number. Eventually he will get the idea, and trashing an e-mail message is easier than dodging a phone call.

Of course, that may seem a bit disingenuous, but one thing about dating hasn't changed: it's still war out there.

Many single people have found that e-mail can be a solution to another age-old dating problem—when to call? Ellen Lavery, a 25-year-old from Manhattan, found herself in that situation a few months ago, the morning after a party where she exchanged phone numbers and e-mail addresses with a man. "The next day, I would have absolutely considered a phone call too soon, too desperate," she said, "a severe violation of the three-day rule. So I shot him off a brief 'we should get together sometime' e-mail. It seemed more acceptable and less threatening, but not overbearing."

Leslie, 31, a publishing executive in Manhattan, has used e-mail as a follow-up to a date. (She and several other people interviewed for this article spoke on the condition that their last names not be used.) "It would be a little too awkward to call, seeing as how you just saw that person the night before, and a letter is too formal, so e-mail comes in handy." 10

And what about that first e-mail note? Traditionally, the first phone call can be more nerve-racking than transporting nuclear weapons across a rope bridge. You have to be on your toes: funny but not obnoxious, charming yet not hammy, deep but not psychotic, all on the spot. An e-mail message, however, can go through multiple drafts; wording and tone can painstakingly be thought out, reviewed, edited and, if it's not quite right, sent back to committee. "I always show my e-mails to friends before I send them out," said Drew Brooks, a 25-year-old in Manhattan. "Involving other people is fun."

Single people who follow up on chance encounters with e-mail are finding that the awkward first stages of a relationship can be made easier online.

One reason relationships can move so far so fast over the Internet is the solitary nature of e-mail. "When you're e-mailing, you can be at home, cozy, in your pajamas," Ms. Amatenstein said. "It's so psychologically inviting, people say things they normally would not say."

Ling, a 23-year-old student in Manhattan who is dating someone she met on the Asian Avenue Web site, found that to be the case.

"We just started talking, and pretty soon we were writing each other   15
every day," she said. "It's like a psychiatrist's office: you get in, and you
feel like you can say anything. It was weird when we first talked to each
other on the phone, because we already knew so much about each other."

Mr. Brooks said that he and many of his friends find it easier to be
themselves behind the veil of e-mail, saying whatever they want without
the risk of a raised eyebrow, a nervous laugh or a dropped jaw. "In e-mail,
your needs and feelings are much more important and apparent," he
said, "because you're basically exchanging a series of monologues."

E-mail is also enabling people to do a little cyberflirting at work off
the radar screen of nosy co-workers: "Although you speak on the phone,
having a little light communication throughout the day can be a rein-
forcement," said Shalu Jaisinghani, 25, a financial consultant from
Hoboken, N.J. "You get that two-second rush, ego boost, when you see
that new-message icon flash across the screen indicating the guy you dig
is thinking about you in the middle of the day."

Not all e-mail from a romantic interest, however, is an ego booster.
Increasingly, people are finding that the distance of e-mail simplifies one
of the potentially messier tasks in a relationship: the breakup. "That's one
great thing about e-mail," Mr. Brooks said. "There's no ramifications for
you in just blowing someone off."

Not everyone sees it that way, though. Brenda Ross, whose former
boyfriend broke up with her via e-mail, after they had talked about the
possibility of marriage, said it was about the "lamest" thing a person
could do. "E-mail is a great way to break up with someone," she said, "if
you're a coward."

Debra A. Klein

Debra A. Klein writes travel and business articles for The New York Times, *where this article originally appeared, in 2001.*

A Reunion? Relax. You're Invisible

A few months ago I was overcome with nostalgia and self-pity. A
former classmate e-mailed me a link to my past. "Click here," he invited.

I did and was instantly transported back two and a half decades, and
light-years in self-esteem. Smiling up at me was my unflattering 1976
graduation picture—my sixth grade graduation picture—posted on the
World Wide Web.

How did my yearbook photo find its way out from under the Snoopy bank in my parents' attic and into the public domain? What would I find next? My Dynamite magazine, Op Sail T-shirt, stockpile of Shrinky Dink art? My mind raced.

Looking for answers, I clicked on Back and stumbled into a time warp: more bucktoothed preteenagers with "One Day at a Time" hairdos. Faces I hadn't thought of in more than 20 years grinned out from atop giant striped collars. Scribbled ink mustaches obscured one or two.

My curiosity morphed to paranoia. My mental Mood Ring turned   5
from green to black. An anonymous e-mail message popped into my In box. "Any chance you can make it?" teased a stranger, offering an Internet address. I took the bait.

An elementary school classmate I could not recall and who I swear must have added himself digitally to our class pictures had created a Web page to organize a reunion of our entire sixth grade. Sometime last year that classmate, Sergio Caplan, now a software entrepreneur, had reconnected in cyberspace with boys I recall mostly as terrors of blacktop dodge ball. One had suggested a get-together in the flesh.

Sergio had turned to the Web to disseminate details about the gathering quickly, but in doing so changed the nature of the event. Had I been invited personally to a private party whose hosts (in my mind) still thought girls had "cooties," I would have declined politely. This cyber-invitation was socially neutral, like a school-sponsored event.

In less than two months the Davis Reunion Web site (www.wertv.com /davis.html) grew from a simple text page into an interactive portal leading to the pale green tiled halls of our youth. One alumna heard about it and scanned in the yearbook photos. Sergio used these as lures.

It was ingenious marketing. Phone calls would have gone unreturned and print invitations unread. But a mysterious e-mail message leading to a customized slice of your own childhood—that was impossible to ignore. Like Magic Rocks, his initial tiny database of three or four e-mail addresses grew tenfold, seemingly overnight. Like the enthusiasts in that old Fabergé shampoo ad, everyone, it seemed, had told two friends.

By the time I logged on to the site two weeks before the party, it was   10
chugging with clickable sections for chatting, leaving messages and seeing who, among the 100 or so alumni, was planning to attend. Noting the large number of people who had already been told of the reunion, I tried not to take it personally that as in the old days of kickball, I seemed to have been notified close to last.

The chat room hummed with exchanges between unlikely gossips; only in cyberspace, I thought, would shy students vent over soap opera plots. The real drama for me, though, came in a private online connection. Using newly acquired e-mail addresses, I was at last able to express condolences to my best friends from kindergarten on the tragic death of their little brother last summer. Although 10 years had passed since we had last spoken, the Internet helped us gracefully sew a gap of a decade and hundreds of miles.

As the reunion date approached, rapid-fire e-mail messages multiplied like Wacky Packages on a denim loose-leaf binder as we all busily recounted 25 years in short bursts. News came in of classmates whom I last remember seeing in parrot skirts and crepe-soled buffalo sandals at graduation.

Sergio, who was not exactly a social butterfly (from what everyone else remembers), was suddenly the Steve Rubell of our exclusive cyber–Studio 54. He let in nerds and popular kids to mingle electronically, flouting the social laws of the jungle gym. In cyberspace, we quickly learned, no one could catch you being uncool.

Despite the huge gap of time, we seemed to be drawn to one another like long-lost siblings because of our intimate shared pasts. And as with siblings, the formalities governing most adult exchanges melted quickly. Our e-mail content spiraled from polite queries to the sort of mischievous missives we passed in class.

For those like me who had moved far from New York and missed the   15 actual night of reunion carousing, the Web page offered intoxicating fun. A classmate posted pictures (with much-needed labels) of unlikely pairings at an East Side bar.

The photos of smiling classmates, beer bottles in hand, revealed a sobering truth. It is easier to exchange light and friendly e-mail banter than it is to converse toe to toe (or in the case of many photos, hip to hip).

Attending a reunion virtually has distinct advantages. There is no need for special hair and makeup, rapid weight loss or figure-flattering jeans. In fact, clothing is optional. As is answering back. You can be button-holed at a reunion, but in cyberspace you can let unwanted e-mail simply wither online.

There are no sticky name tags, or sticky social situations. No moments of panic when you realize you just can't place that face. You can be as verbose as your thesaurus allows, yet never fumble and say the wrong thing. After the party there is no one nearby to eavesdrop on unkind comments (although there is that worry that in cyberspace deleted correspondence can always be retrieved). But there is also no laughter, or clink of glasses or handshakes or hugs, no matter how insincere.

Many of us have since used the Internet to maintain renewed friendships, plan mini-reunions and make business connections online. One sixth-grade friend and I now send each other e-mail incessantly, without teachers to interrupt the free flow of ideas.

Still, there is one classmate with whom I almost never exchange e-   20 mail, and post-reunion that will not change. The one who first sent me the link to our past has been my friend since we sat cross-legged watching "Sesame Street." When we need to connect we turn to a different era's cutting-edge technology: we pick up the phone for the warmth that eludes us in cyberspace.

Topics for Critical Thinking and Writing

1. Refer back to each of the selections in this casebook. Which of them has the most effective opening paragraph? What defines a good opening paragraph?

2. Which of these selections taught you something that you did not know before? For an essay to be successful, must it teach the reader something new? Or might there be other criteria for an essay's effectiveness?

3. Nicholas Negroponte speaks of the "enormous attractions" of e-mail, whereas Rob Nixon describes it as the "supreme distraction of our age." Who makes the more convincing case? What's your view?

4. Do you agree with the person quoted in Judith Kleinfeld's article who says that some kinds of "bad news" should not be delivered by e-mail? Or do you think the e-mail is acceptable for any kind of news, good or bad?

5. Can you imagine life without e-mail? How would your life be better or worse without it?

6. Do you agree with the person quoted in Ed Boland's article who says that e-mail has "changed every aspect of dating"? Do you know anyone who has begun a romance through e-mail? Isn't this a problem? Shouldn't real romance be based on face-to-face contact and communication?

7. Debra A. Klein speaks very positively about the value of e-mail. What are her reasons? How might Rob Nixon reply to her? And what might be her response to him?

8. It is sometimes said that people can "hide" on e-mail. What does this mean? Is this an advantage of e-mail, or a limitation?

9. If you sensed that your roommate was spending too much time reading and sending e-mail, and that this was having a bad effect on his or her life and work, would you be inclined to speak to his or her class dean or someone else in a position of authority? Or should your roommate be left alone?

Stevie Smith

Stevie Smith (1902–71) was born Florence Margaret Smith in England. Her first book was a novel, published in 1936, but she is best known for her several volumes of poetry.

Not Waving but Drowning

Nobody heard him, the dead man,
But still he lay moaning:
I was much further out than you thought
And not waving but drowning.

Poor chap, he always loved larking   5
And now he's dead
It must have been too cold for him his heart gave way,
They said.

Oh, no no no, it was too cold always
(Still the dead one lay moaning)   10
I was much too far out all my life
And not waving but drowning.

 Topics for Critical Thinking and Writing

1. The first line, "Nobody heard him, the dead man," is, of course, literally true. Dead men do not speak. In what other ways is it true?

2. Who are "they" whose voices we hear in the second stanza? What does the punctuation—or lack of it—in line 7 tell us of their feelings for the dead man? What effect is produced by the brevity of line 6? of line 8?

3. In the last stanza, does the man reproach himself, or others, or simply bemoan his fate? What was the cause of his death?

CHAPTER 13

Art and Life

the Checkered House is old,
this as it looked in 1853,
   It was the Headquarters of
General Baum in the revolution
war, and afterwards He used
it as a Hospital,
   then it was a stoping place
for the stage,
   where they changed Horses every
two miles,
   oh we traveled fast in those
   days,

Place de l'Europe, Paris, 1932
Henri Cartier-Bresson

Lila York in Paul Taylor's "Diggity"
Jack Vartoogian

Short Views

Art for art's sake.
Théophile Gautier

What is art, that it should have a sake?
Samuel Butler

Art for art's sake is an empty phrase. Art for the sake of the true, art for the sake of the good and the beautiful, that is the faith I am searching for.
George Sand (Amandine Aurore Lucie Dupin)

Moralists have no place in an art gallery.
Han Suyin

The end of reading is not more books but more life.
Holbrook Jackson

The storyteller's own experience of people and things, whether for good or ill—not only what he has passed through himself, but even events which he has only witnessed or been told of—has moved the writer to an emotion so passionate that he can no longer keep it shut up in his heart. Again and again something in his own life or in that around him will seem to the writer so important that he cannot bear to let it pass into oblivion. There must never come a time, he feels, when people do not know about it.
Lady Murasaki

The artist must say it without saying it.
Duke Ellington

If I had to give young writers advice, I'd say don't listen to writers talking about writing.
Lillian Hellman

Artistic growth is, more than anything else, a refining of the sense of truthfulness. The stupid believe that to be truthful is easy; only the artist, the great artist, knows how difficult it is.
  Willa Cather

There is absolutely everything in great fiction but a clear answer.
  Eudora Welty

Art, it seems to me, should simplify. That, indeed, is very nearly the whole of the higher artistic process; finding what conventions of form and what detail one can do without and yet preserve the spirit of the whole—so that all that one has suppressed and cut away is there to the reader's consciousness as much as if it were in type on the page.
  Willa Cather

I think art, literature, fiction, poetry, what it is, makes justice in the world. That's why it almost always has to be on the side of the underdog.
  Grace Paley

Literature is news that stays news.
  Ezra Pound

The two worst sins of bad taste in fiction are pornography and sentimentality. One is too much sex and the other is too much sentiment.
  Flannery O'Connor

It is easier to understand a nation by listening to its music than by learning its language.
  Anonymous

What's swinging in words? If a guy makes you pat your foot and if you feel it down your back, you don't have to ask anybody if that's good music or not.
  Miles Davis

It started with the moans and groans of the people in the cotton fields. Before it got the name of soul, men were sellin' watermelons and vegetables on a wagon drawn by a mule, hollerin' "watermelon!" with a cry in their voices. And the man on the railroad track layin' crossties—every time they hit the hammer it was with a sad feelin', but with a beat. And the Baptist preacher—he the one who had the soul—he give out the meter, a long and short meter, and the old mothers of the church would reply. This musical thing has been here since America been here. This is trial and tribulation music.

  Mahalia Jackson

If art does not enlarge men's sympathies, it does nothing morally.

  George Eliot

You don't take a photograph, you make it.

  Ansel Adams

A good painter is to paint two main things, namely, man and the working of man's mind. The first is easy, the second difficult, for it is to be represented through the gestures and movements of the limbs.

  Leonardo da Vinci

I like pretty things the best, what's the use of painting a picture if it isn't something nice? So I think real hard till I think of something real pretty, and then I paint it. I like to paint old timey things, historical landmarks of long ago, bridges, mills and hostelries, those old time homes, there are a few left, and they are going fast. I do them all from memory, most of them are day dreams, as it were.

  Grandma Moses

The truest expression of a people is in its dances and its music. Bodies never lie.

  Agnes De Mille

Dancing is like bank robbery, it takes split-second timing.

  Twyla Tharp

Oscar Wilde

Oscar Wilde (1854–1900), born in Dublin, studied classics at Trinity College, Dublin, and then at Oxford. After graduating in 1878 he settled in London, where he achieved fame as a wit and as an advocate of the Aesthetic Movement, whose creed can (with some injustice, of course) be summarized as "Art for Art's Sake." (One contemporary drily asked, "What is art, that it should have a sake?" Two other contemporaries, Gilbert and Sullivan, spoofed the Aesthetic Movement in their comic opera Patience.) *But Wilde was not merely a talker, he was a writer; among his notable works are a witty discussion of the nature of imaginative literature,* The Decay of Lying *(1879); a novel,* The Picture of Dorian Gray *(1891); and several comedies that hold the stage even today,* Lady Windermere's Fan *(1892),* An Ideal Husband *(1895), and his masterpiece* The Importance of Being Earnest *(1895).*

Soon after Earnest *opened, Wilde became involved in a sensational and disastrous court battle. The Marquess of Queensbury (the father of the young man who was Wilde's lover) in effect accused Wilde of homosexuality, and Wilde sued him for libel. During the trial evidence was presented establishing Wilde's homosexuality, and Wilde lost the case. He was then arrested and convicted—homosexual practices were illegal—and he was sentenced to two years in jail at hard labor. Such was his disgrace that his plays were withdrawn from the stage. When Wilde was released he emigrated to France, where he lived his last three years under an assumed name.*

Preface to *The Picture of Dorian Gray*

The artist is the creator of beautiful things.

To reveal art and conceal the artist is art's aim.

The critic is he who can translate into another manner or a new material his impression of beautiful things.

> The highest, as the lowest, form of criticism is a mode of autobiography.

Those who find ugly meaning in beautiful things are corrupt without being charming. This is a fault.   5

> Those who find beautiful meanings in beautiful things are the cultivated. For these there is hope.

> They are the elect to whom beautiful things mean only Beauty.

> There is no such thing as a moral or an immoral book.

> Books are well written, or badly written. That is all.

The nineteenth-century dislike of Realism is the rage of Caliban[1] seeing   10
his own face in a glass.

> The nineteenth-century dislike of Romanticism is the rage of Caliban not seeing his own face in a glass.

The moral life of man forms part of the subject matter of the artist, but the morality of art consists in the perfect use of an imperfect medium. No artist desires to prove anything. Even things that are true can be proved.

> No artist has ethical sympathies. An ethical sympathy in an artist is an unpardonable mannerism of style.

---

[1]**Caliban** a brutish figure in Shakespeare's play *The Tempest* (Editors' note)

No artist is ever morbid. The artist can express everything.

Thought and language are to the artist instruments of an art.   15

Vice and Virtue are to the artist materials for an art.

From the point of view of form, the type of all the arts is the art of the musician. From the point of view of feeling, the actor's craft is the type.

All art is at once surface and symbol.

Those who go beneath the surface do so at their peril.

Those who read the symbol do so at their peril.   20

It is the spectator, and not life, that art really mirrors.

Diversity of opinion about a work of art shows that the work is new, complex, and vital.

When critics disagree the artist is in accord with himself.

We can forgive a man for making a useful thing as long as he does not admire it. The only excuse for making a useless thing is that one admires it intensely.

All art is quite useless.   25

 ## Topics for Critical Thinking and Writing

1. Wilde ends by saying, "all art is quite useless." Do you accept this view? Why or why not? If you think that a novel or a play may be useful because it may teach us something about life, what do you say about other works of art, such as a wordless musical composition, or a still life painting, or a song such as one sung by Eminem or Madonna? What "use" might such a work have?

2. Wilde says (paragraph 4) that "criticism is a mode of autobiography." When you offer criticism—whether in a conversation with a friend about a movie you saw last night, or in a course paper on a story, poem, or play—are you in some measure offering autobiography? In a paragraph explain what Wilde probably means, and in a second paragraph evaluate the idea.

3. "There is no such thing as a moral or an immoral book. Books are well written, or badly written. That is all" (paragraphs 8–9). In an essay of 500 words evaluate the view. Whichever side you take, try to see the opposing point of view, state it as fairly as possible, and then respond to it.

Lou Jacobs Jr.

Lou Jacobs Jr., photographer and the author of several books on photography, is a frequent contributor of essays on the topic to The New York Times, *where this piece originally appeared.*

What Qualities Does a Good Photograph Have?

When amateur and professional photographers get together they often discuss equipment and techniques at some length, but it is not often that photographers take time to consider what makes a good picture.

Many photographic organizations list criteria similar to those described below when judging pictures submitted in a competition. Judges may offer opinions like "The composition is off balance," or "The expressions on peoples' faces tell the story well." But photographic criticism is not an exact art. In the media, critics tend to use esoteric terms that even an "in" group doesn't always grasp.

Therefore it's important to the average photographer that he or she develop a basis for understanding and verbalizing how pictures succeed or fail in their visual way, or how they happen to be a near-miss. The latter term describes an image that has some, but not enough, of the visual virtues discussed below.

Of course "a good picture" is a relative description because it's subjective, as is the judgement of all the qualities mentioned in the list that follows. However, there is enough agreement in the tastes of a variety of people to make certain standards general and valid, though the characteristics of a good picture are subject to flexible interpretation. A little honest controversy about the visual success of a print or slide can be a healthy thing.

Impact: This descriptive word comprises a collection of the qualities that help make a photograph appealing, interesting, impressive, or memorable. For instance, Ansel Adams' "Moonrise, Hernandez, NM" is a famous image that has been selling for astronomical prices at auctions because it has enormous pictorial or visual impact—among other reasons. The picture's impact evolves from many qualities such as the drama of the light, the mood invoked, and the magic sense of realism.

It is possible to translate such qualities into your own photographs when you consider how the subjects were treated, whether landscapes or people. Too seldom do we meet dramatic opportunities in nature as grand as those in "Moonrise," but with a well developed artistic sensitivity, ideal conditions can be captured on film.

Moonrise, Hernandez, New Mexico, 1941
Ansel Adams

Human Interest: Here is another rather general term to encompass emotional qualities, action, and things that people do which appeal to a lot of viewers. A shot of your children laughing or a picture of vendors in a marketplace might both show outstanding human interest. The success of such a photograph depends on how you compose it, on lighting, on timing to catch vivid expressions, and perhaps on camera angle or choice of lens. All of these ingredients of a good picture are coming up on the list.

There is another aspect of human interest in your own or others' photographs. Sometimes the unusualness of a subject and the way it's presented overshadows adequate technique. For instance, a good sports picture showing peak action in a scrimmage or a definitive play in baseball has intrinsic appeal.

A photograph of a pretty girl, a baby, and a sunset are in the same category, because in each case the subject matter grabs the viewer's attention. As a result, a mediocre composition, inferior lighting, a messy background, or other technical or esthetic weaknesses are ignored or excused because the subject is striking.

It's a good feeling when you can distinguish between the subject in a photograph and the way it was treated.

10

Galleries and museums often hang photographs that are "different," but they're not necessarily worthy of distinction. Many offbeat photographs we see are likely not to have lasting visual value, while fine photographs like those of Ansel Adams or Cartier-Bresson will still be admired in future decades.

Effective Composition: Like other qualities that underlie a good picture, composition can be controversial. There are somewhat conventional principles of design that we follow because they seem "natural," like placing the horizon line or a figure off-center to avoid a static effect.

But really effective composition is usually derived from the subject, and generally the urge to keep composition as simple as possible pays off. That's why plain backgrounds are often best for portraits, and if you relate someone to his/her environment, simplicity is also a virtue. Composition may be dynamic, placid, or somewhere between.

Study the compositional tendencies of fine photographers and painters for guidance. Be daring and experimental at times too, because a "safe" composition may also be dull.

Spontaneity: This characteristic of a good picture is related to human interest, realism and involvement. When you are involved with the subject, as you might be in photographing an aged father or mother, you prize most the images that include spontaneous expressions and emotional reactions. Get people involved with each other, too, so they forget the camera and your pictures are likely to be more believable—and credibility is often a pictorial asset.

15

If your camera lens is not fast enough to shoot at let's say 1/60th of a second of f/2.8, then you need flash. But you get more spontaneity when people aren't posed, waiting for the flash to go off. Natural light also adds to the realistic impression you capture of people and places, since flash-on-camera has an unavoidably artificial look in most cases.

Lighting: Certainly we have to shoot sometimes when the light is not pictorial, so we do the best we can. A tripod is often the answer to long exposures and exciting photographs. In some situations the light improves if we have the time and patience to wait. Outdoors plan to shoot when the sun is low in the early morning, and at sunset time. Mountains, buildings and people are more dramatic in low-angle light. Details lost in shadows don't seem to matter when the light quality itself is beautiful.

Lighting also helps to create mood, another element of a good picture. Mood is understandably an ethereal quality which includes mystery, gaiety, somberness, and other emotional aspects. Effective photographs may capitalize on the mood of a place especially when it's dramatic.

Color: In a painting a pronounced feeling of light and shadow is called chiaroscuro, and in photographs such effects are augmented by color which may be in strong contrasts, or part of important forms. Outstanding pictures may also be softly colored in pastels that can be as appealing as bright hues.

We tend to take color in photographs for granted, but we don't have
to settle for literal color when a colored filter or a switch in film may improve a situation. Next time it rains, shoot some pictures through a car
window or windshield, or keep your camera dry and shoot on foot—using indoor color film. The cold blue effects, particularly in slides, are ter-
rific. You may later use an 85B filter to correct the color for normal outdoor or flash use.

Keep in mind that "pretty" or striking color may influence us to
take pictures where there really is no worthwhile image. And when you
view prints and slides, realize that theatrical color can influence your
judgment about the total quality of a picture. A beautiful girl in brightly
colored clothes, or an exotic South Seas beach scene may be photographed with creative skill, or insensitively, no matter how appealing
the color is.

Contrast: Outstanding pictures may be based on the fact that they
contain various contrasting elements, such as large and small, near and
far, old and new, bright and subtle color, etc. In taking pictures and evaluating them, keep the contrast range in mind, although these values are often integral with other aspects of the picture.

Camera Angle and Choice of Lens: If someone standing next to you
shoots a mid-town Manhattan street with a 50mm lens on a 35mm camera,
and you do the same scene with a 35mm or 105mm lens from a crouch
rather than standing, you might get a better picture. You can dramatize a
subject through your choice of camera angle and lens focal length to alter
perspective as well as the relationship of things in the scene. Distortion created this way can be pictorially exciting—or awkward and distracting. You
may get good pictures by taking risks in visual ways, and later deciding if
what you tried seems to work.

Imagination and Creativity: These two attributes of people who take
pictures might have been first on the list if they were not abused words.
Look each one up in the dictionary. Ponder how you would apply the
definitions to your own pictures and to photographs you see in books or
exhibitions.

It takes imagination to see the commonplace in an artistic way, but a
certain amount of imagination and creativity should be involved every
time we press the shutter button. These human capabilities are basic to
understanding the other qualities that make good pictures.

Topics for Critical Thinking and Writing

1. Evaluate the title and the first paragraph.

2. In paragraph 4 Jacobs says, "Of course 'a good picture' is a relative description because it's subjective. . . ." Do you agree? Look, for instance, at Dorothea Lange's photographs of a migrant laborer and her children, on pages 99 and 102–105. Would you be willing to argue that the famous picture (the

one showing the children turned away from the camera) is clearly—objectively—a better picture than one of the other pictures? Explain.

3. In paragraph 5 Jacobs praises Ansel Adams's *Moonrise, Hernandez, NM,* but this picture, showing a cemetery with crosses illumined by a silvery moon, has been disparaged by some critics on the grounds that it is sentimental. How would you define sentimentality? And is it a bad thing in a photograph? Explain.

4. In paragraph 7 Jacobs speaks of "human interest," and he cites a picture of "children laughing or a picture of vendors in a marketplace." Given these examples, what does "human interest" seem to mean? What might be some examples of photographs of people that do *not* have "human interest"?

5. In paragraph 23 Jacobs says that "you can dramatize a subject through your choice of camera angle. . . ." Find an example of such a photo in a newspaper or newsmagazine, or perhaps in this book, and explain how the camera angle "dramatizes" the subject.

6. Take a photo, perhaps one in this book, and in 500 words analyze and evaluate it in Jacobs's terms. Then consider whether Jacobs's essay has helped you to see and enjoy the photograph.

7. Write your own short essay (250–500 words) on "What Qualities Does a Good Photograph Have?" Illustrate it with photocopies of two or three photographs, from this book or from any other source that you wish to draw on. (You may want to choose two examples of good photographs, or one of a good photograph and one of a poor photograph.)

Ben Shahn

Ben Shahn (1898–1969) came to New York City from Lithuania at the age of eight. As a young man he apprenticed in a lithography shop in Manhattan, then studied drawing and painting, and soon established himself as a significant painter. Shahn was also active as a photographer, devoting much of his time in the 1930s to photographing the plight of unemployed workers during the Depression that began in 1929. The two photographs we reproduce were taken in 1936.

Untitled Photographs (New York City)

 Topics for Critical Thinking and Writing

1. The chief differences between the two images are (a) the photographer's distance from his subject, and (b) the tilt of the camera, more evident in the picture at the right than in the one at the left. Is one picture better than the other? If so, why?

2. Take one of these pictures and explain why you think it is a good photograph, a so-so photograph, or a poor photograph.

3. How large a part of your evaluation is based on the ironic contrast between the man, who presumably is weary and despondent, and the advertisement, which shows a rather jaunty figure? If you believe the photo is good, is it because of this forceful contrast? If you believe the photo is not so good, is it because the contrast is too obvious?

4. If you were told that Shahn had posed the man, would your evaluation of the photograph change? Explain.

5. If you were told that the man shielded his face from the camera in an effort to preserve his dignity, would your evaluation of the photograph change? Explain.

6. Let's assume that the man was utterly unaware of the photographer. Do you think it was wrong of the photographer to take his picture without first getting permission? Why?

Mary Beard

Mary Beard, a classicist at Newnham College, Cambridge wrote this essay for a volume called Issues in World Literature. *The book included illustrations, and the essay was intended to help viewers look at unfamiliar works of art.*

Culturally Variable Ways of Seeing: Art and Literature

We tend to take the process of *looking* very much for granted; and we rarely stop to reflect on how we make sense of what we see. It is a striking contrast with our engagement in the process of *reading*. Not only do most of us still remember the struggles of first learning to read, the difficulties of decoding those baffling symbols on the page, but even as well-practiced, adult readers we constantly remind ourselves of the problems of understanding and interpreting texts: when was this text written? Does its age affect our understanding? Who was it written for? Why? What language was it first written in? What difference does the translation make? So, for example, we would hardly try to read the Psalms, the Acts of Buddha, or the Koran without recollecting that these are religious texts, part of a system of beliefs that we perhaps do not share. Nor would we seriously try to read early Chinese love poetry, or attempt to understand the passions of Racine's *Phaedra* or Shakespeare's Prospero without any thought for their historical context: however immediate, even modern, the emotions expressed might at first seem, our reading is almost inevitably affected by the knowledge that "being in love" in ancient China or Elizabethan England may have been quite a different experience (governed by quite different rules and constraints) from "being in love" in the contemporary West.

Compare the very casual approach we take to looking. We are often happy to look without thinking, and to allow ourselves to enjoy images as "pure," with little regard for their context, history, or cultural difference. We may admire, for example, the glittering icons of Byzantium without reflecting on their original purpose as devotional, religious images, just as we often enjoy the luxuriant miniatures of ladies at the Indian court without considering the social and economic circumstances that produced such images. Of course, we are not always so casual. Some images do remain for us firmly rooted in their historical context, or in the ideology that created them. If someone, for example, chose reproductions of Nazi art as home decoration, even now that would be a strident political statement; we would hardly believe any claim that it was just an aesthetic admiration for the paintings. Similarly with Picasso's *Guernica*: few viewers consider the painting without at the same time reflecting on the atrocities of the Spanish Civil War that were its inspiration. But all the same, a glance at most dormitory walls (with their wild juxtapositions of images—postcards of Botticelli next to Salvador Dali, native American textiles next to Hokusai waves) suggests that in the visual field "anything goes."

This atmosphere of free play can be liberating. It allows us to use the images *for ourselves*, without becoming lost in the intricacies of historical context or original purpose; it allows us to fix the images freely into our own personal stories ("This postcard is a souvenir of the time when I . . ." or "This poster reminds me of . . ."). But at the same time the casualness tends to conceal from us the processes which lie behind the ways we make sense of, judge, and rank the images we see. It encourages us not to examine our *rules for looking*. These are the rules that govern things as basic as our classification of artistic production ("major art," "minor arts," "art," "artefact," "craft," "Western art," "tribal art," and so on), the language we use to discuss this production, and the value we choose to give it.

The aim of this essay is to bring out into the open some of these rules for looking. It tries to show not only that such rules do exist, however concealed they may be in everyday life, but also that—as the title suggests—they are *culturally variable*; that is, they are not universal but differ from one culture or cultural subgroup to another. It follows from this variability that the rules themselves may be a source of disagreement or conflict within any society—but particularly within the diffuse amalgam of cultures that makes up modern North America and many other modern-nation states. This essay examines some of the cases where such conflict has become open, even fierce; and it tries to show that these instances of explicit disagreement about our "ways of seeing" are not just peculiar exceptions, but can help us more generally to uncover the rules that underlie our practice of viewing—rules that normally remain concealed, implicit, and unexamined.

The focus of what follows is the museum and art gallery. It is not, of course, the case that art exists only within those institutions. There are all kinds of visual images in private houses, in churches, in dormitories, in hospitals. But nevertheless, over the last two hundred years the museum has become the privileged location for art; the museum is the place we now look to as the guardian of art, the place whose rules play a large part in defining our ways of seeing. As is obvious, the vast majority of the pictures in this book illustrate objects or paintings that (whatever their original location) are now housed in museums.

In the mid 1980s a large exhibition of Hispanic art was shown in various galleries across the United States. It gathered together probably the

5

most comprehensive collection of contemporary paintings and sculptures produced by American artists of Hispanic descent ever to be shown in major national museums. The exhibition's organizers had set out to bring before a wider American public the work of artists normally neglected by mainstream art institutions, and to assert the importance of Hispanic art as part of contemporary American culture. They almost certainly did not foresee the intense controversies that the exhibition would arouse.

The terms of the conflict were very clear. On the one hand there were the well-intentioned, liberal aims of the organizers who saw themselves as expanding the range of the traditional art museum, widening the horizons of the American museum-going public, and at the same time doing justice to Hispanic artists by granting them their rightful place in great national institutions. On the other hand there were those who objected to the cultural imperialism of the mainstream galleries, which (as they saw it) were attempting to take over, domesticate, and so depoliticize Chicano artistic productions. To turn Hispanic art into "Art," to pull murals off street walls and place them as "museum objects" in the institutions of the dominant culture was, so the argument went, to undermine the whole significance of the Hispanic art movement. The rightful place of Hispanic art, in other words, was on the streets, not in the museum.

This debate is part of an irresolvable series of questions about the place of Hispanic art and about how we should look at it. Should Hispanic art always exist on the margins of the dominant artistic culture? How can that dominant culture recognize the work of Hispanic artists without merely appropriating them? Why would Chicano artists *want* to show their work in the Metropolitan Museum? Or why, on the other hand, should they be content never to be shown there? Why should "we" not be free to display and view Hispanic art wherever and however we want? Who has the right to decide where this art belongs? But underlying these questions, even wider issues come into play: namely, the fact that the context in which we view art *matters*; that a painting hung on a museum wall necessarily means something different from the same painting displayed in the street; that we process and understand images in one way when we view them in the calm, quiet, reverent atmosphere of the art museum and in quite other ways when we see them at the back of the parking lot.

It is easy enough to recognize these various options and differences when we are thinking of contemporary art, within the society with which we are most familiar. So even if we do not wholeheartedly agree with the complaints of some of the Chicano artists, we can readily understand what is at stake in their objections. It is rather more difficult to see the force of such issues immediately when we are viewing art that was produced at much greater distance from us—centuries old, perhaps, or from an unfamiliar foreign culture. But here, too, conflict, choices, and options in viewing lie just beneath the surface. How can we recapture them for ourselves?

Imagine that you are in an art museum looking at a painting by an
artist of the Italian Renaissance; let's suppose it is *The Baptism of Christ* by
Piero della Francesca (1416?–1492). How does the museum encourage
you to see and understand this picture? What story does it try to construct around it? Maybe the label beside the painting is very brief, telling
you only the name of the artist, the title, and date of the work of art;
maybe there is not much explicit guidance about "how to look."
Nevertheless the chances are that the whole layout and atmosphere of the
museum has already given you clearer instructions about how and *what*
to see than you realize.

The mere fact that this painting is in a major public gallery has already told you it is "important"—culturally, historically, aesthetically. It is
a chosen object, here for you to admire. And it is surrounded, no doubt,
by other paintings of the Italian Renaissance: a period defined as "great,"
a cultural peak in the history of the West, the age that first recaptured the
genius of classical antiquity. You are here admiring the painting not just
on its own, but also as a symbol of the cultural production of its age. There
are, however, other issues that the museum is encouraging you to bear in
mind. The paintings are arranged in chronological order: you meet fourteenth-century art before fifteenth-century; fifteenth-century art before
sixteenth. You are being asked to assign Piero his place in the *development*
of art, to consider how far his treatment of, say, perspective marks an "advance" on his predecessors; you are being taught to look at this painting
as a representative of the history of artistic style and technique.

What, though, of the subject matter and context? You may already
have reacted somewhat differently to Piero's *Baptism* according to your religious beliefs—Christian, atheist, Moslem, Jew. But what happens if you
discover (or perhaps the museum label tells you) that this picture was originally part of a church altarpiece, that it was painted to be the backdrop of
the most holy Christian ceremonies? What difference does this make to the
way you see it? Instantly then, whatever your own beliefs, you understand
that another way of looking is possible. This painting was once a focus of
religious reverence—not just the *cultural* reverence of today's museum visitor. The scene depicted was a central moment of the Christian faith—not
just (as it is for many viewers today) a matter for intellectual "decoding"
("Baptism: Christ in center, John the Baptist to the side").

It is not, of course, only *one* more way of looking that is possible. The
original viewers may have been no more homogeneous in their attitudes
than we are. Some would perhaps have doubted the Christian faith—and
have found it hard to feel any sense of devotion here. Others, with their
own private conception of Christ, might simply have been disappointed
with Piero's version. The options are almost limitless—although necessarily different from most of the options open to the modern museum-goer.

These considerations are not meant to suggest that the original setting and interpretation of a painting is the only "correct" one. After all,
we could never accurately recover the original interpretations of Piero's
Baptism; we can at best only pretend to be fifteenth-century Italians. We

have necessarily made our own new contexts and meanings for paintings of this type. The questions that have been raised, however, are meant to suggest that we should reflect much more carefully on how our ways of seeing are determined and how they vary. Why do we see as we do? As was so clear in the controversies over the exhibition of Hispanic art, the context of our viewing *makes a difference:* new contexts produce new ways of seeing; new ways of seeing produce new meanings.

An exhibition at the New York Center for African Art in 1987 set out to   15
challenge some of the ways we classify different types of art, and at the same time to reveal the power of museum display in forming our ways of seeing. A prize exhibit was a very cheap, ordinary hunting net from Zaire. It was laid out on its own, on a low platform, under spot-lighting—the kind of treatment usually reserved for the rarest and most precious objects. The questions being posed here were very simple: How do we now classify this net? What happens when we display it as "art" rather than as cheap "arte-fact"? Is it still an "ordinary" hunting net, or has it been transformed? And if it has been transformed, what has brought about the transformation?

This was, of course, in some senses a "trick"—a trick that obviously worked rather well, as several dealers in tribal art were drawn to inquire from the Center where they might acquire another such marvelous net! But, as the questions suggest, it had an important point in highlighting the arbitrariness of our normal division between "native craft" and "art"; and in showing the power of museum display in creating "Art" out of the most humble object. Different styles of display can entirely change the way we see what we see. Imagine how humble the net would have re-mained if it had been displayed in a museum case packed full of other pieces of hunting equipment, and with background information on hunt-ing practices among the Zande people.

These issues of status, valuation, and display are not restricted to the problems of tribal art/craft. They have a much wider resonance in many different areas of the visual arts. Consider, for example, the "master-pieces" of ancient Greek ceramics—the painted vases produced largely in Athens between the sixth and fourth centuries B.C.E., elegantly decorated with scenes drawn from Greek myth and everyday life. These vases are now treated as major works of art: their painters (who sometimes signed their pieces) are discussed by scholars in much the same terms as the painters of the Italian Renaissance; the stylistic details of the painting are minutely compared from vase to vase, influence and imitation from one to another carefully detected; individual vases are given spot-lit, star treatment in most museums. Paradoxically, though, in the ancient world itself the production of these ceramics was a low-grade "craft" activity. Unlike their renowned sculptors or painters on wood or canvas, the men who decorated these vases were, to the Greeks, craftsmen, not artists.

There are various reasons why we have come to value these vase paintings so highly—and so differently from the society that created them. Perhaps the most obvious lies in the accidents of survival: none of the major Greek paintings on wood have survived—we know of them only through the descriptions given by ancient writers; if we want to get any idea of the character of Greek painting, we are *forced* to concentrate on (and so in the process over-value) these paintings on vases. But others might argue that our modern appreciation of these objects as "art" is in fact a proper revaluation of their quality—that the Greeks themselves, in thinking of them as mundane "craft," quite simply failed to recognize their artistic genius. Whatever the underlying reasons, though, it is clear that the modern display of these objects in museums (pride of place in the museum case, shining spotlights onto a single prize specimen) serves to reinforce their high status. The way they are displayed (and so the way that we see them) makes them seem self-evidently "Art."

Could we reverse that valuation? If we consistently displayed these objects in a different way, would we start to think differently about them? Imagine how it would be if they were shown in the case piled one upon another, as if in a cheap china store—not single objects for our admiration. What if we changed their labels and called them "pots," not "vases"? What if we surrounded them with information not about their "artists" or their "painterly technique," but about their domestic use, or about the pottery "industry" in ancient Athens? These changes would, of course, be "tricks," like the "trick" of the Zaire hunting net. But they are tricks that would almost certainly work in making us think quite differently about the objects on display. We would find that we had quite different things to say about these vases or pots, a quite different sense of their value. That in itself should reveal to us how fragile and how variable our judgment of visual objects is.

Explicit conflicts about *how to look* are rare. In other words, the rules we intuit for processing what we see usually do their job very well; they veil from us the sometimes arbitrary, sometimes very loaded choices that we make in classifying and judging the visual world. So, for example, the political agenda that underlies the term "women's craft" or "native craft" (rather than "women's *art*" or "black *art*") is something that most of the time, for most of us, passes unnoticed. But thinking about such conflicts, when they do become explicit, can help to make us aware of the choices that we (or someone on our behalf) are always, necessarily, making when we think about, describe, classify, and *view* works of art.

20

❧ Topics for Critical Thinking and Writing

1. In paragraph 2 Beard suggests that the walls of a dormitory room suggest "the visual equivalent of 'anything goes.'" Think about the walls in your room, whether in a dormitory or not. Is there a unifying taste or theme? Or does the variety itself say something? (In her third paragraph Beard offers a comment that you may find helpful in thinking about these questions.)

2. In paragraph 3 Beard speaks of "art" and of "craft." In your view, what, if anything, is the difference? (See also Beard's paragraphs 16–18.) Consider

such items as a handmade quilt, a handmade chair, flowers made out of beads on wire, beaded moccasins, a braided leather belt.

3. In paragraphs 6–8 Beard tells of the controversy concerning an exhibition of Hispanic art. (By the way, what does *Hispanic* mean? Is a Spanish-speaking Indian from Guatemala a Hispanic person? A Spanish-speaking black from Cuba?) Write a paragraph answering her question, "Why would Chicano artists *want* to show their work in the Metropolitan Museum?" Write a second paragraph answering another of her questions, "Or why, on the other hand, should they be content never to be shown there?"

4. Think about a photograph you like very much, taken by you or by a friend or member of your family. In 250 words answer the question, Is it art? Why, or why not?

John Simon

John Simon, born in Yugoslavia in 1925, received his higher education in the United States. He has written criticism of plays, books, and films for several magazines, as well as a book on Ingmar Bergman. We reprint an article from New York *magazine—a periodical aimed not only at New Yorkers but at all middle-class, general-interest readers.*

Triumph over Death

Why is dance enjoying such all-but-unprecedented popularity in our time? At least partly, I think, because of the withdrawal of the word from our culture—or, more precisely, our withdrawal from the word. Whether in or out of school, Dick and Jane write, read, and express themselves orally with increasing difficulty. One of the consequences is that, among the arts, the wholly or largely nonverbal ones become favored—especially dance, where the body has it all over the mind. In the fine arts and in serious music, the mind seems to make greater demands than in dance, whose only appreciable competition comes from the movies, where the word appears to be undemanding and the visuals are seemingly all that matters. Highly kinetic, then, is what dance and film are: forms, as it were, of body language, which may yet become our lingua franca.

In the domain of dance, ballet is unquestioned king, because it is the least earthbound, the most death-defying, form of dance: it appears to defeat the laws of gravity, defy death itself. The danseur noble[1] at the height of an entrechat or jeté, the ballerina carried aloft but looking more

---

[1]**Danseur noble** is the leading male dancer in a ballet company; an **entrechat** is a leap during which the dancer crosses his feet a number of times, a **jeté** is a leap from one foot to the other, and a **pas de bourrée** is a short running or walking step. (Editors' note)

airborne than handheld, are no longer a little lower than the angels, but fully of their company. Even a simple pas de bourrée, perfectly executed, conveys a skimming along the surface of the earth rather than a walk or run upon it; it is perhaps a water bird skittering along the mirror of a lake. And dancers are always young and beautiful. Just as at a university only the sedentary faculty ages, watching students who are always twentyish come and go, at the ballet only the audience grows old. The faces and bodies may not belong to the same dancers—although, in another way, they do, for the perfectly stylized steps, highly dramatic makeup, and formalized costumes bestow their own uniformity and continuity—but those privileged beings up there are forever beautiful and young.

So our two greatest limitations are overcome before our eyes: we become like unto the angels who need not touch ground, and do not have to die. I think it is no accident that three of the greatest, ever-popular story ballets deal with the triumph over death. In *Swan Lake*, the wicked enchanter and the demanding parent are both bested as the lovers float off into shared immortality. In *Giselle*, the beloved remains faithful to her deceitful lover beyond death, rises from her tomb to save his life, and thus binds him to herself forever. In *The Sleeping Beauty*, Prince Charming awakens the heroine from a sleep perilously resembling death. Even the fourth hardy perennial, *The Nutcracker*, takes us back to the ageless world of childhood, whose animated toys, benign fairies, and transfigured children mortality cannot touch.

It is easier to project ourselves into dancers than into actors. Dancers, especially in ballet, are abstract: they symbolize rather than express, they are mythic rather than specific. The particular words of Shakespeare's Ophelia may leave some audiences cold, but an Ophelia balletically transmuted into a symbol of unfulfilled yearning is an image for everybody. Louis MacNeice's poem, "Les Sylphides," begins, significantly, "Life in a day: he took his girl to the ballet"; stanza three runs: "Now, he thought, we are floating—ageless, oarless—/Now there is no separation, from now on/You will be wearing white/Satin and a real sash/Under the waltzing trees." It seems noteworthy how many extremely obese people there are among balletomanes; they, more than anyone, want to think themselves disembodied sylphs. But all of us, regardless of weight, size, and age, would like to soar, be lighter than air, than care.

⟨ℝ Topics for Critical Thinking and Writing

1. Simon offers no evidence that dance is "enjoying . . . all but unprecedented popularity." Should he have? Explain.

2. In his first paragraph Simon makes a distinction between verbal and nonverbal arts. What are some examples of verbal arts? What are some nonverbal arts other than those he mentions?

3. What contrasts does Simon find between ballet and other forms of dance, and between dance and other theatrical forms?

4. In the first paragraph Simon speaks of "our withdrawal from the word." What does he mean? In the last paragraph he quotes from a poem. How can this apparent inconsistency be explained?

5. How would you characterize the readers Simon addresses in this essay? On what evidence do you base your characterization?

Paul Goldberger

Paul Goldberger, formerly the architecture critic for The New York Times, *has contributed articles to various magazines, and is the author of* The City Observed, *a book about the architecture of Manhattan.*

Quick! Before It Crumbles!
An Architecture Critic Looks at Cookie Architecture

Sugar Wafer (Nabisco)

There is no attempt to imitate the ancient forms of traditional, individually baked cookies here—this is a modern cookie through and through. Its simple rectangular form, clean and pure, just reeks of mass production and modern technological methods. The two wafers, held together by the sugar-cream filling, appear to float, and the Nabisco trademark, stamped repeatedly across the top, confirms that this is a machine-age object. Clearly the Sugar Wafer is the Mies van der Rohe of cookies.

Paul Goldberger, "Quick! Before It Crumbles!" Reprinted by permission of the author.

Fig Newton (Nabisco)

This, too, is a sandwich but different in every way from the Sugar Wafer. Here the imagery is more traditional, more sensual even; a rounded form of cookie dough arcs over the fig concoction inside, and the whole is soft and pliable. Like all good pieces of design, it has an appropriate form for its use, since the insides of Fig Newtons can ooze and would not be held in place by a more rigid form. The thing could have had a somewhat different shape, but the rounded top is a comfortable, familiar image, and it's easy to hold. Not a revolutionary object but an intelligent one.

Milano (Pepperidge Farms)

This long, chocolate-filled cookie summons up contradictory associations. Its rounded ends suggest both the traditional image of stodgy ladyfingers and the curves of Art Deco, while the subtle yet forceful "V" embossed onto the surface creates an abstract image of force and movement. The "V" is the kind of ornament that wishes to appear modern without really being modern, which would have meant banning ornament altogether. That romantic symbolism of the modern was an Art Deco characteristic, of course; come to think of it the Milano is rather Art Deco in spirit.

Mallomar (Nabisco)

This marshmallow, chocolate and cracker combination is the ultimate sensual cookie—indeed, its resemblance to the female breast has been cited so often as to sound rather trite. But the cookie's imagery need not be read so literally—the voluptuousness of the form, which with its nipped waist rather resembles the New Orleans Superdome, is enough. Like all good pieces of design, the form of the cookie is primarily derived from functional needs, but with just enough distinction to make it instantly identifiable. The result is a cultural icon—the cookie equivalent, surely, of the Coke bottle.

Lorna Doone (Nabisco)

Like the Las Vegas casino that is overwhelmed by its sign, image is all in the Lorna Doone. It is a plain, simple cookie (of shortbread, in fact), but a cookie like all other cookies—except for its sign. The Lorna Doone logo, a four-pointed star with the cookie's name and a pair of fleur-de-lis-like decorations, covers the entire surface of the cookie in low relief. Cleverly, the designers of this cookie have placed the logo so that the points of the star align with the corners of the square, forcing one to pivot the cookie forty-five degrees, so that its shape appears instead to be a diamond. It is a superb example of the ordinary made extraordinary.

Oatmeal Peanut Sandwich (Sunshine)

If the Sugar Wafer is the Mies van der Rohe of cookies, this is the Robert Venturi—not pretentiously modern but, rather, eager to prove its ordinariness, its lack of real design, and in so zealous a way that it ends up looking far dowdier than a *really* ordinary cookie like your basic gingersnap. The Oatmeal Peanut Sandwich is frumpy, like a plump matron in a flower-print dress, or an old piece of linoleum. But it is frumpy in an intentional way and not by accident—one senses that the designers of this cookie knew the Venturi principle that the average user of architecture (read eater of cookies) is far more comfortable with plain, ordinary forms that do not require him to adjust radically any of his perceptions.

Topics for Critical Thinking and Writing

1. How seriously do you take these descriptions? Do they have any point, or are they sheer fooling around?

2. Explain, to someone who does not understand them, the references, in context, to Mies van der Rohe, Art Deco, the New Orleans Superdome, and Robert Venturi. If you had to do some research, explain what sources you used and how you located the sources. What difficulties, if any, did you encounter?

3. Explicate Goldberger's final sentence on "Mallomar": "The result is a cultural icon—the cookie equivalent, surely, of the Coke bottle."

4. Write a similar description of some cookie not discussed by Goldberger. Or write a description, along these lines, of a McDonald's hamburger, a BLT, and a hero sandwich. Other possibilities: a pizza, a bagel, and a taco.

Perri Klass

Perri Klass, a physician and a writer of fiction and nonfiction, was born in Trinidad in 1958 and educated in the United States. In the essay that we reprint, from The New York Times, *Klass considers the view that Disney's* The Lion King, *with its themes of patricide and guilt, may be too upsetting for small children.*

King of the Jungle

Last summer, people worried about whether the dinosaurs in *Jurassic Park* were too frightening for children. This summer, some may look at *The Lion King* and wonder if the death of the father lion is too traumatic. In the first case, the worry was that brilliant special effects would leave children frightened of animals they know do not really walk the earth; in the second, that a well-told story would have children identifying with an animated lion cub and his grief and guilt over the loss of his father.

In *The Lion King*, which opened on Wednesday, Mufasa, the king of beasts, is trampled in a wildebeest stampede as he saves his little cub, Simba. Mufasa's evil brother, Scar, who provoked the stampede to kill his brother and take over the lion kingdom, convinces Simba that he killed his father. The distraught cub leaves home, nearly dies and wanders the veldt until he grows up enough to return and challenge his usurping uncle.

Many reviewers have specifically noted the potentially frightening aspects of the movie. Janet Maslin, writing in *The New York Times*, referred to "Mufasa's disturbing on-screen death" and wondered if the film "really warranted a G rating." Terrence Rafferty, writing in *The New Yorker*, said the film dredged up "deep-seated insecurities and terrors." Richard Corliss, in *Time* magazine, said, "Get ready to explain to the kids why a good father should die violently and why a child should have to witness the death." And *Variety* pointed to "scenes of truly terrifying animal-kingdom violence that should cause parents to think twice before bringing along the 'Little Mermaid' set."

Hamlet with fur. An animated movie with the potential to move its audience, adults and children, to make them wonder and worry and cheer and, yes, cry. Isn't that what stories are supposed to do, on the page, on the stage or on the screen?

If children's entertainment is purged of the powerful, we risk homogenization, predictability and boredom, and we deprive children of any real understanding of the cathartic and emotional potentials of narrative. As Marie Antoinette once remarked, "Let them watch Barney." 5

Perri Klass, "King of the Jungle." First published as "Lions and Shadows" in *The New York Times*, June 19, 1994. Copyright © 1994 by Perri Klass. Reprinted by permission of the Elaine Markson Literary Agency.

So this is a Disney cartoon about animals in which a loving parent dies. Surely we've had this discussion before, at some point in our collective cultural pageant. In fact, the world is full of adults who think that the death of Bambi's mother is too upsetting for small children. Too sad. Too scary. There will be parents who feel that *The Lion King* may be too upsetting for children, too; a movie about lions is a little, well, redder in tooth and claw than a movie about a deer. As Timon the meerkat says—and there is no way to convey how much exasperation Nathan Lane gets into his voice—"Carnivores!"

I myself tend to worry more about human villains, both in real life and at the movies. By my standards, *Snow White* is the much more upsetting movie. There is nothing in *The Lion King* that can compare to a wicked queen who wants to kill her stepdaughter for being too beautiful or to a huntsman ordered to kill the girl and cut her heart out. And for that matter, are two lions fighting for control as scary as Cruella De Vil, who, in *101 Dalmatians*, wants to kill the puppies and make them into coats?

Do we really want to protect our children from being saddened or scared or even upset by movies—or by books? Do we want to eliminate surprise, reversal, tragedy, conflict and leave children with stories in which they can be smugly confident that the good will always be rewarded and the bad always punished? Children don't have to sit through "Friday the 13th" at a tender age, but neither do they need an unending diet of wholesomely bland entertainment. A child who is worried, truly worried, about the outcome of a book is a child who is learning to understand what pulls someone into literature, and in fact it is a triumph that in an age of special effects and interactive videos, words on a page still have the power to move children.

Similarly, in an age when cartoons and live action films are full of bang- 'em-on-the-head violence that has no true dramatic impact, this is a movie in which a noble character dies and is truly mourned. And when we talk about children made sad by a movie, we are talking about children being moved by things that are not really happening to real people, and that is what art and drama and literature are all about. Those children are recognizing a character and feeling for that character, and that is a giant step toward empathy.

Maria Tatar, professor of German studies at Harvard and the author   10
of *Off With Their Heads! Fairy Tales and the Culture of Childhood*, points out that stories and folk tales have always offered children a way to consider and even control death and other difficult and forbidden topics. "Kids can handle almost anything if they're authorized to see it, talk about it," she says. "They're much smarter than we give them credit for."

Barry Zuckerman, chairman of the department of pediatrics at Boston City Hospital and an expert on child development, agrees that these stories offer children an opportunity to master troubling issues. "It's not bad for children to be exposed to stressful things. They can cope by having a parent available, so they can cuddle up to a parent who provides safety and security."

And if a child responds to *The Lion King* on some level that is deeper and more intense than a pow-pow Saturday morning cartoon, that is because the people who made this movie are trying for something more complex here, and children know it.

What there is in *The Lion King*, along with sometimes breathtaking animation and well-cast voices, is an interesting mix of *Hamlet, Bambi* and *The Jungle Book,* all shot through with some contemporary sensibility about men who can't grow up. Is this just a late-20th-century take on *Hamlet* imbued with self-help books and actualization therapy? Instead of a young man who could not make up his mind, we have a young man who cannot share his feelings and has trouble with commitment. Still, when the ghost of the dead king appears to the young lion and charges him to depose his treacherous uncle to reclaim the kingdom, you can't help looking around for Rosencrantz and Guildenstern (played here by a wart hog and a meerkat).

Yes, the father dies. And there is a stampede, which is some kind of heroic triumph of animation. But the stampede is not so much scary as it is inexorable, an animal-world event, even if it is provoked by the evil uncle and his hyena henchmen.

Yes, the cub is tortured by guilt, thinking that he started the wildebeests running and is therefore responsible for his father's death. But even small children will have no trouble identifying whose fault it really is; Jeremy Irons gives the evil uncle, Scar, a personality worthy of the long and distinguished line of Disney cartoon villains. And cartoon villains have always had a certain license to be evil, just because they are not real people, and children can see that they are not.

In *The Lion King,* they aren't people at all. It's always a little tricky to know how children absorb animal stories. *Born Free* was the great lion movie of my childhood, another movie about a lion cub who loses a parent, and I can dimly recall discussions of whether the hunting (and eating) scenes were too strong for children. In addition to the loss of Bambi's mother, there is Babar's mother, killed by a wicked hunter on the third page of *The Story of Babar*; within two pages, Babar is consoling himself by buying new clothes. In my experience, children are interested in the death of Babar's mother, and then quickly curious about Babar's new clothes.

I cried when Bambi's mother was shot, but my son, who was then 4, did not; he was interested in what would happen next. Parents are terrified of dying and leaving their child unprotected. For children, the issues are often different.

Note it was Bambi's and Babar's *mothers* who were killed off. Most Disney cartoon features have not included mothers at all; the title character in *The Little Mermaid* has only a father, as do Princess Jasmine in

15

Aladdin and Belle in *Beauty and the Beast*. Snow White and Cinderella, of course, have evil stepmothers. Bambi has a mother, but she dies; Dumbo's mother spends most of the movie locked up.

In *The Lion King*, it is the father who dies. Though this may be dictated by the plot structure of *Hamlet*, it is connected to the movie's 90's-style celebration of the involved dad. Bambi's father, after all, was the archetypal distant father of the 1940's, the kind of stag who would stay out of sight and let his son take the hard knocks, and only show up the end to point the way to manhood. But Mufasa in *The Lion King* is there romping with his cub, offering sensitive advice about what it means to be the King of Beasts: "I'm only brave when I have to be," he tells his admiring son.

Will children see the deeper themes—Disney describes the movie as "allegorical"—or will they simply be entertained by the surface story? Will they understand the central moral, that Simba has to confess the guilt he has been hiding, and has to give up his carefree bachelorhood and accept the responsibilities of leadership? Well, some children will understand some of it. And some of this New-Age-tinged message is there for adults, as are the numerous and clever animated references, from the Busby Berkeley animal acrobatics to the Leni Riefenstahl Nuremberg rally scene in which Scar reviews his hyena troops. You don't have to understand these associations to appreciate the scenes, and, similarly, most of the worrying about Oedipal overtones, guilt and responsibility will be done by parents.

It all comes down to what is real and what is not-real, which can admittedly be a complex question for children. A few months ago my 4-year-old daughter, Josephine, was going to her first opera. Her opera-loving but perhaps overambitious father prepared her as carefully as possible, playing his favorite recording of *La Traviata*, a little each day, explaining the story, showing her a photograph of Maria Callas, and teaching Josephine to listen for her voice of voices. Toward the end of the week, I came into the living room to find Josephine sobbing hysterically on the couch, with the music blaring and her father looking flummoxed.

Why was she crying? "Because Maria Callas is dying!" she wailed. And it was hard to know exactly how to comfort her; when her father told her that no, Callas was just playing the part of a woman who was dying, Josephine promptly asked, "So Maria Callas did not die?" Then, of course, he had to explain that as a matter of fact she was dead—and Josephine was in tears again.

She was eventually comforted, and went on to enjoy the opera tremendously, probably because Maria Callas did not die in our local production.

Children do, in general, understand the difference between real people and cartoon characters. And they understand the difference between people and animals. And these differences give movie makers a certain latitude to explore themes and scenes that they couldn't really touch in a live action movie for children.

20

Are there some children, maybe children under 4, who could be too   25
upset by this movie? Probably.

Will I take Josephine, my own 4-year-old? Certainly, and I would
have taken her a year ago. The bad guys get it most satisfactorily in the
end, and none of the sweet, cute, funny little fellows get hurt—the bird
Zazu is actually endowed with cartoon invulnerability and can emerge
unscathed from a lion's mouth or a boiling pot. Children may be made
sad by the film, as their parents certainly will be, and they may find the
villains scary, but they will also be interested and amused and involved,
and that, after all, is the point of art.

Some children may make it through the death of Mufasa, and then fall
apart at the final apocalyptic battle between lions and hyenas, which goes
on a little too long for the just-keep-your-eyes-closed crowd (the ones
who were traumatized by the wolves in *Beauty and the Beast*). I myself did
not go to see *Jaws* as an adult, since I was a fairly timid ocean swimmer
who did not want to watch images that would make me even more wary.
On the other hand, I had no problem sending my 9-year-old to *Jurassic
Park* last summer; I wouldn't really mind if he ended up very scared of
live dinosaurs.

But let us, for heaven's sake, not start worrying that it's a problem if
children respond to art with sadness or dismay or even fear, as long as
these emotions can be discussed, as long as the sad can be comforted and
the frightened reassured.

And if you do have a child who identifies too completely with Bambi
or Simba, you can practice some reassurances, just to see how they feel.
Then decide which you would be more comfortable saying: "Darling, I
promise, there are no bad men with guns," or "Darling, I promise, there
won't be a wildebeest stampede."

 Topics for Critical Thinking and Writing

1. In her fourth paragraph Klass says that literature is "supposed" to make audiences "wonder and worry and cheer and, yes, cry." Much of Klass's essay is in
   effect addressed to someone whose position might be summarized as saying,
   "Perhaps *adult* literature is supposed to do these things, but not children's literature." List Klass's arguments. Which is the strongest? The weakest? Why?

2. Think back to your childhood and recall a book or film (or perhaps even
   an event at a circus or fair) that in some ways distressed you. Do you
   now feel that you should not have been put through this experience, or
   that an adult should in some way have helped you to cope with it?
   Explain.

3. Evaluate Klass's final paragraph as a concluding paragraph.

Amy Tan

Amy Tan was born in Oakland, California, in 1952, of Chinese immigrant parents. When she was eight, she won first prize among elementary students with an essay entitled "What the Library Means to Me." In due time she attended Linfield College in Oregon, then transferred to San Jose State University where, while working two part-time jobs, she became an honors student and a President's Scholar. In 1973 she earned an M.A. in linguistics, also at San Jose, and she later enrolled as a doctoral student at the University of California, Berkeley, though she left this program after the murder of a close friend. For the next five years she worked as a language development consultant and a project director, and then she became a freelance business writer. In 1986 she published her first short story, and it was reprinted in Seventeen, *where it was noticed by an agent, who encouraged her to continue writing fiction. In 1989* The Joy Luck Club *was published. Other books include* The Kitchen God's Wife *(1991),* The Hundred Secret Senses *(1995), and* The Bonesetter's Daughter *(2001). She has also written two books for children,* The Moon Lady *(1992) and* SAGWA the Chinese Siamese Cat *(1994).*

In the Canon, for All the Wrong Reasons

Several years ago I learned that I had passed a new literary milestone. I had made it to the Halls of Education under the rubric of "Multicultural Literature," also known in many schools as "Required Reading."

Thanks to this development, I now meet students who proudly tell me they're doing their essays, term papers, or master's theses on me. By that they mean that they are analyzing not just my books but me—my grade-school achievements, youthful indiscretions, marital status, as well as the movies I watched as a child, the slings and arrows I suffered as a minority, and so forth—all of which, with the hindsight of classroom literary investigation, prove to contain many Chinese omens that made it inevitable that I would become a writer.

Once I read a master's thesis on feminist writings, which included examples from *The Joy Luck Club*. The student noted that I had often used the number four, something on the order of thirty-two or thirty-six times—in any case, a number divisible by four. She pointed out that there were four mothers, four daughters, four sections of the book, four stories per section. Furthermore, there were four sides to a mahjong table, four directions of the wind, four players. More important, she postulated, my use of the number four was a symbol for the four stages of psychological development, which corresponded in uncanny ways to the four stages of some type of Buddhist philosophy I had never heard of before. The student recalled that the story contained a character called Fourth Wife, symbolizing death, and a four-year-old girl with a feisty spirit, symbolizing regeneration.

Amy Tan, "Required Reading." First appeared in *The Threepenny Review*, Fall 1996. Copyright © 1996 by Amy Tan. Reprinted by permission of the author and the Sandra Dijkstra Literary Agency.

In short, her literary sleuthing went on to reveal a mystical and rather Byzantine puzzle, which, once explained, proved to be completely brilliant and precisely logical. She wrote me a letter and asked if her analysis had been correct. How I longed to say "absolutely."

The truth is, if there are symbols in my work they exist largely by accident or through someone else's interpretive design. If I wrote of "an orange moon rising on a dark night," I would more likely ask myself later if the image was a cliché, not whether it was a symbol for the feminine force rising in anger, as one master's thesis postulated. To plant symbols like that, you need a plan, good organizational skills, and a prescient understanding of the story you are about to write. Sadly, I lack those traits.

All this is by way of saying that I don't claim my use of the number four to be a brilliant symbolic device. In fact, now that it's been pointed out to me in rather astonishing ways, I consider my overuse of the number to be a flaw.

Reviewers and students have enlightened me about not only how I write but why I write. Apparently, I am driven to capture the immigrant experience, to demystify Chinese culture, to point out the differences between Chinese and American culture, even to pave the way for other Asian American writers.

If only I were that noble. Contrary to what is assumed by some students, reporters, and community organizations wishing to bestow honors on me, I am not an expert on China, Chinese culture, mahjong, the psychology of mothers and daughters, generation gaps, immigration, illegal aliens, assimilation, acculturation, racial tension, Tiananmen Square, the Most Favored Nation trade agreements, human rights, Pacific Rim economics, the purported one million missing baby girls of China, the future of Hong Kong after 1997, or, I am sorry to say, Chinese cooking. Certainly I have personal opinions on many of these topics, but by no means do my sentiments and my world of make-believe make me an expert.

So I am alarmed when reviewers and educators assume that my very personal, specific, and fictional stories are meant to be representative down to the nth detail not just of Chinese Americans but, sometimes, of all Asian culture. Is Jane Smiley's *A Thousand Acres* supposed to be taken as representative of all of American culture? If so, in what ways? Are all American fathers tyrannical? Do all American sisters betray one another? Are all American conscientious objectors flaky in love relationships?

Over the years my editor has received hundreds of permissions requests from publishers of college textbooks and multicultural anthologies, all of them wishing to reprint my work for "educational purposes." One publisher wanted to include an excerpt from *The Joy Luck Club*, a scene in which a Chinese woman invites her non-Chinese boyfriend to her parents' house for dinner. The boyfriend brings a bottle of wine as a gift and commits a number of social gaffes at the dinner table. Students were supposed to read this excerpt, then answer the following question: "If you are invited to a Chinese family's house for dinner, should you bring a bottle of wine?"

In many respects, I am proud to be on the reading lists for courses such as Ethnic Studies, Asian American Studies, Asian American Literature, Asian American History, Women's Literature, Feminist Studies, Feminist Writers of Color, and so forth. What writer wouldn't want her work to be read? I also take a certain perverse glee in imagining countless students, sleepless at three in the morning, trying to read *The Joy Luck Club* for the next day's midterm. Yet I'm also not altogether comfortable about my book's status as required reading.

Let me relate a conversation I had with a professor at a school in southern California. He told me he uses my books in his literature class but he makes it a point to lambast those passages that depict China as backward or unattractive. He objects to any descriptions that have to do with spitting, filth, poverty, or superstitions. I asked him if China in the 1930s and 1940s was free of these elements. He said, No, such descriptions are true; but he still believes it is "the obligation of the writer of ethnic literature to create positive, progressive images."

I secretly shuddered and thought, Oh well, that's southern California for you. But then, a short time later, I met a student from UC Berkeley, a school that I myself attended. The student was standing in line at a book signing. When his turn came, he swaggered up to me, then took two steps back and said in a loud voice, "Don't you think you have a responsibility to write about Chinese men as positive role models?"

In the past, I've tried to ignore the potshots. A *Washington Post* reporter once asked me what I thought of another Asian American writer calling me something on the order of "a running dog whore sucking on the tit of the imperialist white pigs."

"Well," I said, "you can't please everyone, can you?" I pointed out   15
that readers are free to interpret a book as they please, and that they are free to appreciate or not appreciate the result. Besides, reacting to your critics makes a writer look defensive, petulant, and like an all-around bad sport.

But lately I've started thinking it's wrong to take such a laissez-faire attitude. Lately I've come to think that I must say something, not so much to defend myself and my work but to express my hopes for American literature, for what it has the potential to become in the twenty-first century—that is, a truly American literature, democratic in the way it includes many colorful voices.

Until recently, I didn't think it was important for writers to express their private intentions in order for their work to be appreciated; I believed that any analysis of my intentions belonged behind the closed doors of literature classes. But I've come to realize that the study of literature does have its effect on how books are being read, and thus on what might be read, published, and written in the future. For that reason, I do believe writers today must talk about their intentions—if for no other reason than to serve as an antidote to what others say our intentions should be.

For the record, I don't write to dig a hole and fill it with symbols. I don't write stories as ethnic themes. I don't write to represent life in general. And I certainly don't write because I have answers. If I knew everything there is to know about mothers and daughters, Chinese and Americans, I wouldn't have any stories left to imagine. If I had to write about only positive role models, I wouldn't have enough imagination left to finish the first story. If I knew what to do about immigration, I would be a sociologist or a politician and not a long-winded storyteller.

So why do I write?

Because my childhood disturbed me, pained me, made me ask foolish questions. And the questions still echo. Why does my mother always talk about killing herself? Why did my father and brother have to die? If I die, can I be reborn into a happy family? Those early obsessions led to a belief that writing could be my salvation, providing me with the sort of freedom and danger, satisfaction and discomfort, truth and contradiction I can't find in anything else in life.

I write to discover the past for myself. I don't write to change the future for others. And if others are moved by my work—if they love their mothers more, scold their daughters less, or divorce their husbands who were not positive role models—I'm often surprised, usually grateful to hear from kind readers. But I don't take either credit or blame for changing their lives for better or for worse.

Writing, for me, is an act of faith, a hope that I will discover what I mean by "truth." I also think of reading as an act of faith, a hope that I will discover something remarkable about ordinary life, about myself. And if the writer and the reader discover the same thing, if they have that connection, the act of faith has resulted in an act of magic. To me, that's the mystery and the wonder of both life and fiction—the connection between two individuals who discover in the end that they are more the same than they are different.

And if that doesn't happen, it's nobody's fault. There are still plenty of other books on the shelf. Choose what you like.

⟨ Topics for Critical Thinking and Writing

1. In paragraph 11 Tan mentions that her books are "required reading" in various courses. What qualities, in your view, should a book of fiction have if it is to be required reading?

2. In paragraph 21 Tan says she doesn't expect her books to influence her readers. Have you ever read a work that has indeed shaped your thoughts or actions in even the slightest degree? If so, explain. If not, explain why you read anything, other than to kill time.

3. The patterns that critics see, Tan says in her first six paragraphs, are not present or, if present, are accidental. Are you convinced, or do you think (1)

she may be speaking tongue-in-cheek, or (2) she may not be aware of how her unconscious mind works? In an essay of 250 words indicate why you do or do not accept at face value her words on this point.

4. Tan says (paragraph 15) that "readers are free to interpret a book as they please." She goes on, however, in paragraph 16 to indicate that she no longer holds this "laissez-faire" attitude. Do you believe that your interpretation of a work should coincide with the author's? In an essay of 250 words, explain why, or why not.

5. In paragraph 18 Tan says she cannot write a story with only "positive role models." Can you think of a work of literature that includes a character from a minority group who is not a "positive" role model? (Many people believe that Shylock in Shakespeare's *The Merchant of Venice* is such an example.) If you are familiar with such a work, do you think that members of the minority group are right to find the depiction offensive? Should such a work not be taught in high school, and perhaps not even in college? Explain, in an essay of 500 words.

Eudora Welty

Eudora Welty (1909–2001), was born in Jackson, Mississippi. Although she earned a bachelor's degree at the University of Wisconsin and spent a year studying advertising in New York City at the Columbia University Graduate School of Business, she lived almost all of her life in Jackson. In the preface to her Collected Stories *she says:*

> I have been told, both in approval and in accusation, that I seem to love all my characters. What I do in writing of any character is to try to enter into the mind, heart and skin of a human being who is not myself. Whether this happens to be a man or a woman, old or young, with skin black or white, the primary challenge lies in making the jump itself. It is the act of a writer's imagination that I set most high.

In addition to writing stories and novels. Welty wrote a book about fiction, The Eye of the Story *(1977), and a memoir,* One Writer's Beginnings *(1984). Here is one of her stories, "A Worn Path," followed by her discussion of the work, in* The Eye of the Story.

A Worn Path

It was December—a bright frozen day in the early morning. Far out in the country there was an old Negro woman with her head tied in a red rag, coming along a path through the pinewoods. Her name was Phoenix Jackson. She was very old and small and she walked slowly in the dark pine shadows, moving a little from side to side in her steps, with the balanced heaviness and lightness of a pendulum in a grandfather clock. She carried a thin, small cane made from an umbrella, and with this she kept tapping the frozen earth in front of her. This made a grave and persistent

---

noise in the still air, that seemed meditative like the chirping of a solitary little bird.

She wore a dark striped dress reaching down to her shoe tops, and an equally long apron of bleached sugar sacks, with a full pocket: all neat and tidy, but every time she took a step she might have fallen over her shoe-laces, which dragged from her unlaced shoes. She looked straight ahead. Her eyes were blue with age. Her skin had a pattern all its own of numberless branching wrinkles and as though a whole little tree stood in the middle of her forehead, but a golden color ran underneath, and the two knobs of her cheeks were illuminated by a yellow burning under the dark. Under the red rag her hair came down on her neck in the frailest of ringlets, still black, and with an odor like copper.

Now and then there was a quivering in the thicket. Old Phoenix said, "Out of my way, all you foxes, owls, beetles, jack rabbits, coons, and wild animals! . . . Keep out from under these feet, little bob-whites. . . . Keep the big wild hogs out of my path. Don't let none of those come running my direction. I got a long way." Under her small black-freckled hand her cane, limber as a buggy whip, would switch at the brush as if to rouse up any hiding things.

On she went. The woods were deep and still. The sun made the pine needles almost too bright to look at, up where the wind rocked. The cones dropped as light as feathers. Down in the hollow was the mourning dove—it was not too late for him.

The path ran up a hill. "Seem like there is chains about my feet, time I   5
get this far," she said, in the voice of argument old people keep to use with themselves. "Something always take a hold of me on this hill—pleads I should stay."

After she got to the top she turned and gave a full, severe look behind her where she had come. "Up through pines," she said at length. "Now down through oaks."

Her eyes opened their widest, and she started down gently. But before she got to the bottom of the hill a bush caught her dress.

Her fingers were busy and intent, but her skirts were full and long, so that before she could pull them free in one place they were caught in another. It was not possible to allow the dress to tear. "I in the thorny bush," she said. "Thorns, you doing your appointed work. Never want to let folks pass—no sir. Old eyes thought you was a pretty little *green* bush."

Finally, trembling all over, she stood free, and after a moment dared to stoop for her cane.

"Sun so high!" she cried, leaning back and looking, while the thick   10
tears went over her eyes. "The time getting all gone here."

At the foot of this hill was a place where a log was laid across the creek.

"Now comes the trial," said Phoenix.

Putting her right foot out, she mounted the log and shut her eyes. Lifting her skirt, levelling her cane fiercely before her, like a festival figure in some parade, she began to march across. Then she opened her eyes and she was safe on the other side.

"I wasn't as old as I thought," she said.

But she sat down to rest. She spread her skirts on the bank around her and folded her hands over her knees. Up above her was a tree in a pearly cloud of mistletoe. She did not dare to close her eyes, and when a little boy brought her a little plate with a slice of marble-cake on it she spoke to him. "That would be acceptable," she said. But when she went to take it there was just her own hand in the air.   15

So she left that tree, and had to go through a barbed-wire fence. There she had to creep and crawl, spreading her knees and stretching her fingers like a baby trying to climb the steps. But she talked loudly to herself: she could not let her dress be torn now, so late in the day, and she could not pay for having her arm or leg sawed off if she got caught fast where she was.

At last she was safe through the fence and risen up out in the clearing. Big dead trees, like black men with one arm, were standing in the purple stalks of the withered cotton field. There sat a buzzard.

"Who you watching?"

In the furrow she made her way along.

"Glad this not the season for bulls," she said, looking sideways, "and the good Lord made his snakes to curl up and sleep in the winter. A pleasure I don't see no two-headed snake coming around that tree, where it come once. It took a while to get by him, back in the summer."   20

She passed through the old cotton and went into a field of dead corn. It whispered and shook and was taller than her head. "Through the maze now," she said, for there was no path.

Then there was something tall, black, and skinny there, moving before her.

At first she took it for a man. It could have been a man dancing in the field. But she stood still and listened, and it did not make a sound. It was as silent as a ghost.

"Ghost," she said sharply, "who be you the ghost of? For I have heard of nary death close by."

But there was no answer—only the ragged dancing in the wind.   25

She shut her eyes, reached out her hand, and touched a sleeve. She found a coat and inside that an emptiness, cold as ice.

"You scarecrow," she said. Her face lighted. "I ought to be shut up for good," she said with laughter. "My senses is gone, I too old. I the oldest people I ever know. Dance, old scarecrow," she said, "while I dancing with you."

She kicked her foot over the furrow, and with mouth drawn down, shook her head once or twice in a little strutting way. Some husks blew down and whirled in streamers about her skirts.

Then she went on, parting her way from side to side with the cane, through the whispering field. At last she came to the end, to a wagon track where the silver grass blew between the red ruts. The quail were walking around like pullets, seeming all dainty and unseen.

"Walk pretty," she said. "This the easy place. This the easy going."   30

She followed the track, swaying through the quiet bare fields, through the little strings of trees silver in their dead leaves, past cabins silver from weather, with the doors and windows boarded shut, all like old women under a spell sitting there. "I walking in their sleep," she said, nodding her head vigorously.

In a ravine she went where a spring was silently flowing through a hollow log. Old Phoenix bent and drank. "Sweet-gum makes the water sweet," she said, and drank more. "Nobody know who made this well, for it was here when I was born."

The track crossed a swampy part where the moss hung as white as lace from every limb. "Sleep on, alligators, and blow your bubbles." Then the track went into the road.

Deep, deep the road went down between the high green-colored banks. Overhead the live-oaks met, and it was as dark as a cave.

A black dog with a lolling tongue came up out of the weeds by the   35
ditch. She was meditating, and not ready, and when he came at her she only hit him a little with her cane. Over she went in the ditch, like a little puff of milk-weed.

Down there, her senses drifted away. A dream visited her, and she reached her hand up, but nothing reached down and gave her a pull. So she lay there and presently went to talking. "Old woman," she said to herself, "that black dog come up out of the weeds to stall you off, and now there he sitting on his fine tail, smiling at you."

A white man finally came along and found her—a hunter, a young man, with his dog on a chain.

"Well, Granny!" he laughed, "what are you doing there?"

"Lying on my back like a June-bug waiting to be turned over, mister," she said, reaching up her hand.

He lifted her up, gave her a swing in the air, and set her down.   40
"Anything broken, Granny?"

"No sir, them old dead weeds is springy enough," said Phoenix, when she had got her breath. "I thank you for your trouble."

"Where do you live, Granny?" he asked, while the two dogs were growling at each other.

"Away back yonder, sir, behind the ridge. You can't even see it from here."

"On your way home?"

"No, sir, I going to town."   45

"Why, that's too far! That's as far as I walk when I come out myself, and I get something for my trouble." He patted the stuffed bag he carried, and there hung down a little closed claw. It was one of the bob-whites, with its beak hooked bitterly to show it was dead. "Now you go on home, Granny!"

"I bound to go to town, mister," said Phoenix. "The time come around."

He gave another laugh, filling the whole landscape. "I know you old colored people! Wouldn't miss going to town to see Santa Claus!"

But something held Old Phoenix very still. The deep lines in her face went into a fierce and different radiation. Without warning, she had seen with her own eyes a flashing nickel fall out of the man's pocket onto the ground.

"How old are you, Granny?" he was saying.   50

"There is no telling, mister," she said, "no telling."

Then she gave a little cry and clapped her hands and said, "Git on away from here, dog! Look! Look at that dog!" She laughed as if in admiration. "He ain't scared of nobody. He a big black dog." She whispered, "Sic him!"

"Watch me get rid of that cur," said the man. "Sic him, Pete! Sic him!"

Phoenix heard the dogs fighting, and heard the man running and throwing sticks. She even heard a gunshot. But she was slowly bending forward by that time, further and further forward, the lids stretched down over her eyes, as if she were doing this in her sleep. Her chin was lowered almost to her knees. The yellow palm of her hand came out from the fold of her apron. Her fingers slid down and along the ground under the piece of money with the grace and care they would have in lifting an egg from under a sitting hen. Then she slowly straightened up, she stood erect, and the nickel was in her apron pocket. A bird flew by. Her lips moved. "God watching me the whole time, I come to stealing."

The man came back, and his own dog panted about them. "Well, I   55
scared him off that time," he said, and then he laughed and lifted his gun and pointed it at Phoenix.

She stood straight and faced him.

"Doesn't the gun scare you?" he said, still pointing it.

"No, sir. I seen plenty go off closer by, in my day, and for less than what I done," she said, holding utterly still.

He smiled, and shouldered the gun. "Well, Granny," he said, "You must be a hundred years old, and scared of nothing. I'd give you a dime if I had any money with me. But you take my advice and stay home, and nothing will happen to you."

"I bound to go on my way, mister," said Phoenix. She inclined her   60
head in the red rag. Then they went in different directions, but she could hear the gun shooting again and again over the hill.

She walked on. The shadows hung from the oak trees to the road like curtains. Then she smelled wood-smoke, and smelled the river, and she saw a steeple and the cabins on their steep steps. Dozens of little black children whirled around her. There ahead was Natchez shining. Bells were ringing. She walked on.

In the paved city it was Christmas time. There were red and green electric lights strung and crisscrossed everywhere, and all turned on in the daytime. Old Phoenix would have been lost if she had not distrusted her eyesight and depended on her feet to know where to take her.

She paused quietly on the sidewalk where people were passing by. A lady came along in the crowd, carrying an armful of red-, green-, and silver-wrapped presents; she gave off perfume like the red roses in hot summer, and Phoenix stopped her.

"Please, missy, will you lace up my shoe?" She held up her foot.

"What do you want, Grandma?"

"See my shoe," said Phoenix. "Do all right for out in the country, but wouldn't look right to go in a big building."

"Stand still then, Grandma," said the lady. She put her packages down on the sidewalk beside her and laced and tied both shoes tightly.

"Can't lace 'em with a cane," said Phoenix. "Thank you, missy. I doesn't mind asking a nice lady to tie up my shoe, when I gets out on the street."

Moving slowly and from side to side, she went into the big building and into a tower of steps, where she walked up and around and around until her feet knew to stop.

She entered a door, and there she saw nailed up on the wall the document that had been stamped with the gold seal and framed in the gold frame, which matched the dream that was hung up in her head.

"Here I be," she said. There was a fixed and ceremonial stiffness over her body.

"A charity case, I suppose," said an attendant who sat at the desk before her.

But Phoenix only looked above her head. There was sweat on her face, the wrinkles in her skin shone like a bright net.

"Speak up, Grandma," the woman said. "What's your name? We must have your history, you know. Have you been here before? What seems to be the trouble with you?"

Old Phoenix only gave a twitch to her face as if a fly were bothering her.

"Are you deaf?" cried the attendant.

But then the nurse came in.

"Oh, that's just old Aunt Phoenix," she said. "She doesn't come for herself—she has a little grandson. She makes these trips just as regular as clockwork. She lives away back off the old Natchez Trace." She bent down. "Well, Aunt Phoenix, why don't you just take a seat? We won't keep you standing after your long trip." She pointed.

The old woman sat down, bolt upright in the chair.

"Now, how is the boy?" asked the nurse.

Old Phoenix did not speak.

"I said, how is the boy?"

But Phoenix only waited and stared straight ahead, her face very solemn and withdrawn into the rigidity.

"Is his throat any better?" asked the nurse. "Aunt Phoenix, don't you hear me? Is your grandson's throat any better since the last time you came for the medicine?"

With her hands on her knees, the old woman waited, silent, erect and motionless, just as if she were in armor.

"You mustn't take up our time this way, Aunt Phoenix," the nurse said. "Tell us quickly about your grandson, and get it over. He isn't dead, is he?"

At last there came a flicker and then a flame of comprehension across her face, and she spoke.

"My grandson. It was my memory had left me. There I sat and forgot why I made my long trip."

"Forgot?" The nurse frowned. "After you came so far?"

Then Phoenix was like an old woman begging a dignified forgiveness for waking up frightened in the night. "I never did go to school. I was too old at the Surrender," she said in a soft voice. "I'm an old woman without an education. It was my memory fail me. My little grandson, he is just the same, and I forgot it in the coming." 90

"Throat never heals, does it?" said the nurse, speaking in a loud, sure voice to Old Phoenix. By now she had a card with something written on it, a little list. "Yes. Swallowed lye. When was it—January—two-three years ago—"

Phoenix spoke unasked now. "No, missy, he not dead, he just the same. Every little while his throat begin to close up again, and he not able to swallow. He not get his breath. He not able to help himself. So the time come around, and I go on another trip for the soothing medicine."

"All right. The doctor said as long as you came to get it, you could have it," said the nurse. "But it's an obstinate case."

"My little grandson, he sit up there in the house all wrapped up, waiting by himself," Phoenix went on. "We is the only two left in the world. He suffer and it don't seem to put him back at all. He got a sweet look. He going to last. He wear a little patch quilt and peep out holding his mouth open like a little bird. I remembers so plain now. I not going to forget him again, no, the whole enduring time. I could tell him from all the others in creation."

"All right." The nurse was trying to hush her now. She brought her a bottle of medicine. "Charity," she said, making a check mark in a book. 95

Old Phoenix held the bottle close to her eyes and then carefully put it into her pocket.

"I thank you," she said.

"It's Christmas time, Grandma," said the attendant. "Could I give you a few pennies out of my purse?"

"Five pennies is a nickel," said Phoenix stiffly.

"Here's a nickel," said the attendant. 100

Phoenix rose carefully and held out her hand. She received the nickel and then fished the other nickel out of her pocket and laid it beside the new one. She stared at her palm closely, with her head on one side.

Then she gave a tap with her cane on the floor.

"This is what come to me to do," she said. "I going to the store and buy my child a little windmill they sells, made out of paper. He going to find it hard to believe there such a thing in the world. I'll march myself back where he waiting, holding it straight up in this hand."

She lifted her free hand, gave a little nod, turned round, and walked out of the doctor's office. Then her slow step began on the stairs, going down.

Topics for Critical Thinking and Writing

1. If you do not know the legend of the phoenix, look it up in a dictionary or, better, in an encyclopedia. Then carefully reread the story to learn whether the story in any way connects with the legend.

2. Characterize the hunter.

3. What would be lost if the episode (with all of its dialogue) of Phoenix falling into the ditch and being helped out of it by the hunter were omitted?

4. Is Christmas a particularly appropriate time in which to set the story? Why or why not?

5. What do you make of the title?

Eudora Welty

Is Phoenix Jackson's Grandson Really Dead?

A story writer is more than happy to be read by students; the fact that these serious readers think and feel something in response to his work he finds life-giving. At the same time he may not always be able to reply to their specific questions in kind. I wondered if it might clarify something, for both the questioners and myself, if I set down a general reply to the question that comes to me most often in the mail, from both students and their teachers, after some classroom discussion. The unrivaled favorite is this: "Is Phoenix Jackson's grandson really *dead?*"

It refers to a short story I wrote years ago called "A Worn Path," which tells of a day's journey an old woman makes on foot from deep in the country into town and into a doctor's office on behalf of her little grandson; he is at home, periodically ill, and periodically she comes for his medicine; they give it to her as usual, she receives it and starts the journey back.

I had not meant to mystify readers by withholding any fact; it is not a writer's business to tease. The story is told through Phoenix's mind as she undertakes her errand. As the author at one with the character as I tell it, I must assume that the boy is alive. As the reader, you are free to think as you like, of course: The story invites you to believe that no matter what happens, Phoenix for as long as she is able to walk and can hold to her purpose will make her journey. The *possibility* that she would keep on even if

---

he were dead is there in her devotion and its single-minded, single-track errand. Certainly the *artistic* truth, which should be good enough for the fact, lies in Phoenix's own answer to that question. When the nurse asks, "He isn't dead, is he?" she speaks for herself: "He still the same. He going to last."

The grandchild is the incentive. But it is the journey, the going of the errand, that is the story, and the question is not whether the grandchild is in reality alive or dead. It doesn't affect the outcome of the story or its meaning from start to finish. But it is not the question itself that has struck me as much as the idea, almost without exception implied in the asking, that for Phoenix's grandson to be dead would somehow make the story "better."

It's *all right*, I want to say to the students who write to me, for things to be what they appear to be, and for words to mean what they say. It's all right, too, for words and appearances to mean more than one thing—ambiguity is a fact of life. A fiction writer's responsibility covers not only what he presents as the facts of a given story but what he chooses to stir up as their implications; in the end, these implications, too, become facts, in the larger, fictional sense. But it is not all right, not in good faith, for things *not* to mean what they say. 5

The grandson's plight was real and it made the truth of the story, which is the story of an errand of love carried out. If the child no longer lived, the truth would persist in the "wornness" of the path. But his being dead can't increase the truth of the story, can't affect it one way or the other. I think I signal this, because the end of the story has been reached before Old Phoenix gets home again: she simply starts back. To the question "Is the grandson really dead?" I could reply that it doesn't make any difference. I could also say that I did not make him up in order to let him play a trick on Phoenix. But my best answer would be: "*Phoenix* is alive."

The origin of a story is sometimes a trustworthy clue to the author—or can provide him with the clue—to its key image; maybe in this case it will do the same for the reader. One day I saw a solitary old woman like Phoenix. She was walking; I saw her, at middle distance, in a winter country landscape, and watched her slowly make her way across my line of vision. That sight of her made me write the story. I invented an errand for her, but that only seemed a living part of the figure she was herself: What errand other than for someone else could be making her go? And her going was the first thing, her persisting in her landscape was the real thing, and the first and the real were what I wanted and worked to keep. I brought her up close enough, by imagination, to describe her face, make her present to the eyes, but the full-length figure moving across the winter fields was the indelible one and the image to keep, and the perspective extending into the vanishing distance the true one to hold in mind.

I invented for my character, as I wrote, some passing adventures—some dreams and harassments and a small triumph or two, some jolts to her pride, some flights of fancy to console her, one or two encounters to scare her, a moment that gave her cause to feel ashamed, a moment to dance and preen—for it had to be a *journey*, and all these things belonged to that, parts of life's uncertainty.

A narrative line is in its deeper sense, of course, the tracing out of a meaning, and the real continuity of a story lies in this probing forward. The real dramatic force of a story depends on the strength of the emotion that has set it going. The emotional value is the measure of the reach of the story. What gives any such content to "A Worn Path" is not its circumstances but its *subject:* the deep-grained habit of love.

What I hoped would come clear was that in the whole surround of this story, the world it threads through, the only certain thing at all is the worn path. The habit of love cuts through confusion and stumbles or contrives its way out of difficulty, it remembers the way even when it forgets, for a dumbfounded moment, its reason for being. The path is the thing that matters.

Her victory—old Phoenix's—is when she sees the diploma in the doctor's office, when she finds "nailed up on the wall the document that had been stamped with the gold seal and framed in the gold frame, which matched the dream that was hung up in her head." The return with the medicine is just a matter of retracing her own footsteps. It is the part of the journey, and of the story, that can now go without saying.

In the matter of function, old Phoenix's way might even do as a sort of parallel to your way of work if you are a writer of stories. The way to get there is the all-important, all-absorbing problem, and this problem is your reason for undertaking the story. Your only guide, too, is your sureness about your subject, about what this subject is. Like Phoenix, you work all your life to find your way, through all the obstructions and the false appearances and the upsets you may have brought on yourself, to reach a meaning—using inventions of your imagination, perhaps helped out by your dreams and bits of good luck. And finally too, like Phoenix, you have to assume that what you are working in aid of is life, not death.

But you would make the trip anyway—wouldn't you?—just on hope.

Topics for Critical Thinking and Writing

1. In paragraph 4 Welty suggests that those who ask the question about the grandson imply "that for Phoenix's grandson to be dead would somehow make the story 'better.'" Why might anyone think this? And *would* the story be better if the grandson were dead? Explain your answer.

2. Did Welty's comment increase your enjoyment and your understanding of her story? If so, offer specific details.

3. Although it seems natural to want to hear what authors have to say about their work, consider the possibility that authors may consciously or unconsciously misrepresent their work. (The painter Claes Oldenburg said that anyone who pays attention to what artists write about their pictures ought

to have his eyes examined.) Do you think, therefore, that we should ignore what writers say about their works? Explain.

W. H. Auden

Wystan Hugh Auden (1907–1973) was born in York, England, and educated at Oxford. In the 1930s his witty left-wing poetry earned him wide acclaim as the leading poet of his generation. He went to Spain during the Spanish Civil War, intending to serve as an ambulance driver for the Republicans in their struggle against Facism, but he was so distressed by the violence of the Republicans that he almost immediately returned to England. In 1939 he came to America, and in 1946 he became a citizen of the United States, though he spent his last years in England. Much of his poetry is characterized by a combination of colloquial diction and technical dexterity.

In the following poem, Auden offers a meditation triggered by a painting in the Museum of Fine Arts in Brussels. The painting, by Pieter Brueghel (c. 1525–1569), is based on the legend of Icarus, told by the Roman poet Ovid (43 B.C.E.–17 C.E.) in his Metamorphoses. *The story goes thus: Daedalus, father of Icarus, was confined with his son on the island of Crete. In order to escape, Daedalus made wings for himself and for Icarus by fastening feathers together with wax, but Icarus flew too near the sun, the wax melted, and Icarus fell into the sea. According to Ovid, the event—a boy falling through the sky—was witnessed with amazement by a ploughman, a shepherd, and an angler. In the painting, however, these figures seem to pay no attention to Icarus, who is represented not falling through the sky but already in the water (in the lower right corner, near the ship), with only his lower legs still visible.*

Musée des Beaux Arts

About suffering they were never wrong.
The Old Masters: how well they understood
Its human position; how it takes place
While someone else is eating or opening a window or just walking
    dully along;
How, when the aged are reverently, passionately waiting   5
For the miraculous birth, there always must be
Children who did not specially want it to happen, skating
On a pond at the edge of the wood;
They never forgot
That even the dreadful martyrdom must run its course   10
Anyhow in a corner, some untidy spot
Where the dogs go on with their doggy life and the torturer's horse
Scratches its innocent behind on a tree.

In Brueghel's *Icarus*, for instance: how everything turns away
Quite leisurely from the disaster; the plowman may   15
Have heard the splash, the forsaken cry.

Landscape with the Fall of Icarus
Pieter Brueghel the Elder, c. 1558

But for him it was not an important failure; the sun shone
As it had to on the white legs disappearing into the green
Water, and the expensive delicate ship that must have seen
Something amazing, a boy falling out of the sky,   20
Had somewhere to get to and sailed calmly on.

 Topics for Critical Thinking and Writing

1. In your own words sum up what, according to the speaker (in lines 1–13), the Old Masters understood about human suffering. (The Old Masters were the great European painters who worked from about 1500 to about 1750.)

2. Suppose the first lines read:

   The Old Masters were never wrong about suffering.
   They understood its human position well.

   What (beside the particular rhymes) would change or be lost?

3. Reread the poem (preferably over the course of several days) a number of times, jotting down your chief responses after each reading. Then, in connection with a final reading, study your notes, and write an essay of 500 words setting forth the history of your final response to the poem. For example, you may want to report that certain difficulties soon were clarified and that your enjoyment increased. Or, conversely, you may want to report

that the poem became less interesting (for reasons you will set forth) the more you studied it. Probably your history will be somewhat more complicated than these simple examples. Try to find a chief pattern in your experience, and shape it into a thesis.

4. Consider a picture, either in a local museum or reproduced in a book, and write a 500-word reflection on it. If the picture is not well known, include a reproduction (a postcard from the museum or a photocopy of a page of a book).

CHAPTER 14

Law and Order

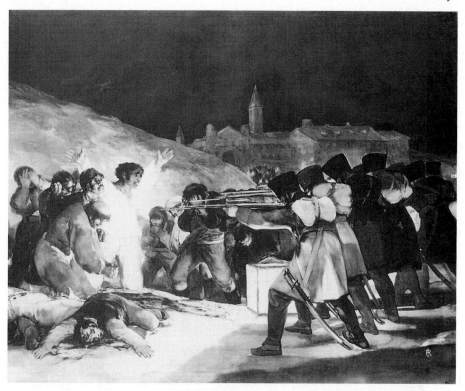

The Third of May, 1808
Francisco Goya

Cell of a Model Prison, U.S.A., 1975
Henri Cartier-Bresson

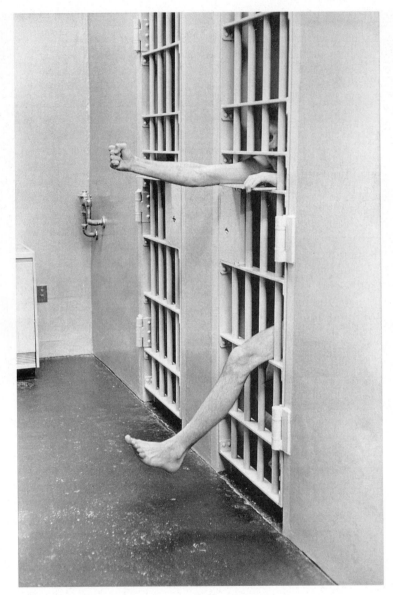

The Problem We All Live With
Norman Rockwell, 1964

Short Views

The trouble for the thief is not how to steal the chief's bugle, but where to blow it.

   African Proverb

Whether there was ever a significant increase in crime and when it might have occurred is puzzling, since the phrase, "the land is full of bloody crimes and the city full of violence," did not appear in a recent Chicago newspaper but in a report on a crime wave in the promised land about 600 B.C. as recorded in Ezekiel VII:23. The logical possibility of an ever-increasing crime wave becomes more doubtful when we consider the biblical origin of humankind: Adam, Eve and Cain committed the worst offenses possible and after Abel was killed, all survivors—or 75 percent of the first four human beings—had criminal records. In spite of all righteous claims to the opposite, this crime wave seems to have subsided, never to reach its biblical heights again. It is simpler and more correct to state that crime has always existed but statistics have not.

   Kurt Weis and Michael F. Milakovich

Whoever desires to found a state and give it laws, must start with assuming that all men are bad and ever ready to display their vicious nature, whenever they may find occasion for it.

   Niccolò Machiavelli

It is questionable whether, when we break a murderer on the wheel, we aren't lapsing into precisely the mistake of the child who hits the chair he bumps into.

   G. C. Lichtenberg

If a man were permitted to make all the ballads, he need not care who should make the laws of a nation.

   Andrew Fletcher

Nature has given women so much power that the law has very wisely given them very little.

   Samuel Johnson

I asked him whether, as a moralist, he did not think that the practice of the law, in some degree, hurt the nice feeling of honesty. JOHNSON. "Why no, Sir, if you act properly. You are not to deceive your clients with false representations of your opinion: you are not to tell lies to a judge." BOSWELL. "But what do you think of supporting a cause which you know to be bad?" JOHNSON. "Sir, you do not know it to be good or bad till the Judge determines it. I have said that you are to state facts fairly; so that your thinking, or what you call knowing, a cause to be bad, must be from reasoning, must be from your supposing your arguments to be weak and inconclusive. But, Sir, that is not enough. An argument which does not convince yourself, may convince the Judge to whom you urge it; and if it does convince him, why, then, Sir, you are wrong, and he is right. It is his business to judge; and you are not to be confident in your own opinion that a cause is bad, but to say all you can for your client, and then hear the Judge's opinion." BOSWELL. "But, Sir, does not affecting a warmth when you have no warmth, and appearing to be clearly of one opinion when you are in reality of another opinion, does not such dissimulation impair one's honesty? Is there not some danger that a lawyer may put on the same mask in common life, in the intercourse with his friends?" JOHNSON. "Why no, Sir. Everybody knows you are paid for affecting warmth for your client; and it is, therefore, properly no dissimulation: the moment you come from the bar you resume your usual behaviour. Sir, a man will no more carry the artifice of the bar into the common intercourse of society, than a man who is paid for tumbling upon his hands will continue to tumble upon his hands when he should walk on his feet."
James Boswell

One law for the ox and the ass is oppression.
William Blake

The law, in its majestic equality, forbids the rich as well as the poor to sleep under bridges, to beg in the streets, and to steal bread.
Anatole France

Decency, security and liberty alike demand that government officials shall be subjected to the same rules of conduct that are commands to the citizen. In a government of laws, existence of the government will be imperilled if it fails to observe the law scrupulously. Our Government is the potent, the omnipresent teacher. For good or for ill, it teaches the whole people by its example. Crime is contagious. If the Government becomes a lawbreaker, it breeds contempt for law; it invites every man to become a law unto himself; it invites anarchy. To declare that in the administration of the criminal law the end justifies the means—to declare that the Government may commit crimes in order to secure the conviction of a private criminal—would bring terrible retribution. Against that pernicious doctrine this Court should resolutely set its face.

> *Louis D. Brandeis*

The trouble about fighting for human freedom is that you have to spend much of your life defending sons of bitches; for oppressive laws are always aimed at them originally, and oppression must be stopped in the beginning if it is to be stopped at all.

> *H. L. Mencken*

Censorship upholds the dignity of the profession, know what I mean?

> *Mae West*

Cathy Booth Thomas

Cathy Booth Thomas, drawing on reporting by Hilary Hylton of Austin, wrote this article for Time *magazine, June 11, 2001.*

A New Scarlet Letter

Gabriel Trevino did a bad, bad thing. Three years ago, at age 31, he fondled the 14-year-old daughter of a friend. For this "slipup," as he calls it, he pleaded no contest and took five years' probation rather than risk a two-to-20-year prison term. Now he thinks prison would have been preferable. These days, people drive by his modest bungalow house, then back up to read the 18-in. by 24-in. sign posted by the little white birdhouse, DANGER, it says. REGISTERED SEX OFFENDER LIVES HERE.

Sitting by the front window in his darkened living room in Corpus Christi, Texas, last week, Trevino was at once defiant and near tears as he talked about this public mortification. "I made my mistake, and I'm paying for it," he said. But, he wondered, why should his wife and two stepdaughters pay too? "I can't even go out and cut my yard. I just stay in the house . . . I was doing good in therapy. How is this helping me?"

The answer is simple, says state District Judge J. Manuel Bañales, who on May 18 ordered Trevino and 13 other "high-risk" sex offenders on probation to post the signs in their yards. "It will keep people like you, sir, honest," he told Trevino last week after denying a request to rescind the order. "Your neighbors will watch you and make sure you're not taking another child into your home." Hours later, Bañales ordered yet another sex offender—No. 15—to put up a sign on release from jail.

In the past decade, all 50 states have passed so-called Megan's laws, requiring sex offenders to alert the community to their presence. Twenty-eight states run Internet sites listing such criminals. In the mid-1990s, judges in Texas, Louisiana, Florida and Oregon began ordering individual sex offenders to post signs outside their homes. But Bañales—who also mandated bumper stickers and even temporary placards for traveling in someone else's car—drew national attention by applying his ruling to so many at one time. His move sparked a debate on the rights of these offenders and the merits of public shaming. "We don't brand people in America," argues Gerald Rogen, president of the Coastal Bend Criminal Defense Lawyers Association. "And we damn sure don't punish the offender's family as well as the offender."

Bañales' judgment, however, was in keeping with a 1999 Texas law—   5
signed by then Governor George W. Bush—permitting judges to impose
public punishment for some crimes. Drunk drivers in the state, for instance, are sometimes made to stand at busy intersections with signs
identifying their transgression. Whether more conventional public notifi-
cations have worked as a deterrent is unclear. A Washington State study
found that such policies didn't keep sex offenders from committing more
crimes, though they did help police find and arrest recidivists more
quickly.

Bañales' extreme version of notification is having immediate consequences for the Corpus Christi 15, as landlords evict them and bosses fire
them. One man attempted suicide after Bañales' ruling. The families also
worry about vigilantes. "I'm scared for my mother's life and myself,"
says Trevino's stepdaughter Ann, 20. Lawyers for the 15 are considering
filing a joint challenge or separate ones in the 13th Court of Appeals, arguing that the signs violate the right to privacy and constitute "cruel and
unusual punishment."

Judge Bañales is unmoved. From a list of nearly 300 adult sex offenders,
he chose 14 of the 15 by working with probation officers and a polygrapher
to pinpoint those who had multiple victims, were not showing progress in
therapy or had failed to show empathy for their victims. Even in court last
week, for instance, Trevino persisted in questioning the judge on why a 14-
year-old could be tried for murder, but could not consent to sex.

Though Bañales, a Democrat, has been accused of issuing his order to
win popularity at the polls next year—his is an elected judgeship—his
cheering section includes probation officers who already see a sobering effect on new probationers. "It's definitely a deterrent now," says Iris Davila,
probation supervisor in the Nueces County Community Supervision and
Correction Department. "Other offenders are saying to us, 'We'll do whatever it takes not to have signs.'"

Topics for Critical Thinking and Writing

1. To what does the title of the article refer? How appropriate or relevant do
   you find the reference?

2. Describe the tone of the first sentence. Would you have advised Thomas to
   revise the sentence, or keep it? Explain.

3. How did Judge Bañales choose the sex offenders who were then ordered to
   put signs in their yards?

4. If you lived in Judge Bañales's district would you be part of what the last
   paragraph calls his "cheering section"? Explain.

5. In paragraph 7, Thomas reports, as a sign that Gabriel Trevino has "failed to
   show empathy for his victim," that "Trevino persisted in questioning the
   judge on why a 14-year-old could be tried for murder, but could not consent

to sex." Do you think it was improper of Trevino to ask this question? If the question were asked of you, what would your answer be?

6.   Several legislators in California have proposed that people who have drunk-driving records be required to use license plates that say "DUI" [Driving Under the Influence]. Your view? In your answer, consider at least the following issues: (a) Should offenders be put to shame? (b) If so, what is the purpose of shaming them? To make them suffer? To rehabilitate them? To safeguard others? To deter others from criminal activity?

7.   A sheriff in Arizona, believing that offenders should be subjected to humiliation, requires prisoners to wear striped uniforms and to serve in chaingangs trimming grass along highways. Your view?

Thomas Jefferson

Thomas Jefferson (1743–1826), governor of Virginia and the third president of the United States, devoted most of his adult life, until his retirement, to the service of Virginia and of the nation. The spirit and the wording of the Declaration are almost entirely Jefferson's.

The Declaration of Independence

In CONGRESS, July 4, 1776.
The Unanimous Declaration of the Thirteen United States of America.

When in the Course of human events, it becomes necessary for one people to dissolve the political bands which have connected them with another, and to assume among the powers of the earth, the separate and equal station to which the Laws of Nature and of Nature's God entitle them, a decent respect to the opinions of mankind requires that they should declare the causes which impel them to the separation.

We hold these truths to be self-evident, that all men are created equal, that they are endowed by their Creator with certain unalienable Rights, that among these are Life, Liberty and the pursuit of Happiness.

That to secure these rights, Governments are instituted among Men, deriving their just powers from the consent of the governed.

That whenever any Form of Government becomes destructive of these ends, it is the Right of the People to alter or to abolish it, and to institute new Government, laying its foundation on such principles and organizing its powers in such form, as to them shall seem most likely to effect their Safety and Happiness. Prudence, indeed, will dictate that Governments long established should not be changed for light and transient causes; and accordingly all experience hath shewn, that mankind are more disposed to suffer, while evils are sufferable, than to right themselves by abolishing the forms to which they are accustomed. But when a long train of abuses and usurpations, pursuing invariably the same

Object evinces a design to reduce them under absolute Despotism, it is their right, it is their duty, to throw off such Government, and to provide new Guards for their future security.

Such has been the patient sufferance of these Colonies; and such is now the necessity which constrains them to alter their former Systems of Government. The history of the present King of Great Britain is a history of repeated injuries and usurpations, all having in direct object the establishment of an absolute Tyranny over these States. To prove this, let Facts be submitted to a candid world.

He has refused his Assent to Laws, the most wholesome and necessary for the public good.

He has forbidden his Governors to pass Laws of immediate and pressing importance, unless suspended in their operation till his Assent should be obtained; and when so suspended, he has utterly neglected to attend to them.

He has refused to pass other Laws for the accommodation of large districts of people, unless those people would relinquish the right of Representation in the Legislature, a right inestimable to them and formidable to tyrants only.

He has called together legislative bodies at places unusual, uncomfortable, and distant from the depository of their public Records, for the sole purpose of fatiguing them into compliance with his measures.

He has dissolved Representative Houses repeatedly, for opposing with manly firmness his invasions on the rights of people.

He has refused for a long time, after such dissolutions, to cause others to be elected; whereby the Legislative powers, incapable of Annihilation, have returned to the People at large for their exercise; the State remaining in the mean time exposed to all the dangers of invasion from without, and convulsions within.

He has endeavoured to prevent the population of these States; for that purpose obstructing the Laws for Naturalization of Foreigners; refusing to pass others to encourage their migrations hither, and raising the conditions of new Appropriations of Lands.

He has obstructed the Administration of Justice, by refusing his Assent to Laws for establishing Judiciary powers.

He has made Judges dependent on his Will alone, for the tenure of their offices, and the amount and payment of their salaries.

He has erected a multitude of New Offices, and sent hither swarms of Officers to harass our people, and eat out their substance.

He has kept among us, in times of peace, Standing Armies without the Consent of our legislatures.

He has affected to render the Military independent of and superior to the Civil power.

He has combined with others to subject us to a jurisdiction foreign to our constitution, and unacknowledged by our laws; giving his Assent to their Acts of pretended Legislation:

For Quartering large bodies of armed troops among us:

For Protecting them, by a mock Trial, from punishment for any 20
Murders which they should commit on the Inhabitants of these States:

For cutting off our Trade with all parts of the world:

For imposing Taxes on us without our Consent:

For depriving us in many cases, of the benefits of Trial by Jury:

For transporting us beyond Seas to be tried for pretended offences:

For abolishing the free System of English Laws in a neighbouring 25
Province, establishing therein an Arbitrary government, and enlarging its
Boundaries so as to render it at once an example and fit instrument for in-
troducing the same absolute rule into these Colonies:

For taking away our Charters, abolishing our most valuable Laws,
and altering fundamentally the Forms of our Governments:

For suspending our own Legislatures, and declaring themselves invested with power to legislate for us in all cases whatsoever.

He has abdicated Government here, by declaring us out of his
Protection and waging War against us:

He has plundered our seas, ravaged our Coasts, burnt our towns, and
destroyed the lives of our people.

He is at this time transporting large Armies of foreign Mercenaries to 30
compleat the works of death, desolation and tyranny, already begun with
circumstances of Cruelty & perfidy scarcely paralleled in the most barbarous ages, and totally unworthy the Head of a civilized nation.

He has constrained our fellow Citizens taken Captive on the high
Seas to bear Arms against their Country, to become the executioners of
their friends and Brethren, or to fall themselves by their Hands.

He has excited domestic insurrections amongst us, and has endeavoured to bring on the inhabitants of our frontiers, the merciless Indian
Savages, whose known rule of warfare, is an undistinguished destruction
of all ages, sexes and conditions. In every stage of these Oppressions We
have Petitioned for Redress in the most humble terms: Our repeated
Petitions have been answered only by repeated injury. A Prince, whose
character is thus marked by every act which may define a Tyrant, is unfit
to be the ruler of a free people. Nor have We been wanting in attentions to
our British brethren. We have warned them from time to time of attempts
by their legislature to extend an unwarrantable jurisdiction over us. We
have reminded them of the circumstances of our emigration and settlement here. We have appealed to their native justice and magnanimity,
and we have conjured them by the ties of our common kindred to dis-
avow these usurpations, which, would inevitably interrupt our connections and correspondence. They too have been deaf to the voice of justice
and of consanguinity. We must, therefore, acquiesce in the necessity,
which denounces our Separation, and hold them, as we hold the rest of
mankind, Enemies in War, in Peace Friends.

We, THEREFORE, the Representatives of the UNITED STATES OF AMERICA, in
General Congress Assembled, appealing to the Supreme Judge of the

world for the rectitude of our intentions, do, in the Name and by Authority of the good People of these Colonies, solemnly publish and declare, That these United Colonies are, and of Right ought to be FREE AND INDEPENDENT STATES; that they are Absolved from all Allegiance to the British Crown, and that all political connection between them and the State of Great Britain, is and ought to be totally dissolved; and that as Free and Independent States, they have full Power to levy War, conclude Peace, contract Alliances, establish Commerce, and to do all other Acts and Things which Independent States may of right do.

And for the support of this Declaration, with a firm reliance on the protection of divine Providence, we mutually pledge to each other our Lives, our Fortunes and our sacred Honor.

◎ Topics for Critical Thinking and Writing

1. What audience is being addressed in the Declaration of Independence? Cite passages in the text that support your answer.

2. The Library of Congress has the original manuscript of the rough draft of the Declaration. This manuscript itself includes revisions that are indicated below, but it was later further revised. We print the first part of the second paragraph of the draft and, after it, the corresponding part of the final version. Try to account for the changes within the draft, and from the revised draft to the final version.

We hold these truths to be ~~sacred & undeniable,~~ *self evident,* that all men are created equal ~~& independent,~~ that ~~from that equal creation they~~ *they are endowed by their creator* ~~derive equal rights some of which are in rights~~ *with* inherent & inalienable *rights; that these* among ~~which~~ are ~~the preservation of~~ life, liberty, & the pursuit of happiness.

We hold these Truths to be self-evident, that all men are created

equal, that they are endowed by their Creator with certain

unalienable Rights, that among these are Life, Liberty and the

pursuit of Happiness.

In a paragraph evaluate the changes. Try to put yourself into Jefferson's mind and see if you can sense why Jefferson made the changes.

3. In a paragraph define *happiness*, and then in a second paragraph explain why, in your opinion, Jefferson spoke of "the pursuit of happiness" rather than of "happiness."

4. In "We Have No 'Right to Happiness'" (page 20) C. S. Lewis discusses the meaning of "the pursuit of happiness" in the Declaration and a current

misinterpretation of the phrase. How does he explain and define the phrase? How does his interpretation differ from what he considers an erroneous interpretation?

5. What assumptions lie behind the numerous specific reasons that are given to justify the rebellion? Set forth the gist of the argument of the Declaration using the form of reasoning known as a *syllogism*, which consists of a major premise (such as "All men are mortal"), a minor premise ("Socrates is a man"), and a conclusion ("Therefore, Socrates is mortal"). For a brief discussion of syllogisms, see page 903 (deduction).

6. In a paragraph argue that the assertion that "all Men are created equal" is nonsense, or, on the other hand, that it makes sense.

7. If every person has an unalienable right to life, how can capital punishment be reconciled with the Declaration of Independence? You need not in fact be a supporter of capital punishment; simply offer the best defense you can think of, in an effort to make it harmonious with the Declaration.

Henry David Thoreau

The essayist, poet, and Transcendental philosopher Henry David Thoreau (1817–62) was born in Concord and spent most of his life (as he put it) "sojourning" in the town and woods nearby and exploring the nearby ponds and rivers. He was educated at Harvard and then taught with his brother John at a school in Concord, but, inspired by his mentor and friend Ralph Waldo Emerson, he began in the late 1830s to keep a detailed journal and embarked on a career as a writer. Early in 1845, he built a small cabin on the shores on Walden Pond, on property that Emerson owned. Thoreau lived there for two years (though he also spent time at the homes of friends and neighbors, and was away for two months in 1846 on a trip to Maine). The record of his experiment in living is the book Walden, *published in 1854. Thoreau lectured frequently and published a number of essays during his lifetime; other essays, as well as book-length collections, including* The Maine Woods *(1864), appeared after his death from tuberculosis in 1862.*

Thoreau wrote "Civil Disobedience," an excerpt from which we give below, in response to being jailed for a night in July 1846 for failing to pay his poll tax, a tax that Thoreau argued meant giving support to the Mexican War. In his antiwar sentiments, he was in the minority, for most Americans endorsed the war, viewing it as a romantic military adventure that would extend America's democratic ideals. Abolitionists, believing that the real goal was the expansion of slavery south and west, criticized the Mexican War and later condemned the peace treaty, signed in 1848, that gave the United States 500,000 square miles of new territory. Thoreau agreed with them from the beginning; he refused to pay his tax, and thought no more about it.

But one day in July, on a trip into Concord to have a shoe repaired, Thoreau was stopped by the town constable Sam Staples, who told him that the tax was overdue. When Thoreau balked at paying it, Staples offered to loan him the money. When Thoreau said no to that too, the constable led him to jail, and he was placed in a cell with another man. Someone, probably Thoreau's Aunt Maria, paid the tax as soon as the family learned what had happened. Thoreau then should have been released, but Staples by then was at home and did not want to go back to the jail. He wasn't released until the next morning.

Thoreau did not produce his famous essay right away. It was not until January 26, 1848, that he lectured at the Concord Lyceum on "the relation of the individual to the State," which with the title "Resistance to Civil Government," was published in 1849 in the volume Aesthetic Papers, *edited by Elizabeth Peabody, an educator, reformer, and Nathaniel Hawthorne's sister-in-law. When it was reprinted after Thoreau's death, it was given the title "Civil Disobedience," by which it is familiarly known.*

"Civil Disobedience" is one of the most influential political essays ever written. The Indian religious and political leader Mohandas K. Gandhi read and translated Thoreau's writings, including "Civil Disobedience," when he campaigned in the 1900s and 1910s for Indian civil rights in South Africa, and he returned to these texts in subsequent decades when he called for Indian independence from the British: "My first introduction to Thoreau's writings was, I think, in 1907, or later, when I was in the thick of the passive resistance struggle. A friend sent me the essay on "Civil Disobedience". It left a deep impression on me." As the literary scholar Perry Miller has observed, "Civil Disobedience" also was a "rallying tract" among resisters of the Nazi occupations in Europe. Martin Luther King Jr. read the essay in college in the 1940s and remembered it in 1955 in the midst of the Montgomery bus boycott: "I became convinced that what we were preparing to do in Montgomery was related to what Thoreau had expressed. We were simply saying to the white community, 'We can no longer lend our cooperation to an evil system.'"

The core of Thoreau's argument is given in the following excerpt. He begins by contending that a person must never support a government whose policies he or she claims to disagree with. Our actions, he insists, should be in accord with our conscience, not at odds with it.

From "Civil Disobedience"

How can a man be satisfied to entertain an opinion merely, and enjoy *it*? Is there any enjoyment in it, if his opinion is that he is aggrieved? If you are cheated out of a single dollar by your neighbor, you do not rest satisfied with knowing that you are cheated, or with saying that you are cheated, or even with petitioning him to pay you your due; but you take effectual steps at once to obtain the full amount, and see that you are never cheated again. Action from principle, the perception and the performance of right, changes things and relations; it is essentially revolutionary, and does not consist wholly with anything which was. It not only divides states and churches, it divides families; ay, it divides the *individual*, separating the diabolical in him from the divine.

Unjust laws exist: shall we be content to obey them, or shall we endeavor to amend them, and obey them until we have succeeded, or shall we transgress them at once? Men generally, under such a government as this, think that they ought to wait until they have persuaded the majority to alter them. They think that, if they should resist, the remedy would be worse than the evil. But it is the fault of the government itself that the remedy *is* worse than the evil. *It* makes it worse. Why is it not more apt to anticipate and provide for reform? Why does it not cherish its wise minority? Why does it cry and resist before it is hurt? Why does it not encourage its citizens to be on the alert to point out its faults, and *do* better than it would have them? Why does it always crucify Christ, and excommunicate Copernicus and Luther, and pronounce Washington and Franklin rebels?

One would think, that a deliberate and practical denial of its authority was the only offence never contemplated by government; else, why has it not assigned its definite, its suitable and proportionate penalty? If a man who has no property refuses but once to earn nine shillings for the State, he is put in prison for a period unlimited by any law that I know, and determined only by the discretion of those who placed him there; but if he should steal ninety times nine shillings from the State, he is soon permitted to go at large again.

If the injustice is part of the necessary friction of the machine of government, let it go, let it go: perchance it will wear smooth,—certainly the machine will wear out. If the injustice has a spring, or a pulley, or a rope, or a crank, exclusively for itself, then perhaps you may consider whether the remedy will not be worse than the evil; but if it is of such a nature that it requires you to be the agent of injustice to another, then, I say, break the law. Let your life be a counter friction to stop the machine. What I have to do is to see, at any rate, that I do not lend myself to the wrong which I condemn.

As for adopting the ways which the State has provided for remedying the evil, I know not of such ways. They take too much time, and a man's life will be gone. I have other affairs to attend to. I came into this world, not chiefly to make this a good place to live in, but to live in it, be it good or bad. A man has not everything to do, but something; and because he cannot do *everything*, it is not necessary that he should do *something* wrong. It is not my business to be petitioning the Governor or the Legislature any more than it is theirs to petition me; and, if they should not hear my petition, what should I do then? But in this case the State has provided no way: its very Constitution is the evil. This may seem to be harsh and stubborn and unconciliatory; but it is to treat with the utmost kindness and consideration the only spirit that can appreciate or deserves it. So is all change for the better, like birth and death, which convulse the body.

I do not hesitate to say, that those who call themselves Abolitionists should at once effectually withdraw their support, both in person and property, from the government of Massachusetts, and not wait till they constitute a majority of one, before they suffer the right to prevail through them. I think that it is enough if they have God on their side, without waiting for that other one. Moreover, any man more right than his neighbors constitutes a majority of one already.

I meet this American government, or its representative, the State government, directly, and face to face, once a year—no more—in the person of its tax-gatherer; this is the only mode in which a man situated as I am necessarily meets it; and it then says distinctly, Recognize me; and the simplest, the most effectual, and, in the present posture of affairs, the indispensablest mode of treating with it on this head, of expressing your little satisfaction with and love for it, is to deny it then. My civil neighbor, the tax-gatherer, is the very man I have to deal with,—for it is, after all, with men and not with parchment that I quarrel,—and he has voluntarily chosen to be an agent of the government. How shall he ever know well what he is and does as an officer of the government, or as a man, until he is obliged to consider whether he shall treat me, his neighbor, for whom he has respect, as a neighbor and well-disposed man, or as a maniac and disturber of the peace, and see if he can get over this obstruction to his neighborliness without a ruder and more impetuous thought or speech

5

corresponding with his action. I know this well, that if one thousand, if one hundred, if ten men whom I could name,—if ten *honest* men only,—ay, if *one* HONEST man, in this State of Massachusetts, *ceasing to hold slaves*, were actually to withdraw from this copartnership, and be locked up in the county jail therefore, it would be the abolition of slavery in America. For it matters not how small the beginning may seem to be: what is once well done is done forever. But we love better to talk about it: that we say is our mission. Reform keeps many scores of newspapers in its service, but not one man. If my esteemed neighbor, the State's ambassador, who will devote his days to the settlement of the question of human rights in the Council Chamber, instead of being threatened with the prisons of Carolina, were to sit down the prisoner of Massachusetts, that State which is so anxious to foist the sin of slavery upon her sister,—though at present she can discover only an act of inhospitality to be the ground of quarrel with her,—the Legislature would not wholly waive the subject the following winter.

Under a government which imprisons any unjustly, the true place for a just man is also a prison. The proper place to-day, the only place which Massachusetts has provided for her freer and less desponding spirits, is in her prisons, to be put out and locked out of the State by her own act, as they have already put themselves out by their principles. It is there that the fugitive slave, and the Mexican prisoner on parole, and the Indian come to plead the wrongs of his race, should find them; on that separate, but more free and honorable ground, where the State places those who are not *with* her, but *against* her,—the only house in a slave State in which a free man can abide with honor. If any think that their influence would be lost there, and their voices no longer afflict the ear of the State, that they would not be as an enemy within its walls, they do not know by how much truth is stronger than error, nor how much more eloquently and effectively he can combat injustice who has experienced a little in his own person. Cast your whole vote, not a strip of paper merely, but your whole influence. A minority is powerless while it conforms to the majority; it is not even a minority then; but it is irresistible when it clogs by its whole weight. If the alternative is to keep all just men in prison, or give up war and slavery, the State will not hesitate which to choose. If a thousand men were not to pay their taxbills this year, that would not be a violent and bloody measure, as it would be to pay them, and enable the State to commit violence and shed innocent blood. This is, in fact, the definition of a peaceable revolution, if any such is possible. If the tax-gatherer, or any other public officer, asks me, as one has done, "But what shall I do?" my answer is, "If you really wish to do anything, resign your office." When the subject has refused allegiance, and the officer has resigned his office, then the revolution is accomplished. But even suppose blood should flow. Is there not a sort of blood shed when the conscience is wounded? Through this would a man's real manhood and immortality flow out, and he bleeds to an everlasting death. I see this blood flowing now.

Topics for Critical Thinking and Writing

1. Do you think that Thoreau really believes, literally, what he says? If you do not, what do you think is the point of the essay?

2. Thoreau emphasizes that each individual must take action—action that bears witness to moral principle. But shouldn't Thoreau also—or instead—stress the importance of individuals joining forces, working together as a morally committed group?

3. On page 752, Thoreau says that if one person alone went to jail, this "would be the abolition of slavery in America." What does Thoreau mean? Does this claim make sense to you?

4. Demonstrators on both sides of the abortion issue, those who support "a woman's right to choose" and those who support "the right to life," have cited Thoreau's essay on "civil disobedience" as a source of inspiration. Can the argument described by Thoreau be applied to opposite positions on a matter of social policy? Would Thoreau find this acceptable, or not?

5. Toward the end of this excerpt, Thoreau refers to the shedding of blood. Is Thoreau conceding that violence might sometimes be the right response to injustice, that an act of moral violence might be needed to counteract immoral violence?

Martin Luther King Jr.

Martin Luther King Jr. (1929–68), clergyman and civil rights leader, achieved national fame in 1955–56 when he led the boycott against segregated bus lines in Montgomery, Alabama. His policy of passive resistance succeeded in Montgomery, and King then organized the Southern Christian Leadership Conference in order to extend his efforts. In 1964 he was awarded the Nobel Peace Prize, but he continued to encounter strong opposition. On April 4, 1968, while in Memphis to support striking sanitation workers, he was shot and killed.

Nonviolent Resistance

Oppressed people deal with their oppression in three characteristic ways. One way is acquiescence: the oppressed resign themselves to their doom. They tacitly adjust themselves to oppression, and thereby become conditioned to it. In every movement toward freedom some of the oppressed prefer to remain oppressed. Almost 2800 years ago Moses set out to lead the children of Israel from the slavery of Egypt to the freedom of the promised land. He soon discovered that slaves do not always welcome their deliverers. They become accustomed to being slaves. They would rather bear those ills they have, as Shakespeare pointed out, than flee to others that they know not of. They prefer the "fleshpots of Egypt" to the ordeals of emancipation.

There is such a thing as the freedom of exhaustion. Some people are so worn down by the yoke of oppression that they give up. A few years ago in the slum areas of Atlanta, a Negro guitarist used to sing almost daily: "Ben down so long that down don't bother me." This is the type of negative freedom and resignation that often engulfs the life of the oppressed.

But this is not the way out. To accept passively an unjust system is to cooperate with that system; thereby the oppressed become as evil as the oppressor. Noncooperation with evil is as much a moral obligation as is cooperation with good. The oppressed must never allow the conscience of the oppressor to slumber. Religion reminds every man that he is his brother's keeper. To accept injustice or segregation passively is to say to the oppressor that his actions are morally right. It is a way of allowing his conscience to fall asleep. At this moment the oppressed fails to be his brother's keeper. So acquiescence—while often the easier way—is not the moral way. It is the way of the coward. The Negro cannot win the respect of his oppressor by acquiescing; he merely increases the oppressor's arrogance and contempt. Acquiescence is interpreted as proof of the Negro's inferiority. The Negro cannot win the respect of the white people of the South or the peoples of the world if he is willing to sell the future of his children for his personal and immediate comfort and safety.

A second way that oppressed people sometimes deal with oppression is to resort to physical violence and corroding hatred. Violence often brings about momentary results. Nations have frequently won their independence in battle. But in spite of temporary victories, violence never brings permanent peace. It solves no social problem; it merely creates new and more complicated ones.

Violence as a way of achieving racial justice is both impractical and   5
immoral. It is impractical because it is a descending spiral ending in destruction for all. The old law of an eye for an eye leaves everybody blind. It is immoral because it seeks to humiliate the opponent rather than win his understanding; it seeks to annihilate rather than to convert. Violence is immoral because it thrives on hatred rather than love. It destroys community and makes brotherhood impossible. It leaves society in monologue rather than dialogue. Violence ends by defeating itself. It creates bitterness in the survivors and brutality in the destroyers. A voice echoes through time saying to every potential Peter, "Put up your sword." History is cluttered with the wreckage of nations that failed to follow his command.

If the American Negro and other victims of oppression succumb to the temptation of using violence in the struggle for freedom, future generations will be the recipients of a desolate night of bitterness, and our chief legacy to them will be an endless reign of meaningless chaos. Violence is not the way.

The third way open to oppressed people in their quest for freedom is the way of nonviolent resistance. Like the synthesis in Hegelian philosophy, the principle of nonviolent resistance seeks to reconcile the truths of two opposites—acquiescence and violence—while avoiding the extremes and immoralities of both. The nonviolent resister agrees with the person who acquiesces that one should not be physically aggressive toward his opponent; but he balances the equation by agreeing with the person of violence that evil must be resisted. He avoids the nonresistance of the former and the violent resistance of the latter. With nonviolent resistance, no individual or group need submit to any wrong, nor need anyone resort to violence in order to right a wrong.

It seems to me that this is the method that must guide the actions of the Negro in the present crisis in race relations. Through nonviolent resistance the Negro will be able to rise to the noble height of opposing the unjust system while loving the perpetrators of the system. The Negro must work passionately and unrelentingly for full stature as a citizen, but he must not use inferior methods to gain it. He must never come to terms with falsehood, malice, hate, or destruction.

Nonviolent resistance makes it possible for the Negro to remain in the South and struggle for his rights. The Negro's problem will not be solved by running away. He cannot listen to the glib suggestion of those who would urge him to migrate en masse to other sections of the country. By grasping his great opportunity in the South he can make a lasting contribution to the moral strength of the nation and set a sublime example of courage for generations yet unborn.

By nonviolent resistance, the Negro can also enlist all men of good will in his struggle for equality. The problem is not a purely racial one, with Negroes set against whites. In the end, it is not a struggle between people at all, but a tension between justice and injustice. Nonviolent resistance is not aimed against oppressors but against oppression. Under its banner consciences, not racial groups, are enlisted. 10

If the Negro is to achieve the goal of integration, he must organize himself into a militant and nonviolent mass movement. All three elements are indispensable. The movement for equality and justice can only be a success if it has both a mass and militant character; the barriers to be overcome require both. Nonviolence is an imperative in order to bring about ultimate community.

A mass movement of militant quality that is not at the same time committed to nonviolence tends to generate conflict, which in turn breeds anarchy. The support of the participants and the sympathy of the uncommitted are both inhibited by the threat that bloodshed will engulf the community. This reaction in turn encourages the opposition to threaten and resort to force. When, however, the mass movement repudiates violence while moving resolutely toward its goal, its opponents are revealed as the instigators and practitioners of violence if it occurs. Then public support is magnetically attracted to the advocates of nonviolence, while those who employ violence are literally disarmed by overwhelming sentiment against their stand.

Only through a nonviolent approach can the fears of the white community be mitigated. A guilt-ridden white minority lives in fear that if the Negro should ever attain power, he would act without restraint or pity to revenge the injustices and brutality of the years. It is something like a parent who continually mistreats a son. One day that parent raises his hand to strike the son, only to discover that the son is now as tall as he is. The parent is suddenly afraid—fearful that the son will use his new physical power to repay his parent for all the blows of the past.

The Negro, once a helpless child, has now grown up politically, culturally, and economically. Many white men fear retaliation. The job of the Negro is to show them that they have nothing to fear, that the Negro understands and forgives and is ready to forget the past. He must convince the white man that all he seeks is justice, *for both himself and the white man.* A mass movement exercising nonviolence is an object lesson in power under discipline, a demonstration to the white community that if such a movement attained a degree of strength, it would use its power creatively and not vengefully.

Nonviolence can touch men where the law cannot reach them. When the law regulates behavior it plays an indirect part in molding public sentiment. The enforcement of the law is itself a form of peaceful persuasion. But the law needs help. The courts can order desegregation of the public schools. But what can be done to mitigate the fears, to disperse the hatred, violence, and irrationality gathered around school integration, to take the initiative out of the hands of racial demagogues, to release respect for the law? In the end, for laws to be obeyed, men must believe they are right. 15

Here nonviolence comes in as the ultimate form of persuasion. It is the method which seeks to implement the just law by appealing to the conscience of the great decent majority who through blindness, fear, pride, or irrationality have allowed their consciences to sleep.

The nonviolent resisters can summarize their message in the following simple terms: We will take direct action against injustice without waiting for other agencies to act. We will not obey unjust laws or submit to unjust practices. We will do this peacefully, openly, cheerfully because our aim is to persuade. We adopt the means of nonviolence because our end is a community at peace with itself. We will try to persuade with our words, but if our words fail, we will try to persuade with our acts. We will always be willing to talk and seek fair compromise, but we are ready to suffer when necessary and even risk our lives to become witnesses to the truth as we see it.

The way of nonviolence means a willingness to suffer and sacrifice. It may mean going to jail. If such is the case the resister must be willing to fill the jail houses of the South. It may even mean physical death. But if

physical death is the price that a man must pay to free his children and
his white brethren from a permanent death of the spirit, then nothing
could be more redemptive.

 ## Topics for Critical Thinking and Writing

1. In the first paragraph, the passage about Moses and the children of Israel is
   not strictly necessary; the essential idea of the paragraph is stated in the
   previous sentence. Why, then, does King add this material? And why the
   quotation from Shakespeare?

2. Pick out two or three sentences that seem to you to be especially effective
   and analyze the sources of their power. You can choose either isolated sentences or (because King often effectively links sentences with repetition of
   words or of constructions) consecutive ones.

3. In a paragraph set forth your understanding of what nonviolent resistance
   is. Use whatever examples from your own experience or reading you find
   useful. In a second paragraph, explain how Maya Angelou's "Graduation"
   (page 145) offers an example of nonviolent resistance.

Linda M. Hasselstrom

*Linda M. Hasselstrom, a South Dakota rancher, writer, and environmentalist, has wielded a gun
as a last resort, but she has never used it. Her essay first appeared in* High Country News *and
later appeared in a somewhat longer form in a collection of her essays,* Land Circle: Writings
Collected from the Land *(Golden, Col.: Fulcrum, 1991).*

*Ms. Hasselstrom has asked us to indicate that her choices for self-defense are based on a
particular set of circumstances, that she does not advocate handgun ownership, and that she is
not a member of any group that advocates handgun use.*

Why One Peaceful Woman
Carries a Pistol

I am a peace-loving woman. But several events in the past 10 years
have convinced me I'm safer when I carry a pistol. This was a personal
decision, but because handgun possession is a controversial subject, perhaps my reasoning will interest others.

I live in western South Dakota on a ranch 25 miles from the nearest
large town: for several years I spent winters alone here. As a free-lance
writer, I travel alone a lot—more than 100,000 miles by car in the last four

years. With women freer than ever before to travel alone, the odds of our encountering trouble seem to have risen. And help, in the West, can be hours away. Distances are great, roads are deserted, and the terrain is often too exposed to offer hiding places.

A woman who travels alone is advised, usually by men, to protect herself by avoiding bars and other "dangerous situations," by approaching her car like an Indian scout, by locking doors and windows. But these precautions aren't always enough. I spent years following them and still found myself in dangerous situations. I began to resent the idea that just because I am female, I have to be extra careful.

A few years ago, with another woman, I camped for several weeks in the West. We discussed self-defense, but neither of us had taken a course in it. She was against firearms, and local police told us Mace was illegal. So we armed ourselves with spray cans of deodorant tucked into our sleeping bags. We never used our improvised Mace because we were lucky enough to camp beside people who came to our aid when men harassed us. But on one occasion we visited a national park where our assigned space was less than 15 feet from other campers. When we returned from a walk, we found our closest neighbors were two young men. As we gathered our cooking gear, they drank beer and loudly discussed what they would do to us after dark. Nearby campers, even families, ignored them; rangers strolled past, unconcerned. When we asked the rangers point-blank if they would protect us, one of them patted my shoulder and said, "Don't worry, girls. They're just kidding." At dusk we drove out of the park and hid our camp in the woods a few miles away. The illegal spot was lovely, but our enjoyment of that park was ruined. I returned from the trip determined to reconsider the options available for protecting myself.

At that time, I lived alone on the ranch and taught night classes in town. Along a city street I often traveled, a woman had a flat tire, called for help on her CB radio, and got a rapist who left her beaten. She was afraid to call for help again and stayed in her car until morning. For that reason, as well as because CBs work best along line-of-sight, which wouldn't help much in the rolling hills where I live, I ruled out a CB.

As I drove home one night, a car followed me. It passed me on a narrow bridge while a passenger flashed a blinding spotlight in my face. I braked sharply. The car stopped, angled across the bridge, and four men jumped out. I realized the locked doors were useless if they broke the windows of my pickup. I started forward, hoping to knock their car aside so I could pass. Just then another car appeared, and the men hastily got back in their car. They continued to follow me, passing and repassing. I dared not go home because no one else was there. I passed no lighted houses. Finally they pulled over to the roadside, and I decided to use their tactic: fear. Speeding, the pickup horn blaring, I swerved as close to them as I dared as I roared past. It worked: they turned off the highway. But I was frightened and angry. Even in my vehicle I was too vulnerable.

Other incidents occurred over the years. One day I glanced out a field below my house and saw a man with a shotgun walking toward a pond full of ducks. I drove down and explained that the land was posted. I politely asked him to leave. He stared at me, and the muzzle of the shotgun began to rise. In a moment of utter clarity I realized that I was alone on the ranch, and that he could shoot me and simply drive away. The moment passed; the man left.

One night, I returned home from teaching a class to find deep tire ruts in the wet ground of my yard, garbage in the driveway, and a large gas tank empty. A light shone in the house; I couldn't remember leaving it on. I was too embarrassed to drive to a neighboring ranch and wake someone up. An hour of cautious exploration convinced me the house was safe, but once inside, with the doors locked, I was still afraid. I kept thinking of how vulnerable I felt, prowling around my own house in the dark.

My first positive step was to take a kung fu class, which teaches evasive or protective action when someone enters your space without permission. I learned to move confidently, scanning for possible attackers. I learned how to assess danger and techniques for avoiding it without combat.

I also learned that one must practice several hours a day to be good at kung fu. By that time I had married George; when I practiced with him, I learned how *close* you must be to your attacker to use martial arts, and decided a 120-pound woman dare not let a six-foot, 220-pound attacker get that close unless she is very, very good at self-defense. I have since read articles by several women who were extremely well trained in the martial arts, but were raped and beaten anyway.   10

I thought back over the times in my life when I had been attacked or threatened and tried to be realistic about my own behavior, searching for anything that had allowed me to become a victim. Overall, I was convinced that I had not been at fault. I don't believe myself to be either paranoid or a risk-taker, but I wanted more protection.

With some reluctance I decided to try carrying a pistol. George had always carried one, despite his size and his training in martial arts. I practiced shooting until I was sure I could hit an attacker who moved close enough to endanger me. Then I bought a license from the county sheriff, making it legal for me to carry the gun concealed.

But I was not yet ready to defend myself. George taught me that the most important preparation was mental: convincing myself I could actually *shoot a person*. Few of us wish to hurt or kill another human being. But there is no point in having a gun—in fact, gun possession might increase your danger—unless you know you can use it. I got in the habit of rehearsing, as I drove or walked, the precise conditions that would be required before I would shoot someone.

People who have not grown up with the idea that they are capable of protecting themselves—in other words, most women—might have to work hard to convince themselves of their ability, and of the necessity. Handgun ownership need not turn us into gun-slingers, but it can be part of believing in, and relying on, *ourselves* for protection.

To be useful, a pistol has to be available. In my car, it's within instant   15
reach. When I enter a deserted rest stop at night, it's in my purse, with my hand on the grip. When I walk from a dark parking lot into a motel, it's in my hand, under a coat. At home, it's on the headboard. In short, I take it with me almost everywhere I go alone.

Just carrying a pistol is no protection; avoidance is still the best approach to trouble. Subconsciously watching for signs of danger, I believe I've become more alert. Handgun use, not unlike driving, becomes instinctive. Each time I've drawn my gun—I have never fired it at another human being—I've simply found it in my hand.

I was driving the half-mile to the highway mailbox one day when I saw a vehicle parked about midway down the road. Several men were standing in the ditch, relieving themselves. I have no objection to emergency urination, but I noticed they'd dumped several dozen beer cans in the road. Besides being ugly, cans can slash a cow's feet or stomach.

The men noticed me before they finished and made quite a performance out of zipping their trousers while walking toward me. All four of them gathered around my small foreign car, and one of them demanded what the hell I wanted.

"This is private land. I'd appreciate it if you'd pick up the beer cans."

"What beer cans?" said the belligerent one, putting both hands on the   20
car door and leaning in my window. His face was inches from mine, and the beer fumes were strong. The others laughed. One tried the passenger door, locked; another put his foot on the hood and rocked the car. They circled, lightly thumping the roof, discussing my good fortune in meeting them and the benefits they were likely to bestow upon me. I felt very small and very trapped and they knew it.

"The ones you just threw out," I said politely.

"I don't see no beer cans. Why don't you get out here and show them to me, honey?" said the belligerent one, reaching for the handle inside my door.

"Right over there," I said, still being polite, "—there, and over there." I pointed with the pistol, which I'd slipped under my thigh. Within one minute the cans and the men were back in the car and headed down the road.

I believe this incident illustrates several important principles. The men were trespassing and knew it; their judgment may have been impaired by alcohol. Their response to the polite request of a woman alone was to use their size, numbers, and sex to inspire fear. The pistol was a response in the same language. Politeness didn't work; I couldn't match them in size or number. Out of the car, I'd have been more vulnerable. The pistol just changed the balance of power. It worked again recently when I was driving in a desolate part of Wyoming. A man played cat-and-mouse with me for 30 miles, ultimately trying to run me off the road. When his car passed mine with only two inches to spare, I showed him my pistol, and he disappeared.

When I got my pistol, I told my husband, revising the old Colt slogan, "God made men *and women,* but Sam Colt made them equal." Recently I have seen a gunmaker's ad with a similar sentiment. Perhaps this is an idea whose time has come, though the pacifist inside me will be saddened if the only way women can achieve equality is by carrying weapons.

25

We must treat a firearm's power with caution. "Power tends to corrupt, and absolute power corrupts absolutely," as a man (Lord Acton) once said. A pistol is not the only way to avoid being raped or murdered in today's world, but, intelligently wielded, it can shift the balance of power and provide a measure of safety.

 ## Topics for Critical Thinking and Writing

1. In her first eight paragraphs, Hasselstrom sketches the kinds of experiences that ultimately caused her to carry a gun. Do you find her account of those experiences persuasive? Do they, in your opinion, justify her decision? If not, why not?

2. In paragraph 13 Hasselstrom introduces an idea that perhaps takes a reader by surprise. Do you think it is true, by and large, that a person who decides to carry a gun must, by means of "rehearsing" prepare himself or herself to use it? Whether or not you think it is true, what is the effect of her introducing this idea? Does it make her account more, or less, persuasive?

3. In paragraphs 17–23 Hasselstrom recounts an episode when her gun frightened off several belligerent and probably slightly intoxicated men. Do you think that this episode serves (as Hasselstrom doubtless thinks it does) as clear support for her position? What counterargument(s) can you imagine?

4. What devices does Hasselstrom use, as a writer, to convince her reader that she is not aggressive or gun-crazy?

Derek Bok

Derek Bok was born in 1930 in Bryn Mawr, Pennsylvania, and was educated at Stanford and Harvard, where he received a law degree. He taught law at Harvard, then served as dean of the law school, and held the office of president of Harvard from 1971 to 1991. The essay that we give here was published in a Boston newspaper, prompted by the display of Confederate flags hung from the window of a dormitory room.

Protecting Freedom of Expression on the Campus

For several years, universities have been struggling with the problem of trying to reconcile the rights of free speech with the desire to avoid racial tension. In recent weeks, such a controversy has sprung up at Harvard. Two students hung Confederate flags in public view, upsetting students who equate the Confederacy with slavery. A third student tried to protest the flags by displaying a swastika.

These incidents have provoked much discussion and disagreement. Some students have urged that Harvard require the removal of symbols that offend many members of the community. Others reply that such symbols are a form of free speech and should be protected.

Different universities have resolved similar conflicts in different ways. Some have enacted codes to protect their communities from forms of speech that are deemed to be insensitive to the feelings of other groups. Some have refused to impose such restrictions.

It is important to distinguish between the appropriateness of such communications and their status under the First Amendment. The fact that speech is protected by the First Amendment does not necessarily mean that it is right, proper, or civil. I am sure that the vast majority of Harvard students believe that hanging a Confederate flag in public view—or displaying a swastika in response—is insensitive and unwise because any satisfaction it gives to the students who display these symbols is far outweighed by the discomfort it causes to many others.

I share this view and regret that the students involved saw fit to behave in this fashion. Whether or not they merely wished to manifest their pride in the South—or to demonstrate the insensitivity of hanging Confederate flags by mounting another offensive symbol in return—they must have known that they would upset many fellow students and ignore the decent regard for the feelings of others so essential to building and preserving a strong and harmonious community.

To disapprove of a particular form of communication, however, is not enough to justify prohibiting it. We are faced with a clear example of

5

Derek Bok, "Protecting Freedom of Expression on the Campus" from *The Boston Globe*, March 25, 1991. Reprinted by permission of the author.

the conflict between our commitment to free speech and our desire to foster a community founded on mutual respect. Our society has wrestled with this problem for many years. Interpreting the First Amendment, the Supreme Court has clearly struck the balance in favor of free speech.

While communities do have the right to regulate speech in order to uphold aesthetic standards (avoiding defacement of buildings) or to protect the public from disturbing noise, rules of this kind must be applied across the board and cannot be enforced selectively to prohibit certain kinds of messages but not others.

Under the Supreme Court's rulings, as I read them, the display of swastikas or Confederate flags clearly falls within the protection of the free-speech clause of the First Amendment and cannot be forbidden simply because it offends the feelings of many members of the community. These rulings apply to all agencies of government, including public universities.

Although it is unclear to what extent the First Amendment is enforceable against private institutions, I have difficulty understanding why a university such as Harvard should have less free speech than the surrounding society—or than a public university.

One reason why the power of censorship is so dangerous is that it is extremely difficult to decide when a particular communication is offensive enough to warrant prohibition or to weigh the degree of offensiveness against the potential value of the communication. If we begin to forbid flags, it is only a short step to prohibiting offensive speakers.   10

I suspect that no community will become humane and caring by restricting what its members can say. The worst offenders will simply find other ways to irritate and insult.

In addition, once we start to declare certain things "offensive," with all the excitement and attention that will follow, I fear that much ingenuity will be exerted trying to test the limits, much time will be expended trying to draw tenuous distinctions, and the resulting publicity will eventually attract more attention to the offensive material than would ever have occurred otherwise.

Rather than prohibit such communications, with all the resulting risks, it would be better to ignore them, since students would then have little reason to create such displays and would soon abandon them. If this response is not possible—and one can understand why—the wisest course is to speak with those who perform insensitive acts and try to help them understand the effects of their actions on others.

Appropriate officials and faculty members should take the lead, as the Harvard House Masters have already done in this case. In talking with students, they should seek to educate and persuade, rather than resort to ridicule or intimidation, recognizing that only persuasion is likely to produce a lasting, beneficial effect. Through such effects, I believe that we act in the manner most consistent with our ideals as an educational institution and most calculated to help us create a truly understanding, supportive community.

Topics for Critical Thinking and Writing

1. In paragraph 8 Bok argues that "the display of swastikas or Confederate flags clearly falls within the protection of the free-speech clause of the First Amendment and cannot be forbidden simply because it offends the feelings of many members of the community." Suppose someone replied thus: "The display of swastikas or of Confederate flags—symbols loaded with meaning—is, to a Jew or an African-American, at least equivalent to a slap in the face. Such a display is, in short, an act of violence." What would you reply, and how would you support your response?

2. Do you find Bok persuasive? Support your answer with evidence about the points of his argument and his techniques of argument.

3. What rules, if any, does your school have concerning limitations of speech? What rules, if any, would you propose?

Stephen Bates

Stephen Bates, Annenberg Senior Fellow, holds a law degree from Harvard Law School. He is the co-author of The Spot: The Rise of Political Advertising on Television *(1984) and the author of* The Media and Congress *(1987),* If No News, Send Rumors: Anecdotes of American Journalism *(1989), and* Battleground: One Mother's Crusade, the Religious Right, and the Struggle for Control of Our Classrooms *(1993). In reading this essay which was first published in 1994, ask yourself whether the uses schools make of the Internet and filters have substantially changed.*

The Internet: The Next Front in the Book Wars

In two suburban Chicago high schools this year, students are analyzing satellite photos of current weather, tracking wildfires in California, questioning atmospheric scientists about their research and collaborating on writing projects with students thousands of miles away. "The Internet is making the school a more integral part of the world," said Barry Fishman, manager of the federally funded CoVis Network which provides the schools' Internet hookup.

But the Internet is also bringing seamier elements of the world into the schoolhouse. Sooner or later, Mr. Fishman and other educators realize, people will complain about what the Internet is making available to schoolchildren and the ceaseless battles over schoolbooks will soar into cyberspace.

The cyberspace battles may prove especially contentious, because the Internet contains a great many works not found on the shelves of most schools. "The School Stopper's Textbook," for instance, tells how to short-circuit electrical wiring, set off explosives in school plumbing and "break into your school at night and burn it down."

"The Big Book of Mischief" features detailed bomb-making instructions.

"Suicide Methods," based in part on Derek Humphry's book "Final Exit," comprehensively analyzes various ways of killing oneself.

A drug archive offers recipes for marijuana brownies and a guide to constructing "bongs, pipes and other wonderful contraptions."

On several archives and Usenet discussion groups, hackers provide tips on breaking into computer networks, telephone systems and cash machines.

Some Usenet groups contain pornographic stories; others have photos of naked men, women and, occasionally, children.

"I don't think parents have ever had quite this challenge before," said Steve Bennett, an author who has developed computer activities for children. "You think your kid is mastering the Internet so he'll be ready for a technically sophisticated job—then you find he's got 'Popular Gynecology' up on the screen."

Schools can keep a pornographic book off the library shelf by not buying it, but they can't keep it from entering the building through cyberspace. The Internet is a headless web of computer networks, designed by Defense Department contractors in the 1960's to withstand nuclear war. Limiting a user's access to material on it is nearly impossible. "The Net interprets censorship as damage and routes around it," said John Gilmore, a leading activist for freedom of speech in cyberspace.

So when educators contemplate bringing the Internet into public schools, "the situation is essentially all or nothing," said Libby Black, director of the Boulder Valley School District's Internet Project in Colorado, which provides Internet accounts to more than 1,600 public school students. Like the fledgling CoVis and other publicly and privately funded networks that provide information services to schools, Boulder Valley excludes the "alt.sex" discussion groups from Usenet's "alternative" hierarchy, but an enterprising user can venture out on the Internet and find a network that does receive them. Even from the confines of an E-mail-only account, a student can instruct several automated systems to send Usenet posts, including those from the alt.sex groups, by return mail. It is the electronic equivalent of interlibrary loan, only beyond the librarian's control.

"You can't prevent it," said Peg Szady, who teaches a course on the Internet at Monta Vista High School in Cupertino, Calif. "There's just no way."

Consequently, schools must rely on discipline and supervision. Early on in the CoVis project, Mr. Fishman sat down with teachers at the two pilot schools. "We attempted to get a sense of how we could educate people to use these tools for good, and minimize people using them for resources not directly related to improving education," he said.

The result is a network-use policy that the student and a parent must sign. The form stipulates that "network use is primarily intended for the support of project work conducted in participating CoVis classes, and far less significantly for other purposes that students and teachers determine to be of educational value."

Other schools send permission forms home with students. The   15
Poudre School District in Fort Collins, Colo., alerts parents to the possibility of "defamatory, inaccurate, abusive, obscene, profane, sexually oriented, threatening, racially offensive, or illegal material" on-line. At Monta Vista, the policy instructs students not to access "areas of cyberspace that would be offensive to any students, teachers, or parents." Many schools limit students' electronic speech, prohibiting profanity, sexually oriented remarks, advertising, political lobbying and "flames" (vituperative verbal attacks). Violators can lose their accounts.

Some systems monitor students' use of the Internet. At Long Island's Oceanside High School, students must fill out a form summarizing each on-line session. Students at several schools in Chicago will soon log onto their Internet accounts using "smartcards," which will record their online movements for subsequent review by teachers. At the Poudre District in Fort Collins, administrators reserve the right to examine users' E-mail and other files. "You really have to do that with kids," said Larry Buchanan, a Poudre educational technologies specialist. "When they know somebody's watching them, they behave differently."

Schools impose such restrictions "to cover their butts," in the view of Russell Smith, a technology consultant for the state of Texas who has reviewed several schools' written policies. "Nobody wants to get sued."

The fear of litigation has a basis. "Some jurisdictions have laws that place a duty on everyone, not just schools, to prevent minors from being exposed to sexually related materials," said Mike Goodwin, online counsel of the Electronic Frontier Foundation. "Even if the material is not legally obscene—for instance, *Playboy* magazine—it may be that a party can be liable for giving that kind of sexually oriented material to a minor." Some states also prohibit "exposing minors to dangerous material or information," he added, but the courts have not definitively ruled on the constitutionality of such laws.

The seamy material on the Internet has not yet generated litigation, or in fact much controversy. At the relatively few schools now offering Internet accounts, students have had their accounts suspended for hacking, abusive E-mail and similar misbehavior more frequently than for accessing objectionable photos and texts.

Even so, educators know that cyberspace has the potential to ignite a   20
sizable controversy. "The nightmare [public school educators] have," Steve Cisler, a senior scientist in the Apple Computer library, wrote in a newsletter last year, "is of some legislator waving around a raunchy [dig-

itized] image 'paid for with tax dollars and found on the State Educational Network,' or reading some choice posting from alt.sex. necrophilia." The furor becomes increasingly likely as more and more schools put students on-line frequently with accounts they can access from home, beyond the scrutiny of school officialdom—and as the public schools' traditional critics begin paying attention to the Internet.

"There's a lot of fundamentalist groups out there," said Mr. Smith, the Texas consultant. "I don't think they know what's up with the Internet yet."

Representatives of three conservative organizations—Concerned Women for America, Focus on the Family and the American Family Association—said they had not yet studied Internet access in public schools.

Conservative Christians won't be the only ones to take offense. Indeed, most protests so far in universities rather than public schools have come from other groups, according to a list prepared by Carl Kadie, coeditor of the electronic periodical *Computers and Academic Freedom News.*

Women have complained about the newsgroups devoted to pornographic photos and sex chatter, and several universities have banned them. In 1989 Stanford banned a Usenet discussion group over a joke that some users deemed anti-Semitic; accused of censorship, the university later backed down. In September of this year, the Education Department's Office for Civil Rights contended that a males-only on-line discussion group at a California junior college violated Federal anti-discrimination law.

Whether the complaints come from the right or the left, the Internet's online community generally supports absolute freedom of inquiry. The phrase "information wants to be free" is a commonplace of Usenet discussions.   25

Mirroring that viewpoint, some civil libertarians have decried efforts to restrict how students use the Internet. In a statement issued in August, the Minnesota Coalition Against Censorship called for all public school students to enjoy unfettered Internet privileges, including access to "information that some have identified as controversial or of potential harm."

Most anti-censorship organizations are still studying the issue. "It's incredibly complex," said Candace Morgan, chairwoman of the American Library Association's Intellectual Freedom Committee. "The most difficult situations are those faced by school libraries."

People for the American Way, a liberal public-interest group, generally takes the position that no library materials should be kept from children, according to Leslie Harris, the organization's director of public policy. But, she added, pornographic images and some other materials on the Internet "may require a different answer."

"We are generally not for restrictions," said Roz Udow of the National Coalition Against Censorship. "But the Internet changes everything—it makes it all so accessible."

Meanwhile, computer engineers are looking for technical fixes. One   30
approach is a "reverse firewall." Whereas a firewall keeps outsiders from
entering a computer system, a reverse firewall would keep users from going beyond a few uncontroversial zones on the Internet, according to
Denis Newman, director of education network systems at BBN Systems
and Technologies. BBN, he said, is at work on a prototype. Other companies are also pursuing technical solutions, according to Nelson Heller,
publisher of a newsletter on educational technology.

Mr. Fishman of CoVis thinks that network architecture won't provide
the answer. "Roadblocks end up taking away what's valuable—the ability of students to perform tasks that their teachers couldn't even conceive
of," he said. In his view, the better approach is for educators to "spend
time up front thinking about what objections people might raise, then try
to defuse those concerns through education."

He hopes that educators succeed in pre-empting the protests.
"Losing the Internet in schools just because of some information on it—
and we're really talking about a small percentage of the total information—it's a pretty bad investment," he said. "If a student was smuggling
dirty pictures in their science textbook, would we take away all the science textbooks?"

 ## Topics for Critical Thinking and Writing

1. It is widely agreed that the government has a compelling interest ("compelling interest" is a common legal term) in protecting children from
   pornography. Does this position in effect mean that schools should not
   make use of the Internet?

2. The final paragraph sets forth an analogy, which is offered as an argument.
   How convincing do you find this argument? Explain.

3. In paragraph 16 Bates says that some schools use a device that monitors
   the student's on-line movement, and that teachers review the account. In
   an essay of 500 words indicate whether you believe this practice is appropriate. Support your position with arguments.

4. In paragraph 17 a technology consultant says—doubtless correctly—that
   schools employ restrictions because they fear they may be sued. But let's
   assume that a school does not have restrictions in place, and a parent sues
   on the grounds that the student has viewed sexually explicit material in
   school. You are a lawyer; take the side of the defense or of the plaintiff—the
   choice is yours—and present your argument to the jury, in about 500
   words.

Barbara L. Keller

Barbara L. Keller, a lawyer, late at night experienced a break-in, but she nevertheless argues that guns, far from being a good means of self-defense, add to the likelihood that the innocent will be harmed.

Frontiersmen Are History

Late on a Friday night, I had a personal introduction to terror. My 11-year-old daughter and I were playing Scrabble. My husband had just phoned to let us know he was grounded in Dallas by bad weather. A moment later my front doorbell rang loudly and repeatedly. I stood up, wondering who in God's name was ringing at 1 o'clock in the morning. Then I heard the sound of shattering glass. Someone was breaking into my house.

As I grabbed my daughter and dashed out the side door to my neighbor's to call the police, she began to cry. "Mom! What about the boys?" My three sons—3, 4 and a mentally handicapped 8-year-old—were asleep upstairs. I had made a split-second decision to leave them and run for help. To go to them, or the phone, would have taken me right into harm's way. Being eight months pregnant, I couldn't carry them two at a time to safety. The minutes it took until the police arrived seemed like years. I wasn't permitted to enter the house until the officers had secured it. I stood on the sidewalk, fearing for my sons' safety and worrying about their reaction if they awoke to find armed policemen trooping through their bedroom. Blessedly, the boys slept through it, and the would-be intruders ran off without entering the house.

In the aftermath of what was for me a horribly traumatic experience, my husband and I considered and once again rejected the idea of buying a gun for protection. Police officers have told me a gun is not a particularly good defense strategy, especially where there are small children in the home. If the gun isn't loaded—or the ammunition isn't very near by—it's not likely to be much help in a situation needing a fast reaction. Yet if it is loaded and handy, it poses a serious threat to children—and others.

Like most residents of Baton Rouge, I have strong views on gun control. Unlike most, I am for it. You have to understand that this is Louisiana. We have been characterized humorously, but I fear accurately, as a society of good ole boys who consider the shotguns displayed in the back of the pickup as a God-given right and a status symbol. We don't much care for being told what to do, especially by the government. During the trial of Rodney Peairs, acquitted of killing a Japanese exchange student who he mistakenly thought was invading his home on Halloween in 1992, a local news program conducted a telephone poll on the question of gun control. At that time, 68 percent of the respondents opposed stricter controls. Such measures routinely fail in our legislature, as they do in Congress.

One result is that we have criminals armed with semiautomatic and assault weapons and a police force that is seriously outgunned. Our options, as I see them, are three: maintain the status quo, make it more difficult for criminals to obtain these weapons, or provide them to the police as well. The status quo is to me unacceptable, and the notion of a police force armed with assault rifles roaming the streets of Baton Rouge does not bring solace to my soul. It terrifies me. That leaves the option of gun control.

Why does this prospect engender such hysteria? I do not propose to outlaw guns—only to make them more difficult to obtain. No one with a criminal record or history of violent mental illness—and no child—should by law be able to purchase a gun. And *no one* has a compelling need to buy an assault weapon.

None of this may make a hill of beans of difference, directly, in the case of a homeowner protecting himself from real or perceived threats. But indirectly it can. We should rethink our cultural heritage and the historical gunslinger's mentality of "a Smith & Wesson beats four aces." We've outgrown the frontier spirit and the need of weapons for survival. In Baton Rouge, I am a definite oddity in not allowing my children, including my normal, rambunctious little boys, to play at shooting people. I don't want my children to think of guns as problem solvers. Nor do I favor the simplistic depictions of good guys versus bad guys.

What really frightens me is that if I were faced with the prospect of imminent harm to myself or my children and had a gun at the ready, I would reach for it, despite my feelings against using firearms for personal protection. Panic is a compelling emotion and basically incompatible with reason. It is tempting fate severely to keep a powerful weapon available to deal with panic-inducing circumstances. The police are trained in when and how to shoot, and innocent people can still fall victim to an officer's adrenaline surge.

I will for a very long time remember the sound of glass breaking and feel all over again the fear mingled with disbelief of that Friday night. If I'd owned a gun, I undoubtedly would have used it—probably to my own detriment. I do not know if the young men who so thoroughly violated my sense of safety were armed. I do know that if I'd had a gun, and had actually confronted them, they would have been more likely to harm me, and my children. It would have been I who escalated the potential for violence, and I would have had to live with the consequences—just like Rodney Peairs.

Although I have felt the terror of helplessness, owning a handgun is something I cannot do. And the "Shoot first, ask questions later" approach is an attitude I don't want to teach my children. Guns are like cars.

We are so inured to their power we tend to treat them irresponsibly. We see them as commodities that we have a right to own and use as we please. Instead, we should limit the "right to bear arms" so that only trained, responsible citizens can buy guns for sport, recreation and protection—while those who would be most likely to use weapons detrimentally will have a much harder time getting them. Most of all, we need to reconsider our entire love affair with guns and the ways that this passion destroys innocent lives.

 Topics for Critical Thinking and Writing

1. Evaluate Keller's first two paragraphs as an opening for her essay.

2. Keller's title ('Frontiersmen Are History') is explained in her seventh paragraph ('We've outgrown the frontier spirit'). Exactly what does she mean? Do you accept the implicit assumption? Why, or why not?

3. If you had been in Keller's position when she heard the doorbell ring and the glass shatter, what would you have done? Loudly announce that you were armed—even if you weren't?

4. In her final paragraph Keller says that "the 'Shoot first, ask questions later' approach is an attitude that I don't want to teach my children." Suppose someone said to you that if you hear an intruder in the house, this lesson is entirely appropriate. In an essay of 500 words set forth your response.

Don B. Kates

Don B. Kates, a civil-liberties lawyer and criminologist, is the editor of Firearms and Violence. *The following essay, arguing that "widespread gun ownership is a net benefit for society," was first published in a conservative magazine,* National Review, *in 1995.*

Shot Down

Criminologists, criminals, and cops all have a professional interest in crime. It is therefore significant that criminological research has generally validated the skepticism of both police and criminals about the effectiveness of gun control. Yet the consensus among these three sets of professionals has received little attention in the popular media.

Surprisingly, in light of the fervent support for stringent gun control that many academics expressed in the 1960s, serious research in this area did not begin until the 1970s. That research demonstrates that no amount of control over mere weaponry can overcome the fundamental socio-cultural and economic determinants of crime. Indeed, the evidence indicates that banning gun possession by the general public is actually counterproductive.

The most prolific researcher in this area is Gary Kleck of Florida State University's School of Criminology. His encyclopedic 1991 book, *Point Blank: Guns and Violence in America*, has won high praise even from academics distressed by its findings. Broadly speaking, those findings are: 1) Gun possession by ordinary citizens is not a problem; the perpetrators of gun crime and accidents are aberrant individuals with histories of substance abuse, violence, felonies, and other dangerous behavior. 2) While outlawing possession of guns by such people is plainly sensible, it can bring at best marginal benefit as long as the fundamental determinants of their behavior remain unchanged. 3) Because guns empower the weak against the strong, and because victims are generally weaker than felons, widespread gun ownership is a net benefit for society.

Based on surveys of both the general populace and incarcerated felons, Kleck finds that gun-armed victims rout criminals three to four times more often than gun-armed criminals attack victims. And a victim who resists with a gun is only half as likely to be injured as a victim who submits—and far less likely to be robbed or raped.

In 1993 the American Society of Criminology declared Kleck's book 5 the single most important contribution to criminological research in the previous three years. Kleck's findings are so unimpeachable that critics often resort to ad hominem attacks. They falsely accuse Kleck of being a National Rifle Association member, minion, or even employee. In fact, Kleck, a liberal Democrat and opponent of the death penalty, is a member not of the NRA but of Amnesty International and the American Civil Liberties Union (ACLU). Moreover, Kleck started out on the other side of the gun-control debate. In a 1991 speech to the National Academy of Sciences, he said:

> When I began my research on guns in 1976, like most academics, I was a believer in the "anti-gun" thesis. . . . It seemed then like self-evident common sense which hardly needed to be empirically tested. . . . [But] the best currently available evidence, imperfect though it is (and must always be), indicates that general gun availability has no measurable net positive effect on rates of homicide, suicide, robbery, assault, rape, or burglary in the U.S. . . . Further, when victims have guns, it is less likely aggressors will attack or injure them and less likely they will lose property in a robbery. . . . The positive associations often found between aggregate levels of violence and gun ownership appear to be primarily due to violence increasing gun ownership, rather than the reverse.

Other scholars have also changed their views. University of Maryland political scientist Ted Robert Gurr and State University of New York criminologist Hans Toch were closely associated with the

Eisenhower Commission, which concluded in the Sixties that "reducing the availability of the handgun will reduce firearms violence." Based on subsequent research, however, each now repudiates this judgment. "When used for protection," Toch writes, "firearms can seriously inhibit aggression and can provide a psychological buffer against the fear of crime. Furthermore, the fact that national patterns show little violent crime where guns are most dense implies that guns do not elicit aggression in any meaningful way. Quite the contrary, these findings suggest that high saturations of guns in places, or something correlated with that condition, inhibit illegal aggression."

Gurr has come to believe that handgun prohibition "would criminalize much of the citizenry but have only marginal effects on criminals," while "overemphasis on such proposals diverts attention from the kinds of conditions that are responsible for much of our crime, such as persisting poverty for the black underclass and some whites and Hispanics." Gurr adds that "guns can be an effective defense," noting that UCLA historian Roger McGrath's evidence from the 19th-century American West "shows that widespread gun ownership deterred" acquisitive crimes. "Modern studies," he writes, "also show that widespread gun ownership deters crime. . . . Convicted robbers and burglars report that they are deterred when they think their potential targets are armed."

Indeed, felons have consistently said that banning handguns would make their lives safer and easier by disarming victims without affecting their own ability to obtain weapons. "Ban guns," said a typical convict interviewed by New York University criminologist Ernest van den Haag in the mid 1970s. "I'd love it. I'm an armed robber."

In 1982 the Chicago suburb of Morton Grove received nationwide publicity for enacting the nation's first handgun ban. Surprisingly little attention was paid to two remarkable responses. One was a letter an inmate in a Florida prison wrote the editor of a local newspaper: "If guns are banned, then I as a criminal feel a lot safer. When a thief breaks into someone's house or property, the first thing to worry about is getting shot by the owner. But now, it seems we won't have to worry about that anymore." Branding it a "fantasy that just because guns are outlawed we, the crooks, can't get guns," the author asserted that "the only people who can't are the ones we victimize. . . . Drugs are against the law. Does that stop us? It's also against the law to rob and steal. But does a law stop us? One more thing: I thank you, the public, for giving me this fine opportunity to further my criminal career."

Similarly, the editor of the inmate newspaper at the Illinois Correctional Center in Menard "made it a point to get the views of those in the real know—convicts here for armed robbery, some of them extremely professional individuals with years of experience in their chosen field. They . . . were unanimous that you in Morton Grove are making things a bit easier for us. . . . [The] law is meaningless and useless in curbing crime. However, it is very effective in curbing the general populace.

10

This coming from 'hardened criminals,' professionals, convicts . . . someone should listen!"

Perhaps the National Institute of Justice did listen. In 1983 it funded a survey of two thousand felons in state prisons across the U.S. In addition to overwhelmingly endorsing the views set out above, 39 per cent of the felons in the NIJ survey said they had aborted at least one crime because they believed the intended victim was armed; 8 per cent had done so "many" times; 34 per cent had been "scared off, shot at, wounded, or captured by an armed victim"; and 69 per cent knew at least one acquaintance who had had such an experience.

Thirty-four per cent of the felons said that in contemplating a crime they either "often" or "regularly" worried that they "might get shot at by the victim." Asked about criminals in general, 56 per cent of the inmates agreed that "a criminal is not going to mess around with a victim he knows is armed with a gun"; 57 per cent agreed that "most criminals are more worried about meeting an armed victim than they are about running into the police"; 58 per cent agreed that "a store owner who is known to keep a gun on the premises is not going to get robbed very often"; and 74 per cent agreed that "one reason burglars avoid houses when people are home is that they fear being shot during the crime."

Since 1976 the District of Columbia has had the country's most extreme gun law: no civilian may buy or carry a handgun, nor may *any* gun be kept loaded or assembled in a home for self-defense. Nevertheless, Washington has one of the highest homicide rates in the country. In 1992 *Washington Post* reporters interviewed the 114 inmates in D.C.'s Lorton Prison who had been convicted of at least one gun crime. The consensus was clear: "Gun control is not the answer, the inmates agreed." And they anticipated no difficulty obtaining an illegal gun. Though many claimed to want to go straight, 25 per cent flatly said they would get a gun as soon as they emerged from prison.

A week later a newspaper in Syracuse found similar opinions when it combined a survey of inmates in a nearby maximum-security prison with a survey of police officers in the local department. The two groups concurred that tougher gun laws would have no effect on crime; neither would banning assault weapons.

This congruence of opinion contradicts the impression that several prominent police chiefs have created that cops generally oppose civilian gun ownership. The truth is that these police chiefs were appointed precisely because their views sharply diverged from their peers'. Furthermore, strong political pressure tends to silence police administrators who oppose gun bans. In the mid 1980s Maurice Turner became Washington, D.C.'s first black police chief. When reporters inquired into the new chief's opinion of D.C.'s severe gun law, he replied that it was not just useless but actually promoted crime, since felons knew it had rendered victims defenseless. When his remarks were reported, he was

15

called on the carpet by Mayor Marion Barry, who told him banning guns was a city policy that he was forbidden to criticize. Thereafter Chief Turner refused to comment on gun control (until he retired, whereupon he reiterated his previous views).

Boston Police Chief Robert DiGrazia, on the other hand, did sincerely champion the banning and confiscation of handguns. In 1976 he had his research division poll police opinion nationwide, hoping the results would support a Massachusetts ballot initiative to ban handguns. Thinking patrol officers would oppose the initiative, he limited the poll to administrators. Yet the survey found "a substantial majority of the respondents looked favorably on the general possession of handguns by the citizenry (excludes those with criminal records [or] history of mental instability). Strong approval was also elicited from the police administrators concerning possession of handguns in the home or place of business." The poll confirmed Chief DiGrazia's views in only one respect: the administrators agreed that officers who dealt with crime on the streets would be even more opposed to banning handguns.

This pattern has been confirmed by subsequent polling. For instance, in *Law Enforcement Technology* magazine's 1991 poll of two thousand cops across the nation, 76 per cent of street officers believed that licenses to carry concealed handguns for protection should be issued to every trained, responsible adult applicant; only 59 per cent of managers agreed. Ninety-one per cent of street officers opposed banning semi-automatic "assault rifles," compared to 66 per cent of top management. On the other hand, 94 per cent of street officers felt that private citizens should keep handguns in their homes and offices for self-defense, and 93 per cent of top management agreed. Over all, 93 per cent of the respondents supported defensive ownership of handguns, 85 per cent felt gun control had little potential to reduce crime, 79 per cent opposed banning "assault weapons," and 63 per cent supported widespread carrying of concealed handguns by trained civilians.

Every year since 1988, the National Association of Chiefs of Police has polled the nation's more than fifteen thousand police agencies, with a response rate of 10 per cent or more. The respondents have consistently said that their departments are understaffed and unable to adequately protect individuals; that law-abiding, responsible adults should have the right to own "any type of firearm" for self-defense; and that banning guns will not reduce crime. In these and other surveys police generally support moderate controls, such as background checks, designed to exclude felons from gun ownership to the extent possible without obstructing defensive ownership by law-abiding citizens.

It's possible, of course, that the cops, the criminals, and the criminologists are mistaken about gun control. But given the remarkable consensus, it's time to reconsider the casual assumption that weapons cause crime.

Topics for Critical Thinking and Writing

1. In his second paragraph Kates says that "no amount" of gun control can "overcome . . . crime." Probably even the most zealous advocates of gun control would agree, and they would explain that it's not a matter of over-coming crime but of reducing it. Do you believe Kates's essay suffers from overstatement? Explain.

2. In his third paragraph Kates calls attention to Gary Kleck's finding that "Gun possession by ordinary citizens is not a problem." But accidents *do* occur; it is not unusual to read a newspaper account of a child who is killed by a loaded gun in the house. *Is* this a "problem"? Explain.

3. Advocates of gun control usually offer, as one of their arguments, evidence that armed homeowners sometimes are injured (or injure family members) by their own weapons. Does Kates face this argument? If so, what is his re-sponse? If not, is his own argument weakened?

4. Let's assume that there is no overwhelming evidence one way or the other concerning crime and laws concerning gun ownership. In an essay of 500 words set forth your own position, explaining why you hold it.

Michael Levin

Michael Levin, educated at Michigan State University and Columbia University, has taught phi-losophy at Columbia and now at City College of the City University of New York. Levin has writ-ten numerous papers for professional journals and a book entitled Metaphysics and the Mind-Body Problem *(1979). The following essay is intended for a general audience.*

The Case for Torture

It is generally assumed that torture is impermissible, a throwback to a more brutal age. Enlightened societies reject it outright, and regimes suspected of using it risk the wrath of the United States.

I believe this attitude is unwise. There are situations in which torture is not merely permissible but morally mandatory. Moreover, these situa-tions are moving from the realm of imagination to fact.

Death: Suppose a terrorist has hidden an atomic bomb on Manhattan Island which will detonate at noon on July 4 unless . . . (here follow the usual demands for money and release of his friends from jail). Suppose, further, that he is caught at 10 A.M. of the fateful day, but—preferring death to failure—won't disclose where the bomb is. What do we do? If we follow due process—wait for his lawyer, arraign him—millions of people

---

Michael Levin, "The Case for Torture." Originally published in *Newsweek*, June 7, 1982. Reprinted by permission of the author.

will die. If the only way to save those lives is to subject the terrorist to the most excruciating possible pain, what grounds can there be for not doing so? I suggest there are none. In any case, I ask you to face the question with an open mind.

Torturing the terrorist is unconstitutional? Probably. But millions of lives surely outweigh constitutionality. Torture is barbaric? Mass murder is far more barbaric. Indeed, letting millions of innocents die in deference to one who flaunts his guilt is moral cowardice, an unwillingness to dirty one's hands. If *you* caught the terrorist, could you sleep nights knowing that millions died because you couldn't bring yourself to apply the electrodes?

Once you concede that torture is justified in extreme cases, you have admitted that the decision to use torture is a matter of balancing innocent lives against the means needed to save them. You must now face more realistic cases involving more modest numbers. Someone plants a bomb on a jumbo jet. He alone can disarm it, and his demands cannot be met (or if they can, we refuse to set a precedent by yielding to his threats). Surely we can, we must, do anything to the extortionist to save the passengers. How can we tell 300, or 100, or 10 people who never asked to be put in danger, "I'm sorry, you'll have to die in agony, we just couldn't bring ourselves to . . . "

Here are the results of an informal poll about a third, hypothetical, case. Suppose a terrorist group kidnapped a newborn baby from a hospital. I asked four mothers if they would approve of torturing kidnappers if that were necessary to get their own newborns back. All said yes, the most "liberal" adding that she would like to administer it herself.

I am not advocating torture as punishment. Punishment is addressed to deeds irrevocably past. Rather, I am advocating torture as an acceptable measure for preventing future evils. So understood, it is far less objectionable than many extant punishments. Opponents of the death penalty, for example, are forever insisting that executing a murderer will not bring back his victim (as if the purpose of capital punishment were supposed to be resurrection, not deterrence or retribution). But torture, in the cases described, is intended not to bring anyone back but to keep innocents from being dispatched. The most powerful argument against using torture as a punishment or to secure confessions is that such practices disregard the rights of the individual. Well, if the individual is all that important—and he is—it is correspondingly important to protect the rights of individuals threatened by terrorists. If life is so valuable that it must never be taken, the lives of the innocents must be saved even at the price of hurting the one who endangers them.

Better precedents for torture are assassination and pre-emptive attack. No Allied leader would have flinched at assassinating Hitler, had that been possible. (The Allies did assassinate Heydrich.) Americans would be angered to learn that Roosevelt could have had Hitler killed in 1943— thereby shortening the war and saving millions of lives—but refused on

5

moral grounds. Similarly, if nation *A* learns that nation *B* is about to launch an unprovoked attack, *A* has a right to save itself by destroying *B*'s military capability first. In the same way, if the police can by torture save those who would otherwise die at the hands of kidnappers or terrorists, they must.

Idealism: There is an important difference between terrorists and their victims that should mute talk of the terrorists' "rights." The terrorist's victims are at risk unintentionally, not having asked to be endangered. But the terrorist knowingly initiated his actions. Unlike his victims, he volunteered for the risks of his deed. By threatening to kill for profit or idealism, he renounces civilized standards, and he can have no complaint if civilization tries to thwart him by whatever means necessary.

Just as torture is justified only to save lives (not extort confessions or   10
recantations) it is justifiably administered only to those *known* to hold innocent lives in their hands. Ah, but how can the authorities ever be sure they have the right malefactor? Isn't there a danger of error and abuse? Won't We turn into Them?

Questions like these are disingenuous in a world in which terrorists proclaim themselves and perform for television. The name of their game is public recognition. After all, you can't very well intimidate a government into releasing your freedom fighters unless you announce that it is your group that has seized its embassy. "Clear guilt" is difficult to define, but when 40 million people see a group of masked gunmen seize an airplane on the evening news, there is not much question about who the perpetrators are. There will be hard cases where the situation is murkier. Nonetheless, a line demarcating the legitimate use of torture can be drawn. Torture only the obviously guilty, and only for the sake of saving innocents, and the line between Us and Them will remain clear.

There is little danger that the Western democracies will lose their way if they choose to inflict pain as one way of preserving order. Paralysis in the face of evil is the greater danger. Someday soon a terrorist will threaten tens of thousands of lives, and torture will be the only way to save them. We had better start thinking about this.

⌖ Topics for Critical Thinking and Writing

1. At the beginning of his essay, Levin presents a number of examples designed to show that torture is sometimes acceptable. Do you agree with his interpretation of these examples?

2. Levin contends: "Torture only the obviously guilty, and only for the sake of saving innocents, and the line between Us and Them will remain clear." Imagine that you are taking the other side in a debate with Levin: How would you reply to his claim?

3. How would you evaluate Levin's essay as a piece of writing? Is his argument clearly stated? Does he support it effectively? Is it convincing, or if not, why not?

4. Whether you agree with Levin or not, can you imagine being the torturer yourself? Or do you think that this job should be performed by someone else? What might be the circumstances that would lead you to feel that torture would be justified?

5. Is it one thing to present an argument like Levin's in an essay, and another to put Levin's ideas into practice? Do you believe that Levin's ideas could ever be put into practice in the United States? Is that fortunate or unfortunate, in your view?

George Orwell

George Orwell (1903–50), an Englishman, adopted this name; he was born Eric Blair, in India. He was educated at Eton, in England, but in 1921 he went to Burma (now Myanmar), where he served for five years as a police officer. He then returned to Europe, doing odd jobs while writing novels and stories. In 1936 he fought in the Spanish Civil War on the side of the Republicans, an experience reported in Homage to Catalonia *(1938). His last years were spent writing in England.*

Shooting an Elephant

In Moulmein, in Lower Burma, I was hated by large numbers of people—the only time in my life that I have been important enough for this to happen to me. I was sub-divisional police officer of the town, and in an aimless, petty kind of way anti-European feeling was very bitter. No one had the guts to raise a riot, but if a European woman went through the bazaars alone somebody would probably spit betel juice over her dress. As a police officer I was an obvious target and was baited whenever it seemed safe to do so. When a nimble Burman tripped me up on the football field and the referee (another Burman) looked the other way, the crowd yelled with hideous laughter. This happened more than once. In the end the sneering yellow faces of young men that met me everywhere, the insults hooted after me when I was at a safe distance, got badly on my nerves. The young Buddhist priests were the worst of all. There were several thousands of them in the town and none of them seemed to have anything to do except stand on street corners and jeer at Europeans.

All this was perplexing and upsetting. For at that time I had already made up my mind that imperialism was an evil thing and the sooner I chucked up my job and got out of it the better. Theoretically—and secretly, of course—I was all for the Burmese and all against their oppressors, the British. As for the job I was doing, I hated it more bitterly than I can perhaps make clear. In a job like that you see the dirty work of the Empire at close quarters. The wretched prisoners huddling in the stinking cages of the lockups, the grey, cowed faces of the long-term convicts, the scarred buttocks of the men who had been flogged with bamboos—all these oppressed me with an intolerable sense of guilt. But I could get nothing into perspective. I was young and ill-educated and I had had to think out my problems in the utter silence that is imposed on every Englishman in the East. I did not even know that the British Empire is dying, still less did I know that it is a great deal better than the younger empires that are going to supplant it. All I knew was that I was stuck between my hatred of the empire I served and my rage against the evil-spirited little beasts who tried to make my job impossible. With one part of my mind I thought of the British Raj as an unbreakable tyranny, as something clamped down, in *saecula saeculorum*,[1] upon the will of prostrate peoples; with another part I thought that the greatest joy in the world would be to drive a bayonet into a Buddhist priest's guts. Feelings like these are the normal by-products of imperialism; ask any Anglo-Indian official, if you can catch him off duty.

One day something happened which in a roundabout way was enlightening. It was a tiny incident in itself, but it gave me a better glimpse than I had had before of the real nature of imperialism—the real motives for which despotic governments act. Early one morning the sub-inspector at a police station at the other end of the town rang me up on the 'phone and said that an elephant was ravaging the bazaar. Would I please come and do something about it? I did not know what I could do, but I wanted to see what was happening and I got onto a pony and started out. I took my rifle, an old .44 Winchester and much too small to kill an elephant, but I thought the noise might be useful *in terrorem*. Various Burmans stopped me on the way and told me about the elephant's doings. It was not, of course, a wild elephant, but a tame one which had gone "must." It had been chained up, as tame elephants always are when their attack of "must" is due, but on the previous night it had broken its chain and escaped. Its mahout, the only person who could manage it when it was in that state, had set out in pursuit, but had taken the wrong direction and was now twelve hours' journey away, and in the morning the elephant had suddenly reappeared in the town. The Burmese population had no weapons and were quite helpless against it. It had already destroyed somebody's bamboo hut, killed a cow and raided some fruit-stalls and devoured the stock; also it had met the municipal rubbish van and, when

---

[1]*Saecula saeculorum* Latin, "For world without end." In the next paragraph *in terrorem* is Latin for "as a warning." (Editors' note)

the driver jumped out and took to his heels, had turned the van over and inflicted violences upon it.

The Burmese sub-inspector and some Indian constables were waiting for me in the quarter where the elephant had been seen. It was a very poor quarter, a labyrinth of squalid bamboo huts, thatched with palmleaf, winding all over a steep hillside. I remember that it was a cloudy, stuffy morning at the beginning of the rains. We began questioning the people as to where the elephant had gone and, as usual, failed to get any definite information. That is invariably the case in the East; a story always sounds clear enough at a distance, but the nearer you get to the scene of events the vaguer it becomes. Some of the people said that the elephant had gone in one direction, some said that he had gone in another, some professed not even to have heard of any elephant. I had almost made up my mind that the whole story was a pack of lies, when we heard yells a little distance away. There was a loud, scandalized cry of "Go away, child! Go away this instant!" and an old woman with a switch in her hand came round the corner of a hut, violently shooing away a crowd of naked children. Some more women followed, clicking their tongues and exclaiming; evidently there was something that the children ought not to have seen. I rounded the hut and saw a man's dead body sprawling in the mud. He was an Indian, a black Dravidian coolie, almost naked, and he could not have been dead many minutes. The people said that the elephant had come suddenly upon him round the corner of the hut, caught him with its trunk, put its foot on his back and ground him into the earth. This was the rainy season and the ground was soft, and his face had scored a trench a foot deep and a couple of yards long. He was lying on his belly with arms crucified and head sharply twisted to one side. His face was coated with mud, the eyes wide open, the teeth bared and grinning with an expression of unendurable agony. (Never tell me, by the way, that the dead look peaceful. Most of the corpses I have seen look devilish.) The friction of the great beast's foot had stripped the skin from his back as neatly as one skins a rabbit. As soon as I saw the dead man I sent an orderly to a friend's house nearby to borrow an elephant rifle. I had already sent back the pony, not wanting it to go mad with fright and throw me if it smelt the elephant.

The orderly came back in a few minutes with a rifle and five cartridges, and meanwhile some Burmans had arrived and told us that the elephant was in the paddy fields below, only a few hundred yards away. As I started forward practically the whole population of the quarter flocked out of the houses and followed me. They had seen the rifle and were all shouting excitedly that I was going to shoot the elephant. They had not shown much interest in the elephant when he was merely ravaging their homes, but it was different now that he was going to be shot. It was a bit of fun to them, as it would be to an English crowd; besides they wanted the meat. It made me vaguely uneasy. I had no intention of shooting the elephant—I had merely sent for the rifle to defend myself if necessary—and it is always unnerving to have a crowd following you. I marched down the hill, looking and feeling a fool, with the rifle over my shoulder and an ever-growing army of people jostling at my heels. At the bottom, when you got away from the huts, there was a metalled road and beyond that a miry waste of paddy fields a thousand yards across, not yet ploughed but soggy from the first rains and dotted with coarse grass. The elephant was standing eight yards from the road, his left side towards us. He took not the slightest notice of the crowd's approach. He was tearing up bunches of grass, beating them against his knees to clean them and stuffing them into his mouth.

I had halted on the road. As soon as I saw the elephant I knew with perfect certainty that I ought not to shoot him. It is a serious matter to shoot a working elephant—it is comparable to destroying a huge and costly piece of machinery—and obviously one ought not to do it if it can possibly be avoided. And at that distance, peacefully eating, the elephant looked no more dangerous than a cow. I thought then and I think now that his attack of "must" was already passing off; in which case he would merely wander harmlessly about until the mahout came back and caught him. Moreover, I did not in the least want to shoot him. I decided that I would watch him for a little while to make sure that he did not turn savage again, and then go home.

But at that moment I glanced round at the crowd that had followed me. It was an immense crowd, two thousand at the least and growing every minute. It blocked the road for a long distance on either side. I looked at the sea of yellow faces above the garish clothes—faces all happy and excited over this bit of fun, all certain that the elephant was going to be shot. They were watching me as they would watch a conjurer about to perform a trick. They did not like me, but with the magical rifle in my hands I was momentarily worth watching. And suddenly I realized that I should have to shoot the elephant after all. The people expected it of me and I had got to do it; I could feel their two thousand wills pressing me forward, irresistibly. And it was at this moment, as I stood there with the rifle in my hands, that I first grasped the hollowness, the futility of the white man's dominion in the East. Here was I, the white man with his gun, standing in front of the unarmed native crowd—seemingly the leading actor of the piece; but in reality I was only an absurd puppet pushed to and fro by the will of those yellow faces behind. I perceived in this moment that when the white man turns tyrant it is his own freedom that he destroys. He becomes a sort of hollow, posing dummy, the conventionalized figure of a sahib. For it is the condition of his rule that he shall spend his life in trying to impress the "natives," and so in every crisis he has got to do what the "natives" expect of him. He wears a mask, and his face grows to fit it. I had got to shoot the elephant. I had committed myself to doing it when I sent for the rifle. A sahib has got to act like a sahib; he has got to appear resolute, to know his own mind and do definite things. To come all that way, rifle in hand, with two thousand people marching at my heels, and then to trail feebly away, having done nothing—no, that was impossible. The crowd would laugh at me. And my whole life, every white man's life in the East, was one long struggle not to be laughed at.

But I did not want to shoot the elephant. I watched him beating his bunch of grass against his knees, with that preoccupied grandmotherly air that elephants have. It seemed to me that it would be murder to shoot him. At that age I was not squeamish about killing animals, but I had never shot an elephant and never wanted to. (Somehow it always seems worse to kill a *large* animal.) Besides, there was the beast's owner to be considered. Alive, the elephant was worth at least a hundred pounds; dead, he would only be worth the value of his tusks, five pounds, possibly. But I had got to act quickly. I turned to some experienced-looking Burmans who had been there when we arrived, and asked them how the elephant had been behaving. They all said the same thing: he took no notice of you if you left him alone, but he might charge if you went too close to him.

It was perfectly clear to me what I ought to do. I ought to walk up to within, say, twenty-five yards of the elephant and test his behavior. If he charged, I could shoot; if he took no notice of me, it would be safe to leave him until the mahout came back. But also I knew that I was going to do no such thing. I was a poor shot with a rifle and the ground was soft mud into which one would sink at every step. If the elephant charged and I missed him, I should have about as much chance as a toad under a steam-roller. But even then I was not thinking particularly of my own skin, only of the watchful yellow faces behind. For at that moment, with the crowd watching me, I was not afraid in the ordinary sense, as I would have been if I had been alone. A white man mustn't be frightened in front of "natives"; and so, in general, he isn't frightened. The sole thought in my mind was that if anything went wrong those two thousand Burmans would see me pursued, caught, trampled on and reduced to a grinning corpse like that Indian up the hill. And if that happened it was quite probable that some of them would laugh. That would never do. There was only one alternative. I shoved the cartridges into the magazine and lay down on the road to get a better aim.

The crowd grew very still, and a deep, low, happy sigh, as of people who see the theatre curtain go up at last breathed from innumerable throats. They were going to have their bit of fun after all. The rifle was a beautiful German thing with cross-hair sights. I did not then know that in shooting an elephant one would shoot to cut an imaginary bar running from ear-hole to ear-hole. I ought, therefore, as the elephant was sideways on, to have aimed straight at his ear-hole; actually I aimed several inches in front of this, thinking the brain would be further forward. 10

When I pulled the trigger I did not hear the bang or feel the kick—one never does when a shot goes home—but I heard the devilish roar of glee that went up from the crowd. In that instant, in too short a time, one would have thought, even for the bullet to get there, a mysterious, terrible change had come over the elephant. He neither stirred nor fell, but every line of his body had altered. He looked suddenly stricken, shrunken, immensely old, as though the frightful impact of the bullet had paralysed him without knocking him down. At last, after what seemed a long time—it might have been five seconds, I dare say—he sagged flabbily to his knees. His mouth slobbered. An enormous senility seemed to have settled upon him. One could have imagined him thousands of years old. I fired again into the same spot. At the second shot he did not collapse but climbed with desperate slowness to his feet and stood weakly upright, with legs sagging and head dropping. I fired a third time. That was the shot that did for him. You could see the agony of it jolt his whole body and knock the last remnant of strength from his legs. But in falling he seemed for a moment to rise, for as his hind legs collapsed beneath him he seemed to tower upward like a huge rock toppling, his trunk reaching skywards like a tree. He trumpeted, for the first and only time. And then down he came, his belly towards me, with a crash that seemed to shake the ground even where I lay.

I got up. The Burmans were already racing past me across the mud. It was obvious that the elephant would never rise again, but he was not dead. He was breathing very rhythmically with long rattling gasps, his great mound of a side painfully rising and falling. His mouth was wide open. I could see far down into caverns of pale pink throat. I waited a long time for him to die, but his breathing did not weaken. Finally I fired my two remaining shots into the spot where I thought his heart must be. The thick blood welled out of him like red velvet, but still he did not die. His body did not even jerk when the shots hit him, the tortured breathing continued without a pause. He was dying, very slowly and in great agony, but in some world remote from me where not even a bullet could damage him further. I felt I had got to put an end to that dreadful noise. It seemed dreadful to see the great beast lying there, powerless to move and yet powerless to die, and not even to be able to finish him. I sent back for my small rifle and poured shot after shot into his heart and down his throat. They seemed to make no impression. The tortured gasps continued as steadily as the ticking of a clock.

In the end I could not stand it any longer and went away. I heard later that it took him half an hour to die. Burmans were bringing dahs and baskets even before I left, and I was told they had stripped his body almost to the bones by the afternoon.

Afterwards, of course, there were endless discussions about the shooting of the elephant. The owner was furious, but he was only an Indian and could do nothing. Besides, legally I had done the right thing, for a mad elephant has to be killed, like a mad dog, if its owner fails to control it. Among the Europeans opinion was divided. The older men said I was right, the younger men said it was a damn shame to shoot an elephant for killing a coolie, because an elephant was worth more than any damn Coringhee coolie. And afterwards I was very glad that the coolie had been killed; it put me legally in the right and it gave me a sufficient pretext for shooting the elephant. I often wondered whether any of the others grasped that I had done it solely to avoid looking a fool.

Topics for Critical Thinking and Writing

1. How does Orwell characterize himself at the time of the events he describes? What evidence in the essay suggests that he wrote it some years later?

2. Orwell says the incident was "enlightening." What does he mean? Picking up this clue, state in a sentence or two the thesis or main point of the essay.

3. Compare Orwell's description of the dead coolie (in the fourth paragraph) with his description of the elephant's death (in the eleventh and twelfth paragraphs). Why does Orwell devote more space to the death of the elephant?

4. How would you describe the tone of the last paragraph, particularly of the last two sentences? Do you find the paragraph an effective conclusion to the essay? Explain.

John

The following story, "The Woman Taken in Adultery," appears in several places in various early manuscripts of the New Testament, for instance in the Gospel according to Luke, after 21:38, in the Gospel according to John, after 7:36, and, in other manuscripts of John, after 7:53. The most famous English translation of the Bible, the King James Version (1611), gives it at John 8:3–11, and so it is commonly regarded as belonging to John. But most biblical scholars agree that the language of this short story differs notably from the language of the rest of this Gospel, and that it is not in any manuscript of John before the sixth century is further evidence that it was not originally part of this Gospel.

    The Gospel according to John was apparently compiled in the late first century. John 21:20–24 says the author, or "the disciple which testifieth of these things," is "the disciple whom Jesus loved, . . . which also leaned on his breast at supper, and said, 'Lord, which is he that betrayeth thee?'" Since the second century the book has traditionally been ascribed to John, one of the inner circle of twelve disciples.

The Woman Taken in Adultery

Jesus went unto the mount of Olives. And early in the morning he came again into the temple, and all the people came unto him; and he sat down, and taught them.

And the scribes and Pharisees[1] brought unto him a woman taken in adultery; and when they had set her in the midst, they say unto him, "Master, this woman was taken in adultery, in the very act. Now Moses in the law commanded us that such should be stoned: but what sayest thou?" This they said, tempting him, that they might have to accuse him. But Jesus stooped down, and with his finger wrote on the ground, as though he heard them not. So when they continued asking him, he lifted

---

[1]**scribes and Pharisees** The scribes were specialists who copied and interpreted the Hebrew law; the Pharisees were members of a sect that emphasized strict adherence to the Mosaic law. (Editors' note)

up himself, and said unto them, "He that is without sin among you, let him first cast a stone at her." And again he stooped down, and wrote on the ground. And they which heard it, being convicted by their own conscience, went out one by one, beginning at the eldest, even unto the last: and Jesus was left alone, and the woman standing in the midst.

When Jesus had lifted up himself, and saw none but the woman, he said unto her, "Woman, where are those thine accusers? Hath no man condemned thee?" She said, "No man, Lord." And Jesus said unto her, "Neither do I condemn thee; go, and sin no more."

Topics for Critical Thinking and Writing

1. Do you interpret the episode of "The Woman Taken in Adultery" to say that crime should go unpunished? Or that adultery is not a crime? Or that a judge cannot punish a crime if he himself is guilty of it? Or what?

2. We read that Jesus wrote with his finger on the ground but we are not told what Jesus wrote. How relevant do you find Jesus' action to the story? Explain.

3. This story is widely quoted and alluded to. Why, in your opinion, has the story such broad appeal?

Mitsuye Yamada

Mitsuye Yamada, the daughter of Japanese immigrants to the United States, was born in Japan in 1923, during her mother's return visit to her native land. Yamada was raised in Seattle, but in 1942 she and her family were incarcerated and then relocated in a camp in Idaho, when Executive Order 9066 gave military authorities the right to remove any and all persons from "military areas." In 1954 she became an American citizen.

To the Lady

The one in San Francisco who asked:
Why did the Japanese Americans let
the government put them in
those camps without protest?

Come to think of it I   5
    should've run off to Canada
    should've hijacked a plane to Algeria
    should've pulled myself up from my

bra straps
and kicked'm in the groin   10
should've bombed a bank
should've tried self-immolation
should've holed myself up in a
woodframe house
and let you watch me   15
burn up on the six o'clock news
should've run howling down the street
naked and assaulted you at breakfast
by AP wirephoto
should've screamed bloody murder   20
like Kitty Genovese[1]

Then
YOU would've
    come to my aid in shining armor
    laid yourself across the railroad track   25
    marched on Washington
    tattooed a Star of David on your arm
    written six million enraged
    letters to Congress

    But we didn't draw the line   30
    anywhere
    law and order Executive Order 9066[2]
    social order moral order internal order

YOU let'm
    I let'm   35
    All are punished.

 Topics for Critical Thinking and Writing

1. Has the lady's question (lines 2–4) ever crossed your mind? If so, what answers did you think of?

2. What, in effect, is the speaker really saying in lines 5–21? And in lines 22–29?

3. Explain the last line.

---

[1]**Kitty Genovese** In 1964 Kitty Genovese of Kew Gardens, New York, was stabbed to death when she left her car and walked toward her home. Thirty-eight persons heard her screams, but no one came to her assistance. (Editors' note)
[2]**Executive Order 9066** An authorization, signed in 1941 by President Franklin D. Roosevelt, allowing military authorities to relocate Japanese and Japanese Americans who resided on the Pacific Coast of the United States. (Editors' note)

CHAPTER 15

Body and Soul

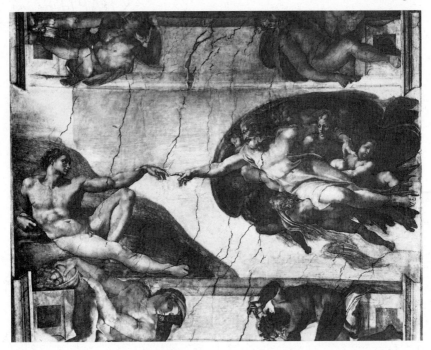

The Creation of Adam
Michelangelo

Priest Kensu Achieving Enlightenment While Catching a Shrimp
Kao, 14th Century

The Gross Clinic
Thomas Eakins

Lifted Lotus
Ken Gray

Short Views

Man can embody truth but he cannot know it.
W. B. Yeats

Anatomy is destiny.
Napoleon

If anything is sacred, the human body is sacred.
Walt Whitman

Man consists of two parts, his mind and his body, only the body
has more fun.
Woody Allen

It is a sign of a dull nature to occupy oneself deeply in matters that
concern the body; for instance, to be over much occupied about exercise, about eating and drinking, about easing oneself, about sexual intercourse.
Epictetus

It is much more difficult to live with one's body than with one's
soul. One's body is so much more exacting: What it won't have it
won't have, and nothing can make bitter into sweet.
D. H. Lawrence

Every man is the builder of a temple, called his body, to the god
he worships, after a style purely his own, nor can he get off by
hammering marble instead. We are all sculptors and painters, and
our material is our own flesh and blood and sinews.
Henry David Thoreau

A sound mind in a sound body, is a short but full definition of a
happy state in this world. He that has these two, has little more to
wish for; and he that wants either of them, will be little the better
for anything else.
John Locke

This soul, or life within us, by no means agrees with the life outside us. If one has the courage to ask her what she thinks, she is
always saying the very opposite to what other people say.
Virginia Woolf

The Soul unto itself
Is an imperial friend—
Or the most agonizing Spy—
An Enemy—could send—
  Emily Dickinson

We are bound to our bodies like an oyster to its shell.
  Plato

Body: The material substance of an animal, opposed to the immaterial soul. Soul: The immaterial and immortal substance of man.
  Samuel Johnson, **Dictionary of the English Language (1755)**

Men cannot be broken if their tormentors cannot invade and violate their souls. . . . The soul that is within me no man can degrade.
  Frederick Douglass

Soul is like electricity—we don't know what it is, but it's a force
that can light a room.
  Ray Charles

The abdomen is the reason why man does not easily take himself
for a God.
  Friedrich Nietzsche

Those who see any difference between soul and body have neither.
  Oscar Wilde

However broken down is the spirit's shrine, the spirit is there all
the same.
  Nigerian Proverb

What shall it profit a man, if he shall gain the whole world, and
lose his own soul?
  Jesus

Anonymous

The following story is told of two nineteenth-century Japanese Zen monks. It may or may not be historically true.

Muddy Road

Two monks, Tanzan and Ekido, were once traveling together down a muddy road. A heavy rain was still falling.

Coming around a bend, they met a lovely girl in a silk kimono and sash, unable to cross the intersection.

"Come on, girl," said Tanzan at once. Lifting her in his arms, he carried her over the mud.

Ekido did not speak again until that night when they reached a lodging temple. Then he no longer could restrain himself. "We monks don't go near females," he told Tanzan, "especially not young and lovely ones. It is dangerous. Why did you do that?"

"I left the girl there," said Tanzan. "Are you still carrying her?"

 Topics for Critical Thinking and Writing

1. The storyteller reports that after several hours Ekido "no longer could restrain himself." What emotion(s) has Ekido been experiencing? Why?

2. Is this story of interest only to persons interested in Zen Buddhism, or does it speak to a wider audience? Explain.

D. T. Suzuki

D[aisetz] T[eitaro] Suzuki (1870–1966) was one of Japan's leading writers on Zen Buddhism. He occasionally visited the United States, where he taught, lectured, and wrote. He is still regarded as the foremost interpreter of Zen Buddhism to the West.

Zen is the Japanese word for a school of Buddhism derived from China, where it was called Ch'an. In this essay Suzuki tries to explain satori, "enlightenment" or "awakening." The awakening is from a world of blind strivings (including those of reason and morality); the awakened being, free from a sense of the self in opposition to all other things, perceives the unity of all things. (When Suzuki was asked how it feels to have attained satori, he replied, "Just like ordinary everyday experience, except about two inches off the ground.")

What Is Zen?

The object of Zen training consists in making us realize that Zen is our daily experience and that it is not something put in from the outside. Tennō Dōgo (T'ien-huang Tao-wu, 748–807) illustrates the point most eloquently in his treatment of a novice monk, while an unknown Japanese swordmaster demonstrates it in the more threatening manner characteristic of his profession. Tennō Dōgo's story runs as follows:

> Dōgo had a disciple called Sōshin (Ch'ung-hsin). When Sōshin was taken in as a novice, it was perhaps natural of him to expect lessons in Zen from his teacher the way a schoolboy is taught at school. But Dōgo gave him no special lessons on the subject, and this bewildered and disappointed Sōshin. One day he said to the master, "It is some time since I came here, but not a word has been given me regarding the essence of the Zen teaching." Dōgo replied, "Since your arrival I have ever been giving you lessons on the matter of Zen discipline."
>
> "What kind of lesson could it have been?"
>
> "When you bring me a cup of tea in the morning, I take it; when you serve me a meal, I accept it; when you bow to me I return it with a nod. How else do you expect to be taught in the mental discipline of Zen?"
>
> Sōshin hung his head for a while, pondering the puzzling words of the master. The master said, "If you want to see, see right at once. When you begin to think, you miss the point."

The swordsman's story is this:

> When a disciple came to a master to be disciplined in the art of swordplay, the master, who was in retirement in his mountain hut, agreed to undertake the task. The pupil was made to help him gather kindling, draw water from the nearby spring, split wood, make fires, cook rice, sweep the rooms and the garden, and generally look after his household. There was no regular or technical teaching in the art. After some time the young man became dissatisfied, for he had not come to work as servant to the old gentleman, but to learn the art of swordsmanship. So one day he approached the master and asked him to teach him. The master agreed.
>
> The result was that the young man could not do any piece of work with any feeling of safety. For when he began to cook rice early in the morning, the master would appear and strike him from behind with a stick. When he was in the midst of his sweeping, he would be feeling the same sort of blow from somewhere, some unknown direction. He had no peace of mind, he had to be always on the *qui vive*. Some years passed before he could successfully dodge the blow from wherever it might come. But the master was not quite satisfied with him yet.
>
> One day the master was found cooking his own vegetables over an open fire. The pupil took it into his head to avail himself of this opportunity. Taking up his big stick, he let it fall over the head of the master, who was then stooping over the cooking pan to stir its contents. But the pupil's stick was

caught by the master with the cover of the pan. This opened the pupil's mind to the secrets of the art, which had hitherto been kept from him and to which he had so far been a stranger. He then, for the first time, appreciated the unparalleled kindness of the master.

The secrets of perfect swordsmanship consist in creating a certain frame or structure of mentality which is made always ready to respond instantly, that is, im-mediately, to what comes from the outside. While technical training is of great importance, it is after all something artificially, consciously, calculatingly added and acquired. Unless the mind that avails itself of the technical skill somewhat attunes itself to a state of the utmost fluidity or mobility, anything acquired or superimposed lacks spontaneity of natural growth. This state prevails when the mind is awakened to a *satori*. What the swordsman aimed at was to make the disciple attain to this realization. It cannot be taught by any system specifically designed for the purpose, it must simply grow from within. The master's system was really no system in the proper sense. But there was a "natural" method in his apparent craziness, and he succeeded in awakening in his young disciple's mind something that touched off the mechanism needed for the mastery of swordsmanship.

Dōgo the Zen master did not have to be attacking his disciple all the time with a stick. The swordsman's object was more definite and limited to the area of the sword, whereas Dōgo wanted to teach by getting to the source of being from which everything making up our daily experience ensues. Therefore, when Sōshin began to reflect on the remark Dōgo made to him, Dōgo told him: "No reflecting whatever. When you want to see, see im-mediately. As soon as you tarry [that is, as soon as an intellectual interpretation or mediation takes place], the whole thing goes awry." This means that, in the study of Zen, conceptualization must go, for as long as we tarry at this level we can never reach the area where Zen has its life. The door of enlightenment-experience opens by itself as one finally faces the deadlock of intellectualization.

We now can state a few things about Zen in a more or less summary way:

1. Zen discipline consists in attaining enlightenment (or *satori*, in Japanese).

2. *Satori* finds a meaning hitherto hidden in our daily concrete particular experiences, such as eating, drinking, or business of all kinds.

3. The meaning thus revealed is not something added from the outside. It is in being itself, in becoming itself, in living itself. This is called, in Japanese, a life of *kono-mama* or *sono-mama*.[1] Kono- or sono-mama means the "isness" of a thing. Reality in its isness.

---

[1]*Kono* is "this," *sono* "that," and *mama* means "as-it-is-ness." Kono-mama or sono-mama thus corresponds to the Sanskrit *tathatā*, "suchness," and to the Chinese *chih-mo* or *shih-mo*.

4. Some may say, "There cannot be any meaning in mere isness." But this is not the view held by Zen, for according to it, isness is the meaning. When I see into it I see it as clearly as I see myself reflected in a mirror.

5. This is what made Hō Koji (P'ang Chü-shih), a lay disciple of the eighth century, declare:

> How wondrous this, how mysterious!
> I carry fuel, I draw water.

The fuel-carrying or the water-drawing itself, apart from its utilitarianism, is full of meaning; hence its "wonder," its "mystery."

6. Zen does not, therefore, indulge in abstraction or in conceptualization. In its verbalism it may sometimes appear that Zen does this a great deal. But this is an error most commonly entertained by those who do not at all know Zen.

7. *Satori* is emancipation, moral, spiritual, as well as intellectual. When I am in my isness, thoroughly purged of all intellectual sediments, I have my freedom in its primary sense.

8. When the mind, now abiding in its isness—which, to use Zen verbalism, is not isness—and thus free from intellectual complexities and moralistic attachments of every description, surveys the world of the senses in all its multiplicities, it discovers in it all sorts of values hitherto hidden from sight. Here opens to the artist a world full of wonders and miracles.

9. The artist's world is one of free creation, and this can come only from intuitions directly and im-mediately rising from the isness of things, unhampered by senses and intellect. He creates forms and sounds out of formlessness and soundlessness. To this extent, the artist's world coincides with that of Zen.

10. What differentiates Zen from the arts is this: While the artists have to resort to the canvas and brush or mechanical instruments or some other mediums to express themselves, Zen has no need of things external, except "the body" in which the Zen-man is so to speak embodied. From the absolute point of view this is not quite correct; I say it only in concession to the worldly way of saying things. What Zen does is to delineate itself on the infinite canvas of time and space the way the flying wild geese cast their shadow on the water below without any idea of doing so, while the water reflects the geese just as naturally and unintentionally.

11. The Zen-man is an artist to the extent that, as the sculptor chisels out a great figure deeply buried in a mass of inert matter, the Zen-man transforms his own life into a work of creation, which exists, as Christians might say, in the mind of God.[2]

---

[2]After writing the above I feel somewhat uneasy lest my readers may not be able to comprehend what Zen means to us of modern time. Everything of life nowadays shows the tendency to turn into a complete routine of mechanization, leaving nothing that will demonstrate the dignity and destiny of human existence.

Topics for Critical Thinking and Writing

1. After telling the swordsman's story, Suzuki uses the word "im-mediately." Why does he add the hyphen? (Check a dictionary if you don't know the Latin origin of the word.)

2. Suzuki in this essay is teaching the meaning of Zen. How does he go about teaching? How successful do you find his methods?

3. In the 9th point in his numbered list Suzuki says that the artist, like the enlightened person, works from "intuition" and is "unhampered by senses and intellect." What do you understand him to mean by intuition? What value does the work of art have for the artist? Does it have the same value for us?

Langston Hughes

Langston Hughes (1902–67), born in Joplin, Missouri, was the first African-American writer to establish an international reputation. Enormously versatile, he wrote poems, plays, stories, novels, children's books, filmscripts, essays, and autobiographies. (The selection printed below is from an autobiographical volume called The Big Sea *[1940]). Hughes also exerted a great influence on American literature by organizing poetry readings for black writers and by founding three theater groups.*

Salvation

I was saved from sin when I was going on thirteen. But not really saved. It happened like this. There was a big revival at my Auntie Reed's church. Every night for weeks there had been much preaching, singing, praying, and shouting, and some very hardened sinners had been brought to Christ, and the membership of the church had grown by leaps and bounds. Then just before the revival ended, they held a special meeting for children, "to bring the young lambs to the fold." My aunt spoke of it for days ahead. That night I was escorted to the front row and placed on the mourners' bench with all the other young sinners, who had not yet been brought to Jesus.

My aunt told me that when you were saved you saw a light, and something happened to you inside! And Jesus came into your life! And God was with you from then on! She said you could see and hear and feel Jesus in your soul. I believed her. I had heard a great many old people say the same thing and it seemed to me they ought to know. So I sat there calmly in the hot, crowded church, waiting for Jesus to come to me.

The preacher preached a wonderful rhythmical sermon, all moans and shouts and lonely cries and dire pictures of hell, and then he sang a song about the ninety and nine safe in the fold, but one little lamb was left out in the cold. Then he said: "Won't you come? Won't you come to Jesus? Young lambs, won't you come?" And he held out his arms to all us young sinners there on the mourners' bench. And the little girls cried. And some of them jumped up and went to Jesus right away. But most of us just sat there.

A great many old people came and knelt around us and prayed, old women with jet-black faces and braided hair, old men with work-gnarled hands. And the church sang a song about the lower lights are burning, some poor sinners to be saved. And the whole building rocked with prayer and song.

Still I kept waiting to *see* Jesus.   5

Finally all the young people had gone to the altar and were saved, but one boy and me. He was a rounder's son named Westley. Westley and I were surrounded by sisters and deacons praying. It was very hot in the church, and getting late now. Finally Westley said to me in a whisper: "God damn! I'm tired o' sitting here. Let's get up and be saved." So he got up and was saved.

Then I was left all alone on the mourners' bench. My aunt came and knelt at my knees and cried, while prayers and songs swirled all around me in the little church. The whole congregation prayed for me alone, in a mighty wail of moans and voices. And I kept waiting serenely for Jesus, waiting, waiting—but he didn't come. I wanted to see him, but nothing happened to me. Nothing! I wanted something to happen to me, but nothing happened.

I heard the songs and the minister saying: "Why don't you come? My dear child, why don't you come to Jesus? Jesus is waiting for you. He wants you. Why don't you come? Sister Reed, what is this child's name?"

"Langston," my aunt sobbed.

"Langston, why don't you come? Why don't you come and be saved?   10
Oh, Lamb of God! Why don't you come?"

Now it was really getting late. I began to be ashamed of myself, holding everything up so long. I began to wonder what God thought about Westley, who certainly hadn't seen Jesus either, but who was now sitting proudly on the platform, swinging his knickerbockered legs and grinning down at me, surrounded by deacons and old women on their knees praying. God had not struck Westley dead for taking his name in vain or for lying in the temple. So I decided that maybe to save further trouble, I'd better lie, too, and say that Jesus had come, and get up and be saved.

So I got up.

Suddenly the whole room broke into a sea of shouting, as they saw me rise. Waves of rejoicing swept the place. Women leaped in the air. My aunt threw her arms around me. The minister took me by the hand and led me to the platform.

When things quieted down, in a hushed silence, punctuated by a few ecstatic "Amens," all the new young lambs were blessed in the name of God. Then joyous singing filled the room.

That night, for the last time in my life but one—for I was a big boy   15
twelve years old—I cried. I cried, in bed alone, and couldn't stop. I buried my head under the quilts, but my aunt heard me. She woke up and told my uncle I was crying because the Holy Ghost had come into my life, and because I had seen Jesus. But I was really crying because I couldn't bear to tell her that I had lied, that I had deceived everybody in the church, and I hadn't seen Jesus, and that now I didn't believe there was a Jesus any more, since he didn't come to help me.

 ## Topics for Critical Thinking and Writing

1. Is the piece amusing, or serious, or both? Explain.

2. How would you characterize the style or voice of the first three sentences? Childlike, or sophisticated, or what? How would you characterize the final sentence? How can you explain the change in style or tone?

3. In the paragraph beginning "Now it was really getting late," why does Hughes bother to tell us that Westley was "swinging his knickerbockered legs and grinning"? Do you think that Westley too may have cried that night? Give your reasons.

4. Is the episode told from the point of view of someone "going on thirteen," or from the point of view of a mature man?

5. One of the Golden Rules of narrative writing is "Show, don't tell." In about 500 words, report an experience—for instance, a death in the family, or a severe (perhaps unjust) punishment, or the first day in a new school—that produced strong feelings. Like Hughes, you may want to draw on an experience in which you were subjected to group pressure. Do not explicitly state what the feelings were; rather, let the reader understand the feelings chiefly through concretely detailed actions. But, like Hughes, you might state your thesis or basic position in your first paragraph and then indicate when and where the experience took place.

Henry David Thoreau

Henry David Thoreau (1817–62) was born in Concord, Massachusetts, where he spent most of his life ("I have travelled a good deal in Concord"). He taught and lectured, but chiefly he observed, thought, and wrote. From July 4, 1845, to September 6, 1847, he lived near Concord in a cabin at Walden Pond, an experience recorded in Walden *(1854).*
We reprint part of the first chapter of Walden.

Economy

The mass of men lead lives of quiet desperation. What is called resignation is confirmed desperation. From the desperate city you go into the desperate country, and have to console yourself with the bravery of minks and muskrats. A stereotyped but unconscious despair is concealed even under what are called the games and amusements of mankind. There is no play in them, for this comes after work. But it is a characteristic of wisdom not to do desperate things.

When we consider what, to use the words of the catechism, is the chief end of man, and what are the true necessaries and means of life, it appears as if men had deliberately chosen the common mode of living because they preferred it to any other. Yet they honestly think there is no choice left. But alert and healthy natures remember that the sun rose clear. It is never too late to give up our prejudices. No way of thinking or doing, however ancient, can be trusted without proof. What everybody echoes or in silence passes by as true to-day may turn out to be falsehood to-morrow, mere smoke of opinion, which some had trusted for a cloud that would sprinkle fertilizing rain on their fields. What old people say you cannot do you try and find that you can. Old deeds for old people, and new deeds for new. Old people did not know enough once, perchance, to fetch fresh fuel to keep the fire a-going; new people put a little dry wood under a pot, and are whirled round the globe with the speed of birds, in a way to kill old people, as the phrase is. Age is no better, hardly so well, qualified for an instructor as youth, for it has not profited so much as it has lost. One may almost doubt if the wisest man has learned anything of absolute value by living. Practically, the old have no very important advice to give the young, their own experience has been so partial, and their lives have been such miserable failures, for private reasons, as they must believe; and it may be that they have some faith left which belies that experience, and they are only less young than they were. I have lived some thirty years on this planet, and I have yet to hear the first syllable of valuable or even earnest advice from my seniors. They have told me nothing, and probably cannot tell me anything to the purpose. Here is life, an experiment to a great extent untried by me; but it does not avail me that they have tried it. If I have any experience which I think valuable, I am sure to reflect that this my Mentors said nothing about.

One farmer says to me, "You cannot live on vegetable food solely, for   3
it furnishes nothing to make bones with;" and so he religiously devotes a
part of his day to supplying his system with the raw material of bones;
walking all the while he talks behind his oxen, which, with vegetable-
made bones, jerk him and his lumbering plough along in spite of every
obstacle. Some things are really necessaries of life in some circles, the
most helpless and diseased, which in others are luxuries merely, and in
others still are entirely unknown.

The whole ground of human life seems to some to have been gone   4
over by their predecessors, both the heights and the valleys, and all things
to have been cared for. According to Evelyn, "the wise Solomon pre-
scribed ordinances for the very distances of trees; and the Roman prætors
have decided how often you may go into your neighbor's land to gather
the acorns which fall on it without trespass, and what share belongs to
that neighbor." Hippocrates has even left directions how we should cut
our nails; that is, even with the ends of the fingers, neither shorter nor
longer. Undoubtedly the very tedium and ennui which presume to have
exhausted the variety and the joys of life are as old as Adam. But man's
capacities have never been measured; nor are we to judge of what he can
do by any precedents, so little has been tried. Whatever have been thy
failures hitherto, "be not afflicted, my child, for who shall assign to thee
what thou hast left undone?"

We might try our lives by a thousand simple tests; as, for instance,   5
that the same sun which ripens my beans illumines at once a system of
earths like ours. If I had remembered this it would have prevented some
mistakes. This was not the light in which I hoed them. The stars are the
apexes of what wonderful triangles! What distant and different beings in
the various mansions of the universe are contemplating the same one at
the same moment! Nature and human life are as various as our several
constitutions. Who shall say what prospect life offers to another? Could a
greater miracle take place than for us to look through each other's eyes for
an instant? We should live in all the ages of the world in an hour; ay, in all
the worlds of the ages. History, Poetry, Mythology!—I know of no reading
of another's experience so startling and informing as this would be.

The greater part of what my neighbors call good I believe in my soul   6
to be bad, and if I repent of anything, it is very likely to be my good behavior. What demon possessed me that I behaved so well? You may say
the wisest thing you can, old man—you who have lived seventy years,
not without honor of a kind,—I hear an irresistible voice which invites me
away from all that. One generation abandons the enterprises of another
like stranded vessels.

I think that we may safely trust a good deal more than we do. We   7
may waive just so much care of ourselves as we honestly bestow elsewhere. Nature is as well adapted to our weakness as to our strength. The
incessant anxiety and strain of some is a well-nigh incurable form of disease. We are made to exaggerate the importance of what work we do; and

yet how much is not done by us! or, what if we had been taken sick? How vigilant we are! determined not to live by faith if we can avoid it; all the day long on the alert, at night we unwillingly say our prayers and commit ourselves to uncertainties. So thoroughly and sincerely are we compelled to live, reverencing our life, and denying the possibility of change. This is the only way, we say; but there are as many ways as there can be drawn radii from one centre. All change is a miracle to contemplate; but it is a miracle which is taking place every instant. Confucius said, "To know that we know what we know, and that we do not know what we do not know, that is true knowledge." When one man has reduced a fact of the imagination to be a fact to his understanding, I foresee that all men will at length establish their lives on that basis.

Let us consider for a moment what most of the trouble and anxiety   8
which I have referred to is about, and how much it is necessary that we be troubled, or at least careful. It would be some advantage to live a primitive and frontier life, though in the midst of an outward civilization, if only to learn what are the gross necessaries of life and what methods have been taken to obtain them; or even to look over the old day-books of the merchants, to see what it was that men most commonly bought at the stores, what they stored, that is, what are the grossest groceries. For the improvements of ages have had but little influence on the essential laws of man's existence; as our skeletons, probably, are not to be distinguished from those of our ancestors.

By the words, *necessary of life*, I mean whatever, of all that man obtains   9
by his own exertions, has been from the first, or from long use has become, so important to human life that few, if any, whether from savageness, or poverty, or philosophy, ever attempt to do without it. To many creatures there is in this sense but one necessary of life. Food. To the bison of the prairie it is a few inches of palatable grass, with water to drink; unless he seeks the Shelter of the forest or the mountain's shadow. None of the brute creation requires more than Food and Shelter. The necessaries of life for man in this climate may, accurately enough, be distributed under the several heads of Food, Shelter, Clothing, and Fuel; for not till we have secured these are we prepared to entertain the true problems of life with freedom and a prospect of success. Man has invented, not only houses, but clothes and cooked food; and possibly from the accidental discovery of the warmth of fire, and the consequent use of it, at first a luxury, arose the present necessity to sit by it. We observe cats and dogs acquiring the same second nature. By proper Shelter and Clothing we legitimately retain our own internal heat; but with an excess of these, or of Fuel, that is, with an external heat greater than our own internal, may not cookery properly be said to begin? Darwin, the naturalist, says of the inhabitants of Tierra del Fuego, that while his own party, who were well clothed and sitting close to a fire, were far from too warm, these naked savages, who were farther off, were observed, to his great surprise, "to be steaming with perspiration at undergoing such a roasting." So, we are told, the

New Hollander goes naked with impunity, while the European shivers in his clothes. Is it impossible to combine the hardiness of these savages with the intellectualness of the civilized man? According to Liebig, man's body is a stove, and food the fuel which keeps up the internal combustion in the lungs. In cold weather we eat more, in warm less. The animal heat is the result of a slow combustion, and disease and death take place when this is too rapid; or for want of fuel, or from some defect in the draught, the fire goes out. Of course the vital heat is not to be confounded with fire; but so much for analogy. It appears, therefore, from the above list, that the expression, *animal life*, is nearly synonymous with the expression, *animal heat*; for while Food may be regarded as the Fuel which keeps up the fire within us,—and Fuel serves only to prepare that Food or to increase the warmth of our bodies by addition from without—Shelter and Clothing also serve only to retain the *heat* thus generated and absorbed.

   The grand necessity, then, for our bodies, is to keep warm, to keep the vital heat in us. What pains we accordingly take, not only with our Food, and Clothing, and Shelter, but with our beds, which are our night-clothes, robbing the nests and breasts of birds to prepare this shelter within a shelter, as the mole has its bed of grass and leaves at the end of its burrow! The poor man is wont to complain that this is a cold world; and to cold, no less physical than social, we refer directly a great part of our ails. The summer, in some climates, makes possible to man a sort of Elysian life. Fuel, except to cook his Food, is then unnecessary; the sun is his fire, and many of the fruits are sufficiently cooked by its rays; while Food generally is more various, and more easily obtained, and Clothing and Shelter are wholly or half unnecessary. At the present day, and in this country, as I find by my own experience, a few implements, a knife, an axe, a spade, a wheelbarrow, etc.; and for the studious, lamplight, stationery, and access to a few books, rank next to necessaries, and can all be obtained at a trifling cost. Yet some, not wise, go to the other side of the globe, to barbarous and unhealthy regions, and devote themselves to trade for ten or twenty years, in order that they may live—that is, keep comfortably warm,—and die in New England at last. The luxuriously rich are not simply kept comfortably warm, but unnaturally hot; as I implied before, they are cooked, of course *à la mode*. 10

   Most of the luxuries, and many of the so-called comforts of life, are not only not indispensable, but positive hindrances to the elevation of mankind. With respect to luxuries and comforts, the wisest have ever lived a more simple and meagre life than the poor. The ancient philosophers, Chinese, Hindoo, Persian, and Greek, were a class than which none has been poorer in outward riches, none so rich in inward. We know not much about them. It is remarkable that *we* know so much of them as we do. The same is true of the more modern reformers and benefactors of their race. None can be an impartial or wise observer of human life but from the vantage ground of what *we* should call voluntary poverty. Of a life of luxury the fruit is luxury, whether in agriculture, or commerce, or 11 literature, or art. There are nowadays professors of philosophy, but not philosophers. Yet it is admirable to profess because it was once admirable to live. To be a philosopher is not merely to have subtle thoughts, nor even to found a school, but so to love wisdom as to live accordingly to its dictates, a life of simplicity, independence, magnanimity, and trust. It is to solve some of the problems of life, not only theoretically, but practically. The success of great scholars and thinkers is commonly a courtier-like success, not kingly, not manly. They make shift to live merely by conformity, practically as their fathers did, and are in no sense the progenitors of a nobler race of men. But why do men degenerate ever? What makes families run out? What is the nature of the luxury which enervates and destroys nations? Are we sure that there is none of it in our own lives? The philosopher is in advance of his age even in the outward form of his life. He is not fed, sheltered, clothed, warmed, like his contemporaries. How can a man be a philosopher and not maintain his vital heat by better methods than other men?

When a man is warmed by the several modes which I have described, what does he want next? Surely not more warmth of the same kind, as more and richer food, larger and more splendid houses, finer and more abundant clothing, more numerous incessant and hotter fires, and the like. When he has obtained those things which are necessary to life, there is another alternative than to obtain the superfluities; and that is, to adventure on life now, his vacation from humbler toil having commenced. The soil, it appears, is suited to the seed, for it has sent its radicle downward, and it may now send its shoot upward also with confidence. Why has man rooted himself thus firmly in the earth, but that he may rise in the same proportion into the heavens above?—for the nobler plants are valued for the fruit they bear at last in the air and light, far from the ground, and are not treated like the humbler esculents, which, though they may be biennials, are cultivated only till they have perfected their root, and often cut down at top for this purpose, so that most would not know them in their flowering season.   12

I do not mean to prescribe rules to strong and valiant natures, who will mind their own affairs whether in heaven or hell, and perchance build more magnificently and spend more lavishly than the richest, without ever impoverishing themselves, not knowing how they live,—if, indeed, there are any such, as has been dreamed; nor to those who find their encouragement and inspiration in precisely the present condition of things, and cherish it with the fondness and enthusiams of lovers,—and, to some extent, I reckon myself in this number; I do not speak to those who are well employed, in whatever circumstances, and they know whether they are well employed or not;—but mainly to the mass of men who are discontented, and idly complaining of the hardness of their lot or of the times, when they might improve them. There are some who complain most energetically and inconsolably of any, because they are, as they say, doing their duty. I also have in my mind that seemingly wealthy,   13 but most terribly impoverished class of all, who have accumulated dross, but know not how to use it, or get rid of it, and thus have forget their own golden or silver fetters.

As for Clothing, to come at once to the practical part of the question, perhaps we are led oftener by the love of novelty and a regard for the opinions of men, in procuring it, than by a true utility. Let him who has work to do recollect that the object of clothing is, first, to retain the vital heat, and secondly, in this state of society, to cover nakedness, and he may judge how much of any necessary or important work may be accomplished without adding to his wardrobe. Kings and queens who wear a suit but once, though made by some tailor or dressmaker to their majesties, cannot know the comfort of wearing a suit that fits. They are no better than wooden horses to hang the clean clothes on. Every day our garments become more assimilated to ourselves, receiving the impress of the wearer's character, until we hesitate to lay them aside, without such delay and medical appliances and some such solemnity even as our bodies. No man ever stood the lower in my estimation for having a patch in his clothes; yet I am sure that there is greater anxiety, commonly, to have fashionable, or at least clean and unpatched clothes, then to have a sound conscience. But even if the rent is not mended, perhaps the worst vice betrayed is improvidence. I sometimes try my acquaintances by such tests as this,—Who could wear a patch, or two extra seams only, over the knee? Most behave as if they believed that their prospects for life would be ruined if they should do it. It would be easier for them to hobble to town with a broken leg than with a broken pantaloon. Often if an accident happens to a gentleman's legs, they can be mended; but if a similar accident happens to the legs of his pantaloons, there is no help for it; for he considers, not what is truly respectable, but what is respected. We know but few men, a great many coats and breeches. Dress a scarecrow in your last shift, you standing shiftless by, who would not soonest salute the scarecrow? Passing a cornfield the other day, close by a hat and coat on a stake, I recognized the owner of the farm. He was only a little more weatherbeaten than when I saw him last. I have heard of a dog that barked at every stranger who approached his master's premises with clothes on, but was easily quieted by a naked thief. It is an interesting question how far men would retain their relative rank if they were divested of their clothes. Could you, in such a case, tell surely of any company of civilized men which belonged to the most respected class? When Madam Pfeiffer, in her adventurous travels round the world, from east to west, had got so near home as Asiatic Russia, she says that she felt the necessity of wearing other than a travelling dress, when she went to meet the authorities, for the "was now in a civilized country, where . . . people are judged of by their clothes." Even in our democratic New England towns the accidental possession of wealth, and its manifestation in dress and equipage alone, obtain for the possessor almost universal respect. But they who yield such

14

respect, numerous as they are, are so far heathen, and need to have a missionary sent to them. Beside, clothes introduced sewing, a kind of work which you may call endless; a woman's dress, at least, is never done.

A man who has at length found something to do will not need to get a new suit to do it in; for him the old will do, that has lain dusty in the garret for an indeterminate period. Old shoes will serve a hero longer than they have served his valet,—if a hero ever has a valet,—bare feet are older than shoes, and he can make them do. Only they who go to soirées and legislative halls must have new coats, coats to change as often as the man changes in them. But if my jacket and trousers, my hat and shoes, are fit to worship God in, they will do; will they not? Who ever saw his old clothes,—his old coat, actually worn out, resolved into its primitive elements, so that it was not a deed of charity to bestow it on some poor boy, by him perchance to be bestowed on some poorer still, or shall we say richer, who could do with less? I say, beware of all enterprises that require new clothes, and not rather a new wearer of clothes. If there is not a new man, how can the new clothes be made to fit? If you have any enterprise before you, try it in your old clothes. All men want, not something to *do with*, but something to *do*, or rather something to *be*. Perhaps we should never procure a new suit, however ragged or dirty the old, until we have so conducted, so enterprised or sailed in some way, that we feel like new men in the old, and that to retain it would be like keeping new wine in old bottles. Our moulting season, like that of the fowls, must be a crisis in our lives. The loon retires to solitary ponds to spend it. Thus also the snake casts its slough, and the caterpillar its wormy coat, by an internal industry and expansion; for clothes are but our outmost cuticle and mortal coil. Otherwise we shall be found sailing under false colors, and be inevitably cashiered at last by our own opinion, as well as that of mankind.

We don garment after garment, as if we grew like exogenous plants by addition without. Our outside and often thin and fanciful clothes are our epidermis, or false skin, which partakes not of our life, and may be stripped off here and there without fatal injury; our thicker garments, constantly worn, are our cellular integument, or cortex; but our shirts are our liber,[1] or true bark, which cannot be removed without girdling and so destroying the man. I believe that all races at some seasons wear something equivalent to the shirt. It is desirable that a man be clad so simply that he can lay his hands on himself in the dark, and that he live in all respects so compactly and preparedly, that, if an enemy take the town, he can, like the old philosopher, walk out the gate empty-handed without anxiety. While one thick garment is, for most purposes, as good as three thin ones, and cheap clothing can be obtained at prices really to suit customers; while a thick coat can be bought for five dollars, which will last as many years, thick pantaloons for two dollars, cowhide boots for a dollar and a half a pair, a summer hat for a quarter of a dollar, and a winter cap

15

16

---

[1]**Liber** Latin for "bark" (Editors' note)

for sixty-two and a half cents, or a better be made at home at a nominal cost, where is he so poor that, clad in such a suit, *of his own earning*, there will not be found wise men to do him reverence?

When I ask for a garment of a particular form, my tailoress tells me   17 gravely, "They do not make them so now," not emphasizing the "They" at all, as if she quoted an authority as impersonal as the Fates, and I find it difficult to get made what I want, simply because she cannot believe that I mean what I say, that I am so rash. When I hear this oracular sentence, I am for a moment absorbed in thought, emphasizing to myself each word separately that I may come at the meaning of it, that I may find out by what degree of consanguinity *They* are related to *me*, and what authority they may have in an affair which affects me so nearly; and finally, I am inclined to answer her with equal mystery, and without any more emphasis of the "they"—"It is true, they did not make them so recently, but they do now." Of what use this measuring of me if she does not measure my character, but only the breadth of my shoulders, as it were a peg to hang the coat on? We worship not the Graces, nor the Parcæ, but Fashion. She spins and weaves and cuts with full authority. The head monkey at Paris puts on a traveller's cap, and all the monkeys in America do the same. I sometimes despair of getting anything quite simple and honest done in this world by the help of men. They would have to be passed through a powerful press first, to squeeze their old notions out of them, so that they would not soon get upon their legs again; and then there would be some one in the company with a maggot in his head, hatched from an egg deposited there nobody knows when, for not even fire kills these things, and you would have lost your labor. Nevertheless, we will not forget that some Egyptian wheat was handed down to us by a mummy.

On the whole, I think that it cannot be maintained that dressing has in   18 this or any country risen to the dignity of an art. At present men make shift to wear what they can get. Like shipwrecked sailors, they put on what they can find on the beach, and at a little distance, whether of space or time, laugh at each other's masquerade. Every generation laughs at the old fashions, but follows religiously the new. We are amused at beholding the costume of Henry VIII., or Queen Elizabeth, as much as if it was that of the King and Queen of the Cannibal Islands. All costume off a man is pitiful or grotesque. It is only the serious eye peering from and the sincere life passed within it which restrain laughter and consecrate the costume of any people. Let Harlequin be taken with a fit of the colic and his trappings will have to serve that mood too. When the soldier is hit by a cannon ball rags are as becoming as purple.

The childish and savage taste of men and women for new patterns   19 keeps how many shaking and squinting through kaleidoscopes that they may discover the particular figure which this generation requires today. The manufacturers have learned that this taste is merely whimsical. Of two patterns which differ only by a few threads more or less of a particular color, the one will be sold readily, the other lie on the shelf, though it frequently happens that after the lapse of a season the latter becomes the most fashionable. Comparatively, tattooing is not the hideous custom which it is called. It is not barbarous merely because the printing is skin-deep and unalterable.

I cannot believe that our factory system is the best mode by which men may get clothing. The condition of the operatives is becoming every day more like that of the English; and it cannot be wondered at, since, as far as I have heard or observed, the principal object is, not that mankind may be well and honestly clad, but, unquestionably, that the corporations may be enriched. In the long run men hit only what they aim at. Therefore, though they should fail immediately, they had better aim at something high. [20]

As for a Shelter, I will not deny that this is now a necessary of life, though there are instances of men having done without it for long periods in colder countries than this. Samuel Laing says that "the Laplander in his skin dress, and in a skin bag which he puts over his head and shoulders, will sleep night after night on the snow ... in a degree of cold which would extinguish the life of one exposed to it in any woollen clothing." He had seen them asleep thus. Yet he adds, "They are not hardier than other people." But, probably, man did not live long on the earth without discovering the convenience which there is in a house, the domestic comforts, which phrase may have originally signified the satisfactions of the house more than of the family; though these must be extremely partial and occasional in those climates where the house is associated in our thoughts with winter or the rainy season chiefly, and two thirds of the year, except for a parasol, is unnecessary. In our climate, in the summer, it was formerly almost solely a covering at night. In the Indian gazettes a wigwam was the symbol of a day's march, and a row of them cut or painted on the bark of a tree signified that so many times they had camped. Man was not made so large limbed and robust but that he must seek to narrow his world, and wall in a space such as fitted him. He was at first bare and out of doors; but though this was pleasant enough in serene and warm weather, by daylight, the rainy season and the winter, to say nothing of the torrid sun, would perhaps have nipped his race in the bud if he had not made haste to clothe himself with the shelter of a house. Adam and Eve, according to the fable, wore the bower before other clothes. Man wanted a home, a place of warmth, or comfort, first of physical warmth, then the warmth of the affections. [21]

We may imagine a time when, in the infancy of the human race, some enterprising mortal crept into a hollow in a rock for shelter. Every child begins the world again, to some extent, and loves to stay out doors, even in wet and cold. It plays house, as well as horse, having an instinct for it. Who does not remember the interest with which, when young, he looked at shelving rocks, or any approach to a cave? It was the natural yearning of that portion of our most primitive ancestor which still survived in us. From the cave we have advanced to roofs of palm leaves, of bark and [22] boughs, of linen woven and stretched, of grass and straw, of boards and shingles, of stones and tiles. At last, we know not what it is to live in the open air, and our lives are domestic in more senses than we think. From the hearth the field is a great distance. It would be well, perhaps, if we were to spend more of our days and nights without any obstruction between us and the celestial bodies, if the poet did not speak so much from under a roof, or the saint dwell there so long. Birds do not sing in caves, nor do doves cherish their innocence in dovecots.

However, if one designs to construct a dwelling house, it behooves him to exercise a little Yankee shrewdness, lest after all he finds himself in a workhouse, a labyrinth without a clue, a museum, an almshouse, a prison, or a splendid mausoleum instead. Consider first how slight a shelter is absolutely necessary. I have seen Penobscot Indians, in this town, living in tents of thin cotton cloth, while the snow was nearly a foot deep around them, and I thought that they would be glad to have it deeper to keep out the wind. Formerly, when how to get my living honestly, with freedom left for my proper pursuits, was a question which vexed me even more than it does now, for unfortunately I am become somewhat callous, I used to see a large box by the railroad, six feet long by three wide, in which the laborers locked up their tools at night; and it suggested to me that every man who was hard pushed might get such a one for a dollar, and, having bored a few auger holes in it, to admit the air at least get into it when it rained and at night, and hook down the lid, and so have freedom in his love, and in his soul be free. This did not appear the worst, nor by any means a despicable alternative. You could sit up as late as you pleased, and, whenever you got up, go abroad without any landlord or house-lord dogging you for rent. Many a man is harassed to death to pay the rent of a larger and more luxurious box who would not have frozen to death in such a box as this. I am far from jesting. Economy is a subject which admits of being treated with levity, but it cannot so be disposed of. A comfortable house for a rude and hardy race, that lived mostly out of doors, was once made here almost entirely of such materials as Nature furnished ready to their hands. Gookin, who was superintendent of the Indians subject to the Massachusetts Colony, writing in 1674, says, "The best of their houses are covered very neatly, tight and warm, with barks of trees, slipped from their bodies at those seasons when the sap is up, and made into great flakes, with pressure of weighty timber, when they are green. . . . The meaner sort are covered with mats which they make of a kind of bulrush, and are also indifferently tight and warm, but not so good as the former. . . . Some I have seen, sixty or a hundred feet long and thirty feet broad. . . . I have often lodged in their wigwams, and found them as warm as the best English houses." He adds that they were commonly carpeted and lined within with well-wrought embroidered mats, and were furnished with various utensils. The Indians had advanced so far as to regulate the effect of the wind by a mat suspended over the hole in the roof and moved by a string. Such a lodge was in the first instance

23

constructed in a day or two at most, and taken down and put up in a few hours; and every family owned one, or its apartment in one.

In the savage state every family owns a shelter as good as the best, and sufficient for its coarser and simpler wants; but I think that I speak within bounds when I say that, though the birds of the air have their nests, and the foxes their holes, and the savages their wigwams, in modern civilized society not more than one half the families own a shelter. In the large towns and cities, where civilization especially prevails, the number of those who own a shelter is a very small fraction of the whole. The rest pay an annual tax for this outside garment of all, become indispensable summer and winter, which would buy a village of Indian wigwams, but now helps to keep them poor as long as they live. I do not mean to insist here on the disadvantage of hiring compared with owning, but it is evident that the savage owns his shelter because it costs so little, while the civilized man hires his commonly because he cannot afford to own it; nor can he, in the long run, any better afford to hire. But, answers one, by merely paying this tax the poor civilized man secures an abode which is a palace compared with the savage's. An annual rent of from twenty-five to a hundred dollars (these are the country rates) entitles him to the benefit of the improvements of centuries, spacious apartments, clean paint and paper, Rumford fireplace, back plastering, Venetian blinds, copper pump, spring lock, a commodious cellar, and many other things. But how happens it that he who is said to enjoy these things is so commonly a *poor* civilized man, while the savage, who has them not, is rich as a savage? If it is asserted that civilization is a real advance in the condition of man,—and I think that it is, though only the wise improve their advantages,—it must be shown that it has produced better dwellings without making them more costly; and the cost of a thing is the amount of what I will call life which is required to be exchanged for it, immediately or in the long run. An average house in this neighborhood costs perhaps eight hundred dollars, and to lay up this sum will take from ten to fifteen years of the laborer's life, even if he is not encumbered with a family,—estimating the pecuniary value of every man's labor at one dollar a day, for if some receive more, others receive less;—so that he must have spent more than half his life commonly before *his* wigwam will be earned. If we suppose him to pay a rent instead, this is but a doubtful choice of evils. Would the savage have been wise to exchange his wigwam for a palace on these terms?

24

Topics for Critical Thinking and Writing

1. What, according to Thoreau (paragraphs 11–20), are the legitimate functions of clothing? What other functions does he reject, or fail to consider?

2. In paragraph 20, beginning "I cannot believe," Thoreau criticizes the factory system. Is the criticism mild or severe? Explain. Point out some of the earlier

passages in which he touches on the relation of clothes to a faulty economic system.

3. List or briefly set forth Thoreau's assumptions (paragraphs 21–24) about architecture.

4. In paragraph 24 Thoreau says: "The cost of a thing is the amount of what I will call life which is required to be exchanged for it, immediately or in the long run." The definition of cost is interesting, but no less so than the definition implicit in "what I will call life." Of what other definitions of cost are you aware? Do they also involve an implicit definition of what Thoreau calls life?

5. Many of Thoreau's sentences mean both what they say literally and something more; often, like proverbs, they express abstract or general truths in concrete, homely language. How might these sentences (from paragraph 14–18) be interpreted?

    a. We know but few men, a great many coats and breeches.
    b. Dress a scarecrow in your last shift, you standing shiftless by, who would not soonest salute the scarecrow?
    c. If you have any enterprise before you, try it in your old clothes.
    d. Every generation laughs at the old fashions, but follows religiously the new.
    e. When the soldier is hit by a cannon ball rags are as becoming as purple.

Phillip Lopate

Phillip Lopate, born in Jamaica, New York, in 1943, is the author of two novels and of three collections of personal essays. Lopate teaches humanities at Hofstra University.

Portrait of My Body

I am a man who tilts. When I am sitting, my head slants to the right; when walking, the upper part of my body reaches forward to catch a sneak preview of the street. One way or another, I seem to be off-center— or "uncentered," to use the jargon of holism. My lousy posture, a tendency to slump or put myself into lazy, contorted misalignments, undoubtedly contributes to lower back pain. For a while I correct my bad habits, do morning exercises, sit straight, breathe deeply, but always an inner demon that insists on approaching the world askew resists perpendicularity.

I think if I had broader shoulders I would be more squarely anchored. But my shoulders are narrow, barely wider than my hips. This has always made shopping for suits an embarrassing business. (Françoise Gilot's *Life with Picasso* tells how Picasso was so touchy about his disproportionate body—in his case all shoulders, no legs—that he insisted the tailor fit him at home.) When I was growing up in Brooklyn, my hero was Sandy Koufax, the Dodgers' Jewish pitcher. In the doldrums of Hebrew choir practice at Feigenbaum's Mansion & Catering Hall, I would fantasize striking out the side, even whiffing twenty-seven batters in a row. Lack of shoulder development put an end to this identification; I became a writer instead of a Koufax.

It occurs to me that the restless angling of my head is an attempt to distract viewers' attention from its paltry base. I want people to look at my head, partly because I live in my head most of the time. My sister, a trained masseuse, often warns me of the penalties, like neck tension, that may arise from failing to integrate body and mind. Once, about ten years ago, she and I were at the beach and she was scrutinizing my body with a sister's critical eye. "You're getting flabby," she said. "You should exercise every day. I do—look at me, not an ounce of fat." She pulled at her midriff, celebrating (as is her wont) her physical attributes with the third-person enthusiasm of a carnival barker.

"But"—she threw me a bone—"you do have a powerful head. There's an intensity . . . " A graduate student of mine (who was slightly loony) told someone that she regularly saw an aura around my head in class. One reason I like to teach is that it focuses fifteen or so dependent gazes on me with such paranoiac intensity as cannot help but generate an aura in my behalf.

I also have a commanding stare, large sad brown eyes that can be   5
read as either gentle or severe. Once I watched several hours of myself on videotape. I discovered to my horror that my face moved at different rates: sometimes my mouth would be laughing, eyebrows circumflexed in mirth, while my eyes coolly gauged the interviewer to see what effect I was making. I am something of an actor. And, as with many performers, the mood I sense most in myself is that of energy-conserving watchfulness; but this expression is often mistaken (perhaps because of the way brown eyes are read in our culture) for sympathy. I see myself as determined to the point of stubbornness, selfish, even a bit cruel—in any case, I am all too aware of the limits of my compassion, so that it puzzles me when people report a first impression of me as gentle, kind, solicitous. In my youth I felt obliged to come across as dynamic, arrogant, intimidating, the life of the party; now, surer of myself, I hold back some energy, thereby winning time to gather information and make better judgments. This results sometimes in a misimpression of my being mildly depressed. Of course, the simple truth is that I have less energy than I once did, and that accumulated experiences have made me, almost against my will, kinder and sadder.

Sometimes I can feel my mouth arching downward in an ironic smile, which, at its best, reassures others that we need not take everything so seriously—because we are all in the same comedy together—and, at its worst, expresses a superior skepticism. This smile, which can be charming when not supercilious, has elements of the bashful that mesh with the worldly—the shyness, let us say, of a cultivated man who is often embarrassed for others by their willful shallowness or self-deception. Many times, however, my ironic smile is nothing more than a neutral stall among people who do not seem to appreciate my "contribution." I hate that pain-in-the-ass half-smile of mine; I want to jump in, participate, be loud, thoughtless, vulgar.

Often I give off a sort of psychic stench to myself, I do not like myself at all, but out of stubborn pride I act like a man who does. I appear for all the world poised, contented, sanguine when inside I may be feeling self-revulsion bordering on the suicidal. What a wonder to be so misread! Of course, if in the beginning I had thought I was coming across accurately, I never would have bothered to become a writer. And the truth is I am not misread, because another part of me is never less than fully contented with myself.

 Topics for Critical Thinking and Writing

1. In describing his body, what does Lopate reveal about his mind and personality?

2. Imitating Lopate, write a three-paragraph portait of your body, beginning with your posture. We find his first sentence, "I am a man who tilts," engaging. See if you can rival it.

Natalie Angier

Natalie Angier, born in New York in 1958, attended the University of Michigan for two years, then transferred to Barnard College, from which she graduated in 1978. In college she studied English, physics, and astronomy, and formed the ambition of writing for nonspecialists about literary and scientific matters. At the age of 22 she was hired by Time Inc. as a member of the staff of a new magazine, Discover, *where she wrote about biology for four years. She has also worked as a science writer for* Time *magazine, and has taught at New York University's Graduate Program in Science and Environmental Reporting. In 1990 she began writing on science-related subjects for* The New York Times, *and the next year she won a Pulitzer prize for her reporting. Angier's most recent book is* Women, an Intimate Geography *(1999).*

The Sandbox: Bully for You: Why Push Comes to Shove

Some people are just fair game for being picked on and put down: lawyers, politicians, journalists, mothers-in-law and, now, bullies. These days, everybody is ganging up on bullies, blaming them for all that ails us.

Bullies and their taunting, arrogant ways are said to have been the driving force behind the student shootings at Columbine and Santana

High Schools. Young bullies supposedly grow into sociopaths, angry drunks, wife abusers or maybe mayors of major East Coast cities.

The victims of bullying are portrayed as emotionally disfigured for life, unable to shake the feeling that they are unlovable wimps, or that everybody is out to get them.

The news bristles with reports that bullies abound. Recently, in one of the largest studies ever of child development, researchers at the National Institutes of Health reported that about a quarter of all middle-school children were either perpetrators or victims (or in some cases, both) of serious and chronic bullying, behavior that included threats, ridicule, name calling, punching, slapping, jeering and sneering.

Another highly contentious study suggested that too much time in day care may predispose a child to bullying: youngsters who spent more than 30 hours a week away from mommy had a 17 percent chance of ending up as garden-variety bullies and troublemakers, compared to only 6 percent of children who spent less than 10 hours a week in day care.

Everywhere, legislators are struggling to beat each other to the punch in demanding that schools stamp out bad behavior. In Colorado, for example, home to Columbine High School, Gov. Bill Owens has just signed legislation requiring all state school districts to develop anti-bullying programs to prevent bullying.

In a similar spirit, the familiar phys-ed game of dodgeball—also known as killerball, prison ball or bombardment—is taking a hit lately, as school authorities nationwide have moved to ban the game on the theory that it fosters hyperaggression and gives the class klutzes an inferiority complex.

Yet even as quick-fix programs with names like "Taking the Bully by the Horns" proliferate across the academic and electronic universe, experts in aggressive behavior warn that there is no easy way to stamp out bullying among children. Short of raising kids in isolation chambers, they say, bullying behaviors can never be eliminated entirely from the sustained hazing ritual otherwise known as growing up.

"Can we get rid of bullying altogether? I don't think so," said Richard J. Hazler, a professor of counselor education at Ohio University in Athens. "We can't eliminate all growing pains, either. It's tough learning to make your way in this world."

Philip C. Rodkin, an assistant professor of educational psychology at the University of Illinois at Urbana-Champaign, pointed out that, despite all the attention being paid to the subject, the root causes of bullying remain a mystery. "This is not a trivial problem," he said. "Bullies have always been with us, and we're only beginning to ask why."

Some researchers say that, despite the hype and handwringing, there is no epidemic of bullying in schools, and in fact the incidence of serious bullying has very likely declined over the years.

"It certainly was a problem when I was in boarding school, but that was ages ago," said Richard Dawkins, a professor at Oxford University who has studied the evolution of aggressive and selfish behavior. "I

believe there is far less bullying now, though there probably will always be a bit."

As an example of how bad it used to be, Professor Dawkins cited a passage from the British poet John Betjeman's 1960 autobiographical poem, "Summoned by Bells."

> *Twelve to one:*
> *What chance had Angus? They surrounded him,*
> *Pulled off his coat and trousers, socks and shoes*

And, wretched in his shirt, they hoisted him
Into the huge waste paper basket; then
Poured ink and treacle on his head. With ropes
They strung the basket up among the beams
And as he soared I only saw his eyes
Look through the slats at us who watched below.

As Frans de Waal, a primatologist at Emory University, sees it, one of the problems in the standard approach to bully analysis is that researchers tend to ignore the subtle dynamics between a bully and the object of a bully's scorn—the scapegoat. "Some individuals may have bully characteristics, and others may have scapegoat characteristics," he said. "The two things need to be studied together, but because personality research is generally done from an individual perspective, they rarely are."

Dr. de Waal has observed that bullying behavior is quite common   15
among most species of monkeys and apes, and that many animals at or near the top of the hierarchy will harass, charge, snap and howl at their subordinates for no other reason than because they can. But at least as striking as the presence of simian bullies, Dr. de Waal said, are the resident scapegoats, the low-ranking individuals who seem to be chosen for the role by other members of the group. Whenever a group is under strain, or when its hierarchy is in doubt, the higher-ranking primates start taking it out on the scapegoat, with the result that any time the beleaguered monkey ventures from its corner, it gets beaten up.

"This is not just a way to release frustration," said Dr. de Waal. "The scapegoat also gives the high-ranking individuals in the group a common enemy, a unifier. By uniting against the scapegoat in moments of tension, it creates a bond."

And while primate research can never be applied directly to human affairs, even when those humans are swinging from monkey bars, bully experts admit that children in groups will often encourage, or at least not discourage, a bully's nasty acts against an underling. In one study of how peers contribute to bullying, researchers from York University studied videotapes of 53 episodes of bullying among elementary school students on the school playground. The researchers found that 54 percent of the time, onlookers stood by passively as the bully picked on the victim, an inactive form of activity that the researchers said ended up reinforcing the bully's behavior. And 21 percent of the time, some of the onlookers joined in on the taunting. Only in 25 percent of the cases did a child attempt to step in and help the victim or call a teacher to help.

But as researchers lately have discovered, many bullies in fact are quite popular. "Some kids may be goaders, cheering the bully on because they want to be accepted," said Laura Hess Olson, an assistant professor of child development at Purdue University in West Lafayette, Ind. "Or they may just stand by and do nothing because they're afraid they might be targeted next." Whatever the case, she added, "We have to realize that everybody is a player in creating the atmosphere in which bullying occurs."

Another point worth noting, said Dr. Olson, is that the old stereotype of the bully as an antisocial and unpopular misfit is false. In one study of third- to fifth-graders in two East Coast schools, she and her colleagues found that, while the students described by their peers and teachers as friendly, outgoing and self-confident were the most popular, the boys known to be bullies were the second-most popular group, way beyond the perceived wimps, eggheads and teacher's pets.

"There are a fair amount of kids in a classroom who think that bullies are cool," said Dr. Rodkin, "especially when they're attractive and athletic."   20

Adding to the challenge of curbing bullies is the fact that, as researchers have learned, many students blame victims of bullying for bringing their troubles on themselves by sulking or whimpering or walking around with their head hanging low. A sizable number of students agree with the premise that bullying can help "toughen" people and teach which behaviors are laudable and which are risible to the group.

In this scenario, then, bullies are neither born nor made, but instead have bulliness thrust upon them. The group needs its whipcracking rulemeister, just as an army boot camp needs its snarling, abusive sergeant if the soft-bellied newcomers are ever to get into fighting trim.

Indeed, it's hard to see how bullying behavior in schools can be eliminated when bullying behavior among adults is not only common but often applauded—at least if it results in wild success. J. P. Morgan, for example, was thought by many of his colleagues and subordinates to be, in the words of Robert M. LaFollette, the Wisconsin progressive, "a beefy, red-faced thick-necked financial bully, drunk with wealth and power." Yet he was also lionized in his day, described by officials at Harvard University as a "prince among merchants," a man of "skill, wisdom and courage." Hey, he was the richest guy in the world, wasn't he?

It's perhaps a bit of delicious paradox that, at a time when the nation is seized with concern over school bullying, the international community views with alarm the recent moves by the United States to scuttle the Kyoto global warming treaty and to promote the construction of a space-based nuclear missile shield. To the rest of the world, it seems, America is the biggest bully of them all.

 Topic for Critical Thinking and Writing

1. How would you describe the tone of Angier's first sentence? Do you find it attractive?

2. When you were in school, were you the victim of bullying, or a bully, or both? Did you observe bullying going on around you? If so, what were your responses to bullying? (Your answer to any of these questions might pro-

vide an excellent topic for an essay of 500 words. Remember to ask yourself: Who? What? When? Where? and—most important—Why?)

3. Do you agree or disagree with the premise offered in paragraph 21 "that bullying can help 'toughen' people and teach which behaviors are laudable and which are risible to the group"? On what do you base your answer? Personal or observed experience? reasoning? reading? or what? Set forth your answer in an essay of 500 words.

4. In one paragraph evaluate Angier's last paragraph as a conclusion to her article. Support your evaluation with evidence.

Bart J. Bok

Bart J. Bok (1906–1983) was born in the Netherlands but spent most of his adult life in the United States, teaching astronomy at Harvard and at the University of Arizona. One of his books, The Milky Way, *which he wrote with his wife Priscilla, has remained a standard work in the field for some forty years. Bok's essay on astrology was first published in a magazine called* The Humanist. *We follow the essay with the replies that the magazine printed in a later issue.*

A Critical Look at Astrology

During the past ten years, we have witnessed an alarming increase in the spread of astrology. This pseudoscience seems to hold fascination especially for people of college age who are looking for firm guideposts in the confused world of the present. It is not surprising that people believe in astrology when most of our daily newspapers regularly carry columns about it and when some of our universities and junior colleges actually offer astrology courses. The public, young and old, has the right to expect from its scientists, especially from astronomers, clear and clarifying statements showing that astrology lacks a firm scientific foundation.

I have spoken out publicly against astrology every ten years or so, beginning in 1941 in "Scientists Look at Astrology," written with Margaret W. Mayall for the now-defunct *Scientific Monthly* (Volume 52). I have softened a bit since my early crusading days, for I have come to realize that astrology cannot be stopped by simple scientific argument only. To some it seems almost a religion. All I can do is state clearly and unequivocally that modern concepts of astronomy and space physics give no support—better said, negative support—to the tenets of astrology.

Bart J. Bok, "A Critical Look at Astrology" as appeared in *The Humanist*, Sept–Oct 1975 is from Bart J. Bok and Lawrence E. Jerome, *Objections to Astrology*, pp. 21–33, (Amherst, NY: Prometheus Books), copyright 1975. Reprinted by permission of Prometheus Books.

Not more than a dozen or so of my fellow astronomers have spoken out publicly on astrology. Twice I suggested to my friends on the Council of the American Astronomical Society that the council issue a statement pointing out that there is no scientific foundation for astrological beliefs. Both times I was turned down, the principal argument being that it is below the dignity of a professional society to recognize that astrological beliefs are prevalent today. To me it seems socially and morally inexcusable for the society not to have taken a firm stand. Astronomers as a group have obviously not provided the guidance that the public sorely needs. Those who live in a free society are entitled to believe in whatever causes they care to espouse. However, I have had more than half a century of day-to-day and night-to-night contacts with the starry heavens, and it is my duty to speak up and to state clearly that I see no evidence that the stars and planets influence or control our personal lives and that I have found much evidence to the contrary.

The Origins of Astrology

Astrology had its origins in the centuries before the birth of Christ. Present-day astrological concepts and techniques largely go back to the period 100 to 200 A.D. It was only natural that early civilizations would consider the stars and planets in the heavens as awesome evidence of supernatural powers that could magically affect their lives. Variety was brought into the picture by the constantly changing aspects of the heavens. No one can blame the Egyptians, the Greeks, the Arabs, or the people of India for having established systems of astrology at times when they were also laying the foundations for astronomy. Right up to the days of Copernicus, Galileo, and Kepler (who was an expert astrologer)—even to the time of Isaac Newton—there were good reasons for exploring astrology.

However, all this changed when the first measurements were made of   5
the distances to the sun, planets, and stars and when the masses of these objects were determined. The foundations of astrology began to crumble when we came to realize how vanishingly small are the forces exerted by the celestial objects on things and people on earth—and how very small are the amounts of radiation associated with them received on earth. The only perceptible and observable effects evident to all of us are produced by the tidal forces caused by the gravity of the moon and sun. To assume that the sun, moon, and planets would exert special critical forces upon a baby at birth—forces that would control the future life of the infant— seems to run counter to common sense. Radiative effects are also dubious. It is even less likely that the stars—each one a sun in its own right and several hundred thousand or more times farther from the earth than our sun—would exercise critical effects on a baby at birth. Some seasonal effects there might well be, for a baby born in northern latitudes in April faces initially a warm summer period; one born in October, a cool winter season.

Before the days of modern astronomy, it made sense to look into possible justifications for astrological beliefs, but it is silly to do so now that we have a fair picture of man's place in the universe.

Horoscopes: Their Preparation and Interpretation

Astrology claims to foretell the future by studying the positions of the sun, moon, and planets in relation to the constellations of stars along the celestial zodiac at the time of the birth of the subject. This is done through the medium of the *horoscope*. Anyone with a knowledge of beginning astronomy and with an American Nautical Almanac on his desk can proceed to draw one. I have found it a not unpleasant pastime on several occasions. Some of our readers may be interested in learning a little about the technical procedures involved in the preparation of a horoscope. Figures 1 and 2, which are reproduced from the previously mentioned *Scientific Monthly* article, may help to illustrate the procedures.

For a given place on earth—the birthplace of the subject—the celestial sphere is drawn in the standard manner favored by teachers of college beginning-astronomy courses. We see in Figure 1 that the local celestial meridian (a great circle passing through the celestial poles, the zenith, and the north and south points on the horizon) and the local celestial horizon (the great circle 90 degrees away from the zenith overhead)

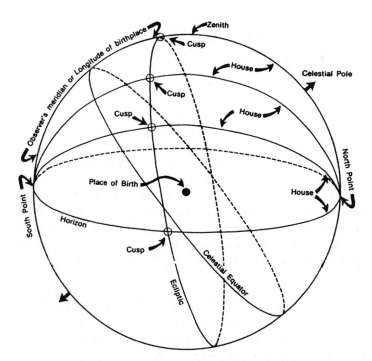

Figure 1. *The Celestial Sphere Divided into Twelve Parts.*

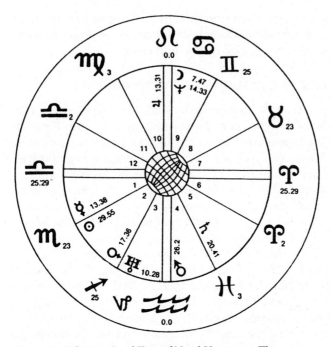

Figure 2. *A Conventional Type of Natal Horoscope. The horoscope is drawn for November 23, 1907, 4 a.m. Eastern-Standard Time, latitude 40°43'N, longitude 73"58'W. The spokes of the wheel mark the limits of the houses; the zodiacal signs and the degrees mark the cusps. The position of the sun, moon, and planets are shown by their symbols.*

divide the sphere into four equal parts. The celestial sphere is further divided by cutting each of the four sections into three equal slices by great circles passing through the north and south points on the local horizon. The ecliptic, which traces the sun's annual path across the sky, is just as it would have been observed at the time and place of birth. The celestial equator at the time and place of birth is also shown, but it plays a small role in horoscope preparation, except to help in plotting the position of the sun, moon, and planets from the Almanac. The intersections between the twelve great circles and the ecliptic circle mark the *cusps* of the twelve *houses*.

We are now ready to draw the horoscope for the subject at the time and place of birth. We see in Figure 2 that the houses and their cusps are drawn on a graph representing the plane of the ecliptic. This is accomplished either with the aid of suitable astrological tables or by the use of some simple spherical trigonometry. The whole business can, if so desired, be prepared nicely as a program for a reasonably fast computer, all of which helps create the impression that astrology is basically scientific in nature. The houses are numbered from 1 to 12 (as shown in Figure 2), with house 1 being the one that is about to rise above the local horizon. Standard tables are then used to mark the positions of the zodiacal constellations in the outer margin of the horoscope wheel. The positions of the sun, moon, and planets are shown by their symbols in the houses where they belong.

To sum up: Figure 2 shows a horoscope in which the twelve houses, with their cusps marked, and the positions of the zodiacal constellations and the sun, moon, and planets are drawn on the plane of the ecliptic, just as they would have been observed at the time and place of birth of the subject.

The type of horoscope shown in figure 2 is a *natal* horoscope. It becomes—according to astrologers—the all-important guide to predicting a person's future. There are other types of horoscopes in use—*judicial* and *honorary* ones, for example—but these need not concern us here.

The abracadabra begins when the astrologer starts to interpret a person's horoscope. The first and most important item is the date of birth, which makes a person an Aries if born between March 21 and April 19, a Taurus if born in the month following, and so on. The date of birth naturally fixes the sign of the zodiac in which the sun is located. It is the important fact that tells whether a person is an Aries, a Pisces, or whatever.

The next important item to note is if the moon or the sun and what planets are in the first house, the one that is about to rise above the horizon at the time and place of birth. The *ascendant* is defined as the sign of the zodiac that is associated with the first house. It is obvious that the time of birth must be precisely known if a proper horoscope is to be prepared.

Third in line are the positions relative to each other of the sun, moon, and planets in the various houses. The so-called *aspects* are noted. These indicate which celestial objects are in conjunction (near to each other in position), and which are 60, 90, 120, or 180 degrees apart in the heavens. These aspects are important for astrological interpretation, as are the positions of the planets in the houses in which they are found.

The astrologer can refine his interpretations to any desired extent— the end product becoming increasingly more expensive as further items are added.

How and by whom were these rules of analysis and interpretation of horoscopes first established? They go back to antiquity, basically to the work of Ptolemy in the second century. Ptolemy wrote two famous books: *Almagest*, the most complete volume on the motions of the planets published during the great days of Greek astronomy, and *Tetrabiblos*, the bible of astrology. The *Almagest* is today treated with respect and admiration by historians of science, and it is clearly one of the great works of the past. However, no astronomer would think of referring to it today when considering problems relating to the motions of the planets. *Tetrabiblos* is still the standard reference guide for the astrologer. Astronomy has been a constantly changing and advancing science, whereas astrology has essentially stood still since the days of Ptolemy, in spite of tremendous advances in our knowledge of the solar system and the universe of stars and galaxies.

A Scientist's View of Astrology

I continue to ask myself why people believe in astrology. I have asked this same question of many who apparently accept its predictions, including some of my young students in beginning-astronomy courses. One answer is simple and straightforward: "It would be nice to know what the future holds; so why not consult astrological predictions?" In addition, some people feel that it is useful to have available certain impersonal rules by which to make personal decisions. Astrology does provide reasonably definite answers and does yield firm guidelines for personal decisions. Many people find this very comforting indeed.

Believers in astrology have a remarkable faculty for remembering the times when predictions come true and ignoring the occasions when the opposite is the case. And when failure of a prediction does stare us in the face, the astrologer who made the prediction can always get out of trouble by citing the famous dictum that the stars *incline* but do not *compel*.

I have learned that many people who take astrology seriously were first attracted to the field by their reading of the regular columns in the newspapers. It is deplorable that so many newspapers now print this daily nonsense. At the start the regular reading is sort of a fun game, but it often ends up as a mighty serious business. The steady and ready availability of astrological predictions can over many years have insidious influences on a person's personal judgment.

For some people astrology has become a religion. I urge them to examine their beliefs with care. At best, astrology can be looked upon as a self-centered approach to religious beliefs, for it deals primarily with daily affairs and with what is best for a particular person. Astrology, when practiced as completely as possible, takes away from each of us our right and duty to make our own personal decisions.

The most complete religious approach is found in people who have "experienced" astrology, who deep inside themselves "know" astrology to be true and who believe profoundly in effects of cosmic rhythms and "vibrations." I do not know how to convince these people that they are on the wrong track, and hence they will have to go their chosen ways.

Many believers in astrology speak glibly of the forces exerted by the sun, moon, and planets. I should mention here that these forces—according to astrology, critically effective only at the precise moment of birth—can hardly be gravitational or radiative in nature. The known forces that the planets exert on a child at the time of birth are unbelievably small. The gravitational forces at birth produced by the doctor and nurse and by

20

the furniture in the delivery room far outweigh the celestial forces. And the stars are so far away from the sun and earth that their gravitational, magnetic, and other effects are negligible. Radiative effects are sometimes suggested as doing the job. First of all, the walls of the delivery room shield us effectively from many known radiations. And, second, we should bear in mind that our sun is a constantly varying source of radiation, radiating at many different wavelength variations that are by themselves far in excess of the radiation received from the moon and all the planets together.

Many believers in astrology have suggested that each planet issues a different variety of special, as-yet-undetected radiations or "vibrations" and that it is the interplay between these mysterious forces, or quantities, that produces strong effects of an astrological nature. If there is one thing that we have learned over the past fifty years, it is that there is apparently conclusive evidence that the sun, moon, planets, and stars are all made of the same stuff, varieties and combinations of atomic particles and molecules, all governed by uniform laws of physics. We have seen samples of the moon that are similar to rocks on earth, and as a result of our space probes we have been able to study the properties of samples from the surface of Mars. It seems inconceivable that Mars and the moon could produce mysterious waves, or vibrations, that could affect our personalities in completely different ways. It does not make sense to suppose that the various planets and the moon, all with rather similar physical properties, could manage to affect human affairs in totally dissimilar fashions.

There are many other questions that we can ask of the astrologers. For example, why should the precise moment of birth be *the* critical instant in a person's life? Is the instant of conception not basically a more drastic event than the precise moment when the umbilical cord is severed? Would one not expect to find in human beings the same cumulative effects that we associate with growth and environment in plants and animals? Astrology demands the existence of totally unimaginable mechanisms of force and action.

I shall not deal here with statistical tests of astrological predictions or with correlations. . . . At one time I thought seriously of becoming personally involved in statistical tests of astrological predictions, but I abandoned this plan as a waste of time unless someone could first show me that there was some sort of physical foundation for astrology.

What specifically can astronomers and scientists in related fields do to make people realize that astrology is totally lacking in a proper scientific foundation? Speaking out firmly whenever the occasion demands is one way to approach the problem. This is the course that I have steadily pursued, and I hope that astronomers, young and old, will follow me on this path. I have frequently recommended that there be one or two lectures on astrology, somewhat along the lines of this essay, in each introductory astronomy course. The students should feel free to bring their questions to the instructor. An interesting experiment has been undertaken in the Natural Science 9 course at Harvard University, in which the

25

instructor, Michael Zeilik, is teaching a section called "Astrology—The Space Age Science?" that involves among other things a laboratory exercise in which natal horoscopes are cast.

The fact that some recent textbooks on astronomy contain sections (or chapters) on astrology is a most encouraging development, as is a chapter on the subject in George Abell's book *Exploring the Universe* (third edition, 1974). I have read a similar chapter in an introductory-astronomy textbook now in preparation. Let us have more of this!

The Psychology of Belief in Astrology

Thirty-five years ago, my good friend and colleague at Harvard University, the late Gordon W. Allport, one of the finest psychologists of his day, drafted at my request a brief statement entitled "Psychologists State Their Views on Astrology." The executive council of the Society for Psychological Study of Social Issues endorsed this statement, which was publicly released, and I wish to close my present essay by reproducing it once again.

> Psychologists find no evidence that astrology is of any value whatsoever as an indicator of past, present, or future trends in one's personal life or in one's destiny. Nor is there the slightest ground for believing that social events can be foretold by divinations of the stars. The Society for the Psychological Study of Social Issues therefore deplores the faith of a considerable section of the American public in a magical practice that has no shred of justification in scientific fact.
>
> The principal reason why people turn to astrology and to kindred superstitions is that they lack in their own lives the resources necessary to solve serious personal problems confronting them. Feeling blocked and bewildered they yield to the pleasant suggestion that a golden key is at hand—a simple solution—an ever-present help in time of trouble. This belief is more readily accepted in times of disruption and crisis when the individual's normal safeguards against gullibility are broken down. When moral habits are weakened by depression or war, bewilderment increases, self-reliance is lessened, and belief in the occult increases.
>
> Faith in astrology or in any other occult practice is harmful insofar as it encourages an unwholesome flight from the persistent problems of real life. Although it is human enough to try to escape from the effort involved in hard thinking and to evade taking responsibility for one's own acts, it does no good to turn to magic and mystery in order to escape misery. Other solutions must be found by people who suffer from the frustrations of poverty, from grief at the death of a loved one, or from fear of economic or personal insecurity.
>
> By offering the public the horoscope as a substitute for honest and sustained thinking, astrologers have been guilty of playing upon the human tendency to take easy rather than difficult paths. Astrologers have done this in spite of the fact that science has denied their claims and in spite of laws in some states forbidding the prophecies of astrology as fraudulent. It is

30

against public interests for astrologers to spread their counsels of flight from reality.

It is unfortunate that in the minds of many people astrology is confused with true science. The result of this confusion is to prevent these people from developing truly scientific habits of thought that would help them understand the natural, social, and psychological factors that are actually influencing their destinies. It is, of course, true that science itself is a long way from a final solution to the social and psychological problems that perplex mankind; but its accomplishments to date clearly indicate that men's destinies are shaped by their own actions in this world. The heavenly bodies may safely be left out of account. Our fates rest not in our stars but in ourselves.

R. G. Dobbins, Kathleen Russo and Carolyn Bermingham, Joseph F. Goodavage, Barbara Koval, Mandrake

The Humanist—*the journal in which Bok's article first appeared*—published the following replies in a later issue.

The Astrologers Reply

Regarding your magazine's recent and highly publicized scurrilous attack on astrology:

Science itself is a highly systematized, rigid series of *learned expectations* that tends to exclude that which it cannot explain. The more highly educated and degreed the scientist, the less likely he is to investigate nonconforming phenomena. . . .

Science is the New Superstition. Astrology has been known for at least 4000 years. Science is about 170 years old. Which is the upstart?. . .

This high-handed, unprovoked attack on an ancient study that interested men of the stature of Newton, Kepler, and Galileo sends cold shivers through the spine of anyone who believes that academic pursuits should be a free and open affair, untainted by acrimony or social pressures to desist from the process of study and learning. The chilling effect of the atmosphere of suspicion and mistrust that will be created as a result of this proclamation on the acquisition of knowledge and the determination of the validity of astrology's propositions is a move back to the time of inquisitions, the burning of books, and the hiding of outlawed knowledge from humanity. It is a step back to the Dark Ages.

R. G. Dobbins
Tempe, Ariz.

... The serious student of astrology does not condone the use of horoscope columns or magazines, since the basis of these prognostications are for sun signs only. The measurable placement of the sun at the time of birth in no way determines the individual choice of career or style of life. Nor is there any relationship between that sign and day-to-day occurrences. Likewise, no astrologer who approaches his study in a rational manner lends any credence to the transit of a particular planet through a certain segment of the zodiac as the causal factor in individual behavior.

The development of astrology is based on the corresponding relationship of cosmic forces to human behavior. The time of birth is an arbitrary standard that the astrologer will work with in order to establish a pattern of behavior related to an astronomical framework. Some astrologers do feel that the time of conception would be a more accurate moment with which to work; however, no method has yet been devised to determine that measurement with reliability. The only choice available, then, is the moment of birth, if recorded precisely. ... In this respect, the position of the planets, sun, moon, the individual place of birth, and their relationship of angularity to one another can give a fairly accurate description of individual potential and behavior traits. The future of the individual, however, is not within the chart. ...

Much of what has been proposed by astrologers in the past and today is without foundation and should be considered "nonsense," but not until further investigation is made by those confronted with the "irrational" and the tendency to "obscurantism," so that intelligent and informed rebuttal can be made. ...

Since we, too, take offense with the irrational, we would rather promote astrology and its study as an instrument of developing a more substantial understanding of each individual and thusly creating a higher awareness of his own potentials. The reflection of fraudulence and incompetence on the contributions of sound astrological practice will only stand in the way of greater human development and thought.

Kathleen Russo, President
Carolyn Bermingham, Vice President
Federation of Scientific Astrologers

The point you've completely overlooked in presenting "Objections to Astrology" [Sept./Oct. 1975] is the possibility of an equally valid viewpoint—one not based on opinion and/or authority (as is most of astrology), but on previously unsuspected real universe data. ...

While writing a science piece on assignment for *True* magazine in 1963, I became interested in the effect of weather on health and joined the American Institute of Medical Climatology. At that time the entire city of Philadelphia was engaged in a three-year study of the moon's influence and effect on rainfall. Under the aegis of the AIMC I began studying the lives of people born at the same time and place to determine whether there was an unaccountable tendency for the same sort of major events to happen to them at the same time or not. If not, then astrology could be discredited once and for all, because it based its credence entirely on the horoscope.

My initial search yielded positive results of "parallelism," which were reported in magazine articles and in my book *Astrology: The Space-Age Science.* Since then, the results have been more refined and specific.

In all fairness—after publishing "Objections to Astrology"—can you refuse to give equal attention to an alternate view that is backed by hard data? I note that neither Bok nor Jerome presented any new evidence or proof to back their assault, but instead relied on opinion and authority— the same mistake they're indirectly accusing the astrologers of committing.

My aim is not to defend astrology, but to present the truth as I have found it. . . . If my cases of parallelism are purely anomalistic and a further study of other genetically unrelated "time twins" yields the exact opposite data, I will be just as satisfied to have it judged once and for all on the facts instead of bias or the emotional opinions of experts who know little or nothing about a subject they're condemning. I hold the same opinion about those who practice and defend astrology without ever checking the basic premise to question its validity.

I agree that astrology has never been conclusively proven on a purely scientific basis, and neither has it been disproven. I'm perfectly willing to present the results of my search in Bart J. Bok's own territory: fifty "time twins" all born at a time of the five-planet conjunction and total solar eclipse (in the zodiacal sign of Aquarius) on February 4 and 5, 1962, in Tucson, Arizona.

I suggest that the locations and identities of the families of those children be given to one or two distinguished or objective observers to be investigated on their own terms. . . .

Now that *The Humanist* has acted as the catalyst of what must by now be a tidal wave of reaction, pro and con, I'm sure that you—as a responsible journal—will want to examine *all* the facts, not just one set of opinions. You can be certain that before long you will receive the signatures of several thousand astrologers to back a set of arguments citing the opinion and authority of experts in *their* field.

Sooner or later, however, the facts will out. I was not prepared to present my data for another eighteen months, but your action prompts me to make this premature announcement.

Joseph F. Goodavage
Whitefield, Maine

Some scientists and other equally misinformed opponents of astrology assign definitions to astrology and practices to astrologers that have no foundation in fact.

A handful of scientists have proclaimed that there is no scientific basis for astrology and offer as proof their opinion that vast distances from here to a star or planet precludes its exerting "gravitational or other effects." Might not astronomy also be criticized on the same basis? Does any astronomer have first-hand knowledge of a star? Has it been proven that telescopes do not distort their data during transmission? What are the "other effects" to which they so mysteriously allude? Physicists prove the existence of infinitesimal particles by their effects. Is this the special privilege of physicists or are other correlations equally valid?

The scientific basis for astrology has been neither proved nor disproved. It has never been thoroughly and scientifically investigated.

Astrology far antedates modern science. Its tenets and beliefs are based on an ancient tradition of symbolic knowledge and empirical verification. Are not the ideas and experiences of men who espoused astrology, from ancient Egypt to the Renaissance, worthy of our consideration?

Astrology is predicated on planetary and stellar correlations, not on   5
their influence. Astrologers believe in an ordered universe, which is cyclical, converging, and synchronized. The pattern of any instant of time is reflected in the angular relationships of heavenly bodies. That pattern permeates the universe, but is simultaneous, not causative. Thus, no legitimate astrologer would advise a client that celestial influences were the cause of his distress. One's reflection in a mirror causes neither a smile nor a frown.

The question of fate vs. free will is not germane in the context of symbolic knowledge. A symbol, though well-defined, has within it a multitude of possibilities. The many facets of a diamond sparkle in countless ways, but a diamond is still a diamond. A human being cannot be other than a human being. Yet, within the framework of his humanness are superb possibilities. Man's free will is augmented by the awareness, nurtured by astrologers, of conditions and potentialities that are internally and externally structured. The individual is not given prescriptions of conduct that are to be followed by all men, nor is he judged by the probabilities of most. He is judged on his own individual potentials, given his own individual solutions and his own individual alternatives. The increasing interest in astrology is the result not of man's weakness but of his reaffirmation of the individual, his power and his uniqueness.

Astrologers do not and cannot predict the future. Man's free will alone determines which solutions and which alternatives he will choose.

Barbara Koval
Reston, Va.

"... Roger Elliot, astrological author and astrologer-in-residence at *TV Times* magazine [said] 'Of course one accepts that there are a great many charlatans about. But surely scientists aren't saying that because something is hard to measure one rejects it? What about Buddhism and Christianity? What about love?'

"'After all I'm not claiming that planets actually *influence* events. I see the process as analogous to the train Departures Board at Victoria Station. It tells you what the trains are going to do, but it doesn't actually control them. Now why, precisely, the planets should fulfill this role is, indeed, a subject for speculation.'

"'Anyway, in the last analysis, even if it emerged that astrology weren't *factually* true, I think it is still valuable if it has a personal truth for the individual. I mean, the truth of, say, David Hockney or Michelangelo will always be essentially personal, won't it?' . . . "—"Mandrake," *London Sunday Telegraph*, Sept. 7, 1975.

Topics for Critical Thinking and Writing

1. Evaluate Bok's first three paragraphs as an opening. If you think they are effective, specify the strengths. If you think they are weak, specify the weaknesses.

2. In paragraph 5 Bok writes:

   > To assume that the sun, moon, and planets would exert special critical forces upon a baby at birth—forces that would control the future life of the infant—seems to run counter to common sense. Radiative effects are also dubious. It is even less likely that the stars—each one a sun in its own right and several hundred thousand or more times farther from the earth than our sun—would exercise critical effects on a baby at birth.

   Do you think Bok here offers convincing objections against astrology?

3. Why, according to Bok, do believers in astrology persist in their belief even when predictions fail to come true? Can you think of other reasons for belief in astrological predictions?

4. In paragraph 20 Bok says that "for some people astrology has become a religion," and in paragraph 21 he says that "the most complete religious approach is found in people who have 'experienced' astrology, who deep inside themselves 'know' astrology to be true and who believe profoundly in effects of cosmic rhythms and 'vibrations.'" Is Bok in effect saying that if a person believes that the planets and stars exert an influence on behavior, he or she takes astrology for a religion? Would it be equally fair, then, to say that if a person believes that genes exert an influence on behavior such a person takes biology for a religion?

5. In paragraphs 22 and 23 Bok offers reasons for rejecting belief in astrology. How compelling do you find the reasons?

6. We reprint some of the letters astrologers wrote in reply to Bok's essay. In your opinion, do any of the responses offer reasonable arguments against Bok's attack on astrology? If so, which ones?

Alfred Meyer

Alfred Meyer was born in 1935. An editor and writer, he has written for the general public on a wide range of subjects.

Do Lie Detectors Lie? All Too Often

About the size of an attaché case and equally portable, the instrument looks fairly innocuous. Dials and knobs cluster neatly at one end, while four inked styluses rest on a roll of paper on the other. Once the tubes, cuffs, and electrodes that are its sensors emerge, however, the instrument appears more sinister, doubly so when a human subject is connected to its serpentine appurtenances. But the hardware inflicts no injury, merely records changes in some rather simple physiological responses: blood pressure, breathing, sweating. On the contrary, it is the software programmed into the instrument's keeper, a sort of wizard of truth, that is menacing. He will be well-dressed, efficient, and maddeningly neutral. In calm tones he will tell you how the instrument works and assure you that it is highly accurate. He will discuss the questions he intends to ask, switch on the instrument, and begin the questioning. Within an hour or two, he will leave, in most cases convinced that, by combining his own observations of your behavior with the readings of his instrument, he knows if you have told the truth.

Limited almost exclusively to law enforcement work and to matters of national security during its formative years in the 1940s and 1950s, the lie detector, or polygraph, today has become a common fixture in American society, almost to an Orwellian degree. In addition to its uses in prisons, the military, police work, FBI and CIA investigations, and pretrial examinations both for the prosecution and the defense, the polygraph has also found its way into corporate America, where it is widely used for detecting white collar crime and for screening potential employees. This year, it is estimated, half a million to a million Americans, for one reason or another, will take a lie detector test. Such extravagant use takes place despite the facts that no state freely admits polygraph evidence in criminal cases (though about 25 do when both prosecution and defense agree in advance of the testing), that innocent persons often fail the polygraph test while guilty ones pass it, and that the scientific foundation of polygraph technology is, if not altogether questionable, as some critics claim, at least open to serious challenge.

Ironically, considering the procedure's inherent piety, the administration of the lie detector test involves a necessary touch of deception.

Alfred Meyer, "Do Lie Detectors Lie? All Too Often," from the June 1982 issue of *Science 82*. Every attempt has been made to locate the author; should contact information be available, please notify Longman Publishers.

Polygraph theory holds that physiological reactions—changes in blood pressure, rate of breathing, sweating of the palms—elicited by a set of questions will reliably betray falsehood. But it is the form and mix of questions that polygraphers claim are the key to their technique. The standard format, known as the Control Question Test, involves interspersing "relevant" questions with "control" questions. Relevant questions relate directly to the critical matter, such as, "Did you participate in the robbery of the First National Bank on September 11, 1981?" Control questions, on the other hand, are less precise, such as, "In the last 20 years, have you ever taken something that didn't belong to you?"

In the pretest interview, the polygrapher reviews all the questions and frames the control questions to produce "no" answers. It is in this crucial pretest phase that the polygrapher's deception comes into play, for he wants the innocent subject to dissemble while answering the control questions during the actual test. For example, pursuing the hypothetical control question above, most people are likely to have taken something that didn't belong to them at some stage in their lives. Yet fear of embarrassment may lead the subjects to deny misdeeds and therefore to answer the control question dishonestly.

The assumption underlying the Control Question Test is that the   5
truthful subject will display a stronger physiological reaction to the control questions, whereas a deceptive subject will react more strongly to the relevant questions.

That is the heart of it. Modern lie detection relies on nothing more than subtle psychological techniques, crude physiological indicators, and skilled questioning and interpretation of the results. It resembles nothing so much as a game of cat and mouse—often played for very high stakes.

But does it work? The answer is, yes, sometimes. As for how well— that depends on who you ask.

In a recent publication, for example, the American Polygraph Association cites studies that yield accuracy rates ranging from 87.2 to 96.2 percent. But such studies, conducted in the lab by criminologists and a handful of psychologists, most of whom make their living as polygraphers, have come under heavy attack. The chief adversary is psychologist David Lykken of the University of Minnesota, who cites other studies, conducted in the field, which yield far lower rates of 64 to 71 percent.

Lykken bases his criticism of lab data on several points. First, he maintains that there is no "specific lie response." The polygraph merely records general emotional arousal. It cannot distinguish anxiety or indignation from guilt. Second—and this is his most telling point—accuracy rates based on lab studies are flawed because they depend on mock crimes using subjects who do not face the real life consequences of being found truthful or deceptive.

Even a stalwart of polygraphy like psychophysiologist David Raskin   10
of the University of Utah acknowledges the difficulty of assessing accuracy rates in real life situations, those where people face criminal charges.

Moreover, he writes, "In a large percentage of criminal investigations, guilt or innocence is never determined conclusively."

Even in field trials, for example, where a panel of polygraph experts independently score the tests of people who have previously been tried and found guilty or not guilty, one can't be sure the outcome is accurate. Such ambiguity makes it virtually impossible to correlate polygraph results with the truth in samples large enough to achieve genuine statistical validity.

When it comes to verifying the truthfulness of innocent subjects, both Raskin and Lykken agree that the lie detector turns up more innocent people found guilty—false positives—than guilty people found innocent. While Raskin believes the chances of a polygraph identifying an innocent person as lying are less than 10 percent, Lykken believes that the chance is closer to 50 percent. He contends that it is impossible to design control questions that will produce the same level of responsiveness in innocent subjects as is produced by the relevant questions in guilty subjects. The discrepancy results from lack of agreement on whether to use lab or field studies as the standard.

Lykken has still other criticisms of the polygraph. He contends, for example, that with some preparation it is possible to defeat the test. To illustrate, he frequently relates the experience of Floyd Fay, convicted of a murder charge—wrongfully, it was later proved—partly on the basis of a failed lie detector test. While imprisoned, Fay took an interest in polygraph technology and, after studying it, claimed to have trained fellow inmates to foil tests administered by prison officials. The inmates reportedly used such countermeasures as placing a tack in a shoe and stamping on it during the control questioning.

Raskin dismisses Fay's training efforts since they were hardly run under controlled conditions. He cites the recent work of psychologist Michael Dawson in California. With the help of the late method actor Lee Strasberg, Dawson invited a large group of students from Strasberg's Actors' Studio in Hollywood to try, with all an actor's cunning control of emotions, a la Stanislavsky, to "beat the test." None did. Yet again, it was an experiment involving a mock rather than a real crime.

Clearly no one has established beyond a doubt the validity and reliability of the lie detector, though many argue that it is better than any of the alternatives, such as expert testimony from psychiatrists or psychologists. Yet polygraphy is fast becoming an American obsession, one, incidentally, not shared by the British or the Europeans or, as far as we know, the Russians. America's increasing dependence on the polygraph reflects its enormous faith in the rational processes of science: Each of us can probably recall a time when our voices sounded funny as we told a fib. Surely, if we can "hear" a lie, science can detect one.

It comes as a surprise, therefore, to learn how fragile polygraphy's scientific foundations are. When Raskin embarked on polygraphy research in Utah in 1970, not a single scientific laboratory had assessed the validity or reliability of the Control Question Test, by then already in wide use. Nor had a single report by a trained scientist evaluating that test appeared in the scientific literature.

Meanwhile, armed rather more with art than with science—and not a little merchandising magic thrown in—the technology is spreading like wildfire, alarming even such advocates as Raskin. Though he and Lykken clash often enough in print on the scientific merits of polygraphy, there is one development that appalls both men equally: use of polygraph tests in pre-employment screening by corporations, banks, fast-food chains, and a number of other commercial enterprises.

Such tests, according to Raskin, often are conducted hastily and haphazardly, resulting in highly questionable accuracy. They seek by vague and general questions to elicit admissions of a personal nature, thereby constituting invasion of privacy, and violate personal freedom by requiring tests that may put a job at stake. Particularly distasteful are tests given to present employees—who can hardly refuse—such as those recently used in the upper echelons of government to try to curb leaks to the media.

For Lykken, such uses merely exacerbate an already intolerable situation. He points to the scant amount of training polygraphers receive before they qualify as technicians of truth. Perhaps as many as a dozen contemporary polygraphers do hold Ph.D. degrees, but the vast majority of the 4,000 to 8,000 practicing examiners have had no significant training in physiology or in psychology, even though lie detection demands extremely subtle—and difficult—psychophysiological interpretations. Most of the 25 or more schools that train examiners provide only an eight-week course of instruction and require two years of college for admission.

While Raskin in his laboratory continues to attempt to make the polygraph more scientifically valid and reliable, Lykken continues to question the ground rules. Where Raskin sees the polygraph as a legitimate tool for protecting society, Lykken fears that the technology poses a greater threat to the innocent than to the guilty and, ultimately, is based on little more than an intimidating mystique that uses the language and trappings of science to sell itself to a trusting public. 20

Most law enforcement officials, however, look on the polygraph not as a technique for intimidating and imprisoning people but for screening out innocent suspects early, thus expediting the legal process. They prefer to talk about truth verification rather than lie detection. But for the present, verifying the truth appears at least as difficult as detecting a lie.

Topics for Critical Thinking and Writing

1. Having read the entire essay, go back and reread the first paragraph. What passages in this paragraph especially indicate the writer's attitude toward the use of lie detectors?

2. What words or phrases in paragraphs 2 and 3 are especially charged with negative connotations?

3. In paragraph 20 Meyer implies that the use of polygraphs relies chiefly on "an intimidating mystique"? What does he mean? Do you agree?

4. In paragraph 15 Meyer calls polygraphy an "American obsession." Why? How does he explain our faith in polygraphy? On the whole, do you agree with his characterization of Americans in this paragraph?

5. List Meyer's arguments against the uses of polygraphs, and then evaluate them. Do you believe that he gives convincing reasons against using polygraphs in examining persons accused of crimes? In examining applicants for jobs?

6. After reading this essay, how would you feel if a prospective employer asked you to submit to a polygraph? What course of action do you think you would follow?

Robert Frost

Robert Frost (1874–1963) was born in California. After his father's death in 1885 Frost's mother brought the family to New England, where she taught in high schools in Massachusetts and New Hampshire. Frost studied for part of one term at Dartmouth College in New Hampshire, then did odd jobs (including teaching), and from 1897 to 1899 was enrolled as a special student at Harvard. He later farmed in New Hampshire, published a few poems in local newspapers, left the farm and taught again, and in 1912 left for England, where he hoped to achieve more popular success as a writer. By 1915 he had won a considerable reputation, and he returned to the United States, settling on a farm in New Hampshire and cultivating the image of the country-wise farmer-poet. By the time of his death he was the nation's unofficial poet laureate. In fact he was well read in the classics, in the Bible, and in English and American literature.

Design

I found a dimpled spider, fat and white,
On a white heal-all,[1] holding up a moth
Like a white piece of rigid satin cloth—
Assorted characters of death and blight
Mixed ready to begin the morning right,   5
Like the ingredients of a witches' broth—
A snow-drop spider, a flower like a froth,
And dead wings carried like a paper kite.

---

[1]**heal-all** a flower, normally blue (Editors' note)

What had that flower to do with being white,
The wayside blue and innocent heal-all? 10
What brought the kindred spider to that height,
Then steered the white moth thither in the night?
What but design of darkness to appall?—
If design govern in a thing so small.

 ## Topics for Critical Thinking and Writing

1. What meanings of the word *design* come to your mind? Which of these meanings are relevant to the poem?

2. The poem is a sonnet (14 lines), divided into an octave (the first eight lines) and a sestet (the next six). How does the structure shape the thought?

CHAPTER 16

Classic Essays

Plato

Plato (427–347 B.C.) in his dialogues often uses the Athenian philosopher Socrates as a mouth-piece for ideas that scholars believe are Platonic, but in the dialogue called Crito *he probably was fairly careful to represent Socrates' own ideas.*

In 399 B.C. Socrates was convicted of impiety and was sentenced to death. Behind the charge of impiety was another, that Socrates had "corrupted the young." It seems clear, however, that the trial was a way of getting rid of a man considered by some to be a troublesome questioner of conventional opinions.

About a month intervened between the trial and Socrates' death because the law prohibited execution until a sacred ship had returned to Athens. Socrates could easily have escaped from prison but made no effort to leave, as we see in this dialogue reporting his decision to abide by the unjust decision of a duly constituted group of jurors.

Crito

(Scene: A room in the State prison at Athens in the year 399 B.C. The time is half an hour before dawn, and the room would be almost dark but for the light of a little oil lamp. There is a pallet bed against the back wall. At the head of it a small table supports the lamp; near the foot of it Crito is sitting patiently on a stool. He is an old man, kindly, practical, simple-minded; at present he is suffering from acute emotional strain. On the bed lies Socrates asleep. He stirs, yawns, opens his eyes and sees Crito.)

Socrates: Here already, Crito? Surely it is still early?

Crito: Indeed it is.

Socrates: About what time?

Crito: Just before dawn.

Socrates: I wonder that the warder paid any attention to you.   5

Crito: He is used to me now, Socrates, because I come here so often; besides, he is under some small obligation to me.

Socrates: Have you only just come, or have you been here for long?

Crito: Fairly long.

Socrates: Then why didn't you wake me at once, instead of sitting by my bed so quietly?

Crito: I wouldn't dream of such a thing, Socrates. I only wish I were   10 not so sleepless and depressed myself. I have been wondering at you, because I saw how comfortably you were sleeping; and I deliberately didn't wake you because I wanted you to go on being as comfortable as you could. I have often felt before in the course of my life now fortunate you are in your disposition, but I feel it more than ever now in your present misfortune when I see how easily and placidly you put up with it.

Socrates: Well, really, Crito, it would be hardly suitable for a man of my age to resent having to die.

Crito: Other people just as old as you are get involved in these misfortunes, Socrates, but their age doesn't keep them from resenting it when they find themselves in your position.

Socrates: Quite true. But tell me, why have you come so early?

Crito: Because I bring bad news, Socrates; not so bad from your point of view, I suppose, but it will be very hard to bear for me and your other friends, and I think that I shall find it hardest of all.

Socrates: Why, what is this news? Has the boat come in from Delos— the boat which ends my reprieve when it arrives?[1]

Crito: It hasn't actually come in yet, but I expect that it will be here today, judging from the report of some people who have just arrived from Sunium and left it there. It's quite clear from their account that it will be here today; and so by tomorrow, Socrates, you will have to—to end your life.

Socrates: Well, Crito, I hope that it may be for the best; if the gods will it so, so be it. All the same, I don't think it will arrive today.

Crito: What makes you think that?

Socrates: I will try to explain. I think I am right in saying that I have to die on the day after the boat arrives?

Crito: That's what the authorities say, at any rate.

Socrates: Then I don't think it will arrive on this day that is just beginning, but on the day after. I am going by a dream that I had in the night, only a little while ago. It looks as though you were right not to wake me up.

Crito: Why, what was the dream about?

Socrates: I thought I saw a gloriously beautiful woman dressed in white robes, who came up to me and addressed me in these words: "Socrates, to the pleasant land of Phthia on the third day thou shalt come."

Crito: Your dream makes no sense, Socrates.

Socrates: To my mind, Crito, it is perfectly clear.

Crito: Too clear, apparently. But look here, Socrates, it is still not too late to take my advice and escape. Your death means a double calamity for me. I shall not only lose a friend whom I can never possibly replace, but besides a great many people who don't know you and me very well will be sure to think that I let you down, because I could have saved you if I had been willing to spend the money; and what could be more contemptible than to get a name for thinking more of money than of your friends? Most people will never believe that it was you who refused to leave this place although we tried our hardest to persuade you.

Socrates: But my dear Crito, why should we pay so much attention to what "most people" think? The really reasonable people, who have more claim to be considered, will believe that the facts are exactly as they are.

Crito: You can see for yourself, Socrates, that one has to think of popular opinion as well. Your present position is quite enough to show that the capacity of ordinary people for causing trouble is not confined to

---

[1] **Delos ... arrives** Ordinarily execution was immediately carried out, but the day before Socrates' trial was the first day of an annual ceremony that involved sending a ship to Delos. When the ship was absent—in this case for about a month—executions could not be performed. As Crito goes on to say, Socrates could easily escape, and indeed he could have left the country before being tried. (All notes are the editors'.)

petty annoyances, but has hardly any limits if you once get a bad name with them.

Socrates: I only wish that ordinary people *had* unlimited capacity for doing harm; then they might have an unlimited power for doing good; which would be a splendid thing, if it were so. Actually they have neither. They cannot make a man wise or stupid; they simply act at random.

Crito: Have it that way if you like; but tell me this, Socrates. I hope that you aren't worrying about the possible effects on me and the rest of your friends, and thinking that if you escape we shall have trouble with informers for having helped you to get away, and have to forfeit all our property or pay an enormous fine, or even incur some further punishment? If any idea like that is troubling you, you can dismiss it altogether. We are quite entitled to run that risk in saving you, and even worse, if necessary. Take my advice, and be reasonable.

Socrates: All that you say is very much in my mind, Crito, and a great deal more besides.

Crito: Very well, then, don't let it distress you. I know some people who are willing to rescue you from here and get you out of the country for quite a moderate sum. And then surely you realize how cheap these informers are to buy off; we shan't need much money to settle them; and I think you've got enough of my money for yourself already. And then even supposing that in your anxiety for my safety you feel that you oughtn't to spend my money, there are these foreign gentlemen staying in Athens who are quite willing to spend theirs. One of them, Simmias of Thebes, has actually brought the money with him for this very purpose; and Cebes and a number of others are quite ready to do the same. So as I say, you mustn't let any fears on these grounds make you slacken your efforts to escape; and you mustn't feel any misgivings about what you said at your trial, that you wouldn't know what to do with yourself if you left this country. Wherever you go, there are plenty of places where you will find a welcome; and if you choose to go to Thessaly, I have friends there who will make much of you and give you complete protection, so that no one in Thessaly can interfere with you.

Besides, Socrates, I don't even feel that it is right for you to try to do what you are doing, throwing away your life when you might save it. You are doing your best to treat yourself in exactly the same way as your enemies would, or rather did, when they wanted to ruin you. What is more, it seems to me that you are letting your sons down too. You have it in your power to finish their bringing up and education, and instead of that you are proposing to go off and desert them, and so far as you are concerned they will have to take their chance. And what sort of chance are they likely to get? The sort of thing that usually happens to orphans when they lose their parents. Either one ought not to have children at all, or one ought to see their upbringing and education through to the end. It strikes me that you are taking the line of least resistance, whereas you ought to make the choice of a good man and a brave one, considering that you pro-

30

fess to have made goodness your object all through life. Really, I am ashamed, both on your account and on ours your friends'; it will look as though we had played something like a coward's part all through this affair of yours. First, there was the way you came into court when it was quite unnecessary—that was the first act; than there was the conduct of the defense—that was the second; and finally, to complete the farce, we get this situation, which makes it appear that we have let you slip out of our hands through some lack of courage and enterprise on our part, because we didn't save you, and you didn't save yourself, when it would have been quite possible and practicable, if we had been any use at all.

There, Socrates; if you aren't careful, besides the suffering there will be all this disgrace for you and us to bear. Come, make up your mind. Really it's too late for that now; you ought to have it made up already. There is no alternative; the whole thing must be carried through during this coming night. If we lose any more time, it can't be done, it will be too late. I appeal to you, Socrates, on every ground; take my advice and please don't be unreasonable!

Socrates: My dear Crito, I appreciate your warm feelings very much—that is, assuming that they have some justification; if not, the stronger they are, the harder they will be to deal with. Very well, then; we must consider whether we ought to follow your advice or not. You know that this is not a new idea of mine; it has always been my nature never to accept advice from any of my friends unless reflection shows that it is the best course that reason offers. I cannot abandon the principles which I used to hold in the past simply because this accident has happened to me; they seem to me to be much as they were, and I respect and regard the same principles now as before. So unless we can find better principles on this occasion, you can be quite sure that I shall not agree with you; not even if the power of the people conjures up fresh hordes of bogies to terrify our childish minds, by subjecting us to chains and executions and confiscations of our property.

Well, then, how can we consider the question most reasonably? Suppose that we begin by reverting to this view which you hold about people's opinions. Was it always right to argue that some opinions should be taken seriously but not others? Or was it always wrong? Perhaps it was right before the question of my death arose, but now we can see clearly that it was a mistaken persistence in a point of view which was really irresponsible nonsense. I should like very much to inquire into this problem, Crito, with your help, and to see whether the argument will appear in any different light to me now that I am in this position, or whether it will remain the same; and whether we shall dismiss it or accept it.

Serious thinkers, I believe, have always held some such view as the one which I mentioned just now: that some of the opinions which people entertain should be respected, and others should not. Now I ask you, Crito, don't you think that this is a sound principle?—You are safe from the prospect of dying tomorrow, in all human probability; and you are not likely to have your judgment upset by this impending calamity. Consider, then; don't you think that this is a sound enough principle, that one should not regard all the opinions that people hold, but only some and not others? What do you say? Isn't that a fair statement?

Crito: Yes, it is.

Socrates: In other words, one should regard the good ones and not the bad?

Crito: Yes.   40

Socrates: The opinions of the wise being good, and the opinions of the foolish bad?

Crito: Naturally.

Socrates: To pass on, then: What do you think of the sort of illustration that I used to employ? When a man is in training, and taking it seriously, does he pay attention to all praise and criticism and opinion indiscriminately, or only when it comes from the one qualified person, the actual doctor or trainer?

Crito: Only when it comes from the one qualified person.

Socrates: Then he should be afraid of the criticism and welcome the   45
praise of the one qualified person, but not those of the general public.

Crito: Obviously.

Socrates: So he ought to regulate his actions and exercises and eating and drinking by the judgment of his instructor, who has expert knowledge, rather than by the opinions of the rest of the public.

Crito: Yes, that is so.

Socrates: Very well. Now if he disobeys the one man and disregards his opinion and commendations, and pays attention to the advice of the many who have no expert knowledge, surely he will suffer some bad effect?

Crito: Certainly.   50

Socrates: And what is this bad effect? Where is it produced?—I mean, in what part of the disobedient person?

Crito: His body, obviously; that is what suffers.

Socrates: Very good. Well now, tell me, Crito—we don't want to go through all the examples one by one—does this apply as a general rule, and above all to the sort of actions which we are trying to decide about: just and unjust, honorable and dishonorable, good and bad? Ought we to be guided and intimidated by the opinion of the many or by that of the one—assuming that there is someone with expert knowledge? Is it true that we ought to respect and fear this person more than all the rest put together; and that if we do not follow his guidance we shall spoil and mutilate that part of us which, as we used to say, is improved by right conduct and destroyed by wrong? Or is this all nonsense?

Crito: No, I think it is true, Socrates.

Socrates: Then consider the next step. There is a part of us which is   55
improved by healthy actions and ruined by unhealthy ones. If we spoil it by taking the advice of nonexperts, will life be worth living when this part is once ruined? The part I mean is the body; do you accept this?

Crito: Yes.

Socrates: Well, is life worth living with a body which is worn out and ruined by health?

Crito: Certainly not.

Socrates: What about the part of us which is mutilated by wrong actions and benefited by right ones? Is life worth living with this part ruined? Or do we believe that this part of us, whatever it may be, in which right and wrong operate, is of less importance than the body?

Crito: Certainly not.

Socrates: It is really more precious?

Crito: Much more.

Socrates: In that case, my dear fellow, what we ought to consider is not so much what people in general will say about us but how we stand with the expert in right and wrong, the one authority, who represents the actual truth. So in the first place your proposition is not correct when you say that we should consider popular opinion in questions of what is right and honorable and good, or the opposite. Of course one might object "All the same, the people have the power to put us to death."

Crito: No doubt about that! Quite true, Socrates; it is a possible objection.

Socrates: But so far as I can see, my dear fellow, the argument which we have just been through is quite unaffected by it. At the same time I should like you to consider whether we are still satisfied on this point: that the really important thing is not to live, but to live well.

Crito: Why, yes.

Socrates: And that to live well means the same thing as to live honorably or rightly?

Crito: Yes.

Socrates: Then in the light of this agreement we must consider whether or not it is right for me to try to get away without an official discharge. If it turns out to be right, we must make the attempt; if not, we must let it drop. As for the considerations you raise about expense and reputation and bringing up children, I am afraid, Crito, that they represent the reflections of the ordinary public, who put people to death, and would bring them back to life if they could, with equal indifference to reason. Our real duty, I fancy, since the argument leads that way, is to consider one question only, the one which we raised just now: Shall we be acting rightly in paying money and showing gratitude to these people who are going to rescue me, and in escaping or arranging the escape ourselves, or shall we really be acting wrongly in doing all this? If it becomes clear that such conduct is wrong, I cannot help thinking that the question whether we are sure to die, or to suffer any other ill effect for that matter, if we stand our ground and take no action, ought not to weigh with us at all in comparison with the risk of doing what is wrong.

Crito: I agree with what you say, Socrates; but I wish you would consider what we ought to *do*.

60

65

70

Socrates: Let us look at it together, my dear fellow; and if you can challenge any of my arguments, do so and I will listen to you; but if you can't, be a good fellow and stop telling me over and over again that I ought to leave this place without official permission. I am very anxious to obtain your approval before I adopt the course which I have in mind; I don't want to act against your convictions. Now give your attention to the starting point of this inquiry—I hope that you will be satisfied with my way of stating it—and try to answer my questions to the best of your judgment.

Crito: Well, I will try.

Socrates: Do we say that one must never willingly do wrong, or does it depend upon circumstance? Is it true, as we have often agreed before, that there is no sense in which wrongdoing is good or honorable? Or have we jettisoned all our former convictions in these last few days? Can you and I at our age, Crito, have spent all these years in serious discussions without realizing that we were no better than a pair of children? Surely the truth is just what we have always said. Whatever the popular view is, and whether the alternative is pleasanter than the present one or even harder to bear, the fact remains that to do wrong is in every sense bad and dishonorable for the person who does it. Is that our view, or not?

Crito: Yes, it is.

Socrates: Then in no circumstances must one do wrong.   75

Crito: No.

Socrates: In that case one must not even do wrong when one is wronged, which most people regard as the natural course.

Crito: Apparently not.

Socrates: Tell me another thing, Crito: Ought one to do injuries or not?

Crito: Surely not, Socrates.   80

Socrates: And tell me: Is it right to do an injury in retaliation, as most people believe, or not?

Crito: No, never.

Socrates: Because, I suppose, there is no difference between injuring people and wronging them.

Crito: Exactly.

Socrates: So one ought not to return a wrong or an injury to any per-   85
son, whatever the provocation is. Now be careful, Crito, that in making these single admissions you do not end by admitting something contrary to your real beliefs. I know that there are and always will be few people who think like this; and consequently between those who do think so and those who do not there can be no agreement on principle; they must always feel contempt when they observe one another's decisions. I want even you to consider very carefully whether you share my views and agree with me, and whether we can proceed with our discussion from the established hypothesis that it is never right to do a wrong or return a wrong or defend one's self against injury by retaliation; or whether you

dissociate yourself from any share in this view as a basis for discussion. I have held it for a long time, and still hold it; but if you have formed any other opinion, say so and tell me what it is. If, on the other hand, you stand by what we have said, listen to my next point.

Crito: Yes, I stand by it and agree with you. Go on.

Socrates: Well, here is my next point, or rather question. Ought one to fulfill all one's agreements, provided that they are right, or break them?

Crito: One ought to fulfill them.

Socrates: Then consider the logical consequence. If we leave this place without first persuading the State to let us go, are we or are we not doing an injury, and doing it in a quarter where it is least justifiable? Are we or are we not abiding by our just agreements?

Crito: I can't answer your question, Socrates; I am not clear in my mind. 90

Socrates: Look at it in this way. Suppose that while we were preparing to run away from here (or however one should describe it) the Laws and Constitution of Athens were to come and confront us and ask this question: "Now, Socrates, what are you proposing to do? Can you deny that by this act which you are contemplating you intend, so far as you have the power, to destroy us, the Laws, and the whole State as well? Do you imagine that a city can continue to exist and not be turned upside down, if the legal judgments which are pronounced in it have no force but are nullified and destroyed by private persons?"—how shall we answer this question, Crito, and others of the same kind? There is much that could be said, especially by a professional advocate, to protest against the invalidation of this law which enacts that judgments once pronounced shall be binding. Shall we say "Yes, I do intend to destroy the laws, because the State wronged me by passing a faulty judgment at my trial"? Is this to be our answer, or what?

Crito: What you have just said, by all means, Socrates.

Socrates: Then what supposing the Laws say, "Was there provision for this in the agreement between you and us, Socrates? Or did you undertake to abide by whatever judgments the State pronounced?" If we expressed surprise at such language, they would probably say: "Never mind our language, Socrates, but answer our questions; after all, you are accustomed to the method of question and answer. Come now, what charge do you bring against us and the State, that you are trying to destroy us? Did we not give you life in the first place? Was it not through us that your father married your mother and begot you? Tell us, have you any complaint against those of us Laws that deal with marriage?" "No, none," I should say. "Well, have you any against the laws which deal with children's upbringing and education, such as you had yourself? Are you not grateful to those of us Laws which were instituted for this end, for requiring your father to give you a cultural and physical education?" "Yes,"

I should say. "Very good. Then since you have been born and brought up and educated, can you deny, in the first place, that you were our child and servant, both you and your ancestors? And if this is so, do you imagine that what is right for us is equally right for you, and that whatever we try to do to you, you are justified in retaliating? You did not have equality of rights with your father, or your employer (supposing that you had had one), to enable you to retaliate; you were not allowed to answer back when you were scolded or to hit back when you were beaten, or to do a great many other things of the same kind. Do you expect to have such license against your country and its laws that if we try to put you to death in the belief that it is right to do so, you on your part will try your hardest to destroy your country and us its Laws in return? And will you, the true devotee of goodness, claim that you are justified in doing so? Are you so wise as to have forgotten that compared with your mother and father and all the rest of your ancestors your country is something far more precious, more venerable, more sacred, and held in greater honor both among gods and among all reasonable men? Do you not realize that you are even more bound to respect and placate the anger of your country than your father's anger? That if you cannot persuade your country you must do whatever it orders, and patiently submit to any punishment that it imposes, whether it be flogging or imprisonment? And if it leads you out to war, to be wounded or killed, you must comply, and it is right that you should do so; you must not give way or retreat or abandon your position. Both in war and in the law courts and everywhere else you must do whatever your city and your country commands, or else persuade it in accordance with universal justice; but violence is a sin even against your parents, and it is a far greater sin against your country"—What shall we say to this, Crito?—that what the Laws say is true, or not?

Crito: Yes, I think so.

Socrates: "Consider, then, Socrates," the Laws would probably continue, "whether it is also true for us to say that what you are now trying to do to us is not right. Although we have brought you into the world and reared you and educated you, and given you and all your fellow citizens a share in all the good things at our disposal, nevertheless by the very fact of granting our permission we openly proclaim this principle: that any Athenian, on attaining to manhood and seeing for himself the political organization of the State and us its Laws, is permitted, if he is not satisfied with us, to take his property and go away wherever he likes. If any of you chooses to go to one of our colonies, supposing that he should not be satisfied with us and the State, or to emigrate to any other country, not one of us Laws hinders or prevents him from going away wherever he likes, without any loss of property. On the other hand, if any one of you stands his ground when he can see how we administer justice and the rest of our public organization, we hold that by so doing he had in fact undertaken to do anything that we tell him; and we maintain that anyone who disobeys is guilty of doing wrong on three separate counts: first because we

95

are his parents, and secondly because we are his guardians; and thirdly because, after promising obedience, he is neither obeying us nor persuading us to change our decision if we are at fault in any way; and although all our orders are in the form of proposals, not of savage commands, and we give him the choice of either persuading us or doing what we say, he is actually doing neither. These are the charges, Socrates, to which we say that you will be liable if you do what you are contemplating; and you will not be the least culpable of your fellow countrymen, but one of the most guilty." If I said "Why do you say that?" they would no doubt pounce upon me with perfect justice and point out that there are very few people in Athens who have entered into this agreement with them as explicitly as I have. They would say "Socrates, we have substantial evidence that you are satisfied with us and with the State. You would not have been so exceptionally reluctant to cross the borders of your country if you had not been exceptionally attached to it. You have never left the city to attend a festival or for any other purpose, except on some military expedition; you have never traveled abroad as other people do, and you have never felt the impulse to acquaint yourself with another country or constitution; you have been content with us and with our city. You have definitely chosen us, and undertaken to observe us in all your activities as a citizen; and as the crowning proof that you are satisfied with our city, you have begotten children in it. Furthermore, even at the time of your trial you could have proposed the penalty of banishment, if you had chosen to do so; that is, you could have done then with the sanction of the State what you are now trying to do without it. But whereas at that time you made a noble show of indifference if you had to die, and in fact preferred death, as you said, to banishment, now you show no respect for your earlier professions, and no regard for us, the Laws, whom you are trying to destroy; you are behaving like the lowest type of menial, trying to run away in spite of the contracts and undertakings by which you agreed to live as a member of our State. Now first answer this question: Are we or are we not speaking the truth when we say that you have undertaken, in deed if not in word, to live your life as a citizen in obedience to us?" What are we to say to that, Crito? Are we not bound to admit it?

Crito: We cannot help it, Socrates.

Socrates: "It is a fact, then," they would say, "that you are breaking covenants and undertakings made with us, although you made them under no compulsion or misunderstanding, and were not compelled to decide in a limited time; you had seventy years in which you could have left the country, if you were not satisfied with us or felt that the agreements were unfair. You did not choose Sparta or Crete—your favorite models of good government—or any other Greek or foreign state; you could not have absented yourself from the city less if you had been lame or blind or decrepit in some other way. It is quite obvious that you stand by yourself above all other Athenians in your affection for this city and for us its Laws;—who would care for a city without laws? And now, after all this, are you not going to stand by your agreement? Yes, you are, Socrates, if you will take our advice; and then you will at least escape being laughed at for leaving the city.

"We invite you to consider what good you will do to yourself or your friends if you commit this breach of faith and stain your conscience. It is fairly obvious that the risk of being banished and either losing their citizenship or having their property confiscated will extend to your friends as well. As for yourself, if you go to one of the neighboring states, such as Thebes or Megara, which are both well governed, you will enter them as an enemy to their constitution[2] and all good patriots will eye you with suspicion as a destroyer of law and order. Incidentally you will confirm the opinion of the jurors who tried you that they gave a correct verdict; a destroyer of laws might very well be supposed to have a destructive influence upon young and foolish human beings. Do you intend, then, to avoid well governed states and the higher forms of human society? And if you do, will life be worth living? Or will you approach these people and have the impudence to converse with them? What arguments will you use, Socrates? The same which you used here, that goodness and integrity, institutions and laws, are the most precious possessions of mankind? Do you not think that Socrates and everything about him will appear in a disreputable light? You certainly ought to think so. But perhaps you will retire from this part of the world and go to Crito's friends in Thessaly? That is the home of indiscipline and laxity, and no doubt they would enjoy hearing the amusing story of how you managed to run away from prison by arraying yourself in some costume or putting on a shepherd's smock or some other conventional runaway's disguise, and altering your personal appearance. And will no one comment on the fact that an old man of your age, probably with only a short time left to live, should dare to cling so greedily to life, at the price of violating the most stringent laws? Perhaps not, if you avoid irritating anyone. Otherwise, Socrates, you will hear a good many humiliating comments. So you will live as the toady and slave of all the populace, literally 'roistering in Thessaly' as though you had left this country for Thessaly to attend a banquet there; and where will your discussions about goodness and uprightness be then, we should like to know? But of course you want to live for your children's sake, so that you may be able to bring them up and educate them. Indeed! by first taking them off to Thessaly and making foreigners of them, so that they may have that additional enjoyment? Or if that is not your intention, supposing that they are brought up here with you still alive, will they be better cared for and educated without you, because of course your friends will look after them? Will they look after your children if you go away to Thessaly, and not if you go away to the next world? Surely if those who profess to be your friends are worth anything, you must believe that they would care for them.

"No, Socrates; be advised by us your guardians, and do not think more of your children or of your life or of anything else than you think of

2**as an enemy to their constitution** as a lawbreaker

what is right; so that when you enter the next world you may have all this to plead in your defense before the authorities there. It seems clear that if you do this thing, neither you nor any of your friends will be the better for it or be more upright or have a cleaner conscience here in this world, nor will it be better for you when you reach the next. As it is, you will leave this place, when you do, as the victim of a wrong done not by us, the Laws, but by your fellow men. But if you leave in that dishonorable way, returning wrong for wrong and evil for evil, breaking your agreements and covenants with us, and injuring those whom you least ought to injure—yourself, your friends, your country, and us—then you will have to face our anger in your lifetime, and in that place beyond when the laws of the other world know that you have tried, so far as you could, to destroy even us their brothers, they will not receive you with a kindly welcome. Do not take Crito's advice, but follow ours."

That, my dear friend Crito, I do assure you, is what I seem to hear 100 them saying, just as a mystic seems to hear the strains of music; and the sound of their arguments rings so loudly in my head that I cannot hear the other side. I warn you that, as my opinion stands at present, it will be useless to urge a different view. However, if you think that you will do any good by it, say what you like.

Crito: No, Socrates, I have nothing to say.

Socrates: Then give it up, Crito, and let us follow this course, since God points out the way.

Topics for Critical Thinking and Writing

1. Socrates argues that because throughout his life he lived in Athens, in effect he established a compact with the city to live by its laws and must therefore now accept the judgment—however mistaken—of a duly constituted court. How convincing is this argument? Suppose this argument were omitted. Would Socrates' conclusion be affected?

2. Socrates argues that just as in matters of caring for the body we heed only experts and not the multitude, so in moral matters we should heed the expert, not the multitude. How convincing is this analogy between bodily health and moral goodness? Socrates sometimes compared himself to an athletic coach, saying he trained people to think. Judging from the dialogue, how did he train a student to think?

3. The personified figure of the laws does not add much to the essential argument. Why, then, is the passage included?

4. The ancient Chinese teacher Confucius asked one of his pupils, "Do you think of me as a man who knows about things as the result of wide study?" When the pupil replied "Yes," Confucius disagreed: "I have one thing, and upon it all the rest is rooted." Exactly what did Confucius mean? In an essay of 500 words explain what Socrates would have said, if he had been asked the question.

Jonathan Swift

Jonathan Swift (1667–1745) was born in Ireland of an English family. He was ordained in the Church of Ireland in 1694, and in 1714 he became dean of St. Patrick's Cathedral, Dublin. He wrote abundantly on political and religious topics, often motivated (in his own words) by "savage indignation." It is ironic that Gulliver's Travels, *the masterpiece by this master of irony, is most widely thought of as a book for children.*

From the middle of the sixteenth century, the English regulated the Irish economy so that it would enrich England. Heavy taxes and other repressive legislation impoverished Ireland, and in 1728, the year before Swift wrote "A Modest Proposal," Ireland was further weakened by a severe famine. Swift, deeply moved by the injustice, the stupidity, and the suffering that he found in Ireland, adopts the disguise or persona of an economist and offers an ironic suggestion on how Irish families may improve their conditions.

A Modest Proposal

For Preventing the Children of Poor People in Ireland from Being a Burden to Their Parents or Country, and for Making Them Beneficial to the Public

It is a melancholy object to those who walk through this great town or travel in the country, when they see the streets, the roads, and cabin doors, crowded with beggars of the female sex, followed by three, four, or six children, all in rags and importuning every passenger for an alms. These mothers, instead of being able to work for their honest livelihood, are forced to employ all their time in strolling to beg sustenance for their helpless infants: who as they grow up either turn thieves for want of work, or leave their dear native country to fight for the pretender in Spain, or sell themselves to the Barbadoes.

I think it is agreed by all parties that this prodigious number of children in the arms, or on the backs, or at the heels of their mothers, and frequently of their fathers, is in the present deplorable state of the kingdom a very great additional grievance; and, therefore, whoever could find out a fair, cheap, and easy method of making these children sound, useful members of the commonwealth, would deserve so well of the public as to have his statue set up for a preserver of the nation.

But my intention is very far from being confined to provide only for the children of professed beggars; it is of a much greater extent, and shall take in the whole number of infants at a certain age who are born of parents in effect as little able to support them as those who demand our charity in the streets.

As to my own part, having turned my thoughts for many years upon this important subject, and maturely weighed the several schemes of our projectors, I have always found them grossly mistaken in their computation. It is true, a child just dropped from its dam may be supported by her milk for a solar year, with little other nourishment; at most not above the value of 2s.,[1] which the mother may certainly get, or the value in scraps, by her lawful occupation of begging; and it is exactly at one year old that I propose to provide for them in such a manner as instead of being a charge upon their parents or the parish, or wanting food and raiment for the rest of their lives, they shall on the contrary contribute to the feeding, and partly to the clothing, of many thousands.

There is likewise another great advantage in my scheme, that it will prevent those voluntary abortions, and that horrid practice of women murdering their bastard children, alas! too frequent among us! sacrificing the poor innocent babes I doubt more to avoid the expense than the shame, which would move tears and pity in the most savage and inhuman breast.

The number of souls in this kingdom being usually reckoned one million and a half, of these I calculate there may be about 200,000 couple whose wives are breeders; from which number I subtract 30,000 couple who are able to maintain their own children (although I apprehend there cannot be so many, under the present distress of the kingdom); but this being granted, there will remain 170,000 breeders. I again subtract 50,000 for those women who miscarry, or whose children die by accident or disease within the year. There only remain 120,000 children of poor parents annually born. The question therefore is, how this number shall be reared and provided for? which, as I have already said, under the present situation of affairs, is utterly impossible by all the methods hitherto proposed. For we can neither employ them in handicraft or agriculture; we neither build houses (I mean in the country) nor cultivate land; they can very seldom pick up a livelihood by stealing, till they arrive at six years old, except where they are of towardly parts; although I confess they learn the rudiments much earlier; during which time they can, however, be properly looked upon only as probationers; as I have been informed by a principal gentleman in the country of Cavan, who protested to me that he never knew above one or two instances under the age of six, even in a part of the kingdom so renowned for the quickest proficiency in that art.

I am assured by our merchants, that a boy or a girl before twelve years old is no saleable commodity; and even when they come to this age they will not yield above 3l. or 3l. 2s. 6d. at most on the exchange; which cannot turn to account either to the parents or kingdom, the charge of nutriment and rags having been at least four times that value.

I shall now therefore humbly propose my own thoughts, which I hope will not be liable to the least objection.

I have been assured by a very knowing American of my acquaintance in London, that a young healthy child well nursed is at a year old a most delicious, nourishing, and wholesome food, whether stewed, roasted, baked, or broiled; and I make no doubt that it will equally serve in a fricassee or a ragout.

---

[1] **2s.** = two shillings. Later in the essay, "£" and "l" stand for pounds and "d" for pence. (Editors' note)

I do therefore humbly offer it to public consideration that of the
120,000 children already computed, 20,000 may be reserved for breed,
whereof only one-fourth part to be males; which is more than we allow to
sheep, black cattle, or swine; and my reason is, that these children are seldom the fruits of marriage, a circumstance not much regarded by our savages; therefore one male will be sufficient to serve four females. That the
remaining 100,000 may, at a year old, be offered in sale to the persons of
quality and fortune through the kingdom; always advising the mother to
let them suck plentifully in the last month, so as to render them plump
and fat for a good table. A child will make two dishes at an entertainment
for friends; and when the family dines alone, the fore or hind quarter will
make a reasonable dish, and seasoned with a little pepper or salt will be
very good boiled on the fourth day, especially in winter.

I have reckoned upon a medium that a child just born will weigh 12
pounds, and in a solar year, if tolerably nursed, will increase to 28 pounds.

I grant this food will be somewhat dear, and therefore very proper for
landlords, who, as they have already devoured most of the parents, seem
to have the best title to the children.

Infant's flesh will be in season throughout the year, but more plentiful
in March, and a little before and after: for we are told by a grave author,
an eminent French physician, that fish being a prolific diet, there are more
children born in Roman Catholic countries about nine months after Lent
than at any other season; therefore, reckoning a year after Lent, the markets will be more glutted than usual, because the number of popish infants is at least three to one in this kingdom: and therefore it will have one
other collateral advantage, by lessening the number of papists among us.

I have already computed the charge of nursing a beggar's child (in
which list I reckon all cottagers, laborers, and four-fifths of the farmers) to be
about 2s. per annum, rags included; and I believe no gentleman would re-
pine to give 10s. for the carcass of a good fat child, which, as I have said, will
make four dishes of excellent nutritive meat, when he has only some particular friend or his own family to dine with him. Thus the squire will learn to
be a good landlord, and grow popular among the tenants; the mother will
have 8s. net profit, and be fit for work till she produces another child.

Those who are more thrifty (as I must confess the times require) may
flay the carcass; the skin of which artificially dressed will make admirable
gloves for ladies, and summer boots for fine gentlemen.

As to our city of Dublin, shambles may be appointed for this purpose
in the most convenient parts of it, and butchers we may be assured will
not be wanting: although I rather recommend buying the children alive,
and dressing them hot from the knife as we do roasting pigs.

A very worthy person, a true lover of his country, and whose virtues I
highly esteem, was lately pleased in discoursing on this matter to offer a refinement upon my scheme. He said that many gentlemen of this kingdom,
having of late destroyed their deer, he conceived that the want of venison
might be well supplied by the bodies of young lads and maidens, not ex-

ceeding fourteen years of age nor under twelve; so great a number of both sexes in every country being now ready to starve for want of work and service; and these to be disposed of by their parents, if alive, or otherwise by their nearest relations. But with due deference to so excellent a friend and so deserving a patriot, I cannot be altogether in his sentiments; for as to the males, my American acquaintance assured me from frequent experience that their flesh was generally tough and lean, like that of our schoolboys by continual exercise, and their taste disagreeable; and to fatten them would not answer the charge. Then as to the females, it would, I think, with humble submission be a loss to the public, because they soon would become breeders themselves: and besides, it is not improbable that some scrupulous people might be apt to censure such a practice (although indeed very unjustly), as a little bordering upon cruelty; which, I confess, has always been with me the strongest objection against any project, how well soever intended.

But in order to justify my friend, he confessed that this expedient was put into his head by the famous Psalmanazar, a native of the island Formosa, who came from thence to London about twenty years ago: and in conversation told my friend, that in his country when any young person happened to be put to death, the executioner sold the carcass to persons of quality as a prime dainty; and that in his time the body of a plump girl of fifteen, who was crucified for an attempt to poison the emperor, was sold to his imperial majesty's prime minister of state, and other great mandarins of the court, in joints from the gibbet, at 400 crowns. Neither indeed can I deny, that if the same use were made of several plump young girls in this town, who without one single groat to their fortunes cannot stir abroad without a chair, and appear at the playhouse and assemblies in foreign fineries which they never will pay for, the kingdom would not be the worse.

Some persons of a desponding spirit are in great concern about that vast number of poor people, who are aged, diseased, or maimed, and I have been desired to employ my thoughts what course may be taken to ease the nation of so grievous an encumbrance. But I am not in the least pain upon that matter, because it is very well known that they are every day dying and rotting by cold and famine, and filth and vermin, as fast as can be reasonably expected. And as to the young laborers, they are now in as hopeful a condition: they cannot get work, and consequently pine away for want of nourishment, to a degree that if at any time they are accidentally hired to common labor, they have not strength to perform it; and thus the country and themselves are happily delivered from the evils to come.

I have too long digressed, and therefore shall return to my subject. I think the advantages by the proposal which I have made are obvious and many, as well as of the highest importance.   20

For first, as I have already observed, it would greatly lessen the number of papists, with whom we are yearly overrun, being the principal breeders of the nation as well as our most dangerous enemies; and who stay at home on purpose to deliver the kingdom to the Pretender, hoping to take their advantage by the absence of so many good Protestants, who have chosen rather to leave their country than stay at home and pay tithes against their conscience to an Episcopal curate.

Secondly, The poor tenants will have something valuable of their own, which by law may be made liable to distress and help to pay their landlord's rent, their corn and cattle being already seized, and money a thing unknown.

Thirdly, Whereas the maintenance of 100,000 children from two years old and upward, cannot be computed at less than 10s, a-piece per annum, the nation's stock will be thereby increased £50,000 per annum, beside the profit of a new dish introduced to the tables of all gentlemen of fortune in the kingdom who have any refinement in taste. And the money will circulate among ourselves, the goods being entirely of our own growth and manufacture.

Fourthly, The constant breeders beside the gain of 8s. sterling per annum by the sale of their children, will be rid of the charge of maintaining them after the first year.

Fifthly, This food would likewise bring great custom to taverns, where the vintners will certainly be so prudent as to procure the best receipts for dressing it to perfection, and consequently have their houses frequented by all the fine gentlemen, who justly value themselves upon their knowledge in good eating; and a skilful cook who understands how to oblige his guests, will contrive to make it as expensive as they please.

Sixthly, This would be a great inducement to marriage, which all wise nations have either encouraged by rewards or enforced by laws and penalties. It would increase the care and tenderness of mothers toward their children, when they were sure of a settlement for life to the poor babes, provided in some sort by the public, to their annual profit instead of expense. We should see an honest emulation among the married women, which of them would bring the fattest child to the market. Men would become as fond of their wives during the time of their pregnancy as they are now of their mares in foal, their cows in calf, their sows when they are ready to farrow; nor offer to beat or kick them (as is too frequent a practice) for fear of a miscarriage.

Many other advantages might be enumerated. For instance, the addition of some thousand carcasses in our exportation of barreled beef, the propagation of swine's flesh, and improvement in the art of making good bacon, so much wanted among us by the great destruction of pigs, too frequent at our table; which are no way comparable in taste or magnificence to a well-grown, fat, yearling child, which roasted whole will make a considerable figure at a lord mayor's feast or any other public entertainment. But this and many others I omit, being studious of brevity.

Supposing that 1,000 families in this city would be constant customers for infants' flesh, besides others who might have it at merry-meetings, particularly at weddings and christenings, I compute that Dublin would take

25

off annually about 20,000 carcasses; and the rest of the kingdom (where probably they will be sold somewhat cheaper) the remaining 80,000.

I can think of no one objection that will possibly be raised against this proposal, unless it should be urged that the number of people will be thereby much lessened in the kingdom. This I freely own, and it was indeed one principal design in offering it to the world. I desire the reader will observe, that I calculate my remedy for this one individual kingdom of Ireland and for no other that ever was, is, or I think ever can be upon earth. Therefore let no man talk to me of other expedients: of taxing our absentees at 5s. a pound: of using neither clothes nor household furniture except what is of our own growth and manufacture: of utterly rejecting the materials and instruments that promote foreign luxury: of curing the expensiveness of pride, vanity, idleness, and gaming in our women: of introducing a vein of parsimony, prudence, and temperance: of learning to love our country, in the want of which we differ even from Laplanders and the inhabitants of Topinamboo: of quitting our animosities and factions, nor acting any longer like the Jews, who were murdering one another at the very moment their city was taken: of being a little cautious not to sell our country and conscience for nothing: of teaching landlords to have at least one degree of mercy toward their tenants: lastly, of putting a spirit of honesty, industry, and skill into our shopkeepers; who, if a resolution could now be taken to buy only our native goods, would immediately unite to cheat and exact upon us in the price, the measure, and the goodness, nor could ever yet be brought to make one fair proposal of just dealing, though often and earnestly invited to it.

Therefore, I repeat, let no man talk to me of these and the like expedients, till he has at least some glimpse of hope that there will be ever some hearty and sincere attempt to put them in practice. 30

But as to myself, having been wearied out for many years with offering vain, idle, visionary thoughts, and at length utterly despairing of success, I fortunately fell upon this proposal; which, as it is wholly new, so it has something solid and real, of no expense and little trouble, full in our own power, and whereby we can incur no danger in disobliging England. For this kind of commodity will not bear exportation, the flesh being of too tender a consistence to admit a long continuance in salt, although perhaps I could name a country which would be glad to eat up our whole nation without it.

After all, I am not so violently bent upon my own opinion as to reject any offer proposed by wise men, which shall be found equally innocent, cheap, easy, and effectual. But before something of that kind shall be advanced in contradiction to my scheme, and offering a better, I desire the author or authors will be pleased maturely to consider two points. First, as things now stand, how they will be able to find food and raiment for 100,000 useless mouths and backs. And secondly, there being a round million of creatures in human figure throughout this kingdom, whose subsistence put into a common stock would leave them in debt 200,000,000 l.

sterling, adding those who are beggars by profession to the bulk of farmers, cottagers, and laborers, with the wives and children who are beggars in effect; I desire those politicians who dislike my overture, and may perhaps be so bold as to attempt an answer, that they will first ask the parents of these mortals, whether they would not at this day think it a great happiness to have been sold for food at a year old in the manner I prescribe, and thereby have avoided such a perpetual scene of misfortunes as they have since gone through by the oppression of landlords, the impossibility of paying rent without money or trade, the want of common sustenance, with neither house nor clothes to cover them from the inclemencies of the weather, and the most inevitable prospect of entailing the like or greater miseries upon their breed for ever.

I profess, in the sincerity of my heart, that I have not the least personal interest in endeavoring to promote this necessary work, having no other motive than the public good of my country, by advancing our trade, providing for infants, relieving the poor, and giving some pleasure to the rich. I have no children by which I can propose to get a single penny; the youngest being nine years old, and my wife past child-bearing.

Topics for Critical Thinking and Writing

1. Characterize the pamphleteer (not Swift but his persona) who offers his "modest proposal." What sort of man does he think he is? What sort of man do we regard him as? Support your assertions with evidence.

2. In the first paragraph, the speaker says that the sight of mothers begging is "melancholy." In this paragraph what assumption does the speaker make about women that in part gives rise to this melancholy? Now that you are familiar with the entire essay, explain Swift's strategy in his first paragraph.

3. Explain the function of the "other expedients" (listed in paragraph 29).

4. How might you argue that although this satire is primarily ferocious, it also contains some playful touches? What specific passages might support your argument?

Elizabeth Cady Stanton

Elizabeth Cady Stanton (1815–1902), born into a prosperous conservative family in Johnstown, New York, became one of the most radical advocates of women's rights in the nineteenth century. In 1840 she married Henry Brewster Stanton, an ardent abolitionist lecturer. In the same year, at the World Anti-Slavery Convention in England—which refused to seat the women delegates—she met Lucretia Mott, and the two women resolved to organize a convention to discuss women's rights. Not until 1848, however, did the convention materialize. Of the three hundred or so people who attended the Seneca Falls convention, sixty-eight women and thirty-two men signed the Declaration of Sentiments, but the press on the whole was unfavorable. Not until 1920, with the passage of the Nineteenth Amendment, did women gain the right to vote. (For further details about her life and times, see Stanton's Eighty Years & More: Reminiscences 1815–1897.*)*

Declaration of Sentiments and Resolutions

When, in the course of human events, it becomes necessary for one portion of the family of man to assume among the people of the earth a position different from that which they have hitherto occupied, but one to which the laws of nature and of nature's God entitle them, a decent respect to the opinions of mankind requires that they should declare the causes that impel them to such a course.

We hold these truths to be self-evident: that all men and women are created equal; that they are endowed by their Creator with certain inalienable rights; that among these are life, liberty, and the pursuit of happiness; that to secure these rights governments are instituted, deriving their just powers from the consent of the governed. Whenever any form of government becomes destructive of these ends, it is the right of those who suffer from it to refuse allegiance to it, and to insist upon the institution of a new government, laying its foundation on such principles, and organizing its powers in such form, as to them shall seem most likely to effect their safety and happiness. Prudence, indeed, will dictate that governments long established should not be changed for light and transient causes; and accordingly all experience hath shown that mankind are more disposed to suffer, while evils are sufferable, than to right themselves by abolishing the forms to which they were accustomed. But when a long train of abuses and usurpations, pursuing invariably the same object, evinces a design to reduce them under absolute despotism, it is their duty to throw off such government, and to provide new guards for their future security. Such has been the patient sufferance of the women under this government, and such is now the necessity which constrains them to demand the equal station to which they are entitled.

The history of mankind is a history of repeated injuries and usurpations on the part of man toward woman, having in direct object the establishment of an absolute tyranny over her. To prove this, let facts be submitted to a candid world.

He has never permitted her to exercise her inalienable right to the elective franchise.

He has compelled her to submit to laws, in the formation of which   5
she had no voice.

He has withheld from her rights which are given to the most ignorant and degraded men—both natives and foreigners.

Having deprived her of this first right of a citizen, the elective franchise, thereby leaving her without representation in the halls of legislation, he has oppressed her on all sides.

He has made her, if married, in the eye of the law, civilly dead.

He has taken from her all right in property, even to the wages she earns.

He has made her, morally, an irresponsible being, as she can commit   10
many crimes with impunity, provided they be done in the presence of her husband. In the covenant of marriage, she is compelled to promise obedience to her husband, he becoming to all intents and purposes, her master—the law giving him power to deprive her of her liberty, and to administer chastisement.

He has so framed the laws of divorce, as to what shall be the proper causes, and in case of separation, to whom the guardianship of the children shall be given, as to be wholly regardless of the happiness of women—the law, in all cases, going upon a false supposition of the supremacy of man, and giving all power into his hands.

After depriving her of all rights as a married woman, if single, and the owner of property, he has taxed her to support a government which recognizes her only when her property can be made profitable to it.

He has monopolized nearly all the profitable employments, and from those she is permitted to follow, she receives but a scanty remuneration. He closes against her all the avenues to wealth and distinction which he considers most honorable to himself. As a teacher of theology, medicine, or law, she is not known.

He has denied her the facilities for obtaining a thorough education, all colleges being closed against her.

He allows her in Church, as well as State, but a subordinate position,   15
claiming Apostolic authority for her exclusion from the ministry, and, with some exceptions, from any public participation in the affairs of the Church.

He has created a false public sentiment by giving to the world a different code of morals for men and women, by which moral delinquencies which exclude women from society, are not only tolerated, but deemed of little account in man.

He has usurped the prerogative of Jehovah himself, claiming it as his right to assign for her a sphere of action, when that belongs to her conscience and to her God.

He has endeavored, in every way that he could, to destroy her confidence in her own powers, to lessen her self-respect, and to make her willing to lead a dependent and abject life.

Now, in view of this entire disfranchisement of one-half the people of this country, their social and religious degradation—in view of the unjust laws above mentioned, and because women do feel themselves aggrieved, oppressed, and fraudulently deprived of their most sacred rights, we insist that they have immediate admission to all the rights and privileges which belong to them as citizens of the United States.

In entering upon the great work before us, we anticipate no small amount of misconception, misrepresentation, and ridicule; but we shall use every instrumentality within our power to effect our object. We shall employ agents, circulate tracts, petition the State and National legislatures, and endeavor to enlist the pulpit and the press in our behalf. We hope this Convention will be followed by a series of Conventions embracing every part of the country.

[The following resolutions were discussed by Lucretia Mott, Thomas and Mary Ann McClintock, Amy Post, Catharine A. F. Stebbins, and others, and were adopted:]

Whereas, The great precept of nature is conceded to be, that "man shall pursue his own true and substantial happiness." Blackstone in his Commentaries remarks, that this law of Nature being coeval with mankind, and dictated by God himself, is of course superior in obligation to any other. It is binding over all the globe, in all countries, and at all times; no human laws are of any validity if contrary to this, and such of them as are valid, derive all their force, and all their validity, and all their authority, mediately and immediately, from this original; therefore,

Resolved, That such laws as conflict, in any way, with the true and substantial happiness of woman, are contrary to the great precept of nature and of no validity, for this is "superior in obligation to any other."

Resolved, That all laws which prevent woman from occupying such a station in a society as her conscience shall dictate, or which place her in a position inferior to that of man, are contrary to the great precept of nature, and therefore of no force or authority.

Resolved, That woman is man's equal—was intended to be so by the Creator, and the highest good of the race demands that she should be recognized as such.

Resolved, That the women of this country ought to be enlightened in regard to the laws under which they live, that they may no longer publish their degradation by declaring themselves satisfied with their present position, nor their ignorance, by asserting that they have all the rights they want.

Resolved, That inasmuch as man, while claiming for himself intellectual superiority, does accord to woman moral superiority, it is preeminently his duty to encourage her to speak and teach, as she has an opportunity, in all religious assemblies.

Resolved, That the same amount of virtue, delicacy, and refinement of behavior that is required of woman in the social state, should also be required of man, and the same transgressions should be visited with equal severity on both man and woman.

Resolved, That the objection of indelicacy and impropriety, which is so often brought against woman when she addresses a public audience, comes with a very ill-grace from those who encourage, by their attendance, her appearance on the stage, in the concert, or in feats of the circus.

Resolved, That woman has too long rested satisfied in the circumscribed limits which corrupt customs and a perverted application of the Scriptures have marked out for her, and that it is time she should move in the enlarged sphere which her great Creator has assigned her.

Resolved, That it is the duty of the women of this country to secure to themselves their sacred right to the elective franchise.   30

Resolved, That the equality of human rights results necessarily from the fact of the identity of the race in capabilities and responsibilities.

Resolved, therefore, That, being invested by the Creator with the same capabilities, and the same consciousness of responsibility for their exercise, it is demonstrably the right and duty of woman, equally with man, to promote every righteous cause by every righteous means; and especially in regard to the great subjects of morals and religion, it is self-evidently her right to participate with her brother in teaching them, both in private and in public, by writing and by speaking, by any instrumentalities proper to be used, and in any assemblies proper to be held; and this being a self-evident truth growing out of the divinely implanted principles of human nature, any custom or authorities adverse to it, whether modern or wearing the hoary sanction of antiquity, is to be regarded as a self-evident falsehood, and at war with mankind.

[At the last session Lucretia Mott offered and spoke to the following resolution:]

Resolved, That the speedy success of our cause depends upon the zealous and untiring efforts of both men and women, for the overthrow of the monopoly of the pulpit, and for the securing to woman an equal participation with men in the various trades, professions, and commerce.

Topics for Critical Thinking and Writing

1. Stanton echoes the Declaration of Independence because she wishes to associate her ideas and the movement she supports with a document and a movement that her readers esteem. And of course she must have believed that if readers esteem the Declaration of Independence, they must grant the justice of her goals. Does her strategy work, or does it backfire by making her essay seem strained?

2. The Declaration claims that women have "the same capabilities" as men (paragraph 32). Yet in 1848 Stanton and the others at Seneca Falls knew, or should have known, that history recorded no example of an outstanding

woman philosopher to compare with Plato or Kant, a great composer to compare with Beethoven or Chopin, a scientist to compare with Galileo or Newton, or a creative mathematician to compare with Euclid or Descartes. Do these facts contradict the Declaration's claim? If not, why not? How else but by different intellectual capabilities do you think such facts are to be explained?

3. Stanton's Declaration is almost 150 years old. Have all of the issues she raised been satisfactorily resolved? If not, which ones remain?

4. In our society, children have very few rights. For instance, a child cannot decide to drop out of elementary school or high school, and a child cannot decide to leave his or her parents in order to reside with some other family that he or she finds more compatible. Whatever your view of children's rights, compose the best Declaration of the Rights of Children that you can.

Virginia Woolf

Virginia Woolf (1882–1941) was born in London into an upper-middle-class literary family. In 1912 she married a writer, and with him she founded the Hogarth Press, whose important publications included not only books by T. S. Eliot but also her own novels.
   This essay was originally a talk delivered in 1931 to the Women's Service League.

Professions for Women

When your secretary invited me to come here, she told me that your Society is concerned with the employment of women and she suggested that I might tell you something about my own professional experiences. It is true I am a woman; it is true I am employed, but what professional experiences have I had? It is difficult to say. My profession is literature; and in that profession there are fewer experiences for women than in any other, with the exception of the stage—fewer, I mean, that are peculiar to women. For the road was cut many years ago—by Fanny Burney, by Aphra Behn, by Harriet Martineau, by Jane Austen, by George Eliot—many famous women, and many more unknown and forgotten, have been before me, making the path smooth, and regulating my steps. Thus, when I came to write, there were very few material obstacles in my way. Writing was a reputable and harmless occupation. The family peace was not broken by the scratching of a pen. No demand was made upon the family purse. For ten and sixpence one can buy paper enough to write all the plays of Shakespeare—if one has a mind that way. Pianos and models, Paris, Vienna and Berlin, masters and mistresses, are not needed by a writer. The

cheapness of writing paper is, of course, the reason why women have succeeded as writers before they have succeeded in the other professions.

But to tell you my story—it is a simple one. You have only got to figure to yourselves a girl in a bedroom with a pen in her hand. She had only
to move that pen from left to right—from ten o'clock to one. Then it occurred to her to do what is simple and cheap enough after all—to slip a
few of those pages into an envelope, fix a penny stamp in the corner, and
drop the envelope in the red box at the corner. It was thus that I became a
journalist; and my effort was rewarded on the first day of the following
month—a very glorious day it was for me—by a letter from an editor containing a check for one pound ten shillings and sixpence. But to show you
how little I deserve to be called a professional woman, how little I know
of the struggles and difficulties of such lives, I have to admit that instead
of spending that sum upon bread and butter, rent, shoes and stockings, or
butcher's bills, I went out and bought a cat—a beautiful cat, a Persian cat,
which very soon involved me in bitter disputes with my neighbors.

What could be easier than to write articles and to buy Persian cats
with the profits? But wait a moment. Articles have to be about something.
Mine, I seem to remember, was about a novel by a famous man. And
while I was writing this review, I discovered that if I were going to review
books I should need to do battle with a certain phantom. And the phantom was a woman, and when I came to know her better I called her after
the heroine of a famous poem, The Angel in the House. It was she who
used to come between me and my paper when I was writing reviews. It
was she who bothered me and wasted my time and so tormented me that
at last I killed her. You who come of a younger and happier generation
may not have heard of her—you may not know what I mean by the Angel
in the House. I will describe her as shortly as I can. She was intensely
sympathetic. She was immensely charming. She was utterly unselfish.
She excelled in the difficult arts of family life. She sacrificed herself daily.
If there was chicken, she took the leg; if there was a draught she sat in it—
in short she was so constituted that she never had a mind or a wish of her
own but preferred to sympathize always with the minds and wishes of
others. Above all—I need not say it—she was pure. Her purity was supposed to be her chief beauty—her blushes, her great grace. In those
days—the last of Queen Victoria—every house had its Angel. And when I
came to write I encountered her with the very first words. The shadow of
her wings fell on my page; I heard the rustling of her skirts in the room.
Directly, that is to say, I took my pen in hand to review that novel by a famous man, she slipped behind me and whispered: "My dear, you are a
young woman. You are writing about a book that has been written by a
man. Be sympathetic; be tender; flatter; deceive; use all the arts and wiles
of our sex. Never let anybody guess that you have a mind of your own.
Above all, be pure." And she made as if to guide my pen. I now record
the one act for which I take some credit to myself, though the credit

rightly belongs to some excellent ancestors of mine who left me a certain sum of money—shall we say five hundred pounds a year?—so that it was not necessary for me to depend solely on charm for my living. I turned upon her and caught her by the throat. I did my best to kill her. My excuse, if I were to be had up in a court of law, would be that I acted in self-defense. Had I not killed her she would have killed me. She would have plucked the heart out of my writing. For, as I found, directly I put pen to paper, you cannot review even a novel without having a mind of your own, without expressing what you think to be the truth about human relations, morality, sex. And all these questions, according to the Angel in the House, cannot be dealt with freely and openly by women; they must charm, they must conciliate, they must—to put it bluntly—tell lies if they are to succeed. Thus, whenever I felt the shadow of her wing or the radiance of her halo upon my page, I took up the inkpot and flung it at her. She died hard. Her fictitious nature was of great assistance to her. It is far harder to kill a phantom than a reality. She was always creeping back when I thought I had dispatched her. Though I flatter myself that I killed her in the end, the struggle was severe; it took much time that had better have been spent upon learning Greek grammar; or in roaming the world in search of adventures. But it was a real experience; it was an experience that was bound to befall all women writers at that time. Killing the Angel in the House was part of the occupation of a woman writer.

But to continue my story. The Angel was dead; what then remained? You may say that what remained was a simple and common object—a young woman in a bedroom with an inkpot. In other words, now that she had rid herself of falsehood, that young woman had only to be herself. Ah, but what is "herself"? I mean, what is a woman? I assure you, I do not know. I do not believe that you know. I do not believe that anybody can know until she has expressed herself in all the arts and professions open to human skill. That indeed is one of the reasons why I have come here—out of respect for you, who are in process of showing us by your experiments what a woman is, who are in process of providing us, by your failures and successes, with that extremely important piece of information.

But to continue the story of my professional experiences. I made one pound ten and six by my first review; and I bought a Persian cat with the proceeds. Then I grew ambitious. A Persian cat is all very well, I said; but a Persian cat is not enough. I must have a motor car. And it was thus that I became a novelist—for it is a very strange thing that people will give you a motor car if you will tell them a story. It is a still stranger thing that there is nothing so delightful in the world as telling stories. It is far pleasanter than writing reviews of famous novels. And yet, if I am to obey your secretary and tell you my professional experiences as a novelist, I must tell you about a very strange experience that befell me as a novelist. And to understand it you must try first to imagine a novelist's state of

5

mind. I hope I am not giving away professional secrets if I say that a novelist's chief desire is to be as unconscious as possible. He has to induce in himself a state of perpetual lethargy. He wants life to proceed with the utmost quiet and regularity. He wants to see the same faces, to read the same books, to do the same things day after day, month after month, while he is writing, so that nothing may break the illusion in which he is living—so that nothing may disturb or disquiet the mysterious nosings about, feelings round, darts, dashes and sudden discoveries of that very shy and illusive spirit, the imagination. I suspect that this state is the same both for men and women. Be that as it may, I want you to imagine me writing a novel in a state of trance. I want you to figure to yourselves a girl sitting with a pen in her hand, which for minutes, and indeed for hours, she never dips into the inkpot. The image that comes to my mind when I think of this girl is the image of a fisherman lying sunk in dreams on the verge of a deep lake with a rod held out over the water. She was letting her imagination sweep unchecked round every rock and cranny of the world that lies submerged in the depths of our unconscious being. Now came the experience, the experience that I believe to be far commoner with women writers than with men. The line raced through the girl's fingers. Her imagination had rushed away. It had sought the pools, the depths, the dark places where the largest fish slumber. And then there was a smash. There was an explosion. There was foam and confusion. The imagination had dashed itself against something hard. The girl was roused from her dream. She was indeed in a state of the most acute and difficult distress. To speak without figure she had thought of something, something about the body, about the passions which it was unfitting for her as a woman to say. Men, her reason told her, would be shocked. The consciousness of what men will say of a woman who speaks the truth about her passions had roused her from her artist's state of unconsciousness. She could write no more. The trance was over. Her imagination could work no longer. This I believe to be a very common experience with women writers—they are impeded by the extreme conventionality of the other sex. For though men sensibly allow themselves great freedom in these respects, I doubt that they realize or can control the extreme severity with which they condemn such freedom in women.

These then were two very genuine experiences of my own. These were two of the adventures of my professional life. The first—killing the Angel in the House—I think I solved. She died. But the second, telling the truth about my own experiences as a body, I do not think I solved. I doubt that any woman has solved it yet. The obstacles against her are still immensely powerful—and yet they are very difficult to define. Outwardly, what is simpler than to write books? Outwardly, what obstacles are there for a woman rather than for a man? Inwardly, I think the case is very different; she has still many ghosts to fight, many prejudices to overcome. Indeed it will be a long time still, I think, before a woman can sit down to write a book without finding a phantom to be slain, a rock to be dashed against.

And if this is so in literature, the freest of all professions for women, how is it in the new professions which you are now for the first time entering?

Those are the questions that I should like, had I time, to ask you. And indeed, if I have laid stress upon these professional experiences of mine, it is because I believe that they are, though in different forms, yours also. Even when the path is nominally open—when there is nothing to prevent a woman from being a doctor, a lawyer, a civil servant— there are many phantoms and obstacles, as I believe, looming in her way. To discuss and define them is I think of great value and importance; for thus only can the labor be shared, the difficulties be solved. But besides this, it is necessary also to discuss the ends and the aims for which we are fighting, for which we are doing battle with these formidable obstacles. Those aims cannot be taken for granted; they must be perpetually questioned and examined. The whole position, as I see it—here in this hall surrounded by women practising for the first time in history I know not how many different professions—is one of extraordinary interest and importance. You have won rooms of your own in the house hitherto exclusively owned by men. You are able, though not without great labor and effort, to pay the rent. You are earning your five hundred pounds a year. But this freedom is only a beginning; the room is your own, but it is still bare. It has to be furnished; it has to be decorated; it has to be shared. How are you going to furnish it, how are you going to decorate it? With whom are you going to share it, and upon what terms? These, I think, are questions of the utmost importance and interest. For the first time in history you are able to ask them; for the first time you are able to decide for yourselves what the answers should be. Willingly would I stay and discuss those questions and answers—but not tonight. My time is up; and I must cease.

 ## Topics for Critical Thinking and Writing

1. How would you characterize Woolf's tone, especially her attitude toward her subject and herself, in the first paragraph?

2. What do you think Woolf means when she says (paragraph 3): "It is far harder to kill a phantom than a reality"?

3. Woolf conjectures (paragraph 6) that she has not solved the problem of "telling the truth about my own experiences as a body." Is there any reason to believe that today a woman has more difficulty than a man in telling the truth about the experiences of the body?

4. In paragraph 7, Woolf suggests that phantoms as well as obstacles impede women from becoming doctors and lawyers. What might some of these phantoms be?

5. This essay is highly metaphoric. What is the meaning of the metaphor of "rooms" in the final paragraph? What does Woolf mean when she says:

"The room is your own, but it is still bare. . . . With whom are you going to share it, and upon what terms?"

6. Evaluate the last two sentences. Are they too abrupt and mechanical? Or do they provide a fitting conclusion to the speech?

May Sarton

May Sarton (1912–95), born in Belgium, was brought to the United States in 1916, and in 1924 she became a citizen. A teacher of writing and a distinguished writer herself, she received numerous awards for her fiction, poetry, and essays.

The Rewards of Living a Solitary Life

The other day an acquaintance of mine, a gregarious and charming man, told me he had found himself unexpectedly alone in New York for an hour or two between appointments. He went to the Whitney and spent the "empty" time looking at things in solitary bliss. For him it proved to be a shock nearly as great as falling in love to discover that he could enjoy himself so much alone.

What had he been afraid of, I asked myself? That, suddenly alone, he would discover that he bored himself, or that there was, quite simply, no self there to meet? But having taken the plunge, he is now on the brink of adventure; he is about to be launched into his own inner space, space as immense, unexplored, and sometimes frightening as outer space to the astronaut. His every perception will come to him with a new freshness and, for a time, seem startlingly original. For anyone who can see things for himself with a naked eye becomes, for a moment or two, something of a genius. With another human being present vision becomes double vision, inevitably. We are busy wondering, what does my companion see or think of this, and what do I think of it? The original impact gets lost, or diffused.

"Music I heard with you was more than music."[1] Exactly. And therefore music *itself* can only be heard alone. Solitude is the salt of personhood. It brings out the authentic flavor of every experience.

"Alone one is never lonely: the spirit adventures, walking/In a quiet garden, in a cool house, abiding single there."

Loneliness is most acutely felt with other people, for with others, even with a lover sometimes, we suffer from our differences of taste, temperament, mood. Human intercourse often demands that we soften the edge of perception, or withdraw at the very instant of personal truth for

[1]**"Music . . . music"** A line from Conrad Aiken's *Bread and Music* (1914). (Editors' note)

fear of hurting, or of being inappropriately present, which is to say naked, in a social situation. Alone we can afford to be wholly whatever we are, and to feel whatever we feel absolutely. That is a great luxury!

For me the most interesting thing about a solitary life, and mine has been that for the last twenty years, is that it becomes increasingly rewarding. When I can wake up and watch the sun rise over the ocean, as I do most days, and know that I have an entire day ahead, uninterrupted, in which to write a few pages, take a walk with my dog, lie down in the afternoon for a long think (why does one think better in a horizontal position?), read and listen to music, I am flooded with happiness.

I am lonely only when I am overtired, when I have worked too long without a break, when for the time being I feel empty and need filling up. And I am lonely sometimes when I come back home after a lecture trip, when I have seen a lot of people and talked a lot, and am full to the brim with experience that needs to be sorted out.

Then for a little while the house feels huge and empty, and I wonder where my self is hiding. It has to be recaptured slowly by watering the plants, perhaps, and looking again at each one as though it were a person, by feeding the two cats, by cooking a meal.

It takes a while, as I watch the surf blowing up in fountains at the end of the field, but the moment comes when the world falls away, and the self emerges again from the deep unconscious, bringing back all I have recently experienced to be explored and slowly understood, when I can converse again with my hidden powers, and so grow, and so be renewed, till death do us part.

Topics for Critical Thinking and Writing

1. The essay opens with an anecdote about an acquaintance of the author's. Why are we told at the outset that he is "a gregarious and charming man"?

2. In paragraph 2 Sarton compares inner space with outer space. And in paragraph 3 she writes, "Solitude is the salt of personhood." How do you interpret these metaphors? How do they enrich her main point, that solitude is rewarding?

3. What does Sarton mean when in her second paragraph she says, "Anyone who can see things for himself with a naked eye becomes, for a moment or two, something of a genius"? Does your own experience confirm her comment? Explain.

4. What phrase in the last paragraph connects the ending with the first paragraph?

5. Drawing on Sarton's essay, in a paragraph explain the distinction between being "alone" and being "lonely."

6. In an essay of about five hundred words explain the difference between loving and being in love.

Martin Luther King Jr.

Martin Luther King Jr. (1929–68), clergyman and civil rights leader, achieved national fame in 1955–56 when he led the boycott against segregated bus lines in Montgomery, Alabama. His policy of passive resistance succeeded in Montgomery, and King then organized the Southern Christian Leadership Conference in order to extend his efforts. In 1963 Dr. King was arrested in Birmingham, Alabama, for participating in a march for which no parade permit had been issued by the city officials. In jail he wrote a response to a letter that eight local clergymen had published in a newspaper. Their letter titled "A Call for Unity" is printed here, followed by King's response. In 1964 he was awarded the Nobel Peace Prize, but he continued to encounter strong opposition. On April 4, 1968, while in Memphis to support striking sanitation workers, he was shot and killed.

Letter from Birmingham Jail

In Response to "A Call for Unity"

A Call for Unity

April 12, 1963

We the undersigned clergymen are among those who, in January, issued "An Appeal for Law and Order and Common Sense," in dealing with racial problems in Alabama. We expressed understanding that honest convictions in racial matters could properly be pursued in the courts, but urged that decisions of those courts should in the meantime be peacefully obeyed.

Since that time there had been some evidence of increased forbearance and a willingness to face facts. Responsible citizens have undertaken to work on various problems which cause racial friction and unrest. In Birmingham, recent public events have given indication that we all have opportunity for a new constructive and realistic approach to racial problems.

However, we are now confronted by a series of demonstrations by some of our Negro citizens, directed and led in part by outsiders. We recognize the natural impatience of people who feel that their hopes are slow in being realized. But we are convinced that these demonstrations are unwise and untimely.

We agree rather with certain local Negro leadership which has called for honest and open negotiation of racial issues in our area. And we believe this kind of facing of issues can best be accomplished by citizens of our own metropolitan area, white and Negro, meeting with their knowledge and experience of the local situation. All of us need to face that responsibility and find proper channels for its accomplishment.

Just as we formerly pointed out that "hatred and violence have no sanction in our religious and political traditions," we also point out that such actions as incite to hatred and violence, however technically peaceful those actions may be,   5 *have not contributed to the resolution of our local problems. We do not believe that these days of new hope are days when extreme measures are justified in Birmingham.*

We commend the community as a whole, and the local news media and law enforcement officials in particular, on the calm manner in which these demonstrations have been handled. We urge the public to continue to show restraint should the demonstrations continue, and the law enforcement officials to remain calm and continue to protect our city from violence.

We further strongly urge our own Negro community to withdraw support from these demonstrations, and to unite locally in working peacefully for a better Birmingham. When rights are consistently denied, a cause should be pressed in the courts and in negotiations among local leaders, and not in the streets. We appeal to both our white and Negro citizenry to observe the principles of law and order and common sense.

C.C.J. Carpenter, D.D., L.L.D., Bishop of Alabama; Joseph A. Durick, D.D., Auxiliary Bishop, Diocese of Mobile-Birmingham; Rabbi Milton L. Grafman, Temple Emanu-El, Birmingham, Alabama; Bishop Paul Hardin, Bishop of the Alabama–West Florida Conference of the Methodist Church; Bishop Nolan B. Harmon, Bishop of the North Alabama Conference of the Methodist Church; George M. Murray, D.D., L.L.D., Bishop Coadjutor, Episcopal Diocese of Alabama; Edward V. Ramage, Moderator, Synod of the Alabama Presbyterian Church in the United States; Earl Stallings, Pastor, First Baptist Church, Birmingham, Alabama.

Letter from Birmingham Jail

April 16, 1963

My Dear Fellow Clergymen:

   While confined here in the Birmingham city jail, I came across your recent statement calling my present activities "unwise and untimely."[1] Seldom do I pause to answer criticism of my work and ideas. If I sought to answer all the criticisms that cross my desk, my secretaries would have little time for anything other than such correspondence in the course of the day, and I would have no time for constructive work. But since I feel that you are men of genuine good will and that your criticisms are sincerely set forth, I want to try to answer your statement in what I hope will be patient and reasonable terms.

---

[1]This response to a published statement by eight fellow clergymen from Alabama (Bishop C.C.J. Carpenter, Bishop Joseph A. Durick, Rabbi Milton L. Grafman, Bishop Paul Hardin, Bishop Nolan B. Harmon, the Reverend George M. Murray, the Reverend Edward V. Ramage, and the Reverend Earl Stallings) was composed under somewhat constricting circumstances. Begun on the margins of the newspaper in which the statement appeared while I was in jail, the letter was continued on scraps of writing paper supplied by a friendly Negro trusty, and concluded on a pad my attorneys were eventually permitted to leave me. Although the text remains in substance unaltered, I have indulged in the author's prerogative of polishing it for publication. [King's note]

I think I should indicate why I am here in Birmingham, since you have been influenced by the view which argues against "outsiders coming in." I have the honor of serving as president of the Southern Christian Leadership Conference, an organization operating in every southern state, with headquarters in Atlanta, Georgia. We have some eighty-five affiliated organizations across the South, and one of them is the Alabama Christian Movement for Human Rights. Frequently we share staff, educational, and financial resources with our affiliates. Several months ago the affiliate here in Birmingham asked us to be on call to engage in a nonviolent direct-action program if such were deemed necessary. We readily consented, and when the hour came we lived up to our promise. So I, along with several members of my staff, am here because I was invited here. I am here because I have organizational ties here.

But more basically, I am in Birmingham because injustice is here. Just as the prophets of the eighth century B.C. left their villages and carried their "thus saith the Lord" far beyond the boundaries of their home towns, and just as the Apostle Paul left his village of Tarsus and carried the gospel of Jesus Christ to the far corners of the Greco-Roman world, so am I compelled to carry the gospel of freedom beyond my own home town. Like Paul, I must constantly respond to the Macedonian call for aid.

Moreover, I am cognizant of the interrelatedness of all communities and states. I cannot sit idly by in Atlanta and not be concerned about what happens in Birmingham. Injustice anywhere is a threat to justice everywhere. We are caught in an inescapable network of mutuality; tied in a single garment of destiny. Whatever affects one directly, affects all indirectly. Never again can we afford to live with the narrow, provincial "outside agitator" idea. Anyone who lives inside the United States can never be considered an outsider anywhere within its bounds.

You deplore the demonstrations taking place in Birmingham. But 5
your statement, I am sorry to say, fails to express a similar concern for the conditions that brought about the demonstrations. I am sure that none of you would want to rest content with the superficial kind of social analysis that deals merely with effects and does not grapple with underlying causes. It is unfortunate that demonstrations are taking place in Birmingham, but it is even more unfortunate that the city's white power structure left the Negro community with no alternative.

In any nonviolent campaign there are four basic steps: collection of the facts to determine whether injustices exist; negotiation; self-purification; and direct action. We have gone through all these steps in Birmingham. There can be no gainsaying the fact that racial injustice engulfs this community. Birmingham is probably the most thoroughly segregated city in the United States. Its ugly record of brutality is widely known. Negroes have experienced grossly unjust treatment in the courts. There have been more unsolved bombings of Negro homes and churches in Birmingham than in any other city in the nation. These are the hard, brutal facts of the case. On the basis of these conditions, Negro leaders sought to negotiate with the city fathers. But the latter consistently refused to engage in good-faith negotiation.

7 Then, last September, came the opportunity to talk with leaders of Birmingham's economic community. In the course of the negotiations, certain promises were made by the merchants—for example, to remove the stores' humiliating racial signs. On the basis of these promises, the Reverend Fred Shuttlesworth and the leaders of the Alabama Christian Movement for Human Rights agreed to a moratorium on all demonstrations. As the weeks and months went by, we realized that we were the victims of a broken promise. A few signs, briefly removed, returned; the others remained.

8 As in so many past experiences, our hopes had been blasted, and the shadow of deep disappointment settled upon us. We had no alternative except to prepare for direct action, whereby we would present our very bodies as a means of laying our case before the conscience of the local and the national community. Mindful of the difficulties involved, we decided to undertake a process of self-purification. We began a series of workshops on nonviolence, and we repeatedly asked ourselves: "Are you able to accept blows without retaliating?" "Are you able to endure the ordeal of jail?" We decided to schedule our direct-action program for the Easter season, realizing that except for Christmas, this is the main shopping period of the year. Knowing that a strong economic-withdrawal program would be the by-product of direct action, we felt that this would be the best time to bring pressure to bear on the merchants for the needed change.

9 Then it occurred to us that Birmingham's mayoralty election was coming up in March, and we speedily decided to postpone action until after election day. When we discovered that the Commissioner of Public Safety, Eugene "Bull" Connor, had piled up enough votes to be in the run-off, we decided again to postpone action until the day after the run-off so that the demonstrations could not be used to cloud the issues. Like many others, we waited to see Mr. Connor defeated, and to this end we endured postponement after postponement. Having aided in this community need, we felt that our direct-action program could be delayed no longer.

10 You may well ask: "Why direct action? Why sit-ins, marches, and so forth? Isn't negotiation a better path?" You are quite right in calling for negotiation. Indeed, this is the very purpose of direct action. Nonviolent direct action seeks to create such a crisis and foster such a tension that a community which has constantly refused to negotiate is forced to confront the issue. It seeks so to dramatize the issue that it can no longer be ignored. My citing the creation of tension as part of the work of the nonviolent resister may sound rather shocking. But I must confess that I am not afraid of the word "tension." I have earnestly opposed violent tension, but there is a type of constructive, nonviolent tension which is necessary for growth. Just as Socrates felt that it was necessary to create a tension in the mind so that individuals could rise from the bondage of myths and half-truths to the unfettered realm of creative analysis and objective appraisal,

so must we see the need for nonviolent gadflies to create the kind of tension in society that will help men rise from the dark depths of prejudice and racism to the majestic heights of understanding and brotherhood.

The purpose of our direct-action program is to create a situation so crisis-packed that it will inevitably open the door to negotiation. I therefore concur with you in your call for negotiation. Too long has our beloved Southland been bogged down in a tragic effort to live in monologue rather than dialogue.

One of the basic points in your statement is that the action that I and my associates have taken in Birmingham is untimely. Some have asked: "Why didn't you give the new city administration time to act?" The only answer that I can give to this query is that the new Birmingham administration must be prodded about as much as the outgoing one, before it will act. We are sadly mistaken if we feel that the election of Albert Boutwell as mayor will bring the millennium to Birmingham. While Mr. Boutwell is a much more gentle person than Mr. Connor, they are both segregationists, dedicated to maintenance of the status quo. I have hope that Mr. Boutwell will be reasonable enough to see the futility of massive resistance to desegregation. But he will not see this without pressure from devotees of civil rights. My friends, I must say to you that we have not made a single gain in civil rights without determined legal and nonviolent pressure. Lamentably, it is an historical fact that privileged groups seldom give up their privileges voluntarily. Individuals may see the moral light and voluntarily give up their unjust posture; but as Reinhold Niebuhr[2] has reminded us, groups tend to be more immoral than individuals.

We know through painful experience that freedom is never voluntarily given by the oppressor; it must be demanded by the oppressed. Frankly, I have yet to engage in a direct-action campaign that was "well timed" in the view of those who have not suffered unduly from the disease of segregation. For years now I have heard the word "Wait!" It rings in the ear of every Negro with piercing familiarity. This "Wait" has almost always meant "Never." We must come to see, with one of our distinguished jurists, that "justice too long delayed is justice denied."[3]

We have waited for more than 340 years for our constitutional and God-given rights. The nations of Asia and Africa are moving with jetlike speed toward gaining political independence, but we still creep at horse-and-buggy pace toward gaining a cup of coffee at a lunch counter. Perhaps it is easy for those who have never felt the stinging darts of segregation to say, "Wait." But when you have seen vicious mobs lynch your mothers and fathers at will and drown your sisters and brothers at whim;

---

[2] **Reinhold Niebuhr** (1892–1971) minister, political activist, author, and professor of applied Christianity at Union Theological Seminary (This and the following notes are the editors'.)
[3] **Justice . . . denied** a quotation attributed to William E. Gladstone (1809–98), British statesman and prime minister

when you have seen hate-filled policemen curse, kick, and even kill your black brothers and sisters; when you see the vast majority of your twenty million Negro brothers smothering in an airtight cage of poverty in the midst of an affluent society; when you suddenly find your tongue twisted and your speech stammering as you seek to explain to your six-year-old daughter why she can't go to the public amusement park that has just been advertised on television, and see tears welling up in her eyes when she is told that Funtown is closed to colored children, and see ominous clouds of inferiority beginning to form in her little mental sky, and see her beginning to distort her personality by developing an unconscious bitterness toward white people; when you have to concoct an answer for a five-year-old son who is asking: "Daddy, why do white people treat colored people so mean?"; when you take a cross-country drive and find it necessary to sleep night after night in the uncomfortable corners of your automobile because no motel will accept you; when you are humiliated day in and day out by nagging signs reading "white" and "colored"; when your first name becomes "nigger," your middle name becomes "boy" (however old you are) and your last name becomes "John," and your wife and mother are never given the respected title "Mrs."; when you are harried by day and haunted by night by the fact that you are a Negro, living constantly at tiptoe stance, never quite knowing what to expect next, and are plagued with inner fears and outer resentments; when you are forever fighting a degenerating sense of "nobodiness"—then you will understand why we find it difficult to wait. There comes a time when the cup of endurance runs over, and men are no longer willing to be plunged into the abyss of despair. I hope, sirs, you can understand our legitimate and unavoidable impatience.

15   You express a great deal of anxiety over our willingness to break laws. This is certainly a legitimate concern. Since we so diligently urge people to obey the Supreme Court's decision of 1954 outlawing segregation in the public schools, at first glance it may seem rather paradoxical for us consciously to break laws. One may well ask: "How can you advocate breaking some laws and obeying others?" The answer lies in the fact that there are two types of laws: just and unjust. I would be the first to advocate obeying just laws. One has not only a legal but a moral responsibility to obey just laws. Conversely, one has a moral responsibility to disobey unjust laws. I would agree with St. Augustine that "an unjust law is no law at all."

16   Now, what is the difference between the two? How does one determine whether a law is just or unjust? A just law is a man-made code that squares with the moral law or the law of God. An unjust law is a code that is out of harmony with the moral law. To put it in the terms of St. Thomas Aquinas: An unjust law is a human law that is not rooted in eternal law and natural law. Any law that uplifts human personality is just. Any law that degrades human personality is unjust. All segregation statutes are unjust because segregation distorts the soul and damages the personality.

It gives the segregator a false sense of superiority and the segregated a false sense of inferiority. Segregation, to use the terminology of the Jewish philosopher Martin Buber, substitutes an "I-it" relationship for an "I-thou" relationship and ends up relegating persons to the status of things. Hence segregation is not only politically, economically, and sociologically unsound, it is morally wrong and sinful. Paul Tillich[4] has said that sin is separation. Is not segregation an existential expression of man's tragic separation, his awful estrangement, his terrible sinfulness? Thus it is that I can urge men to obey the 1954 decision of the Supreme Court, for it is morally right; and I can urge them to disobey segregation ordinances, for they are morally wrong.

Let us consider a more concrete example of just and unjust laws. An unjust law is a code that a numerical or power majority group compels a minority group to obey but does not make binding on itself. This is *difference* made legal. By the same token, a just law is a code that a majority compels a minority to follow and that it is willing to follow itself. This is *sameness* made legal.

Let me give another explanation. A law is unjust if it is inflicted on a minority that, as a result of being denied the right to vote, had no part in enacting or devising the law. Who can say that the legislature of Alabama which set up that state's segregation laws was democratically elected? Throughout Alabama all sorts of devious methods are used to prevent Negroes from becoming registered voters, and there are some counties in which, even though Negroes constitute a majority of the population, not a single Negro is registered. Can any law enacted under such circumstances be considered democratically structured?

Sometimes a law is just on its face and unjust in its application. For instance, I have been arrested on a charge of parading without a permit. Now, there is nothing wrong in having an ordinance which requires a permit for a parade. But such an ordinance becomes unjust when it is used to maintain segregation and to deny citizens the First Amendment privilege of peaceful assembly and protest.

I hope you are able to see the distinction I am trying to point out. In no sense do I advocate evading or defying the law, as would the rabid segregationist. That would lead to anarchy. One who breaks an unjust law must do so openly, lovingly, and with a willingness to accept the penalty. I submit that an individual who breaks a law that conscience tells him is unjust, and who willingly accepts the penalty of imprisonment in order to arouse the conscience of the community over its injustice, is in reality expressing the highest respect for law.

20

---

[4]**Paul Tillich** Tillich (1886–1965), born in Germany, taught theology at several German universities, but in 1933 he was dismissed from his post at the University of Frankfurt because of his opposition to the Nazi regime. At the invitation of Reinhold Niebuhr, he came to the United States and taught at Union Theological Seminary.

21   Of course, there is nothing new about this kind of civil disobedience. It was evidenced sublimely in the refusal of Shadrach, Meshach, and Abednego to obey the laws of Nebuchadnezzar, on the ground that a higher moral law was at stake. It was practiced superbly by the early Christians, who were willing to face hungry lions and the excruciating pain of chopping blocks rather than submit to certain unjust laws of the Roman Empire. To a degree, academic freedom is a reality today because Socrates practiced civil disobedience. In our own nation, the Boston Tea Party represented a massive act of civil disobedience.

22   We should never forget that everything Adolf Hitler did in Germany was "legal" and everything the Hungarian freedom fighters did in Hungary was "illegal." It was "illegal" to aid and comfort a Jew in Hitler's Germany. Even so, I am sure that, had I lived in Germany at the time, I would have aided and comforted my Jewish brothers. If today I lived in a Communist country where certain principles dear to the Christian faith are suppressed, I would openly advocate disobeying that country's anti-religious laws.

23   I must make two honest confessions to you, my Christian and Jewish brothers. First, I must confess that over the past few years I have been gravely disappointed with the white moderate. I have almost reached the regrettable conclusion that the Negro's great stumbling block in his stride toward freedom is not the White Citizen's Counciler or the Ku Klux Klanner, but the white moderate, who is more devoted to "order" than to justice; who prefers a negative peace which is the absence of tension to a positive peace which is the presence of justice; who constantly says: "I agree with you in the goal you seek, but I cannot agree with your methods or direct action"; who paternalistically believes he can set the timetable for another man's freedom; who lives by a mythical concept of time and who constantly advises the Negro to wait for a "more convenient season." Shallow understanding from people of good will is more frustrating than absolute misunderstanding from people of ill will. Lukewarm acceptance is much more bewildering than outright rejection.

24   I had hoped that the white moderate would understand that law and order exist for the purpose of establishing justice and that when they fail in this purpose they become the dangerously structured dams that block the flow of social progress. I had hoped that the white moderate would understand that the present tension in the South is a necessary phase of the transition from an obnoxious negative peace, in which the Negro passively accepted his unjust plight, to a substantive and positive peace, in which all men will respect the dignity and worth of human personality. Actually, we who engage in nonviolent direct action are not the creators of tension. We merely bring to the surface the hidden tension that is already alive. We bring it out in the open, where it can be seen and dealt with. Like a boil that can never be cured so long as it is covered up but must be opened with all its ugliness to the natural medicines of air and

light, injustice must be exposed, with all the tension its exposure creates, to the light of human conscience and the air of national opinion before it can be cured.

In your statement you assert that our actions, even though peaceful, must be condemned because they precipitate violence. But is this a logical assertion? Isn't this like condemning a robbed man because his possession of money precipitated the evil act of robbery? Isn't this like condemning Socrates because his unswerving commitment to truth and his philosophical inquiries precipitated the act by the misguided populace in which they made him drink hemlock? Isn't this like condemning Jesus because his unique God-consciousness and never-ceasing devotion to God's will precipitated the evil act of crucifixion? We must come to see that, as the federal courts have consistently affirmed, it is wrong to urge an individual to cease his efforts to gain his basic constitutional rights because the quest may precipitate violence. Society must protect the robbed and punish the robber.

I had also hoped that the white moderate would reject the myth concerning time in relation to the struggle for freedom. I have just received a letter from a white brother in Texas. He writes: "All Christians know that the colored people will receive equal rights eventually, but it is possible that you are in too great a religious hurry. It has taken Christianity almost two thousand years to accomplish what it has. The teachings of Christ take time to come to earth." Such an attitude stems from a tragic misconception of time, from the strangely irrational notion that there is something in the very flow of time that will inevitably cure all ills. Actually, time itself is neutral; it can be used either destructively or constructively. More and more I feel that the people of ill will have used time much more effectively than have the people of good will. We will have to repent in this generation not merely for the hateful words and actions of the bad people but for the appalling silence of the good people. Human progress never rolls in on wheels of inevitability; it comes through the tireless efforts of men willing to be co-workers with God, and without this hard work, time itself becomes an ally of the forces of social stagnation. We must use time creatively, in the knowledge that the time is always ripe to do right. Now is the time to make real the promise of democracy and transform our pending national elegy into a creative psalm of brotherhood. Now is the time to lift our national policy from the quicksand of racial injustice to the solid rock of human dignity.

You speak of our activity in Birmingham as extreme. At first I was rather disappointed that fellow clergymen would see my nonviolent efforts as those of an extremist. I began thinking about the fact that I stand in the middle of two opposing forces in the Negro community. One is a force of complacency, made up in part of Negroes who, as a result of long years of oppression, are so drained of self-respect and a sense of "somebodiness" that they have adjusted to segregation; and in part of a few middle-class Negroes who, because of a degree of academic and economic security and because in some ways they profit by segregation, have become insensitive to the problems of the masses. The other force is one of bitterness and hatred, and it comes perilously close to advocating violence. It is expressed in the various black nationalist groups that are springing up across the nation, the largest and best-known being Elijah Muhammad's Muslim movement. Nourished by the Negro's frustration over the continued existence of racial discrimination, this movement is made up of people who have lost faith in America, who have absolutely repudiated Christianity, and who have concluded that the white man is an incorrigible "devil."

28   I have tried to stand between these two forces, saying that we need emulate neither the "do-nothingism" of the complacent nor the hatred and despair of the black nationalist. For there is the more excellent way of love and nonviolent protest. I am grateful to God that, through the influence of the Negro church, the way of nonviolence became an integral part of our struggle.

29   If this philosophy had not emerged, by now many streets of the South should, I am convinced, be flowing with blood. And I am further convinced that if our white brothers dismiss as "rabble-rousers" and "outside agitators" those of us who employ nonviolent direct action, and if they refuse to support our nonviolent efforts, millions of Negroes will, out of frustration and despair, seek solace and security in black-nationalist ideologies—a development that would inevitably lead to a frightening racial nightmare.

30   Oppressed people cannot remain oppressed forever. The yearning for freedom eventually manifests itself, and that is what has happened to the American Negro. Something within has reminded him of his birthright of freedom, and something without has reminded him that it can be gained. Consciously or unconsciously, he has been caught up by the *Zeitgeist*,[5] and with his black brothers of Africa and his brown and yellow brothers of Asia, South America, and the Caribbean, the United States Negro is moving with a sense of great urgency toward the promised land of racial justice. If one recognizes this vital urge that has engulfed the Negro community, one should readily understand why public demonstrations are taking place. The Negro has many pent-up resentments and latent frustrations, and he must release them. So let him march; let him make prayer pilgrimages to the city hall; let him go on freedom rides—and try to understand why he must do so. If his repressed emotions are not released in nonviolent ways, they will seek expression through violence; this is not a threat but a fact of history. So I have not said to my people: "Get rid of your discontent." Rather, I have tried to say that this normal and healthy discontent can be channeled into the creative outlet of nonviolent direct action. And now this approach is being termed extremist.

[5]*Zeitgeist* German for "spirit of the age"

31   But though I was initially disappointed at being categorized as an extremist, as I continued to think about the matter I gradually gained a measure of satisfaction from the label. Was not Jesus an extremist for love: "Love your enemies, bless them that curse you, do good to them that hate you, and pray for them which despitefully use you, and persecute you." Was not Amos an extremist for justice: "Let justice roll down like waters and righteousness like an ever-flowing stream." Was not Paul an extremist for the Christian gospel: "I bear in my body the marks of the Lord Jesus." Was not Martin Luther an extremist: "Here I stand; I cannot do otherwise, so help me God." And John Bunyan: "I will stay in jail to the end of my days before I make a butchery of my conscience." And Abraham Lincoln: "This nation cannot survive half slave and half free." And Thomas Jefferson: "We hold these truths to be self-evident, that all men are created equal. . . . " So the question is not whether we will be extremists, but what kind of extremists we will be. Will we be extremists for hate or for love? Will we be extremists for the preservation of injustice or for the extension of justice? In that dramatic scene on Calvary's hill three men were crucified. We must never forget that all three were crucified for the same crime—the crime of extremism. Two were extremists for immorality, and thus fell below their environment. The other, Jesus Christ, was an extremist for love, truth, and goodness, and thereby rose above his environment. Perhaps the South, the nation, and the world are in dire need of creative extremists.

32   I had hoped that the white moderate would see this need. Perhaps I was too optimistic; perhaps I expected too much. I suppose I should have realized that few members of the oppressor race can understand the deep groans and passionate yearnings of the oppressed race, and still fewer have the vision to see that injustice must be rooted out by strong, persistent, and determined action. I am thankful, however, that some of our white brothers in the South have grasped the meaning of this social revolution and committed themselves to it. They are still all too few in quantity, but they are big in quality. Some—such as Ralph McGill, Lillian Smith, Harry Golden, James McBride Dabbs, Ann Braden, and Sarah Patton Boyle—have written about our struggle in eloquent and prophetic terms. Others have marched with us down nameless streets of the South. They have languished in filthy, roach-infested jails, suffering the abuse and brutality of policemen who view them as "dirty nigger-lovers." Unlike so many of their moderate brothers and sisters, they have recognized the urgency of the moment and sensed the need for powerful "action" antidotes to combat the disease of segregation.

33   Let me take note of my other major disappointment. I have been so greatly disappointed with the white church and its leadership. Of course, there are some notable exceptions. I am not unmindful of the fact that each of you has taken some significant stands on this issue. I commend you, Reverend Stallings, for your Christian stand on this past Sunday, in welcoming Negroes to your worship service on a nonsegregated basis. I

commend the Catholic leaders of this state for integrating Spring Hill College several years ago.

34   But despite these notable exceptions, I must honestly reiterate that I have been disappointed with the church. I do not say this as one of those negative critics who can always find something wrong with the church. I say this as a minister of the gospel, who loves the church; who was nurtured in its bosom; who has been sustained by its spiritual blessings and who will remain true to it as long as the cord of life shall lengthen.

35   When I was suddenly catapulted into the leadership of the bus   35 protest in Montgomery, Alabama, a few years ago, I felt we would be supported by the white church. I felt that the white ministers, priests, and rabbis of the South would be among our strongest allies. Instead, some have been outright opponents, refusing to understand the freedom movement and misrepresenting its leaders; all too many others have been more cautious than courageous and have remained silent behind the anesthetizing security of stained-glass windows.

36   In spite of my shattered dreams, I came to Birmingham with the hope that the white religious leadership of this community would see the justice of our cause and, with deep moral concern, would serve as the channel through which our just grievances could reach the power structure. I had hoped that each of you would understand. But again I have been disappointed.

37   I have heard numerous southern religious leaders admonish their worshipers to comply with a desegregation decision because it is the law, but I have longed to hear white ministers declare: "Follow this decree because integration is morally right and because the Negro is your brother." In the midst of blatant injustices inflicted upon the Negro, I have watched white churchmen stand on the sideline and mouth pious irrelevancies and sanctimonious trivialities. In the midst of a mighty struggle to rid our nation of racial and economic injustice, I have heard many ministers say: "Those are social issues, with which the gospel has no real concern." And I have watched many churches commit themselves to a completely otherworldly religion which makes a strange, unbiblical distinction between body and soul, between the sacred and the secular.

38   I have traveled the length and breadth of Alabama, Mississippi, and all the other southern states. On sweltering summer days and crisp autumn mornings I have looked at the South's beautiful churches with their lofty spires pointing heavenward. I have beheld the impressive outlines of her massive religious-education buildings. Over and over I have found myself saying: "What kind of people worship here? Who is their God? Where were their voices when the lips of Governor Barnett dripped with words of interposition and nullification? Where were they when Governor Wallace gave a clarion call for defiance and hatred? Where were their voices of support when bruised and weary Negro men and women decided to rise from the dark dungeons of complacency to the bright hills of creative protest?"

ঋ∿ Yes, these questions are still in my mind. In deep disappointment I have wept over the laxity of the church. But be assured that my tears have been tears of love. There can be no deep disappointment where there is not deep love. Yes, I love the church. How could I do otherwise? I am in the rather unique position of being the son, the grandson, and the great-grandson of preachers. Yes, I see the church as the body of Christ. But, Oh! How we have blemished and scarred that body through social neglect and through fear of being nonconformists.

ঋ∿ There was a time when the church was very powerful—in the time when the early Christians rejoiced at being deemed worthy to suffer for what they believed. In those days the church was not merely a thermometer that recorded the ideas and principles of popular opinion; it was a thermostat that transformed the mores of society. Whenever the early Christians entered a town, the people in power became disturbed and immediately sought to convict the Christians for being "disturbers of the peace" and "outside agitators." But the Christians pressed on, in the conviction that they were "a colony of heaven," called to obey God rather than man. Small in number, they were big in commitment. They were too God-intoxicated to be "astronomically intimidated." By their effort and example they brought an end to such ancient evils as infanticide and gladiatorial contests.   40

ঋ∿ Things are different now. So often the contemporary church is a weak, ineffectual voice with an uncertain sound. So often it is an archdefender of the status quo. Far from being disturbed by the presence of the church, the power structure of the average community is consoled by the church's silent—and often even vocal—sanction of things as they are.

ঋ∿ But the judgment of God is upon the church as never before. If today's church does not recapture the sacrificial spirit of the early church, it will lose its authenticity, forfeit the loyalty of millions, and be dismissed as an irrelevant social club with no meaning for the twentieth century. Every day I meet young people whose disappointment with the church has turned into outright disgust.

ঋ∿ Perhaps I have once again been too optimistic. Is organized religion too inextricably bound to the status quo to save our nation and the world? Perhaps I must turn my faith to the inner spiritual church, the church within the church, as the true *ekklesia* and the hope of the world. But again I am thankful to God that some noble souls from the ranks of organized religion have broken loose from the paralyzing chains of conformity and joined us as active partners in the struggle for freedom. They have left their secure congregations and walked the streets of Albany, Georgia, with us. They have gone down the highways of the South on tortuous rides for freedom. Yes, they have gone to jail with us. Some have been dismissed from their churches, have lost the support of their bishops and fellow ministers. But they have acted in the faith that right defeated is stronger than evil triumphant. Their witness has been the spiritual salt that has preserved the true meaning of the gospel in these troubled times. They have carved a tunnel of hope through the dark mountain of disappointment.

44 I hope the church as a whole will meet the challenge of this decisive hour. But even if the church does not come to the aid of justice, I have no despair about the future. It have no fear about the outcome of our struggle in Birmingham, even if our motives are at present misunderstood. We will reach the goal of freedom in Birmingham and all over the nation, because the goal of America is freedom. Abused and scorned though we may be, our destiny is tied up with America's destiny. Before the pilgrims landed at Plymouth, we were here. Before the pen of Jefferson etched the majestic words of the Declaration of Independence across the pages of history, we were here. For more than two centuries our forebears labored in this country without wages; they made cotton king; they built the homes of their masters while suffering gross injustice and shameful humiliation—and yet out of a bottomless vitality they continue to thrive and develop. If the inexpressible cruelties of slavery could not stop us, the opposition we now face will surely fail. We will win our freedom because the sacred heritage of our nation and the eternal will of God are embodied in our echoing demands.

45 Before closing I feel impelled to mention one other point in your statement that has troubled me profoundly. You warmly commended the Birmingham police force for keeping "order" and "preventing violence." I doubt that you would have so warmly commended the police force if you had seen its dogs sinking their teeth into unarmed, nonviolent Negroes. I doubt that you would so quickly commend the policemen if you were to observe their ugly and inhumane treatment of Negroes here in the city jail; if you were to watch them push and curse old Negro women and young Negro girls; if you were to see them slap and kick old Negro men and young boys; if you were to observe them, as they did on two occasions, refuse to give us food because we wanted to sing our grace together. I cannot join you in your praise of the Birmingham police department.

46 It is true that the police have exercised a degree of discipline in handling the demonstrators. In this sense they have conducted themselves rather "nonviolently" in public. But for what purpose? To preserve the evil system of segregation. Over the past few years I have consistently preached that nonviolence demands that the means we use must be as pure as the ends we seek. I have tried to make clear that it is wrong to use immoral means to attain moral ends. But now I must affirm that it is just as wrong, or perhaps even more so, to use moral means to preserve immoral ends. Perhaps Mr. Connor and his policemen have been rather nonviolent in public, as was Chief Pritchett in Albany, Georgia, but they have used the moral means of nonviolence to maintain the immoral end of racial injustice. As T. S. Eliot has said: "The last temptation is the greatest treason: To do the right deed for the wrong reason."

47 I wish you had commended the Negro sit-inners and demonstrators of Birmingham for their sublime courage, their willingness to suffer, and their amazing discipline in the midst of great provocation. One day the South will recognize its real heroes. They will be the James Merediths,

with the noble sense of purpose that enables them to face jeering and hostile mobs, and with the agonizing loneliness that characterizes the life of the pioneer. They will be old, oppressed, battered Negro women, symbolized in a seventy-two-year-old woman in Montgomery, Alabama, who rose up with a sense of dignity and with her people decided not to ride segregated buses, and who responded with ungrammatical profundity to one who inquired about her weariness: "My feets is tired, but my soul is at rest." They will be the young high school and college students, the young ministers of the gospel and a host of their elders, courageously and nonviolently sitting in at lunch counters and willingly going to jail for conscience's sake. One day the South will know that when these disinherited children of God sat down at lunch counters, they were in reality standing up for what is best in the American dream and for the most sacred values in our Judaeo-Christian heritage, thereby bringing our nation back to those great wells of democracy which were dug deep by the founding fathers in their formulation of the Constitution and the Declaration of Independence.

Never before have I written so long a letter. I'm afraid it is much too long to take your precious time. I can assure you that it would have been much shorter if I had been writing from a comfortable desk, but what else can one do when he is alone in a narrow jail cell, other than write long letters, think long thoughts, and pray long prayers?

If I have said anything in this letter that overstates the truth and indicates an unreasonable impatience, I beg you to forgive me. If I have said anything that understates the truth and indicates my having a patience that allows me to settle for anything less than brotherhood, I beg God to forgive me.

I hope this letter finds you strong in the faith. I also hope that circumstances will soon make it possible for me to meet each of you, not as an integrationist or a civil-rights leader but as a fellow clergyman and a Christian brother. Let us all hope that the dark clouds of racial prejudice will soon pass away and the deep fog of misunderstanding will be lifted from our fear-drenched communities, and in some not too distant tomorrow the radiant stars of love and brotherhood will shine over our great nation with all their scintillating beauty.

50

Yours for the cause of Peace and Brotherhood,

Martin Luther King Jr.

Topics for Critical Thinking and Writing

1. In his first five paragraphs how does King assure his audience that he is not a meddlesome intruder but a man of good will?

2. In paragraph 3 King refers to Hebrew prophets and to the Apostle Paul, and later (paragraph 10) to Socrates. What is the point of these references?

3. In paragraph 11 what does King mean when he says that "our beloved Southland" has long tried to "live in monologue rather than dialogue"?

4. King begins paragraph 23 with "I must make two honest confessions to you, my Christian and Jewish brothers." What would have been gained or lost if he had used this paragraph as his opening?

5. King's last three paragraphs do not advance his argument. What do they do?

6. Why does King advocate breaking unjust laws "openly, lovingly" (paragraph 20)? What does he mean by these words? What other motives or attitudes do these words rule out?

7. Construct two definitions of *civil disobedience*, and explain whether and to what extent it is easier (or harder) to justify civil disobedience, depending on how you have defined the expression.

8. If you feel that you wish to respond to King's letter on some point, write a letter nominally addressed to King. You may, if you wish, adopt the persona of one of the eight clergymen whom King initially addressed.

9. King writes (paragraph 46) that "nonviolence demands that the means we use must be as pure as the ends we seek." How do you think King would evaluate the following acts of civil disobedience: (a) occupying a college administration building in order to protest the administration's unsatisfactory response to a racial incident on campus, or in order to protest the failure of the administration to hire minority persons as staff and faculty; (b) sailing on a collision course with a whaling ship to protest against whaling; (c) trespassing on an abortion clinic to protest abortion? Set down your answer in an essay of five hundred words.

Peter Singer

Peter Singer teaches philosophy at Princeton University. This essay originally appeared in 1973 as a review of Animals, Men and Morals, *edited by Stanley and Roslind Godlovitch and John Harris.*

Animal Liberation

I

We are familiar with Black Liberation, Gay Liberation, and a variety of other movements. With Women's Liberation some thought we had come to the end of the road. Discrimination on the basis of sex, it has been said, is the last form of discrimination that is universally accepted and practiced without pretense, even in those liberal circles which have long prided themselves on their freedom from racial discrimination. But one should always be wary of talking of "the last remaining form of discrimination." If we have learned anything from the liberation movements, we should have learned how difficult it is to be aware of the ways in which we discriminate until they are forcefully pointed out to us. A liberation movement demands an expansion of our moral horizons, so that practices that were previously regarded as natural and inevitable are now seen as intolerable.

Animals, Men and Morals is a manifesto for an Animal Liberation movement. The contributors to the book may not all see the issue this way. They are a varied group. Philosophers, ranging from professors to graduate students, make up the largest contingent. There are five of them, including the three editors, and there is also an extract from the unjustly neglected German philosopher with an English name, Leonard Nelson, who died in 1927. There are essays by two novelist/critics, Brigid Brophy and Maureen Duffy, and another by Muriel the Lady Dowding, widow of Dowding of Battle of Britain fame and the founder of "Beauty Without Cruelty," a movement that campaigns against the use of animals for furs and cosmetics. The other pieces are by a psychologist, a botanist, a sociologist, and Ruth Harrison, who is probably best described as a professional campaigner for animal welfare.

Whether or not these people, as individuals, would all agree that they are launching a liberation movement for animals, the book as a whole amounts to no less. It is a demand for a complete change in our attitudes to nonhumans. It is a demand that we cease to regard the exploitation of other species as natural and inevitable, and that, instead, we see it as a continuing moral outrage. Patrick Corbett, Professor of Philosophy at Sussex University, captures the spirit of the book in his closing words:

> . . . We require now to extend the great principles of liberty, equality and fraternity over the lives of animals. Let animal slavery join human slavery in the graveyard of the past.

The reader is likely to be skeptical. "Animal Liberation" sounds more like a parody of liberation movements than a serious objective. The reader may think: We support the claims of blacks and women for equality because blacks and women really are equal to whites and males—equal in intelligence and in abilities, capacity for leadership, rationality, and so on. Humans and nonhumans obviously are not equal in these respects. Since justice demands only that we treat equals equally, unequal treatment of humans and nonhumans cannot be an injustice.

This is a tempting reply, but a dangerous one. It commits the non-racist and non-sexist to a dogmatic belief that blacks and women really are just as intelligent, able, etc., as whites and males—and no more. Quite possibly this happens to be the case. Certainly attempts to prove that racial or sexual differences in these respects have a genetic origin have

5

not been conclusive. But do we really want to stake our demand for equality on the assumption that there are no genetic differences of this kind between the different races or sexes? Surely the appropriate response to those who claim to have found evidence for such genetic differences is not to stick to the belief that there are no differences, whatever the evidence to the contrary; rather one should be clear that the claim to equality does not depend on IQ. Moral equality is distinct from factual equality. Otherwise it would be nonsense to talk of the equality of human beings, since humans, as individuals, obviously differ in intelligence and almost any ability one cares to name. If possessing greater intelligence does not entitle one human to exploit another, why should it entitle humans to exploit nonhumans?

Jeremy Bentham expressed the essential basis of equality in his famous formula: "Each to count for one and none for more than one." In other words, the interests of every being that has interests are to be taken into account and treated equally with the like interests of any other being. Other moral philosophers, before and after Bentham, have made the same point in different ways. Our concern for others must not depend on whether they possess certain characteristics, though just what that concern involves may, of course, vary, according to such characteristics.

Bentham, incidentally, was well aware that the logic of the demand for racial equality did not stop at the equality of humans. He wrote:

> The day *may* come when the rest of the animal creation may acquire those rights which never could have been withholden from them but by the hand of tyranny. The French have already discovered that the blackness of the skin is no reason why a human being should be abandoned without redress to the caprice of a tormentor. It may one day come to be recognized that the number of the legs, the villosity of the skin, or the termination of the *os sacrum*, are reasons equally insufficient for abandoning a sensitive being to the same fate. What else is it that should trace the insuperable line? Is it the faculty of reason, or perhaps the faculty of discourse? But a full-grown horse or dog is beyond comparison a more rational, as well as a more conversable animal, than an infant of a day, or a week, or even a month, old. But suppose they were otherwise, what would it avail? The question is not, Can they *reason?* nor Can they *talk?* but, Can they *suffer?*[1]

Surely Bentham was right. If a being suffers, there can be no moral justification for refusing to take that suffering into consideration, and, indeed, to count it equally with the like suffering (if rough comparisons can be made) of any other being.

So the only question is: Do animals other than man suffer? Most people agree unhesitatingly that animals like cats and dogs can and do suffer, and this seems also to be assumed by those laws that prohibit wanton cruelty to such animals. Personally, I have no doubt at all about this and

[1] *The Principles of Morals and Legislation*, ch. XVII, sec. 1, footnote to paragraph 4. (All notes are the author's.)

find it hard to take seriously the doubts that a few people apparently do have. The editors and contributors of *Animals, Men and Morals* seem to feel the same way, for although the question is raised more than once, doubts are quickly dismissed each time. Nevertheless, because this is such a fundamental point, it is worth asking what grounds we have for attributing suffering to other animals.

It is best to begin by asking what grounds any individual human has for supposing that other humans feel pain. Since pain is a state of consciousness, a "mental event," it can never be directly observed. No observations, whether behavioral signs such as writhing or screaming or physiological or neurological recordings, are observations of pain itself. Pain is something one feels, and one can only infer that others are feeling it from various external indications. The fact that only philosophers are ever skeptical about whether other humans feel pain shows that we regard such inference as justifiable in the case of humans.

Is there any reason why the same inference should be unjustifiable for other animals? Nearly all the external signs which lead us to infer pain in other humans can be seen in other species, especially "higher" animals such as mammals and birds. Behavioral signs—writhing, yelping, or other forms of calling, attempts to avoid the source of pain, and many others—are present. We know, too, that these animals are biologically similar in the relevant respects, having nervous systems like ours which can be observed to function as ours do.   10

So the grounds for inferring that these animals can feel pain are nearly as good as the grounds for inferring other humans do. Only nearly, for there is one behavioral sign that humans have but nonhumans, with the exception of one or two specially raised chimpanzees, do not have. This, of course, is a developed language. As the quotation from Bentham indicates, this has long been regarded as an important distinction between man and other animals. Other animals may communicate with each other, but not in the way we do. Following Chomsky, many people now mark this distinction by saying that only humans communicate in a form that is governed by rules of syntax. (For the purposes of this argument, linguists allow those chimpanzees who have learned a syntactic sign language to rank as honorary humans.) Nevertheless, as Bentham pointed out, this distinction is not relevant to the question of how animals ought to be treated, unless it can be linked to the issue of whether animals suffer.

This link may be attempted in two ways. First, there is a hazy line of philosophical thought, stemming perhaps from some doctrines associated with Wittgenstein, which maintains that we cannot meaningfully attribute states of consciousness to beings without language. I have not seen this argument made explicit in print, though I have come across it in conversation. This position seems to me very implausible, and I doubt that it would be held at all if it were not thought to be a consequence of a broader view of the significance of language. It may be that the use of a public, rule-governed language is a precondition of conceptual thought.

It may even be, although personally I doubt it, that we cannot meaning-fully speak of a creature having an intention unless that creature can use a language. But states like pain, surely, are more primitive than either of these, and seem to have nothing to do with language.

Indeed, as Jane Goodall points out in her study of chimpanzees, when it comes to the expression of feelings and emotions, humans tend to fall back on non-linguistic modes of communication which are often found among apes, such as a cheering pat on the back, an exuberant em-brace, a clasp of hands, and so on.[2] Michael Peters makes a similar point in his contribution to *Animals, Men and Morals* when he notes that the ba-sic signals we use to convey pain, fear, sexual arousal, and so on are not specific to our species. So there seems to be no reason at all to believe that a creature without language cannot suffer.

The second, and more easily appreciated way of linking language and the existence of pain is to say that the best evidence that we can have that another creature is in pain is when he tells us that he is. This is a dis-tinct line of argument, for it is not being denied that a non-language-user conceivably could suffer, but only that we could know that he is suffer-ing. Still, this line of argument seems to me to fail, and for reasons similar to those just given. "I am in pain" is not the best possible evidence that the speaker is in pain (he might be lying) and it is certainly not the only possible evidence. Behavioral signs and knowledge of the animal's bio-logical similarity to ourselves together provide adequate evidence that animals do suffer. After all, we would not accept linguistic evidence if it contradicted the rest of the evidence. If a man was severely burned, and behaved as if he were in pain, writhing, groaning, being very careful not to let his burned skin touch anything, and so on, but later said he had not been in pain at all, we would be more likely to conclude that he was lying or suffering from amnesia than that he had not been in pain.

Even if there were stronger grounds for refusing to attribute pain to those who do not have a language, the consequences of this refusal might lead us to examine these grounds unusually critically. Human infants, as well as some adults, are unable to use language. Are we to deny that a year-old infant can suffer? If not, how can language be crucial? Of course, most parents can understand the responses of even very young infants better than they understand the responses of other animals, and some-times infant responses can be understood in the light of later development. 15

This, however, is just a fact about the relative knowledge we have of our own species and other species, and most of this knowledge is simply derived from closer contact. Those who have studied the behavior of other animals soon learn to understand their responses at least as well as we understand those of an infant. (I am not referring to Jane Goodall's and other well-known studies of apes.) Consider, for example, the degree

---

[2]Jane van Lawick-Goodall, *In the Shadow of Man* (Boston: Houghton Mifflin, 1971), p. 225.

of understanding achieved by Tinbergen from watching herring gulls.[3] Just as we can understand infant human behavior in the light of adult human behavior, so we can understand the behavior of other species in the light of our own behavior (and sometimes we can understand our own behavior better in the light of the behavior of other species).

The grounds we have for believing that other mammals and birds suffer are, then, closely analogous to the grounds we have for believing that other humans suffer. It remains to consider how far down the evolutionary scale this analogy holds. Obviously it becomes poorer when we get further away from man. To be more precise would require a detailed examination of all that we know about other forms of life. With fish, reptiles, and other vertebrates the analogy still seems strong, with molluscs like oysters it is much weaker. Insects are more difficult, and it may be that in our present state of knowledge we must be agnostic about whether they are capable of suffering.

If there is no moral justification for ignoring suffering when it occurs, and it does occur in other species, what are we to say of our attitudes toward these other species? Richard Ryder, one of the contributors to *Animals, Men and Morals,* uses the term "speciesism" to describe the belief that we are entitled to treat members of other species in a way in which it would be wrong to treat members of our own species. The term is not euphonious, but it neatly makes the analogy with racism. The non-racist would do well to bear the analogy in mind when he is inclined to defend human behavior toward nonhumans. "Shouldn't we worry about improving the lot of our own species before we concern ourselves with other species?" he may ask. If we substitute "race" for "species" we shall see that the question is better not asked. "Is a vegetarian diet nutritionally adequate?" resembles the slave-owner's claim that he and the whole economy of the South would be ruined without slave labor. There is even a parallel with skeptical doubts about whether animals suffer, for some defenders of slavery professed to doubt whether blacks really suffer in the way whites do.

I do not want to give the impression, however, that the case for Animal Liberation is based on the analogy with racism and no more. On the contrary, *Animals, Men and Morals* describes the various ways in which humans exploit nonhumans, and several contributors consider the defenses that have been offered, including the defense of meat-eating mentioned in the last paragraph. Sometimes the rebuttals are scornfully dismissive, rather than carefully designed to convince the detached critic. This may be a fault, but it is a fault that is inevitable, given the kind of book this is. The issue is not one on which one can remain detached. As the editors state in their Introduction:

> Once the full force of moral assessment has been made explicit there can be
> no rational excuse left for killing animals, be they killed for food, science, or

[3]N. Tinbergen, *The Herring Gull's World* (New York: Basic Books, 1961).

sheer personal indulgence. We have not assembled this book to provide the reader with yet another manual on how to make brutalities less brutal.

Compromise, in the traditional sense of the term, is simple unthinking weakness when one considers the actual reasons for our crude relationships with the other animals.

The point is that on this issue there are few critics who are genuinely detached. People who eat pieces of slaughtered nonhumans every day find it hard to believe that they are doing wrong; and they also find it hard to imagine what else they could eat. So for those who do not place nonhumans beyond the pale of morality, there comes a stage when further argument seems pointless, a stage at which one can only accuse one's opponent of hypocrisy and reach for the sort of sociological account of our practices and the way we defend them that is attempted by David Wood in his contribution to this book. On the other hand, to those unconvinced by the arguments, and unable to accept that they are merely rationalizing their dietary preferences and their fear of being thought peculiar, such sociological explanations can only seem insultingly arrogant.

II

The logic of speciesism is most apparent in the practice of experimenting on nonhumans in order to benefit humans. This is because the issue is rarely obscured by allegations that nonhumans are so different from humans that we cannot know anything about whether they suffer. The defender of vivisection cannot use this argument because he needs to stress the similarities between man and other animals in order to justify the usefulness to the former of experiments on the latter. The researcher who makes rats choose between starvation and electric shocks to see if they develop ulcers (they do) does so because he knows that the rat has a nervous system very similar to man's, and presumably feels an electric shock in a similar way.

Richard Ryder's restrained account of experiments on animals made me angrier with my fellow men than anything else in this book. Ryder, a clinical psychologist by profession, himself experimented on animals before he came to hold the view he puts forward in his essay. Experimenting on animals is now a large industry, both academic and commercial. In 1969, more than 5 million experiments were performed in Britain, the vast majority without anesthetic (though how many of these involved pain is not known). There are no accurate U.S. figures, since there is no federal law on the subject, and in many cases no state law either. Estimates vary from 20 million to 200 million. Ryder suggests that 80 million may be the best guess. We tend to think that this is all for vital medical research, but of course it is not. Huge numbers of animals are used in university departments from Forestry to Psychology, and even more are used for commercial purposes, to test whether cosmetics can cause skin damage, or shampoos eye damage, or to test food additives or laxatives or sleeping pills or anything else.

A standard test for foodstuffs is the "LD50." The object of this test is to find the dosage level at which 50 percent of the test animals will die. This means that nearly all of them will become very sick before finally succumbing or surviving. When the substance is a harmless one, it may be necessary to force huge doses down the animals, until in some cases sheer volume or concentration causes death.

Ryder gives a selection of experiments, taken from recent scientific journals. I will quote two, not for the sake of indulging in gory details, but in order to give an idea of what normal researchers think they may legitimately do to other species. The point is not that the individual researchers are cruel men, but that they are behaving in a way that is allowed by our speciesist attitudes. As Ryder points out, even if only 1 percent of the experiments involve severe pain, that is 50,000 experiments in Britain each year, or nearly 150 every day (and about fifteen times as many in the United States, if Ryder's guess is right). Here then are two experiments:

O. S. Ray and R. J. Barrett of Pittsburgh gave electric shocks to the feet of 1,042 mice. They then caused convulsions by giving more intense shocks through cup-shaped electrodes applied to the animals' eyes or through pressure spring clips attached to their ears. Unfortunately some of the mice who "successfully completed Day One training were found sick or dead prior to testing on Day Two." [*Journal of Comparative and Physiological Psychology*, 1969, vol. 67, pp. 110–116]

At the National Institute for Medical Research, Mill Hill, London, W. Feldberg and S. L. Sherwood injected chemicals into the brains of cats—"with a number of widely different substances, recurrent patterns of reaction were obtained. Retching, vomiting, defaecation, increased salivation and greatly accelerated respiration leading to panting were common features." . . . The injection into the brain of a large dose of Tubocuraine caused the cat to jump "from the table to the floor and then straight into its cage, where it started calling more and more noisily whilst moving about restlessly and jerkily . . . finally the cat fell with legs and neck flexed, jerking in rapid clonic movements, the condition being that of a major [epileptic] convulsion . . . within a few seconds the cat got up, ran for a few yards at high speed and fell in another fit. The whole process was repeated several times within the next ten minutes, during which the cat lost faeces and foamed at the mouth." This animal finally died thirty-five minutes after the brain injection. [*Journal of Physiology*, 1954, vol. 123, pp. 148–167]

There is nothing secret about these experiments. One has only to open any recent volume of a learned journal, such as the *Journal of Comparative and Physiological Psychology*, to find full descriptions of experiments of this sort, together with the results obtained—results that are frequently trivial and obvious. The experiments are often supported by public funds.

It is a significant indication of the level of acceptability of these practices that, although these experiments are taking place at this moment on university campuses throughout the country, there has, so far as I know,

25

not been the slightest protest from the student movement. Students have been rightly concerned that their universities should not discriminate on grounds of race or sex, and that they should not serve the purposes of the military or big business. Speciesism continues undisturbed, and many students participate in it. There may be a few qualms at first, but since everyone regards it as normal, and it may even be a required part of a course, the student soon becomes hardened and, dismissing his earlier feelings as "mere sentiment," comes to regard animals as statistics rather than sentient beings with interests that warrant consideration.

Argument about vivisection has often missed the point because it has been put in absolutist terms: Would the abolitionist be prepared to let thousands die if they could be saved by experimenting on a single animal? The way to reply to this purely hypothetical question is to pose another: Would the experimenter be prepared to experiment on a human orphan under six months old, if it were the only way to save many lives? (I say "orphan" to avoid the complication of parental feelings, although in doing so I am being overfair to the experimenter, since the nonhuman subjects of experiments are not orphans.) A negative answer to this question indicates that the experimenter's readiness to use nonhumans is simple discrimination, for adult apes, cats, mice, and other mammals are more conscious of what is happening to them, more self-directing, and, so far as we can tell, just as sensitive to pain as a human infant. There is no characteristic that human infants possess that adult mammals do not have to the same or a higher degree.

(It might be possible to hold that what makes it wrong to experiment on a human infant is that the infant will in time develop into more than the nonhuman, but one would then, to be consistent, have to oppose abortion, and perhaps contraception, too, for the fetus and the egg and sperm have the same potential as the infant. Moreover, one would still have no reason for experimenting on a nonhuman rather than a human with brain damage severe enough to make it impossible for him to rise above infant level.)

The experimenter, then, shows a bias for his own species whenever he carries out an experiment on a nonhuman for a purpose that he would not think justified him in using a human being at an equal or lower level of sentience, awareness, ability to be self-directing, etc. No one familiar with the kind of results yielded by these experiments can have the slightest doubt that if this bias were eliminated the number of experiments performed would be zero or very close to it.

III

If it is vivisection that shows the logic of speciesism most clearly, it is the use of other species for food that is at the heart of our attitudes toward them. Most of *Animals, Men and Morals* is an attack on meat-eating—an attack which is based solely on concern for nonhumans, without reference

30

to arguments derived from considerations of ecology, macrobiotics, health, or religion.

The idea that nonhumans are utilities, means to our ends, pervades our thought. Even conservationists who are concerned about the slaughter of wild fowl but not about the vastly greater slaughter of chickens for our tables are thinking in this way—they are worried about what we would lose if there were less wildlife. Stanley Godlovitch, pursuing the Marxist idea that our thinking is formed by the activities we undertake in satisfying our needs, suggests that man's first classification of his environment was into Edibles and Inedibles. Most animals came into the first category, and there they have remained.

Man may always have killed other species for food, but he has never exploited them so ruthlessly as he does today. Farming has succumbed to business methods, the objective being to get the highest possible ratio of output (meat, eggs, milk) to input (fodder, labor costs, etc.). Ruth Harrison's essay "On Factory Farming" gives an account of some aspects of modern methods, and of the unsuccessful British campaign for effective controls, a campaign which was sparked off by her *Animal Machines* (Stuart: London, 1964).

Her article is in no way a substitute for her earlier book. This is a pity since, as she says, "Farm produce is still associated with mental pictures of animals browsing in the fields . . . of hens having a last forage before going to roost. . . ." Yet neither in her article nor elsewhere in *Animals, Men and Morals* is this false image replaced by a clear idea of the nature and extent of factory farming. We learn of this only indirectly, when we hear of the code of reform proposed by an advisory committee set up by the British government.

Among the proposals, which the government refused to implement on the grounds that they were too idealistic, were: "*Any animals should at least have room to turn around freely.*"

Factory farm animals need liberation in the most literal sense. Veal calves are kept in stalls five feet by two feet. They are usually slaughtered when about four months old, and have been too big to turn in their stalls for at least a month. Intensive beef herds, kept in stalls only proportionately larger for much longer periods, account for a growing percentage of beef production. Sows are often similarly confined when pregnant, which, because of artificial methods of increasing fertility, can be most of the time. Animals confined in this way do not waste food by exercising, nor do they develop unpalatable muscle.

"*A dry bedded area should be provided for all stock.*" Intensively kept animals usually have to stand and sleep on slatted floors without straw, because this makes cleaning easier.

"*Palatable roughage must be readily available to all calves after one week of age.*" In order to produce the pale veal housewives are said to prefer, calves are fed on an all-liquid diet until slaughter, even though they are long past the age at which they would normally eat grass. They develop a

35

craving for roughage, evidenced by attempts to gnaw wood from their stalls. (For the same reason, their diet is deficient in iron.)

"*Battery cages for poultry should be large enough for a bird to be able to stretch one wing at a time.*" Under current British practice, a cage for four or five laying hens has a floor area of twenty inches by eighteen inches, scarcely larger than a double page of the *New York Review of Books*. In this space, on a sloping wire floor (sloping so the eggs roll down, wire so the dung drops through) the birds live for a year or eighteen months while artificial lighting and temperature conditions combine with drugs in their food to squeeze the maximum number of eggs out of them. Table birds are also sometimes kept in cages. More often they are reared in sheds, no less crowded. Under these conditions all the birds' natural activities are frustrated, and they develop "vices" such as pecking each other to death. To prevent this, beaks are often cut off, and the sheds kept dark.

How many of those who support factory farming by buying its produce know anything about the way it is produced? How many have heard something about it, but are reluctant to check up for fear that it will make them uncomfortable? To non-speciesists, the typical consumer's mixture of ignorance, reluctance to find out the truth, and vague belief that nothing really bad could be allowed seems analogous to the attitudes of "decent Germans" to the death camps.

There are, of course, some defenders of factory farming. Their arguments are considered, though again rather sketchily, by John Harris. Among the most common: "Since they have never known anything else, they don't suffer." This argument will not be put by anyone who knows anything about animal behavior, since he will know that not all behavior has to be learned. Chickens attempt to stretch wings, walk around, scratch, and even dustbathe or build a nest, even though they have never lived under conditions that allowed these activities. Calves can suffer from maternal deprivation no matter at what age they were taken from their mothers. "We need these intensive methods to provide protein for a growing population." As ecologists and famine relief organizations know, we can produce far more protein per acre if we grow the right vegetable crop, soy beans for instance, than if we use the land to grow crops to be converted into protein by animals who use nearly 90 percent of the protein themselves, even when unable to exercise.

There will be many readers of this book who will agree that factory farming involves an unjustifiable degree of exploitation of sentient creatures, and yet will want to say that there is nothing wrong with rearing animals for food, provided it is done "humanely." These people are saying, in effect, that although we should not cause animals to suffer, there is nothing wrong with killing them.

There are two possible replies to this view. One is to attempt to show that this combination of attitudes is absurd. Roslind Godlovitch takes this course in her essay, which is an examination of some common attitudes to animals. She argues that from the combination of "animal suffering is to be avoided" and "there is nothing wrong with killing animals" it follows that all animal life ought to be exterminated (since all sentient creatures will suffer to some degree at some point in their lives). Euthanasia is a contentious issue only because we place some value on living. If we did not, the least amount of suffering would justify it. Accordingly, if we deny that we have a duty to exterminate all animal life, we must concede that we are placing some value on animal life.

This argument seems to me valid, although one could still reply that the value of animal life is to be derived from the pleasures that life can have for them, so that, provided their lives have a balance of pleasure over pain, we are justified in rearing them. But this would imply that we ought to produce animals and let them live as pleasantly as possible, without suffering.

At this point, one can make the second of the two possible replies to the view that rearing and killing animals for food is all right so long as it is done humanely. This second reply is that so long as we think that a nonhuman may be killed simply so that a human can satisfy his taste for meat, we are still thinking of nonhumans as means rather than as ends in themselves. The factory farm is nothing more than the application of technology to this concept. Even traditional methods involve castration, the separation of mothers and their young, the breaking up of herds, branding or ear-punching, and of course transportation to the abattoirs and the final moments of terror when the animal smells blood and senses danger. If we were to try rearing animals so that they lived and died without suffering, we should find that to do so on anything like the scale of today's meat industry would be a sheer impossibility. Meat would become the prerogative of the rich.

I have been able to discuss only some of the contributions to this book, saying nothing about, for instance, the essays on killing for furs and for sport. Nor have I considered all the detailed questions that need to be asked once we start thinking about other species in the radically different way presented by this book. What, for instance, are we to do about genuine conflicts of interest like rats biting slum children? I am not sure of the answer, but the essential point is just that we do see this as a conflict of interests, that we recognize that rats have interests too. Then we may begin to think about other ways of resolving the conflict—perhaps by leaving out rat baits that sterilize the rats instead of killing them. 45

I have not discussed such problems because they are side issues compared with the exploitation of other species for food and for experimental purposes. On these central matters, I hope that I have said enough to show that this book, despite its flaws, is a challenge to every human to recognize his attitudes to nonhumans as a form of prejudice no less objectionable than racism or sexism. It is a challenge that demands not just a change of attitudes, but a change in our way of life, for it requires us to become vegetarians.

Can a purely moral demand of this kind succeed? The odds are certainly against it. The book holds out no inducements. It does not tell us that we will become healthier, or enjoy life more, if we cease exploiting animals. Animal Liberation will require greater altruism on the part of mankind than any other liberation movement, since animals are incapable of demanding it for themselves, or of protesting against their exploitation by votes, demonstrations, or bombs. Is man capable of such genuine altruism? Who knows? If this book does have a significant effect, however, it will be a vindication of all those who have believed that man has within himself the potential for more than cruelty and selfishness.

ᘓᘉ Topics for Critical Thinking and Writing

1. Reread Singer's first seven paragraphs carefully, observing how he leads us to see that "animal liberation" is not a joke. It will help you to understand his strategy if for each of his paragraphs you write one sentence either summarizing the paragraph or commenting on what it accomplishes in his argument.

2. What grounds does Singer find for attributing suffering to nonhumans? List the arguments he offers to dismiss the relevance of a developed language. Why does he find it necessary to offer these arguments?

3. Does Singer attribute the capacity to feel pain to all species? Explain.

4. How does Singer define *speciesism*? To what extent does he use the analogy of speciesism to racism?

5. What is vivisection? Why, according to Singer, *must* defenders of vivisection also defend speciesism? Why do many of us who would not be willing to defend speciesism tolerate or even participate in experiments on animals?

6. What use of animals does Singer analyze beginning with paragraph 30? Why does he reserve this discussion for the last part of his essay? Why does he offer more detailed and more concrete examples in this section than in the second part, beginning with paragraph 21?

7. When Singer wrote "Animal Liberation," about 30 years ago, he used language that would now be described as sexist. In paragraph 8, for example, he wrote "Do animals other than man suffer?" where he might today write "Do animals other than human beings suffer?" How would you revise his concluding paragraph to avoid sexist language?

A Writer's Glossary

analogy. An analogy (from the Greek *analogos*, proportionate, resembling) is a kind of comparison. Normally an analogy compares substantially different kinds of things and reports several points of resemblance. A comparison of one city with another ("New York is like Chicago in several ways") does not involve an analogy because the two things are not substantially different. And a comparison giving only one resemblance is usually not considered an analogy ("Some people, like olives, are an acquired taste"). But if we claim that a state is like a human body, and we find in the state equivalents for the brain, heart, and limbs, we are offering an analogy. Similarly, one might construct an analogy between feeding the body with food and supplying the mind with ideas: the diet must be balanced, taken at approximately regular intervals, in proper amounts, and digested. An analogy may be useful in explaining the unfamiliar by comparing it to the familiar ("The heart is like a pump . . . "), but of course the things compared are different, and the points of resemblance can go only so far. For this reason, analogies cannot prove anything, though they are sometimes offered as proof.

analysis. Examination of the parts and their relation to the whole.

argument. Discourse in which some statements are offered as reasons for other statements. Argument, then, like emotional appeal and wit, is a form of persuasion, but argument seeks to persuade by appealing to reason. (See Chapter 4, and *deduction*, page 903.)

audience. The writer's imagined readers. An essay on inflation written for the general public—say, for readers of *Newsweek*—will assume less specialized knowledge than will an essay written for professional economists—say, the readers of *Journal of Economic History*. In general, the imagined audience in a composition course is *not* the instructor (though in fact the instructor may be the only reader of the essay); the imagined audience usually is the class, or, to put it a little differently, someone rather like the writer but without the writer's specialized knowledge of the topic.

cliché. Literally, a *cliché* was originally (in French) a stereotype or an electrotype plate for printing; in English the word has come to mean an oft-repeated expression such as "a sight for sore eyes," "a heartwarming experience," "the acid test," "a meaningful relationship," "last but not least." Because these expressions implicitly claim to be impressive or forceful, they can be distinguished from such unpretentious common expressions as "good morning," "thank you," and "see you tomorrow." Clichés in fact are not impressive or forceful; they strike the hearer as tired, vague, and unimaginative.

compare/contrast. Strictly speaking, to compare is to examine in order to show similarities. (It comes from the Latin *comparare*, "to pair," "to match.") To contrast is to set into opposition in order to show differences. (It comes from the Latin *contra*, "against," and *stare*, "to stand.") But in ordinary usage a comparison may include not only similarities but also differences. (For a particular kind of comparison, emphasizing similarities, see *analogy*.) In comparing and contrasting, a writer usually means not simply to list similarities or differences but to reveal something clearly, by calling attention either to its resemblances to something we might not think it resembles, or to its differences from something we might think it does resemble.

connotation. The association that cluster around a word. *Mother* has connotations that *female parent* does not have, yet both words have the same denotation, or explicit meaning.

convention. An agreed-on usage. Beginning each sentence with a capital letter is a convention.

deduction. Deduction is the process of reasoning from premises to a logical conclusion. Here is the classic example: "All men are mortal" (the major premise); "Socrates is a man" (the minor premise); "therefore Socrates is mortal" (the conclusion). Such an argument, which takes two truths and joins them to produce a third truth, is called a *syllogism* (from Greek for "a reckoning together"). Deduction (from the Latin for "lead down from") moves from a general statement to a specific application; it is, therefore, the opposite of *induction* (page 905), which moves from specific instances to a general conclusion.

Notice that if a premise of a syllogism is not true, one can reason logically and still come to a false conclusion. Example: "All teachers are members of a union"; "Jones is a teacher"; "therefore Jones is a member of a union." Although the process of reasoning is correct here, the major premise is false—all teachers are *not* members of a union—and so the conclusion is worthless. Jones may or may not be a member of the union.

Another point: some arguments superficially appear logical but are not. Let's take this attempt at a syllogism: "All teachers of Spanish know that in Spanish *hoy* means *today*" (major premise); "John knows that in Spanish *hoy* means *today*" (minor premise); "therefore John is a teacher of Spanish" (conclusion). Both of the premises are correct, but the conclusion does not follow. What's wrong? Valid deduction requires that the subject or condition of the major premise (in this case, teachers of Spanish) appear also in the minor premise, but here it does not. The minor premise should be "John is a teacher of Spanish," and the valid conclusion, of course, would be "therefore John knows that *hoy* means *today*."

denotation. The explicit meaning of a word, as given in a dictionary, without its associations. *Daytime serial* and *soap opera* have the same denotation, though *daytime serial* probably has a more favorable connotation (see *connotation*).

description. Discourse that aims chiefly at producing a sensory response (usually a mental image) to, for example, a person, object, scene, taste, smell, and so on. A descriptive essay, or passage in an essay, uses concrete words (words that denote observable qualities such as *hair* and *stickiness*) and it uses specific language (words such as *basketball* rather than *game*, and *steak, potatoes, and salad* rather than *hearty meal*).

diction. Choice of words. Examples: between *car, auto,* and *automobile*, between *lie* and *falsehood*, between *can't* and *cannot*.

euphemism. An expression such as *passed away* for *died*, used to avoid realities that the writer finds unpleasant. Thus, oppressive governments "relocate people" (instead of putting them in concentration camps).

evaluation. Whereas an interpretation seeks to explain the meaning, an evaluation judges worth. After we interpret a difficult piece of writing we may evaluate it as not worth the effort.

explication. An attempt to reveal the meaning by calling attention to implications, such as the connotations of words and the tone conveyed by the brevity or length of a sentence. Unlike a paraphrase, which is a rewording or rephrasing in order to set forth the gist of the meaning, an explication is a commentary that makes explicit what is implicit. If we paraphrased the beginning of the Gettysburg Address (page 626), we might turn "Four score and seven years ago our fathers brought forth" into "Eighty-seven years ago our ancestors established," or some such statement. In an explication, however, we would mention that *four score* evokes the language of the Bible, and that the biblical echo helps to establish the solemnity and holiness of the occasion. In an explication we would also mention that *fathers* initiates a chain of images of birth, continued in *conceived in liberty, any nation so conceived,* and *a new birth.* (see Highet's explication of the Gettysburg Address, page 627.)

exposition. An expository essay is chiefly concerned with giving information—how to register for classes, the causes of the French Revolution, or the tenets of Zen Buddhism. The writer of exposition must, of course, have a point of view (an attitude or a thesis), but because exposition—unlike persuasion—does not assume that the reader's opinion differs from the writer's, the point of view in exposition often is implicit rather than explicit.

general and **specific** (or **particular**). A general word refers to a class or group; a specific (particular) word refers to a member of the class or group. Example: *vehicle* is general compared with *automobile* or with *motorcycle.* But *general* and *specific* are relative. *Vehicle* is general when compared to *automobile,* but *vehicle* is specific when compared to *machine,* for *machine* refers to a class or group that includes not only vehicles but clocks, typewriters, and dynamos. Similarly, although *automobile* is specific in comparison with *vehicle, automobile* is general in comparison with *Volkswagen* or *sportscar.*

generalization. A statement relating to every member of a class or category, or, more loosely, to most members of a class or category. Example: "Students from Medford High are well prepared." Compare: (1) "Janet Kuo is well prepared" (a report of a specific condition); (2) "Students from Medford High are well prepared" (a low-level generalization, because it is limited to one school); (3) "Students today are well prepared" (a high-level generalization, covering many people in many places).

imagery and **symbolism**. When we read *rose,* we may more or less call to mind a picture of a rose, or perhaps we are reminded of the odor or texture of a rose. Whatever in a piece of writing appeals to any of our senses (including sensations of heat and pressure as well as of sight, smell, taste, touch, sound) is an image. In short, images are the sensory content of a work, whether literal (the roses discussed in an essay on rose-growing) or figurative (a comparison, in a poem, of a girl to a rose). It is usually easy to notice images in literature, particularly in poems, which often include comparisons such as "I wandered lonely as a cloud," "a fiery eye," and "seems he a dove? His feathers are but borrowed." In literature, imagery (again, literal as well as figurative) plays a large part in communicating the meaning of the work. For instance, in *Romeo and Juliet* abundant imagery of light and dark reenforces the conflict between life and death. Juliet especially is associated with light (Romeo says, "What light through yonder window breaks? It is the east and Juliet is the sun"), and at the end of the play, when the lovers have died, we are told that the morning is dark: "The sun for sorrow will not show his head."

If we turn from imaginative literature to the essay, we find, of course, that descriptive essays are rich in images. But other kinds of essays, too, may make use of imagery—and not only by literal references to real people or things. Such essays may use figures of speech, as Thoreau does when he says that the imagination as well as the body should "both sit down at the same table." The imagination, after all, does not literally sit down at a table—but Thoreau personifies the imagination, seeing it as no less concrete than the body.

The distinction between an image and a symbol is partly a matter of emphasis and partly a matter of a view of reality. If an image is so insisted on that we feel that the writer sees it as highly significant in itself and also as a way of representing something else, we can call it a symbol. A symbol is what it is, and yet it is also much more. We may feel that a passage about the railroad, emphasizing its steel tracks and its steel cars, its speed and its noise, may be not only about the railroad but also about industrialism and, even further, about an entire way of life—a way of thinking and feeling—that came into being in the nineteenth century.

A symbol, then, is an image so loaded with significance that it is not simply literal, and it does not simply stand as a figure for something else; it is both itself *and* something else that it richly suggests, a kind of manifestation of something too complex or too elusive to be otherwise revealed. Still, having said all of this, one must add that the distinction between *image* and *symbol* is not sharp, and usage allows us even to say such things as, "The imagery of light symbolizes love," meaning that the imagery stands for or represents or is in part about love.

induction. Reasoning from the particular to the general, or drawing a conclusion about all members of a class from a study of some members of the class. Every elephant I have seen is grayish, so by induction (from Latin, "lead into," "lead up to") I conclude that all elephants are grayish. Another example: I have met ten graduates of Vassar College and all are females, so I conclude that all Vassar graduates are females. This conclusion, however, happens to be incorrect; in the mid-1970s Vassar began to admit males, and so although male graduates are relatively few they do exist. Induction is valid only if the sample is representative.

Because one can rarely be certain that it is representative, induced conclusions are usually open to doubt. Still, we live our lives largely by induction; we have dinner with a friend, we walk the dog, we write home for money—all because these actions have produced certain results in the past and we assume that actions of the same sort will produce results consistent with our earlier findings. Nelson Algren's excellent advice must have been arrived at inductively: "Never eat at a place called Mom's, and never play cards with a man called Doc."

interpretation. An explanation of the meaning. If we see someone clench his fist and tighten his mouth, we may interpret these signs as revealing anger. When we say that in the New Testament the passage alluding to the separation of sheep from goats is to be understood as referring to the saved and the damned, we are offering an interpretation.

irony. In *verbal irony*, the meaning of the words intentionally contradicts the literal meaning, as in "that's not a very good idea," where the intended meaning is "that's a terrible idea."

Irony, in distinction from sarcasm, employs at least some degree of wit or wryness. Sarcasm reveals contempt obviously and heavily, usually by asserting the opposite of what is meant: "You're a great guy" (if said sarcastically) means "It's awful of you to do this to me." Notice that the example of irony we began with was at least a trifle more ingenious than this sarcastic remark, for the sarcasm here simply is the opposite of what is meant, whereas our example of verbal irony is not quite the opposite. The opposite of "that's not a very good idea" is "that is a very good idea," but clearly (in our example) the speaker's meaning is something else. Put it this way: sarcasm is irony at its crudest, and finer irony commonly uses overstatement or especially understatement, rather than a simple opposite. (For a brief discussion of the use of irony in satire, see *satire*, pages 907–908.)

If the speaker's words have an unintentional double meaning, the irony may be called *dramatic irony:* a character, about to go to bed, says, "I think I'll have a sound sleep," and dies in her sleep. Similarly, an action can turn dramatically ironic: a character seeks to help a friend and unintentionally harms her. Finally, a situation can be ironic: thirsty sailors are surrounded by water that cannot be drunk.

All these meanings of irony are held together, then, by the sense of a somewhat bitter contrast.

jargon. Technical language used inappropriately or inexactly. *Viable* means *able to survive.* To speak of a *viable building* is to use jargon. "A primary factor in my participation in the dance" is jargon if what is meant is "I dance because. . . "

metaphor. Words have literal meanings: a lemon is a yellow, egg-shaped citrus fruit; to drown is to suffocate in water or other fluid. But words can also have metaphoric meanings: we can call an unsatisfactory automobile a *lemon,* and we can say that we are *drowning* in paperwork. Metaphoric language is literally absurd; if we heed only the denotation it is clearly untrue, for an automobile cannot be a kind of citrus fruit, and we cannot drown in paperwork. (Even if the paper literally suffocated someone, the death could not be called a drowning.) Metaphor, then, uses not the denotation of the word but the associations, the connotations. Because we know that the speaker is not crazy, we turn from the literal meaning (which is clearly untrue) to the association.

myth. (1) A traditional story dealing with supernatural beings or with heroes, often accounting for why things are as they are. Myths tell of the creation of the world, the creation of man, the changes of the season, the achievements of heroes. A Zulu myth, for example, explains that rain is the tears of a god weeping for a beloved slain bird. *Mythology* is a system or group of such stories, and so we speak of Zulu mythology, Greek mythology, or Norse mythology. (2) Mark Schorer, in *William Blake*, defines myth as "a large controlling image that gives philosophic meaning to the facts of ordinary life. . . . All real convictions involve a mythology. . . . Wars may be described as the clash of mythologies." In this sense, then, a myth is not a traditional story we do not believe, but any idea, true or false, to which people subscribe. Thus, one can speak of the "myth" of democracy or of communism.

narration. Discourse that recounts a real or a fictional happening. An anecdote is a narrative, and so is a history of the decline and fall of the Roman Empire. Narration may, of course, include substantial exposition ("four possible motives must be considered") and description ("the horse was an old gray mare"), but the emphasis is on a sequence of happenings ("and then she says to me, . . . ").

parable. A parable is a short narrative from which a moral or a lesson can be drawn. A parable may, but need not, be an allegory wherein, say, each character stands for an abstraction that otherwise would be hard to grasp. Usually the parable lacks the *detailed* correspondence of an allegory.

paradox. An apparent self-contradiction, such as "He was happiest when miserable."

paraphrase. A rewording of a passage, usually in order to clarify the meaning. A paraphrase is a sort of translating within the same language; it can help to make clear the gist of the passage. But one must recognize the truth of Robert Frost's charge that when one paraphrases a line of good writing one puts it "in other and worse English." Paraphrase should not be confused with *explication*, page 904.

parody. A parody (from the Greek *counter song*) seeks to amuse by imitating the style—the diction, the sentence structure—of another work, but normally the parody substitutes a very different subject. Thus, it might use tough-guy Hemingway talk to describe not a bullfighter but a butterfly catcher. Often a parody of a writer's style is a good-natured criticism of it.

persona. The writer or speaker in a role adopted for a specific audience. When Abraham Lincoln wrote or spoke, he sometimes did so in the persona of commander in chief of the Union army, but at other times he did so in the persona of the simple man from Springfield, Illinois. The persona is a mask put on for a performance (*persona* is the Latin word for *mask*). If *mask* suggests insincerity, we should remember that whenever we speak or write we do so in a specific role—as friend, or parent, or teacher, or applicant for a job, or whatever. Although Lincoln was a husband, a father, a politician, a president, and many other things, when he wrote a letter or speech he might write solely as one of these; in a letter to his son, the persona (or, we might say, personality) is that of father, not that of commander in chief. The distinction between the writer (who necessarily fills many roles) and the persona who writes or speaks a work is especially useful in talking about satire, because the satirist often invents a mouthpiece very different from himself. The satirist—say, Jonathan Swift—may be strongly opposed to a view, but his persona (his invented essayist) may favor the view; the reader must perceive that the real writer is ridiculing the invented essayist.

persuasion. Discourse that seeks to change a reader's mind. Persuasion usually assumes that the writer and the reader do not agree, or do not fully agree, at the outset. Persuasion may use logical argument (appeal to reason), but it may also try to win the reader over by other means—by appeal to the emotions, by wit, by geniality.

rhetoric. Although in much contemporary usage the word's meaning has sadly decayed to "inflated talk or writing," it can still mean "the study of elements such as content, structure, and cadence in writing or in speech." In short, in the best sense rhetoric is the study of the art of communicating with words.

satire. A work ridiculing identifiable objects in real life, meant to arouse in the reader contempt for its object. Satire is sometimes distinguished from comedy in that comedy aims simply to evoke amusement, whereas satire aims to bring about moral reform by ridicule. According to Alexander Pope, satire "heals with morals what it hurts with wit." Satire sometimes uses invective (direct abuse), but if the invective is to entertain the reader it must be witty, as in a piling up of ingenious accusations. Invective, however, is probably less common in satire than is irony, a device in which the tone somehow contradicts the words. For instance, a speaker may seem to praise ("well, that's certainly an original idea that you have"), but we perceive that she is ridiculing a crackpot idea. Or the satirist may invent a naive speaker (a persona) who praises, but the praise is really dispraise because a simpleton offers it; the persona is sincere, but the writer is ironic and satiric. Or, adopting another strategy, the writer may use an apparently naive persona to represent the voice of reason; the persona dispassionately describes actions that we take for granted (a political campaign), and through this simple, accurate, rational description we see the irrationality of our behavior. (For further comments on *irony*, see pages 905–906.)

style. A distinctive way of expression. If we see a picture of a man sitting on a chair, we may say that it looks like a drawing for a comic book, or we may say that it looks like a drawing by Rembrandt, Van Gogh, or Andrew Wyeth. We have come to recognize certain manners of expression—independent of the content—as characteristic of certain minds. The content, it can be said, is the same—a man sitting in a chair—but the creator's way of expressing the content is individual.

Similarly, "Four score and seven years ago" and "Eighty-seven years ago" are the same in content; but the styles differ, because "Four score and seven years ago" distinctively reflects a mind familiar with the Bible and an orator speaking solemnly. In fact, many people (we include ourselves) believe that the content is not the same if the expression is not the same. The "content" of "Four score and seven years ago" includes suggestions of the Bible and of God-fearing people not present in "eighty-seven years ago." In this view, a difference in style is a difference in content and therefore a difference in meaning. Surely it is true that in the work of the most competent writers, those who make every word count, one cannot separate style and content.

Let C. S. Lewis have the next-to-last word: "The way for a person to develop a style is (a) to know exactly what he wants to say, and (b) to be sure he is saying exactly that. The reader, we must remember, does not start by knowing what we mean. If our words are ambiguous, our meaning will escape him. I sometimes think that writing is like driving sheep down a road. If there is any gate open to the left or the right the readers will most certainly go into it." And let the Austrian writer Karl Kraus have the last word: "There are two kinds of writers, those who are and those who aren't. With the first, content and form belong together like soul and body; with the second, they match each other like body and clothes."

summary. The word *summary* is related to *sum*, to the total something adds up to. (The Greeks and Romans counted upward, and wrote the total at the top.) A summary is a condensation or abridgment briefly giving the reader the gist of a longer work. Here are a few principles that govern summaries:

1. A summary is much briefer than the original. It is not a paraphrase—a word-by-word translation of someone's words into your own—for a paraphrase is usually at least as long as the original, whereas a summary is rarely longer than one-fourth the original, and may even be much briefer, perhaps giving in a sentence or two an entire essay.

2. A summary usually achieves its brevity by omitting almost all the concrete details of the original, presenting only the sum that the details add up to.

3. A summary is accurate; it has no value if it misrepresents the point of the original.

4. The writer of a summary need not make the points in the same order as that of the original. In fact, a reader is occasionally driven to write a summary because the original author does not present the argument in an orderly sequence; the summary is an attempt to disengage the author's argument from the confusing presentation.

5. A summary normally is written in the present tense, because the writer assumes that although the author wrote the piece last year or a hundred years ago, the piece speaks to us today. (In other words, the summary is explicitly or implicitly prefaced by "He says," and all that follows is in the present tense.)

6. Because a summary is openly based on someone else's views, not your own, you need not use quotation marks around any words that you take from the original.

Here is a summary of this entry on *summary:*

A summary is a condensation or abridgment. These are some characteristics: 1) it is rarely more than one-fourth as long as the original; 2) its brevity is usually achieved by leaving out most of the concrete details of the original; 3) it is accurate; 4) it may rearrange the organization of the original, especially if a rearrangement will make things clearer; 5) it normally is in the present tense; 6) quoted words need not be enclosed in quotation marks.

thesis. The writer's position; the proposition advanced.

thesis statement. A sentence or two summarizing the writer's position or attitude. An essay may or may not have an explicit thesis statement.

tone. The prevailing spirit of an utterance. The tone may be angry, bitter, joyful, solemn, or expressive of any similar mood or emotion. Tone usually reflects the writer's attitude toward the subject, the audience, and the self. (For further comments on tone, see pages 16–17.)

PHOTO ACKNOWLEDGMENTS

Photo services provided by Photo-Search, Inc., New York.

p. 47: William Notman/Buffalo Bill Historical Center, Cody, WY.

p. 95: Bildarchiv Foto Marburg/Art Resource, NY.

pp. 99, 104, 105 (2), 520: Dorothea Lange/FSA Photo/Library of Congress.

pp. 102, 103: The Dorothea Lange Collection, The Oakland Museum of California, City of Oakland. Gift of Paul S. Taylor.

pp. 112, 113: © Robert Doisneau/Rapho/Liaison International.

p. 114: Mark R. Harrington/Courtesy National Museum of the American Indian, Smithsonian Institution.

pp. 115, 309, 310: AP/Wide World.

p. 184: George Hight/Courtesy National Museum of the American Indian, Smithsonian Institution N33190.

p. 185: Ernest C. Withers, Courtesy Panoticon Gallery, Waltham , MA.

p. 186: "Pearblossom Hwy." © David Hockney 1986. Collection of The J. Paul Getty Museum, Los Angeles, CA.

p. 187: Courtesy NASA. Photographed by Neil Armstrong.

p. 222: Krista Niles/NY Times Pictures.

p. 223: © Reuters/New Media/CORBIS.

p. 246 (top): Joanne Leonard/Woodfin Camp.

p. 246: The New Yorker Collection 1990 Roz Chast from cartoonbank.com. All rights reserved.

p. 247: 1973 © Faith Ringgold.

p. 248: "Acrobat's Family with a Monkey," 1905, by Pablo Picasso. Goteborgs, Kunstmuseum © 2000 Estate of Pablo Picasso/Artists Rights Society (ARS), New York.

p. 309: N. Lane/Sipa Press.

p. 322: Dorothea Lange/War Relocation Authority/The National Archives.

p. 323: Marion Post Wolcott/FSA Photo/Library of Congress.

p. 324: Friends of American Art Collection. All rights reserved by The Art Institute of Chicago and VAGA, New York.

p. 325: © Gordon Parks.

p. 378: Courtesy Amy Tan.

p. 401: Pablo Picasso, "Girl Before a Mirror, 1932." (Museum of Modern Art, NY/© The Estate of Pablo Picasso/Artists Rights Society [ARS], New York).

p. 402: Collection of the Frida Kahlo Museum, Mexico City. Photo: Ceniap/INBA, Mexico. Reproduction authorized by the Instituto Nacional de Bellas Artes y Literatura/Courtesy Banco de Mexico,

911